Sources of
English Constitutional History

HARPER'S HISTORICAL SERIES

Under the Editorship of
Guy Stanton Ford

Sources of English Constitutional History

A SELECTION OF DOCUMENTS FROM A.D. 600 TO THE PRESENT

EDITED AND TRANSLATED
BY
CARL STEPHENSON
AND
FREDERICK GEORGE MARCHAM
Cornell University

HARPER & BROTHERS PUBLISHERS
New York and London

SOURCES OF ENGLISH CONSTITUTIONAL HISTORY
Copyright, 1937, by Harper & Brothers
Printed in the United States of America

C-G

To the memory of
CHARLES HENRY HULL

CONTENTS

SECTION I
THE ANGLO-SAXON PERIOD

INTRODUCTORY NOTE	1
1. DOOMS OF AETHELBERHT (601-04)	2
2. DOOMS OF HLOTHAERE AND EADRIC (685-86) . .	4
3. DOOMS OF WIHTRAED (695-96)	5
4. DOOMS OF INE (688-95)	6
5. DOOMS OF ALFRED (871-901)	10
6. DOOMS OF EDWARD THE ELDER (901-24) . . .	12
7. DOOMS OF AETHELSTAN (925-40)	13
8. ANONYMOUS DOOMS	
(A) Concerning Incendiaries and Murderers . .	15
(B) Concerning Ordeals	16
9. DOOMS OF EDMUND (942-46)	17
10. CORONATION OATH OF EDGAR	18
11. DOOMS OF EDGAR (946-63)	18
12. DOOMS OF AETHELRED (980-1016)	20
13. DOOMS OF CANUTE (1020-34)	22
14. CUSTOMARY OATHS	
(A) Oath of a Man to His Lord . . .	25
(B) Oath of an Accuser	25
(C) Oath of One Thus Accused	25
(D) Oath of One Seizing Property	25
(E) Oath in Reply to Such Seizure	25
(F) Oath of an Oath-Helper	25
15. CHARTERS AND WRITS	
(A) Offa, King of Mercia: Grant to Worcester Cathedral (741-96)	25
(B) Aethelred, Alderman of Mercia: Grant to the Monastery of Berkeley (883)	26
(C) Aethelred, Alderman of Mercia, and His Witan: Confirmation of a Title to Land (896) . .	28
(D) Edgar: Grant to the Bishop of Winchester (963) .	29

vii

viii   CONTENTS

(e) Canute: Grant to St. Paul's, London (1036).   .   .   30
(f) Confirmation of a Title to Land in the Shire Court
    of Hereford (1036)   30
(g) Edward the Confessor: Grant to Westminster
    Abbey (1056)   31

SECTION II
THE NORMAN KINGS

INTRODUCTORY NOTE   33
16. WILLIAM I: ORDINANCE CONCERNING TRIALS   .   .   35
17. WILLIAM I: ORDINANCE ON CHURCH COURTS   .   .   35
18. WILLIAM I: TEN (ATTRIBUTED) ARTICLES   .   .   36
19. RECORDS CONCERNING A SUIT (1079-86)
    (a) Writ of William I (1079-83)   38
    (b) Writ of Geoffrey, Bishop of Coutances (1086)   .   38
    (c) Writ of William I (1086)   38
20. WILLIAM I: WRITS CONCERNING INQUESTS AT ELY
    (a) Confirmation of Liberties for the Abbot of Ely
        (c. 1080)   39
    (b) Mandate for a Renewed Inquest (1082)   .   .   39
21. RETURN FROM THE DOMESDAY INQUEST (1086)   .   .   40
22. EXCERPTS FROM DOMESDAY BOOK
    (a) Herefordshire   41
    (b) Cheshire   44
    (c) Berkshire   45
    (d) Worcestershire   45
    (e) Nottinghamshire   46
23. HENRY I: CORONATION CHARTER (1100)   .   .   .   46
24. HENRY I: ORDINANCE ON LOCAL COURTS   .   .   .   49
25. PIPE ROLL OF 31 HENRY I (1130)
    (a) Warwickshire Account   49
    (b) Miscellaneous Entries   52
26. EXCERPTS FROM THE "LAWS OF HENRY I"   .   .   .   54
27. WRITS CONCERNING FEUDAL TENURES
    (a) William I: Grant in Free Alms (1070-71)   .   .   58
    (b) William I: Summons for Military Service
        (1072)   58

CONTENTS

(c) William II: Writ for the Collection of Relief
(1095-96) 59
(D) Henry I: Grant Concerning Scutage (1127) . 59
(E) Henry I: Grant of an Heiress with Lands
(1121) 59
(F) Subinfeudation by Charter (1121-22) . . 60
(G) Exchange and Enfeoffment of Dower Land
(c. 1123) 60
(H) Stephen: Confirmation of a Serjeanty . . 61
28. Grants to Boroughs
(A) William I: Charter to London . . . 61
(B) Henry I: Charter to London 61
(C) Henry I: Charter to Beverley 63
(D) The Liberties of Newcastle 64
29. The Constitution of the King's Household . . 65

SECTION III
HENRY II AND HIS SONS

Introductory Note 71
30. The Constitutions of Clarendon (1164) . . 73
31. The Assize of Clarendon (1166) . . . 76
32. The Assize of Northampton (1176) . . . 80
33. Forms of Original Writs in Glanville
(A) Assize of Mort d'Ancestor 82
(B) Assize of Novel Disseisin 83
(C) Assize Utrum 83
(D) Assize of Darrein Presentment . . . 83
(E) Writ of Right 84
(F) Praecipe 84
(G) De Nativo 84
(H) Pone 84
(I) Prohibe 85
34. The Assize of Arms (1181) 85
35. The Assize of the Forest (1184) . . . 87
36. Baronial Returns (1166)
(A) From the Archbishop of York . . . 89
(B) From the Abbot of St. Albans . . . 90
(C) From the Earl of Essex 90

ix

CONTENTS

(d) From Baderon of Monmouth	91
(e) From Gilbert of Pinkney	91
(f) From Peter de La Mare	91
(g) From William of London	91
37. PIPE ROLL OF 33 HENRY II (1187)	
(a) Entries Concerning Scutage . . .	91
(b) Entries Concerning Tallage . . .	92
(c) Entries Concerning Profits of Justice . .	93
38. ORDINANCE OF THE SALADIN TITHE (1188) . .	95
39. BOROUGH CHARTERS AND RECORDS	
(a) John: Charter to Ipswich (1200) . .	96
(b) Record of Proceedings at Ipswich (1200) .	97
(c) Communal Oath of the Londoners . .	101
(d) Levy of a Municipal Tax at London (1199) .	101
(e) Ordinance for the Defense of London .	103
(f) John: Charter to London (1215) . .	104
40. JUDICIAL RECORDS OF 1194	
(a) Articles for the General Eyre . . .	104
(b) Excerpts from a Court Roll of 6 Richard I .	107
41. LETTERS CLOSE AND PATENT (1205-13)	
(a) Summons to a Great Council (1205) . .	109
(b) Summons of Service from the Cinque Ports (1206)	110
(c) Levy of a Tax on Chattels and Rents (1207) .	110
(d) Military and Naval Preparations (1212) .	111
(e) Summons to a Great Council (1213) . .	112
42. HOUSEHOLD EXPENSE ROLL (1210) . . .	113
43. JOHN: CHARTER TO THE CHURCH (1214) . .	114
44. MAGNA CARTA (1215)	115

SECTION IV
HENRY III AND EDWARD I

INTRODUCTORY NOTE	127
45. HENRY III: CHARTER OF THE FOREST (1217) .	129
46. LETTERS CLOSE AND PATENT (1218-54)	
(a) Collection of Scutage (1218) . . .	133
(b) Summons before the Itinerant Justices (1219)	133

CONTENTS

(c) Collection of Carucage (1220)	134
(d) Collection of a Fifteenth (1225)	135
(e) Election of County Representatives (1227) .	136
(f) Collection of Tallage and Levy of Ships (1227)	137
(g) Collection of a Fortieth (1232)	138
(h) Ordinance for the Preservation of the Peace (1242)	139
(i) Naval Levies (1242)	140
(j) Writs of Summons (1253-54)	141

47. RECORDS OF THE BARONIAL CRISIS (1258-66)

(a) Henry III: Letters Agreeing to Reform (1258)	142
(b) The Provisions of Oxford (1258)	143
(c) The Provisions of Westminster (1259) . .	146
(d) The Decision of Louis IX (1264)	148
(e) The Dictum of Kenilworth (1266) . . .	149

48. HENRY III: LATER WRITS OF SUMMONS

(a) Meeting with Knights of the Shire at Windsor (1261)	150
(b) First Parliament of Simon de Montfort (1264)	150
(c) Second Parliament of Simon de Montfort (1265)	151
(d) Council of 1268	152

49. PARLIAMENTARY AND OTHER WRITS (1275-95)

(a) Parliament of 1275	153
(b) The New Customs (1275)	154
(c) Subsidy of 1282	155
(d) Parliaments of 1283	155
(e) Subsidies of 1294	158
(f) Parliaments of 1295	159

50. MILITARY AND NAVAL RECORDS (1278-97)

(a) Distraint of Knighthood (1278)	161
(b) Commissions of Array	161
(c) Memorandum of Service from the Cinque Ports (1293)	162
(d) General Levy for Service in France (1297) .	163

51. RECORDS CONCERNING PARLIAMENT (1297-1306)

(a) Confirmation of the Charters (1297) . . .	164
(b) Parliamentary Bill of 1301	165
(c) Maltote of 1303	166
(d) Memorandum of Parliament (1306) . . .	167

xi

CONTENTS

52. EDWARD I: STATUTES AND ORDINANCES
   - (A) Statute of Gloucester (1278) 169
   - (B) Statute of Mortmain (1279) 169
   - (C) Ordinance for the Household (1279) 170
   - (D) Statute of Merchants (1283) 172
   - (E) Statute of Winchester (1285) 173
   - (F) Statute of Quia Emptores (1290) 174
   - (G) Ordinance Concerning Judicial Circuits (1293) . 175
   - (H) Articles of 1300 175
53. ROYAL COUNCILLORS' OATHS OF OFFICE
   - (A) Oath of 1257 176
   - (B) Oath of 1307 176
54. JUDICIAL RECORDS (1220-83)
   - (A) Excerpts from the de Banco Roll of 1220 . . 177
   - (B) Excerpts from Assize Rolls of 1221 179
   - (C) Excerpts from Exchequer Plea Rolls of 1236-37 . 180
   - (D) Excerpts from Coroners' Rolls of 1266-67 . . 181
   - (E) Memorandum of Judicial Appointments (1278) . 183
   - (F) Excerpts from the Coram Rege Rolls of 1281 . 184
   - (G) Excerpts from the Parliament Roll of 1283 . . 186
   - (H) Excerpts from Manorial Court Rolls (1246-49) . 187

SECTION V
EDWARD II, EDWARD III, AND RICHARD II

INTRODUCTORY NOTE 190
55. EDWARD II: CORONATION OATH (1308) 192
56. ORDINANCES OF 1311 193
57. EDWARD II: HOUSEHOLD ORDINANCE (1318) . . . 199
58. EDWARD II: STATUTE OF YORK (1322) 204
59. EDWARD II'S ABDICATION (1327) 205
60. EDWARD III: WRITS OF SUMMONS
   - (A) Parliament of 1337 205
   - (B) Great Council of 1353 206
61. PARLIAMENT ROLLS OF EDWARD III
   - (A) Parliament of 1330 207
   - (B) Parliament of 1332 209

xii

CONTENTS

(c) Parliament of 1339 210
(d) First Parliament of 1340 212
(e) Parliament of 1341 213
(f) Parliament of 1343 217
(g) Parliament of 1348 217
(h) Parliament of 1372 218
(i) Parliament of 1376 219

62. EDWARD III: STATUTES AND ORDINANCES
(A) Second Statute of 1 Edward III: Restriction of
Military Levies, Improvement of Justice, etc.
(1327) 223
(B) Second Statute of 14 Edward III: Parliamentary
Control of Direct Taxes (1340) 223
(C) Annulment of the Statute of 1341 (1342) . . 224
(D) Statute of Labourers (1351) 225
(E) Statute of Provisors (1351) 226
(F) Statute of Treasons (1352) 227
(G) Ordinance and Statute of Praemunire (1353) . 227
(H) Ordinance and Statute of the Staple (1353) . 228
(I) Statute of 34 Edward III: On Justices of the Peace
(1361) 230
(J) Statute of 36 Edward III: Regarding Purvey-
ance, Customs, etc. (1362) 231

63. PARLIAMENT ROLLS OF RICHARD II
(A) Parliament of 1377 232
(B) Parliament of 1378 234
(C) Parliament of 1379 235
(D) Parliament of 1380 236
(E) Parliament of 1381 237
(F) Parliament of 1386 237
(G) Parliament of 1388 239
(H) Parliament of 1397 240
(I) Parliament of 1398 241

64. RICHARD II: STATUTES AND ORDINANCES
(A) Appointment of Councillors (1377) . . . 242
(B) Statute of 7 Richard II: For the Improvement of
Justice (1384) 242
(C) Ordinance Concerning Livery and Maintenance
(1390) 243
(D) Ordinance Concerning the King's Council (1390) 244

xiii

xiv CONTENTS

(E) Statute of 15 Richard II: Restriction of Uses
(1391) 245
(F) Second Statute of Praemunire (1393) . . . 246
65. DURHAM HALMOTE ROLLS (1375) 246

SECTION VI
THE HOUSES OF LANCASTER AND YORK

INTRODUCTORY NOTE 249
66. PARLIAMENT ROLLS OF HENRY IV AND HENRY V
    (A) Parliament of 1399 250
    (B) Parliament of 1401 257
    (C) Parliament of 1404 259
    (D) Parliament of 1406 262
    (E) Parliament of 1407 263
    (F) Parliament of 1414 265
67. PARLIAMENT ROLLS OF HENRY VI
    (A) Parliament of 1422 265
    (B) Parliament of 1427 267
    (C) Parliament of 1429 269
    (D) Parliament of 1439 270
    (E) Parliament of 1451 270
    (F) Parliament of 1455 271
68. PARLIAMENT ROLL OF RICHARD III (1483) . . . 272
69. STATUTES (1399-1483)
    (A) 1 Henry IV: Restriction of Appeals (1399) . . 273
    (B) 3 Henry IV: For the Burning of Heretics
    (1401) 274
    (C) 7 Henry IV: On the Succession to the Throne
    and Elections to Parliament (1406) . . . 275
    (D) 1 Henry V: On Elections to Parliament (1413) . 276
    (E) 8 Henry VI: On Elections to Parliament (1429) . 276
    (F) 23 Henry VI: On Elections to Parliament (1445) 277
    (G) 1 Edward IV: Validation of Lancastrian Acts
    (1461) 277
    (H) 1 Richard III: Abolition of Benevolences (1483) 278
70. RECORDS OF THE PRIVY COUNCIL
    (A) Petition and Judgment (1401) 279
    (B) Minutes of December 8, 1406 279

CONTENTS

(c) Minutes of August 18, 1409 280
(d) Memorandum of May 6, 1421 281
(e) Minutes, March to June, 1422 282
(f) Minutes of November 12, 1437 284
(g) Judgment in the Star Chamber (1482) . . 284

71. CASES IN CHANCERY
(a) Petition for General Relief (1399) . . . 285
(b) Petition for Injunction 286
(c) Petition with Regard to a Trust 286
(d) Petition and Judgment Regarding a Mortgage (1456) 287

72. BOROUGH RECORDS
(a) Extracts from the London Liber Albus . . 288
(b) Henry VI: Charter to Nottingham (1448) . 290
(c) Municipal Ordinances at Leicester (1466-67) . 291
(d) Returns of Borough Elections (1437) . . 294

SECTION VII
THE TUDORS

INTRODUCTORY NOTE 296

73. HENRY VII: STATUTES
(a) Act of Succession (1485) 298
(b) Star Chamber Act (1487) 299
(c) Act Concerning Justices of the Peace (1489) . 299
(d) Poyning's Law (1494) 301
(e) Statute of Treason (1495) 301
(f) Statute of Liveries (1504) 302

74. HENRY VIII: STATUTES
(a) Act Concerning the Court of Star Chamber (1529) 303
(b) Act in Restraint of Appeals (1533) . . . 304
(c) Act for the Submission of the Clergy and Restraint of Appeals (1534) 306
(d) Act Concerning Ecclesiastical Appointments and Absolute Restraint of Annates (1534) . . 307
(e) Act Concerning Peter's Pence and Dispensations (1534) 308
(f) First Act of Succession (1534) 310
(g) Supremacy Act (1534) 311

xv

CONTENTS

(H) Statute of Uses (1536)	312
(I) Beggars Act (1536)	313
(J) Act for the Government of Wales (1536) .	314
(K) Statute of Proclamations (1539) . .	316
(L) Act Dissolving the Greater Monasteries (1539)	317
(M) Statute of the Six Articles (1539) . .	319
(N) Third Act of Succession (1543) . .	320
75. ORDER FOR THE COUNCIL OF THE NORTH (1545)	321
76. WILL OF HENRY VIII (1546) . . .	323
77. EDWARD VI: STATUTES	
(A) First Act of Uniformity (1549) . .	325
(B) Second Act of Uniformity (1552) . .	326
78. MARY: STATUTES	
(A) First Statute of Repeal (1553) . .	328
(B) Act Concerning the Regal Power (1554) .	328
(C) Second Statute of Repeal (1555) . .	329
(D) Highways Act (1555)	330
79. PROCEEDINGS OF THE PRIVY COUNCIL (1526–57)	
(A) Regulations for the Council (1526) . .	331
(B) Letters of the Council (1547) . .	332
(C) Minutes of 28–29 April, 1550 . .	333
(D) Report to the Council on Princess Mary (1551)	334
(E) Letters of the Council (1552–53) . .	335
(F) Committees of the Council (1554) . .	335
(G) Letters of the Council (1555–57) . .	336
80. RECORDS OF CASES IN STAR CHAMBER (1505–53)	
(A) The Bishop of Worcester v. Thomasyn and Others (1505)	337
(B) Mulsho v. the Inhabitants of Thingden (1529)	338
(C) Broke v. Spyttul (1534)	340
(D) Petyt v. Jobber and Others (1540–41) .	341
(E) Gerard v. Dodd (1547–53) . . .	342
(F) The King v. a Jury of Lichfield (1551–53)	343
81. ELIZABETH: STATUTES	
(A) Act of Supremacy (1559) . . .	344
(B) Act of Uniformity (1559) . . .	346
(C) Statute of Artificers (1563) . . .	348
(D) Treasons Act (1571)	351
(E) Act Prohibiting Bulls from Rome (1571) .	352
(F) Act against Sectaries (1593) . . .	354

CONTENTS xvii

(G) Act against Papists (1593) 355
(H) Poor Relief Act (1598) 356
82. PROCEEDINGS IN PARLIAMENT (1559-1601)
(A) Opening of Parliament (1559) 358
(B) Procedure on a Bill (1559) 360
(C) Speech of the Lord Keeper on the Administration
    of Justice (1559) 361
(D) A Day's Business in the Commons (1563) . . 363
(E) Procedure on a Request for Supply (1566) . . 363
(F) Debate on Freedom of Speech (1566) . . . 363
(G) Speech of the Queen (1567) 364
(H) Debate on Freedom of Speech (1571) . . . 365
(I) Intervention by the Queen (1572) 366
(J) The Case of Peter Wentworth (1576) . . . 367
(K) The Case of Arthur Hall (1581) 370
(L) Peter Wentworth's Questions on Free Speech
    (1587) 372
(M) Speech of the Lord Keeper on the Privileges of
    the Commons (1593) 372
(N) Speech of Serjeant Heyle (1601) 373
(O) Speeches by Sir Robert Cecil (1601) . . . 374
(P) Speech of the Queen (1601) 375
83. RECORDS CONCERNING THE COUNCIL (1558-1600)
(A) Proceedings on a Case in London (1558-59) . 376
(B) Committees of the Council (1558) . . . 377
(C) Letters on Judicial Matters (1559-66) . . 377
(D) Memorandum on the Statute of Artificers (1565) 378
(E) Memorandum on Appeals from Jersey (1572) . 379
(F) Oath of the Clerk of the Council (1572) . . 379
(G) Miscellaneous Letters (1573-93) 380
(H) Instructions to Local Government Officials
    (1598) 382
(I) John Herbert's Memorandum (1600) . . . 383
84. COMMISSION FOR ECCLESIASTICAL CAUSES (1559) . 384
85. ACTS CONCERNING PRINTING (1530-85)
(A) Proclamation Against Erroneous Books (1530) . 387
(B) Decree in Star Chamber Concerning Books
    (1566) 388
(C) Decree in Star Chamber Concerning Printers
    (1585) 389

CONTENTS

86. LOCAL JUDICIAL RECORDS (1553-96)
   (A) Oath of Office of a Justice of the Peace . . 390
   (B) Persons Summoned to the Staffordshire Quarter
       Sessions (October, 1585) 391
   (C) Staffordshire Quarter Sessions Rolls (1587-96) . 392
   (D) Rolls of Borough Sessions at Nottingham
       (1553-88) 394
87. RECORDS CONCERNING THE MILITIA (1539-77)
   (A) Commission of a Lord Lieutenant (1576) . . 396
   (B) Instructions for General Musters (1572) . . 397
   (C) Certificate of Muster Masters (1539) . . . 399
   (D) Instructions for Training Men in Lancashire
       (1577) 399
88. GRANTS FOR TRADE AND COLONIES (1578-1601)
   (A) Letters Patent to Sir Humphrey Gilbert (1578) . 400
   (B) Charter to the East India Company (1601) . . 401

SECTION VIII
THE EARLY STUARTS

INTRODUCTORY NOTE 404
89. RECORDS OF PARLIAMENT AND TAXES (1604-22)
   (A) James I: Proclamation Concerning Elections
       (1604) 406
   (B) Early Proceedings of the Commons (1604) . . 407
   (C) The Case of Sir Francis Goodwin (1604) . . 410
   (D) The Case of Sir Thomas Shirley (1604) . . 414
   (E) Notes Concerning Procedure in the Commons
       (1604-07) 415
   (F) Message of James I to the Commons (5 June
       1604) 418
   (G) The Apology of the Commons (20 June 1604) . 418
   (H) James I: Levy of Impositions (1608) . . . 424
   (I) Address of the Commons to James I (1610) . 425
   (J) Letter of James I to the Commons (1621) . . 427
   (K) Debates in the Commons on Privilege (1621) . 427
   (L) The King's Dissolution of Parliament (1622) . 429
90. JAMES I: STATUTES
   (A) Succession Act (1604) 431
   (B) Act to Explain the Statute of Artificers (1604) . 432

xviii

CONTENTS   xix

(c) General Act in Shirley's Case (1604) 433
(d) Statute of Monopolies (1624) 434
91. RECORDS OF JUDICIAL CASES (1606-21)
(a) Bates' Case (1606) 435
(b) The Question of Prohibitions (1607) 437
(c) The Case of the Postnati (1608) 438
(d) The Question of Royal Proclamations (1610) . . 441
(e) Council Proceedings on a Judgment in Chancery (1613) 442
(f) The Question of Commendams (1616) 442
(g) Council Proceedings against Sir Edward Coke (1616) 443
(h) Pigg v. Caley (1618) 444
(i) Impeachment of Francis Bacon (1621) 444
92. RECORDS CONCERNING PARLIAMENT (1626-29)
(a) Letter of Charles I to the Commons (1626) . . 447
(b) Charles I: Ordinance for Levying Customs (1626) 447
(c) Proceedings on the Arrest of Certain Lords (1626) 448
(d) Petition of Right (1628) 450
(e) Proceedings on the Petition of Right (1628) . . 453
(f) Resolutions of the Commons (1629) 454
93. ACTS OF THE ROYAL GOVERNMENT (1630-35)
(a) Proclamation for Distraint of Knighthood (1630) 455
(b) Writ for the Collection of Ship Money (1634) . 455
(c) Commission for Levying Fines Under Forest Law (1635) 456
94. RECORDS OF JUDICIAL CASES (1627-38)
(a) The Case of the Five Knights (1627) 457
(b) The Question of Ship Money (1637) 458
(c) The King v. John Hampden (1638) 459
(d) Star Chamber Reports (1631) 462
(e) High Commission Reports (1631) 467
95. RECORDS OF THE SHORT PARLIAMENT (1640)
(a) Speech of the Lord Keeper (13 April) 471
(b) Speech of the Lord Keeper (22 April) 472
(c) Proceedings in the Commons (23-24 April) . . 473
(d) The King's Speech and Its Results (24 April) . 473
(e) Dissolution of Parliament (5 May) 475

CONTENTS

96. RECORDS OF THE LONG PARLIAMENT (1640-42)
    - (A) Triennial Act (1641) 476
    - (B) Act for the Attainder of Strafford (1641) . . 477
    - (C) Act to Continue the Existing Parliament (1641) . 478
    - (D) Tunnage and Poundage Act (1641) . . . 478
    - (E) Act Abolishing Arbitrary Courts (1641) . . 479
    - (F) Act Abolishing the Court of High Commission (1641) 480
    - (G) Act Abolishing Ship Money (1641) . . . 481
    - (H) Act Defining Forests and Forest Law (1641) . 482
    - (I) Act Abolishing Fines for Distraint of Knighthood (1641) 483
    - (J) Reply of Charles I to the Commons' Petition (1641) 483
    - (K) Orders of the Commons with Regard to Printing 485
    - (L) Act Abolishing Temporal Power of the Clergy (1641) 486
    - (M) The Militia Ordinance (1642) 486
    - (N) Royal Proclamation (27 May 1642) . . . 487
    - (O) Declaration of the Lords and Commons (27 May 1642) 488
    - (P) The Nineteen Propositions (1 June 1642) . . 489
97. DECREE OF THE CLERGY ON REGAL POWER (1640) . 491
98. RECORDS OF LOCAL GOVERNMENT 1616-37
    - (A) Speech of James I to the Judges (1616) . . 493
    - (B) The Lord Keeper's Instructions to the Justices (1632) 494
    - (C) Yorkshire Quarter Sessions Records (1610-12) . 495
    - (D) Worcestershire Quarter Sessions Records (1637) 497
99. RECORDS CONCERNING VIRGINIA (1606-25)
    - (A) James I: Charter to the Virginia Company (1606) 499
    - (B) Ordinance of the Virginia Council (1621) . . 500
    - (C) Charles I: Proclamation Concerning Virginia (1625) 501

SECTION IX
THE INTERREGNUM

INTRODUCTORY NOTE 503
100. THE SOLEMN LEAGUE AND COVENANT (1643) . . 504

CONTENTS

101. ORDINANCES OF PARLIAMENT (1644-45)	
(A) Committee for Co-operation with the Scots (1644)	505
(B) The Self-Denying Ordinance (1645)	506
102. THE HEADS OF THE PROPOSALS (1647)	507
103. AN AGREEMENT OF THE PEOPLE (1649)	511
104. RECORDS OF THE TRIAL OF CHARLES I (1649)	
(A) Act Erecting a High Court of Justice (6 January)	516
(B) The King's Refusal to Recognize the Court (21 January)	517
(C) The Sentence of the Court (27 January)	518
105. ACT ESTABLISHING A COUNCIL OF STATE (1649)	519
106. ACT ABOLISHING THE KINGSHIP (1649)	521
107. ACT ABOLISHING THE HOUSE OF LORDS (1649)	522
108. TREASONS ACT (1649)	522
109. ACT ESTABLISHING THE COMMONWEALTH (1649)	523
110. NAVIGATION ACT (1651)	524
111. THE INSTRUMENT OF GOVERNMENT (1653)	525
112. THE HUMBLE PETITION AND ADVICE (1657)	529
113. THE DECLARATION OF BREDA (1660)	532

SECTION X

THE RESTORED STUARTS

INTRODUCTORY NOTE	534
114. CHARLES II: STATUTES	
(A) Act Legalizing the Convention Parliament (1660)	535
(B) Act Abolishing Feudal Tenures (1660)	536
(C) Post Office Act (1660)	537
(D) Navigation Act (1660)	538
(E) Treasons Act (1661)	538
(F) Act Restoring the Temporal Power of the Clergy (1661)	540
(G) Act Against Tumultuous Petitioning (1661)	540
(H) Militia Act (1661)	541
(I) Ecclesiastical Commission Act (1661)	541
(J) Corporation Act (1661)	542
(K) Act of Uniformity (1662)	543

CONTENTS

(L)	Act to Relieve the Poor (1662)	546
(M)	Licensing Act (1662)	548
(N)	Act Regulating Commerce (1663) . .	551
(O)	Triennial Act (1664)	552
(P)	Conventicle Act (1664)	553
(Q)	Five-Mile Act (1665)	554
(R)	First Test Act (1673)	555
(S)	Act Repealing the Statute for the Burning of Heretics (1678)	556
(T)	Second Test Act (1678)	556
(U)	Habeas Corpus Act (1679)	557

115. ROYAL DECLARATION OF INDULGENCE (1672) . . 559

116. PROCEEDINGS IN PARLIAMENT (1668-81)

(A)	On Skinner v. the East India Company (1668-70)	560
(B)	On the Right of the Lords to Amend Money Bills (1671)	563
(C)	On the Declaration of Indulgence (1673) . .	567
(D)	On Shirley v. Fagg (1675)	569
(E)	On the Right of the Lords to Amend Money Bills (1678)	572
(F)	On the Impeachment of Danby (1679) . .	572
(G)	On the Printing of Votes in the Commons (1681)	576

117. RECORDS OF JUDICIAL CASES (1670-88)

(A)	Bushell's Case (1670)	577
(B)	The King v. Henry Carr (1680) . . .	579
(C)	The King v. the City of London (1682) .	581
(D)	Godden v. Hales (1686)	582
(E)	The Case of the Seven Bishops (1688) . .	583

118. RECORDS CONCERNING COLONIES (1660-81)

(A)	Appointment of Committees of the Council (1660)	586
(B)	Instructions for the Council of Trade (1660) . .	587
(C)	Establishment of a Single Committee on Trade and Plantations (1675)	588
(D)	Charles II: Charter to Connecticut (1662) . .	589
(E)	Charles II: Grant to William Penn (1681) . .	590

119. RECORDS OF LEICESTER (1660-88)

(A)	Petition of Nathaniel Hasselwood for the Freedom of the Borough	592

xxii

CONTENTS

(B) Letter Concerning a New Municipal Charter
    (1664) 592
(C) Disputed Election to the Corporation (1665-66) . 593
(D) Memorandum Concerning Conventicles (1671) . 594
(E) Petition of the Stocking-Makers . . . 594
(F) Letter Concerning Elections to Parliament (1677) 596
(G) Chamberlain's Account (1682-83) . . . 597

SECTION XI
WILLIAM III TO GEORGE II

INTRODUCTORY NOTE 598
120. WILLIAM III: STATUTES
    (A) Bill of Rights (1689) 599
    (B) Mutiny Act (1689) 605
    (C) Coronation Oath Act (1689) 606
    (D) Toleration Act (1689) 607
    (E) Triennial Act (1694) 608
    (F) Trials for Treason Act (1696) 609
    (G) Civil List Act (1698) 610
    (H) Act of Settlement (1701) 610
121. ANNE: STATUTES
    (A) Act of Union with Scotland (1707) . . . 612
    (B) Place Act (1707) 615
122. GEORGE I: STATUTES
    (A) Riot Act (1715) 617
    (B) Septennial Act (1716) 618
    (C) Irish Parliament Act (1719) 618
123. PROCEEDINGS IN PARLIAMENT (1695-1745)
    (A) Commons' Resolutions on the Licensing Bill
        (1695) 619
    (B) Resolutions on the Case of Ashby v. White
        (1704) 621
    (C) Minority Protest in the Lords against the Septennial Act (1716) 623
    (D) Commons' Debate on the Printing of Speeches
        (1738) 624
    (E) Discussion of Cabinet Councils (1738-40) . . 627
    (F) Debate on the Removal of Walpole from Office
        (1741) 629
    (G) Sir William Yonge on Annual Parliaments (1745) 634

xxiii

xxiv CONTENTS

124. RECORDS OF JUDICIAL CASES (1691-1710)
  (A) The Case of John Ashton (1691) 637
  (B) Blankard v. Galdy (1693) 638
  (C) Ashby v. White and Others (1702-03) 639
  (D) The Queen v. Paty and Others (1704) 640
  (E) The Queen v. Tutchin (1704) 640
  (F) Impeachment of Sacheverell (1710) 641

125. RECORDS CONCERNING COLONIES (1692-1718)
  (A) Instructions to the Governor of New York (1692) 646
  (B) Order in Council on Colonial Appeals (1696) . 648
  (C) Order on an Appeal from Connecticut (1698) . 648
  (D) Report on Trade and Plantations (1700) . . . 650
  (E) Council Proceedings on Colonial Trade (1705-18) 654

SECTION XII

GEORGE III AND GEORGE IV

INTRODUCTORY NOTE 657

126. GEORGE III: STATUTES
  (A) Stamp Act (1765) 658
  (B) Declaratory Act (1766) 659
  (C) Townshend's Revenue Act (1767) 660
  (D) Quebec Act (1774) 661
  (E) Colonial Tax Repeal Act (1778) 663
  (F) Burke's Place Act (1782) 664
  (G) Irish Appeals Act (1783) 664
  (H) Canadian Constitution Act (1791) 664
  (I) Fox's Libel Act (1792) 666
  (J) Act Suspending Habeas Corpus in Certain Cases (1794) 667
  (K) Treasonable and Seditious Practices Act (1795) . 668
  (L) Seditious Assemblies Act (1795) 668
  (M) Poor Relief Act (1795) 670
  (N) Act of Union with Ireland (1800) 671
  (O) Cotton Industry Arbitration Act (1800) . . . 673
  (P) Combination Act (1800) 674
  (Q) Factory Act (1802) 675

127. GEORGE IV: STATUTES
  (A) Repeal of the Combination Acts (1825) . . . 676

CONTENTS

(B) Repeal of the Test and Corporation Acts (1828) . . . 677
(C) Roman Catholic Emancipation Act (1829) . . 678
128. PROCEEDINGS IN PARLIAMENT (1763-84)
  (A) Proceedings in the Case of John Wilkes (1763) 679
  (B) Minority Protest in the Lords on the Repeal of the Stamp Act (1766) 681
  (C) Proceedings on the Middlesex Election (1769) . 682
  (D) Commons' Debate on the Reporting of Speeches (1778) 685
  (E) Commons' Debate on North's Government (1779) 687
  (F) Commons' Debate on Dunning's Resolutions (1780) 690
  (G) Pitt's Proposals for Reform of Parliament (1783) 692
  (H) Commons' Debate on the Influence of the Crown (1783) 696
  (I) Debates on the Continuance of Pitt's Ministry (1784) 699
129. RECORDS OF JUDICIAL CASES (1763-1820)
  (A) Habeas Corpus Proceedings in Wilkes' Case (1763) 704
  (B) Entick v. Carrington (1765) . . . 705
  (C) Somersett's Case (1772) . . . 710
  (D) Campbell v. Hall (1774) . . . 711
  (E) The Case of the Dean of St. Asaph (1784) . 713
  (F) Grant v. Gould (1792) . . . 715
  (G) The Case of Wolfe Tone (1798) . . . 716
  (H) Wright v. Fitzgerald (1799) . . . 717
  (I) The King v. Burdett (1820) . . . 718

SECTION XIII

WILLIAM IV AND VICTORIA (TO 1880)

INTRODUCTORY NOTE 721

130. WILLIAM IV: STATUTES
  (A) Reform Act (1832) . . . 723
  (B) Privy Council Appeals Act (1833) . . . 725
  (C) Act Abolishing Slavery (1833) . . . 726
  (D) Factory Act (1833) . . . 726
  (E) Poor Law Amendment Act (1834) . . . 728
  (F) Municipal Corporations Act (1835) . . . 729

xxv

xxvi   CONTENTS

131. VICTORIA: STATUTES (1839-76)
    (A) Constables Act (1839) 733
    (B) Defence Act (1842) 734
    (C) Repeal of the Navigation Acts (1849) 735
    (D) County and Borough Police Act (1856) 735
    (E) Petitions of Right Act (1860) 736
    (F) Colonial Laws Validity Act (1865) 737
    (G) British North America Act (1867) 738
    (H) Representation of the People Act (1867) 744
    (I) Education Act (1870) 747
    (J) Ballot Act (1872) 749
    (K) Judicature Act (1873) 750
    (L) Appellate Jurisdiction Act (1876) 753

132. PROCEEDINGS IN PARLIAMENT (1831-66)
    (A) Debates on the Reform Bill (1831) 755
    (B) Debate on Melbourne's Government (1841) . . . 762
    (C) Disraeli on the Work of the Commons (1848) . . 767
    (D) Debate on the Rebellion Losses Bill of Canada
        (1849) 768
    (E) Lord John Russell on Palmerston's Dismissal
        (1852) 772
    (F) Gladstone on the Advance of the Working Class
        (1866) 775

133. RECORDS CONCERNING CANADA (1839-59)
    (A) The Durham Report (1839) 776
    (B) Letter of Howe to Russell (18 September 1839) . 779
    (C) Dispatches of Russell to Poulett Thomson (1839) 780
    (D) Dispatch of Stanley to Bagot (8 October 1841) . 783
    (E) Dispatch of Metcalfe to Stanley (5 August 1843) 785
    (F) Dispatches of Grey to Harvey (1846-47) 786
    (G) Dispatch of Elgin to Grey (1847) 789
    (H) Letter of Grey to Elgin (22 February 1848) . . . 790
    (I) Dispatch of Elgin to Newcastle (26 March 1853) 790
    (J) The Galt Memorandum (1859) 791

134. RECORDS OF JUDICIAL CASES (1832-76)
    (A) Charge to the Bristol Grand Jury (1832) . . . 792
    (B) Stockdale v. Hansard (1839) 794
    (C) The Case of the Sheriff of Middlesex (1840) . . 797
    (D) Wason v. Walter (1868) 798
    (E) Rustomjee v. the Queen (1876) 801

SECTION XIV

VICTORIA (1880) TO GEORGE VI

INTRODUCTORY NOTE 803

135. VICTORIA: STATUTES (1884-1900)
  (A) Representation of the People Act (1884) . . 805
  (B) Redistribution of Seats Act (1885) . . . 805
  (C) Allotments Act (1887) 806
  (D) Local Government Act (1888) 808
  (E) Workmen's Compensation Act (1897) . . . 810
  (F) Commonwealth of Australia Act (1900) . . 811

136. EDWARD VII: STATUTES
  (A) Trade Disputes Act (1906) 817
  (B) Union of South Africa Act (1909) . . . 817

137. GEORGE V: STATUTES
  (A) Parliament Act (1911) 822
  (B) National Insurance Act (1911) 824
  (C) Defence of the Realm Consolidation Act (1914) . 826
  (D) Representation of the People Act (1918) . . 827
  (E) Re-election of Ministers Act (1919) . . . 829
  (F) Sex-Disqualification Removal Act (1919) . . 830
  (G) Church of England Assembly Act (1919) . . 830
  (H) Emergency Powers Act (1920) 832
  (I) Irish Free State Agreement Act (1922) . . 833
  (J) Trade Disputes and Trade Unions Act (1927) . 835
  (K) Equal Franchise Act (1928) 837
  (L) Local Government Act (1929) 837
  (M) Statute of Westminster (1931) 839

138. PROCEEDINGS IN PARLIAMENT (1909-32)
  (A) Debate on the Budget (1909) 841
  (B) Debate on Reform of the House of Lords (1910) 846
  (C) Resolutions of the House of Lords (1910) . . 850
  (D) Debate in the Commons on Cabinet Responsibility (1932) 851

139. RECORDS OF JUDICIAL CASES (1884-1935)
  (A) Bradlaugh v. Gossett (1884) 857
  (B) Kruse v. Johnson (1898) 861
  (C) Local Government Board v. Arlidge (1915) . . 864

xxvii

xxviii   CONTENTS

    (D) The King v. Halliday (1917) 867
    (E) Attorney General v. De Keyser's Royal Hotel
        (1920) 871
    (F) Moore and Others v. the Attorney General of the
        Irish Free State (1935) 875
140. RECORDS OF THE IMPERIAL CONFERENCE (1926) . . 878
141. HIS MAJESTY'S GOVERNMENT (1936) 883
142. RECORDS OF EDWARD VIII's ABDICATION (1936)
    (A) Speech by Prime Minister Baldwin . . . 885
    (B) Declaration of Abdication Act 890
143. GEORGE VI: CORONATION OATH (1937) . . . 891
SAINTS' DAYS AND OTHER FESTIVALS MENTIONED IN THE
    FOREGOING DOCUMENTS 892
GENERAL BIBLIOGRAPHY 894

PREFACE

This book has been designed for use in any course that touches the growth of English institutions, a subject that almost inevitably demands a certain amount of source work. Before now the student has been provided with many collections of documents covering particular phases of English constitutional history. He has not, however, had one volume to illustrate all of it, combining extracts from the whole magnificent series that stretches back from the most recent acts of parliament to the dooms of the Kentish kings. Herewith is presented such a volume, which has been planned and carried out as a joint enterprise. Although Stephenson is mainly responsible for the portion before 1485, and Markham for what follows, it is hoped that the close collaboration of the editors will be apparent from the result.

In organizing a book of this sort, and one that must be kept to a useful size for an elementary course, the most difficult task is that of selection. Possibly half the available space must be assigned to the great monuments that everybody considers essential. But from all the other accumulated records of thirteen centuries just what shall be taken? Constantly faced with the embarrassing duty of excluding one document in order to include another, we have in general sought to be guided by the experience of the class-room—to govern our choice by the needs of the ordinary student. And above all else we have prized direct information concerning the organs of government. Accordingly, we have preferred official to unofficial compositions, passing over most of the latter in order to keep more of the former. No doubt the absence of many a favourite passage from chronicler or essayist will be noted and regretted. Yet our primary concern is not the history of political opinion; and it is a sheer impossibility, in this brief source book, adequately to represent leading comment on English institutions from the Venerable Bede to Harold Laski. Eventually it may seem desirable to undertake some such project in a supplementary volume.

Except for the limitation just stated, our view of constitutional history has been comparatively broad. We have given attention to local as well as central government and, to show the enlarging

xix

PREFACE

interests of the state, we have from time to time included materials that can be classified under ecclesiastical, legal, economic, social, or colonial history. On the other hand, we have made no effort to give by way of examples any full or continuous account of the church, the common law, trade and industry, the classes of the people, or the separate parts of the empire. Nor have we so treated every well-known feature of the constitution narrowly defined. Any selection of documents such as this must emphasize the origin of institutions; from a series of records covering many centuries, the oldest are chosen because they explain the beginning of the governmental organ that produced them. To continue indefinitely with similar extracts would serve no useful purpose. In each succeeding period stress must be laid on the great new developments, while other matters receive illustration in whatever space happens to be left.

For the sake of convenience in study and teaching, we have divided our book into chronological sections, within each of which the documents have to a certain extent been topically arranged. But no analytic plan has been rigorously applied; the instructor will always prefer to select and recombine material to suit his particular needs. Nor has any systematic interpretation of the documents been attempted. The introduction that stands at the head of each section is intended merely as a brief guide to the principal sources of that period and to the pertinent historical literature. Footnotes have been added to explain or supplement the more difficult texts, to provide cross-references, and occasionally to indicate a special article or other commentary. Such references, as well as the citations placed after the separate documents, are abbreviated. For complete bibliographical descriptions the reader may consult the alphabetical list following p. 894. And immediately preceding it he will find a table of the feast days used for dating events in the earlier documents.

Words in parentheses should be read as part of the original text. Often they are quotations in the language of the original; less frequently, when so designated in a footnote, additions from a parallel source. Square brackets, on the contrary, always indicate words supplied for one reason or another by the editors. Omitted passages, without regard to length, are shown by three points (...). Sums in English money are printed in the usual way: with £, s., and d. for pounds, shillings, and pence. To these their council the wisdom and scholarship of others concerned with teaching the history of the English constitution.

The result is, I believe, as near a common denominator of needs to be served as is possible in any selection made from such a wealth of material. The editors have been at special pains to refer to supplementary material and have contributed fresh translations of documents hitherto unavailable or available only in inaccurate renderings.

GUY STANTON FORD.

EDITOR'S FOREWORD

IT MIGHT be thought that this volume enters a field well occupied by many preceding collections of documents. That is true only in the sense that certain periods and phases have had their special collections. Hitherto no selection of documents over the whole range of English constitutional history has been attempted. It is therefore a service to teaching and scholarship to produce a volume that tells in documents the story of mankind's oldest and greatest and most successful experiment in self-government. The most vagrant-minded student into whose hands this volume may fall cannot wholly lose the trail that winds through the centuries from Ine and Canute to the halls of Westminster and the far-flung forums of the British Commonwealth of Nations. The dullest teacher cannot keep living documents like these from gripping the discerning student with a new faith in the mighty force of the coalescing wills of common men. It is a long story from the day when kings initiated self-government by royal command, to paraphrase Professor White, to the day when an abdicating king, speaking across the seven seas over the radio, summed up the intervening centuries: "At long last I am able to say a few words of my own. . . . Until now it has not been constitutionally possible for me to speak."

The story may be long, but I envy the student who is putting it together for himself for the first time. Whether he is to be lawyer, legislator or plain citizen, he will be emboldened to believe that democracy has done and still can do great things as the agency of the common welfare.

The scholars who have edited this collection of basic documents in English constitutional history might well quote the words of Alfred the Great when he compiled the laws of his predecessors: "I have not ventured to place in writing much of my own, being uncertain what might please those who came after us. So I have here collected the dooms that seemed to me most just." Where Alfred adds that he did what he did with the advice of his witan they might say that in selection and annotation they have fortified their own judgment and teaching experience by summoning to in the same way make plain our obligation to the Chetham Society, the Pipe Roll Society, the Royal Historical Society (successor to the Camden Society), the Selden Society, the Society of Antiquaries of Newcastle-upon-Tyne, the Staffordshire Record Society, the Incorporated Council of Law Reporting for England and Wales, the Corporation of the Borough of Nottingham, and the Worcestershire County Council—all of which have been good enough to place at our disposal their valuable publications. Through the courtesy of Messrs. J. E. Neale and G. O. Sayles and the editor of the English Historical Review, we have been able to make use of two documents that originally appeared in that journal. And the following publishers have kindly allowed us to include in our collection the various materials that are here briefly indicated: the Halifax Chronicle, no. 133B; John Murray, no. 133G,I; Longmans Green & Company, no. 87A; Cassell & Company (and Mr. Arthur Bryant), no. 113; the Cambridge University Press, nos. 51D, 59, 72C, 118B, 119; the Manchester University Press, nos. 52C, 57, 61I (in part); and the Oxford University Press, nos. 27F, 28C, 39A-B, 53A, 72D, 83I, 84, 89H, 133D,H.

Lastly, we wish to acknowledge our great indebtedness to those who have read and criticized all or parts of this book in manuscript: especially Dean Guy Stanton Ford, general editor of the series; Professors A. B. White, D. H. Willson, and Faith Thompson, also of the University of Minnesota; Dr. E. F. Bradford of Cornell University; Professors C. H. McIlwain and R. B. Merriman of Harvard University; Professor Paul Knaplund of the University of Wisconsin; and Professor R. L. Schuyler of Columbia University. Mr. H. H. King, Faculty Research Assistant in the Cornell University Library, has performed the invaluable service of verifying our documents from the printed originals. And we have received help in many ways from our departmental assistants, past and present: Messrs. Walter Balderston, Arthur B. Ferguson, Goldwin A. Smith, and Francis D. Wormuth. To these and the other friends whom we have consulted—so many that we shall not attempt to list them all by name—we extend our warmest thanks. Without their practical suggestions our book would have lost much, and without their constant goodwill and encouragement we ourselves should have lost infinitely more.

CARL STEPHENSON
F. G. MARCHAM

abbreviations has been added *m.* for marks. And to avoid the confusion that otherwise would be inevitable, spelling has been made to conform to British rather than purely American usage.

Throughout the latter portion of the book documents are given in their original language, except that, to facilitate study, the spelling, punctuation, capital letters, and paragraphs have been brought into greater harmony with modern practice. The earlier documents are nearly all translated from Anglo-Saxon, Latin, or Old French, and in every case the translation is a new one based directly on the printed record. Even the fifteenth-century writings in English have as a rule been treated in the same way, for otherwise they would be virtually unintelligible to the average student. Only the two royal speeches quoted in no. 66A and the excerpts under no. 72C have been preserved without essential change.

Translation is on the whole fairly literal, and in all passages of real importance an effort has been made to reproduce the meaning of the original with scrupulous care. But since this book is not intended for experts, liberties of a minor sort have often been taken to improve the sense of a text. When merely a verbal change is involved, singulars have sometimes been read as plurals, or vice versa. In many enumerations "and" or its substitutes have been inserted or omitted at will. "The latter," "the former," or occasionally a name in brackets has been put in place of an ambiguous pronoun. And the rhetorical preambles to various writs and charters have been given a decidedly free rendering. Logical uniformity in the translation of proper names is impossible. Christian names have regularly been changed to familiar forms. When the surname is essentially French, it has been given with "de"; when essentially English, with "of"—so Geoffrey de Mandeville and William of London. But inconsistencies are hard to avoid, and many names not easily identified have been left as they stand in the Latin. A little carelessness or inaccuracy in such matters may be pardoned because, in the present connection, it hardly affects the value of the documents.

For permission to incorporate in this volume numerous extracts from statutes, parliamentary proceedings, and other records published by the British government, we wish to express our gratitude to the Controller of H. M. Stationery Office. The precise derivation of such extracts is indicated by the references below them in the text, supplemented by the general bibliography. References given

Sources of
English Constitutional History

SECTION I

THE ANGLO-SAXON PERIOD

OUR most valuable source for early English institutions is the matchless series of Anglo-Saxon dooms, which begin with the enactments of the first Christian king of Kent and end with those of Canute. Spanning close upon five centuries, they cannot be expected to reflect a uniform pattern either of state or of society. Furthermore, it must be remembered that in the main they are fragments of customary law rather than a code. Their tantalizing obscurity is due to the fact that the great body of familiar usages remained unwritten. So, although the present selection is at best a set of meagre excerpts, it is in no more disconnected than the entire compilation. The student may be sure that he has before him all very significant references to the organs of government, especially those statements which are first of their kind. And he will find in addition a number of passages chosen to illustrate the working of the customary law and the status within it of the various social classes.

Compared with the dooms, the charters of the Anglo-Saxon period are of minor importance in the study of English constitutional history. From the great mass of such instruments that have come down to us, only seven are translated in the following pages. They may be regarded as typical examples, showing primarily how legal documents were drafted, how the formal decisions of courts were rendered, and how, through the alienation of public rights, the kings created immunities for their favoured subjects. The definitive edition of the dooms is F. Liebermann's *Gesetze der Angelsachsen*, which is accompanied by a German translation and a wealth of learned comment. Text and English translation of nearly all the following excerpts are available, with useful notes, in F. L. Attenborough's *Laws of the Earliest English Kings* and A. J. Robertson's *Laws of the Kings of England from Edmund to Henry I*. There is, unfortunately, no well-edited general collection of Anglo-Saxon charters. Neither Kemble's *Codex Diplomaticus Aevi Saxonici* nor Birch's *Cartularium Saxonicum*

1

2   THE ANGLO-SAXON PERIOD

is at all adequate to meet the needs of modern scholars. The seven charters here given are all from Thorpe's *Diplomatarium Anglicum Aevi Saxonici*—a convenient volume of documents taken from Kemble's edition and provided with translations from the Anglo-Saxon, free use of which has here been made. For a much wider selection of such material, the student is referred to Miss Robertson's *Anglo-Saxon Charters*.[1]

As may be realized by glancing through the first few of the *Supplementary Studies* by Petit-Dutaillis,[2] the work of Stubbs on the earlier centuries of English constitutional history has been largely superseded; but as yet no single essay has been written to take its place. For the advanced student an indispensable guide to all phases of Anglo-Saxon institutions is provided by Liebermann's exhaustive notes and *Sachglossar* (*Gesetze*, vols. I-II). And any one who hopes to understand the dooms and other pre-Conquest sources should read F. W. Maitland's *Domesday Book and Beyond* and H. M. Chadwick's *Studies on Anglo-Saxon Institutions*. The latter is especially valuable for specific comment on courts, officials, coinage, and social classes. Much illuminating criticism of these same matters will also be found in the chapters by W. J. Corbett in the *Cambridge Medieval History*, vols. II and III. On the controversial subject of the borough two recent books may be consulted: J. Tait, *The Medieval English Borough*, and C. Stephenson, *Borough and Town*. The standard accounts of Anglo-Saxon law are those in Pollock and Maitland, *History of English Law*, I, ch. ii, and W. A. Holdsworth, *History of English Law*, II, bk. i; the earlier works are now antiquated. Other references on special topics are from time to time given in the footnotes.

[1] To be published by the Cambridge University Press.
[2] The first two volumes of these *Studies and Notes Supplementary to Stubbs' Constitutional History* (1908, 1914) are by Petit-Dutaillis; the third (1929) by G. Lefebvre. Since all three are now published as one volume, the work will henceforth be referred to as Petit-Dutaillis and Lefebvre.

1. DOOMS OF AETHELBERHT (601-04)

These are the dooms that King Aethelberht established in the days of Augustine.[1]

[1] The famous Roman missionary and archbishop of Canterbury, who secured the conversion of Aethelberht, king of Kent, and presumably inspired him to have the following dooms written down.

1. DOOMS OF AETHELBERHT

1. [One who steals] the property[2] of God and the church [shall pay] twelvefold compensation:[3] the property of a bishop, elevenfold; the property of a priest, ninefold; the property of a deacon, sixfold; the property of a [lesser] clergyman, threefold. [He who breaks] the peace (*frip*) of the church [shall pay] double compensation; the peace of a public assembly (*maethl*), double compensation.

2. If the king summons his people[4] to him, and if any one there does them wrong, he shall pay double compensation [to the injured person] and 50s. to the king.

3. If the king is drinking in a man's house, and if any one commits any kind of misdeed there, he shall pay double compensation [to the householder].

4. If a freeman steals from the king, he shall pay ninefold compensation [to the king].

5. If a man slays another in a villa[5] of the king, he shall pay 50s. compensation.

6. The King's *mundbyrd*[6] is 50s.

9. If a freeman steals from a freeman, he shall pay threefold compensation [to the latter]; and the king shall have the fine (*wite*) and all the goods [of the thief].

13. If a man slays another in a villa of a nobleman (*eorl*), he shall pay 12s. compensation [to the nobleman].

15. The *mundbyrd* of a *ceorl*[7] is 6s.

17. If a man leads the way in breaking into some one's villa, he shall pay 6s. compensation; the one who next breaks in 3s.; and every one after that 1s.

21. If a man slays another, he shall pay as compensation [to the kindred] the ordinary wergeld (*leodgeld*) of 100s.

24. If any one binds a freeman, he shall pay [him] 20s. compensation.

27. If a freeman commits hedge-breaking,[8] he shall pay 6s. compensation.

---

[2] *Feoh*, which originally meant cattle, but eventually came to be used for movable property in general.

[3] Such compensation as is prescribed in these dooms was normally paid to the injured person or his kindred, in contrast to the fine, *wite*, paid to the king or his agent. The Kentish shilling, like the gold *solidus* of the Merovingians, was reckoned at twenty times the worth of a silver penny, *denarius* or *sceatt*.

[4] *Leode*, a quite general word, which could refer to any of the king's subjects.

[5] *Tun*, from which is derived our word town, was the ordinary term for an agricultural village during the later Anglo-Saxon period. Here, as in articles 13 and 17 below, it evidently refers to a house or an estate.

[6] Literally, right of protection; hence the payment for violating it.

[7] The ordinary freeman, often contrasted with the *eorl*, or nobleman.

[8] That is to say, forcibly enters a man's property surrounded by a hedge. Cf. Alfred, 40 (below, p. 11), and the later *hamsocn* (below, p. 22, n. 1).

4   THE ANGLO-SAXON PERIOD

28. If the man takes any property from inside, he shall pay three-fold compensation . . .[9]

(Anglo-Saxon) Liebermann, *Gesetze*, I, 3 f.

[9] Here follows in the doom an elaborate schedule of compensations for minor injuries: e.g., an ear, 12s.; an eye, 50s.; the chin-bone, 20s.; a front tooth, 6s.; a thumb, 20s.; a forefinger, 9s.; a fingernail, 1s.; a big toe, 10s.

2. DOOMS OF HLOTHAERE AND EADRIC (685-86)

1. If some one's servant[1] slays a man of noble birth, one whose wergeld is 300s., his master shall give up the slayer [to the kindred] and also pay [them] the value of three [ordinary] men.[2]

2. If the slayer escapes, he shall then add the value of a fourth man and shall clear himself with good oath-helpers, [proving] that he was unable to secure the slayer.

3. If some one's servant slays a freeman, one whose wergeld is 100s., his master shall give up the slayer and pay also the value of a second man. . . .

5. If a freeman steals a man, and he returns to accuse [the former], he shall make a personal accusation and the accused man shall then clear himself if he can: every [such] man shall have a number of free-men as oath-helpers, with [at least] one of them from the same vill to which he himself belongs. If he cannot thus clear himself, then he shall pay compensation to the best of his ability.

7. If [presumably] one man steals property from another, and if the owner afterwards seizes it, the accused shall vouch to warranty at the king's hall,[3] presenting, if he can, the man who sold it to him. If he cannot do so, he shall give it up and the owner shall have [legal title].

8. If a man accuses another of a misdeed, and if he meets that [accused] man in an assembly (*medle*) or in a court (*þinge*), the [accused] man must regularly furnish the other with a surety[4] and submit to whatever justice the Kentish doomsmen[5] prescribe. . . .

[1] *Esne*, who was evidently unfree, although the ordinary word for slave in these dooms is *þeuw*. Cf. Wihtraed, 22 (below, p. 6).
[2] Because the slain man's wergeld was thrice that of an ordinary man. Cf. art. 3, below.
[3] *Sele;* cf. art. 16, below. Such a royal hall was apparently not a private residence, but rather an administrative centre in charge of a reeve, as is indicated at London. On the procedure known to the Anglo-Saxons as *team,* and later styled vouching to warranty, see Holdsworth, *History of English Law,* II, 100 f. See also the oaths under no. 14, below.
[4] The surety (*borh*) was a person who, if the accused man escaped, would be legally responsible for his obligations.
[5] *A dema,* whence is derived "deemster," and "dempster," was any one who rendered dooms, legal decisions of any kind. A royal official or judge might be called a *dema,* but in the courts of England and the continent at this time it was the suitors, rather than the presiding magistrate, who declared the law. See Pollock and Maitland, I, 139.

3. DOOMS OF WIHTRAED 5

11. If a man in some one else's house calls another a perjurer, or accosts him insultingly with scandalous words, he shall pay 1s. to the householder, 6s. to the man whom he insulted, and 12s. to the king.

12. If, where men are drinking, one takes the tankard from another without any fault [on the part of the latter], by ancient custom he shall pay 1s. to the householder, 6s. to the man whose tankard he took, and 12s. to the king.

13. If, where men are drinking, one draws his weapon but inflicts no injury with it, he shall pay 1s. to the householder and 12s. to the king.

14. If the house is bloodied, he shall pay the *mundbyrd*⁶ of the householder, and to the king [a fine of] 50s.

15. If any one entertains, as a guest in his own house, a trader or some other man from beyond the border, keeping him for three nights and supplying him with food, and if he then does wrong to some one, the man [of the house] shall bring him to justice or satisfy justice in his place.

16. If a Kentishman buys property in London-wick,⁷ he must have as witnesses two or three reliable freemen or the king's wick-reeve. Then, should any one take it away from the man in Kent, he shall vouch to warranty at the king's hall (*sele*) in [London-]wick the man who sold it to him, if the man is known to him and can be produced for warranty. If he cannot do that, he shall swear on the altar, together with one of his witnesses or with the king's reeve, that he bought the property honestly and by public purchase in [London-]wick, and its value shall then be returned to him. If, however, he cannot justify himself by such lawful process, he must surrender it and the [rightful] owner shall have [legal title].

(Anglo-Saxon) *Ibid.*, I, 9 f.

---
⁶ See above, p. 3, n. 6.
⁷ *Wic* is a common equivalent of *tun*, to designate a settlement, big or little.

3. DOOMS OF WIHTRAED (695-96)

2. The *mundbyrd*¹ of the church shall be, like that of the king, 50s. . . .

16. The word of a bishop or of the king shall be incontestible [even] without an oath.

17. The head of a monastery shall clear himself by the same form as a priest.

18. A priest shall clear himself by his own [unsupported] affirmation: [dressed] in his sacred garments, he shall declare before the altar, *Veritatem dico in Christo; non mentior.*² In the same way shall a deacon clear himself.

19. A [lesser] clergyman shall clear himself with three [oath-

---
¹ See above, p. 3, n. 6.
² Before Christ I speak the truth; I do not lie.

helpers[3] of his own rank. But he alone shall have his hand on the altar; the others shall merely stand by to support the oath.
20. A stranger (*gest*) shall clear himself by his own [unsupported] oath at the altar.[4] In the same way shall a king's thegn clear himself.
21. An ordinary freeman (*ceorlisce man*) shall clear himself at the altar with three oath-helpers of his own rank. . . .
22. If any one accuses a bishop's or a king's servant (*esne*), the latter shall clear himself by the hand of the reeve,[5] so that the reeve shall either clear him or deliver him over [to the complainant] to be beaten. . . .
25. If any one slays a man in the act of theft, let him[6] lie without wergeld.
26. If any one catches a freeman in the act of theft, the king shall determine one of three [penalties]: that he be slain, that he be sold beyond the sea, or that he redeem his life through [payment of] his wergeld. The one who catches and holds him shall have half of what he is worth; or, if he should be slain, he [who captured him] shall be paid 70s.
27. If a slave (*þeuw*) steals and it is proposed to redeem him, 70s. [shall be paid] if the king is willing [to spare him.] . . .
28. If a man coming from afar, or a stranger, leaves the highway and then neither calls out nor blows a horn, he shall be considered a thief, to be slain or to be redeemed [by paying his wergeld].

(Anglo-Saxon *Ibid.*, I, 12 f.

[3] Literally "as a foursome"—counting himself one of the four.
[4] The dooms normally regard a stranger as a suspicious person (cf. art. 28, below). In this instance, however, a man of honourable rank, a guest rather than a vagabond, seems to be thought of, for he is treated like a king's thegn. The latter title becomes increasingly common in the dooms, designating in particular a noble retainer.
[5] That is to say, the reeve of the estate to which the servant is attached may take an oath to clear him.
[6] The slain thief, for whose death the kindred had no right to compensation.

4. DOOMS OF INE (688-95)

I, Ine, by the grace of God king of the West Saxons, with the advice and instruction of Cenred, my father, of Hedde, my bishop, and of Eorcenwold, my bishop, together with all my aldermen,[1] the most distinguished *witan*[2] among my people, and also a great assembly of God's servants, have taken counsel concerning the welfare of our

[1] Royal officials of the highest rank, generally in charge of considerable districts, where they held courts, commanded troops, and performed other duties in the king's name.
[2] Literally "wise men"—the king's chief advisers, both lay and clerical. To what extent they constituted a formal council, with definite powers and privileges, has been a matter of controversy. See Chadwick, *Studies*, ch. ix, and F. Liebermann, *The National Assembly in the Anglo-Saxon Period*; cf. the formulae in the charters under no. 15. below.

4. DOOMS OF INE

souls and the state of our realm, in order that just laws and just royal dooms should be established and assured to all our people, and so that no alderman or subject of ours should henceforth pervert these our dooms. . . .

6. If any one fights in the king's house, he shall forfeit all his inheritance, and it shall be in the king's judgment whether or not he shall lose his life. If any one fights in a monastery, he shall pay 120s. compensation [to the monastery]. If any one fights in the house of an alderman, or of some other distinguished statesman (*witan*), he shall pay 60s. compensation [to the householder] and another 60s. as a fine [to the king]. If, however, he fights in the house of a rent-payer (*gafolgeldan*)[3] or peasant (*gebures*), he shall pay 30s.[4] as a fine and 6s. to the peasant. . . .

8. If any one demands justice before any shireman (*scirman*),[5] or any other judge, and cannot obtain it through default of a pledge [from the accused], he shall pay 30s. compensation [to the plaintiff] and within seven nights do him proper justice.

9. If any one wreaks vengeance [on his enemy] before demanding justice [in court], he shall give back anything he has seized together with as much again [to the injured party], and shall pay 30s. compensation [to the king]. . . .

12. If a thief is captured [in the act of thieving], let him suffer death or redeem his life through payment of his wergeld.

13. . . . By "thieves" (*þeofas*) we mean men up to the number seven; by "a band" (*hloð*) from seven to thirty-five; by "an army," (*here*) above thirty-five.

14. One accused of belonging to [such] a band shall clear himself through [an oath worth] 120 hides[6] or pay an equal amount[7] as compensation.

15. One accused of plundering with [such] an army shall redeem

---

[3] The ordinary meaning of *gafol* was rent, and it was often paid in kind (see no. 15A, below). The text seems to imply that the *gafolgelda* was a kind of *gebur*—the "boor" of our modern speech.

[4] This was apparently the original amount, although most manuscripts have 120. The West Saxon shilling was a weight of silver, at this time reckoned as 1/48 of a pound, but from the eleventh century on as 1/20 of a pound. At all times the pound was supposed to contain 240 silver pence (*denarii*).

[5] In the early dooms *scir* means any administrative district. The alderman was in charge of a large shire—whether or not it corresponded to one of the later counties is doubtful.

[6] Cf. art. 19, below, and Alfred, 39 (below, p. 11). According to this equation, the oaths of a *ceorl*, a six-hundred man, and a twelve-hundred man were computed respectively as 10, 30, and 60 hides. By this means any group of freemen could be quickly assessed at what may be called their swearing-worth. Note also that many dooms required the number of oath-helpers, or the total value of their oaths, to vary in proportion to the gravity of the offence; see especially Edward the Elder, I, 1 (below, p. 12). The determination of such matters was normally left to the doomsmen in the court.

[7] I.e., 120s.

8 THE ANGLO-SAXON PERIOD

his life through [payment of] his wergeld or shall clear himself by [an oath equivalent to] his wergeld.

19. A king's *geneat*,⁸ if his wergeld is 1200s., may swear for 60 hides if he is a regular communicant [at church].

20. If a man from afar, or a stranger, goes through the woods off the highway and neither calls out nor blows a horn, he may be considered a thief, to be slain or to be redeemed [by paying his wergeld].⁹

21. If then any one lays claim to the wergeld of the slain man, the slayer may prove [by an unsupported oath] that he slew the man as a thief; neither the geld-associates¹⁰ nor the lord¹¹ [of the slain man] may avail themselves of an oath [to set aside such proof]....

22. Should your *geneat* steal and then escape you, you may claim the *angyld*¹² from his surety, if you have one for him. If not, you must pay the *angyld*, but he shall not on that account be held guiltless.

23. [The wergeld of] a Welsh rent-payer¹³ [is] 120s.; of his son 100. A Welsh slave [is worth] 60, or sometimes 50. A Welshman's skin [is worth] 12.¹⁴ ...

25. If a trader does business among the people throughout the countryside, he must do so before witnesses. If stolen property is found in the possession of a trader, and if he has not bought it before good witnesses, he must pay a fine of 36s. or clear himself through [an oath equivalent to] the fine, swearing that he was neither the thief nor an accomplice....

32. If a Welshman possesses a hide of land, his wergeld is 120s.; if only half a hide, 80s.; if no land at all, 60s.

33. A Welsh horseman who rides in the king's service has a wergeld of 200s....

36. If some one captures a thief or is given a captured thief [to

⁸ The *geneat* might enjoy relatively high or low status, but was always a man of honourable rank. As described in the later sources, his chief duty was that of riding on errands; cf. no. 15c.
⁹ A re-enactment of Wihtraed, 28 (above, p. 6).
¹⁰ The meaning, obviously, is not "gild-brethren," as was assumed by older writers, but those persons who might have to pay compensation for a man's acts and so would have a claim on any wergeld that might be paid when he was slain. See Gross, *Gild Merchant*, I, 177.
¹¹ *Hlaford*, literally the "bread-keeper," while the lady is the "breadkneader." The term was a vague one that could be used for any person of superior authority: God, the king, a husband, a great noble, one from whom land was held, one having rights of jurisdiction over another, or one to whom a man commended himself (cf. no. 14A). Just what sort of lord may be meant in a particular doom is often hard to determine.
¹² Literally "single payment"—the mere value of the stolen property. On the surety see above, p. 4, n. 4.
¹³ *Gafolgelda*; see above, p. 7, n. 3.
¹⁴ That is to say, he could buy off a beating with this sum. Cf. Alfred, 35 (below, p. 11), where flogging a Saxon *ceorl* involves the payment of 20s. compensation.

4. DOOMS OF INE 9

guard], and then lets the thief go or conceals the theft, he shall pay the thief's wergeld as compensation. If he is an alderman, he shall lose his shire, unless the king will pardon him.

37. If a *ceorl* has often been accused of theft, and is finally proved guilty, either through the cauldron[15] or through being caught in the act, he shall have his hand or his foot cut off.

38. If a *ceorl* and his wife have a child, and the *ceorl* dies, the mother shall keep her child and bring it up. She shall be given 6s. [a year] for its care—a cow in summer and an ox in winter.[16] The relatives shall keep the homestead until the child has grown up.

39. If any one leaves his lord without permission or steals away into another shire[17], and if he is then discovered, he must go back to where he was before and pay his lord 60s.

40. The landed property (*worðig*) of a *ceorl* shall be fenced both winter and summer. If it is not, and if his neighbour's cattle come through an opening that he has left, he shall have no claim to such cattle; he must drive them out and suffer the damage. . . .

42. If free peasants (*ceorlas*) have the task of fencing a common meadow or other land that is divided into strips (*gedálland*),[18] and if some have built their portions of the fence while others have not, and if their common acres or grasslands are eaten [by straying animals], then those responsible for the opening must go and pay compensation to the others, who have done their share of the fencing, for any damage that may have been suffered. . . .

45. [Compensation for] *burhbryce*[19] of the king, or of a bishop anywhere in his diocese, is 120s.; of an alderman 80s.; of a king's thegn 60s.; of a landed nobleman (*gesíðcundes monnes*)[20] 35s.; and according to these values [accusations of such offences] are to be cleared by oath.

50. If a nobleman comes to an agreement with the king or with the king's alderman concerning the misdeeds of his dependants, or with his lord concerning slave or free, he shall have no share of such fines as they may pay through his own failure to restrain them from evil-doing at home.[21]

51. If a nobleman holding land neglects army service (*ferd*), he

---

[15] I.e., the ordeal of hot water; cf. no. 8b, below.

[16] It is not clear from the text whether the two animals were paid as the equivalent of the money or in addition to it. In Alfred, 16, a calf is valued at a shilling; a cow and an ox might well be worth 6s.

[17] See above, p. 7, n. 5; cf. Alfred, 37 (below, p. 11).

[18] The reference is to the division of arable into strips under the open-field system. It is noteworthy that in the present enactment the holder of the strip is styled a *ceorl*, the designation of the ordinary freeman.

[19] In these early dooms the *burh* is the fortified dwelling or estate of an important man; for the later *burh*, see below, p. 14, n. 7.

[20] This term is now substituted for the *eorl* of the Kentish dooms; see Chadwick, *Studies*, chs. iii, x.

[21] The doom seems to refer to some such arrangement as was later called *sac* and *soc*; see below, p. 30, n. 23.

shall pay 120s. and forfeit his land; one who holds no land shall pay 60s.; a *ceorl* shall pay 30s. as fine for neglect of service (*fierdwite*). (Anglo-Saxon) *Ibid.*, I, 88 f.

5. DOOMS OF ALFRED (871-901)

I, then, King Alfred, have collected these [dooms] and ordered [them] to be written down—[that is to say,] many of those which our predecessors observed and which were also pleasing to me. And those which were not pleasing to me, by the advice of my *witan*, I have rejected, ordering them to be observed only as amended. I have not ventured to put in writing much of my own, being uncertain what might please those who shall come after us. So I have here collected the dooms that seemed to me the most just, whether they were from the time of Ine, my kinsman, from that of Offa, king of the Mercians,[1] or from that of Aethelberht, the first of the English to receive baptism; the rest I have discarded. I, then, Alfred, king of the West Saxons, have shown these [dooms] to all my *witan*, who have declared it is the will of all that they be observed. . . .

4. If any one plots against the king's life, either by himself or by harbouring outlaws or their men, he shall forfeit his life and all that he has.[2] If he wishes to clear himself, he must do so through [an oath equal to] the king's wergeld. So likewise we command with regard to all ranks of men, *eorl* or *ceorl*: he who plots against the life of his lord shall forfeit his life and all that he has, or else clear himself through [an oath equal to] his lord's wergeld. . . .

7. If any one fights or draws his weapon in the king's hall (*heall*) and is then caught, at the king's judgment he may be put to death or allowed his life in case the king is willing to forgive him. . . .

15. If any one fights or draws his weapon in the presence of an archbishop, he shall pay 150s. compensation; if this happens in the presence of some other bishop or in that of an alderman, he shall pay 100s. compensation. . . .

22. If any one at the popular court (*folces gemote*) brings an accusation [for theft] before the king's reeve and wishes to withdraw it, let him make his complaint against the right person if he can; if he cannot, he shall lose his *angylde*[3] and also pay a fine. . . .

34. It is further ordained with regard to traders that they shall bring before the king's reeve at the popular court all the men whom they are taking with them, declaring how many there are. And they should take with them such men as [when necessary] they can later bring to justice in the popular court. And in case they need more men

---

[1] The dooms of Offa have not come down to us.
[2] This crime may be called treason, but it should be noted that no idea of *lèse majesté* appears in the doom. As yet the king is treated like any other lord, and he has a wergeld like any other freeman.
[3] See above, p. 8, n. 12.

5. DOOMS OF ALFRED

with them on their journey, as often as such need arises, a similar declaration must be made to the king's reeve in the popular court.

35. One who binds an innocent *ceorl* shall pay [him] 10s. compensation. One who flogs him shall pay [him] 20s. One who puts him under duress[4] shall pay [him] 30s. One who, as a shameful insult, cuts his hair shall pay [him] 10s. One who shears him like a priest, but without binding him, shall pay [him] 30s. One who cuts off his beard shall pay [him] 20s. One who binds him and then shears him like a priest shall pay [him] 60s. . . .

36. If any one wishes to go from one settlement[5] into another to seek a lord, he must first have as witness the alderman in whose shire he was at first a follower. If he does so without such witness, the lord who takes him as a man shall pay a fine of 120s., dividing his payment so that the king will get half in that in the shire where the man was at first a follower and half in that to which he comes. . . .

38. If any one fights at a court before the king's alderman, he shall pay whatever wergeld and fine (*wer ond wite*) may be due, but before that [he must pay] 120s. fine to the alderman. If he disturbs the court by [merely] drawing a weapon, [he shall pay] a fine of 120s. to the alderman. If anything of the sort occurs before a subordinate of the king's alderman, or before a priest of the king, 30s. fine shall be paid.

39. If any one fights in the house of a *ceorl*, he shall pay the *ceorl* 6s. compensation. If he draws his weapon but does not fight, the compensation shall be half as much. If either of these offences is committed in the house of a six-hundred man,[6] the compensation shall be three times that paid to a *ceorl*; if in the house of a twelve-hundred man, the compensation shall be twice that of the six-hundred man.

40. [Compensation for] *burhbryce*[7] of the king is 120s.; of an archbishop 90s.; of any other bishop or of an alderman 60s.; of a twelve-hundred man 30s.; of a six-hundred man 15s. [Compensation for] breaking through the hedge of a *ceorl* [is] 5s. If any of these offences occurs while the army is in the field or during the fast of Lent, the penalty shall be doubled. . . .

41. We now ordain that any one who has bookland[8] left him by his kinsmen is not to give it outside his kindred if there is written or oral evidence (*gewrit oððe gewitnes*) that to do so was forbidden by the man who originally acquired it or by those who gave it to him. And this should be proved in the presence of the kindred, and with the witness of the king or of the bishop, by any one [wishing to annul such an alienation].

[4] *On hengenne*—e.g., locks him up or fastens him in stocks.
[5] Cf. Ine, 39 (above, p. 9).
[6] One whose wergeld is 600s.
[7] Cf. Aethelberht, 27, and Ine, 45 (above, pp. 3, 9).
[8] Land held by book, that is to say, by charter; see the examples under no. 15, below.

42. We also command that any one knowing his enemy to be at home shall not fight him before demanding justice of him [in court]. If [the accuser] has strength to surround and besiege his enemy inside [the latter's house], let him be held there seven nights and not attacked so long as he will remain inside. Then, after seven nights, if the [besieged] enemy will surrender and give up his weapons, let him be kept unharmed for thirty nights while news of him is sent to his kinsmen and friends. . . . If, however, [the accuser] lacks the strength to besiege his enemy, he shall ride to the alderman and ask him for aid; if the latter refuses him aid, he shall ride to the king before beginning a fight. . . . We declare furthermore that one may fight for his lord without incurring blood-feud,[9] if the lord has been attacked. So also the lord may fight for his man. In the same way one may fight for his blood-relative, should the latter be unjustly attacked, except against his own lord—that we do not permit. . . .[10] (Anglo-Saxon) *Ibid*. I, 46 f.

[9] The lawful vengeance of the kindred.

[10] Here follows in the text a detailed schedule of compensations for physical injuries: e.g., an ear, 30s.; an eye, the tongue, a hand, or a foot, 66s. 3⅓d.; the nose, 60s.; a front tooth, 8s.; a molar, 4s.; an eye-tooth, 15s.; a thumb, 30s.; a thumbnail, 5s.; a first finger, 15s.; its nail, 3s.; a little finger 9s.; its nail, 1s.; a big toe, 20s.; a little toe, 5s.

5. DOOMS OF EDWARD THE ELDER (901-24)

1. King Edward's commands to all his reeves: that you deem such right dooms as you know to be most right and as stand in the doombook.[1] Nor for any cause shall you fail to declare the customary law; and [you shall see to it] that a day is set for every cause, when that which you decide concerning it shall be carried out.

1. And I will that every man shall have his warrantor;[2] and that no one shall trade outside a port,[3] but shall have the witness of the portreeve or of other trustworthy men whose word can be relied on. And if any one trades outside a port, he shall be liable for the king's *oferhyrnesse*.[4] . . . A man who wishes to prove lawful title shall bring forward trustworthy witnesses to it, or he shall, if he can, provide an undetermined[5] oath such as shall satisfy the complainant. If, however, he cannot do this, he shall be assigned six men from the

[1] Presumably, as Liebermann suggests, Alfred's collection.

[2] *Getéaman*; see above, p. 4, n. 3.

[3] *Ceapige butan porte*. This is the first appearance in the dooms of the word *port*. Subsequently it is often used as the equivalent of *burh*, and the reeve of a borough was always styled portreeve; see below, p. 14, n. 7. A review of the literature in this connection will be found in C. Stephenson, *Borough and Town*, pp. 65 f.; cf. Tait, *The Medieval English Borough*, pp. 5 f.

[4] A special fine of 120s. for violation of a royal command.

[5] *Ungecorenne*—the term used when the defendant chose his own oath-helpers, as distinguished from the procedure required below.

7. DOOMS OF AETHELSTAN

same *gebuhrscipe*[6] in which he has his home. From these six he shall name [as oath-helper] one for each cow, or the equivalent in lesser beasts; and the number [of oath-helpers] shall be increased, as they are needed, in proportion to the property [in dispute]. . . .

3. Concerning perjurers we further declare that, if their guilt has been proved, whether oaths have failed for them or they have been oversworn [by better oaths], they shall no longer be oath-worthy, but must rely upon the ordeal [for clearing themselves of charges].

II. King Edward admonished his *witan*, when they were at Exeter, that all should consider how the peace of their country could be better kept than it had been; for it seemed to him that what he had previously ordained had not been enforced as it should have been.

1. . . . No man shall refuse justice to another. If he does so, let him pay compensation as has been earlier provided: the first time 30*s.*, the second time the same amount, the third time 120*s.* to the king.

2. And if it is not exacted by the reeve lawfully, with the witness of such men as have been assigned to him for that purpose,[7] he shall pay 120*s.* as my *oferhyrnesse*. . . .

4. It is also my will that every one shall always have on his land men ready to guide those who wish to track their own [cattle]; and that such guides shall in no way obstruct the search for the sake of bribes; nor shall they anywhere willfully or wittingly protect or foster guilt. . . .

6. If, through conviction for theft, any one, deserted by his kindred and knowing no one who will pay compensation in his place, loses his freedom and places himself under the hand of another, then let him be liable for as much slave labour as may be due; and his kindred shall forfeit all claim to his wergeld [should he be slain]. . . .

8. It is my will that each reeve shall hold a court (*gemot*) every four weeks,[8] and that the reeves shall see that every man obtains folkright, and that every case shall have a day set when it is to be decided. And if any one [of my reeves] neglects this [duty], he shall be liable for the compensation already prescribed.

(Anglo-Saxon) *Ibid.*, I, 138 f.

---

[6] Presumably a district with a borough as its administrative centre; in any case, the region in which the accused dwelt.
[7] Probably by the court.
[8] This is the first definite mention of the monthly court which later dooms call the hundred; see below, p. 17, n. 5.

7. DOOMS OF AETHELSTAN (925-40)

II. 1. In the first place, no thief caught in the act is to be spared, [if he is] over twelve years old and [if the stolen property is worth] over 8*d.* . . .

2. And with regard to lordless men from whom no justice is to be obtained, we have ordained that their kindred be commanded to settle

14   THE ANGLO-SAXON PERIOD

them in homes [where they will be subject] to folkright, and to find them lords in the popular court (*folcgemote*). And if, by the day set, the kindred will not or cannot do so, he¹ shall thenceforth be an outlaw, to be treated as a thief by any one who meets him. . . .

3. Should a lord intervene on behalf of his guilty man and [thereby] deny justice [to some one], and should the [latter] man then appeal to the king, [the lord] shall pay [to the complainant] the value of the goods [in question], and to the king 120s. He, however, who appeals to the king before seeking justice [in the local court]² as often as he should, shall pay the same fine as the other would have been liable for had he denied justice. . . .

4. And with regard to betrayal of the lord, we have declared that he who cannot deny it, or [having denied it] is convicted by the threefold ordeal,³ shall forfeit his life.

7. And with regard to the simple ordeal for men who have been often accused of theft, we have ordained that, if they are convicted, they shall be imprisoned and shall be released only on the conditions already stated.⁴ . . .

10. And no one shall exchange any livestock without witness of the reeve,⁵ the priest, the lord of the land (*londhlafordes*), the [lord's] steward, or some other reliable man. If any one does so, he shall pay a fine of 30s. [to the king], and the lord of the land shall seize whatever has been exchanged. . . .

12. And we have ordered that no one shall trade in goods worth more than 20d. outside a port;⁶ but every one shall do his trading inside, with the witness of the portreeve or of some other trustworthy man, or else at the popular court (*folcgemote*) with the witness of the reeves.

13. And we have ordered that every borough (*burh*)⁷ shall be repaired within a fortnight after Rogation. . . .

14. [We have also ordered] that one coinage shall have currency throughout all the king's realm and that no one shall mint [money] except within a port. . . . There shall be seven moneyers at Canterbury: four for the king, two for the archbishop, and one for the abbot. At Rochester [there shall be] three: two for the king and one for the bishop. At London [there shall be] eight, at Winchester six,

---

¹ A lordless man of this sort.
² Cf. Edgar, III, 2 (below, p. 19); Cnute, II, 17 (below, p. 22).
³ See no. 8n.
⁴ When a surety has been found.
⁵ The king's reeve is apparently meant; cf. art. 12, below. That the *hordere* of this passage was an ordinary rural steward, rather than some sort of treasurer, has been shown by R. L. Poole (*The Exchequer in the Twelfth Century*, pp. 22 f.).
⁶ A modification of Edward, I, 1 (above, p. 12).
⁷ This is the first appearance of the word in the dooms to refer to the official centres of defence and administration that are so frequently mentioned in the contemporary Anglo-Saxon Chronicle. It is clear from the following article that such a borough might also be called a port; see above, p. 12, n. 3.

8. ANONYMOUS DOOMS

at Lewes two, at Hastings one, another at Chichester, at Southampton two, at Wareham two, at Dorchester one, at Exeter two, at Shaftsbury two, and besides these one in [each of] the other boroughs (*burgum*) . . . .

20. And if any one thrice neglects attendance at the court (*gemot*), he shall pay the king's *ofer***h***ýrnesse*.⁸ And the holding of the court shall be announced seven days in advance. If, however, he will neither do what is right nor pay the *ofer***h***ýrnesse*, then all the chief (*yldestan*) men who belong to the borough shall ride against him and take all that he has and put him under surety. . . .

23. If any one is obliged to [go to] the ordeal, he shall come three days in advance to the priest in charge of the consecration; and before he does so, he shall feed himself on bread, water, salt, and herbs; and on each of the three days he shall attend mass; and on the day he undergoes the ordeal he shall make an offering and take communion; and then, before he goes to the ordeal, he shall swear an oath that, according to folkright, he is innocent of the charge made against him. And if it is [the ordeal of cold] water, he must sink an ell and a half on the rope [to clear himself].⁹ If it is the [ordeal of] iron, three days must elapse before the hand is uncovered.¹⁰ . . .

25. If, now, any of my reeves will not enforce this [ordinance], or shows less zeal [in the matter] than we have commanded, he must pay my *ofer***h***ýrnesse*, and I shall find another man who will [enforce it].

V, 1. . . . And in the district (*manunge*) of every reeve let there be named as many men as are known to be trustworthy, so that they may serve as witnesses in every suit. And their oaths shall count as those of trustworthy men, [to be numbered] according to the value of the property without selection.¹¹

(Anglo-Saxon) *Ibid.*, I, 150 f.

---

⁸ See above, p. 12, n. 4.

⁹ In this ordeal the accused was tied hand and foot and then lowered on the end of a rope into a pond or other still water. If he sank to the required depth, as marked on the rope, he was declared innocent, on the theory that a guilty person would not be received by the consecrated water. But a psychological factor may be detected in the possibility of a man's struggling to keep himself up.

¹⁰ See below, p. 16, n. 5.

¹¹ See above, p. 7, n. 6; p. 12, n. 5.

8. ANONYMOUS DOOMS¹

(A) CONCERNING INCENDIARIES AND MURDERERS

With regard to incendiaries and murderers,² we have ordered that the difficulty of their oath shall be tripled;³ likewise the iron for

---

¹ To judge from both the language and the subject matter, the two following dooms date from the time of Aethelstan.

² *Morþslyhtum*, those who slew by stealth or tried to conceal their offense; cf. the later *murdrum* (below, p. 36, n. 2).

³ That is to say, the required number of oath-helpers is to be tripled.

15

[trying such persons by] ordeal shall be brought up to three pounds in weight. The accused must go to the ordeal himself; and the accuser shall choose either ordeal by water or ordeal by iron, whichever he may prefer. If [the accused] fails in such oath and so is proved guilty, the chief men who belong to the borough[4] shall decide whether or not he shall be permitted to live.

(Anglo-Saxon) *Ibid.*, I, 388.

(B) CONCERNING ORDEALS

And with regard to the ordeal, according to the commands of God and of the archbishop and of all the bishops, we order that, as soon as the fire has been brought to heat the [iron or water for the] ordeal, no one shall come into the church except the priest and the man to be tried. And [if the ordeal is by iron,] nine feet, according to the feet of the man to be tried, shall be measured from the [starting] post to the [final] mark.[5] If, on the other hand, it is to be [ordeal by] water, that shall be heated until it becomes boiling hot, whether the kettle is of iron or of brass, of lead or of clay. And if the process is "single," the hand shall be plunged in for the stone[6] up to the wrist; if it is "threefold,"[7] up to the elbow. And when the [water for the] ordeal is ready, two men from each party shall go in, and they shall agree that it is as hot as we have ordered.

Then an equal number of men from both parties shall go in and stand along the church on each side of the ordeal, and all of them shall be fasting and shall have held themselves from their wives during the previous night. And the priest shall sprinkle them all with holy water and give them to taste of the holy water; and he shall give them the Book to kiss and [shall] make over them] the sign of Christ's cross. And no one shall build up the fire any more after the consecration has been begun, but the iron shall lie on the embers until the last collect. Then it shall be laid on the [starting] post. And nothing else shall be said inside the church except a prayer to God Almighty that He disclose the fullness of truth. And [after the man has undergone the ordeal,] his hand shall be [bound up and] sealed; and after the third day it shall be inspected to see whether, within the sealed wrapping, it is foul or clean (*ful swa claene*).[8] And if any one breaks these provisions, the ordeal shall be [counted] a failure for him, and he shall pay a fine of 120s. to the king.

(Anglo-Saxon) *Ibid.*, I, 386.

---

[4] Cf. Æthelstan, 20 (above, p. 15).
[5] It is stated below that the iron, when heated, was to be laid on the post. The accused picked up the iron in his bare hand and carried it for the specified distance.
[6] The one placed in the bottom of the kettle for this purpose.
[7] Cf. the previous doom.
[8] The cleanness of the hand was probably determined by its freedom from infection.

9. DOOMS OF EDMUND (942-46)

II. 1. Henceforth, if any man slays another, [we order] that he by himself shall incur the blood-feud,[1] unless he, with the help of his friends, buys it off by paying the full wergeld [of the slain man] within twelve months, no matter of what rank the latter may be. If, however, his kinsmen abandon him, refusing to pay anything in his behalf, then it is my will that the whole kindred, with the sole exception of the actual slayer, be free of the blood-feud so long as they give him neither food nor protection. If, on the other hand, one of his kinsmen later gives him such assistance, the former shall forfeit to the king all that he has, and he shall incur the blood-feud [along with the slayer] because the latter has already been disowned by the kindred. And if any one of the other kindred[2] takes vengeance on any men besides the true slayer, he shall incur the enmity of the king and all of the king's friends, and he shall forfeit all that he has.

III. This is the decree that King Edmund and his bishops, together with his *witan*, formulated at Colyton for the [maintenance of] peace and the swearing of an oath.[3]

1. In the first place [he commands] that all, in the name of God before whom this holy thing is holy, shall swear fealty to King Edmund, as a man should be faithful to his lord, without dissension or betrayal, both in public and in secret, loving what he loves and shunning what he shuns; and from the day on which this oath is sworn that no one shall conceal [the breach of] this [obligation], on the part of a brother or a relative any more than on the part of a stranger.

2. He also wills that, when a man is definitely known to be a thief, [both] twelve-hundred men and two-hundred men[4] shall join in taking him dead or alive, in whichever way they can. And whoever prosecutes a blood-feud against any one who has taken part in this search shall incur the enmity of the king and of all his friends. And if anybody refuses to present himself and give assistance, he shall pay a fine of 120s. to the king and of 30s. to the hundred [court],[5] unless he can prove that he had no knowledge of the affair by an oath of equal value.[6] . . .

---

[1] Cf. Alfred, 42 (above, p. 12).
[2] That of the slain man.
[3] Cf. no. 1A.
[4] Cf. Alfred, 39 (above, p. 11).
[5] This is the first mention of the hundred in the dooms. To what extent the name was new is a matter of controversy, but it was certainly connected with assessment of districts for military purposes in hundreds of hides, and much of this assessment system was the product of the Danish wars. So far as the institution was concerned, it is evident that many of the provisions henceforth applied to the hundred court were repetitions of those already applied to the *folcgemot*. See especially the analysis of the sources and literature in Liebermann, *Gesetze*, II, 516 f.; also Helen M. Cam, in the *English Historical Review*, XLVII. 370 f. On the payment to the hundred, cf. Edgar, I, 1-2 (below, p. 18). Since it is hardly credible that the hundred had a common chest, we must believe that the suitors to the court somehow shared the profits of justice.
[6] I.e., 120s.

7. And every man shall be responsible for his own men and for all who are under his protection and on his land. And all persons of bad repute, or those frequently accused of crime, shall be placed under surety. And reeve or thegn, *eorl* or *ceorl*, who refuses to carry out these orders, or neglects them, shall pay a fine of 120s. and suffer other penalties as stated above.

(Anglo-Saxon and Latin.) *Ibid.*, I, 186 f.

10. CORONATION OATH OF EDGAR

This writing has been copied, letter by letter, from the writing which Archbishop Dunstan gave our lord at Kingston on the day that he was consecrated as king, forbidding him to make any promise save this, which at the bishop's bidding he laid on Christ's altar:—
In the name of the Holy Trinity I promise three things to the Christian people my subjects: first, that God's Church and all Christian people of my realm shall enjoy true peace; second, that I forbid to all ranks of men robbery and all wrongful deeds; third, that I urge and command justice and mercy in all judgments, so that the gracious and compassionate God who lives and reigns may grant us all His everlasting mercy.

(Anglo-Saxon.) *Ibid.*, I, 214 f.

11. DOOMS OF EDGAR (946–63)

1. This is the ordinance as to how the hundred [court][1] shall be held.

1. In the first place, [we command] that they[1] shall assemble every four weeks and that all shall [there] give one another justice.

2. [We also command] that men shall ride forth in pursuit of thieves. If there is pressing need, notice shall be given to the hundred-man, and he shall then inform the tithingmen;[2] and they shall all go forth, whither God may direct them, to find [the criminals]. Justice is to be done to the thief as already ordained by [King] Edmund. And the *ceapgyld*[3] shall be paid to the owner, and the rest [of the thief's property] shall be divided in two, half to the hundred and half to the lord—except the men [who belong to the thief]; they shall go to his lord.

3. And any one who disobeys this [command] and scorns the judgment of the hundred, should his guilt be later determined, shall pay to the hundred 30d., and for the second offence 60d., half to the hundred and half to his lord. If he does it a third time, he shall pay half a pound; on the fourth offence he shall forfeit all that he has

[1] The suitors to the court; cf. Edward, II, 8 (above, p. 13).
[2] The hundredman was the royal official in charge of a hundred; by analogy, the tithing may be understood as a subdivision of the hundred and the tithingman as its head. In this respect, however, the dooms are very obscure. See below, p. 23, n. 6.
[3] The value of the stolen property; cf. *angyld* (above, p. 8, n. 12).

11. DOOMS OF EDGAR

and be outlawed, unless the king shall permit him [to stay in] the land.

4. And we have provided with regard to strange cattle that no one shall keep [any], unless he has the witness of the hundredman or the tithingman and such person is eminently trustworthy. And unless he has one of these [as witness], he shall not be permitted to vouch to warranty.[4]

5. We have also provided that, if a trail of lost cattle leads from one hundred into another, notice shall be given to the hundredman of the latter, and that he shall then join [in the search]. If he fails to do so, he shall pay the king 30s. . . .

7. In the hundred, as in [any] other court, we will that folkright shall be enforced in every suit and that a day shall be set for trying it. And he who fails to appear on this day, unless his absence is caused by a command from his lord, shall pay the king 30s. compensation and on a [newly] set day do what he should have done before.

III, 2. And no one shall appeal to the king on account of any suit unless he has failed to obtain justice at home.[5] If [however] the law is too severe, he may seek mitigation from the king. And no one shall forfeit more than his wergeld for any offence that can be paid for in money.

3. And a doomsman[6] who renders an evil doom against any one shall pay 120s. compensation to the king, unless he can prove by oath that he acted according to the best of his knowledge; and he shall lose forever his rank of thegn, unless he buys it back from the king by whatever payment the latter will allow. And the shire bishop (*scire biscop*) may exact the compensation on behalf of the king. . . .

5. And the hundred court shall be attended as has already been provided. And the borough court (*burhgemot*) shall be held three times a year and the shire court (*scirgemot*) twice.[7] And the shire bishop and the alderman shall be present and shall there administer both ecclesiastical and secular law (*Godes riht ge woruldriht*). . . .

8. And one coinage shall have currency throughout all the king's realm and no one shall refuse it. And there shall be [as a standard]

---

[4] That is to say, only the designated persons could be called on to warrant his lawful possession; see above, p. 4, n. 3.

[5] In the hundred court; cf. Cnute, II, 17 (below, p. 22).

[6] See above, p. 4, n. 5. The provision that the bishop could exact the compensation would indicate the alderman or the reeve as a possible offender. Cf. art. 5, below.

[7] This is the earliest specific mention of either the borough court or the shire court, both of which appear to have been courts of superior jurisdiction. Whether such a court was called *burhgemot* or *scirgemot*, and whether it met twice or three times a year, were perhaps matters of secondary importance. For evidence that at this time the shire was a comparatively large district, see Aethelred, II, 8 (below, p. 20). And on the controversial subject of the borough court, see C. Stephenson, *Borough and Town*, pp. 64-70; Tait, *The Medieval English Borough*, ch. ii.

19

20   THE ANGLO-SAXON PERIOD

one measure (and one weight), as used (at London and) at Winchester.⁸ . . .

IV, 3. My will is then that every one, in borough or out of borough, shall be under surety. And witnesses shall be chosen for every borough and for every hundred: for every [great] borough thirty-six men shall be chosen as witnesses; for a small borough and for every hundred twelve—unless you wish [to have] more.⁹ . . .

6. And under their witness every one shall buy and sell all the goods that he buys and sells either in a borough or in a wapentake.¹⁰ And each of them, when he is first chosen as a witness, shall swear an oath that neither for fee nor for love, nor through fear, will he ever deny anything of which he is a witness or [will he ever] testify to anything but what he has seen or heard. And two or three of the men thus put on oath shall be present as witnesses at every transaction.

7. And he who rides out for the sake of any purchase shall announce to his neighbours what he is going for; and as soon as he comes home, he shall also announce under whose witness he made his purchase.

8. But if, while on some journey, he makes an unexpected purchase, without having made announcement [of it] when he set out, let him announce it when he comes home; and if it is livestock, he shall put it on the common pasture with the witness of his fellow villagers.¹¹ If he does not do so within five nights, the villagers (*tunes men*) shall notify the hundredman and shall [thereby] escape punishment, either for themselves or for their herdsmen. And he who brought the livestock there shall lose it, because he failed to notify his neighbours of it; and the lord of the land (*landrica*) shall take half and the hundred half.

(Anglo-Saxon) *Ibid.*, I, 192 f.

---

⁸ The phrases in parentheses are additions to the original text. The insertion of London proves the growing importance of that city as a commercial centre in the eleventh century.

⁹ Cf. Aethelstan, V, 1 (above, p. 15), which set up a select group of oath-helpers in the district later called the hundred. Note that such an oath-helper was often styled a witness and that a witness to a purchase served as an oath-helper when vouched to warranty; see the oaths under no. 14, below.

¹⁰ A name by which the hundred was often known in Danish regions.

¹¹ *Tunescipe*, our "township." This is the sole appearance of the word in the dooms; see Maitland, *Domesday Book and Beyond*, p. 147.

12. DOOMS OF AETHELRED (980–1016)

II, 8. If any one seizes something that he lost, the man in whose possession it was seized shall give solemn engagement and provide surety that he will present his warrantor whenever formal claim [to the property] is made.¹ If he vouches a living person to

---

¹ See above, p. 4, n. 3.

12. DOOMS OF AETHELRED   21

warranty, and the one thus summoned is in another shire, he shall have as long a time [for his process] as may be necessary. ... If he summons [a warrantor] from across one shire, he shall have a week's time; if he summons [one] from across two shires, he shall have two weeks' time; if he summons [one] from across three shires, he shall have three weeks' time—as many shires as he has to send across, so many weeks' time shall he have.

III. These are the laws (*laga*) that King Aethelred and his *witan* have drawn up at Wantage for the improvement of the peace. ...

3. ... And a court shall be held in every wapentake and there the twelve leading (*yldestan*) thegns,[2] together with the reeve, shall come forward and swear on holy things, to be placed in their hands, that they will neither accuse any innocent man nor spare any guilty one. ...

6. And every accuser shall have the right to choose which [ordeal] he will [have the accused undergo], either water or iron. And every vouching to warranty (*team*) and every ordeal shall be held in a borough of the king. ...

13. And if any man is accused of giving food to a man who has broken our [royal] lord's peace (*grið*), he shall clear himself with thrice twelve [oath-helpers], and the latter shall be named by the reeve [of the king]. ... And that doom shall stand when the thegns [who declare it] are agreed; [or] if they disagree, that [doom] shall stand which is declared by eight of them, and those who are thereby outvoted shall each pay [a fine of] 6 half-marks.[3] ...

IV, 5. They[4] have also declared that, to their eyes, no difference exists between counterfeiters and the merchants who take good money to the counterfeiters and pay them to make [from it] impure money of insufficient weight, and who then trade and bargain with it; [or between counterfeiters] and those who secretly make dies, engraving on them the name of some moneyer other than the guilty party, and who sell them to the counterfeiters. Wherefore it has been decided by all the *witan* that these three [kinds of] men shall be made liable for the same punishment. And if one of them is accused, whether he is English or comes from beyond sea, he shall clear himself through the full ordeal.[5] And they have decided that [convicted] counterfeiters shall [each] lose a hand, which shall be exhibited over the place where they made their coin. And moneyers who work in woods,

---

[2] On the possible connection between this doom and the Norman grand jury, see Pollock and Maitland, I, 139–43. Cf. the lawmen of Domesday and the *scabini* of the Frankish courts; Helen M. Cam, *Local Government in Francia and England*, pp. 31 f.

[3] The mark was a Danish unit of account, normally held to contain 8 ounces or ores of 20*d.* each, and so rated as two-thirds of a pound.

[4] The king's *witan*.

[5] See no. 8A.

or make coin in [other secret] places of the same sort, shall forfeit their lives, unless the king wishes to spare them. . . .

9. And it has been decided that there shall be fewer moneyers than heretofore: there shall be three moneyers in every principal port, and one in every other port.[6] . . .

VI. 31. Let us all, furthermore, give earnest attention to the improvement of the peace and the improvement of the coinage.

32. The improvement of the peace [shall be] such as is best for the husbandman (*bondan*) and worst for the thief. And the coinage shall be so improved that one coinage, free of all false [issue], shall have currency throughout the whole land. And weights and measures shall be made exactly right, to the exclusion in the future of all wrong ones. And the repair of boroughs (*burhbote*) and the repair of bridges (*bricbote*) shall be earnestly pushed in every region;[7] and likewise the maintenance of the army and the fleet, whenever there is need, and as may be ordered in our common necessity.

33. And it is well to have in readiness the ships for the fleet (*fyrdscipa*) soon after Easter in every year. . . .

35. And if any one, without leave, deserts the army when the king is there, he risks losing all his property.

---
[6] Cf. Athelstan, II, 14 (above, p. 14).
[7] On the borough as a fortification, see above, p. 14, n. 7. On the threefold obligation resting with all landholders, cf. Canute, II, 65 (below, p. 24), and the charters under no. 15, below. This was the famous *trimoda necessitas*, on which term see W. H. Stevenson, in the *English Historical Review*, XXIX, 689 f.

13. DOOMS OF CANUTE (1020-34)

(Anglo-Saxon and Latin: *Ibid*, I, 224, f.

II. Here now follows the secular ordinance which, by the counsel of my *witan*, I wish to be obeyed throughout all England. . . .

12. These are the rights which the king enjoys over all men in Wessex: namely, [compensations for] breach of his personal protection (*mundbryce*), housebreaking (*hamsocne*),[1] assault by ambush (*forsteal*), and neglect of army service (*fyrdwite*)—unless he wishes to honour some one in particular [by granting him even these rights.] . . .

14. And in Mercia he [likewise] enjoys the aforesaid rights over all men.

15. And in the Danelaw he enjoys the fines for fighting,[2] neglect of army service, breach of his personal peace (*gryðbryce*), and housebreaking—unless he wishes to honour some one in particular. . . .

17. And no one shall appeal to the king unless he fails to obtain

---
[1] More accurately, unlawful entry upon a person's premises, whether a house or land; cf. Athelberht, 5-27 (above, p. 3), and Alfred, 40 (above, p. 11).
[2] *Flihtewite*, having to do especially with cases involving bloodshed.

13. DOOMS OF CANUTE

justice in his hundred.³ Every one, under pain of fine, must attend his hundred court whenever attendance is demanded by law.

18. And the borough court shall be held three times [a year] and the shire court twice unless there is need to hold it oftener. And the shire bishop and the alderman shall be present and shall there administer both ecclesiastical and secular law.⁴

19. And no one shall seize property [to enforce his rights] either in the shire [court] or outside it, unless he has thrice sought justice in the hundred. If he fails to obtain justice on the third attempt, then, the fourth time, he shall go to the shire court; and the shire shall set him a day for his fourth effort. And if this fails, then he shall secure leave either here or there⁵ to go after his property [in any way he can].

20. It is our will that every freeman above the age of twelve shall be brought within hundred and tithing,⁶ if he wishes to be law-worthy when accused by some one, or wergeld-worthy [when slain]. Otherwise he shall not enjoy any rights as a freeman, whether he is a householder or a member of another's household. Every one shall be brought within a hundred and under surety (*borge*), and his surety shall keep him and see that he performs his legal obligations....

22. And every trustworthy man, who is free of accusations and has never failed in oath or ordeal, shall be law-worthy in the hundred, [clearing himself] through a simple oath.⁷ For an untrustworthy man oath-helpers for the simple oath shall be chosen from three hundreds, and for the threefold oath from [a territory] as wide as belongs to the borough—or he must go to the ordeal. And a simple oath of exculpation shall be introduced by a simple fore-oath [of accusation]; a threefold oath by a threefold fore-oath.⁸ ...

24. And no one, either within a borough or in the open country, shall buy anything worth more than 4*d.*, whether living or not, without the trustworthy witness of four men. . . .

29. And if any one encounters a thief and wilfully lets him go without making an outcry,⁹ he shall pay the thief's wergeld as com-

---

³ Cf. Aethelstan, II, 3 (above, p. 14), and Edgar, III, 2 (above, p. 19).
⁴ A re-enactment of Edgar III, 5 (above, p. 19).
⁵ Following Miss Robertson's suggestion that the hundred and shire courts are referred to.
⁶ Cf. Edgar, I, 2; IV, 3 (above, pp. 18, 20). One group of writers headed by Liebermann, has held that the tithing of this passage refers to a group of ten men combined for the sake of mutual suretyship; another that such a system was a police measure introduced by the Normans and that the tithing here, as in Edgar's dooms, was territorial. For a cogent presentation of the latter argument, see W. A. Morris, *The Frankpledge System*.
⁷ And with oath-helpers chosen by himself, as appears from the following provision.
⁸ See the oaths under no. 14.
⁹ That is to say, without raising hue and cry, as it was known in the later law.

23

pensation, or shall clear himself by a full oath, [swearing] that he did not know him [whom he let go] to be guilty of anything. And if any one hears the outcry and neglects it, he shall pay the king's *oferhyrnesse* or clear himself by a full oath.

30. And if any man appears untrustworthy to the hundred, being discredited by accusations, and if now three men together bring charges against him, he shall have no recourse but to go to the three-fold ordeal. . . .

57. And if any one plots against the king or against his own lord, he shall forfeit his life and all that he has, unless he goes to the threefold ordeal and there clears himself.[10] . . .

65. If any one neglects the repair of boroughs, the repair of bridges, or army service,[11] he shall pay 120s. compensation to the king [in the region] under English law, and in the Danelaw whatever is customary [there] ; or he shall clear himself with eleven oath-helpers out of fourteen named for him [by the court]. All the people shall, according to law, assist in the repair of churches. . . .

70. And if any one, whether through negligence or through sudden death, departs this life without having made a will,[12] his lord shall take no more of his chattels than his lawful heriot. Rather, by his direction, the goods are to be most justly apportioned to the widow, the children, and the near relatives—to each the share that is rightfully his.

71. And heriots shall be fixed in proportion to rank. The heriot of an earl [shall be] what belongs thereto: namely, eight horses, four saddled and four unsaddled ; also four helmets, four shirts of mail, eight spears and as many shields, four swords, and 200 mancuses of gold.[13] For king's thegns, those who live close to him, the heriot shall be four horses, two saddled and two unsaddled ; also two swords, four spears and as many shields, helmets, and shirts of mail ; and 50 mancuses of gold. And for an ordinary thegn [the heriot shall be] his horse with its harness and his weapons, or, in Wessex, his *healsfang*[14] in Mercia £2 and in East Anglia £2. And among the Danes the heriot of a king's thegn who enjoys soke[15] is £4. And if he lives in greater intimacy with the king, [it is] two horses, one saddled and the other unsaddled ; also a sword, two spears, two shields, and 50 mancuses of gold. And for him who is not so well off [the heriot is] £2.

(Anglo-Saxon) *Ibid.*, I, 308 f.

[10] Cf. Alfred, 4 (above, p. 10).
[11] See above, p. 22, n. 7.
[12] Dying intestate was already considered exceptional. Many Anglo-Saxon wills have come down to us from earlier centuries.
[13] *Mancus* is derived from the Arabic and was originally used to designate an Arabic gold coin or an imitation of one. In the dooms, however, it is a weight of gold equal to 30d. in silver.
[14] A term normally used to mean a tenth of the wergeld.
[15] Jurisdictional rights over certain persons, or profits of justice in certain places ; see below, p. 30, n. 23.

14. CUSTOMARY OATHS

(A) OATH OF A MAN TO HIS LORD

By the Lord before whom this holy thing is holy, I will to N.[1] be faithful and true, loving all that he loves and shunning all that he shuns, according to the law of God and the custom of the world; and never by will or by force, in word or in deed, will I do anything that is hateful to him; on condition that he will hold me as I deserve and will furnish all that was agreed between us when I bowed myself before him and submitted to his will.

(B) OATH OF AN ACCUSER

By the Lord before whom this holy thing is holy, I thus bring my charge with full folkright, without deceit and without malice, and without any guile whatsoever, that stolen from me was this property, N., which I claim and which I seized in the possession of N.

(C) OATH OF ONE THUS ACCUSED

By the Lord . . . neither by counsel nor by deed had I knowledge of or part in this, that the property, N., was carried off. On the contrary, I possess the property for this reason, that I lawfully inherited it. . . . that he,[2] having the lawful right to sell it, sold it to me. . . . that it is the offspring of my own animals, my private property raised under my care.

(D) OATH OF ONE SEIZING PROPERTY

By the Lord . . . I seize N. neither through hate nor hostility, nor through unrighteous greed, and I know nothing truer than what my spokesman has said for me, and what I now myself state as truth, that *he* was the thief of my property.

(E) OATH IN REPLY TO SUCH SEIZURE

By the Lord . . . I am guiltless, both in thought and in deed, of the accusation made against me by N.

(F) OATH OF AN OATH-HELPER

By the Lord . . . the oath which N. has sworn is clean and without falsehood.

(Anglo-Saxon) *Ibid.*, I, 396 f.

[1] In these oaths *N.* represents either a person's name or the description of a particular article of property, usually an animal.
[2] Designating the person accused.

15. CHARTERS AND WRITS

(A) OFFA, KING OF MERCIA: GRANT TO WORCESTER CATHEDRAL (741-96)

In the name of our Lord Jesus Christ who reigns throughout all time! I, Offa, for the health of my soul and the souls of my relatives

26 THE ANGLO-SAXON PERIOD

after my death and the soul of my son Egfrith, give to [the church of] Worcester this land at Westbury with all that lawfully pertains to it: namely, sixty hides, and in another place, at Hanbury, twenty hides. [And this land is] lawfully to remain with the same endowment of liberty in all things as when King Aethelbald earlier bestowed it on my grandfather, Eanulf. . . . In the name of Almighty God we command that it shall be free from all power of kings and princes, or of their subordinates, with the exception of these dues, that is to say, the rent (*gafol*)[1] at Westbury: two tuns of clear ale, a coomb of mild ale, a coomb of Welsh ale, seven oxen, six wethers, forty cheeses, . . . [2] thirty ambers of rye corn, and four ambers of meal at the king's manor (*ad regalem vicum*). This, with the advice and consent of my prelates and counsellors, has accordingly been determined by firm covenant: no royal, princely, or secular official shall in the future, by demands great or small, either through force or through requisition, exact anything from them on account of [this] our inheritance, with the sole exception of what is specified in this present charter.

These are the witnesses. . . .[3]

(Latin and Anglo-Saxon) Thorpe, *Diplomatarium*, pp. 39 f.

(B) AETHELRED, ALDERMAN OF MERCIA: GRANT TO THE MONASTERY OF BERKELEY (883)

. . . Wherefore I, Aethelred, alderman, by the heartening grace of God endowed and enriched with a portion of the Mercian realm,[4] for love of God, for the remission of my guilt and sin, for the prayers of the abbot and the congregation [of monks] at Berkeley, and on behalf of all Mercia, free them forever of the *gafol* which they still have to pay into the king's hand, [namely,] from that part of the king's *feorm*[5] that has remained obligatory, whether in clear ale, in beer, in honey, in cattle, in swine, or in sheep. And this I have done for the sake of their godly prayers, and also because they have granted to me in perpetuity a certain portion of their land, that is to say, twelve hides at Stoke. Furthermore, they have given me 30 mancuses of gold[6] so that I shall also free the monastery from

---

[1] See above, p. 7, n. 3.
[2] Certain words at this point are unintelligible.
[3] In the original the clerk wrote the names of the witnesses, together with the variety of forms by which they attested the document. Each witness then added a cross in the appropriate place. The present charter lists eighteen witnesses, including King Offa, his son, an archbishop, a bishop, four abbots, and seven aldermen.
[4] Aethelred was descended from the royal line of Mercia and still held about half of the old kingdom. His wife was the famous Lady of the Mercians, Aethelflaed, daughter of King Alfred.
[5] The regular name for the payments of food owed the king from many of his estates.
[6] See above, p. 24, n. 13.

15. CHARTERS AND WRITS

all dues (*gafolum*) to which the lord of the people⁷ is entitled, great or small, known or unknown, except simple compensation (*angilde*) to others,⁸ and except repair of fortresses (*faestengeweorc*), military service (*fyrdsocne*), and repair of bridges (*brycggeweorce*).⁹ And this I do with the leave and witness of King Alfred, and with [the counsel of] all the Mercian *witan*, both clergy and laity.

Now, moreover, I give that same land at Stoke—namely, twelve hides—to Cynulf, son of Ceoluht, for 60 mancuses of pure gold, to be free of all obligations toward king or alderman or reeve: [that is to say,] of every burden, great or small, except military service, repair of fortresses, repair of bridges, and simple compensation to others, with naught out for *write*. And we enjoin that no one, either relative or stranger, shall in any way rob [Cynulf]¹⁰ of it as long as he lives, for he has deserved it of the Mercian lords through righteous submission [to them].

And we now, in the name of Almighty God, command that this immunity for the monastery of Berkeley, as described above, and also the gift of land which we grant to Cynulf for three men's lives, shall continue unimpaired on this condition, that on the death of Cynulf and his two heirs, without any controversy, the twelve hides of land at Stoke are to be given in perpetual alms to the episcopal see of Worcester on behalf of Aethelred, alderman, and of all the Mercians. Also we beg and implore in the name of the Holy Trinity that, if there should be any man who with evil intent violates aught that is written in this charter, he may know that he does so to the displeasure of God and of all His saints, as well as of all men, both clerical and lay, who can think or will anything rightful; and that he shall make amends before the throne of the Eternal Judge if he has not already [in his lifetime] done so with just reparation to God and man.

Now this munificent grant was made in the year of the Incarnation of the Lord 883 . . . by the consent and attestation of the witnesses whose names are here noted. . . .¹¹

This land, moreover, is bounded by the following bounds: first from Hazlewell in Hazledean, then to Woldeswell; from Woldeswell to Sweordes Stone in Ewcombe; from Ewcombe to Avon's stream; from Avon's stream again up, then to Ridgeley; from Ridgeley then to Penpau; from Penpau then to Severn's stream; from Hazle-

---

⁷ Meaning, of course, the king.

⁸ Cf. the similar phrase below, with the addition of "naught out to *write*." As pointed out by Maitland (*Domesday Book and Beyond*, pp. 290 f.), the charter implies the grant of a judicial immunity: the church was to enjoy the profits of justice, including all fines normally paid to the king, but not including ordinary compensation paid by tenants for injuries to persons other than the grantee.

⁹ See above, p. 22, n. 7.

¹⁰ The text by error has Ceoluht.

¹¹ Besides the king and Aethelred, the list includes three bishops, an abbot, a priest, two aldermen, and eight other persons.

27

well again, then to Leadgedelf; from Leadgedelf to Millpool; from Millpool again to Avon's stream.

(Latin and Anglo-Saxon) *Ibid.*, pp. 129 f.

(C) ÆTHELRED, ALDERMAN OF MERCIA, AND HIS WITAN: CONFIRMATION OF A TITLE TO LAND (896)

Under the dominion of the Saviour Christ our Lord. After 896 winters had passed since His birth, then, in that year, . . . Æthelred, alderman, called together all the Mercian *witan* at Gloucester—bishops, aldermen, and all his magnates—and this he did with the leave and witness of King Alfred. And there they took counsel how, in the sight both of God and of the world, they could most justly rule their people; and [how they] could right [the wrongs of] man, whether clerical or lay, whether in the matter of their lands or of other things that had been withheld from them.

Then Bishop Wærferth complained to the *witan* that he had been deprived of nearly all the woodland belonging to Woodchester, which King Æthelbald had given to [the church of] Worcester in perpetual alms, [namely,] to Bishop Wilferth for mast and wood; and he said that, so far as he could tell, some of it had been taken at Bisley, some at Avening, some at Sherston, and some at Thornbury. Then all the *witan* declared that right should be done to this church as well as to any other. Whereupon Æthelwald at once announced that he would not hinder justice, saying that Bishops Ealhberht and Alhhun had earlier been [concerned] about the same [matter], and promising that he would do his part in giving right to every church. So, with the utmost graciousness, he yielded to the bishop and bade his *geneat*,[12] named Ecgfat, ride with a priest of the Worcester men (*ceastersetna*), named Wulfhun. And he then led him along all the bounds, while he read them to him from the old charters,[13] as King Æthelbald had earlier bounded that [woodland] in his grant. Then Æthelwald expressed the wish that the bishop and the [episcopal] household would kindly allow him to enjoy [the use of] it while he lived and [grant the same privilege] to Alhmund, his son; [so that] they might hold it by lease (*laen*) of [the bishop] and his household, and neither of them, during the time that God gave them [to live], would ever deprive [the bishop] of the mast to which he was entitled at Longridge. And Æthelwald then solemnly declared that only to the displeasure of God should any one but the lord of the church have that [woodland], saving [the rights of] Alhmund; and this only on condition that the latter should hold the same friendly relation with the bishop as he [himself] now held. If, however, it should happen that Alhmund did not hold that friendly relation, or if it should be proved that he was not worthy of the land, or,

[12] See above, p. 8, n. 8.
[13] Since Wulfhun was a priest, it must have been he who read the charters while Ecgfat showed him the boundaries.

15. CHARTERS AND WRITS 29

thirdly, if his end should come, that then the lord of the church should take his land.

Thus the Mercian *witan* decided in the assembly, directing the [present] record concerning the land [to be drawn up] for him.¹⁴ And this was done by the witness of Aethelred the alderman and Aethelbaed,¹⁵ of Aethulf the alderman, Aethelferth the alderman, Alhelm the alderman, Eadnoth, Alfred, Werferth, Aethelwald the priest, and of his own kinsmen, Aethelstan and Aethelhun, as well as of his own son, Alhmund.

And thus the priest of the Worcestermen rode it,¹⁶ and with him Aethelwald's *geneat*: first to Gemythley, and thence to Rodborough itself; thence to Smeethcombe; thence to Sugley; thence to Hardley, [for which] there is another name, Dryganley; so to Nailsworth the smaller, and so to Aethelferth's land. Thus did Aethelwald's man show him the bounds as the old charters provided and indicated. (Anglo-Saxon). *Ibid.*, pp. 139 f.

(D) EDGAR: GRANT TO THE BISHOP OF WINCHESTER (963)¹⁷

Here, in this writing, is made known how King Edgar, with the counsel of his *witan*, confirmed the liberties at Taunton for the Holy Trinity, St. Peter and St. Paul, and the episcopal see of Winchester, as this freedom had earlier been established by King Edward: granting that men in that vill (*hame*) of God, whether two-hundred or twelve-hundred,¹⁸ should enjoy the same rights as his own men enjoyed in his own royal vills; that all causes and rights should be given into the hand of God in the same measure as when they were brought into his own; [that] the [control of] trade in the vill (*tunes cyping*) and the income from [all other] rights in the port¹⁹ should go to the holy see [of Winchester] as they earlier did in the days of my ancestors, and as they were collected for Bishop Aelfeage and for each of those who possessed the land. If any one will increase this liberty, may God increase his welfare during a long life here and in eternity. If, on the contrary, any one, through insolence and the instigation of the devil or his limbs, should seek to violate this liberty or to pervert it, unless he shall make amends before his death, may he with malediction be cut off from the communion of our Lord and of all His saints, and may he suffer eternal torment in hell along with Judas, who was Christ's betrayer.

¹⁴ Presumably the bishop.
¹⁵ See above, p. 26, n. 4.
¹⁶ The boundary of the land in question.
¹⁷ This document exists in two versions, Latin and Anglo-Saxon. The translation has been made from the latter.
¹⁸ Cf. Alfred, 39 (above, p. 11).
¹⁹ See above, p. 12, n. 3. In this case the reference is to the borough of Taunton which, together with all royal rights in market and court, remained in the hands of the bishop until after the Norman Conquest; see Round, in *Victoria History of Somerset*, I, 400 f.

THE ANGLO-SAXON PERIOD

... This was done at Cheddar on the holy Eastertide, in which year 968[20] years had passed since the birth of Christ, and in the tenth year of the reign [of Edgar], by the witness of the *witan* whose names are written below...[21]

(Anglo-Saxon) *Ibid.,* pp. 235 f.

(E) CANUTE: GRANT TO ST. PAUL'S, LONDON (1036)

I, King Canute, give friendly greetings to my bishops, my earls,[22] and all my thegns in the shires where my priests of St. Paul's monastery hold land. And I make known to you my will that they shall enjoy their *sac* and *soc, toll* and *team,*[23] within tide and without tide, as fully and continuously as they best had them in any king's day, in all things, in borough and out of borough. And I will not permit any man in any way to do them wrong. And of this the witnesses are Aegelnoth, archbishop; Aelfric, archbishop; Aelwi, bishop; Aelwine, bishop; Duduc, bishop; Godwine, earl; Leofric, earl; Osgod Clapa, Thored, and many others.

May God curse him who shall pervert this [grant]!

(Anglo-Saxon) *Ibid.,* pp. 319 f.

(F) CONFIRMATION OF A TITLE TO LAND IN THE SHIRE COURT OF HEREFORD (1036)

Here, in this writing, it is made known that a shire court sat at Aegelnoth's Stone in the time of King Canute. There sat Aethelstan, bishop; Ranig, alderman; Edwin, [son] of the alderman; Leofwine, son of Wulfsige; and Thurcil the White (*Hwita*). And thither came Tofig the Proud (*Pruda*) on the king's errand. And there were Bryning the sheriff,[24] Aegelweard of Frome, Leofwine of Frome, Godric of Stoke, and all the thegns of Herefordshire. Then came faring to the court Edwin, son of Enwen, and there claimed as against his own mother a portion of land, namely, Wellington and Cradley. Then the bishop asked who would speak for his mother. Then Thurcil the White answered, saying that he would if he knew

---

[20] The text mistakenly reads 978.

[21] The list includes, besides the king and the queen, the two archbishops, seven bishops, nine abbots, eight aldermen, and nine thegns.

[22] These officials henceforth appear in place of the aldermen; see Chadwick, *Studies,* ch. v.

[23] Such phrases as these now become characteristic of all formal grants of immunity; see Maitland, *Domesday Book and Beyond,* pp. 258 f. *Sac* and *soc* (more properly *sacu* and *socn*) together meant no more than the latter term alone, which ordinarily in modern English is given as *soke* or *soken;* see above, p. 24, n. 15. *Toll,* from the Latin *theloneum,* has come down to us with the spelling and the meaning alike unchanged. *Team* meant vouching to warranty, or the right to collect the fees for it on one's own land or elsewhere; see above, p. 4, n. 3.

[24] The shire-reeve, or sheriff, henceforth attains great importance in local government as the subordinate of the earl, who normally was in charge of several shires.

15. CHARTERS AND WRITS

the defence [that she cared to make]. Since he did not know the defence, three thegns were chosen from the court [to ride to the place] where she was, and that was Fawley. These [thegns] were Leofwine of Frome, Aegelsige the Red (*Reada*), and Winsige Seagthman. And when they had come to her, they asked her about the land which her son claimed. Then she said that she had no land which in aught belonged to him, and she burst into a noble rage against her son. Then she called thither her kinswoman Leofflaed, Thurcil's wife, and before those [present] thus addressed her: "'Here sits Leofflaed, my kinswoman, to whom, after my day, I give both my lands and my gold, both gear and garments, and all that I possess.'" After which she said to the thegns: "'Do nobly and well. Announce my message to the court before all the good men, telling them to whom I have given my land and all my belongings; and [that] to my own son [I have] never [given] anything. And bid them be witness of this [gift].'" And they then did so, riding to the court and declaring to all the good men what she had directed them [to say]. Then Thurcil the White stood up in the court and prayed all the thegns to grant his wife a clean title to all the lands which her kinswoman had given her, and they did so. And Thurcil then rode to St. Aethelberht's monastery, with the leave and witness of all the folk, and caused this [grant] to be set forth in a Christ's book.[25]

(Anglo-Saxon) *Ibid.*, pp. 336 f.

(G) EDWARD THE CONFESSOR: GRANT TO WESTMINSTER ABBEY

(1056)

I, King Edward, give friendly greeting to Bishop Wulfwig, Earl Gyrth, and all my thegns of Oxfordshire. And I make known to you that I have granted to Christ and to St. Peter of Westminster the village where I was born, by name Islip, and half a hide at Marsh, free of *scot* and *gafol*,[26] with all things thereto pertaining, in wood and in field, in meadow and in water, with the church and the churchsoke,[27] as full and as complete and as free as it stood under my own hand, and as Aelfgifa Emma, my mother, gave and bequeathed it to me as a first gift on my birthday. And I grant them moreover *sac* and *soc*, *toll* and *team*, *infangenepeof*, *blodwite*, and *weardwite*, *hamsocn*, *forsteall*, *grybbryce* and *mundbryce*,[28] and all the rights which [there] belong to me. Now I greet well my beloved kinsman, Wigod, at Wallingford, and I bid thee on my behalf ride around these lands [and put them] into the possession of the saint; for I

[25] That is to say, formally recorded by a monastic scribe.
[26] The two words together cover all rents and taxes; see above, p. 7, n. 3. *Scot* also appears in eleventh-century documents as the equivalent of *geld*; see below, p. 38, n. 2.
[27] The territory subjected to the jurisdiction of the church.
[28] *Infangenepeof* was the right to punish thieves caught on the property; *blodwite* the fine for wounding with bloodshed; *weardwite* the fine for neglect of guard duty. For the other terms, see above, pp. 22, 30.

THE ANGLO-SAXON PERIOD

will on no account permit any man there to hold any authority, over anything or at any time, save only the abbot and the brothers for the sake of the monastery's worthy needs.

And whoever shall firmly hold this [grant in] alms, may God and God's Mother hold him in everlasting bliss. And whoever shall turn it aside, may he be turned aside from God to the bitter pains of hell's inmates, unless he be the more painfully shall make amends on this earth.

May God and St. Peter keep you!

(Anglo-Saxon) *Ibid.*, pp. 368 f.

SECTION II

THE NORMAN KINGS

The more important constitutional documents of the Norman period naturally fall into two divisions: those connected with the reign of William I (1066-87) and those connected with the reign of his talented son, Henry I (1100-35). Here included are such ordinances of the Conqueror as have survived, together with a selection of typical writs emanating from his chancery. The great inquest of 1086 is illustrated by the famous Cambridgeshire return, as well as by characteristic excerpts from the final condensation that became known as Domesday Book. Although Henry I's reign is especially noteworthy for the development of a more efficient central government, it has little to offer in the way of formal enactments. His Coronation Charter was, in all probability, never intended to be enforced, and is chiefly significant because it served as a precedent for Magna Carta. We have one brief ordinance, dealing with the shire and hundred courts, but it tells us almost nothing about their composition. For additional details we have to fall back on the wretched compilation misnamed *Leges Henrici Primi*. The few passages translated below (no. 26) are among those which apparently give authentic information on the legal usages of the early twelfth century. With regard to the organization of the exchequer, and the other financial measures now generally attributed to Henry I, our best source is the pipe roll of 1130,[1] so a considerable portion of it has been included in the following pages. And since Henry's reign marked the opening of a new era in British municipal history, three famous records of his activity in that respect have been placed under one heading, together with William I's vague grant to the Londoners.

Throughout the Norman period feudal tenures were established and regulated by oral agreement rather than by charter. We have, however, ample proof that enfeoffment for knight service and serjeanty, as well as in free alms, was extended to all parts of his

---

[1] Originally published by the Record Commission in 1833 and reprinted by the Pipe Roll Society in 1929.

33

THE NORMAN KINGS

conquered kingdom, and that the feudal aids and incidents—perhaps even scutage—were quite familiar features of the system from the beginning. The illustrations here presented have been chosen because they are among the earliest and most specific available. Finally, within the present section, it has seemed well to give a complete English version of the *Constitutio Domus Regis* (no. 29), apparently an official survey of the king's household arrangements drawn up shortly after the death of Henry I. It is a most remarkable document, graphically revealing how, in a feudal age, matters of government and of domestic economy were intimately combined.

An exhaustive catalogue of the acts of William I and William II, with full bibliographical references, will be found in the *Regesta Regum Anglo-Normannorum* of H. W. C. Davis, additional volumes of which are promised in the near future. The original texts of the Conqueror's ordinances, Henry I's Coronation Charter, his writ concerning the shire and hundred courts, and the two charters to London are available, not only in the books of Liebermann and Robertson already cited (above, p. 1), but also in Stubbs, *Select Charters*. Along with the other Anglo-Norman compilations, the *Leges Henrici Primi* are excellently edited, though not translated, in Liebermann's *Gesetze*. The greater part of Domesday Book is translated, and usually provided with valuable introductions, in the appropriate volumes of the *Victoria History of the Counties of England*.

The constitutional history of this period, like that of the one preceding, can no longer be accepted as it appears in the classic pages of Stubbs. The revisions forced by the penetrating criticisms of J. H. Round, F. W. Maitland, Paul Vinogradoff, R. L. Poole, and other scholars have been admirably summarized by Petit-Dutaillis; but since he wrote his *Supplementary Studies* many additional contributions have been made to the subject— prominent among them F. M. Stenton's *First Century of English Feudalism*. On all phases of borough development during this period the student is referred to the books of J. Tait and C. Stephenson cited above (p. 2). More specific references are from time to time given in the footnotes.

So far as legal history is concerned, the chapters in Pollock and Maitland must long remain our chief authority and inspiration.

17. WILLIAM I: ORDINANCE   35

16. WILLIAM I: ORDINANCE CONCERNING TRIALS

William, king, gives friendly greeting to all before whom this writing may come throughout all England, bidding and urging all men throughout all England to observe it, to wit:—

If an Englishman challenges any Frenchman to combat for theft or for manslaughter or for any cause in which combat or judgment (*dom*) is customarily had between two men, he shall have full leave to accept [the challenge]. And if the Englishman rejects combat [as a mode of trial], the Frenchman whom the Englishman has accused shall clear himself by oath against him, with oath-helpers according to Norman law. Furthermore, if a Frenchman challenges an Englishman to combat, for [one of] the same causes, the Englishman shall have full leave to defend himself by combat, or by [the ordeal of] iron, if that suits him better. And if, being infirm, he will not or cannot engage in combat, he shall get him a lawful champion [to take his place]. And if the Frenchman is overcome, he shall give the king £3. And if the Englishman will not defend himself [either] by combat or with oath-helpers, he shall clear himself by [the ordeal of] iron. And in all cases involving outlawry the king ordains that the Englishman shall clear himself by [the ordeal of] iron. And if an Englishman accuses a Frenchman in a cause involving outlawry, and then wishes to prove the charge against him, the Frenchman shall defend himself by combat. And if the Englishman does not dare to challenge him to combat, the Frenchman shall defend himself by an unprescribed (*unforedan*) oath.[1]

(Anglo-Saxon) Liebermann, *Gesetze*, I, 484.

---

[1] One that did not have to be letter-perfect, at least not in Anglo-Saxon.

17. WILLIAM I: ORDINANCE ON CHURCH COURTS

W[illiam], by the grace of God king of the English, to R[alph] Bainard, G[eoffrey] de Mandeville, P[eter] de Valognes, and my other faithful men of Essex, Hertfordshire, and Middlesex, greeting.[1] Be it known to all of you, and to my other faithful men resident in England, that, by the common counsel of the archbishops, bishops, abbots, and all the princes of my realm, I have decided to amend the ecclesiastical law,[2] which up to my own time has not been rightly observed in England, nor in accordance with the holy canons. I ordain and, by my royal authority, command that henceforth, when ecclesiastical law is involved, no bishop or archdeacon shall hold pleas in the hundred [court], nor shall he bring to judgment before laymen any

---

[1] Similar writs were presumably sent to the other shires.

[2] *Leges episcopales*, literally "episcopal laws." For the presence of the bishop in the shire court during the previous period, see Edgar, III, 5 (above, p. 19), and Cnute, II, 18 (above, p. 23). And on the "common counsel" in the earlier part of the sentence, see A. B. White, in the *American Historical Review*, XXV, 15 f.

18. WILLIAM I: TEN (ATTRIBUTED) ARTICLES[1]

(Latin: *Ibid.* I, 485 f.

1. In the first place, he wishes above all else the one God to be venerated throughout his entire kingdom; the one Christian faith always to be kept inviolate; peace and security to be maintained between Englishmen and Normans.

2. We have also ordained that by covenant and oath every freeman shall promise within and without England to be faithful to King William, with him and before him to keep and defend his lands and his honour with all fealty against his foes.

3. It is also my will that all men whom I have brought with me, or who have come after me, shall be under my peace and protection. And if any one of them is slain, his lord[2] shall take the slayer within five days if he can; if, however, he cannot, he shall make a beginning of paying to me 46m.[3] of silver [and shall continue with his payment] as long as the property of that lord shall last. When, moreover, the property of that lord fails, the entire hundred in which the homicide

---

[1] This unofficial compilation apparently summarizes various authentic decrees of the Conqueror that have not come down to us. In some cases the provisions are confirmed by other sources. The parts omitted, for example, are approximate repetitions of no. 16.

[2] In the text as it stands the *eius* seems to refer to the slain man; but it is more likely that William put the responsibility on the slayer's lord, who would almost certainly be an Englishman. This document is our oldest source for the murder fine (*murdrum*), which is frequently heard of in later records; see particularly no. 26, art. 91.

[3] The Norman mark was two-thirds of a pound; see above, p. 21, n. 3.

18. WILLIAM I: TEN ARTICLES 37

was committed shall bear the common responsibility of paying what remains [of the debt].

4. And every Frenchman who was in England during the time of King Edward, my kinsman, [and was there] sharing the customs of Englishmen—what they call being in scot and lot—shall be paid for according to the law of the English.[4] This decree was enacted at Gloucester.

5. We also forbid that any livestock be bought or sold anywhere except within cities,[5] and this before three trustworthy witnesses; nor shall any used thing [be bought or sold] without a surety and a warrantor. And if any one does otherwise, let him pay double the value [of the goods] and afterwards a forfeiture [to us]. . . . .

7. This likewise I wish and enjoin: that in [cases affecting] lands, as in all other matters, all shall keep and hold the law of King Edward, with the addition of those [amendments] which I have made for the benefit of the English people.

8. Every one who wishes to be considered a freeman shall be in pledge, so that his pledge shall hold and keep him for justice should he commit any offence.[6] And should any such [offender] escape, his pledges shall see to the payment of simple compensation toward the claim and shall clear themselves [by oath] of having been cognizant of any fraud in that escape. The hundred and county[7] [courts] shall be attended in accordance with the decrees of our predecessors. And let those who rightly owe attendance, but who refuse to attend, be summoned once. And if they refuse to attend on the second summons, let one ox be taken [as a fine] and let them be summoned a third time. And if they do not attend on the third summons, let a second ox be taken. If, however, they do not attend on the fourth summons, let the amount claimed [in the suit against them]—what is called *ceapgeld*[8]—be given [to the claimant], and to the king his forfeiture in addition.

9. I forbid, on pain of my full forfeiture, that any one shall sell a man outside his native land.

10. I also forbid that any one be slain or hanged for any offence,

---

[4] Such a Frenchman was to be regarded as a naturalized Englishman, for whom compensation had to be paid according to the customary law in force before the Conquest.

[5] The *civitas* of this passage is apparently a mere translation of *port* or *burh*, the official trading centre specified in the dooms since the days of Edward the Elder.

[6] Under the Norman system of frankpledge the lesser freemen throughout the countryside were organized into groups of ten, within which the members were mutually responsible for each other's misdeeds; see the references above, p. 23, n. 6, and no. 26, art. 8. Frankpledge appears prominently in the documents of the next two centuries.

[7] "County" is by derivation a French synonym for the English "shire."

[8] The simple compensation, or *angild*, referred to a few sentences earlier; see above, p. 8, n. 12.

38 THE NORMAN KINGS

but let him be blinded or castrated. And this decree shall not be violated, on pain of my full forfeiture.

(Latin, *Ibid.*, I, 486 f.

19. RECORDS CONCERNING A SUIT (1079-86)

(A) WRIT OF WILLIAM I (1079-83)

William, king of the English, to Lanfranc, archbishop [of Canterbury], and Geoffrey, bishop of Coutances, greeting. See to it that *sac* and *soc*,[1] as between Bishop Wulfstan and Walter, abbot of Evesham, are determined as they were on the day that, in the time of King Edward, geld[2] was last taken for the building of a fleet. And for holding this plea, be you, Geoffrey, president (*praesul*) in my place; and be sure that Bishop Wulfstan fully has what is his right. Also see to it that the bishop justly has the houses in Worcester which he claims as against the abbot, and that all those who hold lands of him are always prepared for my service and his.

Witness, Roger d'Ivry.

(Latin) Bigelow, *Placita Anglo-Normannica*, p. 287.

(B) WRIT OF GEOFFREY, BISHOP OF COUTANCES (1086)

Geoffrey, bishop of Coutances, to Remi, bishop [of Lincoln], and Walter Giffard and Henry de Ferrers and Adam [de Port], and the other barons of the king, greeting. Know that, as I now give testimony, when by the king's precept I held the plea between Bishop Wulfstan and the abbot of Evesham, the bishop proved the three hides at Bengeworth and the houses in the city [of Worcester] to belong to his fief, so that thence the abbot owes him service like his other vassals (*feudati*). And he proved that the *sac* and *soc* of Hampton belong to his hundred of Oswaldslaw; that the pleas [of Hampton] should be heard there; that geld, host,[3] and other lawful services should be rendered to him from those fifteen hides [at Hampton]; and that church-scot[4] and burial fees (*sepulturu*) should be paid at his vill of Croppethorn. This was sworn and proved before me and Urse d'Abetot and Osbern Fitz-Escrop, and other barons of the kingdom, by the judgment and testimony of the whole county [court].

(Latin) *Ibid.* p. 287.

(C) WRIT OF WILLIAM I (1086)

William, king of the English, to Urse, sheriff [of Worcestershire], and Osbern Fitz-Escrop and all men, French and English, of Worces-

---

[1] See above, p. 30, n. 23.
[2] *Geld*, like *scot*, was a general word that could be used to denote any tax or exaction: see above, p. 31, n. 26, and below, no. 27A. More specifically, as in Domesday Book, the term was used to refer to the Danegeld.
[3] *Expeditio*—the Anglo-Saxon *fyrd*, not the feudal service established after the Norman Conquest.
[4] Obscure payments in kind for the support of a local church; see Maitland, *Domesday Book and Beyond*, p. 321.

tershire, greeting. I will and command that Bishop Wulfstan shall have *sac* and *soc* and services and all customs belonging to his hundred and to his lands as fully as he best had them in the time of King Edward. And with regard to the lands which he has proved to be held of his fief by the abbot of Evesham—namely, the four[5] hides at Bengeworth and the houses in the city—I command that, if the abbot wishes to keep them, he must thence do service to the bishop like the other vassals of the latter. And with regard to the fifteen hides at Hampton, whence the bishop has proved soke and geld and host and other services of mine to belong to his hundred, and church-scot and burial fees to belong to his vill, I forbid any one to obstruct his tenure, but command that he shall enjoy all those [services] for my benefit and his, as was by my precept sworn and proved before Bishop Geoffrey and before you. By the witness of the said Bishop Geoffrey and of Roger d'Ivry.

(Latin) *Ibid.*, p. 19.

[5] Either this figure or the one given above is an error.

20. WILLIAM I: WRITS CONCERNING INQUESTS AT ELY

(A) CONFIRMATION OF LIBERTIES FOR THE ABBOT OF ELY (*c.* 1080)

William, king of the English, to all his faithful men and his sheriffs in those counties where the abbey of Ely possesses lands, greeting. I command that, in borough and out of borough, the abbey of Ely shall have all its customs: namely, *sac* and *soc, toll* and *team, infangenepeof, hamsocn, gryðbryce, fihtwite, fyrdwite*,[1] and all other forfeitures within its own land and from its own men. These [liberties], I say, it shall have as it had them on the day that King Edward was alive and dead and as, according to my command, they were proved at Kentford by [the oaths of] various shires in the presence of my barons: namely, Geoffrey, bishop of Coutances; Abbot Baldwin, Ivo Taillebois, Peter de Valognes; Picot, sheriff [of Cambridge]; Tihel de Heluin, Hugh de Hosdeng, Jocelyn of Norwich, and many others.

Witness, Roger Bigod.

(Latin) Hamilton, *Inquisitio Comitatus Cantabrigiensis*, p. xviii.

(B) MANDATE FOR A RENEWED INQUEST (1082).

William, king of the English, to Lanfranc, archbishop [of Canterbury], and Roger, count of Mortain, and Geoffrey, bishop of Coutances, greeting. I command and instruct you that you again cause to be assembled all the shires that were present at the plea held concerning the lands of the church of Ely before my wife last came to Normandy. Let there also be present with them those of my barons who can suitably attend, those men who were at the afore-

[1] Cf. no. 15G.

said plea, and those who hold lands of the same church. When these men have been brought together, let several be chosen of those Englishmen who know how the lands of the said church lay on the day that King Edward died, and let whatever they may say in that connection be testified to on oath. When that is done, let restitution be made to the church of those lands that were in its demesne on the day of Edward's death, except those which men shall claim as having been given them by me. These [lands] then signify to me by letters, [telling] what they are and who holds them. But those holding thegnlands[2] that beyond doubt should be held of the church shall make peace with the abbot as best they may; and if they refuse [to do so], the church shall keep their lands. Let the same be done with regard to those holding *sac* and *soc*. Lastly, order those men to repair the bridge of Ely who up to now, by my disposition and command, have been accustomed so to do.

(Latin) *Ibid.*, p. xviii.

---

[2] Lands that before the Conquest had been held of the church by thegns. Men styled thegns occasionally appear in the Norman documents, but they were generally supplanted by French knights.

21. RETURN FROM THE DOMESDAY INQUEST (1086)

Here is written down the inquisition of the lands [of Cambridgeshire] as made by the king's barons:[1] namely, by the oath of the sheriff of the shire; of all the barons, their Frenchmen, and the whole hundred [court]; of the priest, the reeve, and six villeins of each vill.[2] Then [is set down] how the manor is called, who held it in the time of King Edward, who holds it now, how many hides there are, how many ploughs in demesne, how many ploughs of the men, how many men, how many villeins, how many cotters, how many serfs, how many freemen, how many sokemen, how much woods, how much meadow, how many pastures, how many mills, how many fishponds, how much has been added or taken away, how much it was worth altogether and how much now, and how much each freeman or sokeman had or has there. All this [information is given] three times over: namely, in the time of King Edward, when King William gave it out, and how it is now—and whether more can be had [from it] than is being had.

These men swore. . . .[3]

(Latin) *Ibid.*, pp. 97 f.

---

[1] See Round, *Feudal England*, pp. 3 f., 118 f. On this fundamental criticism all subsequent study of Domesday has been based.

[2] Cf. no. 26, art. 7.

[3] Here follows a long list of names, arranged hundred by hundred. These groups were the juries that made the original returns. Domesday Book is a compilation made by condensing such material and rearranging it, so that the manors are enumerated as land of the king or land of a particular baron.

22. EXCERPTS FROM DOMESDAY BOOK
(A) HEREFORDSHIRE

In the city of Hereford, in the time of King Edward, there were 103 men dwelling together inside and outside the wall, and they had the customs hereinunder noted.[1] If any one of them wished to leave the city, he could, with the consent of the reeve, sell his house to another man who was willing to perform the service owed from it, and the reeve got the third penny from this sale. But if any one, because of his poverty, could not perform the service, he gave up his house without payment to the reeve, who saw to it that the house did not remain vacant and that the king did not lose the service. Every entire messuage (*integra masura*) inside the wall rendered 7½d., and [also] 4d. for the hire of horses; and [the holder] reaped for three days at Marden[2] and spent one day gathering hay wherever the sheriff wished. Whoever had a horse went thrice a year with the sheriff to the pleas and the hundred [court] at Wormelow.[3] When the king engaged in a hunting expedition, one man customarily went from each house to serve as a beater (*ad stabilationem*) in the wood. Other men, who did not have entire messuages, found guards for the [royal] hall when the king was in the city. On the death of a burgess who served with a horse, the king had his horse and arms.[4] From him who had no horse, when he died, the king had either 10s. or his land, together with the houses [on it]. If any one, overtaken by death, had not divided what he possessed, the king had all his chattels (*pecunia*). These customs were had alike by those living in the city and by those dwelling outside the wall, except that an entire messuage outside the wall rendered only 3½d. The other customs were common [to both groups].

Any man's wife who brewed inside or outside the city gave 10d. according to custom. There were six smiths in the city, each of whom gave 1d. for his forge. Each of them made 120 shoes (*ferra*) from the king's iron, and to each of them 3d. was customarily paid on that account, and these smiths were quit of all other custom. Seven moneyers were there; one of them was the bishop's moneyer. When the coinage was changed, each of them gave 18s. to obtain the dies, and from the day on which they returned each of them gave the king 20s. for one month;[5] and in the same way the bishop had 20s. from his moneyer. When the king came to the city, the moneyers

---
[1] On the interpretation of the following entries, see especially Round, in *Victoria History of Herefordshire*, I, 263 f.
[2] A nearby royal manor.
[3] This was south of Hereford, toward the wild region of Archenfield. On such a trip the sheriff needed an armed escort.
[4] The heriot of the ordinary thegn in Canute, II, 71 (above, p. 24). Cf. the moneyers of Hereford, the Welshmen of Archenfield, and the thegns of Nottinghamshire in the following passages.
[5] Presumably a pound a month, for relatively large sums were reported from mints elsewhere.

made for him as many pennies as he wished—that is to say, of the king's silver. And these seven had their *sac* and *soc*. When any moneyer of the king died, the king had 20s. as relief.⁶ But if he died without having divided his cash (*censum*), the king had all of it. If the sheriff went into Wales with an army, these men [of Hereford] went with him. But if any one was summoned to go and did not do so, he paid 40s. fine to the king.

In this city Earl Harold⁷ had 27 burgesses enjoying the same customs as the other burgesses. From this city the reeve rendered £12 to King Edward and £6 to Earl Harold, and he had in his farm all the aforesaid customs.⁸ The king, however, had in his demesne three forfeitures: namely, breach of his peace, house-breaking, and assault by ambush. Whoever committed one of these [offenses] paid the king 100s. fine, whosesoever man he was.⁹ Now the king has the city of Hereford in demesne,¹⁰ and the English burgesses who dwell there have their previous customs. The French burgesses, however, are quit, through [payment of] 12d., of all forfeitures except the three aforesaid.¹¹ This city renders to the king £60 by tale in assayed money.¹² Between the city and the eighteen manors that render their farms in Hereford £335. 18s. are accounted for, besides the pleas of the hundred and county [courts].¹³

In Archenfield the king has three churches. The priests of these churches undertake the king's embassies into Wales, and each of them sings for the king two masses every week. When any one of them dies, the king customarily has 20s. from him. If any Welshman steals a man or a woman, a horse, an ox, or a cow, on being convicted, he first returns what has been stolen and [then] pays 20s. as a fine. For theft of a sheep, however, or of a bundle of sheaves, he pays 2s. fine. If any one kills a man of the king or commits house-breaking, he pays the king 20s. compensation for the man and 100s. as fine. If he kills any thegn's man, he gives 10s. to the lord of the slain man. But if a Welshman kills a Welshman, the relatives of the slain man come together and plunder the slayer and his kin and burn their houses until, toward

---

⁶ The Anglo-Saxon heriot; see n. 4 on the previous page.

⁷ The Normans refused to recognize Harold's title to the throne.

⁸ The borough, including the revenues described above, was farmed by the portreeve for £18 a year, two-thirds to the king and one-third to the earl.

⁹ The list of crown pleas varied from region to region; cf. the customs of Worcestershire and Nottinghamshire below, and Canute, II, 12 (above, p. 22).

¹⁰ Earlier there had been three great border earls who enjoyed all regalian rights within their respective territories: Roger de Montgomery, earl of Shrewsbury; Hugh d'Avranches, earl of Chester; and William Fitz-Osbern, earl of Hereford. Before 1086, however, the third of these earldoms had been forfeited as the consequence of a rebellion.

¹¹ Cf. the entry for Rhuddlan, below.

¹² See below, p. 49, no. 25, n. 1.

¹³ These manors had earlier belonged to Earl William, and so had been brought into a financial organization centering in Hereford.

22. DOMESDAY BOOK

noon on the following day, the body of the slain man is buried. Of this plunder the king has the third part, but they enjoy all the rest of it in peace. He, however, who burns a house in another fashion, on being accused of doing so, defends himself by [the oaths of] forty men. But if he cannot [clear himself], he has to pay 20s. fine to the king. If any one conceals a sester of honey out of a customary payment, and is convicted of it, he renders five sesters for one, should he hold enough land to warrant the payment. If the sheriff calls them to the shire court, six or seven of the better men among them go with him [as escort]. He who is summoned [to the court] and does not go gives the king 2s. or an ox; and whoever stays away from the hundred [court] pays the same amount. He who is commanded by the sheriff to go with him into Wales, and does not do so, pays a similar fine. But if the sheriff does not go, none of them has to go. When the army advances against the enemy, they customarily form the advance guard, and on return [they form] the rear guard. These were the customs of the Welshmen in Archenfield during the time of King Edward.

Here are set down those holding lands in Herefordshire and in Archenfield and in Wales. . . .[14]

The land of the king. . . . The king holds Leominster.[15] Queen Edith held it. . . . In this manor . . . there were 80 hides, and in demesne 30 ploughs.[16] In it were 8 reeves, 8 beadles, 8 ridingmen, 238 villeins, 75 bordars, and 82 serfs and bondwomen.[17] These together had 230 ploughs. The villeins ploughed 140 acres of the lord's land and sowed it with their own seed grain, and by custom they paid £11. 52d. The ridingmen paid 14s. 4d. and 3 sesters of honey; and there were eight mills [with an income] of 73s. and 30 sticks of eels.[18] The wood rendered 24s. besides pannage.[19] Now

---

[14] According to the regular plan, the king heads the list of landholders and is followed by his barons, first the ecclesiastics and after them the laymen. The lands held by each person in the list are then described in turn, manor by manor.

[15] On this "gigantic manor" see Maitland, *Domesday Book and Beyond*, p. 112.

[16] By *caruca* is meant, not merely the plough proper, but also the team of eight oxen. The hide in Domesday is a unit of assessment for geld and other royal services. It was divided into 4 virgates or yardlands, 8 bovates, and 120 acres.

[17] The beadle appears in Domesday as the subordinate of a manorial reeve. The *radcniht* or ridingman seems to have been much the same as a *geneat*; see above, p. 8, n. 8. The *villani* of Domesday, being distinguished from *servi*, were legally free; for it was only later that serfdom and villeinage came to be arbitrarily identified. According to Domesday, the normal villein holding was thirty acres of arable. The bordar or cotter, on the other hand, held only a hut and a garden plot. See especially Maitland, *Domesday Book and Beyond*, pp. 26 f.; Vinogradoff, *Villeinage in England*.

[18] About two dozen eels were counted as a stick. Most of them, obviously, were taken from mill-ponds.

[19] Swine were commonly allowed to run wild in woodland. Rent paid for the privilege was called pannage; see immediately below.

in this manor the king has in demesne 60 hides and 29 ploughs; and 6 priests, 6 ridingmen, 7 reeves, 7 beadles, 224 villeins, 81 bordars, and 25 serfs and bondwomen. Among them all they have 201 ploughs. They plough and sow with their own grain 125 acres, and by custom they pay £7. 14s. 8½d.; also 17s. [worth] of fish, 8s. of salt, and 65s. of honey. In it are eight mills [with an income] of 108s. and 100 sticks of eels less 10. A wood 6 leagues[20] long and 3 leagues wide renders 22s. Of these shillings 5 are paid for buying wood at Droitwich, and thence are obtained 30 mitts of salt.[21] Each villein possessing ten pigs gives one pig for pannage. From woodland brought under cultivation come 17s. 4d. An eyrie of hawks is there. . . . Altogether this revenue, except the eels, is computed at £23. 2s. This manor is at farm for £60 in addition to the maintenance of the nuns. The county[22] says that, if it were freed [of that obligation], this manor would be worth six score, that is to say, £120. . . .

(Latin) Domesday Book, I, 179-83[b].

(B) CHESHIRE

Earl Hugh[23] holds Rhuddlan of the king. There in the time of King Edward lay Englefield, and it was entirely waste. Earl Edwin held it [in the time of King Edward]. It was likewise waste when Earl Hugh received it. Now he has in demesne half the castle that is called Rhuddlan, and it is the administrative centre (*caput*) of this land. There he has eight burgesses and half of the church, half of the mint, half of the mining of iron wherever it may be found in this manor, half of the water of Clwyd in both mills and fisheries that may be conducted there—that is to say, in the part of the river that belongs to the earl's fief—half of the forests that do not belong to any vill of this manor, half of the toll, and half of the vill called Bryn. There is land for three ploughs and they are in demesne, together with seven serfs. . . . Robert of Rhuddlan holds of Earl Hugh half of the same castle and borough, in which Robert himself has ten burgesses. . . .

In this manor of Rhuddlan there was recently built a castle, likewise called Rhuddlan. A new borough is there, and in it [are] eighteen burgesses [divided] between the earl and Robert, as mentioned above. To these burgesses they granted the laws and customs that are [enjoyed] in Hereford and in Breteuil: namely, that during an entire year they shall give for any misdeed no more than 12d., except for homicide, theft, and premeditated house-breaking.[24] In the year of

---

[20] The Domesday league is a mile and a half, but these measurements are only rough approximations.

[21] Salt-wiches are a prominent feature of this region; see Tait, *The Domesday Survey of Cheshire,* pp. 39 f. The wood bought at Droitwich was for the furnaces used in connection with salt-pans. The mitt included two ambers of four bushels each.

[22] I.e., the jury that spoke for it.

[23] See above, p. 42, n. 10; and for illuminating comment on the whole entry, the introduction to Tait's work just cited.

[24] On the significance of these customs, see Mary Bateson, "The Laws of Breteuil," in the *English Historical Review,* vols. XV, XVI; C. Stephenson, *Borough and Town,* pp. 88 f., 120 f.

this description[25] the toll of this borough was placed at farm for 3s. The income of Earl Hugh from Rhuddlan and Englefield is valued at £6. 10s.; Robert's share at £17.

(Latin) *Ibid.,* I, 269.

(C) BERKSHIRE[26]

When geld was given in the time of King Edward, commonly throughout all Berkshire the hide gave 3½d. before Christmas and the same amount at Pentecost. If the king sent an army anywhere, only one soldier went from five hides, and 4s. were given him from each hide as food and pay for two months. This money, indeed, was not sent to the king, but was given to the soldiers. If any one was summoned for an expedition and did not go, he forfeited all his land to the king. But if any one, for the sake of remaining [at home], promised to send another in his place, and yet he remained who was to have been sent, his lord was quit through [payment of] 50s. On the death of a king's household thegn or *cniht,*[27] all his arms, as well as one horse with a saddle and one without, were sent to the king as relief. But if he possessed dogs or hawks, they were given to the king as a present, if the latter was willing to accept them. If any one slew a man enjoying the king's peace, he forfeited to the king both his body and all his substance. He who broke into a city[28] by night paid 100s. fine to the king, not to the sheriff.[29] He who was summoned as a beater for hunting, and did not go, paid the king 50s. fine.

(Latin) *Ibid.,* I, 56ᵇ.

(D) WORCESTERSHIRE

In this county, if any one knowingly breaks the peace which the king has given by his own hand, he is outlawed.[30] If any one knowingly breaks the king's peace given by the sheriff, he pays 100s. fine. He who commits assault by ambush pays 100s. fine. He who commits rape can offer no atonement save judgment upon his body. These forfeitures the king has in the said county except on the land of St. Peter of Westminster, to which King Edward gave whatever [rights] he had there[31]—so the county says. When the king advances against the enemy, any one who is summoned and who remains behind, if he

---

[25] The year of the Domesday inquest, 1086.

[26] Round (in *Domesday Studies,* pp. 77 f.) was the first to explain the significance of the Berkshire custom. For further comment on this and the following entries, see the appropriate volumes of the *Victoria County History.*

[27] See above, p. 41, n. 4. The *cniht* was a sort of lesser thegn; see Gross, *Gild Merchant,* I, 183 f.

[28] Cf. Ine, 45 (above, p. 9); and see above, p. 37, n. 5.

[29] The meaning of this provision and the similar ones below is probably that small fines were included in the sheriff's farm, while more extraordinary ones were not.

[30] Although the present tense is used, the customs described were those of the Anglo-Saxon period.

[31] Cf. no. 15G, above.

is so free a man that he has his *sac* and *soc* and can go with his land whither he pleases,³² is in the king's mercy³³ for all his land. If, however, the freeman of some other lord remains away from the host, and if his lord takes another man in his place, he has to pay 40*s.* to his lord who received the summons. If, however, no one goes for him at all, he shall indeed give to his lord the 40*s.*, but the lord has to pay the same amount to the king.

(Latin) *Ibid.,* I, 172.

(E) NOTTINGHAMSHIRE

. . . In Nottinghamshire and Derbyshire breach of the king's peace, given under [his own] hand or seal, is atoned for by [a fine of] 18 hundreds, each hundred [being] £8.³⁴ Of this fine the king has two parts, the earl the third; that is to say, 12 hundreds go to the king and 6 to the earl. If any one, on conviction of anything, is exiled according to law, no one except the king can restore peace to him. A thegn having more than six manors pays no relief for his land except to the king, [namely,] 3*m.* of silver—wherever he may live, in borough or out of borough. If a thegn having *sac* and *soc* forfeits his land, half of his land and his chattels is shared between the king and the earl; his lawful wife, together with his legitimate heirs if there are any, has the other half.

(Latin) *Ibid.,* I, 280.ᵇ

---

³² That is to say, can commend himself, with his land, to a lord of his own choosing.
³³ See below, p. 48, n. 6.
³⁴ A method of reckoning peculiar to certain Danish regions; see Round, *Feudal England,* p. 73.

23. HENRY I: CORONATION CHARTER (1100)

Henry, king of the English, to Samson, bishop [of Worcester], and to Urse d'Abetot,¹ and to all his barons and faithful men of Worcestershire, both French and English, greeting.

1. Know that by the mercy of God, and by the common counsel of the barons of the whole kingdom of England, I have been crowned king of the same kingdom. And since the kingdom has been oppressed by unjust exactions, I, through fear of God and through the love that I have for you all, in the first place make the Holy Church of God free, so that I will neither sell nor put at farm nor, on the death of an archbishop, bishop, or abbot, take anything from the demesne of a church, or from its men, until a successor enters upon it.² And I henceforth remove all the bad customs through which the kingdom of England has been unjustly oppressed; which bad customs I here in part set down.

---

¹ Sheriff of Worcester. Other forms of address were of course used for the other counties.
² For examples of this feudal usage and of many others abolished or restricted in the Coronation Charter, see Henry's own pipe roll (no. 25).

23. CORONATION CHARTER

2. If any one of my barons, earls, or other men who hold of me dies, his heir shall not redeem his land as he did in the time of my brother, but he shall relieve it by a just and legitimate relief. In the same way, furthermore, the men of my barons shall relieve their lands from their lords by just and legitimate reliefs.

3. And if any one of my barons or other men wishes to give in marriage his daughter, sister, niece, or [other] female relative, let him talk with me about the matter; but I will neither take anything from his property for this permission nor prohibit him from giving her [in marriage], unless he wishes to wed her to an enemy of mine. And if, on the death of a baron or other man of mine, a daughter remains as heiress, I will give her [in marriage], together with her land, by the counsel of my barons. And if, on the death of a husband, his wife survives and is without children, she shall have her dowry and marriage portion,[3] and I will not give her to a husband unless it is in accord with her own wish.

4. If, moreover, the wife survives with children, she shall yet have her dowry and marriage portion so long as she keeps her body legitimately, and I will not give her [in marriage] except in accord with her wish. And the guardian of the land and the children shall be either the widow or another one of the relatives who more rightly ought to be [in that position]. And I command that my barons shall conduct themselves in the same way toward the sons or daughters or wives of their men.

5. The common *monetagium*,[4] which has been collected throughout the cities and counties, and which did not exist in the time of King Edward, I utterly abolish for the future. If [however] any one, whether a moneyer or some one else, is taken with false money, let justice be done in the matter.

6. I pardon all pleas and debts that were owed to my brother, except my lawful farms and except those [payments] which were agreed on for the sake of others' inheritances or of those things that more rightly affected others.[5] But if any one has pledged anything for the sake of his own inheritance, that I pardon, as well as all reliefs that have been agreed on for the sake of rightful inheritances.

7. And if any one of my barons or men becomes infirm, as he himself may bestow his chattels or provide [by will] for their bestowal, so, I grant, shall they be bestowed. But if he, prevented by arms or

---

[3] The marriage portion (*maritagium*) was the land conferred on a woman by her father or other relative; the dowry that given her by her husband. To the former she had an absolute title if she survived her husband; in the latter she had only a life estate. Cf. no. 27E, G.

[4] The *monetagium*, which is obscurely referred to in Domesday, was an exaction introduced in England by William I. On the continent it was usually a tax on sales, paid for a term of years on condition that, during such time, no change in the coinage would be made.

[5] Presumably payments made to secure lands and perquisites that had reverted to the crown through escheat or forfeiture. But the clause might also refer to a sum paid by one man to advance the claim of another. For examples see Henry's pipe roll.

infirmity, has not bestowed his chattels or provided [by will] for their bestowal, his widow or his children or his relatives or his liegemen shall divide them for the good of his soul as may seem to them best.

8. If any one of my barons or men commits an offence, he shall not [be declared] in mercy [and required to] give a pledge from his chattels,[6] as he was in the time of my father and my brother; but he shall pay compensation according to the measure of the offence, as was done before the time of my father, in the time of my other predecessors. But if he is convicted of treason or disgraceful crime,[7] let him make amends as is just.

9. I also pardon all murders[8] [committed] before that day on which I was crowned king, and those that have been committed afterwards are to be paid for by just compensation according to the law of King Edward.

10. By the common counsel of my barons, I have kept in my hands the forests as they were held by my father.[9]

11. To knights who hold their lands by military service (*per loricas*) I grant, of my own gift, the lands of their demesne ploughs[10] quit of all gelds and of all work; so that, inasmuch as they are thus relieved of a heavy burden, they may the better provide themselves with arms and horses, to be fit and ready for my service and the defence of my kingdom.

12. I establish my firm peace throughout the whole kingdom and command that it be henceforth maintained.

13. I restore to you the law of King Edward, together with those amendments by which my father, with the counsel of his barons, amended it.[11]

14. If any one, since the death of my brother William, has taken anything from my property or from the property of any one else, let him at once restore it without penalty; but if any one keeps anything [of that sort], he on whom it may be found shall pay me heavy compensation.

Witnesses: Maurice, bishop of London; William, bishop elect of Winchester; Gerard, bishop of Hereford; Henry, earl [of Warwick]; Simon, earl [of Northampton]; Walter Giffard, Robert de Montfort, Roger Bigot, Odo the Steward, Robert Fitz-Hamon, Robert Malet. At Westminster, when I was crowned. Farewell!

(Latin) Liebermann, *Gesetze*, I, 521 f.

---

[6] This was a promise to abolish the system of amercement, or arbitrary fine, introduced by the Conqueror, and to revert to the older system of *bot* and *wite*, but it was not kept; see Pollock and Maitland, II, 513 f. Many examples of amercement will be found in the following documents.

[7] *Perfidiae vel sceleris*—offences for which there was no lawful compensation in money; cf. Alfred, 4 (above, p. 10), and the subsequent dooms.

[8] See above, p. 36, n. 2.

[9] See no. 35 and the references there given.

[10] Cf. no. 22A. If carried out, the reform would have been equivalent to a heavy reduction of hidage on all baronial manors.

[11] Cf. no. 18, art. 7.

24. HENRY I: ORDINANCE ON LOCAL COURTS

Henry, king of the English, to Samson, bishop [of Worcester], Urse d'Abetot, and all his barons of Worcestershire, French and English, greeting. Know that I grant and command that henceforth [the courts of] my counties and hundreds shall meet in the same places and at the same times as they did in the time of King Edward, and not otherwise. And I am unwilling that my sheriff, on account of any business that peculiarly concerns him, should have them meet in any other way. For I, when I please and on my own decision, will have them adequately summoned for the sake of my royal needs (*dominica necessaria*). And henceforth, if a plea arises concerning the division or occupation of lands, and if it is between my own barons (*dominicos barones meos*), let it be tried in my court.[1] And if it is between vassals of some baron who holds an honour of me, let the plea be tried in the court of their lord. And if it is between vassals of two lords, let it be tried in the county [court]. And this [trial] shall be by combat unless it is given up through their own fault (*nisi remanserit in eis*). Also I will and command that all men of the county shall attend the county [court] and the hundred [courts] as they did in the time of King Edward, and no peace or quittance of mine shall excuse them from following my pleas and judgments according to the usage of that time.[2]

Witnesses: R[ichard], bishop of London; Roger, Bishop [of Salisbury]; Ralph the Chamberlain; Robert, count of Meulan. At Reading.

(Latin) *Ibid.,* I, 524.

---

[1] His feudal court, made up of his vassals.

[2] Nevertheless, specific exemption from suit to shire and hundred courts was not infrequent in royal grants of immunity; e.g., no. 27A. For a general discussion of the principles involved, see Pollock and Maitland, I, 537 f.; and cf. no. 26.

25. PIPE ROLL OF 31 HENRY I (1130)

(A) WARWICKSHIRE ACCOUNT

Geoffrey de Clinton renders account of 44s. 8d. blanch[1] from the old farm. He has paid it into the treasury. And he is quit.

And the same man [renders account] of the new farm. In the treasury £100. 4s. 4d. by weight. And he owes £32. 9s. 4d. blanch.

And the same Geoffrey renders account of 310m. of silver for an office in the treasury at Winchester. In the treasury 100m. of silver. And he owes 210m. of silver.

And the same man owes 40m. of silver on behalf of the earl of Leicester for the debt of Ernald de Vétheuil.

---

[1] Payment by tale was made by counting out 240d. to the pound, as distinguished from payment by weight, when an actual pound of silver was demanded. If, furthermore, sample coins were melted down and an additional sum was thrown in as compensation for proved debasement, payment was said to be blanch. For a description of this procedure and of the whole exchequer system, see R. L. Poole, *The Exchequer in the Twelfth Century.*

And the same man owes 20*m*. of silver and 1*m*. of gold that the king will confirm in a charter for his church of Arden everything that the earl of Warwick gave him for the benefit of the said church.

And the same man owes £7. 13*s*. 8*d*. from the old farm of the land of William de Roumare.

And the same man owes 40*m*. of silver with which he should acquit Nicholas Fitz-Gundewin of Rouen.

Geoffrey Lovet owes £9. 13*s*. 4*d*. for the security that he unjustly took from a certain man; of which [money] the pledges are Geoffrey de Clinton and Robert de Neufbourg.

Osbert of Arden renders account of £10 for the pleas of William Hubold.[2] In the treasury 40*s*. And he owes £8.

And the same sheriff renders account of 100*s*. from old pleas and murders.[3] In pardon by the king's writ to the earl of Warwick 100*s*. And he is quit.

Hugh Fitz-Richard renders account of 200*m*. of silver and one valuable horse (*equo de pretio*) and two war-horses (*dextrariis*) for the land that Geoffrey de Lovet holds of him. In the treasury £30. And by the witness of Miles of Gloucester he has acquitted himself toward the king of the valuable war-horse (*dextrario pretioso*). And he owes 155*m*. of silver and two horses. And thereof [these men] are pledges: the earl of Warwick, 60*m*. of silver; Henry de Sai, 20*m*. of silver; Henry d'Armentières, 20*m*. of silver.

William Fitz-Ralph renders account of 113*s*. 4*d*. and one war-horse that he may have the land of his father. In the treasury 30*s*. And he owes £4. 3*s*. 4*d*. and one war-horse.

Robert Fitz-Ralph renders account of £4 for his portion of his father's land. In the treasury 20*s*. And he owes 60*s*.

The earl of Warwick renders account of £72. 16*s*. 8*d*. and two war-horses for pleas concerning stags;[4] and of 20*m*. of silver for the land which Geoffrey Lovet holds of him; and of 200*m*. of silver that the king will pardon him the surplus hidage of his manor of Brailles.[5] In the treasury £43. 6*s*. 8*d*. And he owes £176. 2*s*. 4*d*.

Guibert, steward of Roger de Mowbray, renders account of 1*m*. of silver from the pleas of Geoffrey de Clinton. He has paid it into the treasury. And he is quit.

Agnes de Clincamp renders account of 40*s*. that her sons may secure the inheritance of their father's land. She has paid it into the treasury. And she is quit.

And the same sheriff renders account of £8. 5*d*. from arrears of Danegeld. In the treasury 70*s*. 5*d*. And in pardons by the king's writ to the chancellor £4. 10*s*. And he is quit.

Walter Croc renders account of 33*s*. 4*d*. from the old rent of the

---

[2] Entries of this sort normally refer to trials held before the king's justices on mission—already an important source of revenue.

[3] See above, p. 36, n. 2.

[4] Violations of forest law. There are many such entries in the roll.

[5] A reduction of hidage would, of course, mean a reduction of Danegeld, which, as this roll testifies, was by now an annual exaction.

25. PIPE ROLL 31 HENRY I

forest during four years. He has paid it into the treasury. And he is quit.

And the same Walter renders account of 10m. of silver from the new rent of the forest. In the treasury 106s. 8d. And he owes 26s. 8d.

And the same man owes 3m. of gold for having his office again; and £13. 11s. 5d. for the land of Richard Chienewe; and £7. 6s. 8d. for the plea of Roger, son of Eli the *scutellarius*;[6] and £18. 5s. from the pleas of William of Gloucester; and 10 horses and 106 oxen and 200 pigs which he took from the forest, and which did not belong to him but to the forester. And he is in the king's mercy unless the king will be his warrantor for the 30s. that he unlawfully took and did not return.

And the same sheriff renders account of £12. 3s. 10d. from arrears of Danegeld. In the treasury 19s. And in pardons by the king's writ: to Ralph the Butler 60s.; to the count of Meulan 24s.; to Geoffrey de Mandeville 60s. 9d.; to Curtis 10s.; to the earl of Warwick £4. 4s. Total £11. 4s. 10d. And he is quit.

And the same sheriff renders acount of 37s. 2d. from arrears of aid from the borough of Tamworth.[7] He has paid it into the treasury. And he is quit.

New Pleas and New Obligations[8]

Robert Tortran renders account of 60m. of silver for the chattels of William de Chenfara that he took. In the treasury 30m. of silver. And he owes 30m. of silver.

Hugh Hall (*de Hella*) renders account of 100s. for the claims of Leofric Lock. In the treasury 30s. And he owes 70s.

Rodbricht of Bradwell renders account of 100s. from the same pleas. In the treasury 30s. And in pardon by the king's writ to the same Rodbricht 20s. And he owes 50s.

Ralph, son of Godwin Hall (*de Halla*) renders account of 10m. of silver from the same pleas. In the treasury 40s. And he owes 7m. of silver.

Fulk of Mauritania renders account of 30m. of silver for the plea concerning the chattels of Matilda of Stafford. In the treasury 5m. of silver. And he owes 25m. of silver.

Ivo, son of Hugh of Leicester, owes 20m. of silver for the grant of the land which belonged to William de Beaumont, and which the earl of Warwick gave him.

And the same sheriff renders account of Danegeld. In the treasury £78. 12s. 1d. And in pardons by the king's writ: to William Comyn 13s.; to the earl of Chester 24s. . . .[9] Total £50. 5d. And he is quit.

---

[6] Probably keeper of the dishes in the royal kitchen; see below, p. 67.

[7] On the annual *auxilia burgorum* that accompanied the Danegeld, see C. Stephenson, *Borough and Town*, pp. 160 f.

[8] *Conventiones* is the regular form, but it covered a variety of payments besides those based on agreement.

[9] Thirty-five other items enumerated.

And the same sheriff owes 30s. from the aid of the borough of Tamworth.

Geoffrey de Clinton renders account of the farm of Wargrave. In the treasury £80. And he is quit.

And the same Geoffrey renders account of £20 from the old farm of Wallop. He has paid it into the treasury. And he is quit.

And the same Geoffrey renders account of the new farm of Wallop. In the treasury £20. And he owes £20.

And the same Geoffrey renders account of the revenues of the abbey of Evesham. In the treasury £40.

(Latin) Pipe Roll of 31 Henry I, pp. 104 f.

(B) MISCELLANEOUS ENTRIES

Oxfordshire. . . . Matthew de Vernon owes 100 *muids*[10] of wine for the settlement of his brother's duel. . . . The cordwainers of Oxford render account of 5 ounces of gold as a bonus (*gersoma*) for having their gild again. In the treasury 30s. in place of 2 ounces of gold. And they owe 3 ounces of gold. . . .

Nottinghamshire and Derbyshire. . . . Robert de Lusors renders account of £8. 6s. 8d. that he may marry the sister of Ilbert de Lacy. . . . Ralph Halselin renders account of 200m. of silver and 1m. of gold for the relief of his father's land. . . .

Wiltshire. . . . Humphrey de Bohun renders account of £22. 10s. for the relief of his father's land; and of 400m. of silver in order to be steward of the king.[11] . . . And the same sheriff owes 41s. 6d. from arrears of Danegeld. And the same sheriff owes £6. 18d. from arrears of the county's aid.[12] . . .

Yorkshire. . . . And the same sheriff owes £27. 10s. 7d. from arrears of the county's aid. . . . Walter de Chauncey renders account of £15 that he may marry a wife of his own choosing. . . . Thomas of York, son of Wulfgeat (*Ulvieti*), owes one hunting dog in order to be alderman of the gild merchant of York. . . .

Cambridgeshire. . . . Hervey, bishop of Ely, renders account of 7½m. of gold for the office of his nephew William. In the treasury £18 in place of 3m. of gold. And he owes 4½m. of gold. . . . And the same bishop owes £240 that the king will quitclaim him of the bishop's surplus of knights and that the abbey of Charteris may be quit of wardpenny.[13] . . .

Surrey. . . . And the same [John Belet] owes 60s. from old aid of his knights.[14] . . .

Essex. . . . And the same [Richard Fitz-Gilbert] owes 200m. of

---

[10] The *modius* seems to have been a large, rather than a small barrel; cf. the *modius* of grain, below, p. 67.

[11] See below, p. 66.

[12] *Auxilium comitatus*—a tax supplementary to the Danegeld, apparently raised through negotiation with the county court.

[13] Cf. no. 27D.

[14] Entries such as this, in the light of the one preceding, would appear to refer to scutage.

25. PIPE ROLL 31 HENRY I

silver for the help that the king gave him in connection with his debt to the Jews. Juliana, wife of William of Hastings, owes £6 from old aid of knights from the fief of Waleran, her grandfather. . . .

Kent. . . . Turgis, [bishop of] Avranches, renders account of 300m. of silver and 1m. of gold and a war-horse for the land and the widow of Hugh d'Auberville and to have wardship over his son until the latter is twenty years old. . . .

Northamptonshire. . . . Osbert of Leicester owes 200m. of silver that the king will pardon him and Osbert, his clerk, for their malevolence. . . . Guy Maufé renders account of one war-horse that he may be justly treated in the court of his lord.[15] In the treasury 40s. in place of one war-horse. And he is quit. . . .

Norfolk. . . . Benjamin renders account of £4. 5s. that he may keep the pleas that belong to the king's crown.[16] In the treasury 56s. 8d. And he owes 28s. 4d.; and [guarantees] to make a profit of 500m. for the king. . . .

Suffolk. . . . William of Middlehall renders account of 4m. of silver from the pleas of Richard Basset. But he cannot be found in the county, nor has he anything. And so he is quit. . . .

Lincolnshire. . . . And the same sheriff renders account of 1m. of gold for the weavers' gild of Lincoln. In the treasury £6 in place of 1m. of gold. And he is quit. . . . Lucy, countess of Chester, renders account of £266. 13s. 4d. for the land of her father. In the treasury £166. 13s. 6d. And she owes £100; also 500m. of silver that she need not take a husband inside five years. And the same countess renders account of 45m. of silver for the same agreement, to be given to whom the king pleases. To the queen 20m. of silver. And she owes 25m. of silver. And the same lady owes 100m. of silver that she may hold justice in her court among her own men. . . . The burgesses of Lincoln render account of 200m. of silver and 4m. of gold that they may hold the city of the king in chief.[17] . . . Lambert Fitz-Peter renders account of one palfrey for the land of his father. In the treasury 30s. in place of one palfrey. And he is quit. . . .

Durham. . . . And the same Geoffrey renders account of the old farm of the bishropic for the previous year. . . . And the same Geoffrey renders account of the new farm of the bishropric.[18] . . .

London and Middlesex. The four sheriffs of London render account of the farm of London. In the treasury £16. 14s. 9d. blanch. And in fixed liveries £8. 2s. 1d. by tale. And in livery to the count of Mortain £12. 12s. 6d. by tale. And in clothes for the same count 65s. by tale. And in liveries to the serjeants who guard the count and to

---

[15] Cf. no. 33E.

[16] Keeping the crown pleas should be distinguished from trying them. The keeper, whose functions were later taken over by the coroner, had charge of a case until the time that it came to trial before a justice.

[17] That is to say, farm the city direct from the king. The grant, presumably, was not in fee, as was that secured by the Londoners; see no. 28B.

[18] Taken into the king's hands during a vacancy despite his Coronation Charter.

watchmen and doorkeepers at the Tower £12. 3s. 4d. by tale. And in livery to the wife of Owen the Naperer[19] 46s. 8d. by tale. And in livery to Geoffrey the Engineer[20] £10. 12s. 11d. by tale. And in livery to Ralph the Arborer[21] £7. 12s. 1d. by tale. And to the goldsmiths of London for charcoal 60s. 10d. by tale. And in oil to burn before the queen's sepulchre 16s. 2½d. And in livery to the archbishop of Rouen and in clothes for the count of Normandy £23. 10s. by tale. And in herrings, unguent, oil, nuts, and transportation to Woodstock £8. 18s. 5d. by tale. And in the purchase of wine and in transportation £45. 6s. 2d. by tale. And in the purchase of pepper, cummin, ginger, towels, basinets, and linen cloth for the king's use £23. 19s. 9d. by tale. And in building two arches of London Bridge £25 by tale. And in work on the Tower of London £17. 6s. by tale. And in repairing the houses that belonged to Othweard (*Otuerus*), [in repairing] the chapel, and in other minor work 22s. 9d. by tale. And in quittances of toll[22] to the merchants of Thierry, count of Provence, 75s. 3d. by tale. And in the purchase of cloth to place on the queen's sepulchre 3s. by tale. And they owe £310. 9s. 2d. blanch. . . . Abraham and Deuslesalt,[23] Jews, render account of 1m. of gold that they may have their debts from Osbert of Leicester. . . . Rabbi Joseph (*Rubi Gotsce*), the Jew, and Jacob and Manasseh render account of 6m. of gold that the king will help them against Richard Fitz-Gilbert in the matter of his debts. . . . The men of London render account of 100m. of silver that they may have a sheriff of their own choosing.[24] . . . The Jews of London render account of £2000 for the infirm man whom they slew. . . . The abbot of Westminster renders account of 1000m. of silver to collect the goods of his church which were unlawfully dispersed, and to have the custody of them when collected. . . .

(Latin) *Ibid.*, pp. 4 f.

---

[19] See below, p. 67.
[20] *Ingeniator*, one in charge of a siege engine.
[21] *Arborarius*, the exact meaning of which remains doubtful.
[22] The tolls collected in the port of London were included in the farm of the city; hence any special pardon of such payments was charged off on the account as a credit to the sheriffs.
[23] *Dieu-le-saut*, the French equivalent of the Hebrew Isaiah.
[24] This liberty was subsequently confirmed by Henry's charter, no. 28B.

26. EXCERPTS FROM THE "LAWS OF HENRY I"[1]

7. Concerning the general pleas of the counties, how and when they should be held. . . . If any one of the king's barons or other men is lawfully present at the county [court],[2] he may acquit all the land that he there has in his demesne. The same is true if his steward is lawfully present. If both are of necessity absent, the reeve, the priest,

---

[1] Not a collection of royal enactments, but a private compilation which is often obscure or inaccurate: see above, p. 33, also Pollock and Maitland, I, 99.
[2] See below, art. 31.

26. "LAWS OF HENRY I"

and four of the better men of the vill shall attend on behalf of all who are not summoned to the court by name.[3] We have decreed the same to be observed in the hundred . . . with regard to the presence of the lord and his steward, or of the priest, the reeve, and the better men. . . .

8. Concerning the holding of the hundreds. If, however, there is need for a specially full session, all freemen shall assemble twice a year in their hundred . . . for the sake of determining, among other matters, whether the tithings are full. . . . The tenth man, indeed, is to be in charge of each group of nine,[4] and one of the better men, likewise, [is to be in charge of] the whole hundred, and he is called the alderman. . . .

15. Concerning Danegeld. If Danegeld, which earlier was given to the house-carls[5]—that is to say, 12*d.* annually from every hide—is not paid on time, compensation is made with a fine (*wita*). . . .

20. Concerning soke.[6] . . . For all soke is either exclusively or jointly held. In the custody [of subordinates], indeed, there is a threefold distinction [of soke]: under the reeves of manors in the appurtenant hall-motes,[7] under the men in charge of hundreds and boroughs, and under the sheriffs. Archbishops, bishops, earls, and other magnates in the lands under their own authority have *sac* and *soc, toll* and *team,* and *infangþeof*[8] over their own men and in their own [property], and occasionally over the men of another, especially when those men are seized or accused in [the act of] misdoing, and then they are to have adequate compensation; moreover, in other [lands], acquired by purchase or exchange or in any [such] way, they have *sac* and *soc* in ordinary cases and [such cases are tried] in the appurtenant hall-motes. Finally, jurisdiction in capital cases over all barons and magnates, clerical or lay, belongs to the king, no matter where they hold land and whether it is soke of the king or not.[9] . . .

25. Concerning the privileges of the nobles of England. If a plea arises between men of any baron having soke, in case of an ordinary action,[10] the plea is tried in the court of their lord. If it is between

---

[3] As Liebermann remarks (*Gesetze,* III, 316), this article may reflect the provisions of a lost ordinance of Henry I. See also Pollock and Maitland, I, 545 f., and cf. no. 21.

[4] The tithing was really a group of ten; see above, p. 37, n. 6, and below, pp. 78, 109, etc.

[5] Here called *þingemanni,* the members of the royal standing guard under Canute and Edward the Confessor.

[6] See above, p. 30, n. 23.

[7] On the nature and origin of these manorial courts, see Maitland, *Domesday Book and Beyond,* pp. 80 f.

[8] Cf. nos. 15G, 20A, 27F.

[9] The meaning is that in crown pleas the great men were personally subject to the king's justice, without regard to the privileges which they might enjoy within their own fiefs.

[10] One not reserved to the king or under ecclesiastical jurisdiction.

men of two lords having soke, the accused man shall respond in the court of his lord,[11] in case of an ordinary action. . . .

29. Those who should be the king's judges.[12] The king's judges are to be barons of the county, who there have freeholds; by them the cases of individuals should be decided on the prosecution of either party. But villeins, cotters, virgators,[13] or poor and mean persons of this sort are not to be included among the judges. . . .

31. Concerning capital pleas. . . . The county [court] should be attended by bishops, earls, and other magnates, who through just deliberation are to define God's laws and worldly concerns.[14] No one is permitted to dispute the record[15] of a court of the king; elsewhere it may be done by credible men of the court. And no one is to be convicted in capital pleas by testimony [alone].[16] . . . Every one ought to be judged by his peers[17] and [by men] of the same province [in which he lives]. . . .

32. That no one should judge his lord. . . . No one shall judge his lord or bring judgment against one of whom he is the liegeman, even if the case belongs to the prince.[18] If a lord brings suit against his man, he can, if necessary, make use of his counsellors as judges.[19]

33. Concerning the trial of a plea. If any one has a plea tried in his court or in any place of judicial business [under him], he shall summon the peers[20] and his neighbours, so that, when judgment is enforced, he may administer justice that is free and not liable to be contradicted by any one. . . .

51. Concerning the summoning of the hundred. . . . Moreover, as aforesaid, the hundred [court] ought to be assembled every month —that is to say, twelve times a year—and the county [court] twice, unless there is need for it more often. . . .

52. Concerning the king's own plea. If any one is impleaded by the king's justice in a crown plea, whosoever man he may be, he ought not to refuse the justice gage of right.[21] . . .

55. Concerning the privilege of a lord with regard to his man. It is lawful for every lord to summon his man for judgment in his court. Even if the man is residing at a more remote manor in the honour of which he holds, he shall go to court when his lord summons him. If the lord holds various fiefs, a man of one honour is not compelled

---

[11] But see Henry I's ordinance, no. 24.

[12] *Iudices regis*, meaning doomsmen or judgment-finders who declare the royal law.

[13] *Ferdingus (feorðing)* designated a man holding a fourth—presumably of a hide, i.e., a virgate. See above, p. 43, n. 16.

[14] A reflection of Edgar, III, 5 (above, p. 19); but see no. 17.

[15] Either written or oral testimony as to a previous action.

[16] Without ordeal, compurgation, or battle.

[17] His social equals; cf. Magna Carta, art. 39 (below, p. 121).

[18] That is to say, unless it is a crown plea.

[19] As well as his vassals who are to be specially summoned; cf. arts. 29, 55.

[20] The vassals who owed suit to the court.

[21] I.e., security for appearing in court and defending the suit.

26. "LAWS OF HENRY I"

by law to go to court in another, unless it is a case affecting some one else to which his lord summons him. If a man holds of various lords and honours, no matter how much he holds of the others, his primary obligation . . . is to the lord whose liegeman he is. Every man owes fealty to his lord for life and limbs and earthly honour and the keeping of counsel in all that is honest and worthy, saving fealty to God and to the prince of the land. Theft, treason, murder, and whatever is opposed to God and the catholic faith are, indeed, to be undertaken and carried out for no one. But fealty is to be kept toward all lords, and especially toward the lord of whom he is the liegeman, saving fealty to those mentioned above. . . .

80. Concerning homicide in the king's court, army, borough, or castle. If any one commits homicide in a house, court, borough, castle, army, or militia of the king, he shall be in the king's mercy[22] for his chattels or limbs. If assault is committed on any one in the king's highway, it is *forsteal*,[23] and compensation of 100*s*. shall be paid to the king. . . . And a royal highway is defined [as a road] which is always open, which no one can close or divert from its termination, and which leads to a royal city, borough, castle, or port. . . .

87. . . . If any one can prove by judgment of hot iron, or battle, or the production of lawful witnesses or oath-helpers, or [other] fit mode of proof, that he was assaulted and was forced to commit homicide in self-defence, such demonstration on his part shall be considered satisfactory and justice shall accordingly be done. . . .

88. . . . And no one shall forfeit his fief to the deprivation of his legitimate heirs except through felony[24] or the voluntary surrender [of the property]. . . .

91. Concerning the payment of murder [fine].[25] If any Frenchman or any Norman or, lastly, any man from beyond the sea is slain, and the affair turns out so calamitously that it is considered murder and the slayer is unknown and eventually flees, so that within seven days he is not handed over to the king's justice for the carrying out of whatever may be right, 46*m*. of silver shall be paid—40*m*. to the king and 6*m*. to the relatives of the slain man. If the relatives have no accusers or provers,[26] these [6*m*.] shall go to him who does prove [who committed] the murder. Where, however, [the slain man] is found, there must investigation be made according to the law, and the alderman of the hundred and [the lord] on whose land [the slain man] lies should give security that he will be paid for. . . . If the murder is discovered in a house or in a hall or in a close, when it comes to paying the aforesaid 46*m*., whatever is in that manor . . .

---

[22] See above, p. 48, n. 6.
[23] See Canute, II, 12 (above, p. 22).
[24] Default of feudal obligations. Because it involved forfeiture, felony was later made to embrace all sorts of crimes under English law; for examples see no. 54.
[25] See above, p. 36, n. 2.
[26] Through whom to determine the guilty party.

should first be sold. . . . And if thereby the 46m. are forthcoming, nothing is to be sought elsewhere; but if there is a deficiency, it is made up by the hundred in common. If, moreover, the manor in which the murder is discovered is of the king's demesne farm, and if the king so orders, composition for it shall be made by the entire hundred. If the murder is discovered in fields that are open and generally accessible, [the money] shall be supplied by the whole hundred in common, and not merely by him to whom the land belongs. If it happens on the boundary, [the obligation] shall fall on both [territories]. If it is on the king's highway, compensation is to be paid by him who owns the adjacent land. . . .

92. . . . [The death of] an Englishman is not regarded or paid for as murder, but only [that of] a Frenchmen; indeed, should there be no one to prove that the slain man is English, he is held to be French. . . . If the hundred wishes to prove concerning some one that he is not a Frenchman and that [accordingly] there is no murder, this [obligation] is to be entrusted to twelve of the better men from the same hundred, swearing [to that effect]. . . .

(Latin) Liebermann, *Gesetze*, I, 553 f.

27. WRITS CONCERNING FEUDAL TENURES[1]

(A) WILLIAM I: GRANT IN FREE ALMS (1070-71)

William, king of England, to Baldwin, sheriff of Devonshire, and to all his barons and ministers of the province, greeting. Know that I have granted to my monks of Battle [Abbey] the church of St. Olave in Exeter, with all the lands of Sherford and Kenbury, and with all other lands and things belonging to that church. Wherefore I will and command that they shall hold it freely and peacefully, and that, as my royal alms (*elemosina dominica*), it shall be exempt from all custom of earthly service: [namely,] from all pleas and plaints and shires and hundreds,[2] and from all geld, scot, aid, gift,[3] Danegeld, and army [service], with *sac* and *soc*, toll and *infangenepeof*, and all work on castles and bridges.

Witnesses: Thomas, archbishop of York; William Fitz-Osbert. At Winchester.

(Latin) Oliver, *Monasticon Dioecesis Exoniensis*, p. 117.

(B) WILLIAM I: SUMMONS FOR MILITARY SERVICE (1072)

William, king of the English, to Aethelwig, abbot of Evesham, greeting. I command you to summon all those who are under your charge and administration[4] that they shall have ready before me at Clarendon on the octave of Pentecost all the knights that they owe

---

[1] See Pollock and Maitland, I, 240 f.

[2] See above, p. 49, n. 2.

[3] *Donum*, a frequent substitute in the pipe rolls for *auxilium* or *tallagium*; cf. no. 37B.

[4] As Round pointed out, the abbot commanded the military forces of a considerable region; his owed service was only five knights.

27. FEUDAL WRITS

me. Come to me likewise yourself on that day, and bring ready with you those five knights that you owe me from your abbey.
 Witness, Eudo the Steward. At Winchester.
(Latin) Round, *Feudal England*, p. 304.

(C) WILLIAM II: WRIT FOR THE COLLECTION OF RELIEF (1095-96)
 William, king of the English, to all French and English who hold free lands of the bishopric of Worcester, greeting. Know that, since the bishop has died, the honour has reverted into my own hand.[5] It is now my will that from your lands you give me such relief as I have assessed through my barons: [namely,] Hugh de Lacy £20; Walter Punther £20; Gilbert Fitz-Turold £5; Robert, bishop [of Hereford], £10; the abbot of Evesham £30; Walter of Gloucester £20; Roger Fitz-Durand £10. . . .[6] And if any one refuses to do this, Urse and Bernard are to take both his lands and his chattels into my hand.
 Witnesses: Ranulf the Chaplain, Odo the Steward, Urse d'Abetoŭ.
(Latin) *Ibid.*, p. 309.

(D) HENRY I: GRANT CONCERNING SCUTAGE (1127)
 Henry, king of the English, to his archbishops, bishops, abbots, earls, etc., greeting. Know that to the church of St. Aetheldreda of Ely, for the love of God, for the souls of my father and mother, for the redemption of my sins, and on the petition of Hervey, bishop of the same church, I have forgiven £40 of those £100 which the aforesaid church was accustomed to give for scutage whenever scutage was assessed throughout my land of England; so that henceforth forever the church shall on that account give no more than £60 when scutage is levied throughout the land. And so let the aforesaid church be quit in perpetuity of the aforesaid [40] pounds.[7]
 Witnesses: Roger, bishop of Salisbury; Geoffrey, my chancellor; Robert, [keeper] of the seal; William de Tancarville; William d'Aubigny, steward; Ralph Basset, Geoffrey de Clinton, William de Pont-de-l'Arche. At Eling during my crossing.
(Latin) *Ibid.*, p. 268.

(E) HENRY I: GRANT OF AN HEIRESS WITH LANDS (1121)
 Henry, king of the English, to his archbishops, bishops, abbots, earls, and sheriffs, to all his barons, French and English, and to all his faithful men of all England and Wales, greeting. Know that to

---

[5] The feudal custom of northern France quite justified the seizure by a lord of a vacant bishopric or abbacy, but not the collection of a relief from the prelate's vassals. Abuses such as this led to Henry I's exaggerated promises on his accession (see no. 23). It is apparent that reliefs from lay baronies were already customary in the time of William II.

[6] Here in the text follow twenty-two other names with amounts ranging down to 20s.

[7] Despite the pious language of this charter, Henry's concession was not gratuitous; see above, p. 52.

Miles of Gloucester I have given and firmly granted Sibyl, daughter of Bernard de Neufmarché, with all the land of her father Bernard and of her mother after their death, or earlier—that is to say, during their lifetime, if they wish—and with this marriage portion:[8] namely, Talgarth, the forest of Ystradyw, the castle of Hay,[9] and the whole land of Bryn as far as the boundaries of the land of Richard Fitz-Pons—that is to say, as far as Cantref Bychan and Cowarne, a certain vill in England—also the fee and service of Roger de Baskerville, the fee and service of William Revell, the fee and service of Robert de Turberville, and the fee and service of Picard. And I will and enjoin that all the tenants of the aforesaid [land given as] marriage portion shall perform liege homage to [the said Miles] as to their lord, saving my fealty. And all the tenants of all the aforesaid land of Bernard shall likewise perform liege homage to him as to their lord, saving my fealty and [saving the rights of] Bernard so long as he wishes to hold the land. And this I give and grant to [the said Miles] as the purchase of Bernard which he has given to me[10]—and this at the request of the said Bernard and of his wife and of his barons.[11] And I will and firmly enjoin that [the said Miles] shall hold it as well and as honourably, as quietly and as freely, as ever Bernard best and most honourably held it.

Witnesses: Roger, bishop of Salisbury; Robert, bishop of Lincoln; Ralph the Chancellor, Robert the King's Son, William de Tancarville, Nigel d'Aubigny, Payn Fitz-John, Geoffrey Fitz-Payn, Geoffrey de Clinton, Ralph Basset, William Brito d'Aubigny. In the same year that the king took in marriage the daughter of the duke of Louvain, between Easter and Pentecost.

(Latin) Round, *Ancient Charters*, p. 8.

(F) SUBINFEUDATION BY CHARTER (1121-22)

William Peverel of Dover to Hamund Peverel, his brother, and to William Peverel, his nephew, and to all his faithful men, French and English, as well as to all his friends, both present and future, greeting. Know that, for his service, I have given to Thurstan, my steward, and to all his heirs Gidding and Daywell, to be held of me and my heirs in fee and inheritance, with *sac* and *soc*, *toll* and *team*, and *infangenepeof*, in wood and in plain, in vill and in street, in fields and in meadows, in waters and in all other places, in return for the service of half a knight. Witnesses. . . .

(Latin) Stenton, *English Feudalism*, p. 273.

(G) EXCHANGE AND ENFEOFFMENT OF DOWER LAND (*c.* 1123)

We desire [hereby] to make known that Walter of Gloucester has given Little Hereford in fee to William de Mare, his nephew, for the service of two knights. But since Walter of Gloucester and Miles,

---

[8] See above, p. 47, n. 3.
[9] *Haia Talliata* (*Haie Taillé*) a trimmed hedge.
[10] So that the king might bestow it on Miles.
[11] Note that the term baron did not as yet refer solely to a vassal of the king.

his son, earlier gave that aforesaid [Little] Hereford in dower to Sibyl, wife of the same Miles, they have given Bardsley in exchange to the same Sibyl, by the favour and grant of the said Miles. Moreover, the said Sibyl, by the counsel of her good men, of her own will and without any compulsion, has gratuitously ceded Little Hereford to William de Mare on account of the above-named exchange, having received, by way of token and testimony, a certain gold ring from the same William.

Now of this grant and donation the witnesses are. . . .

(Latin) Round, *Ancient Charters*, p. 19.

(H) STEPHEN: CONFIRMATION OF A SERJEANTY

Stephen, king of the English, to the archbishop of York, to his barons, sheriffs, and ministers, and to all his faithful men of Yorkshire, French and English, greeting. Know that I have granted and confirmed to John, my larderer of York, and to David, his son, all his land which he holds of me in chief together with his office of larderer and his livery,[12] and all his lands, from whomsoever he holds them, as he was seised of them on the day that King Henry was alive and dead. Wherefore I will and command that he shall hold them well and in peace, freely and quietly, in wood and in plain, in meadows and pastures, in waters, mills, and marshes, in roads and in sown fields, and in all other places, with *sac* and *soc*, *toll* and *team* and *infangenepeof*, and with all the customs and liberties with which he ever held best and most freely in the time of King Henry.

Witnesses: Robert de Vere, Robert Fitz-Richard. At Nottingham.

(Latin) *Calendar of Patent Rolls, 1385-89*, p. 19.

---

[12] See below, p. 67; also Round, *The King's Serjeants and Officers of State*, pp. 233 f. Besides his central larder, the king maintained various local larders, the chief function of which was the preservation of meat from his forests.

28. GRANTS TO BOROUGHS

(A) WILLIAM I: CHARTER TO LONDON

King William gives friendly greeting to William, bishop [of London], to Geoffrey,[1] portreeve [of London], and to all the burgesses (*burhwaru*) of London, both French and English. And I make known to you that I wish you both [French and English] to enjoy all the rights that you enjoyed in the days of King Edward. I will that every child shall be the heir of his father after his father's lifetime. And I will not permit any man to do you any wrong. God keep you!

(Anglo-Saxon) Libermann, *Gesetze*, I, 486.

(B) HENRY I: CHARTER TO LONDON[2]

Henry, by the grace of God king of England, to the archbishop of

---

[1] That the Gosfregð of this charter was Geoffrey de Mandeville, constable of the Tower and sheriff of London, was indicated by Round, *Geoffrey de Mandeville*, p. 439.

[2] For the dating of this charter after 1130, see J. P. S. Tatlock, in *Speculum*, XI, 461 f.

Canterbury, and to the bishops, abbots, earls, barons, justices, sheriffs, and all his faithful men of all England, both French and English, greeting. Know that to my citizens of London I have granted the shrievalty of London and of Middlesex, to be held at farm for £300 on account at the exchequer, by them and their heirs of me and my heirs;[3] so that the said citizens may install a sheriff, whomsoever they please from among themselves, and a justice,[4] whomsoever they please from among themselves, to keep the pleas of my crown and to try them, and no other man is to be justice over the said men of London. And the citizens shall not be impleaded in any plea outside the walls of the city, and they are to be quit of scot and of Danegeld and of murder-fine,[5] and none of them shall wage battle.[6] And if one of the citizens is impleaded in connection with pleas of the crown, as a man of London, he shall prove his case by an oath to be determined in the city. And within the walls of the city no one is to be billeted; neither for one of my household nor for one of any other is lodging to be exacted by force. And all men of London, together with all their goods, are to be quit and free, throughout all England and throughout all the ports of the sea, from toll, passage, lastage, and all other [such] customs.[7] And churches, barons, and citizens shall well and peaceably have and hold all their sokes[8] together with all customs [of the latter]; so that the tenants who are settled in sokes shall owe customs to none except to him whose soke it is, or to his minister whom he may there appoint. And a man of London shall not be adjudged in mercy as regards his chattels except to the amount of his wergeld, namely, 100s.—that is to say, in a plea that concerns chattels (*pecuniam*).[9] And there shall no longer be [judgments of] *miskenning* in the husting, the folkmote, or in other courts within the city.[10] And the husting shall meet once a week, namely, on Mon-

---

[3] The text of the preceding sentence is that given by H. G. Richardson in the *English Historical Review*, XLII, 80 f. This is the earliest known grant of a borough in fee-farm to the burgesses; cf. Lincoln, above, p. 53, n. 17.

[4] See above, p. 53, n. 16.

[5] Exemption from scot and Danegeld would free the burgesses from all arbitrary taxation; see above, p. 38, n. 2. And on the *murdrum*, see above, p. 36, n. 2.

[6] That is to say, be held for trial by combat.

[7] *Passagium* and *lestagium* were particular forms of toll: the former term applied especially to taxes on the carriage of goods overland; the latter to those on the cargoes of ships.

[8] A soke in the mediaeval borough was a sort of manorial island—a territory under seignorial jurisdiction rather than the law of the privileged community.

[9] Cf. Edgar, III, 2 (above, p. 19).

[10] *Miskenning* or *stultiloquium* was the use, either by plaintiff or by defendant, of a wrong formula in a judicial process. The heavy penalty which it carried in Anglo-Saxon law would be especially irksome to the large French-speaking population of London; cf. William's concession to his French barons, above, p. 35, n. 1. The husting was the weekly court for the dispatch of ordinary business; the folkmote, we are told by later documents, met three times a year for extraordinary business, such as watch and ward, fire-prevention, and the election of municipal officials.

day. And I will see to it that my citizens have their lands and pledges and debts inside the city and outside it. And with regard to lands concerning which claims are made to me, I will on their behalf maintain justice according to the law of the city. And if any one takes toll or custom from a London citizen, the London citizens shall, within the city, take from the borough or the vill where the toll or custom was collected as much as the man of London gave for toll and thereby suffered in damage. And all debtors who owe debts to the citizens shall pay the same, or they shall prove in London that they do not owe [the debts]. But if they refuse to pay and do not come to prove their case [in London], then the citizens to whom the debts are owing shall take their pledges within the city, from either the borough or the vill or the county in which the man lives who owes the debt.[11] And the citizens shall have their hunting dogs for hunting, as [they were] best and most fully had by their ancestors—namely, in the Chilterns, in Middlesex, and in Surrey.

Witnesses: the bishop of Winchester, Robert Fitz-Richard, Hugh Bigot, Alfred of Totnes, William d'Aubigny, Hubert the king's chamberlain, William de Montfichet, Hagulf de Tany, John Belet, Robert Fitz-Seward. Given at Westminster.

(Latin) *Ibid.,* I, 524 f.

(C) HENRY I: CHARTER TO BEVERLEY[12]

Henry, king of England, to his archbishops, bishops, justiciars, sheriffs, and all his faithful men, greeting. Know that I have granted and given and by this my charter have confirmed to the men of Beverley their free burgage[13] according to the free laws and customs of the burgesses of York; also their gild merchant,[14] together with their pleas and toll and all their other free customs and liberties in all things, as Archbishop Thurstan has granted and confirmed to them by his charter, inside the vill of Beverley and outside it, as well in wood as in field or in marsh and in other things. And it is my will that they, like the men of York, shall be quit of toll throughout the whole shire of York.

Witnesses: G[eoffrey] the Chancellor; R[obert], count of Meulan. At Woodstock.

(Latin) Gross, *Gild Merchant,* II, 21.

---

[11] For full discussion of this custom, see M. Bateson, *Borough Customs,* II, lii f.

[12] This is the royal confirmation of a grant to Beverley by Thurstan, archbishop of York (Stubbs, *Select Charters,* p. 131). The latter charter, in addition to the liberties mentioned here, farms the borough tolls to the burgesses for 18*m*. a year.

[13] That is to say, the customs and laws pertaining to a free borough, including beyond doubt burgage tenure.

[14] The archbishop's charter has *hans-hus*—the gildhall, in which the burgesses are authorized to enact statutes for the good of the town; see Gross, *Gild Merchant,* I, 192 f.

(D) THE LIBERTIES OF NEWCASTLE

These are the laws and customs which the burgesses of Newcastle-upon-Tyne enjoyed in the time of Henry [I], king of England, and should [now] enjoy.[15]

Burgesses can levy distraint upon foreigners (*foris habitantes*) inside their market and outside it, inside their homes and outside them, and inside their borough and outside it without the licence of the reeve, except when courts are held in the borough and except [when foreigners are summoned thither] for military service or castle-guard. A burgess may not levy distraint upon a [fellow] burgess without the licence of the reeve. If a burgess has lent anything of his to a foreigner, such a debtor must pay [his debt] in the borough if he admits it; if he denies it, he must give justice in the borough. Pleas that arise in the borough must be held and settled there, except those which are crown pleas. If any burgess is accused in any case, he shall not plead outside the borough except through default of [justice in the borough] court. And he need answer only when day and time are set, unless he has already been guilty of *miskenning*[16]—[that is to say,] except in matters pertaining to the crown.

If a ship that wishes to depart [at once] puts in at Tynemouth, the burgesses may buy [from it] whatever they please. If a plea arises between a burgess and a merchant [coming by sea], it must be settled before the third ebb-tide. Whatever merchandise a ship brings [to the borough] by sea should be carried ashore, except salt; and herring should [also] be sold on board the ship. If any one lawfully and without [adverse] claim holds land in burgage for a year and a day, he need not make reply to a claimant unless the claimant has been outside the kingdom of England, or unless he is a child not old enough to speak [in a judicial process]. If a burgess has a son, he shall share his father's liberty if he lives with his father.[17] If a peasant comes to dwell in the borough, and remains there as a burgess for a year and a day, he may permanently remain in the borough,[18] unless he or his lord has made a preliminary statement that he is to remain for a [fixed] term. If any one accuses a burgess of anything, he may not wage battle against the burgess, but the burgess shall defend him-

---

[15] In addition to the principal (or A) text of this document, published by Charles Johnson in *Archaeologia Aeliana*, Fourth Series, I, 170, there are three other versions (*ibid.*, 172 f.). The original record seems to have been made as the result of an inquest under Henry II. In place of the heading here given, the B text reads: "These are the laws and customs which King Henry [I] granted to his burgesses of Newcastle."

[16] See above, p. 62, n. 10.

[17] The A text is corrupt at this point, but the other versions make the meaning clear. B reads: "If a burgess has a son in his own home [eating] at his own table, the son shall have the same liberty as his father."

[18] ... *in burgo ex toto remaneat*. The other versions agree in stating that he shall thenceforth remain there as a burgess. This is obviously a statement of the famous "law of a year and a day," by which the serf could attain freedom by completing a legal residence in a privileged town.

self by compurgation (*per legem*)—unless it is [an accusation of] treason, in which case he should defend himself by battle.[19] Nor can a burgess wage battle against a foreigner unless he has first abandoned his burgage.[20]

No merchant who is not a burgess can buy either wool or hides or other merchandise [in the country] outside the borough,[21] nor [can he buy them] inside the borough except from a burgess. If a burgess commits an offence, he shall give 6 ores[22] to the reeve. In the borough there is neither merchet nor heriot nor *blodwit* nor *stengesdint*.[23] Every burgess may have his own bake-oven and hand-mill if he wishes, saving the rights of the king's oven. If a woman commits a misdeed concerning bread or beer,[24] no one should intervene [in the matter] except the reeve. If she commits the offense twice, let her be punished by her [rightful] forfeiture; if she commits the offence a third time, let justice be done on her [by the common counsel of the burgesses].[25] No one who is not a burgess may buy cloths for dyeing or make them up or cut them.[26] A burgess may give or sell his land and freely and quietly go whither he pleases, unless a [legal] claim stands against him.

(Latin) *Archaeologia Aeliana,* Fourth Series, I, 170.

---

[19] See above, p. 62, n. 6.
[20] That is to say, given up his burgess status and burgage tenure.
[21] Burgesses normally had a monopoly of trade in certain articles within a specified region; in the case of Nottingham, for example, it was Nottinghamshire.
[22] 10s.; see above, p. 21, n. 3.
[23] The general meaning of this whole article is that the ordinary manorial custom has no force in the borough. At this time merchet and heriot were respectively the French *formariage* and *mainmorte*, which were eventually taken by the courts as marks of servile status. *Blodwit* was the old Anglo-Saxon fine for assault with bloodshed, which seems to have become essentially a seignorial perquisite. *Stengesdint* means beating with a stick; its exact implication here is not known.
[24] That is to say, violates the local regulations for baking or brewing.
[25] The phrase in brackets is added from the other versions.
[26] In order to sell by the piece, rather than in quantity.

29. THE CONSTITUTION OF THE KING'S HOUSEHOLD[1]

This is the constitution of the king's household regarding maintenance (*de procurationibus*).[2]

---

[1] Two copies of this document have been preserved: one in the *Liber Niger Scaccarii* (*Black Book of the Exchequer*), edited by Thomas Hearne; the other in the *Red Book of the Exchequer* (III, 807-13), edited by Hubert Hall. Both texts are badly jumbled and in places are almost unintelligible. With the exception of a few phrases, the following translation is based on the former, which is generally superior. For illuminating criticism of the document as a whole, see R. L. Poole, *The Exchequer in the Twelfth Century,* pp. 94 f., and J. H. Round, *The King's Serjeants and Officers of State.*
[2] The *domus regis,* it should be noted, was not merely the king's palace, for his court was still migratory. To eat in the *domus* was to take one's meals with the household. The understanding of many passages will be aided by comparison with the household ordinances of Edward I and Edward II (nos. 52C, 57).

The chancellor [is to have] 5s. a day, one demeine simnel,[3] two common [simnels], one sester of clear wine, one sester of ordinary wine,[4] one big candle (*grossum cereum*), and forty candle-ends. The master of the writing office (*scriptorium*) at first [received] 10d. a day, one common simnel, half a sester of ordinary wine, one big candle, and twelve candle-ends; but King Henry increased [the allowance] for Robert [keeper] of the seal to the extent that, on the day of the king's death, he was having 2s., one sester of ordinary wine, one common simnel, one little candle (*cereolum*), and twenty-four candle-ends. The chaplain[5] and the custodian of the chapel and of the relics [are to have] the allowance of two men, and four serjeants of the chapel [are to have] double food each. Two pack-horses of the chapel [are assigned] 1d. a day each and 1d. a month for shoeing. For the service of the chapel [are provided] two candles on Wednesday, two on the Sabbath, one candle every night [to be placed] before the relics, thirty candle-ends, and a gallon of clear wine for mass; also a sester of ordinary wine for washing the altar on the Day of Absolution,[6] and for communion on Easter a sester of clear wine and one of ordinary wine.

Concerning the stewards: the steward, if he eats outside the household, [is to receive the same] as the chancellor; if [he eats] inside, 3s. 6d., two common simnels, one sester of ordinary wine, and a full allowance of candles (*plenarie candelam*).[7] The clerk of the issue (*expensae*) of bread and wine [is to have] 2s. a day, one common simnel, one sester of ordinary wine, one little candle, and twenty-four candle-ends. Concerning the dispensers of bread: the master dispenser of bread in constant attendance (*assiduus*), if he eats outside the king's household, [is to have] 2s. 10d. a day, one common simnel, one sester of ordinary wine, one little candle, and twenty-four

---

[3] The *simenellus dominicus* is contrasted throughout with the *simenellus sal'* (occasionally *salat'*). The clerks who made the existing copies thus seem to have meant a "salt simnel," although, as remarked by Hubert Hall, one might prefer to find a connection with *salarium*, a salary or stipend, or with the French *salle*, the hall where most of the household ate. In any case, the original record clearly intended to make the same distinction as that found in a charter of William I, which grants to the abbot of Battle and two of his monks that, when summoned to the royal court, they shall have the following livery: two *panes similagines de dominico*, two *panes similagines de communi*, one sester of wine *de dominico*, one sester of wine *de communi*, six dishes of fish "or of whatever else may be at the court," two candles, and ten candle-ends (*Calendar of Charter Rolls*, III, 196; Davis, *Regesta*, no. 60). The later paragraph telling about the four bakers apparently makes the difference between the demeine and the ordinary simnel chiefly a matter of size. The liveries of food, drink, and candles were in addition to the regular meals; cf. no. 57.

[4] *Vinum expensabile*, wine of issue.

[5] Plural in the *Black Book*, singular in the *Red Book*—one of many such discrepancies.

[6] Holy Thursday.

[7] In the text the preceding sentence is obviously out of place, being inserted after the description of the master dispenser.

29. THE KING'S HOUSEHOLD

candle-ends; if, however, [he eats] inside, 2s., half a sester of ordinary wine, and a full allowance of candles. Concerning the dispensers who serve in turn: if [they eat] outside the household, [each is to have] 19d. a day, one common simnel, one sester of ordinary wine, one big candle, and twenty candle-ends; if [they eat] inside, 10d., half a sester of ordinary wine, and a full allowance of candles. Concerning the naperers: the naperer[8] [is to have] the customary food, 1½d. a day for his man, 1d. for a pack-horse, and 1d. a month for shoeing. The usher[9] of the dispensary [is to have] the same amount except [the allowance for] the pack-horse. The counter of bread[10] [is to have] the customary food. Concerning the four bakers who serve together in their turn: the two who serve in the household are to eat in the household; the two who go abroad are to have 40d. for procuring a Rouen *muid*,[11] from which they should supply 40 demeine simnels, 140 common [simnels], and 270 bakery loaves (*panes de pistrino*). A demeine simnel [is] for four men, a common [simnel] for two [men], a loaf for one man. The waferer[12] [is to have] the customary food and 1½d. for his man. The keeper of the tables (*bordarius*) [is to have] the same amount and in addition a pack-horse together with its livery. The bearer of the alms-dish is to eat in the household.

Concerning the dispensers of the larder: the master dispenser of the larder in constant attendance [is to have the same] as the master dispenser of bread and wine and in the same way. Likewise the dispensers of the larder who serve in turn [are to have the same] as the dispensers of bread and wine who serve in turn. The larderers who serve in turn [are to have] the customary food and 1½d. a day for their man. The usher of the larder [is to be treated] in the same way. The butchers [are to have] only the customary food. Concerning the cooks: the cook of the royal kitchen is to eat in the household [and is to have] 1½d. for his man. The keeper of the vessels (*vasarius*) is to eat in the household and [is to have] 1½d. for his man; also a pack-horse together with its livery. The somler[13] of the same kitchen [is to be treated] in the same way. The serjeant of the kitchen [is to have] only the customary food. The cook for the king's private family and the dispenser [are to be treated] in the same way.[14] Ralph de La Marche, who while cook died before the death of the

---

[8] The officer in charge of cloths for the tables and related services.

[9] *Ostiarius*, which at this time still retained its original meaning of doorkeeper.

[10] Evidently, as Round pointed out, the *pannetier*, whose title was eventually corrupted into pantler.

[11] The *modius* was also a measure of wine; see above, p. 52, n. 10. In the present instance it is obvious that a considerable quantity of grain or flour is meant.

[12] *Nebularius*—the maker of the sweet wafers that were the more highly prized in an age when sugar was a great rarity.

[13] *Sumelarius*, French *sommelier*—originally a person in charge of packing utensils or produce; cf. *sumarius*, a pack-horse.

[14] The text of this sentence and of the one following is badly corrupted.

king, ate in the household and [had] 1½d. for his man. Concerning the great kitchen: Owen Polchart[15] [is to have] the customary food and 1½d. for his man. Two cooks [are to have] the customary food each and 1½d. for their man. The serjeants of the same kitchen [are to have] only the customary food. The usher of the spit-house [is to have] the customary food and 1½d. for his man. The turnspit [is to be treated] in the same way and besides [is to have] a pack-horse together with its livery. The carter of the great kitchen [is to have] double food, and the rightful livery for his horse. The carter of the larder [is to be treated] in the same way. The serjeant who receives the venison[16] is to eat inside and [is to have] 1½d. for his man.

Concerning the butlery: the master butler [is to be treated] like the steward; they have the one livery and [receive it] in the same way. The master dispenser of the butlery [is to be treated] like the master dispenser of bread and wine. The dispensers of the butlery who serve in turn [are to be treated] like the dispensers of issue who serve in turn; but they have a larger allowance of candles, for they receive a small candle and twenty-four candle-ends. The usher of the butlery [is to have] the customary food and 1½d. for his man. The keepers of the hose[17] are to eat in the household and [are to have] 3d. each for their men. The keeper of the butts[18] [is to have] the customary food, 3d. for his men, half a sester of ordinary wine, and twelve candle-ends. The workmen under the keeper of the butts [are to have] only the customary food, but the serjeant [is to have] in addition 1½d. for his man and two pack-horses with their liveries. Concerning the cupbearers: four only should serve together in their turn, of whom two are to eat in the household and each [is to have] 1½d. for his man. The other two are to have the customary food and likewise 1½d. [each] for their men. The keepers of the mazers[19] [are to have] only double food. Concerning the fruiterer: the fruiterer is to eat in the household and is to have 3d. for his men. The carter [is to have] the customary food, and livery for his horse.

The master chamberlain is the equal of the steward in livery. The treasurer [is to be treated] like the master chamberlain, if he is at the court and serving as treasurer.[20] William Mauduit is to eat regularly in the household and [is to have] 13d. a day, one big candle, twelve candle-ends, and three pack-horses with their liveries. The porter of the king's litter[21] is to eat in the household and [is to have] 1½d.

---

[15] See Round, *King's Serjeants*, p. 58.
[16] *Venacionem;* see below, p. 87, n. 2.
[17] Probably wine-skins. At any rate, the *hosarii* were somehow connected with the receipt and distribution of wine; see Round, *King's Serjeants*, pp. 177 f.
[18] *Butarius,* presumably the man in charge of the casks in the cellar.
[19] Maple-wood cups.
[20] Originally a subordinate of the chamberlain, now his equal. The rise of this officer is eloquent testimony to the growing importance of financial administration.
[21] The man responsible for carrying the king's bedding when he went on journeys.

29. THE KING'S HOUSEHOLD

for his man and a pack-horse with its livery. The chamberlain who serves in his turn [is to have] 2s. a day, one common simnel, one sester of ordinary wine, one little candle, and twenty-four candle-ends. The chamberlain of the candles [is to have] 8d. a day and half a sester of ordinary wine. The king's tailor is to eat in the household and [is to have] 1½d. for his man. The chamberlains, if they wish, are to eat in the household without other livery. The ewerer[22] [is to have] double food and, when the king makes a journey, 1d. for drying the king's clothes; and when the king bathes, 4d., except on the three annual festivals. Concerning the launderer there is doubt.

The constables are to have liveries like the stewards and in the same way. William Fitz-Odo [is to have] one demeine simnel, one sester of clear wine, one little candle, and twenty-four candle-ends. Henry de la Pomerai, if he eats outside the household, [is to have] 2s. a day, one common simnel, one sester of ordinary wine, one little candle and twenty-four candle-ends. If, however, [he eats] inside, [he is to have] 14d., half a sester of ordinary wine, and a full allowance of candles. Roger d'Oilly [is to be treated] in the same way. The master marshal, namely John, [is to be treated] in the same way; and in addition he ought to have counterfoils for the gifts and liveries that are made from the king's treasury and chamber, and, as witness to everything, he ought to have tallies against all the king's officials. The four marshals who serve the king's household [including] both clerks and knights and also ministers, when they[23] take lodgings or stay outside the court on the king's business, [are to have] 8d. a day, one gallon of ordinary wine, and twelve candle-ends. If [the marshals] remain inside, [they are to have] 3d. a day for their men and a full allowance of candles. But if any one of the marshals is sent on the king's business, [he is to have] only 8d. The serjeant of the marshals, if they are sent on the king's business, are to have 3d. a day each; if not, they are to eat in the king's household. The ushers [who are] knights themselves are to eat in the household and [are to have] 1½d. for each of their men, and eight candle-ends. Gilbert Bonhomme and Ralph are to eat in the household and [are to have] 1½d. for their men. The other ushers, [who are] not knights, are to eat in the household without other livery. The watchmen [are to have] double food, 1½d. for their men, and four candles; and in addition each [is to have] of a morning two loaves, one dish [of meat], and a gallon of beer. The keeper of the hearth is always to eat in the household and, from Michaelmas to Easter, [is to have] 4d. a day for a fire. The usher of the chamber [is to have] 4d. for the king's litter on each day when the king makes a journey.[24] The curtainer[25] is to eat in the household; and when he had the curtains carried, he used to have

---

[22] *Aquarius*, water-bearer.
[23] The members of the household.
[24] Perhaps this and the following sentence are misplaced, belonging rather under the description of the chamber.
[25] *Cortinarius*, the man who cared for the tents and hangings used in connection with a royal progress.

livery for one man [and] one pack-horse. Each of the four trumpeters [is to have] 3*d*. a day. Twenty serjeants [are to have] 1*d*. a day each. The velterers[26] [are to have] 3*d*. a day each; also 2*d*. for their men, and for each greyhound ½*d*. a day. The king's pack (*mueta*) [is assigned] 8*d*. a day. The knights huntsmen [are to have] 8*d*. a day each. The cat-hunters [are to have] 5*d*. each. The leader of the liam-hound [is to have] 1*d*., and ½*d*. for the liam-hound. The berner [is to have] 3*d*. a day. The hunters with harriers [are to have] 3*d*. a day each; and four big harriers should have 1*d*., and six little harriers 1*d*. Two men [are required] for the big harriers and each [is to have] 1*d*. a day. The keepers of the brachs [are to have] 3*d*. a day each. The wolf-hunters [are to have] 20*d*. a day for horses, men, and dogs, and they should have twenty-four coursing dogs and eight greyhounds; also £6 a year for buying horses, but they themselves say £8. Concerning the archers who carry the king's bow: each [is to have] 5*d*. a day, and the other archers [are to have] the same amount. Bernard, Ralph le Robeur, and their fellows [are to have] 3*d*. a day each.

(Latin) *Liber Niger Scaccarii,* pp. 341 f.

---

[26] The berner had charge of the ordinary coursing dogs; the velterers of the larger greyhounds. These two groups both hunted the quarry by sight. The liam-hound, on the other hand, followed a track by scent, like a bloodhound. The brachs were smaller dogs of the same sort. Harriers were apparently used for hunting hares. On this whole subject, see Round, *King's Serjeants,* pp. 268 f.

SECTION III

HENRY II AND HIS SONS

THE signal importance of Henry II's reign (1154-89) in the constitutional history of England is well known to all students of the subject. Such a collection as this can hardly omit the major enactments of a king who restored the lost efficiency of the Norman monarchy, regulated anew the troubled relations of church and state, enormously extended the resources of the crown, and laid the foundations of the English common law. In addition to the more familiar sources, such as the Constitutions of Clarendon and Henry's famous assizes, the present section includes some of the baronial returns that Round made the subject of a characteristically brilliant study.[1] These are supplemented by a series of scutage accounts from the pipe roll of 1187, and further examples of the king's financial measures are provided by entries concerning tallage and items of judicial income. Typical of this reign were also two remarkable essays in Latin: the *Dialogue on the Exchequer*[2] and the *Treatise on the Laws and Customs of England*,[3] attributed respectively to Richard Fitz-Nigel and Ranulf de Glanville. However interesting and authoritative, such lengthy unofficial works cannot be incorporated in a brief volume of documents; only some of the commoner writs quoted by Glanville are given here. For additional illustration and comment on these two works, the student is referred to the scholarly introductions by the editors, to R. L. Poole, *The Exchequer in the Twelfth Century*, and to Pollock and Maitland, *History of English Law*.

Constitutionally, the reigns of Richard and John (1189-1216) were a mere prolongation of their father's reign. It is largely by virtue of more systematic chancery enrolment that we henceforth gain fuller information with regard to the working of the central courts and the activities of local officials. Alongside of the pipe rolls, which are continuous from the second year of Henry II, there appear by 1216 such great compilations as the charter

---

[1] *Feudal England*, pp. 236 f.
[2] Edited by Crump, Hughes, and Johnson (Oxford, 1902); translated in Henderson, *Historical Documents*, pp. 20 f.
[3] Edited by G. E. Woodbine (Yale University Press, 1932).

rolls, patent rolls, close rolls, *curia regis* rolls, and fine rolls. From this formidable mass of material a few extracts are presented to illustrate, not only the general character of the records, but also, when possible, significant phases of legal and constitutional development. In the former connection particular reference should be made to the very helpful criticism of T. F. Tout, *Chapters in the Administrative History of Mediaeval England,* vol. I. In the latter connection the principal guides are the books already cited for the previous section—expecially those of Pollock and Maitland, Petit-Dutaillis, Round, and Stenton.

Thanks to a careful reworking of the pertinent records by a number of scholars,[4] the history of London and the other boroughs is much better known to us than it was to Stubbs. One result of their research has been to enhance our appreciation of Henry I's activity. Despite the increased output of borough charters under the Angevins, which may be readily perceived by a glance at Ballard's collection,[5] actual innovations within the field of municipal privileges were few in the later twelfth century. Lesser towns normally enjoyed customs like those of Newcastle; larger towns commonly received the liberties of London. But under Henry II the latter ceased to include exemption from arbitrary taxation and the right to choose magistrates. It was not until the closing decade of the century that the capital regained some degree of autonomy under an elected mayor and board of aldermen. The more definite of our meagre sources for that advance are given below. Meanwhile Henry II had apparently allowed a few boroughs to have elected reeves, and such arrangements were formally confirmed by Richard in charters which served as precedents for that of John to Ipswich. The latter grant has been selected for translation (no. 39A) because the ensuing action of the Ipswich burgesses is graphically described in a surviving record (no. 39B)—truly an outstanding monument in the history of local self-government.

This section appropriately ends with Magna Carta, which so

---

[4] J. H. Round, *Geoffrey de Mandeville,* pp. 347 f., and *The Commune of London,* pp. 219 f.; Mary Bateson, in the *English Historical Review,* XVII, 480 f.; M. Weinbaum, *Verfassungsgeschichte Londons,* and *London unter Eduard I und II,* vol. II. See also Petit-Dutaillis and Lefebvre, pp. 91 f.; F. M. Stenton, *Norman London;* W. Page, *London;* C. Stephenson, *Borough and Town,* pp. 179 f.; J. Tait, *The Medieval English Borough.*

[5] *British Borough Charters, 1042-1216.*

30. CONSTITUTIONS OF CLARENDON

admirably summarizes the developments of the previous century and introduces those of the century to come. And since the Great Charter has too often been thought of as an inflexible and definitive enactment, it has seemed advisable to indicate, by a sort of gloss on the original text, the changes made in the reissues. A list of the principal works dealing with the wider significance of Magna Carta in the constitutional history of England will be given at the head of the following section. For the moment it will suffice to refer the student to W. S. McKechnie's scholarly monograph, *Magna Carta,* together with the citations made in the footnotes.

30. THE CONSTITUTIONS OF CLARENDON (1164)

In the year 1164 from the Incarnation of the Lord, in the fourth year of the papacy of Alexander [III], and in the twelfth year of Henry II, most illustrious king of the English, there was made, in the presence of the said king, this record and recognition[1] of a certain portion of the customs and liberties and rights of his ancestors—namely, of King Henry his grandfather and of others—which ought to be observed and held in the kingdom. And on account of the dissensions and disputes that had arisen between the clergy and the justices of the lord king and the barons of the realm concerning [such] customs and rights, this recognition was made in the presence of the archbishops, bishops, clergy, earls, barons, and magnates of the realm. Furthermore, Thomas, archbishop of Canterbury, and Roger, archbishop of York, and Gilbert, bishop of London, and Henry, bishop of Winchester, and Nigel, bishop of Ely, and William, bishop of Norwich, and Robert, bishop of Lincoln, and Hilary, bishop of Chichester, and Jocelyn, bishop of Salisbury, and Richard, bishop of Chester, and Bartholomew, bishop of Exeter, and Robert, bishop of Hereford, and David, bishop of St. David's and Roger, [bishop] elect of Worcester, have granted and steadfastly promised, *viva voce* and on their word of truth, that the said customs, recognized by the archbishops, bishops, earls, and barons, and by the nobler and more venerable men of the realm, should be held and observed for the lord king and his heirs in good faith and without evil intent, these being present[2] . . . and many other magnates and nobles of the realm, both clerical and lay.

Now a certain part of the recognized customs and rights of the kingdom are contained in the present writing, of which part these are the chapters:—

1. If controversy arises between laymen, between laymen and

[1] *Recognitio,* the same word as is often used for the verdict of a jury; see, for examples, no. 33.
[2] Here follow in the text thirty-eight names.

clergymen, or between clergymen, with regard to advowson and presentation to churches, it shall be treated or concluded in the court of the lord king.

2. Churches of the lord king's fee[3] may not be given in perpetuity without his assent and grant.

3. Clergymen charged and accused of anything shall, on being summoned by a justice of the king, come into his court, to be responsible there for whatever it may seem to the king's court they should there be responsible for; and [to be responsible] in the ecclesiastical court [for what] it may seem they should there be responsible for—so that the king's justice shall send into the court of Holy Church to see on what ground matters are there to be treated. And if the clergyman is convicted, or [if he] confesses, the Church should no longer protect him.[4]

4. Archbishops, bishops, and parsons of the kingdom are not permitted to go out of the kingdom without the licence of the lord king. And should they go out [of it], they shall, if the king so desires, give security that, neither in going nor in remaining nor in returning, will they seek [to bring] evil or damage to the king or to the kingdom.

5. Excommunicated men should not give security for all future time (*ad remanens*) or take an oath, but [should] merely [provide] security and pledge of standing by the judgment of the church in order to obtain absolution.

6. Laymen should not be accused except through known and lawful accusers and witnesses in the presence of the bishop, [yet] so that the archdeacon shall not lose his right or anything that he should thence have. And if the guilty persons are such that no one wishes or dares to accuse them, the sheriff, on being asked by the bishop, shall have twelve lawful men from the neighbourhood, or the vill, placed on oath before the bishop to set forth the truth in the matter according to their own knowledge.[5]

7. No one who holds of the king in chief, nor any of his demesne ministers, shall be excommunicated; nor shall the lands of any of them be placed under interdict, unless first the lord king, if he is in the land, or his justiciar, if he is outside the kingdom, agrees that justice shall be done on that person—and in such a way that whatever belongs to the king's court shall be settled there, and whatever

---

[3] That is to say, the right of appointing to a living, or advowson, held in fee of the king.

[4] It was over this article that the famous controversy between the king and Thomas Becket took place. For the best interpretation, see Pollock and Maitland, I, 447 f.

[5] The article deals with trials in ecclesiastical courts, of which the lowest was that of the archdeacon. In the final clause we have our first clear reference to the accusation jury, but it is significant that the institution is described as a feature of established custom under Henry I; see Pollock and Maitland, I, 151, and cf. no. 31.

30. CONSTITUTIONS OF CLARENDON

belongs to the ecclesiastical court shall be sent thither to be dealt with there.

8. With regard to appeals, should they arise—they should proceed from the archdeacon to the bishop, and from the bishop to the archbishop. And if the archbishop fails to provide justice, recourse should finally be had to the lord king, in order that by his precept the controversy may be brought to an end in the court of the archbishop; so that it should not proceed farther[6] without the assent of the lord king.

9. If a claim is raised by a clergyman against a layman, or by a layman against a clergyman, with regard to any tenement which the clergyman wishes to treat as free alms, but which the layman [wishes to treat] as a lay fee, let it, by the consideration of the king's chief justice and in the presence of the said justice, be settled through the recognition of twelve lawful men whether the tenement belongs to free alms or to lay fee. And if it is recognized as belonging to free alms, the plea shall be [held] in the ecclesiastical court; but if [it is recognized as belonging] to lay fee, unless both call upon the same bishop or [other] baron, the plea shall be [held] in the king's court. But if, with regard to that fee, both call upon the same bishop or [other] baron, the plea shall be [held] in his court; [yet] so that, on account of the recognition which has been made, he who first was seised [of the land] shall not lose his seisin until proof [of the title] has been made in the plea.[7]

10. If any one in a city, castle, borough, or demesne manor of the lord king is summoned by an archdeacon or a bishop for some offence on account of which he ought to respond to the said persons, and if he refuses satisfaction on their summons, he may well be placed under an interdict; but he should not be excommunicated until the chief minister of the lord king in that vill has been called upon to bring him to justice, so that he may come for satisfaction. And if the king's minister defaults in the matter, he shall be in the mercy of the lord king, and the bishop may then coerce that accused man through ecclesiastical justice.

11. Archbishops, bishops, and all parsons of the realm who hold of the king in chief have their possessions of the king as baronies and are answerable for them to the king's justices and ministers; also they follow and observe all royal laws and customs, and like other barons they should take part with the barons in the judgments of the lord king's court, until the judgment involves death or maiming.[8]

---

[6] Be appealed to the papal court.

[7] The article is obscurely phrased, but its general purport is clear. The preliminary question, whether the land is held in free alms or not, is to be decided in the king's court by a recognition jury—the procedure known as the assize *utrum* (see no. 33c). Jurisdiction over further litigation is to be determined by the jury's verdict.

[8] Clergymen were forbidden by canon law to take life or shed blood.

12. When an archbishopric, bishopric, abbey, or priory within the king's gift becomes vacant, it should be in his hands; and he shall thence take all revenues and income just as from his own demesne. And when it comes to providing for the church, the lord king should summon the greater parsons of the church, and the election should be held in the king's own chapel by the assent of the lord king and by the counsel of those parsons of the kingdom whom he has called for that purpose. And there the man elected should, before being consecrated, perform homage and fealty to the lord king as to his liege lord, for life and limbs and earthly honour,[9] saving the rights of his order.

13. If any of the magnates of the realm forcibly prevent an archbishop, bishop, or archdeacon from administering justice, either by himself or through his men, the lord king should bring them to justice. And if perchance any forcibly prevent the lord king from [administering] his justice, the archbishops, bishops, and archdeacons should bring them to justice, so that they may satisfy the lord king.

14. Chattels of those who have incurred royal forfeiture should not be withheld in any church or churchyard against the king's justice; for they are the king's own, whether they are found inside churches or outside them.

15. Pleas of debt, owed under pledge of faith[10] or without pledge of faith, belong to the king's justice.

16. Sons of peasants should not be ordained without the assent of the lord on whose land they are known to have been born.

Now the [present] record of the aforesaid royal rights and customs was made at Clarendon by the archbishops, bishops, earls, and barons, and by the more noble and venerable men of the realm, on the fourth day before the Purification of the Blessed Virgin Mary, in the presence of the lord Henry, together with his father, the lord king. There are, moreover, other rights and customs, both many and great, of the Holy Mother Church, of the lord king, and of the barons of the realm, which are not contained in this writing; they are to be saved to Holy Church, to the lord king and his heirs, and to the barons of the realm, and are inviolably to be observed forever.

(Latin) Stubbs, *Select Charters*, pp. 163 f.

---

[9] Cf. no. 26, art. 55.
[10] See Pollock and Maitland, II, 189 f.

31. THE ASSIZE OF CLARENDON (1166)

Here begins the Assize[1] of Clarendon made by King Henry, namely the second, with the assent of the archbishops, bishops, abbots, earls, and barons of all England.

---

[1] In this context the word means an ordinance or set of instructions delivered to the king's ministers. The text comes to us on the authority of a chronicler and in many places lacks the precision and clarity that we should expect in a document issued by the royal chancery. See below, p. 80, n. 1.

31. ASSIZE OF CLARENDON

1. In the first place the aforesaid King Henry, by the counsel of all his barons, has ordained that, for the preservation of peace and the enforcement of justice, inquiry shall be made in every county and in every hundred through twelve of the more lawful men of the hundred and through four of the more lawful men of each vill, [put] on oath to tell the truth, whether in their hundred or in their vill there is any man accused or publicly known as a robber or murderer or thief, or any one who has been a receiver of robbers or murderers or thieves, since the lord king has been king. And let the justices[2] make this investigation in their presence and the sheriffs in their presence.

2. And whoever is found by the oath of the aforesaid men to have been accused or publicly known as a robber or murderer or thief, or as a receiver of them since the lord king has been king, shall be seized; and he shall go to the ordeal of water and swear that, to the value of 5s., so far as he knows, he has not been a robber or murderer or thief, or a receiver of them, since the lord king has been king.

3. And if the lord of the man who has been seized or his steward or his men seek [to free] him under pledge, within the third day after he has been seized, let him and his chattels be remanded under pledge until he has made his law.[3]

4. And when robbers or murderers or thieves, or receivers of them, are seized in consequence of the aforesaid oath, if the justices are not soon to come into that county where they were seized, the sheriff shall, through some intelligent man, notify the nearest justices that he has seized such men; and the justices shall send back word to the sheriff that those [accused] are to be brought before them, wherever they please. The sheriff shall then take those [accused] before the justices, and with him he shall take two lawful men from the hundred or the vill where they were seized, to bring the record of the county and the hundred as to why they were seized; and there before the justices they shall make their law.

5. And with regard to those seized in consequence of the aforesaid oath of this assize, no one shall have jurisdiction or judgment or [forfeiture of] chattels but the lord king in his court and in the presence of his justices; and the lord king shall have all their chattels. With respect, however, to those seized otherwise than through this oath, let whatever is customary and right be done.

6. And the sheriffs who have seized them shall take them before the justice without other summons than shall be had from him. And when robbers or murderers or thieves, or receivers of them, whether seized in consequence of the oath or otherwise, are delivered to the sheriffs, the latter shall take them immediately and without delay.

7. And in every county where there are no jails let them be

---

[2] The king's itinerant justices who from time to time held full meetings of the county courts.

[3] That is to say, submitted to ordeal.

made within a borough or some castle of the king—with the king's money and with his wood if that is near at hand, or with some other wood close by, and by view of the king's serjeants—so that the sheriffs may have the seized men guarded in those [jails] by the officials accustomed to do so and by their serjeants.

8. The lord king also wills that all should come to the county [court] for the making of this oath; so that no one, on account of any liberty that he has, or on account of any jurisdiction or soke that he may enjoy, shall abstain from attendance for the making of this oath.[4]

9. And let there be no one, in castle or out of castle, or even in the honour of Wallingford,[5] who forbids the sheriffs to enter upon his jurisdiction or his land for view of frankpledge;[6] and let all men be placed under sureties, and let them be sent before the sheriffs under frankpledge.

10. And within cities or boroughs no one shall have men, or shall receive [men] within his house or his land or his soke for whom he will not be sponsor, [guaranteeing] that he will bring them before the justice, should they be summoned, or that they are under frankpledge.

11. And let there be no persons, either in a city or a borough or a castle, or outside them, or even in the honour of Wallingford, who forbid the sheriffs to enter upon their land or their soke for the purpose of seizing those who have been accused or publicly known as robbers or murderers or thieves, or receivers of them, or outlaws, or those accused under forest [law];[7] on the contrary, [the king] commands them to give assistance in seizing those [suspects].

12. And if any one is seized who possesses [the proceeds] of robbery or theft, should he be a notorious person and have a bad reputation, and should he not have a warrantor, let him not have his law.[8] And if he is not notorious, let him, on account of his [suspicious] possessions, go to the [ordeal of] water.

13. And if any one, in the presence of lawful men or of a hundred [court], has confessed robbery or murder or theft, or the reception of those [who have committed such crimes], and should he then wish to deny it, let him not have his law.

14. The lord king also wills that those who make their law and are cleared by the law, if they are of very bad reputation, being publicly and shamefully denounced by the testimony of many lawful men, shall abjure the lands of the king, so that they shall cross the sea within eight days unless they are detained by the wind; then, with the first [favourable] wind that they have, they shall

---
[4] Cf. no. 24.
[5] An important fief that was declared forfeit by Henry II and thenceforth held by a member of the royal house.
[6] See above, p. 37, n. 6.
[7] See no. 35.
[8] In other words, he is to have no chance of clearing himself.

31. ASSIZE OF CLARENDON

cross the sea and thenceforth not return to England, except at the mercy of the lord king; [so that] they shall there be outlaws and shall be seized as outlaws if they return.

15. And the lord king forbids that any waif (*vaivus*)—that is to say, one wandering or unknown—shall be given lodging anywhere except in a borough; and he should not be given lodging there for more than one night unless he or his horse becomes ill there, so that he can show evident excuse [for his delay].

16. And if [otherwise] he stays there for more than one night, let him be seized and held until his lord may come to give pledge for him, or until he himself may find good sureties; and let him who provided the lodging be likewise seized.

17. And if any sheriff has notified another sheriff that men have fled from his county into the other county as the consequence of robbery or murder or theft, or of receiving those [who have committed such crimes], or of outlawry, or of accusation under the king's forest [law], let the latter [sheriff] seize them. Also, if he knows of himself or through others, that such men have fled into his county, let him seize them and guard them until he has good sureties for them.

18. And all sheriffs shall have the names of all fugitives who have fled from their counties written down, and this they shall do before [the courts of] their counties. And the names of those men, [thus] written down, they shall bring before the justices when first they report to those [justices], so that the latter may make inquiry throughout all England and may seize the chattels [of the fugitives] for the use of the king.

19. And the lord king wills that, as soon as the sheriffs have received the summons of the itinerant justices to come before the latter together with [the courts of] their counties, they shall bring together [the courts of] their counties and make inquiry concerning all who recently, after this assize, have come into their counties; and they shall put those [newcomers] under pledge to appear before the justices, or they shall guard those [newcomers] until the justices come to them, and then they shall bring [the newcomers] before the justices.

20. The lord king also forbids monks or canons or any religious community to receive any one from the lower classes (*de minuto populo*) as a monk or a canon or a brother until it is known of what reputation he may be, unless he is sick unto death.

21. The lord king also forbids that any one in all England shall receive under him within his land or his soke or his house any from the sect of those renegades[9] branded and placed under excommunication at Oxford. And if any one does receive them, he shall be in the mercy of the lord king; and the house in which they resided shall be taken outside the vill and burned. And every

---

[9] Heretics, probably Albigensians; see Pollock and Maitland, II, 547.

sheriff shall take an oath to obey this [command]; and he shall have this sworn by all his officials, by the stewards of barons, and by all knights and freeholders of the county.

22. And the lord king wills that, during his pleasure, this assize shall be observed in the kingdom.

(Latin) *Ibid.*, pp. 170 f.

32. THE ASSIZE OF NORTHAMPTON (1176)[1]

1. If, by the oath of twelve knights of the hundred—or, should knights not be present, by the oath of twelve lawful freemen—and by the oath of four men of every vill in the hundred, any one has been accused in the presence of the lord king's justices of murder or theft or robbery, or of receiving men who have committed such [crimes], or of falsification[2] or arson, he shall go to the ordeal of water; and if he fails [in the ordeal], he shall lose one foot. And to increase the severity of the law, it was added at Northampton that with the foot he should lose his right hand, and that he should abjure the realm and depart from it within forty days. And if he should be cleared by the [ordeal of] water, let him find sureties and remain in the kingdom, unless he has been accused of murder or other disgraceful felony by the community (*commune*) of the county and the lawful knights of his own countryside (*patria*). If [now] he has been accused in the aforesaid manner of this [sort of crime], although he has been cleared by the [ordeal of] water, let him nevertheless go out of the kingdom within forty days and take with him his chattels, saving the rights of his lords; and let him abjure the realm [on pain of being] in the lord king's mercy. This assize, moreover, shall hold good for all the time since the assize was made at Clarendon down to the present, and henceforward during the lord king's pleasure, with regard to murder, treason, and arson, and with regard to all [offenses in] the preceding chapters, except minor thefts and robberies which were committed in time of war, as of horses, oxen, and lesser things.

2. Item, no one, either in a vill or in a borough, shall be permitted to give lodging within his house for more than one night to any stranger for whom he is unwilling to be legally responsible, unless such lodger has a reasonable excuse which the master of the house may prove to his neighbours. And when he leaves, let him leave by day and in the presence of the neighbours.

3. If any one has possessed [the proceeds] of murder or theft or robbery or falsification, or of any other felony that he has committed, and confesses it before the reeve of a hundred or a borough and be-

---

[1] The document, as reported by the chronicler, is headed, "These are the assizes made at Clarendon and afterwards recorded at Northampton." That is to say, the earlier ordinance is regarded as still in effect, with certain amendments. But what is here stated about the Assize of Clarendon does not entirely agree with the text that we have.

[2] *Falsoneria*, meaning either counterfeiting or forgery.

fore lawful men, he may not afterwards deny it before the justices. And if, without [such] possession, he admits anything of the same sort in their presence, this likewise he may not deny before the justices.

4. Item, if any freeholder dies, his heirs shall remain in such seisin as their father had of his fee on the day that he was alive and dead; and they shall have his chattels, with which to carry out the testament of the deceased. And afterwards they shall go to their lord and shall perform to him their obligation for relief and other things owed from their fee. And if the heir is under age, the lord of the fee shall receive his homage and have wardship over him so long as is right. The other lords, if there are several, shall [also] receive his homage and he shall perform to them whatever obligations he owes. And the wife of the deceased shall have her dowry and the portion of his chattels to which she is entitled. And if the lord of the fee denies to the heirs of the deceased the seisin of the said deceased['s property] which they demand, the justices of the lord king shall have recognition made in the matter by twelve lawful men, as to what seisin in this respect the deceased had on the day that he was alive and dead.[3] And according to the recognition thus made, those [justices] shall make restitution to his heirs. And if any one acts contrary to this [command], and is convicted of so doing, let him remain in the king's mercy.

5. Item, the justices of the lord king shall have recognition made of disseisins contrary to the assize from the time that the lord king first came to England after the peace made between him and the king his son.[4]

6. Item, from the first Sunday after Easter to the first Sunday after Pentecost, the justices shall receive oaths of fealty to the lord king from all who wish to dwell in the kingdom: namely, from earls, barons, knights, freeholders, and even peasants. And whoever refuses to swear fealty is to be seized as an enemy of the lord king. The justices are also to command that all those who have not yet performed their homage and allegiance to the lord king shall come at the time assigned them and perform homage and allegiance to the king as to their liege lord.

7. Item, the justices, by writ of the lord king or of those acting in his place, shall enforce all rights and claims pertaining to the lord king and his crown to the amount of half a knight's fee and less, unless the case is so important that it cannot be decided without the lord king or [unless it is] such as, through their own uncertainty, the justices may report to him or to those acting in his place. They should, however, to the best of their ability strive to assure the king's interest. Also they shall hold assize concerning wicked thieves and [other] malefactors of the land—which assize, by the counsel of the

---

[3] This is known in law as the assize *mort d'ancestor*; see no. 33A.

[4] Apparently a reference to the assize of *novel disseisin*, the ordinance establishing which has not come down to us; see no. 33B.

king his son and of his men, is [to be held] throughout the counties to which they shall go.

8. Item, the justices shall see to it that the castles[5] [supposed to have been] razed are totally razed, and that those to be razed are well pulled down. And if they fail to do this, the lord king wishes them brought to judgment in his court as men in contempt of his command.

9. Item, the justices shall make inquiry concerning the escheats, churches, lands, and women[6] who are in the gift of the lord king.

10. Item, the bailiffs[7] of the lord king shall be answerable at the exchequer both for their fixed rents and for all sums acquired within their bailiwicks, except those belonging to the [farm of the] county.

11. Item, the justices shall make inquiry concerning the custody of castles: as to who owe [payments in this connection], how much [is owed], and where [it should be paid]. And afterwards they shall give the information to the lord king.

12. Item, [it is ordered that] a thief, from the time that he is captured, shall be delivered to the sheriff to guard. And if the sheriff is absent, he shall be taken to the nearest castellan,[8] and the latter shall guard him until he is turned over to the sheriff.

13. Item, the justices shall have investigation made, according to the custom of the land, as to those who have left the kingdom; and unless they are willing to return within a stated time and to stand trial in the court of the lord king, they shall then be outlawed; and the names of the outlaws shall be brought to the exchequer at Easter and Michaelmas, and shall thence be sent to the lord king.

(Latin) *Ibid.,* pp. 179 f.

---

[5] The so-called adulterine castles—those built without royal authorization during the anarchy under Stephen.

[6] Heiresses whom the king could bestow in marriage. For examples, see no. 40.

[7] Henceforth the ordinary title of an official in charge of a district less than a county. Bailiffs might be subordinates of the sheriff, but certain boroughs, escheated honours, and the like were regularly farmed as separate units.

[8] The official in charge of a castle, often called a constable.

33. FORMS OF ORIGINAL WRITS IN GLANVILLE

(A) Assize of Mort d'Ancestor

The king to the sheriff, greeting. If G., son of O., will give you security for prosecuting his claim, then summon through good summoners twelve free and lawful men from the neighbourhood of ———, to be before me or my justices on ———, prepared to recognize by oath whether O., father of the aforesaid G., was seised in demesne, as of his fee,[1] of one virgate of land in that vill on the day that he died, if he died after my first coronation, and whether the said G.

---

[1] See no. 32, art. 4. This assize gave redress only when the land was held in fee, rather than, for example, in villeinage or by lease.

is his nearest heir. And in the meantime they shall view that land, and you shall have their names written down. And summon through good summoners R., who holds that land, to be there in order to hear that recognition. And you are to have there the summoners and this writ.

(Latin) Glanville, *Tractatus de Legibus,* xiii, 3.

(B) ASSIZE OF NOVEL DISSEISIN[2]

The king to the sheriff, greeting. Complaint has been made to me by N. that R. has unlawfully and without judgment disseised him of his free tenement in———since my last crossing to Normandy; and so I command you, if the aforesaid N. will give you security for prosecuting his claim, to have restored to that tenement the chattels taken from it and [to let] the said tenement with its chattels remain in peace until———. And in the meantime you shall have twelve free and lawful men of the neighbourhood view that land, and you shall have their names written down. And summon them through good summoners to be before me or my justices, prepared to make recognition concerning it. And place under gage and good pledges the aforesaid R., or his bailiff if he himself cannot be found, to be there in order to hear that recognition. And you are to have there the summoners and this writ.

(Latin) *Ibid.,* xiii, 33.

(C) ASSIZE UTRUM[3]

The king to the sheriff, greeting. Summon through good summoners twelve free and lawful men from the neighbourhood of———, to be before me or my justices on———, prepared to recognize by oath whether the one hide of land, which N., parson of the church in that vill, claims against R. in that vill as free alms of his said church, is lay fee of the said R. or church fee. And in the meantime let them view that land and have their names written down. And summon through good summoners the aforesaid R., who holds that land, to be there in order to hear that recognition. And you are to have there the summoners and this writ.

(Latin) *Ibid.,* xiii, 24.

(D) ASSIZE OF DARREIN PRESENTMENT[4]

The king to the sheriff, greeting. Summon through good summoners twelve free and lawful men from the neighbourhood of———, to be before me or my justices on———, prepared to recognize by oath what patron presented the last parson, now dead, to the church of that vill, which is thus said to be vacant, and of which N. claims the advowson. And have their names written down. And summon through

---

[2] I.e., recent dispossession; see above, p. 81, n. 4.
[3] See no. 30, art. 9.
[4] I.e., last nomination to a benefice; see no. 30, art. 1.

good summoners R., who is deforcing that claim, to be there in order to hear that recognition. And you are to have there the summoners and this writ.

(Latin) *Ibid.,* xiii, 19.

(E) WRIT OF RIGHT

The king to Earl W., greeting. I command you without delay to give full right to N. with regard to the ten carucates of land in Middleton, which he claims to hold of you by the free service of one knight's fee for all service.[5] And unless you act in this matter so that I hear no further complaint as to default of justice, the sheriff of Nottingham will do so.

(Latin) *Ibid.,* xii, 3.

(F) PRAECIPE[6]

The king to the sheriff, greeting. Command N. lawfully and without delay to restore to R. one hide of land in———, of which the same R. complains that the aforesaid N. is deforcing him. And unless he does so, summon him through good summoners to be before me or my justices on——— at———, in order to show good cause for not having done so. And you are to have there the summoners and this writ.

(Latin) *Ibid.,* i, 6.

(G) DE NATIVO

The king to the sheriff, greeting. Complaint has been made to me by R. that N. is drawing him into villeinage, despite the fact that, according to his statement, he is a freeman. And so I command you that, if the said R. will give you security for prosecuting his claim, you shall then bring that suit before me or my justices on———, and in the meantime see that he enjoys peace in this matter. And summon the aforesaid N. through good summoners to be there in order to show cause for drawing him into villeinage. And you are to have there the summoners and this writ.

(Latin) *Ibid.,* v, 2.

(H) PONE

The king to the sheriff, greeting. Bring before me or my justices on——— that suit which is in your county [court] between M. and N. concerning one hide of land in———, which the same M. claims against the aforesaid N. as her legitimate marriage portion.[7] And summon through good summoners the aforesaid N., who holds that

---

[5] Glanville here gives various examples of specific tenures. On the significance of the action, see Pollock and Maitland, I, 385.

[6] In full, *Praecipe quod reddat;* see art. 34 of Magna Carta, below, p. 120.

[7] See above, p. 47, n. 3.

land, to be there with his suit. And you are to have there the summoners and this writ.

(Latin) *Ibid.*, vi, 7.

(I) PROHIBE

The king to the sheriff, greeting. Prohibit R. from proceeding in the court Christian with the plea begun between him and N. concerning the lay fee of the aforesaid R. in———, in which connection he complains that the aforesaid N. is impleading him in the court Christian before———. And if the aforesaid R. will give you security for prosecuting his claim, then place the aforesaid N. under gage and good pledges to be before me or my justices on———, to show cause for impleading him in the court Christian concerning his lay fee in———, although that plea pertains to my crown and dignity.[8]

(Latin) *Ibid.*, xii, 22.

---

[8] See no. 30, art. 9.

34. THE ASSIZE OF ARMS (1181)

1. Whoever possesses one knight's fee shall have a shirt of mail, a helmet, a shield, and a lance; and every knight shall have as many shirts of mail, helmets, shields, and lances as he possesses knight's fees in demesne.[1]

2. Moreover, every free layman who possesses chattels or rents to the value of 16*m.* shall have a shirt of mail, a helmet, a shield, and a lance; and every free layman possessing chattels or rents to the value of 10*m.* shall have a hauberk, an iron cap, and a lance.[2]

3. Item, all burgesses and the whole community of freemen shall have [each] a gambeson,[3] an iron cap, and a lance.

4. Besides, each of them shall swear to have these arms before the feast of St. Hilary, to be faithful to the lord king Henry—namely, the son of the Empress Matilda—and to bear these arms in his service according to his command and in fealty to the lord king and his kingdom. And henceforth no one having these arms shall sell them or pledge them or lend them or alienate them in any other way; nor shall a lord in any way alienate them from his men, either through forfeiture or through gift or through pledge or in any other way.

5. If any one having these arms dies, his arms shall remain to his heir. If, however, the heir is not of age to use arms in time of need, that person who has wardship over him shall also have custody of the arms and shall find a man who can use the arms in the service of the lord king until the heir is of age to bear arms, and then he shall have them.

6. Any burgess who has more arms than he ought to have by this

---

[1] That is to say, as many knights as remain charged against his demesne; cf. no. 36.

[2] Presumably less elaborate armour than that required of the other group.

[3] A padded surcoat.

assize shall sell them, or give them away, or in some way alienate them to such a man as will keep them for the service of the lord king of England. And none of them shall keep more arms than he ought to have by this assize.

7. Item, no Jew shall keep in his possession a shirt of mail or a hauberk, but he shall sell it or give it away or alienate it in some other way, so that it shall remain in the king's service.

8. Item, no one shall carry arms out of England except by the command of the lord king: no one is to sell arms to another to carry out of England; nor shall a merchant or any other man carry them out of England.

9. Item, the justices shall have [a report] sworn by lawful knights, or by other free and lawful men of the hundreds and neighbourhoods and boroughs—as many as they see fit to employ—as to what persons possess chattels to the amount that they should have a shirt of mail, a helmet, a lance, and a shield according to what has been provided; so that they shall separately name for those [justices] all men of their hundreds and neighbourhoods and boroughs who are worth 16m. in either chattels or rents, and likewise those who are worth 10m. And then the justices shall have written down [the names of] all those jurors and other men, [recording] how much in chattels or rents they [each] have and what arms, according to the value of the chattels or rents, they should [each] have. Then, in their presence and in a common assembly of those men, they shall have read this assize regarding the possession of arms, and they shall have those men swear to have arms according to the value of the aforesaid chattels or rents, and to keep them for the service of the lord king according to this aforesaid assize, under the command of and in fealty to the lord king Henry and his kingdom. If, moreover, it should happen that any one of them, who ought to have these arms, is not in the county during the period when the justices are in that county, the justices shall set a time for him [to appear] before them in another county. And if he does not come to them in any county through which they are to go, and is not in that land [at all], they shall set him a time at Westminster toward the octave of St. Michael; so that, as he loves his life and all that he has, he shall be there for swearing his oath. And they shall command him, before the aforesaid feast of St. Hilary, to have arms according to the obligation resting on him.

10. Item, the justices shall have proclamation made in the counties through which they are to go that, with respect to those who do not have such arms as have been specified above, the lord king will take vengeance, not merely on their lands or chattels, but on their limbs.

11. Item, no one who does not possess 16m. [as specified above] or 10m. in chattels is to swear concerning free and lawful men.

12. Item, the justices shall command through all the counties that no one, as he loves his life and all that he has, shall buy or sell any ship to be taken away from England, and that no one shall carry any timber or cause it to be carried out of England. And the lord king

commands that no one shall be received for the oath concerning arms unless he is a freeman.

(Latin) Stubbs, *Select Charters*, pp. 183 f.

35. THE ASSIZE OF THE FOREST (1184)[1]

This is the assize of the lord king Henry, son of Matilda, with regard to his forest and venison[2] in England, [proclaimed] at Woodstock by the counsel and assent of the archbishops, bishops, and barons—earls and nobles—of England.

1. In the first place, he has forbidden that any one shall commit any sort of offence touching his venison and his forests, and he wills that no one shall take confidence from the fact that hitherto those who have committed offences touching his venison and his forests have been declared in mercy [only] as concerned their chattels. For henceforth, if any one commits any [such] offence against him and is convicted of it, he wills that full justice shall be had of that man as was had in the time of King Henry, his grandfather.

2. Item, he has commanded that no one shall have bows, arrows, dogs, or hounds in his forests, unless [such person] has the warrant of the king or of some other man who can [lawfully] be his warrantor.

3. Item, he forbids all persons to give or sell anything to the destruction or waste of their woods, which are within the forest of King Henry;[3] while fully conceding that, without waste, they may take from their woods whatever may be necessary for them, and this by view of the king's forester.

4. Item, he has commanded that all those who have woods within the bounds of the king's forest may put proper foresters in their woods; for which foresters those to whom the woods belong are to be sureties, or they are to provide such proper sureties as can pay compensation, should the foresters commit any offence touching what pertains to the lord king. And those who, outside the bounds of the [forest] visitation, have woods in which the venison enjoys the peace of the lord king are to have no forester unless they will swear [to respect] the king's assize, the peace of his venison, and whatever custodian is put in charge of his woods.[4]

5. Item, the lord king has commanded that his foresters shall exercise care over the forest of knights and others who have woods within the bounds of the king's forest, [to see] that the woods are not destroyed. For if on this account the woods are destroyed, let it be well known to those whose woods are destroyed that compensation

---

[1] On all phases of this assize see the chapters in Petit-Dutaillis and Lefebvre, pp. 149 f., and G. J. Turner's introduction to his *Select Pleas of the Forest* (Selden Society). No really good text of the document has come down to us.

[2] *Venatio*, meaning either game or hunting rights.

[3] The forest was a game preserve which might include all kinds of land, either inhabited or uninhabited. Within it might lie extensive woods that were the property of lay and clerical nobles. Such persons, under royal supervision, were entitled to any reasonable use of their own woods.

[4] Cf. articles 7, 13.

will be exacted from those men themselves or from their lands, and from none other.

6. Item, the lord king has commanded that all his foresters shall swear to the best of their ability to enforce the assize that he has established for his forests, and that they will not disturb knights or other good men in [the enjoyment of] what the king has granted them with regard to their woods.

7. Item, the king has commanded that, in each county where he has venison, twelve knights shall be appointed to guard his vert[5] and venison together with the forest; and four knights shall be appointed to have charge of agistment[6] in his woods, and to receive and keep his pannage. And the king forbids that any one shall provide agistment for his own woods within the bounds of the forest before agistment is provided for the king's woods. And [provision for] the lord king's agistment begins fifteen days before Michaelmas and lasts until fifteen days after Michaelmas.

8. And the lord king has commanded that, when a forester has the lord king's own woods in his charge, if those woods are destroyed and he can by no means show good cause for the destruction of the woods, vengeance shall be taken on the forester's own body and not otherwise.

9. Item, the king forbids all clergymen to commit any offences touching his venison or his forests. He strictly orders his foresters that, if they find such men committing offences, they shall not hesitate to lay hands on those men in order to hold them and put them under attachment;[7] he himself will give full warranty.

10. Item, the king has ordered that his assarts,[8] both new and old, are to be inspected; likewise his purprestures[9] and wastes of forests, and that each [class of offences] is to be recorded by itself.

11. Item, the king has commanded that, on summons of his master forester, archbishops, bishops, earls, barons, knights, freeholders, and all men, as they wish to be protected and not to be declared in the king's mercy, shall come to try the pleas of the lord king touching his forests, and to attend to his other business in the county [court].

12. At Woodstock the king has also commanded that, if any man commits a first offence touching the forest, good pledges shall be accepted from him, and so likewise if he commits a second offense. But if he does wrong a third time, for the third offence no further pledges shall be accepted from him, nor anything other than the body of the misdoer.

13. Item, the king has commanded that every man who is [at least]

---

[5] Green wood, or growing timber.

[6] The putting of animals, especially swine, into the woods to feed. For pannage, see above, p. 43, n. 19.

[7] Restraint either of the person or of his property, to assure his appearance in court.

[8] Clearings made for cultivation or some other purpose.

[9] Unauthorized uses of the royal land.

twelve years of age, and who dwells within the peace of the venison,[10] shall swear that peace; and clergy holding lay fees [shall do the same].

14. Item, he has commanded that the lawing of mastiffs[11] shall be carried out wherever his wild beasts enjoy his peace and have been accustomed to enjoy it.

15. Item, he has commanded that no tanner or bleacher of hides shall dwell in his forests outside a borough.

16. Item, the king has commanded that henceforth no one, either within or without a forest, shall engage in any kind of chase at night for the taking of wild beasts wherever his wild beasts live or enjoy his peace or have been accustomed to enjoy it, on pain of imprisonment for one year and of redeeming themselves by fine at at his pleasure; and that no one, under the same penalty, shall raise against his wild beasts any obstruction, either living or dead, between his forest and the woods or other regions disafforested by him or his ancestors.

(Latin) *Ibid.*, pp. 186 f.

---

[10] The region adjoining the forest, technically known as the purlieu, where hunting was restricted; see Petit-Dutaillis and Lefebvre, pp. 233 f.

[11] Mutilation of the dogs' feet so that they could not chase game; cf. no. 45, art. 6.

36. BARONIAL RETURNS (1166)[1]

(A) FROM THE ARCHBISHOP OF YORK

To his most beloved lord, Henry, by the grace of God king of England, duke of Normandy and of Aquitaine, and count of Anjou, his Roger, by the same grace archbishop of York and legate of the Apostolic See, greeting. Your majesty has commanded that all your faithful men, both clerical and lay, who hold of you in chief within Yorkshire, shall signify to you by their sealed letters patent[2] how many knights each of them has who were enfeoffed by old enfeoffment in the time of King Henry, your grandfather, namely, on the day and in the year that he was alive and dead; and how many he has who were enfeoffed by new enfeoffment after the death of your said grandfather of blessed memory; and how many knights are charged against the demesne of each. And the names of all those men, both of the new enfeoffment and of the old, are to be inscribed in that writ, because you wish that, if there are any who have not yet sworn fealty to you and whose names are not yet inscribed in your roll,

---

[1] On all problems of interpretation raised by these returns, see Round, *Feudal England*, pp. 236 f.; also his *Studies on the Red Book of the Exchequer* for criticism of the edition published in the Rolls Series.

[2] Letters patent had the seal attached to a strip of parchment run through the bottom of the document, so that it might be freely opened. For letters close the strip was run through the folded document, so that it should be read only by the person to whom it was addressed. Cf. no. 41 for examples of the difference in style. What here follows in the archbishop's letter obviously reflects the terms of the king's original mandate.

they should swear fealty to you before the first Sunday of Lent. As one of which [faithful men], being subject in all things to your command, I have with all diligence, and in so far as the brevity of the time would permit, made investigation within my tenement and by the present writing signify to you, my lord, [the results].

Wherefore, my lord, be it known to you in the first place that no knight is charged against the demesne of the archbishopric of York, since we have enough knights enfeoffed through whom to perform all the service that we owe you, as also our predecessors had; and we have more than we owe, as you may see from the present writing. For our predecessors, not through necessity of the service that we owe, but because they wished to provide for their relatives and serjeants, enfeoffed more [knights] than they owed the king. Now these are the names of those enfeoffed from the time of King Henry [I].[3] . . . After the death of King Henry, however, [the following men] were enfeoffed: Peter the Steward with half a knight's fee; Earl Peter with the twentieth of a knight; Geoffrey of Burton with the twelfth of a knight; Gervaise of Bretton with the third of a knight. And since, my lord, of these there are some from whom I demand more service than they are performing, while others are withholding what is said to belong to the table (*mensam*) and demesne of the archbishop rather than to those men themselves, I humbly ask that this writing shall not be held against me or my successors if we are unable to restore or to retain the rights of the church. Fare thee well, my lord!

(Latin) *Liber Niger Scaccarii*, pp. 303 f.

(B) From the Abbot of St. Albans

To his most benign lord, Henry, by the grace of God illustrious king of the English, Brother Robert, humble minister of the church of St. Albans, greeting and faithful service. With regard to the knights, whose number and names you order reported to you in writing, we truthfully give you this information. We have six knights enfeoffed from old enfeoffment of the time of King Henry [I], but from new enfeoffment none. Nor have we any knight who performs the full service of a knight except Hugh Wach, who holds of us one knight's fee.[4] . . . Our demesne, moreover, owes you no [knight]. May Almighty God preserve to you in peace and for long the integrity of your realm!

(Latin) *Ibid.*, p. 244.

(C) From the Earl of Essex

To Henry, king of England, duke of Normandy and of Aquitaine, and count of Anjou, Geoffrey, earl of Essex, greeting and faithful service. Know that the names hereinunder written are those of the knights who hold of me by old enfeoffment. . . . Total of the knights

---

[3] The text here lists 39 tenants with over 41 knight's fees.
[4] Various lesser holdings are enumerated.

by old enfeoffment, ninety-seven knights and the third of a knight. These are the names of the knights by new enfeoffment. . . . Total of those newly enfeoffed.⁵ . . . And my men tell me that I owe the king sixty knights.

(Latin) *Ibid.*, pp. 228 f.

(D) FROM BADERON OF MONMOUTH

To his lord, Henry, king of the English, Baderon of Monmouth, greeting. Lord, I have heard your precept in the county [court] of Hereford: namely, that I should notify you, signifying to you by my letters patent under seal, how many knights I have who were enfeoffed by old enfeoffment. Accordingly, prepared to obey your precept, I have noted their names as follows. . . . These ten are of the old enfeoffment; of [knights] newly enfeoffed I have none. Besides, I am bound to furnish you five [knights] from my demesne.

(Latin) *Ibid.*, p. 152.

(E) FROM GILBERT OF PINKNEY

To his lord, the king, Gilbert of Pinkney gives this notification. It is ascertained that I have eleven and a half knights enfeoffed by old enfeoffment from the time of King Henry [I]: namely. . . . And afterwards, from my demesne, I gave to Henry, my son, one knight's fee; and to Gilbert, my son, half a knight's fee. In addition there remains against my demesne the service of two knights.

(Latin) *Ibid.*, p. 196.

(F) FROM PETER DE LA MARE

To Henry, by the grace of God king of the English, Peter de la Mare, greeting. Be it known to you that, by your grace, I hold Lavington in demesne for the service of two knights; but that I there have no knight enfeoffed, either by old or by new [enfeoffment]. Farewell!

(Latin) *Ibid.*, p. 113.

(G) FROM WILLIAM OF LONDON

To his dearest lord, Henry, by the grace of God king of the English, William of London, greeting. Know that I have no knight enfeoffed, either by old or by new enfeoffment; but that I am bound to defend my fief through the service of my body.

(Latin) *Ibid.*, p. 113.

37. PIPE ROLL OF 33 HENRY II (1187)

(A) ENTRIES CONCERNING SCUTAGE

From the scutage of the knights of Lincolnshire who did not depart with the king for the army of Galloway. The bishop of Lincoln renders account of £60 of scutage for his knights of the old enfeoffment, which he acknowledges he owes the king. . . . Oliver d'Ain-

---

⁵ Twelve knights plus a number of fractions.

court owes £35 of scutage for his knights. Martin Martel renders account of 5s. for the fourth of a knight's fee. . . . William de Berville renders account of 3s. 4d. for the sixth of a knight's fee. . . .

Yorkshire. . . . Laurence, archdeacon of Bedford, and Master Roger Arundel render account of £20 of scutage for the knights of the archbishopric of York, which the archbishop acknowledges he owes the king.[1] They have paid it into the treasury. And they are quit. The same men render account of £27. 9s. 8d. for the knights which the archbishop does not acknowledge he owes the king, but which are accounted for because the archbishopric is in the king's hands. In the treasury £24. 9s. 8d. And they owe 60s. . . .

Gloucestershire. . . . Hugh Bardolf renders account of £327. 3s. of scutage for the knights of the honour of the earl of Gloucester, both of the old enfeoffment and of the new, for which account is rendered because the honour is in the king's hands. In the treasury £207. 8s. 10d. And in pardons by the king's writ.[2] . . . And in demesnes of the king, from which he has tallage, £6. And in pardons by the king's writ to the barons of the said honour enfeoffed in Wales £41. 15s. And he owes £62. 2s. 6d. . . .

Devonshire. . . . The bishop of Exeter renders account of £15. 10s. of scutage for his knights, which he acknowledges he owes the king. He has paid it into the treasury. And he is quit. The same man owes £18. 2s. 4d. for the knights which he does not acknowledge. Walter, abbot of Tavistock, renders account of £16 of scutage for the knights which he acknowledges. . . .

Cornwall. . . . Agnes, who was wife of Walter Hay, renders account of £12. 10s. of scutage for twenty knights: namely, 12s. 6d. for each knight. . . . Nicholas Fitz-Geoffrey renders account of £6. 5s. of scutage for ten knights with small fees. . . . William Fitz-Richard renders account of 62s. 6d. of scutage for five knights in the manner aforesaid. . . .

(Latin) *Pipe Roll of 33 Henry II,* pp. 75 f.

(B) ENTRIES CONCERNING TALLAGE

From the tallage of the king's demesnes and the lands which were then in his hands in Norfolk. The same sheriff renders account of 100s. from the contribution (*donum*) of Cawston.[3] . . . The same sheriff renders account of 4m. from the vill of Eresham. . . . The same sheriff renders account of £7. 10s. from the half-hundred of Eresham. . . . The same sheriff renders account of £25. 13s. 4d. from Yarmouth. . . . The same sheriff renders account of £93. 16s.

---

[1] The barons, especially the great ecclesiastics, refused to admit that they owed any service beyond that anciently charged against their fiefs, no matter how many knights they had subinfeudated. So, as may be seen from the entries below, the king often failed to collect all the assessed scutage, unless the honour was in his hands. See Round, *Feudal England,* pp. 242 f.

[2] Sums totalling £9. 16s. 8d. pardoned to five persons.

[3] About half of the assessed sum is normally paid into the treasury, with the remainder left for the following year.

37. PIPE ROLL 33 HENRY II

8d. from the contribution of Norwich. . . . The same sheriff renders account of 1m. from two men of the king dwelling in Clacklose Hundred. . . .
Suffolk. . . . The same sheriff renders account of 2m. from Holbrook. . . . The same sheriff renders account of 2m. from Dunningworth. . . . The same sheriff renders account of 40s. from Little Framingham. . . . The same sheriff renders account of £20. 16s. 8d. from the contribution of Oreford. . . . The same sheriff renders account of £16 from Ipswich. . . . The same sheriff renders account of £30. 6s. 4d. from Lothingland. . . . The same sheriff renders account of £4. 13s. 4d. from the contribution of Eye. . . . The burgesses of Dunwich [owe] 100m. from the contribution promised by them in common. . . .
Lincolnshire. . . . From the tallage of the demesnes and lands which were then in the king's hands, [assessed] by Geoffrey de Lucy and Jocelyn, archdeacon of Chichester, and William le Vavasseur. The same sheriff renders account of £45. 15s. from the contribution of Grimsby together with the soke. . . . The same sheriff renders account of £31. 6s. 8d. from Caistor together with the soke. . . . The same sheriff renders account of 46s. 8d. from Stallingborough, demesne of the archbishopric [of York]. . . . The same sheriff renders account of 40s. from Benningworth, land of the archbishop. . . . The men of Sixhills and Henton owe 2m. of contribution. The same sheriff renders account of 103s. from Torksey. . . . The same sheriff renders account of 40s. from Surfleet, which belonged to Helpe the Crossbowman. . . . The citizens of Lincoln owe £176. 4s. from the contribution assessed by the justices on individual men. . . .
Yorkshire. . . . The same sheriff renders account of £226. 6s. 4d. from the contribution of the city of York, assessed by the justices on the men of the same city except the moneyers. . . .

(Latin) *Ibid.*, pp. 59 f.

(C) ENTRIES CONCERNING PROFITS OF JUSTICE

Northamptonshire. . . . From the pleas of Ranulf de Glanville, Jocelyn the Archdeacon, Thomas of Hurstbourne, and Michael Belet. The same sheriff renders account of 3s. 4d. from the amercement of Adam of Newton because he did not have the man for whom he was surety. . . . William of Stanford renders account of 8m., because, while he was serjeant of the hundred, he did not present to the sheriff a crown plea that had earlier been presented to him. . . . Ralph of the Churchyard renders account of 4s. 8d. for the flight of Richard. . . . Simon the Dean renders account of ½m. because he detained a [certain] man's slayers who were not in frankpledge. . . . The same sheriff renders account of 35s. from Sutton Hundred for a murder.[4] . . . Richard Blere renders account of 5s. 8d. for purpres-

---
[4] See above, p. 36, n. 2.

ture.⁵ . . . Peter, son of Adam, renders account of 75*m*. for the same and because he took a certain woman and tortured her without the king's licence. . . . The burgesses of Northampton render account of 20*m*. for the concealment of a crown plea.⁶ . . . Reginald, reeve of Weddon, owes ½*m*. because he first denied what he afterwards acknowledged. . . . Ralph of Aldewinc renders account of ½*m*. for a false claim. . . . William Caperum owes ½*m*. for false measure. Ralph, son of Bernard, renders account of ½*m*. because he withdrew [from his suit]. . . . Item, from offerings to the court. Hugh Ridel renders account of £93. 6*s*. 8*d*. to have such seisin of his land of Withering as he had when Peter de Saint-Médard died. . . . Gilbert de Wanleville owes 40*s*. for a recognition against William de Bere concerning sixteen virgates of land as to whether it is gage or fee. Geoffrey Brito renders account of 15*m*. for the wife whom he married without the king's licence when she was in the gift of the king. . . . Robert Reval renders account of 10*m*. that he may have in the king's court his suit against Adam Fitz-Warin concerning eight virgates of land in Cosgrove. . . .

Hampshire. . . . From the pleas of the forest [held] by Geoffrey Fitz-Peter. The same sheriff renders account of 25*s*. from the demesnes of the bishop and the prior of Winchester for transgression of the assize of the forest.⁷ . . . Walter Waleran renders account of 2*s*. for an escape. . . . Robert d'Aumale renders account of 20*s*. for bows and arrows [kept] against the assize. . . . The same sheriff renders account of 56*s*. 10*d*. for wastes, assarts, purprestures, and pleas of the forest of Hampshire. . . . The prioress of Amesbury owes 3*s*. for vert.

London. . . . Bruno the Jew owes £340 of the amercement of 2000*m*. for which he fined with the king at Waltham.⁸ Aaron the Jew of Lincoln owes 500*m*. of the same fine. But he is dead and the king has his chattels. . . . The Jews of England owe 5525½*m*. of amercement for Jurnet of Norwich, whose charters they have in order to acquit him. . . .

Norfolk. . . . Spreggi renders account of 100*m*. for not arresting Robert as the justices ordered. . . . William Fitz-William of Lynn renders account of 2*m*. for a recognition concerning the advowson of the church of Lynn.⁹

Lincolnshire. . . . Benedict Clarizia renders account of 20*m*. of amercement for the hauberk that his wife took in pledge contrary to the prohibition.¹⁰ . . . Robert de Hardre owes 1*m*. of gold for recognition concerning two carucates of land in Hadley, as to whether it is free fee of the church or lay [fee].¹¹ . . .

---

⁵ See above, p. 88, n. 9.
⁶ That is to say, for failure to make presentation.
⁷ For this and the following items, see no. 35.
⁸ In connection with these entries, cf. no. 40A.
⁹ See no. 33D.
¹⁰ See no. 34, art. 7.
¹¹ See no. 33C.

38. SALADIN TITHE

Yorkshire. . . . The bishop of Durham owes 500*m*. because he held in the court Christian a plea concerning the advowson of a certain church.[12] . . . Robert of Sanford owes 40*s*. for recognition of his father's death with regard to the land of Ecclesfield, as against Reginald de Lucy. Ralph de Clare renders account of £80 to have the king's benevolence. . . .

Sussex. . . . Robert of Badbury renders account of £35. 9*s*. 10*d*. for disseisin against the assize. . . . The bishop of Chichester renders account of 10*m*. because he hunted without licence in woods of the king's escheat. . . . Warner de Sumery renders account of 20*s*. for right[13] concerning the service from one virgate of land in Bixley, as against Gilbert of Balliol. . . .

Essex and Hertfordshire. . . . The abbess of Barking owes 20*m*. for 180 oaks cut down in the forest against the assize. . . . Ralph of Dene owes 10*s*. for dogs [kept] against the assize. . . . Edwin Scaldhot renders account of 20*d*. because he unjustly vexed the jurors. . . .

Staffordshire. . . . Guy de Suinfen renders account of 1*m*. for having in the king's court his suit against Henry de Pirie, which was in the county [court]. . . .

Wiltshire. . . . The same sheriff owes 18*d*. from Kinwardstone Hundred for a murder and failure to prove Englishry.[14] . . . Walter de Saint-Germain renders account of 40*s*. for an investigation of the truth concerning the marriage of Margaret, wife of Ralph, his brother. . . .

Berkshire. . . . The same sheriff renders account of 2½*m*. from the vill of Letcombe because it received without frankpledge an unknown man who had slain five men. . . . Midwinter owes 20*s*. because it received a man who was not in frankpledge. . . .

(Latin) *Ibid.*, pp. 103 f., 197 f., etc.

---
[12] See no. 30, art. 1.
[13] See no. 33E.
[14] See no. 26, art. 92.

38. ORDINANCE OF THE SALADIN TITHE (1188)

1. Every one shall give in alms for this year's aid of the land of Jerusalem a tenth of his rents and movables, except the arms, horses, and clothes of knights, and except likewise the horses, books, clothes, vestments, and all sacred furnishings[1] of clergymen, and [except] the precious stones of both clergymen and laymen.

2. Moreover, this money is to be collected within each parish in the presence of the parish priest and the archpriest,[2] one Templar and one Hospitaller, a serjeant of the lord king and a clerk of the king, a serjeant of a baron and his clerk, and a clerk of the bishop—after excommunication has been proclaimed by the archbishops and bishops and by the archpriests, each in his own parish, of every man

---
[1] *Capella*, whatever the priest needed for divine service.
[2] The chief priest of the diocese, otherwise known as the rural dean.

who will not lawfully give the aforesaid tenth in the presence and with the knowledge of those who, as already stated, should be present. And if any one, to the knowledge of these men, gives less than he should, let there be chosen from the parish four or six lawful men who, being sworn, shall determine the amount that he should have declared; then he must make up the deficiency in his contribution.

3. Clergy and knights who have taken the cross, however, shall give nothing toward the said tenth except from their own property and demesnes; whatever their men may owe shall be collected for their use by the aforesaid persons and given to them entire.

4. Moreover, on the day of the Nativity, [the day] of St. Stephen, and [the day] of St. John the bishops shall have announcement made through their letters in each parish of their bishoprics that every one is to assemble the aforesaid tenth at his own home before the Purification of the Blessed Virgin, and on the following day or thereafter pay [it] at the place to which he is summoned and in the presence of the aforesaid persons.

(Latin) Stubbs, *Select Charters*, p. 189.

39. BOROUGH CHARTERS AND RECORDS

(A) JOHN: CHARTER TO IPSWICH (1200)

John, by the grace of God king, etc. Know that we have granted and by our present charter have confirmed to our burgesses of Ipswich our borough of Ipswich, with all its appurtenances and with all its liberties and free customs, to be held of us and our heirs by them and their heirs in hereditary right, paying to our exchequer every year at Michaelmas term, by the hand of the reeve of Ipswich, the just and accustomed farm and, at the same time, the increment of 100s. sterling by tale that they used to pay. We have also granted that all burgesses of Ipswich are to be quit of toll, stallage,[1] lastage, pontage, and all other customs throughout all our land and throughout the ports of the sea. We have granted to them that, with the exception of our officials, none of them shall be impleaded in any plea outside the borough of Ipswich, save only in pleas concerning foreign tenures; and that they shall have their gild merchant and their hanse;[2] that no one shall be lodged or shall take anything by force within the borough of Ipswich; that they shall justly have their lands and their pledges and all their debts, by whomsoever owed; that, with regard to their lands and tenures inside the borough, justice shall be assured them according to the custom of the borough of Ipswich and of our free boroughs; that, with regard to their debts established at Ipswich and their pledges made in the same place, the pleas shall be held at Ipswich; and that none of them shall be adjudged in mercy with respect to his chattels except according to the law of our free boroughs. We also forbid any one in all our land, on pain of £10

---

[1] Rent paid for stalls in a market or fair; not to be confused with tallage. Cf. no. 28B for a number of these privileges.

[2] See above, p. 63, n. 14.

forfeiture to us, to exact toll, stallage, or any other custom from the men of Ipswich. Wherefore we will and straitly command that the aforesaid burgesses shall have and hold the aforesaid liberties and free customs well and in peace, as they have been and are best and most freely enjoyed by the other burgesses of our free boroughs in England, saving in all things to our citizens of London their liberties and free customs.

Furthermore, we will and grant that our said burgesses, by the common counsel of their town, shall elect two of the more lawful and discreet men of their town and present them to our chief justice at our exchequer; which men shall well and faithfully keep the reeveship (*prepdsituram*) of our aforesaid borough of Ipswich. And so long as they well conduct themselves in that office, they shall not be removed except by the common counsel of the aforesaid burgesses. We also will that in the same borough, by the common counsel of the aforesaid burgesses, four of the more lawful and discreet men of the borough shall be elected to keep the pleas of the crown and other matters that pertain to us and to our crown in the same borough,[3] and to see that the reeves of that borough justly treat both rich and poor.

These are the witnesses. . . . May 25, in the second year of our reign.

(Latin) Gross, *Gild Merchant*, II, 115 f.

(B) RECORD OF PROCEEDINGS AT IPSWICH (1200)

On Thursday next after the feast of the Nativity of St. John the Baptist, in the second year of the reign of King John, all the townspeople (*tota villata*) of the borough of Ipswich assembled in the churchyard of St. Mary at the Tower to elect two bailiffs[4] and four coroners in the same borough according to the provision of the aforesaid charter of the lord king, which the same king had recently granted to the burgesses of the aforesaid borough. On which day the same burgesses, by common consent and in unanimity, elected two good and lawful men of their town—namely, John Fitz-Norman and William de Belines—who were sworn to keep the reeveship (*prepositurum*) of the aforesaid borough, and well and faithfully to treat both rich and poor. On the same day, furthermore, they unanimously elected four coroners—namely, John Fitz-Norman, William de Belines, Philip de Porte, and Roger Lew—who were sworn to keep the pleas of the crown and to care for other matters that pertain to the crown in the same borough and to see that the aforesaid bailiffs justly and lawfully treat both rich and poor. On the same day, furthermore, it was ordered by the common counsel of the said town that henceforth there should be sworn in the aforesaid borough twelve chief portmen, as there are in other free boroughs of England, and

---

[3] See above, p. 53, n. 16; cf. no. 40A, art. 20.
[4] See above, p. 82, n. 7. It was obviously a matter of indifference to both king and burgesses whether their magistrates were styled *praepositi* or *ballivi*. For criticism of this whole document, see C. Stephenson, *Borough and Town*, pp. 174 f., and J. Tait, *The Medieval English Borough*, pp. 270 f.

that, for themselves and the whole town, they should have full power of governing and maintaining the aforesaid borough and all the liberties of the aforesaid borough, of rendering the judgments of the town, and also of keeping, ordering, and doing in the same borough whatever ought to be done for the welfare and honour of the said town. And besides it was announced by the aforesaid bailiffs and coroners that all the townspeople should come to the aforesaid churchyard on Sunday next after the coming feast of the Apostles Peter and Paul, to elect the aforesaid twelve chief portmen according to the provision of the same ordinance.

On Sunday next after the feast of the Apostles Peter and Paul, in the aforesaid year, the whole town of Ipswich assembled in the presence of the bailiffs and coroners of the same town, to elect twelve chief portmen in the same town, as previously ordered. And the aforesaid bailiffs and coroners, by the assent of the townspeople, chose four good and lawful men from each parish of the said town, who were sworn to elect twelve chief portmen from the better, more discreet, and more influential men of the aforesaid town, to make ordinances for the welfare of the town, as aforesaid. And the aforesaid sworn men of the parishes met and elected, for themselves and for all the townspeople, these twelve whose names are written below: namely, John Fitz-Norman, William de Belines, Philip de Porte, Roger Lew, Peter Everard, William Gotschalk, Ames Bolle, John of St. George, John le Mayster, Sayer Fitz-Thurstan, Robert Parys, and Andrew Pepper. Which men were sworn in the presence of all the aforesaid townspeople well and faithfully to keep and govern the borough of Ipswich and, to the best of their ability, to maintain all the liberties that had recently been granted to the burgesses of the same borough by the charter of the lord king aforesaid; also to maintain all other liberties and free customs of the aforesaid town and justly to render the judgments of the courts in the same town without respect to the person of any one; and, besides, to order and to do all else that ought to be done for the welfare and honour of the aforesaid town, justly and lawfully treating both rich and poor.

On the same day, as soon as the aforesaid twelve chief portmen had been sworn according to the aforesaid form, they had all the townspeople raise their hands towards the Book and in unison solemnly swear, from that hour onward, to be obedient, attentive, agreeable, and helpful with body and with goods to their bailiffs and coroners, and to all and singular of the twelve chief portmen aforesaid, for preserving and maintaining the aforesaid town of Ipswich and the aforesaid new charter, together with the honour and all the liberties and free customs of the aforesaid town, to the best of their ability as they justly and reasonably should, in all places and against all persons, saving, nevertheless, the king and his royal authority. On the same day it was agreed that the aforesaid new charter of the lord king should be given for safe keeping to two good and lawful men of the same town—namely, John Fitz-Norman and Philip de Porte—who were sworn faithfully to keep the said charter and to deliver it to the aforesaid townspeople whenever that should be necessary and when, on the request of the townspeople, they should be notified to do so. And since there was more to be ordered and done for the welfare and honour of the town than could properly be attended to on this one day, it was agreed that the bailiffs, the coroners, and all the chief portmen aforesaid should come and assemble here on Tuesday next after the feast of the Translation of St. Thomas the Martyr, to order and do whatever ought to be ordered and done for the welfare and honour of the said town.

On Thursday next after the feast of the Translation of St. Thomas the Martyr, in the aforesaid year, the bailiffs, coroners, and other chief portmen assembled to deliberate and ordain concerning the welfare of the town of Ipswich. In the first place, they ordered that all revenues of the aforesaid borough should thenceforth be collected by the hands of the bailiffs and of four good and lawful men of the same borough; and that every year, for the said townspeople, they should pay the right and accustomed farm at the exchequer of the lord king. Furthermore, they ordered that in the said borough two beadles should be sworn to carry out arrests, distraints, and all commands of the bailiffs, coroners, and chief portmen that ought to be carried out in the same borough; that one of the same beadles should be keeper of all prisoners to be placed under arrest by the bailiffs of the borough; and that such keeper should find security for the safe keeping of all his prisoners, etc. Furthermore, they ordered that, by the common counsel of the townspeople, there should be made in the said borough a common seal for use in important business affecting the community of the said borough, also for signing affidavits on behalf of all and singular of the burgesses of the same borough, and for doing all else that ought to be done for the common honour and benefit of the aforesaid town; and that such common seal should be kept by three or four good and lawful men of the aforesaid borough, sworn to do so before the community of the same borough. Furthermore, they ordered that in the said borough, by the common counsel of its townspeople, one good and lawful and fit man should be elected to be alderman of the gild merchant in the same borough; that four good and lawful men of the same borough should be associated with him; and that the alderman and those four should swear well and faithfully to maintain the aforesaid gild and all pertaining to the gild. Furthermore, they ordered that the aforesaid new charter should be sent to the full county [court] of Suffolk and as far as Norwich to the full county [court] of Norfolk; and that the same charter should be publicly read in those counties, so that the liberties contained in the said charter should be generally known and published everywhere in each county. Furthermore, they ordered that no burgess of the aforesaid town should be quit of custom for his merchandise in the same town—that is to say, if he were a merchant—except one in scot and lot with respect to the common aids and obligations of the town.

On Sunday next after the feast of the Nativity of the Virgin Mary, in the aforesaid year, the community of the town of Ipswich assembled before the bailiffs, coroners, and other chief portmen of the same town to hear all the aforesaid ordinances, which were read before the people of the town in the churchyard of St. Mary at the Tower. And to the aforesaid ordinances, when they had there been read, the whole community aforesaid unanimously consented. And afterwards they elected their bailiffs to remain [in office] for the next year to come: namely, John Fitz-Norman and William de Belines. On the same day they elected four men to collect the customs of the town together with the aforesaid bailiffs: namely, Peter Pepper, Norman Halynoth, Clement le Palmer, and Leman de Pont. Likewise on the same day they elected two beadles—namely, John Prikehert and John Hawe—who were sworn well and faithfully to carry out arrests, distraints, and all commands of the bailiffs, coroners, and portmen, and [to do] all that pertained to their office. And the aforesaid John Prikehert was elected to keep the prisoners of the town; and he found sureties to be responsible for the escape of prisoners, should that—which God forbid!—occur: namely, Edmund Marsh (*de Marisco*), Peter Pepper, John Hawe, and Thomas de Horner. And since more could not be attended to on this day, it was agreed that the bailiffs and the whole community should be here on Thursday next after the coming feast of St. Faith, in order to elect an alderman and do the other things that could not at the moment be done. And it was announced by the bailiffs that in the meantime they would have a common seal made, as ordered above.

On Thursday next after the feast of St. Faith, in the aforesaid year, the bailiffs, coroners, and other chief portmen, as well as the whole community, assembled in the church of St. Mary at the Tower. And the bailiffs there showed the common seal of the town which had recently been made. And then three of the more lawful and influential men of the said borough were elected to keep that seal: namely, John Fitz-Norman, William de Belines, and Philip de Porte. Which men were sworn before the community well and faithfully to keep the aforesaid seal and not to sign any letter or other instrument with the same seal unless it was for the common honour and benefit of the town or of the burgesses of the town—and that with the assent of their peers. And besides it was agreed that the common charter of the town should remain in the keeping of the same men. On the same day an alderman was elected by the common counsel of the townspeople, namely, William Gotschalk. And four men were elected to be associated with him: namely, Peter Everard, John le Mayster, Roger Lew, and John of St. George. Which men were sworn, together with the alderman, well and faithfully to govern the gild merchant in the borough of Ipswich and all matters pertaining to the gild, and well and faithfully to treat all brothers of the gild. And afterwards it was announced by the alderman and his four associates, in the presence of the people of the town, that all who were of the liberty of the town should come before the alderman and his associates on a certain day—

when and where to be made known to them—in order to put themselves in the gild and pay their hanse[5] to the same gild. . . .

(Latin) *Ibid.*, II, 116 f.

(C) COMMUNAL OATH OF THE LONDONERS[6]

Oath of the commune in the time of King Richard, while he was held captive in Germany. That they will bear faith to the lord king Richard for their life and limbs and earthly honour against all men and women who can live and die, and that they will keep and aid in keeping his peace. And that, in fealty to the king, they will support the commune and be obedient to the mayor of the city of London and to the *échevins*[7] of the said commune; and that they will follow and observe the decisions of the mayor, the *échevins*, and the good men who shall be [associated] with them, saving the honour of God and Holy Church, saving the fealty of the lord king Richard, and saving in all respects the liberties of the city of London. And that, neither for reward nor for family nor for any other consideration will they abstain from pursuing and maintaining right in all things to the best of their ability and knowledge; and that, in fealty to the lord king Richard, they will together endure good and evil, whether for life or for death. And if any one presumes to disturb the peace of the lord king and his realm, that they, by the counsel of the lady [queen mother][8] and of the lord [archbishop] of Rouen,[9] and of the mayor and of the other justices of the lord king, will support, to the best of their ability and knowledge, the faithful men of the lord king and those who desire to preserve the peace, saving always in all things the liberties of London.

(Latin) Weinbaum, *London*, II, 57.

(D) LEVY OF A MUNICIPAL TAX AT LONDON (1199)

A certain assessment (*assisa*) made to raise money for the lord king, when 3000*m*. were given him for the shrievalty.[10] It has been decided that each of the aldermen[11] and all men of their wards are

---

[5] The word is often used to mean a tax or a fee.

[6] First published and commented on by Round, *Commune of London*, pp. 235 f. For subsequent estimates of its significance, see the works cited above, p. 72, n. 4.

[7] A common name for groups of municipal magistrates in northern France. In this document the term probably applies to the aldermen who, along with the mayor, came to be elected by the citizens.

[8] Eleanor of Aquitaine.

[9] Walter, archbishop of Rouen, was royal justiciar from 1191 to 1193.

[10] An entry in the Fine Roll of 1 John shows that this payment was to secure a charter confirming the liberties of the city, and they, without doubt, included the right to elect magistrates and to farm London and Middlesex.

[11] When first heard of, in the early twelfth century, the aldermen were royal officials in charge of the city wards. By this time they had apparently come to be elected by the citizens assembled in wardmotes (cf. no. 72A)—the assemblies which had probably been used for a century or more to carry out such measures as are described in this and the following document.

to swear that, from rents which they have in the city and the Portsoken and which are in fee,[12] they will give 4s. on the pound, 2s. on 10s., 12d. on 5s., 6d. on 30d., and the proportionate amount on 12d. And from rent of lodgers (*hospitum*) which is not in fee—whether a reed, a rush, or anything else[13]—they will give 2s. on the pound, and so on down to the proportionate amount on 12d. Besides, from all their chattels and other things in their possession, either from what lies in their houses or from other movable property, wherever it may be—whether on this side of the sea or beyond it—they will give 2s. on the pound and so on down to the proportionate amount on 12d. And they are to swear that, on account of this assessment, they have removed chattels neither from their houses nor from anywhere else, and that they will not remove them until they have fully paid toward this assessment whatever may be their obligation. And from all debts known to be owed them, from whatever they know they have, they shall give as much as from their other chattels. And from foreign rents[14] which are held in the city and in the Portsoken and which are in fee, they shall give 4s. on the pound, as provided above, and from others which are not held in fee [they shall give] according to what has been said above; and this should be charged against the foreigners on their reception [in the city]. And they shall swear that they will conceal no one who is of the city or who enjoys a claim (*se advocet*) through the city and who does not make this oath and contribution as established and provided, so that they do not report the fact to the aldermen and the wardens of the chest. Money-lenders, men or women, shall not swear this oath.[15] [The names of] all are to be written down—of those who come to the chest and of those who do not come. And if any wish to swear that they do not have 12d. either in rent or in chattels, let them prove this to the mayor and citizens, and pay amends for [not doing] this. Each man shall swear for himself and for his wife and children, and he shall give the proper amount for them; or, if he prefers, let them come before the mayor and the citizens to swear and pay for themselves. And all the aldermen shall give strict orders to all in their wards that no one shall leave the city, either by a street of the lord [king] or otherwise, until he has acquitted himself and his [family] of this assessment. Moreover, if any of them does otherwise, let his name be recorded and handed over to the mayor and the rest [of the officials], who shall

---

[12] Part of the text is destroyed at this point, and what remains is very bad; but the general meaning can be guessed from what follows concerning foreign debts. The Portsoken was the suburb lying east of the Roman wall to the north of the Tower.

[13] *Arundine vel iunco vel alio*—does this mean that rents were actually paid in reeds and rushes, or is it merely a rhetorical flourish?

[14] That is to say, rents enjoyed by persons who were not citizens of London.

[15] Presumably because the assets of all such persons were carefully set down in official records; cf. no. 40A, art. 24.

seize all that he has, lands and chattels, for the use of the city. And every woman who is engaged in trading, in so far as she is manifestly acting for herself, shall carry out this [same set of instructions].

(Latin) *Ibid.,* II, 51 f.

(E) ORDINANCE FOR THE DEFENCE OF LONDON

A certain provision made for defending the city in the time of King John, at his request and with his approval. Each alderman shall hold his wardmote[16] for all his men who are aged fifteen years and more. And when they have assembled, each shall swear that, for every pound in movable property and in debts that he estimates he has [owed to him], he will give 2d., and for 10s. in movable property 1d. Item, for 20s. in rent each give 3d., and for 10s. [in rent] 1½d. Item, the alderman shall assemble all foreign merchants who are in his ward; and when he has explained to them the city's need, and how they and their chattels are safeguarded by the city, he shall urge them each by free will to contribute as much for the defence of the city as he has received from the city in favour. If, however, [he will] not [contribute], he shall be compelled to give 2d. for every pound in chattels which at the moment he has in the city. Item, from all rent of foreigners 12d. shall be taken for every pound, except from ecclesiastical rents. Item, to collect and receive this money, four good and discreet men shall be elected from each ward, who [in return] for a receipt shall pay that money at the gild-hall to Simon Blund and R. of Antioch.

Item, those persons who knowingly and deliberately break their oaths shall be excommunicated throughout all churches in the city. Item, each man, when his oath has been made, shall pay the money immediately or by the following Sunday at the latest; otherwise [his obligation] will be doubled on the next day.

Item, each alderman shall inspect the arms of all persons in his ward, so that they will have those [arms] ready for the defence of their bodies and their chattels and their city. And if any one is in default with respect to his arms, let his name be immediately enrolled, and let it be explained to the lord mayor and the other barons[17] of the city in what way, against the peace and security of the city, he has defaulted. Item, the alderman in his full wardmote shall command and provide that all have horses who ought to have them. Furthermore, a pennon shall be made in each ward, and the alderman shall have his banner. And when they have had the summons of the alderman, the men of each ward shall follow the banner of their alderman to the place assigned them for the defence of the city.

(Latin) *Ibid.,* II, 82 f.

---

[16] See above, p. 101, n. 11.

[17] An honorary title borne by the citizens of London and of the Cinque Ports. The usage perhaps arose because the burgesses of these towns were the first to hold liberties direct of the crown.

(F) JOHN: CHARTER TO LONDON (1215)

John, by the grace of God king of England, etc. Know that we have granted and by our present charter have confirmed to our barons of our city of London that each year they may elect for themselves from among their own number a mayor who is faithful to us [and is] discreet and fit for the government of the city; so that, when he has been elected, he shall be presented to us, or to our justiciar if we are not present, and shall swear fealty to us. And they shall be permitted to remove him at the end of the year and to substitute another if they will, or they may retain the same man; yet so that he shall be presented to us or to our justiciar if we are absent. We have also granted and by our charter have confirmed to our said barons that well and in peace, freely, quietly, and fully, they shall have all the liberties which they have hitherto enjoyed, as well in the city of London as outside it, both on land and on water, and in all other places, saving to us our chamberlainship.[18] Wherefore we will and straitly command that our aforesaid barons of our city of London shall each year select for themselves from among their own number a mayor in the aforesaid fashion, and that they shall have all the aforesaid liberties well and in peace, fully and completely, with everything pertaining to liberties of this kind, as aforesaid. Witnesses. . . .

(Latin) Stubbs, *Select Charters*, p. 311.

40. JUDICIAL RECORDS OF 1194

(A) ARTICLES FOR THE GENERAL EYRE

In the first place, four knights are to be elected from the entire county, who on oath shall elect two lawful knights from each hundred or wapentake, and these two shall on oath elect ten [additional] knights—or free and lawful men, if knights are not available—from each hundred or wapentake; so that these twelve shall together make response concerning all the [following] articles for the entire hundred or wapentake.

1. Concerning the pleas of the crown, both old and new, and all those which have not yet been determined before the justices of the lord king.

2. Item, concerning all recognitions and all pleas which have been summoned before the justices by writ of the king or of his chief justice, or those which have been sent before them from the principal court of the king.

3. Item, concerning escheats, which now exist, and which occurred after the king set out for the land of Jerusalem, and which were then in the king's hands, and whether or not they are in his hands now; and concerning all escheats of the lord king, if they have been taken out of his hands, how and by whom [it was done] and into whose hands they have come, and who has thence had the revenue and how, what it was, what it has been worth, and what it is worth now;

---

[18] The king reserved the right to appoint to the profitable office of city chamberlain or treasurer.

40. JUDICIAL RECORDS

and if there has been any escheat which belongs to the lord king and which is not in his hands.

4. Item, concerning churches which are in the gift of the lord king.

5. Item, concerning the wardships over children to which the king is entitled.

6. Item, concerning the marriages of girls or widows to which the lord king is entitled.

7. Item, concerning malefactors and their receivers and confederates.

8. Item, concerning falsifiers.[1]

9. Item, concerning the slayers of Jews, who they are; and concerning the pledges of the slain Jews, and their chattels, lands, debts, and charters . . . ; and all the pledges and debts of the slain Jews shall be taken into the king's hands; and those who were present at the slaying of the Jews, and who have not yet fined with the lord king or his justices, shall be arrested and shall be freed only by the lord king or his justices.

10. Item, concerning all aids paid for the ransom of the lord king, who made promises and to what amount, how much he has paid and how much is in arrears.

11. Item, concerning the adherents of Earl John,[2] which ones have fined with the lord king and which have not.

12. Item, concerning the chattels of Earl John or of his adherents, which have not been confiscated for the use of the lord king, how much the sheriffs or their bailiffs have received, and who has bestowed anything contrary to the ancient customs of the kingdom.

13. Item, concerning all the lands of Earl John, his demesnes, wardships, escheats, and grants, and why the grants were made; and such grants of Earl John and all of them shall be taken into the lord king's hands, except those which have been confirmed by the king.

14. Item, concerning debts and fines which were owed to Earl John, and why; and all of them shall be exacted for the use of the lord king.

15. Item, concerning money-lenders who have died, and their chattels.

16. Item, concerning wines sold contrary to the assize and concerning false measures both of wine and of other things.

17. Item, concerning crusaders who died before setting out for Jerusalem, who has had their chattels and what and how many these are.

18. Item, concerning grand assizes,[3] which involve 100s. worth of land, and which less.

---

[1] See above, p. 80, n. 2; and cf. art. 24, below.

[2] The king's brother, who had conspired against him and who had just been driven out of England.

[3] Trials in which a disputed title to land was settled by a jury of knights; see Pollock and Maitland, I, 147.

19. Item, concerning defaults.

20. Furthermore, in each county three knights and a clerk shall be elected as keepers of the crown pleas.[4]

21. And no sheriff shall be justice within his shrievalty or within any county that he has held since the first coronation of the lord king.

22. Furthermore, all the cities, boroughs, and demesnes of the lord king shall be tallaged.[5]

23. Moreover, the justices named[6] . . . shall cause to be summoned the knights of the county named in the roll to come on the day and to the place of which they shall make announcement, and in their presence they shall have those men swear to do all that is lawfully possible to restore the wardships and escheats of the lord king and to evaluate them for the advantage of the lord king, failing to do so for neither hate nor favour nor grace of any one.[7] . . .

24. All debts and pledges of Jews shall be enrolled, [also their] lands, houses, rents, and possessions. Moreover, a Jew who conceals any of these is to incur forfeiture to the lord king of his body and of what he has concealed, as well as of all his possessions and all his chattels. Nor shall it be permitted for the Jew ever to recover what he has concealed. Furthermore, six or seven places shall be provided, where [Jews] are to make their loans. And two lawful Christians, two lawful Jews, and two lawful scribes shall be provided, before whom and the clerk of William of St. Mary's Church and of William de Chimelli the loans are to be made. And the charters for the loans shall be made in the form of a chirograph:[8] one part, sealed with the seal of the borrower, to remain with the Jew; the other to remain in a common chest, on which are three locks. Of the keys to these locks the two Christians shall have one, the two Jews a second, and the clerk of William of St. Mary's Church and of William de Chimelli the third. And besides [there shall be on the chest] three seals; those having the keys shall affix their seals.[9] . . . And henceforth no loan, no payment to Jews, and no change in the charters shall be made except in the presence of the aforesaid men or the majority of them, if all cannot be present. And the two Christians aforesaid shall have one receipt roll for payments henceforth to be made to Jews, and the two Jews shall have one, and the keeper of the roll [shall have] one. Furthermore, every Jew shall swear on his scroll[10] that he will

---

[4] That is to say, coroners. See above, p. 53, n. 16; also nos. 39B, 53D.

[5] See no. 37B.

[6] That is to say, those on eyre in that region.

[7] These knights are to choose twelve lawful men in each region of the county and the twelve are to choose enough of the freer men in each wardship or escheat to meet the needs of the king. From information thus obtained the manors are to be evaluated, restocked whenever necessary, and let to farmers.

[8] Two copies inscribed on one piece of parchment were separated by cutting through letters, such as CHIROGRAPH, written in between the two.

[9] Details follow in the text for enrolling such records and concerning the fees to be paid to the scribes.

[10] Of the Hebrew law.

enroll all his debts, pledges, and rents, and all his goods and possessions, and that he will conceal nothing, as aforesaid; and [that], if he should gain knowledge that any one has concealed anything, he will secretly reveal it to the justices on mission, that he will detect and denounce forgers of charters and clippers of coin whenever he learns of them, and [that he will act] in the same way with regard to the forged charters. . . .

(Latin) *Ibid.,* pp. 250 f.

(B) Excerpts from a Court Roll of 6 Richard I[11]

Wiltshire Pleas and Assizes. . . . The assize comes to make recognition whether Richard le Cras unlawfully and without judgment disseised Walter son of Philip of his free tenement in Melksham after the first coronation of the lord king. The jurors say that they do not know whether or not it is a free tenement. Let him ask other jurors if he wishes. . . .

The assize comes to make recognition whether the prior of Farley unlawfully and without judgment disseised William Burnel of his free tenement in Penly after the first coronation of the lord king. The jurors say that the prior of Farley did disseise him of it. Judgment: William to have seisin of it and the prior [to be] in mercy. . . .

The assize comes to make recognition whether Payn Burnel, uncle of Ralph de Berners, was seised in demesne as of his fee on the day that he died of one virgate of land with its appurtenances in Hillcot, and whether he died after the first coronation of Henry, the king's father, and whether Ralph is his nearest heir—which land is held by Henry de Berners. The jurors say that Payn was not seised of it on the day that he died. Judgment: Henry to hold in peace and Ralph [to be] in mercy for a false claim. . . .

The assize comes to make recognition whether Richard, uncle of William, was seised in demesne as of his fee on the day that he died of one virgate of land in Charlton, and whether he died after the first coronation of Henry, the king's father, and whether William is his nearest heir—which land is held by Isabel of Marlborough and Thomas, her son. And Isabel and Thomas have said that they claim nothing in that land of right,[12] but that they hold it as villeinage of the canons of Charlton, and [that it is] free alms of Reginald de Pavillon who gave that land to the aforesaid canons. And William asks the assize that recognition be made whether that land was free tenement or villeinage when that land was to be inspected and was inspected. The jurors say that, when by the king's writ that land was

---

[11] The first part is a record of civil pleas held before the itinerant justices; the second is a record of the returns made to the articles in the preceding document. See Maitland's introduction to the volume cited below. For the forms of action here illustrated, cf. no. 33.

[12] Since they hold in villeinage, which is not protected by the king's court; see above, p. 82, n. 1.

inspected, Isabel held that land as a free tenement. Judgment: William to have that land and Isabel [to be] in mercy. . . .

Hundred of Calne, inside and outside [the borough]. The jurors say that a certain man was found dead in the fields of Cherhill and it is not known who he was. Murder.[13]

Eli of Stodlegh and the forester of G[eoffry] Fitz-Peter, in the home of Herbert the Chamberlain (*de Camera*), took a certain Matthew who, they said, was an outlaw, and who was handed over to G[eoffrey] Fitz-Peter by writ of the archbishop of Rouen.[14] And the said Herbert was therefore put under gage and pledge. And the jurors say that they made no imputation against the said Herbert besides that reception of Matthew. And Herbert appears and acknowledges that he gave lodging [to Matthew] that one time when he was captured, not knowing that he was a malefactor. Herbert is to be quit.

Tova, wife of Ralph Jagard, has accused Ralph, nephew of Hugh de Brewer, and others of having stolen a certain pig, and she has withdrawn [from her suit]. In mercy.[15] . . .

Berwick is an escheat of the lord king and is worth £15. John Marshal had possession of it and thence took 75*s*. Then Henry de Longchamps had it and thence took £26. 5*s*., and after him the sheriff of Wiltshire thence took £7. 10*s*. . . . Again William de Braose held it and thence took £15, and he still has it. . . .

Richard, son of Elmer, and Alfred the Ploughman fled on account of the robbery of sheep from the castle of Marlborough, and they were in the tithing of Walter. . . . In mercy.[16]

The same [jurors] say that Philip and Arnold of Calne were at the taking of the sheep of Marlborough, together with others who fled, and that Arnold was not in any tithing. And Philip comes and acknowledges that he was there and that Arnold was with him. Philip is to be put under pledge, in case any one wishes to bring suit against him. . . .

Sum of the first aid[17] from the vill of Calne 4*m*., which the sheriff has received. Sum of the second tallage £4. 16*s*. 8*d*., which the sheriff has received.

Sum of the first aid from the hundred outside [the borough] £25. 18*s*. 11*d*., which the clerks of the sheriff have received. Sum of the second aid £4. 6*s*. 8*d*., [which] Thomas the clerk has received. Sum of the hidage £9. 18*d*. Adam, clerk of the sheriff, has received all except 23*s*., which Guy de Dives has received, and [except] 20*s*. from the hidage of Alan Basset. . . .

---

[13] See above, p. 36, n. 2.
[14] See above, p. 101, n. 9.
[15] Marginal notation.
[16] Marginal notation. Walter and his tithing are to be amerced because of the escape; see above, p. 37, n. 6.
[17] The following entries deal with the various taxes levied for Richard's ransom. *Auxilium* and *tallagium* sometimes appear as synonymous terms.

41. LETTERS CLOSE AND PATENT

Manor of Malmesbury. Emma of Summerford was slain in the house of her mother, and Thomas and Richard of Malmesbury were on that account accused. And the whole jury, being interrogated concerning it, said that they did not suspect the aforesaid Thomas and Richard of Malmesbury of the death of the same Emma. And the knights of the whole county said that they did suspect the aforesaid Thomas and Richard, because the same men then proceeded to Gloucester, and they are convinced that the same men proceeded to Gloucester for the sake of there selling the chattels of that woman. Thomas and Richard are to clear themselves by the water.[18]

Sum of the first aid 67s. 6d.; sum of the second aid £5. 10s. 9d.— which [sums] Ralph Fitz-Stephen has received. Sum of the hidage 2s., which Laurence the serjeant of the hundred has received.

Hundred of Sedgelaw. The jurors say that a certain man was slain at Ashley, and his wife on that account accused John and Hugh, serjeants of the abbot of Malmesbury in the vill of Crudwell, and they fled. John was in the tithing of Walter Scarlet of Norton, and Hugh was a clerk. They are to be outlawed.

Fulling, land of Walter Maltravers, is escheat, and it is worth 50s. and is in the hands of Walter of St. Mary's Church.

Countess Margaret is in the gift of the lord king and has the wardship of her son by [grant of] the lord king. . . .

Hundred of Bradford. . . . In the vill of Bradford a certain woman was slain . . . , and Agatha was taken on the appeal of the mother and father of the slain woman and incarcerated at Salisbury. And when Earl J[ohn] broke the jail, then she escaped with the other prisoners and was never seen afterwards. . . . Englishry was presented at the [proper] term.

A certain infant of twelve years was drowned at Broughton, and Englishry was not presented. . . . Accident. . . .

Hundred of Devizes. The churches of Devizes were given to William de Furneaux by Earl John, and they are worth 3½m.

Sum of the first aid for the ransom of the lord king 3m., which Roger Fitz-Everard and Walter Giffard received. Sum of the second [aid] 100s. 7d., which Guy de Dives paid at the exchequer, and for which he has [a receipt].

Concerning the other articles [the jurors report] nothing.

(Latin) Maitland, *Rolls of the King's Court*, pp. 70-109.

---

[18] See no. 31, art. 2.

41. LETTERS CLOSE AND PATENT (1205-13)[1]

(A) SUMMONS TO A GREAT COUNCIL (1205)

The king, etc., to the bishop of Salisbury, etc. We command and pray you that as you cherish us and our honour, avoiding all excuse

---

[1] See above, p. 89, n. 2.

and delay, you come to us at London on Sunday next before the Ascension of the Lord, with us to consider our great and arduous concerns and the common good of our kingdom. And since, with regard to those demands from the king of France which have been brought to us by his messengers and ours[2]—and from which, by the grace of God, we hope to have a favourable outcome—it is needful to have your counsel and that of the other magnates of our land whom we have caused to be convoked on that day and at that place, you shall also cause to be summoned, on our part and on yours, the abbots and conventual priors of your whole diocese; so that, as they cherish us and the common good of the kingdom, they shall be present with us in the aforesaid council.

(Latin) Stubbs, *Select Charters*, p. 277.

(B) SUMMONS OF SERVICE FROM THE CINQUE PORTS (1206)

The king, etc., to all his beloved and faithful barons of Hastings, Dover, Sandwich, Hythe, and Romney, greeting.[3] We command you that as you cherish us and our honour and the peace of our kingdom and yourselves and all that you have, avoiding all excuse and delay, you be with us at Portsmouth on the eve of Pentecost, or as soon as you can, with as much service as you owe us, to go into our service as William of Wrotham, archdeacon of Taunton, will on our part instruct you. . . . May 12. . . .

(Latin) *Rotuli Litterarum Patentium*, I, 64.

(C) LEVY OF A TAX ON CHATTELS AND RENTS (1207)[4]

The king to all, etc. Know that by the common counsel and assent of our council at Oxford, it was provided for the defence of our kingdom and granted for the recovery of our rights that every layman throughout all England, of whosesoever fee he may be, who has rent and chattels in England, shall give us as aid 12*d.* from every mark's worth of annual rent, and 12*d.* from [every mark's worth of] every sort of movable property that he had on the octave of the Purification of the Blessed Mary—namely, at the end of the council—and so in proportion whether more or less. And all stewards and bailiffs of the earls and barons shall swear in the presence of our justices to the value of the rents and movable property of their lords and likewise of their own. And every man besides the earls and barons shall swear to his own rents and chattels according to whatever [plan] our justices dispatched for this purpose shall find best suited to our advantage. . . . February 17.

(Latin) Stubbs, *Select Charters*, pp. 278 f.

---

[2] Having to do, of course, with the war between John and Philip Augustus.

[3] For references to sources and literature concerning these towns, see the recent book of K. M. E. Murray, *Constitutional History of the Cinque Ports;* also cf. no. 50c.

[4] On the significance of this tax, see S. K. Mitchell, *Taxation under John and Henry III*, ch. iii.

41. LETTERS CLOSE AND PATENT

(D) MILITARY AND NAVAL PREPARATIONS (1212)[5]

The king to the bailiffs of ports, etc. We instruct you that henceforth you permit no ship, from whatsoever land it may be, to cross the sea from your bailiwick unless to that effect you have our special precept, in which is set down the number of men and horses that are to cross; and to suit the number of those whom we order to cross, you shall have a ship delivered to them. . . . March 23.

The king to G[eoffrey] Fitz-Peter, greeting. We command you that, on sight of these letters, you immediately send to Portsmouth with the utmost haste all the ships of your bailiwick, and others coming thither from anywhere, which can carry six horses or more, to go into our service as we have elsewhere directed, notwithstanding our last mandate given you, that you should not permit any ship, from whatsoever land it might be, to cross the sea without our special letters. . . . March 25.

Similar letters to all bailiffs of ports.

The king to the reeves and good men of Canterbury, etc. We command you that, as you cherish us, you have well prepared with horses and arms, forty of the solider and better men of our town of Canterbury, that they may well be fit and ready to cross the sea with us in our service when we send you orders, and so that we shall be grateful to you and to them. . . . June 15.[6]

The king to the sheriff of Lincoln, etc. We command you to see that we have from our city of Lincoln, from our demesnes and escheats, from those men who do not join the army with us, and from the abbeys and priories of your bailiwick two hundred good, strong, and vigorous men with axes, and that many among them are such as well know how to put themselves to carpentering, and for whom we shall be grateful to you; so that they shall be fit and ready for entering our service. And see that, by those on whose behalf they are sent, they are provided with victuals for forty days from the day on which they arrive at Chester. And you are to send with them one of your clerks and four serjeants to inspect and record those who have come and how they have come. And you are to inform us of their names and [tell us] on whose behalf they have been sent. . . . July 10.[7]

The king to the sheriff of Northumberland, etc. We command you

---

[5] In the course of this year John planned first a campaign in France and then one in Wales, but eventually all the orders were rescinded.

[6] Similar letters were sent to seventeen other boroughs for 10 men each, to thirteen for 20 men each, to three for 30 men each, to four for 40 men each, and to London for 100.

[7] Similar letters were sent to officials in charge of thirty-three other counties, vacant bishoprics, escheated honours, etc., for quotas of from 100 to 700 men equipped with axes or with spades and hoes.

to be with us at Chester on the Sunday next after the coming feast of the Assumption of the Blessed Mary. And have orders given throughout your whole bailiwick that, from the day on which you come to Chester, there shall be no trading in victuals except for our army. And see to it that, from that day, all dealers in victuals from your bailiwick, as they prize their chattels, follow our army with all sorts of victuals. . . . July 20.

Similar letters to all the sheriffs of England.

The king to the sheriff of Lincoln, etc. We command you to have summoned through good summoners all those who hold of us by serjeanty in your bailiwick, and whose names we have sent to you in another writing, that they are to be with us at Chester on Sunday next after the Assumption of the Blessed Mary, well equipped with horses and arms and provided with victuals for going with us into our service. And have this summons made by such witness that no one shall be able to deny that he was summoned. And have there this writ and the other writ. . . . July 21.

Similar letters to all the sheriffs of England.

The king to G[eoffrey] de Lucy, etc. We command you that, on sight of these letters, you immediately send our eighteen galleys toward Chester on a circuit of the coast of Llewelyn's land, to scatter and destroy the ships, galleys, and boats of our Welsh enemies, and to inflict evil upon them in all ways possible. But you are constantly to beware lest you incur injury from the land or the forces of W[illiam] Earl Marshal.[8] And you are to send to Bristol two galleys with our supplies; and those who bring them are to notify us as soon as they arrive at Bristol. And if you have need of money, you are to let us know. . . . [August 17.]

(Latin) *Rotuli Litterarum Clausarum*, I, 121-33.

(E) SUMMONS TO A GREAT COUNCIL (1213)[9]

The king to the sheriff of Oxford, greeting. We command you that you have all the knights of your bailiwick who were summoned to be with us at Oxford a fortnight after All Saints' Day come [thither] with their arms; and likewise the barons in person, but without arms. And have four discreet knights of your county come thither to us at the same time, to speak with us concerning the affairs of our kingdom. . . . November 7.

Similar letters to all the sheriffs.

(Latin) Stubbs, *Select Charters*, p. 282.

---

[8] The earl of Pembroke, who was then in conflict with the king.

[9] As pointed out by Miss Levett (*English Historical Review*, XXXI, 85 f.), Stubbs wrongly put *homines* for *milites* in the last sentence of this writ. For the best interpretation of the document, see A. B. White, in the *American Historical Review*, XXII, 325 f.

42. EXPENSE ROLL

42. HOUSEHOLD EXPENSE ROLL (1210)[1]

Sunday, at Clarendon. In harness bought for the lord king's use both in the great stable and in the stable of the chamber by Walter de Saint-Ouen and Nicholas of Wells, of which the particulars are endorsed on the roll, 41s. 9½d. To William of London, messenger of the lord bishop of Norwich, going to his lord, 5s., by William Brewer. Item, in alms to a hundred poor people, whom the king fed because he ate twice on Friday next after the feast of the Holy Trinity at Knappe, 9s. 4½d. Item, in alms to a hundred poor people because he ate twice on Friday next before the feast of St. John the Baptist, 9s. 4½d. Item, in alms to a hundred poor people because he ate twice on Friday next after the feast of St. John the Baptist, 9s. 4½d., paid to Brother Thomas. Item, at the same place, in a gift to William Le Pugneur, knight, 3m., by the king. . . .

On Tuesday next after the feast of All Saints, at Nottingham. To William the ewerer,[2] who has ½d. a day for 140 days—that is to say, from June 18 to November 4, both being counted—5s. 10d. To the same William for a bath of the lord king taken at Marlborough, 5d.; for a second bath at Nottingham, 5½d., for a third bath at Northampton, 5½d.; for a fourth bath at Gloucester, 5½d. Item, at the same place, in expenses of Adam and Gervaise, carters of the chamber, and of the man of Thomas the Marshal, and of two sumptermen with five cart-horses, two pack-horses, and a rouncey of Thomas the Marshal, staying with the wardrobe at Northampton and Rockingham for six days by the king's precept, while the lord king made a trip through the forests and river preserves, 18s. Item, in shoeing the said horses and in litter [for them] at Maldon, 4d., paid to Thomas the Marshal. . . .

On Thursday next after the feast of the Conception of the Blessed Mary, at Bristol, we paid to Engelard, sheriff of Gloucester, £400 to be put in the king's treasury. . . .

On the next Sunday, in the same place. In a gift to Walter de Marc, 5s., by the king. In a fur of vair[3] for trimming the tunic of the lord king, 20s. In gris for certain sleeves of the lord king, 9d. To a certain messenger going to the bishop of Winchester with letters concerning rumours about the Roman emperor, 3d. To Roger of the Tower going to Hugh de Neville with letters concerning the same, 3d. In two dozen [sheets of] parchment for making rolls concerning the bishoprics, 18d. . . .

On Sunday next before the [feast of the] Chair of St. Peter, at St. Bridget. In small expenses of Henry, son of the duke of Saxony, 20s., paid to Hugh of Barnwell by the king. In parchment at the same

---

[1] This is the oldest of the *mise* rolls, which anticipate the daily account-books of the later wardrobe; see Tout, *Chapters in Mediaeval Administrative History,* I, 44 f.
[2] See above, p. 69, n. 22.
[3] Vair and gris were two very popular kinds of fur: the former was grey and white, the latter grey.

place, 9*d*. On the same day, in repairs of the lord king's leggings furred with gris, 8*d*. . . . In a sack of cordovan to hold the lord king's robe, 7*s*. In four pairs of boots furred with lamb for the use of the lord king, 7*s*. 8*d*. In one pair of cowhide hose for the use of the lord king, 3*s*. In furbishing two swords of the lord king, 22*d*. In four pairs of iron spurs for the use of the same, 16*d*. . . . In a strap for the sword of the lord king, 8*d*. . . .

On Monday, [the feast of] the Chair of St. Peter, at Tweedmouth. To Philip of Stradley, for buying a horse, 2*m*., by the king. In a fur of gris bought at Winchester for the lord king's overtunic [in which] to get up during the night, 20*s*., by the hand of William the Tailor. . . .

(Latin) *Rotuli de Liberate ac de Misis*, pp. 117-51.

43. JOHN: CHARTER TO THE CHURCH (1214)

John, by the grace of God king of England, lord of Ireland, duke of Normandy and of Aquitaine, and count of Anjou, to archbishops, bishops, earls, barons, knights, bailiffs, and all who may hear or see these letters, greeting. Since, by the grace of God, a full agreement with regard to damages and usurpations during the time of the interdict has been established, of the pure and free will of each party, between us and our venerable fathers—[namely,] Stephen, archbishop of Canterbury, primate of all England, and cardinal of the Holy Roman Church; and the bishops, William of London, Eustace of Ely, Giles of Hereford, Jocelyn of Bath and Glastonbury, and Hugh of Lincoln—we wish, not merely to give them satisfaction to the best, God willing, of our ability, but also to make sound and useful provision for the whole English Church in perpetuity. Accordingly, no matter what sort of custom has hitherto been observed in the English Church, either in our own time or in that of our predecessors, and no matter what right we have hitherto asserted for ourself in the election of any prelates, we [now], on the petition of those [prelates], for the health of our soul and [the souls] of our predecessors and successors, kings of England, of our own pure and free will and by the common assent of our barons, have granted and established and by this our charter have confirmed that in all and singular of the churches, monasteries, cathedrals, and convents of our whole realm of England the elections of whatsoever prelates, both greater and lesser, shall henceforth and forever be free, saving to us and our heirs the custody of vacant churches and monasteries that belong to us. We also promise that we will not hinder, nor will we permit or authorize our men to hinder, the electors in any or all of the aforesaid churches and monasteries, when prelacies become vacant, from freely appointing a pastor over themselves whenever they please, providing, however, that permission to elect has first been sought from us and our heirs—which [permission] we will not deny or delay. And if perchance—which God forbid!—we should deny or delay [permission], the electors shall nevertheless proceed to make

44. MAGNA CARTA

a canonical election. Moreover, after the election has been held, our confirmation is to be requested; which likewise we will not deny, unless we can bring forward and lawfully prove some reasonable cause for which we ought not to give confirmation. Wherefore we will and straitly enjoin that, when churches or monasteries are vacant, no one shall act or presume to act in any way contrary to this our grant and constitution. If, however, any one at any time or in any way shall act contrary to it, may he incur the malediction of Almighty God and our own!

These are the witnesses. . . . November 21, in the sixteenth year of our reign.

(Latin) Stubbs, *Select Charters*, pp. 283 f.

44. MAGNA CARTA (1215)[1]

John, by the grace of God king of England, lord of Ireland, duke of Normandy and of Aquitaine, and count of Anjou, to his archbishops, bishops, abbots, earls, barons, justiciars, foresters, sheriffs, reeves, ministers, and all his bailiffs and faithful men, greeting. Know that, through the inspiration of God, for the health of our soul and [the souls] of all our ancestors and heirs, for the honour of God and the exaltation of Holy Church, and for the betterment of our realm, by the counsel of our venerable fathers[2] . . . , of our nobles[3] . . . , and of our other faithful men—

1. We have in the first place granted to God and by this our present charter have confirmed, for us and our heirs forever, that the English Church shall be free and shall have its rights entire and its liberties inviolate. *And how we wish [that freedom] to be observed appears from this, that of our own pure and free will, before the conflict that arose between us and our barons, we granted and by our charter confirmed the liberty of election that is considered of prime importance and necessity for the English Church,[4] and we obtained confirmation of it from the lord pope Innocent III—which [charter] we will observe ourself and we wish to be observed in good faith by our heirs forever.* We have also granted to all freemen of our

---

[1] John's charter was reissued under Henry III in 1216 and again in 1217, at both times with considerable revision. The second reissue was confirmed with minor changes by Henry III in 1225, after he had been declared of age, and this remained the official Magna Carta of subsequent reigns. Parts of the original charter omitted after 1215 are here printed in italics. It has not been thought necessary to show how the introductory and final clauses were modified in each reissue, but noteworthy alterations of the numbered articles are given in the footnotes. The latter also include explanations of the more obscure words and phrases. For more detailed comment, see McKechnie, *Magna Carta;* and for all points connected with the reissues, see Faith Thompson, *The First Century of Magna Carta.*
[2] Here in the text follow the names of eleven ecclesiastics.
[3] Here in the text follow the names of sixteen lay nobles.
[4] Above, no. 43.

kingdom, for us and our heirs forever, all the liberties hereinunder written, to be had and held by them and their heirs of us and our heirs.

2. If any one of our earls or barons or other men holding of us in chief dies, and if when he dies his heir is of full age and owes relief, [that heir] shall have his inheritance for the ancient relief: namely, the heir or heirs of an earl £100 for the whole barony of an earl; the heir or heirs of a baron £100 for a whole barony; the heir or heirs of a knight 100s. at most for a whole knight's fee.[5] And let whoever owes less give less, according to the ancient custom of fiefs.

3. If, however, the heir of any such person is under age[6] and is in wardship, he shall, when he comes of age, have his inheritance without relief and without fine.[7]

4. The guardian of the land of such an heir who is under age shall not take from the land of the heir more than reasonable issues and reasonable customs and reasonable services, and this without destruction and waste of men or things. And if we entrust the wardship of any such land to a sheriff or to any one else who is to answer to us for its issues, and if he causes destruction or waste of [what is under] wardship, we will exact compensation from him; and the land shall be entrusted to two discreet and lawful men of that fief, who shall answer for the issues to us or the man to whom we may assign them. And if we give or sell the wardship of any such land to any one, and if he causes destruction or waste of it, he shall forfeit that wardship and it shall be given to two discreet and lawful men of that fief, who likewise shall answer to us as aforesaid.

5. Moreover, the guardian, so long as he has wardship of the land, shall from the issues of that same land keep up the houses, parks, preserves, fish-ponds, mills, and other things belonging to that land. And to the heir, when he comes of full age, [the guardian] shall give all his land, stocked with ploughs[8] *and produce*,[9] *according to what crops may be seasonable and to what the issues of the land can reasonably permit.*

6. Heirs shall be married without disparagement; *yet so that,*

---

[5] On the interpretation of this article, see J. H. Round, in *Magna Carta Commemoration Essays*, pp. 46 f.

[6] In the reissues this article ends as follows: "his lord shall not have wardship over him or over his land before receiving his homage. And when such heir, being under wardship, comes of age—that is to say, [attains] his twenty-first year—he shall have his inheritance without relief and without fine; so that, although he may become a knight while he is yet under age, his land shall nevertheless remain under the wardship of his lords until the term aforesaid."

[7] A term often used for an offering or a composition.

[8] In the reissues this article ends as follows: "and with all other things as, at least, he received it. All these [provisions] are to be observed with regard to custody over archbishoprics, bishoprics, abbeys, priories, churches, and vacant prelacies that belong to us, except that rights of this sort ought not to be sold."

[9] *Wainnagium*, by which the context forces us to understand chiefly harvested crops necessary for seed and the upkeep of the estate.

44. MAGNA CARTA

before the marriage is contracted, it shall be announced to the blood-relatives of the said heir.

7. A widow shall have her marriage portion and inheritance immediately after the death of her husband and without difficulty; nor shall she give anything for her dowry or for her marriage portion or for her inheritance—which inheritance she and her husband were holding on the day of that husband's death. And after his death she shall remain in the house[10] of her husband for forty days, within which her dowry shall be assigned to her.[11]

8. No widow shall be forced to marry so long as she wishes to live without a husband; yet so that she shall give security against marrying without our consent if she holds of us, or without the consent of her lord if she holds of another.

9. Neither we nor our bailiffs will seize any land or revenue for any debt, so long as the chattels of the debtor are sufficient to repay the debt;[12] nor shall the sureties of that debtor be distrained so long as the chief debtor is himself able to pay the debt. And if the chief debtor, having nothing with which to pay,[13] defaults in payment of the debt, the sureties shall be responsible for the debt; and, if they wish, they shall have the lands and revenues of the debtor until satisfaction is made to them for the debt which they previously paid on his behalf, unless the chief debtor proves that he is quit of such responsibility toward the said sureties.

10. *If any one has taken anything, whether much or little, by way of loan from Jews, and if he dies before that debt is paid, the debt shall not carry usury so long as the heir is under age, from whomsoever he may hold. And if that debt falls into our hands, we will take only the principal contained in the note.*

11. *And if any one dies owing a debt to Jews, his wife shall have her dowry and shall pay nothing on that debt. And if the said deceased is survived by children who are under age, necessities shall be provided for them in proportion to the tenement that belonged to the deceased; and the debt shall be paid from the remainder, saving the service of the lords. In the same way let action be taken with regard to debts owed to others besides Jews.*

12. *Scutage or aid shall be levied in our kingdom only by the common counsel of our kingdom, except for ransoming our body, for*

---

[10] Changed in the second reissue to "principal dwelling."

[11] See above, p. 47, n. 3. The second reissue adds: "unless it has been assigned to her earlier, or unless that house is a castle. And if she leaves the castle, she shall at once be provided with a suitable house, in which she may honourably dwell until her dowry is assigned to her as aforesaid. And in the meantime she shall have her reasonable estovers of common. Moreover, she shall be assigned as dowry one-third of all the land held by her husband during his lifetime, unless she was endowed with less at the church door." Estovers of common were a share of the produce.

[12] The reissues here insert the clause: "and the debtor is himself ready to satisfy [the debt] from them."

[13] The reissues here insert the clause: "or being unwilling to pay when he can."

knighting our eldest son, and for once marrying our eldest daughter; and for these [*purposes*] only a reasonable aid shall be taken. The same provision shall hold with regard to the aids of the city of London.[14]

13. And the city of London shall have all its ancient liberties and free customs, *both by land and by water*. Besides we will and grant that all the other cities, boroughs, towns,[15] and ports shall have all their liberties and free customs.

14. And in order to have the common counsel of the kingdom for assessing aid other than in the three cases aforesaid, or for assessing scutage, we will cause the archbishops, bishops, abbots, earls, and greater barons to be summoned by our letters individually; and besides we will cause to be summoned in general, through our sheriffs and bailiffs, all those who hold of us in chief—for a certain day, namely, at the end of forty days at least, and to a certain place. And in all such letters of summons we will state the cause of the summons; and when the summons has thus been made, the business assigned for the day shall proceed according to the counsel of those who are present, although all those summoned may not come.

15. In the future we will not grant to any one that he may take aid from his freemen, except for ransoming his body, for knighting his eldest son, and for once marrying his eldest daughter; and for these [*purposes*] only a reasonable aid shall be taken.

16. No one shall be distrained to render greater service from a knight's fee, or from any other free tenement, than is thence owed.

17. Common pleas shall not follow our court, but shall be held in some definite place.

18. Assizes of novel disseisin, of mort d'ancestor, *and of darrein presentment*[16] shall be held only in their counties [of origin] and in this way: we, or our chief justice if we are out of the kingdom, will send two justices through each county[17] *four times a year*; and they, together with four knights of each county elected by the county

---

[14] Literally, "in the same way let it be done. . . ." The Londoners had wanted a guarantee of exemption from forced taxes, but secured only this vague and ambiguous article; see C. Stephenson, *Borough and Town*, p. 183.

[15] The reissues here make specific mention of the barons of the Cinque Ports; see above, p. 103, n. 17.

[16] See no. 33.

[17] The second reissue substitutes the following provisions: "once a year; and they, together with the knights of the counties, shall hold the aforesaid assizes in the counties. And those matters which cannot be concluded during that visit in the county by the aforesaid justices, sent to hold the said assizes, shall be concluded by the same men elsewhere on their eyre. And those matters which, owing to the difficulty of some particulars, cannot be determined by the same men shall be referred to our justices of the bench and there concluded. Assizes of darrein presentment shall always be held before the justices of the bench and there concluded." The court of the bench (*de banco*) was that which became known as the court of common pleas; see Pollock and Maitland, I, 198 f.

44. MAGNA CARTA

[*court*], *shall hold the aforesaid assizes in the county, on the day and at the place* [*set for the meeting*] *of the county* [*court*].

19. *And if within the day* [*set for the meeting*] *of the county* [*court*] *the aforesaid assizes cannot be held, as many knights and free tenants shall remain of those present at the county* [*court*] *on that day as may be needed for holding the trials, according as the business is greater or less.*

20. A freeman shall be amerced for a small offence only according to the degree of the offence; and for a grave offence he shall be amerced according to the gravity of the offence, saving his contenement.[18] And a merchant shall be amerced in the same way, saving his merchandise; and a villein[19] in the same way, saving his wainage[20] —should they fall into our mercy. And none of the aforesaid amercements shall be imposed except by the oaths of good men from the neighbourhood.[21]

21. Earls and barons shall be amerced only by their peers,[22] and only according to the degree of the misdeed.

22. No clergyman shall be amerced with respect to his lay tenement except in the manner of those aforesaid, not according to the value of his ecclesiastical benefice.[23]

23. Neither vill nor man shall be distrained to make bridges on river-banks, except such as by right and ancient custom ought to do so.

24. No sheriff, constable, coroner, or other bailiff of ours shall hold the pleas of our crown.[24]

25. *All counties, hundreds, wapentakes, and trithings*[25] *shall remain at the ancient farms without any increment, with the exception of our demesne manors.*

26. If any one holding a lay fee of us dies, and if our sheriff or bailiff shows our letters patent of summons concerning a debt that the deceased owed to us, our sheriff or bailiff shall be permitted, by view of lawful men, to attach and record such chattels of the deceased as are found on the lay fief to the value of that debt; so that, moreover, nothing shall thence be removed until a debt that is manifestly owed shall be paid to us. And the residue shall be left to the executors for carrying out the will of the deceased. And if nothing is owed us from it, all the chattels shall be yielded to [disposition by] the deceased, saving to his wife and children their reasonable portions.

27. *If any freeman dies intestate, his chattels, under ecclesiastical*

---

[18] Sufficient property to guarantee sustenance for himself and his family.
[19] The second reissue here inserts: "of some one else, not our own."
[20] See above, p. 116, n. 9.
[21] Under such conditions the amercement was said to be afeered.
[22] Social equals.
[23] The wording of this article is changed in the reissues, but without affecting its meaning.
[24] See above, p. 53, n. 16.
[25] Certain large counties were divided into trithings or ridings, and these were subdivided into hundreds or **wapentakes**.

inspection, shall be distributed by the hands of his near relatives and friends, saving to each [*creditor*] the debts that the deceased owed him.

28. No constable or other bailiff of ours shall take grain or other chattels of any one without immediate payment therefor in money, unless by the will of the seller he may secure postponement of that [payment].[26]

29. No constable shall distrain any knight to pay money for castle-guard when he is willing to perform that service himself, or through another good man if for reasonable cause he is unable to perform it himself. And if we lead or send him on a military expedition, he shall be quit of [castle-]guard for so long a time as he shall be with the army[27] *at our command*.

30. No sheriff or bailiff of ours, nor any other person, shall take the horses or carts of any freeman for carrying service,[28] *except by the will of that freeman*.

31. Neither we nor our bailiffs[29] will take some one else's wood for [repairing] castles or for doing any other work of ours, except by the will of him to whom the wood belongs.

32. We will hold the lands of those convicted of felony only for a year and a day, and the lands shall then be given to the lords of the fiefs [concerned].

33. All fish-weirs shall henceforth be entirely removed from the Thames and the Medway and throughout all England except along the sea-coasts.

34. Henceforth the writ called praecipe shall not be issued for any one concerning any tenement whereby a freeman may lose his court.[30]

35. There shall be one measure of wine throughout our entire kingdom, and one measure of ale; also one measure of grain, namely, the quarter of London; and one width of dyed cloth, russet [cloth], and hauberk [cloth],[31] namely, two yards between the borders. With weights, moreover, it shall be as with measures.

36. Nothing henceforth shall be taken or given for the writ of

---

[26] Changed in the second reissue to read: "No constable or his bailiff shall take grain or other chattels of any one who is not of the vill where the castle is situated without immediate payment therefor in money, unless by the will of the seller he may secure postponement of that [payment]. If, moreover, he is of that vill, payment must be made within forty days."

[27] The reissues here substitute: "to perform the service owed from his fief."

[28] The reissues end the clause as follows: "unless he makes the anciently established payment [for such service]: namely, for a two-horse cart 10d. a day and for a three-horse cart 14d. a day. No cart from the demesne of any ecclesiastical parson or knight, or of any lady, shall be taken by the aforesaid bailiffs."

[29] The second reissue here inserts: "nor other men."

[30] That is to say, through which procedure a baron or other freeholder may lose jurisdiction over his men; see no. 33F.

[31] Perhaps cloth to be worn under a hauberk.

inquisition concerning life and limbs,[32] but it shall be issued gratis and shall not be denied.

37. If any one holding of us by fee-farm or by socage or by burgage[33] holds land of some one else by military service, on account of that fee-farm or socage or burgage we are not to have the wardship of the heir or of the land that is another's fee, unless the said [land held by] fee-farm owes military service. By virtue of some little serjeanty held of us by the service of rendering knives or arrows or something of the sort, we are not to have wardship of any one's heir or of land that he holds of another by military service.

38. No bailiff shall henceforth put any one to his law[34] by merely bringing suit [against him] without trustworthy witnesses presented for this purpose.

39. No freeman shall be captured or imprisoned or disseised[35] or outlawed or exiled or in any way destroyed, nor will we go against him or send against him, except by the lawful judgment of his peers or[36] by the law of the land.

40. To no one will we sell, to no one will we deny or delay right or justice.

41. All merchants[37] may safely and securely go away from England, come to England, stay in and go through England, by land or by water, for buying and selling under right and ancient customs and without any evil exactions,[38] except in time of war if they are from the land at war with us. And if such persons are found in our land at the beginning of a war, they shall be arrested without injury to their bodies or goods until we or our chief justice can ascertain how the merchants of our land who may then be found in the land at war with us are to be treated. And if our men are to be safe, the others shall be safe in our land.

42. *Every one shall henceforth be permitted, saving our fealty, to leave our kingdom and to return in safety and security, by land*

---

[32] Also called the writ *de odio et atia*; it was designed to relieve a man of trial by combat when he had been appealed "through spite and hatred." At this point the third reissue inserts: "by him who seeks the inquisition."

[33] These three tenures were alike in being free, though non-military.

[34] See above, p. 77, n. 3. The second reissue expands this phrase to "manifest law or oath." The new provision was probably intended to cover substitutes for the ordeal, which had been abolished by the Lateran Council of 1215.

[35] The second reissue adds: "of any free tenement or liberties or free customs."

[36] Presumably meaning "and"; cf. art. 56. The interpretation is also aided by John's writ of May, 1215 (*Rotuli Litterarum Patentium*, I, 141): "Know that we have granted to our barons who are opposing us that we will neither capture nor disseise them or their men, nor will we go against them with force or with arms, except by the law of our kingdom or by the judgment of their peers in our court. . . ." See McIlwain, in *Magna Carta Commemoration Essays*, pp. 122 f.; and, for another interpretation, M. Radin, *Anglo-American Legal History*, pp. 165 f.

[37] The reissues here insert: "unless they have earlier been given public prohibition."

[38] *Malis toltis* (maltotes); see no. 51c.

or by water, except in the common interest of the realm for a brief period during wartime, and excepting [always] men imprisoned or outlawed according to the law of the kingdom and people from a land at war with us and merchants, who are to be treated as aforesaid.

43. If any one holds of any escheat—such as the honour of Wallingford, Nottingham, Boulogne, Lancaster, or the other escheats that are in our hands and are baronies—and if he dies, his heir shall give only such relief and shall render us only such service as would be due to the baron if that barony were in the hands of the baron; and we shall hold it in the same way that the baron held it.[39]

44. *Men dwelling outside the forest shall no longer, in consequence of a general summons, come before our justices of the forest, unless they are [involved] in a plea [of the forest] or are sureties of some person or persons who have been arrested for [offences against] the forest.*[40]

45. *We will appoint as justiciars, constables, sheriffs, or bailiffs only such men as know the law of the kingdom and well desire to observe it.*

46. All barons who have founded abbeys, concerning which they have charters from kings of England or [enjoy] ancient tenures, shall have the custody of those [abbeys] during vacancies, as they ought to have.[41]

47. *All forests that have been afforested in our time shall at once be disafforested; and the same shall be done with regard to riverbanks which in our time we have placed under ban.*[42]

48. Concerning all bad customs of forest and warrens, of foresters and warreners, of sheriffs and their officers, and of river-banks and their wardens, inquisition shall at once be made in each county through twelve knights of that same county placed under oath, who ought to be elected by the good men of the same county. And within forty days after the inquisition has been made, they shall be utterly abolished by the same [knights], so that they shall never be restored;

---

[39] The second reissue adds: "Nor shall we, by virtue of such barony or escheat, have any escheat or [enjoy] wardship over any of our men unless he who held the barony or escheat [also] held of us in chief elsewhere." And after this a new article is inserted, as follows: "Henceforth no freeman shall give or sell to any one so much of his land that from what remains of it whatever service pertains to the fief cannot adequately be performed for the lord to whom it is owed."

[40] This became art. 2 of the Forest Charter, no. 45.

[41] Changed in the second reissue to read: "All patrons of abbeys who have charters from kings of England concerning their advowson, or [who enjoy] ancient tenure or possession [of that privilege], shall have custody of those [abbeys] when they are vacant, as they ought to have and as has been declared above."

[42] That is to say, reserved for the king's hawking. Part of this article was incorporated in the Forest Charter (no. 45); the rest was made into a new article in the second reissue.

44. MAGNA CARTA

in such fashion [however] that we may have prior notice, or our justiciar [may] if we are not in England.

49. We will immediately restore all hostages and charters which were delivered to us by Englishmen as security for the peace or for faithful service.

50. We will utterly remove from their offices the relatives of Gerard d'Athée, Engelard de Cigogné, Peter and Guy and Andrew de Chanceaux, Guy de Cigogné, Geoffrey de Martigny and his brothers, Philip Marc and his brothers and his nephew Geoffrey, together with all their adherents, so that henceforth they shall have no office in England.

51. And immediately after the restoration of peace we will remove from the kingdom all alien knights, crossbowmen, serjeants, and mercenaries, who have come with horses and arms to the injury of the kingdom.

52. If any one, without the lawful judgment of his peers, has been disseised or deprived by us of his lands, castles, liberties, or rights, we will at once restore them to him. And if a dispute arises in this connection, then let the matter be decided by the judgment of the twenty-five barons, concerning whom provision is made below in [the article on] security for the peace. With regard, however, to all those [possessions] of which any one, without lawful judgment of his peers, was disseised or deprived by King Henry, our father, or by King Richard, our brother—which possessions we have in our hands or which are held by others whose possession we are bound to warrant—we are to have respite for the ordinary term of crusaders,[43] except those [possessions] concerning which suit was brought or inquest was made by our precept before we took the cross. Moreover, when we return from our journey, or if perchance we abandon our journey, we will at once administer full justice in such matters.

53. Moreover, we are to have similar respite and in the same way with regard to the disafforestation or retention of the forests which Henry, our father, or Richard, our brother, afforested; with regard to wardships over lands of another's fee, which sort of wardships we have hitherto enjoyed on account of a fee that any one holds of us by military service,[44] and with regard to abbeys which were founded in a fee other than our own, and over which the lord of the fee has asserted that he has the right. And when we return, or if we abandon our journey, we will at once give full justice to those making complaints in such matters.

54. No one shall be seized or imprisoned on the appeal of a woman for the death of any one but her husband.[45]

---

[43] The three years' grace enjoyed by crusaders in meeting their obligations.
[44] Cf. art. 37.
[45] The second reissue **adds** three new articles:
"Henceforth no county [court] shall be held oftener than once a month; and wherever a longer time [between sessions] has been customary, let it be longer. Nor shall any sheriff or his bailiff make his tourn* through a hundred

55. *All fines which have been made with us unjustly and contrary to the law of the land, and all amercements made unjustly and contrary to the law of the land, are to be entirely pardoned; or decision is thereon to be made by the judgment of the twenty-five barons concerning whom provision is made below in [the article on] security for the peace, or by the judgment of the majority of them, together with the aforesaid Stephen, archbishop of Canterbury, if he can be present, and other men whom he may wish to associate with himself for this purpose—and if he cannot be present, the business shall nevertheless proceed without him; yet so that, if any one or more of the twenty-five barons aforesaid are [involved] in a dispute of this kind, they shall be removed so far as this judgment is concerned, and others, elected and sworn for this purpose, shall be substituted in their places by the rest of the twenty-five.*

56. *If, without the lawful judgment of their peers, we have disseised or deprived Welshmen of their lands, liberties, or other things in England or in Wales, [the same] shall be immediately restored to them. And if a dispute arises in this connection, then decision is thereon to be made in the [Welsh] march by the judgment of their peers—according to the law of England for their tenements in England, according to the law of Wales for their tenements in Wales, and according to the law of the march for their tenements in the march. Welshmen shall act in the same way toward us and our men.*

57. *Moreover, with regard to those [possessions] of which any Welshman, without the lawful judgment of his peers, was disseised or deprived by King Henry, our father, or King Richard, our brother.*[46] ...

58. *We will at once restore the son of Llewelyn and all the [other]*

more often than twice a year; and [then he shall hold the court] only at the due and accustomed place [and time], namely, once after Easter and again after Michaelmas. And view of frankpledge shall without excuse be made then, at that Michaelmas term; and in such a way that every one shall enjoy the liberties which he was accustomed to have in the time of King Henry, our grandfather, or which he has subsequently acquired. The view of frankpledge, moreover, shall be made in this way: namely, so that our peace is maintained, the tithings are [kept] whole as has been accustomed, and the sheriff does not seek excuses [for additional revenue], but is content with what the sheriff was accustomed to have for making his view in the time of King Henry, our grandfather.

"Henceforth no one shall be permitted to give his land to any religious house in such a way as to receive it back, to be held of that house; nor shall any religious house be permitted to accept the land of any one on condition that it be given back, to be held by the man from whom it has been received. If, moreover, any one henceforth grants his land to any religious house in this way and is convicted of so doing, his grant shall be utterly quashed and that land shall be forfeit to the lord of the fief.

"Scutage shall henceforth be taken as it was customarily taken in the time of King Henry, our grandfather."

* See Pollock and Maitland, I, 530 f.
[46] The rest of this article repeats the ending of art. 52.

hostages of *Wales*, together with the charters that were given us as security for the peace.

59. We will act toward Alexander, king of the Scots, in the matter of restoring his sisters and the [other] hostages, together with his liberties and rights in the same way as we act toward our other barons of England,[47] unless by the charters which we have from his father William, one time king of the Scots, the action ought to be otherwise—and this shall be [determined] by the judgment of his peers in our court.

60. Now all these aforesaid customs and liberties, which we have granted, in so far as concerns us, to be observed in our kingdom toward our men, all men of our kingdom, both clergy and laity, shall, in so far as concerns them, observe toward their men.

61. Since moreover for [the love of] God, for the improvement of our kingdom, and for the better allayment of the conflict that has arisen between us and our barons, we have granted all these [liberties] aforesaid, wishing them to enjoy those [liberties] by full and firm establishment forever, we have made and granted them the following security: namely, that the barons shall elect twenty-five barons of the kingdom, whomsoever they please, who to the best of their ability should observe, hold, and cause to be observed the peace and liberties that we have granted to them and have confirmed by this our present charter; so that, specifically, if we or our justiciar or our bailiffs or any of our ministers are in any respect delinquent toward any one or trangress any article of the peace or the security, and if the delinquency is shown to four barons of the aforesaid twenty-five barons, those four barons shall come to us, or to our justiciar if we are out of the kingdom, to explain to us the wrong, asking that without delay we cause this wrong to be redressed. And if within a period of forty days, counted from the time that notification is made to us, or to our justiciar if we are out of the kingdom, we do not redress the wrong, or, if we are out of the kingdom, our justiciar does not redress it, the four barons aforesaid shall refer that case to the rest of the twenty-five barons, and those twenty-five barons, together with the community of the entire country, shall distress and injure us in all ways possible—namely, by capturing our castles, lands, and possessions and in all ways that they can—until they secure redress according to their own decision, saving our person and [the person] of our queen and [the persons] of our children. And when redress has been made, they shall be obedient to us as they were before. And any one in the land who wishes shall swear that, for carrying out the aforesaid matters, he will obey the commands of the twenty-five barons aforesaid and that he, with his men, will injure us to the best of his ability; and we publicly and freely give licence of [thus] swearing to every one who wishes to do so, and to no one will we ever prohibit [such] swearing. Moreover, all those of the land who of

---

[47] The Scottish king held the earldom of Huntingdon and other English fiefs of King John.

themselves and by their own free will are unwilling to take the oath for the twenty-five barons, with them to distress and injure us, we will by our mandate cause to swear [such an oath] as aforesaid. And if any one of the twenty-five barons dies or departs from the land, or in any other way is prevented from carrying out these aforesaid matters, the rest of the twenty-five barons aforesaid shall by their own decision choose another in his place, who is to be sworn in the same way as the others. Moreover, in all the matters entrusted to those twenty-five barons for execution, if perchance the same twenty-five are present and disagree among themselves in some respect, or if certain of those summoned are unwilling or unable to be present, that which the majority of those present may provide or command shall be held as settled and established, just as if all twenty-five had agreed to it. And the aforesaid twenty-five shall swear that they will faithfully observe all that has been set forth above. And neither of ourself nor through others will we procure from any one anything whereby any of these concessions and liberties may be revoked or diminished; and should anything of the sort be procured, it shall be null and void, and we will never make use of it either of ourself or through others.

62. And to all we freely pardon and condone all the ill-will, indignation, and rancour that from the beginning of the conflict have arisen between us and our men, both clergy and laity. Furthermore, to all, whether clergy or laity, we fully pardon and condone, in so far as pertains to us, all trespasses committed on account of the said conflict since Easter in the sixteenth year of our reign until the re-establishment of peace. And besides we have caused to be drawn up for them letters patent of the lord Stephen, archbishop of Canterbury, of the lord Henry, archbishop of Dublin, of the bishops aforesaid, and of Master Pandulf,[48] *in witness of that security and the concessions aforesaid.*

63. Wherefore we wish and straitly enjoin that the English Church shall be free and that the men in our kingdom shall have and hold all the aforesaid liberties, rights, and grants well and in peace, freely and quietly, fully and completely, for themselves and their heirs from us and our heirs, in all things and in all places forever, as aforesaid. Moreover, it has been sworn both on our part and on the part of the barons that all the aforesaid [provisions] shall be observed in good faith and without malicious intent.

By the witness of the aforesaid men and of many others. Given by our hand in the meadow that is called Runnymede between Windsor and Staines, June 15, in the seventeenth year of our reign.

(Latin) *Ibid.,* pp. 292 f., 336 f., 341 f., 350 f.

---

[48] The papal legate.

SECTION IV

HENRY III AND EDWARD I

THAT the period from 1216 to 1307 is one of the most important in the whole constitutional history of England has long been recognized. At the accession of Henry III the royal government was essentially that of his grandfather—an amazingly efficient system for the age, but one still contained within the prescriptive custom of feudalism. At the death of Edward I feudal principles, though by no means forgotten, had ceased to dominate political practice. The framework of what we know as the English constitution had been solidly built. How this development has tended to simplify the task of selecting illustrative material may at once be appreciated by turning to the documents in the following section. Our wealth of sources for the thirteenth century cannot so easily be classified.

One thread that can be followed throughout the confusion is Magna Carta, the reissues of which have already been summarized (no. 44). Intimately associated with them from the outset of Henry III's reign was his Forest Charter, here given in full. Another related document, the Provisions of Oxford, since it was never put into effect, has been considerably abbreviated. The Provisions of Westminster, being largely concerned with details of private law, have been cut down to a few articles. And it has not seemed necessary to retain more than the principal clauses in the famous settlements of 1264 and 1266 (no. 47D, E). Likewise the product of a baronial crisis was Edward I's Confirmation of the Charters, which, however, embodied much more than a reissue of Magna Carta and the Forest Charter. In it there clearly appeared an issue that was long to be of paramount interest—parliamentary control of taxation.

By 1297 the parliament of the ensuing centuries, or at least its constituent elements, had definitely emerged, and precedents had been set with regard to its deliberative, judicial, and fiscal powers. To explain when and how all these complicated developments took place is a difficult problem, to which no complete solution is possible in a brief source book. All that has been attempted here is to illustrate its more significant phases through a number of extracts from the rolls of Henry III and Edward I: principally writs of summons for meetings with the king or his ministers, ordinances for the collection of taxes, and demands for the performance of other service. From such documents it is hoped that the student may obtain a fairly accurate knowledge of how the king made up his greater councils, together with a few revealing glimpses of military, naval, and financial administration. Edward's major statutes are given at least in part, and a good many pages have been devoted to a variety of judicial records.

The materials available under this last heading are so extensive as to defy representative selection within brief scope. No effort has been made to set forth in adequate fashion the growth of the common law. Under no. 54 will be found merely some typical entries in the rolls, illustrating such matters as manorial justice and administration, the beginnings of jury trial in criminal cases, the local activities of the coroner, the gradual differentiation of the central courts, and the adjudication of petitions in parliament. For additional information on these subjects the student is referred, not only to the standard works on English law, but also to the introductions of the volumes published by the Selden Society—a series which includes various kinds of records that have been entirely passed over in the present collection.

Of the enormous mass of other official writings produced in the thirteenth century, lack of space prevents the inclusion of more than a few extraordinary pieces. Thus the selections already given from pipe rolls, household accounts, and similar records must serve to exemplify the continuations of such enrolments in the later age. And in the field of borough institutions an impressive accumulation of charters and customals has also been left to one side. How old privileges were extended to new communities and how more elaborate machinery came to be set up for the government of the greater towns can be readily learned from the second volume of Ballard's *British Borough Charters,* which is provided with an admirable introduction by James Tait. On the other hand, a place has been made for two early forms of the oath taken by royal councillors and for Edward I's Household Ordinance—next to the *Constitutio Domus Regis* (no. 29) the oldest regulation of the sort that has survived.

For the constitutional development of thirteenth-century England the work of Stubbs remains generally valuable, although some of his dominant ideas have now been abandoned by most historians. Among the books that have brought a new approach to the study of parliamentary origins may be mentioned the following:[1] G. B. Adams, *The Origin of the English Constitution;* C. H. McIlwain, *The High Court of Parliament;* D. Pasquet, *Essay on the Origins of the English House of Commons;* A. F. Pollard, *The Evolution of Parliament;* A. B. White, *Self-Government at the King's Command;* Petit-Dutaillis and Lefebvre *Studies and Notes Supplementary to Stubbs' Constitutional History.* This last work is particularly valuable for its concise review of the literature on parliamentary origins, as well as for its chapters on the forest and forest law. T. F. Tout's volumes on *The Administrative History of Mediaeval England* provide much information concerning the more routine phases of the royal government. All the tax levies that appear in the documents grouped under no. 46, together with many others, are considered in detail by S. K. Mitchell in his *Studies in Taxation under John and Henry III.* And Edward I's reorganization of the whole fiscal system has recently acquired fresh significance from the scholarship of our lamented friend, J. F. Willard.[2] As previously, additional references are given in the footnotes.

---

[1] See also the numerous essays by H. G. Richardson and G. Sayles: *Transactions of the Royal Historical Society,* Fourth Series, XI, 137 f.; *Bulletin of the Institute of Historical Research,* V, 129 f., and VI, 71 f.; likewise those cited below, pp. 152, n. 4, 186, n. 18.

[2] *Parliamentary Taxes on Personal Property 1290-1334,* recently published by the Mediaeval Academy of America.

45. HENRY III: CHARTER OF THE FOREST (1217)[1]

Henry, by the grace of God king of England, lord of Ireland, duke of Normandy and of Aquitaine, and count of Anjou, to his archbishops, bishops, abbots, priors, earls, barons, justiciars, foresters, sheriffs, reeves, ministers, and all his faithful men, greeting. Know that[2] . . . we have granted and by this present charter have confirmed, for us and our heirs forever, these liberties hereinunder written, to be held in our kingdom of England forever:—

---

[1] Issued as a supplement to Magna Carta during the minority of Henry III and confirmed by him, with only slight revision, in 1225. For the meaning of many technical words, as well as the general significance of the articles, see no. 35 and the notes to that document.

[2] The introductory clauses are largely copied from Magna Carta.

1. In the first place, all the forests which Henry, our grandfather, afforested shall be visited by good and lawful men; and if he afforested any woodland other than that of his own demesne to the damage of him to whom the woodland belonged, let it be disafforested. And if he afforested his own proper woodland, let it remain forest, saving common of herbage and other things in the same forest to those who were accustomed to have them before.

2. Men dwelling outside the forest shall no longer, in consequence of a general summons, come before our justices of the forest, unless they are [involved] in a plea [of the forest] or are sureties of some person or persons who have been arrested for [offences against] the forest.³

3. All forests, however, which were afforested by King Richard, our uncle, or by King John, our father, down to the time of our first coronation, shall at once be disafforested, excepting our own demesne woodland.

4. Archbishops, bishops, abbots, priors, earls, barons, knights, and [other] freeholders, who have woodlands of theirs in the forests, shall have their woodlands as they had them at the time of the first coronation of the aforesaid King Henry, our grandfather; so that they shall forever be quit of all purprestures, wastes, and assarts made in those woodlands from that time down to the beginning of the second year of our coronation. And whoever henceforth makes any waste, purpresture, or assart in those [woods] without our licence shall be responsible for such wastes and assarts.

5. Our regardors⁴ shall go through the forests for making their regard as was customarily done in the time of the first coronation of the said Henry, our grandfather, and not otherwise.

6. The investigation or view of the lawing of dogs living within the forest shall henceforth be carried out whenever the regard should be made, namely, every three years; and then it should be made by the view and testimony of lawful men and not otherwise. And he whose dog is then found not to be lawed shall give as amercement 3s., and henceforth no ox shall be taken for [default of such] lawing. Moreover, the lawing shall be carried out by common assize as follows: three toes shall be cut off a forefoot without [injuring] the ball [of the foot]; nor shall dogs henceforth be lawed except in the places where they were customarily lawed at the time of the first coronation of King Henry, our grandfather.

7. No forester or beadle shall henceforth levy scotale,⁵ or collect sheaves or oats or any grain or lambs or pigs; nor shall he take up any kind of collection. And by the view and oath of twelve regardors,

---

³ Originally art. 44 of Magna Carta.
⁴ Inspectors, whose duties are described below.
⁵ The exaction of ale, or the equivalent in money, on the pretext of some festivity—a common abuse on the part of public officials.

45. CHARTER OF THE FOREST

when they make their regard, as many foresters shall be appointed to keep the forests as reasonably appear sufficient for keeping them.

8. No swainmote[6] shall henceforth be held in our kingdom oftener than three times a year: namely, at the beginning of the fortnight before the feast of St. Michael, when the agistors meet for the agistment of our demesne woodlands; and about the feast of St. Martin, when our agistors ought to receive our pannage—at which two swainmotes are to assemble the foresters, verderers,[7] and agistors, but no one else by compulsion. And the third swainmote shall be held at the beginning of the fortnight before the feast of St. John the Baptist, for the fawning of our beasts; and for holding that swainmote the foresters and verderers shall assemble, but no others by compulsion. And the verderers and foresters shall also meet every forty days throughout the year to inspect attachments for [offences in] the forest concerning both vert and venison, through presentment by the same foresters and in the presence of those attached. The aforesaid swainmotes, however, are to be held only in the counties where they have been customarily held.

9. Every freeman shall at his own pleasure provide agistment for his woodland in the forest and have his pannage. We also grant that every freeman may freely and without interference drive his swine through our demesne woodland in order to agist them in his own woods or wherever else he pleases. And if the swine of any freeman spend one night in our forest, that shall not be made the excuse for taking anything of his away from him.

10. Henceforth no one shall lose life or limbs on account of our hunting rights; but if any one is arrested and convicted of taking our venison, let him redeem himself by a heavy payment, if he has anything with which to redeem himself. And if he has nothing with which to redeem himself, let him lie in our prison for a year and a day. And if, after the year and the day, he can find sureties, let him be freed from prison; but if he cannot, let him abjure the realm of England.

11. Any archbishop, bishop, earl, or baron who crosses our forest may take one or two beasts by view of the forester, if he is present; if not, let a horn be blown so that this [hunting] may not appear to be carried on furtively.

12. Henceforth every freeman, in his wood or on his land that he has in the forest, may with impunity make a mill, fish-preserve, pond, marl-pit, ditch, or arable in cultivated land outside coverts, provided that no injury is thereby given to any neighbour.

13. Every freeman may in his own woods have eyries of hawks, sparrow-hawks, falcons, eagles, and herons; and he may also have honey that is found in his woods.

14. Hereafter no forester who does not hold in fee, rendering to us

---

[6] Or swanimote—a court of the king's swineherds and other forest employees, with the functions here described.

[7] Men of the knightly class chosen in the county courts; cf. no. 35, art. 7.

a farm for his bailiwick, shall levy any road-tax (*chiminagium*) in his bailiwick. A forester, however, who holds in fee, rendering to us a farm for his bailiwick, may levy road-tax: namely, 2d. on a cart for a half-year, and 2d. for the other half-year; ½d. on a horse that carries loads for a half-year, and ½d. for the other half-year—and this only on those who, from outside his bailiwick, come by his licence into his bailiwick as merchants, to buy wood, timber, bark, or charcoal, and to carry it elsewhere to sell where they please. And road-tax shall not be levied on any other cart or pack-horse. And road-tax shall be taken only in the places where it has been anciently accustomed and owed. Moreover, those men who carry on their backs wood, bark, or charcoal for sale, although they may therefrom make their living, shall henceforth pay no road-tax. Moreover, no road-tax shall be paid to our foresters from the woods of other men, but only from our demesne woods.

15. All men outlawed merely for [offences against] the forest, from the time of King Henry, our grandfather, to our first coronation, may without interference return to our peace and provide good sureties that hereafter they will commit no offence with regard to our forest.

16. No castellan or other man [of the locality] shall hold pleas of the forest, concerning either vert or venison; but every forester holding in fee shall make attachments for pleas of the forest, concerning both vert and venison, and shall present them to the verderers of the provinces; and when they have been enrolled and closed under the seals of the verderers, they shall be presented to our chief forester when he comes into those parts to hold the pleas of the forest; and they shall be brought to conclusion before him.

17. Now these liberties with regard to the forest we have granted to all, saving to the archbishops, bishops, abbots, priors, earls, barons, knights, and other persons both ecclesiastical and lay, [also] to the Templars and the Hospitallers, the liberties and free customs in forests and outside them, in warrens and in other things, that they earlier had. Moreover, all these aforesaid liberties and customs, which we have granted to be observed, in so far as concerns us, toward our men, all persons of our kingdom, both clergy and laity, shall, in so far as concerns them, observe toward their men.

Since indeed we as yet have no seal, we have had the present charter sealed with the seal of our venerable father the lord Gualo, cardinal priest of the title[8] of St. Martin's and legate of the Apostolic See, and that of William Marshal, earl of Pembroke, rector of us and of our kingdom. By the witness of the aforesaid men and many others. Given by the hand of the aforesaid lord legate and of William Marshal at St. Paul's, London, November 6, in the second year of our reign.

(Latin) Stubbs, *Select Charters,* pp. 344 f.

---

[8] I.e., a parish in the city of Rome.

46. LETTERS CLOSE AND PATENT (1218-54)
(A) COLLECTION OF SCUTAGE (1218)

The king to the sheriff of Worcester, greeting. We command you that, on sight of these letters, you immediately distrain all those men of your bailiwick who hold of us in chief, and who have not brought you our letters regarding the collection of their scutage by their own hand,[1] without delay to pay you the scutage owed us, namely, $2m$. from each knight's fee (*scuto*). And as you cherish your life and all that you have, see to it that you have all that scutage at our exchequer on Sunday next after the coming Mid-Lent. You are likewise to distrain all those of your bailiwick who have received our letters regarding the collection of their scutage by their own hand, for which they should have accounted at our exchequer at terms now passed, that on the same day, avoiding all excuse and delay, they account to us at our exchequer, under your inspection, for the scutage which they owe us. And you are there to have with you our letters which they bring you regarding the collection of their scutage by their own hand.

(Latin) *Rotuli Litterarum Clausarum*, I, 377.

(B) SUMMONS BEFORE THE ITINERANT JUSTICES (1219)[2]

The king to the sheriff of York and Northumberland, greeting. Summon through good summoners all archbishops, bishops, abbots, earls, barons, knights, and freeholders of all your bailiwick, also four lawful men and the reeve from every vill and twelve lawful burgesses from every borough throughout your entire bailiwick, together with all other men of your bailiwick who by custom and right should come before our itinerant justices, to be at York before our justices a fortnight after St. Martin's day in order to hear and obey our precept. You are also to have brought before them at that time all pleas of the crown which have not been tried, and which have arisen since the assizes were last held in those parts before itinerant justices in the time of the lord king John, our father; likewise all attachments pertaining to those pleas, and all assizes and all pleas which have been assigned to the first assizes before the justices, together

---

[1] The tax was often passed on to the sub-tenants. See, for example, the royal authorizations of 1223 (*Rotuli Litterarum Clausarum*, I, 570 f.): "The king to the sheriff of Northampton, greeting. Know that we have granted to our beloved and faithful uncle, William, earl of Salisbury, that he may have from his knights who hold of him in your bailiwick his scutage for our army of Wales, in which he now is by our order: namely, $2m$. from a knight's fee. And therefore we command you that you cause him to have the said scutage as aforesaid. . . ." "The king to the sheriff of Middlesex, greeting. Know that we have granted to William, earl of Salisbury, that he may have from his freemen in your bailiwick a reasonable aid for maintaining himself in our service with our army of Wales, in which he now is by our order: namely, $2m$. from a knight's fee. And therefore we command you. . . ."

[2] This is a regular form, found year after year in the rolls.

with the writs for those assizes and pleas—so that, through your default or that of your summons, none of those assizes and pleas shall fail to be held. You are also to have it proclaimed and made known throughout your entire bailiwick that all assizes and all pleas for which a day has been set, but which have not been concluded before our justices at Westminster, shall be brought thither to York before the aforesaid justices in the same state as when, by our precept, they were held over at Westminster. Also summon through good summoners all those who have been sheriffs since the last eyre of the justices into those parts, to be present in the same place before the aforesaid justices, together with the writs concerning assizes and pleas which they received during their own time [of office], and to answer concerning their own time [of office] as should be done in the presence of the itinerant justices. And you are there to have the summoners and this writ. By the witness of W[illiam] Marshal, earl of Pembroke, rector of us and of our kingdom, at Westminster, November 4. In the presence of S[tephen], archbishop of Canterbury; P[eter], bishop of Winchester; and R[obert], bishop of Durham.

Similar letters to all the sheriffs of England except [those of] Gloucester, Worcester, Hereford, Stafford and Shropshire, and Leicester and Warwick; but with variation of place, as recorded on the dorse of the letters patent.[3]

(Latin) *Ibid.*, I, 403.

(C) COLLECTION OF CARUCAGE[4] (1220)

The king to the sheriff of Northampton, greeting. Know that, on account of our great need and the urgent pressure of our debts, and for the sake of preserving our land of Poitou, all the magnates and faithful men of our entire kingdom have of their free will granted in common that a contribution (*donum*) shall be made to us: namely, 2s. from every plough-team, in so far as it was joined by the day after the last preceding feast of St. John the Baptist in the fourth year of our reign, to be collected by your hand and [the hands] of two lawful knights of your county, who shall be elected to do so by the will and counsel of all men of the county in full county [court]. And therefore we command you, firmly and straitly enjoining, that, having convoked your full county [court], you cause to be elected by the will and counsel of those men of the county two of the more lawful knights of the whole county who best have the knowledge, willingness, and ability to carry out this business to our advantage. And you, taking those [knights] with you, shall immediately cause that contribution to be assessed on and collected from every plough-team as aforesaid, excepting the demesnes of the archbishops and bishops and their peasants, and excepting the demesnes of the

---

[3] That is to say, on the reverse side of the patent roll.

[4] A tax levied on the plough-team (*caruca*) or on the plough-land (*carucata*). In the present writ the former is specified; but see Mitchell, *Studies in Taxation under John and Henry III*, p. 133.

46. LETTERS CLOSE AND PATENT

Cistercian order and of the Premonstratensians. And see to it that you are able distinctly and clearly to account to us at London on the day after Michaelmas next how many plough-teams there are in your bailiwick from which we ought to have that contribution. And have the money due therefrom safely collected by the hands of the two knights aforesaid and by your own; and have it sent to London on the aforesaid day under your seal and the seals of the two knights aforesaid, and safely deposited in the house of the New Temple until provision is made as to what ought to be done with it. And as you cherish your life and all that you have, concern yourself with this matter so that, on account of no assessment or collection poorly carried out by you and the aforesaid knights, we shall later need to have severe inquisition made by faithful men sent from our court, to your grave confusion and that of those men associated with you in carrying out the aforesaid assessment and collection. Witness. . . .

Similar letters to all the sheriffs of England.

(Latin) *Ibid.*, I, 437.

(D) COLLECTION OF A FIFTEENTH (1225)

The king to . . . ,[5] greeting. We have assigned you as our justiciars to assess and collect for our use the fifteenth of all movables in the counties of Nottingham and Derby according to this form. Our sheriff of Nottingham and Derby will cause to be assembled before you at Nottingham all the knights of his counties on the Sunday next before Mid-Lent; on which day you shall cause to be elected four lawful knights from each hundred or wapentake—or more or less according to the size of the hundreds and wapentakes—who are to go through every hundred or wapentake to assess and collect the aforesaid fifteenth of all chattels. Nevertheless, from this fifteenth, for the benefit of archbishops, bishops, abbots, priors, and other men of religion, also of earls, barons, knights, and freeholders who are not merchants, are to be exempted their books of all kinds, the ornaments of churches and chapels, riding-horses, draught-horses, pack-horses, arms of all kinds, jewels, vases, utensils, hay, and [the contents of] larders and cellars; also grain bought for supplying castles. Likewise from this fifteenth, for the benefit of merchants who pay a fifteenth from all their merchandise and movables, are to be exempted the arms to which they are sworn,[6] their riding-horses, the utensils in their houses, and [the contents of] their larders and cellars [kept] for their sustenance. Likewise from this fifteenth, for the benefit of villeins, are to be exempted the arms to which they are sworn, their utensils, their meat and fish and drink that are not for sale, and their hay and fodder that are not for sale. Moreover, those knights shall not go into the hundreds or wapentakes of which they are residents, but into other adjacent hundreds or wapentakes. Furthermore, every person, with the exception of earls, barons, and

---

[5] Six collectors are named—one of many groups thus commissioned.
[6] See nos. 34, 46H.

knights, shall swear to the number, quantity, and value of his own movables and also of the movables belonging to two of his nearest neighbours. And if, perchance, dissension thereby arises between him who owns the movables and his neighbours who have sworn concerning the same movables, the said knights shall seek a verdict through the oaths of twelve good and lawful men of the neighbourhood—or as many as they shall deem sufficient for a verdict in this matter—and according to that verdict they shall levy the fifteenth. But the serjeants and reeves of the lands of earls, barons, and knights—or just the reeves, if no serjeants are there—shall in the same way swear the same oath concerning the movables of their lords in each vill.[7] . . . Moreover, you are to follow the same procedure with regard to the fiefs of archbishops, bishops, abbots, priors, and other men of religion, except for their demesnes and their own villeins; so far as these are concerned, the archbishops and bishops shall have the fifteenth assessed and collected in the aforesaid form, and shall account for it to us at the same terms [as prescribed for the regular collectors]. And so we command and straitly enjoin you that, in the fealty by which you are bound to us, you give care and efficacious action to carrying out this matter as set forth above. By witness of the king, at Westminster, February 15.

(Latin) *Patent Rolls, 1216-1225,* pp. 560 f.

(E) ELECTION OF COUNTY REPRESENTATIVES (1227)[8]

The king to the sheriff of Northumberland, greeting. We command you that in your full county [court] you tell the knights and good men of your bailiwick to elect from their own number four of the more lawful and discreet knights, who are to be before us at Westminster three weeks after the feast of St. Michael, there to set forth on behalf of the whole county their quarrel with you, should they have one, regarding the articles contained in the charter of liberty that has been granted to them.[9] And you are to be there yourself to show cause for the demand which in this connection you made upon them. And you are to have there the names of the knights and this writ. [By witness of the king at Northampton, August 13, in the eleventh year of the reign.]

(Latin) *Rotuli Litterarum Clausarum,* II, 213.

---

[7] The writ here gives details concerning the safeguarding of the money and the oaths to be sworn by the knights and justices.

[8] Copies of this writ were sent to the sheriffs of sixteen counties besides Northumberland; the instructions to the sheriffs of nineteen other counties contain additional clauses with regard to the perambulation of the forest. Mandates of the previous year had called for representatives from only eight counties, to meet at Lincoln; but the assembly had been postponed because the king had been unable to be at that city in time. On the significance of these writs of summons, see A. B. White, in the *American Historical Review,* XIX, 735 f.

[9] The reissue of Magna Carta, which the barons had demanded in return for the grant of a fifteenth.

46. LETTERS CLOSE AND PATENT

(F) COLLECTION OF TALLAGE AND LEVY OF SHIPS (1227)

The king to his beloved and faithful, the good men of his towns of Nottingham and Derby, and his other good men of his boroughs and demesnes in the same counties, greeting. Whereas opportunity has been given us of recovering, by the grace of God, our heritage in the lands across the sea, on which account it behooves us, God willing, soon to embark; we have assessed an efficacious aid in our city of London, so that, by the will of all our barons[10] of the said city, we have tallaged all men, whether greater or less, through their own agency (*per se*). And therefore we have provided that similar aid is to be assessed through all our cities, boroughs, and demesnes; so that in every one of our demesnes all men, according to their ability, shall be tallaged through their own agency. Thus we send to you our beloved and faithful William Basset, Eustace of Ludham, and the sheriff of Nottingham and Derby, to assess the tallage in the towns of Nottingham and Derby, and in our other boroughs and demesnes of the aforesaid counties, according to the mode and form described above; and we command and urge you to render us such prompt and efficacious aid in this urgent necessity that through your aid we may the more speedily recover our rights and may recognize ourself forever grateful to you—so that, indeed, as you cherish us and our honour, you let us have half of the aforesaid tallage at our exchequer on the approaching close of Easter in the eleventh year of our reign, and the other half on the feast of St. John the Baptist in the same year. By the witness of the king, at Westminster, January 30.[11]

The king to the bailiffs and good men of Dunwich, greeting. Know that, by the counsel of our faithful men, we are making preparations, God willing, to cross the sea in our own person. Wherefore we command and firmly enjoin you that, in the fealty by which you are bound to us, you have all good ships of your port, besides those which you owe us through your promise,[12] come to Portsmouth well equipped and supplied with arms and victuals; so that at the latest they shall be there on the approaching feast of St. James the Apostle, in the eleventh year of our reign, ready to cross the sea with our body. By witness of the king, at Westminster.[13]

(Latin) *Ibid.*, II, 208, 211.

---

[10] See above, p. 103, n. 17.

[11] Similar letters were sent to most of the other counties; also commissions to the various groups of justices, together with notifications to the sheriffs.

[12] From this writ and other records it appears that various boroughs had, as the result of separate negotiation, granted the king quotas of ships for his war, and in return had been given special concessions with regard to their tallage.

[13] The entry in the roll is rather confusing, but it seems to mean that similar letters were sent to Yarmouth, Ipswich, Oreford, Colchester, Pevensey, Seaford, Lynn, Southampton, Portsmouth, and the Cinque Ports (Dover, Sandwich, Hythe, Winchelsea, Rye, Hastings, and Romney); with the writs to the latter

(G) COLLECTION OF A FORTIETH (1232)

The king to the sheriff of Kent, greeting. Know that the archbishops, bishops, abbots, priors, and clerks having lands that do not belong to their churches, [as well as] the earls, barons, knights, freemen, and villeins[14] of our kingdom, have granted to us as aid the fortieth part of all their evident movables as possessed on the morrow of St. Matthew the Apostle in the sixteenth year of our reign: namely, of grain, ploughs, sheep, cows, swine, studs, and cart-horses assigned to productive work on manors, excepting the property that the aforesaid archbishops, bishops, and other ecclesiastical parsons receive from parish churches belonging to them, from prebendal churches, from prebends, and from lands pertaining to prebends and parochial churches. Moreover, it has been generally provided by our faithful men aforesaid that the said fortieth is to be assessed and collected in this manner: namely, that from each entire vill four of the better and more lawful men shall be elected along with the reeves of those particular vills, and that by their oaths the fortieth of all the aforesaid movables is to be determined and assessed upon each person in the presence of the knights assessors commissioned for that purpose. And afterwards, by the oaths of two lawful men from [each of] the same vills, inquiry and assessment shall be made touching the fortieth of movable property possessed by the said four men and the reeves. And let it be distinctly and plainly recorded to whose barony or liberty each vill in whole or in part belongs.[15] . . . Nothing, however, shall be taken by way of a fortieth from any one who does not have movable property of this sort to the value of at least 40*d*. Now for the assessment and collection of the aforesaid fortieth in your county according to the plan aforesaid, we have assigned[16] . . . , whom, immediately on sight of these letters, you shall summon before you to hear our precept, and to whom you shall at once hand our letters patent which are directed to them for this purpose and which we send you to be handed to them. Moreover, you shall cause to come before them, on the particular days and at the [particular] places which they may then deem most convenient, [the men of] the various vills of your county in order diligently to carry out this matter. . . . By my own witness, at Westminster, September 28.[17]

(Latin) *Close Rolls, 1231-1234*, pp. 155 f.

---

changed to read "besides those which are owed us by way of service." Cf. nos. 41B, 50C.

[14] Presumably a grant by the magnates was held to bind their tenants, free and unfree.

[15] The writ here gives details concerning the collection of the money and the transmission of the records.

[16] Four persons are named.

[17] The roll also includes the forms used for notifying the knights assessors and for commissioning the itinerant justices. Similar letters were sent to all the counties.

46. LETTERS CLOSE AND PATENT

(H) Ordinance for the Preservation of the Peace (1242)[18]

The king to the sheriff of Worcester, greeting. Know that, for the strict maintenance of our peace, it has been provided by our council that watches shall be kept in the various cities and boroughs and in all the other vills of your county from the day of the Ascension of the Lord to the day of St. Michael: namely, in every city by six armed men at each gate; in every borough by twelve men and in every vill by six men similarly armed, or four or less according to the number of the inhabitants. And they shall keep continuous watch throughout the whole night from sunset to dawn: so that, if any foreigner passes by them, they shall hold him until morning; then, if he is trustworthy, he shall be released, but if he is suspicious, he shall be turned over to the sheriff, who is to receive and safeguard him without difficulty or delay. If, however, foreigners of this sort, on passing through, do not allow themselves to be arrested, then the aforesaid watchmen are to raise hue against them on all sides and, with the whole force of the vill and of the neighbouring vills, are to follow them with hue and cry from vill to vill until they are captured. And then they are to be turned over to the sheriff as aforesaid; yet so that no one, on account of such arrest or capture of foreigners, shall be [unjustly] molested by the sheriff or his bailiffs. And the various cities, boroughs, and vills are to be warned to carry out each of the aforesaid watches and pursuits so diligently that, by reason of their default, we shall not have to inflict severe punishment.

It has also been provided that each sheriff, together with two knights especially assigned for that purpose, shall make the circuit of his county from hundred to hundred, [visiting] also the cities and boroughs; and in each hundred or city or borough they shall cause to be assembled before them the citizens, burgesses, freeholders, villeins, and other men aged from fifteen to sixty years. And they shall have them all assessed and sworn to arms according to their [respective] possessions in land and chattels: namely, for land worth £15, a shirt of mail, an iron cap, a sword, a knife, and a horse; for land worth £10, a hauberk, an iron cap, a sword, and a knife; for land worth 100s., a purpoint, an iron cap, a sword, a lance, and a knife; for land worth 40s. or more, up to a value of 100s., a sword, a knife, a bow, and arrows. Whatever persons have less than 40s. value of land are to be sworn to falchions (*falces*), halberds, knives, and other small arms. For chattels worth 60m., [a man shall possess] a shirt of mail, an iron cap, a sword, a knife, and a horse; for chattels worth 40m., a hauberk, an iron cap, a sword, and a knife; for chattels worth 20m., a purpoint, an iron cap, a sword, and a knife; for chattels worth 10m., a sword, a knife, a bow, and arrows; for chattels worth 40s. or more, up to a value of 10m., falchions, knives, halberds, and other small arms. Furthermore, all who, outside the forest, can have bows and arrows are to have them; but those in the forest [are to have] bows

---

[18] Wrongly dated 1252 in Stubbs, *Select Charters*, p. 362. Cf. no. 34.

and bolts.[19] And in the various cities and boroughs all men sworn to arms shall be obedient to their mayors, or to their reeves and bailiffs where there are no mayors.[20] In each of the other vills, moreover, there shall be established one or two constables,[21] according to the number of the inhabitants and the decision of the aforesaid [officials]. Besides, in each hundred there shall be established a chief constable, at whose command all men sworn to arms in his hundred shall be assembled; and to him they shall be obedient in carrying out necessary measures for the conservation of our peace. The chief constables of the various hundreds, moreover, shall be obedient to the sheriff and the two knights aforesaid, in coming at their command and in carrying out necessary measures for the conservation of our peace. . . .[22] By the witness of W[alter], archbishop of York, at Westminster, May 20.

(Latin) *Close Rolls, 1237-1242*, pp. 482 f.

(I) NAVAL LEVIES (1242)[23]

The king to the barons of Hastings, greeting. Whereas, on account of his continuous injuries, we are under no obligation to observe a truce toward the king of France, and whereas war between us has already broken out: we have decided, by your aid and counsel and by that of our other barons of the Cinque Ports, to assail the said king and his men both by sea and by land and to fight him in every way we can. Therefore, especially relying on your manliness and faith for willing and powerful aid in this affair, we command and urge you, in the fealty by which you are bound to us and as you cherish us and our honour, that as quickly as possible you have your ships prepared and well manned; and that, together with our other barons of the Cinque Ports, to whom we have sent the same mandate, you equip yourselves for assailing the said king of France along the coasts of Brittany, Normandy, and Boulogne, both by sea and by land, with fire and with other weapons at your command; yet so that you, on account of this our mandate, shall not presume to cause damage or injury to churches, or to any one who enjoys our protection or safe conduct—saving also to us the fifth which, as you know, belongs to us from booty acquired by you in our wars. . . . In testimony whereof, etc., to continue during our pleasure. By witness of the king, at Xanten, June 8.

Similar letters to the other barons of the Cinque Ports: namely, Sandwich, Dover, Hythe, Romney, Winchelsea, and Rye. Also to the good men of Dunwich. . . .

---

[19] *Pilettos*—apparently some sort of blunt arrows; cf. no. 35, art. 2.
[20] Cf. no. 39E.
[21] This seems to be the inauguration of rural constables as peace officers. On the earlier use of the word, see above, pp. 69, 82, n. 8.
[22] Details follow concerning the enforcement of these measures. Similar letters, together with the proper commissions of knights, were sent to all the counties.
[23] Cf. no. 41B, D.

46. LETTERS CLOSE AND PATENT

The mayor and sheriffs of London are ordered to send 120 footsoldiers with crossbows to Dover—to B[ertram] de Crioyl, constable of Dover [Castle], who on the part of the king will instruct them as to what they are to do. Witnessed as above [August 2].

The bailiffs of Dunwich are ordered with the utmost haste to send to Dover five ships well filled with [sea]men and crossbowmen—as many as they can supply—to do what B[ertram] de Crioyl, constable of Dover [Castle] will instruct them on the part of the king. Witnessed as above.

A similar mandate to the bailiffs of Yarmouth for five ships. Similar mandates to the bailiffs of Ipswich, Oreford, and Blakeney for four ships [each]. Witnessed as above.

(Latin) *Ibid.,* pp. 456, 495 f.

(J) Writs of Summons (1253-54)

The king to B[oniface], archbishop of Canterbury, greeting. Whereas we have to communicate to you certain grave and urgent matters touching our interest and that of our kingdom, which we are unwilling to settle without your counsel and that of our other magnates, we command you that, in the fealty by which you are bound to us and as you cherish us and our honour, you do not fail to be at Westminster a fortnight after St. Hilary next—in the presence of our queen, our brother Richard, earl of Cornwall, others of our council remaining in England, and yet others of our council in Gascony, whom we are about to send for [the meeting on] the same day—to hear our good will and pleasure and, together with our said council, to take up the matters aforesaid. Nor are you to delay your arrival so that you fail promptly to attend on the same day. By witness of Queen Eleanor and of Richard, earl of Cornwall, at Westminster, December 27.

The king to the sheriff of Bedford and Buckingham, greeting.[24] Whereas the earls, barons, and other magnates of our kingdom have steadfastly promised to be at London with horses and arms three weeks from Easter next, prepared and well equipped to advance without delay towards Portsmouth in order to cross the sea to us in Gascony [and to support us] against the king of Castile, who in strength is to make hostile invasion of our land of Gascony next summer; and whereas we have ordered you to distrain for that same [service] all men of your bailiwick who hold land worth £20 of us in chief, or of others who are under age and in our wardship: [therefore] we straitly command you that, besides all those men aforesaid, you summon before our council at Westminster a fortnight after next Easter four lawful and discreet knights from the aforesaid counties, whom the same counties are to elect for this [purpose], to represent all and several of the same counties—namely, two from one county

---

[24] On the significance of this writ, see Pasquet, *Origins of the House of Commons,* pp. 33 f.

and two from the other—to provide, along with knights of the other counties whom we have caused to be summoned for the same day, what sort of aid they will give us in so great an emergency. And to the knights and others of the aforesaid counties you yourself shall explain our needs and the urgency of our business, and you shall induce them to render us efficacious aid that will suffice for the present; so that the four knights aforesaid can make a precise response to our aforesaid council at the aforesaid term with regard to the aforesaid aid on behalf of all men of the aforesaid counties. . . . By witness of the queen and of Richard, earl of Cornwall, at Windsor, February 11.

Similar letters were directed to all the sheriffs of England.

(Latin) *Close Rolls, 1253-1254*, pp. 107, 114.

47. RECORDS OF THE BARONIAL CRISIS (1258-66)

(A) HENRY III: LETTERS AGREEING TO REFORM (1258)

The king to all, etc. You are to know that, through an oath given on our behalf[1] by Robert Waleran, we have granted to the nobles and magnates of our kingdom that, by twelve faithful men of our council already elected and by twelve other faithful men of ours elected on the part of those nobles, who are to convene at Oxford one month after the feast of Pentecost next, the state of our kingdom shall be ordered, rectified, and reformed according to what they shall think best to enact for the honour of God and our faith and the good of our kingdom. And if, perchance, any of those elected on our part are absent, those who are present shall be permitted to substitute others in place of the absentees; and the same shall be done [with regard to those elected] on the part of the aforesaid nobles and faithful men of ours. And whatever is ordained in this matter by the twenty-four elected by both sides and sworn to the undertaking, or by the majority of them, we will inviolably observe, wishing and henceforth straitly enjoining that their ordinance be inviolably observed by all. And whatever security those men, or the majority of them, may provide for the observance of this matter we will fully grant and cause to be granted. We also attest that Edward, our first-born son, through an oath personally taken, has by his letters granted that he will faithfully and inviolably observe, and will cause ever to be observed, all that has been expressed and granted above, so far as in him lies. Furthermore, the said earls and barons have promised that, on the completion of the business noted above, they will strive in good faith to see that a common aid is rendered to us by the community of our kingdom. In testimony whereof, etc. . . . Given at Westminster, May 2.

(Latin) Stubbs, *Select Charters*, p. 372.

---

[1] *In animam nostram;* kings very commonly named proxies to swear for them.

(B) THE PROVISIONS OF OXFORD (1258)

It has been provided that from each county there shall be elected four discreet and lawful knights who, on every day that the county [court] is held, shall assemble to hear all complaints touching any wrongs and injuries inflicted on any persons by sheriffs, bailiffs, or any other men, and to make the attachments that pertain to the said complaints [for keeping] until the first arrival of the chief justiciar in those parts: so that they shall take from the plaintiff adequate pledges for his prosecution [of the case], and from the defendant for his coming and standing trial before the said justiciar on his first arrival; and that the four knights aforesaid shall have all the said complaints enrolled, together with their attachments, in proper order and sequence—namely, for each hundred separately and by itself— so that the said justiciar, on his first arrival, can hear and settle the aforesaid complaints singly from each hundred. And they shall inform the sheriff that they are summoning all his hundredmen and bailiffs before the said justiciar on his next arrival, for a day and a place which he will make known to them: so that every hundredman shall cause all plaintiffs and defendants of his bailiwick to come in succession, according to what the aforesaid justiciar shall bring to trial from the aforesaid hundred; also as many men and such men— both knights and other free and lawful men—as may be required for best proving the truth of the matter. [This, however, is to be done] in such a way that all are not troubled at one and the same time; rather let [only] as many come as can be [used in cases to be] tried and concluded in one day.

Likewise it is provided that no knight of the aforesaid counties, by virtue of an assurance that he is not to be placed on juries or assizes, shall be excused by a charter of the lord king or be exempt from [the obligations of] this provision thus made for the common good of the whole kingdom.

Elected on the part of the lord king: the lord bishop of London; the lord bishop elect of Winchester; the lord H[enry], son of the king of Germany; the lord J[ohn], earl de Warenne; the lord Guy de Lusignan; the lord W[illiam] de Valence; the lord J[ohn], earl of Warwick; the lord John Mansel; Brother J[ohn] of Darlington; the abbot of Westminster; the lord H[enry] of Hengham.

Elected on the part of the earls and barons: the lord bishop of Worcester; the lord Simon, earl of Leicester; the lord Richard, earl of Gloucester; the lord Humphrey, earl of Hereford; the lord Roger Marshal; the lord Roger de Mortimer; the lord J[ohn] Fitz-Geoffrey; the lord Hugh le Bigot; the lord Richard de Gray; the lord W[illiam] Bardulf; the lord P[eter] de Montfort; the lord Hugh le Despenser. And if it should happen that of necessity any one of these cannot be present, the rest of them shall elect whom they please in place of the absentee, namely, another person needful for carrying on that business.

Thus swore the community[2] of England at Oxford. . . .
This is the oath [administered] to the twenty-four. . . .
Thus swore the chief justice of England. . . .
Thus swore the chancellor of England. . . .
This is the oath taken by the wardens of the castles. . . .
These are the men sworn [to be] of the king's council.[3] . . .

The twelve on the king's side have chosen from the twelve on the side of the community the earl Roger Marshal and Hugh le Bigot. And the party of the community has chosen from the twelve who are on the side of the king the earl of Warwick and John Mansel. And these four have power to elect the council of the king; and when they have made the election, they shall designate those [elected] to the twenty-four. And that shall hold on which the majority of these [four] agree.

These are the twelve who have been elected by the barons, on behalf of the whole community of the land, to consider common needs along with the king's council at the three annual parliaments. . . .

These are the twenty-four appointed by the community to consider aid for the king. . . . And if any one of these cannot or will not be present, those who are present shall have power to elect another in his place.

Concerning the state of Holy Church:—It should be remembered that the state of Holy Church is to be amended by the twenty-four chosen to reform the state of the kingdom of England—at what time and place they think best, according to the powers that they hold by writ of the king of England.[4]

Concerning the chief justice:—[It has been decided] furthermore that a chief justice—or two [chief justices]—shall be appointed; also what power he shall have; and that he shall be [in office] for only one year, so that at the end of the year he shall render account of his term before the king and the royal council and before the man who is to follow him [in office].

Concerning the treasurer and the exchequer:—The same [has been decided] with regard to the treasurer; so that he shall render account at the end of the year. And according to the ordinance of the said twenty-four, other good men are to be appointed to the exchequer, whither all the issues of the land are to come, and not elsewhere. And let that be amended which seems in need of amendment.

Concerning the chancellor:—The same [has been decided] with regard to the chancellor; so that he shall render account of his term at the end of the year, and that merely by the king's will he shall

---

[2] *Le commun*—a phrase which is shown by the context to have meant parliament or the baronial party. The oaths, which are here omitted, add nothing to the information given in the following articles.

[3] Fifteen men, of whom eleven were of the twenty-four named above.

[4] No. 47A, preceding.

seal nothing out of course,[5] but shall do so by [the advice of] the council that surrounds the king.

Concerning the power of the justice and of the bailiffs:—The chief justice has power to redress the misdeeds of all other justices, of bailiffs, of earls, of barons, and of all other people, according to the rightful law of the land. And writs are to be pleaded according to the law of the land in the proper places. And [it has been decided] that the justices shall accept nothing unless it is a present of bread and wine and like things: namely, such meat and drink as have been customarily brought for the day to the tables of the chief men. And this same regulation shall be understood [to hold] for all the king's councillors and all his bailiffs. And [it has been ordered] that no bailiff, by virtue of his office or of some plea, shall take any fee, either by his own hand or in any manner through another person. And if he is convicted [of so doing], let him be punished; likewise the man who gives [the fee]. And the king, if it is suitable, shall give [fees] to his justices and to his people who serve him, so that they shall have no need of taking anything from others.

Concerning the sheriffs:—As sheriffs there shall be appointed loyal persons, good men who are landholders; so that in each county there shall be as sheriff a feudal tenant of the same county, who shall well, loyally, and justly treat the people of the county. And [it is ordered] that he shall take no fee; that he shall be sheriff for no more than a year in all; that during the year he shall render his accounts at the exchequer and be responsible for his term [of office]; that the king, from the royal income, shall make [allowance] to him in proportion to his receipts, so that he may rightly keep the county; and that he shall take no fees, neither he nor his bailiffs. And if they are convicted [of such wrongdoing], let them be punished. It should be remembered that, with regard to the Jewry and the wardens of the Jewry, such reforms are to be established as shall carry out the oath in this respect.

Concerning the escheators:—Good escheators are to be appointed. And [it is ordered] that they shall take nothing from goods of deceased persons whose lands ought to be in the king's hands; but that, if a debt is owing to him, the escheators shall have free administration of the goods until they have carried out the king's wishes—and this according to the provision in the charter of liberties.[6] Also [it is ordered] that inquiry shall be made concerning the misdeeds committed there by escheators, and that redress shall be made for such [wrongs]. Nor shall tallage or anything else be taken, except as it should be according to the charter of liberties. The charter of liberties is to be strictly observed.

Concerning the exchange of London:—It should be remembered to establish reforms touching the exchange of London; also touching

---

[5] That is to say, nothing but routine documents.
[6] Art. 26 of Magna Carta, above, p. 119.

the city of London and all the other cities of the king, which have been brought to shame and ruin by tallages and other oppressions.

Concerning the household of the king and queen:—It should be remembered to reform the household of the king and queen.

Concerning the parliaments, as to how many shall be held annually and in what manner:—It should be remembered that the twenty-four have ordained that there are to be three parliaments a year: the first on the octave of St. Michael, the second on the morrow of Candlemas, and the third on the first day of June, that is to say, three weeks before [the feast of] St. John. To these three parliaments the chosen councillors of the king shall come, even if they are not summoned, in order to examine the state of the kingdom and to consider the common needs of the kingdom and likewise of the king; and by the king's command [they shall come] also at other times, whenever it is necessary. So too it should be remembered that the community is to elect twelve good men, who shall come to the three parliaments and at other times, when there is need and when the king and his council summon them to consider the affairs of the king and the kingdom. And [it has been decided] that the community shall hold as established whatever these twelve shall do—and this is to reduce the cost to the community. Fifteen are to be named by these four men—that is to say, by the earl Marshal, the earl of Warwick, Hugh le Bigot, and John Mansel—who have been elected by the twenty-four to name the aforesaid fifteen, who are to form the king's council. And they are to be confirmed by the aforesaid twenty-four, or by the majority of those men. And they shall have the power of advising the king in good faith concerning the government of the kingdom and concerning all matters that pertain to the king or the kingdom; and of amending and redressing everything that they shall consider in need of amendment or redress. And [they shall have authority] over the chief justice and over all other people. And if they cannot all be present, that shall be firm and established which the majority of them shall enact.

These are the names of the principal castles of the king, and of those who have charge of them. . . .

(Latin and French) *Ibid.*, pp. 378 f.

(C) THE PROVISIONS OF WESTMINSTER (1259)

In the year 1259 from the Incarnation of the Lord, the forty-third of the reign of King Henry, son of King John, at a meeting of the lord king and his magnates at Westminster on Michaelmas fortnight, the provisions hereinunder written, by the common counsel and consent of the said king and his magnates, were enacted and published by the same king and his magnates in this form:—

1. With regard to the performance of suit to the courts of the magnates and of other lords who have such courts, it is provided and established by general agreement that no one who is enfeoffed by charter shall henceforth be distrained to perform suit to his lord's

court, unless he is specifically obliged by the tenor of his charter to perform the suit; with the sole exception of those whose ancestors were accustomed to perform suit of this kind, or who themselves [were accustomed so to do], before the first crossing of the said lord king into Brittany—after the time of which crossing twenty-nine and a half years had elapsed down to the time that this constitution was made. And likewise no one enfeoffed without charter since the time of the Conquest, or by other ancient enfeoffment, shall be distrained to perform suit of this kind, unless he or his ancestors were accustomed to perform it before the first crossing of the lord king into Brittany. . . .

4. With regard to the sheriff's tourn,[7] it is provided that, unless their presence is specially demanded, archbishops, bishops, abbots, priors, earls, and barons, or other men of religion, or women, shall not of necessity come thither. . . . And the tourns shall be held according to the form of the king's Great Charter, and as they were customarily held in the time of the kings John and Richard.

5. It is also provided that neither on the eyres of the justices nor in the [courts of the] counties nor in the courts of barons shall fines henceforth be taken from anybody for miskenning,[8] or for avoidance of trouble on that score. . . .

8. Moreover, with regard to charters of exemption and liberty, [to the effect] that those securing them are not to be put on assizes, juries, or recognitions, it is provided that, if their oath is so essential that without it justice cannot be administered . . . , they shall be forced to swear, saving to them their aforesaid liberty and exemption in other respects. . . .

11. Henceforth no one except the lord king and his ministers shall be permitted, for any cause whatsoever, to levy distraints outside his fief, or on a royal or a common highway. . . .

16. Hereafter no one but the king shall hold in his court a plea concerning false judgment rendered in a court of his tenant; for pleas of this sort especially pertain to the crown and dignity of the king. . . .

18. Without the king's writ, no one may henceforth distrain his free tenants to respond concerning their free tenements or anything that pertains to their free tenements. Nor may he cause his free tenants against their will to take oaths; so that no one may do this without the king's precept. . . .

21. Hereafter itinerant justices shall not amerce vills on their eyres because particular twelve-year-old persons do not come before sheriffs and coroners for inquests concerning a man's death or other matters pertaining to the crown; so long as, nevertheless, enough men come from those vills for satisfactorily carrying out such inquests.

22. No judgment of murder[9] shall henceforth be rendered before

---

[7] See above, p. 123, n. 45.
[8] See above, p. 62, no. 10.
[9] Cf. nos. 40B, 54D.

the justices in a case that is adjudged merely one of accident; but [a judgment of] murder shall be proper in the case of a man feloniously slain, and not otherwise. . . .

(Latin) *Ibid.*, pp. 390 f.

(D) THE DECISION OF LOUIS IX (1264)

. . . In the name of the Father and the Son and the Holy Spirit. By our [present] decision or ordinance we quash and annul all the aforesaid provisions, ordinances, statutes, and obligations,[10] however called, and whatever has followed from them or by occasion of them, especially since it appears that the supreme pontiff by his letters has proclaimed them quashed and annulled; ordaining that as well the said king as all the barons and others who have consented to the present arbitration, and who in any way have bound themselves to observe the aforesaid [provisions], shall be utterly quit and absolved of the same. We likewise add that, by virtue or force of the aforesaid provisions or obligations or ordinances, or of any authority already granted by the king on that account, no one shall make new statutes or hold or observe those already made; nor ought any one, through non-observance of the aforesaid [provisions], to be held the enemy, either principal or otherwise, of any one else, or for that reason incur any penalty. . . . We also decree and ordain that the aforesaid king at his own volition may freely appoint, dismiss, and remove the chief justice, chancellor, treasurer, counsellors, lesser justices, sheriffs, and any other officials and ministers of his kingdom and his household, as he was used and able to do before the time of the provisions aforesaid. Furthermore, we repeal and quash the statute made to the effect that the kingdom of England should henceforth be governed by natives and that all aliens should leave the kingdom, never to return, except those whose residence the faithful men of the kingdom commonly agreed to, ordaining by our decision that aliens may safely remain in the said kingdom, and that the king may safely call to his counsel such aliens and natives as shall seem to him useful and loyal, just as he was able to do before the time aforesaid. Likewise we declare and ordain that the said king shall have full power and unrestricted rule within his kingdom and its appurtenances, and shall in all things and in every way enjoy such status and such full power as he enjoyed before the time aforesaid. By the present ordinance, however, we do not wish or intend in any way to derogate from royal privileges, charters, liberties, establishments, and praiseworthy customs of the kingdom of England existing before the time of the same provisions. . . .

Now this our ordinance or decision we have promulgated at Amiens on the morrow of the blessed Vincent the Martyr, A.D. 1263, in the

---

[10] The Provisions of Oxford, concerning which the French king had been called upon to arbitrate the quarrel between Henry III and the opposing party of the baronage.

month of January. In testimony whereof we have caused our seal to be attached to the present letters.

(Latin) *Ibid.*, pp. 396 f.

(E) THE DICTUM OF KENILWORTH (1266)[11]

. . . 1. We declare and provide that the most serene lord prince Henry, illustrious king of England, shall have, fully receive, and freely exercise his dominion, authority, and royal power without impediment or contradiction of any one, whereby, contrary to the approved rights and laws and the long established customs of the kingdom, the regal dignity might be offended; and that to the same lord king and to his lawful mandates and precepts full obedience and humble attention shall be given by all and singular the men of the same kingdom, both greater and lesser. And all and singular shall through writs seek justice in the court of the lord king and shall [there] be answerable for justice, as was accustomed to be done up to the time of the recent disorders.

2. Furthermore, we ask the same lord king and reverently urge his piety that, for doing and rendering justice, he will nominate such men as, seeking not their own [interests] but those of God and the right, shall justly settle the affairs of subjects according to the praiseworthy laws and customs of the kingdom, and shall thereby strengthen with justice and restore the throne of royal majesty.

3. We likewise ask and urge the same lord king fully to guard and observe the liberties of the Church and the charters of liberties and of the forest, to keep and hold which he is expressly bound by his own oath.

4. Also the lord king shall provide that grants which up to the present he has made of his free will, and not under compulsion, shall be observed; and that he will firmly establish other necessary [measures] determined by his men and at his own pleasure. And furthermore the English Church shall be fully restored to its liberties and customs, which it had and rightly held before the time of such disorders, and shall be permitted to enjoy them freely. . . .[12]

37. All henceforth shall maintain firm peace, and none shall commit homicide, arson, robbery, or other transgression against the peace. And if any one does so and is convicted, let him have judgment and law according to the custom of the kingdom.

38. Likewise all interested persons shall swear on the Holy Gospels that, on account of the disorders, no one will take private revenge, nor will he procure or consent or tolerate that private revenge should be taken. And if any one takes private revenge, let him be punished

---

[11] The final settlement of the Barons' War, dictated by a commission of four bishops, two earls, and six other barons appointed for that purpose.

[12] The omitted articles take up in detail the restoration of lawful rights, the cancellation of Simon de Montfort's acts, and the rehabilitation, on various conditions, of those who had been disinherited.

by the court of the lord king, and let those who have injured the Church make satisfaction to it.

39. Also, if any one is unwilling to observe this decision, or to undergo judgment by his peers in the court of the lord king, such persons as thus declare themselves, and are accordingly disinherited, shall have no right of recovering their lands. And if any one holding lands of disinherited men rebels against the decision, he is to have no just claim, by the gift of the lord king, either to the land or to what is paid for redeeming it. Moreover, if any person does not consent to this decision, he is to be a public enemy of the lord king and of his sons and of the community; the people and clergy, in so far as is permitted by canon law, shall prosecute him as an enemy to the peace of the Church and of the kingdom. . . .

Given and published in the castle of Kenilworth on the day before the Kalends of November in the year of grace 1266, the fifty-first year of the reign of the lord Henry, king of England.

(Latin) *Ibid.*, pp. 407 f.

48. HENRY III: LATER WRITS OF SUMMONS

(A) MEETING WITH KNIGHTS OF THE SHIRE AT WINDSOR (1261)

The king to the sheriff of Norfolk and Suffolk, greeting. Whereas, on the part of the bishop of Worcester, the earl of Leicester, the earl of Gloucester, and certain other nobles of our realm, three knights have been summoned from each of our counties to be at St. Albans on the approaching feast of St. Matthew the Apostle, in order with them to deliberate on the common affairs of our kingdom; and [whereas] we and our nobles aforesaid shall come together on the same day at Windsor to treat concerning peace between us and them: we command you on our part to give strict orders to those knights from your bailiwick, who have been summoned before those [nobles] on the aforesaid day, that, avoiding all excuse, they come to us at Windsor on the aforesaid day; and you are also strictly to prohibit them from going elsewhere on the said day, by all means causing them to come before us on the aforesaid day to have a conference with us on the aforesaid matters, so that, as a consequence of this business, they may see and understand that we propose no undertaking but what we know to be for the honour and common benefit of our realm. By witness of the king at Windsor, September 11.

(Latin) *Ibid.*, pp. 394 f.

(B) FIRST PARLIAMENT OF SIMON DE MONTFORT (1264)

The king to Adam of Newmarket, greeting. Whereas the disturbance recently experienced in our kingdom has now subsided and, by the grace of divine co-operation, peace has now been ordained and established between us and our barons; and [whereas], in order that this peace may be inviolably observed throughout our entire kingdom, it has been provided by the counsel and assent of our barons that in each of our counties throughout England keepers of our peace shall be appointed for the defence and security of those parts, until other provision for the state of our kingdom may be made by us and our barons; and whereas, relying on your fidelity as well as your industry, we, by the counsel of our said barons, have assigned you as our keeper in the county of Lincoln during our pleasure: we command and firmly enjoin that, in the fealty by which you are bound to us, you there diligently see to the keeping of our peace and to those matters which pertain to it, as aforesaid. . . .[1] And whereas in our approaching parliament, it is necessary for us to deliberate with our prelates, magnates, and other faithful men concerning our affairs and those of our kingdom: we command you to send to us on behalf of the entire county aforesaid four of the more lawful and discreet knights of the same county elected for that purpose by the assent of that county; so that they shall be with us at London on the octave of the approaching feast of the Holy Trinity at the latest, in order to deliberate with us on the aforesaid affairs. . . . By witness of the king at St. Paul's in London, June 4.

(Latin) *Ibid.*, pp. 399 f.

(C) SECOND PARLIAMENT OF SIMON DE MONTFORT (1265)

Henry, by the grace of God king of England, lord of Ireland, and duke of Aquitaine, to the venerable father in Christ, R[obert], by the same grace bishop of Durham. Whereas, after the grave peril of the disorders recently experienced in our kingdom, Edward, our dearest first-born son, was delivered as a hostage to assure and strengthen the peace of our kingdom; and whereas, now that the aforesaid disorders have—thank God!—been quieted, we must hold a deliberation with our prelates and magnates to make salutary provision for his release, and to establish and consolidate full assurance of peace and tranquillity for the honour of God and the advantage of our whole kingdom, and to consider certain other affairs of our kingdom which we are unwilling to settle without your counsel and that of our other prelates and magnates: [therefore] we command and urge you, in the faith and love by which you are bound to us, that, avoiding all excuse and putting aside all other concerns, you come to us at London on the octave of St. Hilary next, together with us and with our aforesaid prelates and magnates whom we have summoned to the same place, to consider the matters set forth above and to give your counsel [regarding them]. And by no means fail to do this, as you cherish us, our honour, and your own, as well as the common tranquillity of our kingdom. By witness of the king, at Worcester, December 14 [1264]. . . .[2]

Similar mandates to the sheriffs throughout England, that by the

---
[1] The writ here includes details regarding the prevention of crimes and disorders.
[2] Here follow in the roll the names of the prelates and lay barons summoned by the same form.

same form they should cause two of the more lawful, upright, and discreet knights from every county to come to the king at London on the octave aforesaid.

Letters in the same form also to the citizens of York, to the citizens of Lincoln, and to the other boroughs of England, that in the same way they should send two of the more discreet, lawful, and upright citizens or burgesses.

A mandate in the same form to the barons and good men of the Cinque Ports, as is contained in the writ enrolled below. . . .[3]

(Latin) *Reports Touching the Dignity of a Peer,* III, 33 f.

(D) COUNCIL OF 1268[4]

Those same men who were not at Windsor have been ordered to be at Westminster on Wednesday before the quinzime of Easter. . . .[5]

Writs are to be issued for certain persons of the Cinque Ports, whom the lord R[ichard] of Lyburne[6] ought to name, and for certain persons of the cities and boroughs: namely, that the bailiffs and six others of the more discreet, better, and wealthier men in the same —that is to say, the nearer of the cities and boroughs—are to be at London on the quinzime of Easter, to treat and consult with regard to the affairs of the lord king and of the kingdom, which also concern [those men] themselves; and that they should bring with them letters patent of credence addressed to all persons and [respectively] sealed with the communal seals of the same cities and boroughs. . . .

The king to his beloved and faithful his mayor and citizens of York, greeting. Whereas, with regard to arduous affairs concerning us and the estate and community of our kingdom, and especially in the council summoned by the legate[7] at London on the approaching quinzime of Easter, we wish to have a special deliberation and conference with you and the other faithful men of our said kingdom, whom we have caused to be summoned for this purpose, and without whom we are unable to settle those affairs: [therefore] we command and firmly enjoin that in the fealty, homage,[8] and love by which you are bound to us, immediately on sight of these letters and setting aside all other concerns, you cause the said mayor, together with the bailiffs and six of the better and more discreet and more substantial men [of the said city] to come with all haste to us at Westminster, [bringing with them] your letters patent

---

[3] This writ is in substance much the same as the one quoted; each of the Cinque Ports is to send four representatives.

[4] See the article by G. O. Sayles in the review cited below. The following extracts are from a carelessly written memorandum of March, 1268, to which are appended the form of the summons to the boroughs and the form of the letters patent to be returned with the deputies.

[5] Various persons are named as having received the writ.

[6] Constable of Dover Castle and warden of the Cinque Ports.

[7] Ottobono, papal legate.

[8] The wrong form seems inadvertently to have been used by the clerk, for the burgesses owed no homage.

signed with the seal of your community according to the form sent to you enclosed in the present letters; so that they shall be there on the approaching quinzime of Easter at the latest, there in the matters aforesaid to do whatever we shall see fit to provide by the common counsel of our kingdom. And by no means fail to do this. Witness.

[Such letters to] York, Lincoln, Northampton, Stafford, Norwich, Cambridge, Lynn, Oxford, Worcester, Gloucester, Shrewsbury, Hereford, Bristol, Winchester, Southampton, Canterbury, Chichester, Rochester, Bath, Coventry, Lichfield, Exeter, Ely, Bury St. Edmunds, Yarmouth, Ipswich, Dunwich. . . .

To all faithful in Christ before whom these present letters shall come, the mayor, bailiffs, and entire community of the city of York, greeting in the Lord. For the sake of the affairs concerning our lord King H[enry], illustrious king of England, his kingdom, the community of England, and us, [to be considered] in the council called by the legate at London on the approaching quinzime of Easter, we have seen fit to send thither ———, our mayor, and ———, our bailiffs, and ——— our citizens or fellow burgesses, so that full faith may be given to them in everything which, with regard to the aforesaid matters, they shall see fit on our behalf to set forth in the council or on the occasion of the council. And we shall hold as established and accepted whatever on our behalf those men do in the aforesaid matters. In testimony whereof, etc. Given, etc.

(Latin) *English Historical Review*, XL, 583 f.

49. PARLIAMENTARY AND OTHER WRITS (1275-95)

(A) Parliament of 1275

Edward, by the grace of God king of England, lord of Ireland, and duke of Aquitaine, to the sheriff of Middlesex, greeting. Whereas, for certain particular reasons, we have prorogued our general parliament[1] . . . at London with our prelates and the other magnates of our realm . . . until the morrow of the Sunday after Easter next; we command you that you summon to the same place, on the morrow of the Sunday after Easter aforesaid, four knights from your county of the more discreet and lawful, and likewise from each of the cities, boroughs, and trading towns[2] of your bailiwick six or four citizens, burgesses, or other good men, to consider, along with the magnates of our kingdom, the affairs of the said kingdom. On our part also you are without delay to have those letters of ours that are addressed to various persons in your bailiwick given or sent to them. And by no means neglect to do this and to give us full information touching the execution of this mandate at the term afore-

---

[1] Note that in this and the following writs *parliamentum* is used as a synonym of *colloquium*, meaning a conference or deliberation.

[2] *Ville mercatorie*, not market towns; see Ballard and Tait, *British Borough Charters*, II, lii.

said. By my own witness at Woodstock, December 26, in the third year of our reign.

(Latin) Stubbs, *Select Charters,* pp. 441 f.

(B) THE NEW CUSTOMS (1275)

William de Valence, earl of Pembroke, to all faithful in Christ before whom the present writing may come, greeting in the Lord. Whereas the archbishops, bishops, and other prelates of the kingdom of England, as well as the earls and barons, and we and the communities of the said kingdom, at the suggestion and request of the merchants, have for a variety of reasons unanimously granted, for ourselves and our heirs, to the magnificent prince, our dearest lord Edward, by the grace of God illustrious king of England, ½m. for each sack of wool and ½m. for every three hundred wool-fells, which make a sack, and 1m. for each last of hides exported from the kingdom of England and the land of Wales, to be henceforth collected in each port of England and Wales, both within liberties and without: [therefore] we, at the request and suggestion of the aforesaid merchants, grant, for us and our heirs, that the same lord king and his heirs shall have within each of our ports in Ireland, both within liberties and without, ½m. from every sack of wool and ½m. from every three hundred wool-fells, which make a sack, and 1m. from every last of hides exported from the land of Ireland, to be collected by the hands of wardens and bailiffs of the said king; saving to us the forfeitures of those who, without the licence and warrant of the said lord king [given] by his letters patent and signed with the seal provided for that purpose, shall presume to take wool, wool-fells, or hides of this sort through our fiefs, where we enjoy liberties, [for export] out of Ireland. From which [articles] the said lord king and his heirs shall collect and keep the half-mark from wool and wool-fells and the mark from lasts of hides in the manner aforesaid; yet so that in each of our ports, where the writs of the aforesaid king do not run, two of the more discreet and faithful men of those ports shall be elected, and they, having taken an oath with regard to the seizure of wool, wool-fells, and hides in the said ports until the merchants of wool, wool-fells, and hides aforesaid have their warrant under the seal of the lord king provided for that purpose, shall faithfully collect and receive the said custom for the use of the said lord king, and shall therefor be answerable to him. In testimony whereof we have set our seal to the present writing. Given in the general parliament of the lord king aforesaid, at Westminster, on Sunday, the feast of St. Dunstan the Bishop, in the third year of the reign of the same king.[3]

(Latin) *Ibid.,* pp. 443 f.

---

[3] Similar letters were issued by eleven other barons named in the roll, following the language of a royal ordinance which has come down to us in French (Palgrave, *Parliamentary Writs,* I, 1 f.). On the taxes mentioned in this writ, see Gras, *The Early English Customs System,* ch. iii.

49. PARLIAMENTARY WRITS

(C) SUBSIDY OF 1282

The king to the sheriff of Warwick and Leicester, to the citizens, burgesses, merchants, mayors, bailiffs, and commmunities of the cities, boroughs, and trading towns, and to all other men of the aforesaid counties, greeting. Whereas we have sent our beloved John of Kirkby for the sake of orally explaining to you on our part and in our name, and of expediting through you, certain arduous and especial concerns of ours, which we have entrusted to him: we command and firmly enjoin you, in the fealty and affection by which you are bound to us, that you place firm trust in the same John with respect to the said matters and carry them out in all ways. Moreover we have enjoined the same John without delay to inform us concerning your response and your willingness. In testimony whereof, etc. By witness of the king, at Chester, June 19.[4]

The king to his beloved and faithful the mayor and citizens of Hereford, greeting. For the courteous subsidy that you have promised us for the sake of our present expedition into Wales—concerning which we have been informed orally by our clerk, John of Kirkby, whom we sent to you on this account with our letters of credence—we are exceedingly grateful to you, and through the grace of God we will indemnify you in this respect at an opportune time. But since at the present moment we greatly need the money, we command and firmly enjoin you, in the fealty and homage[5] by which you are bound to us, and according to the instructions drawn up under the seal of our clerk aforesaid and delivered to our sheriff of Hereford and to you, to cause the money of the aforesaid subsidy to be levied in all haste and paid to the same sheriff; so that it may be brought to us as we have commanded him through other letters of ours, and so that we may have it by the morrow of All Saints at the latest. And by no means neglect this, as you cherish your bodies and all that you have in the kingdom. And strive especially to prevent such an occurrence as that we and our army should presently retreat from the region of Wales through default of that payment of money, on which we are placing full reliance. By witness of the king, at Denby, October 28.

(Latin) *Ibid.,* pp. 456 f.

(D) PARLIAMENTS OF 1283

The king to the sheriff of Norfolk and Suffolk, greeting. Whereas Llewelyn, son of Griffith, and his accomplices, the other Welshmen, to us enemies and rebels, have so often in our own time and in the times of our progenitors, **kings** of England, disturbed the peace of our kingdom . . . ,[6] we **command** and firmly enjoin you to summon

---

[4] Similar letters were sent to the sheriffs of all the counties but Cornwall; likewise to all abbots, priors, and men of religion in all the counties except Cornwall: Palgrave, *Parliamentary Writs,* I, 384.

[5] See above, p. 152, n. 8.

[6] A number of rhetorical clauses are omitted.

to Northampton on the octave of St. Hilary, before us or before such of our faithful men as we may care to depute for this matter, all those of your bailiwick fit and able to bear arms who have land worth £20 and who are not with us on our Welsh expedition; also four knights from each of the aforesaid counties, having full authority [to act] on behalf of the communities of the same counties; also from each city, borough, or trading town two men similarly empowered on behalf of their communities—in order to hear and do what on our part we shall cause to be explained to them. And you shall not presume, through love, favour, reward, fear, or any other consideration, to grant pardon or postponement to any one of your bailiwick who has arms worth £20 and is fit and able to bear arms. Nor by any means shall you, on the aforesaid account, summon before us, or before our faithful men aforesaid, any one who does not have land worth more than £20, although he may be fit or able to bear arms. And through the four knights aforesaid you are to inform us, or our faithful men aforesaid, on the day and [at the] place aforesaid, of the names of all those whom you thus summon. And you are to have there the names of those four knights and this writ. And as you cherish your life and all that you have, do not fail to attend to all these matters. By witness of the king, at Rhuddlan, November 24 [1282].

Similar mandates to the sheriffs of Nottingham, Derby, Shropshire, Stafford, Cambridge, Huntingdon, Essex, Hertford, Buckingham, Bedford, Somerset, Dorset, Surrey, Sussex, Warwick, Leicester, Oxford, Berkshire, Kent, Middlesex, Northampton, Rutland, Lincoln, Cornwall, Devon, Wiltshire, Hereford, Worcester, Gloucester, and Hampshire, that they should summon, etc., at Northampton. And to the sheriffs of York, Cumberland, Westmorland, Northumberland, and Lancashire that they should summon, etc., at York.

The king to the venerable father in Christ, John, by the same grace archbishop of Canterbury and primate of all England, greeting. Whereas Llewelyn . . . ,[7] we command and urge you to summon to Northampton . . . your suffragans and the abbots, priors, and various other heads of religious houses, as well as proctors from the deans and chapters of your collegiate churches and [those] of the suffragans in your dioceses. And you are to be present on the same day and at the same place to hear and do what in this connection we shall cause to be explained to you and to them for the sake of the public good; also to give us your advice and assistance. . . .

Similar letters of the same date addressed to the archbishop of York, to summon his suffragans, etc., before the king at York on the aforesaid octave, or before faithful men whom the king, etc.

The king to the mayor and sheriffs and the whole community of his city of London, greeting. We are exceedingly grateful to you for having liberally granted to us, as a subsidy for our expedition in

---

[7] Here and immediately below the writ uses the preceding form.

49. PARLIAMENTARY WRITS

Wales, a thirtieth of all your movable goods; aside from those which were excluded from the fifteenth recently granted to us, and excepting [the goods of] those three hundred persons in the aforesaid city who gave us a subsidy[8] for the sake of the warlike expedition aforesaid, on condition that our magnates would decide to grant the same. And we wish you to know that the same magnates, with respect to themselves, have granted and ratified the subsidy of the said thirtieth, as on our part they were requested to do. And since, as you know, we greatly need the money for the sake of our expedition aforesaid, we have assigned . . .[9] to lay and assess the said thirtieth and to collect it through themselves and through you, the mayor and sheriffs aforesaid. And so we command you in the said matter to be obedient, responsive, serviceable, and helpful to the same men . . . , according to the instructions which on our part they will give you. In testimony whereof, etc. Witnessed as above, February 28.

The king to the knights and freemen and the whole community of the county of Hampshire, greeting. We are exceedingly grateful to you for having, through the four knights sent to Northampton on the part of the community of the aforesaid county, courteously agreed to give us a subsidy for the sake of our present expedition in Wales, to the same amount as our magnates should provide and agree upon as a subsidy of this sort. And whereas the same magnates . . . have agreed upon a subsidy to us of a thirtieth . . . , we have assigned . . .[10] to lay and assess the said thirtieth and to collect it by their own agency and with the sheriff of the aforesaid county. And so we command you. . . . By witness of the king at Rhuddlan, February 28.[11]

The king to the mayor, citizens, and sheriffs of London. . . .[12] And since we wish to have a deliberation with our faithful men as to what should be done with the aforesaid David . . . , we command you to cause two of the wiser and fitter citizens of the aforesaid city to be elected, and to send them to us so that they shall come before us at Shrewsbury on the morrow of Michaelmas next, to talk with us concerning this and other matters. And by no means fail to do this. By witness of the king, at Rhuddlan, June 28.[13]

(Latin) Palgrave, *Parliamentary Writs*, I, 10-16.

---

[8] Presumably the subsidy or loan taken to anticipate the parliamentary grant; cf. no. 49c, preceding.

[9] Three collectors are named.

[10] Two collectors are named.

[11] Letters resembling one or the other of these forms were sent to the other counties.

[12] The writ contains a long preamble reciting the crimes of the Welsh and announcing the capture of Prince David.

[13] Similar letters were sent to twenty other boroughs; to nineteen persons requiring their individual attendance; and to the sheriffs of all the counties ordering the election in each of two knights to represent their respective communities at the same *colloquium*.

(E) SUBSIDIES OF 1294

The king to the knights and freeholders and the whole community of the county of Cumberland, greeting. Whereas the earls, barons, knights, and all other men of our kingdom have now courteously and graciously given us as a subsidy for our war . . . a tenth of all their movable goods, with the exception of those exempted from the fifteenth recently granted to us in the same kingdom[14] . . . , we have assigned our beloved and faithful Thomas of Newton, Robert of Whiteridge, or one of them, together with a certain clerk, to lay and assess and to levy and collect the said tenth in the aforesaid county, and to bring it to our exchequer and there pay it at the following terms. . . . And so we command you. . . .[15] By witness of the king at Westminster, November 12, in the twenty-second year of our reign.

The king to his beloved and faithful Robert of Ratford, greeting. Whereas our citizens and good men of London have graciously conceded to us as a subsidy for our war the sixth of their movables,[16] thus setting an example to the other men in our demesne towns for granting a similar subsidy, we have commissioned you to seek a sixth of this sort from each of our demesne cities and other towns in the counties of Kent, Sussex, Surrey, and Hampshire according to the assessment of the tenth already granted in our kingdom. And so we command you that, taking with you the sheriffs of the [respective] regions, you personally go to each of our demesne cities and other towns and on our part diligently urge and effectively induce the men of the said cities and towns—by whatever means you consider desirable—to give us the aforesaid sixth according to the aforesaid assessment. And you are without delay to report to us, or to our treasurer and our barons of the exchequer, what you accomplish in this undertaking. In testimony whereof we have caused to be drawn up these our letters patent. By witness of the venerable father [William, bishop of Bath and Wells], November 21, in the twenty-third year of our reign.[17]

(Latin) Brady, *Treatise of Boroughs*, pp. 63 f.

---

[14] The parliament of this year, like that of 1290, included no representatives of the boroughs, which were dealt with by separate negotiation. In 1290 a fifteenth was obtained both within and without boroughs, but in 1294 the latter were prevailed on to give a sixth, in contradistinction to the tenth of the knights and magnates. On the significance of this precedent, and on the general character of the assemblies concerned, see Willard, *Parliamentary Taxes*, pp. 3 f.; Stubbs, *Constitutional History*, II, 255 f.

[15] The form used is virtually the same as that in the writs of 1283. Similar letters assigned other commissioners in the rest of the counties.

[16] The writ appointing commissioners to levy the sixth in London states that the subsidy has been liberally and freely (*liberaliter et libenter*) granted by the citizens.

[17] Similar letters assigned other groups of collectors in six other regions; see Pasquet, *Origins of the House of Commons*, App. I (added by G. Lapsley).

49. PARLIAMENTARY WRITS

(F) PARLIAMENTS OF 1295

Edward, etc., to the venerable father in Christ, R[obert], by the same grace archbishop of Canterbury and primate of all England, greeting. Whereas, with regard to certain arduous affairs touching us and our kingdom, as well as you and the other prelates of the same kingdom, which we are unwilling to settle without your presence and theirs, we wish to hold our parliament and to have a conference and discussion with you concerning these matters, we command and firmly enjoin you, in the fealty and love by which you are bound to us, to come to us at Westminster on the first day of the month of August next, or in any case within the third day following at the latest, in order with us to consider the said affairs and to give us your counsel. And by no means fail to do this. By my own witness at Whitchurch, June 24. By writ of the privy seal.

Similar mandates to the archbishop of York, to the bishops, abbots, and priors, to the masters of the order of Sempringham and of the Knights of the Temple in England, and to the prior of the Hospital of St. John of Jerusalem in England, as noted below: namely. . . .[18]

The king to his beloved and faithful brother Edmund, earl of Lancaster, greeting. Whereas, with regard to certain arduous affairs touching us and our kingdom, as well as you and the other nobles and magnates of the same kingdom, which, etc. (as above): we command and firmly enjoin you, in the fealty and homage by which you are bound to us, to come to us, etc. (as above to the end). Witnessed as above.

Similar mandates individually by letters close to the following earls and barons: namely. . . .[19]

The king to his beloved and faithful Gilbert of Thornton, greeting. Whereas, with regard to certain arduous affairs touching us and our kingdom, as well as you and others of our council, which, etc. (as above): we command you in the fealty and love by which you are bound to us, etc. (as above in the mandate for the bishops to the end). Witnessed as above.

Similar mandates to the justices of both benches,[20] the itinerant justices, the justices assigned as deans,[21] the men sworn of the council, the barons of the exchequer, and the other clerks of the council whose names are noted below: namely. . . .[22]

The king to the sheriff of Northampton, greeting. Whereas we wish to have a conference and discussion with the earls, barons, and

---

[18] Besides the archbishop and the heads of the great orders, the list includes eighteen bishops, forty-two abbots, and eleven priors.
[19] Ten earls and fifty-three other barons are enumerated.
[20] Later known as the courts of king's bench and common pleas; but cf. no. 54E.
[21] That is to say, chief justices on the circuits; see nos. 52G, 54E.
[22] Besides Gilbert, thirty-eight persons are named.

other nobles of our realm concerning the provision of remedies for the dangers that in these days threaten the same kingdom—on which account we have ordered them to come to us at Westminster on the Sunday next after the feast of St. Martin in the coming winter, there to consider, ordain, and do whatever the avoidance of such dangers may demand—we command and firmly enjoin you that without delay you cause two knights, of the more discreet and more capable of labour, to be elected from the aforesaid county, and two citizens from each city of the aforesaid county, and two burgesses from each borough, and that you have them come to us on the day and at the place aforesaid; so that the said knights shall then and there have full and sufficient authority on behalf of themselves and the community of the county aforesaid, and the said citizens and burgesses on behalf of themselves and the respective communities of the cities and boroughs aforesaid, to do whatever in the aforesaid matters may be ordained by common counsel; and so that, through default of such authority, the aforesaid business shall by no means remain unfinished. And you are there to have the names of the knights, citizens, and burgesses, together with this writ. By witness of the king, at Canterbury, October 3.

Similar letters addressed to each of the sheriffs throughout England under the same date.

The king to the venerable father in Christ, R[obert], by the same grace archbishop of Canterbury and primate of all England. . . .[23] Wherefore, since darts cause less injury when they are foreseen, and since your fortunes, like those of the other citizens of the same kingdom, are greatly concerned in this affair, we command and firmly enjoin you, in the fealty and love by which you are bound to us, that on Sunday next after the feast of St. Martin in the coming winter you personally be present at Westminster; first summoning (*premunientes*) the prior and chapter of your church and the archdeacons and all the clergy of your diocese, the said prior and archdeacons to be present along with you in person, the said chapter [to be represented] by one fit proctor, and the said clergy by two—which proctors are to have full and sufficient authority from the said chapter and clergy to concern themselves, together with us, with the rest of the prelates and magnates, and with other inhabitants of our kingdom, in considering, ordaining, and deciding how such dangers and premeditated evils are to be obviated. By witness of the king, at Wingham, September 30.[24]

The king to his beloved and faithful kinsman, Edmund, earl of

---

[23] The rhetorical preamble includes the famous phrase that "what concerns all should be approved by all," but it is doubtful whether such flourishes had any constitutional significance.

[24] Similar letters were sent to the other bishops and, with the omission of the *premunientes* clause, to the heads of religious houses and the masters of the military orders.

Cornwall, greeting. Whereas we wish to have a conference and discussion with you and with the other magnates of our kingdom to provide ways to meet the dangers that in these days threaten our entire kingdom, we command and firmly enjoin you, in the faith and love by which you are bound to us, to be present in person at Westminster on Sunday next after the feast of St. Martin in the coming winter, in order to consider, ordain, and decide, together with us, the prelates, and the rest of the magnates, and with other inhabitants of our kingdom, how such dangers are to be obviated.

Similar letters to those noted below: namely. . . .[25]

(Latin) Palgrave, *Parliamentary Writs*, I, 28-31.

[25] The roll lists eight earls and forty-one other barons.

50. MILITARY AND NAVAL RECORDS (1278-97)

(A) DISTRAINT OF KNIGHTHOOD (1278)[1]

The king to the sheriff of Gloucester, greeting. We command and firmly enjoin you without delay to distrain all men of your bailiwick possessing land to the value of £20 a year, who hold of us in chief and who ought to be knights but are not, to receive from us the arms of knighthood before the feast of the Lord's Nativity next or on that same day. You are also to distrain without delay all men of your bailiwick from whomsoever they hold, possessing land to the value of £20 or a whole knight's fee worth £20 a year, who ought to be knights but are not, to receive such arms on the same feast or before. And in this connection [see to it] that you obtain from the same men good and sufficient security, and have the names of all those men inscribed in a certain roll by the view of two lawful knights of the aforesaid county, and sent to us without delay under your seal and the seals of the two knights aforesaid. And we wish you to know that we shall make diligent investigation with regard to your conduct in the execution of this mandate, and according to it shall have an appropriate remedy to apply. By my own witness, at Westminster, June 26, in the sixth year of our reign.

(Latin) *Ibid.*, I, 214.

(B) COMMISSIONS OF ARRAY

The king to all his bailiffs and faithful men of the counties of Nottingham and Derby to whom, etc., greeting. Whereas we have sent our beloved and faithful William Wyther into the aforesaid counties there to select, both within and without liberties, three hundred foot-soldiers from those more capable and fit to bear arms, and to lead those men to us as we shall instruct him: [therefore] we command that, when the same William comes to the aforesaid counties to select

[1] Precedents for such action can be found in the rolls of Henry III, but under Edward I the practice was systematized and extended; cf. no. 50D.

the said men as stated above, you are to be serviceable, helpful, attentive, and obedient to him, according to what on our part the same William shall tell you. And as you cherish our interest and honour, and as we trust in your fealty, by no means fail to do this. . . . By witness of the king, at Rhuddlan, December 6 [1282].[2]

The king to the sheriffs of Hampshire, Dorset, and Wiltshire, and to all his faithful men of the same counties, both within and without liberties, greeting. Know that we have assigned our beloved and faithful . . . , together with those whom they shall associate with themselves, to select in the aforesaid counties three thousand men, both archers and crossbowmen, capable for attack and defence and well supplied with arms suited to them; and to have them come to Winchelsea, so that they shall be there on the third or fourth day after the feast of All Saints next, thus equipped and ready to set forth on our fleet. . . . And so we command you. . . . By witness of the king, at Canterbury, October 3 [1295].

(Latin) *Ibid.*, I, 245, 270.

(C) MEMORANDUM OF SERVICE FROM THE CINQUE PORTS (1293)

It is to be remembered that, on the octave of St. Hilary in the twenty-first year of King Edward, son of King Henry, when Stephen of Penchester, then constable of Dover [Castle] and warden of the Cinque Ports,[3] in connection with the account for his aforesaid bailiwick was present in the exchequer before Master William de la Marche, the treasurer, and the barons of the same exchequer, and after the said Stephen had been interrogated at length concerning the aforesaid Cinque Ports—namely, as to which were the ports and which their members, and as to what services the said ports owed the king, and how and in what way [they were owed]—the same Stephen informed the aforesaid treasurer and barons to this effect:—

Sussex. Hastings is a chief port, the members of which are these: Winchelsea, Rye, the lathe[4] of Pevensey, and Bulverhythe in the county of Sussex; Bekesbourne and Grange in the county of Kent. Which port, with its aforesaid members, ought on the king's summons to find twenty-one ships; and in each ship there ought to be twenty-one men, strong, fit, well armed, and prepared for the king's service; but so that, on the king's behalf, summons should thereof be made forty days before. And when the aforesaid ships and the men in them have come to the place whither they have been summoned, they shall there remain in the king's service for fifteen days at their own cost. And if the king needs their service beyond the fifteen days afore-

---

[2] Many similar commissions were issued in this and the following years for foot-soldiers, ditch-diggers, and carpenters, all of whom were normally paid by the king. Cf. no. 41D.

[3] Cf. no. 48D.

[4] An administrative district peculiar to this region.

50. MILITARY AND NAVAL RECORDS

said, or wishes them to remain there longer, those ships with the men in them shall remain in the king's service so long as he pleases and at his cost: that is to say, a master shall receive 6d. per day, a constable 6d. per day, and each of the others 3d. per day.

Kent. Romney is a chief port, and Old Romney and Lydd are members of the same. Which port, with its members, shall find five ships for the king in the manner aforesaid. The port of Hythe owes the king five ships in the manner aforesaid. Dover is a chief port, the members of which are these: Faversham, Folkestone, and Margate. This port, with its aforesaid members, owes twenty-one ships in the manner aforesaid. Sandwich is a chief port, the members of which are Fordwich, Stonor, and Sarre. Which port, with its members, owes the king five ships in the manner aforesaid.

Total service of the Cinque Ports, fifty-seven ships.

(Latin) *Red Book of the Exchequer,* II, 714 f.

(D) GENERAL LEVY FOR SERVICE IN FRANCE (1297)

The king to the sheriff of York, greeting. Whereas by way of careful precaution against the peril and damage that might be incurred by us and our whole kingdom from the plots of our enemies, we recently commanded you to inform all men of your bailiwick possessing land and rent to the value of £20 a year, both within and without liberties, and likewise men having more—those not holding of us in chief as well as those so holding—that they should at once provide themselves with horses and arms and should hold themselves fit and ready to join us and to go with our own person for the safeguarding and defence of themselves and of our whole kingdom aforesaid, as soon as we should issue summons for them; and whereas, on account of the safeguarding aforesaid, we have now decided to set our crossing to the lands beyond the sea: [therefore] we command and firmly enjoin you, in the fealty by which you are bound to us, that on our part you immediately summon all and several of your bailiwick, both within and without liberties, who possess land and rent to the value of £20 a year or more, as aforesaid, from whomsoever they hold, urging and firmly enjoining them, on the first Sunday after the octave of St. John the Baptist next, to come to us at London with horses and arms—that is to say, each of them as befits his condition—prepared to cross the sea with our person to the lands aforesaid, for the honour of God and of themselves, and for the safeguarding and common benefit of the said kingdom. And so you are to devote yourself to the execution of this our mandate with all speed, lest—which God forbid!—our crossing be delayed through your default and we be obliged to chastise you severely. By witness of the king at Loders, May 15.

Similar letters to each of the sheriffs of England.

(Latin) Palgrave, *Parliamentary Writs,* I, 281.

51. RECORDS CONCERNING PARLIAMENT (1297-1306)

(A) CONFIRMATION OF THE CHARTERS (1297)

Edward, by the grace of God king of England, lord of Ireland, and duke of Aquitaine, to all who may see or hear these present letters, greeting. Know that, for the honour of God and of Holy Church and for the benefit of our entire kingdom, we have granted for ourself and for our heirs that the Great Charter of Liberties and the Charter of the Forest, which were drawn up by the common assent of the whole kingdom in the time of King Henry, our father, are to be observed without impairment in all their particulars. And we will that those same charters shall be sent under our seal to our justices—those of the forest as well as the others—to all sheriffs of counties, and to all our other ministers, as well as to all cities throughout the land, together with our writs providing that the aforesaid charters are to be published and announcement is to be made to the people that we have granted these [charters] to be observed in all their particulars; and that our justices, sheriffs, mayors, and other ministers, whose duty it is to administer the law of the land under us and through our agency, shall cause the same charters in all particulars to be admitted in pleas and judgments before them—that is to say, the Great Charter of Liberties as common law and the Charter of the Forest according to the assize of the forest, for the relief of our people. And we will that, if any judgment is henceforth rendered contrary to the particulars of the charters aforesaid by our justices, or by our other ministers before whom pleas are held contrary to the particulars of the charters, it shall be null and void. And we will that these same charters shall be sent under our seal to the cathedral churches throughout the kingdom and shall there remain; and twice a year they shall be read to the people. And [we will] that the archbishops and bishops shall pronounce sentences of greater excommunication against all those who, by deed or aid or counsel, shall violate the aforesaid charters, infringing them in any particular or violating them in any way; and the aforesaid prelates shall pronounce and publish these sentences twice a year. And if the same prelates—the bishops or any of them—prove negligent in making the aforesaid denunciation, by the archbishops of Canterbury and York who at the time hold office, they shall be reproved in a suitable manner and compelled to make this same denunciation in the form aforesaid.

And whereas some people of our kingdom are fearful that the aids and taxes (*mises*), which by their liberality and good will they have heretofore paid to us for the sake of our wars and other needs, shall, despite the nature of the grants, be turned into a servile obligation for them and their heirs because these [payments] may at a future time be found in the rolls, and likewise the prises that in our name have been taken throughout the kingdom by our ministers: [therefore] we have granted, for us and our heirs, that, on account of anything that has been done or that can be found from a roll or in some other way, we will not make into a precedent for the future any such aids, taxes, or prises. And for us and our heirs we have also granted to the archbishops, bishops, abbots, priors, and other folk of Holy Church, and to the earls and barons and the whole community of the land, that on no account will we henceforth take from our kingdom such aids, taxes, and prises, except by the common assent of the whole kingdom and for the common benefit of the same kingdom, saving the ancient aids and prises due and accustomed.[1]

And whereas the greater part of the community all feel themselves gravely oppressed by the maltote on wool—that is to say, 40s. from each sack of wool—and have besought us to relieve them [of the charge], at their prayer we have fully relieved them, granting that henceforth we will take neither this nor any other [custom] without their common assent and good will, saving to us and our heirs the custom on wool, wool-fells, and hides previously granted by the community of the kingdom aforesaid.[2]

In testimony whereof we have caused to be written these our letters patent. Given at Ghent, November 5, in the twenty-fifth year of our reign.

(French) Stubbs, *Select Charters*, pp. 490 f.

(B) PARLIAMENTARY BILL OF 1301

Bill of the prelates and nobles delivered to the lord king on behalf of the whole community in the parliament of Lincoln in the year aforesaid:[3]—

... Thus the said community is of the opinion that, if it please our lord the king, the two charters, of liberties and of the forest, shall henceforth be entirely observed in all particulars. [Response:] It expressly pleases the king.

And statutes contrary to the said charters shall be annulled and voided. [Response:] It expressly pleases.

And the power of the justices assigned to keep the charters in the counties shall be defined by the counsel of the prelates, earls, and barons. [Response:] It tacitly pleases.

---

[1] Cf. the first article in what used to be called the Statute *De Tallagio non Concedendo*, but which seems rather to have been a petition drawn up by the parliamentary opposition during the crisis of 1297: "No tallage or aid shall henceforth be imposed or levied by us or by our heirs in our kingdom except by the will and common assent of the archbishops, bishops, and other prelates, and of the earls, barons, knights, burgesses, and other freemen in our kingdom." On this subject see especially Pasquet, *Origins of the House of Commons*, pp. 109, 237 f. See below, p. 166, n. 6; and cf. no. 56, art. 10.

[2] See no. 49B.

[3] January, 1301. The king had first presented a bill to parliament, asking the latter to assume all responsibility that the new delimitation of the royal forest would not violate his coronation oath, and to provide means whereby the proposed disafforestment could be amended. This parliament bluntly refused to do, sending to the king instead the following articles. On this whole subject see Petit-Dutaillis and Lefebvre, pp. 217 f.; Pasquet, *Origins of the House of Commons*, p. 115.

And the perambulation that has already been made and ridden[4] by view of good men according to the form of the said charter of the forest shall stand and at the same time shall be carried out through prompt disafforestment according to the bounds determined by the perambulators, so that the community may at once be seised of them. [Response:] It expressly pleases.

And offences and trespasses committed by the king's ministers against the tenor of the said charters and prises extortionately taken without consent or payment, against the form of the lord king's statute made at Westminster during Lent just past, shall henceforth cease. [Response:] It expressly pleases.

And any offence by a minister shall be paid for in proportion to the trespass, according to [the judgment of] auditors who are not suspected on account of their past deeds and who are assigned for such purpose by the prelates, earls, and barons of the land, and this matter shall be undertaken at once. [Response:] The lord king wishes to provide another remedy in this connection, rather than through such auditors.

And henceforth sheriffs shall be answerable for their revenues according to the customary practice in the time of his father—which revenues have been and are now to the great impoverishment of the people. And sheriffs shall not be placed under increased charges. [Response:] It pleases the lord king that in this respect a fit remedy shall be provided by common counsel as quickly as is well possible.

And wherever the perambulation has in part been made, but has not been ridden, it shall be done between now and Michaelmas next. [Response:] It expressly pleases.

On condition that the aforesaid matters are carried out and firmly established and accomplished, the people of the realm grant him a fifteenth in place of the twentieth recently granted—yet so that all the matters aforesaid are carried out between now and Michaelmas next; otherwise nothing is to be taken. [Response:] It expressly pleases. . . .

(French and Latin) Palgrave, *Parliamentary Writs*, I, 104 f.

(C) MALTOTE OF 1303[5]

The king to the sheriff of Lincoln, greeting. Whereas we have learned that divers merchants of our kingdom, in order that they may be quit of our prises[6] and may use and enjoy the various liberties granted by us to foreign and alien merchants, are willing to give us from their goods and merchandise certain new payments and customs, which the said foreign and alien merchants give us from their merchandise within our kingdom and dominions: we [therefore],

---

[4] There were two steps in the procedure: juries first determined the theoretic extent of the forest; then commissioners fixed the bounds by riding along them.

[5] See above, p. 121, n. 38.

[6] The exactions of wine and other merchandise to which the king was entitled by ancient custom.

51. PARLIAMENT (1297-1306)

wishing to have a discussion and conference regarding these matters with the merchants of the said kingdom, command you to summon to our exchequer at York two or three citizens from each city, and two or three burgesses from each borough within your bailiwick, so that they shall be there on the morrow of St. John the Baptist next, with full power on behalf of the communities of the cities and boroughs aforesaid, to accept and to do what shall then be ordered in the foregoing connection by the counsel and assent of us and of them and of the merchants of the said kingdom. And you are then and there to have this writ. By witness of the king, at Newcastle-upon-Tyne, May 7.

Similar letters addressed to each of the sheriffs throughout England.

... And the aforesaid Walter, John, and Henry[7] appear for the city of London and ... for Lincoln. For Winchester ... ; for Salisbury ... ; for Exeter ... ; for Northampton ... ; for Oxford ... ; for Leicester ... ; for Bristol ... ; for Huntingdon ... ; for Hertford ... ; for Shrewsbury ... ; for Stafford ... ; for Lichfield ... ; for Coventry ... ; for Warwick ... ; for Worcester ... ; for St. Albans ... ; for Plympton ... ; for Bodmin ... ; for Weymouth ... ; for Canterbury ... ; for Dunhaved ... ; for Liskeard ... ; for Dorchester ... ; for Yarmouth ... ; for Norwich ... ; for Dunwich ... ; for Lynn ... ; for Colchester ... ; for Cambridge ... ; for Melcombe ... ; for Chichester ... ; for Grimsby ... ; for Rochester ... ; for the city of York ... ; for Scarborough ... ; for Nottingham ... ; for Kingston-upon-Hull ... ; for Newcastle-upon-Tyne ... ; for Whitby ... ; for Richmond. ... All of whom, by virtue of the summons in the aforesaid writ, appeared on June 25 before the council of the lord king at York, and said that by their unanimous opinion and will, on behalf both of themselves and of the communities of the cities and boroughs aforesaid, they would by no means agree to an increased maltote or to the customs mentioned in the aforesaid writ as having been granted to the lord king by foreign and alien merchants, but only to the customs anciently due and used.

(Latin) *Ibid.,* I, 134-35.

(D) MEMORANDUM OF PARLIAMENT (1306)

Memorandum that, after the lord king had recently ordered that Edward, his first-born son, should be decorated with the belt of knighthood at the feast of Pentecost in the thirty-fourth year of his reign, mandates were issued for the archbishops, bishops, abbots, priors, earls, barons, and other magnates to come before the lord king and his council at Westminster on the morrow of Holy Trinity next following, in order to deliberate and ordain with regard to giving the

---

[7] Commissioned by the mayor and community of London in a preceding writ. Similar groups of deputies are named from each of the other boroughs.

king an aid for the knighting aforesaid and in order to consent to
those matters which should further be ordained in that connection, or
for them then and there to send procurators or attorneys with sufficient instructions to carry out the aforesaid matters in their place;
also each of the sheriffs of England was commanded to cause two
knights from his county to come to the said place at the said time,
and from each city of his bailiwick two citizens and from each borough of the same bailiwick two burgesses or one, etc., in order to
deliberate, ordain, and consent as aforesaid. [Accordingly] there
came in person before the king and his council at Westminster on that
day[8] . . . ; also through procurators and attorneys[9] . . . ; and there
came likewise two knights from each county of the same kingdom, two
citizens from each city, and two burgesses from each borough, elected
by the communities of the same counties, cities, and boroughs in the
place of the same communities, to deliberate, ordain, and consent as
aforesaid. And when all the aforesaid persons had assembled before
the aforesaid council of the king, and it had been explained to them
by the same council on behalf of the king that by right of the royal
crown aid should be given the lord king on the occasion aforesaid,
and besides that the lord king had incurred multifarious expenses and
many other obligations toward suppressing the rebellion and malice of
Robert Bruce, traitor to the same lord king, and of his adherents
in the parts of Scotland, who were then presuming to make war
against the king in those parts; the same prelates, earls, barons, and
other magnates, as well as the knights of the shires, having discussed
the matter with deliberation, and considering that aid was owed as
aforesaid and that the king had incurred many obligations on account
of the aforesaid war, at length unanimously granted to the lord king
on behalf of themselves and the whole community of the land a thirtieth of all their movable temporal goods which they should happen to
possess on Michaelmas next following, to be taken as a competent
aid to the lord king for the knighting of his aforesaid son and also as
an aid toward the expenditures that should be made in connection
with the aforesaid war. This grant, however, [was made] on condition that it should in no way be held to their own prejudice or to that
of their successors or heirs in future times, and that it should never
be taken as a precedent in a case of this kind; also that in assessing the
aforesaid goods all should be excepted which had been excepted in
assessing the fifteenth granted by the community of the kingdom to
the lord king in the eighteenth year of his reign for exiling the Jews.
Moreover, the citizens and burgesses of the cities and boroughs aforesaid and others of the king's demesnes, being assembled and holding
a discussion on the said matters, in consideration of the obligations
incurred by the lord king as aforesaid, unanimously granted the lord

---

[8] Twenty persons, including the warden of the Cinque Ports "together with certain barons of the same ports."

[9] Twenty-seven named persons "and many other prelates, magnates, and nobles of the realm."

king for the reasons aforesaid the twentieth of their movable goods, to be taken as aforesaid.

(Latin) Pasquet, *Origins of the House of Commons*, pp. 234 f.

52. EDWARD I: STATUTES AND ORDINANCES[1]

(A) STATUTE OF GLOUCESTER (1278)

In the year of grace 1278, the sixth of the reign of King Edward, son of King Henry, at Gloucester in the month of August, the same king, having summoned the more discreet men of his kingdom, both greater and lesser, has made provision for the betterment of his kingdom and the fuller administration of justice, as is demanded by the kingly office. . . .

The sheriffs shall have it commonly proclaimed throughout their bailiwicks—that is to say, in cities, boroughs, trading towns, and elsewhere—that all those who claim to have any franchises by charters of the king's predecessors, kings of England, or by other title, shall come before the king or before the itinerant justices on a certain day and at a certain place to show what sort of franchises they claim to have, and by what warrant[2] [they hold them]. . . . And if those who claim to have such franchises do not come on the day aforesaid, those franchises shall then be taken into the king's hand by the local sheriff in the name of distress; so that they shall not enjoy such franchises until they come to receive justice. . . .

(French) *Statutes of the Realm*, I, 45 f.

(B) STATUTE OF MORTMAIN (1279)

The king to his justices of the bench, greeting. Whereas it was formerly enacted[3] that men of religion should not enter upon the fiefs of any persons without the consent and licence of the principal lords from whom those fiefs were immediately held; and whereas since then men of religion have nevertheless entered upon the fiefs of others as well as their own—by appropriating them, buying them, and sometimes by receiving them through gifts of other men—whereby the services which are owed from fiefs of this sort, and which were originally established for the defence of the kingdom, are wrongfully withheld and the principal lords [are caused to] lose their escheats: [therefore] we, seeking in this connection to provide

---

[1] *Statutum* had not as yet acquired the technical meaning of a legislative enactment in full parliament, as distinguished from an ordinance in council. The word was still vague, being generally applied to especially formal statements of law; see Holdsworth, *History of English Law*, II, 172 f., 244 f.; and cf. the examples cited below, no. 62.

[2] *Quo warranto* here and in the writ employed for legal proceedings of this sort. See especially H. M. Cam, *The Hundred and the Hundred Rolls*, ch. xiv; in which work the student will also find a full account of the inquests that led up to the formulation of this statute—e.g., the Articles of 1274, pp. 248 f.

[3] In the reissue of Magna Carta (above, p. 123, n. 45), somewhat extended by the Provisions of Westminster.

a suitable remedy for the good of the kingdom, by the counsel of the prelates, earls, and other faithful men of our kingdom who are members of our council, have enacted, established, and ordained that no man of religion or any other whatsoever shall buy or sell lands or tenements, or under colour of donation, lease, or other title of any sort shall receive them from any one, or presume artfully and craftily to appropriate them in any way whatsoever, whereby land and tenements of this sort may somehow come into mortmain[4]—under pain of forfeiting the same [lands or tenements]. . . . And so we command you to have the aforesaid statute read in your presence and henceforth strictly held and observed.

By witness of the king, at Westminster, November 25, in the seventh year of our reign.

(Latin) Stubbs, *Select Charters*, pp. 451 f.

(C) ORDINANCE FOR THE HOUSEHOLD (1279)

. . . It is ordained and commanded that the stewards, or one [of them] if both cannot be [there] together, with the treasurer,[5] or the comptroller if the treasurer cannot be [there], one of the marshals of the hall, and the clerks and serjeants of the offices[6] shall be present each night for [drawing up] the account of the household. And there, by the witness of the ushers of the hall, the servings of food in the hall (*mes de la sale*) are to be checked; and according to the number of the servings, the issues from the pantry, butlery, and kitchen are to be checked. And if there is irregularity, let it be corrected and the serjeants be reproved. Each night on the margin of the household roll is to be written the [amount of] wine dispensed during the day; so that, by the testimony of this roll which bears the record of the household, we may two or three times a year audit the account of the tuns of wine [dispensed]. Next the wages of the serjeants, squires, and grooms are to be there examined, as has been accustomed. And if at the account any wrongdoing is presented which is not so bad as to require being brought to the king's attention, let it be punished there at the discretion of the stewards and the treasurer—by the withholding of wages or in some other way according to what they may think best—so that the lord [king] shall not be bothered with affairs that can be settled by those [officials].

The treasurer, having called to him one of the stewards, or both of them, shall once or twice in every year audit the account of the chamberlain of wines; so that he may clearly know how many pieces come from each port and from each ship, and the names of the persons from whom the wines have been taken, parcel by parcel, and

---

[4] Literally, "dead hand"—permanent possession by a church or other corporation.

[5] Of the wardrobe, on which see Tout, *Chapters in Mediaeval Administrative History*, II, 27 f. More detailed information concerning most of the officials mentioned here will be found in the Household Ordinance of 1318, no. 57.

[6] *Mesters* (i.e., *métiers*), such as the pantry, butlery, kitchen, etc.

52. STATUTES AND ORDINANCES

how much is through purchase and how much through prise.[7] And this account is to be audited and checked by the treasurer and one of the stewards in such fashion that the treasurer can present a summary of it in his account at the feast of St. Edmund the King, when he renders his account.

In the same way the treasurer shall draw up the account of the great wardrobe.[8] . . . And it is to be noted that the treasurer shall henceforth have all articles for the great wardrobe bought at three fairs a year by a certain man, who shall be keeper of the great wardrobe and shall go to fairs to make the purchases; and he shall be put on oath to the king for this particular office. And the usher of the wardrobe shall be comptroller for him, going to fairs with him to view his purchases and at the account witnessing liveries [made by him]. . . . And the aforesaid keeper shall not purchase anything or deliver anything to anybody without the special command of the treasurer, and this in the presence of the comptroller. . . .

The usher of the wardrobe should each day have the wax and candle-wicks weighed—what is to be made [into candles] and what is to be kept. And each night [he should] weigh what is given out in livery and on the morrow reweigh what is left; so that through such weights he may know what has been dispensed each night, and the sum of it all at the end of the year. . . . And the chandler shall have nothing in his charge except what is to be dispensed at night, as delivered to him by the usher.

And whereas it is rightful that the household of Madame [the queen] should be regulated according to the ordinance of the king's household, it is ordered that the steward of Madame, or the man who is in charge of her household, shall each night be present at the account for the king's household, together with the pantler, the butler, the chief cook, and the marshal of her chamber. . . .

Furthermore, it is ordained that the marshals, or one of them, shall make the circuit of the household each month of the year, or more often if they see fit, to clear it of rascally men and women, and of horses belonging to them, so that they shall take no hay, or oats, or wages. And [the marshals] shall do the same for the household of Madame. And the marshals of the hall and the ushers shall also see to it that the hall is well cleared of strange people and of rascals who should not eat [there], and that the hall is served well and for the common good (*comunaument*) and that no knight has more than one squire eating in the hall.

The evening livery of wine and candles shall all be made by the king's men, as well for the household of Madame as elsewhere. And the treasurer and the stewards shall see to it that no liveries are made outside except in a proper place, neither of bread nor of wine nor of candles; and each night they shall examine the liveries for the house-

---

[7] See above, p. 166, n. 6.
[8] "So-called not because of its importance, but because it dealt with bulky commodities": Tout, *Place of Edward II in English History*, p. 71.

hold of Madame as well as for other places and for the king's household.

Furthermore, it is ordained that no one shall sleep in the wardrobe except the treasurer; Sire Thomas Gunneys [the comptroller];[9] Master William of Louth, the treasurer's clerk; Master Simon, the surgeon; Orlandino,[10] when he comes to court; William of Blyborough and Sire Stephen of St. George [clerks of the wardrobe]; John Rede, chief usher of the wardrobe, and a footman under him—no others.

And it is ordained that no clerk who holds a benefice of the king shall henceforth receive wages from the king. And it is ordained that no one shall eat in the wardrobe except the under-usher; and the chamberlain, the treasurer, and all the other chamberlains [shall eat] in the hall unless they are lodged apart from the court.

With regard to the king's carriage [service], it is provided that for the wardrobe there shall be three long carts; for the pantry a long cart and a short one, which is to carry the demeine flour and the mills of the saucery;[11] for the butlery a long cart and a short one; for the kitchen a long cart and two short ones.

Twenty men are chosen as serjeants-at-arms . . . , and each is to receive 3½m. a year for robes. . . . Besides, it is ordained that each squire shall receive 10s. a year for robes, and each serving man (*valet de mester*) 1m. And each groom who receives 2d. a day as wages is to have 10s. for robes; and each groom who receives 1½d. a day, and all the others who ought to have robes, are to have ½m. . . .[12]

(French) Tout, *Mediaeval Administrative History*, II, 158 f.

(D) STATUTE OF MERCHANTS (1283)

Whereas merchants heretofore, on lending their goods to various people, have incurred poverty owing to the fact that no suitable law was provided whereby they could speedily recover their debt on the day set for payment; and whereas, on this account, many merchants have ceased coming into this land with their merchandise, to the damage of the merchants and of the whole kingdom: [therefore] the king, by himself and his council, has ordained and established[13] that the merchant who wishes to make sure of his debt shall cause his

---

[9] As appears from other entries in the record.

[10] Of Lucca, the king's banker.

[11] Demeine flour was that of superior quality for the king's use; cf. above, p. 66, n. 3. On the saucery see below, p. 204.

[12] Preceding the ordinance as printed is a memorandum of the wages and liveries enjoyed by the other officials, listed by name. The steward, the marshal, the surgeon, the chaplain, and the chiefs of the wardrobe received 8m. a year for robes, together with various fees, unless they had received lands or benefices. Subordinates usually received 3m. for robes, and wages of 7d. a day.

[13] Despite the phrasing of the act, it was actually drawn up in the assembly of burgesses first summoned to Shrewsbury (above, p. 157) and then transferred to Acton Burnell.

debtor to come before the mayor of London or York or Bristol—[that is to say,] before the mayor and a clerk whom the king shall depute for that purpose—to acknowledge the debt and the day of payment; and the acknowledgment shall be enrolled by the hand of the aforesaid clerk so that it may be known. Moreover, the aforesaid clerk shall with his own hand write out a record of the obligation, to which shall be attached the seal of the debtor, together with the king's seal provided for that purpose, which seal shall remain in the custody of the mayor and the clerk aforesaid. And if the debtor does not pay on the day set for him, let the creditor come to the mayor and the clerk with the record of the obligation; and if it is found by the roll and the record that the debt was acknowledged and that the set day has passed, the mayor shall at once, by view of worthy men, have movables of the debtor sold to the amount of the debt. . . .[14] And to meet the cost of the aforesaid clerk, the king shall take a penny from every pound [of the debt]. This ordinance and establishment the king wishes henceforth to be observed throughout his entire kingdom of England by all persons who shall freely choose to make such acknowledgments, excepting Jews, to whom this establishment does not apply. . . .

Given at Acton Burnell, October 12, in the eleventh year of our reign.

(French) *Statutes of the Realm*, I, 53 f.

(E) STATUTE OF WINCHESTER (1285)

Whereas every day robbery, homicide, and arson are committed more frequently than used to be the case, and felonies escape presentment by the oaths of jurors who would see the felonies committed on strangers pass unpunished rather than accuse the offenders, many of whom are persons of the same country[15] . . . : [therefore] our lord the king, in order to abate the power of felons, has established a penalty in such cases; so that henceforth, through fear of the penalty rather than of the oath, no one will be spared and no felony will be concealed. . . .

Accordingly, inquests shall be held when necessary in a vill by him who is lord of the vill, and afterwards in hundreds, franchises, and counties—sometimes in two, three, or four counties, in cases where felonies are committed on the borders of counties—so that the offenders may be brought to justice. And if the country will not answer for criminals in this way, the penalty shall be such that each country—that is to say, the people living in the country—shall be responsible for the robberies committed and the damages [thus incurred]. . . .

And for better assuring the peace, the king has commanded that

---

[14] The statute includes detailed provisions for the attachment of property in towns other than those mentioned, for imprisonment of debtors with insufficient chattels, and the like.

[15] *Pays* (Latin, *patria*)—the neighbourhood in which a person had his home.

in great towns which are walled the gates shall be closed from sunset to sunrise; and that no man shall be lodged in the suburbs, or in the outskirts of the town, except in the daytime—nor even in the daytime unless his host will be responsible for him. And the bailiffs of towns each week, or at least every fortnight, shall make investigation concerning men lodged in the suburbs or in the outskirts of the towns; and if they find anybody harbouring or otherwise lodging persons suspected of being in any respect violators of the peace, the bailiffs shall have justice done in the matter. And the king has commanded that henceforth all watches shall be kept according to the ancient custom. . . .[16]

Furthermore, it is commanded that highways from one trading town to another shall be enlarged wherever there are woods, hedges, or ditches; so that there shall be neither ditches, underbrush, nor bushes for two hundred feet on the one side and two hundred feet on the other, where men can hide near the road with evil intent; yet so that this statute shall not apply to oaks or to any great trees, so long as they are cleared underneath. . . .

Moreover, it is commanded that every man shall have in his house arms for keeping the peace according to the ancient assize. . . .

Given at Winchester, October 8, in the thirteenth year of the king's reign.

(French) Stubbs, *Select Charters*, pp. 464 f.

(F) Statute of Quia Emptores (1290)

Whereas the buyers of lands and tenements belonging to the fiefs of magnates and other men have in times past frequently entered upon their fiefs to the prejudice of the same [lords], because the freeholders of the said magnates and other men have sold their lands and tenements to such purchasers to be held in fee by themselves and their heirs of the feoffors and not of the principal lords of the fiefs, whereby those same principal lords have often lost the escheats, marriages, and wardships of lands and tenements belonging to their fiefs; and whereas this has seemed very hard and burdensome to those magnates and other lords, being in such cases manifest disinheritance: [therefore] the lord king in his parliament at Westminister [held] after Easter in the eighteenth year of his reign. . . , at the suggestion of the magnates of his realm,[17] has granted, provided, and established that henceforth every freeman shall be permitted to sell his land or tenement, or a part of it, at pleasure; yet so that the feoffee shall hold that land or tenement of the same principal lord [of whom the feoffor held] and by the same services and customs by which the feoffor earlier held. . . .

(Latin) *Ibid.*, p. 473.

---

[16] What is omitted here and in the second paragraph below is largely a repetition of Henry III's ordinance (no. 46h).

[17] The parliament was attended only by prelates and lay barons.

52. STATUTES AND ORDINANCES

(G) ORDINANCE CONCERNING JUDICIAL CIRCUITS (1293)

Whereas the lord king, in his recent statutes at Westminster[18] commanded that in each county certain justices, and no others, should be commissioned for the holding of assizes, juries, and certifications[19] at particular times in those counties; and whereas the justices of the two benches,[20] as well as the itinerant justices assigned to carry out the aforesaid [commissions] for limited periods, have often, when they were not on eyre, been hindered, both by their offices and by precepts of the lord king directed to them, from coming to the [appointed] places on the days announced by them; and whereas, on account of their absence, justice has long been withheld from many persons and misdeeds have gone unpunished: [therefore] the lord king, desirous that, in so far as he can [provide it], speedy justice shall be rendered to every one in his kingdom for the wrongs done to that person, commands that henceforth eight circumspect and discreet justices shall be commissioned to hold assizes, juries, and certifications throughout the whole kingdom of England—namely, two in the counties of York, Northumberland, Westmorland, Cumberland, Lancaster, Nottingham, and Derby; two in the counties of Lincoln, Leicester, Warwick, Stafford, Shropshire, Northampton, Rutland, Gloucester, Hereford, and Worcester; two in the counties of Cornwall, Devon, Somerset, Dorset, Wiltshire, Hampshire, Oxford, Berkshire, Sussex, and Surrey; and two in the counties of Kent, Essex, Hertford, Norfolk, Suffolk, Cambridge, Huntingdon, Bedford, and Buckingham. And the assizes, juries, and recognitions of Middlesex shall be held before the justices of the bench. . . .

(Latin) *Statutes of the Realm*, I, 112.

(H) ARTICLES OF 1300[21]

. . . Moreover, no common pleas shall henceforth be held in the exchequer, contrary to the form of the Great Charter. On the other hand, the king wills that the chancery and the justices of his bench shall follow him; so that he may always have near him certain men expert in the law, who, whenever the need arises, will know how rightfully to dispatch all such business as may come before the court. Henceforth no writ touching the common law shall be issued under the small seal.[22]

(French) *Ibid.*, I, 138 f.

---

[18] The reference is to art. 30 of the lengthy enactment known as the Second Statute of Westminster (1285). The article in question provided that for each county two justices should be commissioned to hold assizes three times a year. See Stubbs, *Const. Hist.*, II, 284.
[19] Certification was a process by which a vague or insufficient verdict was brought before a court for examination.
[20] Cf. 54E.
[21] Issued as an explanatory supplement to the Confirmation of the Charters (no. 51A).
[22] Cf. no. 54G, the last excerpt.

53. ROYAL COUNCILLORS' OATHS OF OFFICE

(A) OATH OF 1257

They have sworn in the first place to provide faithful counsel to the lord king as often as they shall perceive it to be useful. Item, they will reveal the counsel of the lord king to no one to whom it ought not to be revealed, whereby they believe harm might ensue. Item, they will consent to the alienation of none of those things which belong to the ancient demesne of the crown. Item, they will bring it about that justice is administered to all, both rich and poor, both great and small, according to the rightful laws and customs of the kingdom. Item, they will freely permit, with regard to themselves, their friends, and their relatives, that justice shall be provided to every one seeking it. Nor through them shall the administration of justice be impeded for prayer or price, for favour or spite; but they will in good faith strive to have the great and the small judged alike, according to the law and custom of the kingdom. Nor will they, either by word or by deed, support or defend evil-doers in their wrongs. Item, from no one whom they know to have business in the court of the king, or of his bailiffs, will they accept, either of themselves or through others, any gift or service on an occasion of this sort, in any way or by any means whatsoever. Item, should any one in the council discover for certain, or hear from reliable sources, that another councillor has received any reward or gift other than something to eat or drink,[1] he will bring it to the public attention of the whole council. And if [such councillor] is convicted of this [offence], he shall be forever excluded from the council and he shall lose his lands and his rents, or the income from his possessions, for one year. And if he has no such income, he shall be punished according to the decision of the councillors.

(Latin) Baldwin, *The King's Council*, pp. 346 f.

(B) OATH OF 1307

He who is to be sworn of the king's council shall be charged with regard to the particulars hereinunder written; and if he is to be a justice, he shall be charged [especially] with regard to the last particular:—

That well and loyally, according to your knowledge and ability, you will counsel the king. That well and loyally you will keep his counsel; and that you will not accuse another [on account] of anything that he may say in the council. And that, to the best of your ability, you will give and devote your care, aid, and counsel to keep and maintain, to safeguard and restore, the rights of the king and of the crown, in so far as you can without committing wrong. And that, whenever you know things of the crown and rights of the king to be concealed, wrongfully alienated, or withheld, you will bring it to the king's knowledge. And that, to the best of your ability and in loyal fashion, you will support the crown. And that you will take

---

[1] Cf. no. 47B, p. 145.

no part in court or council where the king deprives himself of something belonging to the crown, unless it is an action that you should approve. And that for no one, through love or hate, for good will or ill will, you will abstain from having right and justice done to every man, of whatsoever estate or condition, according to your knowledge and ability. And that you will take nothing from any one for doing wrong or delaying justice. And that, in judging or enforcing right there where you may be assigned, you will spare no one on account of grandeur, poverty, or wealth, so that justice shall not be done. And that, if you have formed an alliance through lordship or otherwise, so that you cannot do these things without breaking such alliance, you will tell the king or have him informed of it. And that henceforth you will make no alliance by oath with any one without the king's permission. And that you will take no gift from any one on account of a plea or anything else that is to be determined before you, unless it is food and drink for the day.

(French) *Statutes of the Realm*, I, 248.

54. JUDICIAL RECORDS (1220-83)

(A) EXCERPTS FROM THE CURIA REGIS ROLL OF 122?

Hugh Hop-over-Humber appeals Thomas of Dean for [the following offense:] that on St. Giles's day, between the first and third hours, in the second year of the king's reign, while he, together with his cousin William of Leigh, was in the park of Cuckfield belonging to the earl de Warenne, for the purpose of guarding that park, the said Thomas came with a band [of accomplices], a multitude of men armed with bows and arrows, and assaulted them, aiming an arrow at the said William and hitting him in the leg, so that within nine days he died of the wound. And that [Thomas] did this wickedly and feloniously and in [violation of] the lord king's peace, [Hugh], as one who was present and saw it, offers to prove by his body, as the court shall decide. He also says that pursuit was made according to the law of the land and that hue was raised; that twelve jurors indicted [Thomas] on account of that death[2] before the itinerant justices on their last visit to these parts; and that the said William, while he was still alive after being wounded, stated that the said Thomas had struck him as aforesaid, and so blamed [Thomas] for his death.

And Thomas appears and denies the entire charge as an ordained clerk. And thereupon Robert of Dean, his brother, appears and presents letters close from the bishop of Chichester, in which it is set forth that the said Thomas has sufficiently proved before him by witnesses, etc., that the said Thomas was in due season promoted to the order of acolyte by Selfrid, one time bishop of Chichester, and that [the bishop] accordingly claims him as a clerk, so that justice may be

---
[1] On the nature of these records see Maitland's introduction; cf. immediately below, no. 54E, F.
[2] See no. 31, art. 1.

administered with respect to him for all who may complain in the ecclesiastical court. Thomas is committed to R[alph], bishop of Chichester, who shall hold him for justice because he is a clerk. And it should be known that the lord [archbishop] of Canterbury, who earlier took the said Thomas into custody, is quit thereof.

William Smallwood[3] appeals Hugh the Large of Walthamstow for having received him together with two horses which he had [taken] from the chamberlain of Baldwin de Guisnes, whom he had slain; so that the said Hugh kept those two horses in his chamber for eight days, and for thus keeping them he received 6s., and a certain woman at the inn [received] 6d. for carrying water to the horses in order that they might not be seen. And that the same [Hugh] knew they were stolen property and received them as stated he offers to prove by his body. And Hugh denies the entire charge against him, [submitting to judgment] as the court shall decide; and he puts himself on the country[4] that he is held to be a trustworthy man. He is committed to the vill of Walthamstow, to be produced on summons.

The same [William] also appeals Nicholas of Trumpington as a receiver. . . . He is committed to the vill of Cheshunt, etc. . . .

The same [William] also appeals Robert Woodcock and William his son as receivers. . . . Let the sheriff take pledges for them.

The same [William] also appeals William, son of Henry Ware, as a receiver, but he is so old that he can hardly move; [evidently] the charge against him is trumped up. And so the matter should be discussed. The jurors say that they know nothing [bad] of him; and so let him go quit because he is old.

The same [William] also appeals John and Adam, sons of the priest, for being his associates and for homicide: namely, that they along with him slew a man of Alfred Gernon, scalding him in the house of Robert Woodcock and taking from him property to the value of £4 sterling. Likewise they killed another man in the same house and a third between Writtle and Chelmsford. Likewise Adam together with him broke into the house of Michael Smallwood, his brother, and robbed it, so that the said Adam [thence] received a blue cloak with a hood of doe-skin worth half a mark. And this he offers to prove by his body, and he takes as his first opponent Adam. And they appear and deny the entire charge word by word, and they put themselves on the country. And the sheriff says that he held an inquest and that, according to the inquest, they are of ill fame. The lawful knights of the county give the same testimony. So the combat is to proceed, in the first place against Adam, whom [William] appeals

---

[3] William, a confessed felon, has turned approver. That is to say, he now has to appeal and vanquish a certain number of persons—often five—in order to secure a pardon. In the present case, however, he is himself vanquished in his first duel. See F. C. Hamil, in *Speculum*, XI, 238 f.

[4] The ordinary phrase for submitting to jury trial, on the beginnings of which in criminal cases see Pollock and Maitland, II, 648 f.

54. JUDICIAL RECORDS

for the death of the aforesaid men and for the robbery of his brother's house and [the theft of] the aforesaid cloak worth 7s., and who denies the entire charge [offering defense] by his body. . . . William Smallwood is vanquished and hanged; Adam and John are dismissed under pledge. . . .

Alice, wife of William Black, confesses that she was present with her husband at the slaying of three men and one woman at Barnet. And so let her be burned. . . .

Thomas of Lyminge, who was captured together with robbers, at St. Albans, appears and says that he has no lord, that he is not in frankpledge, and that he has no pledge [of any kind]. Furthermore, it is testified by the steward of the abbot of St. Albans and by [other] good men that he confessed the robbery in the abbot's court. Furthermore, he stated in the [court of the] bench that he knew no man who was so big a thief as Robert of Bermondsey, the archbishop's steward, and afterwards he withdrew the charge. And since he has nothing in his favour and refuses to put himself on the country, it is decided that he is to be hanged.

(Latin) Maitland, *Select Pleas of the Crown*, pp. 120-34.

(B) Excerpts from Assize Rolls of 1221

Agnes, who was the wife of Robert Wood, appeals Thomas, son of Hubert, for the death of her husband Robert. And because the same [Agnes] has a [second] husband named Robert de Verdun who makes no appeal, she has no power of appealing; so the truth is to be sought by the country. And Thomas appears and denies responsibility for the death, but does not wish to put himself on the country. And the twelve jurors say that he is guilty of that death, and twenty-four knights chosen for this purpose, other than the aforesaid twelve, say the same; and so let him be hanged. The chattels of Thomas [amount to] 34s. 6d., for which the sheriff is answerable.

And the jurors testify that the said Thomas, after that deed, continued to go back and forth from his house to cultivate his land; and [yet] he was not arrested, nor was his land taken into the king's hands until the day before the arrival of the justices. So the sheriff [is to be brought] to judgment. And [Thomas] was a villein and for that reason his land was not taken.[5] And the township[6] of Spernal does not appear; therefore it is in mercy for default, and is to appear tomorrow.

The same Agnes appealed as accessories Henry, son of Hubert; Michael, reeve of Spernal; Simon, the priest's son; Patecoc, son of Simon of Spernal; and Robert of Shortenhall. And none of them appears; and [yet] she sued at a number of county courts after the death of her husband, and [the accused men] were neither attached nor outlawed. So the county [is to be brought] to judgment.

[5] An addition to the record, to explain the sheriff's conduct.
[6] *Villata* meaning the people of the vill or their legal representatives.

Afterwards the township of Spernal appears and confesses that all the aforesaid men were residents in their vill after the death of Robert and were not arrested. So [the township is] in mercy. And all those appealed as accessories have fled, and they were in the frankpledge of the township of Spernal. So [the township is] in mercy. The chattels of Henry [amount to] nothing. The chattels of Michael [amount to] 14s., for which the sheriff is answerable. . . .

Simon of Coughton, on account of drunkenness, fell dead from his horse in the vill of Alcester. And Simon, his son, who was with him, does not appear, nor was he attached; he is not suspected. The township of Alcester confesses that they did not present the death [of Simon] at the county [court] or to the coroners. So the township is in mercy. No one is suspected. Judgment—misadventure. The township of Coughton confesses that the body was carried into their vill and that it was buried without the view of the serjeant [of the hundred] or of the coroners, and that they made no presentment at the county [court]. So [the township is] in mercy. The value of the horse is 1m., for which the sheriff is answerable. . . .

Richard Goky, accused of the death of Henry Lightfoot who was slain at Ling, appears and denies the entire charge and puts himself on the country. And the townships of North Curry, Bridgewater, Creech, and Newton, also the twelve jurors, say on oath that they suspect of that death no one but the same Richard, and they affirm that he slew [Henry]. And so let him be hanged. Inquiry is to be made as to his chattels. And the township of Ling and the twelve jurors in the first place presented a certain Robert Young as having killed [Henry]. And afterwards they appear and confess that they did so on the instance of Roger Baryl, serjeant of the hundred. And so [he is to be put in] custody, and the twelve jurors and the township of Ling are in mercy for their false presentment. The amercement of the jurors is pardoned.

(Latin) Ibid., 99-117.

(C) EXCERPTS FROM EXCHEQUER PLEA ROLLS OF 1236-37

An assize, summoned and attached to make recognition on oath whether Richard of Hinton holds three-fourths of a knight's fee with appurtenances in Eastbury of the king in chief or of Ralph le Moyne, appears before the barons of the exchequer on the morrow of St. Hilary: namely. . . .[7] They declare on oath that the said Richard of Hinton holds the said three-fourths of a knight's fee with appurtenances in Eastbury of Ralph le Moyne in chief; that the said Richard and his ancestors always rendered to the same Ralph and his ancestors the service owed from this [fief]; and that the said Ralph holds that tenement of the lord king. And so it is decided that the said Richard is to be quit of the scutage exacted from him for the said tenement, and that the same Richard shall henceforth render

---

[7] The names of the twelve jurors are omitted.

service for the said tenement to Ralph le Moyne and his heirs as has been accustomed. . . .

Robert Musard has offered himself against Henry of the exchequer with respect to a plea of 6m. for the scutage of Poitou, as is contained in the writ. Henry, having been summoned and attached a number of times, has appeared and has acknowledged that he received from the aforesaid Robert 6m. for the aforesaid scutage of Poitou; and he states that he acquitted the said Robert for 40s. out of the 6m. aforesaid in the county of Nottingham when he was sheriff of Berkshire. And the barons have had inspection made of the account rolls of that county for the fifteenth and sixteenth years, during which the said Henry was sheriff of Berkshire; and from the rolls they have found that nothing was paid by the said Henry on behalf of the aforesaid Robert in the county of Nottingham for the aforesaid scutage, as he has alleged. . . .[8] Finally, however, they have come to an agreement by permission of the barons: to the effect that the same Henry will acquit Robert of the said scutage and will give him 4m. for his trouble and expense. And because the same H[enry] had rendered account in full and had pledged his faith to having rendered an honest account, when [actually] he had not fully accounted for the said scutage, because of his concealment, he is delivered to the marshal as a prisoner. Afterwards he is liberated from prison by the bishop of Carlisle. And the same Henry is in mercy, but is pardoned by the barons. . . .

Hubert of Wick and Walter of Hales, executors of the will of Richard of Brome . . . have appeared and declared that they have in deposit at Langley about 25m. from the goods of the said Richard, and they have undertaken to pay that sum at the exchequer within three weeks after Easter toward satisfaction of the debt that the same Richard owed the lord king. Moreover, they have declared that William Bernehouse, who lives in the county of Suffolk, owed the said Richard 20m.; that Nicholas Crawe, who lives in Norfolk, owed the same Richard 20s.; [and that] Ralph of Selton [owed him] four oxen worth 40s. Besides, as they say, the men of Earl R[oger] Bigot in Ditchling carried off the crop from five acres of corn belonging to the said Richard, worth 1m. And the sheriff is ordered to distrain the said debtors for the said debts to the king's use. . . . Afterwards the said executors paid £17. 4s. of the said debt, and they have declared that they have nothing more of his goods. And so they are acquitted, and the lord king is to recover the remainder of the said debt from the heir of the said Richard of Brome.

(Latin) Jenkinson and Formoy, *Select Cases in the Exchequer*, pp. 7-13.

(D) EXCERPTS FROM CORONERS' ROLLS OF 1266-67

Richard of Eltisley of the parish of Eaton came to the county

---

[8] Henry says he paid the rest of the money into the exchequer and a mistake was made in the tallies, but his explanation is found to be worthless.

[court] of Bedford on Monday next after Epiphany in the fiftieth year of King Henry [III] and appealed William Moring of Staplehoe for [the following offense:] that before the hour of vespers on Sunday next after the Lord's Nativity he came into the house of the said Richard and assaulted the said Richard wickedly, feloniously, and against the peace of the lord king by premeditated assault, striking him on the right shoulder with a willow stick and so knocking him to the ground; afterwards, falling upon the said Richard, [William] seized with his right hand [Richard's] finger—the one called index, next the thumb—and bit it, so that [Richard] believes himself to be maimed. This he offers reasonably to demonstrate and prove as a maimed man can and should, according to the decision of the lord king's court. The said Richard finds pledges for prosecution: [namely,] Henry of Basing from Staplehoe and John Poignant from the same [vill].

Item, at the county [court] of Bedford, on Monday next after the Purification of the Blessed Mary, Richard appears and sues, and the said William, having been called for the first time, does not appear. Item, at the county [court] of Bedford, on Monday next after the feast of St. Matthew the Apostle in the fiftieth year, the aforesaid Richard appears and sues, and William Moring, having been called for the second time, does not appear. Item, at the county [court] of Bedford, on Monday next after the Annunciation of the Blessed Mary in the aforesaid year, Richard appears and sues, and William Moring, being present, denies the entire charge and finds pledges: [namely,] Reginald, son of Walter of Honeydon, and William Allen of Staplehoe. . . .

It happened about bedtime on Sunday next before the feast of St. Bartholomew in the fiftieth year that Henry Colburn of Barford went out of his house in Barford to drink a tankard of beer and did not return that night; but early the next morning Agnes Colburn, his mother, looked for him and found the said Henry dead. And he was wounded in the body about the heart and in the belly with seven knife-wounds, and in the head with four wounds apparently made with a pick-axe, and also in the throat and the chin and the head as far as the brain. The aforesaid Agnes at once raised the hue and pursuit was made. And she finds pledges: [namely,] Humphrey Quarrel and Thomas Quarrel of the same Barford.

Inquest was held before S[imon] Read, the coroner, by four neighbouring townships: Barford, Boxton, Wilden, and Renhold. And they say that Gilbert, son of Margaret, killed the said Henry as aforesaid. They also say that they have suspicion of Hugh Cointerel, Agnes Cointerel, Hugh, son of the same Agnes, and Alice Wrong, who have appeared in the full county [court] and are delivered to G. Read, the sheriff, [to be put] in jail. . . . Gilbert had no chattels. Englishry was presented by Richard, brother [of Henry], on the side of his father and mother; and by Maurice Plane, his uncle, on the side of his father.

54. JUDICIAL RECORDS

It happened in the vill of Wilden on Wednesday next before the feast of Simon and Jude in the fiftieth year that unknown malefactors came to the house of Jordan Hull of Wilden and broke into the said house while the said Jordan was absent. And the said malefactors wounded Agnes, wife of the said Jordan, and killed Emma, his eight-year-old daughter. Afterwards they carried off all the goods from the house. . . . Inquest was held before S[imon] Read, the coroner, by four neighbouring townships . . . , who said what has been reported, and that the malefactors were unknown. . . .

It happened at Eaton on Thursday next after the feast of the Apostles Peter and Paul in the fiftieth year that Reginald Stead of Eaton, reaper of John Francis, went into the meadows of Eaton to guard the meadow of his lord and, being taken with falling sickness, collapsed and died forthwith by misadventure. Alice, his wife, was the first to discover him, and she finds pledges. . . . Inquest was held before S[imon] Read, the coroner, by four neighbouring townships . . . , who say that he died by misadventure of the aforesaid disease, and they know nothing beyond that.

(Latin) Gross, *Select Cases from Coroners' Rolls*, pp. 2-6.

(E) MEMORANDUM OF JUDICIAL APPOINTMENTS (1278)
Justices of the bench for pleas of the king:

Ralph of Hengham, Chief [Justice], who is to receive annually in fee for maintaining himself in the king's service, at two terms, ... 60*m.*
Nicholas of Stapleton, at two terms, ... 50*m.*
Walter of Wimburn, at two terms, ... 40*m.*

Total 150*m.*

Justices of the bench at Westminster:[9]

Thomas of Weyland, Chief [Justice] .... 60*m.*
Walter of Helion .... 50*m.*
John of Lovetoft .... 50*m.*
Roger of Leicester .... 40*m.*
William of Brompton .... till now nothing

Total 200*m.*

Itinerant justices toward the north, namely, in the counties of
 Cumberland, Westmorland, and Northumberland:
The Abbot of Westminster, Chief [Justice][10]
John de Vaux
William of Saham .... 50*m.*
Roger Loveday .... 40*m.*

---
[9] This is the common bench; the court preceding is that of *coram rege*, or king's bench. Cf. no. 52G.
[10] The man heading the circuit, being a beneficed clergyman, receives no salary.

John of Metingham	40*m.*
Master Thomas of Sodington	40*m.*

Itinerant justices toward the south, namely, in the counties of Hertford and Kent:
The bishop of Worcester, Chief [Justice]

John of Reigate	60*m.*
Geoffrey of Leukenore	40*m.*
William of Norburgh	40*m.*
Walter of Hopton	40*m.*
Solomon of Rochester	40*m.*

The aforesaid justices were installed by the king himself and others of his council [at Gloucester]. . . .

(Latin) Palgrave, *Parliamentary Writs*, I, 382.

(F) Excerpts from the Coram Rege Rolls of 1281

Command was given to the mayor and sheriffs of London that they should send to the king here on this day the record and process of the suit recently held before them in their husting of London between Edmund Trentemars, plaintiff, and Master Thomas of Bread Street concerning a messuage with appurtenances in the suburb of London; which same record and process they sent to the following effect. . . . And Edmund, being asked why he had caused the aforesaid record to come here, says it is because the lord king granted by his Statute of Gloucester[11] that, if any one within the city of London vouches any foreigner to warranty, he shall, according to the Statute of Gloucester, sue against his warranty before the justices of the bench, etc. Whereupon the said Thomas Trentemars was adjourned until the next arrival of the itinerant justices at the Tower of London. And thereof he seeks remedy, etc. . . .

The abbot of Fécamp was summoned to answer to the lord king by what warrant he holds the manor of Steyning, which is ancient demesne of the crown of England, as is said, and concerning which William of Pembridge, who sues for the king,[12] says that the lord king Henry, father of the present lord king, was seised of the aforesaid manor, etc. . . . And the abbot now appears by his attorney and says that he holds the aforesaid manor by this warrant: that St. Edward [the Confessor], one time king, gave the aforesaid manor with its appurtenances to the abbot and monks of Fécamp, which same deed was confirmed by William [I], one time king of England, and a certain Henry, king of England. . . . When this charter had been read and understood, the attorney of the same abbot was told that in such connection he might go *sine die*, etc. . . .

The jury [in the suit] between Hugh le Despenser, plaintiff, and Roger le Bigot, earl of Norfolk and marshal of England, having been chosen by the consent of the parties, [comes to make recogni-

---

[11] No. 52A.
[12] That is to say, acting as king's attorney.

54. JUDICIAL RECORDS

tion] whether Alina le Despenser, who was wife of the aforesaid Roger, bore of the same Roger offspring since deceased that was heard to cry or raise its voice within four walls in the manor of Woking, or not; and if so, what kind of voice it raised, and whether that offspring was male or female, and in what house such child was born and in what church it was baptized, and when and at what time and in whose presence, and how long the same child lived, etc. . . .[13]

Command was given to the sheriff that he should cause to come here on this day the appeal which Wenthiliana, daughter of William le Prestre made in his county [court] against William d'Evreux for the death of Adam le Gouth, her husband, and also the appeal which Susan, daughter of Organ, made in the aforesaid county [court] against the aforesaid William for the death of her brother, John son of Organ, together with all appendant matters touching those appeals. . . .[14]

The lord king, by Walter of Wimbourne who sues for him, brings suit against Robert Banaster for the advowson of the church of Wigan with appurtenances. . . .[15]

Command was sent to John de Vaux and his associates, justices of the last eyre in the county of York, that under their seals they should send to the king the record and process of the suit brought before them on the aforesaid eyre by writ of right of the lord king between Peter de Mauley, plaintiff, and the abbot of Whitby, tenant, concerning the manors of Newholm, Stakesby, and Dunsley with their appurtenances. . . . Which same justices sent the record to the following effect. . . .[16]

Agnes Colle appeals Henry le Ternur and Gilbert of Grafham for the death of her son John. And she appeals them for this: that, while her aforesaid son was in the peace of the lord king on Saturday next after the feast of the Nativity of the Blessed Virgin in the eighth year of the present king's reign, at a place called Broneswellbrook between the vill of Offord Cluny and [that of] Offord Darcy, the aforesaid Henry le Ternur and Gilbert came with a certain Henry Nichol of Bedwin, and they held the aforesaid John by his hands and neck while the same Henry struck the aforesaid John with a Cologne sword [wounding him] to the brain, whereof he died. And that they wickedly and by felony aforethought committed the aforesaid felony on the aforesaid day in the aforesaid year she offers, etc. . . .[17]

(Latin) Sayles, *Select Cases in King's Bench*, pp. 74-91.

---

[13] The case did not go to the jury, for Roger surrendered Alina's lands to Hugh, her nearest heir. If she had borne Roger a living heir, he would have had a life estate.

[14] The cases were sent to the hundred court of Archenfield because of that district's ancient liberty.

[15] A jury of twelve awarded the right to Robert.

[16] A jury of twelve gave a verdict for Peter; the abbot was declared in mercy.

[17] The accused denied the charge and put themselves on the country. A day was set for trial.

(G) EXCERPTS FROM THE PARLIAMENT ROLL OF 1283[18]

Aymer de Peche, who is ill, beseeches the lord king graciously to command the escheator to return to him the seisin of the manor of Steeple, the custody of which belongs to him because Hugh son of Otto ended his days holding of the said Aymer by military service the aforesaid manor, with which he had been enfeoffed by the same Aymer, who held the aforesaid manor of the lord king in chief.

[Endorsed:] Let it be restored because [Hugh] held nothing of the king in chief.

The lord William Martin seeks a writ of the lord king to the treasurer and the barons of the exchequer [permitting him] to pay the debt that he owes the king by instalments of £10 a year.

Let him pay 50*m.* a year in two [instalments]. . . .

When our lord the king was at Bristol on the festival of Easter in the eighth year of his reign, the mayor and community [of the town] made to him devout supplication, asking that he regard their condition which, through default of confirmation of the liberties obtained by grant and confirmation from the lord king Henry, father of the present lord king, and from his other ancestors, had been greatly injured by the divers oppressions of justices, sheriffs, and bailiffs; and requesting that the lord king would confirm their charters of liberties aforesaid. And the lord king promised them that he would do so when he first confirmed any liberties. We beseech you, lord chancellor, that you apply your counsel to whatever may be done in this matter for the sake of the community aforesaid.

The king will respond in the next parliament. . . .

The prior of Hexham beseeches the lord king to grant him licence[19] to enter upon land to the value of £20 in North Milburn within the county of Northumberland, which is held of Robert de Stuteville and Eleanor his wife for the service of 6*d.* a year for all service, and concerning which the sheriff of Northumberland was commanded to make diligent investigation as to what damage the lord king would suffer if the said prior took possession of the said land in fee. And the sheriff, having carried out an investigation, made a return in which it was stated that the lord king would thereby suffer no damage, except only to the amount of 6*d.* per year. And when [the result of] this inquest had been seen by the chancellor, the prior was told that he should come to this parliament.

[Endorsed:] The king will not grant the favour asked in the petition.

Thomas de Torneye, who had been in Wales to perform the service that the lord Gilbert de Bulebeke owed to our lord the king in connection with his recent expedition into those parts, was taken, after

---

[18] On the nature of these enrolments see the editors' introduction to the volume cited below; also that of Maitland to his *Memoranda de Parliamento*.

[19] Cf. no. 52B.

returning from Wales, and held in the prison of Aylesbury in the county of Buckingham on suspicion of a robbery suffered by Master John de Saint-Omer, of which he is not guilty; and by letters under the king's privy seal in the possession of the sheriff, to the effect that he is not to be released, he is being held in that prison until the delivery of the same prison.[20] Wherefore he beseeches our lord the king that he may be brought under the common law and have a jury trial;[21] for in the prison he is at the point of death on account of the duress with which he is treated.

[Endorsed:] Let a writ be issued for the two men imprisoned at Aylesbury; it is not to be neglected on account of a mandate under the small seal. Let an inquest be made by the justices through a good [jury of the] country.

(French and Latin) Richardson and Sayles, *Rot. Parl. Anglie*, pp. 17-25.

(H) EXCERPTS FROM MANORIAL COURT ROLLS (1246-49)[22]
Pleas of the manors ... of Bec, Hokeday term, A.D. 1246:—

Bledlow [Buckinghamshire]. ... The court made presentment that Simon Combe has raised a certain fence on the lord's land. Therefore let it be pulled down. ... A day at the next court is given to Alice of Standen for producing her charter and her heir. ...

Tooting [Surrey]. ... The court made presentment that the following persons had encroached on the lord's land. ...[23] Therefore [they are] in mercy. Godwin [is] in mercy because he neglected to do what he was ordered on behalf of the lord. Fine 12d. Roger Reed [is] in mercy for non-payment of rent. Pledge: Jordan of Streatham. Fine 6d. ...

Ruislip [Middlesex]. ... The court makes presentment that Nicholas Breakspeare is not in tithing, and he holds land. Therefore let him be distrained. Breakers of the assize [of beer]. ... .[24] Roger son of Hamo gives 20s. to have seisin of the land that was his father's and to have an inquest by twelve [men] as to a certain croft held by Gilbert Bisuthe. Pledges: Gilbert Lamb, William son of John, and Robert King. ... Richard Maleville [offers to prove] at his law[25] as against the lord that he did not take attached property away from the lord's serjeants to the lord's damage and dishonour [amounting to] 20s. Pledges: Gilbert Bisuthe and Richard Hubert. Hugh Tree [is] in mercy for cattle of his taken in the lord's garden. Pledges: Walter of Hull and William Slipper. Fine 6d. Twelve jurors say that Hugh Cross has title to the bank and hedge over which there was a dispute between him and William White. Therefore let him hold

---
[20] By the itinerant justices.
[21] Literally "have his country (*pays*)"; see above, p. 178, n. 4.
[22] On the nature of these courts and their records, see the famous introduction by the editor, F. W. Maitland.
[23] Seven persons are named, with fines from 6d. to 2s.
[24] Thirteen persons are named, with a normal fine of 6d.
[25] That is to say, by compurgation; see above, p. 77, n. 3.

in peace, and let the said William be distrained for many trespasses. Later he fined for 12d. . . .

Pleas of the manors of Bec, Martinmas term, A.D. 1247:—

Weedon Beck [Northamptonshire]. . . . Elias Deynte resigned his land in full court and seisin of it was given to William Deynte, his son, who swore fealty and found pledges, named above, for his 5s. of relief. Later he paid it. The whole township gives 6m. for the abbot's tallage. . . . William Green and Guy Lawman have gallon measures that are too small. John Mercer will give three hens yearly at the feast of St. Martin to have the lord's patronage,[26] and he is received into a tithing. . . .

Wretham [Norfolk]. . . . Gilbert son of Richard gives 5s. for permission to marry a wife. . . . The following women have been violated and accordingly owe *leyrwite*. . . .[27] From the township 3m. for the abbot's tallage. . . .

Tooting [Surrey]. . . . The whole township gives 2½m. for the abbot's tallage. William Jordan [is] in mercy for badly ploughing the lord's land. Pledge: Arthur. Fine 6d. John Shepherd [is] in mercy for encroaching upon land bordering on his. Pledge: Walter Reeve. Fine 6d. Lucy Reed [is] in mercy for cattle of hers taken in the lord's pasture after ward had been set. . . .[28] Elias of Streatham [is] in mercy for default of autumn [labour] service. Fine 6d. Bartholomew Chaloner, who was at law against Reginald son of Swain, has defaulted in his law. Therefore let him be in mercy and let him satisfy the aforesaid Reginald for the latter's damage and dishonour, namely with 6s. Pledges: William Shoemaker and William Spendlove. Fine 6 gallons [? of beer].

Deveril [Wiltshire]. . . . William Miller [offers to prove] at his law that he was not pledge for William Scut of Hull, whose sheep were taken in the lambs' pasture. Pledges for his law: William Swineherd and Thomas Guner. Arnold Smith is in mercy for not producing the said William Scut, for whom he was pledge. The parson of the church is in mercy for a cow of his taken in the lord's meadow. Pledges: Thomas Guner and William Cook. The township gives 2m. for the abbot's tallage. From William Cobbe, William Cook, and Walter Dogskin 2s. for [neglect of] ward [in the case] of seven pigs belonging to Robert Gentil and for the damage that they did in the lord's corn. From Martin Shepherd 6d. for the wound that he inflicted on Pekin. . . .

Weedon Beck [Northamptonshire]. . . . The court made presentment that William son of Noah is the fugitive bondman of the lord and is living at Dodford. Therefore he is to be sought. They also say that William Askil, John Parsons, and Godfrey Green furtively carried off four geese from the vill of Horepoll. John Witrich [is]

---

[26] Meaning to be received as a manorial tenant.
[27] The fine for unchastity. Five girls are named, with fines from 6d. to 12d.
[28] That is to say, after it had been closed to such use.

54. JUDICIAL RECORDS

in mercy for a colt of his taken in the lord's corn. Pledges: Guy Love and Simon Winbold. . . .

Pleas of the manors of Bec, A.D. 1249:—

Ogbourne [Wiltshire]. . . . Presentment was made that Stephen Shepherd by night struck his sister with a certain knife and badly wounded her. So let him be committed to prison. Later he fined for 2s. Pledge: Walter of Wick. Presentment was made that Robert son of Carter by night invaded [the property of] Peter Burgess and feloniously threw stones at his door, so that the same Peter Burgess raised hue [and cry]. Therefore let the aforesaid Robert be committed to prison. Later he fined for 2s. . . . Adam Moses gives half a sester of wine to have an inquest as to whether Henry Ayulf imputed to him the crime of larceny and used vile and insulting words [concerning him]. Later they came to agreement, and Henry gives security for amercement. Fine 12d. . . . From Ralph Joce ½m. for his son because [the latter] unlawfully took corn from the lord's court. . . . From Ralph Scales 6d. for carrying off timber. From William Cooper 12d. because without licence he ploughed his land with the lord's plough. From Hugh New 12d. for trespass in the wood. From Richard Penant 12d. for the same. From Helen, widow of Little Ogbourne, 6d. for the same. From Nicholas Seward 6d. for a false claim against William Pafey. From William Pafey 12d. for engaging in a fight with the same Nicholas. . . .

(Latin) Maitland, *Select Pleas in Manorial Courts*, pp. 6-20.

SECTION V

EDWARD II, EDWARD III, AND RICHARD II

THE period between the death of Edward I and the accession of Henry IV is chiefly significant for the rapid development of parliamentary institutions. This development involved, not only the definitive organization of a bicameral parliament, but also the assertion by that body of positive constitutional functions, principally directed toward restraint of the crown. And no matter what may have been the legality of such claims under Edward III, the triumph of parliament was assured by the Revolution of 1399.

That most of the materials presented below have a direct bearing upon this issue will be apparent without detailed comment. Edward II's reign is represented by five documents, of which only two run to any great length. The Ordinances of 1311, generally neglected by the compilers of source books, are here reproduced almost entire, because they provide a comprehensive criticism of the royal government and so link the parliamentary contests under Edward III with the baronial uprisings of the previous age. The Household Ordinance of 1318 is even less known.[1] Yet it gives us our most graphic picture of the royal *entourage* at which so many attacks were levelled and, by comparison with the *Constitutio Domus Regis* of about 1135 (no. 29), throws into historical perspective the whole intervening evolution of the English administrative system.

Aside from nos. 60 and 65, the remaining documents in this section fall under two main heads: statutes and ordinances, and excerpts from the rolls of parliament. In so far as possible, records of local government have been grouped in the following section and in those preceding; but the Durham Halmote Rolls are too important to be omitted, and their date necessitates an isolated position here. Although the chief value of the two writs of summons is merely that of typical examples, it should be noted that the great council of 1353 inaugurated some famous

---

[1] The French text, published without emendation by Tout, is corrupt in spots and is difficult throughout. Francis Tate's translation, reprinted by F. J. Furnivall in *Life Records of Chaucer*, Pt. II (Chaucer Society, 1876), is hopelessly inaccurate.

INTRODUCTORY NOTE

legislation (no. 62G, H). Such ordinances and statutes as are here included have been selected, first, on account of their actual provisions, that is to say, their reform or restatement of pre-existing law and custom; secondly, in order to show the methods by which enactments, more or less formal, came to be made. In the latter respect, however, statutes and ordinances serve at most to supplement the parliament rolls, which are unquestionably our best source for the constitutional history of the fourteenth and fifteenth centuries.

How rich and varied is the information supplied by these documents no one can possibly realize until he has worked through formidable volumes of Old French. What is translated in the following pages is, of course, but a small fragment of the whole series; yet the selections are extensive enough to reveal the characteristic features of the record and to illustrate many developments of great significance for the English monarchy. Among them may be mentioned the organization, powers, and procedure of the parliament as a whole and of its two houses separately; private suits, impeachment of ministers, and other judicial business in parliament; the growth of parliamentary control over taxation and expenditure; the constant agitation on the part of both houses for thorough reform of the royal administration; and the relation to all these matters of the king and his council. For it should not be thought that, on account of their name, the parliament rolls deal only with parliament in the modern sense. Throughout the fourteenth century parliament was still what the word originally implied—a specially important meeting of the king and his counsellors, including peers and deputies of the commons alongside of the more permanent advisers. To attempt a logical separation of parliamentary affairs from those of crown and council is futile. And a glance at the substance of the petitions and enactments in parliament will show that they were concerned with virtually all phases of the government, local as well as central.

Mainly because Stubbs was able to draw most of the material for his last six chapters from the parliament rolls, this portion of his *Constitutional History* remains authoritative—an indispensable commentary for one who would understand the purport of the following documents. But inevitably, through the advance of research, some of his views have been modified or superseded;

and the most useful guide in this connection is the volume of *Studies and Notes* by Petit-Dutaillis and Lefebvre, which contains an especially valuable essay on the Revolt of 1381. Particular reference may also be made to T. F. Tout, *Chapters in Mediaeval Administrative History*, vols. II-VI, and *The Place of the Reign of Edward II in English History*; J. C. Davies, *The Baronial Opposition to Edward II*; J. F. Baldwin, *The King's Council in England during the Middle Ages*; C. H. McIlwain, *The High Court of Parliament*; A. F. Pollard, *The Evolution of Parliament*; H. L. Gray, *The Influence of the Commons on Early Legislation*; M. V. Clarke, *Medieval Representation and Consent*; and M. McKisack, *The Parliamentary Representation of the English Boroughs during the Middle Ages*. These and other scholars have likewise published numerous special articles, some of which are cited in the footnotes. An excellent introduction to all this literature and to the problems involved has recently been provided by Eleanor C. Lodge and Gladys A. Thornton in their *English Constitutional Documents, 1307-1485*.

55. EDWARD II: CORONATION OATH (1308)[1]

"Sire, will you grant and keep and by your oath confirm to the people of England the laws and customs given to them by the previous just and god-fearing kings, your ancestors, and especially the laws, customs, and liberties granted to the clergy and people by the glorious king, the sainted Edward, your predecessor?" "I grant and promise them."

"Sire, will you in all your judgments, so far as in you lies, preserve to God and Holy Church, and to the people and clergy, entire peace and concord before God?" "I will preserve them."

"Sire, will you, so far as in you lies, cause justice to be rendered rightly, impartially, and wisely, in compassion and in truth?" "I will do so."

"Sire, do you grant to be held and observed the just laws and customs that the community of your realm shall determine, and will you, so far as in you lies, defend and strengthen them to the honour of God?" "I grant and promise them."

(French) *Statutes of the Realm*, I, 168.

---

[1] This is the form actually followed at the coronation of Edward II, but the record provides an alternative in Latin to be used "if the king is literate." It is also stated that the archbishop of Canterbury put the questions before the king was crowned; and, after he had given his oral responses, he personally swore on the altar that he would keep all his promises. See B. Wilkinson, in *Historical Essays in Honour of James Tait*, pp. 405 f.

56. ORDINANCES OF 1311

... Whereas, through bad and deceitful counsel, our lord the king and all his men have everywhere been dishonoured and his crown in many ways has been debased and ruined, while his lands of Gascony, Ireland, and Scotland are on the point of being lost unless God improves the situation, and his realm of England has been brought to the verge of rebellion through prises[1] and [other] oppressive and destructive measures—which facts are known and proved—our lord the king of his free will has granted to the prelates, earls, and barons, and to the other good men of his realm, that certain persons should be elected to ordain and determine the condition of his household and of his realm, as appears more fully in the commission issued by our lord the king in this connection. Therefore we, Robert, by the grace of God archbishop of Canterbury and primate of all England, and the bishops, earls, and barons elected by virtue of the said commission, do ordain for the honour of God and Holy Church and of the king and his realm in the manner following:—

1. ... In the first place it is ordained that Holy Church shall have all its liberties as heretofore and as it should have them.

2. Item, it is ordained that the king's peace shall be firmly kept throughout the entire kingdom; so that every one may safely go, come, and remain according to the law and custom of the realm.

3. Item, it is ordained that, in order to acquit the king's debts, to relieve his estate,[2] and the more honourably to maintain it, no gift of land, rent, liberty, escheat, wardship, marriage, or office shall be made to any of the said Ordainers during their [tenure of] power under the said ordinance, or to any other person, without the counsel and assent of the said Ordainers or the majority of them—or of six of them at least—but that all sources of profit shall be improved for the benefit of the king until his estate is properly relieved and some other ordinance may be made for the honour and profit of the king.

4. Item, it is ordained that the customs of the kingdom shall be received and kept by men of the kingdom itself, and not by aliens; and that the issues and profits of the same customs, together with all other issues and profits pertaining to the kingdom from any source whatsoever, shall in their entirety come to the king's exchequer and be paid by the treasurer and the chamberlains for maintaining the king's household and [to be spent] in other ways for his benefit; so that the king may live of his own without taking prises other than those anciently due and accustomed. And all others shall cease. ...

6. Item, it is ordained that the Great Charter shall be observed in all its particulars; so that, if there is any point in the said charter that is doubtful or obscure, it shall be interpreted by the said Or-

---
[1] See arts. 4 and 10, below.
[2] The word constantly used throughout these records to denote the king's legal position, including all powers and perquisites of the royal office.

dainers and other men whom they may see fit to call upon for that purpose.³ . . .

7. And besides, since the crown has been so abased and ruined by numerous grants, we ordain that all grants made to the damage of the king and the impoverishment of the crown since the commission was given to us . . . shall be annulled; and we do annul them entirely, so that they shall not be given back to the same persons without the common assent [of the baronage⁴] in parliament. . . .

9. Whereas the king, on account of the many perils that he and his kingdom may incur, ought not to undertake an act of war against any one, or to go out of the kingdom, without the common assent of his baronage, we ordain that henceforth the king shall neither go out of the kingdom nor undertake an act of war against any one without the common assent of his baronage, and that in parliament. . . .

10. And whereas it is feared that the people of the land will rebel on account of the prises and divers oppressions recently established, . . . we ordain that henceforth all prises shall be abolished except the ancient and lawful prises due to the king and to others who are lawfully entitled to them. And if any prises are taken contrary to the ordinance aforesaid by any one whomsoever, no matter of what condition he may be—that is to say, if any one, under colour of purveyance for the use of our lord the king or of some one else, takes grain, wares, merchandise, or other goods against the will of those to whom they belong, and does not immediately give in return money to the true value [of the goods], unless he thereof has respite by the free will of the seller according to the provision in the Great Charter regarding prises taken by constables of castles and their bailiffs,⁵ saving the accustomed prises aforesaid—notwithstanding any commission that may be [issued], pursuit with hue and cry shall be raised against him and he shall be taken to the nearest jail of the king, and the common law shall be enforced against him as against a robber or thief, should he be convicted of such [wrongdoing].

11. Also, [whereas] new customs have been levied and the old [customs] have been increased upon wool, cloth, wines, avoirdupois, and other things—whereby [our] merchants come more rarely and bring fewer goods into the country, while alien merchants reside longer than they used to, and by such residence things become dearer than they used to be, to the damage of the king and his people—we ordain that all manner of customs and maltotes levied since the coronation of King Edward, son of King Henry, are to be entirely removed and utterly abolished forever, notwithstanding the charter which the said King Edward granted to alien merchants, because it

---

³ Cf. art. 38, below.
⁴ Cf. arts. 9, 11, 14, etc.
⁵ Arts. 28-31, above, p. 120.

was issued contrary to the Great Charter and contrary to the liberty of the city of London and without the assent of the baronage. . . .[6]

13. And whereas the king, as aforesaid, has been badly advised and guided by evil councillors, we ordain that all the evil councillors shall be put out and utterly removed, so that neither they nor other such persons shall be near him or shall be retained in any office under the king; and that other persons who are fit shall be put in their places. And the same shall be done in the case of domestics, officials, and other men in the king's household who are not fit.

14. And whereas many evils have been incurred through [the employment of] such councillors and such ministers, we ordain that the king shall appoint the chancellor, the chief justices of both benches, the treasurer, the chancellor[7] and the chief baron of the exchequer, the steward of the household, the keeper of the wardrobe, the comptroller and a fit clerk to keep the privy seal,[8] a chief keeper of the forests on this side of Trent and one on the other side of Trent, also an escheator on this side of Trent and one on the other side, as well as the king's chief clerk of the common bench, by the counsel and assent of the baronage, and that in parliament. And if by some chance it happens that there is need to appoint any of the said ministers before parliament meets, then the king shall make such appointments by the good counsel [of those] whom he shall have near him up to the time of the parliament. And so let it be done henceforth with regard to such ministers whenever there is need.

15. Item, we ordain that the chief wardens of ports[9] and of castles on the sea shall be appointed and installed in the aforesaid manner, and that such wardens are to be of the land itself.[10]

16. And whereas the lands of Gascony, Ireland, and Scotland are in peril of being lost through default of good ministers, we ordain that worthy and fit ministers to keep ward in the said lands shall be named according to the form set forth in the article before the last [preceding].

17. Moreover, we ordain that sheriffs shall henceforth be appointed by the chancellor, the treasurer, and others of the council who are present; and if the chancellor is not present, let them be appointed by the treasurer, the barons of the exchequer, and the justices of the bench. And such men are to be named and installed as are fit and worthy, and as have lands and tenements through which they may be held responsible for their actions to the king or to the people. And

---

[6] Saving to the king the ancient customs from wool and hides; see no. 51A.
[7] When, in the thirteenth century, the chancellor ceased to attend the meetings of the exchequer, his clerk became known as the chancellor of the exchequer.
[8] For further details concerning these and other household officials, see no. 57.
[9] Referring especially to the warden of the Cinque Ports and constable of Dover Castle; see no. 50C.
[10] I.e., England.

only such persons shall be appointed, and they shall have their commissions under the great seal. . . .[11]

24. And whereas the people feel much aggrieved because of divers debts demanded of them for the king's use by summons from the exchequer, of which debts, being actually paid, the people have various acquittances . . . ; we ordain that henceforth in the account of every sheriff, or other minister of the king who is answerable at the exchequer, such tallies, writs, and franchises as are allowable in the account shall be allowed. . . . And if the treasurer and the barons of the exchequer do not act in the manner aforesaid, the plaintiffs shall enjoy [the right of] recovery through petition in parliament.[12]

25. Whereas ordinary merchants and many others of the people are allowed to bring pleas of debt and trespass in the exchequer, through the fact that they are received by the ministers of the said court more favourably than they should be[13]—whereby accounts and other concerns of the king are greatly delayed and, in addition, a large number of people are aggrieved—we ordain that henceforth no pleas shall be held in the said court of the exchequer except pleas touching the king and his ministers: [namely] those answerable at the exchequer by reason of their offices, the ministers of the court itself, and their subordinates and servants who most of the time are with them in those places where the exchequer may be. And if anybody is received by the said court with permission to plead in the manner aforesaid, those impleaded shall have their [right to] recovery in parliament.

26. Item, whereas the people feel much aggrieved because stewards and marshals hold many pleas that do not pertain to their offices, and also because they will not receive attorneys for defendants as well as for plaintiffs, we ordain that henceforth they shall receive attorneys for defendants as well as for plaintiffs, and that they shall hold no pleas of freehold, debt, covenant, or contract, nor any common plea touching men of the people—saving [to their jurisdiction] only trespasses of the household itself and other trespasses committed within the verge,[14] and contracts and covenants which any one of the king's household may make with another of the same household within the household itself and not elsewhere. . . .[15]

28. Whereas the people feel much aggrieved because men are em-

---

[11] The next two articles provide for investigations concerning the misdeeds of forest officials and the enforcement of the Forest Charter (no. 45). Arts. 20-23 impose penalties on Piers Gaveston and three other persons named.

[12] Cf. nos. 54G, 61A.

[13] Cf. no. 54C.

[14] The area distinguished by the king's presence and thereby set apart from the common law.

[15] Various details follow in the text, including remedies at common law provided for aggrieved parties.

boldened to kill and rob by the fact that the king, through evil counsel, so lightly grants them his peace against the provisions of the law; we ordain that henceforth no felon or fugitive shall be protected or defended in any sort of felony by the king's charter granting his peace, except only in case the king can give grace according to his oath, and that by process of law and the custom of the realm. And if any charter is henceforth made and granted to any one in any other manner, it shall be of no avail and shall be held as null. And no recognized malefactor against the crown and the peace of the land is to be aided or maintained[16] by any one.

29. Whereas in the king's court persons find their cases delayed because a party alleges that in the king's absence answer should not be made to demands, and [whereas] also many persons wrongfully suffer injuries from the king's ministers, with regard to which injuries one can secure recovery only in common parliament; we ordain that the king shall hold a parliament once a year, or twice if need be, and that in a convenient place. And [we ordain] that in those parliaments pleas which are delayed in the said manner, and pleas wherein the justices are of different opinions, shall be recorded and settled. And likewise those bills[17] which are brought to parliament shall be settled as heretofore in accordance with law and right.

30. Whereas all the people suffer greatly in many ways whenever a change of money is made in the kingdom, we ordain that, when there is need and the king wishes to make a change [of the money], he shall do so by the common counsel of his baronage, and that in parliament.

31. Item, we ordain that all statutes which were made in amendment of the law and for the benefit of the people by the ancestors of our lord the king shall be kept and maintained as heretofore in accordance with law and right; provided that they are not contrary to the Great Charter or to the Forest Charter or to the ordinances by us made. And if any statute is made contrary to what has been said, it shall be held as null and as utterly void.

32. Whereas, to the great injury of the people, the law of the land and common right have often been delayed by letters issued under the king's privy seal, we ordain that henceforth neither the law of the land nor common right shall be delayed or disturbed by letters under the said seal. And if, through such letters issued under the privy seal contrary to right or to the law of the land, anything is done in any session of the court of our lord the king, it shall be of no avail and shall be held as null.

33. Whereas many of the people other than those known to be merchants feel much aggrieved and injured by the Statute of Merchants made at Acton Burnell,[18] we ordain that hereafter this statute shall

---

[16] Cf. no. 64c.
[17] "Bill" and "petition" were at this time synonymous terms.
[18] No. 52D.

hold only as between merchant and merchant and with regard to dealings made between them. . . .[19]

38. Item, we ordain that the Great Charter of Liberties and the Forest Charter issued by King Henry, son of King John, shall be observed in all their particulars, and that points in the said charters of liberties which are doubtful shall be explained in the next parliament after this by the advice of the baronage, the justices, and other persons learned in the law. And this is to be done because we are unable to attend to the matter during our term [of office].

39. Item, we ordain that the chancellor, the treasurer, the chief justices of both benches, the chancellor of the exchequer, the treasurer of the wardrobe, the steward of the king's household, and all justices, sheriffs, escheators, constables, investigators [named] for any cause whatsoever, and all other bailiffs and ministers of the king, whenever they receive their offices and bailiwicks, shall be sworn to keep and observe all the ordinances made by the prelates, earls, and barons for that purpose elected and assigned—[to maintain] every one of those [ordinances] without contravening them in any particular.

40. Item, we ordain that in each parliament one bishop, two earls, and two barons shall be assigned to hear and determine all plaints of those wishing to complain of the king's ministers, whichever they may be, who have contravened the ordinances aforesaid. And if the said bishop, earls, and barons cannot all attend, or are prevented from hearing and determining the said plaints, then two or three of them shall do so. And those who are found to have contravened the said ordinances, in the interest of the king and in the interest of the plaintiffs, shall be punished at the discretion of the persons thus assigned.

41. Item, we ordain that the aforesaid ordinances are to be maintained and observed in all their particulars, and that our lord the king shall cause them to be issued under his great seal and sent into every county of England, to be published, held, and strictly kept as well within franchises as without. . . .

These ordinances, having been shown to us[20] and published on Monday next before the feast of St. Michael just past, we agree to, accept, and confirm. And we will and grant, for us and our heirs, that all and several of the said ordinances, made according to the form of our letters aforesaid, shall be published throughout our entire realm, henceforth to be strictly maintained and observed. In testimony whereof we have caused these our letters patent to be drawn up.

Given at London, October 5, in the fifth year of our reign.

(French) *Ibid.*, I, 157 f.

---

[19] The seals for authenticating such transactions are to be entrusted to groups of substantial citizens elected in certain specified towns: Newcastle-upon-Tyne, Nottingham, Exeter, Bristol, Southampton, Lincoln, Northampton, London, and Canterbury. The next four articles deal with reforms of the criminal law.

[20] King Edward II.

57. EDWARD II: HOUSEHOLD ORDINANCE (1318)[1]

... The king should have a fit steward of the household, who, if he is a banneret,[2] is to have a knight, three squires, and a clerk for the pleas that pertain to the stewardship, [all of them] eating in the hall. And each night he shall receive for his chamber a sester of wine, twelve candles, two *tortis pur viu*,[3] and one torch, and more when he needs them. And [he is to have] bedding for the whole year and wood for the winter season—from the eve of All Saints to the eve of Easter—[to be obtained] from the usher of the hall. And [he is to have] a livery for his chamberlain: namely, a portion of bread, a gallon of ale, and a general serving (*messe de gros*) from the kitchen. And [he is to have] dinners and suppers when he wants them; and as fees 20m. a year, in equal instalments on the feasts of Christmas and Pentecost. And if he is a simple knight, he shall receive fees and robes like the other simple knights of the household, and shall have two squires and his clerk eating in the hall.

A treasurer of the wardrobe, who is to have a chaplain, a clerk, and two squires eating in the hall. . . .[4]

A chamberlain, who, if he is a banneret, is to have a knight and three squires eating in the hall. . . .

Item, a comptroller, who is to keep a counter-roll against the treasurer of the wardrobe for all receipts and issues pertaining to the same wardrobe; and he is to witness them in the exchequer in connection with the account of the said treasurer. And he shall attend the receipt of wines in gross and shall supervise all the offices of the household, such as the pantry, butlery, cellar, larder, spicery, dispensary of oats (*avenerie*) and other offices, [to see] that the wines and victuals that he finds in the said offices are good and suitable for dispensing in the said household. . . . And he is to go into those same offices every Monday to examine the remainders [of supplies] and to see that they, with the amounts dispensed in the past week, agree with the receipts of the aforesaid week. And he shall be in the kitchen for the cutting of meat and the division of fish. . . . And every day, if he sees reasonable cause, he shall be present at the account,[5] to-

---

[1] The preamble explains that this ordinance was drawn up at the king's request by the steward, the chamberlain, the treasurer, and the comptroller of the wardrobe, to define the duties of the various officials and to establish needed reforms in the administration of the household. On the general significance of the document, see Tout, *Place of Edward II in English History*, ch. v, and *Chapters in Mediaeval Administrative History*, II, pp. 242 f.

[2] The banneret, as opposed to the simple knight or bachelor, had the right to bear a square pennon on his lance.

[3] Large candles "for view (? display)"; see *Oxford English Dictionary* under *tortis*. Henceforth the expression will be translated merely as "great candles."

[4] All the greater officials received liveries similar to that of the steward, but with considerable variation in the particular items. Besides, each normally had his own chamberlain, who was entitled to food and drink.

[5] Drawn up in the wardrobe; see no. 52c.

gether with the steward and the treasurer. And this same comptroller of the wardrobe is to have a clerk and a squire eating in the hall. . . .

Item, a cofferer, who shall be appointed for the treasurer and shall have a clerk eating in the hall. . . .

Item, two clerks of the counting table, well able to write and perform all duties touching the wardrobe and its account under the [direction of the] cofferer. . . .

Item, a fit clerk keeper of the privy seal, who is to have a squire eating in the hall. . . .[6]

Item, a clerk purveyor of the great wardrobe,[7] who should sleep on guard when he is at court. And he shall have a squire eating in the hall. . . .

Item, a clerk of the spicery, chief usher of the wardrobe, who shall receive from the clerk purveyor of the great wardrobe the wax, napery, linen, cloth, canvas, spices, and the other things of all sorts that pertain to his office, [and this] by indenture expressly mentioning price, yardage, weight, and cost.[8] And he shall cause to be weighed the wax which the chandler is to have worked, and shall reweigh it after it has been worked. And he shall oversee and cause to be recorded by his under-clerk the liveries of chandlery made each day in the wardrobe, and on the next day he shall supervise the putting away of the torches, the great candles, and the mortars.[9] Each day he shall record the parcels of all sorts of things delivered and dispensed from his office, as counted since the day before, and he shall answer concerning them at the account of the household. And he shall oversee the carriages belonging to the wardrobe, as well for the coffers and other things of his office as for the beds of the wardrobe clerks which ought to be carried. And he shall make allowance in his roll for the carriage and transportation reasonably used in connection with the king's journeys. . . .[10]

Item, a serjeant under-usher of the wardrobe, who shall live in the wardrobe, sleeping within its door to safeguard all the things inside it. And he shall be answerable if peril is incurred by his default. And he shall obtain from the offices the liveries for all men of the wardrobe, and he shall carry out their orders. . . .

Item, a porter of the wardrobe, who shall carry the coffers and the other furnishings of the wardrobe to the carts, and shall load and unload them. And he shall be on the cart [while it is] on the road. And at night, if the cart is outdoors wandering through the country, he shall remain on watch. . . .

Item, a squire fruiterer, who shall receive and take from the clerk of the spicery confections and other spiceries, and figs and grapes for

---

[6] Also four under-clerks with liveries.

[7] See above, p. 171, n. 8.

[8] This was a newly established reform, as is explained in the next paragraph of the text.

[9] Bowls of oil with floating wicks.

[10] Also an under-clerk to assist him.

the king's mouth. And each day he shall record for the said clerk what has been expended on the previous day: as well the said spiceries and fruit, thus received from the said clerk, as apples, pears, cherries, and other fruits which the said fruiterer shall purvey. . . .

Item, a serjeant chandler, who shall receive the wax and candle-wicks by weight from the clerk of the spicery, and shall have them worked according to the assize contained in the statute. . . .[11]

Item, a confessor of the king and his companion. . . .[12]

Item, a chief chaplain, who is to have a squire eating in the hall . . . and five chaplains . . . and six clerks. . . .

Item, an almoner chaplain, who is to have a squire eating in the hall. . . .[13]

Item, a physician. . . .

Item, a surgeon. . . .

Item, a clerk of the market, coroner of the king's household, who shall enforce the assize of bread, wine, and ale; also the assize of all sorts of measures, weights, and yards within the verge of our lord the king's presence. And he shall have wrongdoers who have broken the assize, or who are found with false measures, punished by imposition or fine. . . .

Item, the king shall have a squire inspector and keeper of viands for his mouth, and an inspector of his table; also a squire to carve before the king and a squire to serve him with his cup. . . .

Item, the king shall have two squires ushers of the chamber, one of whom shall be serjeant purveyor of wood and bedding for the office of the chamber. . . . And the serjeant purveyor shall have a serving-man to help him in making purveyance. . . .

Item, eight footmen of the chamber, who shall serve in the chamber making beds, holding and carrying torches, and [doing] various other things according to the commands of the king's chamberlain. . . .

Item, the king is to have thirty serjeants-at-arms, properly armed and mounted . . . , who shall daily ride armed before the king's person while he is journeying through the country, unless they have other commands from the king or the steward. . . .

Item, a knight chief usher of the hall, who shall have charge of the door of the hall, [seeing] that it is well kept by the serjeants and valets of the usher, as is fit. And he shall take care that the hall is well and honourably served, and that no one eats there except those who rightfully should, saving always that strangers are received and honoured as they ought to be. And each day he should enter and inspect the offices of the household, [to see] that the things sent by the purveyors are sufficient according to the purchase, and that no one is permitted in the same offices except those who ought to be there. And he shall have a squire eating in the hall. . . .

---

[11] I.e., a separate ordinance dealing with these matters. Two serving-men under the chandler worked the wax.

[12] With four horses and three grooms.

[13] Also a clerk and a serving-man.

Item, two serjeants ushers of the hall, of whom one shall be purveyor of wood and of bedding for the service of the hall.[14] . . .

Item, two knights marshals of the hall, of whom one shall have charge of lodgings and the other shall be on duty in the hall. . . .

Item, two serjeants marshals of the hall, of whom one shall have charge of lodgings and the other shall be on duty in the hall. . . .

Item, a serjeant overseer of the sideboard for the hall, who is to advise concerning the places that he serves, according as persons of high estate and others may be seated in the hall. . . .[15]

Item, a chief clerk of the pantry and butlery, who ought to keep the records of his office. And he is to respond each day at the account of the household. . . . He shall be present at the receipt of bread, wine, and ale; and he shall inspect and examine [them, to see] that they are of the proper weight, measure, and value. . . .[16]

Item, a serjeant chief pantler, who shall receive the bread in gross by view of the clerk or the under-clerk, and shall each day be answerable to the chief clerk for the enrolment of what has been dispensed. . . .[17]

Item, a serjeant pantler for the king's mouth, who each day shall receive from the great pantry the bread for the king and for his chamber, and for no other place. . . .[18]

Item, a waferer, who shall serve the king, the hall, and the chamber with wafers, as pertains to him. . . .

Item, a serjeant baker, who shall bake all sorts of bread for dispensing in the king's household—as well round loaves for all the commonalty as demeine loaves for the king's mouth. . . .[19]

Item, a serjeant naperer, who shall perform his office in the king's chamber and in the hall. And he shall receive the napery from the clerk of the spicery and shall be responsible for it at the account whenever he is asked. . . .[20]

Item, a ewerer for the chamber, who shall perform his office in the said chamber. . . .[21]

Item, a launderer for the king's chamber, who shall wash all sorts of linen cut for the king's body . . .[22] and the covers used in the service of the chamber. . . .

---

[14] Under the serjeants were two serving-men; under the knight was a sewer, who had charge of setting the table.

[15] He was assisted by two squires sewers, who served the meals in the hall. Besides, twenty-four squires were on duty in the hall, to carry out the commands of the high officials.

[16] Also an under-clerk, who kept tallies for all bread, wine, and ale received.

[17] Also a serving-man and two porters.

[18] Assisted by a serving-man for the chamber, and one for the rest of the household.

[19] Cf. above, p. 66, n. 3. The baker was assisted by two serving-men, one for the oven and the other for the mill.

[20] Also a serving-man.

[21] Also a serving-man, who acted as ewerer for the hall.

[22] This portion of the text is very corrupt.

57. HOUSEHOLD ORDINANCE

Item, a launderer of napery, who shall wash all sorts of cut linen pertaining to the said office of napery, and the covers from offices connected with the hall. . . .

Item, a chief butler, serjeant purveyor of wines. . . . And he shall do that which pertains to him according to the content of the statute concerning his office below.[23]

Item, a serjeant butler of the household, who shall receive and dispense all wine and ale that are dispensed in the household. . . .

Item, a serjeant butler for the king, who shall receive from the butler of the household all the wine and ale that are dispensed in the king's chamber. . . .[24]

Item, a chief clerk of the kitchen, who ought to make the enrolments pertaining to his office. And every day at the account in the wardrobe before the steward and the treasurer he shall be responsible for the parcels delivered [in the kitchen] and for all other matters pertaining to his office. And he shall be present at the cutting of meat and the division of fish. And he shall oversee the purchase and the cost of meat and fish and of all other things pertaining to his office, with the aid of the comptroller, the knight usher of the hall or the knight marshal, and the sewer of the king's table. . . .[25]

Item, two serjeants cooks for the king's mouth. . . .[26]

Item, two serjeants cooks for the hall. . . .

Item, a serjeant larderer, who shall receive the meat and fish that the buyers cause to be brought to the larder, or which comes as a present; also the venison which comes thither from the king's huntsmen or from any other source. And he shall deliver the aforesaid meat and fish to be dispensed for the household in parcels, and [this] under the inspection of the comptroller, the knight usher of the hall or the knight marshal of the hall, the clerk of the kitchen, the sewer of the king's table, and the chief cook. And he shall keep the food on the sideboard and each day he shall give to the said clerk a record of the parcels of the aforesaid meat and fish dispensed in the manner aforesaid. . . .[27]

Item, a serjeant poulterer, who shall attend to purchases and purveyance of all sorts of things pertaining to his office. . . .[28]

Item, a serjeant of the scullery, who shall buy and purvey wood, charcoal, and all sorts of vessels of brass, iron, and wood that belong

---

[23] A separate ordinance added at the end of the survey.

[24] Also enumerated in the service of the butlery: a serving-man of the cup-house two drawers of ale and wine, a purveyor of ale, two serving-men of the pitcher-house, and two porters.

[25] As assistants he had an under-clerk and two buyers, who were to give money or tallies for anything taken by purveyance.

[26] Under each pair of cooks were five serving-men.

[27] Under him were an usher of the larder and two porters.

[28] Three serving-men assisted him in obtaining poultry and preparing it for the kitchen.

to the kitchen; also the pots and various other things pertaining to his office. . . .[29]

Item, a [second] serjeant of the scullery, who shall receive the silver vessels from the wardrobe by number and weight . . . , and shall keep them and be responsible for them by number and weight in the same wardrobe at the end of the year. . . .

Item, a serjeant of the saucery, who shall buy and purvey flour for all manner of sauces and other things needed for the office of the saucery and the king's household. . . .[29]

Item, a serjeant porter, who shall guard the door where the king sleeps, so that none may enter except those who by right should do so. . . .[29]

Item, a chief clerk of the marshalsea. . . .[30]

(French) Tout, *Edward II in English History*, pp. 270 f.

---

[29] Also two serving-men.

[30] Here the text gives a detailed account of all the services connected with the king's stables. The chief clerk, assisted by a purveyor of oats, had charge of all records pertaining to the office, including tallies given for oats, hay, straw, harness, etc. The actual care of the king's horses—palfreys, chargers, pack-horses, draught-horses, etc.—devolved on two serjeants harbingers and three serjeants marshals, under whom were numerous serving-men, porters, and grooms. The record then describes the officers in charge of the king's hunting, fishing, and fowling, and lists his trumpeters, musicians, messengers, and archers. It ends with a group of particular ordinances to regulate the duties of the chief butler, the arrangement of lodgings for the court, the daily account in the wardrobe, the exclusion from the household of undesirable persons, and many other matters.

58. EDWARD II: STATUTE OF YORK (1322)

Whereas our lord King Edward, son of King Edward, on March 16, in the third year of his reign, granted to the prelates, earls, and barons of his realm . . . ;[1] and whereas the archbishop of Canterbury, primate of all England, and the bishops, earls, and barons chosen for the purpose, drew up certain ordinances that begin as follows . . . , which ordinances our said lord the king caused to be rehearsed and examined in his parliament at York three weeks after Easter in the fifteenth year of his reign . . . ; and whereas, through that examination in the said parliament, it was found that by the ordinances thus decreed the royal power of our said lord the king was wrongfully limited in many respects, to the injury of his royal lordship and contrary to the estate of the crown; and whereas, furthermore, through such ordinances and provisions made by subjects in times past against the royal authority of our lord the king's ancestors, the kingdom has incurred troubles and wars, whereby the land has been imperilled: [therefore] it is agreed and established at the said parliament by our lord the king, by the said prelates, earls,

---

[1] Reciting the preamble to the Ordinances of 1311. On the significance of the following provisions, see G. Lapsley, in the *English Historical Review*, XXVIII, 118 f., and G. L. Haskins, *The Statute of York*.

and barons, and by the whole community of the realm assembled in this parliament, that everything ordained by the said Ordainers and contained in the said ordinances shall henceforth and forever cease [to be valid], losing for the future all title, force, virtue, and effect; and that the statutes and establishments duly made by our lord the king and his ancestors prior to the said ordinances shall remain in force. And [it is decreed] that henceforth and forever at all times every kind of ordinance or provision made under any authority or commission whatsoever by subjects of our lord the king or of his heirs against the royal power of our lord the king or of his heirs, or contrary to the estate of the crown, shall be null and shall have no validity or force whatever; but that matters which are to be determined with regard to the estate of our lord the king and of his heirs, or with regard to the estate of the kingdom and of the people, shall be considered, granted, and established in parliament by our lord the king and with the consent of the prelates, earls, and barons, and of the community of the kingdom, as has been accustomed in times past.[2]

(French) *Statutes of the Realm,* I, 189.

59. EDWARD II'S ABDICATION (1327)

Whereas Sire Edward, recently king of England, of his free will and by the common counsel and assent of the prelates, earls, barons, and other nobles, and of the whole community of the realm, has abdicated the government of the realm; and whereas he has granted and wills that the government of the realm should devolve upon his eldest son and heir, Sire Edward, who should govern, reign, and be crowned king; and whereas all the great men have performed their homage [to the said heir]: we proclaim and publish the peace of our said lord, Sire Edward, the son [of King Edward]; and on his part we command and firmly enjoin each and every one, on pain of disherison and loss of life or members, not to break the peace of our said lord the king; for he is and shall be ready to enforce right for each and every one of the said kingdom in all matters and against all persons, both great and small. So, if any one has some demand to make of another, let him make it by means of [legal] action, without resorting to force or violence.

(French) Lodge and Thornton, *English Constitutional Documents,* p. 21.

60. EDWARD III: WRITS OF SUMMONS

(A) Parliament of 1337

The king to the venerable father in Christ, J[ohn], by the same grace archbishop of Canterbury and primate of all England, greeting. Whereas, on account of divers arduous matters especially affect-

---

[2] The ordinance was sent to all the sheriffs with commands for it to be read in full county court.

ing us and the state of our kingdom, we propose to hold our parliament at York on Monday next after the feast of St. Hilary and to have a conference with you and the other prelates, magnates, and nobles of the said kingdom; we command and enjoin you that, in the fealty and love by which you are bound to us, avoiding all excuse, you be personally present on the said day at the said place, in order with us and with the other prelates, magnates, and nobles aforesaid to discuss the said matters and thereupon give your counsel. And as you cherish us and our honour, as well as the peace and tranquillity of our kingdom, by no means fail to do this; first summoning (*premunientes*) the prior and chapter of your church of Christ at Canterbury and the archdeacons and all the clergy of your diocese, the said prior and archdeacons to be present in person, the said chapter [to be represented] by one fit proctor and the said clergy by two—which proctors are to have full and sufficient authority from the said chapter and clergy—on the said day and at the said place to determine and agree upon those measures which then and there, by the favour of divine clemency, may happen to be ordained through common counsel. By witness of the king of Bothwell, November 29.[1]

By the king himself.

(Latin) *Report Touching the Dignity of a Peer*, IV, 464 f.

(B) GREAT COUNCIL OF 1353[2]

The king to the venerable father in Christ, S[imon], by the same grace archbishop of Canterbury, greeting. Whereas, on account of great and urgent matters recently come upon us, which intimately concern us as well as the condition and rights of our kingdom of England, and for which it behooves us to find a speedy and provident solution, we desire to have a conference and deliberation with you, with the rest of the prelates, magnates, and nobles, and with our other faithful men of the said kingdom, at Westminster on the morrow of the Assumption of the Blessed Virgin next to come: we firmly enjoin and command that, in the fealty, love, and allegiance by which you are bound to us, putting aside all other affairs, you be personally present at the said place on the said day in order, with us, with the rest of the prelates, magnates, and nobles, and with the other men aforesaid, to discuss the said business and thereupon give your counsel. And as you cherish us, our honour, and the salvation, defence, and best interest of our said kingdom, and as you wish to

---

[1] Similar mandates were sent to the archbishop of York, eighteen bishops, and the custodian of one vacant see; without the *premunientes* clause, to twenty-seven abbots and four priors; and with different forms of address, to fifty-eight lay peers and fifteen justices and councillors. Furthermore, by the usual form (see the writs of 1295, no. 49F) the sheriff of each county was ordered to cause the election of two knights of the shire, two citizens from each city, and two burgesses from each borough. The warden of the Cinque Ports was commanded to have two barons elected from each of the ports.

[2] Cf. no. 62G, H.

avoid its subversion, by no means fail to do this, then and there notifying us of the day on which you received these present letters and by whom they were brought to you. By witness of the king at Westminster, July 20.[3]
By the king himself and his council.

(Latin) *Ibid.*, IV, 593 f.

---

[3] Similar mandates were sent to nineteen bishops, the abbot of Westminster, the prior of the Hospital of St. John, thirty-seven lay peers, and sixteen justices and councillors. The sheriff of each county was ordered to have only one knight of the shire elected, so as to avoid disturbing the men engaged in their autumn work. Two citizens were to be elected from London, but only one—on account of the same autumn work!—from York and from each of nine other towns. Two barons were to be elected from the Cinque Ports as a whole.

61. PARLIAMENT ROLLS OF EDWARD III

(A) PARLIAMENT OF 1330

These are the treasons, felonies, and wrongs done to our lord the king and to his people by Roger de Mortimer and others of his following.[1] . . .

Accordingly, for the reasons aforesaid, and for many other reasons which may not all be set forth at present, our said lord the king, by the advice and aid of his privy and intimate councillors, had the said Roger taken in such fashion as he has often described to you. So our said lord the king charges you, earls and barons, the peers of the realm, that, with regard to these matters vitally affecting him and you and all the people of his kingdom, you render for the said Roger such right and lawful judgment as should be incurred by a man of this sort, who, as he believes, is truly guilty of all the crimes set forth above; and [he charges you] that the said matters are notorious and known to be true to you and all the people of the kingdom.

The which earls, barons, and peers, having examined the articles, returned to the king's presence in the same parliament and all declared through one of the peers [as spokesman] that all the matters contained in the said articles were notorious, being known to them and to the people, and especially the article touching the death of Sire Edward, father of our lord the present king. Wherefore, as judges of parliament, the said earls, barons, and peers, by the assent of the king in the same parliament, awarded and adjudged that the said Roger, as a traitor and enemy to the king and to the kingdom, should be drawn[2] and hanged. And thereupon the earl marshal was commanded to carry out the execution of the said judgment; and the mayor, aldermen, and sheriffs of London, also the constable of the Tower and those who had [the prisoner] in custody, [were ordered] to be of assistance to the said earl marshal in carrying out the said execution.

---

[1] See M. V. Clarke, in *Oxford Essays Presented to H. E. Salter*, pp. 164 f.
[2] On a hurdle to the place of execution.

Which execution was carried out and performed on Thursday next after the first day of parliament, namely, November 29. . . .

In the same parliament summoned at Westminster Sir Eblé Lestrange and Alice[3] his wife presented a petition in these words:—

To our lord the king and his council Eblé Lestrange and Alice his wife set forth that all the lands which he held of the inheritance of the said Alice, after the death of Thomas, one time earl of Lancaster . . . , were taken into the hands of the king, father of our lord the present king, and kept in his hands. . . . Wherefore they pray our lord the king that, for the salvation of his father's soul and for that of his own [soul], he will call before him his good council and the good and loyal men who were then in the council of his said father, and will examine them with regard to the matters aforesaid . . . ; and then that of his especial grace he will act toward them as may be his pleasure and as his good conscience may decide for him.

After the petition had been read and heard before our lord the king and the prelates, earls, barons, and other lords[4] of the same parliament, whereas it was testified by some of the said lords, trustworthy men, that the said Alice had then been subjected to such arbitrary will and severity . . . : our lord the king, having regard for good faith and conscience, with the assent of the said prelates, earls, barons, and other lords of the same parliament, granted to the said Sir Eblé and Alice, in order to constitute an estate for them, the lands which were still in their hands, to the value of 500m., and lands of the same inheritance which were then in the king's hands, to the value of 700m., to be had and held in fee forever . . . by the aforesaid Sir Eblé and Alice, and by the heirs of the said Sir Eblé, of our lord the king and his heirs, and of the other chief lords of the fief, for the services due and accustomed. . . . And thereupon our lord the king commanded the bishop of Winchester, his chancellor, to put into execution that which had thus been granted and agreed on. . . .

Item, in the same parliament summoned at Westminster Sir John of Clavering presented a petition in these words. . . .

After which petition had been read and heard before the council in the said parliament, whereas the lords and the other discreet men of the same [parliament] could not then agree on making a final disposition of that [case] ; it was responded that this same petition and all the other petitions presented to the same parliament, together with the inquests returned in the chancery by the escheator . . . and with all the other certifications and memoranda of the exchequer

---

[3] Widow of Thomas, earl of Lancaster. The two following extracts are given as examples of the numerous private petitions introduced in this and the succeeding parliaments. Cf. no. 54G, and, on the jurisdiction of the chancellor, no. 71.

[4] *Granz*, the usual term for members of the original parliament; *seigneurs* came into general use a little later.

touching the said matter, should be remanded to the chancery, and that the chancellor, having summoned thither the discreet men of the king's council, should administer justice in the matter. . . .

(French) *Rotuli Parliamentorum,* II, 52-53, 57, 59.

(B) PARLIAMENT OF 1332

These are the memoranda of the actions taken in the parliament summoned at Westminster on Wednesday, the morrow of the Nativity of Our Lady, in the sixth year of the reign of Edward III after the Conquest:—

. . . On which Thursday they held a discussion and deliberation: that is to say, the said prelates by themselves; and the said earls, barons, and other lords by themselves; and also the knights of the shires by themselves.[5] . . . And they advised for the sake of improvement[6] that our lord the king should remain in England and should betake himself toward the parts of the north, and that he should have with him discreet and forceful men for the salvation of the said kingdom and of his people, in case the men of Scotland or others should wish to invade it for the purpose of evil-doing. And they also advised that the king should send discreet and forceful men to the parts of Ireland, as well as money, to assist his lieges there. And whereas our lord the king could not carry out these matters except by the aid of his people, the said prelates, earls, barons, and other lords, as well as the knights of the shires and all the commons[7]—in order to carry out the said projects, and in order that our lord the king could live of his own and pay his expenses without burdening his people through outrageous prises or otherwise—of their free will granted to our lord the king a fifteenth, to be levied from the community,[8] and a tenth, to be levied from the cities, boroughs, and demesnes of the king. And our lord the king, at the request of the said prelates, earls, barons, and knights of the shires, for the relief of his said people, granted that the commissions recently issued for those appointed to assess a tallage in the said cities, boroughs, and demesnes throughout England should for the present be entirely repealed; and that for this purpose writs should be sent out in due form; and that in the future he would not have such tallage assessed except as had been done in the time of his ancestors and as he rightfully should.[9]

(French) *Ibid.,* II, 66.

---

[5] For the union of the knights and burgesses to form the house of commons, see the procedure in the parliaments of 1339-41 (no. 61C-E) and the definite statements concerning the parliaments of 1343 and 1348 (no. 61F, G).

[6] In the lamentable conditions previously described.

[7] *Tote la commune*—one of many expressions used to denote the members of the lower house.

[8] That is to say, from everybody outside cities and boroughs; see above p. 158, n. 14. For tallage, cf. nos. 37B, 46F.

[9] Despite the vagueness of this promise, tallage was never again levied; cf. no. 62B.

(C) PARLIAMENT OF 1339[10]
Memoranda of the parliament held at Westminster on the quinzime of St. Michael, in the thirteenth year of our lord the king's reign:—
In the first place a general proclamation was made in the great hall of Westminster according to the following form. . . .[11]
And then the reasons for the summons of this parliament were set forth and explained to the lords and to the commons, so that in this connection their counsel and advice might be obtained in the best manner possible. And three reasons were expounded, of which the first was that every one, whether great or small, ought to take up with himself the best way in which peace could and should be more securely preserved within the kingdom. The second reason was how the march of Scotland and the lands to the north could best be guarded and defended against the Scottish enemies. The third reason was how the sea could be guarded against enemies, so that they should do no damage and should not enter the kingdom to destroy it. . . .
And after that exposition[12] had been made, everybody, both great and small, was of the opinion that in this necessity [the king] would have to be aided with a large sum; otherwise he would be shamed and dishonoured, and he and his people would be ruined forever. . . . And afterwards they sought [to decide] how he could best be aided, to the least cost and grievance of his people, to his own greatest profit, and to the most efficacious advancement of the business aforesaid, considering the grave lack of money from which the country was suffering. And among other methods certain members of the council proposed the one that is described below: namely, that within two years each man of the kingdom, of whatever status or condition he might be, should pay to our lord the king a tithe of his sheaves, wool, and lambs, in the same way as he gave [tithe] to Holy Church. And the members of the council who best knew the estate of our lord the king, and his affairs both on this side [of the sea] and on that, were of the opinion that by this [tax] the king could be greatly aided and his said affairs improved and advanced in every way—on which matters there was prolonged discussion. And after that discussion the lords gave their response in the schedule which follows. . . .
This is the grant made by the lords to our lord the king in the present parliament: namely, the tenth sheaf of every sort of grain from their demesne lands, except the lands of their bondmen, [as well as]

---

[10] For a clear sketch of the complicated parliamentary history of the next few years, see Stubbs, *Constitutional History*, II, 400 f.

[11] To prevent riots and disturbances, the king forbids the carrying of arms in or near the palace of Westminster, or in the city of London and its suburbs, by any one except designated officials and except earls and barons, each of whom is entitled to carry a sword unless he is in the presence of the king or in the royal council chamber.

[12] Of the king's needs, made by the archbishop of Canterbury and other councillors. The king asked a large aid for the war in France.

the tenth fleece and the tenth lamb from their demesne stock during
the coming year, to be paid in two years. And the said lords desire
that the maltote, which recently has been levied on wool, shall be
utterly abated and that the ancient custom shall be held to; that they
shall have, by specific charter and by enrolment of parliament, [the
promise] that no such custom [as the maltote] shall further be levied,
and that neither this grant, which they have just made to our lord
the king, nor any other grant made by them in times past shall be
turned to their prejudice as a customary burden. . . .[13]

And the commons gave their response in another schedule, as
follows:—

Lords, the men of the commons who are here at this parliament
have well understood the position of our lord the king and the pressing need that he has of being aided by his people; and they are much
enheartened and greatly comforted by the fact that he has made such
progress in the enterprises which he has undertaken for his own honour and the salvation of his people; and they pray God that He will
give him grace for successful continuation and for victory over his
enemies. . . . And with regard to his need of aid from his people,
the men of the commons who are here well know that he must be
greatly aided, and they are of good disposition to do so, as they
have ever been in times past. But in so far as the aid has to be large,
they do not dare give consent until they have advised and consulted with the communities (*communes*) of their country. Wherefore the said men of the commons pray monseigneur the duke,[14] and
the other lords who are present, that he will be pleased to summon
another parliament on some convenient day; and in the meantime
each [man of the commons] will return to his country. And they
promise loyally, in the fealty which they owe to our lord the king, that
they will all do their best, each in his own country, to obtain good and
proper aid for our lord the king; and they are confident, with God's
help, of a successful outcome. And they furthermore pray that a
writ shall be sent to each sheriff of England [ordering] that two of
the worthiest knights of the shire should be elected and sent to the
next parliament for the commons, and that none of them should be
either a sheriff or other minister.

And the men of the commons also presented two bills: one containing their response in the matters which they were charged to consider—that is to say, the peace of the land and the guarding of the
Scottish march and of the sea—and the other [containing] the graces
which they asked of the king. Of which [bills] the tenor is as follows. . . .[15]

[The commons also pray that] the king through his council will
pardon his commons the murders, escapes, and chattels of fugitives

---

[13] Cf. nos. 49B, 51A, C.
[14] The Black Prince, duke of Cornwall, who had been placed in charge of
the government during the king's absence.
[15] The first bill is omitted.

and felons and all trespasses in the forest of times past. Item, that they be pardoned aids for knighting the son of our lord the king and for marrying his daughter. Item, with regard to those men who, with or without commission, come to take prises either for the great horses of our lord the king or for other purposes, that they be arrested if they do not give immediate payment; and that [otherwise] they be treated as violators of the peace. Item, that pardon be given of all old debts up to the coronation of our lord the present king—as well scutages and reliefs as other debts owed for any reason whatsoever. And the commons pray that the maltote on wool and lead be levied as it used to be of old, since, as we understand, it has been increased without the assent of either commons or lords; and if it is demanded otherwise [than as aforesaid], that each man of the commons may forbid it with impunity; and that explanation be given them concerning the form of the security which they wish to be established for the commons in the aforesaid matters. . . .[16]

(French) *Ibid.*, II, 103-05.

(D) First Parliament of 1340

Memoranda of the parliament summoned at Westminster on the octave of St. Hilary in the thirteenth year of the reign of our lord the king, Edward III after the conquest. . . .

By virtue of which letters[17] the said treasurer, Richard [of Willoughby], John [of Stonor], and John [of St. Paul] had some of the lords and commons, who had arrived by that time, assembled in the Painted Chamber and had the said letters read. And those who had come were further told that, since the [rest of the] prelates, earls, barons, and other lords, as well as the knights of the shires and the citizens and burgesses of cities and boroughs, had been prevented by bad weather from coming on the said day, it would be necessary to await their arrival. And so the said parliament was postponed from day to day until Monday next after the said octave. . . .

On which day the reasons for calling the said parliament were set forth to the commons: namely, to make good and agreeable response concerning the promise which they had made at the last parliament, for giving suitable aid to our lord the king. . . . Upon this exposition they replied that they wished to talk together and consider the matter; and that, with God's help, they would make such response as would be to the pleasure of their liege lord and of all his council. Concerning which matter the commons delayed giving their response until Saturday, February 19.

On which day they offered to aid our lord the king in this necessity with 30,000 sacks of wool, on certain conditions put in the indentures drawn up in that connection and sealed under the seals of the prelates and other lords. . . . And since the matters contained in these indentures so intimately touched the estate of our lord the king, it was

---

[16] See the proceedings of the next parliament and no. 62B.
[17] From the duke of Cornwall naming as deputies the following men.

the opinion of the said council that our lord the king and the privy[18] council close to him should be advised of them. Wherefore it was granted and agreed that the said indentures should be sent to our lord the king, together with the advice of his council on this side [of the sea]; so that he could express his will in that connection. And it should be remembered that on the same day the earls and barons in attendance at the said parliament granted, for themselves and for their peers of the land holding by barony, the tenth sheaf, the tenth fleece, and the tenth lamb from all their demesne lands.

And whereas it was the opinion of the prelates, earls, barons, and other lords that, for carrying out the enterprises of our lord the king both on this side [of the sea] and on that, a large sum of money would have to be raised without delay, particularly for preparing a fleet of ships on the sea and equipping men-at-arms and archers for the defence of the kingdom, and that, if this were not done with haste, very great perils might arise; they asked the men of the commons how the latter wished to meet these perils and provide for their own salvation.

To which question, after a long discussion had taken place, they replied that they would vouchsafe to our lord the king 2500 sacks, to provide for the prompt raising of that [money], with this proviso: that, if the conditions set forth above were pleasing to our lord the king, those 2500 sacks should be counted as partial satisfaction of the said 30,000 sacks; and if not, they would vouchsafe these [2500 sacks] to our lord the king by their gift, as is more fully contained in another indenture made in this connection. . . .

(French) *Ibid.*, II, 107-08.

(E) PARLIAMENT OF 1341

In the first place it was agreed that Sir Thomas of Drayton should be clerk of the parliament.

Item, it was agreed by our lord the king and those of his council who had then arrived that a proclamation should be made against the bearing of arms by any person, according to the fashion customarily observed in other parliaments. . . .

Item, announcement was made that any one who wished to present a petition to our lord the king and to his council should present it between now and the next Saturday, the day stated in the announcement. And the following men were assigned to receive petitions from England: namely. . . .[19] And for petitions from Gascony, Wales, Ireland, Scotland, and the [Channel] Islands. . . . And to hear the petitions from England [the following men] were assigned. . . .[20]

---

[18] *Secrez*—that is to say, the intimate councillors who accompanied the king in France.

[19] Three chancery clerks constituted each group of receivers.

[20] In each case the hearers of petitions were a committee of bishops, earls, and barons, with the chancellor and treasurer as associates if needed.

Item, to hear the petitions from Gascony, Wales, Ireland, Scotland, and the [Channel] Islands, [the following men] were assigned. . . .

Item, it is to be remembered that, on acount of debates arising in connection with certain articles which the lords and commons of the land asked of our lord the king, the parliament was continued day after day from the said Thursday[21] until the next Thursday following. On which Thursday a bill was brought in parliament by the lords of the land, containing certain requests which our lord the king graciously agreed to, as is more fully set forth below.

And whereas, among other matters contained in the petition of the lords, it was provided that peers of the land, whether officials or others, should not be held to answer concerning trespasses with which they had been charged by the king, except in parliament; [and whereas] it was the king's opinion that such provision would be improper and opposed to his rightful estate: therefore the said lords prayed the king to agree that four bishops, four earls, and four barons, together with certain men skilled in the law, should be chosen to consider in what cases the said peers should be held to answer in parliament and nowhere else, and in what cases they should not be; and to report their advice to him. And to do this [the following men] were elected. . . . Which twelve men reported their advice in full parliament on the Monday next following, in a schedule which is transcribed in this form. . . .[22]

Also they presented, before this same Monday, certain petitions affecting all the lords and commons of the realm, a copy of which is as follows:—

. . . That it may please his most high lordship . . . to command that the said Great Charter, together with the other ordinances and statutes made through great deliberation, shall be observed, maintained, and enforced in all particulars; and that the aforesaid persons who have been attached and imprisoned, and the other persons who have been deprived[23] as stated above, shall be fully liberated and restored to their benefices, lands, tenements, possessions, goods, and chattels, so that each may be lawfully tried according to his condition, without recourse in the future to such actions against the law and the tenor of the Great Charter and all the other ordinances and statutes.

Item, that the chancellor, the treasurer, the barons and chancellor of the exchequer, the justices of both benches and all other justices whatsoever, the steward and chamberlain of the king's household, the keeper of the privy seal, and the treasurer of the wardrobe shall, whenever they are installed in office, swear to maintain and keep without infringement the law of the land and the provisions of the

---

[21] When the king's request for aid had been presented to parliament.

[22] The report, guaranteeing the trial of peers in parliament, was embodied in a statute duly sealed by the king; but this was one of the acts annulled by the king in the following year (no. 62c).

[23] Of lands and other possessions, arbitrarily and without due process of law.

61. PARLIAMENT ROLLS

Great Charter and of the other statutes made by the assent of the peers of the land. . . .

Item, the lords and commons of the land . . . pray that certain persons shall be deputed by commission to audit the accounts of all those who have received the wool for our lord the king or the other aids granted to him; and likewise of those who have received and spent his moneys both beyond the sea and here, as well since the beginning of the war as at present; and that the rolls, memoranda, obligations, and other records made beyond [the sea] shall be delivered to the chancery, to be enrolled and recorded, as should be done at such times. . . .

Item, whereas many evils have arisen through bad councillors and ministers, the lords and the commons pray that it may please the king to ordain by the advice of the prelates, earls, and barons, that he will appoint in parliament the chancellor, the chief justices of both benches, the treasurer, the chancellor and the chief baron of the exchequer, the steward of his household, the keeper of the wardrobe, the comptroller, a clerk fit to keep his private seal, and the king's chief clerks of the common bench. And this shall henceforth be done in the case of such ministers whenever there is need, and they shall swear before the peers in parliament to observe the laws, as stated above, and this according to the ordinances previously made in such connection. . . .

And they besought the king that he would graciously make those concessions. And our lord the king, having deliberated on the matter contained in the same petitions, had certain responses made to the same petitions. When these responses, together with the aforesaid petitions, were reported in full parliament before the king and the lords and commons of the realm on the next Wednesday following, it was the opinion of the said lords and commons that the said responses were not so full or sufficient as was proper. Wherefore they besought the king that he would please to add an amendment. And our lord the king, yielding to their prayer, agreed with them that four prelates, four earls, and four barons, together with other men skilled in the law, should be assigned to review the said petitions and responses, and to report their advice to the king. And [the following men] were appointed. . . .

And on the same Wednesday the said archbishops and other prelates brought certain petitions before the king in his said parliament, whereof a copy is as follows. . . .

Responses to the clergy. . . .[24]
Responses to the lords. . . .[25]
Responses to the commons:—As to the first article, it is the will of our lord the king that the Great Charter and other statutes shall be observed in all their particulars. And he wills and grants for him-

---

[24] Made by the king after the prelates had declared earlier answers unsatisfactory.

[25] Dealing with only one important article; much the same as that below.

self and his heirs that, if any person does anything in the future contrary to the Great Charter, the statutes, or the rightful laws, he shall answer in parliament, or wherever else he should answer under the common law, as stated above. . . . And as to the oaths of ministers, it pleases the king that his ministers shall be sworn according to the form of the petition. . . .

Item, as to the second article—that is to say, with regard to the auditing of accounts from those who have received the king's wool, other aids, etc.—it pleases the king that the matter shall be attended to by good men deputed for the purpose, provided that the treasurer and the chief baron [of the exchequer] are added to them. And it shall be done in this case as has been ordained on previous occasions; and the lords [of the commission] shall be elected in this parliament. Furthermore, all rolls, memoranda, and obligations made beyond the sea shall be delivered into the chancery. . . .

It pleases the king that, if one of the king's great officials named in the petition is removed from office by death or other cause, he will secure the agreement of the lords who may be found nearest in the country, together with [that of] the good council which he shall have about him, and will place another fit man in the said office. And [such appointee] shall be sworn at the next parliament in accordance with the petition. And at every parliament their offices shall be taken into the king's hands and they [shall be held] to answer to those who may see fit to complain against them. And if complaint of any misdeed is made concerning any minister, and if he is thereof convicted in parliament, he shall be removed and shall be punished by the judgment of the peers, and another fit man shall be appointed to that [office]. And in such matters the king without delay will have execution pronounced and carried out according to the judgment of the peers in parliament.

It is to be remembered that, upon the aforesaid responses as well to the petitions of the lords as to those of the commons and of the clergy, the statutes hereinunder written were made by the said lords and commons and shown to our lord the king, together with certain conditions that the lords and commons asked of the king for the grant made to him of 30,000 sacks of wool in lieu of the ninth sheaf, lamb, and fleece of the second year.[26] Which statutes and conditions were then read before the king. And the chancellor, the treasurer, certain judges of both benches, the steward of the king's household, the chamberlain, and various others were sworn on the cross of Canterbury to hold and keep those [enactments] in so far as pertained to them. But the said chancellor, treasurer, and certain judges protested that they assented neither to the making nor to the form of the said statutes, and that they could not keep them in case the said statutes were contrary to the laws and usages of the realm, which they were sworn to preserve. And afterwards the same statutes and

---

[26] Cf. no. 62B.

conditions were sealed with the king's great seal and delivered to the lords and the knights of the shires. . . .[27]

(French) *Ibid.*, II, 126-31.

(F) PARLIAMENT OF 1343

. . . Item, it is to be remembered that on the next Wednesday—namely, the last day of April—our lord the king and the archbishop aforesaid came into the Painted Chamber, together with the bishops . . . , and the earls . . . , and the other lords and commons there assembled. And the reasons for the summoning of parliament were explained to them by the chancellor of our lord the king in the manner following. . . . Whereupon the said prelates and lords were charged to meet by themselves in the White Chamber until Thursday, May 1, in order to treat, consult, and agree among themselves as to whether or not our lord the king should send messages to the court of Rome, setting forth and explaining his rights there before the said holy father the pope, as aforesaid. And in the same way the knights of the shires and the commons were charged to meet in the Painted Chamber in order to treat, consult, and agree among themselves on the same matter, and to report their answer and assent in parliament on the said Thursday. . . .

Item, it is granted and agreed that the statute made at Westminster on the quinzime of Easter, in the fifteenth year of the reign of our lord the king, shall be entirely repealed and annulled and shall lose the name of statute, as being prejudicial and contrary to the laws and usages of the realm and to the rights and prerogatives of our lord the king. But because certain articles were included in the same statute which are reasonable and in accord with law and right, it is agreed by our lord the king and his council that such articles and the others granted in this present parliament shall, by the advice of the justices and other learned men, be made into a new statute and held forever. . . .[28]

(French) *Ibid.*, II, 135-39.

(G) PARLIAMENT OF 1348

. . . Whereupon the knights of the shires and the others of the commons were told that they should withdraw together and take good counsel as to how, for withstanding the malice of the said enemy and for the salvation of our said lord the king and his kingdom of England, our lord the king could be aided to his greatest advantage and to the least burdening of his people; and that, as soon as they had come to a decision, they should notify our lord the king and the lords of his council. The which knights and others of the commons

---

[27] Cf. no. 62c.

[28] Cf. no. 62c. No articles from the annulled statute are included in the statute of this year.

took counsel on the matter day after day and at last gave their response to the following effect:[29]—

... Thus the said poor commons, to their own excessive hurt, grant to our lord the king three fifteenths, to be levied during three years, beginning at Michaelmas next; on condition that in each of these years one fifteenth, and nothing in addition, shall be levied in equal portions at two terms of the year, Michaelmas and Easter, and that this aid shall be assigned and kept solely for the war of our lord the king and shall in no way be assigned to [pay] old debts. ...

And afterwards the said commons were told that all individual persons who wished to present petitions in this parliament should present them to the chancellor; and that the petitions touching the commons [in general] should be presented to the clerk of the parliament. The which commons presented their petitions to the said clerk in the manner following:—

... Item, the commons pray that the petitions presented in the last parliament by the said commons and fully answered and granted by our said lord the king and the prelates and lords of the land, shall be observed; and that, by no bill presented in this parliament in the name of the commons or of any one else, shall the responses already granted be changed: for the commons acknowledge no such bill as may be presented by any one to effect the contrary. Response: At an earlier time the king, by the advice of the prelates and lords of the land, made answer to the petitions of the commons regarding the law of the land, [to the effect] that neither the laws held and accustomed in times past nor the process of the same [law of the land] so accustomed in the past could be changed without making a new statute—to do which the king could not then and cannot now see his way. But as soon as he can see his way [to do so], he will bring the lords and the skilled men of his council before him and by their advice and counsel will ordain concerning such articles and others that involve amendment of the law; so that right and equity shall be enforced for all and each of his lieges and subjects. ...

(French) *Ibid.*, II, 200 f.

(H) PARLIAMENT OF 1372

... The petitions that the commons presented in Parliament and the responses to them were read, and also an ordinance made in the same parliament to the following effect:—

Whereas men of the law, who pursue a variety of business in the king's courts for the sake of individuals with whom they are [as-

---

[29] The address of the commons begins with a long list of the outrageous taxes and impositions laid upon them in the past contrary to the king's promises. Then follow a large number of specific conditions, including guarantees against other forms of taxation, restoration of 20,000 sacks of wool previously borrowed by the king, immediate settlement by commissioners of petitions left over from the last parliament, respite from all judicial eyres for three years, and the formal entry of these conditions in the roll of parliament.

sociated], take numerous petitions and have them presented before parliament in the name of the commons, although the latter are not at all concerned with them . . . ; and whereas sheriffs, who are the common ministers of the people and ought to stay by their offices to do right to every one, are named . . . and returned to parliament as knights of the shire by the sheriffs themselves: [therefore] it is agreed and granted in this parliament that henceforth no man of the law, pursuing business in the king's courts, or sheriff during such time as he is sheriff, shall be returned or accepted as a knight of the shire; nor shall those men of the law and sheriffs, who are at present returned to parliament, have wages. But the king wishes that the worthiest knights and serjeants of the country shall be returned as knights in parliament, and that they shall be elected in the full county [court].

And afterwards permission was given to the knights of the shires to depart and to sue for their writs of expenses. And so they departed. But the citizens and burgesses who had come to parliament were for certain reasons commanded to remain. To which citizens and burgesses, assembled on the very next day in a chamber near the White Chamber, it was shown how in the previous year a subsidy had been granted for a certain term to assure safe convoy of ships and merchandise coming to this country and leaving it by sea—that is to say, 2s. from each tun of wine coming to this country and 6d. from every pound of any merchandise whatsoever, either imported or exported[30]—[and how] this term had already passed. [So they were asked] that, considering the perils and mischiefs which might be incurred by their ships and merchandise from enemies on the sea, they would grant for the said causes a similar subsidy to continue for one year. Which subsidy they granted to the king, to be taken and levied in the same way as it had been taken and levied during the previous year. And so they departed.

(French) *Ibid.*, II, 310.

(I) PARLIAMENT OF 1376

. . . On the said morrow the prelates, the duke [of Cornwall], the earls, barons, and other lords, as well as the commons, justices, serjeants-at-law, and others, assembled in the Painted Chamber, where, before the king himself and all the others, Sir John Knyvett, knight, the chancellor of England, announced the causes for the summoning of the present parliament. . . . And in conclusion the chancellor besought them on behalf of the king that they would take diligent counsel regarding these matters—that is to say, the prelates and lords by themselves and the commons by themselves—and that, for the sake of prompter action by parliament, they would make good response in this connection as soon as they well might. And thereupon certain

---

[30] This tax, known as tunnage and poundage, was formally granted for two years by parliament in 1373: Stubbs, *Constitutional History*, II, 444 f., 556 f.

prelates and lords were assigned to be triers, and certain clerks to be receivers of bills in parliament, whose names here follow. . . .

Item, after the said prelates, lords, and commons had assembled in parliament, the said commons were told on behalf of the king that they should retire by themselves to their ancient place [of meeting], in the chapter house of the abbot of Westminster, and should there discuss and take counsel among themselves with regard principally to those matters of which, as stated above, declaration had been made in parliament on behalf of the king. And the prelates and lords on their part were likewise to hold a discussion; and they were told that report should be made from one group to the other concerning the acts and intentions of each. And so the commons departed to their said place [of meeting].[31]

(French) *Ibid.,* II, 321 f.

. . . And on the said second day all the knights and commons aforesaid assembled and went into the chapter house and seated themselves about [the room] one next another. And they began to talk about their business, the matters before the parliament, saying that it would be well at the outset for them to be sworn to each other to keep counsel regarding what was spoken and decided among them, and loyally and without concealment to deliberate and ordain for the benefit of the kingdom. And to do this all unanimously agreed, and they took a good oath to be loyal to each other. Then one of them said that, if any of us knew of anything to say for the benefit of the king and the kingdom, it would be well for him to set forth among us what he knew and then, one after the other, [each of the rest could say] what lay next his heart.

Thereupon a knight of the south country rose and went to the reading desk in the centre of the chapter house so that all might hear and, pounding on the said desk, began to speak in this fashion: "*Jube domine benedicere, etc.*[32] My lords, you have heard the grievous matters before the parliament—how our lord the king has asked of the clergy and the commons a tenth and a fifteenth and customs on wool and other merchandise for a year or two. And in my opinion it is much to grant, for the commons are so weakened and impoverished by the divers tallages and taxes which they have paid up to the present that they cannot sustain such a charge or at this time pay it. Besides, all we have given to the war for a long time we have lost because it has been badly wasted and falsely expended. And so it would be well to consider how our lord the king can live and govern his kingdom and maintain the war from his demesne property, and not

---

[31] The official roll is here interrupted for the sake of inserting a portion of an anonymous chronicle preserved at St. Mary's Abbey, York. This account is especially valuable as our earliest description of procedure at a separate meeting of the commons, including the election of a speaker. See the remarks of the editor, V. H. Galbraith, p. xliv.

[32] He begins and ends his speech with a conventional Latin grace.

hold to ransom his liegemen of the land. Also, as I have heard, there are divers people who, without his knowledge, have in their hands goods and treasure of our lord the king amounting to a great sum of gold and silver; and they have falsely concealed the said goods, which through guile and extortion they gained in many ways to the great damage of our lord the king and the kingdom. For the present I will say no more. *Tu autem domine meserere nostris.*" And he went back to his seat among his companions.

Thereupon another knight arose and went to the reading desk and said: "My lords, our companion has spoken to good purpose, and now, as God will give me grace, I will tell you one thing for the benefit of the kingdom. You have heard how it was ordained by common counsel in parliament that the staple of wool and other merchandise should be wholly at Calais, to the great advantage of our lord the king; and then the said town was governed and ruled by merchants of England, and they took nothing by way of payments to maintain the war or for the government of the said town. And afterwards the said staple was suddenly removed to divers cities and towns of England, and the merchants were ousted from Calais, together with their wives and their households, without the knowledge or consent of parliament, but for the benefit of a few, illegally and against the statute thereupon made; so that the lord of Latimer and Richard Lyons of London and others could have advantages.[33] And by concealment they took great sums of the maltote, which rightfully the king should have, because each year, to keep the town, the king spends sums amounting to £8000 of gold and silver, without getting anything there, where no expense used to be necessary. Wherefore it would be well to provide a remedy by advising that the staple should be restored to Calais." And he would say no more, but went back to his seat.

And the third man rose and went to the reading desk and said: "My lords, our companions have spoken very well and to good purpose. But it is my opinion that it would not be profitable or honourable for us to deliberate on such great affairs and such grievous matters for the benefit of the kingdom without the counsel and aid of those greater and wiser than we are, or to begin such procedure without the assent of the lords. Wherefore it would be well at the outset to pray our lord the king and his wise council in the parliament that they may grant and assign to us certain bishops and certain earls, barons, and bannerets, such as we may name, to counsel and aid us and to hear and witness what we shall say." And to this all agreed. Then two or three more arose in the same manner, one after the other, and spoke on various subjects. . . .

About the same time a knight from the march of Wales, who was steward to the earl of March and was named Sir Peter de la Mare, began to speak where the others had spoken, and he said: "My lords, you have well heard what our companions have had to say and what

---

[33] Cf. no. 62H.

they have known and how they have expressed their views; and, in my opinion, they have spoken loyally and to good purpose." And he rehearsed, word for word, all the things that they had said, doing so very skilfully and in good form. And besides he advised them on many points and particulars, as will be more fully set forth below. And so they ended the second day.

Then on the third day all the knights and commons assembled in the said chapter house and day after day until the next Friday held discussion concerning various matters and [particularly] the extortions committed by divers persons, through treachery, as they were advised. During which discussion and counsel, because the said Sir Peter de la Mare had spoken so well and had so skilfully rehearsed the arguments and views of his companions, and had informed them of much that they did not know, they begged him on their part to assume the duty of expressing their will in the great parliament before the said lords, as to what they had decided to do and say according to their conscience. And the said Sir Peter, out of reverence to God and his good companions and for the benefit of the kingdom, assumed that duty. . . .[34]

(French) *Anonimalle Chronicle*, pp. 80 f.

And thereupon the following prelates and lords were assigned in parliament . . . to go to the said commons and be of aid to them, joining with them and discussing the said matters that had been declared to them, as aforesaid. . . .[35]

Item, the commons, considering the sufferings of the land . . . , pray that the council of our lord the king may be afforced with lords of the land, prelates, and others, to remain constantly at the number of ten or twelve according to the king's will; so that no important business shall there pass or be determined without the advice and consent of all. . . . And our lord the king, believing the said request to be honourable and of good advantage to him and all his kingdom, has granted it. . . .

And afterwards the said commons came into parliament and made open protestation. . . .[36] Then the said commons made complaint in parliament especially of the persons mentioned below, affirming that many deceits and other wrongs had been inflicted upon the king and his kingdom, as appears below. . . .[37]

[34] The chronicle continues with a long and interesting account of the ensuing debates in parliament.

[35] The roll next records a grant of subsidy and certain ordinances concerning the council, although these enactments were presumably made after the protestation of the commons and the presentation of their petitions.

[36] Through their speaker, although the fact is not stated in the roll. The address summarized the complaints earlier made during the meeting of the commons, especially the restoration of the staple to Calais and the wasting of the royal revenues through the dishonesty of the king's advisers.

[37] Here the roll describes at length the impeachment of Lyons, Latimer, and others.

Hereafter follow the petitions presented in writing to the parliament by the commons, together with the responses made to those petitions in the same parliament. . . .[38]

(French) *Rotuli Parliamentorum*, II, 322-57.

[38] There were 140 of them; see Stubbs, *Constitutional History*, II, 453 f.

62. EDWARD III: STATUTES AND ORDINANCES

(A) SECOND STATUTE OF 1 EDWARD III: RESTRICTION OF MILITARY LEVIES, IMPROVEMENT OF JUSTICE, ETC. (1327)

. . . Item, the king wills that henceforth no one shall be charged to arm himself otherwise than was accustomed in the time of his ancestors, kings of England; and that no one shall be distrained to go outside his county except in case of necessity owing to the sudden invasion of enemy aliens into the kingdom, and such procedure shall then be followed as has been accustomed in times past for the defence of the kingdom. . . .

Likewise, whereas commissions[1] have been issued to certain people of the counties for arraying men-at-arms, and for taking them to the king in Scotland, in Gascony, or elsewhere at the cost of the counties—[for] up to this time the king has not provided wages for the said arrayers and commanders, or for the men-at-arms whom they have taken—whereby the commonalty of the counties has been greatly burdened and impoverished: the king wills that this shall no longer be done. . . .

Item, whereas the king wishes that common law should be administered to all, the poor as well as the rich, he commands and enjoins that none of his councillors or of his household or of his other ministers, nor any lord of the land . . . , nor any other man of the kingdom, small or great, shall undertake the maintenance of quarrels or suits in the country, to the disturbance of the common law. . . .

Item, for better keeping and preserving the peace, the king wills that in each county good and loyal men—such as are not maintainers of evil and fraud in the country—shall be assigned as keepers of the peace.[2] . . .

(French) *Statutes of the Realm*, I, 255 f.

(B) SECOND STATUTE OF 14 EDWARD III: PARLIAMENTARY CONTROL OF DIRECT TAXES (1340)

. . . Whereas the prelates, earls, barons, and commons of our realm, in our present parliament summoned at Westminster . . . , of their free will and grace have granted us, in aid of advancing the great enterprises that we have before us both on this side of the sea

[1] Cf. no. 50B.
[2] Cf. nos. 46H, 52E.

and beyond it, the ninth sheaf, the ninth fleece, and the ninth lamb[3] . . . ; and [whereas] the citizens of cities and the burgesses of boroughs [have granted] the true ninth of all their goods; and [whereas] foreign merchants and other[4] men who live neither from trade nor from flocks of sheep, [have granted] the fifteenth of their goods, rightly [assessed] according to value: we, desirous of providing indemnity for the said prelates, earls, barons, and others of the said commonalty, and also for the citizens, burgesses, and merchants aforesaid, will and grant for us and our heirs to the same prelates, earls, barons, and commons, [and to the same] citizens, burgesses, and merchants, that this grant now chargeable shall not at another time be treated as a precedent or work to their prejudice in the future; and that henceforth they shall be neither charged nor burdened to make common aid or to sustain charge except by the common assent of the prelates, earls, and barons, and of the other lords and commons of our said realm of England, and this in parliament; and that all profits arising from the said aid, and from wardships, marriages, customs, and escheats, together with other profits arising from the kingdom of England, shall be devoted and spent to maintain the safeguarding of our said kingdom of England and [to advance] our wars in Scotland, France, and Gascony, and nowhere else during the [continuance of] the said wars. . . .[5]

And whereas the said prelates, earls, barons, and commons, for the sake of the great enterprises which we have undertaken, have granted at our request that we may levy 40s. on each sack of wool passing beyond sea from now until the feast of Pentecost next; and 40s. on every three hundred wool-fells; and 40s. on a last of leather: we . . . have granted that, after the said feast of Pentecost to come in one year, neither we nor our heirs shall demand, assess, levy, or cause to be levied more than half a mark of custom on a sack of wool throughout all England, half a mark on three hundred wool-fells, and one mark on a last of leather. . . .

(French) *Ibid.*, I, 289-91.

(C) ANNULMENT OF THE STATUTE OF 1341[6] (1342)

The king to the sheriff of Lincoln, greeting. Whereas, in our parliament summoned at Westminster on the quinzime of Easter last, certain articles expressly contrary to the laws and customs of our kingdom of England, and to our royal rights and prerogatives, were drawn up in the form of a statute on the pretence that they had been granted by us: we, considering how we were bound by oath to observe and defend such laws, customs, rights, and prerogatives, and desiring

---

[3] Substituted for the tenth sheaf, lamb, etc., in the second parliament of 1340; see above, pp. 210 f.

[4] That is to say, other than those of cities and boroughs.

[5] The act continues with a general pardon of old debts, according to the commons' petition of 1339 (above, p. 211).

[6] Cf. no. 61E, F.

providently to revoke what had been improvidently done [and to restore conditions] to their proper state, thereupon held a council and deliberation with the earls, barons, and other skilled men of our said realm. [To them it was explained that] we never consented to the drawing up of the said pretended statute, but secured beforehand protests for the revocation of the said statute, should it proceed *de facto*;[7] and then, to avoid the dangers which we feared such a denial would provoke, we dissembled, as behooved us, promising that the said pretended statute should be sealed for the time being, since otherwise the said parliament would have been dissolved in bad feeling with nothing accomplished, and so—which God forbid!— our grave enterprises would in all likelihood have been ruined. [Therefore] it appeared to the said earls, barons, and skilled men that, because the said statute did not proceed of our free will, it was null and ought not to have the name or force of a statute. And so, by their counsel and assent, we have decreed the said statute to be null, considering that it ought to be annulled in so far as it proceeded *de facto*; wishing, nevertheless, that the articles in the said pretended statute which have already been approved in other statutes of ours, or [in those] of our ancestors, kings of England, should in all respects be observed according to the form of the said statutes, as is proper. And we do this solely to conserve and reintegrate the rights of our crown, as we are bound [to do]; and not in any way to oppress or burden our subjects, whom we desire to rule in kindness. And therefore we command you to have all these matters publicly proclaimed in such places within your bailiwick as you shall think best. By witness of the king at Westminster, October 1, in the fifteenth year [of our reign].

By the king himself and his council.

(Latin) *Ibid.*, I, 297.

(D) STATUTE OF LABOURERS (1351)

Whereas, to curb the malice of servants who after the pestilence were idle and unwilling to serve without securing excessive wages, it was recently ordained by our lord the king, with the assent of the prelates, nobles, and other men of his council, that such servants, both men and women, should be bound to serve in return for the salaries and wages that were customary in those places where they were obligated to serve during the twentieth year of the reign of our said lord the king, that is to say, five or six years earlier; and whereas the same servants, on refusing to serve in any manner, were to be punished by imprisonment of their bodies, as is more clearly set forth in the same ordinance . . . ; and whereas our lord the king has now, by the petition of the commons in this present parliament, been given to understand that the said servants have no regard for the said ordinance, but, to suit their ease and their selfish desires,

---

[7] That is to say, not of right, since the king had never really assented to it.

refrain from serving the lords or other men unless they receive double or triple that which they were accustomed to have in the said twentieth year and earlier, to the great damage of the lords and the impoverishment of all men of the said commons, who now pray for remedy of these matters: therefore in the same parliament, by the assent of the prelates, earls, barons, and the other lords, and of the same commons there assembled, the following measures are ordained and established to curb the malice of the said servants. . . .[8]

(French) *Ibid.,* I, 311.

(E) STATUTE OF PROVISORS (1351)

. . . Our lord the king, perceiving the mischief and damage mentioned above, and having regard to the said statute made in the time of his said grandfather[9] . . . , and also giving attention to the grievous complaints made to him by his people in various parliaments held in times past . . . , with the assent of all the lords and commons of his said kingdom, for the honour of God and the benefit of the said Church of England and [the welfare] of all his kingdom, has ordained and established that the free elections of archbishops and bishops, and [the elections to] all other dignities and benefices that are elective in England, shall continue to be held in such fashion as when they were granted by the ancestors of our said lord the king or founded by the ancestors of other lords; that all prelates and men of Holy Church, who hold advowsons of any benefices by gift of our lord the king and of his ancestors, or of other lords and donors . . . , shall freely have their collations and presentations according to the terms of the enfeoffment by the donors. And in case reservation, collation, or provision is by the court of Rome made of any archbishopric, bishopric, dignity, or other benefice whatsoever, to the disturbance of the elections, collations, or presentations aforesaid, [it is ordained] that, at the very time of the vacancies when such reservations, collations, or provisions should take effect, our lord the king and his heirs are to have and enjoy, for the time being, the collations to archbishoprics, bishoprics, and other elective dignities that are under his advowry, just as his ancestors had them before free election was granted. . . .[10]

(French) *Ibid.,* I, 317 f.

[8] The ordinance (*Statutes of the Realm,* I, 307) had fixed wages as here stated, at the same time prohibiting increased prices for victuals above the standard of the same years, forbidding alms to sturdy beggars, etc. The statute merely added details concerning the wages of agricultural labourers and of artisans, together with measures intended to secure the enforcement of the ordinance. See B. H. Putnam, *The Enforcement of the Statutes of Labourers.*

[9] The reference is to the Statute of Carlisle (1307) and the parliamentary petition against encroachments by the see of Rome: Stubbs, *Constitutional History,* II, 163.

[10] Similar enactment is made with regard to papal provision in religious houses; other lay patrons besides the king are given the same kind of protection; and means of enforcement is prescribed.

62. STATUTES AND ORDINANCES

(F) STATUTE OF TREASONS (1352)

. . . Item, whereas until now there have been various opinions as to which cases should be called treason and which not, the king, at the request of the lords and the commons, has made the following declarations:—

If a man compasses or imagines the death of our lord the king, of our lady his consort, or of their eldest son and heir; or if a man violates the king's consort, the king's eldest daughter being as yet unmarried, or the consort of the king's eldest son and heir; or if a man makes war against our said lord the king in his kingdom, or is an adherent of enemies to our lord the king in the kingdom, giving them aid or comfort in his kingdom or elsewhere . . . ; or if a man counterfeits the great or the privy seal of the king or his money; or if a man, for the sake of trading or making payments in deceit of our said lord the king or of his people, brings into this kingdom false coin, counterfeit of the money of England, . . . knowing it to be false; or if a man slays the chancellor, treasurer, or justice of our lord the king . . . while [such official is] in his place and attending to his office—these cases specified above, it must be understood, are to be adjudged treason against our lord the king and his royal majesty; and in such [cases of] treason forfeiture of property pertains to our lord the king, as well lands and tenements held of another as those held of [the king] himself. . . .[11]

(French) *Ibid.,* I, 319 f.

(G) ORDINANCE AND STATUTE OF PRAEMUNIRE (1353)[12]

Our lord the king, with the assent and by the prayer of the lords and commons of his kingdom of England, in his great council[13] held at Westminster on Monday next after the feast of St. Matthew the Apostle, in the twenty-seventh year of his reign—that is to say in England; in France the fourteenth—for the improvement of his said kingdom and for the maintenance of its laws and usages, has ordained and established the measures hereinunder written:—

First, whereas our lord the king has been shown by the clamorous and grievous complaints of his lords and commons aforesaid how numerous persons have been and are being taken out of the kingdom to respond in cases of which the cognizance pertains to the court of our lord the king; and also how the judgments rendered in the same court are being impeached in the court of another, to

---

[11] The statute also defines "another kind of treason"—the commission of similar offenses against a lord other than the king. The distinction is that known in law as between high and petit treason.

[12] Technically, this ordinance became a statute when it was confirmed by the parliament of the ensuing year; cf. the next document. For the name, see no. 64F; for interpretation, see W. T. Waugh, in the *English Historical Review,* XXXVII, 173 f., and E. B. Graves, in *Anniversary Essays by Students of C. H. Haskins,* pp. 57 f.

[13] Cf. nos. 60B, 62H (last paragraph).

the prejudice and disherison of our lord the king and of his crown and of all the people of his said kingdom, and to the undoing and annulment of the common law of the same kingdom at all times customary: therefore, after good deliberation held with the lords and others of the said council, it is granted and agreed by our said lord the king and by the lords and commons aforesaid that all persons of the king's allegiance, of whatever condition they may be, who take any one out of the kingdom in a plea of which the cognizance pertains to the king's court or in matters regarding which judgments have been rendered in the king's court, or who bring suit in the court of another to undo or impede the judgments rendered in the king's court, shall be given a day . . . [on which] to appear before the king and his council, or in his chancery, or before the king's justices in their courts, either the one bench or the other, or before other justices of the king who may be deputed for the purpose, there to answer to the king in proper person regarding the contempt involved in such action. And if they do not come in proper person on the said day to stand trial, let them, their procurators, attorneys, executors, notaries, and supporters, from this day forth be put outside the king's protection, and let their lands, goods, and chattels be forfeit to the king, and let their bodies, wherever they may be found, be taken and imprisoned and redeemed at the king's pleasure. . . .

(French) *Ibid.*, I, 329.

(H) Ordinance and Statute of the Staple (1353)

On Monday next after the feast of St. Matthew the Apostle, in the twenty-seventh year of the reign of our lord, King Edward III . . . , a great council was summoned at Westminster. . . .[14] On which Friday the prelates, dukes, earls, barons, and commons, assembled in the White Chamber of our lord the king, were told . . . the cause for the summons of the said council. . . .[15] Considering which mischief, our lord the king, by the assent of certain prelates and lords of his said kingdom . . . had ordained that the staple of wool, wool-fells, leather, and lead should be held in certain places within his kingdom of England and his lands of Wales and Ireland. And by the assent and advice of the said prelates and lords he had ordained for the maintenance and good government of the same staple certain particulars, which he caused to be read aloud before the prelates, lords, and commons, in order to obtain their assent. And [it was said] also that, if they wished to make any additions or subtractions, they should show [their desire] in writing. And thereupon the commons asked for a copy of the said particulars, which was given them—that is to say, one [copy] for the knights of the shires and another for the citizens

---

[14] Cf. no. 60B. The meeting was postponed from Monday until Friday.

[15] Principally the king's decision to change the staple, as is recited in the ordinance. On the procedure followed in drafting this statute, see H. L. Gray, *The Influence of the Commons on Early Legislation*, pp. 250 f.

62. STATUTES AND ORDINANCES

and burgesses. And they, after long deliberation among themselves, presented their opinion to the council in writing. And after this writing had been read and debated by the lords, the ordinances of the staple were drawn up in the form following:—

Edward, by the grace of God king of England and France and lord of Ireland, to all our sheriffs, mayors, bailiffs, ministers, and other faithful men to whom these present letters may come, greeting. Whereas good deliberation has been held with the prelates, dukes, earls, barons, knights of the shires—that is to say, one from each for the whole shire—and commons of cities and boroughs of our kingdom of England, summoned to our great council held at Westminster . . . , concerning the damages which have been notoriously incurred by us and by the lords, as well as by the people of our kingdom of England and our lands of Wales and Ireland, because the staple of wool, leather, and wool-fells for our said kingdom and lands has been kept outside the said kingdom and lands; and also concerning the great profits that would accrue to our said kingdom and lands if the staple should be held within them and nowhere else: so, for the honour of God and the relief of our kingdom and lands aforesaid, and for the sake of avoiding the perils that otherwise may arise in times to come, by the counsel and common assent of the said prelates, dukes, earls, barons, knights, and commons aforesaid, we have ordained and established the measures hereinunder written, to wit:—

First, that the staples of wool, leather, wool-fells and lead grown or produced within our kingdom and lands aforesaid shall be perpetually held in the following places: namely, for England at Newcastle-upon-Tyne, York, Lincoln, Norwich, Westminster, Canterbury, Chichester, Winchester, Exeter, and Bristol; for Wales at Carmarthen; and for Ireland at Dublin, Waterford, Cork, and Drogheda, and nowhere else. . . .[16]

. . . For which grant our lord the king thanked the lords and commons. And then the said commons prayed the king that their petitions, which they had drawn up concerning divers grievances as well as benefits of his commons, should be answered. Which petitions our lord the king caused to be read and answered by the prelates, lords, and other men of his council in the following manner:—

. . . Item, whereas certain articles touching the state of the king and the common benefit of his kingdom have been agreed and assented to by him, and by the prelates, lords, and commons of his land in this council just held; the said commons pray that the aforesaid articles shall be recited at the next parliament and entered in the roll of the same parliament, with the intent that the ordinances and

---

[16] The following articles provide that all the said products, before being exported, must be taken to one of the staple towns, where they are to be officially weighed, sealed, and taxed. The prescribed customs are those of 1275 (no. 49B), except that 20s. worth of lead is to pay 3d., and that aliens are taxed at a higher rate.

agreements made in councils shall not be of record as if they had been made by a common parliament. . . .

As to the tenth article, it is the king's pleasure that all the ordinances made concerning the staple shall be published and proclaimed in each county of England, and in each place where a staple is [situated], so that they may be firmly kept; and at the next parliament, for the sake of greater stability, they shall be rehearsed and entered in the roll of parliament. . . .

Also the said commons in this parliament[17] prayed that the ordinances of the staple, and all the other ordinances made at the last council . . . , which they had examined with great care and deliberation, and which seemed to them good and advantageous for our lord the king and all his people, should be confirmed in this parliament and held as a statute to endure forever. To which prayer the king and all the lords unanimously agreed; to the effect that, whenever anything was to be added [to that statute], it should be added [in parliament], or whenever anything was to be subtracted, it should be subtracted in parliament, no matter at what time the need should arise, and never in any other fashion.

(French) *Rotuli Parliamentorum*, II, 246, 253, 257.

(I) STATUTE OF 34 EDWARD III: ON JUSTICES OF THE PEACE (1361)

These are the measures which our lord the king, the prelates, the lords, and the commons have ordained in this present parliament, held at Westminster on Sunday next before the feast of the Conversion of St. Paul, to be observed and publicly proclaimed throughout the kingdom, to wit:—

First, that for the keeping of the peace, there shall be assigned in each county of England one lord, and with him three or four of the most worthy men of the county together with certain men skilled in the law,[18] and they shall have power to restrain evil-doers, rioters, and all other miscreants; to pursue, arrest, capture, and chastise them according to their trespass or offence; to have them imprisoned and duly punished according to the law and custom of the kingdom, and according to what [the justices] may think best to do at their discretion and good advisement. Also [they shall have power] to inform themselves and to make inquiry concerning all those who have been pillagers and robbers in the regions beyond [the sea], and who have now returned to become vagrants, refusing to work as they used to in times past; and to take and arrest all whom they can find on indictment or suspicion, and to put them in prison. . . . Also [they shall have power] to hear and determine, at the king's suit, all manner of felonies and trespasses committed in the

---

[17] Of the next year, 1354.

[18] Cf. no. 62A, above; and for a résumé of the subject, together with citation of the pertinent literature, see Lodge and Thornton, *Constitutional Documents*, pp. 325 f.

same county, according to the laws and customs aforesaid. . . . And the fine to be assessed before the justices, because of trespass committed by any person, shall be just and reasonable, according to the gravity of the offence and as the causes leading to it are taken into account. . . .

Item, it is agreed that the men assigned to keep the peace shall have power to make inquiry concerning measures and also weights, according to the statute thereupon made in the twenty-fifth year of our lord the king's reign. . . .

Item, it is agreed in this present parliament that the Statute of Labourers earlier made shall stand in all its particulars, with the exception of the pecuniary penalty, in which connection it is agreed that henceforth labourers shall not be punished by fine and redemption. . . .

Item, with regard to labourers and artisans who run away from their [owed] services into another vill or county, [it is provided] that the [aggrieved] party shall have his suit before the justices [of the peace]. . . .

(French) *Statutes of the Realm*, I, 364 f.

(J) STATUTE OF 36 EDWARD III: REGARDING PURVEYANCE, CUSTOMS, ETC. (1362)

For the honour and gratification of God, for the reform of the outrageous wrongs and oppressions suffered by the people, and for the relief of their condition, King Edward, in his parliament held at Westminster on the quinzime of St. Michael in the thirty-sixth year of his reign, at the request of his commons and by their petition presented to him in the said parliament, with the assent of the prelates, dukes, earls, barons, and other lords assembled in the said parliament, has granted for him and his heirs forever the articles hereinunder written:—

First, that the Great Charter, the Charter of the Forest, and the other statutes made in his own time and in the times of his ancestors shall be well and firmly observed in all particulars.

Item, on account of the grievous complaint that has been made concerning purveyors of victuals for the households of the king, the queen, their eldest son, and other lords and ladies of the kingdom, the king, of his own will and without compulsion of lords or commons, has granted and ordained for the relief of his people that henceforth no man of the said kingdom shall take any prise except solely for [the king] himself and for the queen his consort. Furthermore, with the assent aforesaid, it is ordained and established that, in case of such purveyances to be henceforth made for the households of the king and the queen, prompt payment in hand shall be rendered—that is to say, the price at which such victuals are commonly sold in the neighbouring markets. [It is also ordained] that the heinous name of purveyor shall be changed to buyer; and if the buyer cannot well agree with the seller of that for which there is need, then the prises which are made for the said two households shall be made by the view, testimony, and appraisal of the lords, or of their bailiffs and constables, and four good men of each vill, and this through indenture to be made between the buyers and the said lords, or bailiffs and constables, and four good men, stating the amount of what has been taken, its price, and the persons from whom it was taken. And [it is ordained] that the prises shall be made in a proper and easy manner, without duress, compulsion, threats, or other villainy; that the prises and purchases shall be made in the regions and places where there is greatest plenty, and this at a convenient time; and that no more shall be taken than is needful at that season for the said two households. . . .[19]

Item, [it is ordained] that, with the exception of the king and queen, no lord of England or other man of the said kingdom, of whatsoever estate or condition, shall of himself or through any of his servants in any way take prises of any sort of victuals; but they shall buy what they need from those who of their own free will wish to sell, and for these [victuals] they shall pay promptly in hand according to what they may agree upon with the seller. . . .

Item, to maintain the said articles and statutes, and to redress divers mischiefs and grievances that recur day after day, parliament shall be held every year, as was earlier ordained by statute.

Item, by the assent aforesaid, the king, considering the great subsidy which the commons have granted him earlier in this parliament, to be levied for three years on wool, leather, and wool-fells, wills and grants that, after the said term has passed, nothing shall be taken or asked of the said commons except only the ancient custom of half a mark;[20] that neither the grant just made nor any that has heretofore been made shall be turned into a precedent or burden for the said commons in time to come; that resident as well as foreign merchants may pass with their wool free of restraint; and that henceforth no subsidy or other charge shall be levied or granted on wool either by merchants or by any other persons without the assent of parliament. . . .

(French) *Ibid.,* I, 371 f.

---

[19] The statute gives long and elaborate provisions for the commissioning of buyers, the prevention of abuses, etc.
[20] Cf. no. 49B.

63. PARLIAMENT ROLLS OF RICHARD II

(A) PARLIAMENT OF 1377

. . . And afterwards the commons came before the king in parliament, and there Sir Peter de la Mare, knight, who acted as speaker for the commons,[1] made his protestation, that what he had to say was not said on his own personal account, but by the initiative, as-

---

[1] See above, p. 222.

63. PARLIAMENT ROLLS

sent, and express will of all the commons there assembled.[2] . . . And since our lord the king—whom God save!—is at present innocent and of tender age, the said commons, for the redress of the wrongs aforesaid, as well as of others, and for the salvation of the kingdom, which at present is in great peril and more so than ever before, besought our lord the king and the lords of parliament with regard to three matters in particular:—

First, that it might please them to ordain and appoint in this present parliament eight fit persons of different estates, to remain continually along with the king's officials in council [to consult] on the needs of the king and the kingdom. . . .

Item, that it might please them to ordain and appoint in this parliament those who were to surround the person of our same lord the king, who is of such tender age. . . . And that it should also be ordained that our same lord the king and his household should be governed with good moderation of expenses, to be met solely from the [ordinary] revenues of the kingdom and from the other rights of his crown and his dominions; and that, for the aid and relief of his commons aforesaid, all which is or may be granted for his wars shall be used and expended in the wars and not otherwise.

Item, that the common law, as well as the special laws, statutes, and ordinances of the land made in earlier times for the common benefit and salutary governance of the kingdom, should in their entirety be kept, ratified, and confirmed. . . . Request is also made to the lords of parliament that whatever is ordained in this parliament shall not be repealed without [consent of] parliament. . . .

And thereupon answer was given that on these matters the prelates and lords would consult together; and the commons were instructed to return to their place and by themselves to consider their other business from now until the next Thursday. On which day they were commanded to return to parliament to hear the responses made to their aforesaid requests.

As to the first request presented by the said commons to our lord the king and to the lords of parliament, . . . our lord the king . . . has granted it, provided always that the chancellor, the treasurer, the keeper of the privy seal, the justices of both benches, and all the other officials of the king may perform and carry through the duties pertaining to their offices without the presence of such councillors. And our lord the king, for certain reasons that influence him at present, by the advice of the lords of parliament, wishes to have nine persons as such councillors for this present year only, and has had them elected in parliament: namely. . . . And as to the second request of the commons, . . . the lords of parliament respond, saying that to them it seems too severe and burdensome a request that any person should be placed near their lord the king other than one well pleasing to him for various reasons, or to remove

---

[2] The commons complained especially of the evils then being suffered by the knights and the merchants.

any of his officials or servants except by the express will of the said king. . . .[3] And as to the third and last request, it seems reasonable to all the lords that for the present it should be conceded and granted.

Item, the lords and commons of the kingdom of England, clearly perceiving the great peril of the kingdom . . . , of their free will have granted to our same lord the king two fifteenths outside cities and boroughs and two tenths within the same cities and boroughs.[4] . . . And it is the humble prayer [of the commons] to their liege lord and to the other lords of the parliament that for these moneys, as well as for the moneys from the tithes recently granted by the clergy of England and also for the moneys arising from the subsidies of wool, certain fit persons should be assigned on the part of the king to be treasurers or wardens, to such effect that these moneys shall be entirely devoted to the expenses of the war, and by no means to anything else. And it is to be remembered that this request was granted to them by the king. . . . And thereupon our lord the king had William Walworth and John Philipot, merchants of London, assigned to be wardens of the said sums to be used as aforesaid, and to render faithful account of their receipts and expenditures in such fashion as should be reasonably ordained by our lord the king and his said great council. . . .[5]

(French) *Rotuli Parliamentorum*, III, 5-7.

(B) PARLIAMENT OF 1378

. . . And thereupon the commons, after some little deliberation, made another request of our lord the king, that it might please him to have demonstration made to his said commons how and in what way the said great sums thus given and ordered for the said war had been expended.[6] . . . To which it was replied by the said Sir Richard[7] . . . that, although it was unheard of that, for any subsidy or other grant made to the king by the commons in parliament or out of parliament, account should afterwards be rendered to the commons or to anybody besides the king and his officials, nevertheless, to please the commons, our said lord the king willed and commanded of his own initiative, without doing so as of right or through coercion on account of the said request recently made to him, that the said William Walworth,[8] there present, together with certain other persons from the council of our lord the king to be assigned

---

[3] But, they think, those about the king should be warned not to impose on him for their own selfish ends, and the officers of the household should be talked to about moderation of expenses.
[4] To be levied according to the ancient custom; see no. 61B.
[5] Sixty-nine petitions of the commons follow.
[6] This was after the commons had refused further aid and the king had protested their refusal.
[7] Richard le Scrope, steward of the king's household.
[8] See the preceding document.

for this duty by the king, should clearly show you in writing the receipts and expenditures made of those [sums]—on the understanding that this [action] should not thereafter be held a precedent, on the ground that it was taken otherwise than solely by the initiative and command of our lord the king, as aforesaid. . . .

Item, they prayed that five or six of the prelates and lords should come to the commons to discuss with them jointly the said matters concerning which they were charged.[9] And to this request the lords replied, saying that they were neither obliged nor willing to do this; for such manner of procedure had never been used in any parliament except in the last three parliaments recently held. But they said and declared that it had well been accustomed for the lords to choose from among themselves a certain small number, six or ten, and for the commons [to choose] another small number from among themselves; and for these lords and commons thus elected to meet together in easy manner, without murmurs, cries, and noise. And so by motions made among them they would quickly arrive at some good decision, which would then be reported to their companions of one or the other group. And in such fashion the lords would henceforth proceed, and in none other. . . . And thereupon the commons readily assented that certain lords and commons, a small and reasonable number, should be elected, as had anciently been accustomed. . . .[10]

(French) *Ibid.*, III, 35-36.

(C) PARLIAMENT OF 1379

. . . These are the names of the prelates and lords assigned on the request of the commons to examine the estate of the king: namely, . . .[11] First, [they are] to examine the revenues arising from the subsidy on wool, those received since the feast of St. Michael last and those presumably to be received before the feast of St. Michael next; item, to examine as well all the revenues of the kingdom received since the said time . . . and those which presumably can be received and levied before the said feast of St. Michael . . . ; item, to examine what sort of fees or wages the great and petty officers of the king were accustomed to have in the early days of King Edward, grandfather of our present king. . . .[12] And it should be remembered that the said lords thus assigned have the command of the same king in parliament to enter . . . the offices and courts of the king as may be necessary for this investigation, together with the officials and keepers of the same; and there, together with the

---

[9] See above, p. 222.
[10] The commons examined the royal accounts and approved them, except for a protest that too much had been spent outside the kingdom. Finally they granted the usual subsidy on wool.
[11] Three bishops, three earls, and three barons.
[12] Also annuities being paid by the king's grant, the furniture of the household, and other matters.

said officials, to search the rolls, accounts, and any other records that are concerned in this matter . . . ; and to make a distinct report to our said lord the king and to his council as to what they have done and have found, together with their good advice in this connection. . . .

Item, the lords and commons of the kingdom of England assembled in this parliament have granted for themselves and for the whole community of England the subsidy on wool, wool-fells, and leather; also another subsidy, to be taken from the goods of certain persons throughout the kingdom according to a certain form and in a certain manner prescribed in a schedule made in that connection and already presented in parliament, of which the tenor is word for word as follows. . . .[13]

(French) *Ibid.*, III, 57.

(D) PARLIAMENT OF 1380

. . . In the first place the lords and commons have agreed that, to meet the aforesaid necessities, every lay person[14] of the kingdom who has passed the age of fifteen years, whether male or female, of whatsoever condition or estate, both inside and outside franchises, shall give three groats[15]—with the exception of actual beggars, who are to be charged nothing—always providing that the levy shall be made under the regulation and form that each lay person is to be equally charged according to his ability and in the manner following: that is to say, in raising the total sum to be accounted for in each vill, the well-to-do shall according to their ability aid the lesser folk; yet so that the wealthiest man shall not pay more than the sum of sixty groats for himself and his wife and that no person shall pay less than a groat for himself and his wife. And no one shall be charged for payment except in the place where he and his wife and his children have their residence, or in the place where he remains in service. . . . And commissions shall be given to fit persons, as well in the counties as in the cities and boroughs, to be collectors and comptrollers of the aforesaid sum; and they are to be sworn well and loyally to perform their office. And it is the intention of the said commons to make the present grant solely for the support of the earl of Buckingham and the other lords and men of his company in the parts of Brittany, for the defence of the kingdom, and for the safeguarding of the sea.

(French) *Ibid.*, III, 90.

---

[13] The added subsidy was a graduated poll-tax, according to which dukes were to pay 10*m*.; royal justices £5; earls and the mayor of London £4; barons, bannerets, serjeants-at-law, aldermen of London, and mayors of larger towns £2; bachelors, squires, apprentices-at-law, mayors of smaller towns, and great merchants £1; other merchants, franklins, artisans, and the mass of the people lesser sums down to 4*d*.

[14] The clergy made a separate grant of £100,000.

[15] A silver coin worth 4*d*.

(E) PARLIAMENT OF 1381

. . . And the king commanded Sir Richard le Scrope, knight, the newly created chancellor of England, to rehearse for them the same charge touching the points aforesaid.[16] And so he clearly did; and especially with regard to the repeal thus made of the grant of freedom and manumission to the serfs and villeins of the land, it was again on the king's behalf plainly asked of all those present in full parliament whether this repeal pleased them or no.

To which the prelates and temporal lords, as well as the knights, citizens, and burgesses, unanimously responded that this repeal had been well made; adding that such [grant of] manumission or freedom could not be made without the assent of those who had the greatest interest. And to this they had never assented of their free will; nor would they have ever done so except to live and die all in one day.[17] And they—that is to say, the prelates and lords, as well as the commons—humbly besought our lord the king that these manumissions and enfranchisements, thus made and granted through coercion, to their disherison and the destruction of the kingdom, should be quashed and annulled by the authority of this parliament, and that the said repeal should be affirmed as one well and justly made. And this was then unanimously granted and agreed to by all. . . .

And it is to be noted that afterwards, when the king had secured advice from the lords of the kingdom and from his council with regard to these requests made to him [by the commons], as it truly appeared to him to be for his benefit and for that of his said kingdom, he willed and granted that certain prelates, lords, and other men should be assigned to survey and examine in privy council the estate and governance of our said lord the king's person, as well as of his said household, and to advise themselves of sufficient remedies, should he proceed with the matter [of reform], and thereupon to make report to the king aforesaid. And the lords in parliament then declared it seemed to them that, if reform of the government was to be made throughout the kingdom, attention should first be given to its principal member—namely, the king himself—and then [pass] from person to person, as well those of Holy Church as others, and from place to place, from the highest degree to the lowest, sparing no person, degree, or place.

And to do this for the said household, the following lords were elected. . . .[18]

(French) *Ibid.*, III, 100 f.

(F) PARLIAMENT OF 1386

. . . In this parliament all the commons, assembled as one body

---

[16] This was done at the request of the speaker of the commons.

[17] *Pur vivre et mourir touz en un jour;* the meaning obviously is "under threat of immediate death."

[18] The duke of Lancaster and seventeen others.

and with a single purpose, came before the king, the prelates, and the lords in the parliament chamber and made bitter complaint concerning the last chancellor of England, Michael de la Pole, earl of Suffolk, who was there present; accusing him by word of mouth in the manner following. . . . And on all these articles the commons asked the judgment of parliament. To which the said earl replied in the manner following. . . . And thereupon, after the response of the said earl to the accusations of the said commons, and the replies made to these [arguments] by the one side and the other, the said earl, at the request of the said commons, on account of the gravity of the offences thus charged against him, was arrested by the king's order and committed to the custody of the constable of England, and then released on bail. . . . And for the misdeeds and offences aforesaid, of which the said earl through the insufficiency of his said responses has thus been convicted, it is adjudged that he is to be committed to the king's prison, to remain there during the king's pleasure; and he shall not be liberated from the said prison until he has paid fine and redemption at the king's pleasure. . . .

The lords and commons of the realm assembled in this present parliament, for the defence of the kingdom and of the sea, and for the protection of trading, granted to our lord the king in full parliament certain subsidies and aids on certain conditions, according to the form and in the words that follow. . . .[19] And in addition the said lords and commons have for the said reasons granted another half a tenth and half a fifteenth, to be levied from laymen at the quinzime of St. Michael next, on a certain condition: namely, that the aforesaid grants, except the said latter half a tenth and half a fifteenth, together with the other income of the king, may [be made to] suffice for the charges and defences of the kingdom during the coming year, through the care and good administration of . . .[20], who have been ordained and assigned by our lord the king under his commission sealed with the great seal . . . to be of the continual council of our lord the king; and that until then the same latter half a tenth and half a fifteenth shall under no circumstances be levied or collected by any one in any way. . . .[21]

Item, the commons very humbly pray that, for the honour of God, for the maintenance of your crown, for your own profit and that of all the prelates and lords, and for the relief of the poor commons of your realm, it may please you to ordain and appoint in this present parliament fit officials: namely, the chancellor, the treasurer, the keeper of the privy seal, the steward of your household, and also

---

[19] The grant was of half a tenth and half a fifteenth, and of tunnage and poundage until the end of the next year.

[20] The dukes of York and Gloucester, two archbishops, two bishops, one abbot, one earl, one baron, two knights, the chancellor, the treasurer, and the keeper of the privy seal.

[21] Other provisions follow, prohibiting substitutions on the commission, interference with the members, etc.

the other lords of your great and continual council. [And they petition] that the said lords and officials may have power to correct and amend all the defects that so greatly blemish your crown . . . ; likewise that a statute be made that no one, of whatsoever dignity, estate, nation, or condition, shall in private or in public be so bold as to effect or counsel the contravention of what the said lords and officials see fit to decide, and this under severe penalty. Which matters, through your benignity, you have partially put into execution; it is prayed that at present you may please to carry out the remainder. . . . Response: The king so wills, providing that the commission and statutes asked in this petition shall be in effect for no more than one entire year. And as to the steward of his household, he will install a fit man by the advice of his council. . . .

It should be remembered that the king in full parliament, before its close, made public protest by personal word of mouth that, on account of anything done in the said parliament, he was unwilling that prejudice should be incurred by himself or by his crown, and that his prerogative and the liberties of his said crown should be saved and guarded. . . .

(French) *Ibid.*, III, 216-24.

(G) PARLIAMENT OF 1388[22]

. . . At the last parliament, on account of the great damages and terrible dangers which had been incurred through the bad government [of those] surrounding the king during all his earlier reign— [namely,] Alexander, then archbishop of York; Robert de Vere, then duke of Ireland; Michael de la Pole, then earl of Suffolk; Robert Tressilian, one time justice; Nicholas Brember, knight; and their adherents and others—whereby the king and all his kingdom had been almost wholly ruined and destroyed, . . . ordinance was made by statute and a commission was given to various lords for the benefit, honour, and salvation of the king, his royal authority, and all his realm, the tenor of which commission and statute is as follows. . . . And thereupon the aforesaid Alexander, Robert, Michael, Robert, and Nicholas, and their aforesaid adherents and others . . . devised, plotted, and proposed various horrid treasons and wrongs against the king, the aforesaid lords thus assigned, and all the other lords and commons who had agreed to set up the aforesaid ordinance and commission, [thus conspiring] for the defeasance of the king, his royal authority, and all his realm.

Whereupon Thomas, duke of Gloucester, uncle of our lord the king, and son of King Edward—whom God assoil!—Richard, earl of Arundel, and Thomas, earl of Warwick, perceiving the evil purposes of the traitors aforesaid, assembled in force to safeguard their persons, to show and declare the said treasons and evil purposes, and to provide remedy according to the will of God. And they came

---

[22] The following recitation constitutes the preamble to the petition, which is here placed in the third paragraph.

into the presence of our aforesaid lord the king and appealed the said five traitors for high treason committed by the latter against the king and his kingdom. Upon which appeal, our said lord the king adjourned the aforesaid parties until this present parliament. . . .[23] Which five traitors were attainted in this present parliament of the treasons and wrongs aforesaid, at the suit and appeal of the said duke of Gloucester, the said earls of Derby, Arundel, and Warwick, and the earl marshal.

[Therefore] may it please our said highly respected lord the king to accept, approve, and confirm in this present parliament all that was done in the last parliament, as set forth above, and whatever has been done since the said last parliament through force of the statute, ordinance, or commission aforesaid, as well as what has been done by the aforesaid duke of Gloucester, earls of Derby, Arundel, and Warwick, and earl marshal. Response: Our lord the king, considering the matter of the said petition to be true and the request of his said commons in this affair to be for the honour of God and to his own advantage and that of his realm, by assent of the prelates, dukes, earls, barons, and all others in this present parliament, granted the request of the said commons in all particulars according to the form of the said petition. . . .[24]

(French) *Ibid.*, III, 248 f.

(H) PARLIAMENT OF 1397

. . . Item, with regard to the fourth article,[25] concerning the expense of the king's household and the residence of bishops and ladies in his company, the king was greatly aggrieved and offended at the fact that the commons, his lieges, should take unto themselves or presume [to make] any regulation or government of the king's person, or of his household, or of any person of the state whom he pleased to have in his company. And it seemed to the king that the commons herein committed a great offence against his regality and his royal majesty and the liberty both of himself and of his honourable progenitors, which he had held and by the aid of God would maintain and support. Wherefore the king commanded the said lords spiritual and temporal on the following Saturday morning fully to show and declare the king's will in this matter to the said commons. Furthermore, the king, hearing how the said commons had been moved and excited by a bill presented before them to express and demonstrate the said last article, commanded the duke of Guienne and Lancaster to charge Sir John Bussy, speaker of the commons, by

---

[23] The record here recites how the said traitors violated the king's protection by open revolt, and how the Lords Appellant were forced to take arms against them.

[24] Here follow a complete pardon for the Lords Appellant and the royal assent to various other petitions providing for punishment of the traitors, the purification of the government, etc.

[25] In the address by the speaker of the commons.

the fealty [owed to the king] to report to him the name of the man who had presented the said bill before the commons.

Item, on Saturday, the morrow of Candlemas, the lords spiritual and temporal were [assembled] together with the commons, to whom they explained the will and command of the king; and the said commons delivered the said bill to the lords, with the name of the man who had presented it to them, that is to say, Sir Thomas Haxey. Which bill was afterwards at the king's command delivered by the clerk of parliament to the clerk of the crown. Then, by the king's order, the commons came before the king in parliament; and there, with all the humility and obedience of which they were capable, they expressed deep grief, as appeared from their demeanour, that the king had formed such an opinion of them. And they humbly besought the king to hear and accept their apology: that it had never been their intention or will to express, present, or do anything which would offend or displease the king's royal majesty, or would contravene his royal estate and liberty, either in this matter concerning his own person and the government of his household, [in that] concerning the lords and ladies in his company, or in any other matter touching [the king] himself; for they well knew and understood that such matters pertained to them not at all, but solely to the king himself and to his [power of] ordinance. . . .[26]

(French) *Ibid.*, III, 339.

(I) PARLIAMENT OF 1398[27]

. . . Item, on the same Thursday the commons prayed the king that, since they had before them divers petitions, as well for individual persons as others, which had been neither read nor answered, and also since numerous other matters and proposals had been brought up in the king's presence, which for lack of time they could not at present well terminate, it might be the king's pleasure to commit full power to certain lords and such other persons as should please him, to examine, answer, and determine the said petitions and the matters and proposals aforesaid and all related questions. To which prayer the king agreed. And thereupon, by the authority and assent of parliament, he appointed and assigned. . . .[28]

Item, on the same day the commons of the realm, by the assent of the lords spiritual and temporal, granted to the king the subsidy on wool, wool-fells, and leather for his lifetime; also a fifteenth and

---

[26] The commons formally submitted to the royal grace, which was granted through the chancellor. The king personally promised not to request tenths and fifteenths just for himself and his household.

[27] First summoned at Westminster, September, 1397; adjourned to Shrewsbury, January, 1398. During the first session the statute and commission of 1388 were repealed and the Lords Appellant convicted of high treason. See J. G. Edwards, in the *English Historical Review*, XL, 321 f.

[28] Twelve peers, or six of them, and six knights, or three of them, with power as aforesaid.

tenth and half a fifteenth and half a tenth, in the manner and form following. . . .[29]

(French) *Ibid.,* III, 368.

[29] They were thanked and dismissed by the king on the same day.

64. RICHARD II: STATUTES AND ORDINANCES

(A) APPOINTMENT OF COUNCILLORS (1377)

The king to all who shall see these letters, greeting. By the assent of the prelates, dukes, earls, barons, and others assembled beside us in our council held at Westminster on the morrow of our coronation, we recently ordained that twelve persons—that is to say, two bishops, two earls, two barons, two bannerets, and four bachelors—should be elected by us and them as our councillors to aid our chancellor and treasurer in affairs touching the estate, honour, and advantage of us, and of our kingdom, lordships, and lands; and that the said councillors thus to be elected should have, after their election, our letters patent [commissioning them] to carry out and execute the said matters; and that the said chancellor and treasurer should duly enforce the measures ordained by them and by the said elected [councillors], or by the majority of them. Whereupon [the following men] were elected by us and by the prelates and lords aforesaid. . . . And in our presence they were sworn as our councillors, to carry out and execute the said matters according to the form stated above so long as it should be our pleasure. We, wishing the said ordinance to be put into effect, have constituted and assigned the aforesaid men, thus elected, as our councillors to carry out and execute the said matters according to the form of the ordinance aforesaid.[1] . . . And so we shall hold firm and good whatever the said elected [councillors], together with the aforesaid chancellor and treasurer, or the majority of them, shall do in our name as stated above and in each and all of the aforesaid matters, and we will that it be strictly observed. In testimony whereof we have caused to be drawn up these our letters patent, to continue at our pleasure. Given at our palace of Westminster, July 20.

By writ of the king himself under the signet.

(French) *Ibid.,* III, 386.

(B) STATUTE OF 7 RICHARD II: FOR THE IMPROVEMENT OF JUSTICE (1384)

. . . Item, it is agreed and established that no man of law shall henceforth be justice of assize or of common jail delivery in his own country (*patria*), and that the chief justice of the common bench, among others, shall be assigned to hold assizes of this sort and to deliver jails; but with regard to the chief justice of the king's bench,

[1] They were especially commissioned to borrow money for the king's immediate needs.

let such action be taken as has been customary for the greater part of the past hundred years.

Item, . . . after the said ordinance [of Edward III] had been recited in parliament, it was agreed and established that no justice of the king's bench or of the common bench, or any baron of the exchequer, so long as he held the office of justice or baron, should henceforth take, either by himself or through others, whether openly or in secret, any robe, fief, pension, gift, or reward from anybody except the king; nor [should he take] any present from anybody except one of food and drink which is not of great value. And [it is established] that henceforth [such justices and barons] shall not give counsel to any one, whether great or small, in causes or concerns to which the king is a party or which in any way touch the king; and that they are not to be of counsel to any one in any case, plea, or dispute pending before themselves or in any other great court or tribunal of the king, on penalty of forfeiting office and of paying fine and ransom to the king.[2]

Item, on complaint made by the same commons to the lord king in parliament, to the effect that great disherison of people had been caused in times past, and might yet be caused, through false entry of pleas, erasure of rolls, and alteration of verdicts, it was agreed and established that any one, whether judge or clerk, properly convicted before the king and his council . . . of an offence of this sort . . . should be punished by fine and redemption at the king's pleasure and should satisfy the party [defrauded]. . . .

Item, whereas various pleas which touch the common law, and which ought to be discussed and determined according to the common law, are now by way of innovation coming to be drawn before the constable and the marshal of England,[3] to the serious damage and disturbance of the people: it is agreed and established that all pleas and disputes which touch the common law of the land, and which ought to be discussed and determined according to the common law, shall henceforth by no means be drawn or held before the aforesaid constable and marshal; but that the court of the same constable and marshal shall have [jurisdiction over] that which pertains to the said court, and the common law that which pertains to it; and let such action and usage continue as was customary in the time of the lord king's ancestors.

(Latin) *Statutes of the Realm*, II, 36 f.

(C) ORDINANCE CONCERNING LIVERY AND MAINTENANCE (1390)

Whereas . . . in many of our parliaments previously held . . . grievous complaint and great clamour has been made to us by the lords spiritual and temporal, as well as by the commons of our kingdom, concerning the great and outrageous oppression of maintenance, carried on to the damage of us and our people in various parts of

---

[2] Cf. no. 53.
[3] Cf. no. 56, art. 26.

the same kingdom by divers supporters . . . of suits and inquests . . . , among whom many are the more encouraged and emboldened in their aforesaid maintenance and wrongdoing because they are in the retinues of lords and others of our said kingdom [and are provided] with fees, robes, and other liveries called company liveries:[4] [therefore] by the advice of our great council, we have ordained and straitly enjoined that neither prelate nor other man of Holy Church, nor bachelor, nor squire, nor other man of less estate shall bestow any sort of such livery as is called company livery; and that no duke, earl, baron, or banneret shall bestow such company livery on knight or squire, unless he is retained for the term of his life during peace and war and through indenture [made] without fraud or malice, or unless he is a domestic and family retainer living in the household; nor [shall such a nobleman bestow such livery] on any valet called "yeoman archer," or on any person of less estate, unless he is similarly a family retainer living in the household. . . . And [it is ordained] that no lord spiritual or temporal or other person, who has or shall have men in his retinue, shall suffer any who are with him to be in any way supporters . . . of suits and inquests in the localities; but, as aforesaid, he shall oust them from his service and retinue as soon as it can be perceived [that they are wrongdoers of this sort] . . . ; and that none of our lieges, great or small, of whatsoever condition he may be, whether he is the retainer of some lord or is any other sort of person belonging to no retinue, shall undertake any quarrel other than his own or shall maintain it, by himself or through others, either openly or in secret; and that all those who, contrary to this our ordinance, use or wear such livery as is called company livery shall utterly abandon it within ten days after the proclamation of this same ordinance. . . . Given under our great seal at Westminster, May 12.

By the king himself and the council.

(French) *Ibid.*, II, 74 f.

(D) ORDINANCE CONCERNING THE KING'S COUNCIL (1390)

In the first place, the lords of the council shall take pains to appear at the council by eight or nine o'clock at the latest.

Item, the affairs of the king and the kingdom are to be examined in preference to all others when the greater men of the council and the other officers are present.

Item, matters touching the common law are to be sent for determination before the justices.

Item, matters touching the office of chancellor are to be sent for determination before him in the chancery.

Item, matters touching the office of treasurer are to be sent for determination before him in the exchequer.

---

[4] This ordinance was one of many futile efforts to check the practice of keeping bands of uniformed retainers, organized like the notorious free companies in the French wars.

Item, all other matters, which cannot be settled without the special grace and permission of the king, are to be laid before him in order thereon to have his opinion and pleasure.

Item, no gift or grant that may be turned to the diminution of the king's profit shall be passed without the advice of the council and the assent of the dukes of Guienne, York, and Gloucester and of the chancellor, or of two of them.

Item, all other matters presented to the council in order to have their advice, and other matters of great weight, are to be determined by those of the council who are present, together with the officers.

Item, all other bills of less weight from the people[5] are to be examined and determined before the keeper of the privy seal and others of the council who may be present at the time.

Item, ordinances previously made by the assent of the king and of his council with regard to offices in his gift are to be held and observed.

Item, no steward or justice is henceforth to be appointed for the term of his life.

Item, bachelors who are of the king's council shall have reasonable wages for the time spent in work connected with the same council.

Item, lords who are of the same council shall receive consideration for their labour and expense by the advice of the king and his council.

Item, after one matter has beeen introduced in the council, they shall not pass on to any other matter until an answer has been given in the matter first introduced.

On March 8, in the thirteenth year, etc., this ordinance was made at Westminster in the presence of the king, there being in attendance the duke of Guienne, the duke of York, the earl of Salisbury, the earl of Northumberland, the earl of Huntingdon, the chancellor, the treasurer, the [keeper of the] privy seal, the steward, Lovell, Stury, and Dalynrigg.

(French) Nicolas, *Proceedings of the Privy Council*, I, 18a f.

(E) STATUTE OF 15 RICHARD II: RESTRICTION OF USES[6] (1391)

... Item, whereas it is contained in the statute *De Religiosis*[7] that no man of religion or other man whatsoever shall buy or sell, or under colour of gift or lease or other title of any sort shall receive from any one or in any way, by artifice or strategem, cause lands or tenements to be appropriated to himself from any one . . . , so that the said lands and tenements come into mortmain: . . . it is granted and agreed that all those who are possessed of lands, tenements, fiefs, advowsons, or other possessions by enfeoffment or in other fashion for the use of men of religion or of other spiritual persons . . . shall, between now and the feast of St. Michael next, have them amortized

---

[5] That is to say, private petitions; see, for example, no. 70.
[6] On the law of uses, see Holdsworth, *History of English Law*, IV, 407 f.
[7] The Statute of Mortmain, no. 52B.

by licence of the king and the lords [of the lands]; or, otherwise, [the holders] shall sell them and alienate them for another use between now and the said feast, on pain of their being forfeit to the king and the lords as tenements purchased by men of religion, according to the form of the statute *De Religiosis*. And from this time on, under the same penalty, no such purchase shall be made, so that such men of religion or other spiritual persons shall thereof enjoy the profits as aforesaid. And this same statute shall extend to and hold for all lands, tenements, fiefs, advowsons, and other possessions purchased or to be purchased for the use of gilds or fraternities.[8] . . .

(French) *Statutes of the Realm,* II, 79 f.

(F) SECOND STATUTE OF PRAEMUNIRE (1393)[9]

. . . Wherefore our said lord the king, by the assent aforesaid and at the prayer of his said commons, has ordained and established that, if any one purchases or pursues, or causes to be purchased or pursued, in the court of Rome or elsewhere, any such translations,[10] processes, sentences of excommunication, bulls, instruments, or anything else touching our lord the king that is inimical to him, his crown, his regality, or his aforesaid kingdom, as aforesaid; or if any one brings them into the kingdom, receives them, or thereof makes notification or any other execution, either within the said kingdom or outside it; such persons, their notaries, procurators, partisans, supporters, abettors, and counsellors are to be put outside the protection of our said lord the king, and their lands, tenements, goods, and chattels are to be forfeit to our lord the king. And [it is ordained] that, if they can be found, they are to be bodily attached and taken before the king and his council, there to respond in the cases aforesaid; or that process shall be brought against them by *praemunire facias*[11] in the manner provided by other statutes concerning provisors and other men who, in derogation of our lord the king's regality, bring suit in the court of another.

(French) *Ibid.,* II, 85 f.

[8] The prohibition also extended to municipalities.
[9] The extremely long preamble is omitted.
[10] Removals of ecclesiastics from one office to another.
[11] The special writ after which the statute came to be named; cf. no. 62G.

65. DURHAM HALMOTE ROLLS (1375)[1]

Pittington. . . . Inquest: it was proved by oath . . . that Thomas, son of John Widowson of West Rainton, is a freeman of free condition and of free status and not a bondman of the said lord prior.

Ferry. It was ordered[2] that no cotters of the vill should leave the vill while any of the tenants had work to be done. . . .

[1] On the significance of these records see Pollock and Maitland, I, 624 f.; and cf. no. 54H.
[2] *Ordinatum est*—the usual form used to introduce a local ordinance or by-law. Before too much communal self-government is read into these extracts, it

65. DURHAM HALMOTE ROLLS

Wallsend. From Alan of Durham and John del Rawe 2s. for breach of the peace in gathering peasecods. And it was ordered that no tenants of the vill should gather peasecods except for their own use, and not for sale at Newcastle—and this in the place ordered by the reeve. . . .

Westoe. Increase of rent 6d.: John Gray took a cottage last in the holding of Thomas Wright, to have and to hold at the will of the lord, at annual rent of 2s. Catherine of Brenklaw took half a cottage, last in the holding of William Souter, to have and to hold at the will of the lord, at annual rent of 18d. . . .

Coupon. It was ordered that no tenants of the vill should enter the park without licence. . . .

Aycliffe. It was ordered that all cotters, and all other tenants of the lord who had no corn of their own to harvest, should reap with the lord at Ketton, on pain of 40d. . . . And it was ordered that William Power, the reeve, and the forester should have all such tenants, servants, and labourers of the vill stopped from going outside the vill for harvesting, except with the lord and his tenants, on pain of 20s. William Power, John Taylor, Gilbert Randolf, and Thomas Watson were made constables of the vill. . . .

Willington. From the tenants of Willington and Wallsend 2s. amercement because they did not have a common smith as they had been ordered in many halmotes. It was ordered that [the men] of this vill and township should have a common smith before the feast of St. Martin and that henceforth none of them should work on ploughshares, under penalty of 20s. . . .

Hebburn. John of Hedworth rendered homage and fealty in the church of Jarrow to the lord Robert, prior of the church of Durham . . . , for his land which he holds of the aforesaid [prior] in Hebburn. Item, John Wiley rendered homage and fealty to the same lord Robert in his court at Harton. . . .

Aycliffe. It was ordered for all tenants of the vill, namely for brewers, that they should not sell a gallon of beer for more than 1½d. . . .

West Merrington. It was ordered that no tenants of the vill should insult one another by word or deed.

Mid Merrington. . . . It was ordered that no tenants of the vill should cut down thorns in the fields of Mid Merrington. . . .

Moorsley. Presentment was brought that Alice, daughter of John Hudson, was married on free land; therefore let inquiry be made whether the same Alice should give merchet[3] or not. John son of Roger was claimed as the lord's bondman of the vill of Little Haswell. And he says he is a freeman; so he shall swear not to remove himself before the next court. . . .

Coupon. Little-Stephen took a cottage once in the holding of Geoffrey Ladman. Gilbert son of John was elected to the office of reeve, and John de Raw is his associate. And they were sworn.

---

should be noted that the village obligations, though declared "by common assent," often carried a penalty of 20s. for disobedience. See the entries below.

[3] A fine for permission to marry, at this time a mark of servile condition.

Aycliffe. It was ordered by common assent that they should have a common harvester[4] before the feast of St. Cuthbert in March, on pain of 20*s*.; also that they should have a common harvester before the feast of St. Helen, on pain of 20*s*.; also that no tenant of the said vill should do wrong to the said harvester or unlawfully take from him animals under pledge or remove animals from his fold without the licence of the said harvester, on pain of 20*s*.; also that every tenant should act toward the shepherds of the vill as was agreed in common. . . .

Ferry. It was ordered that no tenants of that vill or of the townships of East Merrington, Mid Merrington, West Merrington, and Chilton should implead one another in any court except the court of the prior, that is to say, in his lay and secular [court]. . . .

West Rainton. . . . From Thomas Rois 18*d*., because his dog ate a pea-hen. . . .

Hedworth. . . . It was ordered that no tenant of the vill should permit his wife to vilify or insult any persons of the neighbourhood. . . .

Hesleden. . . . It was ordered by common assent that everything gathered in the field, whether corn or herbs, should be brought openly through the centre of the vill and not secretly behind the gardens. . . . It was ordered that all women of the vill should hold their tongues and should not scold or curse any one.

Dalton. From Joan, wife of William Smith, 12*d*. for merchet. From Margaret, servant of the farmer, 12*d*. for *leyrwite*[5] [incurred] with two men. From Joan Woodcock 6*d*. for the same. From the wife of John Dawson 6*d*. for breach of the assize of beer. . . . Marjory, widow of John Dawson, deceased, took a kiln built by the same John in the lord's waste, to have and to hold for the term of her life, at annual rent of 12*d*., but the lord prior of his grace remitted to the aforesaid Marjory all but 8*d*., to be paid annually during the life of the said Marjory. And she gave as fine 12*d*., which was pardoned except 3*d*. Item, the aforesaid Marjory took a villein tenement (*terram husbandorum*) : namely, a messuage and eighteen acres of land with appurtenances, which the said John Dawson, formerly husband of the said Marjory, once held, to have and to hold for the term of her life, and paying annually the ancient farm. And within a year she will build a house at her own expense. And she gives as fine 13*s*. 4*d*., which is pardoned except 40*d*. . . . John, son of John Dawson, took two villein tenements, each containing eighteen acres, which the said John Dawson earlier held, to have and to hold for the term of nine years, rendering annually the ancient farm. And he gives 40*d*. as fine for the said term of nine years. . . .

(Latin) *Halmota Prioratus Dunelmensis,* pp. 126-32.

---

[4] *Messor*—apparently a superintendent of the harvest who incidentally acted as keeper of the pound.

[5] See above, p. 188, n. 27.

SECTION VI

THE HOUSES OF LANCASTER AND YORK

IN THIS section, as in the one before it, pre-eminence has been accorded to statutes and excerpts from the rolls of parliament; so what has been said of those sources in the previous introduction is to a large degree applicable here also. With particular regard to the following selection, it need only be remarked that the bulk of the material is drawn from the early Lancastrian period, when so many important precedents were established for subsequent ages. Emphasis has thus been placed on the Revolution of 1399, its formal justification and its immediate results (no. 66A); parliamentary control of the council and the household (nos. 66c, D; 67A, B); parliamentary appropriation and audit (no. 66D, E); and the assertion by the commons of various rights and privileges—that redress should precede supply (no. 66B, E); that grants of money should originate in the lower house (no. 66E); that petitions agreed to in parliament should not be changed without parliamentary consent (no. 66F); that election returns should not be tampered with by officials (no. 66c); that members should enjoy freedom of petition (no. 66A), freedom of discussion (nos. 66B, 67c), and, to a certain extent, freedom from arrest (nos. 66c, 67c). No. 67E is included as an example of the parliamentary attainders that became all too common in the later fifteenth century. Finally, the acts of Richard III's parliament have been summarized in order to show the development of what we know as bill procedure (no. 68).

On some of these matters additional information is provided by the acts of the privy council, which henceforth attain increasing importance as a source for constitutional history. Under no. 70 will be found a variety of excerpts: a few chosen, as just remarked, because they supplement the parliament rolls; others because they are typical of the council's daily work, administrative or judicial. And a comparison of the entries under nos. 70 and 71 will quickly show how vague and fluctuating was as yet the distinction between justice in council and justice in chancery. The technicalities of equitable procedure, like those of the common law, must here be passed over; nevertheless, several cases are presented as instances of appeal to the chancellor's conscience when no remedy could be had in the ordinary courts, and of the discretionary authority retained by the king in council—the basis of an enhanced star chamber jurisdiction under the Tudors.

Concluding this section are a number of documents concerning the boroughs. A few excerpts from the *Liber Albus,* in default of a better source, reveal the growing complexity of the London government. Henry VI's charter to Nottingham is typical of the formal acts of incorporation then being secured by the greater towns. The Leicester ordinances are homely examples of municipal by-laws. The indentures for the parliament of 1437 illustrate the varieties of electoral processes that prevailed in England until the Reform Act of 1832. Although an indefinite amount of other such material could be assembled, it would include little that was fundamentally new. In the history of English municipal institutions the formative period is the twelfth, rather than the fifteenth century. And the maturing of the local administrative system in other respects can well be left for more vivid portrayal in connection with the reorganization of the Tudors.

The list of authorities cited for the preceding section may likewise be taken for the present one, with the addition of several works that deal specifically with fifteenth-century institutions: F. B. Chrimes, *English Constitutional Ideas in the Fifteenth Century;* T. F. T. Plucknett, "The Lancastrian Constitution," in *Tudor Studies;* and numerous special articles, some of which, as usual, are referred to in footnotes. Lastly, attention should be called to the contemporary account of the English constitution, or what the author thought it should be, in Sir John Fortescue's *Governance of England* (ed. Plummer)—one of the many famous books which the present collection is, for lack of available space, forced to neglect.

66. PARLIAMENT ROLLS OF HENRY IV AND HENRY V

(A) Parliament of 1399

At the parliament summoned and held at Westminster by King Henry IV on Monday, the day of St. Faith the Virgin . . . , in the presence of the same king seated on his royal throne in the great hall of Westminster, and of all the lords spiritual and temporal, and of the commons who had come thither by virtue of their summons

66. PARLIAMENT ROLLS

to parliament, and of many other gentlemen and commoners there present in large numbers, Thomas of Arundel, archbishop of Canterbury, related how King Richard II after the Conquest had summoned his parliament to be held there on the previous Tuesday . . . ; which summons was without force and effect through the acceptance of the renunciation made by the same King Richard, and through the deposition of the same King Richard made on the aforesaid Tuesday, as more fully appears in the record and process drawn up in this connection and enrolled in this roll of parliament. . . .

Here follow the record and process of the renunciation by King Richard II after the Conquest, and of the acceptance of the same renunciation; likewise of the deposition of the same King Richard. . . .[1] On the next day, however . . . , in the great hall at Westminster, honourably prepared for the holding of parliament, in the presence of the said archbishops of Canterbury and York, of the duke of Lancaster, of other dukes and lords both spiritual and temporal whose names are inscribed below, and of the people of the said kingdom then and there assembled in a very great multitude for the sake of [witnessing] the deeds of parliament, while the aforesaid duke of Lancaster occupied the place due and accustomed to his estate and while the royal throne, solemnly prepared with cloth of gold, stood vacant in the absence of any presiding officer whatsoever, the aforesaid archbishop of York . . . had the said cession and renunciation read by another, first in Latin and then in English. And immediately it was asked of the estates and the people then and there present[2] . . . whether for their own interest and for the benefit of the kingdom, they wished to accept the same renunciation and cession. And the same estates and people, considering, for the reasons specified by the king himself in his aforesaid renunciation and cession, that to do so would be highly expedient, all singly and in common with the people unanimously and with one accord accepted such renunciation and cession. After this acceptance, however, it was then publicly set forth that, besides the renunciation and cession accepted as aforesaid, it would in many ways be expedient and advantageous for the said kingdom if, in order to obviate all scruple and evil suspicion, the many crimes and defaults frequently committed by the said king in connection with the bad government of his kingdom—on account of which, as he himself had asserted in the cession made by him, he merited deposition—should be written down in the form of articles, to be publicly read and declared to the people. And so a large part

---

[1] The long account of Richard's abdication and how it was brought to parliament is here omitted. On the significance of this whole proceeding, see M. V. Clarke and V. H. Galbraith, "The Deposition of Richard II," in *Bulletin of the John Rylands Library*, XIV, 125 f.; also G. Lapsley, in the *English Historical Review*, XLIX, 423 f., 577 f.

[2] The archbishop of Canterbury was first asked for his opinion; then, apparently, the others were interrogated one after the other.

of those articles was then publicly read, of all which articles the tenor is as follows. . . .[3]

Item, in the parliament recently held at Shrewsbury[4] the same king, proposing to oppress his people, subtly procured and caused it to be granted that, by the counsel of all the estates of his realm, the power of parliament to decide certain petitions, which had been presented in the same parliament but on which no progress had as yet been made, should devolve upon certain persons. By colour of which concession the persons thus deputed proceeded with other matters of common concern to that parliament—and this at the will of the king and in derogation of the estate of parliament, to the great damage of the entire kingdom, and [by way of setting] a pernicious example. And in order that [these persons] might seem to have a certain colour of authority for such deeds, the king had the rolls of parliament deleted and changed to suit himself and contrary to the terms of the aforesaid concession. . . .

Item, when the king of England was able, without oppressing his people, to live honourably from the issues of his kingdom and from the patrimony belonging to his crown, since the kingdom was not burdened with the expense of wars, the same king, while truces between the kingdom of England and his adversaries continued during almost his entire reign, not only gave the greater part of his said patrimony to unworthy persons, but also, on that account, threw such burdens of taxation on his subjects in nearly every year of his reign that he widely and outrageously oppressed his people, to the impoverishment of his kingdom. And the income thus obtained was not used for the benefit and advantage of the kingdom of England, but was prodigally dissipated for the sake of his own ostentation, pomp, and vainglory. And great sums of money were owed in his kingdom for the victuals of his household and other purchases of his, although, more than any of his progenitors, he enjoyed an abundance of treasure and riches. Item, the same king, refusing to keep and defend the just laws and customs of his kingdom, but [wishing] at his own arbitrary will to do whatever appealed to his desires, sometimes—and very often when the laws of the kingdom had been declared and explained to him by his justices and others of his council, and when, according to those laws, he was to administer justice to those seeking it—expressly said, with an austere and determined countenance, that his laws were in his own mouth or, occasionally, in his own breast; and that he alone could establish and change the laws of his realm. And he, seduced by that opinion, would not permit justice to be done to many of his lieges, but by threats and intimidation compelled many to abstain from the pursuit of common justice. . . .

Item, although, according to the statutes and custom of his realm,

---

[3] The record here inserts the coronation oath (no. 55) and then justifies the deposition by thirty-three articles, of which five are translated below.
[4] See no. 63 I.

his people in all the counties of the kingdom ought, on the summoning
of every parliament, to be free to elect and depute knights on behalf of such counties to attend parliament, explain their grievances,
and in that connection sue for remedies as may seem best to them;
nevertheless, the aforesaid king, in order that he might be able the
more freely to carry out his own headstrong will, very often sent
mandates to his sheriffs that they should cause certain persons,
nominated as knights of the shires by the king himself, to come to
his parliaments. And these knights, since they favoured the same
king, he was able to induce—as he very often did, sometimes by
divers threats and intimidation and sometimes by rewards—to support matters prejudicial to the kingdom and extremely burdensome
to the people, especially the grant to the same king of a subsidy on
wool for the term of his life and another subsidy for a number of
years, to the excessive oppression of his people. . . .

Item, although the lands, tenements, goods, and chattels of every
freeman, according to the laws of the realm accustomed throughout
all times past, ought not to be seized unless they have been [law-
fully] forfeited, nevertheless the said king, proposing and determining to undo such laws, in the presence of very many lords and of
other men from the commonalty of the realm, often said and affirmed
that the life of every one of his lieges, together with the lands, tenements, goods, and chattels of such men, was subject to his own pleasure, apart from any [lawful] forfeiture—which is wholly contrary
to the laws and customs of his kingdom aforesaid.

Item, although it is established and ordained that no freeman shall
be seized, etc., or in any way destroyed, and that the king will neither
go against him nor send against him, except by the lawful judgment
of his peers, or by the law of the land;[5] nevertheless, by the will,
mandate, and order of the said king, very many of his lieges, maliciously accused of having publicly or secretly said something that
might lead to the slander, shame, or humiliation of the said king's person, were seized and imprisoned and taken to a military court before the
constable and marshal of England. . . . Wherefore, since the aforesaid king wilfully contravened such statute of his realm, it is not to
be doubted that he thereby committed perjury. . . .

And since it seemed to all these estates, thereupon interrogated
singly and in common, that those statements of his crimes and defaults were notoriously sufficient for deposing the same king, considering also his own confession with regard to his incompetence and
other matters contained in the said renunciation and cession which
had been openly published, all the estates aforesaid unanimously
agreed that the deposition of the said king was abundantly justified in
order to secure the greater safety and tranquillity of the people and
the good of the kingdom. . . .[6]

---

[5] Art. 39 of Magna Carta, above, p. 121.

[6] A commission was then appointed to draw up the formal deposition of Richard and, in the name of all, to withdraw the homage and fealty of his subjects.

And immediately, as it appeared from the foregoing [actions] and their result that the kingship of England, together with its appurtenances, was vacant, the aforesaid Henry, duke of Lancaster, rising from his place and standing so erect that he could be well seen by all the people, humbly signing himself on the brow and breast with the symbol of the Cross and first invoking Christ by name, laid claim to the said kingship of England, thus declared vacant, together with the crown and all its members and appurtenances; [and this he did] in his mother tongue by the form of words following:—

"In the name of Fadir, Son, and Holy Gost, I, Henry of Lancaster chalenge this rewme of Yngland and the corone with all the membres and the appurtenances, als I that am disendit be right lyne of the blode comyng fro the gude lorde Kyng Henry Therde, and thorghe that ryght that God of his grace hath sent me, with the helpe of my kyn and of my frendes, to recover it—the whiche rewme was in poynt to be undone for defaut of governance and undoyng of the gode lawes."

After which declaration and claim the lords both spiritual and temporal, and all the estates there present, were asked singly and in common what they thought of that declaration and claim; and the same estates, together with all the people, unanimously agreed without difficulty or delay that the aforesaid duke should reign over them. And immediately . . . the aforesaid archbishop, taking the said King Henry by the right hand, led him to the royal throne aforesaid. And after the said king, kneeling before the said throne, had made a short prayer, the same archbishop of Canterbury, with the assistance of the aforesaid archbishop of York, placed the said king and caused him to sit on the aforesaid royal throne, while the people in their excessive joy loudly applauded. And then the said archbishop of Canterbury, when silence had with difficulty been obtained, on account of the joy of all the bystanders, preached a brief sermon, speaking in these words. . . . And when this sermon had been ended, the said Lord King Henry, in order to put at rest the minds of his subjects, in the same place publicly spoke the following words:—

"Sires, I thank God and yowe, spiritual and temporal and all the astates of the lond, and do yowe to wyte[7] it is noght my will that no man thynk that be waye of conquest I wold disherit any man of his heritage, franches, or other ryghtes that hym aght to have, no put hym out of that that he has and has had by the gude laws and customs of the rewme—except thos persons that has ben agan the gude purpose and the commune profyt of the rewme."

. . . On Monday, which was the day of St. Edward the King and Confessor, the said King Henry was crowned at Westminster with all due honour and solemnity; and certain lords and others, in accordance with their tenures, severally performed their service to the same

---

[7] Would have you know.

King Henry after the fashion accustomed at the time of such coronation.

Item, on the following Tuesday, the commons of the realm presented to the king Sir John Cheyne as their speaker and procurator in parliament, to whom the king well agreed. . . .[8]

Item, on the same Wednesday, the said commons set forth to our lord the king that on Monday next after the feast of the Exaltation of the Holy Cross, in the twenty-first year of the reign of the recent King Richard, a parliament was summoned and held at Westminster and then adjourned to Shrewsbury,[9] at which town, by the authority of parliament, certain power was committed to various persons to proceed with divers articles and matters contained in the roll of parliament made in that connection, as appears from the said roll. In which parliament, also by the aforesaid authority, divers statutes, judgments, ordinances, and establishments were made, ordained, and rendered, erroneously and very grievously, to the great disherison and to the ultimate destruction and undoing of numerous honourable lords and other lieges of the kingdom and of their heirs for all time. Wherefore the same commons prayed our lord the king, and all the lords spiritual and temporal in this present parliament, that it might please them by their common assent to revoke, annul, quash, delete, and repeal everything whatsoever that had been done in that same parliament held in the said twenty-first year or [enacted] by its authority. . . . Whereupon our said lord the king, having deliberated and advised with all the lords spiritual and temporal, severally examined in full parliament with regard to the matters aforesaid, by the common assent of the same lords, adjudged the said parliament held in the said twenty-first year and the authority thereby given as described above, together with all its other consequences and effects, to be of no force or validity. . . .[10]

Item, on the same Wednesday the said commons prayed our said lord the king that the [acts of the] parliament held at Westminster in the eleventh year of the said King Richard,[11] which parliament was held for the great honour and common profit of the whole kingdom, should be of full force and validity. To which prayer the king, by the common assent of all the lords aforesaid, severally examined in parliament concerning the matter, has well agreed; and he wills that the [acts of the] said parliament, held in the said eleventh year, shall be observed and kept in all particulars. . . .

On Monday, the morrow of All Souls, which was the third day of November, the commons made their protestation in the same manner as at the opening of the parliament; and besides they set forth

---

[8] On Wednesday the speaker made his usual address and the commons voted various customs for three years as well as a tenth and fifteenth.

[9] See no. 63 I.

[10] Richard II's statute of treasons was also repealed, leaving the law as it had been established in 1352 (no. 62F).

[11] See no. 63G.

to the king that, whereas the judgments of parliament pertained solely to the king and to the lords, and not to the commons except in case it pleased the king of his special grace to show them the same judgments for their satisfaction, no record should be made in parliament concerning the said commons to the effect that they are or shall be parties to any judgments henceforth to be given in parliament. To which, at the king's command, response was made by the archbishop of Canterbury, to the effect that the commons are petitioners and demandants, and that the king and the lords have always had and of right shall have the [rendering of] judgments in parliament, after the manner described by the same commons; except that the king especially wishes to have their advice and assent in the making of statutes, or of grants and subsidies, or [other] such matters for the common good of the realm. . . .

Item, since divers statutes and ordinances have been framed in times past . . . touching provisions [made] at the court of Rome,[12] the commons of the realm of England assembled in parliament, through the great trust which they have in the person of our lord the king, in his most excellent sense and discretion, and in the great tenderness and affection which above all others he has for his crown and its rights and the salvation of his royal estate, have of their free will agreed in full parliament that our said lord the king, with the consent and advice of such wise men and worthy persons as in this connection it may please him to call upon for counsel, shall have power to effect such permission, ordinance, and moderation with regard to the said statute as may seem to him most reasonable and advantageous for the satisfaction of God and the salvation of Holy Church; and even to quash, repeal, delete, and wholly annul the same statute according to his high discretion and according to what shall seem to him for the honour of God and most expedient and necessary for the honour and profit of his royal estate, of his said realm, and of his people. . . .

Item, it is to be remembered that Thomas of Haxey, clerk, presented to our lord the king in parliament a petition in the following words:[13]—

To our most respected lord the king and to his lords of parliament your poor clerk, Thomas Haxey, sets forth that the said Thomas, in the parliament held at Westminster on the day of St. Vincent in the twentieth year of King Richard II, presented a bill to the commons of the said parliament for the honour and profit of the said king and of all his realm, on account of which bill, at the desire of the said king, the said Thomas was adjudged traitor and forfeited everything that he had, in violation of right and of the usage that had hitherto prevailed in parliament (and to the undoing of the customs of the commons). Therefore may it please your very gracious

---

[12] See nos. 62E, 64E.
[13] Cf. no. 63H. Two versions of this petition are included in the roll. The clauses given below in parentheses are added by the second version.

lordship to have the record and process of the said judgment, together with all appendant matters, brought before this present parliament, to have that judgment quashed and annulled as erroneous, and to have the same Thomas entirely restored to his rank, estate, goods, chattels, farms, annuities, pensions, lands, tenements, rents, offices, advowsons, and possessions of all sorts, together with their appurtenances . . . ; and that he may hold them for himself and his heirs as he held them on the day that the said bill was drawn up . . . (as well for the enforcement of right as for the salvation of the liberties of the said commons).

Response: When this petition, together with the record and process of that [judgment], had been read and heard, our same lord the king, by the advice and consent of all the lords spiritual and temporal, ordained and decided that the judgment rendered against the said Thomas in the parliament held at Westminster in the said twentieth year of Richard, recently king, should be utterly quashed, reversed, repealed, and annulled, and be held as of no force or effect; that the said Thomas should be restored to his name and fame, and that he and his heirs should be entitled to seek, demand, and have their inheritance as heirs of their ancestors in such fashion as the said Thomas was [seised] before the said judgment thus rendered against him, notwithstanding the same judgment, according to which the [right of inheritance by] blood was broken as between the said Thomas, together with his heirs, and any of their ancestors.[14]

(Latin, French, English) *Rotuli Parliamentorum,* III, 415-34.

(B) PARLIAMENT OF 1401

It is to be remembered that, in the parliament held at Westminster on Thursday, the octave of St. Hilary, which was the twentieth day of January, in the second year of King Henry IV since the Conquest, the knights of the shires, the citizens of the cities, and the burgesses of the boroughs, who had come by virtue of summons to parliament, were proclaimed by their names in the chancery of the king within the hall of Westminster and in the presence of the chancellor of England and of the steward of the king's household. And on their appearance the same parliament, for certain good reasons affecting the king, was adjourned until the next Friday. . . . On Friday, January 21, Sir William Thirning, chief justice of the common bench, at the king's command declared the cause for the summoning of parliament, in the form that follows:[15]—

. . . And, finally, the king wills and commands that no lord, knight of the shire, citizen, or burgess, who has come to parliament by virtue of summons, shall absent himself from the same parlia-

---

[14] The reference is to the so-called corruption of blood resulting from conviction of treason; cf. the attainder of John Cade, no. 67E.

[15] The chief cause was financial: the great expense of the government and the cost of restoring the kingdom, putting down rebellions, defending the frontiers, etc.

ment or depart from it out of the city until it is finished; and that they shall come on time every day to their places assigned for the parliament; and that forthwith the said commons shall among themselves effect the election of their common speaker and, according to custom, bring him into the [king's] presence on next Saturday at ten o'clock. . . .

On Saturday, January 22, the commons of the realm presented to the king Sir Arnold Savage as their speaker and procurator in parliament, to whom the king well agreed. . . .[16]

Item, on the same day[17] the said commons set forth to our lord the king that, in connection with certain matters to be taken up among themselves, one of their number, in order to please the king and to advance himself, might perchance tell our lord the king of such matters before they had been determined and discussed, or agreed on by the same commons, whereby our same lord the king might be grievously moved against the said commons or some of them. Therefore they very humbly prayed our lord the king that he would not receive any such person for the relating of any such matters. . . . To which it was responded on behalf of the king that he wished the same commons to have deliberation and advisement in treating all their affairs among themselves, in order at their convenience to arrive at the best end and conclusion for the welfare and honour of him and of all his kingdom; and that he would not listen to any such person or give him credence until such matters had been presented to the king by the advice and consent of all the commons, according to the purpose of their said petition. . . .

Item, on the same Saturday the said commons prayed our lord the king that the business done and to be done in this parliament should be enacted and engrossed before the departure of the justices, and while they had it in their memory. To which it was replied that the clerk of parliament should, by the advice of the justices, do his duty in enacting and engrossing the substance of [the proceedings of] parliament, and then show it to the king and to the lords of parliament in order to know their opinion. . . .

Item, on the same Saturday the said commons set forth to our said lord the king that in several parliaments during times past their common petitions had not been answered before they had made their grant to our lord the king of some aid or subsidy. And therefore they prayed our same lord the king that, for the great ease and comfort of the said commons, our lord the king might be pleased to grant to the same commons that they could have knowledge of the responses to their said petitions before any such grant had thus been made. To which it was replied that the king wished to confer on this matter with the lords of the parliament and thereupon do what seemed best to him by the advice of the said lords. And afterwards,

---

[16] The speaker then made his address and the commons voted tunnage and poundage for two years, together with a tenth and fifteenth.

[17] Tuesday, January 25.

66. PARLIAMENT ROLLS

that is to say, on the last day of the parliament, the response was given that such procedure had been unknown and unaccustomed in the time of any of his progenitors or predecessors—[namely] that they should have any answer to their petitions, or knowledge of it, before they had set forth and completed all their other business in parliament, whether it was the making of any grant or something else. And, in conclusion, the king wished in no way to change the good customs and usages of ancient times. . . .[18]

(French) *Ibid.,* III, 454-58.

(C) PARLIAMENT OF 1404

. . . Item, upon certain prayers and requests earlier made by the commons at various times regarding the removal of divers persons, as well aliens as others . . . , it was in particular agreed by the said lords that four persons—namely, the king's confessor, the abbot of Dore, Master Richard Durham, and Crosby of the chamber—should be entirely ousted and removed from the king's household. Whereupon, on Saturday, February 9, the said confessor, Master Richard, and Crosby came before the king and the lords in parliament. And there the king, excusing the said four persons, said openly that, so far as he was concerned, he knew of no special reason or occasion why they should be removed from his household. Nevertheless, our same lord the king, well understanding that what the said lords or commons should do or ordain was for his good and that of the kingdom, and, finally, wishing to conform to their desires, he well agreed to the same ordinance and charged the said confessor, Master Richard, and Crosby to leave his said household. And a similar charge would have been given to the said abbot if he had been present. And our same lord the king further said that he would act in the same way with regard to any one else near his royal person, should that one incur the hatred or indignation of his people. . . .

Item, on the same Saturday the said commons prayed our said lord the king that, in the ordinance to be drawn up for the household of our same lord the king, nomination and appointment should be made of honest, virtuous, and reputable persons, concerning whom notice might be given to the said lords and commons in this parliament; and that such an ordinance should be made as might be pleasing to God and be of honour and advantage to the estate of the king and of his kingdom. . . .

Item, with regard to the commission of array[19] . . . of which a copy was delivered to the said commons, so that they might be advised concerning it and might correct it according to their desires, the same commons, having thereupon deliberated and consulted, caused to be cancelled certain clauses and words contained in it. And they prayed the king that henceforth no commission of array should

---

[18] How the commons largely gained their point by voting subsidies on the last day of parliament is illustrated below, p. 263.
[19] Cf. no. 50B.

be issued otherwise, or in other words than were contained in the same copy. . . . Which prayer our said lord the king, by the advice of the lords and after consultation on the matter with the judges of the realm, very graciously granted in parliament. Of which copy the tenor follows in these words. . . .

Item, it should be remembered that, on March 1, it was granted by the king and the lords spiritual and temporal in parliament that certain farms, revenues, issues, profits, and emoluments, specified in the enrolment of the letters patent below, should be devoted to and spent for the expenses of the king's household. . . .[20]

Item, on Saturday, March 1, in the presence of the king and the lords of parliament, the archbishop of Canterbury at the king's command explained to the said lords our same lord the king's intention regarding his government. . . . He told them that it was our said lord the king's desire that the laws should be kept and observed; that equal right and justice should be administered to poor and rich alike; that, on account of any letters under the secret seal[21] or the privy seal, or on account of any command or signed instruction whatsoever, the common law should not be disturbed, or the people in any way delayed in their pursuit [of justice]. And besides, our same lord the king, wishing that good administration should be maintained in his household, prayed the said lords that they would give their aid and care to placing it under good and satisfactory government, and one by a suitable number [of persons]; so that the people could be paid for their victuals and for the [other] expenses of his said household. . . . And it was furthermore our same lord the king's will that, with regard to the grant to be made in this present parliament by the lords and commons for the wars and for the defence of the kingdom, certain treasurers for the same grant should be appointed by the advice of the said lords and commons, so that the money thence arising should be expended for the wars and for nothing else. . . .

Item, for the sake of good and just government and of a remedy to be provided for the numerous complaints, grievances, and mischiefs shown to our lord the king in this parliament, our same lord the king, in reverence to God and in response to the very insistent and especial requests brought to him at various times in this parliament by the commons of his realm, for the ease and comfort of all his people has appointed certain lords and other persons, hereinunder written, to be of his great and continual council: namely, the archbishop of Canterbury; the bishop of Lincoln, chancellor of England; the bishop of Rochester, the bishop of Worcester, the bishop of Bath, the bishop of Bangor, the duke of York, the earl of Somerset, the earl of Westmorland; the lord of Roos, treasurer of England; the keeper of the privy seal, the lord of Berkeley, the lord of Willoughby, the lord of

---

[20] The total amount was £12,100, drawn from seven specified sources.

[21] Normally used for the king's personal correspondence. One form of the secret seal became known as the signet in the fifteenth century; see Tout, *Chapters in Mediaeval Administrative History*, V, 195 f.

66. PARLIAMENT ROLLS 261

Furnivall, the lord of Lovell, Sir Piers Courteney, Sir Hugh Waterton, Sir John Cheyne, Sir Arnold Savage, John Northbury, John Durward, John Curson.

Item, whereas the writ of summons to parliament returned by the sheriff of Rutland was not satisfactory or properly returned, as the said commons understood, the same commons prayed our lord the king and the lords in parliament that this matter might be properly examined in parliament, and that, in case default was therein discovered, such punishment should thereof be made as should serve for an example to others against trespass in such ways on some other occasion. Whereupon our said lord the king, in full parliament, commanded the lords of parliament to examine the said matter and at their discretion to deal with it as they thought best. And thereupon the said lords caused to come before them in parliament as well the said sheriff as William Ondeby, who had been returned by the said sheriff as one of the knights of the said shire, and also Thomas of Thorpe, who had been elected in full county [court] as one of the knights of the same shire for the said parliament and had not been returned by the said sheriff. And after the same parties had been duly examined and their cases well heard in the said parliament, it was decided by the same lords that, whereas the same sheriff had not satisfactorily made return of the said writ, he should amend the same return and should return the said Thomas as one of the knights, since the latter had been elected to the parliament in the county [court]; and besides that the said sheriff, on account of this default, should be discharged from his office and committed to Fleet Prison, and that he should be subjected to fine and redemption at the king's pleasure. . . .

May it please our most excellent and respected lord the king to grant to your poor commons of the parliament held at Westminster on the morrow of St. Hilary, in the fifth year of your reign, the following petitions for their relief:—

. . . Item, the commons pray that, whereas all the lords, knights, citizens, and burgesses attending parliament by the king's writ, together with their servants, are under royal protection while coming, remaining, and returning; and [whereas] the said lords, knights, citizens, burgesses, and their household servants have at the aforesaid times often suffered numerous mischiefs and molestations, such as murder, mayhem, and battery, from men lying in ambush or otherwise, for which due remedy has never been provided. . . .[22] : may it please [the king] to ordain sufficient remedy in this matter and in other similar cases, so that the punishment may serve as a terrible example to others who commit such misdeeds in times to come—that is to say, if any one kills or murders a man who has thus come to parliament under your protection, he shall be adjudged [guilty of]

---

[22] The petition then describes in detail the "horrible battery" recently suffered by Richard Cheddar while coming to parliament as knight of the shire for Somerset.

treason; if any one maims or disfigures such a man thus come under your protection, he shall lose a hand; and if any one assaults or beats such a man thus come, he shall be subjected to a year's imprisonment as well as fine and redemption to the king. And [the commons pray] that it may please you of your special grace henceforth to abstain from grants of pardon in such cases, unless the parties concerned have come to full agreement. . . .[23]

(French) *Ibid.*, III, 523-42.

(D) PARLIAMENT OF 1406

. . . Item, on Saturday, May 22, the commons came before the king and the lords in parliament, and there the said Sir John[24] related how, at the opening of parliament and afterwards, he had petitioned the king with regard to a satisfactory government; and he prayed our same lord the king to proceed with its establishment. And he also related how the archbishop of Canterbury had reported to them that the king wished to be counselled by the wisest lords of the realm, who were to have the supervision of everything that should be done for the good government of his kingdom. To do which the king agreed; and he declared by his own mouth that it was wholly his pleasure [so to do]. And thereupon a bill was drawn up by the king himself and of his own will was read, with the names of the lords who were to be of his council. Of which bill the tenor follows. . . .[25]

And thereupon the said lords prayed the king that, since this bill was the king's desire and [resulted] from his own initiation and not at all from their suit, the said bill might be entered as of record in the roll of parliament. And they also prayed that all matters contained within the said bill might be executed according to its provisions. Which [requests] the king granted. Furthermore, the king commanded that, as requested by the said lords, the said bill should well be enacted and enrolled in the same roll of parliament. . . .

Item, on the same day,[26] the said Sir John Tibetot, in the name of the said commons, prayed our said lord the king and all the lords in parliament that certain lords spiritual and temporal, whom they should be pleased to name, and also certain of the commons whose names he had written on a schedule in parliament . . . , might be assigned to be present at the enactment and engrossing of the roll of parlia-

---

[23] The king replies that the assailant is to be summoned before the king's bench; if he does not come, he is to pay double damages and be subject to ransom at the king's pleasure. Similar action is to be taken in future cases of the same sort.

[24] Tibetot, speaker of the commons.

[25] The list of councillors includes three prelates, six peers, three knights, the chancellor, the treasurer, the keeper of the privy seal, the steward, and the chamberlain. Instructions to all officials must be drawn up in council or endorsed by some of the members. Certain specified actions can be taken only by the advice of the council. Note this early example of what was to become known as bill procedure; cf. nos. 51B, 70B.

[26] December 22.

ment. And he further asked that this prayer and petition should be enacted as of record in the roll of parliament. Which prayers the king graciously conceded. . . .

In reverence to God and for the great love and affection that your poor commons of your realm of England have for you, our very sovereign and very gracious lord the king, and on account of the great trust that your said commons have in the lords recently elected and ordained for your council in order to provide better government than has been had, your said poor commons, by the assent of the lords spiritual and temporal, on December 22 of the eighth year of your reign, grant to you, most sovereign lord, for the salvation and defence of your kingdom of England against all enemies and rebels . . . , an entire fifteenth and tenth to be levied from laymen in the accustomed manner. . . .[27] [And this grant is made] on condition that the said fifteenth and tenth, the said subsidies, and all that remains unspent of the previous grant made at Coventry shall, by the advice of the lords and officials named and elected to the council by our lord the king in this present parliament, be disbursed and expended in the most advantageous places for the defence of the kingdom and the safeguarding of the sea, and in no other way. . . .[28]

(French) *Ibid.*, III, 568, 572-85.

(E) PARLIAMENT OF 1407

. . . Item, on Wednesday, November 9, the commons came before the king and the lords in parliament, and there Thomas Chaucer, speaker for the said commons, made protestation. . . .[29] To which the chancellor of England replied, saying that with regard to all these matters the same chancellor had already accounted to them in the refectory, the place assigned to the said commons for this proceeding— first orally and then in writing, by means of a schedule presented to the said commons voluntarily by the said lords of the council and at neither the instance nor the request of the said commons, [explaining] how and in what manner the said tenth and fifteenth, as well as the subsidy and the tunnage and poundage, had been spent. . . .

Item, on Friday, December 2, which was the last day of the parliament, the commons came before the king and the lords in parliament and there, by the king's command, a schedule of indemnity was read touching a certain altercation that had arisen between the lords and the commons; and at the command of our same lord the king the same schedule was entered as of record in the roll of parliament. Of which schedule the tenor is as follows:—

It is to be remembered that on Monday, November 21, while our

---

[27] Also tunnage and poundage and the ordinary customs on wool, etc., for one year.

[28] Although recorded toward the beginning of the roll, this grant was made at the end of the session; cf. no. 66B.

[29] In this address, the usual formality, he reminded the king of promised reform in the government, the reconstitution of the council, etc.

sovereign lord the king was in the council chamber within the abbey of Gloucester, and while the lords spiritual and temporal assembled for this present parliament were there before him, a conference was held among them regarding the state of the kingdom and the defence of the same. . . . And thereupon the aforesaid lords were asked by way of interrogation what aid would be necessary and [how much] might suffice in this case. To which demand and question the same lords severally responded that, in consideration on the one hand of the king's need and on the other of the poverty of his people, less aid would not suffice than a tenth and a half [a tenth] from the cities and boroughs and a fifteenth and a half [a fifteenth] from other laymen, and besides this an extension of the subsidy from wool, leather, and wool-fells, and of [tunnage and poundage at] 3s. the tun and 12d. the pound, from the feast of St. Michael next to the feast of St. Michael two years hence. Whereupon, by the command of our said lord the king, word was sent to the commons of this present parliament to cause a certain number of persons from their membership to appear before our said lord the king and the said lords, in order to hear and to report to their companions what they might have by way of command from our said lord the king. And thereupon the said commons sent into the presence of our said lord the king, and of the said lords, twelve of their members, to whom, at the command of our same lord the king, the aforesaid question was set forth, together with the response severally made to it by the lords aforesaid. Which response, it was the pleasure of our said lord the king, they should report to the rest of their companions in order that action might be taken to conform as nearly as possible with the opinion of the lords aforesaid. When this report had thus been made to the said commons, they were thereby greatly disturbed, saying and affirming that it was to the great prejudice and derogation of their liberties. And as soon as our said lord the king had heard this, desirous that neither at the present time nor in that to come anything should be done that in any way could be turned against the liberty of the estate [of the commons], under which they had come to parliament, or against the liberties of the lords aforesaid, willed, granted, and declared, by the advice and consent of the same lords, to the following effect: namely, that in the present parliament and in all those to come the lords may well confer among themselves in the king's absence regarding the state of the kingdom and the remedies thereby demanded, and that in the same way the commons on their part may well confer among themselves with regard to the state and remedies aforesaid; always provided that neither the lords on their part nor the commons on their part shall make any report to our said lord the king of any grant made by the commons and assented to by the lords, or of the discussions in connection with the said grant, until the same lords and commons are of one mind and accord in this matter, and then [the report shall be made] in the manner and form accustomed, that is to say, by the mouth of the speaker of the said commons for the time being, so that the said lords and commons may hear the pleasure of our said lord the king. Furthermore, our said lord the king, by the assent of the lords aforesaid, wills that the conference held in this present parliament, as aforesaid, shall not be made a precedent for times to come or be turned to the prejudice or derogation of the liberty of the estate, under which the same commons are now in attendance—neither in this present parliament, nor in any other throughout the future. . . .[30]

(French) *Ibid.*, III, 609-11.

(F) PARLIAMENT OF 1414

Item, it is to be remembered that in this parliament the commons presented to our most sovereign lord the king a petition of which the tenor is word for word as follows:—

Our sovereign lord, your humble and true lieges who have come on behalf of the commons of your land pray your righteousness that— whereas it has ever been their liberty and freedom that no statute or law should be made unless they have thereto given their assent, and in consideration of the fact that the commons of your land, who now are and ever have been a member of your parliament, have the power of assenting as well as of petitioning—from this time forward, on complaint by the commons asking remedy for any mischief either by the mouth of the speaker of the commons or else by written petition, no law shall thereupon be made and engrossed as a statute and a law with either additions or subtractions which in any particular or particulars change the meaning and intent as requested by the mouth of the speaker or the aforesaid petitions drawn up in writing after the manner aforesaid, without the assent of the aforesaid commons. It is to be understood, our sovereign lord, that if the commons either orally or in writing make two or three requests of you, or as many as please them, they have no intention whatsoever but that it shall always be in the freedom of your high regality to grant whichever of them you please and to refuse the rest.

Response: The king grants of his especial grace that, in connection with the petitions of his commons, nothing contrary to their request shall henceforth be enacted, whereby they shall be bound without their assent; saving always to our liege lord his real prerogative to grant and deny what may please him of their petitions and requests aforesaid. . . .

(French and English) *Ibid.*, IV, 22.

67. PARLIAMENT ROLLS OF HENRY VI

(A) PARLIAMENT OF 1422

. . . It is to be remembered that, on the twenty-seventh day of this parliament, in consideration of the tender age of our most honoured lord, King Henry VI after the Conquest—on which account he could

---

[30] A parliamentary grant in the regular form follows.

not for the time being personally see to the protection and defence of his kingdom of England and of the English Church—the same lord king, fully trusting in the wisdom and industry of his dearest uncles, John, duke of Bedford, and Humphrey, duke of Gloucester, by the advice and consent of the lords both spiritual and temporal assembled in the present parliament, and also by the assent of the commons of the English realm assembled in the same, ordained and constituted his said uncle, the duke of Bedford, now absent in foreign parts, as protector and defender of his kingdom and the English Church aforesaid, and as chief councillor of the said lord king; and [he ordered] that the said duke, when he returned to England and came into the king's presence, and for so long a time as he there remained and it was pleasing to our same lord the king, should be and should be styled protector and defender of the same kingdom and chief councillor of the said king. And furthermore the same lord king, by the advice and consent aforesaid, in the absence of his aforesaid uncle, the duke of Bedford, ordained and constituted his aforesaid uncle, the duke of Gloucester, who was then present in his said kingdom of England, as protector and defender of his said kingdom of England and the English Church, and as chief councillor of the said lord king; and [he ordered] that the same duke of Gloucester should be and should be styled protector and defender of the same kingdom of England and the Church aforesaid during the king's pleasure, and besides that letters patent of the said lord king should be drawn up in the form here following. . . .

Now when this act had thus been drawn up and the commission had been secured, and after their contents had been read and recited in the presence of the said lord duke of Gloucester, as well as of the aforesaid lords spiritual and temporal, the same lord duke of Gloucester, having thereupon deliberated, agreed to assume, in so far as pertained to him, the obligation and exercise of such office for the honour of God, for the benefit of the king and the kingdom aforesaid, and at the request of the aforesaid lords; and he then and there did assume it according to the form of the act aforesaid—protesting, nevertheless, that such assumption of his, or consent in this matter, should in no way serve to the prejudice of his aforesaid brother, but that the same brother might freely deliberate and decide for himself whether or not to assume such responsibility. . . .[1]

Be it known that afterwards . . . , on the request of the said commons, and by the advice and consent of all the lords aforesaid, certain persons of rank, both spiritual and temporal, were named and elected as councillors to assist in the government, whose names, written in a small schedule and publicly read in this parliament, here follow: the duke of Gloucester, the archbishop of Canterbury, the bishop of London, the bishop of Winchester, the bishop of Norwich, the

---

[1] Here follows a memorandum limiting the discretionary authority of the protector to minor appointments in church and state; all important offices were to be filled only by the advice of the council.

bishop of Worcester, the duke of Exeter, the earl of March, the earl of Warwick, the earl marshal, the earl of Northumberland, the earl of Westmorland, Lord Fitz-Hugh, Sir Ralph Cromwell, Sir Walter Hungerford, Sir John Tiptoft, Sir Walter Beauchamp.

And be it known also that the same persons, thus named and elected as assistant councillors, after this nomination and election, agreed to accept such assistance in the government in the manner and form set forth in a schedule written in English on paper, containing not only all their names, but also five special articles presented in this same parliament by the same persons named as assistant councillors; of which schedule the tenor is as follows. . . .[2]

(Latin and French) *Ibid.*, IV, 174-76.

(B) PARLIAMENT OF 1427

. . . It is to be remembered that, on March 3 of the present year, the illustrious prince, my lord Humphrey, duke of Gloucester . . . immediately after the opening of the same parliament, among other matters, declared that he, in the absence of the illustrious prince, my lord John, duke of Bedford, his dearest brother, acted as protector and defender of the kingdom of England and chief councillor of the lord king, and that, through the relation of certain persons, he had heard there were diverse opinions concerning his authority and power. The aforesaid duke of Gloucester, therefore desirous of being more fully informed in this matter of his power and authority, particularly urged and requested all the lords spiritual and temporal assembled in the present parliament that they, through the good discretion and advisement of all, would discuss and consider such power and authority of his and with all possible speed give him sure information in that matter, stating that he would absent himself from the chamber of the parliament aforesaid until response should be made to him in this connection. When this declaration and request had been heard . . . , all and singular of the lords spiritual and temporal had a certain response drawn up in writing and put into an indenture, which afterwards . . . was delivered to the aforesaid duke of Gloucester by the venerable father, Henry, archbishop of Canterbury; of which response the tenor follows in these words:—

High and mighty prince, my lord of Gloucester, we, lords spiritual and temporal assembled by command of the king our sovereign lord in this his present parliament, well remember how[3]. . . , in the first

---

[2] These articles specify that the council is to have control of appointments to financial offices and the leasing of wardships, marriage rights, etc. A record is to be kept of the councillors present each day and nothing is to be done without the agreement of at least four of them; a majority is required for important matters. A new election was made in the parliament of the next year and eight additional articles were passed, further defining the necessary procedure of the council.

[3] The address first recites the parliamentary action of 1422; see the previous document.

parliament held at Westminster by our sovereign lord the king who now is, you desired to have the government of this land, affirming that it belonged to you of right, as well by virtue of your birth as by the last will of the late king, your brother—whom God assoil! . . . Whereupon the lords spiritual and temporal then assembled in parliament . . . held great and long deliberation and advisement, sought precedents in the government of the land for similar times and cases when kings of this land had been of tender age, also obtained information concerning the laws of the land from such persons as were notably learned therein, and finally found your said desire unjustified and groundless according to precedent and the law of the land, which the late king during his lifetime could not alter, change, or abrogate by his last will or otherwise without the consent of the three estates;[4] nor could he commit or grant to any person the government or rule of this land for a longer term than that of his own life. . . . Nevertheless, to preserve peace and tranquillity, and in order to ease and appease you, it was ordained and established by the authority of the king with the assent of the three estates of this land that, in the absence of my lord your brother of Bedford, you should be chief of the king's council; and accordingly a title was devised for you different from that of the other councillors—not the title of tutor, lieutenant, governor, or regent, nor any title that would imply authority of government over the land, but the title of protector and defender, which implies a personal duty of attending to the actual defence of the land, as well against outward enemies, if the case requires, as against inward rebels, should there be any—which God forbid! And therewith you were granted certain power, which is specified and contained in an act of the said parliament, to continue as long as might be the king's pleasure. And if the intent of the said estates had been for you to have more power or authority, more would have been expressed therein. . . .[5] With all our hearts we marvel that, considering the open declaration of the authority and power belonging to my lord of Bedford, to you in his absence, and to the king's council, to which [declaration] both my lord of Bedford aforesaid and you purely and simply subscribed, you should in any way be stirred or moved not to content yourself therewith, or to lay claim to any other. . . . Accordingly, considering the facts and causes aforesaid and many others too long for enumeration, we, the lords aforesaid, pray, exhort, and require you to content yourself with the power set forth and declared above . . . and that you neither desire nor exercise any larger power; giving you, as our answer to your aforesaid demand, that which is above written, and which without variance or change we will keep and abide by. . . .

Item, on March 25, which was the last day of this present parliament, another petition was presented to our lord the king in the said

---

[4] The lords spiritual and temporal and the commons.
[5] The address then relates at length how the duke had agreed to all these earlier arrangements.

parliament by the commons of the same, the tenor of which petition here follows:—

May it please our sovereign lord the king, considering how, in order to obtain suitable remedies, numerous petitions have been introduced and presented to your most noble highness by the commons of this present parliament, and how they have not as yet been settled, to ordain by the advice of the lords spiritual and temporal, and by the consent of the aforesaid commons, that the said petitions may be delivered to the lords of your most wise council, who, calling unto themselves, if need be, the justices and other persons skilled in your law, shall have power through the authority of the said parliament between now and the coming feast of the Nativity of St. John the Baptist to hear and determine the said petitions; and that the latter, thus determined by the advice and consent aforesaid, may be enacted, enrolled, and placed as of record in the roll of your same parliament.

Response: *Le roi le voet*.[6]

Afterwards, that is to say, on June 15 next following, in the presence of divers lords of our lord the king's council[7] . . . assembled in the Star Chamber[8] at Westminster, a number of the said petitions . . . were read and heard; and by virtue of the authority given to the said lords, as aforesaid, they were answered and determined, as is more clearly set forth in the endorsement of the same petitions. . . .

(Latin, French, English) *Ibid.*, IV, 326-34.

(C) PARLIAMENT OF 1429

The commons pray that—whereas one William Larke, servant to William Melrede, attending your present court of parliament for the city of London, through the subtle imagination and conjecture of one Margery Janyns, and while he was then in the service of the said William Melrede, was arrested by the local officers in the court of piepowder[9] belonging to the abbot of Westminster and, at the suit of the said Margery, was thence removed to your [court of] common bench . . . , and by the justices of your said bench was committed to your Fleet Prison and there detained in prison until the present . . . —it may please your royal majesty, considering how the said William Larke was in the service of the said William Melrede at the time of the said arrest and truly supposed that, by the privilege of your court of parliament, he was quit of all arrest during [the session of] your said court except for treason, felony, or surety of the peace, to ordain by the authority of your same parliament that the said

---

[6] The king so wills—the form still used for the royal assent to an act of parliament.

[7] Seven bishops, five lay peers, the justices of both benches, the chief baron and two other barons of the exchequer.

[8] Cf. no. 70G.

[9] A corruption of *pied poudré*, dusty foot. The court was so called because it was held to settle the disputes of those attending a fair.

William Larke shall be liberated from your Fleet Prison, notwithstanding the said condemnation, judgment, and execution, or anything thereby pending against or upon him; saving always to the said Margery and her executors their right to execute the said judgment against the said William Larke after the end of the same parliament. And [the commons pray the king] also to grant, by the aforesaid authority, that none of your said lieges—that is to say, lords, knights of your shires, citizens, or burgesses in your parliaments to come, together with their servants or menials—shall in any way be arrested or detained in prison during the time of your parliaments, except for treason, felony, or surety of the peace, as aforesaid.

Response: The king, by the advice of the lords spiritual and temporal, and at the especial request of the commons assembled in this present parliament, and also with the assent of the counsel of the Margery Janyns named in this petition, wills and grants by the authority of the said parliament that William Larke, named in the said petition, shall for the time being be liberated from Fleet Prison. . . .[10] And as to the remainder of the petition, *le roi s'avisera*.[11]

(French) *Ibid.,* IV, 357-58.

(D) PARLIAMENT OF 1439

. . . Item, by command of the said lord king, a certain schedule or bill was presented and delivered to the commons in words to this effect. . . .[12] To which schedule or bill and the matter therein contained the said commons gave their assent in these words: To this bill the commons have assented. When this schedule or bill and the assent thereto had been read and fully made known before the same lord king in his aforesaid parliament and the lords spiritual and temporal there assembled, the same lord king, having thereon had mature and careful deliberation with the same lords, by the advice and consent of the same lords and commons, on the authority of the aforesaid parliament, granted all and singular of the matters specified and contained in the aforesaid bill or schedule and the assent thereto, and he willed and granted that they should be enacted as of record in the aforesaid parliament. . . .

(Latin and French) *Ibid.,* V, 8-9.

(E) PARLIAMENT OF 1451

. . . Your commons of this present parliament pray that—whereas the false traitor John Cade, who named himself John Mortimer and

---

[10] Details follow with regard to the execution of the judgment after the termination of parliament and the recommitment of Larke to prison.

[11] The king will deliberate—the form that became customary for a royal denial of a petition.

[12] Here follows a formal act in English to provide greater income for the household and so to relieve the people of continued exactions from royal purveyors. Compare this procedure with what had become customary by 1483 (no. 68).

was lately called captain of Kent, on July 8 in the twenty-eighth year
of your reign at Southwark in the shire of Surrey, and on July 9
of the year aforesaid at Dartford and Rochester in the shire of Kent,
also at Rochester aforesaid and elsewhere on July 10 and 11 next
following, within this your noble realm of England falsely and
traitorously imagined your death and the destruction and subversion
of this your said realm, by gathering and raising a great number of
your people and inciting them falsely and traitorously to rise against
you in the places aforesaid and at the times aforesaid, contrary to
your royalty, crown, and dignity, and then and there made and raised
war falsely and traitorously against you and your highness; and
whereas, although dead and mischieved, he has not yet been punished
by the law of your said land—you consider the premises and warn
such traitors against so doing in times to come and, for the salvation
of yourself and your said realm, by the advice of your lords spiritual
and temporal in this your present parliament assembled and by authority of the said parliament, ordain that he be attainted of these
treasons, that by the authority aforesaid he forfeit to you all goods,
lands, tenements, rents, and possessions which he had on the said
July 8 or thereafter, that his blood be corrupted and disabled forever, and that he be called false traitor within your said realm forever-
more.

Response: *Le roi le voet.* . . .

(English) *Ibid.*, V, 224.

(F) PARLIAMENT OF 1455

To the right wise and discreet commons in this present parliament
assembled Thomas Young humbly makes this prayer:—[13]

Whereas, having of late been one of the knights for the shire and
town of Bristol[14] in divers parliaments held before this time, in his
speech at the same [parliaments] he conducted himself as well and
faithfully, and with all such true and diligent labour, as in his sim-
plicity he could or might, for the welfare of the king our sovereign
lord and of this his noble realm; and whereas, notwithstanding the
fact that, by the ancient liberty and freedom held, enjoyed, and prescribed by the commons of this land from time out of mind, all such
persons as for the moment are assembled for the same commons in
any parliament ought to have their freedom to speak and say in the
house of their assembly whatever they think convenient or reasonable
without in any way incurring any sort of challenge, charge, or punishment, nevertheless, through false and sinister reports made to the
king's highness concerning him, your said petitioner, on account of
matters presented by him in the house customarily used by the

---

[13] Recorded among the petitions of the commons and endorsed: "To be presented to the lords."

[14] Bristol and the environs had been created a separate county in 1373; since
then its two representatives had been ranked as knights of the shire. Cf. no.
72B.

commons in the said parliament, was taken, arrested, and rigorously and publicly led to the Tower of London, where, contrary to the said liberty and freedom, he was grievously and in great duress imprisoned for a long time, and was put in great fear of unbearable punishment of his body and in dread of the loss of his life, without any indictment, presentment, appeal, due original, accusation, or lawful cause held or sworn against him . . . , whereby he not only suffered great hurt, pain, and discomfort of body, but was . . . put to excessive loss and expense of goods amounting to the sum of 1000*m.* and much more: [therefore] may it please you in your great wisdom to give sympathetic consideration to the premises and thereupon to pray the king our sovereign lord that his highness and most noble grace will be pleased to grant and provide, by the advice of the lords spiritual and temporal in this present parliament, that for the said losses, costs, damages, and imprisonment your said petitioner shall have sufficient and reasonable compensation, as is required by good faith, truth, and conscience.

Response: The king wills that the lords of his council shall act and provide for the said petitioner in this matter as at their discretion they shall think convenient and reasonable.

(French and English) *Ibid.,* V, 337.

68. PARLIAMENT ROLL OF RICHARD III (1483)

. . . It is to be remembered that a certain bill was presented before the lord king in the aforesaid parliament to this effect.[1] . . . Which bill was taken to the commons of the realm of England assembled in the said parliament, and to it the same commons gave their assent in these words: To this bill the commons have assented. When this bill and the assent thereto had been read, heard, and fully made known before the king in the aforesaid parliament, by assent of the lords spiritual and temporal likewise assembled in the said parliament, and of the commons aforesaid, and by the authority of the same parliament, it was pronounced, decreed, and declared that all and singular of the contents of the aforesaid bill were true and undoubted; and the same lord king, by the assent of the said three estates of the realm, and by the authority aforesaid, granted all and singular of the premises contained in the aforesaid bill, pronouncing, decreeing, and declaring them all to be true and undoubted. . . .

Item, a certain petition with a certain schedule attached to it was presented to the same lord king in the said parliament by Henry Percy, now earl of Northumberland, in these words.[2] . . . When this petition and this schedule had been read, heard, and fully made known in the aforesaid parliament, by the advice and consent of the lords

---

[1] A recapitulation of the king's title and settlement of the crown on him and his heirs. The same procedure was used for an act of resumption, an act of attainder against all his enemies, and others.

[2] The extract is typical of numerous private petitions introduced in this same parliament.

spiritual and temporal, and of the commons of the realm of England assembled in the same parliament, answer was made to them in these words: Let it be done as is desired. . . .

Item, a certain other petition was presented to the aforesaid lord king in the said parliament by the commons of the realm of England on behalf of the inhabitants of the town of Croyland in Lincolnshire, to the following purport.[3] . . . When this petition had been read, heard, and fully made known in the aforesaid parliament, by the assent of the lords spiritual and temporal, and of the aforesaid commons assembled in the said parliament, and by the authority of the same persons, answer was made to it in the following form: *Le roi le voet*. . . .

It is to be remembered that the commons of the realm of England assembled in the present parliament appeared before the lord king in the full parliament aforesaid on February 20 of the aforesaid year—that is to say, on the last day of the present parliament—and declared through William Catesby, their speaker, that they, by the assent of the lords spiritual and temporal assembled in the parliament aforesaid, granted to the aforesaid lord king certain subsidies, to be levied from both natives and aliens according to the form specified in a certain indenture drawn up in that connection, the contents of which were then and there exhibited to the same lord king. The tenor of which indenture follows in these words. . . .[4]

Response: Our lord the king, thanking his commons for their kindness in making the aforesaid grants, has accepted those grants and has conceded everything specified in the aforesaid indenture, with the provisions here following. . . .[5]

(Latin, French, English) *Ibid.*, VI, 238-63.

---

[3] This is the form used for the commons' petitions, of which some fifteen are entered in the statute roll of Richard III; e.g., no. 69H.

[4] A formal grant of tunnage and poundage and of customs on wool, woolfells, and hides for the king's lifetime, but with many restrictions set forth in great detail.

[5] Clauses saving the privileges in England of the German Hansa and of the merchants from Spain.

69. STATUTES (1399-1483)

(A) 1 HENRY IV: RESTRICTION OF APPEALS (1399)

14. Item, on account of the many great inconveniences and mischiefs that have occurred in consequence of the numerous appeals[1] heretofore made in the kingdom of England, it is ordained and established that henceforth all appeals for acts accomplished within the kingdom shall be tried and determined according to the good laws of the kingdom made and used in the time of the most noble progenitors of our said lord the king; and that all appeals for acts accomplished outside the kingdom shall be tried and terminated before the constable and marshal of England for the time being. And besides it is granted

---

[1] That is to say, for felony and treason; cf. no. 63G.

and agreed that henceforth no appeals shall in any way or at any time be made or pursued in parliament. . . .

(French) *Statutes of the Realm*, II, 116.

(B) 3 HENRY IV: FOR THE BURNING OF HERETICS (1401)

15. . . . With regard to which innovations and excesses,[2] set forth above, the prelates and clergy aforesaid, and also the commons of the said realm assembled in the same parliament, prayed the said lord king that his royal highness would in the said parliament deign to make provision for a suitable remedy. The same lord king then . . . , by the assent of the magnates and other nobles of the said realm assembled in parliament, has granted, ordained, and established . . . that no one within the said kingdom or the other dominions subject to his royal majesty shall presume to preach in public or in secret without having first sought and obtained the licence of the local diocesan,[3] always excepting curates in their own churches, persons who have hitherto enjoyed the privilege, and others to whom it has been granted by canon law; and that henceforth no one either openly or secretly shall preach, hold, teach, or impart anything, or compose or write any book, contrary to the catholic faith or the decisions of Holy Church, or anywhere hold conventicles or in any way have or maintain schools for such a sect and its nefarious doctrines and opinions; and also that in the future no one shall favour anybody who thus preaches, holds such or similar conventicles, has or maintains such schools, composes or writes such a book, or in any such fashion teaches, instructs, or excites the people.[4] . . . And if any person within the said kingdom and dominions is formally convicted before the local diocesan or his commissioners of the said nefarious preachings, doctrines, opinions, [holding of] schools, and heretical and erroneous instruction, or any of them, and if he refuses properly to abjure the same . . . , or, after abjuration has been made by the same person, he is declared by the local diocesan or his commissioners to have relapsed, so that according to the sacred canons he ought to be relinquished to the secular court . . . , then the sheriff of the local county and the mayor and sheriffs or sheriff, or the mayor and bailiffs of the city, town, or borough of the same county nearest the said diocesan or his said commissioners . . . , shall, after the pronouncement of such sentences, receive those persons and every one of them and shall have them burned before the people in some prominent place, so that such punishment shall inspire fear in the minds of others and prevent such nefarious doctrines and heretical and erroneous opinions,

---

[2] Of the Lollards, "a certain new sect," accused in the long preamble of holding damnable opinions concerning the sacraments and the authority of the Church and of doing all the things which the statute proceeds to forbid.

[3] That is to say, the bishop.

[4] Such persons are to be subjected to canonical trial in the episcopal court and, if convicted, to imprisonment in ecclesiastical prison as well as to royal fine.

69. STATUTES (1399-1483)

or their authors and protagonists in the said kingdom and dominions, from being supported or in any way tolerated against the catholic faith, the Christian religion, and the decisions of Holy Church—which God forbid! And in all and singular of the aforesaid matters regarding the said ordinance and statute, the sheriffs, mayors, and bailiffs of the counties, cities, towns, and boroughs aforesaid are to be attentive, helpful, and favourable to the said diocesans and their commissioners. . . .

(Latin) *Ibid.*, II, 126-28.

(C) 7 HENRY IV: ON SUCCESSION TO THE THRONE AND ELECTIONS TO PARLIAMENT (1406)

2. Item, it is ordained and established in the said parliament at the request and by the assent of the said lords and commons that the inheritance of the crown and of the kingdoms of England and France and of all the other dominions of our said lord the king beyond the sea, together with all their appurtenances, shall be settled upon and shall remain with the person of our same lord the king and the heirs of his body. And at the request and by the assent aforesaid it is especially ordained, established, pronounced, decreed, and declared that my lord Prince Henry, eldest son of our said Lord the king, is to be heir apparent of our same lord the king to succeed him in [the possession of] the aforesaid crown, kingdoms, and dominions, and, after the death of our said lord the king, to have them with all their appurtenances for himself and the heirs of his body. And if he dies without heir of his body, then the aforesaid crown, kingdoms, and dominions, together with their appurtenances, shall all remain to my lord Thomas, second son of our said lord the king, and to the heirs of his body. And if he dies without heir of his body, then the aforesaid crown, kingdoms, and dominions, together with their appurtenances, shall all remain to my lord John, third son of our same lord the king, and the heirs of his body. And if he dies without heir of his body, then the aforesaid crown, kingdoms, and dominions, together with their appurtenances, shall all remain to my lord Humphrey, fourth son of our said lord the king, and to the heirs of his body. . . .

15. Item, on the grievous complaint of the commons regarding improper election to parliament of knights of the shires, which, to the great scandal of the counties and to the retardation of the business of the community in the said courts, is sometimes made through the favouritism of the sheriffs or in other ways contrary to the writs directed to the said sheriffs, our sovereign lord the king, wishing to provide a remedy for these [abuses], by the assent of the lords spiritual and temporal and of all the commons in this present parliament, has ordained and established that henceforth elections of such knights shall be carried out according to the form that follows. That is to say, at the next county [court] to be held after the delivery of the writ for [elections to] parliament, proclamation shall be made in the full county [court] of the day and the place of the parliament;

and all who are there present, as well suitors duly summoned for this purpose as others, shall attend to the election of their knights for the parliament, then freely and impartially proceeding with that election, any command or request to the contrary notwithstanding. And after the election has been held, whether the persons elected are present or absent, their names are to be written in an indenture under the seals of all who elected them, and [this indenture is to be] attached to the said writ for parliament. Which indenture, thus sealed and attached, shall be kept [by the sheriff] for return of the said writ when it comes to [certifying] the knights of the shire.[5] . . .

(French) *Ibid.*, II, 151-56.

(D) 1 Henry V: On Elections to Parliament (1413)

First, that the statutes made concerning the election of knights of the shires to attend parliament shall be held and kept in all particulars, with the addition that henceforth in each county no knights of the shire shall be elected unless, on the date of the writ of summons to parliament, they are resident within the county where they are thus to be elected; and that the knights, squires, and others who are to be electors of such knights of the shires shall also be residents within the same counties in the manner and form aforesaid. And it is furthermore ordained and established that men, citizens, and burgesses resident, domiciled, and enfranchised in the same cities and boroughs are to be elected as citizens and burgesses of cities and boroughs [to attend parliament], and by no means any others. . . .

(French) *Ibid.*, II, 170.

(E) 8 Henry VI: On Elections to Parliament (1429)

7. Item, whereas in many counties the elections of knights of the shires, those chosen to attend the king's parliaments, have of late been carried out by too great and excessive a number of people dwelling within those same counties, of whom the larger part have been people of little substance or of no worth, each pretending to have the same voice in such elections as the most worthy knights or squires dwelling in the same counties, whereby homicides, riots, assaults, and feuds are very likely to arise among the gentlefolk and other people of the same counties unless a suitable remedy is provided in this connection: [therefore] our lord the king, considering the premises, has provided and ordained by the authority of this parliament that knights of the shires, elected to attend parliaments hereafter to be held in the kingdom of England, shall be chosen in each county by persons dwelling and resident therein, each of whom shall have a freehold to the value of at least 40*s*. a year beyond the charges [on the estate][6] . . . ;

---

[5] Cf. no. 72D.

[6] That is to say, clear annual income. The act then repeats the requirement of the preceding statutes, that knights of the shire must be resident in the county and that the sheriff must make returns by indenture.

and that every sheriff of England shall, by the aforesaid authority, have power to examine on the Holy Gospels each such elector, [to determine] how much he is able to spend annually.[7] . . .

(French) *Ibid.*, II, 243 f.

(F) 23 HENRY VI: ON ELECTIONS TO PARLIAMENT (1445)

14. Item, . . .[8] the king, considering the premises, has ordained by the aforesaid authority that the said statutes shall be duly kept and observed in all particulars; and furthermore that each sheriff, after the delivery to him of every such writ [for elections to parliament], shall without fraud draw up and deliver a sufficient precept under his seal to each mayor and bailiff, or to the bailiffs or bailiff where there is no mayor, of the cities and boroughs within his county, reciting the same writ and commanding them by the same precept to have two citizens elected to attend parliament by the citizens of the same city, in case it is a city, or [two] burgesses in the same way, in case it is a borough[9] . . . ; and that the knights of the shires henceforth to be elected to parliament shall be notable knights of the same counties from which they are elected, or else such notable squires of those counties, gentlemen by birth, as are able to be knights;[10] and that no man who is of the rank of valet or lower is to be such knight [of the shire]. . . .

(French) *Ibid.*, II, 340-42.

(G) 1 EDWARD IV: VALIDATION OF LANCASTRIAN ACTS (1461)

. . . First—for the avoidance of ambiguities, doubts, and differences of opinion that might arise, ensue, or be entertained concerning the judicial acts . . . made or secured in the time of Henry IV, of his son Henry V, and of his son Henry VI, recently in succession *de facto* and not rightful kings of England, or any of them—our said lord the king, by the advice and consent of the lords spiritual and temporal, and at the special request of the said commons in the said parliament assembled, and by the authority of the same, has declared, established, and enacted in the same parliament that all fines and final concords[11] levied or made concerning any lands, tenements, possessions, rents,

---

[7] Enforcement is provided through the justices of assize, with a penalty of £100 on the sheriff for a false return.

[8] A long preamble recites the statutes of 1413 and 1429, enumerating their defects and the misdeeds of the sheriffs.

[9] The mayors and bailiffs are to make return by indenture to the sheriff; the latter is to make similar return to the king. Heavy penalties are provided for infraction of the law; also new legal remedies for persons aggrieved in fraudulent elections.

[10] That is to say, persons having the requisite income; distraint of knighthood (see no. 50A) had by now pretty well lapsed.

[11] Sums of money paid in the king's courts in order to secure legal records of agreements.

inheritances, or other things, and all judicial acts, recoveries, and processes . . . made or secured in any court or courts of record . . . during the pretended reign of any of the said recent kings *de facto* and not of right[12] . . . shall have the same force, validity, and effect as if the said fines, final concords, acts, recoveries, processes, and other premises . . . were begun, sued, had, or determined in the time of any king lawfully reigning in this kingdom and obtaining the crown of the same by just title. And [it is ordained] also that all letters patent made by any of the pretended kings to any person or persons for the creation, appointment, or promotion of any of them to any estate, dignity, or pre-eminence shall have, for the said person or persons or for such of their heirs as are specified in the said letters patent, the same force, validity, and effect with regard to such creation, appointment, or promotion as if the same letters patent had been made or granted to any of them by any king lawfully reigning in this kingdom and obtaining the crown of the same by just title; and that persons thus created, appointed, or promoted shall have from the king new grants of annuities for the support of their estates as has been anciently accustomed; always excepting the persons, and each of them, whom our said lord the king considers and holds as rebels or enemies. . . .

(French) *Ibid.*, II, 380 f.

(H) 1 Richard III: Abolition of Benevolences (1483)

. . . Item, our lord the king, remembering how the commons of this his realm, through new and unlawful inventions and inordinate avarice, against the law of the realm have been subjected to great servitude and unbearable charges and exactions, and especially so through a new imposition called benevolence, whereby in divers years the subjects and commons of this land have, against their will and freedom, paid great sums of money to their almost complete ruin—for many and divers honourable men of this realm were on that account compelled of necessity to break up their households and to live in great penury and wretchedness, with their debts unpaid and their children unpreferred, and such memorials as they had ordered for their souls' health were set at naught, to the great displeasure of God and the destruction of this realm—therefore wills and ordains by the advice and consent of his said lords and commons in the said parliament assembled, and by the authority of the same, that henceforth his subjects and the commonalty of this his realm shall in no way be burdened with any such charge or imposition called benevolence, or anything like it; and that such exactions called benevolences as before this time have been taken shall not be held as a precedent for placing such or similar charges upon any of his said subjects of this realm in the future, but that they are to be condemned and annulled forever.

(French) *Ibid.*, II, 478.

---

[12] Judicial acts in parliament are excepted from the force of this statute.

70. RECORDS OF THE PRIVY COUNCIL

(A) PETITION AND JUDGMENT (1401)

To the most wise council of our lord the king his poor chaplain, Nicholas Hogonona of the land of Ireland, humbly prays [as follows] :—

Since, by reason of certain vows that he had made, he recently decided to go on a pilgrimage to the court of Rome, he so came into England; and when he had come to Oxford, he took as companion an Austin friar, to whom he gave 40d. and expenses to conduct him to London; and he also delivered to the said friar 40d. to keep [for him]. And when they had come to London, the said poor chaplain asked for the delivery of his said money, and would have sued for his writ of passage;[1] but in the meantime the said friar went to certain people of London and made a false allegation, stating that he was a "wild Irishman"[2] and an enemy to our said lord the king—and this with the intent of having his said money and his book called a *porthous*,[3] which is still retained [by the said friar], together with part of his money. On account of which statement he was taken and committed to prison, and is there detained in great duress, trouble, and discomfort, although he is a loyal man and a supporter of our said lord the king, as he can well prove if he may come to answer [for himself]. [Accordingly] may it please the said most wise council to grant and command that the said poor chaplain may come before you to give answer to all that any one shall wish to charge against him; and afterwards [may it please you] to ordain concerning his liberation as in your wise discretion may seem demanded by reason and good faith, for the sake of God and as a work of charity.

[Endorsed:] August 25 of the second year, etc. It was agreed by the council—attended by my lords the chancellor, the bishops of Durham, Hereford, and Bangor, the earl of Northumberland, the treasurer, and Master John Prophet—that a writ should be issued to the sheriffs of London for the release from prison of the petitioner in the record, if he is therein detained for the cause here stated and for no other.

(French) Leadam and Baldwin, *Select Cases before the Council*, pp. 85 f.

(B) MINUTES OF DECEMBER 8, 1406[4]

On December 8 of the eighth year, etc., in the afternoon, assembled in council at Westminster my lord the honorable Prince [Henry] and my lords the archbishop of Canterbury, the bishop of Durham, chancellor, the duke of York, and the earl of Somerset; also the

---
[1] The license to cross the sea required of ordinary travellers.
[2] Such persons, as distinguished from law-abiding subjects of the king, had been excluded from England by act of parliament.
[3] A portable breviary.
[4] Cf. no. 66D.

treasurer, and the steward, chamberlain, and treasurer of the household—where they had certain ordinances drawn up.

And in the first place, with regard to the good government of our lord the king's household, it seemed to the council most expedient that good and loyal officers should be placed and ordained in the said household; and especially that there should be a good comptroller, and for that [office] were named Sir Thomas Bromflete and Sir Arnold Savage, one of whom, if it pleased the king, should be comptroller. And since the said council lacked advice for the nomination of other fit persons to be appointed to other offices in the said household according as there might be need for them, the said steward and treasurer were requested to advise them of such fit persons, whose names could be presented to our said lord the king and his said council.

Item, [it was decided] that provision should be made of a certain sum appropriate for the expenses of the said household against the approaching feast of Christmas.

Item, it seemed necessary that, after the said feast, the king should be pleased to withdraw to some convenient place where, by the advice and deliberation of himself and his council and his officials, such moderate government could be ordained for the said household as should henceforth continue to the pleasure of God and of the people.

(French) Nicolas, *Proceedings of the Privy Council*, I, 295 f.

(C) MINUTES OF AUGUST 18, 1409

Matters to be considered by the council: First, regarding the response to be given to the messages from Prussia.[5]

Item, regarding the conference to be held with the king of Castile and the sending of commissioners and deputies on the part of our lord the king to the said conference; also the estates of the great commissioners, etc.—that is to say, a bishop, a baron, a knight, and a clerk, if it please the king.

Item, regarding the land of Ireland.

Item, regarding my lord John, son of the king, and the state of the east march against Scotland.

Item, regarding the truces lately established between our lord the king and the Scots.

Item, regarding the regions of Guienne.

Item, regarding the steward of Guienne.

Item, regarding the dispute between the said steward and the man of La Motte.

Item, regarding Master John Bordin in connection with his office as lieutenant of the constable of Bordeaux and as chancellor of the regions of Guienne.

Item, regarding the Sire de Barde, whose petition has been granted by the advice of the council.

---

[5] Having to do with prises unjustly taken from Prussian merchants—as appears from subsequent minutes.

70. PRIVY COUNCIL RECORDS

Item, regarding William Brewer, captain of Trawe Castle.

Item, regarding the finding of proper security by the Scot, Richard Maughlyn, who desires to be English; to whom the king has granted for this purpose 20m. a year, to be taken from the issues of the county of York, in case he will agree to it.

Item, regarding charters of pardon for murder.

(French) *Ibid.*, I, 319 f.

(D) MEMORANDUM OF MAY 6, 1421[6]

Sum of all the custom, subsidy, and revenue aforesaid, £55,743. 10s. 10d.; out of which [the following expenditures must be made] for annual upkeep, to wit:—

For guarding the kingdom of England, annually 8000m.

Item, for Calais and the march of the same in wartime, £19,119. 5s. 10d.

Item, for guarding the east march and the west march of Scotland, together with Roxburgh Castle in wartime, £19,500.

Item, for guarding the land of Ireland, 2500m.

Item, for guarding Fronsac Castle, 1000m.

Item, for the fees of the treasurer, the keeper of the privy seal, the justices of both benches, the barons of the exchequer, and other officials of the king's court, £3002. 17s. 6d.

Item, to the collectors and comptrollers of the king's customs and subsidies in the various ports of England, for their annual rewards enjoyed by virtue of their offices and received at the exchequer, £547.

Item, to divers dukes, earls, knights, and squires, to the abbess of Shene, and to divers other persons for their annuities enjoyed yearly and received at the exchequer, £772. 12s. 7½d.

Item, to divers persons for their annuities yearly enjoyed from divers customs in the various ports of England, £4374. 4s. 3d.

Item, for the fees of the collectors and comptrollers of customs in the various ports of England yearly allocated to them at the exchequer on account of their offices, £274. 3s. 4d.

Sum of the total annual obligation, £52,235. 16s. 10½d. And so the sum of the aforesaid income exceeds the aforesaid obligation [by] £3700. 13s. 11¾d. From which amount provision must be made [for the following needs] to wit:—

For the chamber of the king and the queen.

Item, for the household of the king and the queen.

Item, for the wardrobe of the king and the queen.

Item, for the king's works.

Item, for the construction of a new tower at Portsmouth.

Item, for the office of clerk of the king's ships.

Item, for keeping the king's lions and the fee of the constable of the Tower of London.

---

[6] Submitted on this date to the king and his council. Only a fragment remains of the itemized statement of receipts.

Item, for artillery and divers other matters ordained for the king's wars.
Item, for the custody and support of the king's prisoners.
Item, for the king's embassies.
Item, for divers messengers, parchments, and other expenses and necessities.
Item, for the expenses of the duchess of Holland.
And no provision has as yet been made [for the following matters], to wit:—
For the old debts of the city of Harfleur.
Item, for the old debts of the city of Calais.
Item, for the old debts of the king's wardrobe.
Item, for the old debts of the king's household.
Item, for the old debts pertaining to the office of clerk of the king's ships.
Item, for the old debts pertaining to the office of clerk of the king's works.
Item, for arrears of annual fees.
Item, for executing the will of King Henry IV with regard to the debts of the same king.
Item, for the debts of the king while he was prince.

(French) *Ibid.*, II, 312 f.

(E) MINUTES, MARCH TO JUNE, 1422

On March 9 in the ninth year, it was advised and agreed by the council that the keeper of the king's great wardrobe[7] should provide for the clothing of all those crossing with the lady queen to the king in the parts of France. . . .

Memorandum that, on March 1 in the ninth year of our sovereign lord Henry V after the Conquest, Ralph, son of Nicholas of Langford, knight, set forth to the lords of the council of our said lord the king how Margaret of Langford . . . , mother of the said Ralph, had, as well by indenture as otherwise, given and delivered to the prior of Gisburn divers things, goods, and jewels to keep for the use and profit of the said Ralph; which prior was unwilling to deliver the said things, goods, and jewels to the said Ralph, according to his allegation; wherefore he prayed the said lords for remedy.[8] . . .

On March 30 in the tenth year,[9] it was agreed by the council that the persons designated below should have, in the name of reward for their crossing to France with the lady queen, the following sums: namely, Lady Margaret of Roos, 100*m.*; Elizabeth Fitz-Hugh, £20; Catherine Chideok, 40*m.* And on the same day £10 were also granted to Friar Walden, newly elected confessor, for his crossing to the king.

---

[7] See above, p. 171, n. 8.

[8] The prior was summoned to appear before the council and to bring with him the articles in question. He did so through an attorney. The articles were delivered to Ralph in return for his copy of the indenture.

[9] Henry V's regnal year ended on March 20, the day of his father's death.

70. PRIVY COUNCIL RECORDS

On May 6 in the tenth year, the lord of Willoughby, [appearing] in person before the lords of the council at Westminster, promised that, by indenture between the king and himself, he would retain for a year's service thirty men-at-arms with the usual quota of archers, that is to say, three to the lance. . . .

On the same day Robert Scot, esquire, undertook to be lieutenant keeper of the Tower of London and of all the prisoners therein contained, for the faithful performance of which [duty] he was personally sworn on holy things at Westminster, and the aforesaid custody was straitly committed to him. . . .

On May 16, in the presence of the lords at Westminster, certain dies (*ferra*) for making the king's coinage in his town of Calais were delivered to a certain William Latchford, servant of Richard Buckland, the treasurer of Calais: namely, one die for the gold noble, another for the half-noble, and another for the gold farthing, as well as a die for coining the silver groat, another for the half-groat, another for the penny, another for the halfpenny, and another for the silver farthing—[placed] in divers sealed bags, which in the same place the same [William] promised to convey with all possible haste to the said town of Calais.

On May 17 it was agreed by the lords that the seigneur de Gaucourt should be transferred to Pontefract Castle . . . in the custody of Robert of Waterton, esquire.

Item, on the same day it was ordained that John Mortimer, knight, should be committed to the king's castle of Pevensey in the custody of John Pelham, knight. . . .

On May 25, in the presence of the lord [duke] of Gloucester and the other lords at Westminster, John, bishop of Hereford, took the oath of fealty that he owed to the king. . . .

On May 28 in the tenth year, in the case [pending] before the lords between John Middlemore, plaintiff, and Richard Clodeshalle, defendant, concerning the manor of Edgebaston with its appurtenances in the county of Warwick . . . , the aforesaid parties were dismissed by the lords to prosecute [their case] at common law if they saw fit.[10]

On the same day the case between the mayor and community of the city of York, plaintiffs, and the lord archbishop of York, defendant, was continued *in statu quo* until the quinzime of Michaelmas next. . . .

On June 29, in the aforesaid year, it seemed to all the lords, being individually examined and making individual responses with regard to the fine that should be paid to the king by Lady Clarence for the demesne of Holderness, once belonging to the lord duke of Clarence,

---

[10] This agreement was reached after the defendant, a tenant of the duke of Bedford, had promised not to allege the king's special protection or to make any other "frivolous or exorbitant" claim by which the case should be excluded from the ordinary courts.

her husband, that one year's income from the said demesne would be sufficient as fine therefrom to be paid by the said Lady Clarence.

On June 30 William Wynart presented before the lords an indenture with an attached schedule, containing the names of the king's prisoners taken in the market of Meaux in France and sent by the king . . . to England for safekeeping there—who, according to what is stated in the said indenture . . . , are to the number of 151. . . .

(Latin and French) Ibid., II, 328-35.

(F) Minutes of November 12, 1437

November 12 in the sixteenth year, etc., in the presence of the king at the hospital of St. John near Clerkenwell, [the following persons] being in attendance: the lord duke of Gloucester, the lord cardinal [Beaufort], the archbishop of York; the bishops of London, Lincoln, Salisbury, Norwich, and Worcester; the earls of Huntingdon, Stafford, Northumberland, Salisbury, and Suffolk; the lords of Hungerford, Tiptoft, and Fanhope; the chancellor, the treasurer, the keeper of the privy seal, and William Philip, knight.

[It is agreed that] they who were of the council before are to be of the council now; [and that the following men are] also to be of the council: the bishop of St. David's, the earl of Salisbury, the keeper of the wardrobe, Sir John Stourton. And the king wills that the present councillors of the king are to have such power as King Henry IV gave to his councillors, according to a schedule passed in parliament during the time of the same king, which [schedule] was read there [in the council]. . . .[11]

The keeper of the privy seal and others have sworn and given their faith to the king, to counsel him well and truly in such matters as shall come before them by way of the king's council, to keep secret the king's counsel, and in short to counsel and do all that good councillors should counsel and do for the king their sovereign lord. . . .[12]

(French and English) Ibid., V, 71 f.

(G) Judgment in the Star Chamber[13] (1482)

In the Star Chamber at Westminster, on May 2 in the twenty-second year of the reign of our sovereign lord King Edward IV—being present my lords the archbishop of York, chancellor of England; the bishops of Lincoln, [lord] privy seal, and of Worcester, Norwich, Durham, and Llandaff; the earl Rivers; the lords Dudley, Ferrers, and Beauchamp; Sirs Thomas Burgh, William Parr, Thomas Vaughan, and Thomas Grey, knights—the judgment and decree earlier rendered by the lords of our said sovereign lord's council for the cause of Richard Whele, otherwise called Richard Pierson . . .

---

[11] Cf. no. 66D. This act, at least in theory, marked the resumption of personal government by the king; see Baldwin, *The King's Council*, pp. 184 f.
[12] Cf. no. 53.
[13] Cf. no. 67B, last paragraph.

against John Fortescue, esquire, . . . was openly read in full and plenary council. . . . The said John Fortescue alleges and says that the said Richard is a Scot born and is under allegiance to the king of Scots, and as such [the said John] has taken him and holds him prisoner. The said Richard [denies this], evidently proving the contrary, that he is an Englishman born and no Scot. . . .[14] And after each of the said parties . . . had at divers times been diligently heard in all that they could or would allege and say in their behalf, it appeared to the lords of the said council that the said Richard Whele, otherwise called Pierson, is and was an Englishman born and no Scot. . . . And therefore it is considered, adjudged, and decreed by the same lords that the same Richard is so to be held, taken, and reputed among all the king's liege people and subjects; he is to be regarded and treated in all places as the king's liegeman and not otherwise; and he is to be wholly free to do whatever he thinks good for a king's subject to do, without trouble, let, or impeachment. And the said John Fortescue is to be commanded, and was so commanded, to perpetual silence in respect to any further . . . vexation of the said Richard in any way and at any time to come for the cause alleged above. . . .

(English) Leadam and Baldwin, *Select Cases before the Council*, pp. 117 f.

[14] The case had been argued at length in the Star Chamber on the previous November 21.

71. CASES IN CHANCERY

(A) PETITION FOR GENERAL RELIEF (1399)

To the most reverend father in God and most gracious lord, the bishop of Exeter, chancellor of England, Simon Hilgay, parson of the church of Hilgay, humbly makes petition [as follows]:—

Whereas he has charge and cure of souls in the same parish and is menaced by one Robert of Wesnam and by . . . ,[1] associates and confederates of the same Robert, who daily menace him to the extent that, through fear of unmerited death, he does not dare to approach the said parsonage to hear the confessions of his parishioners in this most holy time of Lent . . . ; and whereas, furthermore, the said Robert of Wesnam, with so many miscreants for associates and confederates, has such horrid maintenance that the said petitioner will never be able at common law to secure recovery against him and the rest without your most gracious aid: [therefore] may it please your most gracious lordship to consider the aforesaid matter and therein, at your most wise discretion, to provide remedy for the said petitioner —for the sake of God and as a work of charity.

[Endorsed:] By virtue of this petition the herein named Simon Hilgay, parson of the church of Hilgay, obtains four writs directed to the herein named persons, [summoning them] to appear before the said king and his council in his chancery on Tuesday next after

[1] Six other persons named.

the coming feast of St. Gregory, to make answer regarding the content [of the said petition].

(Latin and French) Baildon, *Select Cases in Chancery*, pp. 44 f.

(B) PETITION FOR INJUNCTION

To the most reverend father in God and most gracious lord, the bishop of Exeter, chancellor of England, Esmond Francis, grocer and citizen of London, humbly makes petition [as follows] :—

Whereas, on account of a certain debt owed to him . . . , the said Esmond for the past two years has been executor over certain lands and tenements within the parish of Madesden in the county of Gloucester, once belonging to John Madesden, dyer of London, of which lands and tenements, according to the requirement of the common law, he had livery by the king's writ; and whereas it now happens that, through the maintenance and conspiracy of James Clifford and Hugh Bisley of the same county, no man or farmer of the said county . . . dares to occupy or administer the said lands and tenements for the use and profit of the said Esmond: [therefore] may it please your most noble and gracious lordship to grant a writ of our lord the king directed to the sheriff of the said county and to the justices of the peace in the same locality, instructing them, on behalf of our said lord the king, to charge and command the same James and Hugh, on peril of the consequences, to permit the said Esmond and his servants and farmers to occupy and administer the said lands and tenements thus delivered to him by the law, without any interference or disturbance by the said James and Hugh; so that the said Esmond may have his profit from the said lands and tenements as awarded to him under the law—for the sake of God and as a work of charity.

(French) *Ibid.*, pp. 68 f.

(C) PETITION WITH REGARD TO A TRUST

To the chancellor of England John Horsemonger humbly makes petition as follows:—

Whereas one John Peckham enfeoffed, among others, Reginald Pympe and Walter Judde with certain lands and tenements in the county of Kent on certain conditions, among which was contained the wish of the said John Peckham that, when the said lands were sold, he who was next of blood to the said John Peckham, and to whom the inheritance of the lands and tenements would have descended, was to have £40 to relieve his estate; [and whereas] the said lands and tenements have now been sold by the said feoffees for 500*m.*, which sum the said Reginald has in his own possession, and, although the said petitioner, as kinsman and heir of the said John Peckham . . . , has often requested the said Reginald to pay and deliver to him the said £40 according to the wish of the said John Peckham, [the said Reginald] is nevertheless unwilling to pay him a penny of it, to the great damage of the said petitioner: [there-

fore] may it please your most gracious lordship, for the honour of
God and the cause of righteousness, to grant writs summoning the
said Walter and Reginald to appear before you in the king's chancery, which is a court of conscience, there to make answer in this
matter, as is demanded by reason and conscience; otherwise the said
petitioner is and shall be without remedy—which God forbid!

(French) Ibid., pp. 120 f.

(D) PETITION AND JUDGMENT REGARDING A MORTGAGE (1456)

To the right reverend and worshipful father in God, the archbishop of Canterbury, chancellor of England, Robert Bodenham
humbly makes petition [as follows] :—

Whereas he lately borrowed £80 from John Hall of Salisbury,
for which [sum] the said John, through subtle promises, caused
the said Robert, on May 1 in the thirty-third year of the reign of
our sovereign lord the present king,[2] trustingly to enfeoff the said
John with the manor of Shipton-Bellinger in the shire of Suffolk, to
have and to hold for the said John and his heirs and assigns, on
condition that, if the said Robert or his heirs or executors would pay
to the said John or his assigns £100 at the feast of St. John the
Baptist in the year of our lord 1461, the said feoffment should then
be void,[3] as plainly appears from an indentured deed made in that
connection, so that the said John thereby intends to receive and have
the issues of the said manor until the said day of payment, which
will amount to the sum of 85m., and also £100 by way of usury for
the loan of the said £80, or else the said manor is to be lost and forfeited [by the said Robert]; [and whereas,] moreover, the said John,
imagining further deceit for the injury of the said Robert, by subtlety
caused himself to be bound to the said Robert by an obligation for
£300 under the law merchant of Salisbury dated on the second day
of the said month of May, which [obligation] the said Robert delivered to one John Gardner to keep until satisfactory indentures
in defeasance thereof were made by learned men between the said
Robert and John, that the said condition should be performed;[4]
and [whereas], although the said indentures are not yet made and
the said obligation remains with the said John Gardner, the said John
Hall has sued for execution upon the said obligation for the said £300
and by virtue thereof has taken the said Robert and straitly imprisoned him at Salisbury, so that the said John intends to have from
the said Robert £450 and more for the lending of £80, against right
and conscience and to the utter ruin of the said Robert, who in this
matter has no remedy at common law: [therefore] may it please

---

[2] 33 Henry VI, 1455.
[3] This transaction constituted the mortgage, on the law of which see Holdsworth, *History of English Law*, III, 108 f.
[4] That is to say, Robert signed in favour of John a bond for £300, which
was to be cancelled when further agreements had been drawn up in connection
with the mortgage. On the law merchant, see *ibid.*, II, 158 f.

your gracious lordship to summon the said John by a writ of *sub poena* to appear before you on a certain day to make answer to the premises; and [may it please] you thereupon to execute justice as required by good faith and conscience—for the love of God and as a work of charity.

This is the answer of John Hall to the bill of Robert Bodenham. . . .

This is the replication of Robert Bodenham to the answer of John Hall to the bill of the said Robert. . . .

This is the rejoinder of John Hall to the replication of Robert Bodenham.[5] . . .

[Endorsed:] Memorandum that, on February 18 in the thirty-fourth year of the reign of King Henry VI after the Conquest, after the matters in the herein-written petition . . . , as well as the matters in the answer, replication, and rejoinder . . . , had been fully read and made known in the said chancery, and after deliberation and advisement . . . had been held with the lord king's justices of both benches and with divers serjeants-at-law and other persons then and there appearing as counsel for the parties aforesaid, by the advice of the said justices, it was then and there decided that, in so far as the said Robert then and there in the same chancery paid to the said John Hall the said £80 . . . , the same John Hall should cause the same Robert to be liberated from prison . . . and should quash, annul, and cancel the said obligation [for £300]; and that the said John Hall should re-enfeoff the said Robert with the said manor and its appurtenances. . . .

(Latin and English) *Ibid.*, pp. 137 f.

---

[5] In the course of this debate, the regular procedure in such cases, John admitted at least the principal transaction and advanced little more than trifling arguments in defense. Robert offered to repay the £80 in court, together with reasonable costs, for the recovery of the manor and the quashing of the bond.

72. BOROUGH RECORDS

(A) EXTRACTS FROM THE LONDON LIBER ALBUS[1]

. . . It has been the custom that . . . the commoners, on being summoned for such an election [of a mayor], and after the occasion for the summons has been explained to them by the recorder on behalf of the mayor and aldermen, cross to the other end of the hall[2] . . . and there nominate two aldermen, each of whom has served as sheriff and has proved his fitness for the office of mayor. Having done so, they return and by their common spokesman present to the mayor and aldermen the names of the two men . . . , asking them

---

[1] I.e., White Book, composed by John Carpenter, city clerk, in 1419. This customal contains some fanciful explanation of earlier constitutional history, but in the main was based on authentic records and Carpenter's expert knowledge.

[2] The chamber in the gildhall that was used for sessions of the husting. Cf. nos. 28B, 39D-F.

to admit whichever of the two they please to the office of mayor for the ensuing year. The mayor and the aldermen, mounting to the upper part of the chamber, then choose one of the two by majority vote, with the common clerk noting the result under the supervision of the recorder; and then, once more descending, they announce through their recorder to the people in the gildhall who has been elected mayor for the next year. . . .

Now this has been the process used in holding a wardmote at London. The alderman, after receiving a warrant, orders his beadle to summon all men possessing houses, as well as all paid servants, within his ward to come before him on a certain day at a certain hour and in a certain place . . . within the same ward for the meeting of the wardmote. The names of which persons, after they have been summoned, the beadle shall have inscribed in a certain roll: that is to say, [the names of] the freemen dwelling in that ward of the city by themselves, and [the names of] the paid servants, not freemen,[3] by themselves. And when they have assembled at the assigned hour, with the alderman and the more substantial men of the ward seated in the proper places, the alderman's clerk shall order the beadle on behalf of the alderman to proclaim peace.[4] . . . And by the alderman and the good men of the ward, and also by the jurors at the said wardmote, should be elected the constables, scavagers, aleconners,[5] beadle, and other officers, who shall take suitable oaths of office at the general court. . . .

In electing an alderman it has been the custom for the mayor to go to the ward that has been vacated[6] and, if he pleases, have all free inhabitants of the aforesaid ward summoned through the beadle to the place where the wardmote of that ward is customarily held; and there, at once if it is possible and desirable, or else on a day to be set, the alderman should be elected by the major and better part of those men; yet so that fifteen days shall not be exceeded in making an election, for then the mayor, with the advice of the aldermen, his associates, ought and has been accustomed to install an honest, rich, and discreet man as alderman of that ward. . . .

This is the method of holding the common council. On the day before it is to meet, the mayor and the aldermen, through the servants of the chamber, should cause a certain number of the wiser and wealthier men to be summoned from each ward of the city to meet at the gildhall on the next day—sixteen, twelve, eight, or four, according as the ward is large or small. And no one, unless he has been

---

[3] That is to say, men who did not enjoy the freedom of the city. They had no right of voting at elections; see immediately below.

[4] A jury empanelled by the constables then carries out an inquest to present various offenses for subsequent trial before the city courts.

[5] The scavagers collected "showage," dues paid for displaying goods in the market. The aleconners were inspectors of brewing.

[6] The aldermen enjoyed life tenure of their offices.

summoned, is to come or is to presume to attend such council under pain of imprisonment. . . .

For the purpose of electing sheriffs, the mayor, recorder, aldermen, and commons are to be assembled on the day of St. Matthew the Apostle in such manner as is ordained for the election of the mayor. And first of all, the mayor shall of his own free will choose a worthy freeman of the city to be one of the sheriffs for the ensuing year, on whose behalf he is willing to be responsible for half the farm of the city, should he who is chosen by the mayor be in default. But if the mayor chooses the man by the counsel and consent of the aldermen, they must share his responsibility. And those elected to the common council . . . shall choose for the commons another sheriff, on whose behalf all the commons should be responsible for the other half of the farm owed to the king, if he should be in default. . . .

(Latin and French) *Munimenta Gildhallae Londoniensis,* I, 20-47.

(B) HENRY VI: CHARTER TO NOTTINGHAM (1448)[7]

. . . Furthermore, of our richer grace, on our own initiative, and from our certain knowledge, we have granted and by our present letters have confirmed for us and for our heirs and successors in perpetuity to the existing burgesses of the same town of Nottingham, which has now and has long had a certain corporate form,[8] and to the heirs and successors of the same burgesses, being burgesses of that town, that the said town, [consisting] of a mayor and burgesses, shall henceforth and forever be incorporate, and that the same mayor and burgesses and their successors, being mayors and burgesses of that town thus incorporated, are to be a community perpetually incorporate in fact and in name, known as the Mayor and Burgesses of the Town of Nottingham, and having perpetual succession; and that the mayor and burgesses of that town and their aforesaid successors shall, under that same name, be competent and able to prosecute and defend all manner of pleas, suits, complaints, and demands . . . in any courts whatsoever of us, or of our heirs or successors, or of any other persons whatsoever. . . .

Furthermore . . . we have granted . . . that the same town of Nottingham and the precincts thereof . . . , which now exist and are contained within the county of Nottingham, shall be forever separated . . . from that county . . . ; that the same town of Nottingham and its precincts . . . shall forever be known as the county of the town of Nottingham; that the said burgesses of the same town and their successors . . . shall forever have two sheriffs . . . , to be elected from among themselves in place of the two bailiffs . . . ; that here-

---

[7] These provisions follow a detailed confirmation of Henry V's charter and various subsequent grants. Henry VI's own charter covers some ten pages of print; only the merest skeleton is given here.

[8] The larger boroughs had long been *de facto* corporations; the charters of the fifteenth century only confirmed the status in the formal language of that age: see the forthcoming book on the subject by M. Weinbaum.

72. BOROUGH RECORDS

after each burgess . . . to be elected mayor of that town . . . shall be escheator for us and our heirs and successors[9] . . . ; and that the same existing burgesses of that town and their successors forever shall there have a court [for the settlement] at their pleasure of all and singular contracts, agreements, transgressions made against the peace as well as otherwise, and all other things, causes, and matters whatsoever in any way arising or happening within the same town or its precincts . . . , to be held from time to time in the gildhall of the same town before the mayor . . . and sheriffs of that town for the time being. . . .

Furthermore . . . we have granted . . . that the same burgesses and their heirs and successors may from time to time elect from among themselves seven aldermen, of whom a certain one is to be elected as mayor of that town . . . ; that the aldermen thus elected shall remain in such offices . . . during their lifetimes . . . ; and that the aldermen of the same town for the time being shall be justices for us and our heirs and successors to keep the peace within the same town and its liberty and precincts . . . , having full power and authority for investigating, hearing, and determining all felonies, murders, trespasses, and misprisions, as well as all sorts of other causes, complaints, contempts, and misdeeds, and everything else pertaining to other justices of the peace within our kingdom of England. . . .[10]

(Latin) Stevenson, *Records of the Borough of Nottingham*, II, 186 f.

(C) MUNICIPAL ORDINANCES AT LEICESTER (1466-67)

Hit was ordeyned and agreed at a comen hall[11] holden at Leycestre the xxv day of Octobre, the 6te yere of the regne of the kyng oure sovereyne lord Edward the IIII^{te}, in the time of mairaltie of Roger Wygston than beyng maire of the seyd towne of Leycestre, by a generall assent and agrement as wele of the same maire, his brethern,[12] and all the comens of the same toune then being at the forsaid comen hall, that from that tyme forth no man presume to entre into the gilde hall, otherwise cald the maires hall, at eny comen hall ther holden or to be holden but oonly thoes and siche as ben fraunchest, that is to say, men entred into the marchaundes gild; on payne of

---

[9] London and Middlesex had been combined under one government since before the Norman Conquest (see above, nos. 25B, 28B). Bristol had been made a county in 1373, York in 1398, Norwich in 1404, Lincoln in 1409, and Southampton in 1448. For a much more complete statement of what was involved in such a grant, the student is referred to Edward III's charter to Bristol, clearly translated by N. D. Harding in *Bristol Charters*, pp. 119 f. See also McKisack, *Parliamentary Representation of English Boroughs*, pp. 32, 48 f.

[10] The judicial revenue accruing through acts of the justices of the peace was to go to the town; other revenue collected by the escheator and sheriffs as county officers was reserved by the king.

[11] I.e., the general court.

[12] The twenty-four jurats who had long formed what amounted to a closed corporation for governing the town; see M. Bateson's introduction.

inprisonment as long as the maire lykes forthwith doon upon every suche persone doing the contrary at eny comen hall. . . .

The ordenance made by Richarde Gillot, maire of the town of Leycestre, and his brethern, and by the advise and assent of all the comons of the same town, at a comon halle holden at Leycestre the Thursday next afore the feste of Symonde day and Jude, in the yere of the reigne of our soverayen lorde Kyng Edwarde the Fourth after the Conquest off Ynglond the vii.

The maire commaundeth, on the kynges behalfe, that all maner of men kepe the pees of our soverayn lorde the kyng, and that no man disturbull hit withynne the fraunches of this town as be armour or wepon beryng, as halbergon, salett,[13] bylle, swyrd, longe staff, or dager, or any other maner of wepon, where thurgh the kynges pees should be disturbelyd or lettyd,[14] yn payne of forfeture of his wepon and his body to preson, sauf in supportacion of the maire, but yf hit be a knyght or a squyer a swyrde borne after hym; and that every man of the contrary that bryng any wepon to the town leve hit at his in and bere hit not withynne this town, neyther swyrde, bille, ne long staffe, but in the supportacion of the mayre aforesaid, in payne of forfeiture of his wepon and his body to preson as long as the mayre lykes; and that no man walke after ix of the belle be streken in the nyght withoute lyght, or withoute cause resonable, in payne of inpresonment.

Also, alle bakers that bake shall bake symnell, wastell, coket lovys[15] iiii for a peny of good paste, good bulture,[16] and well baken . . . ; and of all other kyndes of breed sesonable and of good weyght and pryse after the form aforsaid. . . .

Also, that alle brewers that brewe shall brewe good ale and se that it be neyther rawe, roppy, ne red, but holsum for mannys body, selling a galon of the best for i*d*., *ob*.,[17] a galon of the secunde for i*d*., and a galon of the thirde for *ob*.; and that they selle non by measure unlawfull nor unseled,[18] in payne of inprisonment. . . .

Also, that every bocher of the cuntray that bryng flesshe to the market bryng the skynnes and talowe of the same flesshe with hem, in payne of forfetyng theroff; and that no bocher bryng no flesshe to selle withinne this town that is corupte with eny maner of sekenes, in payne of forfeture of the same flesshe and there bodyes to preson as long as the mayre lykes. . . .

Also, that no man ley owte no muke at his dore—stokkys ne stoyns, tymbre ne clay, ne non other maner of thing to the anuysauns of the

---

[13] A halbergon, or halberd, was a combined lance and battle-axe; a sallet was an iron head-piece.

[14] Obstructed.

[15] Simnel, wastel, and cocket were three varieties of first-class bread, but exactly what each term designated is not known; cf. above, p. 66, n. 3.

[16] I.e., well-bolted flour.

[17] *Obulus*, the Latin word for a halfpenny.

[18] Without the official seals that designated true measures.

72. BOROUGH RECORDS

kynges peple, but yf hit be a bygger[19] in the stretes of the town—neyther withinne the iiii yates ne withinne the iiii stretes of the subberbis, but yf hit be remeved withinne iii dayes, in payne of imprisonment as long as the maire likes, etc.

Also, that no man nor woman suffre no corrypcion to lye before his dore, ne keste non owte of his dore by nyght ne by day—that is to say hors, swyn, dogge, ne catte, nor non other corypcion—withinne the iiii yates, ne withinne the iiii stretes of the subbarbys, but voyde hit forthe into the fylde from the course of the peple, yn payne of inprisonment while the mair lykes, etc.

Also, that no man ne woman, ne non other persone, swepe ne throwe owte swepynges whan hit rayneys upon his neghbour for disturbelyng of his neybur, in payne of inprisonment as long as the mayre lykes of the persone or persones that is founden so gylty.

Also, that no man of the town nor of the cuntray play withinne the fraunchys of this town for sylver at no unlaufull gamons . . . , that is for to sey, at dyce, haserdyng, tenes, bowlys, pykking with arowes, coytyng with horsshon, penypryk, foteball, ne cheker in the myre,[20] in payne of inprisonment. And the owner of the hows, gardens, or placez where the plays been used, as often as hit is so founden and used, shall paye to the chamberlens iiii*d*., and every player vi*d*. to the same chamberlens, to the use of the comons. . . .

Also, that no woman use to wasshe no clothes ne none other corripcion at the comon wellys of the town ne in the hye strete, in payne of inprisonment.

Also, that alle maner scholdys that are dwellyng withinne this town, man or woman, that are founde defectyf by sworne men before the maire presented, that than hit shall be lefull to the same mayre for to ponyssh them on a cukstool[21] afore there dore as long as hym lyketh and thanne so to be caried forth to the iiii yates of the town. . . .

Also, all maner men, women, and children that bryngeth any hors or mares to the market laden with corne or other vitaill, that they, after the tyme they be unladen, to lede them owte of the markett place to the innes, in payne of every best ii*d*., to by levied by the chamberlens to the use of the comons. . . .

Also, that no man latt no swyne ne neet[22] goo abrode, neythere before the herde[23] goo afylde ne after he come hom, but kepe them inne tyll the herde come, in payne of losying of every best ii*d*., and that to be levied by the chamberlens to the use of the comons. . . .

Also, that no dukkes be letyn abrode in any stret withinne the iiii yates of the town, on payne of forfeture of every duk *ob*., that to be

---

[19] Builder.
[20] Picking with arrows was apparently throwing darts at a target; quoiting with horseshoes is obvious; in penny-prick the players threw at a penny; checker in the mire remains unidentified.
[21] A chair in which the culprit was bound before being ducked or otherwise punished.
[22] Cattle.
[23] Herdsman.

levied by the chamberlens to the use of the town as ofte as eny dukkes been founden or takyn goyng abroad withinne the said stretes of the town.

Also, that no man in the town dwellyng, fraunchysed ne unfraunchesed, drawe to no conventicles, ryotes, ne assembles withinne the town, ne rydyng withoute, agayen the kinges pees; ne take no lyveres, gownyng ne hodyng, of no man of non astate ne degre for maintenaunce of no man ne of no maner matire; but that they gyf assistence to the maire in sustentacion of the kynges pees, good rule, and honoure of this town. . . .

Also, whatsomever persone or persones that dysobeyeth the maire and his officers and wil nott come to hym when he is sent for, that than hit shall be lefull to the same maire, with all the powre that he can make, to fecche hym, and yf he close his dore, to breeke hit oppen & than to enprison hym whiles the maire lyketh. . . .

Bateson, *Records of the Borough of Leicester,* II, 285 f.

(D) RETURNS OF BOROUGH ELECTIONS (1437)[24]

This indenture, made between Richard Sherwood and William Burton, sheriffs of the city of York, on the one part, and . . . ,[25] citizens of the aforesaid city, on the other part, testifies that the aforesaid sheriffs, in the presence of the aforesaid county[26] at the last county [court] of the aforesaid city held there immediately after the receipt of a certain writ of the lord king, which is sewed to this indenture—namely, at the county [court] of the aforesaid city held there on Monday, Christmas eve, in the fifteenth year of the reign of King Henry VI after the Conquest of England—made proclamation of a certain parliament of the lord king to be held at Westminster on January 21 next to come, and in the same court they caused to be elected two of the more discreet and substantial citizens of the aforesaid city—namely, William Bowes, jr., and Richard Louth—having full and sufficient authority, for themselves and the community of the city aforesaid, to attend the aforesaid parliament and to do and agree to whatever then and there may happen, God willing, to be ordained. In testimony whereof the aforesaid parties have individually placed their seals on portions of this indenture.

Given at York on the day and in the year aforesaid.

This indenture, made between Richard Winsley, bailiff of the liberty of the abbot of Reading at Leominster, on the one part, and John Walter, bailiff of the borough of Leominster, and . . . ,[27] burgesses of the aforesaid borough, on the other part, testifies that the aforesaid burgesses, with the assent of the whole community of the same borough, on Friday next before the feast of Epiphany in the fifteenth year of the reign of King Henry VI after the Conquest,

---

[24] Cf. no. 69c.
[25] Fifteen names.
[26] Of the city of York; see above, p. 291, n. 9.
[27] Eleven names.

72. BOROUGH RECORDS

in the gildhall of the same borough elected William Rabys and John Crewe, burgesses of the aforesaid borough, to attend the parliament of the lord king which is to be held at Westminster on January 21 next to come, having full and sufficient authority, for themselves and the community of the same borough, to consider, advise, and agree to whatever may happen, God willing, to be ordained by the common council of the king of England concerning matters there to be considered and moved. In testimony whereof the aforesaid burgesses have in turn placed their seals on this portion of the indenture.

Given on the day and in the year aforesaid.

This indenture, made in the full county [court] of Devon—held in the castle of the lord king in the city of Exeter on Tuesday, December 28, in the fifteenth year of the reign of King Henry VI—between Thomas Beaumont, knight, sheriff of the aforesaid county, on the one part, and William Wonard, John Copleston . . . ,[28] [on the other part,] by virtue of a certain writ of the lord king, directed to the said sheriff and [now] sewed to this indenture . . . ,[29] testifies that the aforesaid William Wonard, John Copleston, and others have elected John Speke and Roger Champernoun, knights, to attend the aforesaid parliament on the day and at the place aforesaid on behalf of the community of the aforesaid county; also Thomas Cook and Walter Pope, citizens of the city of Exeter; John Searle and Richard Strode, burgesses of the borough of Plympton; Thomas Aysheldon and John Walsh, burgesses of the borough of Tavistock; John Worthy and John Wick, burgesses of the borough of Totnes; John Bearl and Hugh Champernoun, burgesses of the borough of Barnstaple—[all elected] according to the provisions of the said writ.[30] In testimony whereof the aforesaid William Wonard, John Copleston, and all the others named below, who were present at that election, have attached their seals to the present letters. To the other portion of this same indenture, remaining with the aforesaid sheriff, the aforesaid sheriff has attached his seal.

Given on the day and in the place and year aforesaid.

(Latin) McKisack, *Representation of English Boroughs*, pp. 158 f.

---

[28] Seventeen others.
[29] The text here states the substance of the writ of summons.
[30] That is to say, by the men of their respective boroughs and so reported to the sheriff.

SECTION VII

THE TUDORS

The present section is a long one for good reason. England was ruled by the Tudor house for well over a hundred years, from 1485 to 1603, and during all but a few of these years the throne was occupied by masterful and energetic sovereigns. Furthermore, this was an age when the rapid diffusion of wealth and of Renaissance learning within the upper and middle classes led them to take a livelier interest in the study of government and the discharge of its responsibilities. As a consequence, a collection of only the more important constitutional sources must include a relatively large proportion of Tudor documents.

The primary object of the new dynasty was to restore a monarchy that had been weakened by the disorders of the previous age. Henry VII accomplished this first task by re-establishing the traditional authority of the crown. Building upon his success, Henry VIII and Elizabeth greatly extended the royal prerogatives. Yet, though the Tudors developed and controlled a strong royal government, they were by no means tyrannical in their methods. Above all else they desired the actualities of power. Accordingly, they sought to invigorate existing institutions rather than to create an entirely new system. They constantly appealed to ancient custom and the rule of law. They preserved the old governmental agencies, both central and local, with but slight formal change. Occasionally they resorted to frankly despotic measures, but generally they were content with putting to new uses constitutional practices that depended upon the co-operation of the people. Thus the Tudors strengthened the administration of the common law as well as of more arbitrary justice through special courts. They increased the efficiency, not only of their council, but also of their parliament. Even while accomplishing a revolutionary settlement for the Church of England, they anxiously cited precedent and legalized innovation by statute.

Nevertheless, whatever their content, the Tudor records are pervaded by a spirit of newness. For one thing, they were composed in a vigorous English which, despite some archaic expres-

INTRODUCTORY NOTE 297

sions, is essentially our own. Thanks to a familiar language, we come more intimately to know the kings and queens of the sixteenth century, their ministers and justices, the members of their parliaments, even their humbler subjects in town and country. Perhaps it is mainly due to this fact that the documents henceforth seem to reveal more vivid personalities. But there is another factor to be taken into account—the improved education of the sixteenth century. Inspired by the constant encouragement as well as by the example of their sovereigns, Englishmen turned with enthusiasm to the writing of books and the making of speeches upon matters affecting the public life. Such a development stimulated political discussion and led to the keeping of better records.

After the plan followed in previous sections, the materials for the Tudor period have been grouped according to the nature of the documents, rather than according to an attempted analysis of contents. The chronological lists of statutes thus include a variety of formal enactments, and they are supplemented by a few characteristic ordinances for the guidance of courts and the regulation of printing (nos. 75, 84, 85). The excerpts placed under nos. 79 and 83 have been selected, in default of earlier examples, to illustrate the routine work of the privy council and to bring out the diversity of its activities. The star chamber records under no. 80 are of somewhat the same sort—a typical collection of matters brought before that court soon after its reorganization. The lively character of the journals, which in the middle sixteenth century take the place of the older rolls of parliament, can be judged from the extracts under no. 82. Henceforth the procedure of the houses—especially the motions, debates, and speeches in the commons—attain increasing prominence in the annals of the nation. It should, however, be noted that part of the original journals of the Tudor period have not come down to us. All but one of the extracts under no. 82 have been taken from the abstract of the journals made by Sir Simonds D'Ewes in the seventeenth century.

As already stated, no effort has been made to group all documents or parts of documents that deal with local government or social reform. Nos. 86-87 include merely a few illustrative records concerning the militia and the justices of the peace. And to them have been added two famous grants that served as models for the commercial and colonial enterprises of the next century.

From this material reference should be made to the statutes on local justice and administration (notably nos. 73C, 74I, 78D, 81C, H) and to the numerous excerpts from the proceedings of parliament and the acts of the privy council.

In this as in earlier sections it has proved impossible to find room for contemporary writings on political institutions. Indeed, the difficulty becomes doubly apparent for the Tudor period, when such writings appeared in unprecedented numbers. Among them the most famous are Sir Thomas More's *Utopia*, Sir Thomas Elyot's *The Governour*, Sir Thomas Smith's *De Republica Anglorum*, and William Lambarde's *Eirenarcha*, the best editions of which are given in the general bibliography. There are two excellent collections of documents for the Tudor period, both edited with useful notes: J. R. Tanner, *Tudor Constitutional Documents, 1485-1603*; and G. W. Prothero, *Select Statutes and other Constitutional Documents Illustrative of the Reigns of Elizabeth and James I*. These books reproduce in full some of the acts that are here abbreviated. All the great statutes concerning the Church are also printed in Gee and Hardy, *Documents Illustrative of English Church History*. Unfortunately, we have no general constitutional history for the sixteenth century corresponding to that of Stubbs for the earlier period, but K. Pickthorn's *Early Tudor Government* contains an especially valuable treatment of the reigns of Henry VII and Henry VIII. The constitutional issues of the later Tudor period are discussed in E. P. Cheyney's *History of England from the Defeat of the Spanish Armada to the Death of Elizabeth*. Although the footnotes to the following documents cite a number of pertinent monographs and special articles, they are only a small part of the literature concerning Tudor constitutional history. For a complete list of works on the subject, see Conyers Read, *Bibliography of British History, Tudor Period*.

73. HENRY VII: STATUTES

(A) ACT OF SUCCESSION (1485)

Henry, by the grace of God, king of England and of France and lord of Ireland, at the parliament holden at Westminster the seventh day of November, in the first year of the reign of King Henry VII after the Conquest. To the pleasure of Almighty God, the wealth, prosperity, and surety of this realm of England, to the singular comfort of all the king's subjects of the same and in avoiding of all ambiguities and questions: be it ordained, established,

73. HENRY VII: STATUTES

and enacted by authority of this present parliament that the inheritances of the crowns of the realms of England and of France, with all the pre-eminence and dignity royal to the same pertaining, and all other seignories to the king belonging beyond the sea, with the appurtenances thereto in any wise due or pertaining, be, rest, remain, and abide in the most royal person of our now sovereign lord, King Henry VII, and in the heirs of his body lawfully coming, perpetually with the grace of God so to endure, and in none other.

Statutes of the Realm, II, 499: 1 Henry VII, c. 1.

(B) STAR CHAMBER ACT (1487)[1]

An act giving the court of star chamber authority to punish divers misdemeanours. The king, our sovereign lord, remembereth how, by unlawful maintenances, giving of liveries, signs, and tokens, and retainders by indenture, promises, oaths, writing, or otherwise, embraceries of his subjects, untrue demeanings of sheriffs in making of panels and other untrue returns, by taking of money by juries, by great riots and unlawful assemblies, the policy and good rule of this realm is almost subdued, and for the none punishment of this inconvenience and by occasion of the premises nothing or little may be found by inquiry; whereby the laws of the land in execution may take little effect, to the increase of murders, robberies, perjuries, and unsureties of all men living, and losses of their lands and goods, to the great displeasure of Almighty God: be it therefore ordained for reformation of the premises by the authority of this parliament that the chancellor and treasurer of England for the time being and keeper of the king's privy seal, or two of them, calling to [them] a bishop and temporal lord of the king's most honourable council and the two chief justices of the king's bench and common pleas for the time being, or other two justices in their absence, upon bill or information put to the said chancellor for the king or any other against any person for any misbehaving afore-rehearsed, have authority to call before them by writ or privy seal the said misdoers, and them and other by their discretions to whom the truth may be known to examine, and such as they find therein defective to punish them after their demerits, after the form and effect of statutes thereof made, in like manner and form as they should and ought to be punished if they were thereof convict after the due order of the law. . . .

Ibid., II, 509 f.: 3 Henry VII, c. 1.

(C) ACT CONCERNING JUSTICES OF THE PEACE (1489)[2]

An act for justices of peace for the due execution of their commissions. The king our sovereign lord considereth that, by the negligence

---

[1] Cf. nos. 67B (last paragraph), 70G. See A. F. Pollard, "Council, Star Chamber, and Privy Council under the Tudors," in the *English Historical Review,* XXXVII-XXXVIII.

[2] Cf. no. 62 I.

and misdemeaning, favour, and other inordinate causes of the justice of peace in every shire of this his realm, the laws and ordinances made for the politic weal, peace, and good rule of the same, and for perfect security and restful living of his subjects of the same, be not duly executed according to the tenor and effect that they were made and ordained for; wherefore his subjects be grievously hurt and out of surety of their bodies and goods, to his great displeasure; for to him is nothing more joyous than to know his subjects to live peaceably under his laws and to increase in wealth and prosperity: and to avoid such enormities and injuries, so that his said subjects may live more restful under his peace and laws to their increase, he will that it be ordained and enacted by the authority of this present parliament that every justice of the peace within every shire of this his said realm, within the shire where he is justice of peace, do cause openly and solemnly to be proclaimed yearly, four times in a year in four principal sessions, the tenor of this proclamation to this bill annexed; and that every justice of peace being present at any of the said sessions, if they cause not the said proclamation to be made in form abovesaid, shall forfeit to our said sovereign lord at every time 20s.

. . . And his grace considereth that a great part of the wealth and prosperity of this land standeth in that, that his subjects may live in surety under his peace in their bodies and goods; and that the husbandry of this land may increase and be upholden, which must be had by due execution of the said laws and ordinances: [wherefore he] chargeth and commandeth all the justices of the peace . . . to endeavour them to execute . . . the said laws and ordinances ordained for subduing of the premises, as they will stand in the love and favour of his grace, and in avoiding of the pains that be ordained if they do the contrary. . . . And over this, he chargeth and commandeth all manner of men, as well the poor as the rich (which be to him all one in due ministration of justice) that is hurt or grieved in anything that the said justice of peace may hear or determine or execute in any wise, that he [who is] so grieved make his complaint to the justice of peace that next dwelleth unto him, or to any of his fellows, and desire a remedy. And if he then have no remedy, if it be nigh such time as his justices of assizes come into that shire, that then he so grieved show his complaint to the same justices. And if he then have no remedy, or if the complaint be made long afore the coming of the justices of assize, then he so grieved [may] come to the king's highness, or to his chancellor for the time being, and show his grief. And his said highness then shall send for the said justices to know the cause why his said subjects be not eased and his laws executed; whereupon, if he find any of them in default of executing of his laws in these premises according to this his high commandment, he shall do him so offending to be put out of the commission, and further to be punished according to his demerits. And over that, his said highness shall not let for any favour, affection, cost, charge, nor none other cause, but that he shall see his laws to have plain and due execution.

and his subjects to live in surety of their lands, bodies, and goods, according to his said laws, and the said mischiefs to be avoided, that his said subjects may increase in wealth and prosperity to the pleasure of God.

Ibid., II, 536 f.: 4 Henry VII, c. 12.

(D) POYNING'S LAW (1494)

An act that no parliament be holden in this land [of Ireland] until the acts be certified into England. . . . Item, at the request of the commons of the land of Ireland, be it ordained, enacted, and established that . . . no parliament be holden hereafter in the said land, but at such season as the king's lieutenant and council there first do certify [to] the king, under the great seal of that land, the causes and considerations, and all such acts as them seemeth should pass in the same parliament; and [after] such causes, considerations, and acts affirmed by the king and his council to be good and expedient for that land, and his licence thereupon, as well in affirmation of the said causes and acts, as to summon the said parliament under his great seal of England [are] had and obtained . . . , a parliament [is] to be had and holden after the form and effect above rehearsed. And if any parliament be holden in that land hereafter contrary to the form and provision aforesaid, it [shall] be deemed void and of none effect in law.

Statutes at Large, Ireland, I, 44: 10 Henry VII, c. 4.

(E) STATUTE OF TREASON (1495)[3]

An act that no person going with the king to the wars shall be attaint of treason. The king our sovereign lord, calling to his remembrance the duty of allegiance of his subjects of this his realm, and that they by reason of the same are bounden to serve their prince and sovereign lord for the time being in his wars for the defence of him and the land against every rebellion, power, and might reared against him, and with him to enter and abide in service in battle if the case so require; and . . . that it is not reasonable but against all laws, reason, and good conscience that the said subjects going with their sovereign lord in wars attending upon him in his person, or being in other places by his commandment within this land or without, anything should lose or forfeit for doing their true duty and service of allegiance: it be therefore ordained, enacted, and established by the king our sovereign lord, by advice and assent of the lords spiritual and temporal and commons in this present parliament assembled, and by authority of the same, that from henceforth no manner of person nor persons, whatsoever he or they be, that attend upon the king and sovereign lord of this land for the time being in his person, and do him true and faithful service of allegiance in the same, or be in other places by his commandment, in his wars within this land or without, that for the same

---
[3] Cf. no. 62F.

deed and true service of allegiance he or they be in no wise convict or attaint of high treason nor of other offences for that cause by act of parliament or otherwise by any process of law, whereby he or any of them shall . . . forfeit life, lands, tenements, rents, possessions, hereditaments, goods, chattels, or any other things, but to be for that deed and service utterly discharged of any vexation, trouble, or loss; and if any act or acts or other process of the law hereafter thereupon for the same happen to be made contrary to this ordinance, that then that act or acts or other processes of the law, whatsoever they shall be, stand and be utterly void.

Provided alway that no person nor persons shall take any benefit of advantage by this act which shall hereafter decline from his or their said allegiance.

Statutes of the Realm, II, 568: 11 Henry VII, c. 1.

(F) STATUTE OF LIVERIES (1504)

De retentionibus illicitis. The king our sovereign lord calleth to his remembrance that, where before this time divers statutes for punishment of such persons that give or receive liveries, or that retain any person or persons or be retained with any person or persons . . . , have been made and established . . . ,[4] and little . . . is or hath been done for the punishment of the offenders in that behalf: wherefore our sovereign lord the king, by the advice of the lords spiritual and temporal and of his commons of his realm in this parliament being, and by the authority of the same, hath ordained, stablished, and enacted that all his [such] statutes and ordinances afore this time made . . . be . . . put in due execution. And over that . . . , the king ordaineth, stablisheth, and enacteth, by the said authority, that no person, of what estate or degree or condition he be . . . , privily or openly give any livery or sign or retain any person, other than such as he giveth household wages unto without fraud or colour, or that he be his manual servant or his officer or man learned in the one law or in the other,[5] by any writing, oath, promise, livery, sign, badge, token, or in any other manner . . . unlawfully retain; and if any do the contrary, that then he run and fall in the pain and forfeiture for every such livery and sign, badge, or token, 100s., and the taker and accepter of every such livery, badge, token, or sign [is] to forfeit and pay for every such livery and sign, badge or token, so accepted, 100s. . . .

Moreover, the king, our sovereign lord, by the advice, assent, and authority aforesaid, hath ordained, stablished, and enacted that every person that will sue or complain before the chancellor of England or the keeper of the king's great seal in the star chamber, or before the king in his bench, or before the king and his council attending upon his most royal person wheresoever he be—so that there be three of

---

[4] Cf. no. 64c.
[5] That is to say, the civil or the canon law.

the same council at the least, of the which two shall be lords spiritual
or temporal—against any person or persons offending or doing against
the form of this ordinance or any other of the premises, be admitted
by their discretion to give information . . . ; and that upon the same
all such persons be called by writ, subpoena, privy seal, or otherwise,
and the said chancellor [etc.] . . . [are] to have power to examine
all persons defendants . . . as well by oath as otherwise, and to
adjudge him or them convict or attaint, as well by such examination
as otherwise in such penalties . . . as the case shall require. . . .
And also the same party, plaintiff, or informer shall have such reasonable reward of that that by his complaint shall grow to the king as shall
be thought reasonable by the discretion of the said chancellor [etc.] . . .
   And also it is enacted by the said authority that the said chancellor
[etc.] . . . have full authority and power by this statute to . . . send
by writ, subpoena, privy seal, warrant, or otherwise by their discretion,
for any person or persons offending or doing contrary to the premises,
without any suit or information made or put before them or any of
them; and the same person or persons to examine by oath or otherwise by their discretions, and to adjudge all such persons as shall be
found guilty in the premises by verdict, confession, examination,
proofs, or otherwise, in the said forfeitures and pains as the case
shall require, as though they were condemned therein after the course
of the common law; and to commit such offenders to ward, and to
award execution accordingly. . . .

Ibid., II, 658 f.: 19 Henry VII, c. 14.

74. HENRY VIII: STATUTES

(A) ACT CONCERNING THE COURT OF STAR CHAMBER (1529)

   An act that the president of the king's council shall be associate
with the chancellor and treasurer of England and the keeper of the
king's privy seal. Where . . . , in the same good and profitable
statute[1] the president of the king's most honourable council for the time
being attending upon his most noble and royal person is omitted, and
not named . . . to be one of the said persons that should have authority to call before them such misdoers so offending the king's laws in
any of the premises as is before rehearsed: be it therefore . . . enacted
that from henceforth the chancellor, treasurer of England, and the
president of the king's most honourable council attending upon his
most honourable person for the time being, and the keeper of the
king's privy seal, or two of them, calling unto them one bishop and
one temporal lord of the king's most honourable council and the
two chief justices of the king's bench and the common pleas for the
time being, or other two of the king's justices in their absence, upon
any bill or information hereafter to be put in . . . , for any misbehaving before rehearsed . . . , have full power and authority to call be-

---

[1] 3 Henry VII, c. 1 (no. 73B).

fore them by writ of privy seal such misdoers, and them and other by their discretion by whom the truth may be known to examine; and such as they shall find defective to punish them after their demerits after the form and effect of the said former statute, and of all other statutes thereof tofore made and not repealed nor expired, in like manner and form as they should and ought to be punished if they were thereof convicted after the due order in the king's laws. . . .

Ibid., III, 304: 21 Henry VIII, c. 20.

(B) ACT IN RESTRAINT OF APPEALS (1533)

An act that the appeals in such cases as have been used to be pursued to the see of Rome shall not be from henceforth had nor used but within this realm. Where, by divers sundry old authentic histories and chronicles, it is manifestly declared and expressed that this realm of England is an empire, and so hath been accepted in the world, governed by one supreme head and king having the dignity and royal estate of the imperial crown of the same, unto whom a body politic, compact of all sorts and degrees of people divided in terms and by names of spiritualty and temporalty, be bounden and owe to bear next to God a natural and humble obedience (he being also institute and furnished by the goodness and sufferance of Almighty God with plenary, whole, and entire power, pre-eminence, authority, prerogative, and jurisdiction to render and yield justice and final determination to all manner of folk residents or subjects within this his realm, in all causes, matters, debates, and contentions happening to occur, insurge, or begin within the limits thereof, without restraint or provocation to any foreign princes or potentates of the world . . .); and whereas the king his most noble progenitors, and the nobility and commons of this said realm, at divers and sundry parliaments as well in the time of King Edward I, Edward III, Richard II, Henry IV, and other noble kings of this realm, made sundry ordinances, laws, statutes, and provisions for the entire and sure conservation of the prerogatives, liberties, and pre-eminences of the said imperial crown of this realm, and of the jurisdictions spiritual and temporal of the same, to keep it from the annoyance as well of the see of Rome as from the authority of other foreign potentates attempting the diminution or violation thereof, as often and from time to time as any such annoyance or attempt might be known or espied; and [whereas,] notwithstanding the said good statutes and ordinances . . . , divers and sundry inconveniences and dangers not provided for plainly by the said former acts . . . have risen and sprung by reason of appeals sued out of this realm to the see of Rome, in causes testamentary, causes of matrimony and divorces, right of tithes, oblations, and obventions . . . : in consideration whereof, the king's highness, his nobles, and commons, considering the great enormities, dangers, long delays, and hurts that as well to his highness as to his said nobles, subjects, commons, and residents of this his realm in the

74. HENRY VIII: STATUTES

said causes . . . do daily ensue, doth therefore by his royal assent, and by the assent of the lords spiritual and temporal and the commons in this present parliament assembled and by authority of the same, enact, establish, and ordain that all causes testamentary, causes of matrimony and divorces, rights of tithes, oblations, and obventions . . . , whether they concern the king our sovereign lord, his heirs, or successors, or any other subjects or residents within the same of what degree soever they be, shall be from henceforth heard . . . and definitively adjudged and determined within the king's jurisdiction and authority and not elsewhere. . . .

And it is further enacted . . . that, if any person or persons . . . do attempt, move, purchase, or procure from or to the see of Rome, or from or to any other foreign court or courts out of this realm, any manner foreign process, inhibitions, appeals, sentences, summons, citations, suspensions, interdictions, excommunications, restraints, or judgments, of what nature, kind, or quality soever they be, or execute any of the same process, or do any act or acts to the let, impediment, hindrance, or derogation of any process, sentence, judgment, or determination had, made, done, or hereafter to be had, done, or made in any courts of this realm or the king's said dominions or marches of the same for any of the causes aforesaid . . . , that then every person or persons so doing . . . , being convict of the same, for every such default shall incur and run in the same pains, penalties, and forfeitures ordained and provided by the Statute of Provision and Praemunire made in the sixteenth year of the reign of . . . King Richard II. . . .[2]

And furthermore, in eschewing the said great enormities, inquietations, delays, charges, and expenses hereafter to be sustained in pursuing of such appeals and foreign process . . . [they] do therefore . . . ordain and enact that, in such cases where heretofore any of the king's subjects or residents have used to pursue, provoke, or procure any appeal to the see of Rome . . . , they . . . shall from henceforth take, have, and use their appeals within this realm and not elsewhere, in manner and form as hereafter ensueth and not otherwise: that is to say, first from the archdeacon or his official, if the matter or cause be there begun, to the bishop diocesan of the said see . . . ; and likewise, if it be commenced before the bishop diocesan or his commissary, from the bishop diocesan or his commissary, within fifteen days next ensuing the judgment or sentence thereof there given, to the archbishop of the province of Canterbury, if it be within his province, and if it be within the province of York, then to the archbishop of York; and so likewise to all other archbishops in other the king's dominions as the case by the order of justice shall require, and there to be definitively and finally ordered, decreed, and adjudged according to justice, without any other appellation or provocation to any other person or persons, court or courts. And if the matter or contention

---

[2] No. 64F.

for any of the causes aforesaid be or shall be commenced . . . before the archdeacon of any archbishop or his commissary, then the party grieved shall or may take his appeal, within fifteen days next after judgment or sentence there given, to the court of the arches or audience of the same archbishop or archbishops, and from the said court of the arches or audience, within fifteen days then next ensuing after judgment or sentence there given, to the archbishop of the same province, there to be definitively and finally determined without any other or further process or appeal thereupon to be had or sued. . . .

And in . . . any cause, matter, or contention . . . which hath, doth, shall, or may touch the king, his heirs, or successors, kings of this realm . . . , the party grieved . . . shall or may appeal . . . to the spiritual prelates and other abbots and priors of the upper house assembled and convocate by the king's writ in the convocation being or next ensuing within the province or provinces where the same matter of contention is or shall be begun; so that every such appeal be taken by the party grieved within fifteen days next after the judgment or sentence thereupon given or to be given. And . . . whatsoever be done or shall be done and affirmed, determined, decreed, and adjudged by the foresaid prelates, abbots, and priors of the upper house of the said convocation as is aforesaid, appertaining, concerning, or belonging to the king, his heirs, or successors, in any of these foresaid causes of appeals, shall stand and be taken for a final decree, sentence, judgment, definition, and determination, and the same matter so determined never after to come in question and debate, to be examined in any other court or courts. . . .

Ibid., III, 427 f.: 24 Henry VIII, c. 12.

(C) ACT FOR THE SUBMISSION OF THE CLERGY AND RESTRAINT OF APPEALS (1534)

. . . Be it therefore now enacted by authority of this present parliament, according to the said submission and petition of the said clergy, that [neither] they nor any of them from henceforth shall presume to attempt, allege, claim, or put in ure[3] any constitutions or ordinances, provincial or synodal, or any other canons; nor shall enact, promulge, or execute any such canons, constitutions, or ordinance provincial, by whatsoever name or names they may be called, in their convocations in time coming (which alway shall be assembled by authority of the king's writ), unless the same clergy may have the king's most royal assent and licence . . . , upon pain . . . to suffer imprisonment and make fine at the king's will. . . . Provided alway that no canons, constitutions, or ordinance shall be made or put in execution within this realm by authority of the convocation of the clergy which shall be contrariant or repugnant to the king's prerogative royal or the customs, laws, or statutes of this realm—anything contained in this act to the contrary hereof notwithstanding. . . .

---

[3] Practice.

And be it further enacted by authority aforesaid that, from the feast of Easter . . . 1534, no manner of appeals shall be had, provoked, or made out of this realm . . . to the bishop of Rome . . . , but that all manner of appeals . . . shall be made and had . . . after such manner, form, and condition as is limited for appeals to be had . . . in causes of matrimony, tithes, oblations, and obventions by a statute thereof made and established since the beginning of this present parliament. . . .[4]

And for lack of justice at or in any the courts of the archbishops of this realm, or in any the king's dominions, it shall be lawful to the parties grieved to appeal to the king's majesty in the king's court of chancery; and that, upon every such appeal, a commission shall be directed under the great seal to such persons as shall be named by the king's highness, his heirs, or successors, like as in case of appeal from the admiral's court, to hear and definitively determine such appeals and the causes concerning the same. . . .

Ibid., III, 460 f.: 25 Henry VIII, c. 19.

(D) ACT CONCERNING ECCLESIASTICAL APPOINTMENTS AND ABSOLUTE RESTRAINT OF ANNATES (1534).

An act restraining the payment of annates, etc. . . . And forasmuch as in the said act[5] it is not plainly and certainly expressed in what manner and fashion archbishops and bishops shall be elected, presented, invested, and consecrated within this realm and in all other the king's dominions: be it now therefore enacted . . . that the said act and everything therein contained shall be and stand in strength, virtue, and effect; except only that no person nor persons hereafter shall be presented, nominated, or commended to the said bishop of Rome, otherwise called the pope, or to the see of Rome, to or for the dignity or office of any archbishop or bishop within this realm or in any other the king's dominions, nor shall send nor procure there for any manner of bulls, briefs, palls, or other things requisite for an archbishop or bishop, nor shall pay any sums of money for annates, first fruits, or otherwise, for expedition of any such bulls, briefs, or palls; but that by the authority of this act such presenting, nominating, or commending to the said bishop of Rome or to the see of Rome, and such bulls, briefs, palls, annates, first fruits, and every other sums of money heretofore limited, accustomed, or used to be paid at the said see of Rome for procuration or expedition of any such bulls, briefs, or palls, or other thing concerning the same, shall utterly cease and no longer be used within this realm or within any the king's dominions—anything contained in the said act aforementioned, or any use, custom, or prescription to the contrary thereof notwithstanding.

---

[4] The preceding document.

[5] 23 Henry VIII, c. 20, which had provisionally restrained the payment of annates.

And furthermore be it ordained and established by the authority aforesaid that, at every avoidance of any archbishopric or bishopric within this realm or in any other the king's dominions, the king our sovereign lord, his heirs, and successors, may grant unto the prior and convent, or the dean and chapter of the cathedral churches or monasteries where the see of such archbishopric or bishopric shall happen to be void, a licence under the great seal, as of old time hath been accustomed, to proceed to election of an archbishop or bishop of the see so being void, with a letter missive containing the name of the person which they shall elect and choose; by virtue of which licence the said dean and chapter, or prior and convent, to whom any such licence and letters missives shall be directed, shall with all speed and celerity in due form elect and choose the said person named in the said letters missives to the dignity and office of the archbishopric or bishopric so being void, and none other; and if they do defer or delay their election above twelve days next after such licence and letters missives to them delivered, that then for every such default the king's highness, his heirs, and successors, at their liberty and pleasure shall nominate and present, by their letters patents under their great seal, such a person to the said office and dignity so being void as they shall think able and convenient for the same. . . .

And be it further enacted by the authority aforesaid that, if the prior and convent of any monastery, or dean and chapter of any cathedral church, where the see of any archbishop or bishop is within the king's dominions, after such licence as is afore rehearsed shall be delivered to them, proceed not to election and signify the same according to the tenor of this act within the space of twenty days next after such licence shall come to their hands, or else . . . , after any such election, nomination, or presentation shall be signified unto them by the king's letters patents, shall refuse and do not confirm, invest, and consecrate, with all due circumstance as is aforesaid, every such person as shall be so elected, nominate, or presented . . . within twenty days next after the king's letters patents of such signification or presentation shall come to their hands . . . , that then every . . . person . . . so offending . . . shall run into the dangers, pains, and penalties of the Statute of the Provision and Praemunire made in the twenty-fifth year of the reign of King Edward III and in the sixteenth year of King Richard II.[6]

Ibid., III, 462 f.: 25 Henry VIII, c. 20.

(E) ACT CONCERNING PETER'S PENCE AND DISPENSATIONS (1534)

An act for the exoneration from exactions paid to the see of Rome. Most humbly beseech your most royal majesty your obedient and faithful subjects the commons of this your present parliament, assembled by your most dread commandment, that, where your subjects of this your realm, and of other countries and dominions being under

---

[6] No. 64F.

your obeisance, by many years past have been and yet be greatly decayed and impoverished by such intolerable exactions of great sums of money as have been claimed and taken . . . out of this your realm, and other your said countries and dominions, by the bishop of Rome called the pope . . . , pretending . . . that he hath full power to dispense with all human laws, uses, and customs of all realms in all causes which be called spiritual (which matter hath been usurped and practised by him and his predecessors by many years in great derogation of your imperial crown and authority royal, contrary to right and conscience, for where this your grace's realm, recognizing no superior under God but only your grace, hath been and is free from subjection to any man's laws, but only to such as have been devised, made, and ordained within this realm for the wealth of the same, or to such other as by sufferance of your grace and your progenitors the people of this your realm have taken at their free liberty by their own consent to be used amongst them, and have bound themselves by long use and custom to the observance of the same) . . . ; [and whereas], therefore, . . . your royal majesty and your lords spiritual and temporal and commons, representing the whole state of your realm in this your most high court of parliament, have full power and authority not only to dispense but also to authorize some elect person or persons to dispense with those and all other human laws of this your realm and with every one of them, as the quality of the persons and matter shall require, and also the said laws and every of them to abrogate, annul, amplify, or diminish, as it shall be seen unto your majesty and the nobles and commons of your realm present in your parliament meet and convenient for the wealth of your realm . . . :—

It may therefore please your most noble majesty . . . , forasmuch as your majesty is supreme head of the Church of England, as the prelates and clergy of your realm representing the said Church in their synods and convocations have recognized, in whom consisteth full power and authority upon all such laws as have been made and used within this realm, to ordain and enact, by the assent of your lords spiritual and temporal and the commons in this your present parliament assembled, and by authority of the same, that no person or persons of this your realm or of any other your dominions shall from henceforth pay any pensions, censes, portions, Peter pence, or any other impositions to the use of the said bishop or of the see of Rome . . . ; but that all such pensions [etc.] . . . shall from henceforth clearly surcease and never more be levied, taken, perceived, nor paid to any person or persons in any manner of wise—any constitution, use, prescription, or custom to the contrary thereof notwithstanding. . . .

Provided always that [neither] this act nor any thing or things therein contained shall be hereafter interpreted or expounded that your grace, your nobles, and subjects, intend by the same to decline or vary from the congregation of Christ's Church in any things concerning the very articles of the catholic faith of Christendom, or in any other things declared by Holy Scripture and the word of God necessary for your and their salvations; but only to make an ordinance by policies necessary and convenient to repress vice and for good conservation of this realm in peace, unity, and tranquillity from ravin and spoil, ensuing much the old ancient customs of this realm in that behalf, not minding to seek for any reliefs, succours, or remedies for any worldly things or human laws in any cause of necessity but within this realm at the hands of your highness, your heirs, and successors, kings of this realm, which have and ought to have an imperial power and authority in the same and not [be] obliged in any worldly causes to any other superior. . . .

Ibid., III, 464 f.: 25 Henry VIII, c. 21.

(F) First Act of Succession (1534)

An act for the establishment of the king's succession. . . . Your said most humble and obedient subjects, the nobles and commons of this realm . . . , do . . . most humbly beseech your highness . . . that it may be enacted . . . that the marriage heretofore solemnized between your highness and the lady Katherine, being before lawful wife to Prince Arthur your elder brother, which by him was carnally known (as doth duly appear by sufficient proof in a lawful process had and made before Thomas, by the sufferance of God now archbishop of Canterbury and metropolitan and primate of all this realm), shall be by authority of this present parliament definitively, clearly, and absolutely declared, deemed, and adjudged to be against the laws of Almighty God, and also accepted, reputed, and taken of no value nor effect, but utterly void and annulled . . . ; and that the lawful matrimony had and solemnized between your highness and your most dear and entirely beloved wife, Queen Anne, shall be established and taken for undoubtful, true, sincere, and perfect ever hereafter. . . .

And also be it enacted by authority aforesaid that all the issue had and procreate, or hereafter to be had and procreate, between your highness and your said most dearly and entirely beloved wife Queen Anne shall be your lawful children, and be inheritable and inherit, according to the course of inheritance and laws of this realm, the imperial crown of the same, with all dignities, honours, pre-eminences, prerogatives, authorities, and jurisdictions to the same annexed or belonging, in as large and ample manner as your highness to this present time hath the same as king of this realm. . . .[7]

And be it further enacted by authority aforesaid that . . . proclamations shall be made in all shires within this realm of the tenor and contents of this act. And if any person or persons . . . , subject or resident within this realm, or elsewhere within any the king's dominions . . . , by writing or imprinting or by any exterior act or deed maliciously procure or do, or cause to be procured or done, any thing or things to the peril of your most royal person, or maliciously give

---

[7] The king's heirs are enumerated in exact order of succession: first the heirs male and then the heirs female, beginning with Elizabeth.

occasion by writing, print, deed, or act whereby your highness might be disturbed or interrupted of the crown of this realm, or by writing, print, deed, or act procure or do, or cause to be procured or done, any thing or things to the prejudice, slander, disturbance, or derogation of the said lawful matrimony solemnized between your majesty and the said Queen Anne, or to the peril, slander, or disherison of any the issues and heirs of your highness being limited by this act to inherit and to be inheritable to the crown of this realm in such form as is aforesaid—whereby any such issues or heirs of your highness might be destroyed, disturbed, or interrupted in body or title of inheritance to the crown of this realm as to them is limited in this act in form above rehearsed—that then every such person and persons, of what estate, degree, or condition they be of, subject or resident within this realm, and their aiders, counsellors, maintainers, and abettors, and every of them, for every such offence shall be adjudged high traitors, and every offence shall be adjudged high treason, and the offender and their aiders [etc.] . . . , being lawfully convict of such offence by presentment, verdict, confession, or process according to the laws and customs of this realm, shall suffer pains of death as in cases of high treason. . . .

And be it further enacted by authority aforesaid that, if any person or persons . . . , by any words without writing, or any exterior deed or act, maliciously and obstinately publish, divulge, or utter any thing or things to the peril of your highness, or to the slander or prejudice of the said matrimony solemnized between your highness and the said Queen Anne, or to the slander or disherison of the issue and heirs of your body begotten and to be gotten of the said Queen Anne, or any other your lawful heirs which shall be inheritable to the crown of this realm, as is afore limited by this act, that then every such offence shall be taken and adjudged for misprision of treason. . . .

Ibid., III, 471 f.: 25 Henry VIII, c. 22.

(G) SUPREMACY ACT (1534)

An act concerning the king's highness to be supreme head of the Church of England and to have authority to reform and redress all errors, heresies, and abuses in the same. Albeit the king's majesty justly and rightfully is and ought to be the supreme head of the Church of England, and so is recognized by the clergy of this realm in their convocations; yet, nevertheless, for corroboration and confirmation thereof, and for increase of virtue in Christ's religion within this realm of England, and to repress and extirp all errors, heresies, and other enormities and abuses heretofore used in the same, be it enacted by authority of this present parliament that the king, our sovereign lord, his heirs, and successors, kings of this realm, shall be taken, accepted, and reputed the only supreme head in earth of the Church of England called *Anglicana Ecclesia,* and shall have and enjoy, annexed and united to the imperial crown of this realm, as well the title and style thereof as all honours, dignities, pre-eminences, jurisdictions, privileges, authorities, immunities, profits, and commodities to the said dignity of supreme head of the same Church belonging and appertaining; and that our said sovereign lord, his heirs, and successors, kings of this realm, shall have full power and authority from time to time to visit, repress, redress, reform, order, correct, restrain, and amend all such errors, heresies, abuses, offences, contempts, and enormities, whatsoever they be, which by any manner spiritual authority or jurisdiction ought or may lawfully be reformed, repressed, ordered, redressed, corrected, restrained, or amended, most to the pleasure of Almighty God, the increase of virtue in Christ's religion, and for the conservation of the peace, unity, and tranquillity of this realm—any usage, custom, foreign laws, foreign authority, prescription, or any other thing or things to the contrary hereof notwithstanding.

Ibid., III, 492: 26 Henry VIII, c. 1.

(H) STATUTE OF USES (1536)[8]

Where, by the common laws of this realm, lands, tenements, and hereditaments be not devisable by testament, nor ought to be transferred from one to another but by solemn livery and seisin . . . , yet, nevertheless, divers and sundry imaginations, subtle inventions, and practices have been used whereby the hereditaments of this realm have been conveyed from one to another by fraudulent feoffments, fines, recoveries, and other assurances craftily made to secret uses, intents, and trusts, and also by wills and testaments sometime made by . . . words, sometime by signs and tokens, and sometime by writing . . . ; for the extirping and extinguishment of all such . . . , and to the intent that the king's highness or any other his subjects of this realm shall not in any wise hereafter . . . be deceived, damaged, or hurt by reason of such trusts, uses, or confidences . . . : it may please the king's most royal majesty that it may be enacted by his highness, by the assent of the lords spiritual and temporal and the commons in this present parliament assembled, and by authority of the same . . . , that, where any person or persons stand or be seised or at any time hereafter shall happen to be seised of and in any honours, castles, manors, lands, tenements, rents, services, reversions, remainders, or other hereditaments, to the use, confidence, or trust of any other person or persons, or of any body politic, by reason of any bargain, sale, feoffment, fine, recovery, covenant, contract, agreement, will, or otherwise . . . , in every such case all and every such person and persons and bodies politic . . . shall from henceforth stand and be seised, deemed, and adjudged in lawful seisin, estate, and posses-

---

[8] See no. 64E; and for comment on the law of uses, Holdsworth, *History of English Law*, IV, 449-73.

sion of and in the same honours [etc.] . . . to all intents, constructions, and purposes in the law . . . ; and that the estate, right, title, and possession that was in such person or persons that were or shall be hereafter seised of any lands, tenements, or hereditaments to the use, confidence, or trust of any such person or persons, or of any body politic, be from henceforth clearly deemed and adjudged to be in him or them that have or hereafter shall have such use, confidence, or trust. . . .[9]

Ibid., III, 539 f.: 27 Henry VIII, c. 10.

(I) BEGGARS ACT (1536)

An act for punishment of sturdy vagabonds and beggars. . . . And forasmuch as it was not provided in the said act[10] how and in what wise the said poor people and sturdy vagabonds should be ordered at their repair and at their coming into their countries, nor how the inhabitants of every hundred should be charged for the relief of the same poor people, nor yet for the setting and keeping in work and labour of the aforesaid valiant vagabonds at their said repair into every hundred of this realm: it is therefore now ordained and established and enacted . . . that all the governors and ministers of . . . cities, shires, towns, hundreds, wapentakes, lathes, rapes, ridings, tithings, hamlets, and parishes, as well within liberties as without, shall not only succour, find, and keep all and every of the same poor people by way of voluntary and charitable alms . . . , in such wise as none of them of very necessity shall be compelled to wander idly and go openly in begging to ask alms in any of the same cities, shires, towns, and parishes, but also to cause and to compel all and every the said sturdy vagabonds and valiant beggars to be set and kept to continual labour, in such wise as by their said labours they and every of them may get their own livings with the continual labour of their own hands. . . .

Item, it is ordained and enacted . . . that all and every the mayors, governors, and head officers of every city, borough, and town corporate and the churchwardens or two others of every parish of this realm shall in good and charitable wise take such discreet and convenient order, by gathering and procuring of such charitable and voluntary alms of the good Christian people within the same with boxes every Sunday, holy day, and other festival day or otherwise among themselves, in such good and discreet wise as the poor, impotent, lame, feeble, sick, and diseased people, being not able to work, may be provided, holpen, and relieved; so that in no wise they nor none of them be suffered to go openly in begging, and that such as be lusty, or

---

[9] Other articles make specific application of this principle and establish a number of exceptions.
[10] 22 Henry VIII, c. 12.

having their limbs strong enough to labour, may be daily kept in continual labour, whereby every one of them may get their own substance and living with their own hands. . . .

And for the avoiding of all such inconveniences and infections as oftentime have and daily do chance amongst the people by common and open doles, and that most commonly unto such doles many persons do resort which have no need of the same, it is therefore enacted . . . that no manner of person or persons shall make or cause to be made any such common or open doles, or shall give any ready money in alms, otherwise than to the common boxes and common gatherings . . . , to and for the putting in . . . due execution . . . this present act, upon pain to . . . forfeit ten times the value of all such ready money as shall be given in alms contrary to the tenor and purport of the same; and that every person or persons of this realm, bodies politic corporate, and others that be bound or charged yearly, monthly, or weekly to give or to distribute any ready money, bread, victual, or other sustentation to poor people in any place within this realm, shall . . . give and distribute the same money or the value of all such bread, victual, or sustentation unto such common boxes, to the intent the same may be employed towards the relieving of the said poor, needy, sick, sore, and indigent persons, and also towards the setting in work of the said sturdy and idle vagabonds and valiant beggars. . . .

Ibid., III, 558 f.: 27 Henry VIII, c. 25.

(J) ACT FOR THE GOVERNMENT OF WALES (1536)

An act for laws and justice to be ministered in Wales in like form as it is in this realm. Albeit the dominion, principality, and country of Wales justly and righteously is and ever hath been incorporated, annexed, united, and subject to and under the imperial crown of this realm as a very member and joint of the same, wherefore the king's most royal majesty of . . . very right is very head, king, lord, and ruler; yet, notwithstanding, because that in the same country, principality, and dominion divers rights, usages, laws, and customs be far discrepant from the laws and customs of this realm, and also because that the people of the same dominion have and do daily use a speech nothing like nor consonant to the natural mother tongue used within this realm, some rude and ignorant people have made distinction and diversity between the king's subjects of this realm and his subjects of the said dominion . . . of Wales, whereby great discord . . . and sedition hath grown between his said subjects: his highness, therefore, of a singular zeal, love, and favour that he beareth towards his subjects of his said dominion of Wales, minding and intending to reduce them to the perfect order, notice, and knowledge of his laws of this his realm, and utterly to extirp all and singular the sinister uses and customs differing from the same, and to bring his said subjects of this his realm and of his said dominion of Wales to an amicable concord and unity, hath by the deliberate advice, consent, and agreement of the lords spiritual and temporal and the commons in this present parliament assembled, and by the authority of the same . . . , established that his said country or dominion of Wales shall be, stand, and continue forever from henceforth incorporated, united, and annexed to and with this his realm of England; and that all and singular person and persons born and to be born in the said . . . dominion of Wales shall have, enjoy, and inherit all and singular freedoms, liberties, rights, privileges, and laws within this realm and other the king's dominions, as other the king's subjects naturally born within the same have, enjoy, and inherit; and that all and singular person and persons inheritable to any manors, lands, tenements, rents, reversions, services, or other hereditaments which shall descend after the feast of All Saints next coming within the said . . . dominion of Wales, or within any particular lordship part or parcel of the said . . . dominion of Wales, shall forever from and after the said feast of All Saints inherit and be inheritable to the same manors [etc.] . . . after the English tenure, without division or partition, and after the form of the laws of this realm of England, and not after any tenure nor after the form of any Welsh laws or customs; and that the laws, ordinances, and statutes of this realm of England forever, and none other laws . . . , from and after the said feast of All Saints . . . , shall be had, used, practised, and executed in the said . . . dominion of Wales and every part thereof in like manner, form, and order as they are and shall be . . . executed in this realm and in such like manner and form as hereafter by this act shall be further established and ordained. . . .[11]

Also be it enacted . . . that all justices, commissioners, sheriffs, coroners . . . , and their lieutenants, and all other officers and ministers of the laws, shall proclaim and keep the sessions, courts, hundreds, leets, sheriff's courts, and all other courts in the English tongue, and all oaths of officers, juries, and inquests, and all other affidavits, verdicts, and wagers of law to be given and done in the English tongue; and also that from henceforth no person or persons that use the Welsh speech or language shall have or enjoy any manner office or fees within the realm of England, Wales, or other the king's dominions, upon pain of forfeiting the same offices or fees, unless he or they use and exercise the speech or language of English. . . .[12]

Ibid., III, 563 f.: 27 Henry VIII, c. 26.

---

[11] The next fifteen sections describe the organization of counties, lordships, towns, parishes, and the like in the different parts of Wales.

[12] Section 22 provides for the representation of Welsh counties and boroughs in the English house of commons, allotting two knights to the county of Monmouth, one knight to each of the other counties, and one burgess to each of the county towns except Merioneth.

(K) STATUTE OF PROCLAMATIONS (1539)[13]

An act that proclamations made by the king shall be obeyed. Forasmuch as the king's most royal majesty, for divers considerations, by the advice of his council hath heretofore set forth divers and sundry his grace's proclamations, as well for and concerning divers and sundry articles of Christ's religion as for an unity and concord to be had amongst the loving and obedient subjects of this his realm and other his dominions, and also concerning the advancement of his commonwealth and good quiet of his people (which nevertheless divers and many froward, wilful, and obstinate persons have wilfully contemned and broken, not considering what a king by his royal power may do, and for lack of a direct statute and law to coerce offenders to obey the said proclamations . . .); considering also that sudden causes and occasions fortune many times which do require speedy remedies, and that by abiding for a parliament in the meantime might happen great prejudice to ensue to the realm; and weighing also that his majesty, which by the kingly and regal power given him by God may do many things in such cases, should not be driven to extend the liberty and supremacy of his regal power and dignity by wilfulness of froward subjects: it is therefore thought in manner more than necessary that the king's highness of this realm for the time being, with the advice of his honourable council, should make and set forth proclamations for the good and politic order and governance of this his realm of England, Wales, and other his dominions, from time to time for the defence of his regal dignity and the advancement of his commonwealth and good quiet of his people, as the cases of necessity shall require; and that an ordinary law should be provided, by the assent of his majesty and parliament, for the due punishment, correction, and reformation of such offences and disobediences. Be it therefore enacted . . . that always the king for the time being, with the advice of his honourable council, whose names hereafter followeth, or with the advice of the more part of them, may set forth at all times by authority of this act his proclamations, under such penalties and pains and of such sort as to his highness and his said honourable council or the more part of them shall see [m] necessary and requisite; and that those same shall be obeyed, observed, and kept as though they were made by act of parliament for the time in them limited, unless the king's highness dispense with them or any of them under his great seal.

Provided always that the words, meaning, and intent of this act be not understood, interpretate, construed, or extended that by virtue of it any of the king's liege people . . . should have any of his or their inheritances, lawful possessions, offices, liberties, privileges, fran-

---

[13] Repealed immediately after the death of Henry VIII as a bid for popularity on the part of Edward VI's council. On the significance of the statute, see E. R. Adair, in the *English Historical Review*, XXXII, 34 f.; also Pickthorn, *Early Tudor Government, Henry VIII*, pp. 414 f.

chises, goods, or chattels taken from them . . . , nor by virtue of
the said act suffer any pains of death, other than shall be hereafter
in this act declared; nor that, by any proclamation to be made by
virtue of this act, any acts, common laws, standing at this present
time in strength and force, nor yet any lawful or laudable customs
of this realm . . . shall be infringed, broken, or subverted; and
specially all those acts standing this hour in force which have been
made in the king's highness's time; but that every such person . . .
shall stand and be in the same state and condition, to every respect
and purpose, as if this act or proviso had never been had or made
. . . , except such persons which shall offend any proclamation
to be made by the king's highness, his heirs, or successors, for and
concerning any kind of heresies against Christian religion. . . .

And be it further enacted . . . that, if any person or persons . . .
at any time hereafter do wilfully offend and break, or obstinately
not observe and keep, any such proclamation . . . , then all and
every such offender or offenders—being thereof . . . convicted by
confession or lawful witness and proofs before the archbishop of
Canterbury, metropolitan, the chancellor of England, the lord treasurer of England, the president of the king's most honourable council,
the lord privy seal, the great chamberlain of England, [the] lord
admiral, [the] lord steward or grand master, [the] lord chamberlain of the king's most honourable household, two other bishops being
of the king's council (such as his grace shall appoint for the same),
the secretary, the treasurer, and [the] controller of the king's most
honourable household, the master of the horse, the two chief judges,
and the master of the rolls for the time being, the chancellor of the
augmentations, the chancellor of the duchy, the chief baron of the
exchequer, the two general surveyors, the chancellor of the exchequer, the under-treasurer of the same, the treasurer of the king's
chamber for the time being, in the star chamber at Westminster or
elsewhere, or at least before the half of the number afore rehearsed,
of which number the lord chancellor, the lord treasurer, the lord
president of the king's most honourable council, the lord privy seal,
the chamberlain of England, the lord admiral, the two chief judges
for the time being, or two of them, shall be two—shall lose and
pay such penalties, forfeitures of sums of money . . . , and also
suffer such imprisonment of his body, as shall be expressed, mentioned, and declared in any such proclamation. . . .

Ibid., III, 726 f.: 31 Henry VIII, c. 8.

(L) ACT DISSOLVING THE GREATER MONASTERIES (1539)

An act for dissolution of abbeys. Where divers and sundry abbots,
priors, abbesses, prioresses, and other ecclesiastical governors and
governesses of divers monasteries, abbacies, priories, nunneries, colleges, hospitals, houses of friars, and other religious and ecclesiastical houses and places within this our sovereign lord the king's

realm of England and Wales, of their own free and voluntary minds, good wills, and assents, without constraint, coercion, or compulsion of any manner of person or persons, since the fourth day of February, the twenty-seventh year of the reign of our now most dread sovereign lord, by the due order and course of the common laws of this his realm of England, and by their sufficient writings of record under their convent and common seals, have severally given, granted, and by the same their writings severally confirmed all their said monasteries [etc.] . . . , and all their sites, circuits, and precincts of the same, and all and singular their manors, lordships, granges, meses, lands, tenements, meadows, pastures, rents, reversions, services, woods, tithes, pensions, portions, churches, chapels, advowsons, patronage, annuities, rights, entries, conditions, commons, leets, courts, liberties, privileges, and franchises, appertaining or in any wise belonging to any such monastery [etc.] . . . , to have and to hold all the said monasteries [etc.] . . . , and all other the premises, to our said sovereign lord, his heirs and successors, forever; and the same their said monasteries [etc.] . . . , and other the premises, voluntarily, as is aforesaid, have renounced, left, and forsaken . . . : be it therefore enacted . . . that the king, our sovereign lord, shall have, hold, possess, and enjoy to him, his heirs, and successors, forever all and singular such late monasteries [etc.] . . . , which since the said fourth day of February . . . have been dissolved . . . , or by any other mean come to his highness; and by the same authority and in like manner shall have, hold, possess, and enjoy all the . . . hereditaments which appertained or belonged to the said late monasteries [etc.] . . . in as large and ample manner and form as the late abbots, priors, abbesses, prioresses, and other ecclesiastical governors and governesses of such late monasteries [etc.] . . . had, held, or occupied . . . their said late monasteries [etc.] . . . at the time of the said dissolution . . . , or by any other manner of mean coming of the same to the king's highness since the fourth day of February above specified.

And it is further enacted by the authority abovesaid that, not only all the said late monasteries [etc.] . . . , but also all other monasteries [etc.] . . . which hereafter shall happen to be dissolved . . . , and also all the . . . hereditaments, whatsoever they be, belonging or appertaining to the same or any of them, whensoever and as soon as they shall be dissolved . . . , shall be vested, deemed, and adjudged by authority of this present parliament in the very actual and real seisin and possession of the king our sovereign lord, his heirs, and successors, forever. . . .

And be it also enacted by authority aforesaid that all the said late monasteries [etc.] . . . which be dissolved . . . , except such thereof as be come to the king's hands by attainder or attainders of treason, and all the said monasteries [etc.] . . . which hereafter shall happen to be dissolved . . . , and all . . . hereditaments, whatsoever they be, belonging to the same or to any of them, except such thereof which shall happen to come to the king's highness by attainder or attainders of treason, shall be in the order, survey, and governance of our said sovereign lord the king's court of augmentations of the revenues of his crown. . . .

Ibid., III, 733 f.: 31 Henry VIII, c. 13.

(M) STATUTE OF THE SIX ARTICLES (1539)

An act abolishing diversity in opinions. Where the king's most excellent majesty is by God's law supreme head immediately under Him of this whole Church and Congregation of England, intending the conservation of the same Church and Congregation in a true, sincere, and uniform doctrine of Christ's religion . . . , and . . . hath therefore caused and commanded this his most high court of parliament, for sundry and many urgent causes and considerations, to be at this time summoned, and also a synod and convocation of all the archbishops, bishops, and other learned men of the clergy of this his realm to be in like manner assembled; and forasmuch as in the said parliament, synod, and convocation there were certain articles, matters, and questions proponed and set forth touching Christian religion . . . : whereupon, after a great and long deliberate and advised disputation and consultation had and made concerning the said articles, as well by the consent of the king's highness as by the assent of the lords spiritual and temporal and other learned men of his clergy in their convocation, and by the consent of the commons in this present parliament assembled, it was and is finally resolved, accorded, and agreed in manner and form following—that is to say, first, that in the most blessed sacrament of the altar, by the strength and efficacy of Christ's mighty word, it being spoken by the priest, is present really, under the form of bread and wine, the natural body and blood of our Saviour Jesu Christ, conceived of the Virgin Mary, and that after the consecration there remaineth no substance of bread and wine, nor any other substance but the substance of Christ, God and man; secondly, that communion in both kinds is not necessary *ad salutem* by the law of God to all persons, and that it is to be believed and not doubted of but that in the flesh under form of bread is the very blood, and with the blood under form of wine is the very flesh, as well apart as though they were both together; thirdly, that priests, after the order of priesthood received as afore, may not marry by the law of God; fourthly, that vows of chastity or widowhood by man or woman made to God advisedly ought to be observed by the law of God, and that it exempteth them from other liberties of Christian people which without that they might enjoy; fifthly, that it is meet and necessary that private masses be continued and admitted in this the king's English Church and Congregation, as whereby good Christian people ordering themselves accordingly do receive both godly and goodly consolations and benefits, and it is agreeable also to God's law; sixthly, that auricular confession is expedient and necessary to be retained and continued, used, and frequented, in the Church of God. . . .

And be it further enacted . . . that, if any person or persons . . . contemn or contemptuously refuse, deny, or abstain to be confessed at the time commonly accustomed within this realm and Church of England, or contemn or contemptuously refuse, deny, or abstain to receive the holy and blessed sacrament abovesaid at the time commonly used and accustomed for the same, that then every such offender . . . shall suffer such imprisonment and make such fine and ransom to the king our sovereign lord and his heirs as by his highness or by his or their council shall be ordered and adjudged in that behalf; and if any such offender . . . do eftsoons[14] . . . refuse . . . to be confessed or to be communicate . . . , that then every such offence shall be deemed and adjudged felony, and the offender . . . shall suffer pains of death, and lose and forfeit all his . . . goods, lands, and tenements, as in cases of felony. . . .

Ibid., III, 739 f.: 31 Henry VIII, c. 14.

(N) THIRD ACT OF SUCCESSION (1543)[15]

An act concerning the establishment of the king's majesty's succession in the imperial crown of the realm. . . . Forasmuch as our said most dread sovereign lord the king, upon good and just grounds and causes, intendeth by God's grace to make a voyage royal in his majesty's most royal person into the realm of France against his ancient enemy the French king, his highness, most prudently and wisely considering and calling to his remembrance how this realm standeth at this present time in the case of succession . . . , recognizing and knowledging also that it is the only pleasure and will of Almighty God how long his highness or his said entirely beloved son Prince Edward shall live, and whether the said prince shall have heirs of his body lawfully begotten or not, or whether his highness shall have heirs begotten and procreated between his majesty and his said most dear and entirely beloved wife, Queen Katherine that now is, or any lawful heirs and issues hereafter of his own body begotten by any other his lawful wife; and albeit that the king's most excellent majesty, for default of such heirs as be inheritable by the said act, might . . . give and dispose the said imperial crown and other the premises by his letters patents under his great seal, or by his last will in writing signed with his most gracious hand, to any person or persons of such estate therein as should please his highness to limit and appoint; yet to the intent that his majesty's disposition and mind therein should be openly declared and manifestly known and notified as well to the lords spiritual and temporal

---

[14] Again.

[15] A second Act of Succession (1536), necessitated by the king's marriage to Jane Seymour, had included additional provisions, some of which are here rehearsed.

as to all other his loving and obedient subjects of this his realm, to the intent that their assent and consent might appear to concur with thus far as followeth of his majesty's declaration in this behalf: his majesty therefore thinketh convenient, afore his departure beyond the seas, that it be enacted . . . that, in case it shall happen to the king's majesty and the said excellent prince, his yet only son . . . and heir apparent, to decease without heir of either of their bodies lawfully begotten (as God defend!) . . . , that then the said imperial crown and all other the premises shall be to the lady Mary, the king's highness's daughter and to the heirs of the body of the same lady Mary lawfully begotten, with such conditions as by his highness shall be limited by his letters patents under his great seal, or by his majesty's last will in writing signed with his gracious hand; and for default of such issue, the said imperial crown and other the premises shall be to the lady Elizabeth, the king's second daughter, and to the heirs of the body of the said lady Elizabeth lawfully begotten, with such conditions [etc.] . . .[16]

Ibid., III, 955: 35 Henry VIII, c. 1.

[16] In default of the heirs mentioned, the king might determine the succession by his letters patent or will, as provided in the act of 1536 (cf. no. 76).

75. ORDER FOR THE COUNCIL OF THE NORTH (1545)[1]

His majesty, much desiring the quietness and good governance of the people there, and for speedy and indifferent administration of justice to be had between party and party, intendeth to continue his right honourable council called the King's Council in the North Parts. And his highness, knowing the approved truth, wisdom, and experience of the said archbishop of York, with his assured discretion and dexterity in executing of justice, hath first appointed him to be president of the said council so established, and by these presents do give unto him the name and title of lord president of the said council; and with the said name, power and authority to call all such others as shall be named of the said council, at this time or hereafter, together, at all such seasons as he shall think the same expedient; and otherwise by his letters, when they shall be absent, to appoint them and every of them to do such things for the advancement of justice and for the repression and punishment of malefactors as, by the advice of such part of the said council as then shall be present with him, he shall think meet for the furtherance of his grace's affairs and the due administration of justice between his highness's subjects. And further, his majesty by these presents giveth unto the said lord president, in all counsel where things shall be debated at length for the bringing out of the most perfect sentence—which his majesty's pleasure is shall be observed in all cases where the same shall be such as may abide advisement and consultation—a voice negative, to the intent nothing shall pass but by his express

[1] See especially R. R. Reid, *The King's Council in the North*.

commandment, consent, and order. And his highness also willeth and commandeth that all and every of the said councillors to be hereafter named shall exhibit to the said lord president as much honour, obedience, and reverent behaviour in all things (kneeling only excepted) as they would exhibit unto his own person if he were there present amongst them; and in like sort receive and execute all his precepts and commandments to be addressed unto them or any of them, for any matter touching his majesty or any process or thing to be done or served in his grace's name.

And to the intent the said president, being thus established as head and director of such council as his highness hath erected and established there for the purposes abovesaid, may be furnished with such assistants and members as be of wisdom, experience, gravity, and truth, meet to have the name of his grace's councillors, his majesty upon good advisement and deliberation hath elected and chosen these persons whose names ensue hereafter to be his councillors joined in the said council in the north parts with the said president. . . .[2]

His majesty ordaineth that [ten of these] . . . shall give their attendance at their own pleasure; that is to say, go and come when their will is, unless they shall be otherwise by the said president appointed, saving only at four general sittings, where every of the said council shall be present unless they have some just necessary impediment to the contrary. And because it shall be convenient that a number shall be continually abiding with the said president, to whom he may commit the charge and hearing of such matters as shall be exhibited unto him for the more expedition of the same, by these presents his highness doth also ordain that [four of the sixteen] . . . shall give their continual attendance upon the said president, or at the least two of them; so as none of this number appointed to give his continual attendance shall in any wise depart at any time from the said president without his special licence, and the same not to extend above six weeks at one season. . . .[3]

And to furnish the said president and council in all things with authority sufficient and ready to execute justice, as well in causes criminal as in matters of controversy between party and party, his majesty hath commanded two commissions to be made out under his great seal of England, by virtue whereof they shall have full power and authority in either case to proceed as the matter occurrent shall require. And for the more speedy expedition to be used in all cases of justice, his majesty's pleasure is that the said president and council shall cause every complainant and defendant that shall have to do before them to put their whole matter in their bill of complaint and answer, without replication, rejoinder, or other delay to be had or used therein. . . . To which president and council the king's majesty by these presents doth give full power and authority, as well to

---
[2] Sixteen men are named.
[3] Salaries, lodgings, and servants are assigned to the councillors.

punish such persons as in anything shall neglect or contemn their
commandments, as all other that shall speak any seditious words,
invent rumours, or commit any such offences, not being treason,
whereof any inconvenience might grow, by pillory, cutting their
ears, wearing of papers, or otherwise at their discretions; and to
poor suitors having no money, at their discretions to appoint counsel
and other requisites without paying of any money for the same.
And likewise his highness giveth full power and authority to the
said president and council being with him, to cess fines of all persons that shall be convict of any riots, how many soever they be in
number, unless the matter of such riot shall be thought unto them of
such importance as the same shall be meet to be signified unto his
majesty, and punished in such sort, by the order of his council attendant upon his person, as the same may be noted for an example
to others, and semblably, his grace giveth full power and authority
unto them by their discretions to award costs and damages, as well
to the plaintiff as to the defendants, and execution of their decrees;
all which decrees the said secretary shall be bounden, incontinently
upon the promulgation of every of the same, to write or cause to be
written fair in a book, which book shall remain in the hands and
custody of the said president. . . .

And if it shall chance that the said president and council shall be
variant in opinion, either in law or for any order to be taken upon
any fact, that like as if the case be not of very great importance,
that part wherein shall be the greater number of the councillors appointed to give continual attendance shall determine, or else, if they
be of like number, that part whereunto the president shall consent
and lean, who in all causes as is aforesaid shall ever have a voice
negative; so being the case of great importance, if the question be
of the law, the said president and council shall signify the case to
the judges at Westminster, who shall with diligence advertise them
again of their opinions in it. And if it be an order to be taken upon
the fact, the said president and council shall in that case advertise
the king's majesty, or his council attendant upon his person, upon
the same; whereupon they shall have knowledge how to use themselves in that behalf. . . .

State Papers, Henry VIII, V, 402 f.

76. WILL OF HENRY VIII (1546)[1]

Henry R. In the name of God and of the glorious and blessed
Virgin, our Lady Saint Mary, and of all the holy company of heaven,
we, Henry, by the grace of God king of England, France, and Ireland,
Defender of the Faith, and in earth immediately under God the
supreme head of the Church of England and Ireland, of that name

---

[1] On the authenticity of this document, see Pollard, *Protector Somerset*, pp. 3 f.

the eighth, calling to our remembrance the great gifts and benefits of Almighty God given to us in this transitory life, give unto Him our most lowly and humble thanks, acknowledging ourself insufficient in any part to deserve or recompense the same, but fear that we have not worthily received the same. . . .

We will by these presents that, immediately after our departure out of this present life, our said son Edward shall have and enjoy the said imperial crown and realm of England and Ireland, our title to France, with all dignities, honours, pre-eminences, prerogatives, authorities, and jurisdictions, lands and possessions, to the same annexed or belonging to him and to his heirs of his body lawfully begotten.

And for default of such issue of our said son Prince Edward's body lawfully begotten, we will the said imperial crown and other the premises, after our two deceases, shall wholly remain and come to the heirs of our body lawfully begotten of the body of our entirely beloved wife, Queen Katherine, that now is, or of any other our lawful wife that we shall hereafter marry. And for lack of such issue and heirs . . . , the said imperial crown and all other the premises shall wholly remain and come to our said daughter Mary and the heirs of her body lawfully begotten; upon condition that our said daughter Mary, after our decease, shall not marry nor take any person to her husband without the assent and consent of the privy councillors and others appointed by us to our dearest son Prince Edward aforesaid to be of council. . . . We will that, after our decease, and for default of issue of . . . our daughter Mary, the said imperial crown and other the premises shall wholly remain and come to our said daughter Elizabeth and to the heirs of her body lawfully begotten; upon condition [etc.] . . .[2]

Also we, being now at this time (thanks be to Almighty God!) of perfect memory, do constitute and ordain these personages following our executors and performers of this our last will and testament. . . .[3] And all these we will to be our executors and councillors of the privy council with our said son Prince Edward, in all matters concerning both his private affairs and public affairs of the realm. . . . Whom we ordain, name, and appoint, and by these presents signed with our hand do make and constitute of privy council with our said son; and will that they have the government of our most dear son Prince Edward and of all our realms, dominions, and subjects, and of all the affairs public and private, until he shall have fully completed the eighteenth year of his age. . . .

Rymer, Foedera, XV, 110-15.

---

[2] Here follow similar provisions establishing the succession to the crown in favour of his nieces, Frances and Eleanor; and, should they have no lawful issue, in favour of "the next rightful heirs."

[3] The archbishop of Canterbury, the lord chancellor, and fourteen others.

77. EDWARD VI: STATUTES
(A) First Act of Uniformity (1549)

An act for the uniformity of service and administration of the sacraments throughout the realm. Where of long time there hath been had in this realm of England and Wales divers forms of common prayer . . . , and besides the same now of late much more divers and sundry forms and fashions have been used in the cathedral and parish churches of England and Wales, as well concerning the matins or morning prayer and the evensong, as also concerning the holy communion commonly called the mass, with divers and sundry rites and ceremonies concerning the same, and in the administration of other sacraments of the Church; and as the doers and executors of the said rites and ceremonies in other form than of late years they have been used were pleased therewith, so other not using the same rites and ceremonies were thereby greatly offended; and albeit the king's majesty, with the advice of his most entirely beloved uncle, the lord protector and other of his highness's council, hath heretofore divers times essayed to stay innovations or new rites concerning the premises, yet the same hath not had such good success as his highness required in that behalf: whereupon his highness by the most prudent advice aforesaid, being pleased to bear with the frailty and weakness of his subjects in that behalf, of his great clemency hath not been only content to abstain from punishment of those that have offended in that behalf—for that his highness taketh that they did it of a good zeal—but also to the intent a uniform, quiet, and godly order should be had concerning the premises, hath appointed the archbishop of Canterbury and certain of the most learned and discreet bishops and other learned men of this realm to consider and ponder the premises, and thereupon, having as well eye and respect to the most sincere and pure Christian religion taught by the Scripture as to the usages in the primitive Church, should draw and make one convenient and meet order, rite, and fashion of common and open prayer and administration of the sacraments, to be had and used in his majesty's realm of England and in Wales. The which at this time, by the aid of the Holy Ghost, with one uniform agreement is of them concluded, set forth, and delivered to his highness, to his great comfort and quietness of mind, in a book entitled The Book of the Common Prayer and Administration of the Sacraments and other Rites and Ceremonies of the Church after the Use of the Church of England: wherefore the lords spiritual and temporal and the commons in this present parliament assembled . . . do give to his highness most hearty and lowly thanks for the same, and humbly pray that it may be ordained and enacted by his majesty, with the assent of the lords and commons in this present parliament assembled and by the authority of the same . . . , that all and singular ministers in any cathedral or parish church, or other place within this realm of England, Wales, Calais, and marches of the same, or other the king's dominions, shall from and after the feast of Pentecost next coming be bounden to say and use the matins, evensong, celebration of the Lord's Supper commonly called the mass, and administration of each of the sacraments, and all their common and open prayer, in such order and form as is mentioned in the said book and none other or otherwise.

And albeit that the same be so godly and good that they give occasion to every honest and conformable man most willingly to embrace them, yet lest any obstinate person who willingly would disturb so godly order and quiet in this realm should not go unpunished . . . , [be it] ordained and enacted by the authority aforesaid that, if any manner of parson, vicar, or other whatsoever minister that ought or should sing or say common prayer mentioned in the said book or minister the sacraments, shall after the said feast of Pentecost next coming refuse to use the said common prayers or to minister the sacraments in such cathedral or parish church or other places as he should use or minister the same . . . , [he] shall lose and forfeit to the king's highness, his heirs, and successors, for his first offence the profit of such one of his spiritual benefices or promotions as it shall please the king's highness to assign or appoint coming and arising in one whole year next after his conviction; and also that the same person so convicted shall for the same offence suffer imprisonment by the space of six months without bail or mainprise. . . .

And it is ordained and enacted by the authority abovesaid that, if any person or persons whatsoever, after the said feast of Pentecost next coming, shall in any interludes, plays, songs, rhymes, or by other open words, declare or speak anything in the derogation, depraving, or despising of the same book or of anything therein contained or any part thereof . . . , then every person being thereof lawfully convicted in form abovesaid shall forfeit to the king our sovereign lord, his heirs, and successors, for the first offence £10. . . .

Provided always that it shall be lawful to any man that understandeth the Greek, Latin, and Hebrew tongue, or other strange tongue, to say and have the said prayers heretofore specified of matins and evensong in Latin or any such other tongue, saying the same privately as they do understand; and for the further encouraging of learning in the tongues in the universities of Cambridge and Oxford, to use and exercise in their common and open prayer in their chapels, being no parish churches or other places of prayer, the matins, evensong, litany, and all other prayers, the holy communion commonly called the mass excepted, prescribed in the said book . . . in Greek, Latin, or Hebrew—anything in this present act to the contrary notwithstanding. . . .

Statutes of the Realm, IV, 37 .: 2-3 Edward VI, c. 1.

(B) SECOND ACT OF UNIFORMITY (1552)

An act for the uniformity of common prayer and administration of the sacraments. . . . Be it enacted . . . that, from and after the feast

77. EDWARD VI: STATUTES

of All Saints next coming, all and every person and persons inhabiting within this realm or any other the king's majesty's dominions, shall diligently and faithfully, having no lawful or reasonable excuse to be absent, endeavour themselves to resort to their parish church or chapel accustomed, or upon reasonable let thereof to some usual place where common prayer and such service of God shall be used in such time of let, upon every Sunday and other days ordained and used to be kept as holy days, and then and there to abide orderly and soberly during the time of the common prayer, preachings, or other service of God there to be used and ministered; upon pain of punishment by the censures of the Church.

And for the due execution hereof the king's most excellent majesty, the lords temporal, and all the commons in this present parliament assembled doth in God's name earnestly require and charge all the archbishops, bishops, and other ordinaries[1] that they shall endeavour themselves to the uttermost of their knowledge that the due and true execution hereof may be had throughout their dioceses and charges, as they will answer before God for such evils and plagues wherewith Almighty God may justly punish His people for neglecting this good and wholesome law. . . .

And because there hath arisen in the use and exercise of the foresaid common service in the Church heretofore set forth divers doubts for the fashion and manner of the ministration of the same, rather by the curiosity of the minister, and mistakers, than of any other worthy cause: therefore, as well for the more plain and manifest explanation hereof as for the more perfection of the said order of common service, in some places where it is necessary to make the same prayers and fashion of service more earnest and fit to stir Christian people to the true honouring of Almighty God, the king's most excellent majesty, with the assent of the lords and commons in this present parliament assembled and by the authority of the same, hath caused the foresaid order of common service entitled The Book of Common Prayer to be faithfully and godly perused, explained, and made fully perfect; and by the foresaid authority hath annexed and joined it so explained and perfected to this present statute, adding also a form and manner of making and consecrating archbishops, bishops, priests, and deacons, to be of like force, authority, and value as the same like foresaid book entitled The Book of Common Prayer was before, and to be accepted, received, used, and esteemed in like sort and manner, and with the same clauses of provisions and exceptions to all intents, constructions, and purposes, as by the act of parliament made in the second year of the king's majesty's reign was ordained and limited, expressed and appointed, for the uniformity of service and administration of the sacraments throughout the realm. . . .

Ibid., IV, 130: 5-6 Edward VI, c. 1.

---

[1] Persons possessing jurisdiction in their own right.

78. MARY: STATUTES

(A) First Statute of Repeal (1553)

An act for the repeal of certain statutes made in the time of the reign of King Edward VI. Forasmuch as, by divers and several acts hereafter mentioned, as well the divine service and good administration of the sacraments as divers other matters of religion which we and our forefathers found in this Church of England, to us left by the authority of the Catholic Church, be partly altered and in some part taken from us; and in place thereof new things imagined and set forth by the said acts, such as a few of singularity have of themselves devised; whereof hath ensued amongst us in very short time numbers of divers and strange opinions and diversities of sects, and thereby grown great unquietness and much discord, to the great disturbance of the commonwealth of this realm, and in very short time like to grow to extreme peril and utter confusion of the same, unless some remedy be in that behalf provided, which thing all true, loving, and obedient subjects ought and are bounden to foresee and provide to the uttermost of their power . . . : [nine ecclesiastical statutes of Edward VI's reign are totally repealed].

And be it further enacted by the authority aforesaid that all such divine service and administration of sacraments as were most commonly used in the realm of England in the last year of the reign of our late sovereign lord, King Henry VIII, shall be . . . used and frequented through the whole realm of England and all other the queen's majesty's dominions; and that no other kind nor order of divine service nor administration of sacraments be after the said 20th day of December used or ministered in any other manner, form, or degree within the said realm of England or other the queen's dominions than was most commonly used, ministered, and frequented in the said last year of the reign of the said late King Henry VIII. . . .

Ibid., IV, 202: 1 Mary, st. 2, c. 2.

(B) Act concerning the Regal Power (1554)

An act declaring that the regal power of this realm is in the queen's majesty as fully and absolutely as ever it was in any of her most noble progenitors, kings of this realm. Forasmuch as the imperial crown of this realm, with all dignities, honours, prerogatives, authorities, jurisdictions, and pre-eminences thereunto annexed, united, and belonging, by the divine providence of Almighty God is most lawfully, justly, and rightfully descended and come unto the queen's highness that now is, being the very true and undoubted heir and inheritrix thereof, and invested in her most royal person, according unto the laws of this realm . . . : be it declared and enacted by the authority of this present parliament that the law of this realm is and ever hath been, and ought to be understood, that the kingly or regal office of the realm, and all dignities [etc.] . . . thereunto annexed, united, or belonging, being invested either in male or female, are and be and ought to be as fully, wholly, absolutely, and entirely deemed, judged, accepted, invested, and taken in the one as in the other; so that what or whensoever statute or law doth limit and appoint that the king of this realm may or shall have, execute, and do anything as king, or doth give any profit or commodity to the king, or doth limit or appoint any pains or punishment for the correction of offenders or transgressors against the regality and dignity of the king or of the crown, the same the queen . . . may by the same authority and power likewise have, exercise, execute, punish, correct, and do, to all intents, constructions, and purposes, without doubt, ambiguity, scruple, or question—any custom, use, or scruple, or any other thing whatsoever to be made to the contrary notwithstanding.

Ibid., IV, 222: 1 Mary, st. 3, c. 1.

(C) SECOND STATUTE OF REPEAL (1555)

An act repealing all statutes, articles, and provisions made against the see apostolic of Rome since the twentieth year of King Henry VIII, and also for the establishment of all spiritual and ecclesiastical possessions and hereditaments conveyed to the laity. Whereas, since the twentieth year of King Henry VIII of famous memory, father unto your majesty, our most natural sovereign and gracious lady and queen, much false and erroneous doctrine hath been taught, preached, and written . . . , by reason whereof as well the spiritualty as the temporalty of your highness's realms and dominions have swerved from the obedience of the see apostolic and declined from the unity of Christ's Church, and so have continued until such time as, your majesty being first raised up by God and set in the seat royal over us and then by His divine and gracious providence knit in marriage with the most noble and virtuous prince, the king our sovereign lord your husband, the pope's holiness and the see apostolic sent hither unto your majesties . . . and to the whole realm the most reverend father in God, the lord cardinal Pole, legate *de latere*, to call us home again into the right way . . . ; and we . . . , seeing by the goodness of God our own errors, have acknowledged the same unto the said most reverend father, and by him have been . . . received and embraced into the unity and bosom of Christ's Church . . . , upon our humble submission and promise . . . to repeal and abrogate such acts and statutes as had been made in parliament since the said twentieth year of the said King Henry VIII against the supremacy of the see apostolic . . . : [therefore, all such statutes are hereby repealed].

And finally, where certain acts and statutes have been made in the time of the late schism concerning the lands and hereditaments of archbishoprics and bishoprics, the suppression and dissolution of monasteries, abbeys, priories, chantries, colleges, and all other the goods and chattels of religious houses; since the which time the right and dominion of certain lands and hereditaments, goods and chattels, belonging to the same be dispersed abroad and come to the hands and possessions of divers and sundry persons who by gift, purchase, exchange, and other means, according to the order of the laws and statutes of this realm for the time being, have the same: for the avoiding of all scruples that might grow by any the occasions aforesaid or by any other ways or means whatsoever, it may please your majesties to be intercessors and mediators to the said most reverend father, Cardinal Pole, that all such causes and quarrels as by pretence of the said schism or by any other occasion or mean whatsoever might be moved, by the pope's holiness or see apostolic or by any other jurisdiction ecclesiastical, may be utterly removed and taken away; so as all persons having sufficient conveyance of the said lands and hereditaments, goods and chattels, as is aforesaid by the common laws, acts, or statutes of this realm, may without scruple of conscience enjoy them, without impeachment or trouble by pretence of any general council, canons, or ecclesiastical laws, and clear from all dangers of the censures of the Church. . . .

Ibid., IV, 246 f.: 1-2 Philip & Mary, c. 8.

(D) HIGHWAYS ACT (1555)

An act for the amending of highways. For amending of highways, being now both very noisome and tedious to travel in and dangerous to all passengers and carriages, be it enacted . . . that the constables and churchwardens of every parish within this realm shall yearly, upon the Tuesday or Wednesday in Easter Week, call together a number of the parochians[1] and shall then elect and choose two honest persons of the parish to be surveyors and orderers for one year of the works for amendment of the highways in their parish leading to any market town, the which persons shall have authority by virtue hereof to order and direct the persons and carriages that shall be appointed for those works by their discretions; and the said persons so named shall take upon them the execution of their said offices upon pain of every of them making default to forfeit 20s. And the said constables and churchwardens shall then also name and appoint four days for the amending of the said ways before the feast of the Nativity of St. John Baptist then next following, and shall openly in the church, the next Sunday after Easter, give knowledge of the same four days; and upon the said days the parochians shall endeavour themselves to the amending of the said ways, and shall be chargeable thereunto as followeth: that is to say, every person, for every ploughland in tillage or pasture that he or she shall occupy in the same parish, and every other person keeping there a draught or plough, shall find and send, at every day and place to be appointed for the amending of the ways in that parish as is aforesaid, one wain or cart furnished after the custom of the country with oxen, horses,

---

[1] Parishioners.

or other cattle, and all other necessaries meet to carry things convenient for that purpose, and also two able men with the same, upon pain of every draught making default 10s.; and every other householder, and also every cottager and labourer of that parish able to labour and being no hired servant by the year, shall by themselves, or one sufficient labourer for every of them, upon every of the said four days work and travail in the amendment of the said highways, upon pain of every person making default to lose for every day 12d. And if the carriages of the parish, or any of them, shall not be thought needful by the supervisors to be occupied upon any of the said days . . . , then every such person that should have sent any such carriage shall send to the said work for every carriage so spared two able men there to labour for that day, upon pain to lose for every man not so sent to the said work 12d. And every person and carriage abovesaid shall have and bring with them such shovels, spades, picks, mattocks, and other tools and instruments as they do make their own ditches and fences withal, and such as be necessary for their said work; and all the said persons and carriages shall do and keep their work, as they shall be appointed by the said supervisors or one of them, eight hours of every of the said days, unless they shall be otherways licensed by the said supervisors or one of them. . . .

Ibid., IV, 284 f.: 2-3 Philip & Mary, c. 8

79. PROCEEDINGS OF THE PRIVY COUNCIL (1526-57)

(A) REGULATIONS FOR THE COUNCIL (1526)

. . . To the intent that as well matters of justice and complaints touching the griefs of the king's subjects and disorder of his realm and otherwise . . . as also other great occurrences concerning his own particular affairs may be the better ordered and with his grace more ripely debated, digested, and resolved from time to time, as the case shall require; it is ordered and appointed by his highness, that a good number of honourable, virtuous, sad, wise, expert, and discreet persons of his council shall give their attendance upon his most royal person, whose names hereafter follow: that is to say, the lord cardinal, chancellor of England; the duke of Norfolk, treasurer of England; the bishop of London, keeper of the king's privy seal; the duke of Suffolk, marshal of England; the marquess Dorset; the marquess Exeter; the earl of Shrewsbury, steward of the king's household; the lord chamberlain; the bishop of Bath; the bishop of Lincoln; Lord Sandys; Sir William Fitz-William, treasurer of the king's household; Sir Henry Guilford, comptroller; the secretary; Sir Thomas More, chancellor of the duchy; the dean of the king's chapel; Sir Henry Wyat, treasurer of the king's chamber; the vice-chamberlain; the captain of the guard; Doctor Wolman.

And forasmuch as the said lord cardinal, the lord treasurer of England, lord privy seal, lord steward, and divers other lords and personages before mentioned, by reason of their attendance at the terms for administration of justice and exercising of their offices and other reasonable impediments, shall many seasons fortune to be absent from the king's court, and specially in term times; to the intent the king's highness shall not be at any season unfurnished of an honourable presence of councillors about his grace, with whom his highness may confer upon the premises, at his pleasure: it is ordered that the persons hereafter mentioned shall give their continual attendance in the causes of his said council, unto what place soever his highness shall resort—that is to say, the lord chamberlain, the bishop of Bath, the treasurer and comptroller of the king's household, the secretary, the chancellor of the duchy of Lancaster, the dean of the king's chapel, the vice-chamberlain, the captain of the guard; and (for ordering of poor men's complaints and causes) Doctor Wolman.

And because . . . it may chance some of these aforenamed persons to be absent for some reasonable cause; be it always provided and foreseen that either the bishop of Bath, the secretary, Sir Thomas More, and the dean of the chapel, or two of them at the least, always be present, except the king's grace give licence to any of them of the contrary. Which said councillors, so appointed for continual attendance, shall apply themselves effectually, diligently, uprightly, and justly in the premises; being every day, in the forenoon by ten of the clock at the furthest and at afternoon by two of the clock, in the king's dining-chamber, or in such other place as shall fortune to be appointed for the council chamber, there to be in readiness, not only in case the king's pleasure shall be to commune or confer with them upon any cause or matter, but also for hearing and direction of poor men's complaints on matters of justice; which direction well observed, the king's highness shall always be furnished of an honourable presence of councillors about his grace, as to his high honour doth appertain.

Nicolas, Proceedings of the Privy Council, VII, v-viii.

(B) LETTERS OF THE COUNCIL (1547)

[24 March.] Letters to my lord Wharton: that, being advertised by his letters of a late raid of the Scots . . . , the lords here thought good . . . to require him that, by one letter apart, he should inform them of the very certainty of their number and damage done by them at that time as truly as he himself was instructed therein; and by another letter to enlarge the matter, describing their number to have been upon seven hundred, and that they burned three or four villages on our borders, took notable Grays,[1] prisoners, and cattle away, with such other aggravations of that their raid as his wisdom in that behalf could set forth.

---

[1] Presumably men by that name.

79. PROCEEDINGS OF THE COUNCIL

[28 August.] To Sir Thomas Chenye, lord warden of the Cinque Ports: to recommend Sir John Baker so to those that have the naming of knights of the shire as at the next parliament he may be made knight of the shire of Kent accordingly.

[28 September.] To the sheriff of Kent: that, where the lords wrote to him afore to the end to make his friends for the election of Sir John Baker to be knight of the shire, understanding that he did abuse towards those of the shire their request into a commandment, their lordships advertise him that, as they meant not nor mean to deprive the shire by any their commandment of their liberty of election whom they should think meet, so nevertheless if they would in satisfaction of their lordship's request grant their voices to Mr. Baker, they would take it thankfully. A like letter written to the lord warden of the Cinque Ports with this addition, that, being informed he should abuse their request to menace them of the shire of Kent, as they would not believe it, so they advised him to use things in such sort as the shire might have free election.

Acts of the Privy Council, N.S., II, 461, 516, 518 f.

(C) MINUTES OF 28-29 APRIL 1550

At the star chamber. The lord chancellor, the lord high treasurer, the lord privy seal, the bishop of Ely, the lord Paget, the lord Mountague, Sir John Baker, Sir John Gage, Sir Edward North. . . .

Complaint was made by certain clothiers that the Merchants Adventurers by agreement had set such a price upon their cloths that, without the loss of 20s. in a piece, they could not utter them; for the more perfect knowledge whereof all manner of clothiers that then were in London appeared in the star chamber by commandment, where the more part denied to be privy or of counsel with the said complaint, finding great fault with the multitude of clothiers lately increased in the realm, affirming that, as long as every man that would had liberty to be a clothier, as they have now, it was impossible to have good cloth made in the realm. For he that is not bred up in that faculty must trust his factors, and so is commonly deceived; and now the good making is decayed, the cloths are out of estimation, by reason whereof the prices must also decay. Wherefore it was concluded that some device should be had for a law that none should meddle with cloth-making but such as have been apprentices to the occupation.

For the clothiers' matter the Merchants Adventurers were called before the council, for whom the mayor of London with certain of the chiefest of the company appeared, and to the complaint of the clothiers answered that they agreed not together to hinder the clothiers' prices; but the truth is that there lie at Antwerp such a number of our cloths unsold, that till they were uttered these here would not well be bought, which, together with the naughtiness of the making, hindered the prices; and besides that it was commonly not used to ship any between Easter and Whitsuntide.

Further divers reasons were made by them touching the decay of our money by exchange, with other devices touching the commonwealth, which they were commanded to put in writing. . . .

Upon a letter received from the mayor and citizens of Newcastle, declaring the restraint made for uttering of coal into strange parts, and desiring now to know whether they might sell any to such Frenchmen as were already come thither for them: it was agreed that for the present time, to the intent we should not seem uncourteous to the French upon the conclusion of this peace,[2] they therefore that were there might carry coals away; nevertheless, forasmuch as the price of coal is wonderfully increased within the realm, and will daily be dearer if strangers may carry it oversea, therefore the restraint shall continue, and warning be given to the Frenchmen that be there now to come no more, and to warn their countrymen not to lose their travail; with further commandment to the mayor and his brethren to write the names of the carriers and the quantity of the coal that should be sent to Calais or Dover, that if it be transported otherwise the parties may be punished, for the more surety whereof they that do ship it shall at their return bring a testimony in writing where and how they have delivered it. . . .

Ibid., III, 19 f.

(D) REPORT TO THE COUNCIL ON PRINCESS MARY (1551)[3]

First having received commandment and instructions from the king's majesty, we repaired to the said Lady Mary's house . . . , where shortly after our coming I, the lord chancellor, delivered his majesty's letters unto her, which she received upon her knees, saying that, for the honour of the king's majesty's hand wherewith the said letters were signed, she would kiss the letter, and not for the matter contained within them. "For the matter," said she, "I take to proceed not from his majesty but from you of the council." In reading of the letter, which she did read secretly to herself, she said these words in our hearing: "Ah! Good Master Cecil took much pain here." . . . We told her . . . that the king's majesty's pleasure was we should give straight charge to her chaplains that none of them should presume to say any mass or other divine service than is set forth by the laws of the realm. . . . Hereunto her answer was this: first, she protested that to the king's majesty she was, is, and ever will be his majesty's most humble and most obedient subject and poor sister, and would most willingly obey all his commandments in anything, her conscience saved; yea, and would willingly and gladly suf-

---

[2] Signed 24 March 1550.

[3] Made by commissioners who had been sent by the council to warn her to obey the law concerning religious usages.

79. PROCEEDINGS OF THE COUNCIL

fer death to do his majesty good. But rather than she would agree to use any other service than was used at the death of the late king her father, she would lay her head on a block and suffer death. "But," said she, "I am unworthy to suffer death in so good a quarrel. When the king's majesty," said she, "shall come to such years that he may be able to judge these things himself, his majesty shall find me ready to obey his orders in religion; but now in these years, although he, good sweet king, had more knowledge than any other of his years, yet is it not possible that he can be a judge in these things. . . ."

Finally, when we had said and done as is aforesaid and were gone out of the house, tarrying there for one of her chaplains who was not with the rest when we gave the charge aforesaid unto them, the lady Mary's grace sent to us to speak with her one word at a window. When we were come into the court, notwithstanding that we offered to come up to her chamber, she would needs speak out of the window, and prayed us to speak to the lords of the council that her comptroller might shortly return. "For," said she, "since his departing I take the account myself of my expenses and learn how many loaves of bread be made out of a bushel of wheat, and I wis my father and my mother never brought me up with baking and brewing; and, to be plain with you, I am weary with my office, and therefore, if my lords will send my officer home, they shall so give me pleasure. . . . And I pray God to send you to do well in your souls, and your bodies, too, for some of you have but weak bodies."

Ibid., III, 347 f.

(E) LETTERS OF THE COUNCIL (1552-53)

[19 January 1552.] A letter to the sheriff of Essex and Hertfordshire: to elect a new knight of that shire in lieu of Sir Henry Parker, deceased, at the next county day; and to use the matter in such sort as Mr. Sadlier may be elected and returned, for that he seemeth most fittest of any other person thereabouts.

[31 December 1552.] A letter to Thomas Gresham: to take order for the sending over of the king's majesty fustians by piecemeal by forty or fifty bales at once; so as thereby the matter may be so warily and circumspectly handled as the prices of the same fustians may be in any wise furthered to the king's majesty's best advantage.

[15 March 1553.] A letter to the lord treasurer: to suffer Thomas Galiard to transport beyond the seas 200,000 pair of old shoes; providing that under colour thereof he do convey beyond the seas nothing prohibited to be carried out of the realm.

Ibid., III, 459; IV, 199, 236.

(F) COMMITTEES OF THE COUNCIL (1554)

The names of all such as be appointed for the purposes following. To call in debts and provide for money: my lord chancellor, my lord Paget, my lord chamberlain, Mr. Comptroller. To give order for supply of all wants at Calais, Guisnes, and all other pieces of those marches; to give like order for Berwick and other places upon the borders of the north; to give like order for Ireland, Portsmouth, the Isle of Wight, and the islands: my lord treasurer, my lord steward, my lord privy seal, my lord of Sussex, my lord of Pembroke, Sir John Bourne, master of the horse, Sir Richard Southwell, Sir Thomas Cornewalles. To give order for the ships and to appoint captains and others to serve in them: my lord admiral. To give order for victuals necessary to be sent to Calais, Berwick, etc.: Mr. Comptroller, Sir Thomas Cornewalles, Sir William Drury. To consider what laws shall be established in this parliament and to name men that shall make the books thereof: my lord chancellor, my lord treasurer, my lord of Durham, my lord Paget, Mr. Petre, Mr. Baker, Mr. Hare. To appoint men to continue in the examination of the prisoners: [left blank]. To consider what lands shall be sold and who shall be in commission for that purpose: [left blank]. To moderate the excessive charges: my lord steward, etc., for the household; my lord chamberlain, etc., for the chamber. To consider the patents and annuities payable in sundry places, so as the same may be paid all in one place: my lord chancellor, my lord treasurer, my lord steward, Mr. Baker, my lord Paget, Mr. Petre. To appoint a council to attend and remain at London: my lord Riche, Mr. Peckham, the master of the rolls, Sir Thomas Pope, Sir John Mordant, the lieutenant of the Tower.

Ibid., IV, 397 f.

(G) LETTERS OF THE COUNCIL (1555-57)

[3 May 1555.] A letter to George Colte and Thomas Danyell: to make search for John Barnarde and John Walshe, who have used to repair to Sudbury and, carrying the bones of one Pygott that was burned about them, do show the same to the people as relics and persuade them to stand in their error; and upon their apprehension to examine them and, if they be found faulty herein, to commit them to ward; and further to order them according to the laws, and to signify their doings hither.

[29 June 1555.] Several letters to the sheriffs of Kent, Bucks, Berks, and Oxon: to make search for one Francis Baringden, who is thought to lurk in those counties with the wife of one Fallowfelde, merchant of London, whom he hath enticed from her husband; and to apprehend them both and to commit them to ward, and to signify what they shall have done herein hither.

[7 January 1556.] A letter to the mayor and aldermen of the city of Coventry: to cause some Catholic and grave man to be chosen to their mayor for this year coming; and for that the queen's majesty is advertised that John Fitzherbert, Richard Whestler, and one Colman, of the said city, are Catholic and honest persons, they are required to give their voices to one of them to be mayor.

[14 January 1556.] A letter to the lord mayor and sheriffs of London: to give substantial order that, when any obstinate man condemned by order of the laws shall be delivered to be punished for heresy, that there be a good number of officers and other men appointed to be at the execution, who may be charged to see such as shall misuse themselves, either by comforting, aiding, or praising the offenders, or otherwise use themselves to the ill example of others, to be apprehended and committed to ward; and besides to give commandment that no householder suffer any of his apprentices or other servants to be abroad, other than such as their masters will answer for. . . .

[27 June 1557.] A letter to John Fuller, mayor of Canterbury: of thanks for his diligence in the apprehending and committing of the players to ward, whom they are willed to keep so until they shall receive further order from hence; and in the mean[time] their lewd play book is committed to the consideration of the king and queen majesty's learned counsel, who are willed to declare what the same weigheth unto in the law, whereupon they shall receive further order from hence touching the said players.

[18 October 1557.] A letter to the master of the horse, the lord chief justice of the king's bench, Sir Richard Southwell, and Mr. Newdigate: to call before them one Newport and his man, remaining presently in Newgate, and one Cowley, remaining in the king's bench, and to examine them by the best means and ways they can touching certain counterfeit crowns taken with the said Newport, and to put them to the torture if they shall think so convenient.

Ibid., V, 120, 154, 218, 224; VI, 110, 187.

80. RECORDS OF CASES IN STAR CHAMBER (1505-53)[1]

(A) THE BISHOP OF WORCESTER v. THOMASYN AND OTHERS (1505)

To the king our sovereign lord. Humbly showeth unto your highness your faithful chaplain and continual orator Sylvester, bishop of Worcester, that, where at a law-day and court holden for your suppliant at Stratford-upon-Avon, in your county of Warwick, election was made, by the twelve men sworn at the same law-day and court, of two constables for the conservation of your peace within the precinct of the same town, and of a bailiff, there to be for the year following . . . : one Thomas Thomasyn, of the said town yeoman, which of his own presumptuous mind would have been bailiff there for this year, not pleased with the said election, assembled with one Richard Bentley and John Staffordshire of the same, yeoman, and

---
[1] Cf. nos. 73B, 74A; and on the general character of these records, see Leadam's introduction to *Select Cases in Star Chamber*, vol. I.

other misruled persons to the number of twelve, with bills, clubs, stones, and swords, came riotously to the house where the said lawday and court was held; and then and there would have slain one John Elys, deputy steward, sitting and keeping the said court; and there with exclamation said that William Cottoun, which was elected bailiff as is aforesaid, should not be bailiff there, whosoever should say nay; and with assaults and exclamations riotously kept the said deputy steward, bailiff, and twelve men till it was past ten of the clock in the night, to the great disturbance of your peace and in contempt of your highness, and of your laws, to the perilous example of misdoers unless they may have due punishment therefor. . . .

This is the answer of Thomas Thomas[yn], Richard Bentley, and John Staffordshire to the bill of complaint of Sylvester, bishop of Worcester. They say that, at the said law-day held at the town of Stratford-upon-Avon . . . , such twelve men that there should be sworn have been used out of time of mind to be twelve of the most substantial and honest persons of the same town, to the intent that they should choose substantial men and men of honest conversation to be constables and bailiffs of the same town for the year ensuing; and one John Elys, being steward deputy of the same town, to the intent that he would make bailiffs and constables of the said town such as him should please, caused the jury to be made of the most silliest and simplest persons of the said town—and some of them were but men's servants—and left the substantial men out of the same jury; and after the said jury was sworn, they could not agree upon one of the bailiffs; and, they so being not agreed, the said John Elys proclaimed bailiffs and constables at large in the said town such as him pleased, as though the same jurors had been fully agreed upon the same, without the assent or agreement of the said twelve men and before any verdict by them given; and then Richard Bentley and John Staffordshire came to the said John Elys and showed him that they did not well to proclaim the said officers before the said jury were agreed upon them, but advised him to put the said jury in a house until they were agreed. And the said Thomas Thomas[yn] says that, in the morning of the same day out of the court and long before the court began, the same John Elys and the said Thomas Thomas[yn] fell at words for an entry made by the said John Elys in the name of the said bishop into certain lands of Thomas and his wife, by occasion whereof the same John Elys was about to draw his knife at the said Thomas Thomas[yn]. . . .

Leadam, *Select Cases in Star Chamber*, I, 230 f.

(B) MULSHO V. THE INHABITANTS OF THINGDEN (1529)

To the king our sovereign lord. In full humble wise showeth unto your highness your faithful subject, John Mulsho of Thingden in the county of Northampton, esquire, that, where the same John Mulsho was and is seised of . . . the manor of Thingden . . . in the

80. CASES IN STAR CHAMBER

said county of Northampton . . . in his demesne as of fee, and so . . . hath inhabited himself in the said town of Thingden, using there great husbandry, sometimes with four ploughs and sometimes with three and with two at the least, and yet doth: the said John Mulsho, being lord of the said manor as is before said, having no several grass there to maintain his . . . beasts necessary and convenient for the maintenance there of the said husbandry . . . , lawfully improved and enclosed twenty-six acres of lea ground in Thingden aforesaid, being not ploughed many years before, and fourteen acres of arable ground, all which arable ground and leas were parcel of the demesne of the manor belonging to the said John Mulsho, with ditches and hedges quickset with oak, ash, elm, willow, sallow, maple, crab tree, and thorn, to the intent he would have increase of wood there for necessary fuel for his house, because the said town of Thingden is six or seven miles from any forest or great wood. Which enclosure was in several closes divided, and no house of husbandry [was] by the same decayed, and the freeholders, tenants, and inhabitants of the town, notwithstanding the said enclosure, had and yet have sufficient common pasture for all their cattle in the residue of the field of Thingden aforesaid after rate and quantity of their tenures. All which closes the said John Mulsho hath peaceably kept in severalty without let . . . , till now of late that by the sinister labour of the tenants-at-will and copyholders of the said John Mulsho of Thingden and other inhabitants of the same town made to Thomas, lord cardinal, late chancellor of England . . . , who in the king's name granted a writ out of the chancery to Sir William Fitz-William, knight . . . , sheriff of the county of Northampton, commanding him . . . to take the power of the said county with him to throw down the said hedges and ditches about the said closes made by the said John Mulsho, without calling the said John Mulsho by any ordinary process to make answer to the same . . . ; whereupon the said Sir William Fitz-William . . . , taking with him the power of the same county, hath thrown down the said hedges and ditches . . . to the great decay of the husbandry of the said John Mulsho and to his utter undoing. . . . And the said tenants and inhabitants of the said town of Thingden, not contented with the throwing down of the said ditches and hedges and destroying of the wood . . . , riotously assembled themselves and with force and arms hewed and cut up the gate-posts and supports of the gates that belonged to the said closes whereof the said hedges and ditches were thrown down as is aforesaid. And after the sheriff with the power of the shire were departed from thence, and had executed and done as much as the king's writ had commanded them . . . , divers . . . riotous persons to the number of three score . . . riotously assembled themselves . . . with force and arms, that is to say, with bills, hatchets, clubs, piked staves, pitchforks, shovels, and spades, riotously dug up the roots of all such willows . . . and of all other trees which the said John Mulsho had there set for the increase of wood necessary for fuel for his house, and so daily continued riotously by the space of eight days together, with knelling of bells, hooting, and shouting in most riotous manner that the like thereof hath not been seen in these parts. . . .

Ibid., II, 38 f.

(C) BROKE V. SPYTTULL (1534)

To the king our sovereign lord. Whereas your subject Ralph Broke, gentleman, 8th December in this 26th year of your reign, came to a certain pasture . . . belonging to John Broke, father of your beseecher, called the Newe Rudding, to see to such cattle as he then had in the same . . . : at which time Hugh Spyttull of the Mere in the said county, husbandman; Sir William Spyttull of Enfield in the said county, priest; Richard Humphrey Taylor, otherwise Wilcox; John Taylor, otherwise Wilcox; Thomas Spyttull, John Watkes, William Tyrry, and Thomas Kyrkham came to him, by the procurement of Hugh, Humphrey Spyttull, and John Spyttull, in forcible manner and riotously assaulted your subject and Michael Broke, his brother, and Thomas Bailey, then in his company, and sore threatened them, by means of which fear your subjects suffered the said riotous persons to approach nigh to them. And the said persons beat the said Ralph to the ground and sore wounded him, and Thomas Bailey by hard means escaped and came to the town called the Mere and raised hue and cry that his master and Michael his brother were in point to be slain. . . . Whereupon Sir Thomas Dasshefen, priest, Nicholas Moseley, John Dasshefen, and others, minding to keep the peace, came to the said assault. Then the said misdemeaned persons, perceiving that company, kept your said subject in their ward, and feigned that the said Ralph, Michael, and Thomas came to break their hedges about a ground called Small Heath, otherwise Clareheys. Wherefore they said they would justify the beating of them, and imprison them till they found surety that they would break no hedges; where of truth your subjects broke no hedges, although the said Clareheys ought to lie in common to the townships of Lutley and the Mere, [and was] lately enclosed by the said Hugh Spyttull and others, contrary to right. Of which assault the said misdemeaned persons have been, before the justices of the peace in county Stafford, indicted. In consideration whereof, please your highness to grant your writ of *subpoena* to the said persons, commanding them to appear before you, etc. . . .

To our sovereign lord the king. We, Walter Wrottesley, esquire, and John Gravenour, gentleman, commissioners assigned by your writ of *dedimus potestatem* directed to us to hear and examine witnesses concerning the matter in variance in the books hereunto annexed contained, between Ralph Broke and others, plaintiffs, and Hugh Spyttull and others, defendants, certify your highness that we, by force of your writ, the Monday after the feast of St. John the Baptist last, sat at Tresull and called before us the said parties; and the plaintiffs brought before us divers persons hereunder named, who, then examined, deposed as hereunto annexed appears:—

Thomas Lea of the Woo, gentleman, aged 28 years. He saw Ralph Broke's head broken. He saw no hedges broken nor moved. He examined John Watkes, one of the parties with Spyttull, who said he saw not the said Broke within the said Clareheys. The said Thomas Bailey made hue and cry at the Mere, and Sir Thomas Dasshefen, John Dasshefen, Lewes Clare, and Nicholas Moseley came to the rescue. Clareheys is a mile from Enfield. The said Ralph and others say that they were led thither against their wills. On the night of the affray there was no hedge or ditch broken. He saw them as whole as they were the morning before.

William Byllyngesley of Ludston, aged 49 years. . . . On the Wednesday before the fray in Hampton the said Hugh Spyttull and Ralph Broke quarrelled. Further, for forty years past he knew Clareheys lie common, and never knew it enclosed till William Bulwardyn enclosed it and held it sometimes closed and sometimes open for three years or thereabouts.

Thomas Woorwood of Morff, gentleman, aged 88 years. He has known Clareheys lie open for eighty years past until, about sixteen or seventeen years since, William Bulwardyn enclosed it. . . .

Thomas Dasshefen of Enfield, aged 47 years, says that there were nine persons at the said affray, and Hugh Spyttull and Sir William Spyttull had bows and arrows, and the others had staves; and that Ralph Broke had his head broken. . . .

Nicholas Moseley of the Mere, aged 43 years, says that William Tyrry, being at the affray and therefore indicted of riot, said that Ralph Broke had no cause to indict him; for when he, the said William, had the said Ralph by one arm and Humphrey Taylor had him by the other, if he had not pulled the said Ralph back, Richard Spyttull would have slain him. At the same assault they did hit by command of Humphrey Spyttull. Thomas Bailey made hue and cry at the township of the Mere, by reason whereof this deponent, Sir Thomas Dasshefen, and Sir John Dasshefen came to the house of Beves Clares in the Mere, where the said Ralph and Michael were in custody. . . .

Collections for a History of Staffordshire, 1912, pp. 71 f.

(D) PETYT V. JOBBER AND OTHERS (1540-41)

To the king our sovereign lord: your orator, John Petyt, of Chebsey, county Stafford, gentleman. Whereas your orator, 8th May last, was at Chebsey, John Jobber, husbandman [and thirteen others] . . . , with force and arms made assault on your said orator; may it please you to grant your writs of *subpoena* to be directed to them, to appear before you to answer the premises.

The answer of John Jobber, William Palmer, and Robert Stedeman to the bill of complaint of John Petyt. The said bill of complaint is untrue. . . . The town of Chebsey, wherein the pretended offences are supposed to be done, is held of the honour of Tutbury, parcel of the duchy of Lancaster, and all riots there done are determinable before the chancellor of the said duchy. There is a custom in the manor of Chebsey that, if any beasts and cattle or other distress have been taken for any cause . . . , the same distress be impounded in the same manor; and if the takers thereof have been about to drive the same to any other place, the tenants thereof have been used to resist the same. Further, the defendants say that the plaintiff, John Hille of the Pype, John Petyt the younger, and John Bradley, arrayed in forcible manner, with other gentlemen of county Stafford, took and distrained four oxen of Robert Stedeman and would have driven them out of the lordship, whereupon the defendants resisted the same, which is the riot supposed by the plaintiff's bill.

Ibid., p. 140.

(E) GERARD v. DODD (1547-53)

To the king our most dread sovereign lord: your subject, Sir Thomas Gerard, knight, and William Hunt, servant to your said suppliant. Whereas your subject and all his ancestors have been seised by lawful title of descent of the manor of Bromley in the parish of Ecclessall, county Stafford, parcel of which manor is wood called Willibrydge Parke, in which wood for a long time there have eyried sparrowhawks by the space of sixty years last, and this present year the said hawk eyried there and had five young hawks, and your said subject commanded his said servant to make him a cabin in the said wood to keep and watch the said hawks there: so it is that John Dodd of Clorley, county Salop, esquire, enticed Robert Parkes, yeoman, his household servant; Thomas Taylor of Pyxley, county Salop, bailiff to the said John Dodd; and Richard Emys, otherwise Enys, of Drayton in Hales, county Salop, shearman; to convey away the said hawks. By force whereof, 27th June last, they assembled in riotous manner at the said woodside and entered the said wood with vizors upon their faces, hoods upon their heads, and otherwise disguised, one hour after sunrise, and made assault on the said William Hunt, then being within his cabin, and after took him and bound him to a tree, and after, with like force, took away five young hawks out of the nest of the said sparrowhawk and conveyed them to the house of John Dodd, to the loss of your suppliant and the utter undoing of William Hunt, who has consumed all he has in surgery and, by reason of his beating, is not able to serve again. In consideration whereof, please your highness to grant your writ of *subpoena* to be directed to the said John Dodd and Robert Parkes, commanding them to appear before you to make answer to the premises.

The answer of John Dodd, esquire. The said bill is uncertain. . . .

80. CASES IN STAR CHAMBER 343

If it were true, as it is not, it is determinable at the common law. As to the riot, entry, etc., he is not guilty. . . .

The answer of Robert Parkes. As to any riot . . . or other misdemeanours in the said surmised bill alleged, he is not guilty.

Ibid., p. 180.

(F) THE KING v. A JURY OF LICHFIELD (1551-53)

The answer of John Pyllysworth [and ten others]. The said Rowlande Orme and William Fowler do, and at the time of the said verdict did, dwell two miles out of the city of Lichfield, and never dwelt there; and the rest of the defendants do, and at the time of the making of the said verdict did, dwell within the said town. The said Harry Oliver was indicted in the said town before the coroner there for murdering the said John Wescote, and was arraigned before the bailiff and recorder of the town at the said jail-delivery held within the said city, whereunto he pleaded not guilty; which they know to be true, because the said indictment was read to them when they, with the said Raufe Bagnolde, were sworn to try the said Harry. At the time of the said jail-delivery they came to the place where it was held, not thinking to be sworn to try the said Harry, and they, with the said Raufe Bagnolde, were sworn before the said justices to try the said Harry. Proclamation was made that, if any man would give evidence against the same prisoner, that he should come forth and be heard; but, notwithstanding, no man came to give any evidence, and so the said defendants with Raufe Bagnolde went to commune together of their verdict. And as they were going from the bar, one said that he could give evidence concerning the same matter. The recorder of the town asked him if he was not of another jury for life and death, and he said yes; so he could not be sworn to give any evidence. Therefore the said defendants had no evidences given them to find the said Harry guilty. They made their verdict plainly, without favour, and found the said Harry not guilty of the said murder; without that, that they were corrupted by John Ferrers and William Wescote and other their friends to acquit the said Harry, or that they had knowledge themselves how the said murder was committed, or that they found their verdict contrary to their conscience and knowledge. . . .

William Corpson, of Lichfield, spurrier . . . , says that John Wescote was slain in the open street at Lichfield on Ash Wednesday last, being fair day there, and by common report Harry Oliver killed the said Wescote and was indicted for the same, but how many times he knew not. . . . He denies that any labour was made to him to be of the inquest on the trial of the said Harry; nor any sum of money given to him or promised by any person to be favourable to the said Harry Oliver at his arraignment. . . . The said Wescote was slain indeed, and no other person but Harry Oliver was accused of his death and therefore he thinks the said Harry Oliver killed him; but how he knows not, nor had any evidence given thereof. . . .[2]

Ibid., pp. 194 f.

[a] Five other jurymen, being interrogated, say the same.

81. ELIZABETH: STATUTES

(A) Act of Supremacy (1559)

An act restoring to the crown the ancient jurisdiction over the state ecclesiastical and spiritual and abolishing all foreign power repugnant to the same. Most humbly beseech your most excellent majesty your faithful and obedient subjects, the lords spiritual and temporal and the commons in this your present parliament assembled, that, where in time of the reign of your most dear father of worthy memory, King Henry VIII, divers good laws and statutes were made and established, as well for the utter extinguishment and putting away of all usurped and foreign powers and authorities out of this your realm and other your highness's dominions and countries, as also for the restoring and uniting to the imperial crown of this realm the ancient jurisdictions, authorities, superiorities, and pre-eminences to the same of right belonging and appertaining; by reason whereof we, your most humble and obedient subjects, from the five-and-twentieth year of the reign of your said dear father, were continually kept in good order, and were disburdened of divers great and intolerable charges and exactions before that time unlawfully taken and exacted by such foreign power and authority as before that was usurped, until such time as all the said good laws . . . in the first and second years of the reigns of the late King Philip and Queen Mary . . . were . . . repealed . . . ;[1] by reason of which act of repeal your said humble subjects were eftsoons brought under an usurped foreign power and authority, and yet do remain in that bondage, to the intolerable charges of your loving subjects, if some redress by the authority of this your high court of parliament with the assent of your highness be not had and provided: may it therefore please your highness, for the repressing of the said usurped foreign power and the restoring of the rights, jurisdictions, and pre-eminences appertaining to the imperial crown of this your realm, that it may be enacted by the authority of this present parliament that the said act . . . and all and every branch, clauses, and articles therein contained, other than such branches, clauses, and sentences as hereafter shall be excepted, may from the last day of this session of parliament, by authority of this present parliament, be repealed, and shall from thenceforth be utterly void and of none effect. . . .[2]

And to the intent that all usurped and foreign power and authority,

---

[1] No. 78c.

[2] The following three sections revive Henry VIII's statutes declaring the supremacy of the crown in ecclesiastical affairs.

spiritual and temporal, may forever be clearly extinguished and never to be used nor obeyed within this realm or any other your majesty's dominions or countries, may it please your highness that it may be further enacted by the authority aforesaid that no foreign prince, person, prelate, state, or potentate, spiritual or temporal, shall at any time after the last day of this session of parliament use, enjoy, or exercise any manner of power, jurisdiction, superiority, authority, pre-eminence, or privilege, spiritual or ecclesiastical, within this realm or within any other your majesty's dominions or countries that now be or hereafter shall be, but from thenceforth the same shall be clearly abolished out of this realm and all other your highness's dominions forever, any statute, ordinance, custom, constitutions, or any other matter or cause whatsoever to the contrary in any wise notwithstanding . . . ; and that your highness, your heirs, and successors, kings or queens of this realm, shall have full power and authority . . . to exercise . . . all manner of jurisdictions, privileges, and pre-eminences in any wise touching or concerning any spiritual or ecclesiastical jurisdiction within these your realms. . . .

And for the better observation and maintenance of this act, may it please your highness that it may be further enacted by the authority aforesaid that all and every archbishop, bishop, and all and every other ecclesiastical person and other ecclesiastical officer and minister, of what estate, dignity, pre-eminence, or degree soever he or they be or shall be, and all and every temporal judge, justicer, mayor, and other lay or temporal officer and minister, and every other person having your highness's fee or wages within this realm or any your highness's dominions shall make, take, and receive a corporal oath upon the Evangelist, before such person or persons as shall please your highness, your heirs or successors, under the great seal of England to assign and name to accept and take the same, according to the tenor and effect hereafter following, that is to say—

"I, A. B., do utterly testify and declare in my conscience that the queen's highness is the only supreme governor of this realm and of all other her highness's dominions and countries, as well in all spiritual or ecclesiastical things or causes as temporal, and that no foreign prince, person, prelate, state, or potentate hath or ought to have any jurisdiction, power, superiority, pre-eminence, or authority, ecclesiastical or spiritual, within this realm; and therefore I do utterly renounce and forsake all foreign jurisdictions, powers, superiorities, and authorities, and do promise that from henceforth I shall bear faith and true allegiance to the queen's highness, her heirs, and lawful successors, and to my power shall assist and defend all jurisdictions, pre-eminences, privileges, and authorities granted or belonging to the queen's highness, her heirs, and successors, or united or annexed to the imperial crown of this realm: so help me God and by the contents of this Book." . . .[3]

---

[3] Persons refusing to take this oath were to be debarred from offices in church and state.

And for the more sure observation of this act and the utter extinguishment of all foreign and usurped power and authority, may it please your highness that it may be further enacted by the authority aforesaid that, if any person or persons dwelling or inhabiting within this your realm or in any other your highness's realms or dominions . . . , shall by writing, printing, teaching, preaching, express words, deed, or act, advisedly, maliciously, and directly affirm, hold, stand with, set forth, maintain, or defend the authority, pre-eminence, power, or jurisdiction, spiritual or ecclesiastical, of any foreign prince, prelate, person, state, or potentate whatsoever, heretofore claimed, used, or usurped within this realm or any dominion or country being within or under the power, dominion, or obeisance of your highness, or shall advisedly, maliciously, or directly put in ure or execute anything for the extolling, advancement, setting forth, maintenance, or defence of any such pretended or usurped jurisdiction, power, pre-eminence, or authority, or any part thereof, that then every such person and persons so doing and offending, their abettors, aiders, procurers, and counsellors, being thereof lawfully convicted and attainted according to the due order and course of the common laws of this realm [shall suffer specified penalties, culminating in punishment for high treason on the third offence]. . . .

Provided always, and be it enacted by the authority aforesaid, that such person or persons to whom your highness, your heirs, or successors, shall hereafter by letters patents under the great seal of England give authority to have or execute any jurisdiction, power, or authority spiritual, or to visit, reform, order, or correct any errors, heresies, schisms, abuses, or enormities by virtue of this act, shall not in any wise have authority or power to order, determine, or adjudge any matter or cause to be heresy but only such as heretofore have been determined, ordered, or adjudged to be heresy by the authority of the canonical Scriptures, or by the first four general councils or any of them, or by any other general council wherein the same was declared heresy by the express and plain words of the said canonical Scriptures, or such as hereafter shall be ordered, judged, or determined to be heresy by the high court of parliament of this realm, with the assent of the clergy in their convocation—anything in this act contained to the contrary notwithstanding. . . .

Statutes of the Realm, IV, 350 f.: 1 Elizabeth, c. 1.

(B) ACT OF UNIFORMITY (1559)

An act for the uniformity of common prayer and divine service in the Church, and the administration of the sacraments. . . . And further be it enacted . . .[4] that all and singular ministers in any cathedral or parish church or other place within this realm of England, Wales, and the marches of the same, or other the queen's dominions, shall, from and after the feast of the Nativity of St. John Baptist next

---

[4] The first section repeals Mary's statute of 1553 (no. 78A).

coming, be bounden to say and use the matins, evensong, celebration of the Lord's Supper and administration of each of the sacraments, and all their common and open prayer, in such order and form as is mentioned in the . . . book so authorized by parliament in the . . . fifth and sixth year of the reign of King Edward VI,[5] with one alteration or addition of certain lessons to be used on every Sunday in the year, and the form of the litany altered and corrected, and two sentences only added in the delivery of the sacrament to the communicants, and none other or otherwise; and that, if any manner of parson, vicar, or other whatsoever minister that ought or should sing or say common prayer mentioned in the said book or minister the sacraments . . . refuse to use the said common prayers or to minister the sacraments . . . in such order and form as they be mentioned and set forth in the said book, or shall wilfully or obstinately . . . use any other rite, ceremony, order, form, or manner of celebrating of the Lord's Supper openly or privily, or matins, evensong, administration of the sacraments, or other open prayers, than is mentioned and set forth in the said book . . . , or shall preach, declare, or speak anything in the derogation or depraving of the said book or anything therein contained, or of any part thereof, and shall be thereof lawfully convicted according to the laws of this realm by verdict of twelve men, or by his own confession, or by the notorious evidence of the fact . . . , [he shall suffer fine or imprisonment—life imprisonment for the third offence].

And it is ordained and enacted by the authority abovesaid that, if any person or persons whatsoever after the said feast . . . shall in any interludes, plays, songs, rhymes, or by other open words, declare or speak anything in the derogation, depraving, or despising of the same book, or of anything therein contained, or any part thereof, or shall by open fact, deed, or by open threatenings, compel or cause or otherwise procure or maintain any parson, vicar, or other minister in any cathedral or parish church or in chapel or in any other place to sing or say any common or open prayer or to minister any sacrament otherwise or in any other manner and form than is mentioned in the said book, or that by any of the said means shall unlawfully interrupt or let any parson, vicar, or other minister in any cathedral or parish church, chapel, or any other place to sing or say common and open prayer, or to minister the sacraments or any of them, in such manner and form as is mentioned in the said book, that then every such person, being thereof lawfully convicted in form above-said . . . , [shall suffer fine or imprisonment—life imprisonment for the third offence].

And . . . from and after the said feast . . . all and every person and persons inhabiting within this realm or any other the queen's majesty's dominions shall diligently and faithfully, having no lawful or reasonable excuse to be absent, endeavour themselves to resort to

---

[5] No. 77B.

their parish church or chapel accustomed, or upon reasonable let thereof, to some usual place where common prayer and such service of God shall be used in such time of let, upon every Sunday and other days ordained and used to be kept as holy days; and then and there . . . abide orderly and soberly during the time of the common prayer, preachings, or other service of God there to be used and ministered, upon pain of punishment by the censures of the Church, and also upon pain that every person so offending shall forfeit for every such offence 12d., to be levied by the churchwardens of the parish where such offence shall be done, to the use of the poor of the same parish. . . .

Provided always, and be it enacted, that such ornaments of the Church and of the ministers thereof shall be retained and be in use as was in the Church of England by authority of parliament in the second year of the reign of King Edward VI, until other order shall be therein taken by the authority of the queen's majesty, with the advice of her commissioners appointed and authorized under the great seal of England for causes ecclesiastical or of the metropolitan of this realm; and also that, if there shall happen any contempt or irreverence to be used in the ceremonies or rites of the Church by the misusing of the orders appointed in this book, the queen's majesty may, by the like advice of the said commissioners or metropolitan, ordain and publish such further ceremonies or rites as may be most for the advancement of God's glory, the edifying of His Church, and the due reverence of Christ's holy mysteries and sacraments.

And be it further enacted by the authority aforesaid that all laws, statutes, and ordinances wherein or whereby any other service, administration of sacraments, or common prayer is limited, established, or set forth to be used within this realm, or any other the queen's dominions or countries, shall from henceforth be utterly void and of none effect.

Ibid., IV, 355 f.: 1 Elizabeth, c. 2.

(C) STATUTE OF ARTIFICERS (1563)

An act containing divers orders for artificers, labourers, etc. Although there remain and stand in force presently a great number of acts and statutes concerning the retaining, departing, wages, and orders of apprentices, servants, and labourers, as well in husbandry as in divers other arts, mysteries, and occupations, yet, partly for the imperfection and contrariety that is found and do appear in sundry of the said laws, and for the variety and number of them, and chiefly for that the wages and allowances limited and rated in many of the said statutes are in divers places too small and not answerable to this time, respecting the advancement of prices of all things belonging to the said servants and labourers, the said laws cannot conveniently, without the great grief and burden of the poor labourer and hired man, be put in good and due execution; and as the said several acts

81. ELIZABETH: STATUTES

and statutes were at the time of the making of them thought to be very good and beneficial for the commonwealth of this realm, as divers of them yet are, so if the substance of as many of the said laws as are meet to be continued shall be digested and reduced into one sole law and statute, and in the same an uniform order prescribed and limited concerning the wages and other orders for apprentices, servants, and labourers, there is good hope that it will come to pass that the same law, being duly executed, should banish idleness, advance husbandry, and yield unto the hired person both in the time of scarcity and in the time of plenty a convenient proportion of wages . . . : be it . . . enacted that no person which shall retain any servant shall put away his or her said servant, and that no person retained according to this statute shall depart from his master, mistress, or dame before the end of his or her term . . . , unless it be for some reasonable and sufficient cause or matter to be allowed before two justices of peace, or one at the least, within the said county, or before the mayor or other chief officer of the city, borough, or town corporate wherein the said master, mistress, or dame inhabiteth, to whom any of the parties grieved shall complain; which said justices or justice, mayor or chief officer, shall have and take upon them or him the hearing and ordering of the matter between the said master, mistress, or dame, and servant according to the equity of the cause. . . .

And for the declaration and limitation what wages servants, labourers, and artificers, either by the year or day or otherwise, shall have and receive, be it enacted . . . that the justices of peace . . . shall yearly, at every general sessions first to be holden and kept after Easter . . . , assemble themselves together; and they so assembled, calling unto them such discreet and grave persons of the said county or of the said city or town corporate as they shall think meet, and conferring together respecting the plenty or scarcity of the time and other circumstances necessary to be considered, shall have authority . . . to limit, rate, and appoint the wages . . . of . . . artificers, handicraftsmen, husbandmen, or any other labourer, servant, or workman . . . , and shall . . . certify the same, engrossed in parchment with the considerations and causes thereof under their hands and seals, into the queen's most honourable court of chancery, whereupon it shall be lawful to the lord chancellor of England . . . , upon declaration thereof to the queen's majesty, her heirs, or successors, or to the lords and others of the privy council for the time being attendant upon their persons, to cause to be printed and sent down . . . into every county, to the sheriff and justices of peace there . . . , ten or twelve proclamations or more, containing in every of them the several rates appointed by the said justices . . . , with commandment by the said proclamations to all persons in the name of the queen's majesty . . . straitly to observe the same, and to all justices, sheriffs, and other officers to see the same duly and severely observed. . . .

Provided always, and be it enacted . . . , that in the time of hay or corn harvest, the justices of peace and every of them, and also the constable or other head officer of every township, upon request and for the avoiding of the loss of any corn, grain, or hay, shall and may cause all such artificers and persons as be meet to labour . . . to serve by the day for the mowing, reaping, shearing, getting, or inning of corn, grain, and hay, according to the skill and quality of the person; and that none of the said persons shall refuse so to do, upon pain to suffer imprisonment in the stocks by the space of two days and one night. . . .

And be it further enacted . . . that two justices of peace, the mayor . . . of any city, borough, or town corporate, and two aldermen . . . shall and may, by virtue hereof, appoint any such woman as is of the age of twelve years and under the age of forty years and unmarried and forth of service, as they shall think meet to serve, to be retained or serve by the year or by the week or day, for such wages and in such reasonable sort and manner as they shall think meet. And if any such woman shall refuse so to serve, then it shall be lawful for the said justices of peace, mayor, or head officers to commit such woman to ward until she shall be bounden to serve as aforesaid.

And be it further enacted that, if any person shall be required by any householder, having and using half a ploughland at the least in tillage, to be an apprentice and to serve in husbandry or in any other kind of art, mystery, or science before expressed, and shall refuse so to do, that then, upon the complaint of such housekeeper made to one justice of peace of the county wherein the said refusal is or shall be made . . . , the said justice or the said mayor . . . shall have power and authority by virtue hereof, if the said person refuse to be bound as an apprentice, to commit him unto ward, there to remain until he be contented and will be bounden to serve as an apprentice should serve, according to the true intent and meaning of this present act.

And if any such master shall misuse or evil intreat his apprentice, or . . . the said apprentice shall have any just cause to complain, or the apprentice do not his duty to his master, then the said master or prentice being grieved and having cause to complain shall repair unto one justice of peace within the said county, or to the mayor . . . of the city, town corporate, market town, or other place where the said master dwelleth, who shall by his wisdom and discretion take such order and direction between the said master and his apprentice as the equity of the cause shall require. And if for want of good conformity in the said master, the said justice of peace or . . . mayor . . . cannot compound and agree the matter between him and his apprentice, then the said justice or . . . mayor . . . shall take bond of the said master to appear at the next sessions then to be holden in the said county or . . . town . . . , and, upon his appearance and hearing of the matter before the said justices or the said mayor . . . , if it be thought meet unto them to discharge the said apprentice of his apprenticehood, that then the said justices or four of them at the least . . . , or the said mayor . . . , with the consent of three other of his brethren or men of best reputation within the said . . . town . . . , shall have power . . . , in writing under their hands and seals, to pronounce and declare that they have discharged the said apprentice of his apprenticehood, and the cause thereof; and the said writing, so being made and enrolled by the clerk of the peace or town clerk amongst the records that he keepeth, shall be a sufficient discharge for the said apprentice against his master, his executors, and administrators. . . . And if default shall be found to be in the apprentice, then the said justices or . . . mayor . . . , with the assistants aforesaid, shall cause such due correction and punishment to be ministered unto him as by their wisdom and discretions shall be thought meet. . . .

Ibid., IV, 414 f.: 5 Elizabeth, c. 4.

(D) TREASONS ACT (1571)[6]

An act whereby certain offences be made treason. . . . Be it enacted, declared, and established . . . that, if any person or persons whatsoever, at any time after the last day of June next coming during the natural life of our most gracious sovereign lady, Queen Elizabeth . . . , shall, within the realm or without, compass, imagine, invent, devise, or intend the death or destruction, or any bodily harm tending to death, destruction, maim, or wounding of the royal person of the same our sovereign lady, Queen Elizabeth; or to deprive or depose her of or from the style, honour, or kingly name of the imperial crown of this realm or of any other realm or dominion to her majesty belonging, or to levy war against her majesty within this realm or without, or to move or to stir any foreigners or strangers with force to invade this realm or the realm of Ireland or any other her majesty's dominions being under her majesty's obeisance, and such compasses, imaginations, inventions, devices, or intentions, or any of them, shall maliciously, advisedly, and expressly utter or declare by any printing, writing, ciphering, speech, words, or sayings; or if any person or persons whatsoever, after the said last day of June, shall maliciously, advisedly, and directly publish, declare, hold opinion, affirm or say by any speech, express words, or sayings that our said sovereign lady, Queen Elizabeth, during her life is not or ought not to be queen of this realm of England and also of the realms of France and Ireland, or that any other person or persons ought of right to be king or queen of the said realms . . . , during her majesty's life, or shall by writing, printing, preaching, speech, express words, or sayings maliciously, advisedly, and directly publish, set forth, and affirm that . . . our said sovereign lady, Queen Elizabeth, is an heretic, schismatic, tyrant, infidel, or an usurper of

---

[6] Cf. no. 73E. For comment on the treason acts passed between 1495 and 1571, see Tanner, *Tudor Constitutional Documents,* pp. 378-81.

the crown of the said realms or any of them; that then all and every such said offence or offences shall be taken, deemed, and declared, by the authority of this act and parliament, to be high treason; and that as well the principal offender or offenders therein as all and every the abettors, counsellors, and procurers to the same offence or offences, and all and every aiders and comforters of the same offender or offenders . . . shall suffer pains of death and also forfeit unto the queen's majesty, her heirs, and successors, all and singular lands, tenements, and hereditaments, goods, and chattels, as in cases of high treason by the laws and statutes of this realm at this day of right ought to be forfeited and lost. . . .

And be it further enacted that, if any person shall in any wise hold and affirm or maintain that the common laws of this realm not altered by parliament ought not to direct the right of the crown of England; or that our said sovereign lady . . . , with and by the authority of the parliament of England, is not able to make laws and statutes of sufficient force and validity to limit and bind the crown of this realm and the descent, limitation, inheritance, and government thereof; or that this present statute, or any part thereof, or any other statute to be made by the authority of the parliament of England with the royal assent of our said sovereign lady . . . for limiting of the crown, or any statute for recognizing the right of the said crown and realm to be justly and lawfully in the most royal person of our said sovereign lady . . . is not, are not, or shall not or ought not to be forever of good and sufficient force and validity to bind, limit, restrain, and govern all persons . . . whatsoever; every such person, so holding, affirming, or maintaining during the life of the queen's majesty, shall be judged a high traitor, and suffer and forfeit as in cases of high treason is accustomed. . . .

Ibid., IV, 526 f.: 13 Elizabeth, c. 1.

(E) ACT PROHIBITING BULLS FROM ROME (1571)[7]

An act against the bringing in and putting in execution of bulls and other instruments from the see of Rome. Where, in the parliament holden at Westminster in the fifth year of the reign of our sovereign lady the queen's majesty that now is, by one act and statute then and there made . . . it is among other things very well ordained and provided, for the abolishing of the usurped power and jurisdiction of the bishop of Rome and of the see of Rome heretofore unlawfully claimed and usurped within this realm and other the dominions to the queen's majesty belonging, that no person or persons shall hold or stand with to set forth, maintain, defend, or extol the same usurped power, or attribute any manner jurisdiction,

---

[7] Passed in reply to Pius V's bull of the previous year declaring Elizabeth a usurper and freeing her subjects from their allegiance.

authority, or pre-eminence to the same, to be had or used within
this realm or any the said dominions, upon pain to incur the danger,
penalties, and forfeitures ordained and provided by the Statute of
Provision and Praemunire made in the sixteenth year of the reign
of King Richard II . . . ; and yet, nevertheless, divers seditious
and very evil-disposed people . . . have lately procured and obtained
to themselves from the said bishop of Rome and his said see divers
bulls and writings, the effect whereof hath been and is to absolve
and reconcile all those that will be contented to forsake their due
obedience to our most gracious sovereign lady the queen's majesty,
and to yield and subject themselves to the said feigned, unlawful,
and usurped authority . . . : be it enacted . . . that, if any person
or persons, after the first day of July next coming, shall use or put
in ure in any place within this realm or in any the queen's dominions
any such bull, writing, or instrument . . . of absolution or reconciliation at any time heretofore obtained and gotten, or at any time
hereafter to be obtained and gotten, from the said bishop of Rome
or any his successors, or from any other person or persons authorized or claiming authority by or from the said bishop of Rome, his
predecessors, or successors, or see of Rome; or if any person or
persons, after the said first day of July, shall take upon him or
them, by colour of any such bull [etc.] . . . , to grant or promise
to any person or persons within this realm or any other the queen's
majesty's dominions any such absolution or reconciliation by any
speech, preaching, teaching, writing, or any other open deed; or if
any person or persons within this realm or any the queen's dominions,
after the said first day of July, shall willingly receive and take any
such absolution or reconciliation; or else if any person or persons
have obtained or gotten, since the last day of parliament holden in
the first year of the queen's majesty's reign, or after the said first
day of July shall obtain or get from the said bishop of Rome or
any his successors or see of Rome any manner of bull [etc.] . . . ,
containing any thing, matter, or cause whatsoever, or shall publish
or by any ways or means put in ure any such bull [etc.] . . . ; that
then all and every such act and acts, offence and offences, shall be
deemed and adjudged by the authority of this act to be high treason,
and the offender and offenders therein, their procurers, abettors, and
counsellors . . . , shall be deemed and adjudged high traitors to the
queen and the realm, and, being thereof lawfully indicted and attainted . . . , shall suffer pains of death, and also lose and forfeit
all their lands, tenements, hereditaments, goods, and chattels, as in
cases of high treason by the laws of this realm ought to be lost and
forfeited. . . .

And be it further enacted by the authority aforesaid that, if any
person or persons shall at any time after the said first day of July
bring into this realm of England or any the dominions of the same
any token or tokens . . . , crosses, pictures, beads, or suchlike vain
and superstitious things from the bishop or see of Rome . . . and

... shall deliver or offer or cause to be delivered the same or any of them to any subject of this realm, or of any the dominions of the same, to be worn or used in any wise; that then as well the same person and persons so doing as also all and every other person or persons which shall receive and take the same to the intent to use or wear the same, being thereof lawfully convicted and attainted . . . , shall incur into the dangers, penalties, pains, and forfeitures ordained and provided by the Statute of Praemunire and Provision made in the sixteenth year of the reign of King Richard II. . . .

Ibid., IV, 528 f.: 13 Elizabeth, c. 2.

(F) ACT AGAINST SECTARIES (1593)

An act to retain the queen's subjects in obedience. For the preventing and avoiding of such great inconveniences and perils as might happen and grow by the wicked and dangerous practices of seditious sectaries and disloyal persons: be it enacted by the queen's most excellent majesty, and by the lords spiritual and temporal and the commons in this present parliament assembled, and by the authority of the same, that, if any person or persons above the age of sixteen years . . . shall obstinately refuse to repair to some church, chapel, or usual place of common prayer to hear divine service established by her majesty's laws and statutes in that behalf made . . . , [and] shall . . . by printing, writing, or express words or speeches advisedly and purposely practise or go about to move or persuade any of her majesty's subjects . . . to deny, withstand, and impugn her majesty['s] power and authority in causes ecclesiastical, united and annexed to the imperial crown of this realm, or to that end or purpose shall advisedly and maliciously move or persuade any other person whatsoever to forbear or abstain from coming to church to hear divine service, or to receive the communion according to her majesty's laws and statutes aforesaid, or to come to or to be present at any unlawful assemblies, conventicles, or meetings under colour or pretence of any exercise of religion contrary to her majesty's said laws and statutes; or if any person or persons . . . shall . . . willingly join or be present at any such assemblies, conventicles, or meetings . . . ; that then every such person so offending as aforesaid and being thereof lawfully convicted shall be committed to prison, there to remain without bail or mainprise until they shall conform and yield themselves to come to some church, chapel, or usual place of common prayer and hear divine service according to her majesty's laws and statutes aforesaid. . . .[8]

---

[8] The subsequent articles, among other provisions, establish penalties for offenders who refuse to conform, and an oath to be taken by those who submit to the law.

Ibid., IV, 841: 35 Elizabeth, c. 1.

(G) ACT AGAINST PAPISTS (1593)[9]

An act against popish recusants. For the better discovering and avoiding of all such traitorous and most dangerous conspiracies and attempts as are daily devised and practised against our most gracious sovereign lady, the queen's majesty, and the happy estate of this commonweal by sundry wicked and seditious persons, who, terming themselves Catholics and being indeed spies and intelligencers, not only for her majesty's foreign enemies, but also for rebellious and traitorous subjects born within her highness's realms and dominions, and hiding their most detestable and devilish purposes under a false pretext of religion and conscience, do secretly wander and shift from place to place within this realm to corrupt and seduce her majesty's subjects and to stir them to sedition and rebellion: be it ordained and enacted . . . that every person above the age of sixteen years, born within any the queen's majesty's realms or dominions or made denizen, being a popish recusant . . . and having any certain place of dwelling and abode within this realm, shall within forty days next after the end of this session of parliament . . . repair to their place of dwelling where they usually heretofore made their common abode, and shall not any time after pass or remove above five miles from thence. . . .

Provided always, and be it further enacted by the authority aforesaid, that all such persons as . . . aforesaid shall within twenty days next after their coming to any of the said places, as the case shall happen, notify their coming thither and present themselves and deliver their true names in writing to the minister or curate of the same parish and to the constable, headborough, or tithingman of the town; and thereupon the said minister or curate shall presently enter the same into a book to be kept in every parish for that purpose. And afterward the said minister or curate and the said constable, headborough, or tithingman shall certify the same in writing to the justices of the peace of the same county at the next general or quarter sessions to be holden in the said county; and the said justices shall cause the same to be entered by the clerk of the peace in the rolls of the same sessions.

And to the end that the realm be not pestered and overcharged with the multitude of such seditious and dangerous people as is aforesaid, who, having little or no ability to answer or satisfy any competent penalty for their contempt and disobedience of the said laws and statutes and being committed to prison for the same, do live for the most part in better case there than they could if they were abroad at their own liberty . . . : if any such person or persons, being a popish recusant . . . , shall not . . . repair to their place of usual dwelling [etc.] . . . as is aforesaid . . . , and shall not . . . conform themselves to the obedience of the laws and statutes of this realm in coming usually to the church to hear divine

---

[9] An earlier act, 1585, had banished Jesuits and seminary priests.

service, and in making such public confession and submission as hereafter in this act is appointed . . . , such offender . . . shall, upon his . . . corporal oath before any two justices of the peace or coroner of the same county, abjure this realm of England and all other the queen's majesty's dominions forever.

Ibid., IV, 843 f.: 35 Elizabeth, c. 2.

(H) POOR RELIEF ACT (1598)[10]

An act for the relief of the poor. Be it enacted by the authority of this present parliament that the churchwardens of every parish and four substantial householders there . . . , who shall be nominated yearly in Easter week under the hand and seal of two or more justices of the peace in the same county . . . dwelling in or near the same parish, shall be called overseers of the poor of the same parish; and they, or the greater part of them, shall take order from time to time, by and with the consent of two or more such justices of peace, for setting to work of the children of all such whose parents shall not by the said persons be thought able to keep and maintain their children, and also all such persons married or unmarried as, having no means to maintain them, use no ordinary and daily trade of life to get their living by; and also to raise weekly or otherwise, by taxation of every inhabitant and every occupier of lands in the said parish in such competent sum and sums of money as they shall think fit, a convenient stock of flax, hemp, wool, thread, iron, and other necessary ware and stuff to set the poor on work, and also competent sums of money for and towards the necessary relief of the lame, impotent, old, blind, and such other among them being poor and not able to work, and also for the putting out of such children to be apprentices, to be gathered out of the same parish according to the ability of the said parish; and to do and execute all other things, as well for disposing of the said stock as otherwise concerning the premises, as to them shall seem convenient. Which said churchwardens and overseers so to be nominated, or such of them as shall not be let by sickness or other just excuse, to be allowed by such two justices of peace or more, shall meet together at the least once every month in the church of the said parish, upon the Sunday in the afternoon after divine service, there to consider of some good course to be taken and of some meet orders to be set down in the premises; and shall, within four days after the end of their year . . . , make and yield up to such two justices of peace a true and perfect account of all sums of money by them received . . . , upon pain that every one of them absenting them-

---

[10] The provision in this act that local officials should supply the poor with raw materials had appeared in a statute of 1576 to supplement Henry VIII's Beggars Act (no. 74 I). The present statute was re-enacted in 1601 with extension of the tax-paying group and other minor changes. Later poor laws normally cite the revised act.

selves without lawful cause as aforesaid from such monthly meeting for the purpose aforesaid, or being negligent in their office or in the execution of the orders aforesaid, being made by and with the assent of the said justices of peace, to forfeit for every such default 20s.

And be it also enacted that, if the said justices of peace do perceive that the inhabitants of any parish are not able to levy among themselves sufficient sums of money for the purposes aforesaid . . . , the said justices shall and may tax, rate, and assess as aforesaid any other [persons] of other parishes, or out of any parish within the hundred where the said parish is . . . , [and] pay such sum and sums of money to the churchwardens and overseers of the said poor parish for the said purposes as the said justices shall think fit, according to the intent of this law. And if the said hundred shall not be thought to the said justices able and fit to relieve the said several parishes not able to provide for themselves as aforesaid, then the justices of peace at their general quarter sessions, or the greater number of them, shall rate and assess as aforesaid . . . other parishes . . . , as in their discretion shall seem fit. . . .

And to the intent that necessary places of habitation may more conveniently be provided for such poor impotent people, be it enacted by the authority aforesaid that it shall and may be lawful for the said churchwardens and overseers, or the greater part of them, by the leave of the lord or lords of the manor whereof any waste or common within their parish is or shall be parcel . . . , to erect, build, and set up . . . in such waste or common, at the general charges of the parish or otherwise of the hundred or county as aforesaid . . . , convenient houses of dwelling for the said impotent poor; and also to place inmates or more families than one in one cottage or house. . . .

And be it further hereby enacted that the mayors, bailiffs, or other head officers of every corporate town within this realm, being justice or justices of peace, shall have the same authority by virtue of this act within the limits and precincts of their corporations, as well out of sessions as at their sessions, as is herein limited, prescribed, and appointed to any of the justices of peace in the county for all the uses and purposes in this act prescribed, and no other justice of peace to enter or meddle there. . . .

And forasmuch as all begging is forbidden by this present act, be it further enacted by the authority aforesaid that the justices of peace of every county or place corporate, or the more part of them, in their general sessions to be holden next after the end of this session of parliament, or in default thereof at the quarter sessions to be holden about the feast of Easter next, shall rate every parish to such a weekly sum of money as they shall think convenient; so as no parish be rated above the sum of sixpence nor under the sum of an halfpenny weekly to be paid, and so as the total sum of such taxation of the parishes in every county amount not above the rate of twopence for every parish in the said county. Which sums so taxed shall be yearly assessed by the agreement of the parishioners within themselves, or in default thereof by the churchwardens and constables of the same parish or the more part of them, or in default of their agreement by the order of such justice or justices of peace as shall dwell in the same parish or, if none be there dwelling, in the parts next adjoining. . . .

Ibid., IV, 896 f.: 39 Elizabeth, c. 3.

82. PROCEEDINGS IN PARLIAMENT (1559-1601)

(A) OPENING OF PARLIAMENT (1559)[1]

[25 January.] The knights, citizens, and burgesses of the house of commons remained sitting in their own house till notice was brought them . . . that her majesty, the lords spiritual and temporal, and the residue were set in the upper house expecting their repair thither. Whereupon they went up immediately unto the said house and . . . Sir Nicholas Bacon, lord keeper . . . , went and stood behind the cloth of estate on the right hand and there spake as followeth, *viz.*: "My lords and masters all, the queen's most excellent majesty, our natural and most gracious sovereign lady, having as you know summoned hither her high court of parliament, hath commanded me to open and declare the chief causes and considerations that moved her highness thereunto. . . . The immediate cause of this summons and assembly be consultations, advice, and contentation. For although divers things that are to be done here in parliament might by means be reformed without parliament, yet the queen's majesty . . . , reposing herself not a little in your fidelities, wisdoms, and discretions, meaneth not at this time to make any resolutions in any matter of weight before it shall be by you sufficiently and fully debated, examined, and considered. Now the matters and causes whereupon you are to consult are chiefly and principally three points. Of those the first is of well-making of laws, for the according and uniting of these people of the realm into an uniform order of religion, to the honour and glory of God, the establishing of the Church, and tranquillity of the realm. The second [is] for the reforming and removing of all enormities and mischiefs that might hurt or hinder the civil orders and policies of this realm. The third and last is advisedly and deeply to weigh and consider the estate and condition of this realm and the losses and decays that have happened of late to the imperial crown thereof; and therefore to advise the best remedies to supply and relieve the same. . . ."

Whereupon, the knights, citizens, and burgesses, departing to their own house, did there take their several places; and, most remaining

---

[1] The following extracts are taken from the journals of the two houses as edited by Sir Simonds D'Ewes. For the sake of preserving the chronological order, a section from the commons' journal is here inserted between two sections of the lords' journal.

82. PROCEEDINGS IN PARLIAMENT

silent or speaking very submissively, Mr. Treasurer of the queen's house, standing up uncovered, did first put the house in remembrance of the lord keeper's late speech, and of his declaration of her majesty's pleasure, that they should choose a speaker. And therefore, in humble obedience to her majesty's said pleasure, seeing others remain silent, he thought it his duty to take that occasion to commend to their choice Sir Thomas Gargrave, knight, one of the honourable council in the north parts, a worthy member of the house, and learned in the laws of this realm; by which commendations of his, of the aforesaid worthy member of the house to their consideration, he said he did not intend to debar any other there present from uttering their free opinions and nominating any other whom they thought to be more fitting; and therefore desired them to make known their opinions. Who thereupon did with one consent and voice allow and approve of Mr. Treasurer's nomination, and elected the said Sir Thomas Gargrave to be the prolocutor or speaker of the said house.

The said Sir Thomas Gargrave, being thus elected speaker, after a good pause made, stood up uncovered; and, having in all humility disabled himself, as being unfurnished with that experience and other qualities which were required for the undertaking and undergoing of so great a charge, did conclude with an humble request to the house, to proceed to the new election of some other more able and worthy member amongst them. But, the house still calling upon him to take his place of Mr. Speaker, the before-mentioned Mr. Treasurer and Mr. Comptroller of her majesty's household . . . did rise from their places and, going unto the said Sir Thomas Gargrave unto the place where he sat, did each of them take him, one by the right arm and the other by the left, and led him to the chair at the upper end of the house of commons, and there placed him. Where having sat a while covered, he arose and so, standing bare-headed, he returned his humble thanks unto the whole house for their good opinion of him, promising his best and uttermost endeavour for the faithful discharge of that weighty place to which they had elected him.

[28 January.] The knights, citizens, burgesses, and barons of the house of commons, having notice about one of the clock in the afternoon . . . that her majesty, the lord keeper, and divers lords spiritual and temporal were set in the upper house expecting their attendance, they repaired immediately thither with Sir Thomas Gargrave, knight, their speaker elect. . . . The said Sir Thomas Gargrave was led up to the rail or bar at the lower end of the said house . . . , where, after three reverences made to her majesty, he modestly and submissively excused himself as being unable to undergo the many and great difficulties of that place to which . . . he had been chosen. . . . But, notwithstanding all these reasons and excuses according to the usual form . . . , Sir Nicholas Bacon . . . , by her majesty's commandment . . . , assured him of the queen's acceptance and admission of him. . . .

Upon which speech of the lord keeper's, Sir Thomas Gargrave humbly submitting himself to the undergoing of the charge . . . , made a discreet and submissive answer. . . . Then he proceeded to many hearty prayers and feeling expressions of the good success of the parliament. . . . And lastly he came, according to the usual form, first to desire liberty of access for the house of commons to the queen's majesty's presence upon all urgent and necessary occasions. Secondly . . . , if in anything himself should mistake or misreport or over-slip that which should be committed unto him to declare, that it might, without prejudice to the house, be better declared, and that his unwilling miscarriage therein might be pardoned. Thirdly, that they might have liberty and freedom of speech in whatsoever they treated of, or had occasion to propound and debate in the house. The fourth and last, that all the members of the house, with their servants and necessary attendants, might be exempted from all manner of arrests and suits during the continuance of the parliament and the usual space, both before the beginning and after the ending thereof, as in former times hath always been accustomed. . . .

To which speech of the said speaker the lord keeper, without any long pausing, replied again in manner and form following: . . . "To these petitions the queen's majesty hath commanded me to say unto you that her highness is right well contented to grant them unto you, as largely, as amply, and as liberally as ever they were granted by any her noble progenitors; and to confirm the same with as great an authority. Marry, with these conditions and cautions: first, that your access be void of importunity, and for matters needful, and in time convenient; for the second, that your diligence and carefulness be such, Mr. Speaker, that the defaults in that part be as rare as may be, whereof her majesty doubteth little; for the third, which is for liberty of speech, therewith her highness is right well contented, but so as they be neither unmindful or uncareful of their duties, reverence, and obedience to their sovereign; for the last, great heed would be taken that no evil-disposed person seek of purpose that privilege for the only defrauding of his creditors and for the maintenance of injuries and wrongs. These admonitions being well remembered, her majesty thinketh all the said liberties and privileges well granted. . . ."

D'Ewes, Journal, pp. 11-40.

(B) PROCEDURE ON A BILL (1559)

[3 February.] . . . The clerk of the said house, having read the title and the bill aforesaid, standing, kissing his hand, delivered the same, with a breviate containing the substance of the bill annexed unto it, unto the speaker; who thereupon, standing up uncovered and reading both the title and the breviate, said, "This is the second reading." And then, having paused a while, and . . . none speaking against the bill, he put the question for the committing thereof, as followeth, *viz.*: "As many as do think fit this bill should be committed say Yea"; and after the affirmative voice given, "As many as shall think the contrary say No." And then . . . the speaker, judging that the affirmative voice was the greatest, did put the house in mind to name committees. And thereupon every one of the house that listed did name such other members of the same, to be of the committee, as they thought fit. . . . And when a convenient number of the committees named were set down by the clerk, then did the speaker move the house to name the time and place when and where they should meet, which the clerk did also doubtless then take a note of, and did also (silence being made in the house) read out of that book or paper (in which he entered them) the committees' names, with the time and place of their meeting. . . .

[7 February.] The clerk of the house, standing up, read the title and the bill aforesaid and, kissing his hand, delivered the same unto the speaker. Who, standing up uncovered, read again the title of the said bill and opened shortly the effects thereof, and then said, "This is the third reading of this bill"; and told them further that with their favour he would now put it to the question for the passing, but paused a while to see if any member of the house would speak unto it. . . . And whether any of the said house spake unto the said bill or not doth not appear. But the speaker, holding the bill in his hand, made the question for the passing of it in this sort, *viz.*: "As many as are of the mind that the bill shall pass say Yea." Which being answered accordingly by the house, or the greatest part of them, the bill passed; and so he delivered it again unto the clerk who, because the bill was originally begun and first passed in the house of commons, wrote within the said bill, on top of it towards the right hand, these words, *viz.*: *Soit baillé aux seigneurs*.[2]

Ibid., pp. 44 f.

(C) SPEECH OF THE LORD KEEPER ON THE ADMINISTRATION OF JUSTICE (1559)

. . . Is it not great fondness, trow you, for men to use their endeavours to make good laws to govern men's doings and to weed out those that be evil in the commonwealth, and thereupon to bind them fair in books, and to lay them up without seeing to the execution of those laws? Yes, surely. Wherefore ye see that, as there hath been used by you great wisdom and discretion in devising of some, so it is very necessary that like diligence and pains be taken by you and others to see the good execution of all. The effect of which charge consisteth principally in three points: the first in conservation of the queen's peace; the second in administration of justice between subject and subject; and the third in the observation of one uniform order in religion according to the laws now established.

For the first, ye are to foresee all manner of frays, forces, riots, and routs, and the discovering and repealing in time of all manner of

---

[2] Let it be delivered to the lords.

conspiracies, confederacies, and conventicles. And in this part also you are to provide for the swift and speedy appeasing of all manner of tumults, stirs, and uproars, if any happen; and for the diligent searching out and severe punishment of all manner of felonies, burglaries, and all other like enormities—matters, as you know, against the queen's majesty's peace, crown, and dignity. For the well-doing whereof two things are chiefly to be eschewed: the one is slothfulness; the other is uncarefulness. For how can justice banish these enormities, where her ministers be so slothful that they will never creep out of their doors to any courts, sessions, or assizes for the due administration thereof, except they be drawn thereunto with some matters of their own; nor cannot endure to have their ears troubled with the hearing of controversies of their neighbours, for the good appeasing of the same? Or how can the uncareful man that maketh no account of any of the common causes of his country, but respecteth only his private matters and commodities, become a just and diligent searcher out, follower, and corrector of felonies, murders, and suchlike common enemies to the commonwealth? And yet true it is that such careless and slothful men do daily colour and cloak these their faults with the title of quietness. . . .

For the second, you are to provide that all embracers, maintainers, and champerties,[3] which be utter enemies to the due execution of justice between subject and subject, be neither committed by any of you nor, as near as you can, be suffered to be committed by any other—a very behoveful matter to be both carefully and earnestly looked unto, as the root and seed of all justice, and especially if any of these faults light upon any person that hath authority or rule in the country or hath any office of justice to execute among the people. Is it not, trow you, a monstrous disguising to have a justicer a maintainer; to have him, that should by his oath and duty set forth justice and right, against his oath and duty to offer injury and wrong; to have him, that is specially chosen amongst a number by the prince to appease all brablings and controversies, to be a sower and maintainer of strife and sedition, amongst them seeking his reputation and opinion by leading and swaying of juries according to his will—acquitting some for gain, indicting others for malice; bearing with him as his servant, overthrowing the other as his enemy; procuring all questmongers to be of his livery, or otherwise in his danger, that his winks, frowning, and countenance may direct all inquests? Surely, surely, it is true that these be they that be subverters and perverters of all laws and orders; yea, that make daily the laws, that of their own nature be good, to become instruments of mischief. These indeed be they of whom such examples would be made and the founders and maintainers of all enormities. And these be those, whom if you can-

---

[3] A champertor was a man who supported a litigant for a share in the proceeds of the suit.

82. PROCEEDINGS IN PARLIAMENT

not reform for their greatness, yet ought you to complain of their villainies. And thus much for the due administration of justice. . . .

Ibid., pp. 33 f.

(D) A DAY'S BUSINESS IN THE COMMONS (1563)

[8 March.] On Monday, the 8th day of March, three bills had each of them one reading; of which the first, being the bill that St. Katherine's Church shall be a parish church, and the second, for the repairing and mending of highways, were read the third time and passed the house, and were sent up to the lords by Mr. Comptroller. Mr. Attorney brought from the lords three bills, of which one was the bill for denizens' children. The bill also against the unlawful taking of fish, deer, or hawks was read the third time and passed. *Post Meridiem.* In the afternoon eight bills had each of them one reading; of which one was the bill for the subsidy of the clergy. Richard Parrott, gentleman, burgess for Sandwich, for his sickness was licensed to be absent.

Ibid., p. 87.

(E) PROCEDURE ON A REQUEST FOR SUPPLY (1566)

[17 October.] . . . Sir Edward Rogers, knight, comptroller of her majesty's household, moved the house to have consideration of the queen's majesty's late great and extraordinary expenses, to proportion out some supply accordingly. And thereupon Sir William Cecil, knight, her highness' principal secretary, made an excellent declaration of the queen's great charges in defending New Haven in France, in repairing and increasing the navy and munition, her charges also against John O'Neill in Ireland. And immediately thereupon all the privy council being members of this house, the master of the rolls, and forty others of the house, whose names are omitted through the negligence of the clerk, were nominated and appointed to consider of the rate and payment of some supply and aid to be given to her majesty, and ordered to meet to-morrow in the afternoon, in the star chamber.

Ibid., p. 124.

(F) DEBATE ON FREEDOM OF SPEECH (1566)[4]

[9 November.] . . . Sir Francis Knolles, knight, her majesty's vice-chamberlain, declared the queen's majesty's express commands to this house that they should no further proceed in their suit, but to satisfy themselves with her highness' promise of marriage. After whom Mr. Secretary Cecil and Mr. Comptroller severally rehearsed the like matter. . . .

[11 November.] . . . Paul Wentworth, a burgess of the house,

---
[4] See J. E. Neale, "The Commons' Privilege of Free Speech in Parliament," in *Tudor Studies,* pp. 257 f.

by way of motion desired to know whether the queen's command and inhibition, that they should no longer dispute of the matter of succession . . . , were not against the liberties and privileges of the said house. And thereupon arose divers arguments, which continued from nine of the clock in the morning till two of the clock in the afternoon. But then, because the time was far spent, all further debate and reasoning was deferred until the next morning. . . .

[12 November.] Mr. Speaker, being sent for to attend upon the queen's majesty at the court, about nine of the clock, sent word to the house where he was, requiring the house to have patience; and at his coming, after ten of the clock, began to show that he had received a special command from her highness to this house, notwithstanding her first commandment, that there should not be further talk of that matter in the house (touching the declaration of a successor, in case that her majesty should die without issue), and if any person thought himself not satisfied, but had further reasons, let him come before the privy council and there show them. . . .

[25 November.] . . . Mr. Speaker, coming from the queen's majesty, declared her highness' pleasure to be that, for her good will to the house, she did revoke her two former commandments, requiring the house no further to proceed at this time in the matter. Which revocation was taken of all the house most joyfully, with most hearty prayer and thanks for the same. . . .

Ibid., pp. 128-30.

(G) SPEECH OF THE QUEEN (1567)

[2 April.] . . . Then the queen, standing up, said (after she had given her royal assent unto nineteen public acts, and thirteen private): "My lords and others the commons of this assembly, although the lord keeper hath, according to order, very well answered in my name, yet as a periphrasis I have a few words further to speak unto you, notwithstanding I have not been used nor love to do it in such open assemblies. Yet now, not to the end to amend his talk, but remembering that commonly princes' own words be better printed in the hearers' memory than those spoken by her command, I mean to say thus much unto you. I have in this assembly found so much dissimulation, where I always professed plainness, that I marvel thereat—yea, two faces under one hood (and the body rotten) being covered with two vizors, succession and liberty, which they determined must be either presently granted, denied, or deferred. In granting whereof, they had their desires; and denying or deferring thereof (those things being so plaudable as indeed to all men they are) they thought to work me that mischief which never foreign enemy could bring to pass, which is the hatred of my commons. But, alas, they began to pierce the vessel before the wine was fined; and began a thing, not foreseeing the end, how by this means I have seen my well-willers from mine enemies, and can, as me seemeth, very well divide the house into four: first, the broachers and workers thereof, who are in the greatest fault; secondly, the speakers, who by eloquent tales persuaded others, are in the next degree; thirdly, the agreers, who, being so light of credit that the eloquence of the tales so overcame them, that they gave more credit thereunto than unto their own wits; and lastly, those that sat still mute and meddled not therewith, but rather wondered, disallowing the matter, who in my opinion are most to be excused.

"But do you think that either I am unmindful of your surety by succession, wherein is all my care, considering I know myself to be mortal? No, I warrant you. Or that I went about to break your liberties? No, it was never in my meaning; but to stay you before you fell into the ditch. For all things have their time. And although perhaps you may have after me one better learned or wiser; yet, I assure you, none more careful over you. And therefore henceforth, whether I live to see the like assembly or no, or whoever it be, yet beware however you prove your prince's patience, as you have now done mine. And now to conclude, all this notwithstanding (not meaning to make a Lent of Christmas), the most part of you may assure yourselves that you depart in your prince's grace." . . .

Ibid., pp. 116 f.

(H) DEBATE ON FREEDOM OF SPEECH (1571)

[20 April.] . . . Mr. Wentworth, very orderly, in many words remembered the speech of Sir Humphrey Gilbert delivered some days before. He proved his speech (without naming him) to be an injury to the house; he noted his disposition to flatter and fawn on the prince, comparing him to the chameleon, which can change himself into all colours saving white. "Even so," said he, "this reporter can change himself to all fashions but honesty." He showed further the great wrong done to one of the house by a misreport made to the queen (meaning Mr. Bell); he showed his speech to tend to no other end than to inculcate fear into those which should be free. He requested care for the credit of the house and for the maintenance of free speech (the only means of ordinary proceedings), and to preserve the liberties of the house, to reprove liars, inveighing greatly out of the Scriptures and otherwise against liars—as this of David, "Thou, O Lord, shalt destroy liars," etc.

Mr. Treasurer signified his desire to have all things well, saying he could not enter into judgment of any; but he said it was convenient ill speeches should be avoided, and the good meaning of all men to be taken, without wresting or misreporting, and the meaning of all men to be showed in good sort without unseemly words.

Mr. Speaker endeavoured an agreement and unity in the house, making signification that the queen's majesty had in plain words declared unto him that she had good intelligence of the orderly proceeding among us; whereof she had as good liking as ever she had of any parliament since she came unto the crown, and wished we should give her no other cause than to continue the same; and added further her majesty's pleasure to be to take order for licences, wherein she had been careful, and more careful would be.

Mr. Carleton, with a very good zeal and orderly show of obedience, made signification how that a member of the house was detained from them (meaning Mr. Strickland), by whose commandment or for what cause he knew not. But forasmuch as he was not now a private man, but to supply the room, person, and place of a multitude specially chosen and therefore sent, he thought that neither in regard of the country, which was not to be wronged, nor for the liberty of the house, which was not to be infringed, we should permit him to be detained from us; but, whatsoever the intendment of this offence might be, that he should be sent for to the bar of that house, there to be heard, and there to answer.

Mr. Treasurer in some case gave advertisement to be wary in our proceedings, and neither to venture further than our assured warrant might stretch nor to hazard our good opinion with her majesty on any doubtful cause. Withal, he wished us not to think worse than there was cause. "For the man," quoth he, "that is meant is neither detained nor misused; but on considerations is required to expect the queen's pleasure upon certain special points"—wherein he said he durst to assure that the man should neither have cause to dislike or complain, since so much favour was meant unto him as he reasonably could wish. He further said that he was in no sort stayed for any word or speech by him in that place offered, but for the exhibiting of a bill into the house against the prerogative of the queen; which was not to be tolerated. Nevertheless, the construction of him was rather to have erred in his zeal and bill offered than maliciously to have meant anything contrary to the dignity royal. And lastly, he concluded that oft it had been seen that speeches have been examined and considered of. . . .

Ibid., p. 175.

(I) INTERVENTION BY THE QUEEN (1572)

[22 May.] . . . Upon declaration made unto this house by Mr. Speaker from the queen's majesty, that her highness' pleasure is that from henceforth no bills concerning religion shall be preferred or received into this house, unless the same should be first considered and liked by the clergy; and further, that her majesty's pleasure is to see the two last bills read in this house touching rites and ceremonies: it is ordered by the house that the same bills shall be delivered unto her majesty by all the privy council that are of this house, Mr. Heneage, and Mr. Doctor Wilson, master of the requests, or by any four of them. . . .

[23 May.] Mr. Treasurer reported to the house the delivery of the two bills of rites and ceremonies to her majesty, together with the humble request of this house, most humbly to beseech her highness not to conceive ill opinion of this house if it so were that her majesty should not like well of the said bills, or of the parties that preferred them; and declared further that her majesty seemed utterly to mislike of the first bill, and of him that brought the same into the house, and that her highness' express will and pleasure was that no preacher or minister should be impeached or indicted, or otherwise molested or troubled, as the preamble of the said bill did purport; adding these comfortable words farther, that her majesty, as defender of the faith, will aid and maintain all good Protestants to the discouraging of all Papists. . . .

Ibid., p. 213 f.

(J) THE CASE OF PETER WENTWORTH (1576)[5]

[8 February.] . . . Peter Wentworth, esquire, one of the burgesses for the borough of Tregony in the county of Cornwall, was, for unreverent and undutiful words uttered by him in this house of our sovereign lady the queen's majesty, sequestered, that the house might proceed to conference and consideration of his said speech [which in part follows] :—

"Mr. Speaker, I find written in a little volume these words in effect: 'Sweet is the name of liberty, but the thing itself a value beyond all inestimable treasure.' So much the more it behooveth us to take care lest we, contenting ourselves with the sweetness of the name, lose and forgo the thing, being of greatest value that can come unto this noble realm. The inestimable treasure is the use of it in this house. . . .

"I was never of parliament but the last, and the last session [of this parliament]; at both which times I saw the liberty of free speech, the which is the only salve to heal all the sores of this commonwealth, so much and so many ways infringed, and so many abuses offered to this honourable council, as hath much grieved me even of very conscience and love to my prince and state. Wherefore, to avoid the like, I do think it expedient to open the commodities that grow to the prince and whole state by free speech used in this place—at the least so much as my simple wit can gather of it, the which is very little in respect of that that wise heads can say therein; and so it is of the more force.

"First, all matters that concern God's honour through free speech, shall be propagated here and set forward, and all things that do hinder it removed, repulsed, and taken away.

"Next, there is nothing commodious, profitable, or any way beneficial for the prince or state, but faithful and loving subjects will offer it in this place.

"Thirdly, all things discommodious, perilous, or hurtful to the

---

[5] See J. E. Neale, "Peter Wentworth," in the *English Historical Review*, XXXIX, 36 f., 175 f.

prince or state shall be prevented—even so much as seemeth good to our merciful God to put into our minds, the which no doubt shall be sufficient if we do earnestly call upon Him and fear Him; for Solomon saith, 'The fear of God is the beginning of wisdom.' Wisdom, saith he, breatheth life into her children, receiveth them that seek her, and will go beside them in the way of righteousness; so that our minds shall be directed to all good, needful, and necessary things, if we call upon God with faithful hearts.

"Fourthly, if the envious do offer anything hurtful or perilous to the prince or state in this place, what incommodity doth grow thereby? Verily I think none. Nay, will you have me to say my simple opinion therein, much good cometh thereof. How forsooth? For by the darkness of the night the brightness of the sun showeth more excellent and clear. And how can truth appear and conquer until falsehood and all subtleties that should shadow and darken it be found out? For it is offered in this place a piece of fine needlework unto them that are most skilful therein; for there cannot be a false stitch (God aiding us) but will be found out.

"Fifthly, this good cometh thereof: a wicked purpose may the easier be prevented when it is known.

"Sixthly, an evil man can do the less harm when it is known.

"Seventhly, sometime it happeneth that a good man will in this place (for argument sake) prefer an evil cause, both for that he would have a doubtful truth to be opened and manifested, and also the evil prevented; so that to this point I conclude that in this house, which is termed a place of free speech, there is nothing so necessary for the preservation of the prince and state as free speech. And without, it is a scorn and mockery to call it a parliament house; for in truth it is none, but a very school of flattery and dissimulation, and so a fit place to serve the devil and his angels in, and not to glorify God and benefit the commonwealth. . . .

"Now to the impediments thereof. . . . Amongst other, Mr. Speaker, two things do great hurt in this place, of the which I do mean to speak. The one is a rumour which runneth about the house, and this it is: 'Take heed what you do; the queen's majesty liketh not such a matter; whosoever prefereth it, she will be offended with him'—(or the contrary) 'Her majesty liketh of such a matter; whosoever speaketh against it she will be much offended with him.' The other: sometimes a message is brought into the house either of commanding or inhibiting, very injurious to the freedom of speech and consultation. I would to God, Mr. Speaker, that these two were buried in hell—I mean rumours and messages; for wicked undoubtedly they are. The reason is the devil was the first author of them, from whom proceedeth nothing but wickedness. Now I will set down reasons to prove them wicked. . . .

"The queen's majesty is the head of the law and must of necessity maintain the law; for by the law her majesty is made justly our queen and by it she is most chiefly maintained. Hereunto agreeth the most excellent words of Bracton, who saith, 'The king hath no peer nor equal in his kingdom.' He hath no equal, for otherwise he might lose his authority of commanding, sithence that an equal hath no rule of commandment over his equal. The king ought not to be under man, but under God and under the law, because the law maketh him a king. Let the king therefore attribute that to the law which the law attributeth unto him: that is, dominion and power; for he is not a king in whom will and not the law doth rule. And therefore he ought to be under the law. . . ."

Upon this speech, the house, out of a reverend regard of her majesty's honour, stopped his further proceeding before he had fully finished his speech. . . . Mr. Wentworth being sequestered the house as aforesaid for his said speech, it was agreed and ordered by the house upon the question, after sundry motions and disputations had therein, that he should presently be committed to the serjeant's ward as prisoner and, so remaining, should be examined upon his said speech, for the extenuating of his fault therein, by all the privy council being of this house, the master of the requests, the captain of the guard, Mr. Treasurer of the Chamber, the master of the jewelhouse, the master of the wardrobe, Mr. Lieutenant of the Tower, Sir Thomas Scott, Sir Rowland Hayward, Mr. Attorney of the Duchy, Mr. Henry Knolles the elder, Mr. Sampoole, Mr. Randall, Mr. Birched, Mr. Marsh—who were appointed to meet this afternoon between two and three of the clock at the star chamber, and to make report at this house to-morrow next. . . .

Committee . . . : "Here you have uttered certain rumours of the queen's majesty. Where and of whom heard you them?"

Wentworth: "If your honours ask me as councillors to her majesty, you shall pardon me: I will make you no answer. I will do no such injury to the place from whence I came; for I am now no private person. I am a public, and a councillor to the whole state in that place where it is lawful for me to speak my mind freely, and not for you as councillors to call me to account for anything that I do speak in the house. And therefore, if you ask me as councillors to her majesty, you shall pardon me: I will make no answer. But if you ask me as committees from the house, I will make you the best answer I can."

Committee: "We ask you as committees from the house."

Wentworth: "I will then answer you. . . ."

[9 February.] This day Mr. Treasurer, in the name of all the committees yesterday appointed for the examination of Peter Wentworth, burgess for Tregony, declared that all the said committees did meet yesterday in the afternoon in the star chamber according to their commission; and there, examining the said Peter Wentworth touching the violent and wicked words yesterday pronounced by him in this house touching the queen's majesty, made a collection of the same words, which words, so collected, the said Peter Wentworth did acknowledge and confess. And then did the said Mr.

Treasurer read unto the house the said note of collection. Which being read, he declared further that the said Peter Wentworth, being examined what he could say for the extenuating of his said fault and offence, could neither say anything at all to that purpose, neither yet did charge any other person as author of his said speech; but did take all the burden thereof unto himself. And so the said Mr. Treasurer thereupon moved for his punishment and imprisonment in the Tower as the house should think good and consider of. Whereupon, after sundry disputations and speeches, it was ordered upon the question that the said Peter Wentworth should be committed close prisoner to the Tower for his said offence, there to remain until such time as this house should have further consideration of him. And thereupon, immediately, the said Peter Wentworth, being brought to the bar by the serjeant, received his said judgment accordingly by the mouth of Mr. Speaker in form above-recited. And so Mr. Lieutenant of the Tower was presently charged with the custody of the said Peter Wentworth. But the said Peter Wentworth was shortly, by the queen's special favour, restored again to his liberty and place in the house. . . .

Ibid., pp. 236-44.

(K) THE CASE OF ARTHUR HALL (1581)[6]

[4 February.] . . . Upon a motion made to this house by Mr. Norton, in which he declared that some person of late had caused a book to be set forth in print (not only greatly reproachful against some particular good members of this house of great credit, but also very much slanderous and derogatory to the general authority, power, and state of this house, and prejudicial to the validity of the proceedings of the same in making and establishing of laws: charging this house with drunkenness, as accompanied in their councils with Bacchus; and then also with choler, as those which had never failed to Anticyra; and the proceedings of this house to be *opera tenebrarum*) and further that, by the circumstance of the residue of the discourse of the said book, he conjectured the same to be done and procured by Mr. Arthur Hall, one of this house; and so prayed thereupon the said Mr. Hall might be called by this house to answer, and the matter further to be duly examined as the weight thereof, in due consideration of the gravity and wisdom of this house and of the authority, state, and liberty of the same, requireth: it is resolved that the said Mr. Hall be forthwith sent for by the serjeant-at-arms attending upon this house, to make his appearance here in that behalf accordingly.

And then immediately Mr. Secretary Wilson did thereupon signify unto this house that the said Mr. Hall had, upon his examination therein before the lords of the council, heretofore confessed in the hearing of the said Mr. Secretary that he did cause the said

---

[6] See H. Wright, *Arthur Hall*.

82. PROCEEDINGS IN PARLIAMENT

book to be printed indeed. Upon relation whereof, and after some speech then also uttered unto this house by Mr. Chancellor of the Exchequer, of the dangerous and lewd contents of the book, the serjeant was forthwith, by order of this house, sent to apprehend the said Arthur Hall, and presently assisted for that purpose with Sir Thomas Scott and Sir Thomas Browne, by the appointment of this house. . . .

[14 February.] Mr. Vice-Chamberlain, for himself and the residue of the committees appointed to examine Mr. Hall, the printer, the scrivener, and all other persons privy to the setting forth and publishing of the book, declared that they had charged the said Mr. Hall with contempt against this house the last session. . . . Unto all which things . . . the said Mr. Hall could make no reasonable answer or denial. . . .

Mr. Hall was brought to the bar, where, after some reverence done by him (though not yet in such humble and lowly wise as the state of one in that place to be charged and accused requireth), whereof being admonished by Mr. Speaker and further by him charged with sundry of the said parts collected out of the said book, he submitted himself to the house, refusing to make any answer or defence at all in the matter; but, acknowledging his error, prayed pardon of the whole house with all his heart; and, that done, was sequestered.

After which, upon sundry motions and arguments had touching the quality and nature of his faults, and of some proportionable forms of punishment for the same (as imprisonment, fine, banishment from the fellowship of this house, and an utter condemnation and retraction of the said book), it was upon the question resolved by the whole house, without any one negative voice, that he should be committed to prison. And upon another question [it was] likewise resolved that he should be committed to the prison of the Tower, as the prison proper to this house. And upon another question it was in like manner resolved that he should remain in the said prison of the Tower by the space of six months, and so much longer as until himself should willingly make a retractation of the said book to the satisfaction of this house, or of such order as this house shall take for the same during the continuance of this present parliament. And upon another question it was also in like manner resolved that a fine should be assessed by this house, to the queen's majesty's use, upon the said Mr. Hall for his said offence. And upon another question it was also resolved in like manner that the said fine should be 500m. And upon another question also it was likewise resolved that the said Mr. Hall should presently be severed and cut off from being a member of this house any more during the continuance of this present parliament; and that Mr. Speaker, by authority of this house, should direct a warrant from this house to the clerk of the crown-office in the chancery for awarding of the queen's majesty's writ to the sheriff of the said county of Lincoln, for a new burgess to be returned into this present parliament for the said borough of Grantham in lieu and stead of the said Arthur Hall, so as before disabled any longer to be a member of this house. . . .

Ibid., pp. 291 f.

(L) PETER WENTWORTH'S QUESTIONS ON FREE SPEECH (1587)

On Wednesday, the first day of March, Mr. Wentworth delivered unto Mr. Speaker certain articles which contained questions touching the liberties of the house . . . :—

Whether this council be not a place for any member of the same here assembled, freely and without controlment of any person or danger of laws, by bill or speech to utter any of the griefs of this commonwealth whatsoever touching the service of God, the safety of the prince, and this noble realm. Whether that great honour may be done unto God, and benefit and service unto the prince and state without free speech in this council which may be done with it. Whether there be any council which can make, add to, or diminish from the laws of the realm, but only this council of parliament. Whether it be not against the orders of this council to make any secret or matter of weight, which is here in hand, known to the prince or any other, concerning the high service of God, prince, or state, without the consent of the house. Whether the speaker or any other may interrupt any member of this council in his speech used in this house, tending to any of the forenamed high services. Whether the speaker may rise when he will, any matter being propounded, without consent of the house or not. Whether the speaker may overrule the house in any matter or cause there in question, or whether he is to be ruled or overruled in any matter or not. Whether the prince and state can continue, stand, and be maintained without this council of parliament, not altering the government of the state.

At the end, lastly, of the said speech and questions is set down this short note or memorial ensuing; by which it may be perceived both what Serjeant Puckering, the speaker, did with the said questions after he had received them, and what became also of this business. . . . These questions Mr. Puckering pocketed up and showed Sir Thomas Heneage, who so handled the matter that Mr. Wentworth went to the Tower and the questions [were] not at all moved. . . .

Ibid., p. 411.

(M) SPEECH OF THE LORD KEEPER ON THE PRIVILEGES OF THE COMMONS (1593)

. . . Her gracious majesty is well pleased to grant them so far as they be grantable. She saith there be two things in a man most behoveful if they be well used, and most deadly if they be ill used: wit and tongue, they are those. They be most happy possessions and needful helps, and all as they be placed. Having therefore especial care that that may never hurt you, which she by her grant doth yield you, she wills you take good heed in what sort she permits it. She would be sorry that folly past should by new redouble the faults, and chargeth you, Mr. Speaker, if any shall deliver to you any bill that passeth the reach of a subject's brain to mention, that same you receive not, but with purpose to show it where it best becometh you. Next, if any speech undecent or matter unfit for that place be used, remember them of this lesson: your petitions . . . must be ruled, and that thus her majesty granteth you liberal but not licentious speech; liberty therefore, but with due limitation. For even as there can be no good consultation where all freedom of advice is barred, so will there be no good conclusion where every man speak what he listeth, without fit observation of persons, matters, times, places, and other needful circumstances. It shall be meet, therefore, that each man of you contain his speech within the bounds of loyalty and good discretion, being assured that, as the contrary is punishable in all men, so most of all in them that take upon them to be counsellors and procurators of the commonwealth. For liberty of speech her majesty commandeth me to tell you that, to say yea or no to bills, God forbid that any man should be restrained or afraid to answer according to his best liking, with some short declaration of his reason therein, and therein to have a free voice, which is the very true liberty of the house; not, as some suppose, to speak there of all causes as him listeth, and to frame a form of religion or a state of government as to their idle brains shall seem meetest. She saith no king fit for his state will suffer such absurdities; and, though she hopeth no man here longeth so much for his ruin as that he mindeth to make such a peril to his own safety, yet, that you may better follow what she wisheth, she makes of her goodness you the partakers of her intent and meaning.

English Historical Review, XXXI, 136.

(N) SPEECH OF SERJEANT HEYLE (1601)

[9 November.] . . . Then Serjeant Heyle stood up and made a motion, saying: "Mr. Speaker, I marvel much that the house will stand upon granting of a subsidy, or the time of payment, when all we have is her majesty's; and she may lawfully at her pleasure take it from us. Yea, she hath as much right to all our lands and goods as to any revenue of her crown." At which all the house hemmed and laughed and talked. "Well," quoth Serjeant Heyle, "all your hemming shall not put me out of countenance." So Mr. Speaker stood up and said, "It is a great disorder that this should be used; for it is the ancient use of every man to be silent when any one speaketh, and he that is speaking should be suffered to deliver his mind without interruption." So the said serjeant proceeded and, when he had spoken a little while, the house hemmed again; and so he sat down. In his latter speech he said he could prove his former position by precedent in the times of Henry III, King John, King Stephen; which was the occasion of their hemming. . . .

D'Ewes, Journal, p. 633.

(O) SPEECHES BY SIR ROBERT CECIL (1601)

[24 November.] . . . Upon some loud confusion in the house touching some private murmur of monopolies, Mr. Secretary Cecil said: "The duty I owe and the zeal to extinguish monopolies makes me to speak now, and to satisfy their opinions that think there shall be no redress of these monopolies. Order is attended with these two handmaids, gravity and zeal; but zeal with discretion. I have been (though unworthy) a member of this house in six or seven parliaments; yet never did I see the house in so great confusion. I believe there never was in any parliament a more tender point handled than the liberty of the subject; that, when any is discussing this point, he should be cried and coughed down—this is more fit for a grammar school than a court of parliament. I have been a councillor of state this twelve years; yet did I never know it subject to construction of levity and disorder. Much more ought we to be regardful in so great and grave an assembly. Why, we have had speeches upon speeches, without either order or discretion. One would have had us proceed by bill and see if the queen would have denied it; another, that the patents should be brought here before us and cancelled—and this were bravely done! Others would have us to proceed by way of petition, which course doubtless is best; but for the first, and especially for the second, it is so ridiculous, that I think we should have as bad success as the devil himself would have wished in so good a cause. Why, if idle courses had been followed, we should have gone forsooth to the queen with a petition to have repealed a patent of monopoly of tobacco pipes (which Mr. Wingfield's note had) and I know not how many conceits. But I wish every man to rest satisfied till the committees have brought in their resolutions according to your commandments." . . .

[25 November.] . . . Mr. Secretary Cecil stood up and said: "I fear we are not secret within ourselves. Then must I needs give you this for a future caution: that whatsoever is subject to public expectation cannot be good, while the parliament matters are ordinary talk in the street. I have heard myself, being in my coach, these words spoken aloud: 'God prosper those that further the overthrow of these monopolies! God send the prerogative touch not our liberty!' I will not wrong any so much as to imagine he was of this assembly. Yet let me give you this note: that the time was never more apt to disorder and make ill interpretation of good meaning. I think those persons would be glad that all sovereignty were converted into popularity. We, being here, are but the popular branch, and our liberty [is] the liberty of the subject. And the world is apt to slander most especially the ministers of government...."

Ibid., pp. 651, 653.

(P) SPEECH OF THE QUEEN (1601)

[30 November.] In the afternoon, about three of the clock, some sevenscore of the house met at the great chamber before the council chamber in Whitehall. At length the queen came into the council chamber where, sitting under the cloth of state at the upper end, the speaker with all the company came in and, after three low reverences made, he spake to this effect.... And, after three low reverences made, he with the rest kneeled down, and her majesty began thus to answer herself, *viz.*: "Mr. Speaker, we have heard your declaration and perceive your care of our state by falling into the consideration of a grateful acknowledgment of such benefits as you have received; and that your coming is to present thanks unto us, which I accept with no less joy than your loves can have desire to offer such a present. I do assure you that there is no prince that loveth his subjects better, or whose love can countervail our love. There is no jewel, be it of never so rich a prize, which I prefer before this jewel; I mean your love. For I do more esteem it than any treasure or riches; for that we know how to prize, but love and thanks I count inestimable. And though God hath raised me high, yet this I count the glory of my crown, that I have reigned with your loves. This makes me that I do not so much rejoice that God hath made me to be a queen, as to be a queen over so thankful a people. Therefore I have cause to wish nothing more than to content the subject, and that is a duty which I owe. Neither do I desire to live longer days than that I may see your prosperity, and that's my only desire. And as I am that person that still, yet under God, hath delivered you, so I trust, by the almighty power of God, that I still shall be His instrument to preserve you from envy, peril, dishonour, shame, tyranny, and oppression; partly by means of your intended helps, which we take very acceptably, because it manifesteth the largeness of your loves and loyalties unto your sovereign. Of myself I must say this: I never was any greedy, scraping grasper, nor a strait fast-holding prince, nor yet a waster. My heart was never set on worldly goods, but only for my subjects' good. What you do bestow on me, I will not hoard it up, but receive it to bestow on you again. Yea, mine own properties I count yours to be expended for your good. Therefore render unto them from me I beseech you, Mr. Speaker, such thanks as you imagine my heart yieldeth, but my tongue cannot express."

Note that all this while they kneeled. Whereupon her majesty said, "Mr. Speaker, I would wish you and the rest to stand up, for I shall yet trouble you with longer speech." So they all stood up and she went on in her speech, saying: ". . . I know the title of a king is a glorious title; but assure yourself that the shining glory of princely authority hath not so dazzled the eyes of our understanding but that we will know and remember that we also are to yield an account of our actions before the Great Judge. To be a king and wear a crown is more glorious to them that see it, than it is pleasure to them that bear it. For myself, I was never so much enticed with the glorious name of a king, or royal authority of a queen, as delighted that God hath made me this instrument to maintain His truth and glory, and to defend this kingdom, as I said, from peril, dishonour, tyranny, and oppression. There will never queen sit in my seat with more zeal to my country, care to my subjects, and that will sooner with willingness yield and venture her life for your good and safety than myself. And though you have had and may have many princes more mighty and wise sitting in this seat, yet you never had or shall have any that will be more careful and loving. . . . And so I commit you all to your best fortunes and further counsels. And I pray you, Mr. Comptroller, Mr. Secretary, and you of my council, that, before these gentlemen depart into their countries, you bring them all to kiss my hand."

Ibid., pp. 659 f.

83. RECORDS CONCERNING THE COUNCIL (1558-1600)

(A) PROCEEDINGS ON A CASE IN LONDON (1558-59)

[3 December.] Where the chief justice of the king's bench did of late make out an attachment against the judge of the admiralty, upon pretence that he had intermeddled in his jurisdiction in a matter depending between one Adam Wyntropp of London and John Combes, a Frenchman: it was this day ordered by my lords of the council, upon the hearing of both the said judges and what either of them could allege for himself, that as well the process awarded out against the said judge of the admiralty as the said matter in controversy between the said Wyntropp and Combes shall be stayed until their lordships, upon consideration of what hath been alleged on both sides for the maintenance of their several jurisdictions, shall take some further order therein; for the better doing whereof they were commanded to bring to my said lords of the council a note in writing of the cases wherein they have or may contend for their said jurisdictions, so as thereupon their lordships may determine some stay and order between them according to equity and justice. The said Wyntropp, being this day brought before my lords, was commanded that he shall not any further proceed in the matter between Combes and him until their lordships shall take further order therein, upon pain of double the sums of the action that is taken against him.

[27 February.] A letter to Alderman Marten, Thomas Hunt, Thomas Huett, William Holland, and Edward Castelin of London, merchants; with a supplication enclosed and exhibited unto the lords

83. COUNCIL RECORDS

of the council containing matter of variance of long depending between one Adam Wyntropp and one John Combes, Frenchman: by which letter the said alderman and the others are authorized to call the parties before them from time to time and to hear and determine all matters of controversy between them, and to take such final order in the same as may both be agreeable to equity and the good quiet also of the parties hereafter, wherein they be required to travail and take some pains and to certify thereupon what they shall have done in the premises.

Acts of the Privy Council, N. S., VII, 12, 62.

(B) COMMITTEES OF THE COUNCIL (1558)

[23 December.] For care of the north parts towards Scotland and Berwick: the earl of Arundel, the earl of Shrewsbury, the earl of Bedford, the earl of Pembroke, the lord admiral, Sir Ambrose Cave. To survey the office of the treasurer of the chamber and to assign order of payment: the lord chamberlain, Mr. Comptroller, Mr. Secretary, Sir Walter Mildmay. For Portsmouth and the Isle of Wight: marquess of Winchester, the earl of Arundel, the earl of Pembroke, the lord admiral, the captain of Portsmouth, Richard Wurseley, Peter Smith. For consideration of all things necessary for the parliaments: the lord great seal, the judges, the serjeants-at-law, Mr. Attorney, Mr. Solicitor, Sir Thomas Smith, Mr. Goodericke. To understand what lands have been granted from the crown in the late queen's time: the marquess of Winchester, the lord great seal, the lord Rich, the lord North, Mr. Mildmay.

Ibid., VII, 27 f.

(C) LETTERS ON JUDICIAL MATTERS (1559-66)

[15 March 1559.] A letter to the lieutenant of the Tower: that, where there remaineth in his custody the bodies of one Pytt and Nycholles, for the robbing of a widow called Bate in Saint Ellyn's in London, he is required to call the knight marshal unto him in this matter; and, upon examination of the parties, if they shall obstinately persist in the denial of their fact,[1] he is willed to cause them to be brought to the rack and to feel the smart thereof as they by their discretions shall think good for the better bolting out of the truth of this matter.

[25 February 1565.] A letter to Sir John Rogers, knight, George Rogers, Thomas Morton, Robert Coker, John Lewsten, esquires, or to two of them: to cause one Agnes Mondaye, of the county of Dorset, to be apprehended and committed to ward, to be further ordered according to the quality of her fault; and further to make search in her house or other resorting places for all such things as they think may tend to witchcraft, and to advertise hither what they

---
[1] Deed.

shall do herein—which Agnes, besides many other devilish parts, hath of late bewitched one Mistress Chettell that she hath been in peril of her life.

[16 March 1565.] A letter to the commissioners in Cornwall: that they should proceed to the execution of three pirates indicted of piracy, unless by the justices of assize it should be thought otherwise good; and also to send up the twelve men that acquitted one Akers, being indicted also of piracy, and with them their bonds and evidences against the said Akers, to the end the matter shall be heard the first day of the next term in the star chamber.

[20 October 1566.] A letter to the judge of the admiralty, signifying unto him that the queen's majesty, upon information given to her highness that John Hawkins of Plymouth hath prepared a ship to be sent into the king of Spain's Indias, did give order that the said ship should be stayed and the said Hawkins commanded to repair hither to answer his doings in this behalf. Forasmuch as the said Hawkins, being now come hither for that purpose, hath affirmed that he meaneth not to send any ship of his, or by his setting forth, to any of those places that are suspected, the said judge is willed to take sufficient bonds of him, not only that he shall forbear to send any ship or ships to any of those ports of the Indias which are privileged to any person or persons by the king of Spain, but also that neither he nor any other that shall go in any ship of his, or of his setting forth, shall rob, spoil, or evil-handle any of the queen's majesty's subjects, allies, confederates, or friends; and thereupon to signify hither what he shall have done herein, to the end order may be taken to cause his said ship to be set at liberty.

Ibid., VII, 66, 200, 206, 315.

(D) MEMORANDUM ON THE STATUTE OF ARTIFICERS (1565)[2]

[8 July.] Where, according to the statute made in the fifth year of the queen's majesty's reign for the limiting and appointing of wages for artificers, husbandmen, and any other labourer, servant, or workman, it was ordered that the justices of each county of this realm should yearly certify before the twelfth of July, under their hands and seals, what they thought meet to be allowed unto every of them, with the causes and considerations thereof, into the chancery; and that thereupon the lord chancellor or lord keeper should make declaration of the same to the queen's majesty or her highness's privy council, and so cause it to be published by print, as in the said statute more at large appeareth: this day the lord keeper of the great seal showed unto their lordships such certificates as he hath received in this matter, which his lordship was by their lordships desired to

---

[2] No. 81c.

cause to be imprinted and sent abroad according to the tenor of the said act.

Ibid., VII, 230.

(E) MEMORANDUM ON APPEALS FROM JERSEY (1572)

[13 May.] Where certain petitions have been exhibited to my lords of the council by . . . one of the jurats and justices [of the isle of Jersey] . . . for the reformation of certain inconveniences arising in some point of the laws of that isle, and the manner of prosecuting the same . . . , it was commanded by my said lords that an order touching those petitions and for reformation in those cases to be had should be written down in the council book in manner and form following . . . : first, that no appeal be admitted . . . from any sentence or judgment in any matter . . . not exceeding the value . . . of £7 sterling . . . ; that no appeal in any cause . . . be permitted . . . before the same . . . be fully examined and ended by definitive sentence . . . ; that every appeal shall be prosecuted within three months next ensuing the sentence or judgment given therein, except there be just cause of . . . impediment . . . ; [but] no appeal be hereafter received without the copy as well of the sentence or judgment as also of the whole process of the cause closed together under the seal of the isle; and, that there may be no let to the appellant in having thereof, it is ordered by the said lords that the bailiff and jurats of the isle from whom the appeal shall be made, shall, upon request made to them, deliver . . . to the said party appellant the said copy within eight days after such request.

Ibid., VIII, 75 f.

(F) OATH OF THE CLERK OF THE COUNCIL (1572)[3]

The oath of Robert Beale, esquire, to be one of the clerks of the privy council. You shall swear to be a true and faithful servant unto the queen's majesty as one of the clerks of her highness's privy council. You shall not know or understand of any manner thing to be attempted, done, or spoken against her majesty's person, honour, crown, or dignity royal, but you shall let or withstand the same to the uttermost of your power, and either do or cause it to be revealed either to her majesty's self or to her privy council. You shall keep secret all matters committed and revealed unto you, or that shall be treated of secret in council, and if any of the same treaties or counsels shall touch any of the same counsellors, you shall not reveal the same unto him, but shall keep the same until such time as, by consent of her majesty or the council, publication shall be made thereof. You shall to your uttermost bear faith and true allegiance to the queen's majesty, her heirs and lawful successors, and shall assist and defend all jurisdictions, pre-eminences, and authorities granted to her majesty and annexed to her crown [against] all foreign princes, persons, prel-

---

[3] This is virtually the same as the privy councillor's oath of office; cf. no. 53.

ates, or potentates, etc., by act of parliament or otherwise; and generally in all things you shall do as a faithful and true servant and subject ought to do to her majesty. So help you God and the holy contents of this Book.

Ibid., VIII, 78 f.

(G) MISCELLANEOUS LETTERS (1573-93)

[7 June 1573.] A letter to the justices of assizes in the county of Kent: to make an agreement betwixt Antony Parkehurst and his father that meaneth to disinherit him, or to return in whom the fault is.

[24 October 1576.] A letter to Sir Henry Nevill, knight, Richard Ward, esquire, cofferer of her majesty's household, and Richard Lovelace, esquire: to examine a complaint exhibited by one Humphrey Kerry of London, merchant, that, being robbed in a thicket near Maidenhead, hue and cry being raised and followed to the said town, they made not such pursuit after the offenders as by law they were bound; and if upon examination of the matter any default shall appear in the officers, to commit them until they should hear further; and besides, the information being true, to advise how the said Kerry might be recompensed for his losses according to law.

[25 October 1576.] A letter to the customers, comptrollers, and searchers, and other officers of the port of London: to release certain of Holland ordinarily bringing in victuals for the provision of the city of London, who were stayed by them, and that also they may be permitted to pass and repass to and fro from time to time as they shall have occasion for the bringing in of any such victuals; and because the same is a great relief to the poor people of London, they shall from henceforth freely suffer all such as trade hither with victuals to come and return until they shall be further directed from the lords in that behalf.

[6 March 1577.] A letter to the lord president in the north, signifying unto him that, where this last year there was a voyage taken in hand by Martin Frobisher for discovery of some parts of the world unknown, wherein there is great likelihood that the continuance thereof will be beneficial both to the whole realm and particularly to such as are venturers in the same, and for that some encouragement might be given for the following thereof, her majesty is pleased to contribute largely towards such charges as are now to be employed. Wherefore their lordships, understanding that divers merchants in the city of York, towns of Newcastle, Hull, and other places under his lordship's jurisdiction would also be willing to venture somewhat in the said voyage, so as they might be assured of her majesty's and their lordships' good liking . . . , his lordship would signify to the inhabitants thereabouts that, if any merchant or others shall be willing to contribute and adventure any portion of money in this matter at this time, he shall rateably be admitted to the profit thereof as others are. Only their lordships require of them that some expedition be made in the certifying of the names and abilities of such persons as shall be found willing to contribute anything, to the intent the voyage now shortly intended might neither be hindered nor they anywise disappointed. And what shall be done herein their lordships desire to be advertised. The like letter to the mayor and his brethren of the city of Bristol.

[6 March 1577.] A letter to the commissioners for the restraint of grain in the county of Essex, requiring them to suffer Walter Persons and Henry Pometell, bakers . . . , to transport out of the said county eighty quarters of wheat which they have already bargained for . . . , which said wheat is to be employed in biscuit necessary for the furniture of certain barks of Martin Frobisher and others now intending a voyage to the seas; and that bonds be taken of the said bakers or their factors that they shall return certificates from the customer of London that the said wheat hath been brought to London and employed as aforesaid.

[26 February 1579.] To the lord mayor of London: that, whereas their lordships were informed that one Beton, a surgeon, entertained in a ship called *The Thomas of Ipswich* in a voyage towards the northwest, had entered an action before him against Thomas Bonham, owner of the said ship, and that the mariners of the said ship intend to do the like, and that the misdemeanours of the said mariners in the said voyage hath been such as they rather deserve punishment than wages; and, the matter not yet examined and determined, their lordships pray him to give order that all suit in any of his courts may be forborne, as well of the said Beton as of all others for this cause, until the matter may be farther considered and ordered according to right.

[19 February 1581.] A letter unto Barnard Randall, Thomas Gardner, and the constable: that, where it pleased the queen's majesty for certain good considerations to grant unto Jacomo Vertolini under the great seal of England a privilege to erect a glass-house and to make drinking glasses, prohibiting thereby that no person whatsoever should to the prejudice of his said grant make and erect any glass-houses and make glasses of that kind within the realm; forasmuch as complaint is made unto their lordships by the said Jacomo that one Sebastian Orlandini and one John Smith have very lately set up a furnace at the gunpowder mill by Ratcliffe intending to make glasses . . . , they are therefore required forthwith, upon the receipt hereof, to repair unto the said gunpowder mill and there, by virtue of these their lordships' letters, to cause the said furnace to be presently defaced in their own presence before they do depart from the place, and to enjoin them both in her majesty's name that they forbear to attempt the like hereafter, upon pain to receive such punishment for their contempt as by her majesty's said grant is prescribed. . . .

[29 July 1593.] A letter to the vice-chancellor of Cambridge: whereas the two universities of Cambridge and Oxford are the nurseries to bring up youth in the knowledge and fear of God and in all manner of good learning and virtuous education, whereby after they may serve their prince and country in divers callings; for which respect a special care is to be had of those two universities that all means may be used to further the bringing up of the youth that are bestowed there in all good learning, civil education, and honest manners, whereby the state and commonwealth may receive hereafter great good . . . : we therefore as councillors of estate to her majesty, amongst other things concerning the good government of this realm, cannot but have a more especial regard of these principal places, being the fountains from whence learning and education doth flow and so is derived into all other parts of the realm. And for that cause, understanding that common players do ordinarily resort to the university of Cambridge, there to recite interludes and plays, some of them being full of lewd example and most of vanity, besides the gathering together of multitudes of people whereby is great occasion also of divers other inconveniences, we have thought good to require you, the vice-chancellor, with the assistance of the heads of the colleges, to take special order that hereafter there may no plays or interludes of common players be used . . . , either in the university or in any place within the compass of five miles . . . , nor any shows of unlawful games that are forbidden by the statutes of this realm. . . .

The like letter to vice-chancellor and heads of the houses and several colleges in Oxford.

Ibid., VIII, 111; IX, 218 f., 302 f.; XI, 59; XII, 336; XXIV, 427 f.

(H) INSTRUCTIONS TO LOCAL GOVERNMENT OFFICIALS (1598)[4]

[25 March.] A minute of letters directed unto the high sheriff and justices of the peace in the several counties of the realm. . . . Although we doubt not but the justices of the assize in their several circuits have had special regard . . . to admonish you and other justices at the last assizes to have extraordinary care for the due execution of divers good statutes yet in force, and especially of those lately made this last parliament for the good and benefit of the whole state of the realm concerning the relief of poor people, maimed soldiers, the punishment of vagabonds and rogues, and maintenance of tillage, the care whereof is specially recommended to you by the said statutes: nevertheless, considering the remissness that hath been used generally by the justices of the peace in many parts of the realm and the great good that may ensue by the due execution of so good

---

[4] Cf. nos. 73c, 74 I, 81H, 82c.

and necessary laws, her majesty . . . hath commanded us very earnestly . . . to recommend unto your better and more due regard that which belongeth to your duties and the law requireth of you. . . .

To which end it is thought meet that at the next general sessions after Easter you do assemble together and take special order amongst yourselves for one strict and uniform course to be holden for the due observing . . . of the same laws and statutes; and further that you do from thenceforth, from time to time so often as it shall be found requisite . . . , assemble within your several limits to take account of the constables and other under-officers of their proceedings to be informed of those abuses that are to be reformed. . . . Which service if you shall effect according to the trust reposed in you, and with that care which public officers ought to use, and according to her majesty's most earnest desire, yourselves and the whole country shall be partakers of the benefit of the same and her majesty receive that satisfaction which she looketh for. But if you shall neglect the same, her majesty cannot but account you to be unmeet and unworthy for the authority and places which you hold under her. And because her majesty hath had report diversely made unto her that, although there are a great number commonly in every county of the realm by common made justices of the peace, whereof some sort of them do not give their attendance but at times when they have special causes of their own or their friends to treat upon, her majesty, meaning to be more certainly informed of that abuse, commandeth you that shall be present at these sessions next after Easter to certify unto her council who shall they be that should be present to attend the service, so as thereby it may be understood who shall be absent, and they to answer thereunto; whereby her majesty shall be pleased with your service and shall enter into consideration how to reform the negligence of the others. . . .

Ibid., XXVIII, 388 f.

(I) JOHN HERBERT'S MEMORANDUM (1600)

Titles of matters whereof I am charged to have regard as a councillor and secretary: first, to inform myself of all treaties with foreign princes . . . , to be acquainted with the particular actions and negotiations of ambassadors to her majesty and from her; to inform myself of the power and form of proceeding at the council of the marches in Wales and the council in the north, and to understand the manner of the warden's government; to be well informed of the state of Ireland, both the yearly charge of the army and the extraordinary, the state of revenue there and the state of the undertakers, the charge of the Low Country wars, the charges of the French king, the state of their debts to the queen, what the assurances are and where they are; to oversee the order of the council-book and muster-book of the realm; to have the custody of letters from foreign princes to the queen and answers made to them; to have care to the intelligences abroad.

Memorandum, that all causes to be treated on in council and resolved are either only for her majesty or betwixt party and party or betwixt some party, either subject or stranger, and the queen's majesty. The first doth handle principally questions and consultations of state growing from foreign advertisements or some extraordinary accidents within the realm. The second, between party and party, are very seldom heard particularly, but rather ended by overruling an obstinate person who is made to acknowledge his fault; or else the parties are remitted to some court of justice or equity, or recommended by some letters to some justices in the country to compound the differences either by consent of the parties or by direction; or if the cause be great, then to write letters to some principal persons, to have some circumstances better understood and examined concerning matter of fact whereof the council cannot be so well informed when they have only the suggestions of one party against another, upon which report it often happeneth that quarrels and differences are taken up by the council when it appears clearly who is in default. When there is anything in question wherein the queen is a party, it is commonly either by the breach of peace or for some other title. If there be breach of peace, the lords do either punish the offender by commitment or do refer the matter to be further proceeded in the star chamber, where great riots and contempts are punished. If it be matter of title, then the lords refer it to the queen's learned counsel and recommend the same to the judges' care. If there be some suits to the queen of poor men, then do the lords endorse their petitions with their opinions and recommend the dispatch to the secretary or for the poorer sort to the master of the requests.

Prothero, Constitutional Documents, pp. 166 f.

84. COMMISSION FOR ECCLESIASTICAL CAUSES (1559)[1]

Elizabeth, by the grace of God, etc., to the reverend father in God, Mathew Parker, nominated bishop of Canterbury; and Edmond Grindall, nominated bishop of London; and to our right trusted and right well-beloved councillors, Francis Knowles, our vice-chamberlain and Ambrose Cave, knights; and to our trusty and well-beloved Anthony Cooke and Thomas Smyth, knights; William Bill, our almoner; Walter Haddon and Thomas Sackford, masters of our requests; Rowland Hill and William Chester, knights; Randoll Cholmely and John Southcote, serjeants-at-the-law; William May, doctor of law; Francis Cave, Richard Gooderick, and Gilbert Gerrard, esquires; Robert Weston and Thomas Huick, doctors of law; greeting.

Where, at our parliament holden at Westminster the 25th day of January and there continued and kept until the 8th of May then next following, amongst other things there was two acts and statutes made and established . . . ; and where divers seditious and slanderous

---

[1] This is but one of many such commissions that were issued; see R. G. Usher, *The Rise and Fall of the High Commission*.

84. ECCLESIASTICAL COMMISSION

persons do not cease daily to invent and set forth false rumours, tales, and seditious slanders, not only against us and the said good laws and statutes, but also have set forth divers seditious books within this our realm of England, meaning thereby to move and procure strife, division, and dissension amongst our loving and obedient subjects, much to the disquieting of us and our people: wherefore we, earnestly minding to have the same acts before mentioned to be duly put in execution, and such persons as shall hereafter offend in anything contrary to the tenor and effect of the said several statutes to be condignly punished, and having especial trust and confidence in your wisdoms and discretions, have authorized, assigned, and appointed you to be our commissioners;[2] and by these presents do give our full power and authority to you, or six of you . . . , from time to time hereafter during our pleasure to inquire, as well by the oaths of twelve good and lawful men as also by witnesses and all other ways and means ye can devise, for all offences, misdoers, and misdemeanours done and committed and hereafter to be committed or done contrary to the tenor and effect of the said several acts and statutes and either of them, and also of all and singular heretical opinions, seditious books, contempts, conspiracies, false rumours, tales, seditions, misbehaviours, slanderous words or showings, published, invented or set forth . . . by any person or persons against us or contrary or against any the laws or statutes of this our realm, or against the quiet governance and rule of our people and subjects in any . . . place or places within this our realm of England, and of all and every of the coadjutors, counsellors, comforters, procurers, and abettors of every such offender.

And further, we do give power and authority to you, or six of you . . . , from time to time hereafter during our pleasure, as well to hear and determine all the premises as also to inquire, hear, and determine all and singular enormities, disturbances, and misbehaviours done and committed . . . in any church or chapel, or against any divine service, or the minister or ministers of the same, contrary to the laws and statutes of this realm; and also to inquire of, search out, and to order, correct, and reform all such persons as hereafter shall or will obstinately absent themselves from church and such divine service as by the laws and statutes of this realm is appointed to be had and used.

And also we do give and grant full power and authority unto you, and six of you . . . , from time to time and at all times during our pleasure to visit, reform, redress, order, correct, and amend in all places within this our realm of England all such errors, heresies, crimes, abuses, offences, contempts, and enormities spiritual and ecclesiastical wheresoever, which by any spiritual or ecclesiastical power, authority, or jurisdiction can or may lawfully be reformed, ordered, redressed, corrected, restrained, or amended, to the pleasure of Al-

---

[2] Cf. no. 85B. The two statutes referred to are no. 81A, B.

mighty God, the increase of virtue, and the conservation of the peace and unity of this our realm, and according to the authority and power limited, given, and appointed by any laws or statutes of this realm.

And also that you, or six of you . . . , shall likewise have full power and authority from time to time to inquire of and search out all masterless men, quarrellers, vagrant and suspect persons within our city of London, and ten miles compass about the same city, and of all assaults and affrays done and committed within the same city and compass aforesaid.

And also we give full power and authority unto you, and six of you . . . , summarily to hear and finally determine, according to your discretions and by the laws of this realm, all causes and complaints of all them, which in respect of religion, or for lawful matrimony contracted and allowed by the same, were injuriously deprived, defrauded, or spoiled of their lands, goods, possessions, rights, dignities, livings, offices, spiritual or temporal; and them so deprived, as before, to restore into their said livings and to put them in possession, amoving the usurpers in convenient speed, as it shall seem to your discretions good. . . .

And further we do give power and authority unto you, and six of you . . . , not only to hear and determine the same and all other offences and matters before mentioned and rehearsed, but also all other notorious and manifest adulteries, fornications, and ecclesiastical crimes and offences within this our realm, according to your wisdoms, consciences, and discretions; willing and commanding you, or six of you . . . , to use and devise all such politic ways and means for the trial and searching out of all the premises as . . . shall be thought most expedient and necessary. And upon due proof had, and the offence or offences before specified, or any of them, sufficiently proved against any person or persons by confession of the party, or by lawful witnesses, or by any due mean . . . , then you or six of you, as aforesaid, shall have full power and authority to award such punishment to every offender by fine, imprisonment, or otherwise, by all or any of the ways aforesaid, and to take such order for the redress of the same, as to your wisdoms and discretions [shall be thought meet and convenient].

[And further we do give full power and authority unto you,] or six of you . . . , to call before you . . . all and every offender or offenders, and such as [to] you . . . shall seem to be suspect persons in any of the premises; and also all such witnesses as you . . . shall think [meet] to be called before you or six of you as aforesaid and them and every of them to examine upon their corporal oath for the better trial and opening of the premises or any part thereof.

And if you or six of you, as aforesaid, shall find any person or persons obstinate or disobedient either in their [appearance] before you . . . at your calling or commandment, or else not accomplishing or not obeying your order, decrees, and commandments in anything touching the premises or any part thereof . . . , then you . . . shall

85. ACTS CONCERNING PRINTING

have full power and authority to commit the same person or persons so offending to ward, there to remain until he or they shall be by you . . . enlarged and delivered. . . .

And more, we will and command all and singular justices of the peace, mayors, sheriffs, bailiffs, constables, and other our officers, ministers, and faithful subjects, to be aiding, helping, and assisting and at your commandment in the due execution hereof, as they tender our pleasure, and will answer to the contrary at their utmost perils. . . .

Ibid., pp. 227 f.

85. ACTS CONCERNING PRINTING (1530-85)
(A) PROCLAMATION AGAINST ERRONEOUS BOOKS (1530)

The king, our most dread sovereign lord, studying and providing daily for the weal, benefice, and honour of this his most noble realm, well and evidently perceiveth that, partly through the malicious suggestions of our ghostly enemy, partly by the evil and perverse inclination . . . of sundry persons, divers heresies and erroneous opinions have been late sown and spread among his subjects of this his said realm by blasphemous and pestiferous English books, printed in other regions and sent into this realm to the intent as well to pervert and withdraw the people from the catholic and true faith of Christ, as also to stir and incense them to sedition and disobedience against their princes, sovereigns, and heads, as also to cause them to condemn and neglect all good laws, customs, and virtuous manners, to the final subversion and desolation of this noble realm . . . : whereupon the king's highness . . . hath invited and called to him the primates of this his grace's realm, and also a sufficient number of discreet . . . and well-learned personages in divinity . . . , giving unto them liberty to speak . . . their . . . determinations concerning as well the approbation or rejecting of such books as be in any part suspected as also the admission and divulgation of the Old and New Testament translated into English.

Whereupon his highness in his own royal person, calling to him the said primates and divines, hath seriously . . . discussed the premises and finally by all their free assents . . . determined that these books ensuing . . .[1] and divers other books made in the English tongue . . . do contain in them pestiferous errors and blasphemies, and for that cause shall from henceforth be reputed and taken of all men for books of heresy. . . . The king's said highness therefore straitly chargeth . . . all and every his subjects . . . that they from henceforth do not buy, receive, or have any of the books before named, or any other book being in the English tongue and printed beyond the sea of what matter soever it be, or any copy written [and] drawn out of the same, or the same books in the French or Dutch

---
[1] Five books are named.

tongue. . . . [Offenders against this proclamation are to be brought] to the king's highness and his most honourable council, where they shall be corrected and punished for their contempt and disobedience to the terrible example of other like transgressors.

Moreover, his highness commandeth that no manner of person or persons take upon him or them to print any book or books in the English tongue concerning Holy Scripture, not before this time printed within this his realm, until such time as the same book or books be examined and approved by the ordinary of the diocese, where the said books shall be printed; and that the printer thereof, upon every of the said books being so examined, do set the name of the examiner or examiners, with also his own name upon the said books, as he will answer to the king's highness at his uttermost peril. . . .

If it shall hereafter appear to the king's highness that his said people do utterly abandon and forsake all perverse, erroneous, and seditious opinions, with the New Testament and the Old corruptly translated into the English tongue now being in print, and that the same books and all other books of heresy . . . be clearly exterminated and exiled out of this realm of England forever, his highness intendeth to provide that the Holy Scripture shall be by great and learned and catholic persons translated into the English tongue, if it shall then seem to his grace convenient to be. . . .

Wilkins, *Concilia*, III, 740.

(B) DECREE IN STAR CHAMBER CONCERNING BOOKS (1566)

I. That no person should print, or cause to be printed, or bring or procure to be brought into the realm printed, any book against the force and meaning of any ordinance, prohibition, or commandment, contained in any the statutes or laws of this realm, or in any injunctions, letters patents, or ordinances passed or set forth, or to be passed or set forth, by the queen's grant, commission, or authority.

II. That whosoever should offend against the said ordinances should forfeit all such books and copies; and from thenceforth should never use or exercise, or take benefit by any using or exercising, the feat of printing, and to sustain three months' imprisonment without bail or mainprise.

III. That no person should sell or put to sale, bind, stitch, or sew any such books or copies, upon pain to forfeit all such books and copies, and for every book 20s.

IV. That all books so forfeited should be brought into Stationers' Hall; and there one moiety of the money forfeited to be reserved to the queen's use, and the other moiety to be delivered to him or them that should first seize the books or make complaint thereof to the warden of the said company; and all the books so to be forfeited to be destroyed or made waste paper.

85. ACTS CONCERNING PRINTING

V. That it should be lawful for the wardens of the company for the time being or any two of the said company thereto deputed by the said wardens, as well in any ports or other suspected places to open and view all packs, dryfats, maunds,[2] and other things wherein books or paper shall be contained, brought into this realm, and make search in all work-houses, shops, warehouses, and other places of printers, booksellers, and such as bring books into the realm to be sold, or where they have reasonable cause of suspicion; and all books to be found against the said ordinances to seize and carry to the Hall to the uses abovesaid, and to bring the persons offending before the queen's commissioners in causes ecclesiastical.

VI. Every stationer, printer, bookseller, merchant, using any trade of book-printing, binding, selling, or bringing into the realm, should, before the commissioners or before any other persons thereto to be assigned by the queen's privy council, enter into several recognizances of reasonable sums of money to her majesty, with sureties or without, as to the commissioners should be thought expedient, that he should truly observe all the said ordinances, well and truly yield and pay all such forfeitures, and in no point be resisting but in all things aiding to the said wardens and their deputies for the true execution of the premises.

Upon the consideration before expressed and upon the motion of the commissioners, we of the privy council have agreed this to be observed and kept upon the pains therein contained. At the star chamber.

Strype, *Life of Parker*, I, 442 f.

(C) DECREE IN STAR CHAMBER CONCERNING PRINTERS (1585)

Imprimis, that every printer and other person . . . which at this time present hath erected . . . any printing-press, roll, or other instrument for imprinting of books, charts, ballads, portraitures, paper called damask paper, or any such things or matters whatsoever, shall bring a true note or certificate of the said presses . . . already erected, within ten days next coming after the publication hereof, and of the said presses . . . hereafter to be erected or set up from time to time, within ten days next after the erecting or setting up thereof, unto the master and wardens of the Company of Stationers of the city of London for the time being; upon pain that every person failing or offending herein shall have all and every the said presses . . . utterly defaced and made unserviceable for imprinting forever, and shall also suffer twelve months' imprisonment. . . .

Item, that no printer of books nor any other person or persons whatsoever shall set up, keep, or maintain any press or presses . . . , but only in the city of London or the suburbs thereof (except one press in the university of Cambridge and one other press in the university of Oxford and no more) ; and that no person shall hereafter

---

[2] Wooden and wicker containers.

erect, set up, or maintain in any secret or obscure corner or place any such press . . . , but that the same shall be in such open place or places in his or their houses as the wardens of the said company of stationers for the time being, or such other person or persons as by the said wardens shall be thereunto appointed, may from time to time have ready access unto to search for and view the same. And that no printer . . . shall at any time hereafter withstand or make resistance to . . . any such view or search, nor deny, to keep secret, any such press. . . .

Item, that no person or persons shall imprint or cause to be imprinted or suffer by any means to his knowledge his press, letters, or other instruments to be occupied in printing of any book, work, copy, matter, or thing whatsoever except the same . . . hath been heretofore allowed, or . . . be first seen and perused by the archbishop of Canterbury and bishop of London for the time being, or one of them. . . .

Item, that it shall be lawful to or for the said wardens for the time being, or any two by them appointed . . . , to enter into any house, workhouse, warehouse, shop, or other place or places, and to seize, take, and carry away all presses, letters, and all other printing instruments set up, used, or employed contrary to the true meaning hereof, to be defaced and made unserviceable. . . .

Strype, *Life of Whitgift*, III, 160 f.

86. LOCAL JUDICIAL RECORDS (1553-96)[1]

(A) OATH OF OFFICE OF A JUSTICE OF THE PEACE

Ye shall swear that, as justices of the peace in the county of Kent, in all articles in the queen's commission to you directed ye shall do equal right to the poor and to the rich after your cunning, wit, and power, and after the laws and customs of the realm and the statutes thereof made; and ye shall not be of counsel with any quarrel hanging before you; and that ye hold your sessions after the form of statutes thereof made; and the issues, fines, and amercements that shall happen to be made, and all forfeitures which shall fall before you, ye shall cause to be entered without any concealment or embezzling and truly send them to the queen's exchequer. Ye shall not let for gift or other cause, but well and truly ye shall do your office of justice of the peace in that behalf; and that you take nothing for your office of justice of the peace to be done, but of the queen, and fees accustomed, and costs limited by the statute; and ye shall not direct nor cause to be directed any warrant by you to be made to the parties, but ye shall direct them to the bailiffs of the said county or other the queen's officers or ministers, or other indifferent persons,

---

[1] For other documents dealing with the justices of the peace and their activities, see nos. 73C; 81C, F, G, H; 82C; 83H.

86. LOCAL JUDICIAL RECORDS

to do execution thereof. So help you God and by the contents of this Book.

Lambarde, *Eirenarcha*, p. 59.

(B) PERSONS SUMMONED TO THE STAFFORDSHIRE QUARTER SESSIONS (October, 1585)

[Justices]

Thos. Bromley, knt., lord chancellor
Wm. Lord Burghley, lord treasurer
George, earl of Shrewsbury
Robt., earl of Leicester, master of the horse
Wm., bishop of Coventry and Lichfield
Edward, Lord Stafford
Edward, Lord Dudley
Jas. Crofte, knt., controller of the household
Gilbert Gerrard, knt., master of the rolls
Francis Wyndham, one of the justices of the bench
Edward Flowerdew, one of the barons of the exchequer

John Littleton, knt.
Walter Aston, knt.
Ralph Egerton, knt.
Thos. Trentham, esq.
Walter Harecourte, esq.
Ralph Sneid, esq.
Thos. Grasley, esq.
Wm. Bassett, esq.
Edward Aston, esq.
Edward Littleton, esq.
Ralph Aderley, esq.
Robt. Stanford, esq.

Humphrey Ferrers, esq.
John Chetwin, esq.
John Bowes, esq.
Walter Leveson, esq.
Ric. Bagott, esq.
John Grey, esq.
Henry Griffin, esq.
Thos. Lane, esq.
Thos. Rudyer, esq.
Ric. Crompton, esq.
Thos. Waringes, esq.
Wm. Madder, esq.

Coroners

Wm. Greene, gent.
John Jarvice, gent.
George Warner, gent.

Chief Constables

Thos. Corbett, gent. } chief constables of Pirehill Hundred
Hugh Fodon, gent. }
Humphrey Minors, gent., Offlow Hundred
Thos. Warner, gent., Tottmonslow Hundred
Ric. Mills, gent., Cutleston Hundred
Thos. Rickthorne, gent., Seisdon Hundred

Bailiffs of the Liberties

Robt. Whytall, liberty of the duchy of Lancaster
Thos. Ayre, liberty of Robt., earl of Essex, of Lichfield
Robt. Persall, gent., liberty of Wm., bishop of Coventry and Lichfield

THE TUDORS

Bailiffs of the Hundreds
Wm. Pedley, Tottmonslow Hundred
John Marten, Pirehill Hundred
Thos. Harpur, Seisdon Hundred
Wm. Bennett, Offlow Hundred
Ric. Suker, Cudleston

Bailiffs Itinerant
Thurston Garter
Geoffrey Lightwood
Ric. Chauner
Jas. Arendale
John More
Robt. Burges
John Grene
Robt. Mole[2]

Collections for a History of Staffordshire, 1929, pp. 105 f.

(C) STAFFORDSHIRE QUARTER SESSIONS ROLLS (1587-96)

[1587. Writ of restitution] tested by Robert, earl of Essex, at Uttoxeter, 26 July . . . : that, whereas by inquisition . . . at Uttoxeter . . . before Richard Bagot, Ralph Adderly, and Philip Okeover esquire, justices of the peace, it was presented by twelve jurors that George Partridge [and four others] . . . have entered a messuage and close called Ridware Park, the free tenement of Thomas Fitzherbert, knight . . . , and as yet hold him out of it, contrary to the form of the statute of 8 Henry VI, the sheriff is ordered to make reseisin of the premises and restore to Thomas his former possession. [Return by the sheriff]: 29 July . . . I have made reseisin of the premises and restored to Thomas Fitzherbert his former possession. . . .

[1589] Before Edward Leghe, esquire, J. P., 15 February . . . : Richard Painter of Wolverhampton, husbandman, to appear at the next general sessions after Easter; sureties, the said Richard £5. John Creswell of Wolverhampton, gentleman, £5. . . .

Before Richard Crompton esquire, J. P., 17 January: John Lebarne of the city of Lichfield, labourer, to appear at the next general sessions after Easter and in the meantime to keep the peace against James Toye of Walton, county Derby, husbandman; sureties, the said John, £20, Thomas Hardyne of the city of Lichfield, shoemaker, £10, John Smabrydge of the same, dyer, £10. [Added in another hand:] Discharged by the court because agreed. . . .

10 March . . . , Richard Prichard of Fradswell and William Emery

---

[2] Of the persons summoned, there appeared three justices, two coroners, three chief constables, two bailiffs of the liberties, five bailiffs of the hundreds, and six bailiffs itinerant.

of the same, to appear at the next general sessions after Easter and to keep the peace; surety, each man for the other £10. . . .

[1591. Articles] exhibited to the justices by Richard Aukers and Thomas Collye, constables of the town of Wolverhampton, against John Greene of the same, 13 April. . . . First, the said John Green is a common drunkard, a common brawler, quarreller, and breaker of her majesty's peace. Item, he keepeth common ale-selling and usually lodgeth and receiveth persons of ill behaviour, etc. Item, where about Easter last there was a stranger apprehended at Wolverhampton by one Mr. Richards upon suspicion for stealing an old cloak off a hedge; and where thereupon, for the better examination of that fact, the said Aukers went with the said stranger and a servant of the said Mr. Richards to Mr. John Grey, one of the justices of the peace for the said county; and where upon examination of the said stranger it pleased Mr. Grey, for that no person would directly charge the said stranger with the said felony, to remit him: the said Greene at Wolverhampton aforesaid repaired to the said Aukers, most spitefully reviling him and most undutifully exclaiming against the said Mr. Grey, calling the said Mr. Grey villain and false knave, affirming openly it were a good deed he were hanged; whereupon the said constable, willing the said Greene to satisfy himself and not to give out such unseemly speeches, he thereupon reviled most impudently the said constable.

Item, where thereupon the said constable that evening, seeing the unruliness of the said Greene and the violent assaulting of him, the said constable, did therefore put him into the stocks; the said Greene in the night-time with force [did] break open the said stocks, cut them in pieces and took away the ironwork thereof, and, not so satisfied, then and in the night-time came to the door of the dwelling-house of the said constable bragging he was out of the stocks and . . . calling for a fresh pair of stocks. Item, the said Greene hath of late threatened to set fire in the house of the said constable and . . . to kill the said constable with his dagger. Item, the said Greene hath of late threatened to set fire in the house of one Mr. Wats. . . . Item . . . , being for these misdemeanours committed by the said Mr. Grey to the jail at Stafford, the said Greene hath procured himself out of prison by what mean is not known; and upon his return to Wolverhampton upon Easter even, got into his hat upon the one side a feather and upon [the] other side the *mittimus* by which [he] was committed by the said Mr. Grey . . . , and the same openly did wear in his said hat. . . .

Item, upon Easter day the said Greene, coming into the church . . . with the said feather in his hat, seeing the said constable there, in derision . . . made very low obeisance to the said constable . . . ; so looking over his shoulder went out of the church and, putting on a blue coat, [made] the like obeisance in derision of the said constable and his said office. The premises considered, ready all to be proved to your worships, it would please you to take such order that not only the said Greene may be punished for the said misdemeanours and ordered to re-edify the said stocks, but also that he might be bound to his good behaviour hereafter; whereby the said inhabitants may stand more secure from such the violent and unlawful purposes of the said Greene. . . .

[Information] of William Kinge of Lowborowe, county Leicester, draper, against Francis Hilton, servant of the said William, taken 2 December 1596 before Richard Bagot, esq., J. P.: who saith that, Monday the 29th of November last, he sent one Richard Evenson, his son-in-law, to Shrewsbury to buy clothes, accompanied with the said Francis Hilton, and delivered unto the said Richard £30 in money to pay for the said clothes; which money was carried in a bag of malt containing a bushel or thereabouts for more safety. And the said Richard and Francis, travelling together as far as Norton by Cannocke in the county of Stafford, [did] there lodge all night. And Francis Hilton, rising in the morning before the said Richard, took the said £30 out of the said bag, to which the said Richard afterwards coming . . . , missed the same, together with the said party. Whereupon he caused the constable there to be sent for, who, after examination of the matter, raised the said town and sent both horsemen and footmen with billets to every constable for the attaching the said party, who was apprehended at Haywood the next day following; upon whom the most part of the money was found, viz., £29 or thereabouts.

Ibid., 1929, 196, 334 f.; 1930, 110 f.; 1932, 244 f.

(D) ROLLS OF BOROUGH SESSIONS AT NOTTINGHAM (1553-88)

[Presentments of the Mickletorn jury, 27 April 1553.] . . . We present George Taylor (12*d*.) for staking of willows in the Lene, and so letteth the course of the water. We present the schoolmaster that should teach the free school, for there hath been divers men before us and hath complained of him; wherefore we desire you to have him changed. We present Bartholmew Chettel (3*s*. 4*d*.) as a man not worthy to have the office [of common pavior] which he hath, for misbehaving of himself in taking of excess toll, and for because he doth not call of the chamberlains for sand and stone, considering so greatly as this town doth go in decay for fault of paving and by his negligence. . . . We present the cow pasture for the overlying of it; wherefore we desire you that there may be a certainty how many shall be taken in. And we think the number of five score is sufficient, and no burgess to have above two. . . . If any such default be taken, to pay 3*s*. 4*d*. . . .

[Presentments by the constables of the town of Nottingham, 8 October 1566.] We present Robert Parke (8*d*.) for brewing and tippling, being not bound. We present Master Caterne's daughter (4*d*.) and Charles Overay wife (4*d*.), for buying butter and eggs

86. LOCAL JUDICIAL RECORDS

without the Chapel Bar. We present Richard Bredun (4*d*.), Robert Rede (4*d*.), John Freeman (4*d*.) for digging down the common ditch unto the Wishing Stairs for getting of worms. . . .

[Presentments by the constables of the town of Nottingham, 20 July 1573.] We present Edward Backhouse for selling of fruit . . . to men's apprentices . . . ; which we think is not convenient. We present Robert Allyng (40*d*.) for lodging of vagabonds contrary to the constables' mind. We present Mistress Cockyng, widow, for calling the constables knaves and villains when they come for post-horses. . . .

[Presentments of the Mickletorn jury, 28 October 1579.] . . . We present to have an usher for the free school, a thing very needful for this town, and to give him £10 a year to have a good one; it will be a credit to have a good master and a good usher in one school. We present that the burgesses may hear the end and reckoning of any subsidy when any is; also that they may hear the accounts both of the bridgemasters and the wardens of the free school. We present that the Red Book[3] may be openly read at every sessions in the hearing of the burgesses, or at the least such things as shall be most needful, that burgesses may the better discharge their oath and their duty for the common weal of this town. We present to have two sworn men to view the market every Saturday, for the countrymen buy both barley and other corn great store; and they should bring to the market to sell as much of other corn as they buy, or else let the advantage of the statute to be shown upon such offenders, for they hurt our market very sore. . . .

Master Mayor, we request you and your brethren that, according as we have a grant for two fairs in the year by our charter, that there may be some building made on the Timber Hill with the town's money and in short time (by good provision made, the town may reap a great rent for the same and other places as well), and that the continuance of the fair may be proclaimed in every market and fair three months before the fair.

[Presentments of the Mickletorn jury, 22 April 1588.] . . . We have thought good, forasmuch as we have a most godly exercise of preaching on the Friday once a week, and lest the same should decay amongst us through our negligence, in not coming as we ought to do, and specially of the chiefest of our town . . . , it shall be very good not only for yourself, Master Mayor, with the rest of your brethren, but also that the whole council, with the clothing[4] of this town, most reverently to observe the same by some special order set down by you and that the same be duly kept. We present William Hodgkinson for setting part of his house on the common ground in the Holmes (12*d*.). We present the free school to lack

[3] The official record of the by-laws.
[4] Livery company.

repairs, and that the school is greatly annoyed for lack of casements. We present the new bridge to lack a rail. We present the Long Butts to be in decay.

Stevenson, Records of the Borough of Nottingham, IV, 105-223.

87. RECORDS CONCERNING THE MILITIA (1539-77)

(A) COMMISSION OF A LORD LIEUTENANT (1576)[1]

Elizabeth, by the grace of God of England, France, and Ireland queen . . . , to our trusty and well-beloved councillor, Sir Christopher Hatton, knight, our vice-chamberlain, greeting. Know ye that, for the great and singular trust . . . we have in your approved fidelity . . . , we have assigned . . . you to be our lieutenant within our county of Northampton and all corporate and privileged places within the limits . . . of the same county, as well within liberties as without. And [we] do by these presents give full power and authority unto you that you from time to time may levy, gather, or call together all . . . our subjects . . . dwelling . . . within our said county . . . , meet and apt for the wars; and them to try, array, and put in readiness, and them also . . . , after their abilities . . . , sufficiently to cause to be armed and weaponed; and to take the musters of them from time to time in places most meet for that purpose after your good discretion: and also the same our subjects, so arrayed, tried, and armed, as well men-of-arms as other horsemen, archers, and footmen . . . meet and apt for the wars, to conduct and lead, as well against all . . . enemies as also against all . . . rebels, traitors, and other offenders and their adherents . . . , from time to time so often as need shall require by your discretion; and with the said enemies . . . to fight, and them to invade, resist, repress, and subdue, slay, kill, and put to execution of death by all ways and means . . . ; and to . . . execute and use against the said enemies . . . , as necessity shall require by your discretion, the law called the martial law. . . . And further we give you full power and authority, for the execution of this our commission, to appoint and assign in our said county . . . muster masters and one provost marshal. Which provost marshal shall execute and use the martial law, in case of any invasion or rebellion, in conducting any numbers of men of war against the said invaders, traitors, or rebels. . . . And forasmuch as it may be there shall be instant cause, as now there is, for you to be attendant upon our person, or to be otherwise employed in our service, whereby this our service of lieutenancy committed to your fidelity cannot be by you in person executed in such force as we have appointed the same: therefore we give unto you . . . authority to appoint, assign, and constitute by your writing, under your hand and seal, our trusty and well-beloved Sir John Spencer,

---

[1] Less elaborate commissions of this kind had been issued since the reign of Edward VI. For an excellent discussion of the subject, see Miss Thomson's work cited below.

87. MILITIA RECORDS

knight, Sir Richard Knightley, knight, and Sir Edward Montague, knight, to be your deputies in this said service in our said county of Northampton. . . . And by this . . . commission we give unto the said [Spencer, Knightley, and Montague] . . . , or any two of them, full power of authority in your absence to do and execute in our said county of Northampton . . . every thing and things before by this our commission assigned and appointed by you to be done and executed. . . . And further we will and command . . . our justices of the peace, mayors, sheriffs, bailiffs, constables, headboroughs, and all other our officers, ministers, and subjects, meet and apt for the wars within our said county of Northampton . . . , that they and every one of them, with their power and servants, from time to time shall be attendant, aiding, and assisting, counselling, helping, and at the commandment as well of you as of your said deputies . . . , as they and every of them tender our pleasure and will answer for the contrary at their uttermost perils.

Thomson, *Lords Lieutenants in the Sixteenth Century*, pp. 153 f.

(B) INSTRUCTIONS FOR GENERAL MUSTERS (1572)

Instructi ns . . . for general musters and training of all manner of persons able for the wars to serve as well on horseback as on foot. The principal intent of the queen's majesty . . . is to have perfect knowledge of the numbers, qualities, abilities, and sufficiency of all her subjects in that county . . . , from the age of sixteen years upward, that may be found able to bear armour or to use weapon on horseback or on foot; and out of that . . . number, being viewed, mustered, and registered, to have a . . . sufficient number of the most able to be chosen and collected, to be by the reasonable charge of the inhabitants in every shire tried, armed, and weaponed, and so consequently taught and trained . . . for the service and defence of her majesty, her crown, and realm against all attempts both inward and outward. . . .

Articles of the instructions to the commissioners. It is necessary that, by your precept to the constable of the hundreds or other officers thereto requisite . . . , all able persons from sixteen upwards which are within the limits of this your commission in any parish, hamlet, or village, be summoned to appear at days and places certain and meet for the musters; so none, being able of any degree, be forborne to be warned and called to the same general musters. . . . And therefore it shall be well done to command in your precept that the names and surnames of all persons in every parish . . . , able to bear armour or to use weapons . . . , be immediately collected and put in writing . . . ; naming in the said writing or note every householder by himself, with his sons, servants, apprentices, journeymen, or any other sojourners or indwellers remaining in their houses . . . ; and that the said householders be charged to bring all the said persons by name with their armour and weapons at such several times and places as shall be thereto limited. And so, after the return to the commissioners of the said writing containing their names, the said commissioners shall call for the persons and proceed to the musters of them, and register the names of such as shall appear with notes of their armours and weapons. And when some shall not have armour or weapons meet there, it shall be noted to what kind of service for the wars every of the said persons shall seem meet; wherein is meant not to omit to note what number of them may serve for labourers or pioneers, and who are also carpenters, smiths, or suchlike artificers, so as there may be some use had of their abilities for service of their country as cause shall require. . . .

Item, the commissioners shall upon the first musters consider particularly all the imperfections in the persons appearing, and in the armours, weapons, and suchlike, and shall give particular instructions and charge how to remedy the same . . . , and shall appoint certain persons . . . to see to and give order for the reformation thereof against the time of the next musters.

Item, where always of very ancient time there hath been and still are a number certain of soldiers furnished of armour and weapons to be found of the common charge of every town or parish, over and besides such particular persons as are by the late statutes chargeable by reason of their own private possessions or goods to find soldiers, armour, and weapons: the commissioners shall do well, upon the registering of the general musters, to cause special entries to be made apart of the numbers found by the parishes in the musterbooks distinct from the others. . . .

Item, because the training and exercise of a multitude of people in their armour and weapons, and namely archers and harquebusiers, may seem costly and chargeable, and that it shall not seem necessary in many places to have the whole numbers of the able people to be armed and weaponed: therefore [the commissioners] . . . shall therein use their discretions . . . , and shall consider and determine what were or may be a convenient number in every part of the shire to be collected out of the total number, meet to be sorted in bands, and to be trained and exercised in such sort as may . . . reasonably be borne by a common charge of the whole country. . . .

And because, in the choice of the numbers to be trained and exercised, divers of the soldiers inhabiting in many towns shall be forborne and not appointed to be of the trained number, and yet the service of the persons chosen and trained doth appertain to the weal of the whole shire; there shall be consideration had, in the collection of the charges to maintain the said training and exercise, that every town and parish of the shire and inhabitants thereof be rateably charged without burdening some more than other. . . .

Grose, *Military Antiquities*, I, 79 f.

87. MILITIA RECORDS

(C) CERTIFICATE OF MUSTER MASTERS (1539)

This is the certificate of Sir George Gresley, knight, John Vernon and William Wyrley, esquires, three of the king's commissioners . . . appointed for the trial and the view of all persons armed within the hundred of Ofelaw in the county of Stafford, above sixteen years, as well horsemen, footmen, bowmen, and billmen within the said hundred, whose names with their surnames and their weapons severally appeareth; and have given monition to every of them . . . to be ready with their horse and harness, and to have their harness according to the king's statute thereof made. In witness we have subscribed our names and set to our seals the 27th day of April, 1539. . . .[2]

Elford and Hasulhowre

Richard Huddilston—horse, harness, bill; able
John Hervy—harness, without a horse, a bill; able
Richard Wryght ⎫
Rauf Massye ⎪
Petur Foleshist ⎪
John Janens ⎬ —bowmen, able; without horse or harness
John Melburne ⎪
Thomas Smyth ⎪
Alexander Hodson ⎭
Philipp Wright—a bowman, not able

Collections for a History of Staffordshire, 1901, p. 217.

(D) INSTRUCTIONS FOR TRAINING MEN IN LANCASHIRE (1577)

To our very good lords, the earl of Derby and Lord Mounteagle, and to the rest of the commissioners appointed in the fifteenth year of her majesty's reign for the taking of the general musters in the county of Lancashire: after our hearty commendations. Whereas it pleased the queen's majesty . . . to direct her commission . . . unto you for the taking of views and musters of her loving subjects of the county of Lancashire . . . , we would have wished that you had set them down in writing more particularly, according to such direction as was contained in the said instruction. For want whereof we are first to require you . . . you would certify your former musterings somewhat more orderly, according to a schedule which we send you herewith enclosed . . . ; and further, forasmuch upon some considerations . . . it is thought requisite that out of the total number then mustered in that county the number of three hundred should be selected and trained, the same number being so small it is not doubted but the country is very well able to bear the charges of the training (for which cause both her majesty and we assure ourselves that as heretofore you have showed yourselves very forward in executing her majesty's commandment tending to so good an

---

[2] A list similar to the one following is given for each township within the hundred.

end), so now also in respect of some small charges or pains, which the country is to be at, you will not fail to employ your best endeavours for the executing thereof as appertaineth to good and dutiful subjects. And yet our meaning is not, by this present preparation of this small number of shot,[3] but that also . . . all the rest of the serviceable men which were before mustered . . . otherwise to supply and continue in readiness, so as they may be ready to be mustered, as you shall have further commission; by which is meant that the footmen shall be mustered about the month of May and the horsemen about July, whereof we require you to have some consideration in giving warning now aforehand. . . . And so we bid you heartily farewell. Westminster [20 March 1577]. Your loving friends: William Burleigh, Robert Leicester, Francis Bedford, Francis Knowles, Ambrose Warwick, Thomas Sussex, James Crofte, Francis Walsingham.

J. Harland, *Lancashire Lieutenancy*, I, 91 f.

---

[3] Men armed with bows or firearms.

88. GRANTS FOR TRADE AND COLONIES (1578-1601)

(A) LETTERS PATENT TO SIR HUMPHREY GILBERT (1578)

Elizabeth, by the grace of God, queen of England, etc. . . . Know ye that . . . we have given and granted . . . , for us, our heirs, and successors . . . , to our trusty and well-beloved servant, Sir Humphrey Gilbert of Compton . . . , and to his heirs and assigns forever, free liberty and licence . . . at all times forever hereafter to discover, find, search out, and view such remote, heathen, and barbarous lands, countries, and territories, not actually possessed of any Christian prince or people, as to him . . . shall seem good; and the same to have . . . and enjoy to him, his heirs and assigns forever, with all commodities, jurisdictions, and royalties both by sea and land; and the said Sir Humphrey, and all such as from time to time by licence of us [etc.] shall go and travel thither, to inhabit or remain there, to build and fortify at the discretion of the said Sir Humphrey [etc.] . . .

And further that he, the said Humphrey [etc.] . . . , shall have . . . and enjoy to him [etc.] . . . all the soil of all such lands, countries, and territories so to be discovered or possessed as aforesaid . . . , to be had or used with full power to dispose thereof, and of every part thereof in fee simple or otherwise according to the order of the laws of England, as near as the same conveniently may be . . . ; paying unto us for all services, duties, and demands the fifth part of all the ore of gold and silver that . . . shall be there gotten. . . .

And for uniting in more perfect league and amity of such countries, lands, and territories so to be possessed and inhabited as aforesaid with our realms of England and Ireland, and for the better encouragement of men to this enterprise, we do by these presents

88. GRANTS FOR TRADE

grant and declare that all such countries, so hereafter to be possessed and inhabited as aforesaid, from thenceforth shall be of the allegiance of us, our heirs, and successors, and we do grant to the said Sir Humphrey [etc.] . . . , and to all and every other person and persons being of our allegiance . . . that with the assent of the said Sir Humphrey [etc.] . . . shall now in this voyage for discovery, or in the second journey for conquest, hereafter travel to such lands . . . as aforesaid . . . , that they . . . shall and may have . . . all the privileges of free denizens and persons native of England and within our allegiance. . . .

And forasmuch as, upon the . . . inhabiting of such remote lands . . . , it shall be necessary for the safety of all men . . . to determine to live together in Christian peace and civil quietness each with other . . . , we . . . are likewise pleased . . . [to] grant to the said Sir Humphrey [etc.] . . . that he and they . . . may from time to time . . . within the said mentioned remote lands . . . have full and mere power and authority to correct, punish, pardon, govern, and rule by their . . . good discretions and policies, as well in causes capital or criminal as civil . . . , all such our subjects and others as shall . . . hereafter adventure themselves in the said . . . voyages . . . or . . . inhabit any such lands . . . , according to such statutes, laws, and ordinances as shall be by him, the said Sir Humphrey [etc.] . . . , devised or established for the better government of the said people . . . ; so always that the said statutes [etc.] . . . may be, as near as conveniently may, agreeable to the form of the laws and policy of England, and also that they be not against the true Christian faith or religion now professed in the Church of England. . . .

Hakluyt, Principal Navigations, VIII, 17 f.

(B) CHARTER TO THE EAST INDIA COMPANY (1601)

Elizabeth, by the grace of God, etc. . . . Whereas our most dear and loving cousin, George, earl of Cumberland, and our well-beloved subjects, Sir John Hart, of London, knight, [and 217 others] have . . . been petitioners unto us for our royal assent and licence to be granted unto them, that they, at their own adventures, costs, and charges . . . , might adventure and set forth one or more voyages, with convenient number of ships and pinnaces, by way of traffic and merchandise to the East Indies, in the countries and parts of Asia and Africa, and to as many of the islands, ports, cities, towns and places thereabouts as where trade and traffic may by all likelihood be . . . had; divers of which countries and many of the islands, cities and ports thereof, have long since been discovered by others of our subjects, albeit not frequented in trade of merchandise: know ye therefore that we, greatly tendering the honour of our nation, the wealth of our people, and the encouragement of them and others of our loving subjects in their good enterprises, for the increase of our navigation and the advancement of lawful traffic to the benefit of our commonwealth, have . . . granted . . . unto our said loving subjects . . . that they . . . from henceforth be . . . one body corporate and politic, in deed and in name, by the name of the Governor and Company of Merchants of London Trading into the East Indies . . . ; and that by the same name . . . they shall have succession; and that they and their successors . . . shall be at all times hereafter . . . capable in law to have . . . and retain lands, rents, privileges, liberties, jurisdictions, franchises, and hereditaments of whatsoever kind . . . , and also to give . . . and dispose lands, tenements, and hereditaments, and to do and execute all . . . other things, by the same name, that to them shall appertain to do; and that they and their successors . . . may plead and be impleaded . . . in whatsoever courts and places . . . in all . . . actions . . . , causes, and demands whatsoever. . . .

And . . . we do ordain that there shall be from henceforth one of the same company . . . , which shall be called the governor of the said company; and that there shall be from henceforth twenty-four of the said company . . . , which shall be called the committee of the said company, who, together with the governor . . . , shall have the direction of the voyages of or for the said company, and the provision of the shipping and merchandises thereto belonging, and also the sale of all merchandises returned in the voyages . . . , and the managing and handling of all other things belonging to the said company. And for the better execution of this our will and grant in this behalf, we have assigned . . . and make the said Thomas Smith, alderman of London, to be the first and present governor of the said company . . . ; and also we have assigned . . . and make the said Paul Banning [and twenty-three others] to be the twenty-four first and present committees of the said company. . . .

And further we will . . . that it shall . . . be lawful to and for the said governor and company . . . present at any public assembly, commonly called the court, holden for the said company . . . to elect . . . one of the said company to be deputy to the said governor. . . . And further we will and grant . . . unto the said governor and company . . . that they . . . shall . . . have authority and power yearly . . . to elect and nominate one of the said company which shall be governor . . . for one whole year. . . .[1]

And further we . . . grant unto the said governor and company . . . that they . . . and all the sons of them . . . , at their several ages of one-and-twenty years or upwards, and further all such the apprentices, factors, and servants of them . . . , which hereafter shall be employed by the said governor and company . . . , may, by the space of fifteen years . . . , freely traffic and use the trade of merchandise by seas, in and by such ways and passages . . . as they shall esteem and take to be fittest, into and from the said East Indies, in the countries and parts of Asia and Africa . . . in such

---

[1] Members of the committee were also to be annually elected.

88. GRANTS FOR TRADE

order . . . as shall be from time to time at any public assembly or court held by or for the said governor and company . . . limited and agreed, and not otherwise . . . ; so always the same trade be not undertaken nor addressed to any country . . . or place already in the lawful and actual possession of any such Christian prince or state as at this present is or at any time hereafter shall be in league or amity with us, our heirs, or successors, and who doth not or will not accept of such trade, but doth overtly declare . . . the same to be utterly against his or their goodwill and liking.

And further . . . we do grant . . . that it shall and may be lawful to and for the said governor and company . . . to hold court for the said company and the affairs thereof; and that also it shall and may be lawful to and for them . . . to make, ordain, and constitute such and so many reasonable laws . . . as to them . . . shall seem necessary and convenient for the good government of the same company and of all factors, masters, mariners, and other officers employed or to be employed in any of their voyages . . . ; so always as the said laws . . . be reasonable and not contrary to the laws, statutes, or customs of this our realm. . . .

And we . . . grant to the said governor and company . . . that the said East Indies . . . shall not be visited . . . by any of the subjects of us . . . during the said term of fifteen years, contrary to the true meaning of these presents. And by virtue of our prerogative royal, which we will not in that behalf have argued or brought in question, we straitly charge . . . all the subjects of us . . . that none of them, directly or indirectly, do visit . . . or trade . . . into or from any of the said East Indies, or into or from any the . . . places aforesaid, other than the said governor and company . . . , unless it be by . . . licence and agreement of the said governor. . . .[2]

Charters Granted to the East India Company, pp. 3 f.

---

[2] Other articles provide penalties and allow for the revocation or continuance of the charter.

SECTION VIII

THE EARLY STUARTS

THE period from 1603 to 1642, though little more than a third of a century, is here represented by another long series of documents. The reason, of course, is the extraordinary interest of the constitutional struggle under James I and Charles I. And since the struggle was from the beginning concentrated in parliament, it has seemed best to arrange the pertinent materials according to certain convenient divisions of parliamentary history. In this way the various letters and speeches of the kings, as well as the formal resolutions, debates, and other proceedings of parliament, have been kept together in chronological order.

As in previous sections, a number of judicial records have been included for illustrative purposes—especially the reports of ordinary business in the courts of star chamber and high commission. But most of the cases under nos. 91 and 94 have a greater significance: they raised problems concerning the fundamentals of English government. Frequently the judgments by which they were concluded became political issues of first magnitude. Judges of the king's central courts now began to rival his ministers and generals in public fame.

The remaining documents in the present section require few words of comment. No. 97 is particularly valuable for its statement of the doctrine of divine right as officially set forth by some of the clergy. Under no. 98 a series of typical records from the counties show how, despite the rising conflict between crown and parliament, English local government continued its normal routine and constantly extended its activity. Lastly, in the three documents given under no. 99, may be seen the precedents set by the early Stuarts in colonial organization.

The constitutional developments of these momentous years cannot be explained in a short introductory note, but a word may be said with regard to certain important features of parliamentary history. With the first session in 1604, controversy between the king and his critics suddenly became acute. In Elizabeth's reign only a few members of the commons had been given to political agitation, and they had often been opposed by a majority of their fellows. Most argument concerning crown and parliament had then been couched in general terms. In 1604 the champions of parliamentary rights led a strong party in the commons and formulated a detailed programme. Under their guidance, the house drew up the Apology of the Commons, setting forth in large measure the issues that dominated the ensuing struggle. As controversy proceeded, those who spoke for the commons gradually strengthened the position of the house. They gave close attention to parliamentary procedure and marshalled legal precedents to vindicate their privileges and lawful powers—as may be seen by comparing the Apology with the Petition of Right. To refute their arguments, the king elaborated a more cogent statement of the monarchical cause, matching their proofs with his own. During the sessions of 1606-11 and 1621-29 the issues dividing the two camps thus came to be more sharply defined. If this development were to be fully illustrated, the whole series of parliamentary records would have to be drawn upon. For present purposes, however, examples of procedure have been taken from the years 1604-11, when many new practices came into use.

Before 1640 the struggle between king and parliament brought little change in the structure of English government, but with the opening of the Long Parliament the way was cleared for swift legislative action. The new laws (no. 96A-I) struck down the prerogative courts, set further limits to the king's fiscal rights, and assured the regular calling of parliament. This constitutional reform, one of the greatest in English history, was effected in the year 1641 and had the general support of the English public. A considerable party, however, made two additional demands: reorganization of the English Church according to Puritan principles, and extension of parliamentary control over the executive government. These demands (here reflected in no. 96J-P) led to the outbreak of civil war in the summer of 1642.

The great interest of the educated classes in constitutional problems under the early Stuarts had expression in two significant ways: the assiduous reporting of debates by ordinary members of parliament, and the historical study of English institutions. The first is best presented to the reader in the diaries edited by

W. Notestein and his associates;[1] the second in the works of Sir Edward Coke, Sir Simonds D'Ewes, and John Selden.

There are three standard collections of documents for the early Stuart period provided with valuable notes and introductions: G. W. Prothero, *Select Statutes and Other Constitutional Documents Illustrative of the Reigns of Elizabeth and James I;* J. R. Tanner, *Constitutional Documents of the Reign of James I;* S. R. Gardiner, *Constitutional Documents of the Puritan Revolution, 1625-1660.* For general exposition of constitutional history, the student is referred to S. R. Gardiner, *History of England, 1603-1642;* J. R. Tanner, *English Constitutional Conflicts of the Seventeenth Century;* and E. R. Turner, *The Privy Council of England in the Seventeenth and Eighteenth Centuries.* The fundamentals of English constitutional law—a subject given prominence in this and the following sections—will be found clearly introduced in A. V. Dicey, *The Law of the Constitution,* and W. R. Anson, *The Law and Custom of the Constitution.* The volume of *Cases in Constitutional Law* by Keir and Lawson also contains much valuable comment. A full bibliography on all constitutional topics is supplied by G. Davies, *Bibliography of British History: Stuart Period, 1603-1714,* sections i and ix.

---

[1] *Commons Debates, 1621,* edited by W. Notestein, F. H. Relf, and H. Simpson; *Common Debates for 1629,* edited by W. Notestein and F. H. Relf; *The Journal of Sir Simonds D'Ewes,* edited by W. Notestein. See also his "Winning of the Initiative by the House of Commons," in *Proceedings of the British Academy,* 1924.

89. RECORDS OF PARLIAMENT AND TAXES (1604-22)

(A) JAMES I: PROCLAMATION CONCERNING ELECTIONS (1604)

. . . We do hereby straitly charge and admonish all persons interested in the choice of knights for the shires, first, that the knights for the county be selected out of the principal knights or gentlemen of sufficient ability within that county wherein they are chosen; and, for the burgesses, that choice be made of men of sufficiency and discretion without any partial respects or factious combination. . . . Next and above all things, considering that one of the main pillars of this estate is the preservation of unity in the profession of sincere religion of Almighty God, we do also admonish that there be great care taken to avoid the choice of any persons either noted for their superstitious blindness one way, or for their turbulent humours other ways; because their disorderly and unquiet spirits will disturb all the discreet and modest proceeding in that greatest and gravest council. Further, we do command that an express care be had that there be not chosen any persons bankrupts or outlawed, but men of known good behaviour and sufficient livelihood, and such as are not only taxed to the payment of subsidies and other like charges, but also have ordinarily paid and satisfied the same . . . ; next, that all sheriffs be charged that they do not direct any precept for electing and returning of any burgesses to or for any ancient borough-town within their counties being so utterly ruined and decayed that there are not sufficient residents to make such choice, and of whom lawful election may be made; also to charge all cities and boroughs and the inhabitants of the same, that none of them seal any blanks, referring or leaving to any others to insert the names of any citizens or burgesses to serve for any such city or borough, [but that they] do make open and free election according to the law, and set down the names of the persons whom they choose before they seal the certificate. Furthermore, we notify by these presents that all returns and certificates of knights, citizens, and burgesses ought and are to be brought to the chancery, and there to be filed of record. And if any shall be found to be made contrary to this proclamation, the same is to be rejected as unlawful and insufficient, and the city or borough to be fined for the same; and if it be found that they have committed any gross or wilful default and contempt in their election, return, or certificate, that then their liberties according to the law are to be seized into our hands as forfeited. And if any person take upon him the place of a knight, citizen, or burgess, not being duly elected, returned, and sworn according to the laws and statutes in that behalf provided, and according to the purport, effect, and true meaning of this our proclamation, then every person so offending [is] to be fined and imprisoned for the same. . . .

Given at our honour of Hampton Court, the 11th day of January.

Rymer, *Foedera*, XVI, 561 f.

(B) EARLY PROCEEDINGS OF THE COMMONS (1604)

[22 March.] . . . Mr. Speaker with all submissive reverence to his majesty taking leave, he with the commons departed to their usual place. And there being assembled, the first motion was made by Sir William Fleetwood, one of the knights returned for the county of Buckingham on the behalf of Sir Francis Goodwin, knight, who, upon the first writ of summons directed to the sheriff of Buckingham, was elected the first knight for that shire; but, the return of his election being made, it was refused by the clerk of the crown, *quia utlagatus*,[1] and because Sir John Fortescue, upon a second writ, was elected and entered in that place. His desire was that this return might be examined and Sir Francis Goodwin received as a member of the house. The house gave way to the motion; and, for a more deliberate and judicial proceeding in a case of privilege so important to the house, ordered that the serjeant, the proper officer of the house,

---

[1] Because he had been outlawed; see below, p. 410.

should give warning to the clerk of the crown to appear at the bar at eight o'clock the next morning, and to bring with him all the writs of summons, indentures, and returns of elections for the county of Buckingham made and returned for this parliament; and to give warning also to Sir Francis Goodwin to attend in person, whom their pleasure was to hear . . . deliver the state of his own cause and the manner and reasons of the proceeding in the election of the knights of the shire for that county.

This, being a motion tending to matter of privilege, was seconded with another by Mr. Serjeant Shirley, touching an arrest made the 15th of March last, the day of his majesty's solemn entrance through London, and four days before the sitting of the parliament, upon the body of Sir Thomas Shirley, elected one of the burgesses for the borough of Steyning in the county of Sussex, at the suit of one Giles Sympson, a goldsmith, dwelling in Lombard Street, London, by one William Watkins, a serjeant-at-mace and Thomas Aram, his yeoman. And [it was] prayed that the body of the said Sir Thomas might be freed according to the known privilege of the house. Hereupon the house, in affirmation of their own privilege, assented, and ordered that a warrant, according to the ancient form, should be directed under the hand of Mr. Speaker to the clerk of the crown, for the granting of a writ of *habeas corpus* to bring the body of the said Sir Thomas into the house upon Tuesday next at eight o'clock in the morning. . . .

Sir George Moore, allowing these grave and advised resolutions in point of privilege, for the better advancement thereof and for a more deliberate and due proceeding in these and the like cases best beseeming the gravity and honour of that assembly, moved that a select committee might be appointed to consider of all cases of returns and privileges during the time of parliament. This is an usual motion in the beginning of every parliament.

[23 March.] This day may be called *dies juridicus*, the first day of business; the other were but of form and ceremony, yet ever usual and necessary in respect of the magnificence and state of such an assembly. *Principium a Deo:* the beginning was with prayers to God for good success; and such prayers as have been ordinary in former parliaments in the reign of the late queen, and are placed in the front of the Book of Common Prayer, were read by the clerk of the house, to whose place that service anciently appertains. And one other special prayer, fitly conceived for that time and purpose, was read by Mr. Speaker; which was voluntary and not of duty or necessity, though heretofore of late time the like hath been done by other speakers. . . .

After prayers ended and the house settled, with expectation of what should be propounded for the weal of the common subject; Sir Robert Wroth, one of the knights of the shire returned for the county of Essex, moved that matters of most importance might first

89. PARLIAMENT AND TAXES

be handled; and to that purpose offered to the consideration of the house these particulars: *viz.,* (1) confirmation of the Book of Common Prayer; (2) the wardship of men's children, as a burden and servitude to the subjects of this kingdom; (3) the general abuse and grievance of purveyors, and cart-takers, etc.; (4) particular and private patents, commonly called monopolies; (5) dispensations in penal statutes; (6) transportation of ordnance; (7) the writ of *quo titulo ingressi,* etc., abuses of the exchequer, etc.

This motion for the time passed with silence; and Sir Edward Montague, one of the knights for Northamptonshire, proceedeth in another; expressing three main grievances of his country and praying some care to be had of remedy for them: *viz.,* the burden, vexation, and charge of commissaries' courts; (2) the suspension of some learned and grave ministers for matters of ceremony and for preaching against popish doctrine; (3) depopulations by enclosure.

Sir Thomas Crompton, doctor of the civil law, and the king's advocate, being one of the burgesses returned for the university of Oxford by virtue of a new charter granted by his majesty that now is, with some length of speech examined the circumstances and approveth the general purpose of the former motion.

Another learned and good member of the house, taking occasion as well from Sir Thomas Shirley's case, opened the last sitting-day, as from the course begun in these foresaid motions, prayeth generally a consideration of the honour and privilege of this house; which, he said, ought to be kept sacred and inviolable. And thereof a true member of the body ought to be sensible and careful; but unnatural and strange members could not be so tender of the welfare of the whole. And therefore it were fit to examine whether every one here did hold his place by a lawful and just election and return, and were a true member of the body; that, if any were found otherwise, he might be cut off and dismissed, as incompatible for the service of this so honourable and well-compounded an assembly.

A third grave person, and an ancient parliament-man, remembereth and alloweth the motions made by Sir Robert Wroth and Sir Edward Montague; but moveth that nothing might be offered in a general and vanishing speech, without a bill ready framed and exhibited to the house by the mover.

Hereupon the motion was continued that a select committee might be named for the consideration of the particulars mentioned by Sir Robert Wroth; and to that purpose were called and set down by name. . . .[2] And the same committees [are] to make report of their proceeding in all or any of these from time to time, as they shall find fit or as the house shall direct them. And for their first meeting [they] are appointed to assemble themselves the same day at two o'clock in the afternoon in the exchequer chamber.

For the three grievances opened by Sir Edward Montague, were

---

[2] Forty-seven members of the house.

named. . . .³ And [they] were appointed to meet on Monday following . . . at two o'clock in the afternoon in the star chamber. . . .

Journals of the Commons, I, 149-51.

(C) THE CASE OF SIR FRANCIS GOODWIN (1604)

[23 March.] . . . Sir George Coppyn, knight, clerk of the crown in the chancery, this day, according to former order, being attended by the serjeant of the house with his mace, appeared at the bar and produced all the writs of summons, indentures, and returns made of the knights for Buckinghamshire for this parliament; which were severally read by the clerk of the house. And then the clerk of the crown [was] commanded to retire to the door; and after, Sir Francis Goodwin himself, whom it specially concerned, attending to know the pleasure of the house, was called in. . . .

In this meantime the whole case was at large opened and argued *pro et contra* by sundry learned and grave members of the house, and after much dispute the question was agreed upon and made, whether Sir Francis Goodwin were lawfully elected and returned one of the knights for Buckinghamshire and ought to be admitted and received as a member of this house. Upon this question it was resolved in the affirmative, that he was lawfully elected and returned and *de jure* ought to be received. Hereupon the clerk of the crown was commanded to file the first indenture of return, and order was given that Sir Francis should presently take the oath of supremacy usual and his place in the house; which he did accordingly. . . .

[29 March.] . . . Mr. Speaker relateth what he had delivered to the king by warrant from the house the day before touching their proceeding in Sir Francis Goodwin's case, and his majesty's answer. . . . He said he first delivered (1) the manner and the matter; (2) then such precedents as had been vouched and stood upon; (3) he opened the body of the law for election. . . . For the matter of outlawry . . . , Sir Francis has since been chosen, admitted, and served as a member of this house in . . . several parliaments. . . . The outlawry remained in the hustings; so, as the law could not take notice of it, neither was it pleadable. . . .

His majesty answered he was loath he should be forced to alter his tune, and that he should now change it into matter of grief by way of contestation. He did sample it to the murmur and contradiction of the people of Israel. He did not attribute the cause of his grief to any purpose in the house to offend him, but only to a mistaking of the law. For matters of fact, he answered them all particularly that, for his part, he was indifferent which of them were chosen, Sir John or Sir Francis; that they could suspect no special affection in him, because this was a counsellor not brought in by himself. That he had no purpose to impeach their privilege; but, since

---

³ All privy councillors in the house and fifty-nine others.

they derived all matters of privilege from him, and by his grant, he expected they should not be turned against him. [He said] that there was no precedent did suit this case fully; precedents in the times of minors, of tyrants, of women, of simple kings, [were] not to be credited, because [such were] for some private ends. By the law, this house ought not to meddle with returns, being all made into the chancery; and are to be corrected or reformed by that court only into which they are returned. [In] 35 Henry VI it was the resolution of all the judges that matter of outlawry was a sufficient cause of dismission of any member out of the house; that the judges have now resolved that Sir Francis Goodwin standeth outlawed according to the laws of this land. In conclusion, it was his majesty's special charge unto us that, first, the course already taken should be truly reported; (2) that we should debate the matter and resolve amongst ourselves; (3) that we should admit of conference with the judges; (4) that we should make report of all the proceedings unto the council. . . .

[30 March.] . . . Upon the conclusion of this debate . . . ,[4] the house proceeded to question. . . . First question: whether the house was resolved in the matter. And the question was answered by general voice that the whole house was resolved. Second question: whether the reasons of their proceeding shall be set down in writing. Resolved that they shall be set down in writing; and ordered further that a committee should be named for that purpose. . . . The committees were instantly named, *viz.* . . .

The house being resolved upon the question that the reasons of their precedent resolution touching the return, admittance, and retaining of Sir Francis Goodwin as a member of this house should be set down in writing, these committees were specially appointed to perform that service; and have warrant from the house to send for any officer, to view and search any record or other thing of that kind which may help their knowledge or memory in this particular service. And, having deliberately by general consent set down all such reasons, they are to bring them in writing into the house, there to be read and approved, as shall be thought fit.

[2 April.] . . . It was then moved that committees might be named to take the examination of the sheriff of Buckinghamshire, who was by former order sent for and now come. . . . The examination was presently taken by these committees and returned in this form:—

Interrogation 1: Why he removed the county [court] from Aylesbury to Brickhill. He saith it was by reason of the plague being at Aylesbury, the county [court] being the 25th of January, at which time three were dead of the plague there. This was [the] only motive of removing his county [court]. Interrogation 2: Whether he

---

[4] The house had debated the case of Goodwin since the speaker's report on the previous day.

were present at the first election. Saith he was present, and was as faithful to wish the second place to Sir Francis Goodwin as the first to Sir John Fortescue; sent Sir Francis Goodwin word before the election he should not need to bring any freeholders, for the election, he thought, would be without scruple for them both: first to Sir John, second to Sir Francis. About eight of the clock he came to Brickhill [and] was then told by Sir George Throckmorton and others that the first voice would be given for Sir Francis. He answered he hoped it would not be so and desired every gentleman to deal with his freeholders. After eight of the clock [he] went to the election, a great number there being children never at the county [court]. After the writ read, he first intimated the points of the proclamation; then jointly propounded Sir John Fortescue and Sir Francis Goodwin. The freeholders cried first, "A Goodwin! A Goodwin!" Every justice of peace on the bench said, "A Fortescue! A Fortescue!"; and came down from the bench before they named any for a second place and desired the freeholders to name Sir John Fortescue for the first. Sir Francis Goodwin, being in a chamber near, was sent for by the sheriff and justices; and he came down and earnestly persuaded with the freeholders, saying Sir John was his good friend; had been his father's; and that they would not do Sir John that injury. Notwithstanding, the freeholders would not desist, but still cried, "A Goodwin! A Goodwin!": some crying, "A Fortescue!" to the number of sixty or thereabouts; the other, for Sir Francis Goodwin, being about two or three hundred. And Sir Francis Goodwin, to his thinking, dealt very plainly and earnestly in this matter for Sir John Fortescue; for that Sir Francis Goodwin did so earnestly protest it unto him. . . .

[3 April.] . . . The reasons of the proceeding of the house in Sir Francis Goodwin's case penned by the committee were, according to former order, brought in by Mr. Francis Moore and read by the clerk, directed in form of a petition:—

To the king's most excellent majesty: The humble answer of the commons house of parliament to his majesty's objections in Sir Francis Goodwin's case. . . . There were objected against us by your majesty and your reverend judges four things to impeach our proceedings in receiving Francis Goodwin, knight, into our house. . . . The first [was] that we assumed to ourselves power of examining of the elections and returns of knights and burgesses, which belonged to your majesty's chancery and not to us. . . . Our humble answer is that until the seventh year of King Henry IV all parliament writs were returnable into the parliament. . . . In which year a statute was made that thenceforth every parliament writ . . . should have this clause. . . . By this, although the form of the writ be somewhat altered, yet the power of parliament to examine and determine of elections remaineth; for so the statute hath been always expounded . . . to this day. . . . And also the commons, in the begin-

89. PARLIAMENT AND TAXES 413

ning of every parliament, have ever used to appoint special committees all the parliament time for examining controversies concerning elections and returns of knights and burgesses; during which time the writs and indentures remain with the clerk of the crown, and after the parliament ended, and not before, are delivered to the clerk of the petty bag in chancery, to be kept there. Which is warranted by reason and precedents; reason, for that it is fit that the returns should be in that place examined, where the appearance and service of the writ is appointed. The appearance and service is in parliament; therefore the return [is] examinable in parliament. . . .[5]

[5 April.] Mr. Speaker excuseth his absence, by reason he was commanded to attend upon his majesty, and bringeth message from his majesty to this effect: that the king had received a parchment from the house. Whether it were an absolute resolution or reason to give him satisfaction he knew not; he thought it was rather intended for his satisfaction. His majesty protested, by that love he bare to the house, as his loving and loyal subjects, and by the faith he did ever owe to God, he had as great a desire to maintain their privileges as ever any prince had, or as they themselves. He had seen and considered of the manner and the matter; he had heard his judges and council; and . . . he was now distracted in judgment. Therefore, for his further satisfaction, he desired and commanded, as an absolute king, that there might be a conference between the house and the judges; and that, for that purpose, there might be a select committee of grave and learned persons out of the house; that his council might be present, not as umpires to determine, but to report indifferently on both sides.

Upon this unexpected message, there grew some amazement and silence; but at last one stood up and said: "The prince's command is like a thunderbolt; his command upon our allegiance like the roaring of a lion. To his command there is no contradiction; but how, or in what manner, we should now proceed to perform obedience, that will be the question." Another answered: "Let us petition to his majesty that he will be pleased to be present, to hear, moderate, and judge the case himself." Whereupon Mr. Speaker proceeded to this question: . . . whether to confer with the judges in the presence of the king and council. Which was resolved in the affirmative, and a select committee [was] presently named for the conference. . . .

These committees were selected and appointed to confer with the judges of the law touching the reasons of proceeding in Sir Francis Goodwin's case set down in writing and delivered to his majesty, in the presence of the lords of his majesty's council, according to his highness' pleasure, signified by Mr. Speaker this day to the house. It was further resolved and ordered by the house, upon the motion to that end by Mr. Lawrence Hyde, that the foresaid committees should

---

[5] The address then cites precedents and continues the argument to meet the other objections raised by the king.

insist upon the fortification and explaining of the reasons and answers delivered unto his majesty, and not proceed to any other argument or answer, what occasion soever moved in the time of that debate. . . .

[11 April.] . . . Sir Francis Bacon . . . reporteth what had passed in conference in the presence of his majesty and his council. The king said . . . that our privileges were not in question. . . . He granted it was a court of record and a judge of returns. He moved that neither Sir John Fortescue nor Sir Francis Goodwin might have place. . . .

Upon this report, a motion was made that it might be done by way of warrant. . . . Question: whether Sir John Fortescue and Sir Francis Goodwin shall both be secluded and a warrant for a new writ directed. And upon the question [it was] resolved that a writ should issue for a new choice, and a warrant [was] directed accordingly. . . .

Ibid., I, 151-68.

(D) THE CASE OF SIR THOMAS SHIRLEY (1604)

[27 March.] This day the writ of *habeas corpus*, formerly awarded by order of the house, for the bringing in of the body of Sir Thomas Shirley, one of the members of the house and prisoner in the Fleet, was returned by the warden of the Fleet. The prisoner himself [was] brought to the bar; and Simpson, the goldsmith, and Watkins, the serjeant-at-mace, as delinquents, [were] brought in by the serjeant of the house. The writ and return was read by the clerk. . . .

Mr. Speaker proposed divers questions to be answered by the said offenders by whose relation it was averred that the writ of execution was taken forth the 30th of January [and] was delivered to the serjeant the 11th of February, before Sir Thomas was elected burgess; that Simpson and the serjeant, in the interim before the arrest, had no conference or privity one with the other; that the serjeant knew nothing at all of Sir Thomas his election, but understood by his majesty's proclamation that no person outlawed for treason, felony, debt, or any other trespass ought to be admitted a member of the parliament, and was thereupon induced to think that Sir Thomas Shirley, standing outlawed, should not be elected or admitted a burgess; which if he had known or suspected, he would have been very careful not to have given offence to this honourable house by any such arrest.

To this Sir Thomas was admitted to answer, who affirmed that the arrest was made the 15th day of March, the day of his majesty's first and solemn entrance through London; at what time he was going by commandment to wait upon his majesty; whereof, upon the first offer to touch him, he wished the serjeant to take knowledge, as also that he was elected a burgess for the borough of Steyning in the county of Sussex to serve at this present parliament; that, notwith-

89. PARLIAMENT AND TAXES

standing, they persisted in the arrest and carried his body to the prison of the Compter. ...

And the whole case, after long dispute, [was] summarily considered in three particulars: *viz.*, first, privilege to a member; (2) interest reserved to a stranger; (3) punishment of the offender. Which being the grounds of all the subsequent arguments in this case, the dispute ended for this day; with caution that the house should so proceed as they gave not way and encouragement to others to practise to be arrested upon execution with a purpose, by pretence of privilege, to discharge the debt; and a motion that a special committee might be named for the consideration of all the questions and doubts in this case. ...

[16 April.] Moved that a bill might be drawn in the matter of Sir Thomas Shirley, wherein was to be considered only two things: justice of privilege and justice to the party. For better information of the house and direction to the committees, certain ancient precedents of petitions to the kings of this realm, with answer and assent from the said kings in the very point of privilege, and of arrest upon execution, taken out of the parliament records in the Tower, upon this occasion were produced and read in the house, in number three, as followeth. ...[6]

After these precedents read, and some consideration had what was to be done, the house agreed upon three questions: (1) whether Sir Thomas Shirley shall have privilege; (2) whether presently or [to] be deferred till further order; (3) whether we shall be petitioners to his majesty, according to former precedents, for some course of securing the debt to the party and saving harmless the warden of the Fleet. These questions, being severally put, were all resolved in the affirmative; and so left for this day. ...[7]

Ibid., I, 155-75.

(E) NOTES CONCERNING PROCEDURE IN THE COMMONS (1604-07)

[26 March 1604.] ... Note that committees, being once named and a place appointed for their meeting by the house, may from time to time, until the report of their proceedings be made, adjourn and alter their place and time of meeting and select such sub-committees from amongst themselves as they shall find cause, for any particular purpose or service, to be assigned by themselves or the house upon their report. ...

Note, as an ancient rule of the house, that upon any conference the number of the commons named for the said conference are always double to those of the lords; and the place and time of meeting [are] appointed by the lords. ...

[14 April 1604.] ... In the matter formerly proposed touching

---
[6] The commons cite Larke's case (no. 67c) and two later instances.
[7] Cf. no. 90c.

the abuses of purveyors, it was now argued whether it were fittest to proceed by way of petition to his majesty or by bill, by Mr. Martin, Mr. Hoskins, and Mr. Hyde, and, lastly, by Sir Henry Jenkins, who was observed to mistake the question and therefore, to prevent the idle expense of time, was interrupted by Mr. Speaker. And thereupon a rule [was] conceived that, if any man speak impertinently or besides the question in hand, it stands with the orders of the house for Mr. Speaker to interrupt him and to know the pleasure of the house, whether they will further hear him. . . .

[27 April 1604.] Sir Francis Bacon reporteth from the committee touching the union[8] that they had digested their resolutions into heads and assigned several parts to several persons of several qualities as they conceived fit . . . :—

Matter of generality or common reason, two parts: (1) that there is no cause of change, Sir Francis Bacon; (2) that there is no precedent of like change, Sir Edwin Sandys.

Matter of estate inward and of law: Mr. Serjeant Hobart, Serjeant Dodridge, Serjeant Tanfield, Mr. Attorney of the Wards.

Matter of estate foreign or matter of intercourse: Sir Henry Nevill, Sir Richard Spencer, Sir John Hollis, Sir Arthur Atye, Sir Christopher Perkins, Sir Lewis Lewknor, Sir George Carey, master of the chancery.

Matter of honour and reputation: Sir Francis Hastings, Sir Maurice Berkley, Sir George Moore, Sir Herbert Crofts, Mr. Martin, Mr. Yelverton, Sir John Savill, Sir Robert Wingfield, Sir Oliver St. John, Sir Robert Wroth, Mr. Crewe, Sir Edward Hobby, Mr. Hyde. . . .

[12 May 1604.] . . . The commissioners for the union [were] named by the house and a several question [was] put upon every name. Privy councillors, two: Sir John Stanhope, knight, vice-chamberlain to the king; Sir John Harbert, second secretary to his majesty. Common lawyers, four: Sir Francis Bacon, one of his majesty's counsel learned; Sir Thomas Hesketh, knight, attorney of the wards; Sir Lawrence Tanfield, knight, serjeant-at-law; Sir Henry Hobart, knight, serjeant-at-law. Civilians, two: Sir John Bennett, knight, doctor of the laws; Sir Daniel Dun, knight, doctor of the laws. Merchants, four: Sir Henry Billingsley, Mr. Robert Askwith, Mr. Thomas James, Mr. Henry Chapman. Ambassadors, two: Sir Edward Stafford, Sir Henry Nevill. Gentlemen of several qualities and parts of the kingdom, [sixteen]. . . .

[19 May 1604.] . . . A motion [was] made that there might be a special place built and assigned for the keeping of the register and records and papers of the house, etc.; and for the clerk and his servants to attend and write in for the service of the house. The lord

---

[8] The proposed union of England and Scotland, vainly urged by James I during these years.

89. PARLIAMENT AND TAXES

treasurer [was] to be moved in this. For this purpose a warrant was conceived in this form:—

... Whereas it is thought fit and so ordered by the commons house of parliament that all acts, resolutions, and judgments of the house, which are there entered and registered by their common servant, the clerk, should be written and engrossed in one fair register book, and that to be kept by the clerk for the use and direction of the said house; as also that all bills, whether passed or rejected, papers, notes, and other entries and proceedings of the house be preserved and kept in safety: it is required, on the behalf of the said house, that a room or place be provided near at hand with convenient presses and shelves, for the disposing and preserving of the said register, papers, and entries, and for the clerk and his servants to attend upon all occasions for the service of the said house; and this to be performed before the next session of this present parliament. Ed. Phelipps, speaker.

[8 June 1604.] ... Concluded and resolved, upon a double question, (1) that the great committee [for matters of religion] shall select a sub-committee amongst themselves to search, view, and consider of all such precedents as have warranted or may warrant this house to intermeddle with matters ecclesiastical; (2) to consider of the frame of a petition to be exhibited to his majesty for dispensation, with some learned and faithful ministers, in matters indifferent and of ceremony. And if they shall not think it meet to be done by way of petition, to report their opinion to the house. . . .

[26 June 1607.] ... The amendments and provisions annexed to the bill of hostile laws sent down from the lords were secondly read and committed to the great committee named upon the second reading of the bill itself in this house. And [it was] moved that Mr. Speaker might depart, and the committee being compounded of the whole house ... might, for saving of time, presently enter into consideration of their charge. Which, after some dispute whether it were fit or no, being without precedent, seldom moved, and carrying with it no decorum in respect of Mr. Speaker's ordinary and necessary attendance upon the house till eleven o'clock, grew to a question, *viz.*, whether the committee should now sit or in the afternoon. And [it was] resolved upon question they should meet in the afternoon and not now. . . .[9]

Ibid., I, 153, 154, 171, 188, 208, 215, 387.

---

[9] Robert Bowyer's diary (edited by D. H. Willson, pp. 350 f.) gives the following version of these proceedings: "Mr. Speaker did put the house in mind that there is but three courses: 'Either,' said he, 'you must be pleased to dispute it, or to commit it, or to put it to the question.' Whereupon it was committed, the whole house to be committees in this place this afternoon, but not upon a question. Sir William Stroude moved that, being but ten of the clock, the speaker might depart and the house presently to proceed by committee. Of this point divers opinions arose, whereupon the question was made whether now

(F) MESSAGE OF JAMES I TO THE COMMONS (5 JUNE 1604)

... Mr. Speaker delivereth from the king a message, of three parts: the motives of his majesty's unkindness; matter of his relation to us; of his princely satisfaction. When he looked into the gravity and judgment of this house, and of the long continuance of the parliament—[that] so few matters of weight [had been] passed and that matter of privilege had taken much time (which, notwithstanding, he was as careful to preserve as we ourselves)—he was moved with jealousy that there was not such proceeding as, in love, he expected. This [was] the cause of [his] unkindness ... ; we should not think this declaration to us was any condemnation of our ingratitude or forgetfulness of him, but by way of commemoration and admonition, as a father to his children. Neither did he tax us, but only [did] remember us of expedition omitted and desired. Lastly ... , he is resolved we have not denied anything which is fit to be granted. ... He had divers arguments of our good affections: (1) our doubt of his displeasure; (2) our desire to give him satisfaction, which he accepteth as a thing done because desired by us; (3) he observeth the difference of our proceeding, sithence his speech unto us, with greater expedition in those things desired to be effected by him than before. He giveth us thanks and wisheth we would not trouble ourselves with giving him satisfaction. And he giveth what time we desire for finishing the matters of importance depending. ...

Ibid., I, 232 f.

(G) THE APOLOGY OF THE COMMONS (20 JUNE 1604)

The form of apology and satisfaction to be presented to his majesty, penned and agreed by a former select committee, was now reported and delivered into the house by Sir Thomas Ridgeway, one of the committees. . . .

To the king's most excellent majesty: from the house of commons assembled in parliament. Most gracious sovereign, we cannot but with much joy and thankfulness of mind acknowledge your majesty's great graciousness in declaring lately unto us, by the mouth of our speaker, that you rested now satisfied with our doings. Which satisfaction ... yet proceeding merely from your majesty's most gracious disposition and not from any justification which on our behalf hath been made, we ... could not ... but tender in humble sort this further satisfaction. . . . With these minds, dread sovereign, your commons of England, represented now in us their knights, citizens, and burgesses, do come with this humble declaration to your

---

or in the afternoon. . . . It was put to the question and, the voices being doubtful and the question put again, the No prevailed. . . . After dinner members assembled in the house. The voice, as I and others conceived, was for Mr. Fuller to take the chair and some on Mr. Attorney. Mr. Fuller modestly refusing . . . , Mr. Attorney offered himself to it. . . ."

highness and in great assurance of your most gracious disposition, that your majesty with benignity of mind correspondent to our dutifulness, will be pleased to peruse it.

We know, and with great thankfulness to God acknowledge, that He hath given us a king of such understanding and wisdom as is rare to find in any prince in the world. Howbeit, seeing no human wisdom, how great soever, can pierce into the particularities of the rights and customs of people, or of the sayings and doings of particular persons, but by tract of experience and faithful report of such as know them . . . , what grief, what anguish of mind hath it been unto us at some times in presence to hear and see, in other things to find and feel by effect, your gracious majesty, to the extreme prejudice of this house of the commons, thereof so greatly wronged by information. . . ! We have been constrained, as well in duty to your royal majesty, whom with faithful hearts we serve, as to our dear country, for which we serve in this parliament . . . , freely to disclose unto your majesty the truth of such matters concerning your subjects, the commons, as heretofore by misinformation have been suppressed or perverted. Wherein . . . we shall reduce these misinformations to three principal heads: first, touching the cause of the joyful receiving of your majesty into this your kingdom; secondly, concerning the liberties and rights of your subjects of England and the privileges of this house; thirdly, touching the several actions and speeches passed in the house.

It has been told us to our faces by some of no small place, and the same spoken also in the presence of your majesty, that, on the 24th of March was twelvemonth,[10] we stood in so great fear that we would have given half we were worth for the security wherein we now stand. . . . We contrariwise most truly protest the contrary, that we stood not at that time, nor of many a day before, in any doubt or fear at all. We . . . , standing clear in our own consciences touching your majesty's right, were both resolute with our lives and all other abilities to have maintained the same against all the world. . . . But the true cause of our extraordinary great cheerfulness and joy in performing that day's duty was the great and extraordinary love which we bare towards your majesty's most royal and renowned person and a longing thirst to enjoy the happy fruits of your most wise, religious, just, virtuous, and gracious heart. Whereof not rumours, but your majesty's own writings, had given us a strong and undoubted assurance. . . .

Now concerning the ancient right of the subjects of this realm, chiefly consisting in the privileges of this house of the parliament, the misinformation openly delivered to your majesty hath been in three things: first, that we hold not our privileges of right, but of grace only, renewed every parliament by way of donative upon petition, and so to be limited; secondly, that we are no court of record,

---

[10] The day of Elizabeth's death.

nor yet a court that can command view of records, but that our proceedings here are only to acts and memorials, and that the attendance with the records is courtesy, not duty; and, lastly, that the examination of the returns of writs for knights and burgesses is without our compass, and due to the chancery. Against which assertions . . . , tending directly and apparently to the utter overthrow of the very fundamental privileges of our house—and therein of the rights and liberties of the whole commons of your realm of England, which they and their ancestors from time immemorial have undoubtedly enjoyed under your majesty's noble progenitors—we, the knights, citizens, and burgesses in the house of commons assembled in parliament, and in the name of the whole commons of the realm of England, with uniform consent for ourselves and our posterities, do expressly protest, as being derogatory in the highest degree to the true dignity, liberty, and authority of your majesty's high courts of parliament, and consequently to the right of all your majesty's said subjects, and the whole body of this your kingdom; and desire that this our protestation may be recorded to all posterity. And contrariwise . . . , we most truly avouch that our privileges and liberties are our rights and due inheritance no less than our very lands and goods; that they cannot be withheld from us, denied, or impaired, but with apparent wrong to the whole state of the realm; and that our making of request in the entrance of parliament to enjoy our privileges is an act only of manners and doth not weaken our right, no more than our suing to the king for our lands by petition. . . .

From these misinformed positions . . . the greatest part of our troubles, distrust, and jealousy have arisen; having apparently found that in this first parliament of the happy reign of your majesty the privileges of our house, and therein the liberties and stability of the whole kingdom, have been more universally and dangerously impugned than ever, as we suppose, since the beginnings of parliaments. For although it may be true that in the latter times of Queen Elizabeth some one privilege now and then were by some particular act attempted against . . . , yet was not the same ever by so public speech nor by positions in general denounced against our privileges. Besides that in regard to her sex and age which we had great cause to tender, and much more upon care to avoid all trouble, which by wicked practice might have been drawn to impeach the quiet of your majesty's right in the succession, those actions were then passed over, which we hoped, in succeeding times of freer access to your highness' so renowned grace and justice, to redress, restore, and rectify. Whereas, contrariwise, in this parliament . . . , by reason of those misinformations, not only privileges but the whole freedom of the parliament and realm have from time to time, upon all occasions, been mainly hewed at; the freedom of our persons in election hath been impeached; the freedom of our speech prejudiced by often reproofs; thirdly, particular persons noted with taunt and disgrace, who have spoken their consciences in matters proposed to the house, but with all due respect and reverence to your majesty. . . .

What cause we, your poor commons, have to watch over our privileges is manifest in itself to all men. The prerogatives of princes may easily and do daily grow; the privileges of the subject are for the most part at an everlasting stand. They may be by good providence and care preserved; but, being once lost, are not recovered but with much disquiet. If good kings were immortal as well as kingdoms, to strive so for privilege were vanity perhaps and folly. But, seeing the same God, who in His great mercy hath given us a most wise king and religious, doth also sometimes permit hypocrites and tyrants in His displeasure and for sins of people, from hence hath the desire of rights, liberties, and privileges, both for nobles and commons, had his just original; by which an harmonical and stable state is framed, each member under the head enjoying that right, and performing that duty, which for the honour of the head and happiness of the whole is requisite. Thus much touching the wrong done to your majesty by misinformation touching our privileges. The last kind of misinformation made to your majesty hath been touching the actions and speeches of particular persons used in the house. . . . It is very clear unto us, by the effect, that divers things spoken in the house have been perverted and very untruly reported to your majesty. . . .

And now, most gracious sovereign, these necessary grounds of our cause and defence being truly laid . . . , the justification of . . . particulars we trust will be plain and expedite. . . .

1. The gentleman usher's fault in depriving by his unaccustomed neglect a great part of our house from hearing your majesty's speech the first day of the parliament we could not . . . but complain of in decent sort among ourselves, and further we proceeded not. Your majesty's extraordinary great grace and favour, in rehearsing the day following your former admirable speech, did give us content with abundant increase of joy.

2. The yeomen of the guard's words were very opprobrious, and howsoever they might have been not unfitly applied to the peasants of France or boors of Germany, yet could they not be other than very reproachful and injurious to the great dignities and honour of the commons of this realm, who contain not only the citizens, burgesses, and yeomanry, but also the whole inferior nobility of the kingdom, and knights, esquires, and gentlemen; many of which are come immediately out of the most noble families, and some other of their worth advanced to high honour of your majesty's privy council, and otherwise have been employed in very honourable service. In sum, the sole persons of the higher nobility excepted, they contain the whole flower and power of your kingdom; with their bodies your wars, with their purses your treasures, are upheld and supplied. Their hearts are the strength and stability of your royal seat. All these, amounting to many millions of people, are representatively

present in us of the house of commons. The wrong done to us doth redound to the whole land and will so be construed. We could not therefore do less in duty to the realm than to advertise such a delinquent of the unseemliness of this fault; neither yet could we do more in duty to your majesty than upon his acknowledgment thereof to remit it.

3. The right of the liberty of the commons of England in parliament consisteth chiefly in these three things: first, that the shires, cities, and boroughs of England . . . have free choice of such persons as they shall put in trust to represent them; secondly, that the persons chosen during the time of the parliament, as also of their access and recess, be free from restraint, arrest, and imprisonment; thirdly, that in parliament they may speak freely their consciences without check or controlment, doing the same with due reverence to the sovereign court of parliament—that is, to your majesty and to both the houses, who all in this case make but one politic body, whereof your highness is the head. . . .

7. For matter of religion, it will appear by examination of truth and right that your majesty should be misinformed, if any man should deliver that the kings of England have any absolute power in themselves, either to alter religion (which God forfend should be in the power of any mortal man whatsoever!) or to make any laws concerning the same, otherwise than in temporal causes by consent of parliament. We have and shall at all times by our oaths acknowledge that your majesty is sovereign lord and supreme governor in both. Touching our own desires and proceedings therein, they have not been a little misconceived and misreported. We have not come in any Puritan or Brownist spirit to introduce their purity, or to work the subversion of the state ecclesiastical, as now it stands—things so far and so clear from our meaning as that, with uniform consent in the beginning of this parliament, we committed to the Tower a man who out of that humour had, in a petition exhibited to our house, slandered the bishops. But according to the tenor of your majesty's writ of summons directed to the counties from which we came, and according to the ancient and long-continued use of parliaments, as by many records from time to time appeareth, we came with another spirit, even the spirit of peace. We disputed not of matters of faith and doctrine; our desire was peace only, and our device of unity: how this lamentable and long-lasting dissension amongst the ministers (from which both atheism, sects, and ill life have received such encouragement and so dangerous increase) might at length, before help come too late, be extinguished. And for the ways of this peace, we are not addicted at all to our own inventions, but ready to embrace any fit way that may be offered. Neither desire we so much that any man, in regard of weakness of conscience, may be exempted after parliament from obedience to laws established, as that in this parliament such laws may be enacted as, by relinquishment of some few ceremonies of small importance, or by any way better,

a perpetual uniformity may be enjoined and observed. Our desire has been also to reform certain abuses crept into the ecclesiastical state, even as into the temporal; and, lastly, that the land might be furnished with a learned, religious, and godly ministry, for the maintenance of whom we would have granted no small contribution, if in these, as we trust, just and religious desires we had found that correspondency from other which was expected. . . .

9. . . . A general, extreme, unjust, crying oppression is in the cart-takers and purveyors. . . .[11] We have not in this parliament sought anything against them but execution of those laws which are in force already. We demand but that justice which our princes are sworn neither to deny, delay, nor sell.[12] That we sought into the accounts of your majesty's expense was not our presumption, but upon motion from the lords of your majesty's council and offer from your officers of your highness' household; and that upon a demand of a perpetual yearly revenue in lieu of the taking away of these oppressions—unto which composition neither knew we well how to yield, being only for justice and due right, which is unsalable, neither yet durst we impose it by law upon the people, without first acquainting them, and having their counsel unto it. But if your majesty might be pleased in your gracious favour to treat of composition with us for some grievance which is by law and just, how ready should we be to take that occasion and colour to supply your majesty's desire concerning these also, we hold for unjust, should appear, we nothing doubt, to your majesty's full satisfaction.

10. And therefore we come, lastly, to the matter of wards, and such other just burdens (for so we acknowledge them) as to the tenures of [in] capite and knight's service are incident. We cannot forget (for how were it possible?) how your majesty, in a former most gracious speech in your gallery at Whitehall, advised us for unjust burdens to proceed against them by bill; but for such as were just, if we desired any ease, that we should come to yourself by way of petition, with tender of such countervailable composition in profit as for the supporting of your royal estate was requisite. According unto which your majesty's most favourable grant and direction, we prepared a petition to your most excellent majesty for leave to treat with your highness touching a perpetual composition, to be raised by yearly revenue out of the lands of your subjects for wardships and other burdens depending upon them or springing with them. Wherein we first entered into this dutiful consideration, that this prerogative of the crown, which we desire to compound for, was a matter of mere profit and not of any honour at all or princely dignity. . . . Our sayings have always been that this burden was just, that the remitting thereof must come from your majesty's grace, and that the denying of the suit were no wrong unto us. . . .

---

[11] Cf. no. 62J.
[12] Art. 40 of Magna Carta (above, p. 121).

There remaineth ... yet one part more of our duty at this present. ... Let your majesty be pleased to receive public information from your commons in parliament as well of the abuses in the church as in the civil estate and government; for private informations pass often by practice. The voice of the people in things of their knowledge is said to be as the voice of God. And if your majesty shall vouchsafe at your best pleasure and leisure to enter into gracious consideration of our petitions, for ease of those burdens under which your whole people have long time mourned, hoping for relief by your majesty, then may you be assured to be possessed of their hearts; and, if of their hearts, then of all they can do or have. And we, your majesty's most humble and loyal subjects, whose ancestors have with great loyalty, readiness, and joyfulness, served your famous progenitors, kings and queens of this realm, shall with like loyalty and joy, both we and our posterity serve your majesty and your most royal issue forever with our lives, lands, and goods, and all other our abilities; and by all means endeavour to procure your majesty's honour with all plenty, tranquillity, joy, and felicity.[13]

Ibid., I, 243.

(H) JAMES I: LEVY OF IMPOSITIONS (1608)[14]

James, by the grace of God king ... , to our right trusty and right well-beloved councillor, Robert, earl of Salisbury, our high treasurer of England, greeting. It is well known unto all men of judgment ... that the care imposed upon princes to provide for the ... welfare of their subjects is accompanied with so heavy a charge as all the circumstances belonging thereunto can hardly fall under the conceit of any other than of those who are acquainted with the carriage of public affairs. And therefore this special power and prerogative, amongst many others, hath both by men of understanding in all ages and by the laws of all nations been yielded and acknowledged to be proper and inherent in the persons of princes, that they may according to their several occasions raise to themselves such fit and competent means by levying of customs and impositions upon merchandises transported out of their kingdoms or brought into their dominions, either by the subjects born under their allegiance or by strangers ... , as to their wisdoms and discretions may seem convenient, without prejudice of trade and commerce, sufficiently to supply and sustain the great ... expense incident unto them in the maintenance of their crowns and dignities. So we at this time, out of many ... weighty considerations, as well for the exonerating of

---

[13] The official journal contains only the beginning of this document; the rest of the preceding version has been transcribed from *State Papers Domestic, James I,* viii, fol. 60 f. For evidence that the Apology was actually presented to the king, see Notestein, Relf, and Simpson, *Commons Debates, 1621,* V, 433.

[14] This was a general order issued by the king as the result of his victory in Bates' case (no. 91A).

89. PARLIAMENT AND TAXES

the crown of divers just . . . debts as for the supply of many other our . . . important occasions known to us and our council, and now particularly for the service of Ireland . . . , have been forced to resort to some such course of raising profit upon merchandise passing outward and inward as in former times hath been usual, not only by our progenitors, kings and princes of this realm, but also often in practice among other nations. . . . And although we have resolved to lay some kind of impositions both upon many foreign merchandises brought into this our realm and also upon divers native commodities and merchandises . . . , yet, to the intent it may appear what care we have in all things of this nature to avoid the least inconvenience or grievance that may arise to our people, we have . . . given special charge in the levying of the same to . . . exempt all such merchandises as are requisite for the food and sustenance of our people, or which contain matter of munition necessary for the defence of our realms . . . , or any other . . . materials fit . . . for the maintenance and enlargement of trade and navigation. . . .

Know ye therefore that, for the considerations aforesaid . . . , we have . . . ordained . . . that there shall be forever, from and after the 29th day of September next ensuing . . . , levied, taken, and received by way of imposition now newly set, over and besides the customs, subsidies, and other duties heretofore due and payable unto us, upon all merchandises . . . which . . . shall be either brought from any part beyond the seas unto this our realm . . . or which shall be transported . . . forth of the same . . . , just so much for the said new imposition as hath been and is now answered and paid unto us for the subsidy of the said merchandises, and neither more nor less . . . ; excepting such merchandises only as in a schedule hereunto annexed are expressed, which are either altogether . . . exempted from payment of any of the said new impositions or else are appointed . . . to pay the same in such proportion as is either more or less than the subsidy payable for the same, as in the said schedule is more plainly . . . expressed. Wherefore we do . . . command you that forthwith . . . you give order . . . unto all customers or collectors . . . and other our officers and ministers of all our ports . . . that they shall . . . take of all Englishmen, aliens . . . , and all persons . . . which shall bring into this our realm . . . or . . . carry forth . . . of the same . . . any goods, wares or merchandises . . . so much for and by way of the said new imposition as hath been and now is answered and paid unto us for the subsidy of the said merchandises. . . .

Prothero, Constitutional Documents, pp. 353 f.

(I) ADDRESS OF THE COMMONS TO JAMES I (1610)

Most gracious sovereign: Whereas your majesty's most humble subjects, the commons assembled in parliament, have received, first by message and since by speech from your majesty, a commandment of restraint from debating in parliament your majesty's right of imposing upon your subjects' goods exported or imported out of or into this realm; yet allowing us to examine the grievance of those impositions in regard of quantity, time, and other circumstances of disproportion thereto incident: we your said humble subjects, nothing doubting but that your majesty had no intent by that commandment to infringe the ancient and fundamental right of the liberty of the parliament in point of exact discussing of all matters concerning them and their possessions, goods, and rights whatsoever (which yet we cannot but conceive to be done, in effect, by this commandment), do with all humble duty make this remonstrance to your majesty:—

First, we hold it an ancient, general, and undoubted right of parliament to debate freely all matters which do properly concern the subject and his right or state; which freedom of debate being once foreclosed, the essence of the liberty of parliament is withal dissolved.

And whereas, in this case, the subjects' right on the one side and your majesty's prerogative on the other cannot possibly be severed in debate of either: we allege that your majesty's prerogatives of that kind, concerning directly the subjects' right and interest, are daily handled and discussed in all courts at Westminster, and have been ever freely debated upon all fit occasions both in this and all former parliaments without restraint; which being forbidden, it is impossible for the subject either to know or to maintain his right and propriety to his own lands and goods, though never so just and manifest.

It may farther please your most excellent majesty to understand that we have no mind to impugn, but a desire to inform ourselves of, your highness' prerogative in that point, which, if ever, is now most necessary to be known; and though it were to no other purpose, yet to satisfy the generality of your majesty's subjects, who, finding themselves much grieved by these new impositions, do languish in much sorrow and discomfort.

These reasons, dread sovereign, being the proper reasons of parliament, do plead for the upholding of this our ancient right and liberty. Howbeit, seeing it hath pleased your majesty to insist upon that judgment in the exchequer[15] as being direction sufficient for us without further examination, upon great desire of leaving your majesty unsatisfied in no one point of our intents and proceedings, we profess, touching that judgment, that we neither do nor will take upon us to reverse it; but our desire is to know the reasons whereupon the same was grounded, and the rather for that a general conceit is had that the reasons of that judgment may be extended much farther, even to the utter ruin of the ancient liberty of this kingdom, and of your subjects' right of propriety of their lands and goods. . . .

We therefore, your highness' loyal and dutiful commons, not

---

[15] Bates' case (no. 91A).

89. PARLIAMENT AND TAXES

swerving from the approved steps of our ancestors, most humbly and instantly beseech your gracious majesty that, without offence to the same, we may, according to the undoubted right and liberty of parliament, proceed in our intended course of a full examination of these new impositions. . . .[16]

Journals of the Commons, I, 431 f.

(J) Letter of James I to the Commons (1621)

Mr. Speaker: We have heard by divers reports, to our great grief, that our distance from the houses of parliament, caused by our indisposition of health, hath emboldened some fiery and popular spirits of some of the house of commons to argue and debate publicly of the matters far above their reach and capacity, tending to our high dishonour and breach of prerogative royal. These are therefore to command you to make known, in our name, unto the house that none therein shall presume henceforth to meddle with anything concerning our government or deep matters of state; and, namely, not to deal with our dearest son's match with the daughter of Spain, nor to touch the honour of that king or any other our friends and confederates, and also not to meddle with any man's particulars which have their due motion in our ordinary courts of justice. And whereas we hear they have sent a message to Sir Edward[17] Sandys to know the reasons of his late restraint, you shall in our name resolve them that it was not for any misdemeanour of his in parliament. But, to put them out of doubt of any question of that nature that may arise among them hereafter, you shall resolve them, in our name, that we think ourself very free and able to punish any man's misdemeanours in parliament, as well during their sitting as after—which we mean not to spare hereafter upon any occasion of any man's insolent behaviour there that shall be ministered unto us. And if they have already touched any of these points, which we have forbidden, in any petition of theirs which is to be sent unto us, it is our pleasure that you shall tell them that, except they reform it before it come to our hands, we will not deign the hearing nor answering of it.

Rushworth, *Historical Collections,* I, 43 f.

(K) Debates in the Commons on Privilege (1621)

. . . Here again, the speaker going out of the chair, the grand committee falleth into debate of the privileges of the house. Mr.

---

[16] No clear statement of the royal reply to this petition is contained in the official journal of the house, but a private diary of the period (Gardiner, *Parliamentary Debates in 1610,* pp. 41 f.) gives the following report: ". . . For our petition, he granted it as we had set it down ourselves, but he put us in mind to observe three things therein contained: (1) not to impugn his prerogative; (2) to seek his content and satisfaction; (3) to endeavour to unite and confirm his subjects' hearts unto him—protesting that he never meant to abridge us of any liberties appertaining unto us, which he hoped we would not abuse."

[17] A mistake for Edwin.

Alford would have a select committee appointed to consider of the points of such of our privileges as are impeached, and to draw a protestation for the same privileges in particular and also of all the rest in general. Mr. Thomas Crewe saith that, though the calling of a parliament and the continuing, prorogation, and dissolving of it be in the king's sole power, yet, when we are called, we are without limitation to deal in what business ourselves think best; for otherwise shall we not be able to do their business for whom we come hither, which is that of the country. He would not have this committee to insist so much on particulars as on the generality of our privileges. Sir Edward Coke would not have us here at this time, in the handling and debating of our privileges, to meddle with war or marriage; and would have a sub-committee appointed for this; and this sub-committee shall consider of all those matters which are mentioned in the writ of parliament, and also of our liberty of speech and of our power to punish those that speak too lavishly, and of our power to meddle and debate of what we shall of ourselves think fit.

The heads to be considered of by the sub-committee for privileges: (1) concerning freedom of speech; and therein to treat *de arduis et urgentibus negotiis regni* according to the writ of summons, whether it be concerning the king or otherwise; (2) touching the liberty of this house to punish the misdemeanours of any parliament-man in parliament for things whereof this house hath cognizance, whether he ought not to be censured here by the house only; (3) whether, when we receive commandment from the king, the house shall thereon desist, and not proceed notwithstanding such command in any business; (4) whether our privileges be not our right and inheritance; (5) that the sub-committee shall consider of anything else incident to the liberty of the house; (6) that the sub-committee shall consider whether it be not fit for us to make an expression here in the house, that it is an ancient privilege of parliament that no member of this house shall presume to acquaint the king with any business in debate here but by order from the whole house or from the speaker.

It is ordered at this grand committee that a sub-committee shall reduce all these heads which have been propounded into the form of a protestation; and that they shall render an account and their reasons of such things as they shall think not fit to be reduced into a protestation. And the sub-committee is appointed accordingly, and is to sit this afternoon in the committee chamber.

The speaker being in the chair, it is ordered that the speaker shall attend here at four of the clock this afternoon; that, the sub-committee having drawn the foresaid heads into the form of a protestation and made a report thereof to the grand committee, the house may, if occasion be, confirm the protestation; because otherwise it may be the king will command the house to be adjourned before such protestation be made in the house, and so may we endanger the validity of our privileges and liberties in those points wherein

89. PARLIAMENT AND TAXES

they have seemed to be impeached at this our meeting, *viz.*, in those heads before ordered to be considered of by the sub-committee. . . .

The sub-committee bring the draught of a protestation of the grand committee, which containeth as followeth:—

The commons, now assembled in parliament, being justly occasioned thereunto, concerning sundry liberties, franchises, and privileges of parliament amongst others not herein mentioned, do make this protestation following: That the liberties, franchises, privileges and jurisdictions of parliament are the ancient and undoubted birthright and inheritance of the subjects of England; and that the arduous and urgent affairs concerning the king, state, and the defence of the realm, and of the Church of England, and the making and maintenance of laws, and redress of mischiefs and grievances, which daily happen within this realm, are proper subjects and matter of counsel and debate in parliament; and that in the handling and proceeding of those businesses every member of the house hath and of right ought to have freedom of speech to propound, treat, reason, and bring to conclusion the same; that the commons in parliament have like liberty and freedom to treat of those matters in such order as in their judgments shall seem fittest; and that every such member of the said house hath like freedom from all impeachment, imprisonment, and molestation (other than by the censure of the house itself) for or concerning any bill, speaking, reasoning, or declaring of any matter or matters touching the parliament or parliament business; and that, if any of the said members be complained of and questioned for anything said or done in parliament, the same is to be showed to the king by the advice and assent of all the commons assembled in parliament before the king give credence to any private information.

The speaker being in the chair, it is ordered, by question in the house, that this protestation shall be here entered forthwith in the book of the house, and there to remain as of record. And accordingly it was here entered, sitting the house, between five and six of the clock at night by candle-light.[18]

Nicholas, *Proceedings in the Commons in 1620 and 1621*, II, 357 f.

(L) The King's Dissolution of Parliament (1622)

Albeit the assembling, continuing, and dissolving of parliaments be a prerogative so peculiarly belonging to our imperial crown, and the times and seasons thereof so absolutely in our own power, that we need not give account thereof unto any; yet, according to our continual custom to make our good subjects acquainted with the reasons of all our public resolutions and actions, we have thought it expedient at this time to declare, not only our pleasure and resolution therein, grounded upon mature deliberation with the advice and

---

[18] In the margin of the journal, where this entry had been made, is the memorandum: "King James in council with his own hand rent out this protestation" (*Journals of the Commons*, I, 668, note a).

uniform consent of our whole privy council, but therewith also to note some especial proceedings moving us to this resolution. . . .

This parliament was by us called, as for making good . . . laws, so more especially, in this time of miserable distraction throughout Christendom, for the better settling of peace and religion and restoring our children to their ancient and lawful patrimony. . . . This parliament, beginning in January last, proceeded some months with such harmony between us and our people as cannot be paralleled by any former time; for, as the house of commons at the first, both in the manner of their supply and otherwise, showed greater love and more respect than ever any house of commons did to us or, as we think, to any king before us, so we upon all their complaints have afforded them such memorable and rare examples of justice as many ages past cannot show the like. . . . And although, after their first recess at Easter, we found that they misspent a great deal of time . . . , yet we gave them time and scope for their parliamentary proceedings and prolonged the session to an unusual length. . . .

But, during the time of this long recess having to our great charges mediated with the emperor by the means of our ambassador, the lord Digby, and having found those hopes to fail . . . , we, in confidence of the assistance of our people thus freely promised and protested in parliament, did . . . reassemble our parliament the 20th day of November last, and made known unto them the true state and necessity of our children's affairs. . . . Wherein, howbeit we are well satisfied of the good inclination of most part of our house of commons, testified by their ready assent to the speedy payment of a subsidy newly to be granted; yet, upon this occasion, some particular members of that house took such inordinate liberty, not only to treat of our high prerogatives and of sundry things that, without our special direction, were no fit subjects to be treated of in parliament, but also to speak with less respect of foreign princes, our allies, than was fit for any subject to do of any anointed king, though in enmity and hostility with us. And when, upon this occasion, we used some reprehension towards those miscarriages, requiring them not to proceed but in such things as were within the capacity of that house according to the continual custom of our predecessors; then, by the means of some evil-affected and discontented persons, such heat and distemper was raised in the house that, albeit themselves had sued unto us for a session and for a general pardon, unto both which at their earnest suit we assented, yet after this fire kindled they rejected both and, setting apart all businesses of . . . weight, notwithstanding our . . . earnest pressing them to go forward, they either sat as silent or spent the time in disputing of privileges, descanting upon the words and syllables of our letters and messages. . . . And notwithstanding the sincerity of our protestations not to invade their privileges, yet, by persuasion of such as had been the cause of all these distempers, they fall to carve for themselves and, pretending causelessly to be occasioned thereunto, in an unseasonable hour of the

day and a very thin house, contrary to their own customs in all
matters of weight, conclude and enter a protestation for their liberties,
in such ambiguous and general words as might serve for future times
to invade most of our . . . prerogative annexed to our imperial crown;
whereof, not only in the times of other our progenitors but in the
blessed reign of our late predecessor, that renowned queen, Elizabeth, we found our crown actually possessed—an usurpation that
the majesty of a king can no means endure. By all which may appear
that, howsoever in the general proceedings of that house there are
many footsteps of . . . well-affected duty towards us, yet some
ill-tempered spirits have sowed tares among the corn, and thereby frus-
trated the hope of that plentiful . . . harvest which might have multi-
plied the wealth and welfare of this whole land, and by their cunning
diversions have imposed upon us a necessity of discontinuing this
present parliament without putting unto it the name or period of
a session.

And therefore, whereas the said assembly of parliament was by
our commission adjourned until the 8th day of February now next
ensuing, we, minding not to continue the same any longer . . . , have
thought fit to signify this our resolution, with the reasons thereof,
unto all our subjects inhabiting in all parts of this realm; willing
and requiring the said prelates, noblemen, and states, and also the
said knights, citizens, and burgesses, and all others to whom in this
case it shall appertain, that they forbear to attend at the day and
place prefixed by the said adjournment. . . . And albeit we are at
this time enforced to break off this convention of parliament, yet
our will and desire is that all our subjects should take notice, for
avoiding of all sinister suspicions and jealousies, that our . . . full
resolution is to govern our people in the same manner as our progenitors and predecessors, kings and queens of this realm, of best government, have heretofore done . . . ; and that we shall be as glad
to lay hold on the first occasion in . . . convenient time, which we
hope shall not be long, to . . . assemble our parliament with confidence
of the . . . hearty love . . . of our subjects, as either we or any of
our progenitors have at any time heretofore.

Rymer, Foedera, XVII, 344.

90. JAMES I: STATUTES

(A) Succession Act (1604)

A most joyful and just recognition of the immediate, lawful, and undoubted succession, descent, and right of the crown. . . . We . . . ,
your most humble and loyal subjects, the lords spiritual and temporal
and the commons in this present parliament assembled, do from the
bottom of our hearts yield to the divine majesty all humble thanks
and praises . . . , and in most humble and lowly manner do beseech
your most excellent majesty that, as a memorial to all posterities
amongst the records of your high court of parliament forever to

endure, of our loyalty, obedience, and hearty and humble affection, it may be published and declared in this high court of parliament, and enacted by authority of the same, that we, being bounden thereunto both by the laws of God and man, do recognize and acknowledge, and thereby express our unspeakable joys, that immediately upon the dissolution and decease of Elizabeth, late queen of England, the imperial crown of the realm of England, and of all the kingdoms, dominions, and rights belonging to the same, did, by inherent birthright and lawful and undoubted succession, descend and come to your most excellent majesty, as being lineally, justly, and lawfully next and sole heir of the blood royal of this realm as is aforesaid; and that, by the goodness of God Almighty and lawful right of descent, under one imperial crown, your majesty is of the realms and kingdoms of England, Scotland, France, and Ireland the most potent and mighty king. . . .

Statutes of the Realm, IV, 1017 f.: 1 James I, c. 1.

(B) ACT TO EXPLAIN THE STATUTE OF ARTIFICERS (1604)[1]

An act . . . for the explanation of the statute . . . concerning labourers. . . . Whereas the said act hath not, according to the true meaning thereof, been duly put in execution . . . , by reason that ambiguity and question have risen and been made whether the rating of all manner of artificers . . . , other than such as by some statute and law have been rated or else such as did work about husbandry, should or might be rated by the said law: forasmuch as the said law hath been found beneficial for the commonwealth, be it enacted by authority of this present parliament that the said statute, and the authority by the same statute given to any person or persons for assessing and rating of wages . . . , shall be expounded and construed, and shall by force of this act give authority to all persons having any such authority to rate wages of any labourers, weavers, spinsters, and workmen or workwomen whatsoever, either working by the day, week, month, year, or taking any work at any person or persons' hand whatsoever, to be done in great or otherwise. . . .

And furthermore be it enacted . . . that, if any clothier or other shall refuse to obey the said order, rate, or assessment of wages as aforesaid, and shall not pay so much or so great wages to their weavers, spinsters, workmen, or workwomen as shall be so set down, rated, and appointed . . . , that then every clothier and other . . . persons so offending shall forfeit . . . for every such offence, to the party aggrieved, 10*s*.; and that, if the . . . offence and offences of not paying so much or so great wages to their . . . workmen, workwomen, and others shall be confessed by the offender, or . . . the same shall be proved by two sufficient and lawful witnesses before the justices of peace in their quarter sessions . . . , the justices

---
[1] No. 81c.

of assize in their sessions, or before any two justices of the peace . . . , then every such person shall forthwith stand and be in law convicted thereof. . . .

Provided, nevertheless, . . . that no clothier, being a justice of peace in any precinct or liberty, shall be any rater of any wages for any weaver, tucker, spinster, or other artisan that dependeth upon the making of cloth; and in case there be not above the number of two justices of peace within such precinct or liberty but such as are clothiers, that in such case the same wages shall be rated and assessed by the major part of the common council of such precinct or liberty, and such justice or justices of peace, if any there be, as are not clothiers.

Ibid., IV, 1022 f.: 1 James I, c. 6.

(C) GENERAL ACT IN SHIRLEY'S CASE (1604)[2]

An act for new executions to be sued against any which shall hereafter be delivered out of execution by privilege of parliament, and for discharge of them out of whose custody such persons shall be delivered. Forasmuch as heretofore doubt hath been made, if any person being arrested in execution and by privilege of either of the houses of parliament set at liberty, whether the party at whose suit such execution was pursued be forever after barred and disabled to sue forth a new writ of execution in that case: for the avoiding of all further doubt and trouble which in like cases may hereafter ensue, be it enacted by the king's most excellent majesty, by the lords spiritual and temporal, and by the commons in this present parliament assembled that from henceforth the party at or by whose suit such writ of execution was pursued, his executors, or administrators, after such time as the privilege of that session of parliament in which such privilege shall be so granted shall cease, may sue forth and execute a new writ or writs of execution in such manner and form as by the law of this realm he or they might have done if no such former execution had been taken forth and served; and that from henceforth no sheriff, bailiff, or other officer, from whose arrest or custody any such person so arrested in execution shall be delivered by any such privilege, shall be charged or chargeable with or by any action whatsoever for delivering out of execution any such privileged person so as is aforesaid by such privilege of parliament set at liberty—any law, custom, or privilege heretofore to the contrary notwithstanding. Provided always that this act or anything therein contained shall not extend to the diminishing of any punishment to be hereafter by censure in parliament inflicted upon any person which hereafter shall make or procure to be made any such arrest as is aforesaid.

Ibid., IV, 1029: 1-2 James I, c. 13.

---

[2] Cf. no. 89D.

(D) STATUTE OF MONOPOLIES (1624)

An act concerning monopolies and dispensations with penal laws and the forfeiture thereof. Forasmuch as your most excellent majesty, in your royal judgment and of your blessed disposition to the weal and quiet of your subjects, did, in the year of our Lord God 1610, publish in print to the whole realm and to all posterity that all grants of monopolies and of the benefit of any penal laws, or of power to dispense with the law or to compound for the forfeiture, are contrary to your majesty's laws, which your majesty's declaration is truly consonant and agreeable to the ancient and fundamental laws of this your realm; and whereas your majesty was further graciously pleased expressly to command that no suitor should presume to move your majesty for matters of that nature; yet, nevertheless, upon misinformations and untrue pretences of public good, many such grants have been unduly obtained and unlawfully put in execution, to the great grievance and inconvenience of your majesty's subjects, contrary to the laws of this your realm and contrary to your majesty's royal and blessed intention so published as aforesaid: for avoiding whereof and preventing of the like in time to come, may it please your most excellent majesty . . . that it may be declared and enacted, and be it declared and enacted . . . , that all monopolies and all commissions, grants, licences, charters and letters patents . . . to any person . . . , bodies politic or corporate whatsoever . . . , for the sole buying, selling, making, working, or using of anything within this realm or the dominion of Wales, or of any other monopolies, or of power . . . to dispense with any others, or to give licence or toleration to do . . . anything against the tenor . . . of any law or statute . . . , and all proclamations, inhibitions, restraints, warrants of assistance, and all other . . . things whatsoever any way tending to the instituting . . . or countenancing of the same . . . , are altogether contrary to the laws of this realm, and so are and shall be utterly void and of none effect. . . .

And be it further . . . enacted . . . that all monopolies and all such commissions, grants . . . , and all other . . . things tending as aforesaid . . . ought to be and shall be forever hereafter . . . tried and determined . . . according to the common laws of this realm, and not otherwise. . . .

Provided nevertheless . . . that any declaration before mentioned shall not extend to any letters patents and grants of privilege for the term of one-and-twenty years or under, heretofore made of the sole working or making of any manner of new manufacture within this realm to the first and true inventor or inventors of such manufactures, which others, at the time of the making of such letters patents and grants, did not use, so they be not contrary to the law, nor mischievous to the state by raising of the prices of commodities at home or hurt of trade, or generally inconvenient; but that the same shall be of such force as they were or should be if this act had not been made. . . .

Provided also, and be it . . . enacted, that any declaration before mentioned shall not extend to any letters patents and grants of privilege for the term of fourteen years or under, hereafter to be made, of the sole working or making of any manner of new manufactures within this realm, to the true and first inventor and inventors of such manufactures. . . .

Ibid., IV, 1212 f.: 21-22 James I, c. 3.

91. RECORDS OF JUDICIAL CASES (1606-21)

(A) BATES' CASE (1606)[1]

Clark: . . . It seemeth to me strange that any subjects would contend with the king in this high point of prerogative; but such is the king's grace that he had showed his intent to be that this matter shall be disputed and adjudged by us according to the ancient law and custom of the realm. And because that the judgment of this matter cannot be well directed by any learning delivered in our books of law, the best directions herein are precedents of antiquity and the course of this court, wherein all actions of this nature are to be judged; and the acts of parliament recited in arguments of this case prove nothing to the purpose. . . . The precedents of every court ought to be a direction to that court to judge of matters which are aptly determinable therein: as in the king's bench for matters of the crown, in the common pleas for matters of inheritance and civil contracts, and in the exchequer for matters of the king's prerogative, his revenue and government. And as it is not a kingdom without subjects and government, so he is not a king without revenues; for without them he cannot preserve his dominions in peace, he cannot maintain war, nor reward his servants according to the state and honour of a king. And the revenue of the crown is the very essential part of the crown; and he who rendeth that from the king pulleth also the crown from his head, for it cannot be separated from the crown. And such great prerogatives of the crown, without which it cannot be, ought not to be disputed; and in these cases of prerogative the judgment shall not be according to the rules of the common law, but according to the precedents of this court, wherein these matters are disputable and determinable. . . .[2]

And so much for precedents. And now for statutes. The statute of Magna Carta, c. 30 . . . , was objected—that thereby all merchants

---

[1] In 1606 John Bates, a merchant trading with the Levant, refused to pay a custom of 5*s.* a hundredweight imposed by James I in addition to the poundage of 2*s.* 6*d.* established by parliament (cf. no. 89H). For this refusal Bates was brought to trial before the court of the exchequer, which, after lengthy arguments on both sides, upheld the legality of the king's imposition. The following extracts are from the opinions of Baron Clark and Chief Baron Fleming.

[2] Here Clark cites a number of precedents for the king's laying of impositions.

may have safe, etc., to buy and sell without ill toltes—but there is a saving, *viz.*, by the ancient and old customs. The statute of Articuli super Cartas, c. 2, hath a saving in the end of it . . . [regarding] ancient prises due and accustomed.³ So are all the other statutes of purveyors. The statute of . . . 45 Edward III, c. 4,⁴ which has been so much urged—that no new imposition shall be imposed upon woolfells, wool, or leather, but only the custom and subsidy granted to the king—this extends only to the king himself and shall not bind his successors; for it is a principal part of the crown of England, which the king cannot diminish. . . . As to that which was objected, that the defendant had paid poundage granted by the statute . . . , that is nothing to this purpose, for that is a subsidy and not a custom. For when any imposition is granted by parliament, it is only a subsidy and not a custom, for the nature thereof is changed. . . .

The writ of *ne exeat regnum* comprehends a prohibition to him to whom it is directed, that he shall not go beyond the seas; and this may be directed at the king's pleasure to any man who is his subject. And so, consequently, may he prohibit all merchants. And as he may prohibit the persons, so may he prohibit the goods of any man, *viz.*, that he shall export or import at his pleasure. And if the king may generally inhibit that such goods shall not be imported, then by the same reason may he prohibit them upon condition . . . , that, if they import such goods, that then they shall pay, etc. . . .

And so, for all these reasons, judgment shall be given for the king.

Fleming, Chief Baron: . . . The state of the question is touching a new custom. The impositions or customs are duties or sums of money newly imposed by the king without parliament upon merchandise for the augmentation of his revenues. . . . To the king is committed the government of the realm and his people. . . . The king's power is double, ordinary and absolute; and they have several laws and ends. That of the ordinary is for the profit of particlar subjects— for the execution of civil justice . . . , and this is exercised by equity and justice in ordinary courts, and by the civilians is nominated *ius privatum*, and with us common law. And these laws cannot be changed without parliament . . . The absolute power of the king is not that which is converted or executed to private use, to the benefit of any particular person, but is only that which is applied to the general benefit of the people . . . , as the people is the body and the king the head. And this power . . . is most properly named policy and government. And as the constitution of this body varieth with the time, so varieth this absolute law according to the wisdom of the king for the common good. . . .

The matter in question is material matter of state and ought to be ruled by the rules of policy. And if it be so, the king hath done well to execute his extraordinary power. All customs, be they old or new,

---

³ Nos. 44, 51A.
⁴ A re-enactment of no. 62J.

are no other but the effects and issues of trades and commerce with foreign nations. But all commerce and affairs with foreigners, all wars and peace, all acceptance and admitting for current foreign coin, all parties and treaties whatsoever, are made by the absolute power of the king; and he who hath power of causes hath power also of effects. . . . It is said that an imposition may not be upon a subject without parliament. . . . It is not here the question if the king may impose upon the subject or his goods. But the impost here is not upon a subject; but here it is upon Bates as upon a merchant who imports goods within this land charged before by the king. And at the time when the impost was imposed upon them they were the goods of the Venetians, and not the goods of a subject nor within the land. . . .

And whereas it is said that, if the king may impose, he may impose any quantity what he pleases, true it is that this is to be referred to the wisdom of the king, who guideth all under God by his wisdom, and this is not to be disputed by a subject. . . . To prove the power of the king by precedents of antiquity in a case of this nature may easily be done. And if it were lawful in ancient times it is lawful now; for the authority of the king is not diminished, and the crown hath the same attributes that then it had. . . .

All these statutes[5] prove expressly that the king had power to increase the impost, and that upon commodities of the land; and that he continually used this power notwithstanding all acts of parliament against it. And so much for commodities of this land. But for foreign commodities it appears by no act of parliament or other precedent that ever any petition or suit was made to abate the impost of foreign commodities, but of them the impost was paid without denial. . . . Wherefore I think that the king ought to have judgment. . . .

Howell, State Trials, II, 382-94.

(B) THE QUESTION OF PROHIBITIONS (1607)[6]

. . . Upon complaint made to him by Bancroft, archbishop of Canterbury concerning prohibitions, the king was informed that, when the question was made of what matters the ecclesiastical judges have cognizance, either upon the exposition of the statutes concerning tithes or any other thing ecclesiastical, or upon the statute of 1 Elizabeth concerning the high commission, or in any other case in which there is not express authority in law, the king himself may decide it in his royal person; and that the judges are but the delegates of the king, and that the king may take what causes he shall please to determine from the determination of the judges and may determine them himself. And the archbishop said that this was clear in

---

[5] A long list of acts under Edward I, Edward III, and Richard II.
[6] The question arose through complaints by the archbishop of Canterbury that the ecclesiastical courts were being unjustly interfered with through writs of prohibition (see above, no. 33 I). Coke, as chief justice of the king's bench, warmly defended the common law practice, as appears from the following excerpt from his reports.

divinity, that such authority belongs to the king by the word of God in the Scripture. To which it was answered by me, in the presence and with the clear consent of all the judges of England and barons of the exchequer, that the king in his own person cannot adjudge any case, either criminal ... or betwixt party and party ...; but this ought to be determined and adjudged in some court of justice according to the law and custom of England. ...

Then the king said that he thought the law was founded upon reason, and that he and others had reason as well as the judges. To which it was answered by me that true it was that God had endowed his majesty with excellent science and great endowments of nature; but his majesty was not learned in the laws of his realm of England, and causes which concern the life or inheritance or goods or fortunes of his subjects are not to be decided by natural reason, but by the artificial reason and judgment of law—which law is an act which requires long study and experience, before that a man can attain to the cognizance of it—and that the law was the golden metwand and measure to try the causes of the subjects, and which protected his majesty in safety and peace. With which the king was greatly offended, and said that then he should be under the law—which was treason to affirm, as he said. To whom I said that Bracton saith *quod rex non debet esse sub homine, sed sub Deo et lege.*[7]

Coke, *Reports,* XII, 64.

(C) THE CASE OF THE POSTNATI (1608)[8]

[Chief Justice Coke:] ... There is a diversity between a conquest of a kingdom of a Christian king and the conquest of a kingdom of an infidel. For, if a king come to a Christian kingdom by conquest ..., he may at his pleasure alter and change the laws of that kingdom; but, until he doth make an alteration of those laws, the ancient laws of that kingdom remain. ... But if a Christian king should conquer a kingdom of an infidel and bring them under his subjection, there *ipso facto* the laws of the infidel are abrogated; for that they be, not only against Christianity, but against the law of God and of nature contained in the Decalogue. ... But if a king

---

[7] That the king ought not to be under man, but under God and the law.
[8] The origin of this case was an assize of *novel disseisin* (see no. 33B) sought by the guardians of Robert Calvin against Richard and Nicholas Smith regarding a certain freehold in London. The defendants argued that they were not bound to reply in such action, because Robert Calvin was an alien, having been born in Scotland in the year 1606. The question raised was therefore whether a Scot born after (*postnatus*) the accession of James I to the English throne was entitled to bring suit in an English court concerning English lands. As the question was a new one, which came to involve actions both in common law and equity, the case was transferred to the court of exchequer chamber to be argued by all judges of the central courts. The following extracts are from, first, the report of Coke, chief justice of the common pleas, and, secondly, the opinion of Lord Chancellor Ellesmere.

hath a kingdom by title of descent, there seeing by the laws of that kingdom he doth inherit the kingdom, he cannot change those laws of himself without consent of parliament. Also, if a king hath a Christian kingdom by conquest, as Henry II had Ireland—after John had given unto them, being under his obedience and subjection, the laws of England for the government of that country, no succeeding king could alter the same without parliament. And in that case, while the realm of England and that of Ireland were governed by several laws, any that was born in Ireland was no alien to the realm of England. . . .⁹

Whosoever are born under one natural ligeance and obedience, due by the law of nature to one sovereign, are natural-born subjects. . . . Whosoever is born within the king's power or protection is no alien. . . . Whatsoever is due by the law or constitution of man may be altered, but natural ligeance or obedience to the sovereign cannot be altered. . . . Lastly, whosoever at his birth cannot be an alien to the king of England cannot be an alien to any of his subjects of England. . . .

The judgment in the said case, as entered on record, etc. Whereupon all and singular the premises being seen, and by the court of the lord the now king here diligently inspected and examined, and mature deliberation being had thereof; for that it appears to the court of the lord the now king here that the aforesaid plea of the said Richard Smith and Nicholas Smith, above pleaded, is not sufficient in law to bar the said Robert Calvin from having an answer to his aforesaid writ: therefore it is considered by the court of the lord the now king here that the aforesaid Richard Smith and Nicholas Smith to the writ of the said Robert do further answer.

[Lord Chancellor Ellesmere:] . . . King James hath now the kingdoms of England, Scotland, and Ireland, and the isles of Guernsey and Jersey by descent. All these be his dominions and under his subjection and obedience. . . . If at this time subjects born in Ireland or Guernsey and Jersey be no aliens, but capable of lands in England, then, by an analogical interpretation, why should not subjects born in Scotland be at this time in like degree? . . . ¹⁰

In this new learning there is one part of it so strange and of so dangerous consequent as I may not let it pass: *viz.*, that the king is as a king divided in himself, and so as two kings of two several kingdoms; and that there be several allegiances and several subjec-

---

⁹ Coke goes on to discuss at great length the precedents earlier set in connection with Guienne, Normandy, the Isle of Man, and other non-English possessions of the English king. Then follow his conclusions drawn alike from history and natural reason.

¹⁰ The chancellor here reviews the matter of historical precedent, only to agree with the opinions already delivered by Coke and other judges. Then, coming to the objections raised by the attorneys for the defence, he continues with the argument that follows.

tions due unto him respectively in regard of his several kingdoms, the one not participating with the other. This is a dangerous distinction between the king and the crown, and between the king and the kingdom. It reacheth too far; I wish every good subject to beware of it. . . . Upon this subtle and dangerous distinction of faith and allegiance due to the king and of faith and allegiance due to the crown and to the kingdom—which is the only basis and fundamental main reason to disable the plaintiff and all *postnati*—there follow too many gross and foul absurdities; whereof I will touch some few, and so conclude that in law and reason this subtle but absurd and dangerous distinction ought not to be allowed. This bond of allegiance whereof we dispute is *vinculum fidei*; it bindeth the soul and conscience of every subject severally and respectively to be faithful and obedient to the king. And, as a soul or conscience cannot be framed by policy, so faith and allegiance cannot be framed by policy, nor put into a politic body. An oath must be sworn by a natural body; homage and fealty must be done by a natural body, a politic body cannot do it. Now then, since there is but one king and sovereign, to whom this faith and allegiance is due by all his subjects of England and Scotland, can any human policy divide this one king and make him two kings? . . .

I said there was another general rule for expounding of laws, which I reserved to be last spoken of. I will now but touch it; for I will not stand to examine by human reasons whether kings were before laws or laws before kings, nor how kings were first ordained, nor whether the kings or the people did first make laws, nor the several constitutions and frames of states and commonweals, nor what Plato or Aristotle have written of this argument. . . . They were born and lived in Greece, and in popular states; they were enemies, or at least mislikers, of all monarchies . . . ; they accounted all the world barbarous but their own country of Greece; their opinions, therefore, are no canons to give laws to kings and kingdoms, no more than Sir Thomas More's *Utopia* or such pamphlets as we have at every mart. . . .

If this question seem difficult—that neither direct law, nor examples and precedents, nor application of like cases, nor discourse or reason, nor the grave opinion of the learned and reverend judges can resolve it—here is a true and certain rule how, both by the civil law and the ancient common law of England, it may and ought to be decided: that is by sentence of the most religious, learned, and judicious king that ever this kingdom or island had. But this case is so clear as this needeth not at all. And in this I would not be misunderstood, as though I spake of making of new laws or of altering the laws now standing. I mean not so; but I speak only of interpretation of the law in new questions and doubts, as now in this present case. Neither do I mean hereby to derogate anything from the high court of parliament—far be it from my thought! . . . But certain it is it hath been the wisdom of the kings of this realm to reserve in themselves that supreme power to call their nobles, clergy, and commons together, when they saw great and urgent causes, and by that great council to make edicts and statutes for the weal of their people and safety of the kingdom and state. . . .

Thus I have here delivered my concurrence in opinion with my lords the judges, and the reasons that induce and satisfy my conscience that Robert Calvin, and all the *postnati* in Scotland are in reason and by the common law of England natural-born subjects . . . of the king of England, and enabled to purchase and have freehold and inheritance of lands in England and to bring real actions for the same in England. . . .

Howell, State Trials, II, 638-96.

(D) THE QUESTION OF ROYAL PROCLAMATIONS (1610)[11]

. . . The lord chancellor said that every precedent had first a commencement and that he would advise the judges to maintain the power and prerogative of the king, and in cases in which there is no authority and precedent to leave it to the king to order in it, according to his wisdom and for the good of his subjects, or otherwise the king would be no more than the duke of Venice; and that the king was so much restrained in his prerogative that it was to be feared the bonds would be broken. And the lord privy seal said that the physician was not always bound to a precedent, but to apply his medicine according to the quality of the disease. And all concluded that it should be necessary at that time to confirm the king's prerogative with our opinions, although that there were not any former precedent or authority in law; for every precedent ought to have a commencement. To which I answered that true it is that every precedent hath a commencement; but, when authority and precedent is wanting, there is need of great consideration before that anything of novelty shall be established, and to provide that this be not against the law of the land. For I said that the king cannot change any part of the common law, nor create any offence by his proclamation which was not an offence before, without parliament. . . .

It was resolved by the two chief justices, chief baron, and Baron Altham, upon conference betwixt the lords of the privy council and them, that the king by his proclamation cannot create any offence which was not an offence before; for then he may alter the law of the land by his proclamation in a high point. For, if he may create an offence where none is, upon that ensues fine and imprisonment. Also the law of England is divided into three parts: common law, statute law, and custom. But the king's proclamation is none of them. . . . Also it was resolved that the king hath no prerogative but that which the law of the land allows him. But the king, for prevention of offences, may by proclamation admonish his subjects

---

[11] Cf. no. 74K.

that they keep the laws and do not offend them, upon punishment to be inflicted by the law, etc. . . .

Coke, *Reports*, XII, 74 f.

(E) COUNCIL PROCEEDINGS ON A JUDGMENT IN CHANCERY (1613)

The lords having this day heard Sir Henry Billingsley, knight, and Edmund Mathewes, esquire, between whom a controversy hath long depended in the high court of chancery concerning great sums of money due by Mathewes unto the said Billingsley, to the payment whereof sundry his lands and possessions were liable, which the said Billingsley did humbly desire he might, with their lordships' favours, dispose of towards his own satisfaction, according to a solemn decree in chancery given on his behalf; their lordships being nevertheless favourably inclined for Mr. Mathewes' relief . . . , being a gentleman of a good house, and whose distressed estate doth move them to compassion to make some such agreement betwixt them as that the land might be sold to the best advantage and Sir Henry Billingsley satisfied his debt with the moneys arising thereupon, the residue (if any be) to remain unto Mr. Mathewes, provided that the same might be accomplished in such convenient time as Sir Henry Billingsley his estate and occasion might well suffer without much prejudice; and finding the same not possible to be effected by any overtures or motions which their lordships could make unto them, as was desired, the cause is dismissed from this table and Sir Henry Billingsley left unto the validity of his decree and conveyances, to make such use thereof as he shall see cause, and in the meantime Mr. Mathewes required, neither by himself or any other on his behalf, to importune the lords or any of them with further petitions.

Acts of the Privy Council, 1613-1614, p. 87.

(F) THE QUESTION OF COMMENDAMS (1616)[12]

His majesty and the lords [of the council] thought good to ask the judges severally their opinion, the question being put in this manner: whether, if at any time in a case depending before the judges which his majesty conceived to concern him either in power or profit, and thereupon required to consult with them and that they should stay proceedings in the meantime, they ought not to stay accordingly. They all (the lord chief justice only except) yielded that

---

[12] During the course of a trial in the common pleas the question arose whether the king had the right to present a man to an ecclesiastical living *in commendam*—that is to say, to make a temporary appointment. James, wishing to delay the judgment in order to have a preliminary discussion of the problem, caused Bacon, his attorney general, to summon the judges before him for that purpose. At the instance of Coke, now chief justice of the king's bench, they replied that they were bound by oath not to delay a case and that the summons of the attorney general was illegal. But the king compelled them to appear before him in the council and, on bended knees, to listen to his arguments. Whereupon proceedings continued as described in the following account.

they would, and acknowledged it to be their duty so to do. Only the lord chief justice of the king's bench said for answer that when that case should be, he would do that should be fit for a judge to do. And the lord chief justice of the common pleas, who had assented with the rest, added that he would ever trust the justness of his majesty's commandment.

After this was put to a point, his majesty thought fit, in respect of the further day of argument appointed the Saturday following for the *commendams*, to know from his judges what he might expect from them concerning the same. Whereupon, the lord [archbishop] of Canterbury breaking the case into some questions, his majesty did require his judges to deal plainly with him, whether they meant in their argument to touch the general power of granting *commendams*, yea or no. Whereupon all his said judges did promise and assure his majesty that in the argument of the said case of *commendams* they would speak nothing which should weaken or draw into doubt his majesty's prerogative for the granting of them; but intended particularly to insist upon the point of the lapse and other individual points of this case, which they conceive to be of a form differing from all other *commendams* which have been practised. The judges also went further, and did promise his majesty that they would not only abstain from speaking anything to weaken his majesty's prerogative of *commendams*, but would directly and in plain terms affirm the same and correct the erroneous and bold speeches which had been used at the bar in derogation thereof. Also, all the judges did in general acknowledge and profess with great forwardness that it was their duty, if any counsellor at the bar presumed at any time to call in question his majesty's high prerogatives and regalities, that they ought to reprehend them and silence them; and promised so to do hereafter.

Ibid., 1615-1616, pp. 607 f.

(G) COUNCIL PROCEEDINGS AGAINST SIR EDWARD COKE (1616)

Sir Edward Coke, knight, chief justice of the king's bench, presenting himself this day at this board upon his knees, Mr. Secretary Winwood signified unto him that their lordships had made report to his majesty of that which passed on Wednesday last at Whitehall, where he was charged by his majesty's solicitor with certain things wherein his majesty was much unsatisfied. . . . Which being delivered in writing and in his princely judgment duly weighed and considered of, his majesty was no way satisfied with his answers to any of those three points, wherewith he stood charged (*viz.*, neither in that which he made concerning the bond and defeasance upon the installment of a debt of Sir Christopher Hatton, late lord chancellor of England; nor yet in that which he maketh concerning his speeches of high contempt, uttered as he sat in the seat of justice, concerning the overthrow of the common law; nor, lastly, in the answer he offereth to excuse his uncivil and indiscreet carriage before his majesty, assisted with his privy council and his judges), but that the charge lieth still upon him, notwithstanding anything contained in his said answers.

Nevertheless, such is his majesty's clemency and goodness as he is pleased not to proceed heavily against him, but rather to look upon the merit of his former services, and accordingly hath decreed: first, that he be sequestered from the council table until his majesty's pleasure be further known; secondly, that he do forbear to ride this summer's circuit as justice of assize; lastly, that during this vacation . . . he take into his consideration and review his book of reports, wherein (as his majesty is informed) there be many exorbitant and extravagant opinions set down and published for positive and good law. And if, in the review and reading thereof, he find anything fit to be altered or amended, the correcting thereof is left to his discretion. Amongst other things, his majesty was not well pleased with the title of those books, wherein he styled himself lord chief justice of England, whereas he could challenge no more than chief justice of the king's bench. And having corrected what in his discretion he found meet in those reports, his majesty's pleasure was that he should bring the same privately to himself, that he might consider thereof as in his princely judgment should be found expedient. . . .

Hereunto the lord chief justice made answer that he did in all humility prostrate himself to his majesty's good pleasure; that he acknowledged the decree to be just. . . .

Ibid., 1615-1616, pp. 648-50.

(H) PIGG V. CALEY (1618)[13]

Pigg brought an action of trespass against Caley for taking his horse, etc. Caley said that he is seised of the manor of D. to which Pigg is a villein regardant; and that and all those, etc., have been seised of the plaintiff and his ancestors. The plaintiff said that he is free, etc.; *absque hoc*, that the defendant, etc., were seised of the plaintiff, etc., as of villein regardant. And the issue is found for the plaintiff. And upon motion in arrest of judgment, it is ruled that the traverse is well taken. . . .

Noy, *Reports,* p. 27.

(I) IMPEACHMENT OF FRANCIS BACON (1621)[14]

[15 March.] Sir Robert Phillips reporteth from the committee for

---

[13] This brief report of an action before the king's bench is included here because it is the last recorded trial concerning villeinage in an English court. Caley's argument was that Pigg, being his villein attached to his manor, had no right to sue him for trespass. Such status was denied (the implication of the *absque hoc*) by Pigg. And since the jury rendered a verdict in his favour, his action was allowed to stand. See Holdsworth, *History of English Law,* III, 502 f.

[14] Only the crucial points in this famous trial are given here: the formal accusation as shown from the commons journals, supplemented by the contemporary notes of Edward Nicholas, and the final judgment delivered by the lords, as recorded in the journals of that house.

91. JUDICIAL CASES (1606-21)

courts of justice three parts: person against whom, the matter, and opinion of the committee—with desire of further direction.

The person, the lord chancellor . . . ; the matter, corruption; the parties accusing, Awbrey and Egerton. Awbrey complaineth that, wearied in his cause in chancery, he was advised by his counsel, to expedite his business, to present the lord chancellor with £100. He got at use £100; goeth with Sir George Hastings and Mr. Jenkyns to York House. There they two went [in], and returned to him with thanks from my lord and hopes of better success in his cause than formerly. . . . The next, Edward Egerton, [declares] that, having many suits, he first presented my lord with a basin and ewer of £52 . . . ; that he sold tithes, raised £400, carried it to Whitehall to my lord chancellor's lodging, called for Sir George and Sir Richard Yong, and by them sent in this gold in a purse . . . to my lord, who started at it, saying it was too much; that thanks [were] returned to him from my lord. . . .

Journals of the Commons, I, 554.

[19 March.] Sir Robert Phillips reporteth that he acquainted their lordships from this house that we have received a complaint and information against some noble lord of that house, and that therefore we of this house desire a conference with their lordships to acquaint them with the particulars of the complaint and the circumstances; that their lordships have appointed the conference for this afternoon, at two of the clock, the number to be the whole house.

The heads and circumstances of the accusation against the lord chancellor [by Awbrey and Egerton] are set down in writing and are read here in the house; but are to be delivered by word of mouth by Sir Robert Phillips this afternoon at a conference with the lords. . . .

Nicholas, *Proceedings in the Commons,* I, 194 f.

[20 March.] The lord treasurer reported the conference yesterday with the commons. At which conference was delivered the desire of the commons to inform their lordships of the great abuses of the courts of justice. . . . The lord chancellor is accused of great bribery and corruption committed by him in this eminent place, whereof two cases were alleged: the one concerning Christopher Awbrey, the other concerning Edward Egerton. . . .

[24 April.] . . . Their lordships resolved that the lord chancellor should be charged particularly with the briberies and corruptions complained of against him and that his lordship should make a particular answer thereunto. . . . Memorandum that, during the time the whole house was a committee, the collections of corruptions charged upon the lord chancellor and the proofs thereof made by the three committees . . . was read by Mr. Attorney General. . . . Here followeth the said collection. . . .[15]

[30 April.] . . . The lord chief justice . . . signified that he had received from the lord chancellor a paper roll sealed up, which was

---

[15] Twenty-three instances of corrupt practices are enumerated.

delivered to the clerk, and, being opened and found directed to their lordships, it was . . . read; which follows in these words: "To the right honourable the lords spiritual and temporal in the high court of parliament assembled: the confession and humble submission of me, the lord chancellor. Upon advised consideration of the charge, descending into my own conscience and calling my memory to account, so far as I am able, I do plainly and ingenuously confess that I am guilty of corruption and do renounce all defence, and put myself upon the grace and mercy of your lordships. The particulars I declare and confess to be as followeth. . . ."

[3 May.] . . . It was put to the question whether the lord chancellor be guilty of the matters wherewith he is charged or no, and it was agreed by all . . . that he was thereof guilty. . . .

The lords, having agreed upon the sentence to be given against the lord chancellor, did send a message to the house of commons . . . , that the lords are ready to give judgment against the lord viscount St. Albans, lord chancellor, if they with their speaker will come to demand it. In the meantime the lords put on their robes and, answer being returned of this message, the commons come. The speaker came to the bar and, making three low obeisances, said: "The knights, citizens, and burgesses of the commons' house of parliament have made complaint unto your lordships of many exorbitant offences of bribery and corruption committed by the lord chancellor. We understand that your lordships are ready to give judgment upon him for the same. Wherefore I, their speaker, in their name do humbly demand and pray judgment against him, the lord chancellor, as the nature of his offence and demerits do require."

The lord chief justice answered: "Mr. Speaker, upon the complaint of the commons against the lord viscount St. Albans, lord chancellor, this high court hath thereby, and by his own confession, found him guilty of the crimes and corruptions complained of by the commons and of sundry other crimes and corruptions of like nature. And therefore this high court (having first summoned him to attend, and having received his excuse of not attending by reason of infirmity and sickness; which he protested was not feigned or else he would most willingly have attended), doth nevertheless think fit to proceed to judgment. And therefore this high court doth adjudge: (1) that the lord viscount St. Albans, lord chancellor of England, shall undergo fine and ransom of £40,000; (2) that he shall be imprisoned in the Tower during the king's pleasure; (3) that he shall forever be incapable of any office, place, or employment in the state or commonwealth; (4) that he shall never sit in parliament nor come within the verge of the court. This is the judgment and resolution of this high court."

The prince his highness was entreated by the house that, accompanied with divers of the lords of this house, he would be pleased to present this sentence given against the late lord chancellor unto his majesty. His highness was pleased to yield unto this request. . . .

Journals of the Lords, III, 53-106.

92. RECORDS CONCERNING PARLIAMENT (1626-29)

(A) LETTER OF CHARLES I TO THE COMMONS (1626)

Trusty and well-beloved, we greet you well. Our house of commons cannot forget how often and how earnestly we have called upon them for the speeding of that aid which they intended unto us for our great and weighty affairs concerning the safety and honour of us and our kingdoms; and now, the time being so far spent that, unless it be presently concluded, it can neither bring us money nor credit by the time which themselves have prefixed—which is the last of this month—and being further deferred would be of little use. We being daily advertised from all parts of the great preparations of the enemy, ready to assail us, we hold it necessary by these our letters to give them our last and final admonition, and to let them know that we shall account all further delays and excuses to be express denials. And therefore we will and require you to signify unto them that we do expect that they forthwith bring forth their bill of subsidy to be passed without delay or condition, so as it may fully pass that house by the end of the next week at the furthest—which if they do not, it will force us to take other resolutions. But let them know that, if they finish this according to our desire, that we are resolved to let them sit together for the dispatch of their other affairs and, after their recess, to bring them together again the next winter. And if by their denial or delay anything of ill consequence shall fall out either at home or abroad, we may call God and man to witness that we have done our part to prevent it by calling our people together to advise with us, by opening the weight of our occasions unto them, and by requiring their timely help and assistance in those actions wherein we stand engaged by their own counsels. And we will and command you that this letter be publicly read in the house. [9 June, 1626.]

Ibid., III, 670.

(B) CHARLES I: ORDINANCE FOR LEVYING CUSTOMS (1626)[1]

Charles, by the grace of God king of England, Scotland, France, and Ireland, defender of the faith, etc., to our lord treasurer of England . . . , the commissioners of our treasury . . . , to our chancellor and under-treasurer of our exchequer . . . , to our chief baron and the rest of the barons of our exchequer . . . , to the customers, comptrollers, searchers, and all other the officers and ministers of our ports or belonging to our customs . . . , and to all other our officers, ministers, and loving subjects . . . to whom these presents shall come, greeting.

Whereas the lords and others of our privy council have taken into their serious consideration the present state of our revenue arising by

---
[1] In the previous year the commons had drawn up a bill giving Charles tunnage and poundage for one year—instead of for life as had been customary for over a century (see above, p. 273, n. 1). But parliament was dissolved before the bill was passed by the lords, and no agreement on the matter was reached by the parliament of 1626.

customs, subsidy, and impost upon goods and merchandise to be exported and imported out of and into this our realm of England and dominion of Wales and port and town of Berwick, and, finding that it hath been constantly continued for many ages, and is now a principal part of the revenue of our crown and is of necessity to be so continued for the supportation thereof—which in the two last parliaments hath been thought upon, but could not there be settled by authority of parliament as from time to time by many ages and descents past it hath been, by reason of the dissolution of those parliaments before those things which were there treated of could be perfected—have therefore. . . specially ordered that all those duties upon goods and merchandises, called by the several names of customs, subsidy, and imposts, should be levied, collected, and received for our use in such manner and form as the same were levied, collected, and received in the time of our late dear father, King James of blessed memory . . . ; and forasmuch as, through the want of a parliamentary course to settle the payment of those duties, many inconveniences may arise which would tend to the impairing of our revenue of that nature, if in convenient time some settled course should not be taken for the prevention thereof:—

Know ye therefore that we . . . , by the advice of the lords and others of our privy council, do by these presents declare our will and pleasure to be that all those duties upon goods and merchandises . . . shall be levied, collected, and received in such manner and form as the same were levied, collected, and received at the time of the decease of our said late father. . . . And if any person or persons whatsoever shall refuse or neglect to pay the duties, customs, subsidies, or imposts aforesaid . . . , we do further grant by these presents unto the lords and others of our privy council . . . , or unto the lord treasurer of England or chancellor of our exchequer . . . , full power and authority to commit all and every such person and persons to prison. . . .

And for the better execution of this our will and pleasure herein, and to the end that all our officers and subjects may take notice hereof, our will and pleasure is that these our letters patents shall be transcribed and several copies thereof made and sent into every part of this realm. . . .

Witness ourself at Westminster, the 26th day of July.

Rymer, Foedera, XVIII, 737 f.

(C) PROCEEDINGS ON THE ARREST OF CERTAIN LORDS (1626)

[14 March.] . . . The earl of Arundel, being committed by the king to the Tower, sitting the parliament, the house was moved to take the same into their consideration and so to proceed therein as they might give no just offence unto his majesty and yet preserve the privilege of parliament. The lord keeper thereupon signified to the house that he was commanded to deliver this message from his majesty unto their lordships: *viz.*, that the earl of Arundel was restrained for a misdemeanour which was personal unto his majesty and lay in the proper knowledge of his majesty and had no relation to matters of parliament. . . .

[30 March.] . . . The petition of the earl of Bristol for his writ of summons being referred to the lords' committees for privileges, etc., the earl of Hertford reported the same, on this manner, *viz.*: "My lords, whereas the earl of Bristol hath preferred a petition unto this house, thereby signifying that his writ of summons is withheld from him . . . , this petition being referred unto the committee for privileges, and after diligent search no precedent being found that any writ of summons hath been detained from any peer that is capable of sitting in the house of parliament; and considering withal how far it may trench into the right of every member of this house, whether sitting by ancient right of inheritance or by patent, to have their writs detained: the lords' committees are all of opinion that it will be necessary for this house humbly to beseech his majesty that a writ of summons may be sent to this petitioner, and to such other lords to whom no writ of summons hath been directed for this parliament, excepting such as are made incapable to sit in parliament by judgment of parliament or any other legal judgment." Whereupon the duke of Buckingham signified unto the house that, upon the earl of Bristol's petition, the king had sent him his writ of summons. . . .

[19 April.] The lord president reported the petition of the earl of Bristol . . . : "To the right honourable the lords of the higher house of parliament, the humble petition of John, earl of Bristol, humbly showing unto your lordships that he hath lately received his writ of parliament . . . , but jointly with it a letter from my lord keeper, commanding him in his majesty's name to forbear his personal attendance. And although he shall ever obey the least intimation of his majesty's pleasure, yet he most humbly offereth to your lordships' wise considerations . . . how far this may trench upon the liberty and safety of the peers." . . .

The lord president also reported the remonstrance and petition of the peers concerning the claim of their privileges from arrests and imprisonments. . . . May it please your majesty: we, the peers of this your realm assembled in parliament, finding the earl of Arundel absent from his place . . . [therefore called for] his presence. . . . But hereupon a message was delivered unto us from your majesty by the lord keeper, that the earl of Arundel was restrained for a misdemeanour which was personal to your majesty and lay in the proper knowledge of your majesty and had no relation to matter of parliament. This message occasioned us to inquire into the acts of our ancestors . . . ; and, after diligent search both of all [hi]stories, statutes, and records that might inform us in this case, we find it to be an undoubted right and constant privilege of parliament that no lord of parliament, sitting the parliament, or within the usual times of privilege of parliament, is to be imprisoned or restrained without sentence or order of the house, unless it be for treason or felony or for refusing to give surety for the peace. . . . Wherefore we, your majesty's loyal subjects and servants, the whole body of the peers now assembled in parliament, most humbly beseech your majesty that the earl of Arundel, a member of this body, may presently be admitted, with your gracious favour, to come, sit, and serve your majesty and the commonwealth in the great affairs of this parliament. . . .

This remonstrance and petition being read, it was generally approved of by the whole house, and agreed to be presented unto his majesty by the whole house. . . .[2]

Journals of the Lords, III, 526-64.

(D) PETITION OF RIGHT (1628)

The petition exhibited to his majesty by the lords spiritual and temporal, and commons in this present parliament assembled, concerning divers rights and liberties of the subjects, with the king's majesty's royal answer thereunto in full parliament.

To the king's most excellent majesty: Humbly show unto our sovereign lord the king the lords spiritual and temporal, and commons in parliament assembled, that, whereas it is declared and enacted by a statute made in the time of the reign of King Edward the First, commonly called *Statutum de Tallagio non Concedendo*,[3] that no tallage or aid should be laid or levied by the king or his heirs in this realm without the goodwill and assent of the archbishops, bishops, earls, barons, knights, burgesses, and other the freemen of the commonalty of this realm; and, by authority of parliament holden in the five-and-twentieth year of the reign of King Edward III, it is declared and enacted that from thenceforth no person should be compelled to make any loans to the king against his will, because such loans were against reason and the franchise of the land; and by other laws of this realm it is provided that none should be charged by any charge or imposition, called a benevolence,[4] or by such like charge; by which the statutes before mentioned, and other the good laws and statutes of this realm, your subjects have inherited this freedom, that they should not be compelled to contribute to any tax, tallage, aid, or other like charge not set by common consent in parliament: yet, nevertheless, of late divers commissions directed to sundry commissioners in several counties with instructions have issued, by means whereof your people have been in divers places assembled and required to lend certain sums of money unto your majesty; and many of them, upon their refusal so to do, have had an oath administered

---

[2] Eventually Bristol was permitted to return to the house, where charges were brought against him by the king. In the case of Arundel, however, the king delayed a specific answer until the parliament was dissolved in June. Both peers occupied their regular places in the next parliament.

[3] See above, p. 165, n. 1.

[4] Cf. no. 69H.

unto them, not warrantable by the laws or statutes of this realm, and have been constrained to become bound to make appearance and give attendance before your privy council and in other places; and others of them have been therefor imprisoned, confined, and sundry other ways molested and disquieted; and divers other charges have been laid and levied upon your people in several counties by lord lieutenants, deputy lieutenants, commissioners for musters, justices of peace, and others, by command or direction from your majesty or your privy council, against the laws and free customs of the realm.

And where also, by the statute called the Great Charter of the Liberties of England, it is declared and enacted that no freeman may be taken or imprisoned, or be disseised of his freehold or liberties or his free customs, or be outlawed or exiled or in any manner destroyed, but by the lawful judgment of his peers or by the law of the land; and in the eight-and-twentieth year of the reign of King Edward III it was declared and enacted by authority of parliament that no man, of what estate or condition that he be, should be put out of his land or tenements, nor taken, nor imprisoned, nor disherited, nor put to death, without being brought to answer by due process of law: nevertheless, against the tenor of the said statutes and other the good laws and statutes of your realm to that end provided, divers of your subjects have of late been imprisoned without any cause showed; and when for their deliverance they were brought before your justices by your majesty's writs of *habeas corpus*, there to undergo and receive as the court should order, and their keepers commanded to certify the causes of their detainer, no cause was certified, but that they were detained by your majesty's special command, signified by the lords of your privy council; and yet were returned back to several prisons, without being charged with anything to which they might make answer according to the law.

And whereas of late great companies of soldiers and mariners have been dispersed into divers counties of the realm, and the inhabitants against their wills have been compelled to receive them into their houses, and there to suffer them to sojourn, against the laws and customs of this realm, and to the great grievance and vexation of the people: and whereas also, by authority of parliament in the five-and-twentieth year of the reign of King Edward III, it is declared and enacted that no man should be forejudged of life or limb against the form of the Great Charter and the law of the land; and, by the said Great Charter and other the laws and statutes of this your realm, no man ought to be adjudged to death but by the laws established in this your realm, either by the customs of the same realm or by acts of parliament; and whereas no offender of what kind soever is exempted from the proceedings to be used, and punishments to be inflicted by the laws and statutes of this your realm: nevertheless of late divers commissions under your majesty's great seal have issued forth, by which certain persons have been assigned and appointed commissioners, with power and authority to proceed within the land according to the justice of martial law against such soldiers or mariners, or other dissolute persons joining with them, as should commit any murder, robbery, felony, mutiny, or other outrage or misdemeanour whatsoever, and by such summary course and order as is agreeable to martial law and as is used in armies in time of war, to proceed to the trial and condemnation of such offenders, and them to cause to be executed and put to death according to the law martial; by pretext whereof some of your majesty's subjects have been by some of the said commissioners put to death, when and where, if by the laws and statutes of the land they had deserved death, by the same laws and statutes also they might, and by no other ought to have been, adjudged and executed; and also sundry grievous offenders, by colour thereof claiming an exemption, have escaped the punishments due to them by the laws and statutes of this your realm, by reason that divers of your officers and ministers of justice have unjustly refused or forborne to proceed against such offenders according to the same laws and statutes, upon pretence that the said offenders were punishable only by martial law and by authority of such commissions as aforesaid; which commissions and all other of like nature are wholly and directly contrary to the said laws and statutes of this your realm.

They do therefore humbly pray your most excellent majesty that no man hereafter be compelled to make or yield any gift, loan, benevolence, tax, or such like charge without common consent by act of parliament; and that none be called to make answer, or take such oath, or to give attendance, or be confined, or otherwise molested or disquieted concerning the same, or for refusal thereof; and that no freeman, in any such manner as is before mentioned, be imprisoned or detained; and that your majesty would be pleased to remove the said soldiers and mariners; and that your people may not be so burdened in time to come; and that the foresaid commissions for proceeding by martial law may be revoked and annulled; and that hereafter no commissions of like nature may issue forth to any person or persons whatsoever, to be executed as aforesaid, lest by colour of them any of your majesty's subjects be destroyed or put to death, contrary to the laws and franchise of the land (all of which they most humbly pray of your most excellent majesty as their rights and liberties according to the laws and statutes of this realm); and that your majesty would also vouchsafe and declare that the awards, doings, and proceedings to the prejudice of your people in any of the premises shall not be drawn hereafter into consequence or example; and that your majesty would be also graciously pleased, for the further comfort and safety of your people, to declare your royal will and pleasure that in the things aforesaid all your officers and ministers shall serve you according to the laws and statutes of this realm, as they tender the honour of your majesty and the prosperity of this kingdom.

Statutes of the Realm, V, 23 f.

92. PARLIAMENT (1626-29)

(E) Proceedings on the Petition of Right (1628)

[2 June.] His majesty, being seated on his royal throne, delivered unto the clerk of parliament his answer unto the Petition of Right, exhibited by the lords and commons this parliament. The commons, with their speaker, came. His majesty made a short speech unto the lords and commons. The lord keeper then conferred with his majesty and declared unto the lords and commons. . . . The lord keeper having ended his speech, the clerk of the crown read the Petition of Right . . . , and the clerk of the parliament the king's answer, *in haec verba, viz.*: "The king willeth that right be done according to the laws and customs of the realm; and that the statutes be put in due execution, that his subjects may have no cause to complain of any wrongs or oppressions, contrary to their just rights and liberties, to the preservation whereof he holds himself . . . as well obliged as of his prerogative. . . ."

[7 June.] The king's majesty being placed in his royal throne, the lords in their robes, and the commons with their speaker present; the lord keeper, standing in his place as a peer, spoke as followeth, *viz.*: "May it please your most excellent majesty, the lords spiritual and temporal and commons assembled in parliament, taking into their considerations that the good intelligence betwixt your majesty and your people doth much depend upon your majesty's answer unto their Petition of Right, formerly presented with an unanimous consent unto your majesty, do now become most humble suitors unto your majesty that you will be pleased to give a clear and satisfactory answer thereunto in full parliament."

This being spoken by the lord keeper, his majesty said: "The answer I have already given you was made with so good deliberation, and approved by the judgment of so many wise men, that I could not have imagined but that it should have given you full satisfaction; but, to avoid all ambiguous interpretations and to show you that there is no doubleness in my meaning, I am willing to please you in words as well as in the substance. Read your petition, and you shall have such an answer as I am sure will please you."

Then the clerk of the crown read the said Petition of Right. And the clerk of the parliament read and pronounced the king's answer, *viz.*: "Soit droit fait come est désiré."[5]

[26 June.] His majesty being placed in his royal throne, the commons were sent for, to hear his royal answer to the bills. The commons being come, his majesty made this speech, *viz.*: "My lords and gentlemen, it may seem strange that I come so suddenly to end this session. Wherefore, before I give my assent to the bills, I will tell you the cause; though I must avow that I owe an account of my actions to none but to God alone. It is known to every one that a

---

[5] "Let right be done as is desired." On the significance of this whole proceeding, see F. H. Relf, *The Petition of Right*.

while ago the house of commons gave me a remonstrance—how acceptable every man may judge. And for the merit of it, I will not call that in question; for I am sure no wise man can justify it. Now, since I am certainly informed that a second remonstrance is preparing for me, to take away my profit of tunnage and poundage—one of the chief maintenances of the crown—by alleging that I have given away my right thereof by my answer to your petition, this is so prejudicial unto me that I am forced to end this session some few hours before I meant it, being willing not to receive any more remonstrances to which I must give an harsh answer. And since I see that even the house of commons begins already to make false constructions of what I granted in your petition; lest it might be worse interpreted in the country, I will now make a declaration concerning the true meaning thereof. The profession of both houses, in time of hammering this petition, was by no ways to entrench upon my prerogative, saying they had neither intention or power to hurt it. Therefore it must needs be conceived that I have granted no new, but only confirmed the ancient, liberties of my subjects. Yet, to show the clearness of my intentions, that I neither repent nor mean to recede from anything I have promised you, I do here declare that those things which have been done—whereby men had some cause to suspect the liberty of the subjects to be trenched upon, which indeed was the first and true ground of the petition—shall not hereafter be drawn into example for your prejudice; and in time to come—in the word of a king—you shall not have the like cause to complain. But as for tunnage and poundage, it is a thing I cannot want and was never intended by you to ask, never meant, I am sure, by me to grant. To conclude, I command you all that are here to take notice of what I have spoken at this time, to be the true intent and meaning of what I granted you in your petition. But you, my lords the judges . . . , to you only under me belongs the interpretation of the laws; for none of the house of commons, joint or separate, what new doctrine soever may be raised, have any power either to make or declare a law without my consent."

Journals of the Lords, III, 835-79.

(F) RESOLUTIONS OF THE COMMONS (1629)[6]

(1) Whosoever shall bring in innovation of religion, or by favour or countenance seek to extend or introduce popery or Arminianism, or other opinion disagreeing from the true and orthodox church, shall be reputed a capital enemy to this kingdom and commonwealth.

(2) Whosoever shall counsel or advise the taking and levying of the subsidies of tunnage and poundage, not being granted by parliament, or shall be an actor or instrument therein, shall be likewise reputed an innovator in the government, and a capital enemy to the kingdom and commonwealth.

---

[6] Passed while the speaker was held in his chair and the king waited to dissolve parliament.

93. ROYAL GOVERNMENT (1630-35)

(3) If any merchant or person whatsoever shall voluntarily yield or pay the said subsidies of tunnage and poundage, not being granted by parliament, he shall likewise be reputed a betrayer of the liberties of England, and an enemy to the same.

Rushworth, *Historical Collections*, I, 660.

93. ACTS OF THE ROYAL GOVERNMENT (1630-35)

(A) PROCLAMATION FOR DISTRAINT OF KNIGHTHOOD (1630)[1]

Whereas we have heretofore granted our commission under the great seal of England to sundry of the lords and others of our privy council to treat and compound with such of our loving subjects as by law ought to make their fines with us for not making their appearance at the time and place by our writs appointed for receiving the order of knighthood—wherein our commissioners have so far proceeded that many have compounded with them and paid their fines agreed upon accordingly—and we are resolved constantly to hold the like course with all others who are liable by law to pay the like fines: nevertheless, because many parts of this our kingdom are so remote from our city of London as the travel from thence thither would be very chargeable and troublesome and at this time dangerous . . . , in favour of our good and loving subjects whom it concerneth, we have resolved to send our commissions to the several counties of this our realm, to whom they may with more ease and safety repair for their dispatch; whereof we have thought fit by these presents to give notice to all whom it may concern, hereby letting them know that, if they shall neglect this our grace and not attend our commissioners in their several counties where they dwell and with them make agreement on our behalf . . . , we shall leave them to the just proceedings of our laws, and to that end to attend our commissioners at Whitehall or our court of exchequer. And if it shall so fall out to be more charge or trouble unto them, they shall have just cause to lay the blame upon themselves, and to acknowledge our grace and favour if in time it had been accepted. Given at our court at Westminster, the 13th day of July.

Rymer, *Foedera*, XIX, 175 f.

(B) WRIT FOR THE COLLECTION OF SHIP MONEY (1634)[2]

Carolus rex, etc., to the mayor, commonalty, and citizens of our city of London, and to the sheriffs of the same city and good men in the said city and in the liberties and members of the same, greet-

---

[1] Cf. no. 50A.
[2] In this year writs like the one given here were sent only to seaports; but in 1635 and 1636 the system was extended throughout all the counties of England and Wales. The modified writs dispatched for this purpose demanded quotas of ships from all communities, both urban and rural, and ordered the sheriffs to raise the necessary money by assessing lands within their bailiwicks. For the judicial problems involved, see no. 94B, C; and for historical precedent, ɪf. nos. 41D, 46F, I.

ing. Because we are given to understand that certain thieves, pirates, and robbers of the sea, as well Turks, enemies of the Christian name, as others . . . [are] wickedly taking by force and spoiling the ships and goods and merchandises, not only of our subjects, but also of the subjects of our friends in the sea, which hath been accustomed anciently to be defended by the English nation; . . . also, the dangers considered which on every side do hang over our heads, that it behooveth us and our subjects to hasten the defence of the sea and kingdom with all expedition or speed that we can; . . . and, although that charge of defence which concerneth all men ought to be supported by all . . . , you, constituted in the sea-coasts . . . , are chiefly bound to set your helping hand: we command firmly, enjoining you . . . that you cause to be prepared and brought to the port of Portsmouth before the first day of March now next ensuing one ship of war of the burden of 900 tons, with 350 men at the least, as well expert masters as very able and skilful mariners; one other ship of war of the burden of 800 tons, with 260 men at the least . . . ; four other ships of war, every of them of the burden of 500 tons and every of them with 200 men at the least . . . ; and one other ship of war of the burden of 300 tons, with 150 men. . . . And also every of the said ships [is to be equipped] with ordnance, as well greater as lesser, gunpowder and spears and weapons and other necessary arms sufficient for war, and with double tackling and with victuals until the said first of March competent for so many men; and from that time for twenty-six weeks at your charges as well in victuals as men's wages and other things necessary for war. . . . Also we have assigned you, the aforesaid mayor and aldermen of the city aforesaid . . . , to assess all men in the said city and in the liberties and members of the same . . . to contribute to the expenses about the necessary provision of the premises. . . .

Witness myself at Westminster, the 20th day of October in the tenth year of our reign.

Rushworth, *Historical Collections*, II, 257 f.

(C) COMMISSION FOR LEVYING FINES UNDER FOREST LAW (1635)[3]

Charles, by the grace of God king . . . , to our right trusty and right well-beloved cousin and councillor, Henry, earl of Holland; lord chief justice and justice in eyre of all our forests, chases, parks, and warrens on this side Trent, [and to the chancellor of the exchequer, the chief justices of king's bench and common pleas, the attorney general, the solicitor general, and a serjeant-at-law,] greeting. Whereas we are pleased for the ease and benefit of our subjects, upon reasonable fines and compositions to be paid into our exchequer to our use, to pardon and discharge them of all encroachments, purprestures, damages, detriments, trespasses, and offences whatsoever by them committed or done as well in our forest of Dean in

---

[3] Cf. nos. 35, 45.

our county of Gloucester as also in our forest of Essex in our county of Essex, and the perambulations, meets, bounds, and purlieus thereof . . . , and for the time to come to free them and exempt them, their lands, tenements, possessions, leases, and hereditaments of and from all common or depasturing of our deer, laws, liberties, officers, and jurisdictions of forest, and to disafforest the same . . . : know ye therefore that we . . . by these presents do assign, make, and constitute you to be our commissioners, and we do hereby give full power and authority unto you, or any three or more of you . . . , in our name and behalf to compound, contract, and agree with all such persons as shall desire the same for pardons, releases and discharges . . . concerning all and all manner of encroachments, purprestures, damages, detriments, trespasses, and offences whatsoever by them in any wise committed or done in our said several forests . . . ; and also for grants and charters . . . for the fully, clearly, and absolutely disafforesting, discharging, releasing, freeing, and exempting of them, their heirs . . . , and their . . . hereditaments whatsoever of and from our deer and their commoning . . . or depasturing there, and of and from all laws, liberties, privileges, jurisdictions, assize, and ordinances of forest whatsoever, and of and from the view, cognizance, or jurisdiction of all swanimote courts, justice seats, courts or pleas to be holden before justices itinerant, and of and from the view or jurisdictions of justices itinerant, verderers, foresters, regardors, and other officers or ministers of forest. . . .

Rymer, Foedera, XIX, 688 f.

94. RECORDS OF JUDICIAL CASES (1627-38)

(A) THE CASE OF THE FIVE KNIGHTS (1627)[1]

. . . This is a case of very great weight and great expectation, and it had been fit we should have used more solemn arguments of it than now for the shortness of the time we can do. . . . I am sure you expect justice from hence, and God forbid we should sit here but to do justice to all men according to our best skill and knowledge, for it is our oaths and duties so to do. . . . We are sworn to maintain all prerogatives of the king; that is one branch of our oath. And we are likewise sworn to administer justice equally to all people. . . . That which is now to be judged by us is this: whether

---

[1] Following up his demand for a forced loan, Charles I in 1627 imprisoned various persons who had refused to contribute. Five of the prisoners—Sir Thomas Darnel, Sir John Corbet, Sir Walter Earl, Sir John Heveningham, and Sir Edmund Hampden—thereupon sued for writs of *habeas corpus* from the court of king's bench. The writs, thus being granted, were returned by the warden of the Fleet Prison with the statement that he had acted by virtue of a warrant from two members of the privy council ordering the prisoners committed "by the special command of his majesty." The points at issue, as well as the judgment of the court, are clearly stated by Chief Justice Hyde.

any one that is committed by the king's authority, and no cause declared of his commitment, according as here it is upon this return—whether we ought to deliver him by bail or to remand him back again. . . .

The exceptions which have been taken to this return were two: the one for the form, the other for the substance. . . . In our case the cause of the detention is sufficiently answered, which is the demand of the writ; and therefore we resolve that the form of this return is good. The next thing is the main point in law, whether the substance or matter of the return be good or no—wherein the substance is this: he doth certify that they are detained in prison by the special command of the king. And whether this be good in law or no, that is the question. . . .[2]

The precedents are all against you, every one of them. And what shall guide our judgments, since there is nothing alleged in this case but precedents? That, if no cause of the commitment be expressed, it is to be presumed to be a matter of state, which we cannot take notice of. You see we find none—no, not one that hath been delivered by bail in the like cases, but by the hand of the king or his direction. . . . Now here I shall trouble you with no more precedents; and you see your own, what conclusion they produce. And as to those strong precedents alleged on the other side, we are not wiser than they that went before us. And the common custom of the law is the common law of the land, and that hath been the continual common custom of the law, to which we are to submit; for we come not to change the law, but to submit to it. . . .

But the question now is whether we may deliver this gentleman or not. . . . Mr. Attorney hath told you that the king hath done it, and we trust him in great matters. And he is bound by law, and he bids us proceed by law as we are sworn to do, and so is the king. And we make no doubt but the king, if you seek to him . . . , will have mercy. But we leave that. If in justice we ought to deliver you, we would do it; but upon these grounds and these records, and the precedents and resolutions, we cannot deliver you, but you must be remanded. . . . I have endeavoured to give the resolutions of us all.

Howell, *State Trials*, III, 51-59.

(B) THE QUESTION OF SHIP MONEY (1637)[3]

. . . We, desirous to avoid such inconveniences, and out of our princely love and affection to all our subjects, being willing to prevent such errors as any of our loving subjects may happen to run into,

---

[2] The chief justice here takes up in detail the precedents cited by attorneys for the prisoners.

[3] In connection with the writs for the levy of ship money already issued (no. 93B), Charles I directed to his judges the letter which in part follows. And he received the answer which is quoted in full.

have thought fit in a case of this nature to advise with our judges, who, we doubt not, are all well studied and informed in the right of our sovereignty. And because the trial in our several courts, by the formality in pleading, will require a long protraction, we have thought it expedient, by this our letter directed to you all, to require your judgments in the case, as is set down in the enclosed paper, which will not only gain time but also be of more authority to overrule any prejudicate opinions of others in the point. Given under our signet at our court at Whitehall, the 2nd day of February, in the twelfth year of our reign. . . .[4]

May it please your most excellent majesty: We have, according to your majesty's command—every man by himself and all of us together—taken into consideration the case and question signed by your majesty and enclosed in your royal letter. And we are of opinion that, when the good and safety of the kingdom in general is concerned and the whole kingdom is in danger, your majesty may, by writ under the great seal of England, command all the subjects of this your kingdom at their charge to provide and furnish such number of ships, with men, munition, and victuals, and for such time as your majesty shall think fit, for the defence and safeguard of the kingdom from such danger and peril; and that by law your majesty may compel the doing thereof in case of refusal or refractoriness. And we are also of opinion that in such case your majesty is the sole judge both of the danger and when and how the same is to be prevented and avoided. John Bramston. John Finch. Humphrey Davenport. John Denham. Richard Hutton. William Jones. George Crooke. Thomas Trevor. George Vernon. Francis Crawley. Robert Berkeley. Richard Weston.

Ibid., III, 843 f.

(C) THE KING V. JOHN HAMPDEN (1638)[5]

Robert Berkeley: . . . The grand question is shortly this: whether . . . in this special case . . . the charges imposed by the king upon his subjects for provision of shipping, without common consent in parliament, be good in law—yea or no. . . . I hope that

---
[4] The substance of the king's question is repeated in the judges' answer.
[5] John Hampden, a freeholder of Buckinghamshire, refused to pay 20s. assessed upon his land as ship money in accordance with the king's writ of 1636 (see above, p. 455, n. 2). On being summoned before the court of exchequer to show cause for non-payment, Hampden through his attorneys declared the levy illegal; and, as a test case, the matter was taken into exchequer chamber to be discussed before all the justices of the central courts. After twelve days of argument by counsel on the two sides, the court, by a vote of seven to five, gave judgment against Hampden. How these five—Crooke, Hutton, Denham, Davenport, and Bramston—thus came to differ from the view to which they had earlier subscribed is explained in the second of the following opinions, that of George Crooke. The first, in which the majority of the court concurred, is that of Robert Berkeley. Both men were justices of the king's bench.

none doth imagine that it either is or can be drawn by consequence to be any part of the question in this case whether the king may at all times and upon all occasions impose charges upon his subjects in general without common consent in parliament. If that were made the question, it is questionless that he may not. The people of the kingdom are subjects, not slaves—freemen, not villeins to be taxed *de alto et basso*. Though the king of England hath a monarchical power and hath *jura summae majestatis* and hath an absolute trust settled in his crown and person for the government of his subjects, yet his government is to be *secundum leges regni*. . . . By those laws the subjects are not tenants at the king's will of what they have. . . . They have a birthright in the laws of the kingdom. No new laws can be put upon them; none of their laws can be altered or abrogated without common consent in parliament. Thus much I speak to avoid misapprehensions and misreports upon that which I shall say in this case, not as if there were cause of saying so much upon anything challenged on the king's side. . . .[6]

It is to be observed that the principal command in the shipping-writ is not to levy money; it is to provide a ship—which ship being to be provided at the charge of a multitude . . . , the thing cannot be done any manner of way but by . . . money. Therefore, the instructions in the shipping-writ are not only apt but necessary. . . . And thereupon it may be said that the sum assessed upon every one, and in our case upon Mr. Hampden, is . . . a duty to be performed as a means conducing to the principal end; the refusal of performance of which duty is a refusal to obey the principal thing commanded . . . , being of a kind concerning the commonwealth. The king, who is the head, the sovereign of the commonwealth, and who hath as incident to his regal office power of coercion, is by law to exercise such his power of coercion to enforce such as refuse to join with others in performance of that which is commanded for the commonwealth. . . .

I would be loath to irritate any differing in opinion from me with provoking or odious terms; but I cannot more fully express myself . . . than in saying that it is a dangerous tenet, a kind of Judaizing opinion to hold that the weal public must be exposed to the peril of utter ruin and subversion, rather than such a charge as this, which may secure the commonwealth, may be imposed by the king upon the subject without common consent in parliament. . . . All know that the Jews were so strict that they would not use means for defence of themselves and their country upon their Sabbath. Their enemies took the advantage and ruined their state. . . .

Mr. Holbourne[7] supposed a fundamental policy in the creation of the frame of this kingdom that, in case the monarch of England

---

[6] Berkeley here reviews the long series of precedents cited by Hampden's counsel.
[7] Counsel for Hampden

should be inclined to exact from his subjects at his pleasure, he should be restrained, for that he could have nothing from them but upon a common consent in parliament. He is utterly mistaken herein. I agree the parliament to be a most ancient and supreme court, where the king and peers, as judges, are in person, and the whole body of the commons representatively. There peers and commons may . . . , amongst other things, make known their grievances, if there be any, to their sovereign and humbly petition him for redress. But the former fancied policy I utterly deny. The law knows no such king-yoking policy. The law is itself an old and trusty servant of the king's; it is his instrument or means which he useth to govern his people by. I never read nor heard that Lex was Rex; but it is common and most true that Rex is Lex, for he is . . . a living, a speaking, an acting law. . . .

There are two maxims of the law of England which plainly disprove Mr. Holbourne's supposed policy. The first is that the king is a person trusted with the state of the commonwealth. The second of these maxims is that the king cannot do wrong. Upon these two maxims the *jura summae majestatis* are grounded, with which none but the king himself—not his high court of parliament without leave—hath to meddle: as, namely, war and peace, value of coin, parliament at pleasure, power to dispense with penal laws, and divers others; amongst which I range . . . also . . . power to command provision—in case of necessity—of means from the subjects, to be adjoined to the king's own means for the defence of the commonwealth. . . . Otherwise I do not understand how the king's majesty may be said to have the majestical right and power of a free monarch. . . .

And so I have done at this time. And what I have said I have spoken to the best of my understanding and in discharge of my conscience. . . . And, it being high time now for me to give over, I conclude upon all my reasons and authorities cited that, as this case is upon the pleading of it, the charge of 20s. imposed on Mr. Hampden towards the provision of a ship commanded by the writ . . . is consonant to law, and consequently that judgment ought to be given against him. . . .

Sir George Crooke: . . . That which hath moved me most and maketh me distrust my own judgment in this case is that my brothers that have argued before me . . . have all argued one way; with whose opinions I should willingly have concurred if I could have satisfied my own judgment with their reasons. But, not being satisfied, I have learned that I must not come with a multitude against mine own conscience. . . . And therefore I shall show reasons and leave myself to the judgment of my lords and others my brethren. And whatsoever shall be adjudged I must submit unto, and so do with all others; and do now declare my opinion to be that, as this case is, judgment ought to be given for the defendant. My reasons and grounds that I shall insist upon are these: (1) that the command by this writ ... for to have ships at the charge of the inhabitants of the county ... is illegal and contrary to the common laws, not being by authority of parliament; (2) that, if at the common laws it had been lawful, yet now this writ is illegal, being expressly contrary to divers statutes prohibiting a general charge to be laid upon the commons in general without consent in parliament; (3) that it is not to be maintained by any prerogative or power royal, nor allegation of necessity or danger; (4) admitting it were legal to lay such a charge upon maritime ports, yet to charge any inland county, as the county of Bucks is, with making ships and furnishing them with masters, mariners, and soldiers at their charge ... is illegal and not warranted by any former precedent. ... .[8]

To this opinion I confess I then, with the rest of the judges, subscribed my hand; but I then dissented to that opinion and then signified my opinion to be that such a charge could not be laid by any such writ but by parliament. And so absolutely in that point one other did agree with me, and dissented from that opinion; and four others in some other particulars from that which was subscribed. But the greater part seeming absolutely to be resolved upon that opinion—some of them affirming that they had seen divers records and precedents of such writs satisfying them to be of that judgment—I was pressed to subscribe with them. ... And this by more ancient judges than myself was affirmed to be the continual practice; and that it was not fit—especially in a case of this nature, so much concerning the service of the king—for some to subscribe and some to forbear their subscriptions; and that, although we did subscribe, it did not bind us, but that in point of judgment, if the case came in question judicially before us, we should give our judgments as we should see cause. ...

Ibid., III, 1089-1145.

(D) STAR CHAMBER REPORTS (1631)[9]

In the star chamber, Trinity term of the seventh year of King Charles: in the council of the lord king at that same place, before Thomas, lord of Coventry, lord keeper of the great seal; Henry, earl of Manchester, lord keeper of the privy seal; John, earl of Bridgewater; William, bishop of London; Richard, bishop of Winchester; Nicholas Hyde, knight, lord chief justice of the king's bench; Thomas Richardson, knight, lord chief justice of the [common] bench.

Between John Smith, plaintiff, and Benjamin Crokew and Thomas Wright, defendants. The plaintiff's bill showed that there had been

---

[8] Crooke here refers to the answer given by the judges in the previous February.

[9] The following cases are taken from various sessions of the court, each of which is preceded by a list of those present similar to the one that is given here. These lists are normally in Latin.

94. JUDICIAL CASES (1627-38)

a long suit in the chancery between the plaintiff Smith and the defendant Crokew about lands belonging to the free school of [Wooton Underedge] in Gloucestershire, and this suit was directed to be there sued by the judges of the common law. And this was heard so far: the possession was decreed to the school, and all other estates to be cancelled, and the school's estate to be surrendered to the king with purpose to grant the same back again to the school. It was ordered further that, whereas Smith had been in possession of the manor or lordship of Wallens Court, being his own fee simple, and his lands lying intermixed with the school lands, he should have a lease . . . of the said lands in question. The king made a new grant by his letters patents and founded the school; and the lease is made to Mr. Smith accordingly. That divers good ordinances were made for the ordering of the school, 40*m*. per annum raised for the master and £4 a year for four poor scholars going to the university; that Mr. Smith hath improved it to the payment of £4 more to a poor scholar. That the defendant Crokew had—to the scandal of the court of chancery, of the late lord chancellor, of the lord keeper, and the king's counsel—printed and divulged a scandalous book to the number of 400 copies, divulged them in Somersetshire and Gloucestershire and London; and Wright the defendant, being a bookseller in Bristol, sold many of the books. And [the plaintiff] complained particularly that the said book contained a scandalous frontispiece and twelve principal slanders and scandalous passages in the book, naming the several pages; and that it was also to the scandal of the plaintiff Smith. The bill prayed the calling in of this scandalous libel to be burnt, and for repair of the plaintiff's reputation.

The defendants made no defence by counsel but, after an affidavit read for serving of the subpoena . . . , the defendants' answers were read. Crokew answered that there had been many unjust suits between the plaintiff and him, wherein the plaintiff had wronged him; that he caused a brief relation of all to be printed to inform the court of parliament, and kept his book, being printed, from publishing till the parliament was sitting, and then gave some of them to his friends. He intended not to lay scandal upon any, but to lay the fault upon the plaintiff only, and he hath not put to sale any of the books—and so not guilty.

Thomas Wright answered that Crokew told this defendant he had printed such books and would desire him to sell some of them for him; and after thirty books were sent by the carrier to him; that he sold them, not thinking they were scandalous, and he thought they were not when he read the book—and so not guilty.

The plaintiff's counsel showed the scandals of the book and the frontispiece: A True Relation of the Strange Passages in Causes between Smith and Crokew, especially in a Cause about the Statute of 43 of Elizabeth of Charitable Uses—wherein Smith hath abused his majesty that late was, my lord bishop of Canterbury, my lord chancellor, my lord keeper, in getting the possession of the said school lands, for which Crokew hath a bill now depending in the parliament. . . . The defendant Crokew confessed he caused it to be penned, and it was done by a servant of the now master of the court of wards, and agreed with one for £9 to print them, etc.

The court in their sentence condemned this book for a libellous and scandalous book, and declared that to print or write briefs of a cause before the hearing and to divulge and publish them is to be accounted scandalous and libellous, because it tendeth to make a private information of the cause. The court therefore ordered that this book, as many of them as could be gotten, should be brought to the public assizes at Gloucester and there burnt; Crokew to pay £500 fine to the king; and Wright £100 for selling some of the books (for if libels are printed, it is not warrant enough to any bookseller to put them to sale); and both to be imprisoned according to the course of the court; and the sentences to be drawn up to clear Smith in his reputation. . . .

Between Richard Waterhouse, plaintiff, and Sir Arthur Ingram, defendant. . . . The plaintiff's counsel opened the bill, consisting of three several charges: (1) for forging a deed of assignment of an old lease . . . of certain lands at Halifax in Yorkshire . . . ; (2) . . . for procuring a release of the said lands in question from Robert Waterhouse . . . while the said Robert was *non compos mentis*; (3) . . . for endorsing the plaintiff's name as a witness to a deed of indenture . . . whereas the plaintiff was no witness to the same deed. It was confessed by the plaintiff's counsel that two of these charges were mistaken . . . ; but for the third charge they showed that divers trials at the law there had been and verdicts and judgments for the plaintiff. . . .

The defendant justified his purchase and denied the forgery and the other crimes and justified an assignment by one Miller dated 1612 . . . , and produced the same to this court. . . .

The sentence of the court was that Sir Arthur Ingram was clear of the forgery and other crimes; that the bill should be taken off the file; that the plaintiff should pay a fine of £100 to the king *pro falso clamore*, and £500 damages to Sir Arthur Ingram; and the plaintiff to make confession of his fault at the assizes at York, standing upon a stool, and at the block at Halifax. . . .

Between Keld, plaintiff, and Fairside, defendant. . . . The plaintiff brought his bill charging the defendants of perjury, subornation of perjury, and confederacy to indict the plaintiff of high treason at York for saying these words . . . : "If it were the king's pleasure that these exactions be made, then we must needs think he is a very beggarly prince. . . ." That the grand jury found an *ignoramus*.[10]

The defendant was a constable and demanded benevolence[11] of

---

[10] A refusal to indict.
[11] One of the levies made by James I; cf. no. 69H.

94. JUDICIAL CASES (1627-38)

the plaintiff for the king, and the defendant answered upon his oath that the plaintiff did speak these words unto him upon his second coming to him from Sir Thomas Hobby for a larger contribution; and confessed he did give evidence to the grand jury to this purpose, yet the jury would not find the bill.

The court was opinioned the words were spoken, though the jury in favour of life would not take notice of it by a single witness. And therefore, if this man should be punished for this, it would be a dangerous precedent; for that every single witness must run upon this rock, either to be perjured or punished. The plaintiff's bill was therefore dismissed and he was fined £20 *pro falso clamore*. ...

One Archer of Southchurch in Essex was brought *ore tenus*,[12] being then charged by Mr. Attorney General for keeping in his corn and consequently for enhancing the price of corn the last year; which offence Mr. Attorney affirmed to be of high nature and evil consequence, to the undoing of the poor and *malum in se*, and then desired his examination taken before the lord keeper might be read. His examination purported that he had seen at the time of his examining a presentment that was made against him by the grand jury at the last assizes in Essex before Justice Vernon for the said offence of keeping in his corn and enhancing; and for that he had made a bargain to sell the poor of the town where he dwelt rye for 7s. a bushel, and afterwards refused to perform his bargain unless he might have 9s. a bushel. He denied this bargain, but for his excuse said he sold to the towns about him, for the poor, wheat at 7s. and 8s. a bushel, and at the latter end of the year for 5s.; and rye for 7s. and 6s., etc., and some for 3s. and 6d. the bushel. He confessed he kept in his corn till June, and that he had 8 quarters of wheat, 60 quarters of rye, and 100 quarters of oats; and that his family were himself and his wife and daughters, two maids, and a man. He confessed that he sold none or very little of his corn in Rochford Hundred where he dwelt, though he were commanded so to do by the earl of Warwick. Yet for his defence he further alleged that his barn was not visited by any justices or officers according to his majesty's late proclamation and orders for that purpose. ...

Justice Harvey ... was of opinion that this man's punishment and example will do a great deal more good than all their orders which they might have made at the sessions. And therefore he declared his offence to be very great and fit to be punished in this court; and adjudged him to pay 100m. fine to the king and £10 to the poor, and to stand upon the pillory in Newgate Market an hour with a paper, wherein the cause of his standing there was to be written, put upon his hat—"For enhancing the price of corn"—and then to be led through Cheapside to Leadenhall Market, and there likewise to stand upon the pillory one hour more with the same

---

[12] To answer in person.

paper upon his hat, and after this to be sent to Chelmsford, and there likewise in the market to stand upon the pillory.

Sir Thomas Richardson affirmed this offence to be an offence at the common law long before the king's proclamation and orders, and also against some statutes. . . . He therefore condemned the said Archer to be guilty . . . and agreed in his said fine to the king. . . . The bishop of London observed, with Mr. Attorney, that this was *malum in se*, and that this Archer was guilty of a most foul offence. . . . The earl of Danby consented to the sentence in all. . . . The earl of Dorset concurred in his sentence with the earl of Danby. . . . Lord privy seal gave his sentence in few words, that Archer was guilty by his own confession of a very great offence and well worthy the sentence aforesaid. . . . The lord keeper did affirm that it was indeed a good work to bring this man forth to be here sentenced. . . . His said lordship consented to the highest censure against the said Archer . . . and committed Archer to the Fleet. . . .

The king's attorney general, plaintiff; Charley Moody, Richard Strode . . . and others, defendants. The bill set forth that his majesty, being seised of divers lands and waste grounds called the Fens . . . surrounded with water and barren . . . , by advice of his council took order with Sir Cornelius Vermuyden for the draining of the Fens, if it might be. And articles of agreement were made between his majesty and the said Sir Cornelius Vermuyden . . . for the doing thereof; and a special provision [was made] that those that had any title of common should repair to the commissioners appointed for that purpose by commission and, upon their showing their title or interest, they should have full recompense. The king's letters were sent to warn them to come to the commission and demand their recompense. . . . The king provided workmen, the work was brought to good forwardness, and divers ditches and banks made, and Sir Cornelius Vermuyden was at great charge thereabouts. . . . The defendants with others came together in companies to throw down and demolish what was done: although divers proclamations were made, and no right they could pretend. . . . They made their assemblies by hundreds and five-hundreds; they demolish the work; they . . . burn the spades, shovels, wheelbarrows, planks, and beat the workmen; set up a pair of gallows for to terrify the workmen; threw some of them into the water and held them under a while. They had a signal to assemble themselves by, sometimes by a bell, sometimes by an horn. They threatened to kill the workmen if they came thither to work again. . . . They had fourteen several times in riotous and rebellious manner assembled themselves and done these riots, etc., to the slander of his majesty's government, to the hindrance of the work, and to the damage of Sir Cornelius Vermuyden £5000. . . . Some of them put those that served the king's process out of this court upon them into the stocks.

The defendants' answers some were read and the rest opened by

94. JUDICIAL CASES (1627-38)

counsel. They all claimed their common of pasture with all manner of cattle and common of turbary at all times of the year. . . . They never agreed with Sir Cornelius Vermuyden. . . . The country receiveth no profit by the work. The grounds are made rather worse. They confess, some of them, that they did with others enter into their grounds to go to their cattle there depasturing; that they cut down the banks and ditches and levelled them for stopping their way. This they did to claim their right, which they hope this court will maintain; seeing they have had possession and seisin . . . time out of mind. And as to the unlawful assemblies, riots, routs, plots, confederacies, woundings, beatings, etc., not guilty. . . .

It was unanimously declared by the whole court that his majesty proceeded herein legally and rightfully for the benefit of his crown and people. . . . And many of the defendants were found guilty of the several riots charged in the bill: namely, Toxie, James Moody, Henry Scott, and Hezekias Browne, who were fined £1000 apiece; the widow Smith, who married the minister after the riots, £500; and the several women who were proved to be at the said riots, 500m. apiece. And they were adjudged to pay for damages to Sir Cornelius Vermuyden, the relator, £2000. . . .

Gardiner, *Cases in Star Chamber and High Commission*, pp. 37-65.

(E) HIGH COMMISSION REPORTS (1631)

In the court of high commission, Thursday, 20th October, 1631; before George, archbishop of Canterbury; William, bishop of London; Thomas, bishop of Coventry and Lichfield; Theophilus, bishop of St. David's; Francis, bishop of Norwich; John, bishop of Rochester; Sir Dudley Digges, knight; Sir Henry Martin, knight, doctor of law; Sir John Lambe, knight, doctor of law; Sir Nathaniel Brittaine, knight, doctor of law—commissioners.

The cause against Samuel Pretty, clerk. [Article 1:] That the said Samuel, being a minister, was commonly reported for the space of two years last past as a schismatical man. [Answer:] He confesseth himself to be a minister, but denieth that other part of the article. [Article 2:] That he had within twelve months last past preached in the church called St. Michael Pater Noster Royal, London, without licence of the bishop of that diocese. [Answer:] He confesseth that he hath preached in the said church and that he had licence from the late bishop of London. [Article 3:] That the said Samuel in his sermon there delivered these erroneous doctrines and assertions following, *viz.*, that Christians cannot, as touching their reconciliation with God, be too secure—nay, they ought to sing all care away. [Answer:] He saith that he hopeth these words may be spoken, because a favourable construction may be made of them. . . .[13]

The archbishop: "Pretty, tell me, if you had been in Jerusalem

---

[13] Three other articles charge Pretty with doctrinal errors and these charges are supported by three witnesses.

in the Temple among the buyers and sellers, would not Christ have whipped you out with them? What think you?" Samuel Pretty: "If there were not favourable construction of my words to be made, I think I should have been whipped out if I had been there." Then he fell down upon his knees and acknowledged he had given just offence, as by the articles was alleged; and humbly desired mercy of the court.

The archbishop then would only have imprisoned and suspended him from his ministerial office; but it was moved by the bishop of London[14] that he might undergo the censure of the court . . . , for that he and others were minded to degrade him. . . .[15] The archbishop concluded, briefly but sharply reproving him for his phrase of singing all care away. "Yea," saith the archbishop, "drink it away, too; but to what purpose then are all those rules of mortification and growing in sanctification, as 'The night is past, the day is at hand; let us therefore cast away the works of darkness,' etc." And [he] gave his sentence thus: "Let him be imprisoned, suspended, degraded, and kept in prison till he bring in his licence."

[24 November 1631.] A cause against Dr. Hooke, parson of Nettleham in Yorkshire, came to be heard this day. The articles against Dr. Hooke were six or seven: (1) for saying he resigned his archdeaconry because he would be rid of those caterpillars and cankerworms, the ecclesiastical officers; (2) for delivering his opinion at York before the justices of assize that he held it unlawful for priests to exercise any temporal jurisdiction; (3) for making licences for marriages without publishing any banns at his vicarage of Castor . . . and that he used a little seal, and that he married some himself and took money of them for the licences, etc.; (4) he was accused of six or seven several adulteries, he himself being a married man; (5) he was charged with the simoniacal resignation and bestowing of his vicarage of Castor upon a young man, a minister that was no party to this suit; (6) he was articled against for a contempt offered to this court by words, etc. . . .[16]

I give my sentence against this man, for his making of lawless churches, to be suspended three years. For his saying against the officers that they are caterpillars, I let that pass. For his simony I vehemently suspect him, and therefore [he is] to purge himself *septima manu*.[17] For the matters of adultery, it seemeth to me a wondrous thing that a man of his years should so carry himself to be subject to suspicion. These may be pardoned . . . ; I think him not guilty of these obliquities. . . . But for the other thing, that no clergyman may be so much as a justice of peace, this is fantastical and

---

[14] William Laud, subsequently archbishop of Canterbury.

[15] All but one member of the court spoke in favour of his degradation.

[16] After long argument, the members of the court gave their opinions and the archbishop of Canterbury delivered the following sentence.

[17] With six oath-helpers; see immediately below. Cf. no. 14F.

94. JUDICIAL CASES (1627-38)

makes such a breach in the church that he cannot easily make satisfaction. . . . Well, sir, I must admonish you for your contempt . . . ; you are to pay the charges of the suit and to be committed. . . .

[26 April 1632.] Dr. Hooke maketh faith that the certificate of the purgation to be made this day by him was read in the parish church of Nettleton. . . . Then he produced his compurgators: by name, John Shiboy, doctor of divinity; Francis Bradshaw, Thomas Holt, Dennis Squire, Matthew Miller, Thomas Clare, bachelors of divinity. Dr. Hooke and the rest came in their cloaks, and the said Holt in a careless ruff and his hair somewhat long. For which their coming they were chidden, and especially Mr. Holt. And they were rejected till they should come as divines in their gowns. And they went and got them gowns and scarfs; and Mr. Holt had another ruff and a black satin night-cap on. And they appeared again, and then the cause was opened by the doctors both on the one side and the other. The promoter's counsel showed the accusations and the proofs against the doctor, and his counsel showed his defence. Which done, Dr. Hooke took his oath, swearing that he was not guilty of the crimes laid against him, nor any of them. And the said compurgators were first demanded severally whether they, notwithstanding all that had been said, thought the doctor to be clear and innocent. And they all did answer severally Yes. Then they took their oaths, swearing that they thought in their consciences that Dr. Hooke had taken a true oath. . . .

[3 May 1632.] This day were brought to the court out of prison divers persons . . . which were taken on Sunday last at a conventicle met at the house of Barnett, a brewer's clerk, dwelling in the precinct of Black Friars. . . .

Then came in Mr. Latropp, who is asked what authority he had to preach and keep this conventicle. And saith the bishop of London: "How many women sat cross-legged upon the bed whilst you sat on one side and preached and prayed most devoutly?" Latropp: "I keep no such evil company; they were not such women." London: "Are you a minister?" . . . He answered that he was a minister. London: "How and by whom qualified? Where are your orders?" Latropp: "I am a minister of the gospel of Christ, and the Lord hath qualified me." "Will you lay your hand on the Book and take your oath?" said the court. He refuseth the oath. . . .

Samuel Eaton and two women and a maid appeared, who were demanded why they were assembled in that conventicle when others were at church. Eaton: "We were not assembled in contempt of the magistrate." London: "No, it was in contempt of the Church of England." Eaton: "It was in conscience to God. . . ." Canterbury: "What did you?" "We read the Scriptures and catechized our families," said Eaton; "and may it please this honourable court to hear us speak the truth, we will show you what was done . . . ; we did nothing but what you will allow us to do." London: "Who can free you? These are dangerous men; they are a scattered company sown in all the city. . . . Hold them the Book." Eaton: "I dare not swear nor take this oath. . . . I know not what I shall swear to." King's advocate: "It is to give a true answer to articles put into the court against you, or that shall be put in touching this conventicle of yours and divers your heretical tenets, and what words and exercises you used, and things of this nature." Eaton: "I dare not." . . .[18] Archbishop of Canterbury: "Take them away." So they were all committed to the New Prison.

[14 June 1632.] . . . Sound, Hollingsworth, Gerard, John Osborne, and Thomas Pocock, having answered for setting up and continuing the seats above the communion table in St. Austin's Church by Paul's, they being churchwardens and parishioners there, Dr. Duck, the chancellor of London, moved that their answers and their cause might be considered, and they ordered to take down and remove their seats newly set up above the communion table. London: "You say you have not room for your parishioners, and therefore you must have seats above God Almighty and above Christ in His own house. Judge you, is it reason? The church of St. Leonard's, Foster Lane, is in the same case; but I made them pull down their seats. And so I will you. . . ." Parishioners: "If the court will order us to take them down, we will; or else we dare not, for the vestry hath ordered it that they shall be built upon the old foundation." . . . Rochester: "The power of vestries and churchwardens, this is to hatch a lay presbytery."

[21 June, 1632.] . . . Ralph Grafton, an upholsterer, dwelling in Cornhill, London, was required to take his oath to answer the articles. He was said to be a principal ringleader of those conventiclers that met at Black Friars. King's advocate: "This is a rich man, dwelling within the city. My motion is that your grace and the court would set a fine upon this man if he shall refuse to answer, that others may be warned for contemning of the court." London: "Mr. Advocate. I thank you for this motion." King's advocate: "I require you and the court requireth you to take your oath to answer to matters of your own fact, as far as you know and are bound by law." Grafton: "An oath is a matter of an high nature and must not be taken rashly. I dare not, therefore, take this oath. We have done nothing against the law. It was no conventicle. There was nothing spoken against the king, nor against the state. I dare not take the oath and I am no ringleader of any to evil." Canterbury: "You met without law; you had no authority. . . ." Wherefore the court for his contempt in refusing the oath set a fine of £200 upon him and committed him to prison. Grafton: "I have bail here ready; if you please to take

---

[18] The other prisoners also refused to take the oath.

it, I tender it to you." . . . Canterbury: "No, away with him to prison!" . . .

Ibid., pp. 181 f., 246 f., 276 f., 306 f., 315 f.

95. RECORDS OF THE SHORT PARLIAMENT (1640)
(A) SPEECH OF THE LORD KEEPER (13 APRIL)

My lords, and you, the knights, citizens, and burgesses of the house of commons: . . . I doubt not but you rejoice at this day's meeting . . . ; and good reason you have so to do, and with all humbleness of heart to acknowledge the great goodness of his majesty who, sequestering the memory of all former discouragements in preceding assemblies, is now, out of a fatherly affection to his people and a confidence that they will not be failing in their duty to him, pleased graciously to invite you and all his loving subjects to a sacred unity of hearts and affection in the service of him and of the commonwealth, and in execution of those counsels that tend only to the honour of his majesty and to the good preservation of you all. His majesty's kingly resolutions are seated in the ark of his sacred breast, and it were a presumption of too high a nature for any Uzzah, uncalled, to touch it. Yet his majesty is now pleased to lay by the shining beams of majesty . . . , that the distance between sovereignty and subjection should not bar you of that filial freedom of access to his person and counsel. Only let us . . . ever remember that, though the king sometimes lays by the beams and rays of majesty, he never lays by majesty itself.

In former parliaments you have been advised for the preventing and diverting of those dangers which by foreign and remote counsels might have tended to the ruin and to the dishonour of this nation. Therein his majesty's great wisdom and providence hath, for many years, eased you of that trouble; his majesty having with great judgment and prudence, not only foreseen and prevented our dangers, but kept up the honour and splendour of the English crown, of which we all this day find a happy and comfortable experience. . . . But what avails this the kingdom? . . . You are now summoned to counsels and resolutions that more nearly concern you—to prevent a danger and dishonour that knocks at our gates, and that moves from such from whom we had little reason to suspect it. . . .

When his majesty had most reason to expect a grateful return of loyalty and obedience from all the Scottish nation, some men of Belial, some Shebahs, have blown the trumpet there, and by their insolencies and rebellious actions drawn many after them, to the utter desertion of his majesty's government. . . . They have taken up arms against the Lord's anointed, their rightful prince and undoubted sovereign . . . ; they have seized on the trophies of honour and invested themselves with the regal power and authority—such and so many acts of disloyalty and disobedience as, let their pretences be what they will be, no true English Christian heart but must acknowledge them to be the effects of foul and horrid treasons. . . .

His majesty doth therefore desire you, upon these pressing and urgent reasons, that you will for a while lay aside all other debates, and that you would pass an act for such and so many subsidies as you, in your hearty affections to him and to the common good, shall think fit and convenient for so great an action; and withal that you would hasten the payment of it as soon as may be, with a proviso in the act that his majesty's royal assent shall not determine this session. . . . And his majesty is most graciously pleased to give you his royal word that . . . he will give you time for considering of such petitions as you shall conceive to be good for the commonwealth. . . .

Journals of the Lords, IV, 46 f.

(B) SPEECH OF THE LORD KEEPER (22 APRIL)

This day the lord keeper delivered to the house the effect of what was yesterday delivered, by the command of his majesty, at the meeting of the lords spiritual and temporal and the house of commons at Whitehall, *viz.*: ". . . That which I then delivered was, by his majesty's command, to this purpose—to put your lordships and the house of commons in mind of the cause of the calling of this parliament, which was for the supply of his majesty. . . . His majesty hath taken notice of some scruples that did remain in men's minds touching the shipping business. And for the clearing of those doubts and scruples . . . , it was declared to your lordships, first, that the king never had it in his thought or heart to make any revenue of the shipping business, nor to make the least penny of profit or advantage to himself; that *de facto* he had not done it. . . . He hath no ends or aims for himself, nor hath he any thought but to keep up the glory and honour of this nation. . . . His majesty is not wedded to this particular way. . . . If your lordships and the house of commons will think of any other way to maintain him in such a manner as is fit for his majesty . . . to live in, put it into what way you please; settle it with as much security and safety as you can invent, that you may be sure there can come nothing to the king but in that way, that you may be sure it shall be employed for your good and safety. . . . Nothing shall be propounded for the securing of the propriety of your estates and the liberties of your persons but his majesty will as graciously and readily grant the same as it is possible for you to ask it. His majesty doth bring with him wishes and royal desires that this may prove a happy and blessed parliament, and was pleased to put you into the way how to make it so; which was by putting obligations and trust and confidence upon his royal word, which it becomes us in duty and good manners fit for subjects to take from our king. . . . For there is a trust that must always be reposed in a king; and, when the king is pleased to declare himself so gracious and so free that he will perform this trust to the uttermost with royal heaped measure,

95. THE SHORT PARLIAMENT

it is the greatest security. No security of law, no other security that parliament can invent, can match it. . . ."

Ibid., IV, 62 f.

(C) PROCEEDINGS IN THE COMMONS (23-24 APRIL)

Mr. Lenthall reported from the committee of the whole house that the committee had resolved upon the question that we shall consult with the lords to prevent innovation in matter of religion and concerning the property of our goods and liberties and privileges of parliament, the better to give a present supply to his majesty. Upon this report it was ordered, upon the question, that we shall consult with the lords, to prevent innovation in matter of religion and concerning the property of our goods and liberties and privileges of parliament, the better to prepare us to give an answer to his majesty touching supply. . . .

These heads following were by the committee, according to yesterday's order, brought in as inducements and matter for the conference to be desired with the lords . . . :

I. Concerning innovation in matter of religion. (1) The commission that was lately granted to the convocation house. . . . (2) The complaints arising from petitions brought in from the several counties by the members of the house against innovations in religion. (3) The molesting and depriving of godly and conformable ministers for not yielding to matters enjoined without warrant of law. (4) The publishing of papist tenets in licensed books, sermons, and disputations. (5) Restraining of conformable ministers from preaching in their own charges.

II. Concerning propriety of goods. (1) Monopolies and restraint of trade. (2) Ship money. (3) Enlarging the bounds of forests. . . . (4) Military charges: namely, coat and conduct money, wages, arms taken from the owners, forcing the countries to buy or provide at their charges horses and carts by way of tax. (5) The denial of justice in the courts at Westminster to the subject's prejudice in point of the propriety of his goods. (6) Frequent imprisonments and vexations for non-payment of unwarrantable taxes and not submitting to unlawful monopolies.

III. Liberties and privileges of parliament. (1) Punishing men out of parliament for things done in parliament. (2) That which is already voted in the house concerning privilege of parliament. . . .

Journals of the Commons, II, 10 f.

(D) THE KING'S SPEECH AND ITS RESULTS (24-29 APRIL)

"My lords: The necessity of calling this parliament makes me to come this day hither contrary to expectation. You remember what the lord keeper said concerning the occasion of this meeting the first and second days. . . . The house of commons did seem to take into consideration my weighty affairs; but they have in a manner concluded the contrary and, instead of preferring my occasions in the first place, they have held consultation of innovation of religion, property of goods, and privileges of parliament, and so have put the cart before the horse. If it were a time to dispute, I should not much stand upon it; but my necessities are so urgent that there can be no delay. If the house of commons will trust me, I will make good what I have promised by my lord keeper. As for religion, my heart and conscience with the religion now established in the Church of England shall go together. For the ship money, God is my witness I never converted any of it to my own profit, but to the end of preserving the dominion of the seas. . . . As for property of goods, it is a thing I never but intended; and it is my desire to be king of a free and rich people; and if no property in goods, no rich people. I told the commons that, if they would speedily supply my occasions for the present, I would give them further time at winter to present and debate all their just grievances. If they will not trust me first, all my business this summer will be lost; and before the year goeth about I must be trusted at last, for in the winter I must call them to give me a greater supply. If the house of commons will not join to prefer my occasions before their grievances, I conjure your lordships to consider your own honours and mine, and the preposterous course of the house of commons; and desire that your lordships will not join with them, but leave them to themselves. . . . If the supply come not in time, I will not say what mischief may and must follow."

. . . Their lordships taking into consideration that which his majesty delivered to them this morning . . . , these two questions were agreed upon to be proposed to the house:—

First, as many of your lordships as are of opinion his majesty's supply should have precedency and be resolved of before any other matter whatsoever say Content.

[Second,] as many of your lordships as think fit there should be a conference desired with the house of commons to dispose them thereunto say Content. . . .

Then the first question was put and carried by the Contents; and likewise the second question carried in like manner.

The lord keeper reported the conference with the house of commons . . . to this effect. Mr. Pym did say he was commanded by the knights, citizens, and burgesses of the house of commons to represent to your lordships their desire and care to preserve a union and correspondence with your lordships. . . . The great privileges belonging to this high court of parliament are not airy and matters of pomp, but have in them reality and efficacy; whereby this great council of the kingdom is enabled to perform all those noble functions which belong to them in respect of the legislative power and conciliary power. . . . As there are general privileges belonging to

95. THE SHORT PARLIAMENT

the whole body, so there are others more peculiar belonging to either house. . . . Among these peculiar privileges there is one great privilege which was acknowledged by your lordships in the last conference—that the matter of subsidy and supply ought to begin in the house of commons. . . . Yet, after, you were pleased to declare that you have voted in your lordships' house that it was most necessary and fit that matter of supply should have the precedency of all other business and, this being done, your lordships would freely join with them in all things concerning matter of religion, propriety of goods, and liberty of parliament. Now, my lords, if you have voted this, you have not only meddled with matter of supply but, as far as in you lies, you have concluded both the matter and order of proceeding—which the house of commons takes to be a breach of their privilege; for which he was commanded to desire reparation from your lordships. . . .

Journals of the Lords, IV, 66-73.

(E) Dissolution of Parliament (5 May)

His majesty came this day in person to the house, apparelled in his regal robes, and, having ascended his royal throne, the lords spiritual and temporal sitting in their robes uncovered, the house of commons were called in with their speaker. And being all present, his majesty was pleased to express his pleasure to them in these words following . . . :—

"My lords: For my own part, I hope you remember what the first day of the parliament the lord keeper said to you in my name, what he said . . . at the banqueting house at Whitehall, and what I said the last day myself. I named it to you, not in any doubt that you do not remember, but to show you that I never said anything that way in favour to my people but, by the grace of God, I will punctually and really perform it. . . . My lords, you know at the first I expressed myself by my lord keeper that delay was worse danger than refusing. I would not put this fault on all the whole house; I will not judge so uncharitably. But it hath been some few cunning and some ill-affected men that have been the cause of this misunderstanding. I shall only end as I began, giving your lordships thanks for the care you have had of my honour and affairs, desiring you to go on and assist me for the maintaining of government and the liberties of the people that they so much start at. For, my lords, no king in the world shall be more careful to maintain the propriety of their goods, the liberties of their persons, and true religion than I shall be. And now, my lord keeper, do as I have commanded you."

Then the lord keeper said: "My lords, and ye knights, citizens, and burgesses of the house of commons, the king's majesty doth dissolve this parliament."

Ibid., IV, 81.

96. RECORDS OF THE LONG PARLIAMENT (1640-42)

(A) TRIENNIAL ACT (1641)

An act for the preventing of inconveniences happening by the long intermission of parliaments. Whereas by the laws and statutes of this realm the parliament ought to be holden at least once every year for the redress of grievances, but the appointment of the time and place for the holding thereof hath always belonged, as it ought, to his majesty and his royal progenitors; and whereas it is by experience found that the not holding of parliaments accordingly hath produced sundry and great mischiefs and inconveniences to the king's majesty, the church, and commonwealth: for the prevention of the like mischiefs and inconveniences in time to come, be it enacted by the king's most excellent majesty, with the consent of the lords spiritual and temporal and the commons in this present parliament assembled, that the said laws and statutes be from henceforth duly kept and observed. And your majesty's loyal and obedient subjects, in this present parliament now assembled, do humbly pray that it be enacted, and be it enacted accordingly by the authority of this present parliament, that, in case there be not a parliament summoned by writ under the great seal of England and assembled and held before the 10th day of September which shall be in the third year next after the last day of the last meeting and sitting in this present parliament . . .—and so from time to time and in all times hereafter, if there shall not be a parliament assembled and held before the 10th day of September which shall be in the third year next after the last day of the last meeting and sitting in parliament before that time assembled and held . . . —that then . . . the parliament shall assemble and be held in the usual place at Westminster in such manner and by such means only as is hereafter in this present act declared and enacted, and not otherwise, on the second Monday which shall be in the month of November then next ensuing. And in case this present parliament now assembled and held, or any other parliament which shall at any time hereafter be assembled and held . . . , shall be prorogued or adjourned . . . until the 10th day of September which shall be in the third year next after the last day of the last meeting and sitting in parliament . . . , that then . . . every such parliament so prorogued or adjourned . . . shall from the said 10th day of September be thenceforth clearly and absolutely dissolved, and the lord chancellor of England, the lord keeper of the great seal of England, and every commissioner and commissioners for the keeping of the great seal of England, for the time being, shall within six days after the said 10th day of September, in every such third year as aforesaid, in due form of law and without any further warrant or direction from his majesty, his heirs, or successors, seal, issue forth, and send abroad several and respective writs to the several and respective peers of this realm, commanding every such peer that he personally be at the parliament to be held at Westminster on the second Monday which shall be in Novem-

96. THE LONG PARLIAMENT

ber next following the said 10th day of September . . . ; and shall also seal and issue forth . . . several and respective writs to the several and respective sheriffs of the several and respective counties, cities, and boroughs of England and Wales . . . , and to all and every other officers and persons to whom writs have used to be directed, for the electing of the knights, citizens, barons, and burgesses of and for the said counties, cities, Cinque Ports, and boroughs of England and Wales respectively, in the accustomed form, to appear and serve in parliament to be held at Westminster on the said second Monday, which shall be in November aforesaid; which said peers, after the said writs received, and which said knights, citizens, barons, and burgesses chosen by virtue of the said writs, shall then and there appear and serve in parliament accordingly. And the said lord chancellor, lord keeper, commissioner and commissioners aforesaid, shall respectively take a solemn oath upon the Holy Evangelists for the due issuing of writs according to the tenor of this act. . . .[1]

And it is lastly provided and enacted, that his majesty's royal assent to this bill shall not thereby determine this present session of parliament, and that all statutes and acts of parliament which are to have continuance unto the end of this present session shall be of full force after his majesty's assent, until this present session be fully ended and determined. And if this present session shall determine by dissolution of this present parliament, then all the acts and statutes aforesaid shall be continued until the end of the first session of the next parliament.

Statutes of the Realm, V, 54 f.; 16 Charles I, c. 1.

(B) ACT FOR THE ATTAINDER OF STRAFFORD (1641)

An act for the attainder of Thomas, earl of Strafford, of high treason. Whereas the knights, citizens, and burgesses of the house of commons in this present parliament assembled, have, in the name of themselves and of all the commons of England, impeached Thomas, earl of Strafford, of high treason for endeavouring to subvert the ancient and fundamental laws and government of his majesty's realms of England and Ireland and to introduce an arbitrary and tyrannical government against law in the said kingdoms, and for exercising a tyrannous and exorbitant power above and against the laws of the said kingdoms over the liberties, estates, and lives of his majesty's subjects, and likewise for having by his own authority commanded the laying and sessing of soldiers upon his majesty's subjects in Ireland, against their consents, to compel them to obey his unlawful summons and orders, made upon paper petitions in causes between party and party, which accordingly was executed upon divers of his

---

[1] Elaborate provision is made for the assembling of parliament even should such royal officials fail to carry out their oath. Penalties are established for disobedience. And it is provided that this act shall be read annually in local courts and assizes.

majesty's subjects in a warlike manner within the said realm of Ireland; and [whereas] in so doing [he] did levy war against the king's majesty and his liege people in that kingdom; and also for that he, upon the unhappy dissolution of the last parliament, did slander the house of commons to his majesty and did counsel and advise his majesty that he was loose and absolved from rules of government, and that he had an army in Ireland which he might employ to reduce this kingdom—for which he deserveth to undergo the pains and forfeitures of high treason—and [whereas] the said earl hath also been an incendiary of the wars between the two kingdoms of England and Scotland; all which offences hath been sufficiently proved against the said earl upon his impeachment: be it therefore enacted by the king's most excellent majesty and by the lords and commons in this present parliament assembled, and by authority of the same, that the said earl of Strafford, for the heinous crimes and offences aforesaid, stand and be adjudged attainted of high treason, and shall suffer such pains of death, and incur the forfeitures of his goods and chattels, lands, tenements, and hereditaments of any estate of freehold or inheritance in the said kingdoms of England and Ireland, which the said earl or any other to his use, or in trust for him, have or had the day of the first sitting of this . . . parliament, or at any time since. . . .

Ibid., V, 177 f.: 16 Charles I, c. 38.

(C) ACT TO CONTINUE THE EXISTING PARLIAMENT (1641)

An act to prevent inconveniences which may happen by the untimely adjourning, proroguing, or dissolving of this present parliament. . . . Be it declared and enacted by the king our sovereign lord with the assent of the lords and commons in this present parliament assembled, and by the authority of the same, that this present parliament now assembled shall not be dissolved unless it be by act of parliament to be passed for that purpose, nor shall be, at any time or times during the continuance thereof, prorogued or adjourned, unless it be by act of parliament to be likewise passed for that purpose; and that the house of peers shall not at any time or times during this present parliament be adjourned, unless it be by themselves or by their own order; and in like manner, that the house of commons shall not, at any time or times during this present parliament, be adjourned, unless it be by themselves or by their own order; and that all and every thing or things whatsoever done or to be done for the adjournment, proroguing, or dissolving of this present parliament contrary to this act shall be utterly void and of none effect.

Ibid., V, 103 f.: 16 Charles I, c. 7.

(D) TUNNAGE AND POUNDAGE ACT (1641)

A subsidy granted to the king of tunnage, poundage, and other sums of money payable upon merchandise exported and imported. Whereas, upon examination in this present parliament of divers of the farmers, customers, and collectors of the customs upon merchandise, and likewise upon their own confession, it appeared that they have taken divers great sums of money of his majesty's subjects, and likewise of merchants aliens for goods imported and exported by the names of a subsidy of tunnage and poundage, and by colour of divers other impositions laid upon merchandise, which have been taken and received against the laws of the realm, in regard the said sums of money and impositions were not granted by common consent in parliament . . . : be it therefore declared and enacted by the king's most excellent majesty and the lords and commons in this present parliament assembled, and it is hereby declared and enacted, that it is and hath been the ancient right of the subjects of this realm that no subsidy, custom, impost, or other charge whatsoever ought or may be laid or imposed upon any merchandise exported or imported by subjects, denizens, or aliens without common consent in parliament.

Yet, nevertheless, the commons . . . , taking into their consideration the great peril that might ensue to this realm by the not guarding of the seas and the other inconveniences which might follow in case the said sums of money should upon the sudden be forborne to be paid, by and with the advice of the lords in this present parliament assembled and by the authority of the same, do give and grant to our supreme liege lord and sovereign one subsidy called tunnage—that is to say, of every tun of wine that is or shall come into this realm or any his majesty's dominions by way of merchandise the sum of 3s. . . .—and also one other subsidy called poundage—that is to say, of all manner of goods and merchandise of every merchant, denizen, and alien carried or to be carried out of this realm, or any his majesty's dominions, or to be brought into the same by way of merchandise, of the value of every 20s. of the same goods and merchandise 12d. . . .[2]—to have, take, enjoy, and perceive the subsidies aforesaid, and other the forementioned sums and every of them . . . from the five-and-twentieth of May, 1641, to the fifteenth of July next ensuing. . . .

Ibid., V, 104: 16 Charles I, c. 8.

(E) ACT ABOLISHING ARBITRARY COURTS (1641)

An act for the regulating the privy council and for taking away the court commonly called the star chamber. . . . Forasmuch as all matters examinable or determinable . . . in the court commonly called the star chamber may have their proper remedy and redress and their due punishment and correction by the common law of the land and in the ordinary course of justice elsewhere; and forasmuch as the reasons and motives inducing the erection and con-

---

[2] The poundage on tin was double the normal rate. Wool, wool-fells, and woolen cloth were excepted from the force of this article, being taxed according to a separate schedule placed in the article following. Finally, it was provided that tobacco from the English plantations should pay only 2d. on the pound.

tinuance of that court do now cease, and the proceedings, censures, and decrees of that court have by experience been found to be an intolerable burden to the subjects and the means to introduce an arbitrary power and government; and forasmuch as the council table hath of late times assumed unto itself a power to intermeddle in civil causes and matters only of private interest between party and party, and have adventured to determine of the estates and liberties of the subject contrary to the law of the land and the rights and privileges of the subject, by which great and manifold mischiefs and inconveniences have arisen and happened, and much uncertainty by means of such proceedings hath been conceived concerning men's rights and estates: for settling whereof and preventing the like in time to come, be it ordained and enacted by the authority of this present parliament that the said court commonly called the star chamber, and all jurisdiction, power, and authority belonging unto or exercised in the same court, or by any the judges, officers, or ministers thereof, be from the first day of August, in the year of our Lord God 1641, clearly and absolutely dissolved, taken away, and determined. . . .

And be it likewise enacted that the like jurisdiction now used and exercised in the court before the president and council in the marches of Wales; and also in the court before the president and council established in the northern parts; and also in the court commonly called the court of the duchy of Lancaster, held before the chancellor and council of the court; and also in the court of exchequer of the county palatine of Chester, held before the chamberlain and council of that court . . . shall, from the said first day of August, 1641, be also repealed and absolutely revoked and made void. . . .

Be it likewise declared and enacted by authority of this present parliament, that neither his majesty nor his privy council have or ought to have any jurisdiction, power, or authority by English bill, petition, articles, libel, or any other arbitrary way whatsoever, to examine or draw into question, determine, or dispose of the lands, tenements, hereditaments, goods, or chattels of any the subjects of this kingdom, but that the same ought to be tried and determined in the ordinary courts of justice and by the ordinary course of the law.

Ibid., V, 110: 16 Charles I, c. 10.

(F) Act Abolishing the Court of High Commission (1641)

An act for the repeal of a branch of a statute . . . concerning commissioners for causes ecclesiastical. Whereas in the parliament holden in the first year of the reign of the late Queen Elizabeth . . . there was an act made . . . ;[3] and whereas, by colour of some words in the foresaid . . . act whereby commissioners are authorized to execute their commission according to the tenor and effect of the king's

---

[3] Here is recited the clause in the statute of 1559 (no. 81A) establishing the court of high commission.

96. THE LONG PARLIAMENT

letters patents and by letters patents grounded thereupon, the said commissioners have, to the great and insufferable wrong and oppression of the king's subjects, used to fine and imprison them, and to exercise other authority not belonging to ecclesiastical jurisdiction restored by that act, and divers other great mischiefs and inconveniences have also ensued to the king's subjects by occasion of the . . . commissions issued thereupon and the executions thereof: therefore, for the repressing and preventing of the foresaid abuses, mischiefs, and inconveniences in time to come, be it enacted by the king's most excellent majesty and the lords and commons in this present parliament assembled, and by the authority of the same, that the foresaid branch, clause, article, or sentence contained in the said act . . . shall from henceforth be repealed . . . and utterly made void forever. . . .

And be it also enacted by the authority aforesaid that no archbishop, bishop . . . , nor any other person or persons whatsoever exercising spiritual or ecclesiastical power, authority, or jurisdiction . . . shall from and after the first day of August, which shall be in the year of our Lord God 1641, award, impose or inflict any pain, penalty, fine, amercement, imprisonment, or other corporal punishment upon any of the king's subjects for any contempt, misdemeanour, crime, offence, matter, or thing whatsoever belonging to spiritual or ecclesiastical cognizance or jurisdiction, or shall *ex officio*, or at the instance or promotion of any other person whatsoever . . . , minister unto any . . . person whatsoever any corporal oath, whereby he or she shall or may be charged or obliged to make any presentment of any crime or offence, or to confess or to accuse him or herself of any crime, offence, delinquency, or misdemeanour, or any neglect . . . , or thing whereby, or by reason whereof, he or she shall or may be liable or exposed to any censure, pain, penalty, or punishment whatsoever. . . .[4]

And be it further enacted that, from and after the said first day of August, no new court shall be erected, ordained, or appointed within this realm of England or dominion of Wales which shall or may have the like power, jurisdiction, or authority as the said high commission court now hath or pretendeth to have; but that all and every such letters patents, commissions, and grants made or to be made by his majesty, his heirs, or successors, and all powers and authorities granted or pretended or mentioned to be granted thereby, and all acts, sentences, and decrees to be made by virtue or colour thereof shall be utterly void and of none effect.

Ibid., V, 112 f.: 16 Charles I, c. 11.

(G) Act Abolishing Ship Money (1641)

An act for the declaring unlawful and void the late proceedings touching ship money and for the vacating of all records and process

---

[4] See above, p. 470.

concerning the same. Whereas divers writs of late time issued under the great seal of England, commonly called ship writs, for the charging of the ports, towns, cities, boroughs, and counties of this realm respectively to provide and furnish certain ships for his majesty's service; and whereas, upon the execution of the same writs . . . , process hath been thence made against sundry persons pretended to be charged by way of contribution for the making up of certain sums assessed for the providing of the said ships, and in especial . . . against John Hampden, esquire . . . ;[5] and whereas some other actions and process depend . . . against other persons for the like kind of charge grounded upon the said writs commonly called ship writs, all which writs and proceedings as aforesaid were utterly against the law of the land: be it therefore declared and enacted by the king's most excellent majesty and the lords and the commons in this present parliament assembled, and by the authority of the same, that the said charge imposed upon the subject for the providing and furnishing of ships commonly called ship money . . . , and the said writs . . . and the said judgment given against the said John Hampden, were and are contrary to and against the laws and statutes of this realm, the right of property, the liberty of the subjects, former resolutions in parliament, and the Petition of Right made in the third year of the reign of his majesty that now is.

And it is further declared and enacted . . . that all . . . particulars prayed or desired in the said Petition of Right shall from henceforth be put in execution accordingly, and shall be firmly and strictly holden and observed as in the same petition they are prayed and expressed; and that all . . . the records . . . of all . . . the judgment, enrolments . . . , and proceedings as aforesaid, and all . . . the proceedings whatsoever, upon or by pretext . . . of any of the said writs commonly called ship writs . . . , shall be deemed . . . to be utterly void. . . .

Ibid., V, 116 f.: 16 Charles I, c. 14.

(H) ACT DEFINING FORESTS AND FOREST LAW (1641)

An act for the certainty of forests and of the meers, metes, limits, and bounds of the forests.[6] . . . Be it declared and enacted by the king's most excellent majesty and the lords and commons in this present parliament assembled, and by the authority of the same, that from henceforth the metes . . . and bounds of all and every the forests respectively shall be to all intents and purposes taken, adjudged, and deemed to extend no further respectively than the metes . . . and bounds . . . were commonly known, used, or taken to be the metes . . . and bounds of the said forests respectively in the twentieth year of the reign of our late sovereign lord, King James, and not beyond in any wise—any perambulation or perambu-

---

[5] The preamble here reviews the proceedings in Hampden's case (no. 94c).
[6] The preamble recites the recent abuses in this connection; cf. no. 93c.

lations, presentments, extents, surveys, judgments, records, decrees, or other matter or thing whatsoever to the contrary notwithstanding— and that all and every the presentments since the said twentieth year made . . . and all and every judgment and award upon or by reason or pretext of any such presentment or presentments . . . , and all and every fine and fines, and amercement and amercements, upon or by reason or colour of any such presentment or presentments shall from henceforth be adjudged, deemed, and taken to be utterly void and of no force or effect—any law, statute, record, or pretence whatsoever to the contrary notwithstanding.

And be it further enacted by the authority aforesaid that no place or places within this realm of England or dominion of Wales, where no such justice seat, swainmote, or court of attachment have been held or kept, or where no verderers have been chosen or regard made, within the space of sixty years next before the first year of his majesty's reign that now is, shall be at any time hereafter judged, deemed, or taken to be forest or within the bounds or metes of the forests; but the same shall be from henceforth forever disafforested and freed and exempted from the forest laws. . . .[7]

Ibid., V, 119: 16 Charles I, c. 16.

(I) ACT ABOLISHING FINES FOR DISTRAINT OF KNIGHTHOOD (1641)

An act for the prevention of vexatious proceedings touching the order of knighthood.[8] . . . Be it declared and enacted by the king's most excellent majesty and the lords and commons in this parliament assembled, and by the authority of the same, that from henceforth no person or persons of what condition, quality, estate, or degree soever, shall at any time be distrained or otherwise compelled by any writ or process of the court of chancery or court of exchequer, or otherwise by any means whatsoever, to receive or take upon him or them respectively the order or dignity of knighthood; nor shall suffer or undergo any fine, trouble, or molestation whatsoever by reason or colour of his or their having not received or not taken upon him or them the said order or dignity . . . ; and that all and every process, proceeding, and charge now depending by reason or colour of the said pretended custom or writs aforesaid, or of any the dependants thereof, shall from henceforth cease, and stand, be, and remain discharged and utterly void—any former law or custom, or any pretence of any former law or custom, or any other matter whatsoever to the contrary in any wise notwithstanding.

Ibid., V, 131: 16 Charles I, c. 20.

(J) REPLY OF CHARLES I TO THE COMMONS' PETITION (1641)[9]

We having received from you soon after our return out of Scot-

---

[7] Other articles provide for inquests under parliamentary commission to enforce these enactments.

[8] The preamble recites the recent exactions made for this purpose; see no. 93A.

[9] This royal letter, dated December 23, was made in answer to a petition of

land a long petition consisting of many desires of great moment, together with a declaration of a very unusual nature annexed thereunto, we had taken some time to consider of it, as befitted us in a matter of that consequence, being confident that your own reason and regard to us, as well as our express intimation by our comptroller to that purpose, would have restrained you from the publishing of it till such time as you should have received our answer to it; but, much against our expectation finding the contrary, that the said declaration is already abroad in print by directions from your house, as appears by the printed copy, we must let you know that we are very sensible of the disrespect. Notwithstanding, it is our intention that no failing on your part shall make us fail in ours of giving all due satisfaction to the desires of our people in a parliamentary way; and therefore we send your this answer to your petition, reserving ourself in point of the declaration, which we think unparliamentary, and shall take a course to do that which we shall think fit in prudence and honour.

To the petition we say that . . . there are divers things in the preamble of it which we are so far from admitting that we profess we cannot at all understand them—as of "a wicked and malignant party prevalent in the government," of "some of that party admitted to our privy council and to other employments of trust and nearest to us and our children," of "endeavours to sow among the people false scandals and imputations to blemish and disgrace the proceedings of the parliament"—all or any of them, did we know of, we should be as ready to remedy and punish as you to complain of; so that the prayers of your petition are grounded upon such premises as we must in no wise admit. Yet, notwithstanding, we are pleased to give this answer to you.

To the first, concerning religion . . . , we say that, for preserving the peace and safety of this kingdom from the design of the popish party, we have and will still concur with all the just desires of our people in a parliamentary way; that for the depriving of the bishops of their votes in parliament, we would have you consider that their right is grounded upon the fundamental law of the kingdom and constitution of parliament. . . . As for the abridging of the inordinate power of the clergy, we conceive that the taking away of the high commission court hath well moderated that; but if there continue any usurpations or excesses in their jurisdictions, we therein neither have nor will protect them. Unto that clause which concerneth corruptions (as you style them) in religion, in church government,

the house of commons, dated December 1, that accompanied the Grand Remonstrance. The latter document was a long enumeration of parliamentary grievances alleging in particular a "malignant and pernicious design of subverting the fundamental laws and principles of government" on the part of papists, certain members of the clergy, and unscrupulous courtiers. The articles of the petition, which was designed to meet the evils thus enumerated, are clearly rehearsed in the king's reply.

and in discipline and the removing of such unnecessary ceremonies as weak consciences might check at . . . , for any illegal innovations which may have crept in, we shall willingly concur in the removal of them. . . . If our parliament shall advise us to call a national synod, which may duly examine such ceremonies as give just cause of offence to any, we shall take it into consideration and apply ourself to give due satisfaction therein. . . .

To the second prayer of the petition, concerning the removal and choice of councillors, we know not any of our council to whom the character set forth in the petition can belong. . . . By those whom we had exposed to trial, we have already given you sufficient testimony that there is no man so near unto us in place or affection, whom we will not leave to the justice of the law, if you shall bring a particular charge and sufficient proofs against him. And of this we do again assure you; but in the meantime we wish you to forbear such general aspersions as may reflect upon all our council, since you name none in particular. That for the choice of our councillors and ministers of state, it were to debar us that natural liberty all freemen have; and as it is the undoubted right of the crown of England to call such persons to our secret counsels, to public employment, and our particular service as we shall think fit, so we are and ever shall be very careful to make election of such persons in those places of trust as shall have given good testimonies of their abilities and integrity, and against whom there can be no just cause of exception whereon reasonably to ground a diffidence. And to choices of this nature we assure you that the mediation of the nearest unto us hath always concurred.

To the third prayer of your petition, concerning Ireland, we understand your desire of not alienating the forfeited lands thereof to proceed from much care and love, and likewise that it may be a resolution very fit for us to take. But whether it may be seasonable to declare resolutions of that nature before the events of a war be seen, that we much doubt of. Howsoever, we cannot but thank you for this care and your cheerful engagement for the suppression of that rebellion. . . .

Rushworth *Historical Collections*, IV, 452 f.

(K) ORDERS OF THE COMMONS WITH REGARD TO PRINTING

[13 February 1641.] Ordered that the sub-committee heretofore appointed by the grand committee for religion concerning abuses in licensing and printing of books be now made a committee from the house and enlarged to take into consideration and **examine** all abuses in printing, licensing, importing, and suppressing of books of all sorts, and in denying licence to some books and expunging several passages out of other books. . . .

[28 March 1642.] Resolved upon the question that what person soever shall print, [publish, or] sell any act or passages of this house under the name of a diurnal or otherwise, without particular licence of this house, shall be reputed a high contemner and breaker of the privilege of parliament, and so punished accordingly. . . .

Journals of the Commons, II, 84, 501.

(L) ACT ABOLISHING TEMPORAL POWER OF THE CLERGY (1641)

An act for disenabling all persons in holy orders to exercise any temporal jurisdiction or authority. Whereas bishops and other persons in holy orders ought not to be entangled with secular jurisdiction, the office of the ministry being of such great importance that it will take up the whole man; and for that it is found by long experience that their intermeddling with secular jurisdictions hath occasioned great mischiefs and scandal both to church and state: his majesty, out of his religious care of the church, and souls of his people, is graciously pleased that it be enacted, and by authority of this present parliament be it enacted, that no archbishop or bishop or other person that now is or hereafter shall be in holy orders, shall . . . have any seat or place, suffrage, or voice, or use, or execute any power or authority in the parliaments of this realm, nor shall be of the privy council of his majesty, his heirs, or successors, or justice of the peace . . . or execute any temporal authority by virtue of any commission; but shall be wholly disabled and be incapable to have, receive, use, or execute any of the said offices, places, powers, authorities, and things aforesaid. . . .

Statutes of the Realm, V, 138: 16 Charles I, c. 27.

(M) THE MILITIA ORDINANCE (1642)[10]

An ordinance of parliament for the safety and defence of the kingdom of England and dominion of Wales. Whereas there hath been of late a most dangerous and desperate design upon the house of commons, which we have just cause to believe to be an effect of the bloody counsels of papists and other ill-affected persons, who have already raised a rebellion in the kingdom of Ireland; and [whereas] by reason of many discoveries we cannot but fear they will proceed not only to stir up the like rebellion and insurrections in this kingdom of England but also to back them with forces from abroad: for the safety, therefore, of his majesty's person, the parliament, and kingdom in this time of imminent danger, it is ordained by the lords and commons now in parliament assembled, that Henry, earl of Holland, shall be lieutenant of the county of Berks; Oliver, earl of Bolingbroke, shall be lieutenant of the county of Bedford. . . .[11] And [they] shall severally and respectively have power to assemble and call together all and singular his majesty's subjects within the said several and respective counties and places, as well within liberties as

---

[10] When the king refused to sign this enactment in the form of a bill, it was turned into an ordinance of parliament.
[11] Similar appointments are made for the other counties.

without, that are meet and fit for the wars, and them to train and
exercise and put in readiness, and them after their abilities and faculties well and sufficiently from time to time to cause to be arrayed
and weaponed, and to take the muster of them in places most fit for
that purpose; and . . . shall severally and respectively have power
. . . to nominate and appoint such persons of quality as to them
shall seem meet to be their deputy lieutenants, to be approved of
by both houses of parliament; and . . . shall have power to make
colonels and captains and other officers . . . as they shall think fit
for that purpose; and . . . shall have power to lead, conduct and
employ the persons aforesaid arrayed and weaponed, for the suppression of all rebellions, insurrections, and invasions that may happen within the several and respective counties and places; and shall
have power and authority to lead, conduct, and employ the persons
aforesaid arrayed and weaponed, as well within their said several and
respective counties and places as within any other part of this realm
of England or dominion of Wales, for the suppression of all rebellions, insurrections, and invasions that may happen, according as
they from time to time shall receive directions. . . .

Journals of the Lords, IV, 587.

(N) ROYAL PROCLAMATION (27 MAY 1642)

. . . Whereas we understand that, expressly contrary to the . . .
laws of this our kingdom, under colour . . . of an ordinance of parliament, without our consent or any . . . warrant from us, the trained
bands and militia of this kingdom have been lately, and are intended
to be, put in arms and drawn into companies in a warlike manner,
whereby the peace and quiet of our subjects is or may be disturbed:
we, being desirous . . . to prevent that some malignant persons in
this our kingdom do not by degrees seduce our good subjects from
their due obedience to us and the laws of this our kingdom . . . , do
therefore, by this our proclamation, expressly charge and command
all our sheriffs, and all colonels, lieutenant-colonels, sergeant-majors,
captains, officers, and soldiers belonging to the trained bands of this
our kingdom, and likewise all high and petty constables and other
our officers and subjects whatsoever, upon their allegiance and as
they tender the peace of this our kingdom, not to muster, levy, raise,
or march, or to summon or warn, upon any warrant, order or ordinance from one or both our houses of parliament, whereunto we
have not, or shall not, give our express consent, any of our trained
bands or other forces to rise, muster, march, or exercise without
express warrant under our hand or warrant from our sheriff of the
county, grounded upon a particular writ to that purpose under our
great seal. And in case any of our trained bands shall rise or gather
together contrary to this our command, we shall then call them in
due time to a strict account and proceed legally against them as
violators of the laws and disturbers of the peace of this kingdom.

Ibid., V, 111 f.

(O) DECLARATION OF THE LORDS AND COMMONS (27 MAY 1642)

The lords and commons, having perused his majesty's proclamation forbidding all his majesty's subjects belonging to the trained bands or militia of this kingdom, to rise, march, muster, or exercise, by virtue of any order or ordinance of one or both houses of parliament without consent or warrant from his majesty, upon pain of punishment according to the laws, do thereupon declare that . . . it is acknowledged that the king is the fountain of justice and protection; but the acts of justice and protection are not exercised in his own person, nor depend upon his pleasure, but by his courts and by his ministers, who must do their duty therein though the king in his own person should forbid them. And therefore, if judgments should be given by them against the king's will and personal command, yet are they the king's judgments. The high court of parliament is not only a court of judicature, enabled by the laws to adjudge and determine the rights and liberties of the kingdom against such patents and grants of his majesty as are prejudicial thereunto, although strengthened both by his personal command and by his proclamation under the great seal; but it is likewise a council to provide for the necessities, prevent the imminent dangers, and preserve the public peace and safety of the kingdom, and to declare the king's pleasure in those things as are requisite thereunto. And what they do herein hath the stamp of the royal authority although his majesty, seduced by evil counsel, do in his own person oppose or interrupt the same; for the king's supreme and royal pleasure is exercised and declared in this high court of law and council, after a more eminent and obligatory manner than it can be by personal act or resolution of his own.

Seeing therefore the lords and commons, which are his majesty's great and high council, have ordained that, for the present and necessary defence of the realm, the trained bands and militia of this kingdom should be ordered according to that ordinance . . . , the lords and commons do require and command all constables, petty constables, and all other his majesty's officers and subjects whatsoever to muster, levy, raise, march, and exercise, or to summon or warn any, upon warrants from the lieutenants, deputy lieutenants, captains, or other officers of the trained bands, and all others, according to the said ordinance of both houses; and [they] shall not presume to muster, levy, raise, march, or exercise by virtue of any commission or other authority whatsoever, as they will answer the contrary at their perils. And in their so doing they do further declare that they shall be protected by the power and authority of both houses of parliament; and that whosoever shall oppose, question, or hinder them in the execution of the said ordinance, shall be proceeded against as violators of the laws and disturbers of the peace of the kingdom.

Ibid., V, 112 f.

96. THE LONG PARLIAMENT

(P) THE NINETEEN PROPOSITIONS (1 JUNE 1642)

Your majesty's most humble and faithful subjects, the lords and commons in parliament, having nothing in their thoughts and desires more precious and of higher esteem—next to the honour and immediate service of God—than the just and faithful performance of their duty to your majesty and this kingdom . . . , do in all humility and sincerity present to your majesty their most dutiful petition and advice, that out of your princely wisdom . . . you will be pleased to grant and accept these their humble . . . propositions, as the most necessary effectual means, through God's blessing, of removing those jealousies and differences which have unhappily fallen betwixt you and your people . . . :—

1. That the lords and others of your majesty's privy council and . . . great officers and ministers of state, either at home or beyond the seas, may be put from your privy council and from those offices and employments, excepting such as shall be approved of by both houses of parliament; and that the persons put into the places and employments of those that are removed may be approved of by both houses of parliament; and that all privy councillors shall take an oath for the due execution of their places in such form as shall be agreed upon by both houses of parliament.

2. That the great affairs of the kingdom may not be concluded or transacted by the advice of private men, or by any unknown or unsworn councillors; but that such matters as concern the public and are proper for the high court of parliament, which is your majesty's great and supreme council, may be debated, resolved, and transacted only in parliament, and not elsewhere. And such as shall presume to do anything to the contrary shall be reserved to the censure and judgment of parliament. And such other matters of state as are proper for your majesty's privy council shall be debated and concluded by such of the nobility and others as shall from time to time be chosen for that place, by approbation of both houses of parliament. And that no public act concerning the affairs of the kingdom, which are proper for your privy council, may be esteemed of any validity, as proceeding from the royal authority, unless it be done by the advice and consent of the major part of your council, attested under their hands. And that your council may be limited to a certain number, not exceeding twenty-five, nor under fifteen. And if any councillor's place happen to be void in the intervals of parliament, it shall not be supplied without the assent of the major part of the council; which choice shall be confirmed at the next sitting of parliament, or else to be void.

3. That the lord high steward of England, lord high constable, lord chancellor, or lord keeper of the great seal, lord treasurer, lord privy seal, earl marshal, lord admiral, warden of the Cinque Ports, chief governor of Ireland, chancellor of the exchequer, master of the wards, secretaries of state, two chief justices, and chief baron,

may always be chosen with the approbation of both houses of parliament. . . .

4. That he or they unto whom the government and education of the king's children shall be committed shall be approved of by both houses of parliament. . . .

5. That no marriage shall be concluded or treated for any of the king's children with any foreign prince or other person whatsoever, abroad or at home, without the consent of parliament. . . .

6. That the laws in force against Jesuits, priests, and popish recusants be strictly put in execution, without any toleration or dispensation to the contrary. . . .

7. That the votes of popish lords in the house of peers may be taken away. . . .

8. That your majesty would be pleased to consent that such a reformation be made of the church government and liturgy as both houses of parliament shall advise. . . .

9. That your majesty will be pleased to rest satisfied with that course that the lords and commons have appointed for ordering the militia until the same shall be further settled by a bill; and that your majesty will recall your declarations and proclamations against the ordinance made by the lords and commons concerning it.

10. That such members of either house of parliament as have, during this present parliament, been put out of any place and office may either be restored to that place and office or otherwise have satisfaction for the same, upon the petition of that house whereof he or they are members.

11. That all privy councillors and judges may take an oath, the form whereof to be agreed on and settled by act of parliament, for the maintaining of the Petition of Right and of certain statutes made by this parliament, which shall be mentioned by both houses of parliament. . . .

12. That all the judges and all the officers placed by approbation of both houses of parliament may hold their places *quam diu bene se gesserint*.[12]

13. That the justice of parliament may pass upon all delinquents, whether they be within the kingdom or fled out of it. . . .

14. That the general pardon offered by your majesty may be granted, with such exceptions as shall be advised by both houses of parliament.

15. That the forts and castles of this kingdom may be put under the command and custody of such persons as your majesty shall appoint with the approbation of your parliament. . . .

16. That the extraordinary guards and military forces now attending your majesty may be removed and discharged; and that for the future you will raise no such guards or extraordinary forces, but according to the law, in case of actual rebellion or invasion.

---

[12] During good behaviour.

97. DECREE OF THE CLERGY

17. That your majesty will be pleased to enter into a more strict alliance with the states of the United Provinces, and other neighbouring princes and states of the Protestant religion. . . .

18. That your majesty will be pleased, by act of parliament, to clear the lord Kimbolton and the five members of the house of commons[13] in such manner that future parliaments may be secured from the consequence of that evil precedent.

19. That your majesty will be graciously pleased to pass a bill for restraining peers made hereafter from sitting or voting in parliament, unless they be admitted thereunto with the consent of both houses of parliament.

And these our humble desires being granted by your majesty, we shall forthwith apply ourselves to regulate your present revenue in such sort as may be for your best advantage; and likewise to settle such an ordinary and constant increase of it as shall be sufficient to support your royal dignity in honour and plenty, beyond the proportion of any former grants of the subjects of this kingdom to your majesty's royal predecessors. . . .

Ibid., V, 97 f.

---

[13] The five members whom Charles had tried to arrest in the famous scene on 4 January 1642.

97. DECREE OF THE CLERGY ON REGAL POWER (1640)

Whereas sundry laws, ordinances, and constitutions have been formerly made for the acknowledgment and profession of the most lawful and independent authority of our dread sovereign lord, the king's most excellent majesty, over the state ecclesiastical and civil: we, as our duty in the first place binds us and so far as to us appertaineth, enjoin them all to be carefully observed by all persons whom they concern, upon the penalties in the said laws and constitutions expressed. And for the fuller and clearer instruction and information of all Christian people within this realm in their duties in this particular, we do further ordain and decree that every parson, vicar, curate, or preacher, upon some one Sunday in every quarter of the year at morning prayer, shall in the place where he serves treatably and audibly read these explanations of the regal power here inserted:—

The most high and sacred order of kings is of divine right, being the ordinance of God Himself, founded in the prime laws of nature, and clearly established by express texts both of the Old and New Testaments. A supreme power is given to this most excellent order by God Himself in the Scriptures, which is that kings should rule and command in their several dominions all persons of what rank or estate soever, whether ecclesiastical or civil, and that they should restrain and punish with the temporal sword all stubborn and wicked doers. . . . For any person or persons to set up, maintain, or avow in any their said realms or territories respectively, under any pretence whatsoever, any independent coactive power either papal or popular, whether directly or indirectly, is to undermine their great royal office and cunningly to overthrow that most sacred ordinance which God Himself hath established; and so is treasonable against God as well as against the king. For subjects to bear arms against their kings, offensive or defensive upon any pretence whatsoever, is at the least to resist the powers which are ordained of God; and though they do not invade but only resist, St. Paul tells them plainly they shall receive to themselves damnation. And although tribute and custom, and aid and subsidy, and all manner of necessary support and supply be respectively due to kings from their subjects by the law of God, nature, and nations, for the public defence, care, and protection of them; yet, nevertheless, subjects have not only possession of, but a true and just right, title, and property to and in all their goods and estates and ought so to have. And these two are so far from crossing one another that they mutually go together for the honourable and comfortable support of both; for, as it is the duty of the subjects to supply their king, so is it part of the kingly office to support his subjects in the property and freedom of their estates.

And if any parson, vicar, curate, or preacher shall voluntarily or carelessly neglect his duty in publishing the said explications and conclusions, according to the order above prescribed, he shall be suspended by his ordinary till such time as, upon his penitence, he shall give sufficient assurance or evidence of his amendment. And in case he be of any exempt jurisdiction, he shall be censurable by his majesty's commissioners for causes ecclesiastical. And we do also hereby require all archbishops, bishops, and all other inferior priests and ministers, that they preach, teach, and exhort their people to obey, honour, and serve their king; and that they presume not to speak of his majesty's power in any other way than in this canon is expressed. And if any parson, vicar, curate, or preacher, or any other ecclesiastical person whatsoever, any dean, canon, or prebendary of any collegiate or cathedral church, any member or student of college or hall, or any reader of divinity or humanity in either of the universities, or elsewhere, shall in any sermon, lecture, commonplace, determination, or disputation, either by word or writing, publicly maintain or abet any position or conclusion in opposition or impeachment of the aforesaid explications, or any part or article of them, he shall forthwith by the power of his majesty's commissioners for causes ecclesiastical be excommunicated till he repent, and suspended two years from all the profits of his benefice, or other ecclesiastical, academical or scholastical preferments. And if he so offend a second time, he shall be deprived from all his spiritual promotions, of what nature or degree soever they be. Provided always, that if the offence aforesaid be given in either of the universities by men not having any benefice or ecclesiastical preferment, that then the delinquent shall be censured by the ordinary authority in such cases of that university respectively where the said fault shall be committed.

Laud, *Works*, V, pt. ii, 613 f.

98. RECORDS OF LOCAL GOVERNMENT (1616-37)

(A) SPEECH OF JAMES I TO THE JUDGES (1616)

. . . Let the judges be never so careful and industrious, if the justices of peace under them put not to their helping hands, in vain is all your labour; for they are the king's eyes and ears in the country. It was an ancient custom that all the judges, both immediately before their going to their circuits and immediately upon their return, repaired to the lord chancellor of England, both to receive what directions it should please the king by his mouth to give unto them, as also to give him an account of their labours, who was to acquaint the king therewith. And this good ancient custom hath likewise been too much slacked of late. And therefore, first of all, I am to exhort and command you that you be careful to give a good account to me and my chancellor of the duties performed by all justices of peace in your circuits. Which government by justices is so laudable and so highly esteemed by me that I have made Scotland to be governed by justices and constables as England is. And let not gentlemen be ashamed of this place, for it is a place of high honour and great reputation, to be made a minister of the king's justice in service of the commonwealth. Of these are two sorts, as there is of all companies, especially where there is a great number: that is, good and bad justices. For the good, you are to inform me of them, that I may know them, thank them, and reward them as occasion serves. For I hold a good justice of peace in his country to do me as good service as he that waits upon me in my privy chamber, and as ready will I be to reward him. . . . I esteem the service done me by a good justice of peace three hundred miles—yea, six hundred miles—out of my sight as well as the service done me in my presence. For, as God hath given me large limits, so must I be careful that my providence may reach to the farthest parts of them. . . . Therefore let none be ashamed of this office, or be discouraged in being a justice of peace, if he serve worthily in it. . . .

The good justices are careful to attend the service of the king and country for thanks only of the king and love to their country, and for no other respect. The bad are . . . idle slow-bellies, that abide always at home, given to a life of ease and delight, liker ladies than men, and think it is enough to contemplate justice; whenas . . . contemplative justice is no justice, and contemplative justices are fit to be put out. Another sort of justices are busybodies, and will have all men dance after their pipe and follow their greatness, or else will not be content. . . . These proud spirits must know that the country is ordained to obey and follow God and the king, and not them. Another sort are they that go seldom to the king's service, but when it is to help some of their kindred or alliance; so as when they come it is to help their friends or hurt their enemies, making justice to serve for a shadow to faction and tumultuating the country. Another sort are gentlemen of great worth in their own conceit, and cannot be content with the present form of government; but must have a kind of liberty in the people, and must be gracious lords and redeemers of their liberty; and in every cause that concerns prerogative give a snatch against a monarchy, through their Puritanical itching after popularity. Some of them have shown themselves too bold of late in the lower house of parliament; and when all is done, if there were not a king, they would be less cared for than other men.

McIlwain, *Political Works of James I,* pp. 339 f.

(B) The Lord Keeper's Instructions to the Justices (1632)

My lords the judges: The time draweth near that you are now to enter upon your several circuits, before which I am, according to my place and duty, to declare unto you his majesty's pleasure in four things especially. . . .

First, his majesty is informed that papists and recusants that have great estates in the country have the greater favour, contrary to that which is right; which his majesty would have you to look unto, and accordingly to instruct the people of your counties in your charges.

The second thing his majesty would have you to regard and to commend to noblemen and gentlemen in the counties is that you inform them of the grounds and reasons of his majesty's now present proclamation, ready to come forth, commanding their repair to their houses in the country, and not to lie about the cities of London and Westminster, and the places adjacent. And this is necessary in these days, wherein men dispute upon proclamations, whether they should be obeyed. You know that such a thing as the pleasure of the king made known in this court was sufficient; but I persuade myself, for the ground and reasons of this his majesty's command at this time, you know better than myself what they are. Yet for the present occasion I shall name some of them. . . .

There are a multitude of precedents whereby the kings of this realm have, upon due considerations, commanded their subjects to dwell at their own houses. . . . The sheriff of every shire takes his oath to be present in his county and there dwelling. And justices of peace take such an oath that, if they be non-resident, they cannot perform. It is no discharge from their oath to live at London; but they remove hither to London, where they must of necessity live idle. They cannot govern here—that the charter of London inhibiteth. And what do they, their wives, and servants? Themselves go from ordinaries to dicing houses, and from thence to playhouses. Their wives dress themselves in the morning, visit in the afternoon, and perhaps make a journey to Hyde Park, and so home again. Their servants [go] to playhouses, brothel-houses, drunkenness, to any vice. . . . This appeareth to be an offence against many laws, and very hurtful to the common good. It is therefore a great and a gracious providence to take care to prevent it, as his majesty doth. I pray give the countries warning of this; and his majesty will give no more warning in this kind, but expecteth all men to be left without excuse by this his proclamation, if they offend against it.

There is another [proclamation], and that is for the observation of Lent and fish-days, touching which likewise he will give this as his last warning. . . . Some pretend that one meat is not holier than another, and some that their stomachs will not endure fish and therefore they are to be excused. . . . Their stomachs will not bear it, but they can sit all day long at sack and tobacco. Nay, I have heard of some that must needs drink tobacco on the bench; but, if I understand of any such hereafter, they shall not sit upon the bench any more. Some pretend that there is not fish enough. It is truth that the scarcity of fish cometh by the discouragement of fishermen. The king therefore hath very providently set out this proclamation at this time; that men may not pretend shortness of warning, but have fit time to furnish themselves, and the fishermen to provide that there may be plenty. The unsufferable resort and residence of multitudes to the city of London hath heretofore been one means to make fish the scarcer. This is intended to be remedied, and commandment shall be given to the lord mayor and aldermen that they shall see the fishmongers sell at reasonable prices. Therefore your lordships are to give a strict charge and warning that the offenders against these good laws and proclamations shall be strictly dealt withal, both here and in other courts; and you in your assizes are to deal strictly with them.

Another thing there is to be remembered: that, whereas his majesty lately set forth . . . certain orders for the execution of the laws against idle vagrants and rogues . . . , unless execution be done in all, it will but drive them from one county to another. Therefore you are likewise to enforce this upon the justices of peace and other officers, and take care it be observed.

And one thing more you are to look unto in the middle shires of the kingdom: that you suffer no enclosures tending to depopulation.

For all other things, you are to do universal justice, that his majesty may have honour and his people comfort and quiet by your industry.

Gardiner, *Cases in Star Chamber and High Commission*, pp. 176 f.

(C) YORKSHIRE QUARTER SESSIONS RECORDS (1610-12)

The oath of a high constable. You shall well and truly exercise your office of high constable within the wapentake of A, and duly and truly shall keep your petty sessions and receive and take all informations and presentments to you made and presented, and return and certify the same accordingly. All manner of bloodsheds, assaults, affrays, and outcries done and committed within the same wapentake according to your best knowledge you shall present; all manner of

writs, warrants, and precepts to you lawfully directed you shall duly
and truly execute. You shall diligently endeavour to take felons and
vagabonds and do your office upon them according to the laws and
statutes made and provided in that behalf. You shall inquire of the
faults in all under-constables within the said wapentake and the same
with their names certify to the sessions of peace next following after
the same inquiry had. The king's majesty's peace in your own person you shall, as much as in you lieth, conserve and keep. And in all
other things that appertain to your office you shall well and truly
behave yourself. So help you God and the contents of this Book.

Petty constable's oath. You shall duly exercise your office of constable of the township of A, and well and truly present all manner of
bloodsheds, assaults, and affrays, and outcries there . . . committed
against the king's majesty's peace. All manner of writs, warrants,
and precepts to you lawfully directed you shall truly execute. The
king's majesty's peace in your own person you shall conserve and
keep, as much as in you lieth. And in all other things that appertain
to your office you shall well and truly behave yourself. So help you
God and the contents, etc.

High constables. All and every the high constables within the North
Riding shall keep precisely the orders presented unto them in calling
the churchwardens and petty constables at convenient times before
them between every quarter sessions, and give them several copies
of the said orders or articles for 8d. a copy. And [they are] to take
their presentments to every the several articles upon their
oaths . . . ; and if any difficulty happen in any of their presentments,
to let it be censured by the justices at the next sessions. And if there
be default of presentment in any of the offices abovesaid . . . , then
the same defaulters [are] to be presented by the high constables at
every general quarter sessions. And the head constables for every
division [are] to enter in a fair book all such presentments as they
shall so receive of the petty constables from time to time; and [they]
shall attend some of the justices of the division with the said book
of presentments and of defaults of petty constables and churchwardens and overseers of the poor one month before every sessions, to
the end that such justices, upon consideration thereof, may give order
to enjoin such of the offenders to appear at the then next sessions as
they shall think fit to be ordered, as to justice shall appertain. And
it is ordered that every of the said officers and ministers shall carefully behave themselves therein for the good example of the commonwealth . . . , freeing the good subjects from oppression and
reforming common disorders, at their . . . perils.

Orders made, etc. [at Helmsley.] Ordered that all such freeholders
as hereafter shall be summoned to appear at the quarter sessions and
do make default shall be fined, the gentlemen to 40s. and yeomen to
30s. apiece. By the general consent of all the justices here assembled,

98. LOCAL GOVERNMENT

the next general quarter sessions for the body of the whole North Riding shall be holden at Topcliffe upon Tuesday, the 2nd day of October next; and all surveyors [and] collectors for bridges [are] then to make their account there. The several proportions for the rates of these bridges underwritten, due within Richmondshire: *viz.*, for Whitby Bridge £46. 13/4; Yafforth Bridge, £3. 6/8; Isell Bridge, £3. 6/8; Yeddingham Bridge, £3. 6/8—amounting in all to £90, with the proportion of Richmondshire for Katherick Bridge being £33. 6/8. And further it is ordered that the other £10, to make up £100, shall be paid forth of Birdforth. . . .

Whereas the sessions have been holden these two days past and adjourned with a continuance to be held and concluded tomorrow, being the twelfth day at Allerton, these are to direct clerks of the peace to be there attendant for those services. And forasmuch as the sheriff's deputy here present hath refused to disburse his majesty's allowance to the justices now present for their wages, we do therefore, and in respect of his contempt in this behalf, with one consent set upon Mr. Sheriff's head, for a fine to be presently estreated, the sum of £10—and this to be entered amongst the orders of this sessions. . . .

Orders made at this said sessions holden at Thirske. . . . Forasmuch as it doth appear unto them, upon perusal of divers sundry former orders in the sessions . . . , that there was nothing effectually performed for the erecting of the house of correction formerly intended by the said orders . . . to be seated within the town of Richmond: therefore we, his majesty's said justices, do this day further order that all former orders touching the said house shall be resumed; and that all and every of us, and as many other of the justices of peace of the North Riding as will be pleased to be present at Helmsley upon Wednesday, the 27th day of May next, by eight of the clock in the forenoon of the same day, shall then give their meeting there further to consult and conclude in what place the said house of correction shall be erected and established, with all such further due consideration both for orders, governors, ministers, and taxing, assessing, and levying of sums of money and all other things whatsoever requisite and necessary for the full accomplishment and finishing of the aforesaid house of correction, according to his majesty's laws in that case formerly made and provided. . . .

Atkinson, *Quarter Sessions Records*, I, 118, 182 f., 193-95, 254-55.

(D) WORCESTERSHIRE QUARTER SESSIONS RECORDS (1637)

[Presentment of Henry Brian, constable of Bayton.] *Imprimis*, I present Humphrey Cooke for a recusant. Item, John Timberlett doth sell ale and doth keep good order in his house, as far as rightly known. Item, our poor are provided for according to the law. Item, our highways are in good repair. Item, we have punished rogues and vagrants and presented their names to the justices of the peace at our monthly meeting. To the rest of the articles I have not any matter worthy of presentment. . . .

[Presentment by John Hunt and Nicholas Rindon, constables of Chadgsley Corbett.] For recusants we do present Richard Leayght; Mary Bach, widow; and Mary Hunt, widow; Parnell, the wife of Gregory Munk; Elizabeth, the wife of William Leight; and Elizabeth Jordan. Our poor are well and sufficiently provided for. Our highways and bridges are in good repair. Rogues and vagabonds have been punished according to law. Riots or routs or unlawful assemblies we know none. Cards and dicing or other unlawful gaming we know none. Our alehouses are all licensed. For other matters worthy to present, we know none at the present time. . . .

[Presentment of Henry Hewes and John Finchar, constables, and Robert Bolton and Thomas Hewes, churchwardens, of Feckenham and Home.] We have punished one George Stevens of Derby as a rogue and sent him away with a pass according to the law. We have punished one Matthew Garrette of Birmingham as a rogue and sent him away with a pass according to the law. We present these persons hereunder written that absent themselves from church. . . .

[Presentment by Humphrey Wright, constable of Astley.] For recusants, we have none in our parish. John Highley, the younger, sells ale without licence. For our highways, they are in repair. Our poor are well provided for according to the statute. . . .

[Presentment by Thomas Harvey, constable of Inkbarrow.] We keep watch and warding duly. Our poor are provided for by a weekly contribution. Our alehouses do keep very good order. Common drunkards we have none. I present . . for recusants. Our bridges and highways are sufficiently repaired. No tobacco planted. . . .

[Presentment by Humphrey Brian, constable of Bayton.] I do present Humphrey Cooke as a recusant. That Edward Griffen, and Robert Brian, and John Timberlette sell ale. Robert Brian hath been fined in 20s. for selling ale and he yet doth continue selling of ale, but there could be no distress found worth 20s. Our poor are relieved according to the law. Our highways are in good repair. I have punished rogues and vagrants; presented their names to the justices of the peace at our monthly meetings. I do present Humphrey Winwood and Edward Winwood for making assault and affray and bloodshed upon me, being constable about the king's business, and swearing many grievous oaths they would beat me blind. Our watch and ward hath been duly kept, but William Whopper and Humphrey Winwood, being warned by me to watch, told me they would not and were as good as their words. I do present Edward Ashcrofte and John Hill for an affray and bloodshed. . . .

[Presentment by the constable of the township of St. John Bedwardine.] That there are no taverners, vintners, nor cooks; nor any baker that sell above the rate of thirteen to the dozen. That there are none that exceed the rate of 2s. a meal for the master, or above 8d. a meal for his servant attending him. That no unlawful games are used in the victualling houses, as far as our knowledge extends to know. That no inn-keeper exceeds the rate of 6d. a peck for oats, or 2d. for standing a horse at hay for the space of a day. That we know of none that doth harbour or lodge any vagabond rogues or suspected persons within our township. That no rogues or vagabonds do wander, to our knowledge, or do pass unpunished. That watch and ward hath been duly kept, as far as we know. That George Wigfall, Richard Frewin, Philip Callow, John Deakins, and Widow Hopkins are licensed ale-sellers, and John Webb unlicensed. That no victuallers do suffer any drinking in the time of divine service, or unreasonable times in the night. That we know of no inordinate haunts of tippling or drinking within our township. . . . That the highways and bridges are sufficiently mended and repaired within our township. That no loafers have passed unpunished through our default or neglect.

Worcestershire Quarter Sessions Papers, I, 638-45.

99. RECORDS CONCERNING VIRGINIA (1606-25)

(A) JAMES I: CHARTER TO THE VIRGINIA COMPANY (1606)

James, by the grace of God king of England, Scotland, France, and Ireland, defender of the faith, etc. Whereas our loving and well-disposed subjects, Sir Thomas Gates and Sir George Somers, knights; Richard Hackluit, clerk, prebendary of Westminster; and Edward Maria Wingfield, Thomas Hanham, and Ralegh Gilbert, esquires; William Parker and George Popham, gentlemen, and divers others of our loving subjects have been humble suitors unto us that we would vouchsafe unto them our licence to make habitation, plantation, and to deduce a colony of sundry of our people into that part of America commonly called Virginia . . . , situate, lying, and being all along the sea-coasts between four-and-thirty degrees of northerly latitude from the equinoctial line and five-and-forty degrees of the same latitude . . . ; and to that end, and for the more speedy accomplishment of their said intended plantation and habitation there, are desirous to divide themselves into two several colonies and companies—the one consisting of certain knights, gentlemen, merchants, and other adventurers of our city of London and elsewhere . . . , which do desire to begin their plantation and habitation in some fit and convenient place between four-and-thirty and one-and-forty degrees of the said latitude alongst the coasts of Virginia and the coasts of America aforesaid; and the other consisting of sundry knights, gentlemen, merchants, and other adventurers of our cities of Bristol and Exeter, and of our town of Plymouth, and of other places . . . , which do desire to begin their plantation and habitation in some fit and convenient place between eight-and-thirty degrees and five-and-forty degrees of the said latitude . . . .—we, greatly commending . . . so noble a work . . . , do by these our letters patent graciously accept of and agree to their humble and well-intended desires. . . .

And we do also ordain, establish, and agree, for us, our heirs, and successors, that each of the said colonies shall have a council, which shall govern and order all matters and causes which shall arise, grow, or happen to or within the same several colonies, according to such laws, ordinances, and instructions as shall be, in that behalf, given and signed with our hand or sign manual and pass under the privy seal of our realm of England; each of which councils shall consist of thirteen persons, to be ordained, made, and removed from time to time, according as shall be directed and comprised in the same instructions . . . ; and that also there shall be a council established here in England which shall . . . consist of thirteen persons to be for that purpose appointed by us, our heirs, and successors, which shall be called our Council of Virginia, and shall from time to time have the superior managing and direction . . . for all matters that shall or may concern the government as well of the said several colonies as of . . . any other . . . place within the aforesaid precincts. . . .

Also we do, for us, our heirs, and successors, declare by these presents that all and every the persons, being our subjects, which shall dwell and inhabit within every or any of the said several colonies and plantations, and every of their children which shall happen to be born within any of the limits and precincts of the said several colonies and plantations, shall have and enjoy all liberties, franchises and immunities within any of our other dominions to all intents and purposes as if they had been abiding and born within this our realm of England, or any other of our said dominions. . . .

Poore, *Constitutions*, II, 1888 f.

(B) ORDINANCE OF THE VIRGINIA COUNCIL (1621)

An ordinance and constitution of the treasurer, council, and company in England, for a council of state and general assembly. To all people to whom these presents shall come . . . the treasurer, council, and company of adventurers and planters for the city of London for the first colony of Virginia send greeting. Know ye that we . . . , taking into our careful consideration the present state of the said colony of Virginia and intending by the divine assistance to settle such a form of government there as may be to the greatest benefit and comfort of the people . . . , have thought fit to make our entrance by ordering and establishing such supreme councils as may not only be assisting to the governor for the time being . . . , but also by their vigilant care and prudence may provide as well for a remedy of all inconveniences . . . as also for advancing of increase, strength, stability, and prosperity of the said colony.

We therefore . . . , by authority directed to us from his majesty under the great seal . . . , do hereby order and declare that from henceforward there shall be two supreme councils in Virginia. . . . The one of which councils, to be called the council of state—and whose office shall chiefly be assisting with their care, advice, and circumspection to the said governor—shall be chosen, nominated, placed, and displaced ... by us, the said treasurer, council, and company ... , and this council to be always or for the most part residing about or near the governor. The other council, more generally to be called by the governor once yearly, and no oftener but for very extraordinary and important occasions, shall consist for the present of the said council of state, and of two burgesses out of every town, hundred, or other particular plantation, to be respectively chosen by the inhabitants; which council shall be called the general assembly, wherein, as also in the said council of state, all matters shall be decided ... by the greater part of the voices then present, reserving to the governor always a negative voice. And this general assembly shall have free power to treat, consult, and conclude as well of all emergent occasions concerning the public weal of the said colony ... as also to make, ordain, and enact such general laws and orders for the behoof of the said colony ... as shall ... appear necessary or requisite. ... We require the said general assembly, as also the said council of state, to imitate and follow the policy of the form of government, laws, customs, and manner of trial, and other administration of justice used in the realm of England as near as may be. ...

Provided that no law or ordinance made in the said general assembly shall be or continue in force or validity unless the same shall be solemnly ratified and confirmed in a general quarter court of the said company here in England. ...

Stith, *History of Virginia,* App. 4.

(C) CHARLES I: PROCLAMATION CONCERNING VIRGINIA (1625)

Whereas the colony of Virginia, planted by the hands of our most dear father of blessed memory for the propagation of Christian religion, the increase of trade, and the enlarging of his royal empire, hath not hitherto prospered so happily as was hoped and desired ... , and therefore his late majesty ... did desire to resume that popular government and accordingly the letters patent ... were ... questioned and thereupon judicially repealed and adjudged to be void ... ; and whereas we continue the like care of those colonies and plantations as our late dear father did, and ... are of the same judgment that our said father was of for the government of that colony of Virginia ... : we have thought fit to declare, and by our royal proclamation to publish, our own judgment and resolution in these things ... , and therefore we ... declare ... that we hold those territories of Virginia and of the Summer Islands, as also that of New England, where our colonies are already planted ... , to be a part of our royal empire descended upon us and undoubtedly belonging and appertaining unto us ... ; and that our full resolution is that there may be one uniform course of government in and through all our whole monarchy; that the government of the colony of Virginia shall immediately depend upon ourself, and not be committed to any company or corporation—to whom it may be proper to trust matters of trade and commerce, but cannot be fit or safe to communicate the ordering of state affairs, be they of never so mean consequence. . . .

We do hereby declare that we are resolved . . . to establish a council consisting of a few persons of understanding and quality, to whom we will give trust for the immediate care of the affairs of that colony . . . ; also . . . another council to be resident in Virginia, who shall be subordinate to our council here for that colony. . . .

Rymer, Foedera, XVIII, 72 f.

SECTION IX

THE INTERREGNUM

The documents of the years 1642-60, though relatively few, are entitled to occupy a section by themselves because they represent a period unique in English history. Civil conflict and revolutionary government mark off the Interregnum as a gap in an otherwise unbroken story of constitutional growth, and impart to the pertinent documents a novelty that will be obvious even to the beginning student.

The war not only compelled the adoption of such practical measures as those placed under nos. 100 and 101, but also inspired the condemnation of the king and the abolition of the monarchical system (nos. 104, 106, 107). At the same time these revolutionary enactments called forth arguments for their justification and induced the parliamentary leaders to make noteworthy experiments in constructive reform. For the first and only time in English history, the state was given a written constitution—the Instrument of Government, led up to by a number of suggestions (among them nos. 102, 103, 105) and eventually amended by the Humble Petition and Advice in 1657. Short-lived as it was, this work of political innovation deserves careful study—if for no other reason, because it somewhat anticipated such measures as the great Reform Act of 1832. To the Commonwealth and Protectorate were also due the first governmental union of England, Wales, Scotland, and Ireland; the first establishment within them of even partial religious toleration; and the first practical recognition of economic solidarity between the mother country and the colonies—by the Navigation Act of 1651. Therefore, when viewed in perspective from the present day, the acts of the Interregnum have their place in the institutional development of England.

By the year 1642 it was already an established tradition for Englishmen to be interested in all phases of government. The Interregnum, being an age of violent partisanship and of revolutionary change, naturally roused that interest to a new height. The result was a profusion of memoirs, diaries, books, and pamphlets of all sorts. Among them are many works—especially those of John Milton, James Harrington, and Thomas Hobbes—that occupy commanding places in the history of political thought.

Much of this literature, as well as the contemporary activity in practical government and administration, is treated in the following monographs: E. Jenks, *The Constitutional Experiments of the Commonwealth;* T. C. Pease, *The Leveller Movement;* G. P. Gooch, *English Democratic Ideas in the Seventeenth Century;* and C. H. Firth, *The House of Lords during the Civil War.* The constitutional history of the Interregnum also falls within the scope of more general books, such as Gardiner's *History of the Great Civil War* and *History of the Commonwealth and Protectorate;* Firth's *Last Years of the Protectorate;* and the numerous biographies of Oliver Cromwell. The two standard collections of pertinent sources are Gardiner, *Constitutional Documents of the Puritan Revolution,* and Firth and Rait, *Acts and Ordinances of the Interregnum.*

100. THE SOLEMN LEAGUE AND COVENANT (1643)

A solemn league and covenant for reformation and defence of religion, the honour and happiness of the king, and the peace and safety of the three kingdoms of England, Scotland, and Ireland. We, noblemen, barons, knights, gentlemen, citizens, burgesses, ministers of the Gospel, and commons of all sorts in the kingdoms of England, Scotland, and Ireland, by the providence of God living under one king and being of one reformed religion . . . , for the preservation of ourselves and our religion from utter ruin and destruction according to the commendable practice of these kingdoms in former times and the example of God's people in other nations, after mature deliberation, resolved and determined to enter into a mutual and solemn league and covenant wherein we all subscribe; and each one of us for himself, with our hands lifted up to the most high God, do swear :—

That we shall sincerely, really, and constantly, through the grace of God, endeavour in our several places and callings the preservation of the reformed religion . . . ; and we shall endeavour to bring the churches of God in the three kingdoms to the nearest conjunction and uniformity in religion, confession of faith, form of church government, directory for worship, and catechizing. . . . That we shall . . . endeavour the extirpation of popery, prelacy (that is, church government by archbishops, bishops, their chancellors and commissaries, deans, deans and chapters, archdeacons, and all other ecclesiastical officers depending on that hierarchy), superstition . . . , and whatsoever shall be found to be contrary to sound doctrine and power of godliness. . . . We shall . . . endeavour . . . to preserve the rights and privileges of the parliaments and the liberties of the kingdoms, and to preserve and defend the king's majesty's person and authority in the preservation and defence of the true religion and liberties of the kingdoms, that the world may bear witness . . . that we have no thoughts or intentions to diminish his majesty's power and greatness. . . . And whereas the happiness of a blessed peace between these kingdoms . . . is by the good providence of God granted to us, and hath been lately concluded and settled by both parliaments, we shall . . . endeavour that they may remain conjoined in a firm peace and union to all posterity. . . .

Rushworth, *Historical Collections*, V, 478 f.

101. ORDINANCES OF PARLIAMENT (1644-45)

(A) COMMITTEE FOR CO-OPERATION WITH THE SCOTS (1644)

An ordinance for the appointing a committee of both houses of parliament to join with the committees and commissioners of Scotland for the better managing the affairs of both nations in the common cause, according to the ends expressed in the late covenant and treaty between the two nations of England and Scotland. Whereas, by the covenant and treaty ratified and established between the two kingdoms, both nations are engaged in one common cause against the enemies of their religion and liberties, and . . . are firmly united in a joint posture of arms for their own necessary defence, and for the attaining the ends expressed in the covenant and treaty; and whereas both kingdoms have thought it necessary that they should be joined in their counsels as well as in their forces, and in pursuance thereof the convention of the estates of Scotland have appointed committees residing in Scotland and in the Scottish army, and have sent some of the said committees as commissioners for the purposes aforesaid to repair unto and to reside near the parliament . . . : in consideration hereof the lords and commons do nominate, ordain, and appoint Algernon, earl of Northumberland, [and twenty others] . . . , or any six of them, whereof one lord and two commoners, to treat with the committees and commissioners appointed by our brethren of Scotland in such things as shall by them be propounded from and in the name of the kingdom of Scotland for the ends aforesaid; as likewise to propound to the committees and commissioners of Scotland whatever they shall receive in charge from both houses, and from time to time to advise and consult concerning the same and report the results to both houses. And further power and authority is hereby given to them . . . , as a joint committee with the committee and commissioners of Scotland, to advise, consult, order, and direct concerning the carrying on and managing of the war for the best advantage of the three kingdoms, and the keeping a good intelligence between the three kingdoms, their forces, committees, and counsels; and likewise with power to hold good correspondency and intelligence with foreign states, and further to advise and consult of all things in pursuance of the ends in the late covenant and treaty.

Provided always that nothing in this ordinance shall authorize the committee hereby appointed to advise, treat, or consult concerning any cessation of arms or making peace, without express directions from both houses of parliament. And, lastly, the said committee are to observe such orders and directions as they from time to time shall receive from both houses of parliament. Provided also that this ordinance shall continue for three months and no longer.

Journals of the Lords, VI, 430.

(B) THE SELF-DENYING ORDINANCE (1645)

An ordinance of the lords and commons assembled in parliament for the discharging of the members of both houses from all offices, both military and civil. Be it ordained by the lords and commons assembled in parliament that all and every of the members of either house of parliament shall be and by authority of this ordinance are discharged, at the end of forty days after the passing of this ordinance . . . , from . . . every office or command, military or civil . . . , conferred by both or either of the said houses of this present parliament, or by any authority derived from both or either of them since the 20th day of November, 1640.

And be it further ordained that all other governors and commanders of any island, town, castle, or fort, and all other colonels and officers inferior to colonels in the several armies, not being members of either of the houses of parliament, shall, according to their respective commissions, continue in their several places and commands wherein they were employed and entrusted the 20th day of March, 1644, as if this ordinance had not been made; and that the vice-admiral, rear-admiral, and all other captains and other inferior officers in the fleet shall, according to their several and respective commissions, continue in their several places and commands wherein they were employed and entrusted the said 20th day of March, as if this ordinance had not been made.

Provided always, and it is further ordained and declared, that during this war the benefit of all offices, being neither military nor judicial, hereafter to be granted or any way to be appointed to any person or persons by both or either house of parliament or by authority derived from thence, shall go and inure to such public uses as both houses of parliament shall appoint. And the grantees and persons executing all such offices shall be accountable to the parliament for all the profits and perquisites thereof, and shall have no profit out of any such office, other than a competent salary for the execution of the same, in such manner as both houses of parliament shall order and ordain.

Provided that this ordinance shall not extend to take away the power and authority of any lieutenancy or deputy-lieutenancy in the several counties, cities, or places, or of any *custos rotulorum*, or of any commission for justices of peace, or sewers, or any commission of oyer and terminer or jail-delivery.

Provided always, and it is hereby declared, that those members of either house, who had offices by grant from his majesty before this parliament, and were by his majesty displaced sitting this parliament, and have since by authority of both houses been restored, shall not by this ordinance be discharged from their said offices or profits thereof, but shall enjoy the same—anything in this ordinance to the contrary thereof notwithstanding.

Rushworth, *Historical Collections*, VI, 16.

102. THE HEADS OF THE PROPOSALS (1647)

The heads of the proposals agreed upon by his excellency Sir Thomas Fairfax and the council of the army, to be tendered to the commissioners of parliament residing with the army and with them to be treated on by the commissioners of the army. . . . That . . . a certain period may by act of parliament be set for the ending of this parliament, such period to be put within a year at most, and in the same act provision to be made for the succession and constitution of parliaments in future, as followeth:—

1. That parliaments may biennially be called and meet at a certain day, with such provision for the certainty thereof as in the late act was made for triennial parliaments,[1] and what further or other provision shall be found needful by the parliament to reduce it to more certainty. And upon the passing of this, the said act for triennial parliaments [is] to be repealed.

2. Each biennial parliament [is] to sit 120 days certain, unless adjourned or dissolved sooner by their own consent; afterwards to be adjournable or dissolvable by the king. And no parliament [is] to sit past 240 days from their first meeting, or some other limited number of days now to be agreed on; upon the expiration whereof each parliament [is] to dissolve of course, if not otherwise dissolved sooner.

3. The king, upon advice of the council of state, in the intervals between biennial parliaments, [is] to call a parliament extraordinary; provided it meet above 70 days before the next biennial day and be dissolved at least 60 days before the same, so as the course of biennial elections may never be interrupted.

4. That this parliament and each succeeding biennial parliament, at or before adjournment or dissolution thereof, may appoint committees to continue during the interval for such purposes as are in any of these proposals referred to such committees.

5. That the elections of the commons for succeeding parliaments may be distributed to all counties, or other parts or divisions of the kingdom, according to some rule of equality of proportion; so

---
[1] No. 96A.

as all counties may have a number of parliament members allowed to their choice proportionable to the respective rates they bear in the common charges and burdens of the kingdom, [or] according to some other rule of equality or proportion, to render the house of commons, as near as may be, an equal representative of the whole. And in order thereunto, that a present consideration be had to take off the elections of burgesses for poor, decayed, or inconsiderable towns, and to give some present addition to the number of parliament members for great counties that have now less than their due proportion, to bring all . . . , as near as may be, to such a rule of proportion as aforesaid.

6. That effectual provision be made for future freedom of elections, and certainty of due returns.

7. That the house of commons alone have the power from time to time to set down further orders and rules for the ends expressed in the two last preceding articles, so as to reduce the elections of members for that house to more and more perfection of equality in the distribution, freedom in the election, order in the proceeding thereto, and certainty in the returns. . . .

8. That there be a liberty for entering dissents in the house of commons, with provision that no member be censurable for aught said or voted in the house further than to exclusion from that trust —and that only by the judgment of the house itself.

9. That the judicial power, or power of final judgment in the lords and commons . . . may be cleared; and that no officer of justice, minister of state, or other person adjudged by them, may be capable of protection or pardon from the king without their advice or consent.

10. That the right and liberty of the commons of England may be cleared and vindicated as to a due exemption from any judgment, trial, or other proceeding against them by the house of peers, without the concurring judgment of the house of commons—as also from any other judgment, sentence, or proceeding against them, other than by their equals or according to the law of the land.

11. The same act [is] to provide that grand-jurymen may be chosen by and for several parts or divisions of each county respectively, in some equal way . . . ; and that such grand-jurymen for their respective counties may at each assize present the names of persons to be made justices of the peace from time to time, as the county hath need for any to be added to the commission; and at the summer assize [they are] to present the names of three persons, out of whom the king may prick one to be sheriff for the next year.

For the future security of parliament and the militia in general, in order thereunto, that it be provided by act of parliament:—

1. That the power of the militia by sea and land during the space of ten years next ensuing shall be ordered . . . by the lords and

102. HEADS OF THE PROPOSALS

commons assembled . . . in the parliament or parliaments of England by such persons as they shall . . . appoint for that purpose. . . .

2. That the said power shall not be ordered, disposed, or exercised by the king's majesty that now is, or by any person or persons by an authority derived from him, during the said space; or at any time hereafter by his said majesty without the advice and consent of the said lords and commons, or of such committees or council in the intervals of parliament as they shall appoint.

3. That during the same space of ten years the said lords and commons may by bill or ordinance raise and dispose of what moneys and for what forces they shall from time to time find necessary, as also for payment of the public debts and damages, and for all other the public uses of the kingdom.

4. And to the end the temporary security intended by the three particulars last precedent may be the better assured, it may therefore be provided that no subjects that have been in hostility against the parliament in the late war shall be capable of bearing any office of power or public trust in the commonwealth during the space of five years without the consent of parliament or of the council of state; or to sit as members or assistants of either house of parliament until the second biennial parliament be passed.

For the present form of disposing the militia in order to the peace and safety of this kingdom and the service of Ireland:—

1. That there be commissioners for the admiralty, with the vice-admiral and rear-admiral now to be agreed on, with power for the forming, regulating, appointing of officers and providing for the navy. . . .

2. That there be a general for command of the land forces that are to be in pay both in England, Ireland, and Wales, both for field and garrison.

3. That there be commissioners in the several counties for the standing militia of the respective counties . . . , with power for the proportioning, forming, regulating, training, and disciplining of them.

4. That there be a council of state, with power to superintend and direct the several and particular powers of the militia last mentioned for the peace and safety of this kingdom and of Ireland.

5. That the same council may have power, as the king's privy council, for and in all foreign negotiations; provided that the making of war or peace with any other kingdom or state shall not be without the advice and consent of parliament.

6. That the said power of the council of state be put into the hands of trusty and able persons now to be agreed on, and the same persons to continue in that power . . . for the certain term not exceeding seven years.

7. That there be a sufficient establishment now provided for the salary forces both in England and Ireland, the establishment to

continue until two months after the meeting of the first biennial parliament.

That an act be passed for disposing the great offices for ten years by the lords and commons in parliament . . ., and after ten years they [are] to nominate three and the king out of that number [is] to appoint one for the succession upon any vacancy. . . .

That an act be passed for confirmation of the treaties between the two kingdoms of England and Scotland, and for appointing conservators of the peace betwixt them. . . .

An act to be passed to take away all coercive power, authority, and jurisdiction of bishops and all other ecclesiastical officers whatsoever extending to any civil penalties upon any. . . .

That there be a repeal of all acts or clauses in any act enjoining the use of the Book of Common Prayer and imposing any penalties for neglect thereof; as also of all acts or clauses in any act imposing any penalty for not coming to church, or for meetings elsewhere for prayer or other religious duties, exercises, or ordinances; and some other provision [is] to be made for discovering of papists and popish recusants, and for disabling of them and of all Jesuits or priests from disturbing the state.

That the taking of the Covenant be not enforced upon any, nor any penalties imposed on the refusers, whereby men might be restrained to take it against their judgments or consciences. . . .

That—the things herebefore proposed being provided, for settling and securing the rights, liberties, peace and safety of the kingdom—his majesty's person, his queen, and royal issue may be restored to a condition of safety, honour, and freedom in this nation, without diminution to their personal rights, or further limitation to the exercise of the regal power than according to the particulars foregoing. . . .

Next to the proposals aforesaid for the present settling of a peace, we shall desire that no time may be lost by the parliament for dispatch of other things tending to the welfare, ease, and just satisfaction of the kingdom, and in special manner that the just and necessary liberty of the people to represent their grievances and desires by way of petition, may be cleared and vindicated. . . . That . . . the common grievances of this people may be speedily considered of and effectually redressed, and in particular (1) that the excise may be taken off from such commodities whereon the poor people of the land do ordinarily live, and a certain time to be limited for taking off the whole; (2) that the oppressions and encroachments of forest laws may be prevented for the future; (3) all monopolies, old or new, and restraints to the freedom of trade to be taken off; (4) that a course may be taken and commissioners appointed to . . . settle the proportion for land rates to more equality throughout the kingdom . . . ; (5) the present unequal, troublesome, and contentious way of ministers' maintenance by tithes to be considered of, and some remedy applied; (6) that the rules and course of law, and the officers of it, may be so reduced and reformed as that all suits and questions of right may be more clear and certain in the issues, and not so tedious nor chargeable in the proceedings as now . . . ; (7) . . . that the estates of all men may be some way made liable to their debts . . . , whether they be imprisoned for it or not . . . ; (8) some provision to be made that none may be compelled by penalty or otherwise to answer unto questions tending to the accusing of themselves or their nearest relations in criminal causes, and no man's life to be taken away under two witnesses; (9) that consideration may be had of all statutes, and the laws or customs of corporations, imposing any oaths, either to repeal or else to qualify . . . the same, so far as they may extend . . . to the molestation or ensnaring of religious and peaceable people merely for nonconformity in religion. . . .

That provision may be made for payment of arrears to the army and the rest of the soldiers of the kingdom who have concurred with the army in the late desires and proceedings thereof; and in the next place for payment of the public debts and damages of the kingdom; and that to be performed, first to such persons whose debt or damages . . . are great, and their estates small, so as they are thereby reduced to a difficulty of subsistence; in order to all which . . . we shall speedily offer some further particulars . . . , which we hope will be of good use towards public satisfaction. . . .

Ibid., VII, 731 f.

103. AN AGREEMENT OF THE PEOPLE (1649)

An agreement of the people of England and the places therewith incorporated for a secure and present peace upon grounds of common right, freedom, and safety. Having, by our late labours and hazards, made it appear to the world at how high a rate we value our just freedom, and God having so far owned our cause as to deliver the enemies thereof into our hands, we do now hold ourselves bound, in mutual duty to each other, to take the best care we can for the future to avoid both the danger of returning into a slavish condition and the chargeable remedy of another war. For, as it cannot be imagined that so many of our countrymen would have opposed us in this quarrel if they had understood their own good, so may we hopefully promise to ourselves that, when our common rights and liberties shall be cleared, their endeavours will be disappointed that seek to make themselves our masters. Since, therefore, our former oppressions and not-yet-ended troubles have been occasioned, either by want of frequent national meetings in council, or by the undue or unequal constitution thereof, or by rendering those meetings ineffectual, we are fully agreed and resolved, God willing, to provide that hereafter our representatives be neither left to an uncertainty for times nor be unequally constituted, nor made useless to the ends for which they are intended. In order whereunto we declare and agree:—

First, that, to prevent the many inconveniences apparently arising from the long continuance of the same persons in supreme authority, this present parliament end and dissolve upon or before the last day of April, 1649.

Secondly, that the people of England—being at this day very unequally distributed by counties, cities, and boroughs for the election of their representatives—be indifferently proportioned; and, to this end, that the representative of the whole nation shall consist of 400 persons, or not above; and in each country and the places thereto subjoined there shall be chosen, to make up the said representative at all times, the several numbers here mentioned. . . .[1] Provided that the first or second representative may, if they see cause, assign the remainder of the 400 representers, not hereby assigned, or so many of them as they shall see cause for, unto such counties as shall appear in this present distribution to have less than their due proportion. Provided also that, where any city or borough, to which one representer or more is assigned, shall be found in a due proportion not competent alone to elect a representer or the number of representers assigned thereto, it is left to future representatives to assign such a number of parishes or villages near adjoining to such city or borough, to be joined therewith in the elections, as may make the same proportionable.

Thirdly, that the people do of course choose themselves a representative once in two years, and shall meet for that purpose upon the first Thursday in every second May, by eleven in the morning; and the representatives so chosen [are] to meet upon the second Thursday in the June following at the usual place in Westminster, or such other place as, by the foregoing representative or the council of state in the interval, shall be from time to time appointed and published to the people, at the least twenty days before the time of election; and [are] to continue their sessions there or elsewhere until the second Thursday in December following, unless they shall adjourn or dissolve themselves sooner, but [are] not to continue longer. The election of the first representative [is] to be on the first Thursday in May, 1649; and that and all future elections [are] to be according to the rules prescribed for the same purpose in this agreement, viz.:—(1) That the electors in every division shall be natives or denizens of England; not persons receiving alms, but such as are assessed ordinarily towards the relief of the poor; not servants to, and receiving wages from, any particular person; and in all elections, except for the universities, they shall be men of twenty-one years of age or upwards and housekeepers, dwelling within the division for which the election is. . . .[2] (4) That, to the end all officers of state may be certainly accountable and no factions made to maintain corrupt interests, no member of a

---

[1] Quotas are assigned to all constituencies of England and Wales.

[2] Men who have assisted the king in war are disqualified from voting or being elected for the next seven years.

council of state, nor any officer of any salary-forces in army or garrison, nor any treasurer or receiver of public money, shall, while such, be elected to be of a representative; and in case any such election shall be, the same [is] to be void; and in case any lawyer shall be chosen into any representative or council of state, then he shall be incapable of practice as a lawyer during that trust. (5) For the more convenient election of representatives, each county wherein more than three representers are to be chosen, with the towns corporate and cities . . . within the compass thereof to which no representers are herein assigned, shall be divided by a due proportion into so many and such parts as each part may elect two, and no part above three representers. . . .[3]

Fourthly, that 150 members at least be always present in each sitting of the representative, at the passing of any law or doing of any act whereby the people are to be bound; saving that the number of 60 may make a house for debates or resolutions that are preparatory thereunto.

Fifthly, that each representative shall, within twenty days after their first meeting, appoint a council of state for the managing of public affairs until the tenth day after the meeting of the next representative, unless that next representative think fit to put an end to that trust sooner. And the same council [is] to act and proceed therein according to such instructions and limitations as the representative shall give, and not otherwise.

Sixthly, that in each interval betwixt biennial representatives the council of state, in case of imminent danger or extreme necessity, may summon a representative to be forthwith chosen and to meet; so as the session thereof continue not above eighty days, and so as it dissolve at least fifty days before the appointed time for the next biennial representative. And upon the fiftieth day so preceding it shall dissolve of course, if not otherwise dissolved sooner.

Seventhly, that no member of any representative be made either receiver, treasurer, or other officer during that employment, saving to be a member of the council of state.

Eighthly, that the representatives have . . . the supreme trust in order to the preservation and government of the whole; and that their power extend, without the consent or concurrence of any other person or persons, to the erecting and abolishing of courts of justice and public offices, and to the enacting, altering, repealing, and declaring of laws, and the highest and final judgment concerning all natural or civil things, but not concerning things spiritual or evangelical. Provided that, even in things natural and civil, these six particulars next following are . . . excepted and reserved from our representatives, *viz.*:—(1) We do not empower them to impress or constrain any

---

[3] Elaborate provisions are made for electoral procedure. In all constituencies sheriffs or similar officials are to certify lists of qualified voters, to conduct elections when ordered, make returns of persons elected, etc.

person to serve in foreign war, either by sea or land, nor for any military service within the kingdom; save that they may take order for the forming, training, and exercising of the people in a military way, to be in readiness for resisting of foreign invasions, suppressing of sudden insurrections, or for assisting in execution of the laws. And [they] may take order for the employing and conducting of them for those ends, provided that, even in such cases, none be compellable to go out of the county he lives in, if he procure another to serve in his room. (2) That, after the time herein limited for the commencement of the first representative, none of the people may be at any time questioned for anything said or done in relation to the late wars or public differences, otherwise than in execution or pursuance of the determinations of the present house of commons, against such as have adhered to the king or his interest against the people; and saving that accountants for public moneys received, shall remain accountable for the same. (3) That no securities given or to be given by the public faith of the nation, nor any engagements of the public faith for satisfaction of debts and damages, shall be made void or invalid by the next or any future representatives; except to such creditors as have or shall have justly forfeited the same: and saving that the next representative may confirm or make null, in part or in whole, all gifts of lands, moneys, offices, or otherwise, made by the present parliament to any member or attendant of either house. (4) That, in any laws hereafter to be made, no person, by virtue of any tenure, grant, charter, patent, degree, or birth, shall be privileged from subjection thereto, or from being bound thereby, as well as others. (5) That the representative may not give judgment upon any man's person or estate, where no law hath before provided; save only in calling to account and punishing public officers for abusing or failing in their trust. (6) That no representative may in any wise render up or give or take away any of the foundations of common right, liberty, and safety contained in this agreement, nor level men's estates, destroy property, or make all things common; and that, in all matters of such fundamental concernment, there shall be a liberty to particular members of the said representatives to enter their dissents from the major vote.

Ninthly, concerning religion, we agree as followeth:—(1) It is intended that the Christian religion be held forth and recommended as the public profession in this nation; which we desire may, by the grace of God, be reformed to the greatest purity in doctrine, worship, a d discipline, according to the word of God. The instructing the people thereunto in a public way, so it be not compulsive, as also the maintaining of able teachers for that end and for the confutation or discovery of heresy, error, and whatsoever is contrary to sound doctrine, is allowed to be provided for by our representatives; the maintenance of which teachers may be out of a public treasury, and, we desire, not by tithes—provided that popery or prelacy be not held forth as the public way or profession in this nation. (2) That

103. AGREEMENT OF THE PEOPLE

to the public profession so held forth, none be compelled by penalties or otherwise, but only may be endeavoured to be won by sound doctrine and the example of a good conversation. (3) That such as profess faith in God by Jesus Christ, however differing in judgment from the doctrine, worship, or discipline publicly held forth, as aforesaid, shall not be restrained from, but shall be protected in, the profession of their faith and exercise of religion according to their consciences in any place except such as shall be set apart for the public worship—where we provide not for them, unless they have leave—so as they abuse not this liberty to the civil injury of others or to actual disturbance of the public peace on their parts. Nevertheless, it is not intended to be hereby provided that this liberty shall necessarily extend to popery or prelacy. (4) That all laws, ordinances, statutes, and clauses in any law, statute, or ordinance to the contrary of the liberty herein provided for, in the two particulars next preceding concerning religion, be and are hereby repealed and made void.

Tenthly, it is agreed that whosoever shall by force of arms resist the orders of the next or any future representative—except in case where such representative shall evidently render up, or give, or take away the foundations of common right, liberty, and safety contained in this agreement—he shall forthwith . . . lose the benefit and protection of the laws and shall be punishable with death as an enemy and traitor to the nation. Of the things expressed in this agreement—the certain ending of this parliament, as in the first article; the equal or proportionable distribution of the number of the represeners to be elected, as in the second; the certainty of the people's meeting to elect for representatives biennial, and their freedom in elections, with the certainty of meeting, sitting, and ending of representatives so elected, which are provided for in the third article; as also the qualifications of persons to elect or be elected, as in the first and second particulars under the third article; also the certainty of a number for passing a law or preparatory debates, provided for in the fourth article; the matter of the fifth article, concerning the council of state; and of the sixth, concerning the calling, sitting, and ending of representatives extraordinary; also the power of representatives to be, as in the eighth article, and limited, as in the six reserves next following the same; likewise the second and third particulars under the ninth article concerning religion; and the whole matter of the tenth article—all these we do account and declare to be fundamental to our common right, liberty, and safety; and therefore do both agree thereunto and resolve to maintain the same, as God shall enable us. The rest of the matters in this agreement we account to be useful and good for the public. And the particular circumstance of numbers, times, and places expressed in the several articles we account not fundamental; but we find them necessary to be here determined for the making the agreement certain and practicable, and do hold these most convenient that are here set down, and therefore do positively agree thereunto. By the appointment of his excellency the lord general and his general council of officers.

Cobbett, *Parliamentary History of England*, III, 1267 f.

104. RECORDS OF THE TRIAL OF CHARLES I (1649)

(A) Act Erecting a High Court of Justice (6 January)

The act of the commons of England assembled in parliament for erecting of a high court of justice for the trying and judging of Charles Stuart, king of England. Whereas it is notorious that Charles Stuart, the now king of England, not content with those many encroachments which his predecessors had made upon the people in their rights and freedoms, hath had a wicked design totally to subvert the ancient and fundamental laws and liberties of this nation and in their place to introduce an arbitrary and tyrannical government, and that, besides all other evil ways and means to bring this design to pass, he hath prosecuted it with fire and sword, levied and maintained a cruel war in the land against the parliament and kingdom . . . : for prevention therefore of the like or greater inconveniences, and to the end no chief officer or magistrate whatsoever may hereafter presume traitorously and maliciously to imagine or contrive the enslaving or destroying of the English nation, and to expect impunity for so doing; be it ordained and enacted by the commons in parliament, and it is hereby ordained and enacted by the authority thereof, that Thomas Lord Fairfax, Oliver Cromwell, Henry Ireton [and others] shall be and are hereby appointed and required to be commissioners and judges for the hearing, trying, and adjudging of the said Charles Stuart. And the said commissioners, or any twenty or more of them, shall be . . . constituted an high court of justice to meet and sit at such convenient time and place as by the said commissioners . . . under their hands and seals shall be appointed and notified by public proclamation in the Great Hall or Palace Yard at Westminster . . . ; and to take order for the charging of him, the said Charles Stuart, with the crimes and treasons above mentioned, and for the receiving of his personal answer thereunto, and for the examination of witnesses upon oath . . . or otherwise, and taking any other evidence concerning the same; and thereupon, or in default of such answer, to proceed to final sentence according to justice and the merit of the cause, and such final sentence to execute or cause to be executed speedily and impartially. . . .

And Thomas Lord Fairfax, the general, and all officers and soldiers under his command, and all officers of justice and other well-affected persons, are hereby authorized and required to be aiding and assisting unto the said court in the due execution of the trust hereby committed. Provided that this act, and the authority hereby granted, do continue in force for the space of one month from the making hereof, and no longer.

Firth and Rait, *Acts and Ordinances*, I, 1253 f.

104. TRIAL OF CHARLES I

(B) THE KING'S REFUSAL TO RECOGNIZE THE COURT (21 JANUARY)

Having already made my protestations, not only against the illegality of this pretended court, but also that no earthly power can justly call me, who am your king, in question as a delinquent, I would not any more open my mouth upon this occasion more than to refer myself to what I have spoken, were I in this case alone concerned; but the duty I owe to God in the preservation of the true liberty of my people will not suffer me at this time to be silent. For how can any free-born subject of England call life or anything he possesseth his own, if power without right daily make new and abrogate the old fundamental laws of the land—which I now take to be the present case? . . .

There is no proceeding just against any man but what is warranted either by God's laws or the municipal laws of the country where he lives. Now I am most confident this day's proceeding cannot be warranted by God's laws; for, on the contrary, the authority of obedience unto kings is clearly warranted and strictly commanded in both the Old and New Testament. . . . Then for the law of this land, I am no less confident that no learned lawyer will affirm that an impeachment can lie against the king, they all going in his name. And one of their maxims is that the king can do no wrong. . . .

How the house of commons can erect a court of judicature, which was never one itself (as is well known to all lawyers), I leave to God and the world to judge. And it were full as strange that they should pretend to make laws without king or lords' house, to any that have heard speak of the laws of England. And admitting, but not granting, that the people of England's commission could grant your pretended power, I see nothing you can show for that; for certainly you never asked the question of the tenth man in the kingdom; and in this way you manifestly wrong even the poorest ploughman, if you demand not his free consent. . . .

Thus you see that I speak not for my own right alone . . . , but also for the true liberty of all my subjects—which consists, not in the power of government, but in living under such laws, such a government, as may give themselves the best assurance of their lives and property of their goods . . . Besides all this, the peace of the kingdom is not the least in my thoughts. And what hope of settlement is there so long as power reigns without rule or law, changing the whole frame of that government under which this kingdom hath flourished for many hundred years? . . . And believe it, the commons of England will not thank you for this change; for they will remember how happy they have been of late years under the reigns of Queen Elizabeth, the king my father, and myself, until the beginning of these unhappy troubles, and will have cause to doubt that they shall never be so happy under any new. And by this time it will be too sensibly evident that the arms I took up were only to defend the fundamental laws of this kingdom against those who have supposed my power hath totally changed the ancient government.

Thus, having showed you briefly the reasons why I cannot submit to your pretended authority without violating the trust which I have from God for the welfare and liberty of my people, I expect from you either clear reasons to convince my judgment . . . , or that you will withdraw your proceedings.

This I intended to speak in Westminster Hall on Monday, January 22; but against reason was hindered to show my reasons.

Rushworth, *Historical Collections*, VII, 1403.

(C) The Sentence of the Court (27 January)

. . . The commons of England assembled in parliament have by their late act . . . authorized and constituted us an high court of justice for the trying and judging of . . . Charles Stuart for the crimes and treasons in the said act mentioned; by virtue whereof the said Charles Stuart hath been three several times convented before this high court. . . . The first day . . . a charge of high treason and other high crimes was, in the behalf of the people of England, exhibited against him and read openly unto him, wherein he was charged that he . . . , being admitted king of England and therein trusted with a limited power to govern by and according to the law of the land and not otherwise . . . , nevertheless, out of a wicked design to erect and uphold in himself an unlimited and tyrannical power to rule according to his will and to overthrow the rights and liberties of the people . . . , hath traitorously and maliciously levied war against the present parliament and people therein represented . . . ; and that, by the said cruel and unnatural war so levied, continued, and renewed, much innocent blood of the free people of this nation hath been spilt, many families undone, the public treasure wasted, trade obstructed and miserably decayed, vast expense and damage to the nation incurred, and many parts of the land spoiled, some of them even to desolation. . . . Whereupon the proceedings and judgment of this court were prayed against him as a tyrant, traitor, and murderer, and public enemy to the commonwealth, as by the said charge more fully appeareth. To which charge . . . he, the said Charles Stuart, was required to give his answer, but he refused so to do . . . ; upon which his several defaults, this court might justly have proceeded to judgment against him. . . . Yet, nevertheless, this court, for its own clearer information and further satisfaction, have thought fit to examine witnesses upon oath and take notice of other evidences touching the matters contained in the said charge. . . .

Now, therefore . . . , this court is in judgment and conscience satisfied that he, the said Charles Stuart, is guilty of levying war against the said parliament and people and maintaining and continuing the same, for which in the said charge he stands accused; and, by the general course of his government, counsels, and practices . . . , this court is fully satisfied in their judgments and consciences that he has been and is guilty of the wicked design and endeavours in the said charge set forth. . . . For all which treasons and crimes this court doth adjudge that he, the said Charles Stuart, as a tyrant, traitor, murderer, and public enemy to the good people of this nation, shall be put to death by severing of his head from his body.

Ibid., VII, 1418 f.

105. ACT ESTABLISHING A COUNCIL OF STATE (1649)

An act of this present parliament for constituting a council of state for the commonwealth of England. Be it ordained and enacted by this present parliament that Basil, earl of Denbigh . . . [and forty others], or any nine of them, shall be a council of state and have hereby power and are authorized to put in execution these following instructions:—

1. You are hereby authorized and required to oppose and suppress whomsoever shall endeavour or go about to set up or maintain the pretended title of Charles Stuart, eldest son to the late king, or any other of the said late king's issue, or claiming under him or them; or the pretended title or claim of any other single person whomsoever to the crown of England or Ireland, dominion of Wales, or to any of the dominions or territories to them or either of them belonging.

2. You are hereby authorized and empowered to order and direct all the militias and forces both by sea and land of England and Ireland and the dominions to them or either of them belonging, [for] preserving the peace or safety thereof and for preventing, resisting, and suppressing all tumults and insurrections that shall happen to rise in them or either of them, or any invasions of them from abroad; and also, upon any emergencies, to raise and arm such forces as you shall judge necessary for the ends above expressed; and to give commissions under the seal of the council to such officers as you shall judge necessary for the leading, conducting, and commanding of the said forces, and for the prosecution and pursuance of these instructions, or of any other instructions you shall receive from the parliament.

3. You are hereby authorized and required to use all good ways and means for the reducing of Ireland, the isles of Jersey, Guernsey, Scilly, and the Isle of Man, and all other parts and places belonging to the commonwealth of England, not yet reduced.

4. You shall take care that the stores and magazines of all military provisions both for the land service and for the sea be from time to time well and sufficiently furnished, and that the same be issued as you shall by warrant direct; and you are also from time to time to take care of the repair of the shipping belonging to the commonwealth of England, and to build such others as you shall judge necessary for the defence and safety thereof.

5. You are to use all good ways and means for the securing,

advancement, and the encouragement of the trade of England and Ireland and the dominions to them belonging, and to promote the good of all foreign plantations and factories belonging to this commonwealth or any of the natives thereof.

6. You shall advise, order, and direct concerning the entertaining, keeping, renewing, or settling of amity and a good correspondency with foreign kingdoms and states, and for preserving the rights of the people of this nation in foreign parts and composing of their differences there; and you are hereby authorized to send ambassadors, agents, or messengers to any foreign kingdom or state, and to receive ambassadors, agents, or messengers from them for the ends aforesaid.

7. You are to advise and consult of anything concerning the good of this commonwealth and report your opinions concerning the same as you find occasion to the parliament.

8. You are hereby authorized to send for any person or persons whatsoever to advise with them in pursuance of these or any other instructions that shall be given you by the [parliament].

9. You have hereby power and are authorized to send for any records, writings, accounts, books, or papers that you shall think fit for your information in any cause, matter, or thing in agitation before you, in pursuance of these or any other instructions that shall be given you by the parliament.

10. You have hereby power and are authorized, in case of danger to the commonwealth, to administer an oath to any person or persons for the discovery of the truth.

11. You are hereby authorized and empowered to send for and imprison, or otherwise to secure by taking bond in recognizance, any such person or persons as shall be offenders against these or any other instructions which you shall receive from the parliament; and all such as shall contemn or be refractory to any of your commands, directions, or orders in pursuance of the said instructions.

12. You have hereby power and are authorized to charge the public revenue by warrant under the seal of the council with such sum or sums of money from time to time as you shall find necessary for defraying all charges of foreign negotiations, intelligence, and other incidencies, and for the salary of such subordinate officers and attendants as you shall judge fit to employ, and for the effectual carrying on of the service by these instructions committed to you, or by any other instructions hereafter to be given you from the parliament.

13. You are also to observe and put in execution such further orders as you shall receive from time to time from the parliament.

14. The power hereby committed to this council of state shall continue for the space of one year from the day of passing hereof, unless it be otherwise ordered by the parliament.

15. You have also hereby power to appoint committees or any person or persons for examinations, receiving of informations, and preparing of business for your debates or resolutions.

16. You are to meet at Derby House at four of the clock this

afternoon, and from time to time and from place to place as you shall see cause, and in such manner as you shall think fit for the execution of your instructions.

Firth and Rait, *Acts and Ordinances,* II, 2 f.

106. ACT ABOLISHING THE KINGSHIP (1649)

An act for the abolishing the kingly office in England, Ireland, and the dominions thereunto belonging. . . .[1] Whereas it is and hath been found by experience that the office of a king in this nation and Ireland . . . is unnecessary, burdensome, and dangerous to the liberty, safety, and public interest of the people; and that for the most part use hath been made of the regal power and prerogative to oppress and impoverish and enslave the subject; and that usually and naturally any one person in such power makes it his interest to encroach upon the just freedom and liberty of the people and to promote the setting up of their own will and power above the laws, that so they might enslave these kingdoms to their own lust: be it therefore enacted and ordained by this present parliament, and by authority of the same, that the office of a king in this nation shall not henceforth reside in or be exercised by any one single person. . . .[2]

And whereas, by the abolition of the kingly office provided for in this act, a most happy way is made for this nation, if God see it good, to return to its just and ancient right of being governed by its own representatives or national meetings in council, from time to time chosen and entrusted for that purpose by the people: it is therefore resolved and declared by the commons assembled in parliament that they will put a period to the sitting of this present parliament and dissolve the same so soon as may possibly stand with the safety of the people that hath betrusted them, and with what is absolutely necessary for the preserving and upholding the government now settled in the way of a commonwealth; and that they will carefully provide for the certain choosing, meeting, and sitting of the next and future representatives, with such other circumstances of freedom in choice and equality in distribution of members to be elected thereunto as shall most conduce to the lasting freedom and good of this commonwealth.

And it is hereby further enacted and declared, notwithstanding anything contained in this act, no person or persons of what condition and quality soever within the commonwealth of England and Ireland, dominion of Wales, the islands of Guernsey and Jersey, and town of Berwick-upon-Tweed shall be discharged from the obedience and subjection which he and they owe to the government of this nation, as it is now declared; but all and every of them shall

---

[1] The first article of the act takes from the descendants of Charles I all royal powers and dignities, and releases their subjects from all allegiance.

[2] Attempts to restore the rights of the late king's issue are declared high treason.

in all things render and perform the same, as of right is due unto the supreme authority hereby declared to reside in this and the successive representatives of the people of this nation, and in them only.

Ibid., II, 18 f.

107. ACT ABOLISHING THE HOUSE OF LORDS (1649)

An act for the abolishing the house of peers. The commons of England assembled in parliament, finding by too long experience that the house of lords is useless and dangerous to the people of England to be continued, have thought fit to ordain and enact, and be it ordained and enacted by this present parliament and by the authority of the same, that from henceforth the house of lords in parliament shall be and is hereby wholly abolished and taken away; and that the lords shall not from henceforth meet or sit in the said house called the lords' house, or in any other house or place whatsoever, as a house of lords, nor shall sit, vote, advise, adjudge, or determine of any matter or thing whatsoever as a house of lords in parliament. Nevertheless it is hereby declared that neither such lords as have demeaned themselves with honour, courage, and fidelity to the commonwealth, nor their posterities who shall continue so, shall be excluded from the public councils of the nation; but shall be admitted thereunto and have their free vote in parliament, if they shall be thereunto elected, as other persons of interest elected and qualified thereunto ought to have. And be it further ordained and enacted by the authority aforesaid that no peer of this land, not being elected, qualified, and sitting in parliament as aforesaid, shall claim, have, or make use of any privilege of parliament, either in relation to his person, quality, or estate—any law, usage, or custom to the contrary notwithstanding.

Ibid., II, 24.

108. TREASONS ACT (1649)

An act declaring what offences shall be adjudged treason. Whereas the parliament hath abolished the kingly office in England and Ireland, and in the dominions and territories thereunto belonging, and hath resolved and declared that the people shall for the future be governed by its own representatives or national meetings in council, chosen and entrusted by them for that purpose; [and] hath settled the government in the way of a commonwealth and free state without king or house of lords: be it enacted by this present parliament and by the authority of the same, that, if any person shall maliciously or advisedly publish, by writing, printing, or openly declaring, that the said government is tyrannical, usurped, or unlawful, or that the commons in parliament assembled are not the supreme authority of this nation; or shall plot, contrive, or endeavour to stir up or raise force against the present government, or for the subversion or alteration of the same, and shall declare the same by any open deed; that then every such offence shall be taken, deemed, and adjudged by authority of this parliament to be high treason.

And whereas the keepers of the liberty of England and the council of state, constituted and to be from time to time constituted by authority of parliament, are to be, under the said representatives in parliament, entrusted for the maintenance of the said government with several powers and authorities limited, given, and appointed unto them by the parliament: be it likewise enacted by the authority aforesaid that, if any person shall maliciously and advisedly plot or endeavour the subversion of the said keepers of the liberty of England or the council of state, and the same shall declare by any open deed; or shall move any person or persons for the doing thereof; or stir up the people to rise against them or either of them, their or either of their authorities; that then every such offence and offences shall be taken, deemed, and declared to be high treason.

And whereas the parliament, for their just and lawful defence, hath raised and levied the army and forces now under the command of Thomas, Lord Fairfax, and are at present necessitated, by reason of the manifold distractions within this commonwealth and invasions threatened from abroad, to continue the same, which under God must be the instrumental means of preserving the well-affected people of this nation in peace and safety: be it further enacted by the authority aforesaid that, if any person, not being an officer, soldier, or member of the army, shall plot, contrive, or endeavour to stir up any mutiny in the said army, or withdraw any soldiers or officers from their obedience to their superior officers, or from the present government as aforesaid; or shall procure, invite, aid, or assist any foreigners or strangers to invade England or Ireland; or shall adhere to any forces raised by the enemies of the parliament or commonwealth, or keepers of the liberty of England; or if any person shall counterfeit the great seal of England, for the time being used and appointed by authority of parliament; that then every such offence and offences shall be taken, deemed, and declared by authority of this parliament to be high treason, and every such persons shall suffer pains of death, and also forfeit unto the keepers of the liberty of England, to and for the use of the commonwealth, all and singular his and their lands, tenements, and hereditaments, goods and chattels, as in case of high treason hath been used by the laws and statutes of this land to be forfeit and lost.

Ibid., II, 120 f.

109. ACT ESTABLISHING THE COMMONWEALTH (1649)

An act declaring and constituting the people of England to be a commonwealth and free state. Be it declared and enacted by this present parliament and by the authority of the same that the people of England, and of all the dominions and territories thereunto belonging, are and shall be, and are hereby constituted, made, established, and confirmed, to be a commonwealth and free state, and shall from henceforth be governed as a commonwealth and free state by the supreme authority of this nation—the representatives of the people in parliament, and by such as they shall appoint and constitute as officers and ministers under them for the good of the people, and that without any king or house of lords.

Ibid., II, 122.

110. NAVIGATION ACT (1651)

An act for increase of shipping and encouragement of the navigation of this nation. For the increase of the shipping and the encouragement of the navigation of this nation, which under the good providence and protection of God is so great a means of the welfare and safety of this commonwealth, be it enacted by this present parliament and the authority thereof that, from and after the first day of December, 1651 . . . , no goods or commodities whatsoever of the growth, production, or manufacture of Asia, Africa, or America, or of any part thereof, or of any islands belonging to them . . . , as well of the English plantations as others, shall be imported or brought into this commonwealth of England, or into Ireland, or any other lands, islands, plantations, or territories to this commonwealth belonging . . . in any other ship or ships . . . but only in such as do . . . belong only to the people of this commonwealth or the plantations thereof . . . , and whereof the master and mariners are also for the most part of them of the people of this commonwealth, under the penalty of the forfeiture and loss of all the goods that shall be imported contrary to this act, as also of the ship . . . in which the said goods or commodities shall be so brought in and imported—the one moiety to the use of the commonwealth, and the other moiety to the use and behoof of any person or persons who shall seize the said goods or commodities and shall prosecute the same in any court of record within this commonwealth.

And it is further enacted . . . that no goods or commodities of the growth, production, or manufacture of Europe, or of any part thereof, shall after the first day of December, 1651, be imported or brought into this commonwealth of England, or into Ireland, or any other lands, islands, plantations, or territories to this commonwealth belonging or in their possession, in any ship or ships, vessel or vessels whatsoever, but in such as do truly and without fraud belong only to the people of this commonwealth . . . ; and in no other, except only such foreign ships and vessels as do truly and properly belong to the people of that country or place of which the said goods are the growth, production, or manufacture, or to such ports where the said goods can only be or most usually are first shipped for transportation. . . .[1]

Ibid., II, 559 f.

---

[1] The following articles provide that fish imported into English lands must

111. THE INSTRUMENT OF GOVERNMENT (1653)

The government of the commonwealth of England, Scotland, and Ireland, and the dominions thereunto belonging.

1. That the supreme legislative authority of the commonwealth of England, Scotland, and Ireland, and the dominions thereunto belonging, shall be and reside in one person and the people assembled in parliament; the style of which person shall be the Lord Protector of the Commonwealth of England, Scotland, and Ireland.

2. That the exercise of the chief magistracy and the administration of the government over the said countries and dominions, and the people thereof, shall be in the lord protector, assisted with a council, the number whereof shall not exceed twenty-one nor be less than thirteen.

3. That all writs, process, commissions, patents, grants, and other things, which now run in the name and style of the keepers of the liberty of England by authority of parliament, shall run in the name and style of the lord protector; from whom, for the future, shall be derived all magistracy and honours in these three nations. And [he shall] have the power of pardons, except in case of murders and treason, and benefit of all forfeitures for the public use; and shall govern the said countries and dominions in all things by the advice of the council, and according to these presents and the laws.

4. That the lord protector, the parliament sitting, shall dispose and order the militia and forces, both by sea and land, for the peace and good of the three nations by consent of parliament; and that the lord protector, with the advice and consent of the major part of the council, shall dispose and order the militia for the ends aforesaid in the intervals of parliament.

5. That the lord protector, by the advice aforesaid, shall direct in all things concerning the keeping and holding of a good correspondency with foreign kings, princes, and states; and also, with the consent of the major part of the council, have the power of war and peace.

6. That the laws shall not be altered, suspended, abrogated, or repealed, nor any new law made, nor any tax, charge, or imposition laid upon the people, but by common consent in parliament, save only as is expressed in the thirtieth article.

7. That there shall be a parliament summoned to meet at Westminster upon the 3rd day of September, 1654, and that successively a parliament shall be summoned once in every third year, to be accounted from the dissolution of the present parliament.

8. That neither the parliament to be next summoned nor any successive parliaments shall, during the time of five months to be ac-

---

have been caught from English-owned ships and cured by Englishmen; and that fish oil (including whale oil) thus imported must have been extracted by Englishmen from fish similarly caught. Furthermore, after 1 February 1653, no fish were to be exported from English lands except in English-owned ships.

counted from the day of their first meeting, be adjourned, prolonged, or dissolved, without their own consent.

9. That as well the next as all other successive parliaments shall be summoned and elected in manner hereafter expressed: that is to say, the persons to be chosen within England, Wales, the isles of Jersey, Guernsey, and the town of Berwick-upon-Tweed to sit and serve in parliament shall be, and not exceed, the number of 400; the persons to be chosen within Scotland . . . the number of 30; and the persons to be chosen . . . for Ireland . . . the number of 30.

10. That the persons to be elected to sit in parliament from time to time . . . shall be according to the proportions and numbers hereafter expressed. . . .[1]

14. That all and every person and persons who have aided, advised, assisted, or abetted in any war against parliament since the first day of January, 1641—unless they have been since in the service of the parliament and given signal testimony of their good affection thereunto—shall be disabled and incapable to be elected or to give any vote in the election of any members to serve in the next parliament or in the three succeeding triennial parliaments.

15. That all such who have advised, assisted, or abetted the rebellion of Ireland shall be disabled and incapable forever to be elected or give any vote in the election of any member to serve in parliament; as also all such who do or shall profess the Roman Catholic religion. . . .

17. That the persons who shall be elected to serve in parliament shall be such, and no other than such, as are persons of known integrity, fearing God, and of good conversation, and being of the age of twenty-one years.

18. That all and every person and persons seised or possessed to his own use, of any estate, real or personal, to the value of £200, and not within the aforesaid exceptions, shall be capable to elect members to serve in parliament for counties. . . .[2]

23. That the lord protector, with the advice of the major part of the council, shall at any other time than is before expressed, when the necessities of the state shall require it, summon parliaments in manner before expressed; which shall not be adjourned, prorogued, or dissolved without their own consent during the first three months of their sitting. And in case of future war with any foreign state a parliament shall be forthwith summoned for their advice concerning the same.

24. That all bills agreed unto by the parliament shall be presented

---

[1] From one to thirteen members are assigned to each shire and borough of England and Wales. The allotment of representation in Scotland and Ireland is left to the protector and his council. The following articles deal with electoral procedure and the duties of local officials.

[2] The next four articles provide detailed rules for the summoning of parliament or its meeting in default of such summons.

to the lord protector for his consent; and in case he shall not give his consent thereto within twenty days after they shall be presented to him, or give satisfaction to the parliament within the time limited, that then, upon declaration of the parliament that the lord protector hath not consented nor given satisfaction, such bills shall pass into and become laws, although he shall not give his consent thereunto—provided such bills contain nothing in them contrary to the matters contained in these presents.

25. That Henry Lawrence [and 14 others] . . . , or any seven of them, shall be a council for the purposes expressed in this writing. And upon the death or other removal of any of them, the parliament shall nominate six persons of ability, integrity, and fearing God, for every one that is dead or removed, out of which the major part of the council shall elect two, and present them to the lord protector, of which he shall elect one. . . . And in case of corruption or other miscarriage in any of the council in their trust, the parliament shall appoint seven of their number, and the council six, who, together with the lord chancellor, lord keeper, or commissioners of the great seal for the time being, shall have power to hear and determine such corruption and miscarriage, and to award and inflict punishment, as the nature of the offence shall deserve; which punishment shall not be pardoned or remitted by the lord protector. . . .

26. That the lord protector and the major part of the council aforesaid may, at any time before the meeting of the next parliament, add to the council such persons as they shall think fit, provided the number of the council be not made thereby to exceed twenty-one, and the quorum to be proportioned accordingly by the lord protector and the major part of the council.

27. That a constant yearly revenue shall be raised, settled, and established for maintaining of 10,000 horse and dragoons and 20,000 foot in England, Scotland, and Ireland, for the defence and security thereof; and also for a convenient number of ships for guarding of the seas; besides £200,000 *per annum* for defraying the other necessary charges of administration of justice and other expenses of the government—which revenue shall be raised by the customs, and such other ways and means as shall be agreed upon by the lord protector and the council, and shall not be taken away or diminished, nor the way agreed upon for raising the same altered, but by the consent of the lord protector and the parliament.

28. That the said yearly revenue shall be paid into the public treasury, and shall be issued out for the uses aforesaid. . . .

30. That the raising of money for defraying the charge of the present extraordinary forces both at sea and land, in respect of the present wars, shall be by consent of parliament and not otherwise; save only that the lord protector, with the consent of the major part of the council, for preventing the disorders and dangers which might otherwise fall out both by sea and land, shall have power, until the meeting of the first parliament, to raise money for the purposes afore-

said; and also to make laws and ordinances for the peace and welfare of these nations where it shall be necessary, which shall be binding and in force until order shall be taken in parliament concerning the same. . . .

32. That the office of lord protector over these nations shall be elective and not hereditary and, upon the death of the lord protector, another fit person shall be forthwith elected to succeed him in the government; which election shall be by the council. . . . And until the aforesaid election be past, the council shall take care of the government and administer in all things as fully as the lord protector, or the lord protector and council, are enabled to do.

33. That Oliver Cromwell, captain-general of the forces of England, Scotland, and Ireland, shall be and is hereby declared to be lord protector of the commonwealth of England, Scotland, and Ireland, and the dominions thereto belonging, for his life.

34. That the chancellor, keeper or commissioners of the great seal, the treasurer, admiral, chief governors of Ireland and Scotland, and the chief justices of both the benches, shall be chosen by the approbation of parliament; and, in the intervals of parliament, by the approbation of the major part of the council, to be afterwards approved by the parliament.

35. That the Christian religion, as contained in the Scriptures, be held forth and recommended as the public profession of these nations; and that, as soon as may be, a provision less subject to scruple and contention, and more certain than the present, be made for the encouragement and maintenance of able and painful teachers, for instructing the people, and for discovery and confutation of error, heresy, and whatever is contrary to sound doctrine; and that, until such provision be made, the present maintenance shall not be taken away nor impeached.

36. That to the public profession held forth none shall be compelled by penalties or otherwise; but that endeavours be used to win them by sound doctrine and the example of a good conversation.

37. That such as profess faith in God by Jesus Christ, though differing in judgment from the doctrine, worship, or discipline publicly held forth, shall not be restrained from, but shall be protected in, the profession of the faith and exercise of their religion; so as they abuse not this liberty to the civil injury of others and to the actual disturbance of the public peace on their parts; provided this liberty be not extended to popery nor prelacy, nor to such as, under the profession of Christ, hold forth and practice licentiousness. . . .

41. That every successive lord protector over these nations shall take and subscribe a solemn oath, in the presence of the council and such others as they shall call to them, that he will seek the peace, quiet, and welfare of these nations, cause law and justice to be equally administered, and that he will not violate or infringe the matters and things contained in this writing, and in all other things will, to his

power and to the best of his understanding, govern these nations according to the laws, statutes, and customs thereof.

42. That each person of the council shall, before they enter upon their trust, take and subscribe an oath, that they will be true and faithful in their trust, according to the best of their knowledge, and that in the election of every successive lord protector they shall proceed therein impartially, and do nothing therein for any promise, fear, favour, or reward.

Ibid., II, 813 f.

112. THE HUMBLE PETITION AND ADVICE (1657)

To his highness, the lord protector of the commonwealth of England, Scotland, and Ireland, and the dominions thereto belonging, the humble petition and advice of the knights, citizens, and burgesses now assembled in the parliament of this commonwealth. We, the knights, citizens, and burgesses in this present parliament assembled, taking into our most serious consideration the present state of these three nations, joined and united under your highness' protection, cannot but in the first place, with all thankfulness, acknowledge the wonderful mercy of Almighty God in delivering us from that tyranny and bondage . . . which the late king and his party designed to bring us under . . . ; and also that it hath pleased the same gracious God to preserve your person in many battles, to make you an instrument for preserving our peace. . . . We consider likewise the continual danger which your life is in from the . . . malignant and discontented party . . .—it being a received principle amongst them that, no order being settled in your lifetime for the succession in the government, nothing is wanting to bring us into blood and confusion, and them to their desired ends, but the destruction of your person. . . . Upon these considerations, we have judged it a duty incumbent upon us to present and declare these our most just and necessary desires to your highness:—

1. That your highness will be pleased, by and under the name and style of lord protector . . . , to hold and exercise the office of chief magistrate of these nations, and to govern, according to this petition and advice, in all things therein contained, and in all other things according to the laws of these nations, and not otherwise; that your highness will be pleased during your lifetime to appoint and declare the person who shall immediately after your death succeed you in the government of these nations.

2. That your highness will for the future be pleased to call parliaments consisting of two houses, in such manner and way as shall be more particularly afterwards agreed and declared in this petition and advice, once in three years at furthest, or oftener as the affairs of the nation shall require. . . .

3. That the ancient and undoubted liberties and privileges of parliament . . . be preserved and maintained; and that you will not break or interrupt the same, nor suffer them to be broken or inter-

rupted; and, particularly, that those persons who are legally chosen by a free election of the people to serve in parliament may not be excluded from sitting in parliament to do their duties, but by judgment and consent of that house whereof they are members.

4. . . . And that these qualifications[1] may be observed, and yet the privilege of parliament maintained, we desire that it may be by your highness' consent ordained that forty-one commissioners be appointed by act of parliament, who, or any fifteen or more of them, shall be authorized to examine and try whether the members to be elected for the house of commons in future parliament be capable to sit, according to the qualifications mentioned in this petition and advice; and in case they find them not qualified accordingly, then to suspend them from sitting until the house of commons shall, upon hearing of their particular cases, admit them to sit. . . . That the number of persons to be elected and chosen to sit and serve in parliament for England, Scotland, and Ireland, and the distribution of the persons so chosen within the counties, cities, and boroughs of them respectively, may be according to such propositions as shall be agreed upon and declared in this present parliament.

5. That your highness will consent that none be called to sit and vote in the other house, but such as are not disabled, but qualified according to the qualifications mentioned in the former article, being such as shall be nominated by your highness, and approved by this house, and that they exceed not seventy in number, nor be under the number of forty . . . , who shall not give any vote by proxies; and that, as any of them do die or be legally removed, no new ones be admitted to sit and vote in their rooms, but by consent of the house itself. That the other house do not proceed in any civil causes, except in writs of error, in cases adjourned from inferior courts into the parliament for difficulty, in cases of petitions against proceedings in courts of equity, and in cases of privileges of their own house; that they do not proceed in any criminal causes whatsoever against any person criminally, but upon an impeachment of the commons assembled in parliament, and by their consent; that they do not proceed in any cause, either civil or criminal, but according to the known laws of the land, and the due course and custom of parliament; that no final determinations or judgments be by any members of that house, in any cause there depending, either civil, criminal, or mixed, as commissioners or delegates, to be nominated by that house; but all such final determinations and judgments to be by the house itself—any law or usage to the contrary notwithstanding.

6. That in all other particulars which concern the calling and hold-

---

[1] In the preceding clauses the article excludes from voting or from being elected those disenabled by articles 14 and 15 of the Instrument of Government (above, p. 526); also atheists, revilers of religion, persons who deny the authority of Scripture, profaners of the Lord's day, cursers, drunkards, frequenters of taverns, and persons who marry Roman Catholic wives or permit their children to be brought up in that faith or to marry Roman Catholics.

ing of parliaments, your highness will be pleased that the laws and statutes of the land be observed and kept; and that no laws be altered, suspended, abrogated, or repealed, or new law made but by act of parliament.

7. And to the end there may be a constant revenue for support of the government, and for the safety and defence of these nations by sea and land, we declare our willingness to settle forthwith a yearly revenue of £1,300,000 whereof £1,000,000 for the navy and army, and £300,000 for the support of the government, and no part thereof to be raised by a land tax; and this not to be altered without the consent of the three estates in parliament; and to grant such other temporary supplies, according as the commons assembled in parliament shall from time to time adjudge the necessities of these nations to require. And [we] do pray your highness that it be enacted and declared that no charge be laid, nor no person be compelled to contribute to any gift, loan, benevolence, tax, tallage, aid, or any other like charge without common consent by act of parliament—which is a freedom the people of these nations ought by the laws to inherit.

8. That none may be added or admitted to the privy council of your highness or successors, but such as are of known piety and undoubted affection to the rights of these nations and a just Christian liberty in matters of religion, nor without consent of the council to be afterwards approved by both houses of parliament . . . ; after your highness' death, the commander-in-chief under your successors of such army or armies as shall be necessary to be kept in England, Scotland, or Ireland, as also all such field officers at land or generals at sea which after that time shall be newly made and constituted by your successors, be [so made] by the consent of the council and not otherwise. And that the standing forces of his commonwealth shall be disposed of by the chief magistrate, by consent of both houses of parliament, sitting the parliament; and in the intervals of parliament, by the chief magistrate, by the advice of the council. And also that your highness and successors will be pleased to exercise your government over these nations by the advice of your council.

9. And that the chancellor, keeper or commissioners of the great seal of England, the treasurer or commissioners of the treasury there, the admiral, the chief governor of Ireland, the chancellor, keeper or commissioners of the great seal of Ireland, the chief justices of both the benches, and the chief baron in England and Ireland, the commander-in-chief of the forces in Scotland, and such officers of state there as by act of parliament in Scotland are to be approved by parliament, and the judges in Scotland hereafter to be made, shall be approved of by both houses of parliament. . . .

11. That the true Protestant Christian religion, as it is contained in the Holy Scriptures of the Old and New Testament, and no other, be held forth and asserted for the public profession of these nations; and that a confession of faith, to be agreed by your highness and the parliament, according to the rule and warrant of the Scriptures, be

asserted, held forth, and recommended to the people of these nations; that none may be suffered or permitted, by opprobrious words or writing, maliciously or contemptuously to revile or reproach the confession of faith to be agreed on as aforesaid. . . .[2]

18. And in case your highness shall not be satisfied to give your consent to all the matters and things in this humble petition and advice, that then nothing in the same be deemed of force, to oblige the people of these nations in any particulars therein contained.

Ibid., II, 1048 f.

---

[2] Through an elaboration of articles 35-37 of the Instrument of Government (above, p. 528), toleration is extended to all who accept the doctrine of the Trinity and recognize the Old and New Testaments as the revealed word of God. Ministers who accept the confession of faith, but differ in matters of worship and discipline, are to be eligible for any trust, promotion, or employment to which ministers are eligible. But no ministers or preachers may hold civil office. Article 12 confirms the earlier abolition of archbishoprics, bishoprics, and other cathedral offices, together with the disposal made of lands and properties thereto attached.

113. THE DECLARATION OF BREDA (1660)

Charles, by the grace of God, king of England, Scotland, France, and Ireland, defender of the faith, etc., to all our loving subjects, of what degree or quality soever, greeting. If the general distraction and confusion which is spread over the whole kingdom doth not awaken all men to a desire and longing that those wounds which have so many years together been kept bleeding, may be bound up, all we can say will be to no purpose. However, after this long silence, we have thought it our duty to declare how much we desire to contribute thereunto; and that, as we can never give over the hope in good time to obtain possession of that right which God and nature hath made our due, so we do make it our daily suit to the Divine Providence that He will, in compassion to us and our subjects after so long misery and sufferings, remit and put us into a quiet and peaceable possession of that our right, with as little blood and damage to our people as is possible. Nor do we desire more to enjoy what is ours than that all our subjects may enjoy what by law is theirs by a full and entire administration of justice throughout the land, and by extending our mercy where it is wanted and deserved.

And to the end that the fear of punishment may not engage any conscious to themselves of what is past to a perseverance in guilt for the future, by opposing the quiet and happiness of their country in the restoration both of king, peers, and people to their just, ancient, and fundamental rights, we do by these presents declare that we do grant a free and general pardon to all our subjects, of what degree or quality soever, who, within forty days after the publishing hereof, shall lay hold upon this our grace and favour and shall, by any public act, declare their doing so and that they return to the loyalty and obedience of good subjects—excepting only such persons as shall hereafter be excepted by parliament. Those only excepted, let all our subjects, how faulty soever, rely upon the word of a king, solemnly given by this present declaration, that no crime whatsoever, committed against us or our royal father before the publication of this, shall ever rise in judgment or be brought in question against any of them to the least endamagement of them, either in their lives, liberties, or estates, or—as far forth as lies in our power—so much as to the prejudice of their reputations by any reproach or term of distinction from the rest of our best subjects; we desiring and ordaining that henceforth all notes of discord, separation, and difference of parties be utterly abolished among all our subjects, whom we invite and conjure to a perfect union among themselves under our protection, for the resettlement of our just rights and theirs in a free parliament, by which, upon the word of a king, we will be advised.

And because the passion and uncharitableness of the times have produced several opinions in religion, by which men are engaged in parties and animosities against each other—which, when they shall hereafter unite in a freedom of conversation, will be composed or better understood—we do declare a liberty to tender consciences and that no man shall be disquieted or called in question for differences of opinion in matter of religion, which do not disturb the peace of the kingdom; and that we shall be ready to consent to such an act of parliament as, upon mature deliberation, shall be offered to us for the full granting that indulgence.

And because, in the continued distractions of so many years and so many and great revolutions, many grants and purchases of estates have been made to and by many officers, soldiers, and others, who are now possessed of the same and who may be liable to actions at law upon several titles, we are likewise willing that all such differences and all things relating to such grants, sales, and purchases shall be determined in parliament, which can best provide for the just satisfaction of all men who are concerned.

And we do further declare that we will be ready to consent to any act or acts of parliament to the purposes aforesaid and for the full satisfaction of all arrears due to the officers and soldiers of the army under the command of General Monk; and that they shall be received into our service upon as good pay and conditions as they now enjoy.

Bryant, *Letters of Charles II*, pp. 84 f.

SECTION X

THE RESTORED STUARTS

This section represents another brief period set off by clearly marked limits: the acquisition of the throne by Charles II in 1660 and the loss of it by his brother, James II, in 1689. The two reigns thus lay between two revolutions. Through reaction against the one, the Stuarts regained the crown and for a time enjoyed great prestige—only to bring on the other by carrying reaction too far. During these years the fortunes of the restored dynasty turned on constitutional issues, and at least part of the dramatic story should be apparent from the following documents.

Even a hasty glance at the contents of the section cannot fail to show one of its salient features—the astonishing volume of legislation completed within twenty years. Of the statutes here included, the greater part are unmistakably concerned with the work of restoration, which did not end with the recognition of the king and the resumption of monarchical customs. The power of the crown was strengthened by modifying several acts of the Long Parliament (no. 114E, H, O) and by placing restrictions on petitioning and publishing (no. 114G, M). Furthermore, parliament re-established the Anglican Church and, by a series of repressive laws, sought to enforce absolute uniformity within it and to exclude dissenters—Catholic or Protestant—from civil offices and other influential positions (no. 114F, J, K, P, Q, R, T). But Charles II's statutes were not wholly reactionary. Such acts as those abolishing feudal tenures, providing for post offices, extending the economic policies of the Commonwealth, improving the poor law, repealing the penalty of burning for heretics, and assuring freer recourse to the writ of *habeas corpus* may be properly called progressive legislation.

Among the extracts under no. 116 will be found, not merely illustrations of parliamentary procedure, but also examples of debates in the commons and statements of constitutional principle. Sometimes the latter were inspired by conflict between king and parliament; more often, in this period, by disputes between the two houses. Particular attention may be called to the lords' treatment of money bills, a question to be raised again in the twentieth century; and to the discussion of the king's fund for secret service (no. 116F), an anticipation of political controversy under George III.

The phases of English constitutional development illustrated by the other documents in this section will be clear without elaborate explanation. All the more important state trials of the Restoration period are given in brief under no. 117. Next are grouped several ordinances with regard to the colonial administration in England, together with two significant charters of Charles II. One, to Connecticut, was the first directly obtained from the crown by a community of American colonists. The other, to William Penn, is typical of the later and more detailed grants to colonial proprietors. Lastly, under no. 119, are placed a variety of typical borough records—taken from Leicester because they are available in a scholarly edition and because they are well introduced by earlier extracts from the same series (no. 72C).

There is no general book dealing especially with the constitutional history of this period. In addition to what is given in well-known political histories, the student may profitably consult the notes in two collections of documents: D. O. Dykes, *Source Book of Constitutional History from 1660*, and C. G. Robertson, *Select Statutes, Cases, and Documents*. Other valuable comment will be found in the books of Dicey and Anson cited above (p. 406); W. A. Shaw's introduction to the *Calendar of Treasury Books, 1660-1689;* A. B. Keith, *Constitutional History of the First British Empire;* and the volumes on *English Local Government* by Sidney and Beatrice Webb.

114. CHARLES II: STATUTES

(A) ACT LEGALIZING THE CONVENTION PARLIAMENT (1660)

An act for removing and preventing all questions and disputes concerning the assembling and sitting of this present parliament. For the preventing all doubts and scruples concerning the assembling, sitting, and proceeding of this present parliament, be it declared and enacted, and it is declared and enacted, by the king our sovereign lord and by the lords and commons in parliament assembled, and by authority of the same, that the parliament begun and holden at Westminster the third day of November in the sixteenth year of the reign of the late King Charles of blessed memory is fully dissolved and determined, and that the lords and commons now sitting at Westminster in this present parliament are the two houses of parliament and so shall be, and are hereby declared, enacted, and adjudged to be, to all intents, constructions, and purposes whatsoever—notwithstanding any want of the king's majesty's writ or writs of summons, or any defect or alteration of or in any writ or writs of summons, or any other defect or default whatsoever—as if this parliament had been summoned by writ or writs in his majesty's name according to the usual form, and as if his majesty had been present in person at the assembling and commencement of this present parliament. Provided always that this present parliament may be dissolved by his majesty after the usual manner, as if the same had been summoned by writ or writs in his majesty's name. Provided also, and it is hereby enacted, that his majesty's royal assent to this bill shall not determine this present session of parliament.

Statutes of the Realm, V, 179: 12 Charles II, c. 1.

(B) ACT ABOLISHING FEUDAL TENURES (1660)

An act taking away the court of wards and liveries, and tenures *in capite* and by knight's service, and purveyance, and for settling a revenue upon his majesty in lieu thereof. Whereas it hath been found by former experience that the courts of wards and liveries and tenures by knight's service either of the king or others . . . and the consequents upon the same have been much more burdensome . . . to the kingdom than they have been beneficial to the king . . . : be it therefore enacted . . . that the court of wards and liveries, and all wardships, liveries . . . , and forfeitures of marriages by reason of any tenure of the king's majesty or of any other by knight's service . . . , and all other gifts, grants, charges . . . by reason of any tenure of the king's majesty, or of any other, by knight's service and . . . all fines for alienation . . . , tenure by homage, and all charges . . . by reason of . . . tenure by knight's service . . . be . . . taken away and discharged from the . . . 24th day of February, 1645 . . . ; and all tenures of any honours, manors, lands, tenements, or hereditaments of any estate of inheritance at the common law held either of the king or of any other person or persons . . . are hereby enacted to be turned into free and common socage to all intents and purposes from the said day. . . .

And be it further enacted that no pre-emption shall be allowed or claimed in the behalf of his majesty, or of any his heirs or successors, or of any the queens of England, or of any the children of the royal family for the time being, in market or out of market; but that it be hereafter free to all and every of the subjects of his majesty to sell, dispose, or employ his said goods to any other person or persons as him listeth—any pretence of making provision or purveyance[1] of victual, carriages, or other thing for his majesty, his heirs or succes-

---
[1] Cf. no. 62J.

sors . . . , the said queens or children, or any pretence of pre-emption in their . . . behalfs notwithstanding. . . .²

And now—to the intent and purpose that his majesty, his heirs, and successors, may receive a full and ample recompense and satisfaction, as well for the profits of the said court of wards and the tenures . . . and other the premises and perquisites incident thereunto . . . , as also for all . . . purveyance and provisions herein before mentioned . . .—be it therefore enacted by the authority aforesaid that there shall be paid unto the king's majesty, his heirs and successors, forever hereafter . . . the several rates, impositions, duties, and charge hereinafter expressed and in manner and form following. . . .³

Ibid., V, 259 f.: 12 Charles II, c. 24.

(C) POST OFFICE ACT (1660)

An act for erecting and establishing a post office. Whereas, for the maintenance of mutual correspondencies and prevention of many inconveniences happening by private posts, several public post offices have been heretofore erected for carrying and recarrying of letters by posts to and from all parts and places within England, Scotland, and Ireland, and several parts beyond the seas, the well ordering whereof is a matter of general concernment and of great advantage as well for preservation of trade and commerce as otherwise: to the end therefore that the same may be managed so that speedy and safe dispatches may be had . . . , be it therefore enacted . . . that there be from henceforth one general letter office erected . . . within the city of London, from whence all letters and packets whatsoever may be with speed . . . sent unto any part of the kingdoms of England, Scotland, and Ireland, or any other of his majesty's dominions, or unto any . . . country beyond the seas, at which said office all returns and answers may be likewise received; and that one master of the said general letter office shall be from time to time appointed by the king's majesty . . . , by the name and style of his majesty's postmaster general, which said master . . . and his deputy and deputies . . . , and no other person or persons whatsoever, shall . . . have the receiving, taking up, ordering, dispatching . . . , and delivering of all letters and packets whatsoever which shall . . . be sent to and from all . . . parts of . . . his majesty's dominions and to and from all . . . countries beyond the seas . . . , except such letters as shall be sent by coaches, common known carriers of goods, by carts, wagons, or pack-horses. . . .

And be it further enacted . . . that it shall . . . be lawful . . . for such postmaster general . . . to demand . . . and take for the

---

² Heavy penalties are imposed for infraction.

³ Here is set forth a schedule of excises on ale, beer, cider, perry, mead, spirits, coffee, tea, and chocolate; together with import duties on ale, beer, cider, perry, and spirits.

portage and conveyance of all such letters which he shall so convey, carry, or send post . . . according to the several rates and sums of lawful English money hereafter mentioned, and not to exceed the same. . . .[4]

Ibid., V, 297 f.: 12 Charles II, c. 35.

(D) NAVIGATION ACT (1660)[5]

An act for the encouraging and increasing of shipping and navigation. . . . Be it enacted . . . that from and after the first day December, 1660 . . . , no goods or commodities whatsoever shall be imported into or exported out of any lands, islands, plantations, or territories to his majesty belonging . . . in Asia, Africa, or America in any other ship or ships, vessel or vessels, whatsoever but in such ships or vessels as do truly and without fraud belong only to the people of England or Ireland, dominion of Wales or town of Berwick-upon-Tweed . . . and whereof the master and three-fourths of the mariners at least are English, under the penalty of the forfeiture and loss of all the goods and commodities . . . , as also of the ship or vessel. . . .

And it is further enacted . . . that no goods or commodities whatsoever of the growth, production, or manufacture of Africa, Asia, or America . . . be imported into England [etc.] . . . in any other ship . . . [than as aforesaid].

And it is further enacted . . . that no goods or commodities that are of foreign growth, production, or manufacture, and which are to be brought into England [etc.] . . . in English-built shipping or other shipping belonging to some of the aforesaid places and navigated by English mariners as abovesaid, shall be shipped or brought from any other place or places . . . but only from those of their said growth, production, or manufacture, or from those ports where the said goods and commodities can only [be] or are or usually have been first shipped for transportation. . . .[6]

Ibid., V, 246 f.: 12 Charles II, c. 18.

(E) TREASONS ACT (1661)[7]

An act for safety and preservation of his majesty's person and government against treasonable and seditious practices and attempts. . . .

---

[4] Here follows a schedule of postal rates for inland and foreign mail, beginning with 2*d.* for a letter of one sheet to a place not more than eighty miles distant; also elaborate provision for the administration of the postal service.

[5] Cf. no. 110.

[6] The following articles provide that fish and fish-products (including whale oil) not caught on English-owned vessels or produced by English labour are to be charged double customs; that, with certain exceptions, vessels of aliens may not carry goods from one English port to another; and that various other imports must pay special duties.

[7] Cf. no. 62F.

Be it enacted ... that, if any person ... whatsoever ... during the natural life of our most gracious sovereign lord the king ... shall, within the realm or without, compass, imagine, invent, devise, or intend death or destruction, or any bodily harm tending to death or destruction, maim or wounding, imprisonment or restraint of the person of the same our sovereign lord the king; or to deprive or depose him from the style, honour, or kingly name of the imperial crown of this realm, or of any other of his majesty's dominions or countries; or to levy war against his majesty within this realm or without; or to move or stir any foreigner or strangers with force to invade this realm, or any other his majesty's dominions or countries, being under his majesty's obeisance—and such compassings, imaginations, inventions, devices, or intentions, or any of them, shall express, utter, or declare by any printing, writing, preaching, or malicious and advised speaking—being legally convicted thereof upon the oaths of two lawful and credible witnesses upon trial, or otherwise convicted or attainted by due course of law, then every such person and persons so as aforesaid offending shall be deemed, declared, and adjudged to be traitors and shall suffer pains of death, and also lose and forfeit as in cases of high treason.

And be it further enacted by the authority aforesaid that, if any person ... during his majesty's life shall maliciously and advisedly publish or affirm the king to be an heretic or a papist, or that he endeavours to introduce popery; or shall maliciously and advisedly, by writing, printing, preaching, or other speaking, express, publish, utter, or declare any words, sentences, or other thing or things to incite or stir up the people to hatred or dislike of the person of his majesty or the established government; then every such person and persons, being thereof legally convicted, shall be disabled to have ... any place, office, or promotion ecclesiastical, civil, or military, or any other employment in church or state, other than that of his peerage, and shall likewise be liable to such further and other punishments as by the common laws or statutes of this realm may be inflicted in such cases. ...

Be it ... further enacted by the authority aforesaid that, if any person or persons ... shall maliciously and advisedly, by writing, printing, preaching, or other speaking, express, publish, utter, declare, or affirm that the parliament begun at Westminster upon the third day of November, in the year of our Lord 1640, is not yet dissolved, or is not determined, or that it ought to be in being, or hath yet any continuance or existence; or that there lies any obligation upon him or any other person from any oath, covenant, or engagement whatsoever to endeavour a change of government, either in church or state; or that both houses of parliament or either house of parliament have or hath a legislative power without the king, or any other words to the same effect; that then every such person and persons so as aforesaid offending shall incur the danger and penalty of a *praemunire* mentioned in a statute made in the sixteenth year of the reign of King

Richard II.[8] And it is hereby also declared that the oath usually called the Solemn League and Covenant[9] was in itself an unlawful oath, and imposed upon the subjects of this realm against the fundamental laws and liberties of this kingdom, and that all orders and ordinances, or pretended orders and ordinances, of both or either houses of parliament, for imposing of oaths, covenants, or engagements, levying of taxes, or raising of forces and arms, to which the royal assent, either in person or by commission, was not expressly had or given, were in the first creation and making, and still are, and so shall be taken to be, null and void to all intents and purposes whatsoever. . . .

Provided always, and be it enacted, that no person or persons shall be indicted, arraigned, condemned, convicted, or attainted for any of the treasons or offences aforesaid, unless the same offender or offenders be thereof accused by the testimony and deposition of two lawful and credible witnesses upon oath; which witnesses, at the time of the said offender or offenders' arraignment, shall be brought in person before him or them face to face, and shall openly avow and maintain upon oath what they have to say against him or them concerning the treason or offences contained in the said indictment, unless the party or parties arraigned shall willingly without violence confess the same. . . .

Ibid., V, 304 f.: 13 Charles II, st. 1, c. 1.

(F) Act Restoring the Temporal Power of the Clergy (1661)

An act for repeal of an act of parliament entitled An Act for Disenabling All Persons in Holy Orders to Exercise Any Temporal Jurisdiction or Authority.[10] Whereas at the parliament begun at Westminster the third day of November in the sixteenth year of the reign of our late sovereign lord, King Charles of blessed memory, since deceased, an act of parliament was made, entitled [as above] . . . ; which act hath made several alterations prejudicial to the constitution and ancient rights of parliament and contrary to the laws of this land, and is by experience found otherwise inconvenient: be it enacted . . . that the said act . . . and every clause, matter, and thing therein contained shall be and is hereby from henceforth repealed, annulled, and made void to all intents and purposes whatsoever.

Ibid., V, 306: 13 Charles II, st. 1, c. 2.

(G) Act against Tumultuous Petitioning (1661)

An act against tumults and disorders, upon pretence of preparing or presenting public petitions or other addresses to his majesty or the parliament. . . . Be it enacted . . . that no person or persons whatsoever shall from and after the first of August, 1661, solicit, labour, or procure the getting of hands or other consent of any per-

---

[8] No. 64F.
[9] No. 100.
[10] No. 96L.

sons above the number of twenty or more to any petition, complaint, remonstrance, declaration, or other addresses to the king, or both or either houses of parliament, for alteration of matters established by law in church or state, unless the matter thereof have been first consented unto and ordered by three or more justices of that county, or by the major part of the grand jury of the county . . . ; and that no person or persons whatsoever shall repair to his majesty, or both or either of the houses of parliament, upon pretence of presenting or delivering any petition . . . accompanied with excessive number of people, nor at any one time with above the number of ten persons; upon pain of incurring a penalty not exceeding the sum of £100 in money, and three months' imprisonment. . . .

Ibid., V, 308: 13 Charles II, st. 1, c. 5.

(H) MILITIA ACT (1661)[11]

An act declaring the sole right of the militia to be in the king and for the present ordering and disposing the same. Forasmuch as within all his majesty's realms and dominions the sole supreme government, command, and disposition of the militia and of all forces by sea and land and of all forts and places of strength is and by the laws of England ever was the undoubted right of his majesty and his royal predecessors, kings and queens of England, and that both or either of the houses of parliament cannot nor ought to pretend to the same, nor can nor lawfully may raise or levy any war offensive or defensive against his majesty, his heirs, or lawful successors . . . ; and whereas an act is under consideration for exercising the militia with most safety and ease to the king and his people, which act cannot yet be perfected: be it therefore enacted . . . that the militia and land forces of this kingdom and of the dominion of Wales . . . now under the power of lieutenants or their deputies shall be exercised . . . until 25 March next ensuing in such manner as the same now is actually exercised . . . according to such commissions and instructions as they formerly have or . . . shall receive from his majesty. . . .

Provided that neither this act nor any . . . thing therein contained shall be . . . taken to extend to the giving or declaring of any power for the transporting of any the subjects of this realm, or any way compelling them to march out of this kingdom otherwise than by the laws of England ought to be done.

Ibid., V, 308 f.: 13 Charles II, st. 1, c. 6.

(I) ECCLESIASTICAL COMMISSION ACT (1661)

An act for explanation of a clause contained in the act of parliament made in the seventeenth year of the late King Charles. . . .[12] Whereas, in an act of parliament made in the seventeenth year of

---
[11] Cf. no. 96M.
[12] No. 96F.

the late King Charles . . . , it is amongst other things enacted that no archbishop, bishop . . . , nor any other person or persons whatsoever exercising spiritual or ecclesiastical power, authority, or jurisdiction . . . , shall . . . award, impose, or inflict any pain, penalty, fine, amercement, imprisonment, or other corporal punishment upon any of the king's subjects for any contempt, misdemeanour, crime, offence, matter, or thing whatsoever belonging to spiritual or ecclesiastical cognizance or jurisdiction; whereupon some doubt hath been made, that all ordinary power of coercion and proceedings in causes ecclesiastical were taken away, whereby the ordinary course of justice in causes ecclesiastical hath been obstructed: be it . . . enacted by the king's most excellent majesty, by and with the advice and consent of the lords and commons in this present parliament assembled, and by the authority thereof, that . . . archbishops, bishops, or any other person or persons named as aforesaid . . . may proceed, determine, sentence, execute, and exercise all manner of ecclesiastical jurisdiction and all censures and coercions appertaining and belonging to the same . . . , according to the king's majesty's ecclesiastical laws used and practised in this realm . . . , as they did and might lawfully have done before the making of the said act.

And be it further enacted by the authority aforesaid that the afore-recited act . . . and all the matters and clauses therein contained, excepting what concerns the high commission court, or the new erection of some such like court by commission, shall be and is hereby repealed to all intents and purposes whatsoever—any thing, clause, or sentence in the said act contained to the contrary notwithstanding. . . .

Provided . . . that it shall not be lawful for any archbishop, bishop . . . , or any other person having or exercising spiritual or ecclesiastical jurisdiction to tender or administer unto any person whatsoever . . . any . . . oath whereby such person . . . may be charged or compelled to confess or accuse or to purge him or herself of any criminal matter or thing, whereby he or she may be liable to any censure or punishment. . . . Provided always that this act or anything therein contained shall not . . . be construed . . . to abridge or diminish the king's majesty's supremacy in ecclesiastical matters and affairs. . . .

Ibid., V, 315 f.: 13 Charles II, st. 1, c. 12.

(J) Corporation Act (1661)

An act for the well governing and regulating of corporations. Whereas questions are likely to arise concerning the validity of elections of magistrates and other officers and members in corporations, as well in respect of removing some as placing others during the late troubles contrary to the true intent and meaning of their charters and liberties; and to the end that the succession in such corporations may be most probably perpetuated in the hands of persons well affected to his majesty and the established government . . . : be it enacted . . . that no charter of any corporation cities, towns boroughs, Cinque Ports and their members, and other port towns in England or Wales . . . shall at any time hereafter be avoided for or by reason of any act or thing done or omitted to be done before the first day of this present parliament.

And be it further enacted by the authority aforesaid that all persons who, upon the four-and-twentieth day of December, 1661, shall be mayors, aldermen, recorders, bailiffs, town clerks, common-councilmen, and other persons then bearing any office or offices of magistracy or places or trusts or other employment relating to or concerning the government of the said respective cities, corporations, and boroughs . . . shall . . . take the oaths of allegiance and supremacy and this oath following: "I, A. B., do declare and believe that it is not lawful upon any pretence whatsoever to take arms against the king, and that I do abhor that traitorous position of taking arms by his authority against his person or against those that are commissioned by him; so help me God." And also at the same time [he] shall publicly subscribe . . . this following declaration: "I, A. B., do declare that I hold that there lies no obligation upon me or any other person from the oath commonly called the Solemn League and Covenant, and that the same was in itself an unlawful oath and imposed upon the subjects of this realm against the known laws and liberties of the kingdom." . . .[13]

Provided also, and be it enacted by the authority aforesaid, that, from and after the expiration of the said commissions, no person or persons shall forever hereafter be placed, elected, or chosen in or to any the offices or places aforesaid that shall not have within one year next before such election or choice taken the sacrament of the Lord's Supper according to the rites of the Church of England; and that every such person and persons so placed, elected, or chosen shall likewise take the aforesaid three oaths and subscribe the said declaration at the same time when the oath for the due execution of the said places and offices respectively shall be administered. And in default hereof, every such placing, election, and choice is hereby enacted and declared to be void. . . .

Ibid., V, 321 f. : 13 Charles II, st. 2, c. 1.

(K) Act of Uniformity (1662)

An act for the uniformity of public prayers and administration of sacraments and other rites and ceremonies, and for establishing the form of making, ordaining, and consecrating bishops, priests,

---

[13] A royal commission is to be appointed to supervise the making of these tests and to remove from office all persons who refuse them; as well as any others, even if they have taken the tests, should it be deemed "expedient for the public safety." The commissioners are also empowered to restore officeholders who have been illegally removed.

and deacons, in the Church of England. Whereas in the first year of the late Queen Elizabeth there was one uniform order of common service and prayer . . . compiled by the reverend bishops and clergy, set forth in one book, entitled The Book of Common Prayer and Administration of Sacraments and Other Rites and Ceremonies in the Church of England, and enjoined to be used by act of parliament, holden in the said first year of the said late queen . . . ;[14] and yet, this notwithstanding, a great number of people in divers parts of this realm . . . do wilfully and schismatically abstain and refuse to come to their parish churches and other public places where common prayer, administration of the sacraments, and preaching of the word of God is used upon the Sundays and other days ordained and appointed to be kept and observed as holy days; and whereas, by the great and scandalous neglect of ministers in using the said order or liturgy so set forth and enjoined as aforesaid, great mischiefs and inconveniences during the times of the late unhappy troubles have arisen and grown, and many people have been led into factions and schisms, to the great decay and scandal of the reformed religion of the Church of England and to the hazard of many souls; for prevention whereof in time to come, for settling the peace of the Church, and for allaying the present distempers which the indisposition of the time hath contracted, the king's majesty . . . granted his commission under the great seal of England to several bishops and other divines to review the Book of Common Prayer and to prepare such alterations and additions as they thought fit to offer; and afterwards the convocations of both the provinces of Canterbury and York, being by his majesty called and assembled, and now sitting, his majesty hath been pleased to authorize and require . . . the bishops and clergy of the same to review the said Book of Common Prayer and the Book of the Form and Manner of the Making and Consecrating of Bishops, Priests, and Deacons, and that after mature consideration they should make such additions and alterations in the said books respectively, as to them should seem meet and convenient, and should exhibit and present the same to his majesty in writing for his further allowance or confirmation; since which time, upon full and mature deliberation, they . . . have accordingly reviewed the said books and have made some alterations which they think fit to be inserted to the same, and some additional prayers to the said Book of Common Prayer to be used upon proper and emergent occasions, and have exhibited and presented the same unto his majesty in writing, in one book entitled The Book of Common Prayer and Administration of the Sacraments . . . and the Form or Manner of Making, Ordaining, and Consecrating of Bishops, Priests, and Deacons; all of which his majesty, having duly considered, hath fully approved . . . and recommended to this present parliament. . . .

---

[14] No. 81B.

Now, in regard that nothing conduceth more to the settling of the peace of this nation . . . , nor to the honour of our religion and the propagation thereof, than an universal agreement in the public worship of Almighty God . . . , be it enacted . . . that all and singular ministers in any cathedral, collegiate or parish church, or chapel, or other place of public worship within this realm of England, dominion of Wales, and town of Berwick-upon-Tweed, shall be bound to say and use . . . the public and common prayer in such order and form as is mentioned in the said book annexed and joined to this present act. . . . And . . . be it further enacted . . . that every parson, vicar, or other minister whatsoever, who now hath or enjoyeth any ecclesiastical benefice or promotion within the realm of England or places aforesaid, shall, in the church, chapel, or place of public worship belonging to his said benefice or promotion . . . , openly and publicly before the congregation there assembled declare his unfeigned assent and consent to the use of all things in the said book contained and prescribed, in these words, and no other: "I, A. B., do here declare my unfeigned assent and consent to all and everything contained and prescribed in and by the book entitled The Book of Common Prayer . . . and the Form or Manner of Making, Ordaining, and Consecrating of Bishops, Priests, and Deacons." And [it is enacted] that all and every such person who shall . . . neglect or refuse to do the same within the time aforesaid . . . shall *ipso facto* be deprived of all his spiritual promotions. . . .[15]

And be it further enacted by the authority aforesaid that every dean, canon, and prebendary of every cathedral or collegiate church, and all masters and other heads, fellows, chaplains, and tutors of or in any college, hall, house of learning, or hospital, and every public professor and reader in either of the universities, and in every college elsewhere, and every parson, vicar, curate, lecturer, and every other person in holy orders, and every schoolmaster keeping any public or private school, and every person instructing or teaching any youth in any house or private family as a tutor or schoolmaster . . . shall . . . subscribe the declaration or acknowledgement following, *scilicet*: "I, A. B., do declare that it is not lawful, upon any pretence whatsoever, to take arms against the king, and that I do abhor that traitorous position of taking arms by his authority against his person or against those that are commissionated by him, and that I will conform to the liturgy of the Church of England as it is now by law established; and I do declare that I do hold there lies no obligation upon me or any other person, from the oath commonly called the Solemn League and Covenant, to endeavour any change or alteration of government either in church or state, and that the same was in itself

---

[15] The same provision is extended to persons who may be appointed to such livings in the future.

an unlawful oath and imposed upon the subjects of this realm against the known laws and liberties of this kingdom." . . .[16]

And be it further enacted by the authority aforesaid that no person whatsoever shall . . . be capable to be admitted to any parsonage, vicarage, benefice, or other ecclesiastical promotion or dignity whatsoever, nor shall presume to consecrate and administer the holy sacrament of the Lord's Supper, before such time as he shall be ordained priest according to the form and manner in and by the said book prescribed, unless he have formerly been made priest by episcopal ordination, upon pain to forfeit for every offence the sum of £100. . . .

And be it further enacted . . . that no person shall be . . . received as a lecturer, or permitted . . . to preach as a lecturer or to preach or read any sermon . . . in any church, chapel, or other place of public worship . . . unless he be first approved and thereunto licensed by the archbishop of the province or bishop of the diocese . . . , and shall in the presence of the same archbishop or bishop . . . read the nine-and-thirty articles of religion mentioned in the statute of the thirteenth year of the late Queen Elizabeth, with declaration of his unfeigned assent to the same; and . . . the first time he preacheth . . . shall openly, publicly, and solemnly read the common prayers and service in and by the said book appointed to be read for that time of the day, and then and there publicly and openly declare his assent unto and approbation of the said book. . . . And be it further enacted by the authority aforesaid that, if any person who is by this act disabled to preach any lecture or sermon shall, during the time that he shall continue and remain so disabled, preach any sermon or lecture, that then for every such offence the person . . . so offending shall suffer three months' imprisonment in the common jail without bail. . . .

Ibid., V, 364 f.: 14 Charles II, c. 4.

(L) ACT TO RELIEVE THE POOR (1662)

An act for the better relief of the poor of this kingdom. Whereas the necessity, number, and continual increase of the poor . . . through the whole kingdom of England and dominion of Wales is very great and exceeding burdensome . . . ; [and] whereas, by reason of some defects in the law, poor people are not restrained from going from one parish to another . . . , to settle themselves in those parishes where there is the best stock, the largest commons, or wastes to build cottages, and the most woods for them to burn and destroy . . . , to the great discouragement of parishes to provide stocks where it is liable to be devoured by strangers: be it therefore enacted . . . that it shall and may be lawful, upon complaint made by the churchwardens or overseers of the poor of any parish to any justice of

---

[16] Persons failing to make such declaration by a certain time shall forfeit their offices, or be ineligible for appointment.

peace within forty days after any such person or persons coming so to settle as aforesaid in any tenement under the yearly value of £10, for any two justices of the peace . . ., of the division where any person or persons that are likely to be chargeable to the parish shall come to inhabit, by their warrant to remove and convey such person or persons to such parish where he or they were last legally settled, either as a native, householder, sojourner, apprentice, or servant, for the space of forty days at the least, unless he or they give sufficient security for the discharge of the said parish, to be allowed by the said justices.

Provided always that all such persons who think themselves aggrieved by any such judgment of the said two justices may appeal to the justices of the peace of the said county at their next quarter sessions, who are hereby required to do them justice according to the merits of their cause. Provided also that . . . it shall . . . be lawful for any person or persons to go into any county, parish, or place to work in time of harvest, or at any time to work at any other work, so that he or they carry with him or them a certificate from the minister of the parish and one of the churchwardens and one of the overseers for the poor for the said year, that he or they have a dwelling-house or place in which he or they inhabit, and hath left wife and children, or some of them there . . ., and is declared an inhabitant or inhabitants there. . . .

And whereas the laws and statutes for the apprehending of rogues and vagabonds have not been duly executed, sometimes for want of officers, by reason lords of manors do not keep court-leets[17] every year for the making of them: be it therefore enacted . . . that, in case any constable, headborough, or tithingman shall die or go out of the parish, any two justices of the peace may make and swear a new constable, headborough, or tithingman, until the said lord shall hold a court or until next quarter sessions, who shall approve of the said officers so made and sworn as aforesaid, or appoint others as they shall think fit; and if any officer shall continue above a year in his or their office, that then in such case the justices of peace in their quarter sessions may discharge such officers and may put another fit person in his or their place until the lord of the said manor shall hold a court as aforesaid. . . .

And be . . . it enacted . . . that it shall and may be lawful to and for any justice of peace, to whom any rogue, vagabond, or sturdy beggars . . . shall be brought, to reward any person or persons that shall apprehend any rogue, vagabond, or sturdy beggar, by granting unto such person or persons an order or warrant under his hand and seal to the constable, headborough, or tithingman of such parish where such rogue, vagabond, or sturdy beggar passed through unapprehended, requiring him to pay such person or persons the sum

---

[17] Manorial courts; cf. nos. 54H, 65.

of 2s. for every rogue, vagabond, or sturdy beggar which shall be so apprehended. . . .

And whereas constables, headboroughs, or tithingmen are or may be at great charge in relieving, conveying with passes, and in carrying rogues, vagabonds, and sturdy beggars to houses of correction or . . . workhouses . . . , and as yet have no power by law to make rates to reimburse themselves, be it therefore enacted . . . that all constables, headboroughs, and tithingmen so out of purse as aforesaid, together with the churchwardens and overseers of the poor and other inhabitants of the said parish, shall hereby have power and authority to make an indifferent rate and to tax all the occupiers of lands and inhabitants, and all other persons chargeable by the statute of the three-and-fortieth of Elizabeth[18] concerning the office and duty of overseers for the poor within the said parish; which rate being confirmed under the hands and seals of any two justices of peace as aforesaid, the said constable, headborough, or tithingmen shall have power by warrant, under the hands and seals of two justices of peace, to levy by distress and sale of the goods of any person or persons refusing to pay the same, rendering the overplus to the owner if any shall be. . . .

Provided always, and be it enacted . . . , that it shall and may be lawful for the justices of peace in any of the counties of England and Wales, in their quarter sessions assembled . . . , to transport or cause to be transported such rogues, vagabonds, and sturdy beggars as shall be duly convicted and adjudged to be incorrigible to any of the English plantations beyond the seas. . . .

Ibid., V, 401 f.: 14 Charles II, c. 12.

(M) LICENSING ACT (1662)[19]

An act for preventing the frequent abuses in printing seditious, treasonable, and unlicensed books and pamphlets, and for regulating of printing and printing-presses. Whereas the well-government and regulating of printers and printing-presses is matter of public care and of great concernment—especially considering that by the general licentiousness of the late times many evil-disposed persons have been encouraged to print and sell heretical, schismatical, blasphemous, seditious, and treasonable books, pamphlets, and papers, and still do continue such their unlawful and exorbitant practice, to the high dishonour of Almighty God, the endangering the peace of these kingdoms, and raising a disaffection to his most excellent majesty and his government—[and whereas] for prevention thereof no surer means can be advised than by reducing and limiting the number of printing-presses, and by ordering and settling the said art or mystery of printing by act of parliament, in manner as hereinafter is expressed: the king's most excellent majesty by and with the consent and advice

---

[18] See above, p. 356, n. 10.
[19] Cf. no. 85. This act was continued from time to time until 1695; see **no. 123A**.

of the lords spiritual and temporal and commons in this present parliament assembled, doth therefore ordain and enact . . . that no person or persons whatsoever shall presume to print, or cause to be printed, either within this realm of England or any other of his majesty's dominions or in the parts beyond the seas, any heretical, seditious, schismatical, or offensive books or pamphlets, wherein any doctrine or opinion shall be asserted or maintained which is contrary to the Christian faith or the doctrine or discipline of the Church of England, or which shall or may tend or be to the scandal of religion, or the church, or the government or governors of the church, state, or commonwealth, or of any corporation or particular person or persons whatsoever; nor shall import, publish, sell, or disperse any such book or books, or pamphlets; nor shall cause . . . any such . . . to be bound, stitched, or sewed together.

And be it further ordained . . . that no private person or persons whatsoever shall at any time hereafter print or cause to be printed any book or pamphlet whatsoever, unless the same book and pamphlet, together with all and every the titles, epistles, prefaces, proems, preambles, introductions, tables, dedications, and other matters and things thereunto annexed, be first entered in the book of the register of the Company of Stationers of London, except acts of parliament, proclamations, and such other books and papers as shall be appointed to be printed by virtue of any warrant under the king's majesty's sign-manual, or under the hand of one or both of his majesty's principal secretaries of state, and unless the same book and pamphlet, and also all and every said titles . . . [etc.] thereunto annexed, or therewith to be imprinted, shall be first lawfully licensed and authorized to be printed by such person and persons only as shall be constituted and appointed to license the same, according to the direction and true meaning of this present act hereinafter expressed, and by no other: that is to say, that all books concerning the common laws of this realm shall be printed by the special allowance of the lord chancellor, or lord keeper of the great seal of England for the time being, the lords chief justices, and lord chief baron for the time being . . . , or one or more of their appointments; and that all books of history concerning the state of this realm, or other books concerning any affairs of state, shall be licensed by the principal secretaries of state for the time being, or one of them . . . ; and that all books to be imprinted concerning heraldry, titles of honour, and arms, or otherwise concerning the office of earl marshal, shall be licensed by the earl marshal for the time being or by his appointment . . . ; and that all other books to be imprinted or reprinted—whether of divinity, physic, philosophy, or whatsoever other science or art—shall be first licensed and allowed by the lord archbishop of Canterbury and lord bishop of London for the time being or one of them, or by their or one of their appointments. . . .

And be it enacted . . . that every person and persons who . . . are . . . authorized to license the imprinting of books, or reprinting thereof with any additions or amendments, as aforesaid, shall have one written copy of the same book or books which shall be so licensed . . . with the titles [etc.] . . . thereunto annexed . . . ; and upon the said copy licensed to be imprinted he or they, who shall so license the same, shall testify under his or their hand or hands that there is not anything in the same contained that is contrary to the Christian faith or the doctrine or discipline of the Church of England, or against the state or government of this realm, or contrary to good life or good manners, or otherwise as the nature and subject of the work shall require—which licence or approbation shall be printed in the beginning of the same book, with the name or names of him or them that shall authorize or license the same, for a testimony of the allowance thereof. . . .[20]

And be it further enacted . . . that no person or persons within the city of London or the liberties thereof, or elsewhere, shall erect or cause to be erected any press or printing-house, nor shall knowingly demise or let or willingly suffer to be held or used any house, vault, cellar, or other room whatsoever to or by any person or persons for a printing-house . . . , unless he or they . . . shall first give notice to the master or wardens of the said Company of Stationers for the time being, of the erecting of such press. . . .[21]

And for the better discovering of printing in corners without licence, be it further enacted . . . that one or more of the messengers of his majesty's chamber, by warrant under his majesty's sign-manual, or under the hand of one or both of his majesty's principal secretaries of state, or the master and wardens of the said Company of Stationers, or any one of them, shall have power and authority, with a constable . . . , to search all houses and shops where they shall know, or upon some probable reason suspect, any books or papers to be printed, bound, or stitched . . . , and to view there what is imprinting, binding, or stitching, and to examine whether the same be licensed, and to demand a sight of the said licence; and if the said book . . . shall not be licensed, then to seize upon so much thereof as shall be found imprinted, together with the several offenders, and to bring them before one or more justices of the peace, who are hereby . . . required to commit such offenders to prison, there to remain until they shall be tried and acquitted, or convicted and punished for the said offences; and in case the said searchers shall . . . find any book or books . . . which they shall suspect to contain matters therein contrary to the doctrine or discipline of the Church of England, or against the state and government, then upon such suspicion to seize upon such book or books . . . and to bring the same unto the said lord archbishop of Canterbury and lord bishop of London . . . , or to the secretaries of state . . . , who shall take

---

[20] Distribution of books printed abroad is closely restricted.
[21] The act continues with regulation of the printing trade.

up such further course for the suppressing thereof as to them or any of them shall seem fit. . . .

And be it further enacted . . . that every printer shall reserve three printed copies of the best and largest paper of every book new printed, or reprinted by him with additions, and shall, before any public vending of the said book, bring them to the master of the Company of Stationers and deliver them to him; one whereof shall be delivered to the keeper of his majesty's library, and the other two to be sent to the vice-chancellors of the two universities respectively, for the use of the public libraries of the said universities.

Provided always that nothing in this act contained shall . . . extend to the prejudice or infringing of any the just rights and privileges of either of the two universities of this realm touching and concerning the licensing or printing of books in either of the said universities.

Provided always that no search shall be at any time made in the house or houses of any the peers of this realm, or of any other person or persons not . . . using any of the trades in this act before mentioned, but by special warrant from the king's majesty under his sign-manual, or under the hand of one or both of his majesty's principal secretaries of state, or for any other books than such as are in printing, or shall be printed after the 10th of June, 1662—anything in this act to the contrary thereof in any wise notwithstanding. . . . Provided that this act shall continue and be in force for two years to commence from the 10th of June, 1662, and no longer.

Ibid., V, 428 f.: 14 Charles II, c. 33.

(N) ACT REGULATING COMMERCE (1663)

An act for the encouragement of trade. Forasmuch as the encouraging of tillage ought to be in an especial manner regarded and endeavoured; and the surest and effectualest means of promoting and advancing any trade, occupation, or mystery being by rendering it profitable to the users thereof; and great quantities of land within this kingdom lying in a manner waste . . . , which might . . . be improved . . . and thereby much more corn produced, greater numbers of people, horses, and cattle employed, and other land also rendered more valuable: be it therefore enacted . . . that . . . , when the prices of corn and grain . . . do not exceed the rates hereafter following at the havens or places where the same shall be shipped or loaded . . . ,[22] that then it shall be lawful for all and every person and persons to ship, load, carry, and transport any of the said corns or grains . . . unto any parts beyond the seas as merchandise . . .[23]

---

[22] Quarter of wheat, 48*s.*; of barley or malt, 28*s.*; of buckwheat, 28*s.*; of oats, 13*s.* 4*d.*; of rye, 32*s.*; of peas or beans, 32*s.*

[23] Paying only whatever duties are provided by the present grant of tunnage and poundage. When prices reached the stated level, such grains could be exported only by paying custom at an increased rate.

And in regard his majesty's plantations beyond the seas are inhabited and peopled by his subjects of this his kingdom of England, for the maintaining a greater correspondence and kindness between them and keeping them in a firmer dependence upon it and rendering them yet more beneficial and advantageous unto it in the further employment and increase of English shipping and seamen, vent of English woolen and other manufactures and commodities, rendering the navigation to and from the same more safe and cheap, and making this kingdom a staple, not only of the commodities of those plantations, but also of the commodities of other countries and places for the supplying of them . . . : be it enacted that . . . no commodity of the growth, production, or manufacture of Europe shall be imported into any land . . . to his majesty belonging . . . but what shall be *bona fide* . . . laden and shipped in England, Wales, and the town of Berwick-upon-Tweed and in English-built shipping. . . .[24]

Ibid., V, 449 f.: 15 Charles II, c. 7.

(O) TRIENNIAL ACT (1664)

An act for the assembling and holding of parliaments once in three years at the least. . . . Whereas the act made in the parliament begun at Westminster the third day of November, in the sixteenth year of the reign of our late sovereign lord, King Charles of blessed memory . . . ,[25] is in derogation of his majesty's just rights and prerogative inherent to the imperial crown of this realm for the calling and assembling of parliaments, and may be an occasion of manifold mischiefs and inconveniences and much endanger the peace and safety of his majesty and all his liege people of the realm: be it therefore enacted . . . that the said act . . . and all and every the articles, clauses, and things therein contained . . . are hereby . . . declared to be null and void to all intents and purposes whatsoever. . . .

And because, by the ancient laws and statutes of this realm made in the reign of King Edward III, parliaments are to be held very often . . . : be it declared and enacted . . . that hereafter the sitting and holding of parliaments shall not be intermitted or discontinued above three years at the most; but that, within three years from and after the determination of this present parliament, and so from time to time within three years after the determination of any other parliament or parliaments, or if there be occasion more often, your majesty, your heirs, and successors, do issue out your writs for calling, assembling, and holding of another parliament, to the end there may be a frequent calling, assembling, and holding of parliaments once in three years at the least.

Ibid., V, 513: 16 Charles II, c. 1.

---

[24] Detailed provisions follow for the enforcement of the act. Cf. no. 110.
[25] No. 96A.

(P) CONVENTICLE ACT (1664)

An act to prevent and suppress seditious conventicles. Whereas an act made in the five-and-thirtieth year of the reign of our late sovereign lady, Queen Elizabeth . . . ,[26] hath not been put in due execution by reason of some doubt of late made whether the said act be still in force, although . . . the said act is still in force and ought to be put in due execution; for providing therefore of further and more speedy remedies against the growing and dangerous practices of seditious sectaries and other disloyal persons . . . , be it enacted . . . that, if any person of the age of sixteen years or upwards, being a subject of this realm . . . , shall be present at any assembly, conventicle, or meeting under colour or pretence of any exercise of religion in other manner than is allowed by the liturgy or practice of the Church of England in any place within the kingdom of England, dominion of Wales, or town of Berwick-upon-Tweed, at which conventicle, meeting, or assembly, there shall be five persons or more assembled together over and above those of the same household, then it shall and may be lawful . . . for any two justices of the peace, of the county . . . wherein the offence aforesaid shall be committed . . . , and they are hereby required and enjoined—upon proof . . . made of such offence, either by confession of the party or oath of witnesses or notorious evidence of the fact . . . —to make a record of every such offence and offences . . . ; which record so made as aforesaid shall to all intents and purposes be in law taken and adjudged to be a full and perfect conviction. . . . And thereupon the said justices . . . shall commit every such offender so convicted . . . to the jail or house of correction, there to remain without bail . . . for any time not exceeding the space of three months, unless such offender shall pay down to the said justices . . . such sum of money, not exceeding £5, as the said justices . . . shall fine the said offender at . . .[27]

And be it enacted . . . that every person who shall wittingly and willingly suffer any such conventicle, unlawful assembly, or meeting aforesaid to be held in his or her house, outhouse, barn or room, yard or backside, woods or grounds, shall incur the same penalties and forfeitures as any other offender against this act. . . .

And be it enacted . . . that the justices of the peace . . . shall and may, with what aid, force, and assistance they shall think fit for the better execution of this act, after refusal or denial, enter into any house or other place where they shall be informed any such conventicle as aforesaid is or shall be held. . . .[28]

Ibid., V, 516 f.: 16 Charles II, c. 4.

---

[26] No. 81F.

[27] The penalty for a second offence is to be six months' imprisonment or a fine not exceeding £10; for a third offence transportation for seven years.

[28] Most of these provisions, originally enacted as temporary measures, were incorporated in the Second Conventicle Act of 1670. The latter statute, however,

(Q) FIVE-MILE ACT (1665)

An act for restraining non-conformists from inhabiting in corporations. Whereas divers . . . persons in holy orders have not declared their unfeigned assent and consent to the use of all things contained and prescribed in the Book of Common Prayer . . . , or have not subscribed the declaration or acknowledgment contained in a certain act of parliament made in the fourteenth year of his majesty's reign . . . ,[29] or any other subsequent act; and whereas they, or some of them, and divers other person and persons not ordained according to the form of the Church of England, and as have, since the Act of Oblivion,[30] taken upon them to preach in unlawful assemblies, conventicles, or meetings, under colour or pretence of exercise of religion, contrary to the laws and statutes of this kingdom, have settled themselves in divers corporations in England, sometimes three or more of them in a place, thereby taking an opportunity to distil the poisonous principles of schism and rebellion into the hearts of his majesty's subjects, to the great danger of the church and kingdom: be it therefore enacted . . . that the said . . . persons in holy orders or pretended holy orders, or pretending to holy orders, and all . . . persons who have been possessed of any ecclesiastical or spiritual promotion . . . , who have not declared their unfeigned assent and consent as aforesaid, and subscribed the declaration aforesaid, and shall not take and subscribe the oath following . . . ,[31] and all such person and persons as shall take upon them to preach in any unlawful assembly, conventicle, or meeting, under colour or pretence of any exercise of religion, contrary to the laws and statutes of this kingdom, shall not at any time . . . , unless only in passing upon the road, come or be within five miles of any city or town corporate or borough that sends burgesses to the parliament, within his majesty's kingdom of England, principality of Wales, or of the town of Berwick-upon-Tweed, or within five miles of any parish, town, or place wherein he or they have since the Act of Oblivion been parson, vicar, curate, stipendiary, or lecturer, or taken upon them to preach in any unlawful assembly, conventicle, or meeting . . . , upon forfeiture of every such offence the sum of £40 of lawful English money. . . .

Provided always . . . that it shall not be lawful for any person or persons restrained from coming to any city, town corporate, borough, parish, town, or place, as aforesaid, or for any other person or persons as shall not first take and subscribe the said oath,

---

more definitely proscribed conventicles held in the open; imposed a heavy fine upon preachers and teachers in conventicles; and reduced the penalty for first attendance at such a meeting to 5s.

[29] No. 114K.
[30] The general amnesty to all but specified persons granted by statute in 1660.
[31] This is the oath prescribed in the Corporation Act (above, p. 543) with the added promise not to attempt any alteration in church or state.

and as shall not frequent divine service established by the laws of this kingdom and carry him or herself reverently, decently, and orderly there, to teach any public or private school, or to take any boarders or tablers that are taught or instructed by him or herself, or any other, upon pain for every such offence to forfeit the sum of £40. . . .

Ibid., V, 575: 17 Charles II, c. 2.

(R) First Test Act (1673)

An act for preventing dangers which may happen from popish recusants. For preventing dangers which may happen from popish recusants and quieting the minds of his majesty's good subjects: be it enacted . . . that all and every person or persons, as well peers as commoners, that shall bear any office or offices civil or military; or shall receive any pay, salary, fee, or wages by reason of any grant from his majesty; or shall have command or place of trust from or under his majesty or from any of his majesty's predecessors . . . within the realm of England, dominion of Wales, or town of Berwick-upon-Tweed, or in his Majesty's navy, or in the several islands of Jersey and Guernsey; or shall be of the household or in the service or employment of his majesty or of his royal highness the duke of York, who shall inhabit, reside, or be within the city of London or Westminster or within thirty miles distant from the same . . . ; the said person and persons shall personally appear . . . in his majesty's high court of chancery or in his majesty's court of king's bench, and there in public . . . take the several oaths of supremacy and allegiance. . . . And the said respective officers aforesaid shall also receive the sacrament of the Lord's Supper according to the usage of the Church of England . . . in some parish church upon some . . . Sunday immediately after divine service and sermon. . . .[32]

And be it further enacted . . . that all . . . that do . . . refuse to take the said oaths and sacrament in the said courts and places . . . shall be *ipso facto* adjudged incapable and disabled in law . . . to have . . . the said office or offices. . . . And be it further enacted that all . . . that shall . . . refuse to take the said oaths or the sacrament as aforesaid . . . , and yet after such neglect and refusal shall execute any of the said offices or employments after the said times expired . . . , and being thereupon lawfully convicted . . . , shall be disabled from thenceforth to sue or use any action, bill, plaint, or information in course of law, or to prosecute any suit in any court of equity or to be guardian of any child or executor or administrator of any person or capable of any legacy or deed of gift, or to bear any office within this realm of England, dominion of Wales, or town of Berwick-upon-Tweed; and shall forfeit the sum of £500, to be recovered by him that shall sue for the same. . . .

---

[32] The next article provides similar tests to be taken by every new appointee to such office within stated times after his appointment.

And be it further enacted that, if any person or persons, not bred up by his or their parent or parents from their infancy in the popish religion and professing themselves to be popish recusants, shall breed up, instruct, or educate his or their child or children, or suffer them to be instructed or educated, in the popish religion, every such person, being thereof convicted, shall be thenceforth disabled of bearing any office or place of trust or profit in church or state. . . .

And be it further enacted . . . that at the same time when the persons concerned in this act shall take the aforesaid oaths of supremacy and allegiance, they shall likewise make and subscribe this declaration following, under the same penalties and forfeitures as by this act is appointed: "I, A.B., do declare that I do believe that there is not any transubstantiation in the sacrament of the Lord's Supper, or in the elements of bread and wine, at or after the consecration thereof by any person whatsoever."

Ibid., V, 782 f.: 25 Charles II, c. 2.

(S) ACT REPEALING THE STATUTE FOR THE BURNING OF HERETICS (1678)[33]

An act for taking away the writ *de heretico comburendo*. Be it enacted . . . that the writ commonly called *breve de heretico comburendo*, with all process and proceedings thereupon . . . , and all punishment by death in pursuance of any ecclesiastical censures be from henceforth utterly taken away and abolished—any law, statute, canon, constitution, custom, or usage to the contrary . . . in any wise notwithstanding. Provided always that nothing in this act shall extend or be construed to take away or abridge the jurisdiction of Protestant archbishops or bishops or any other judges of any ecclesiastical courts, in cases of atheism, blasphemy, heresy, or schism, and other damnable doctrines and opinions, but that they may proceed to punish the same, according to his majesty's ecclesiastical laws, by excommunication, deprivation, degradation, and other ecclesiastical censures not extending to death. . . .

Ibid., V, 850: 29 Charles II, c. 9.

(T) SECOND TEST ACT (1678)

An act for the more effectual preserving the king's person and government, by disabling papists from sitting in either house of parliament. Forasmuch as divers good laws have been made for preventing the increase and danger of popery in this kingdom, which have not had the desired effects, by reason of the free access which popish recusants have had to his majesty's court, and by reason of the liberty which of late some of the recusants have had and taken to sit and vote in parliament: wherefore, and for the safety of his majesty's royal person and government, be it enacted . . . that . . . no person that now is or hereafter shall be a peer of this realm, or member of

---

[33] No. 60B.

the house of peers, shall vote or make his proxy in the house of peers, or sit there during any debate in the said house of peers—nor any person that now is or hereafter shall be a member of the house of commons shall vote in the house of commons or sit there during any debate in the said house of commons after their speaker is chosen—until such peer or member shall from time to time respectively, and in manner following, first take the several oaths of allegiance and supremacy, and make, subscribe, and audibly repeat this declaration following: "I, A.B., do solemnly and sincerely in the presence of God profess, testify, and declare that I do believe that in the sacrament of the Lord's Supper there is not any transubstantiation of the elements of bread and wine into the body and blood of Christ at or after the consecration thereof by any person whatsoever, and that the invocation or adoration of the Virgin Mary or any other saint and the sacrifice of the mass, as they are now used in the Church of Rome, are superstitious and idolatrous. And I do solemnly in the presence of God profess, testify, and declare that I do make this declaration and every part thereof in the plain and ordinary sense of the words read unto me, as they are commonly understood by English Protestants; without any evasion, equivocation, or mental reservation whatsoever; and without any dispensation already granted me for this purpose by the pope or any other authority or person whatsoever; or without any hope of any such dispensation from any person or authority whatsoever; or without thinking that I am or can be acquitted before God or man, or absolved of this declaration or any part thereof, although the pope, or any other person or persons, or power whatsoever, should dispense with or annul the same, or declare that it was null or void from the beginning." . . .[34]

Ibid., V, 894 f.: 30 Charles II, st. 2, c. 1.

(U) Habeas Corpus Act (1679)[35]

An act for the better securing the liberty of the subject and for prevention of imprisonments beyond the seas. Whereas great delays have been used by sheriffs, jailers, and other officers, to whose custody any of the king's subjects have been committed for criminal or supposed criminal matters, in making returns of writs of *habeas corpus* to them directed . . . to avoid their yielding obedience to such writs, contrary to their duty and the known laws of the land; whereby many of the king's subjects have been . . . long detained in prison in such cases where by law they are bailable, to their great charge

---

[34] The following articles establish various measures for the enforcement of these tests, including penalties to be assessed upon violators. But special exemption is made in favour of Portuguese servants of the queen, not exceeding nine in all; of such other persons as should, by order of the privy council, be given licence to reside at court for a space of no more than ten days; and of the duke of York.

[35] Cf. nos. 94A, 117A.

and vexation: for the prevention whereof and the more speedy relief of all persons imprisoned for any such criminal or supposed criminal matters, be it enacted . . . that, whensoever any person or persons shall bring any *habeas corpus* directed unto any sheriff or sheriffs, jailer, minister, or other person whatsoever for any person in his or their custody, and the said writ shall be served upon the said officer or left at the jail or prison with any of the under-officers . . . of the said officers or keepers . . . , the said officer or officers, his or their under-officers . . . , shall within three days after the service thereof as aforesaid—unless the commitment aforesaid were for treason or felony plainly and specially expressed in the warrant of commitment—. . . make return of such writ or bring or cause to be brought the body of the party so committed or restrained unto or before the lord chancellor, or lord keeper of the great seal of England for the time being, or the judges or barons of the said court from whence the said writ shall issue, or unto or before such other person . . . before whom the said writ is made returnable according to the command thereof; and shall likewise then certify the true causes of his detainer or imprisonment. . . .[36]

And for the prevention of unjust vexation by reiterated commitments for the same offence, be it enacted . . . that no person or persons, which shall be delivered or set at large upon any *habeas corpus*, shall at any time hereafter be again imprisoned or committed for the same offence by any person or persons whatsoever other than by the legal order and process of such court wherein he or they shall be bound by recognizance to appear, or other court having jurisdiction of the cause. . . .

Provided always and be it further enacted that, if any person or persons shall be committed for high treason or felony, plainly and specially expressed in the warrant of commitment . . . , [and] shall not be indicted some time in the next term sessions . . . after such commitment, it shall and may be lawful to and for the judges of the court of king's bench and justices of oyer and terminer or general jail-delivery, and they are hereby required—upon motion to them made in open court the last day of the term sessions . . . either by the prisoner or any one in his behalf—to set at liberty the prisoner upon bail, unless it appears to the judges and justices upon oath made that the witnesses for the king could not be produced the same term sessions. . . . And if any person or persons committed as aforesaid . . . shall not be indicted and tried the second term sessions . . . after his commitment . . . , he shall be discharged from his imprisonment. . . .

And for preventing illegal imprisonments in prisons beyond the

---

[36] If the place of commitment is more than twenty miles, but not over a hundred, from the place to which return is to be made, ten days are allowed; for a distance above a hundred miles, twenty days. The next article provides means whereby a prisoner may secure *habeas corpus* during the vacation of a court.

seas, be it further enacted . . . that no subject of this realm . . . shall or may be sent prisoner into Scotland, Ireland, Jersey, Guernsey, Tangier, or into any parts . . . beyond the seas which are . . . within or without the dominions of his majesty, his heirs, or successors, and that every such imprisonment is hereby enacted and adjudged to be illegal. . . .

Ibid., V, 935 f.: 31 Charles II, c. 2.

115. ROYAL DECLARATION OF INDULGENCE (1672)

Our care and endeavours for the preservation of the rights and interests of the church have been sufficiently manifested to the world by the whole course of our government since our happy restoration, and by the many and frequent ways of coercion that we have used for reducing all erring or dissenting persons and for composing the unhappy differences in matters of religion, which we found among our subjects upon our return. But, it being evident by the sad experience of twelve years that there is very little fruit of all those forcible courses, we think ourselves obliged to make use of that supreme power in ecclesiastical matters which is not only inherent in us but hath been declared and recognized to be so by several statutes and acts of parliament. And therefore we do now accordingly issue out this our royal declaration, as well for the quieting the minds of our good subjects in these points, for inviting strangers in this conjuncture to come and live under us, and for the better encouragement of all to a cheerful following of their trades and callings—from whence we hope, by the blessing of God, to have many good and happy advantages to our government—as also for preventing for the future the danger that might otherwise arise from private meetings and seditious conventicles.

And in the first place, we declare our express resolution, meaning, and intention to be that the Church of England be preserved and remain entire in its doctrine, discipline, and government, as now it stands established by law; and that this be taken to be, as it is, the basis, rule, and standard of the general and public worship of God; and that the orthodox conformable clergy do receive and enjoy the revenues belonging thereunto; and that no person, though of different opinion or persuasion, shall be exempt from paying his tithes or other dues whatsoever. And further we declare that no person shall be capable of holding any benefice, living, or ecclesiastical dignity or preferment of any kind in this kingdom of England, who is not exactly conformable.

We do in the next place declare our will and pleasure to be that the execution of all and all manner of penal laws in matters ecclesiastical against whatsoever sort of nonconformists or recusants be immediately suspended, and they are hereby suspended. And all judges of assize and jail-delivery, sheriffs, justices of the peace, mayors, bailiffs, and other officers whatsoever, whether ecclesiastical or civil, are to take notice of it, and pay due obedience thereunto; and, that there may be no pretence for any of our subjects to continue their illegal meetings and conventicles, we do declare that we shall from time to time allow a sufficient number of places, as shall be desired, in all parts of this our kingdom, for the use of such as do not conform to the Church of England to meet and assemble in, in order to their public worship and devotion—which places shall be open and free to all persons. But to prevent such disorders and inconveniences as may happen by this our indulgence, if not duly regulated, and that they may be better protected by the civil magistrate, our express will and pleasure is that none of our subjects do presume to meet in any place until such place be allowed and the teacher of that congregation be approved by us. And lest any should apprehend that this restriction should make our said allowance and approbation difficult to be obtained, we do further declare that this our indulgence as to the allowance of public places of worship, and approbation of teachers, shall extend to all sorts of nonconformists and recusants, except the recusants of the Roman Catholic religion; to whom we shall no ways allow in public places of worship, but only indulge them their share in the common exemption from the executing the penal laws and the exercise of their worship in their private houses only. And if, after this our clemency and indulgence, any of our subjects shall presume to abuse this liberty and shall preach seditiously, or to the derogation of the doctrine, discipline, or government of the established church, or shall meet in places not allowed by us, we do hereby give them warning and declare we will proceed against them with all imaginable severity. . . .

Cobbett, *Parliamentary History*, IV, 515 f.

116. PROCEEDINGS IN PARLIAMENT (1668-81)
(A) ON SKINNER V. THE EAST INDIA COMPANY (1668-70)[1]

To the honourable the commons of England in parliament assembled: The humble petition of the governor and company of the Merchants of London Trading to the East Indies humbly showeth that Thomas Skinner lately exhibited a petition to the right honourable the lords spiritual and temporal in parliament assembled against your petitioners . . . for injuries pretended to be done by your

[1] In 1661 Thomas Skinner, an independent merchant engaged in oriental trade, petitioned the king with regard to various injuries which he alleged he had suffered at the hands of the East India Company. After long delay, in 1666, his case was referred to a committee of the privy council. This body failed to arrange a settlement between the parties; and so, on the king's order, the matter was brought to the attention of the house of lords. The latter, having examined a petition addressed to them by Skinner, awarded him damages. Meanwhile the case had become the subject of political controversy, as may be seen from the following excerpts: (1) the petition of the East India Company to the house of commons; (2) a resolution in this connection by the lords; (3) subsequent proceedings in the commons; (4) the final action taken on the king's command.

petitioners' factors in the East Indies . . . ; that, though the petitioners did humbly tender a plea to their lordships for that the petition was in nature of an original complaint concerning commoners only and not brought to their lordships by writ of error . . . or any way of appeal, and that the matters therein were relievable in the courts of Westminster Hall . . . , yet their lordships have been pleased, not only to give a hearing to all the matters in the said petition contained, but have denied to grant the petitioners a commission, or so much as time to send for their witnesses now inhabiting upon the place where the injuries were pretended to be done, and without whose testimony it was impossible for the petitioners to make their defence; that, upon the said hearing, their lordships were further pleased to appoint a committee to assess damages against your petitioners, which committee is now proceeding thereon accordingly, whereby several members of this honourable house who are of the said company as well as other your petitioners may be highly detrimented. All which proceedings, as your humble petitioners humbly submit to your honourable judgments, are against the laws and statutes of this nation and custom of parliament. In tender consideration whereof, and forasmuch as these unusual and extraordinary proceedings of their lordships are not only grievous to your petitioners at present, but may also be a precedent of ill consequence to all the commons of England hereafter; and forasmuch as your petitioners have no way of relief in this case otherwise than by making their humble addresses to this honourable house: your petitioners do therefore most humbly pray that your honours will be pleased to take the premises into your grave considerations and to interpose with their lordships for your petitioners' relief therein, in such way and manner as to your great wisdoms shall seem meet. . . .

Howell, State Trials, VI, 721 f.

[7 May 1668.] . . . The house [of lords] after this took into consideration the two previous votes reported from the committee for privileges, which being read and after debate thereof, it was resolved upon the question that the house of commons' entertaining the scandalous petition of the East India Company against the lords' house of parliament and their proceedings, examinations, and votes thereupon had and made are a breach of the privileges of the house of peers, and contrary to the fair correspondency which ought to be between the two houses of parliament, and unexampled in former times. Then the second vote was read. . . . Upon this it was resolved upon the question that the house of lords' taking cognizance of the cause of Thomas Skinner, merchant—a person highly oppressed and injured in East India by the governor and company of merchants of London trading thither—and overruling the plea of the said company and adjudging £5000 damages thereupon against the said governor and company is agreeable to the laws of the land and well warranted by the law and custom of parliament and justified by many parliamentary precedents, ancient and modern. . . .

Reports of Historical MSS. Commission, VIII, App., pt. 1, 172 f.

[2 May 1668.] Sir Robert Howard reports from the committee, to whom it was referred to consider of the whole matter of the debate upon the resolves returned from the committee to which the petition of the Merchants of London Trading to the East Indies was committed, and to bring in the votes altered and drawn up according to the debate and sense of the house, that the committee had drawn up the resolves accordingly; which he read and after delivered the same in at the clerk's table. And the votes were twice read and, upon the question, severally agreed; which are as followeth, *viz.*:—

That the lords' taking cognizance of and their proceeding upon the matter set forth and contained in the petition of Thomas Skinner, merchant, against the governor and company of Merchants of London Trading to the East Indies . . . , and their lordships' overruling the plea of the said governor and company . . . , being a common plea, is not agreeable to the laws of the land and tending to deprive the subject of his right, ease, and benefit due to him by the said laws. . . . That Thomas Skinner, merchant, in commencing and prosecuting a suit by petition in the house of lords against the company of Merchants Trading to the East Indies, wherein several members of this house are parties concerned with the said company in their particular interests and estates, and in procuring judgment therein . . . , is a breach of the privilege of this house. . . .

[9 May 1668.] Resolved, etc., that whosoever shall be aiding or assisting in putting the order or sentence of the house of lords in the case of Thomas Skinner against the East India Company in execution shall be deemed a betrayer of the rights and liberties of the commons of England and an infringer of the privileges of this house. . . .

[4 December 1669.] . . . The house of commons, being informed that Sir Samuel Bernardiston, a commoner of England, has been called before the house of lords and hath had a judgment passed upon him and a fine imposed . . . , resolved, etc., that a conference be desired of the lords upon the matter aforesaid . . . and also upon the proceedings concerning Thomas Skinner and the East India Company. Resolved, etc., that a committee be appointed to prepare and draw up reasons to be insisted upon at the conference to be had with the lords touching the matter aforesaid. . . .

[8 December, 1669.] The house then resumed the consideration of the report of Sir Robert Howard of the heads and proposals brought in from the committee appointed to draw up reasons to be insisted on at the conference to be had with the lords. . . . The first head was twice read and, with the addition of the word "of," upon the question agreed to. . . .[2] The fifth proposition was read twice and upon the question agreed.

---

[2] Various amendments are made to the other propositions.

1. That it is an inherent right of every commoner of England to prepare and present petitions to the house of commons in case of grievance, and of the house of commons to receive the same.
2. That it is the undoubted right and privilege of the house of commons to judge and determine touching the nature and matter of such petitions, how far they are fit or unfit to be received.
3. That no court whatsoever hath power to judge or censure any petition prepared for, or presented to, and received by the house of commons, unless transmitted from thence or the matter is complained of by them.
4. That, whereas a petition by the governor and company of Merchants Trading to the East Indies was presented to the house of commons by Sir Samuel Bernardiston and others complaining of grievance therein, which the lords have censured as a scandalous paper or libel, the said censure and proceedings of the lords against the said Sir Samuel Bernardiston are contrary to and in subversion of the rights and privileges of the house of commons, and liberties of the commons of England.
5. That the continuance upon record of the judgment given by the lords and complained of by the house of commons in the last session of this parliament, in the case of Thomas Skinner and the East India Company, is prejudicial to the rights of the commons of England. . . .

Hatsell, Precedents, III, 184-203.

[22 February 1670.] . . . Resolved that an entry be made in the journal of this house of his majesty's gracious speech, which is as followeth, viz.:—

"My lords and gentlemen: I did very earnestly recommend to you the other day that you would not suffer any differences between yourselves to be revived; and I think it of so great importance that I have sent for you again upon the said subject. I remember very well that the case of Skinner was first sent by me to the lords. I have, therefore, thought myself concerned to offer to you what I judge the best and safest way to put an end to the difference; and, indeed, I can find no other. I will myself give present order to raze all records and entries in this matter both in the council books and in the exchequer; and do desire you to do the like in both houses, that no memory may remain of this dispute between you. And then, I hope, all future apprehensions will be secured."

Resolved that, in obedience to his majesty's command in his speech, a razure or vacat be made in the journals of this house of all the matters therein contained relating to the business between the East India Company and Skinner. Which was accordingly done in the house. . . .

Journals of the Commons, IX, 126.

(B) ON THE RIGHT OF THE LORDS TO AMEND MONEY BILLS (1671)

. . . Mr. Attorney General reports [to the commons] the conference had with the lords. Resolved, etc., that the lords' reasons and the answer of this house be entered in the journal of this house; which are as followeth, *viz.*:—

Thursday, April 20. This conference was desired by their lordships upon the subject matter of the last conference, concerning the bill for impositions on merchandise, etc., wherein the commons communicated to the lords, as their resolution, that there is a fundamental right in that house alone in bills of rates and impositions on merchandise as to the matter, the measure, and the time. And, though their lordships had neither reason nor precedent offered by the commons to back that resolution, but were told that this was a right so fundamentally settled in the commons that they could not give reasons for it . . . , yet the lords in parliament, upon full consideration thereof . . . , are come to this resolution . . . : that the power exercised by the house of peers, in making the amendments and abatements in the bill entitled An Act for an Additional Imposition on Several Foreign Commodities . . . , both as to the matter, measure, and time concerning the rates and impositions on merchandise, is a fundamental, inherent, and undoubted right of the house of peers; from which they cannot depart.

Reasons, etc. The great happiness of the government of this kingdom is that nothing can be done in order to the legislature but what is considered by both houses before the king's sanction be given unto it; and the greatest security to all the subjects of this kingdom is that the houses, by their constitution, do not only give assistance but are mutual checks to each other.

Secondly, consult the writs of summons to parliament, and you will find the lords are excluded from none of the great and arduous affairs of the kingdom and Church of England, but are called to treat and give their counsel upon them all without exception.

Thirdly, we find no footsteps in record or history for this new claim of the house of commons. We would see that charter or contract produced, by which the lords divested themselves of this right and appropriated it to the commons with an exclusion of themselves. Till then we cannot consent to shake or remove foundations, in the laying whereof it will not be denied that the lords and grandees of the kingdom had the greatest hand.

Fourthly, if this right should be denied, the lords have not a negative voice allowed them in bills of this nature. For, if the lords, who have the power of treating, advising, giving counsel, and applying remedies, cannot amend, abate, or refuse a bill in part, by what consequence of reason can they enjoy a liberty to reject the whole? When the commons shall think fit to question it, they may pretend the same grounds for it.

Fifthly, in any case of judicature—which is undoubtedly and indisputably the peculiar right and privilege of the house of lords—if their lordships send down a bill to the commons for giving judgment in a legislative way, they allow and acknowledge the same right in the commons, to amend, change, and alter such bills as the lords have exercised in this bill of impositions sent up by the commons.

Sixthly, by this new maxim of the house of commons, a hard and ignoble choice is left to the lords—either to refuse the crown supplies when they are most necessary or to consent to ways and proportions of aid which neither their own judgment or interest nor the good of the government and people can admit.

Seventhly, if positive assertion can introduce a right, what security have the lords that the house of commons shall not in other bills—pretended to be for the general good of the commons, whereof they will conceive themselves the fittest judges—claim the same peculiar privilege . . . when they shall judge it necessary or expedient?

Eighthly, and whereas you say this is the only poor thing which you can value yourselves upon to the king, their lordships have commanded us to tell you that they rather desire to increase than anyways to diminish the value and esteem of the house of commons, not only with his majesty, but with the whole kingdom; but they cannot give way that it should be raised by the undervaluing of the house of peers . . . , by the denying unto it those just powers which the constitution of this government and the law of the land hath lodged in it for service and benefit of both. . . .[3]

Saturday, 22 April. The commons have desired this conference to preserve a good correspondence with the house of peers. . . . The commons are not without hopes of giving your lordships full satisfaction in the point in question. . . . The commons confess that the best rule for deciding questions of right between the two houses is the law and usage of parliament, and that the best evidences of that usage and custom of parliament are the most frequent and authentic precedents. Therefore the commons will first examine the precedents your lordships seem to rely upon; then they will produce those by which their right is asserted; and, in the last place, they will consider the reasons upon which your lordships ground yourselves. . . .[4]

Thus, an uninterrupted possession of this privilege ever since 9 Henry IV, confirmed by a multitude of precedents both before and after, not shaken by one precedent for these three hundred years, is now required to be delivered up, or an end put to all further discourse. Which opinion, if it be adhered to, is—as much as in your lordship lies—to put an end to all further transactions between the houses in matter of money. . . . Because there appears not to the commons any colour, from the precedents cited by your lordships, why your opinions should be so fixed in this point, we suppose the main defence is in the reasons . . . given for it. . . .

1. Your lordships' first reason is from the happiness of the constitution, that the two houses are mutual checks upon each other Answer: So they are still; for your lordships have a negative to the

---

[3] Here the lords cite numerous precedents.
[4] Here the commons cite two folio pages of precedents.

whole. But, on the other side, it would be a double check upon his majesty's affairs if the king may not rely upon the *quantum* when once his people have given it. . . .

2. Your lordships' reasons drawn from the writ of summons is as little concluding. For, though the writ do not exclude you from any affairs, yet it is only *de quibusdam arduis negotiis*, and must be understood of such as by course of parliament are proper; else the commons, upon the like ground, may entitle themselves to judicature. . . .

3. Your lordships proceed to demand: "Where is that record or contract in parliament to be found, where the lords appropriate this right to the commons in exclusion of themselves?" Answer: To this rhetorical question the commons pray they may answer by another question, "Where is that record or contract by which the commons submitted that judicature should be appropriated to the lords in exclusion of themselves?" Wherever your lordships find the last record they will show the first endorsed upon the back of the same roll. Truth is, precedents there are where both sides do exercise those several rights; but none how either side came by them.

4. If the lords may deny the whole, why not a part? Else the commons may at last pretend to bar a negative voice. Answer: The king must deny the whole of every bill or pass it; yet this takes not away his negative voice. The lord and commons must accept the whole general pardon or deny it; yet this takes not away their negative. . . .

5. Your lordships say: "Judicature is undoubtedly ours, yet in bills of judicature we allow the commons to amend and alter. Why should not the commons allow us the same privilege in bills of money?" Answer: If contracts were now to be made for privileges, the offer might seem fair. But yet the commons should profit little by it; for your lordships do now industriously avoid all bills of that nature, and choose to do many things by your own power which ought to be done by the legislative. . . .

6. Your lordships say you are put to an ignoble choice, either to refuse the king's supplies when they are most necessary or to consent to such ways and proportions which neither your own judgment nor the good of the government or people can admit. Answer: We pray your lordships to observe that this reason, first, makes your lordships' judgment to be the measure of the welfare of the commons of England; secondly, it gives you power to raise and increase taxes as well as to abate. . . . But it is a very ignoble choice put upon the king and his people, that either his majesty must demand and the commons give so small an aid as can never be diminished or else run the hazard of your lordships' re-examination of the rates, whose proportions in all taxes, in comparison to what the commonality pay, is very inconsiderable.

7. If positive assertion can introduce right, the lords have no security, but the commons may extend a right as they judge it necessary or expedient. Answer: We hope no assertions or denials, though never so positive, shall give or take away a right; but we rely upon

usage on our side, and non-usage on your lordships' part, as the best evidences by which your lordships or we can claim any privilege.

8. Your lordships profess a desire to raise our esteem with his majesty and the whole kingdom, but not by the undervaluation of the house of peers. Answer: We have so great confidence in his majesty's goodness that we assure ourselves nothing can lessen his majesty's esteem of our dutiful affections to him. . . .

It was unanimously resolved that the thanks of the house be returned to Mr. Attorney General for his great pains and care in preparing and drawing up the reasons delivered to the lords in answer to their reasons; which was by him performed to the great satisfaction of this house in vindication of their privilege and [the] just and undoubted right of the commons of England. . . .[5]

Ibid., IX, 239-44.

(C) ON THE DECLARATION OF INDULGENCE (1673)[6]

[14 February.] . . . Mr. Powle reports from the committee appointed to prepare and draw up a petition and address to his majesty the said petition and address; which he read in his place and, after, delivered the same in at the clerk's table. And the same, being again twice read, is as followeth, *viz.*:—

Most gracious sovereign We, your majesty's most loyal and faithful subjects, the commons assembled in parliament, do in the first place, as in all duty bound, return your majesty our most humble and hearty thanks for the many gracious promises and assurances, which your majesty hath several times during this present parliament given to us, that your majesty would secure and maintain unto us the true reformed Protestant religion, our liberties, and properties; which most gracious assurances your majesty hath out of your great goodness been pleased to renew unto us more particularly at the opening of this present session of parliament. And further we crave leave humbly to represent that we have with all duty and expedition taken into our consideration several parts of your majesty's last speech to us, and withal the declaration therein mentioned for indulgence to dissenters, dated the 15th of March last. And we find ourselves bound in duty to inform your majesty that penal statutes in matter ecclesiastical cannot be suspended but by act of parliament. We therefore, the knights, citizens, and burgesses of your majesty's house of commons, do most humbly beseech your majesty that the said laws may have their free course until it shall be otherwise provided for by act of parliament; and that your majesty would graciously be pleased to give such directions herein, that no apprehensions or jealousies may remain in the hearts of your majesty's good and faithful subjects.

Resolved, etc., that this house doth agree with the committee in the

---

[5] While this dispute was still going on, the king prorogued the parliament. Cf. document E, below.
[6] No. 115.

petition and address by them drawn up to be presented to his majesty....

[24 February.] ... Mr. Secretary Coventry reports and presents in writing from his majesty his answer to the humble petition and address of this house, which ... is as followeth, *viz.*:—

Charles R. His majesty hath received an address from you, and he hath seriously considered of it, and returneth you this answer: that he is very much troubled that that declaration which he put out for ends so necessary to the quiet of his kingdom, and especially in that conjuncture, should have proved the cause of disquiet in this house of commons and give occasion to the questioning of his power in ecclesiastics; which he finds not done in the reigns of any of his ancestors. He is sure he never had thoughts of using it otherwise than as it hath been entrusted in him—to the peace and establishment of the Church of England and the ease of all his subjects in general. Neither doth he pretend to the right of suspending any laws wherein the properties, rights, or liberties of any of his subjects are concerned, nor to alter anything in the established doctrine or discipline of the Church of England; but his only design in this was to take off the penalties the statutes inflict upon the dissenters, and which he believes, when well considered of, you yourselves would not wish executed according to the rigour and letter of the law. Neither hath he done this with any thought of avoiding or precluding the advice of his parliament; and, if any bill shall be offered him which shall appear more proper to attain the aforesaid ends and secure the peace of the church and kingdom, when tendered in due manner to him, he will show how readily he will concur in all ways that shall appear good for the kingdom....

[26 February.] ... Mr. Powle reports ... an answer agreed by the committee ..., which ... is as followeth, *viz.*:—

Most gracious sovereign: We, your majesty's most humble and loyal subjects, the knights, citizens, and burgesses in this present parliament assembled, do render to your sacred majesty our most dutiful thanks for that, to our unspeakable comfort, your majesty hath been pleased so often to reiterate unto us those gracious promises and assurances of maintaining the religion now established and the liberties and properties of your people. And we do not in the least measure doubt but that your majesty had the same gracious intentions in giving satisfaction to your subjects by your answer to our last petition and address. Yet, upon a serious consideration thereof, we find that the said answer is not sufficient to clear the apprehensions that may justly remain in the minds of your people by your majesty's having claimed a power to suspend penal statutes in matters ecclesiastical, and which your majesty does still seem to assert ... to be entrusted in the crown and never questioned in the reigns of any your ancestors—wherein we humbly conceive your majesty hath been very much misinformed; since no such power was ever claimed or exercised by any of your majesty's predecessors, and, if it should be admitted, might tend to the interrupting of the free course of the laws and altering the legislative power, which hath always been acknowledged to reside in your majesty and your two houses of parliament. We do therefore, with an unanimous consent, become again most humble suitors unto your sacred majesty that you would be pleased to give us a full and satisfactory answer to our said petition and address, and that your majesty would take such effectual order that the proceedings in this matter may not for the future be drawn into consequence or example.

. . . Resolved, etc., that the whole address be agreed to as it was brought in by the committee. . . .

Ibid., IX, 252, 256, 257.

[8 March.] . . . His majesty sitting in his royal throne, adorned with his crown and regal ornaments, commanded the gentleman usher of the black rod to give notice to the house of commons that they attend his majesty presently. The commons being come with their speaker, his majesty made this short speech following: "My lords and gentlemen: . . . If there be any scruple remain with you concerning the suspension of penal laws, I here faithfully promise you that what hath been done in that particular shall not for the future be drawn either into consequence or example. . . ."

Next the lord chancellor reported . . . that his majesty had the last night, in pursuance of what he then intended and declared this morning concerning the suspension of penal laws not being for the future drawn either into consequence or example, caused the original declaration under the great seal to be cancelled in his presence; whereof himself and several other lords of the council were witnesses. . . .

Journals of the Lords, XII, 549.

(D) ON SHIRLEY V. FAGG (1675)[7]

[14 May.] . . . Whereas Thomas Shirley, esquire, his majesty's physician in ordinary, hath a cause depending in this house by way of appeal against Sir John Fagg, a member of the house of commons, and by the law and course of parliament ought to have privilege and freedom from arrest: it is ordered by the lords spiritual and temporal in parliament assembled that the said Thomas Shirley

---

[7] This protracted quarrel between the two houses of parliament began over an appeal in a case of equity brought before the lords by Thomas Shirley against Sir John Fagg, a member of the commons. The original protest of the commons raised the issue of parliamentary privilege only; but, as further appeals of the same sort came to be made, the commons extended their claim of privilege to deny the equitable jurisdiction of the upper house. This latter phase of the dispute, interrupted by the summer prorogation, was revived in November, when the king once more prorogued parliament. Eventually, since the lords persisted in their course, the commons allowed the matter to drop.

be . . . privileged and protected accordingly by the authority of this house during the depending of his said cause in this house; and all persons whatsoever are hereby prohibited from arresting or otherwise molesting the said Thomas Shirley upon any pretence whatsoever. . . .

Ibid., XII, 692.

[20 May.] Sir Thomas Lee reports from the committee appointed to draw up reasons to be offered at the conference to be had with the lords upon the privileges of this house . . . ; which were . . . severally agreed to . . . as followeth, *viz.*:—

1. That by the laws and usage of parliament privilege of parliament belongs to every member of the house of commons in all cases except treason, felony, and breach of the peace; which hath often been declared in parliament without any exception of appeals before the lords.

2. That the reason of that privilege is that the members of the house of commons may freely attend the public affairs in that house without disturbance or interruption; which doth extend as well to appeals before the house of peers as to proceedings in other courts.

3. That, by the constant course and usage of parliament, no member of the house of commons can attend the house of lords without the especial leave of that house first obtained, much less be summoned or compelled so to do.

4. If the lords shall proceed to hear and determine any appeal where the party neither can nor ought to attend, such proceedings would be contrary to the rules of justice.

5. That the not determining of an appeal against a member of the house of commons is not a failure of justice, but only a suspension of proceedings in a particular case during the continuance of that parliament, which is but temporary.

6. That, in case it were a failure of justice, it is not to be remedied by the house of lords alone, but it may be by act of parliament. . . .

[3 June.] . . . Mr. Vaughan reports that the lord privy seal did manage the conference . . . , which Mr. Vaughan did report to the house to the effect following, *viz.*:—

. . . The lords in parliament [are the court] where his majesty is highest in his royal estate and where the last resort of judging upon writs of error and appeals in equity, in all causes and over all persons, is undoubtedly fixed and permanently lodged. It is an unexampled usurpation and breach of privilege against the house of peers that their orders or judgments should be disputed or endeavoured to be controlled, or the execution thereof obstructed, by the lower house of parliament, who are no court nor have authority to administer an oath or give any judgment. It is a transcendent invasion on the right and liberty of the subject and against Magna Carta, the Petition of Right, and many other laws, which have provided that no freeman shall be imprisoned or otherwise restrained of his liberty but by due process of law. This tends to the subversion of the government of this kingdom, and to the introducing of arbitrariness and disorder, because it is in nature of an injunction from the lower house who have no authority nor power of judicature over inferior subjects, much less over the king and lords against the orders and judgments of the supreme court. . . .

A debate arising thereupon, resolved, etc., that a conference be desired with the lords upon the subject matter of the last conference. . . .

[4 June.] . . . Sir Thomas Lee reports from the committee the reasons agreed to be offered at the conference to be had with the lords . . . ; which were . . . severally agreed and are as followeth, *viz.*:—

. . . 'Tis not against the king's dignity for the house of commons to punish by imprisonment a commoner that is guilty of violating their privileges—that being according to the known laws and custom of parliament and the right of their privileges declared by the king's royal predecessors in former parliaments, and by himself in this. But your lordships' claiming to be the supreme court, and that his majesty is highest in his royal estate in the court of judicature there, is a diminution of the dignity of the king who is highest in his royal estate in full parliament. . . . The commons did not infringe any privileges of the house of peers, but only defend and maintain their own. On the other side, your lordships do highly entrench upon the rights and privileges of the house of commons, denying them to be a court or to have any authority or power of judicature; which, if admitted, will leave them without any authority or power to preserve themselves. As to what your lordships call a transcendent invasion of the rights and liberty of the subject . . . , the house of commons presume that your lordships know that neither the Great Charter, the Petition of Right, nor any other laws do take away the law and custom of parliament, or of either house of parliament. . . . But the commons cannot find, by Magna Carta or by any other law or ancient custom of parliament, that your lordships have any jurisdiction in cases of appeal from courts of equity. . . .

[19 November.] . . . Whereas this house hath been informed of several appeals depending in the house of lords from courts of equity, to the great violation of the rights and liberties of the commons of England, it is this day resolved and declared that whosoever shall solicit, plead, or prosecute any appeal against any commoner of England from any court of equity before the house of lords shall be deemed and taken a betrayer of the rights and liberties of the commons of England and shall be proceeded against accordingly.

Resolved, etc., that copies of this resolution and declaration be forthwith publicly affixed upon the door of the lobby of this house and Westminster Hall gate . . . , to the end all persons concerned may take notice thereof. . . .

Journals of the Commons, IX, 342 f., 352, 354, 380 f.

[20 November.] . . . Whereas this day was appointed for hearing the cause at the bar upon the appeal of Dr. Thomas Shirley against Sir John Fagg . . . , it is ordered by the lords spiritual and temporal in parliament assembled that this house will hear the said cause by counsel at the bar on Monday the 22d instant. . . .

The lord Grey of Rolleston acquainted the house that this morning he did see a paper affixed up at Westminster Hall gate tending much to the dishonour of this house and derogatory to its judicature. . . . Ordered . . . that the paper . . . , posted up in several places and signed "Will. Goldsborough, Clerk of the House of Commons," against the judicature of the house of peers in cases of appeals from courts of equity is illegal, unparliamentary, and tending to the dissolution of the government. . . .

Journals of the Lords, XIII, 32 f.

(E) ON THE RIGHT OF THE LORDS TO AMEND MONEY BILLS (1678)

. . . Mr. Solicitor General reports from the committee, to whom it was, amongst other things, referred to prepare and draw up a state[ment] of the rights of the commons in granting of money, a vote agreed by the committee; which he read in his place, and afterwards delivered the same in at the clerk's table, where the same was read and upon the question agreed, and is as followeth, *viz.*:—

Resolved, etc., that all aids and supplies . . . to his majesty in parliament are the sole gift of the commons, and all bills for the granting of any such aids and supplies ought to begin with the commons; and that it is the undoubted and sole right of the commons to direct, limit, and appoint in such bills the ends, purposes, considerations, conditions, limitations, and qualifications of such grants, which ought not to be changed or altered by the house of lords.

Journals of the Commons, IX, 509.

(F) ON THE IMPEACHMENT OF DANBY (1679)[8]

[20 March.] . . . Resolved . . . that a message be sent to the lords to put them in mind of the impeachment of high treason exhibited against Thomas, earl of Danby, in the name of the commons of

---

[8] At the end of the previous year the earl of Danby, principal minister of Charles II, had been impeached for alleged traitorous designs in his conduct of foreign policy. The king had at once intervened to save his minister by dissolving parliament. The following proceedings took place in the new parliament, which, for the same reason, was dissolved shortly after its prorogation on 27 May.

England, and to desire that he may be forthwith committed to safe custody.

Resolved, etc., that it be referred to the committee of secrecy to draw up further articles against Thomas, earl of Danby. . . .

[7 May.] . . . A message from the lords by Mr. Justice Atkins and Mr. Justice Dolben:—

Mr. Speaker, we are commanded by the lords to acquaint this house with an order yesterday made concerning the earl of Danby, *viz.*: Whereas the earl of Danby hath adhered to the plea of his pardon and prayed to be heard by his counsel to make good the validity of his pardon; and whereas the commons have, by their speaker in proper person, demanded judgment against the said earl, as conceiving his pardon to be illegal and void: it is ordered by the lords spiritual and temporal in parliament assembled that Saturday next be appointed for hearing of the earl of Danby to make good his said plea. And we are further to acquaint you with the resolve also yesterday passed, *viz.*: Resolved by the lords spiritual and temporal in parliament assembled that the five lords in the Tower . . .[9] shall be brought to their trials upon the impeachment against them this day seven-night. . . .

[22 May.] . . . Ordered that a committee be appointed to inspect the journals of this house and take an account thereout of all proceedings relating, as well to the impeachment against the earl of Danby, as the impeachment against the other lords in the Tower. . . .

[23 May.] . . . Mr. Papillon reports from the committee, appointed to inspect the journals of this house, a report agreed upon by the committee . . . of all the proceedings relating, as well to the impeachment and bill against the earl of Danby, as to the impeachments against the other lords in the Tower; which he read to the house.

Ordered that Sir Stephen Fox do forthwith produce to this house his ledger book, cash book, and journal, and his receipts for money by him paid for secret service. . . .

[24 May.] . . . Sir Francis Winnington reports from the committee appointed to draw up further articles and prepare evidence against the earl of Danby several informations given to the said committee of moneys paid for secret service to the members of the last parliament. . . .[10]

Ibid., IX, 572, 614, 629, 631.

[23 May.] . . . Sir Stephen Fox: I came but just now from my lodgings by water, and I was told of the order. . . . I know not whether I can do what you command me in any time. I have paid

---

[9] The peers accused of complicity in the Popish Plot.

[10] In connection with these proceedings the official journal is supplemented from the report of debates made by Anchitell Grey, at that time a member of the house. It should be noted that by the king's secret service money is meant the fund used for building up a political following.

much money for secret service, but for these four years I have paid none. I have paid it as the king's bounty and under such other titles. . . .

Mr. Sacheverell: I desire to know of him, during the time he paid money for secret service, whether he cannot remember a name. If he cannot, I can.

The speaker: Who did you pay money to, of the members of the last parliament, for secret service?

Sir Stephen Fox: These are hard circumstances I am under—either to disobey the house or to divulge a secret by the king's command. I can name so few persons that it will give no satisfaction to the house. . . . Upon my memory, I cannot tell who I paid money to for secret service and who upon other accounts. I humbly pray that I may not be put to answer.

Sir Robert Peyton: Fox has receipts from the persons, and those will justify him. Possibly some of the persons may be in his eye. . . .[11]

Mr. Seymour: . . . I would have Fox answer you whether I received any money before I was speaker. In the presence of God I speak it, I never directly nor indirectly disposed of any money for secret service. I told the king that my fortune was not sufficient for that service [of the speakership], and I was paid the money out of the exchequer. But that was so troublesome I desired it might be paid another way; and it was the only favour Lord Danby ever did me, to let me receive it out of the money appointed for secret service. . . .

[24 May.] . . . Sir Francis Winnington . . . : I have brought every particular information, and you shall see whether your members have any wrong. There was £20,000 per annum paid quarterly by the commissioners of excise for secret service to members, etc. . . . ; whereof no account was given to the exchequer but for secret service. . . . Though Sir Stephen Fox has taken a great deal of matter out of my hands, yet there are some more than he has acquainted you with who have received money: *viz.*, to Sir Richard Wiseman and one Knight . . . , each of them £400 per annum; Mr. Roberts, at one or two payments, £500, and Mr. Price £400. Sir John Fowell, at twice, had £500 of Fox. . . . The book of £20,000 was increased by Danby in his time, for formerly it was not above £12,000 per annum for pensions. . . . Before the parliament did sit, there were greater sums paid than at other times. The paper the committee took, etc., mentions other persons. . . .

Sir Thomas Clarges: I move that persons who have received any

---

[11] After further discussion, the clerk was ordered to read the names of the members of the previous parliament. Fox then asserted that the speaker, Mr. Seymour, had received from him £1500 at the end of each session, and that twenty-seven other members had been annually paid sums ranging from £200 to £1000.

money the last parliament may be incapacitated of any trust in the government and refund what they have had.

Sir Francis Winnington: When such a report is brought in, it must be read at the table and I am to be discharged of the papers, and then I shall make motion for your service. . . . Another business has intervened. . . . I move therefore that there may be some way or method to know the bottom of this, whether you will call witnesses to the bar or to the committee. Apply your remedy when you know the disease. I do say that, if any man takes money to sell his country, I would use the utmost power of punishment, that parliaments may not be lost. . . .

Colonel Titus: It is no crime at all to have money nor pension, but to have it for an ill use. Therefore, let every member concerned be heard in his place. He may justify himself. . . .

Colonel Whitley: I am one under that unfortunate list of pensions. I was one of those . . . for the farming of the excise, etc. . . . I had in all £900 which I received at several times. This is the true state of the case. If I did betray my country, etc., I am not only fit to be turned out of the house, but out of the world. I have had money a long time due to me, and can get none of it. Be pleased to examine what relates to me as publicly as you please. . . .

Mr. Bennet: Pray, let us speak with a bounty-man.

Sir Philip Howard: If my case be distinct from others, I hope I shall be so judged. I am one of those to be considered under the head of farmers of the excise, and I desire I may come under the head of those who came in upon a valuable consideration.

Mr. Harbord: This may well admit of a distinction, but not till you have farther heard the matter. If you find that the king's bounty went to one sort of parliament-men and not to another, you may guess by that; for I could in the last parliament have told you how the question would go. If a pensioner went not well, slash!—he was put out of his pension. . . .

Grey, Debates of the Commons, VII, 316-31.

[26 May.] . . . Mr. Sacheverell reports from the committee appointed to draw up reasons why this house cannot proceed to the trial of the lords before judgment given upon the earl of Danby's plea of his pardon . . . that the committee had agreed upon an answer to be returned to the last message of the house of peers . . . , which he read in his place and afterwards delivered the same in at the clerk's table, where the same were again read and, with some amendments made at the table . . . , agreed; and are as followeth, *viz.*:—

. . . The commons therefore are obliged not to proceed to the trial of any of the five lords . . . , but to adhere to their former vote; and for their so doing . . . do offer you these reasons following:—

(1) Because your lordships have received the earl of Danby's plea of his pardon with a very long and unusual protestation, wherein he

hath aspersed his majesty by false suggestions; as if his majesty had commanded or countenanced the crimes he stands charged with. . . . (2) The setting up a pardon to be a bar of an impeachment defeats the whole use and effect of impeachments. For, should this point be admitted . . . , it would totally discourage the exhibiting any for the future; whereby the chief institution for the preservation of the government would be destroyed and, consequently, the government itself. And therefore the case of the said earl, which in consequence concerns all impeachments, ought to be determined before that of the said five lords, which is but their particular case. . . . The house of commons, an excellent conserver of liberty, is solely entrusted with the first propositions concerning the levies of moneys and the impeaching of those who for their own ends—though countenanced by any surreptitiously gotten command of the king—have violated that law which he is bound, when he knows it, to protect. . . . And the lords, being entrusted with the judicatory power, are an excellent screen and bank between the prince and the people, to assist each against any encroachments of the other and by just judgment to preserve that law which ought to be the rule of every one of the three. Therefore, the power legally placed in both houses is more than sufficient to preserve and restrain the power of tyranny. (3) Until the commons of England have right done them against this plea of pardon, they may justly apprehend that the whole justice of the kingdom, in the case of the five lords, may be obstructed and defeated by pardons of the like nature. . . .

Journals of the Commons, IX, 631 f.

(G) ON THE PRINTING OF VOTES IN THE COMMONS (1681)

[24 March.] . . . Sir John Hotham: Mr. Speaker, what I am about to move concerns us all. The last parliament, when you were moved to print your votes, it was for the security of the nation and you found it so. It prevented ill representations of us to the world by false copies of our votes, and none doubted your honour in the care of it. And I am confident that this house will be no more ashamed of their actions than the last was. Printing our votes will be for the honour of the king and the safety of the nation. I am confident, if it had been necessary, you would have had petitions from the parts I come from, that your actions might be made public. As I came hither, everybody almost that I met upon the road cried, "God bless you!" I move, therefore, that your votes may be ordered to be printed with the rest of your proceedings. . . .

Mr. Secretary Jenkins: I beg pardon if I consent not to the motion of printing the votes, etc. Consider the gravity of this assembly. There is no great assembly in Christendom that does it. It is against the gravity of this assembly and it is a sort of appeal to the people. It is against your gravity and I am against it.

Mr. Boscawen: If you had been a privy council, then it were fit what you do should be kept secret; but your journal books are open and copies of your votes in every coffee-house. And if you print them not, half-votes will be dispersed to your prejudice. This printing is like plain Englishmen, who are not ashamed of what they do, and the people you represent will have a true account of what you do. You may prevent publishing what parts of your transactions you will and print the rest.

Mr. Leveson Gower: I find that those who write our votes and transactions and send them all England over are favoured, and I believe that no gentleman in the house will be against printing them but Jenkins. I hope you will not be ashamed of what you do; therefore I am for printing your votes.

Colonel Mildmay: By experience we have found that, when former parliaments have been prorogued or dissolved, they have been sent away with a declaration against them. If our actions be naught, let the world judge of them; if they be good, let them have their virtue. It is fit that all Christendom should have notice of what you do, and posterity of what you have done; and I hope they will do as you do. Therefore I am for printing the votes.

Sir Francis Winnington: Because what has been said by Jenkins is a single opinion, for he says, "Printing is an appeal to the people," I hope the house will take notice that printing our votes is not contrary to law. But pray who sent us hither? The privy council is constituted by the king, but the house of commons is by the choice of the people. I think it not natural nor rational that the people, who sent us hither, should not be informed of our actions. In the Long Parliament it was a trade amongst clerks to write votes, and it was then said by a learned gentleman that it was no offence to inform the people of votes of parliament, etc., and they ought to have notice of them. The Long Parliament were wise in their generation to conceal many things they did from the people, and the clerk who dispersed the votes was sent away and nothing done to him. . . .

Grey, *Debates of the Commons*, VIII, 292 f.

[24 March.] . . . Resolved that the votes and proceedings of this house be printed, and that the care of the printing thereof and the appointment of the printers be committed to Mr. Speaker. . . .

Journals of the Commons, IX, 708.

117. RECORDS OF JUDICIAL CASES (1670-88)

(A) Bushell's Case (1670)[1]

The king's writ of *habeas corpus* . . . issued out of this court, directed to the then sheriffs of London to have the body of Edward

---

[1] In 1670 Edward Bushell, together with eleven other members of a jury, was committed to prison for having acquitted certain persons—among them the famous William Penn—charged with riotous assembly. The legality of this imprisonment then came before the court of king's bench through *habeas corpus*

Bushell, by them detained in prison, together with the day and cause of his caption and detention . . . , before this court, to do and receive as the court should consider. . . . The writ of *habeas corpus* is now the most usual remedy by which a man is restored again to his liberty if he have been against law deprived of it. . . .

In the present case it is returned that the prisoner, being a juryman among others charged at the sessions court of the Old Bailey to try the issue between the king and Penn and Mead upon an indictment for assembling unlawfully and tumultuously, "did *contra plenam et manifestam evidentiam* openly given in court acquit the prisoners indicted, in contempt of the king," etc.

The court hath no knowledge, by this return, whether the evidence given were full and manifest or doubtful, lame, and dark, or indeed evidence at all material to the issue; because it is not returned what evidence in particular . . . was given. . . . Another fault in the return is that the jurors are not said to have acquitted the persons indicted against full and manifest evidence corruptly and knowing the said evidence to be full and manifest against the persons indicted; for, how manifest soever the evidence was, if it were not manifest to them . . . , it was not a finable fault, nor deserving imprisonment—upon which difference the law of punishing jurors for false verdicts principally depends. . . .

I would know whether anything be more common than for two men—students, barristers or judges—to deduce contrary and opposite conclusions out of the same case in law. And is there any difference that two men should infer distinct conclusions from the same testimony? . . . And this often is the case of the judge and jury.

I conclude, therefore, that this return, charging the prisoners to have acquitted Penn and Mead against full and manifest evidence . . . , without saying that they did know and believe that evidence to be full and manifest against the indicted persons, is no cause of fine or imprisonment. . . .

We come now to the next part of the return, *viz.*: "That the jury acquitted those indicted against the direction of the court in matter of law, openly given and declared to them in court." The words, "that the jury did acquit against the direction of the court in matter of law," literally taken . . . , are insignificant and not intelligible. For no issue can be joined of matter in law; no jury can be charged with the trial of matter in law barely; no evidence ever was or can be given to a jury of what is law, or not; nor no such oath can be given to, or taken by, a jury, to try matter in law; nor no attaint can lie for such a false oath. Therefore we must take off this veil and colour of words, which make a show of being something and in truth are nothing.

If the meaning of these words, "finding against the direction of

---

proceedings (cf. no. 114U), as a result of which the prisoners were discharged. The following excerpts are from the judgment by Chief Justice Vaughan.

the court in matter of law," be that—if the judge, having heard the evidence given in court (for he knows no other), shall tell the jury upon this evidence, "The law is for the plaintiff (or for the defendant) and you are under the pain of fine and imprisonment to find accordingly"—then the jury ought of duty so to do, every man sees that the jury is but a troublesome delay, great charge, and of no use in determining right and wrong, and therefore the trials by them may be better abolished than continued; which were a strange new-found conclusion, after a trial so celebrated for many hundreds of years. For if the judge, from the evidence, shall by his own judgment first resolve upon any trial what the fact is, and so, knowing the fact, shall then resolve what the law is and order the jury penally to find accordingly, what either necessary or convenient use can be fancied of juries, or to continue trials by them at all? . . .

True it is . . . , the jury being ready to give their verdict . . . , if . . . the judge shall declare, "The matter of fact being by you so found to be, the law is for the plaintiff and you are to find accordingly for him," [and] if, notwithstanding, they find for the defendant, this may be thought a finding in matter of law against the direction of the court. For in that case the jury first declare the fact, as it is found by themselves; to which fact the judge declares how the law is consequent. And this is ordinary: when the jury find unexpectedly for the plaintiff or defendant, the judge will ask, "How do you find such a fact in particular?" And upon their answer he will say then it is for the defendant, though they found for the plaintiff (or *e contrario*); and thereupon they rectify their verdict. And in these cases the jury, and not the judge, resolve and find what the fact is. Wherefore, always in discreet and lawful assistance of the jury, the judge his direction is hypothetical and upon supposition, and not positive and upon coercion. . . . But in the case propounded by me, where it is possible in that special manner the jury may find against the direction of the court in matter of law, it will not follow they are therefore finable. . . .

No case can be offered . . . that ever a jury was punished by fine and imprisonment by the judge for not finding according to their evidence. . . . Sure this latter age did not first discover that the verdicts of juries were many times not according to the judge's opinion and liking. But the reasons are, I conceive, most clear that the judge could not nor can fine and imprison the jury in such cases. . . .

Howell, *State Trials,* VI, 999-1010.

(B) THE KING V. HENRY CARR (1680)[2]

. . . The present case it stands thus. Mr. Carr, here is an information brought against him for publishing a printed pamphlet called

---

[2] In this case Henry Carr was charged with publishing a "false, scandalous, and malicious book" entitled *The Weekly Packet of Advice from Rome,* in which the government was attacked for failing to enforce the laws against papists. Carr

The Packet of Advice from Rome; and in it there are recited some particulars which were observed to you before. . . . The question is whether he was the author or publisher of this. You hear he is thought the author; but, say his counsel, it is not plain—and that is true. But it seems by their own witnesses, to any man's understanding, that they looked upon him as the author. . . . Now it remains for you to consider what proofs you have as to this particular book against which the information lies. . . . Even for men's lives, you have very often not a direct proof of the fact, of the act, or of the actual killing; but yet you have evidence by presumption as seems reasonable to conscience. If there be a known case in men's lives, certainly that should govern in offences . . . of a nature that reflect upon the government.

As for those words, *"illicite, maliciose,* unlawful," for that I must recite . . . what all the judges of England have declared under their hands. . . . When, by the king's command, we were to give in our opinion what was to be done in point of the regulation of the press, we did all subscribe that [without licence] to print or publish any newsbooks or pamphlets of news whatsoever is illegal; that it is a manifest intent to the breach of the peace; and they may be proceeded against by law for an illegal thing. Suppose now that this thing is not scandalous, what then? If there had been no reflection in this book at all, yet it is *illicite*, and the author ought to be convicted for it. And that is for a public notice to all people, and especially printers and booksellers, that they ought to print no book or pamphlet of news whatsoever, without authority. So as he is to be convicted for it as a thing *illicite* done, not having authority.

And I will assure you, if you find any of those papers, I shall be more merciful in the consideration of their punishment, if it be inoffensive. But if so be they will undertake to print news foolishly, they ought to be punished; and shall be punished if they do it without authority, though there is nothing reflecting on the government as an unlawful thing. The reason is plain: so fond are men in these days that, when they will deny their children a penny for bread, they will lay it out for a pamphlet. . . . And the temptations were so great that no man could keep two-pence in his pocket because of the news. But still they never repented of laying out their money till they found there was nothing against the government. "This is not worth a farthing; there is nothing of treason in it; we will not give a farthing for it." Therefore this book, if it be made by him to be published, it is unlawful, whether it be malicious or not. . . .

Now we come to the more principal matter of fact according to reason and the probable evidence of things: that this person is taken to be the author, and that it was his boy that brought these papers

---

was brought to trial in the court of king's bench and was found guilty by a jury. The following excerpts are from the charge to the jury delivered by Chief Justice Scroggs.

to be printed. . . . The printer says he had been often discoursing with him; that his boy brought them, and that he knew no other person in the world that had any pretensions to be the author; and if he were the author, no doubt but he is the publisher. Whether or no anybody else had an hand in this we do not know. If you are satisfied in your consciences that you believe he is not the author, you must acquit him. . . .

Ibid., VII, 1126-30.

(C) THE KING V. THE CITY OF LONDON (1682)[3]

Mr. Attorney General hath exhibited an information in this court against the mayor, commonalty, and citizens of London, and thereby charges them for usurping upon the king without any warrant or royal grant . . . divers liberties and franchises within the city of London: namely, to be of themselves a body corporate and politic by the name of Mayor, Commonalty, and Citizens of the City of London, and by that name to plead and be impleaded, with several other liberties which, because not now expressly in judgment before us, I shall not mention.

To this the defendants plead that the city of London is and was, time out of mind, an ancient city, and that the citizens of that city are and, for the time aforesaid, have been a body corporate in deed and name. . . . Then they plead the confirmation of their liberties by Magna Carta and other charters of several kings, and amongst others of his majesty that now is; and conclude by that warrant they claim and have used for all the time in the information that liberty and franchise to be a body politic by that name. . . .

To this Mr. Attorney, taking by protestation that the citizens were not a corporation time out of mind . . . , says that the mayor, commonalty, and citizens, assuming upon themselves to be a body politic . . . , did upon pretext thereof . . . assume an unlawful power to levy money of the king's subjects to their own use . . . ; that, by pretext of this law, they have for their own private lucre exacted and levied yearly £5000 of the king's subjects and converted the same to their own use, and this is alleged to be in subversion of the good government of the city, to the oppressing and impoverishing of the king's subjects coming to the markets, to the raising of the prices of necessary provisions, and the disinheriting of the king and his crown, and contrary to the trust reposed in them as a body politic.

[3] This case came to trial before the court of king's bench on *quo warranto* proceedings brought against the mayor and citizens of London. As may be seen from the judgment pronounced by Justice Jones, the king's right was upheld and the city was condemned to forfeit all its liberties. As a matter of fact, however, Charles had merely adopted this method of humbling the Londoners and, after forcing them to make complete submission to his mercy, he restored their ancient rights on condition that they should henceforth install no officials without his confirmation in writing. See D. Ogg, *Reign of Charles II*, II, 636 f.

Mr. Attorney further charges that, whereas the king, the 10th of January in the thirty-second year of his reign, had prorogued the parliament then sitting to the 20th of the same January . . . , the mayor, commonalty, and citizens of the city of London in common council assembled, the 13th of the same January, unlawfully, maliciously, advisedly, and seditiously took upon them to censure the king . . . ; that they ordered a petition to be presented to the king containing this malicious, seditious, and scandalous matter. . . . And this Mr. Attorney alleges to be done in contempt and scandal of the king and his government . . . , and concludes that for these crimes the mayor, commonalty, and citizens of the city of London have forfeited the liberty and franchise of being a body politic and yet since have usurped the franchise upon the king. . . .

I shall therefore briefly deliver the resolution of us all upon all or the most material points debated in the arguments of this case. First, then, as to the great preliminary point—whether a corporation aggregate, such as the city is, may be forfeited or seized into the king's hands—we are of opinion that it may, upon breach of that condition which the law annexes to it, which is a trust for the good government of the king's subjects committed by the king to the corporation. . . .

To the second point, we are of opinion that the assuming a power by the mayor, commonalty, and citizens of London to make by-laws to levy money upon the subject, and the levying vast sums of money thereby, is a great oppression upon the people; and consequently a breach of that trust in law, which is reposed in a body politic for the welfare of the people, and so a just cause of forfeiture.

Thirdly, we are of opinion that the charge touching the ordering, exhibiting, and printing the petition, so scandalous to the king and government, so dangerously tending to the seduction of his subjects to a dislike and hatred of his person and government, and so evidently tending to sedition thereby and rebellion, is another just cause of forfeiture. . . .

And, lastly, [we are of opinion] that upon this whole record, both for the matter and substance of it and the form of pleading, judgment ought to be given, and it is the judgment of this court, that the franchise and liberty of London be taken into the king's hands.

Ibid., VIII, 1268 f.

(D) GODDEN V. HALES (1686)[4]

. . . In the case of Godden and Hales, wherein the defendant pleads a dispensation from the king, it is doubted whether or no the

---

[4] Sir Edward Hales, a colonel in the royal army, having neglected to take the oaths of supremacy and allegiance prescribed by the Test Act (no. 114R), was duly indicted for such neglect and convicted at the Rochester assizes. Thereupon Arthur Godden brought suit according to the provisions of the act for the sum of £500 forfeited by Hales. Actually the entire affair was prearranged, so

king had such a prerogative. Truly, upon the argument before us, it appeared as clear a case as ever came before this court; but, because men fancy I know not what difficulty when really there is none, we were willing to give so much countenance to the question in the case as to take the advice of all the judges of England. They were all assembled at Serjeants' Inn, and this case was put to them. . . . And I must tell you that there were ten upon the place that clearly delivered their opinions. . . . My brother Powell said he was inclined to be of the same opinion, but he would rather have some more time to consider of it. But he has since sent by my brother Holloway to let us know that he does concur with us. To these eleven judges there is one dissenter, brother Street, who yet continues his opinion that the king cannot dispense in this case. But that's the opinion of one single judge against the opinion of eleven.

We were satisfied in our judgments before and, having the concurrence of eleven out of twelve, we think we may very well declare the opinion of the court to be that the king may dispense in this case. And the judges go upon these grounds:—(1) that the kings of England are sovereign princes; (2) that the laws of England are the king's laws; (3) that therefore 'tis an inseparable prerogative in the kings of England to dispense with penal laws in particular cases and upon particular necessary reasons; (4) that of those reasons and those necessities, the king himself is sole judge; and then, which is consequent upon all, (5) that this is not a trust invested in, or granted to, the king by the people, but the ancient remains of the sovereign power and prerogative of the kings of England; which never yet was taken from them, nor can be. And therefore, such a dispensation appearing upon record to come [in] time enough to save him from the forfeiture, judgment ought to be given for the defendant.

Ibid., XI, 1197 f.

(E) The Case of the Seven Bishops (1688)[5]

To the king's most excellent majesty: The humble petition of William, archbishop of Canterbury, and of divers of the suffragan bishops of that province, now present with him, in behalf of themselves and

---

that the defendant could plead in defence that he had the king's letters patent dispensing with the oaths in his case. How the matter was decided by the court of king's bench will appear from the judgment delivered by Chief Justice Herbert.

[5] In 1687 James II issued a Declaration of Indulgence modelled on that of his brother (no. 115), and in the next year he commanded all bishops to have copies of the declaration distributed throughout their dioceses, so that it might be publicly read in all churches. As a consequence, the archbishop of Canterbury, together with six bishops of his province, petitioned the king not to insist upon obedience to his command. For this they were arrested on a charge of publishing a seditious libel and brought to trial before a jury in the court of king's bench. Eventually, in the midst of great popular enthusiasm, they were acquitted. The following excerpts from the records are, first, the bishops' petition and, secondly, the charge to the jury by Chief Justice Wright and his fellow justices.

others of their absent brethren, and of the clergy of their respective dioceses, humbly showeth that the great averseness they find in themselves to the distributing and publishing in all their churches your majesty's late declaration for liberty of conscience proceedeth neither from any want of duty and obedience to your majesty . . . , nor yet from any want of due tenderness to dissenters, in relation to whom they are willing to come to such a temper as shall be thought fit, when the matter shall be considered and settled in parliament and convocation; but, amongst many other considerations, from this especially, because that declaration is founded upon such a dispensing power as hath been often declared illegal in parliament, and particularly in the years 1662 and 1672, and in the beginning of your majesty's reign, and is a matter of so great moment and consequence to the whole nation, both in church and state, that your petitioners cannot in prudence, honour, or conscience, so far make themselves parties to it as the distribution of it all over the nation and the solemn publication of it once and again, even in God's house and in the time of His divine service, must amount to, in common and reasonable construction. Your petitioners therefore most humbly and earnestly beseech your majesty that you will be graciously pleased not to insist upon their distributing and reading your majesty's said declaration. And your petitioners, as in duty bound, shall ever pray, etc.

Lord Chief Justice: . . . Gentlemen, thus stands the case: it is an information against my lords the bishops, his grace my lord of Canterbury, and the other six noble lords; and it is for preferring, composing, making, and publishing, and causing to be published a seditious libel. The way that the information goes is special, and it sets forth that the king was graciously pleased, by his royal power and prerogative, to set forth a declaration of indulgence for liberty of conscience in the third year of his reign; and afterwards, upon the 27th of April in the fourth year, he comes and makes another declaration; and afterwards, in May, orders in council that this declaration should be published by my lords the bishops in their several dioceses. And after this was done, my lords the bishops come and present a petition to the king, in which were contained the words which you have seen. . . .

Gentlemen, upon the point of the publication, I have summed up all the evidence to you; and if you believe that the petition which these lords presented to the king was this petition, truly, I think, that is a publication sufficient. If you do not believe it was this petition, then my lords the bishops are not guilty of what is laid to their charge in this information, and consequently there needs no inquiry whether they are guilty of a libel. But if you do believe that this was the petition they presented to the king, then we must come to inquire whether this be a libel.

Now, gentlemen, anything that shall disturb the government, or make mischief and a stir among the people, is certainly within the case of *Libellis Famosis*;[a] and I must in short give you my opinion: I do take it to be a libel. Now this being a point of law, if my brothers have anything to say to it, I suppose they will deliver their opinions.

Justice Holloway: Look you, gentlemen, it is not usual for any person to say anything after the chief justice has summed up the evidence; it is not according to the course of the court. But this is a case of an extraordinary nature and, there being a point of law in it, it is very fit everybody should deliver their own opinion. The question is whether this petition of my lords the bishops be a libel or no. Gentlemen, the end and intention of every action is to be considered; and likewise, in this case, we are to consider the nature of the offence that these noble persons are charged with. It is for delivering a petition, which, according as they have made their defence, was with all the humility and decency that could be; so that, if there was no ill intent and they were not (as it is not nor can be pretended they were) men of evil lives or the like, to deliver a petition cannot be a fault—it being the right of every subject to petition. If you are satisfied there was an ill intention of sedition, or the like, you ought to find them guilty; but if there be nothing in the case that you find but only that they did deliver a petition to save themselves harmless, and to free themselves from blame, by showing the reason of their disobedience to the king's command, which they apprehended to be a grievance to them, and which they could not in conscience give obedience to, I cannot think it is a libel. It is left to you, gentlemen; but that is my opinion. . . .

Justice Powell: Truly I cannot see, for my part, anything of sedition, or any other crime, fixed upon these reverend fathers, my lords the bishops. For, gentlemen, to make it a libel, it must be false, it must be malicious, and it must tend to sedition. As to the falsehood, I see nothing that is offered by the king's counsel, nor anything as to the malice; it was presented with all the humility and decency that became the king's subjects to approach their prince with. Now, gentlemen, the matter of it is before you; you are to consider of it, and it is worth your consideration. They tell his majesty it is not out of averseness to pay all due obedience to the king, nor out of a want of tenderness to their dissenting fellow subjects, that made them not perform the command imposed upon them; but they say that, because they do conceive that the thing that was commanded them was against the law of the land, therefore they do desire his majesty that he would be pleased to forbear to insist upon it, that they should perform that command which they take to be illegal. Gentlemen, we must

---

[a] The case *De Libellis Famosis* in Coke's reports, earlier stated by the chief justice in these words: "If any person have slandered the government in writing, you are to examine the . . . slander which it imports to the king or government; and, be it never so true, yet if slanderous to the king or the government, it is a libel and to be punished. In that case the right or wrong is not to be examined, or if what was done by the government be legal or no; but whether the party have done such an act."

consider what they say is illegal in it. They say they apprehend the declaration is illegal because it is founded upon a dispensing power, which the king claims, to dispense with the laws concerning ecclesiastical affairs. Gentlemen, I do not remember, in any case in all our law—and I have taken some pains upon this occasion to look into it—that there is any such power in the king, and the case must turn upon that. In short, if there be no such dispensing power in the king, then that can be no libel which they presented to the king, which says that the declaration, being founded upon such a pretended power, is illegal. Now, gentlemen, this is a dispensation with a witness; it amounts to an abrogation and utter repeal of all the laws; for I can see no difference, nor know of none in law, between the king's power to dispense with laws ecclesiastical, and his power to dispense with any other laws whatsoever. If this be once allowed of, there will need no parliament; all the legislature will be in the king—which is a thing worth considering, and I leave the issue to God and your consciences.

Justice Allybone: . . . I think, in the first place, that no man can take upon him to write against the actual exercise of the government unless he have leave from the government, but he makes a libel, be what he writes true or false. . . . Then, I lay down this for my next position: that no private man can take upon him to write concerning the government at all. For what has any private man to do with the government, if his interest be not stirred or shaken? . . . When I intrude myself into other men's business that does not concern my particular interest, I am a libeller. . . . Now then, let us consider further, whether, if I will take upon me to contradict the government, any specious pretence that I shall put upon it shall . . . give it a better denomination. And truly I think it is the worse because it comes in a better dress . . . ; so that, whether it be in the form of a supplication or an address or a petition, if it be what it ought not to be, let us call it by its true name . . . —it is a libel. . . . Then, gentlemen, consider what this petition is. This is a petition relating to something that was done and ordered by the government. Whether the reasons of the petition be true or false, I will not examine that now; nor will I examine the prerogative of the crown; but only take notice that this relates to the act of the government. . . . And shall or ought anybody to come and impeach that as illegal which the government has done? Truly, in my opinion, I do not think he should or ought; for by this rule may every act of the government be shaken when there is not a parliament . . . sitting.

Ibid., XII, 318 f., 422 f.

118. RECORDS CONCERNING COLONIES (1660-81)

(A) APPOINTMENT OF COMMITTEES OF THE COUNCIL (1660)

[4 July.] Upon a petition presented to his majesty by divers merchants and others interested in and trading to the English plantations in America, exposing the good behaviour and great merit of Colonel

James Russell, late governor of the island of Nevis in the West Indies, and humbly beseeching his majesty to grant his commission for the continuance of him, the said Colonel Russell, in the government of the said island: his majesty, this day sitting in council, hath appointed the lord chamberlain, the earl of Southampton, the earl of Leicester, the lord viscount Say and Seal, the lord Roberts, Mr. Denzil Holles, Mr. Secretary Nicholas, Mr. Secretary Morice, Mr. Arthur Annesley, and Sir Anthony Ashley Cooper, or any three or more of them, to meet and sit as a committee every Monday and Thursday at three of the clock in the afternoon, to receive, hear, examine, and deliberate upon any petitions, propositions, memorials, or other addresses which shall be presented or brought in by any person or persons concerning the plantations as well in the continent as islands of America, and from time to time make their report to this board of their proceedings. . . .

[17 August.] The Turkey [Company], the Merchant Adventurers, the East India, Greenland, and Eastland Companies, and likewise the incorporated traders for Spain, France, Portugal, Italy, and the West India plantations [are] to present unto his majesty the names of four of their most knowing, active men—of whom when his majesty shall have chosen two, and unto this number of merchants added some other able and well-experienced persons, dignified also with the presence and assistance of some of his majesty's privy council—all these [are] to be by his majesty appointed, constituted, and authorized by commission under the great seal as a standing committee to inquire into and certify all things tending to the advancement of trade and commerce. . . .

Acts of the Privy Council, Colonial Series, I, 295, 297 f.

(B) INSTRUCTIONS FOR THE COUNCIL OF TRADE (1660)

1. You shall take into your consideration the inconveniences which the English trade hath suffered in any parts beyond the seas, and are to inquire into such articles of former treaties as have been made with any princes or states in relation to trade, and to draw out such observations . . . as may be necessary for us to advise or insist upon in any foreign leagues or alliances, that such evils as have befallen these our kingdoms through want of good information . . . may be provided against in time to come.

2. You are to consider how and by whom any former articles or treaties have been neglected or violated; what new capitulations are necessary either to the freedom of sale to your commodities of all sorts . . . , to the best expedition of justice, to the recovery of debts . . . , or to the prevention of those interruptions which the trade and navigation of our kingdoms have suffered by embargoes of foreign princes or states. . . .

3. You are to consider well the interest of all such trades as are or shall be incorporated by our royal charters, and what jurisdictions

are necessary to be obtained . . . for the more regular management . . . of the trade and of the members of those our corporations in foreign factories.

4. You are to consider the several manufactures of these our kingdoms, how and by what occasions they are corrupted . . . and by what probable means they may be restored and maintained in their ancient goodness and reputation, and how they may be farther improved . . . by a just regulation and standard of weight, length, and breadth. . . .

5. You are also to take into your consideration all the native commodities . . . of these our kingdoms, and how they may be ordered, nourished, increased, and manufactured to the employment of our people and to the best advantage of the public.

6. You are specially to consider of the whole business of the fishings of these our kingdoms or any other of our distant dominions or plantations, and to consult of some effectual means for the re-enforcing, encouraging, and increasing, and for the regulating and carrying on of the trade in all the parts thereof. . . .

7. You are seriously to consider . . . whether the importation of foreign commodities do not overbalance the exportation of such as are native, and how it may be so ordered . . . that we may have more sellers than buyers in every part abroad. . . .

11. You are to consider the general state . . . of our foreign plantations and of the navigation, trade, and several commodities arising thereupon . . . and you are also, in all matters wherein our foreign plantations are concerned, to take advice or information . . . from the council appointed and set apart by us to the more particular inspection, regulation, and care of our foreign plantations. . . .

Cunningham, Growth of English Industry and Commerce, II, 913 f.

(C) ESTABLISHMENT OF A SINGLE COMMITTEE ON TRADE AND PLANTATIONS (1675)

The right honourable the lord keeper of the great seal of England this day acquainted the board by his majesty's command that his majesty, having been pleased to dissolve and extinguish his late council of trade and foreign plantations . . . ,[1] had thought fit to commit what was under their inspection and management to the committee of this board appointed for matters relating to trade and his foreign plantations, *viz.*: the lord treasurer, lord privy seal, duke of Lauderdale, duke of Ormond, marquis of Worcester, earl of Ossory, lord chamberlain, earl of Bridgewater, earl of Essex, earl of Carlisle, earl of Craven, Viscount Fauconberg, Viscount Halifax, Lord Berkeley, Lord Holles, Mr. Vice-Chamberlain, Mr. Secretary Coventry,

---

[1] The committees set up in 1660 (no. 118A) had been superseded by, first, two councils and, later, one council of trade and foreign plantations, which were distinct from the privy council. The direct control of the privy council was restored by this present order.

Mr. Secretary Williamson, Mr. Chancellor of the Exchequer, Mr. Chancellor of the Duchy, and Mr. Speaker. And [he] did particularly order that the lord privy seal, the earl of Bridgewater, earl of Carlisle, earl of Craven, Viscount Fauconberg, Viscount Halifax, Lord Berkeley, Mr. Vice-Chamberlain, and Mr. Chancellor of the Exchequer should have the immediate care and intendency of those affairs, in regard they had been formerly conversant and acquainted therewith . . . ; and that their lordships meet constantly at least once a week and make report to his majesty in council of their results and proceedings from time to time; and that they have power to send for all books, papers, and other writings concerning any of his majesty's said plantations. . . .

Acts of the Privy Council, Colonial Series, I, 619 f.

(D) CHARLES II: CHARTER TO CONNECTICUT (1662)

Charles . . . , etc., to all to whom these presents shall come, greeting. . . . Whereas we have been informed by the humble petition of our trusty and well-beloved John Winthrop [and eighteen others] . . . , being persons principally interested in our colony or plantation of Connecticut in New England that the same colony, or the greatest part thereof, was purchased and obtained for great and valuable considerations . . . : now know ye . . . , in regard the said colony is remote from other the English plantations . . . , and to the end the affairs and business which shall from time to time happen or arise concerning the same may be duly ordered and managed, we have thought fit . . . , at the humble petition of the persons aforesaid . . . , to create and make them a body politic and corporate with the powers and privileges hereinafter mentioned. . . .

We . . . do ordain, constitute, and declare that they, the said John Winthrop . . . and all such others as now are or hereafter shall be admitted and made free of the company and society of our colony of Connecticut in America, shall . . . forever hereafter be one body corporate and politic . . . by the name of Governor and Company of the English Colony of Connecticut in New England in America. . . . And further we will and ordain . . . that, for the better ordering and managing of the affairs and business of the said company and their successors, there shall be one governor, one deputy governor, and twelve assistants, to be from time to time constituted, elected, and chosen out of the freemen of the said company . . . in such manner and form as hereafter in these presents is expressed. . . . And further we . . . do ordain and grant that the governor . . . or . . . deputy governor . . . shall and may from time to time . . . give order for the assembling of the said company . . . to consult and advise of the business and affairs of the said company; and that forever hereafter, twice in every year . . . or oftener in case it shall be requisite, the assistants and freemen of the said company, or such of them . . . who shall be from time to time thereunto elected or deputed by the major part of the freemen of the respective towns, cities, and places . . . , shall have a general meeting or assembly, then and there to consult and advise in and about the affairs and business of the said company. . . . And we do hereby . . . establish and ordain that once in the year forever hereafter . . . the governor, deputy governor, and assistants of the said company, and other officers of the said company . . . shall be in the said general court and assembly . . . newly chosen for the year ensuing by such greater part of the said company . . . then and there present. . . .

And further . . . we do . . . ordain, declare, and grant . . . that all and every the subjects of us, our heirs or successors, which shall go to inhabit within the said colony, and every of their children . . . shall have and enjoy all liberties and immunities of free and natural subjects within any the dominions of us, our heirs, or successors. . . . And we do further of our especial grace . . . give and grant . . . that it shall and may be lawful to and for the governor or deputy governor and such of the assistants of the said company . . . as shall be assembled in any of the general courts aforesaid . . . to erect and make such judicatories for the hearing and determining of all actions, causes, matters, and things happening within the said colony or plantation and which shall be in dispute . . . as they shall think fit and convenient; and also from time to time to make, ordain, and establish all manner of wholesome and reasonable laws, statutes, ordinances, directions, and instructions, not contrary to the laws of this realm of England. . . .

Thorpe, Constitutions, I, 529 f.

(E) Charles II: Grant to William Penn (1681)

Charles . . . , etc., to all [to] whom these presents shall come, greeting. Whereas our trusty and well-beloved subject, William Penn, esquire . . . , out of a commendable desire to enlarge our English empire and promote such useful commodities as may be of benefit to us and our dominions, as also to reduce the savage natives by gentle and just manners to the love of civil society and Christian religion, hath humbly besought leave of us to transport an ample colony unto a certain country hereinafter described in the parts of America not yet cultivated and planted . . . : know ye therefore that we . . . do give and grant unto the said William Penn, his heirs, and assigns all that tract or part of land in America. . . .[2] And him, the said William Penn, his heirs, and assigns, we do by this our royal charter . . . make, create, and constitute the true and absolute proprietary of the country aforesaid . . . ; saving always to us, our heirs, and successors the faith and allegiance of the said William Penn . . . and of all other proprietaries, tenants, and inhabitants that are or shall be within the territories and precincts aforesaid; and saving also unto us, our heirs, and successors the sovereignty of the aforesaid country—

---

[2] As specifically bounded in the charter.

to have, hold, possess, and enjoy the said tract of land . . . , as of our castle of Windsor in our county of Berks, in free and common socage . . . , yielding and paying therefor to us, our heirs, and successors two beaver skins, to be delivered at our said castle of Windsor on the first day of January in every year, and also the fifth part of all gold and silver ore which shall . . . happen to be found within the limits aforesaid. . . . And of our further grace . . . we have thought fit to erect . . . the aforesaid country . . . into a province and seignory and do call it Pennsylvania, and so from henceforth we will have it called.

And . . . know ye . . . that we, reposing special trust and confidence . . . in the said William Penn . . . , do grant free, full, and absolute power . . . to him and his heirs . . . to ordain, make, and enact . . . any laws whatsoever for the raising of money for the public use of the said province, or for any other end appertaining either unto the public state, peace, or safety of the said country, or unto the private utility of particular persons, according unto their best discretions, by and with the advice, assent, and approbation of the freemen of the said country . . . or of their delegates or deputies; whom, for the enacting of the said laws . . . , we will that the said William Penn and his heirs shall assemble in such sort and form as to him and them shall seem best. . . .

And we do likewise give and grant unto the said William Penn and his heirs . . . full power and authority to appoint and establish any judges and justices, magistrates and officers whatsoever, for what causes soever . . . within the precincts aforesaid . . . ; also to remit, release, pardon, and abolish . . . all crimes and offences whatsoever committed within the said country against the said laws, treason and wilful and malicious murder only excepted. . . .

We enjoin, require, and command . . . that all the liege people and subjects of us, our heirs, and successors do keep the same [laws] inviolable in those parts. . . . Provided, nevertheless, that the said laws be consonant to reason and be not repugnant or contrary—but, as near as conveniently may be, agreeable—to the laws and statutes and rights of this our kingdom of England; and saving and reserving to us, our heirs, and successors the receiving, hearing, and determining of the . . . appeals of all . . . persons of, in, or belonging to the territories aforesaid. . . . Our further will and pleasure is that a transcript or duplicate of all laws . . . made and published within the said province shall, within five years after the making thereof, be transmitted and delivered to the privy council. . . . And if any of the said laws, within the space of six months after that they shall be so transmitted . . . , be declared by us, our heirs, or successors, in our or their privy council inconsistent with the sovereignty or lawful prerogative of us, our heirs, or successors, or contrary to the faith and allegiance due . . . from the said William Penn or his heirs or the planters and inhabitants of the said province . . . , such laws . . .

shall become void; otherwise, the said laws so transmitted shall remain and stand in full force. . . .

Ibid., V, 3036 f.

119. RECORDS OF LEICESTER (1660-88)

(A) Petition of Nathaniel Hasselwood for the Freedom of the Borough

Showeth that the petitioner, being formerly a soldier and quartering in this town about eight years, took to wife one Margaret Sneape, a town-born child; where they have continued ever since, himself only having a dependence upon the army until the 25th of April, 1660. . . . Being disbanded . . . , the petitioner was appointed to pass from the headquarters in Scotland into this county, there to follow any lawful calling for his livelihood . . . ; which he hath hitherto endeavoured to do in an honest way, as he humbly conceives. But being informed that he cannot be permitted so to do, in regard he is not made a freeman of the town, most humbly therefore he craves this assembly[1] would . . . permit him to continue in the way he now is . . . or . . . admit him to be a freeman. This petition granted.

Stocks, *Records of Leicester, 1603-1688*, p. 477.

(B) Letter concerning a New Municipal Charter (1664)[2]

. . . We desire you to take up so much money . . . as Mr. Johnson, Mr. Deighton, Mr. Attorney's clerk, and yourself shall think necessary to do our whole business this and next term. . . . We have sent you the last charter past the privy signet under the clerk of the signet's hand; whereof entreat Mr. Johnson and Mr. Deighton to be careful, for we desire it may now pass in the same words as then it was granted by his late majesty without any diminution, but with addition of the things hereinafter mentioned. . . . That on our Saturday market we may also have a horse market, and that foreigners of all trades that market day may depart in summer at seven of the clock and in winter at five of the clock, and not stay all night in town as now they do to prejudice the burgesses. . . . And that all our parishes, suburbs, and fields may be continued within the regulation of Mr. Mayor and the corporation . . . ; and that the encroachment of the country justices, stewards, sheriff, and foreign jurisdictions may be restrained. . . . Sir, we pray [you to] inform Mr. Attorney's clerk herein and get a draft prepared for our charter that we may see it and consider thereof till next term . . . ; and the next term we shall attend Mr. Attorney and pay all fees and perfect our business. . . .

Ibid., pp. 490 f.

---

[1] The court of common hall (see above, p. 291, n. 11), which apparently admitted him as a freeman.

[2] Written by the mayor and some of his associates to a Mr. Browne, who was acting as agent for the corporation in London.

119. RECORDS OF LEICESTER

(C) DISPUTED ELECTION TO THE CORPORATION (1665-66)[3]

[26 December 1665.] It is ordered and agreed at this meeting that the refusing of Edward Billers, William Warburton, and William Orton to renounce the Covenant and subscribe the declaration mentioned in the act for regulating corporations[4] shall be signified to the council according to the order of his majesty. . . .

For the mayor, bailiffs, and burgesses of the borough of Leicester against Edward Billers, William Warburton, and William Orton. The effect of your petition to the council: That the mayor and aldermen of the said borough . . . were wont, upon the death or removal of any of them or of the company of forty-eight called the common council, to elect other in their stead; that three of the said company of forty-eight being lately dead, the mayor and aldermen duly elected the defendants in their places, who, taking advantage of a clause in the late act of parliament for regulating corporations, refused to renounce the Covenant—whereby their election is declared void. Therefore they pray such order as his majesty should think fit. . . . [On] 29 November last, by an order of the council . . . , the said parties are ordered to submit . . . by taking the usual oaths. . . . The corporation under their common seal certify the tender both of the oath and subscription, but they persist in their refusal. Thereupon an order of this February . . . requires the defendants to take the oaths and subscribe, or pay such fines as the corporation shall impose. . . .

Before this order could be procured to be signed . . . , the defendants, having by some means intelligence thereof, came up and are ordered to stand committed before they be heard. They allege in excuse: (1) that they are young men, no householders, and keep no apprentices or servants; (2) that they offered to pay such fines as the corporation should impose; (3) that they offered to submit to their election. Answer: (1) They are all shopkeepers and of very good trades and estates, and there are very few of like ability with them, considering the late regulation; (2) the corporation, if they should impose fines, have no power . . . to recover them . . . ; (3) it is true they did offer to submit to their election by taking the oaths, but would never be persuaded to subscribe to renounce the Covenant, and by that means their election is void by the act.

[6 April 1666.] . . . Memorandum that . . . the aforesaid Edward Billers, William Warburton, and William Orton came to Mr. Mayor and desired they might be put in bond for payment of their fines, and that they might have the discharge for being elected of the company of the eight-and-forty, etc. . . . All which was granted them. . . .

Ibid., pp. 498 f.

---

[3] The corporation consisted of the mayor and the two companies: one of the aldermen, called the four-and-twenty; the other of the common council, called the eight-and-forty. The following excerpts are from the records of the common hall.

[4] No. 114J.

(D) MEMORANDUM CONCERNING CONVENTICLES (1671)

Upon the 12th day of February last, being Sunday, Thomas Ludlam, one of the constables of the borough of Leicester, John Vesey and Thomas Laxton, churchwardens of the parish of All Saints in the said borough, being informed of a conventicle or meeting to be held in a house in the said parish, about two of the clock in the afternoon of the same day went to the said house, where they found several persons met together—and of those two men and eight women, whose names they learned, being then and there sitting and standing in the said house; but they heard no praying or preaching by any person. The mayor of the said borough humbly prays your lordship's judgment and advice, whether this meeting may be accounted a conventicle according to act of parliament.[5]

This was delivered to Judge Wyndham by Mr. Recorder upon the bench at the gildhall of the borough of Leicester. . . . His lordship's opinion was it was not a conventicle within the statute if nothing more appeared; and, if Mr. Mayor and justices should make a warrant of distress, there might be an action of distress brought against the officers.

Ibid., pp. 522 f.

(E) PETITION OF THE STOCKING-MAKERS

Showeth that the petitioners have for divers years last past employed themselves in the buying and combing of wool and in getting the same to be spun and knit up into stockings, to be sold to hosiers and other retailers, by which means they have wrought up yearly about 200 tods of wool, used great quantities of oil and soap, and kept constantly at work about 2000 poor people, men, women, and children of the town of Leicester and adjacent villages—to the great advantage of the town and country, to the support of the petitioners and their families and to the enabling of them to bear a great part of the public taxes. And although the employment before mentioned is no trade within any statute, nor any man by law prohibited the exercise thereof in any city or town corporate of England; yet divers freemen of Leicester, perceiving that the petitioners have brought the said employment to a considerable manufacture, do now endeavour to engross the same wholly to themselves and to turn it into a monopoly, and by unjustifiable ordinances to exclude the petitioners from the free exercise of their calling. And albeit that, at the general sessions of the peace lately holden for the said borough, it was after serious advice and consultation with the grand jury adjudged that it was lawful for the petitioners to keep on their said employment, and ordered that they should not be molested therein; yet several of the said freemen do attempt the procuring of some order of this common hall to hinder the petitioners from the further exercise of their calling.

---

[5] See no. 114P.

And for the accomplishing of their designs [they] do use these false suggestions: that the petitioners do not give the spinners and knitters sufficient wages, and so the work is slightly done and the commodity brought into discredit; but, if the petitioners may be prohibited and some of the freemen only use the calling, they will give greater wages. They will employ none but the best spinners and knitters, and they will have all the yarn wound on clock reels, that so it may be perceived whether good or not and no stockings made but such as shall be very good. To which the petitioners do answer and humbly offer these following considerations:—

1. That it is improbable that, when a very great number of those that set the poor on work shall be restrained, those few which are left shall give greater wages to the poor than are given now when the work-folks will be as many still and fewer masters to employ them.

2. If the goodness of the work be the thing the freemen aim at, they may now take the best work-folks, give greater wages if they please, make better work, and outsell the petitioners, and none can hinder them.

3. If none but the best work-folks be set on work, then the children can never be taught, and the manufacture in short time will perish.

4. It is not the curious making of a few stockings, but the general making of many that is most for the public good; for that sets more people on work, as well children as others, and, when the stockings are made up and sorted, there are amongst them some for all sorts of people, and the buyer is able to judge of them and to give prices accordingly. If none but fine stockings be made, the poor must go without.

5. And as to the clock reels, there will be great inconveniency in them; for every workman is to buy such a reel, which many are not able to do. . . .

6. The viewing of the yarn in the skein is altogether needless, for any man in doubling the yarn from off the spools can judge of the work sufficiently.

7. That driving the petitioners out of the town, if it could be effected, would be much to the damage of the town and hinder above 1000 of the poor people of the work they now have. . . .

8. Divers persons, who by reason of some disasters and losses have been forced to leave off their trades . . . , have learned and taken up this employment . . . ; which advantage or privilege will be taken away if the employment be confined to a small number. . . .

9. If there be no law extant by which the petitioners can be restrained, how safe can it be to contrive ordinances or by-laws to hinder the public good?

10. If the increasing of a manufacture to the height be everywhere

adjudged a public profit, that ought to be advanced rather than the gratifying of a few because freemen.

The premises considered, the petitioners humbly pray that this assembly will not act anything which may tend to the prohibiting of the petitioners from the exercising of the said calling.

Ibid., pp. 536 f.

(F) LETTER CONCERNING ELECTIONS TO PARLIAMENT (1677)[6]

Mr. Mayor and gentlemen: . . . I have again discoursed, not only Mr. Finch, but some other great persons of quality who wish you had not disobliged my lord Huntingdon's tender of Mr. Finch. . . . To which, for you all, I answered you had prudently hitherto behaved yourselves, and none of your twenty-four or forty-eight were anywise engaged against him or on either side, but reserved your liberty of your own votes till the election. . . . But yet, for all this, I still perceive there is unkindness taken, which I will endeavour to mollify as much as I can. But I perceive, if you shall choose any that opposed Mr. Finch, it will not be forgotten. And truly, for my own part, I will neither oppose Mr. Gray or Mr. Finch; though all say here, if you shall choose one of your own members or myself, no offence can be justly taken on either side.

. . . I clearly know . . . and believe the parliament will determine the election is in the mayor, aldermen, common council, and burgesses that are sworn freemen and in none other; though in Sir John Prettyman's election . . .[7] the question was only whether the twenty-four and forty-eight alone should elect as formerly, which was carried in the negation. But had the question been merely betwixt burgesses and no burgesses, the case had been otherwise resolved; for the poorest burgess hath his vote . . . , but those which are no burgesses are no members of the corporation of Leicester, though they dwell in Leicester . . .

Now, gentlemen, I will study how I may to keep us all quiet; and 'tis in the power of the Hall to admonish and rule the burgesses for the welfare of the corporation. . . . Therefore you that govern must be unanimous and first rule yourselves, and the rest when they know it, will obey you. . . . As for the expense of a noble treat to the whole corporation upon the election, no man will deny it; but to hire or engage votes unduly by drinking on any side is so great a crime 'tis not to be suffered. But all other civilities which must occasion some expense will not be scrupled. . . .

Ibid., pp. 545 f.

---

[6] Written by Robert Harding, recorder of the borough, to the mayor and corporation.

[7] In 1661 there was a disputed election: the aldermen and councillors returning one candidate, a tumultuous assembly of burgesses returning another. The house of commons decided in favour of the latter, Sir John Prettyman.

119. RECORDS OF LEICESTER

(G) CHAMBERLAIN'S ACCOUNT (1682-83)

... Item, paid at Mr. Pares' for ale and tobacco, when Mr. Mayor, several aldermen, and common-councilmen met to agree with John Brookes for setting up and building the North Gates and for his earnest of the bargain the same time, 7s.

Item, paid for wine at the White Lyon, when Mr. Mayor and several aldermen and others met about the Abhorrence[8] to be presented to his majesty, 5s. 6d.

Item, paid to Mr. Mayor and aldermen for defraying their charges when they went to London to present the Abhorrence to his majesty from the town, £14. 15s. 6d.

Item, paid for horse-hire and charges of Mr. Beckett and Mr. Goodall when they went to the earl of Rutland with the Abhorrence, 15s. 8d.

Item, paid Mr. Wagstaffe for two bottles of canary and a bottle of claret when Mr. Recorder, Mr. Steward, and Mr. Solicitor met about drawing the Abhorrence, 5s. ...

Ibid., p. 559.

---

[8] One of the Tory petitions "abhorring" the Whig demand for the calling of a new parliament.

SECTION XI

WILLIAM III TO GEORGE II

Between the years 1689 and 1760 the growth of the English constitution was largely governed by a single event—often called by the men of that age the Happy Revolution (see no. 124F). As an episode in political history, this Revolution has been the subject of considerable argument. As an affirmation of public law, it cannot be a matter of doubt; the Bill of Rights is the Revolution. The six enactments that follow it under no. 120 were all closely related to it—as was the refusal of the commons to renew the Licensing Act (no. 123A). The Act of Settlement, which still regulates succession to the British crown, was by its own words a supplement to the fundamental statute of 1689. To assure the acceptance of that settlement by the Scots, the union of the two kingdoms was negotiated and made law under Queen Anne. As a consequence, George of Hanover acceded to the throne of Great Britain in 1714. And the fact that he, as well as his son after him, reigned as foreigners, from time to time threatened by Stuart pretenders, definitively shaped the British constitution of the eighteenth century.

The Revolution of 1689 established the principle of parliamentary sovereignty. It was left for the Hanoverian succession to give parliament effective control over the executive by completing what we know as the cabinet system of government. Since the working of the system depends upon political usage rather than legal forms, to illustrate its development from official documents is impossible. The present section, however, includes a few debates that touch upon the prime minister's relations with the king, with parliament, and with his associates in the privy council (no. 123E, F). Other extracts under the same heading set forth contemporary opinions on the responsibility of the house of commons to the people.

On the whole, these documents reveal a peaceful age of great constitutional advance. The violence and unrest of the earlier Stuart reigns had subsided with the Revolution settlement. Among the trials briefly reported under no. 124, only one was really sensational—the impeachment of Sacheverell, which was coloured by the partisan conflict of Whigs and Tories. The rest, however controversial the issues, were typical of the orderly routine that now characterized British justice. So too, the records in the last group are chiefly interesting as normal products of colonial administration: such as instructions to provincial governors, decisions on appeal from American courts, and regulation of overseas trade. All this passes very quietly; of the antagonisms that were to wreck the imperial constitution there is as yet no hint.

The entire period from 1689 to 1760 has not been covered in any recent book on constitutional history, though phases of the subject are surveyed in such well-known studies as Trevelyan's *England under Queen Anne* and Lecky's *England in the Eighteenth Century*. In addition to the works by Anson, Dicey, Turner, Robertson, and Dykes cited in previous introductions (above, pp. 406, 535), special mention may here be made of the following: M. T. Blauvelt, *The Development of Cabinet Government;* H. W. V. Temperley, "Inner and Outer Cabinet and Privy Council," in the *English Historical Review*, XXVII, 682 f.; A. S. Turberville, *The House of Lords in the Eighteenth Century;* A. V. Dicey and R. S. Rait, *Thoughts on the Union between England and Scotland*. An excellent bibliography on constitutional problems affecting the empire is to be found in the appendix to the *Cambridge History of the British Empire*, I, 855 f., 861 f.

120. WILLIAM III: STATUTES

(A) BILL OF RIGHTS (1689)

An act declaring the rights and liberties of the subject and settling the succession of the crown. Whereas the lords spiritual and temporal and commons assembled at Westminster, lawfully, fully, and freely representing all the estates of the people of this realm, did upon the 13th day of February, in the year of our Lord 1688,[1] present unto their majesties, then called and known by the names and style of William and Mary, prince and princess of Orange, being present in their proper persons, a certain declaration in writing made by the said lords and commons in the words following, *viz.*:—[2]

---

[1] New style, 1689.

[2] In order to understand the statute called the Bill of Rights, these facts must be borne in mind. In December, 1688, James II fled to France. The Convention Parliament, referred to in the opening sentences of this act, met on 22 January 1689 and drew up the declaration which ends at the break in the text on p. 602. On 13 February William and Mary accepted the declaration and were proclaimed

Whereas the late King James II, by the assistance of divers evil counsellors, judges, and ministers employed by him, did endeavour to subvert and extirpate the Protestant religion and the laws and liberties of this kingdom by assuming and exercising a power of dispensing with and suspending of laws and the execution of laws without consent of parliament, by committing and prosecuting divers worthy prelates for humbly petitioning to be excused from concurring to the said assumed power, by issuing and causing to be executed a commission under the great seal for erecting a court called the court of commissioners for ecclesiastical causes, by levying money for and to the use of the crown by pretence of prerogative for other time and in other manner than the same was granted by parliament, by raising and keeping a standing army within this kingdom in time of peace without consent of parliament and quartering soldiers contrary to law, by causing several good subjects being Protestants to be disarmed at the same time when papists were both armed and employed contrary to law, by violating the freedom of election of members to serve in parliament, by prosecutions in the court of king's bench for matters and causes cognizable only in parliament, and by divers other arbitrary and illegal courses;

And whereas of late years partial, corrupt, and unqualified persons have been returned and served on juries in trials, and particularly divers jurors in trials for high treason, which were not freeholders, and excessive bail hath been required of persons committed in criminal cases to elude the benefit of the laws made for the liberty of the subjects, and excessive fines have been imposed, and illegal and cruel punishments inflicted, and several grants and promises made of fines or forfeitures before any conviction or judgment against the persons upon whom the same were to be levied, all which are utterly and directly contrary to the known laws and statutes and freedom of this realm;

And whereas the said late King James II having abdicated the government, and the throne being thereby vacant, his highness the prince of Orange (whom it hath pleased Almighty God to make the glorious instrument of delivering this kingdom from popery and arbitrary power) did, by the advice of the lords spiritual and temporal and divers principal persons of the commons, cause letters to be written to the lords spiritual and temporal being Protestants, and other letters to the several counties, cities, universities, boroughs, and Cinque Ports for the choosing of such persons to represent them as were of right to be sent to parliament to meet and sit at Westminster . . . , in order to [provide] such an establishment as that their

king and queen. On 22 February the Convention Parliament was legalized by an act similar to that passed in 1660 (no. 114A). Finally, on 16 December, the present statute was formally enacted. In the following year a newly elected parliament confirmed all legislation of the Convention Parliament.

religion, laws, and liberties might not again be in danger of being subverted, upon which letters elections having been accordingly made:

And thereupon the said lords spiritual and temporal and commons, pursuant to their respective letters and elections being now assembled in a full and free representative of this nation, taking into their most serious consideration the best means for attaining the ends aforesaid, do in the first place (as their ancestors in like case have usually done) for the vindicating and asserting their ancient rights and liberties, declare that the pretended power of suspending of laws or the execution of laws by regal authority without consent of parliament is illegal; that the pretended power of dispensing with laws or the execution of laws by regal authority, as it hath been assumed and exercised of late, is illegal; that the commission for erecting the late court of commissioners for ecclesiastical causes and all other commissions and courts of like nature are illegal and pernicious; that levying money for or to the use of the crown by pretence of prerogative without grant of parliament, for longer time or in other manner than the same is or shall be granted, is illegal; that it is the right of the subjects to petition the king, and all commitments and prosecutions for such petitioning are illegal; that the raising or keeping a standing army within the kingdom in time of peace, unless it be with consent of parliament, is against law; that the subjects which are Protestants may have arms for their defence suitable to their conditions and as allowed by law; that election of members of parliament ought to be free; that the freedom of speech and debates or proceedings in parliament ought not to be impeached or questioned in any court or place out of parliament; that excessive bail ought not to be required, nor excessive fines imposed, nor cruel and unusual punishments inflicted; that jurors ought to be duly impanelled and returned, and jurors which pass upon men in trials for high treason ought to be freeholders; that all grants and promises of fines and forfeitures of particular persons before conviction are illegal and void; and that, for redress of all grievances and for the amending, strengthening, and preserving of the laws, parliaments ought to be held frequently.

And they do claim, demand, and insist upon all and singular the premises as their undoubted rights and liberties, and that no declarations, judgments, doings, or proceedings to the prejudice of the people in any of the said premises ought in any wise to be drawn hereafter into consequence or example. To which demand of their rights they are particularly encouraged by the declaration of his highness the prince of Orange, as being the only means for obtaining a full redress and remedy therein. Having therefore an entire confidence that his said highness the prince of Orange will perfect the deliverance so far advanced by him and will still preserve them from the violation of their rights which they have here asserted and from all other attempts upon their religion, rights, and liberties, the said lords spiritual and temporal and commons assembled at Westminster do resolve that William and Mary, prince and princess of Orange, be and be declared king and queen of England, France, and Ireland, and the dominions thereunto belonging, to hold the crown and royal dignity of the said kingdoms and dominions to them, the said prince and princess, during their lives and the life of the survivor of them; and that the sole and full exercise of the regal power be only in and executed by the said prince of Orange in the names of the said prince and princess during their joint lives, and after their deceases the said crown and royal dignity of the said kingdoms and dominions to be to the heirs of the body of the said princess, and for default of such issue to the princess Anne of Denmark and the heirs of her body, and for default of such issue to the heirs of the body of the said prince of Orange. And the lords spiritual and temporal and commons do pray the said prince and princess to accept the same accordingly; and that the oaths hereafter mentioned be taken by all persons, of whom the oaths of allegiance and supremacy might be required by law, instead of them; and that the said oaths of allegiance and supremacy, be abrogated:—

"I, A. B., do sincerely promise and swear that I will be faithful and bear true allegiance to their majesties King William and Queen Mary. So help me God."

"I, A. B., do swear that I do from my heart abhor, detest, and abjure as impious and heretical this damnable doctrine and position, that princes excommunicated or deprived by the pope or any authority of the see of Rome may be deposed or murdered by their subjects or any other whatsoever. And I do declare that no foreign prince, person, prelate, state, or potentate hath or ought to have any jurisdiction, power, superiority, pre-eminence, or authority ecclesiastical or spiritual within this realm. So help me God."——

Upon which their said majesties did accept the crown and royal dignity of the kingdoms of England, France, and Ireland and the dominions thereunto belonging, according to the resolution and desire of the said lords and commons contained in the said declaration; and thereupon their majesties were pleased that the said lords spiritual and temporal and commons, being the two houses of parliament, should continue to sit and, with their majesties' royal concurrence, make effectual provision for the settlement of the religion, laws, and liberties of this kingdom, so that the same for the future might not be in danger again of being subverted; to which the said lords spiritual and temporal and commons did agree and proceed to act accordingly:

Now, in pursuance of the premises, the said lords spiritual and temporal and commons in parliament assembled, for the ratifying, confirming, and establishing the said declaration and the articles, clauses, matters, and things therein contained by the force of a law made in due form by authority of parliament, do pray that it may be declared and enacted that all and singular the rights and liberties asserted and claimed in the said declaration are the true, ancient, and indubitable rights and liberties of the people of this kingdom and so shall be esteemed, allowed, adjudged, deemed, and taken to be; and that all and every the particulars aforesaid shall be firmly and strictly holden and observed as they are expressed in the said declaration, and all officers and ministers whatsoever shall serve their majesties and their successors according to the same in all times to come. And the said lords spiritual and temporal and commons, seriously considering how it hath pleased Almighty God, in His marvellous providence and merciful goodness to this nation, to provide and preserve their said majesties' royal persons most happily to reign over us upon the throne of their ancestors . . . , do truly, firmly, assuredly, and in the sincerity of their hearts think, and do hereby recognize, acknowledge, and declare that King James II, having abdicated the government and their majesties having accepted the crown and royal dignity as aforesaid, their said majesties did become, were, are, and of right ought to be by the laws of this realm our sovereign liege lord and lady, king and queen of England, France, and Ireland, and the dominions thereunto belonging; in and to whose princely persons the royal state, crown, and dignity of the said realms with all honours, styles, titles, regalities, prerogatives, powers, jurisdictions, and authorities to the same belonging and appertaining are most fully, rightly, and entirely invested and incorporated, united and annexed.

And for preventing all questions and divisions in this realm by reason of any pretended titles to the crown, and for preserving a certainty in the succession thereof, in and upon which the unity, peace, tranquillity, and safety of this nation doth under God wholly consist and depend, the said lords spiritual and temporal and commons do beseech their majesties that it may be enacted, established, and declared that the crown and regal government of the said kingdoms and dominions, with all and singular the premises thereunto belonging and appertaining, shall be and continue to their said majesties and the survivor of them during their lives and the life of the survivor of them; and that the entire, perfect, and full exercise of the regal power and government be only in and executed by his majesty in the names of both their majesties during their joint lives; and after their deceases the said crown and premises shall be and remain to the heirs of the body of her majesty, and, for default of such issue, to her royal highness the princess Anne of Denmark and the heirs of her body and, for default of such issue, to the heirs of the body of his said majesty. And thereunto the lords spiritual and temporal and commons do, in the name of all the people aforesaid, mostly humbly and faithfully submit themselves, their heirs, and posterities forever; and do faithfully promise that they will stand to maintain and defend their said majesties, and also the limitation and succession of the crown herein specified and contained, to the utmost of their powers with their lives and estates against all persons whatsoever that shall attempt anything to the contrary.

And whereas it hath been found by experience that it is inconsistent with the safety and welfare of this Protestant kingdom to be governed by a popish prince or by any king or queen marrying a papist, the said lords spiritual and temporal and commons do further pray that it may be enacted that all and every person and persons that is, are, or shall be reconciled to, or shall hold communion with, the see or Church of Rome, or shall profess the popish religion, or shall marry a papist shall be excluded and be forever incapable to inherit, possess, or enjoy the crown and government of this realm and Ireland and the dominions thereunto belonging or any part of the same, or to have, use, or exercise any regal power, authority, or jurisdiction within the same. And in all and every such case or cases the people of these realms shall be and are hereby absolved of their allegiance. And the said crown and government shall from time to time descend to and be enjoyed by such person or persons, being Protestants, as should have inherited and enjoyed the same in case the said person or persons . . . were naturally dead. And . . . every king and queen of this realm, who at any time hereafter shall come to and succeed in the imperial crown of this kingdom, shall on the first day of the meeting of the first parliament next after his or her coming to the crown—sitting in his or her throne in the house of peers, in the presence of the lords and commons therein assembled, or at his or her coronation before such person or persons who shall administer the coronation oath to him or her . . . —make, subscribe, and audibly repeat the declaration mentioned in the statute made in the thirtieth year of the reign of King Charles II. . . .[3] But if it shall happen that such king or queen upon his or her succession to the crown shall be under the age of twelve years, then every such king or queen shall make, subscribe, and audibly repeat the said declaration at his or her coronation, or the first day of the meeting of the first parliament as aforesaid which shall first happen after such king or queen shall have attained the said age of twelve years.

All which their majesties are contented and pleased shall be declared, enacted, and established by authority of this present parliament; and shall stand, remain, and be the law of this realm forever. And the same are by their said majesties, by and with the advice and consent of the lords spiritual and temporal and commons in parliament assembled and by the authority of the same, declared, enacted, and established accordingly. And be it further declared and enacted by the authority aforesaid that, from and after this present session of parliament, no dispensation . . . of or to any statute, or any part thereof, shall be allowed; but that the same shall be held void and of no effect—except a dispensation be allowed of in such statute, and except in such cases as shall be specially provided for by one or more bill or bills to be passed during this present session of parliament. Provided that no charter or grant or pardon granted before the three-and-twentieth day of October, in the year of our Lord 1689, shall be

---

[3] No. 114T.

anyways impeached or invalidated by this act; but that the same shall be and remain of the same force and effect in law and no other than as if this act had never been made.

Statutes of the Realm, VI, 142 f.: 1 William & Mary, st. 2, c. 2.

(B) MUTINY ACT (1689)

An act for punishing officers or soldiers who shall mutiny or desert their majesties' service. Whereas the raising or keeping a standing army within this kingdom in time of peace, unless it be with consent of parliament, is against law; and whereas it is judged necessary by their majesties and this present parliament that during this time of danger several of the forces which are now on foot should be continued and others raised for the safety of the kingdom . . . ; and whereas no man may be forejudged of life or limb, or subjected to any kind of punishment by martial law, or in any other manner than by the judgment of his peers and according to the known and established laws of this realm; yet nevertheless, it being requisite for retaining such forces as are or shall be raised during this exigence of affairs in their duty [that] an exact discipline be observed, and that soldiers who shall mutiny or stir up sedition or shall desert their majesties' service be brought to a more exemplary and speedy punishment than the usual forms of law will allow: be it therefore enacted . . . that . . . every person being in their majesties' service in the army and being mustered and in pay as an officer or soldier, who shall . . . excite, cause, or join in any mutiny or sedition in the army, or shall desert their majesties' service in the army, shall suffer death or such other punishment as by a court-martial shall be inflicted.

And it is hereby further enacted and declared that their majesties, or the general of their army for the time being, may by virtue of this act have full power and authority to grant commissions to any lieutenants general or other officers, not under the degree of colonels, from time to time to call and assemble court-martials for punishing such offences as aforesaid. And it is hereby further enacted and declared that no court-martial, which shall have power to inflict any punishment by virtue of this act for the offences aforesaid, shall consist of fewer than thirteen, whereof none to be under the degree of captains.

Provided always that no field officer be tried by other than field officers; and that such court-martial shall have power and authority to administer an oath to any witness in order to the examination or trial of the offences aforesaid. Provided always that nothing in this act contained shall extend or be construed to exempt any officer or soldier whatsoever from the ordinary process of law. Provided always that this act or anything therein contained shall not . . . extend to or concern any the militia forces of this kingdom. Provided also that this act shall continue and be in force until [10 November 1689] . . . and no longer. . . . And no sentence of death shall be given against any offender in such case by any court-martial unless nine of the thirteen officers present shall concur therein. And if there be a greater number of officers present, then the judgment shall pass by the concurrence of the greater part of them. . . .

Ibid., VI, 55 f.: 1 William & Mary, c. 5.

(C) Coronation Oath Act (1689)

An act for establishing the coronation oath. Whereas, by the law and ancient usage of this realm, the kings and queens thereof have taken a solemn oath upon the Evangelists at their respective coronations to maintain the statutes, laws, and customs of the said realm, and all the people and inhabitants thereof in their spiritual and civil rights and properties;[1] but forasmuch as the oath itself on such occasion administered hath heretofore been framed in doubtful words and expressions with relation to ancient laws and constitutions at this time unknown: to the end thereof that one uniform oath may be in all times to come taken by the kings and queens of this realm, and to them respectively administered at the times of their . . . coronation, may it please your majesties that it may be enacted, and be it enacted . . . , that the oath herein mentioned and hereafter expressed shall and may be administered to their most excellent majesties King William and Queen Mary—whom God long preserve—at the time of their coronation, in the presence of all persons that shall be then and there present at the solemnizing thereof, by the archbishop of Canterbury or the archbishop of York, or either of them, or any other bishop of this realm whom the king's majesty shall thereunto appoint, and who shall be hereby thereunto respectively authorized; which oath followeth and shall be administered in this manner, that is to say:—

The archbishop or bishop shall say: "Will you solemnly promise and swear to govern the people of this kingdom of England and the dominions thereto belonging according to the statutes in parliament agreed on and the laws and customs of the same?" The king and queen shall say: "I solemnly promise so to do." Archbishop or bishop: "Will you to your power cause law and justice in mercy to be executed in all your judgments?" King and queen: "I will." Archbishop or bishop: "Will you to the utmost of your power maintain the laws of God, the true profession of the Gospel, and the Protestant reformed religion established by law? And will you preserve unto the bishops and clergy of this realm, and to the churches committed to their charge, all such rights and privileges as by law do or shall appertain unto them or any of them?" King and queen: "All this I promise to do." After this, the king and queen, laying his and her hand upon the Holy Gospels, shall say, king and queen: "The things which I have here before promised I will perform and keep; so help me God." Then the king and queen shall kiss the Book.

[4] Cf. no. 55.

And be it further enacted that the said oath shall be in like manner administered to every king or queen who shall succeed to the imperial crown of this realm. . . .

Ibid., VI, 56 f.: 1 William & Mary, c. 6.

(D) TOLERATION ACT (1689)

An act for exempting their majesties' Protestant subjects, dissenting from the Church of England, from the penalties of certain laws.[5] . . .

And be it . . . enacted . . . that all . . . persons that shall . . . take the said oaths and make and subscribe the declaration aforesaid shall not be . . . prosecuted in any ecclesiastical court for or by reason of their non-conforming to the Church of England.

Provided always . . . that, if any assembly of persons dissenting from the Church of England shall be had in any place for religious worship with the doors locked, barred, or bolted during any time of such meeting together, all . . . persons that shall come to be at such meeting shall not receive any benefit from this law. . . . Provided always that nothing herein contained shall . . . exempt any of the persons aforesaid from paying of tithes or other parochial duties, or any other duties to the church or minister; nor from any prosecution in any ecclesiastical court, or elsewhere for the same. . . .

And be it further enacted . . . that no person dissenting from the Church of England in holy orders, or pretended holy orders, or pretending to holy orders, nor any preacher or teacher of any congregation of dissenting Protestants that shall make and subscribe the declaration aforesaid and take the said oaths . . . , and shall also declare his approbation of and subscribe the articles of religion mentioned in the statute made in the thirteenth year of the reign of the late Queen Elizabeth . . .[6] shall be liable to any of the pains or penalties mentioned in an act made in the seventeenth year of the reign of King Charles II . . . , nor the penalties mentioned in the . . . act made in the two-and-twentieth year of his said late majesty's reign, for or by reason of such persons preaching at any meeting for the exercise of religion; nor to the penalty of £100 mentioned in an act made in the thirteenth and fourteenth of King Charles II . . . for officiating in

---

[5] The laws enumerated in the statute are Elizabeth's Act of Uniformity (no. 81B), her Act against Sectaries (no. 81F), the Second Conventicle Act of Charles II (see p. 553, n. 28), and four others. In order that "some ease to scrupulous consciences in the exercise of religion may be an effectual means to unite their majesties' Protestant subjects in interest and affection," it is provided that the enumerated laws shall not extend to any dissenter who shall take the oaths prescribed in the Bill of Rights (above, p. 602) and make the declaration prescribed in the Second Test Act (above, p. 557).

[6] The act prescribing the Thirty-Nine Articles for the Anglican Church. The present statute waives for such persons subscription to three articles and part of a fourth.

any congregation for the exercise of religion permitted and allowed by this act. . . .[7]

And be it further enacted . . . that every teacher or preacher in holy orders, or pretended holy orders . . . , that shall take the oaths herein required and make and subscribe the declaration aforesaid, and also subscribe such of the aforesaid articles of the Church of England as are required by this act . . . , shall be thenceforth exempted from serving upon any jury, or from being chosen or appointed to bear the office of churchwarden, overseer of the poor, or any . . . other office in any hundred . . . , shire, city, town, parish, division, or wapentake. . . .

And whereas there are certain other persons, dissenters from the Church of England, who scruple the taking of any oath, be it enacted by the authority aforesaid, that every such person shall make and subscribe the aforesaid declaration, and the declaration of fidelity following . . . ; and shall subscribe a profession of their Christian belief in these words. . . .[8]

Provided always . . . that all the laws made and provided for the frequenting of divine service on the Lord's day, commonly called Sunday, shall be still in force and executed against all persons that offend against the said laws, except such persons come to some congregation or assembly of religious worship allowed or permitted by this act. . . .

Provided always that no congregation or assembly for religious worship shall be permitted or allowed by this act until the place of such meeting shall be certified to the bishop . . . , or to the archdeacon . . . , or to the justices of the peace at the general or quarter sessions. . . .

Ibid., VI, 74 f.: 1 William & Mary, c. 18.

(E) Triennial Act (1694)[9]

An act for the frequent meeting and calling of parliaments. Whereas, by the ancient laws and statutes of this kingdom, frequent parliaments ought to be held; and whereas frequent and new parliaments tend very much to the happy union and good agreement of the king and people: . . . it is hereby declared and enacted . . . that from henceforth a parliament shall be holden once in three years at the least. And be it further enacted by the authority aforesaid that, within three years at the farthest from and after the dissolution of this present parliament, and so from time to time forever hereafter within three years at the farthest from and after the determination

---

[7] The acts referred to above are respectively the Five-Mile Act (no. 114Q), the Second Conventicle Act (p. 553, n. 28), and the Act of Uniformity (no. 114K).

[8] The declaration of fidelity in substance repeats the prescribed oaths. The profession of Christian belief affirms the Trinitarian creed and the divine inspiration of the Old and New Testaments.

[9] Cf. no. 114 o.

of every other parliament, legal writs under the great seal shall be issued by directions of your majesties, your heirs, and successors for assembling and holding another new parliament. And be it further enacted by the authority aforesaid that from henceforth no parliament whatsoever . . . shall have any continuance longer than for three years only at the farthest, to be accounted from the day on which by the writs of summons the said parliament shall be appointed to meet. . . .

Ibid., VI, 510: 6-7 William & Mary, c. 2.

(F) Trials for Treason Act (1696)

An act for regulating of trials in cases of treason and misprision of treason. Whereas nothing is more just and reasonable than that persons prosecuted for high treason and misprision of treason . . . should be justly and equally tried . . . : be it enacted . . . that . . . all . . . persons whatsoever that shall be accused and indicted for high treason, whereby any corruption of blood may . . . be made to any such . . . offenders or to any the . . . heirs of any such . . . offenders, or for misprision of such treason, shall have a true copy of the whole indictment, but not the names of the witnesses, delivered unto them . . . five days at the least before . . . they shall be tried for the same, whereby to enable them . . . to advise with counsel thereupon, to plead and make their defence . . . ; and that every such person so accused and indicted . . . shall be received and admitted to make his . . . full defence by counsel learned in the law and to make any proof that he . . . can produce by lawful . . . witnesses. . . . And in case any person . . . so accused or indicted shall desire counsel, the court before whom such person . . . shall be tried . . . is hereby authorized and required, immediately upon his . . . request, to assign . . . such . . . counsel, not exceeding two, as the person or persons shall desire, to whom such counsel shall have free access at all seasonable hours—any law or usage to the contrary notwithstanding.

And be it further enacted that . . . no person . . . whatsoever shall be indicted, tried, or attainted of high treason . . . but by and upon the oaths and testimony of two lawful witnesses . . . , unless the party indicted and arraigned or tried shall willingly, without violence, in open court confess the same, or shall stand mute or refuse to plead. . . . And be it further enacted that no evidence shall be admitted or given of any overt act that is not expressly laid in the indictment. . . .

Provided always that neither this act nor anything therein contained shall anyways extend . . . to any impeachment or other proceedings in parliament. . . . Provided also that [neither] this act nor anything therein contained shall anyways extend to any indictment of high treason . . . for counterfeiting his majesty's coin, his great seal or privy seal, his sign-manual or privy signet.

Ibid., VII, 6 f.: 7-8 William III, c. 3.

(G) Civil List Act (1698)

An act for granting to his majesty a further subsidy of tunnage and poundage towards raising the yearly sum of £700,000 for the service of his majesty's household . . . during his majesty's life. Your majesty's most dutiful and loyal subjects, the commons of England in parliament assembled, being deeply sensible of the great blessings which, by the goodness of Almighty God, we . . . do fully enjoy under your majesty's most auspicious government, and being desirous to make a grateful acknowledgment of your majesty's unparalleled grace and favour . . . , have therefore freely and unanimously resolved to increase your majesty's revenue . . . and do give and grant . . . the further rates, duties, and sums of money hereinafter mentioned; and do humbly beseech your majesty that it may be enacted, and be it enacted . . . , that, over and above all subsidies of tunnage and poundage . . . and above all additional duties . . . already due or payable . . . , there shall be raised . . . one other subsidy called tunnage . . . and one further subsidy called poundage. . . .

And whereas it is intended that the yearly sum of £700,000 shall be supplied to his majesty for the service of his household and family, and for other his necessary expenses and occasions, out of the hereditary rates, and duties of excise . . . , and out of the moneys which . . . shall arise by the further subsidies and duties hereby granted: be it therefore further enacted . . . , that, if the said . . . revenues . . . shall produce in clear money more than the yearly sum of £700,000 . . . , then the overplus of such produce . . . shall not be . . . applied to any use . . . without the authority of parliament.

Ibid., VII, 382 f.: 9 William III, c. 23.

(H) Act of Settlement (1701)

An act for the further limitation of the crown and better securing the rights and liberties of the subject. Whereas, in the first year of the reign of your majesty . . . , an act of parliament was made entitled An Act for Declaring the Rights and Liberties of the Subject and for Settling the Succession of the Crown . . . ;[10] and it being absolutely necessary, for the safety, peace, and quiet of this realm, to obviate all doubts and contentions in the same by reason of any pretended titles to the crown, and to maintain a certainty in the succession thereof . . . : therefore, for a further provision of the succession of the crown in the Protestant line . . . , be it enacted and declared . . . that the most excellent princess Sophia, electress and duchess dowager of Hanover, daughter of the most excellent princess Elizabeth, late queen of Bohemia, daughter of our late sovereign lord, King James I of happy memory, be and is hereby declared to be the next in succession in the Protestant line to the imperial crown and

---

[10] The act here recites the clauses in the Bill of Rights (no. 120A) relating to the succession.

dignity to the said realms of England, France, and Ireland, with the dominions thereunto belonging, after his majesty and the princess Anne of Denmark, and in default of issue of the said princess Anne and of his majesty respectively; and that, from and after the deceases of his said majesty . . . and of . . . the princess Anne of Denmark, and for default of issue of the said princess Anne and of his majesty respectively, the crown and regal government of the said kingdoms of England, France, and Ireland, and of the dominions thereunto belonging, with the royal state and dignity of the said realms and all the honours, styles, titles, regalities, prerogatives, powers, jurisdictions, and authorities to the same belonging and appertaining, shall be, remain, and continue to the said most excellent princess Sophia and the heirs of her body being Protestants. . . .

Provided always, and it is hereby enacted, that . . . every person . . . who shall . . . inherit the said crown by virtue of . . . this present act, and is . . . or shall . . . hold communion with the . . . Church of Rome, or shall profess the popish religion, or shall marry a papist, shall be subject to such incapacities as in such case . . . are by the said recited act provided, enacted, and established; and that every king and queen of this realm who shall come to and succeed in the imperial crown of this kingdom by virtue of this act shall have the coronation oath administered to him, her, or them at their respective coronations according to the act of parliament made in the first year of the reign of his majesty . . . ,[11] and shall make, subscribe, and repeat the declaration in the act first above recited, mentioned, or referred to in the manner and form thereby prescribed.

And whereas it is requisite and necessary that some further provision be made for securing our religion, laws, and liberties from and after the death of his majesty and the princess Anne of Denmark, and in default of issue of the body of the said princess and of his majesty respectively: be it enacted . . . that whosoever shall hereafter come to the possession of this crown shall join in communion with the Church of England as by law established; that, in case the crown and imperial dignity of this realm shall hereafter come to any person not being a native of this kingdom of England, this nation be not obliged to engage in any war for the defence of any dominions or territories which do not belong to the crown of England without the consent of parliament; that no person who shall hereafter come to the possession of the crown shall go out of the dominions of England, Scotland, and Ireland without the consent of parliament; that . . . all matters and things relating to the well governing of this kingdom, which are properly cognizable in the privy council by the laws and customs of this realm, shall be transacted there, and all resolutions taken thereupon shall be signed by such of the privy council as shall advise and consent to the same; that . . . no person born out of the kingdoms of England, Scotland,

---

[11] No. 120C.

or Ireland or the dominions thereunto belonging . . . , except such as are born of English parents, shall be capable to be of the privy council or a member of either house of parliament or to enjoy any office or place of trust, either civil or military, or to have any grant of lands, tenements, or hereditaments from the crown to himself or to any other or others in trust for him; that no person who has an office or place or profit under the king or receives a pension from the crown shall be capable of serving as a member of the house of commons; that . . . judges' commissions be made *quam diu se bene gesserint*,[12] and their salaries ascertained and established, but upon the address of both houses of parliament it may be lawful to remove them; that no pardon under the great seal of England be pleadable to an impeachment by the commons in parliament. . . .[13]

Ibid., VII, 636 f.: 12-13 William III, c. 2.

---

[12] That is to say, they shall be appointed to hold office during good behaviour.
[13] Cf. no. 116F.

121. ANNE: STATUTES

(A) ACT OF UNION WITH SCOTLAND (1707)

An act for the union of the two kingdoms of England and Scotland. . . . Whereas articles of union were agreed on the 22d day of July in the fifth year of your majesty's reign by the commissioners nominated on behalf of the kingdom of England . . . and the commissioners nominated on the behalf of the kingdom of Scotland . . . to treat of and concerning an union of the said kingdoms; and whereas an act hath passed in the parliament of Scotland . . . , wherein 'tis mentioned that the estates of parliament, considering the said articles of union of the two kingdoms, had agreed to and approved of the said articles of union with some additions and explanations, and that your majesty, with advice and consent of the estates of parliament . . . , had passed in the same session of parliament an act entitled Act for Securing of the Protestant Religion and Presbyterian Church government within that kingdom . . . shall be inserted in any act ratifying the treaty . . . :[1] be it enacted . . . that all and every the said articles of union . . . and also the said act of parliament of Scotland for establishing the Protestant religion and Presbyterian Church government within that kingdom . . . shall be, and the said articles and act are hereby, forever ratified, approved, and confirmed. . . .

And whereas, since the passing the said act in the parliament of Scotland for ratifying the said articles of union, one other act, entitled Act Settling the Manner of Electing the Sixteen Peers and Forty-five Members to Represent Scotland in the Parliament of Great Britain, hath likewise passed in the said parliament of Scot-

---

[1] At this point the statute inserts the articles of union and the act of the Scottish parliament just referred to. For the sake of clarity they are placed below.

land . . . :[2] be it therefore further enacted and declared by the authority aforesaid that the said . . . act . . . shall be, and the same is hereby declared to be, as valid as if the same had been part of and engrossed in the said articles of union. . . .

[Articles of union.] Article I. That the two kingdoms of England and Scotland shall, upon the first day of May which shall be in the year 1707, and forever after, be united into one kingdom by the name of Great Britain. . . .

Article II. That the succession to the monarchy of the united kingdom of Great Britain and of the dominions thereto belonging, after her most sacred majesty and in default of issue of her majesty, be, remain, and continue to the most excellent princess Sophia, electress and duchess dowager of Hanover, and the heirs of her body being Protestants, upon whom the crown of England is settled by an act of parliament. . . .

Article III. That the united kingdom of Great Britain be represented by one and the same parliament, to be styled the parliament of Great Britain.

Article IV. That all the subjects of the united kingdom of Great Britain shall, from and after the union, have full freedom and intercourse of trade and navigation to and from any port or place within the said united kingdom and the dominions and plantations thereunto belonging; and that there be a communication of all other rights, privileges, and advantages which do or may belong to the subjects of either kingdom, except where it is otherwise expressly agreed in these articles. . . .

Article VI. That all parts of the united kingdom forever from and after the union shall have the same allowances, encouragements, and drawbacks, and be under the same prohibitions, restrictions, and regulations of trade, and liable to the same customs and duties on import and export. And that the allowances, encouragements, and drawbacks, prohibitions, restrictions, and regulations of trade, and the customs and duties on import and export settled in England when the union commences shall from and after the union take place throughout the whole united kingdom. . . .

Article XVI. That from and after the union the coin shall be of the same standard and value throughout the united kingdom as now in England. . . .

Article XVII. That from and after the union the same weights and measures shall be used throughout the united kingdom, as are now established in England. . . .

Article XVIII. That the laws concerning regulation of trade . . . be the same in Scotland from and after the union as in England. And that all other laws in use within the kingdom of Scotland do after the union . . . remain in the same force as before, except such as are contrary to or inconsistent with this treaty; but alterable by

---

[2] This is the third document immediately following.

the parliament of Great Britain, with this difference . . . : that the laws which concern public right, policy, and civil government may be made the same throughout the whole united kingdom, but that no alteration be made in laws which concern private right except for evident utility of the subjects within Scotland.

Article XIX. That the court or session or college of justice do after the union . . . remain . . . within Scotland as it is now constituted by the laws of that kingdom, and with the same authority and privileges as before the union; subject, nevertheless, to such regulations for the better administration of justice as shall be made by the parliament of Great Britain. . . . And that all other courts now in being within the kingdom of Scotland do remain, but subject to alterations by the parliament of Great Britain. And that all inferior courts within the said limits do remain subordinate as they are now to the supreme courts of justice within the same in all time coming. And that no causes in Scotland be cognizable by the courts of chancery, queen's bench, common pleas, or in any other court in Westminster Hall. And that the said courts, or any other of the like nature after the union, shall have no power to . . . review or alter the acts or sentences of the judicatures within Scotland or stop the execution of the same. And that there be a court of exchequer in Scotland after the union for deciding questions concerning the revenues of customs and excises, there having the same power and authority in such cases as the court of exchequer has in England. . . .

Article XX. That all heritable offices . . . , heritable jurisdictions, offices for life, and jurisdictions for life be reserved to the owners thereof as rights of property in the same manner as they are now enjoyed by the laws of Scotland. . . .

Article XXI. That the rights and privileges of the royal burghs in Scotland, as they now are, do remain entire after the union. . . .

Article XXII. That, by virtue of this treaty, of the peers of Scotland at the time of the union sixteen shall be the number to sit and vote in the house of lords, and forty-five the number of the representatives of Scotland in the house of commons of the parliament of Great Britain. . . .

Article XXV. That all laws and statutes in either kingdom, so far as they are contrary to or inconsistent with the terms of these articles or any of them, shall from and after the union cease and become void. . . .

[Act for securing of the Protestant religion and Presbyterian Church government.] Our sovereign lady and the estates of parliament considering that, by the late act of parliament for a treaty with England for an union of both kingdoms, it is provided that the commissioners for that treaty should not treat of or concerning any alteration of the worship, discipline, and government of the Church of this kingdom as now by law established . . . ; and it being rea-

sonable and necessary that the true Protestant religion as presently
professed within this kingdom, with the worship, discipline, and
government of this Church should be effectually and unalterably secured; therefore her majesty, with advice and consent of the said
estates of parliament, doth hereby establish and confirm the said true
Protestant religion and worship, discipline, and government of this
Church to continue without any alteration to the people of this land
in all succeeding generations. . . .

And it is hereby . . . ordained that this act of parliament, with
the establishment therein contained, shall be held and observed in
all time coming as a fundamental and essential condition of any
treaty or union to be concluded betwixt the two kingdoms without
any alteration thereof or derogation thereto in any sort forever; as
also that this act of parliament and settlement therein contained shall
be insert and repeated in any act of parliament that shall pass for
agreeing and concluding the foresaid treaty or union betwixt the
two kingdoms; and that the same shall be therein expressly declared
to be a fundamental and essential condition of the said treaty or
union in all time coming. . . .

[Act settling the manner of electing the sixteen peers and forty-
five members to represent Scotland in the parliament of Great
Britain.] Our sovereign lady considering that, by the twenty-second
article of the treaty of union . . . , it is provided that . . . of the
peers of Scotland at the time of the union sixteen shall be the number
to sit and vote in the house of lords, and forty-five the number of
the representatives of Scotland in the house of commons of the
parliament of Great Britain, and that the said sixteen peers and
forty-five members . . . be named and chosen in such manner as
by a subsequent act in this present session of parliament in Scotland should be settled . . . : therefore her majesty, with advice
and consent of the estates of parliament . . . , enacts and ordains
that the said sixteen peers . . . shall be named by the said peers of
Scotland . . . out of their own number, and that by open election
and plurality of voices of the peers present and of the proxies for
such as shall be absent . . . ; and that of the said forty-five representatives . . . thirty shall be chosen by the shires or stewardries
and fifteen by the royal boroughs as follows. . . .[3]

Ibid., VIII, 566 f.: 6 Anne, c. 11.

(B) PLACE ACT (1707)

An act for the security of her majesty's person and government
and of the succession to the crown of Great Britain in the Protestant
line. . . .[4]

---

[3] The act concludes with detailed regulation of constituencies and electoral
procedure.

[4] In large part a re-enactment of a statute passed two years earlier, but altered
so as to apply to the united kingdom. The first two articles reaffirm the Protestant

And be it further enacted . . . that this present parliament, or any other parliament which shall hereafter be summoned . . . by her majesty, Queen Anne, her heirs, or successors, shall not be determined or dissolved by the death . . . of her said majesty, her heirs, or successors; but such parliament shall . . . continue and is hereby empowered and required, if sitting at the time of such demise, immediately to proceed to act . . . for and during the term of six months, and no longer, unless the same shall be sooner prorogued or dissolved by such person to whom the crown of this realm of Great Britain shall come. . . . And be it further enacted . . . that, in case there is no parliament in being at the time of such demise . . . , then the last preceding parliament shall immediately convene and sit at Westminster and be a parliament to continue as aforesaid. . . .

And be it further enacted . . . that the privy council of her majesty, her heirs, or successors for the kingdom of Great Britain shall not be determined or dissolved by the death . . . of her majesty, her heirs, or successors; but such privy council shall continue and act as such by the space of six months next after such demise, unless sooner determined by the next successor. . . . Nor shall any office, place, or employment, civil or military, within the kingdoms of Great Britain or Ireland, dominion of Wales, town of Berwick-upon-Tweed, isles of Jersey, Guernsey, Alderney, and Sark, or any of her majesty's plantations become void by reason of the . . . death of her present majesty, her heirs, or successors . . . ; but . . . every . . . person . . . in any of the offices, places, and employments aforesaid shall continue . . . for the space of six months next after such death . . . , unless sooner removed . . . by the next in succession as aforesaid.

And be it further enacted . . . that, whensoever her majesty . . . shall happen to demise . . . without issue of her body, the privy council for Great Britain in being at the time of such demise . . . shall with all convenient speed cause the next Protestant successor . . . to be openly and solemnly proclaimed in Great Britain and Ireland . . . ; and that all and every member and members of the said privy council wilfully neglecting or refusing to cause such proclamation to be made shall be guilty of high treason. . . .

And be it further enacted . . . that no person who shall have . . . any new office or place of profit whatsoever under the crown, which at any time since the 25th of October, 1705, have been created or erected or hereafter shall be created or erected . . . ,[5] nor any person having any pension from the crown during pleasure, shall be capable of being elected, or of sitting or voting, as a member of the house of commons in any parliament which shall be hereafter sum-

---

succession and impose the penalties for high treason upon any one who maintains the contrary in writing or by advised speaking.

[5] At this point the act mentions a number of other offices, the holding of which was a bar to election. From time to time the list was modified by later statutes.

moned. . . . Provided always that, if any person being chosen a member of the house of commons, shall accept of any office of profit from the crown during such time as he shall continue a member, his election shall be and is hereby declared to be void, and a new writ shall issue for a new election. . . . Provided, nevertheless, that such person shall be capable of being again elected. . . .

Ibid., VIII, 738 f.: 6 Anne, c. 41.

122. GEORGE I: STATUTES

(A) Riot Act (1715)

An act for preventing tumults and riotous assemblies and for the more speedy and effectual punishing the rioters. Whereas of late many rebellious riots and tumults have been in divers parts of this kingdom, to the disturbance of the public peace and the endangering of his majesty's person and government . . . : therefore . . . be it enacted . . . that, if any persons to the number of twelve or more, being unlawfully, riotously, and tumultuously assembled together to the disturbance of the public peace . . . , and being required or commanded by any one or more justice or justices of the peace, or by the sheriff of the county, or his under-sheriff, or by the mayor, bailiff, or bailiffs, or other head officer, or justice of the peace of any city or town corporate . . . , by proclamation to be made in the king's name in the form hereinafter directed, to disperse themselves and peaceably to depart to their habitations or to their lawful business, shall . . . unlawfully, riotously, and tumultuously remain or continue together by the space of one hour after such command or request . . . , that then such continuing together . . . shall be adjudged felony without benefit of clergy, and the offenders therein shall be adjudged felons, and shall suffer death as in case of felony without benefit of clergy.

And be it further enacted . . . that the order and form of the proclamation . . . shall be as hereafter followeth: that is to say, the . . . person authorized by this act to make the said proclamation shall, among the said rioters or as near to them as he can safely come, with a loud voice command, or cause to be commanded silence to be while proclamation is making, and after that shall openly and with loud voice make or cause to be made proclamation in these words, or like in effect: "Our sovereign lord the king chargeth and commandeth all persons, being assembled, immediately to disperse themselves and peaceably to depart to their habitations or to their lawful business, upon the pains contained in the act made in the first year of King George for preventing tumults and riotous assemblies. God Save the King!" . . .

And be it further enacted . . . that, if such persons . . . shall continue together and not disperse themselves within one hour, that then it shall be . . . lawful to and for every justice of the peace . . . and other peace officer . . . , and for such other . . . persons as shall be commanded to be assisting unto any such justice of the peace . . . or other head officer aforesaid . . . to seize and apprehend such persons so unlawfully, riotously, and tumultuously continuing together . . . and forthwith to carry the persons so apprehended before one or more of his majesty's justices of the peace . . . in order to their being proceeded against for such their offences according to law; and that, if the persons so unlawfully, riotously, and tumultuously assembled, or any of them, shall happen to be killed, maimed, or hurt . . . by reason of their resisting the persons so dispersing, seizing, or apprehending . . . them, that then every such justice of the peace . . . or other peace officer, and all and singular persons, being aiding and assisting to them . . . , shall be free, discharged, and indemnified . . . of, for, or concerning the killing, maiming, or hurting of any such person or persons. . . .

Statutes at Large, XIII, 142 f.; 1 George I, st. 2, c. 5.

(B) SEPTENNIAL ACT (1716)[1]

An act for enlarging the time of continuance of parliaments. . . . Whereas, in and by act of parliament made in the sixth year of the reign of their late majesties King William and Queen Mary . . . ,[2] it was among other things enacted that from henceforth no parliament whatsoever . . . should have any continuance longer than for three years . . . ; and whereas it hath been found by experience that the said clause hath proved very grievous and burdensome, by occasioning much greater and more continued expenses in . . . elections of members to serve in parliament, and more violent and lasting heats and animosities among the subjects of this realm . . . ; and [whereas] the said provision, if it should continue, may probably at this juncture, when a restless and popish faction are designing and endeavouring to renew the rebellion within this kingdom and an invasion from abroad, be destructive to the peace and security of the government: be it enacted . . . that this present parliament and all parliaments that shall at any time hereafter be called . . . , shall . . . have continuance for seven years and no longer . . . , unless this present or any such parliament hereafter to be summoned shall be sooner dissolved by his majesty, his heirs, or successors.

Ibid., XIII, 282: 1 George I, st. 2, c. 38.

(C) IRISH PARLIAMENT ACT (1719)[3]

An act for the better securing the dependency of the kingdom of Ireland upon the crown of Great Britain. Whereas the house of lords of Ireland have of late against law assumed to themselves a power and jurisdiction to examine, correct, and amend the judgments and decrees of the courts of justice in the kingdom of Ire-

---

[1] Cf. no. 123C.
[2] No. 120E.
[3] Cf. no. 73D.

land: therefore, for the better securing of the dependency of Ireland upon the crown of Great Britain . . . , be it declared by the king's most excellent majesty, by and with the advice and consent of the lords spiritual and temporal and commons in this present parliament assembled . . . , that the said kingdom of Ireland hath been, is, and of right ought to be subordinate unto and dependent upon the imperial crown of Great Britain, as being inseparably united and annexed thereunto; and that the king's majesty, by and with the advice and consent of the lords spiritual and temporal, and commons of Great Britain in parliament assembled, had, hath, and of right ought to have full power and authority to make laws and statutes of sufficient force and validity to bind the kingdom and people of Ireland. And be it further declared and enacted . . . that the house of lords of Ireland have not nor of right ought to have any jurisdiction to judge of, affirm, or reverse any judgment, sentence, or decree, given or made in any court within the said kingdom; and that all proceedings before the said house of lords upon any such judgment, sentence, or decree are and are hereby declared to be utterly null and void to all intents and purposes whatsoever.

Ibid., XIV, 204 f.: 6 George I, c. 5.

123. PROCEEDINGS IN PARLIAMENT (1695-1745)

(A) COMMONS' RESOLUTIONS ON THE LICENSING BILL (1695)[1]

The commons cannot agree to the clause marked A: (1) Because it revives and re-enacts a law which in no wise answered the end for which it was made, the title and preamble of that act being to prevent printing seditious and treasonable books, pamphlets, and papers; but there is no penalty appointed for offenders therein, they being left to be punished at common law, as they may be without that act; whereas there are great and grievous penalties imposed by that act for matters wherein neither church nor state is any ways concerned.

(2) Because that act gives a property in books to such persons as such books are, or shall be, granted to by letters patents, whether the crown had or shall have any right to grant the same, or not, at the time of such grant.

(3) Because that act prohibits printing anything before entry thereof in the register of the Company of Stationers, except proclamations, acts of parliament, and such books as shall be appointed under the sign-manual, or under the hand of a principal secretary of state; whereby both houses of parliament are disabled to order anything to be printed, and the said company are empowered to hinder the printing all innocent and useful books and have an op-

---

[1] Passed by the house on report of a committee to consider the revival of the earlier statute (114M). Clause A was a portion of the bill sent down from the house of lords. As a result of this action by the commons, the Licensing Act lapsed.

portunity to enter a title to themselves and their friends for what belongs to and is the labour and right of others.

(4) Because that act prohibits any books to be imported without special licence into any port in England, except London; by which means the whole foreign trade of books is restrained to London, unless the lord archbishop of Canterbury, or the lord bishop of London shall, in interruption of their more important affairs in governing the church, bestow their time gratis in looking over catalogues of books and granting licences; whereas the commons think the other ports of the kingdom have as good right as London to trade in books, as well as other merchandises.

(5) Because that act leaves it in the power either of the Company of Stationers, or of the archbishop of Canterbury and bishop of London, to hinder any books from being imported, even into the port of London; for if one or more of the Company of Stationers will not come to the custom-house, or that those reverend bishops shall not appoint any learned man to go thither and be present at the opening and viewing books imported, the custom-house officer is obliged to detain them.

(6) Because that act appoints no time wherein the archbishop or bishop of London shall appoint a learned man, or that one or more of the Company of Stationers shall go to the custom-house to view imported books; so that they or either of them may delay it till the importer may be undone by having so great a part of his stock lie dead, or the books, if wet, may rot and perish.

(7) Because that act prohibits any custom-house officer, under the penalty of losing his office, to open any packet wherein are books until some or one of the Company of Stationers, and such learned man as shall be so appointed, are present; which is impracticable, since he cannot know there are books until he has opened the packet.

(8) Because that act confirms all patents of books granted and to be granted—whereby the sole printing of all or most of the classic authors are and have been for many years past, together with a great number of the best books and of most general use, monopolized by the Company of Stationers—and prohibits the importing any such books from beyond sea; whereby the scholars in this kingdom are forced, not only to buy them at the extravagant price they demand, but must be content with their ill and incorrect editions and cannot have the more correct copies which are published abroad, nor the useful notes of foreigners or other learned men upon them.

(9) Because that act prohibits anything to be printed till licensed, and yet does not direct what shall be taken by the licenser for such licence; by colour whereof great oppression may be and has been practised.

(10) Because that act restrains men bred up in the trade of printing and founding of letters from exercising their trade, even in an innocent and inoffensive way, though they are freemen of the Com-

pany of Stationers, either as masters or journeymen—the number of workmen in each of those trades being limited by that act.

(11) Because that act compels master-printers to take journeymen into their service, though they have no work or employment for them.

(12) Because that act restrains all men who are not licensed by the bishop from selling innocent and inoffensive books, though never so useful, in any part of England, except freemen of the Company of Stationers, who may sell without such licence; so that neither church nor state is taken care of thereby, but the people compelled to buy their freedom of trade in all parts of England from the Company of Stationers in London.

(13) Because that act prohibits any one, not only to print books whereof another has entered a claim of property in the register of the Company of Stationers, but to bind, stitch, or put them to sale—and that under a great pecuniary penalty, though it is impossible for a bookbinder, stitcher, or seller to know whether the book brought to him were printed by the proprietor or another.

(14) Because that act prohibits smiths to make any ironwork for any printing-press without giving notice to . . . [the] Company of Stationers, under the penalty of £5; whereas he may not know to what use the iron bespoke of him, and forged by him, may be put.

(15) Because that act prohibits printing and importing, not only heretical, seditious, and schismatical books, but all offensive books, and doth not determine what shall be adjudged offensive books; so that, without doubt, if the late King James had continued in the throne till this time, books against popery would not have been deemed offensive books.

(16) Because that act subjects all men's houses—as well peers' as commoners'—to be searched at any time, either by day or night, by a warrant under the sign-manual, or under the hand of one of the secretaries of state, directed to any messenger, if such messenger shall, upon probable reason, suspect that there are any unlicensed books there; and the houses of all persons free of the Company of Stationers are subject to the like search on a warrant from the master and wardens of the said company or any one of them.

(17) Because the penalties for offences against that act are excessive—it being in the power of the judges or justices of the peace to inflict what punishment they please, not extending to life or member.

Journals of the Commons, XI, 305 f.

(B) RESOLUTIONS ON THE CASE OF ASHBY v. WHITE (1704)[2]

Resolved that it is the opinion of this committee that, according

---

[2] See no. 124c. The first extract below is from the proceedings of the commons (24 January); the second, from those of the lords (27 March).

to the known laws and usage of parliament, it is the sole right of the commons of England in parliament assembled, except in cases otherwise provided for by act of parliament, to examine and determine all matters relating to the right of election of their own members.

Resolved that it is the opinion of this committee that, according to the known laws and usage of parliament, neither the qualification of any elector or the right of any person elected is cognizable or determinable elsewhere than before the commons of England in parliament assembled, except in such cases as are specially provided for by act of parliament.

Resolved that it is the opinion of this committee that the examining and determining the qualification or right of any elector, or any person elected to serve in parliament, in any court of law or elsewhere than before the commons of England in parliament assembled —except in such cases as are specially provided for by act of parliament—will expose all mayors, bailiffs, and other officers, who are obliged to take the poll and make a return thereupon, to multiplicity of actions, vexatious suits, and insupportable expenses, and will subject them to different and independent jurisdictions and inconsistent determinations in the same case, without relief.

Resolved that it is the opinion of this committee that Matthew Ashby, having in contempt of the jurisdiction of this house commenced and prosecuted an action at common law against William White and others, the constables of Aylesbury, for not receiving his vote at an election of burgesses to serve in parliament for the said borough of Aylesbury, is guilty of a breach of the privilege of this house.

Resolved that it is the opinion of this committee that whosoever shall presume to commence or prosecute any action, indictment, or information at common law, which shall bring the right of the electors, or persons elected to serve in parliament, to the determination of any other jurisdiction than that of the house of commons, except in cases specially provided for by act of parliament, such person and persons, and all attorneys, solicitors, counsellors, and serjeants-at-law, soliciting, prosecuting, or pleading in any such case, are guilty of a high breach of the privilege of this house.

The first, second, third, and fourth resolutions, being severally read a second time, were, upon the question severally put thereupon, agreed unto by the house. The fifth resolution being read a second time, an amendment was proposed to be made thereunto, by leaving out "at common law." And the same was, upon the question put thereupon, agreed unto by the house: resolved that the house doth agree with the committee in the said resolution, so amended. . . .

Ordered, that the said resolutions be fixed upon Westminster Hall gate, signed by the clerk.

Ibid., XIV, 308.

This state of the case being read and approved of, the house [of lords] came to the following resolutions, *viz.*:—

It is resolved by the lords spiritual and temporal in parliament assembled that, by the known laws of this kingdom, every freeholder or other person having a right to give his vote at the election of members to serve in parliament, and being wilfully denied or hindered so to do by the officer who ought to receive the same, may maintain an action in the queen's courts against such officer, to assert his right and recover damages for the injury.

It is resolved . . . that the asserting that a person, having right to give his vote at an election and being hindered so to do by the officer who ought to take the same is without remedy for such wrong by the ordinary course of law, is destructive of the property of the subject, [is] against the freedom of elections, and manifestly tends to encourage corruption and partiality in officers who are to make returns to parliament, and to subject the freeholder and other electors to their arbitrary will and pleasure.

It is resolved . . . that the declaring Matthew Ashby guilty of a breach of privilege of the house of commons for prosecuting an action against the constables of Aylesbury for not receiving his vote at an election, after he had in the known and proper methods of law obtained a judgment in parliament for recovery of his damages, is an unprecedented attempt upon the judicature of parliament, and is in effect to subject the law of England to the votes of the house of commons.

It is resolved . . . that the deterring electors from prosecuting actions in the ordinary course of law, where they are deprived of their right of voting, and terrifying attorneys, solicitors, counsellors, and serjeants-at-law, from soliciting, prosecuting, and pleading in such cases, by voting their so doing to be a breach of privilege of the house of commons, is manifest assuming a power to control the law, to hinder the course of justice, and subject the property of Englishmen to the arbitrary votes of the house of commons.

Journals of the Lords, XVII, 534 f.

(C) MINORITY PROTEST IN THE LORDS AGAINST THE SEPTENNIAL ACT (1716)[3]

. . . Then the question was put whether the said bill shall be committed. It was resolved in the affirmative. Dissentient:—

1. Because we conceive that frequent and new parliaments are required by the fundamental constitution of the kingdom, and the practice thereof for many ages . . . is a sufficient evidence and proof of this constitution.

2. Because it is agreed that the house of commons must be chosen by the people and, when so chosen, they are truly the representatives of the people; which they cannot be so properly said to be

---

[3] Signed by thirty-one peers. Cf. no. 122B.

when continued for a longer time than that for which they were chosen. For, after that time, they are chosen by the parliament and not the people; who are thereby deprived of the only remedy which they have against those who either do not understand or, through corruption, do wilfully betray the trust reposed in them—which remedy is to choose better men in their places.

3. Because the reasons given for this bill, we conceive, were not sufficient to induce us to pass it in subversion of so essential a part of our constitution.... We conceive this bill is so far from preventing expenses and corruptions that it will rather increase them. For the longer a parliament is to last, the more valuable to be purchased is a station in it, and the greater also is the danger of corrupting the members of it. For, if ever there should be a ministry who shall want a parliament to screen them from the just resentment of the people or from a discovery of their ill practices to the king, who can't otherwise or so truly be informed of them as by a free parliament, it is so much the interest of such a ministry to influence the elections, which by their authority and the disposal of public money they of all others have the best means of doing, that 'tis to be feared they will be tempted and not fail to make use of them. And even when the members are chosen, they have greater opportunity of inducing very many to comply with them than they could have if, not only the sessions of parliament, but the parliament itself were reduced to the ancient and primitive constitution and practice of frequent and new parliaments. For, as a good ministry will neither practise nor need corruption, so it cannot be any lord's intention to provide for the security of a bad one.

4. We conceive that whatever reasons may induce the lords to pass this bill to continue this parliament for seven years will be at least as strong and may, by the conduct of the ministry, be made much stronger, before the end of seven years, for continuing it still longer and even to perpetuate it; which would be an express and absolute subversion of the third estate of the realm.

Ibid., XX, 331 f.

(D) COMMONS' DEBATE ON THE PRINTING OF SPEECHES (1738)

The speaker informed the house that it was with some concern he saw a practice prevailing which a little reflected upon the dignity of that house; what he meant was the inserting an account of their proceedings in the printed newspapers, by which means the proceedings of the house were liable to very great misrepresentations; that he had in his hands a printed newspaper which contained his majesty's answer to their late address before the same had been reported from the chair, the only way of communicating it to the public; that he thought it his duty to inform the house of these practices, the rather because he had observed them of late to have run into very great abuses; and therefore he hoped that gentlemen would propose some method of stopping it.

123. PROCEEDINGS IN PARLIAMENT

Sir William Yonge: ... There is, indeed, a resolution on our journals against printing or publishing any of the proceedings of this house, but by authority of the chair; but people had generally run away with the notion that this prohibition is in force only during the time we are sitting, and that, as soon as the session ends, they are at liberty to print and publish what they please. ...

Sir William Windham: ... I say, sir, we ought to be very cautious in what manner we form a resolution; for it is a question so nearly connected with the liberty of the press that it will require a great deal of tenderness to form a resolution which may preserve gentlemen from having their sense misrepresented to the public, and at the same time guard against all encroachments upon the liberty of the press. On the other hand, sir, I am sensible that there is a necessity of putting a stop to this practice of printing what are called the speeches of this house, because I know that gentlemen's words in this house have been mistaken and misrepresented. I do not know, sir, but I have some reason of complaint myself upon that head. I have, indeed, seen many speeches of gentlemen in this house that were fairly and accurately taken; and no gentleman, when that is the case, ought to be ashamed that the world should know every word he speaks in this house. For my own part, I never shall; for I hope never to act or speak in this house anything that I shall be ashamed to own to all the world. But of late, sir, I have seen such monstrous mistakes in some gentlemen's speeches, as they have been printed in our newspapers, that it is no wonder if gentlemen think it high time to have a stop put to such a practice. Yet, still, sir, there are two considerations which, I own, weigh very much with me upon this occasion. That this house has a right to prohibit the publication of any of its proceedings during the time we are sitting is past all doubt, and there is no question but that, by the resolutions that now stand upon our votes and are renewed every session, the printers of the papers you have in your hand are liable to the censure of this house. But I am not at all so clear as to the right we may have of preventing any of our proceedings from being printed during our recess. At least, sir, I am pretty sure that people without doors are strongly possessed with that notion, and therefore I should be against our inflicting any censure at present for what is past of that kind. If gentlemen are of opinion, which I do own I am not, that we have a power to prevent any account of our proceedings and debates from being communicated to the public, even during our recess, then, as this affair has been mentioned, they will no doubt think it very proper to come to a resolution against that practice, and to punish it with a very severe penalty. But if we have no such power, sir, I own I do not see how you can form any resolution upon this head that will not be liable to very great censure.

The other consideration that weighs very much, sir, with me upon this occasion is the prejudice which the public will think they sustain, by being deprived of **all knowledge** of what passes in this house otherwise than by the printed votes, which are very lame and imperfect for satisfying their curiosity of knowing in what manner their representatives act within doors. They have been long used to be indulged in this and they may possibly think it a hardship to be deprived of it now. Nay, sir, I must go farther: I do not know but they may have a right to know somewhat more of the proceedings of this house than what appears upon your votes; and if I were sure that the sentiments of gentlemen were not misrepresented, I should be against our coming to any resolution that could deprive them of a knowledge that is so necessary for their being able to judge of the merits of their representatives within doors. If gentlemen, however, are of opinion that they can frame a resolution which will put a stop to all impositions, and yet leave the public some room for having just information of what passes within these walls, I shall be extremely glad to give it my concurrence. But I am absolutely against our stretching our power farther than it will go consistently with the just rights of parliament. Such stretches rather weaken than give any strength to the constitution; and I am sure no gentleman will care to do what may not only look like our claiming powers unknown to our constitution, but what, in its consequences, may greatly affect the liberty of the press. If we shall extend this resolution to the recess of parliament, all political writing, if the authors shall touch upon anything that passed in the preceding session, may be affected by it; for I do not know that anybody would venture to publish anything that might bring upon them the censure of this house. In the meantime, sir, I am as willing as any gentleman in this house that a stop be put to the practice you have taken notice of from the chair. It has grown to such a pitch that I remember some time ago there was a public dispute in the newspapers betwixt two printers or booksellers of two pamphlets, which of them contained the true copy of a certain honourable gentleman's speech in this house. It is therefore high time for gentlemen to think of somewhat to be done for that purpose, and I make no doubt but that any resolution this house shall think fit to come to, will put an effectual stop to it.

Mr. Thomas Winnington: . . . If we do not put a speedy stop to this practice, it will be looked upon without doors that we have no power to do it; for the public will very justly think that, if we had such a power, we would exercise it. And then, sir, what will be the consequence? Why, sir, you will have every word that is spoken here by gentlemen misrepresented by fellows who thrust themselves into our gallery. You will have the speeches of this house every day printed, even during your session. And we shall be looked upon as the most contemptible assembly on the face of the earth. . . .

Then the speaker having drawn up the question, it was unanimously resolved that it is an high indignity to and a notorious breach of the privilege of this house for any news-writer, in letters or other papers (as minutes, or under any other denomination), or for any printer or publisher of any printed newspaper of any denomination, to presume to insert in the said letters or papers or to give therein any account of the debates or other proceedings of this house or any committee thereof, as well during the recess as the sitting of parliament; and that this house will proceed with the utmost severity against such offenders.

Cobbett, Parliamentary History, X, 800-12.

(E) DISCUSSION OF CABINET COUNCILS (1738-40)[4]

Mr. Pulteney [3 March 1738] : . . . I wonder to hear him oppose calling for any papers, or any one paper that can be supposed to have the least relation to the subject of complaint now under our consideration. If I were to advise him—and I speak it with the utmost sincerity—I would advise him, for his own sake as well as for the sake of the nation, to advise laying the affair fully before the parliament, in order to have the advice of parliament upon such an important occasion. We have in this kingdom several councils; we have a privy council, a cabinet council, and, for what I know, a more secret and less numerous council still, by which the other two are directed. But the parliament is his majesty's great and chief council; it is the council which all ministers ought, both for their own sakes and their master's, to advise his majesty to consult with upon every affair of great weight and importance. For from all our histories we shall find that those kings have been the most happy and glorious who have often consulted with their parliaments; and that those ministers have always gone through their administration with the greatest ease and applause and have divested themselves of their power with the greatest safety to themselves, which seldom happens to any but those who have advised their masters to depend chiefly upon the advice of their parliaments.

In our privy council, sir, in our cabinet council, and in any more secret council, if there be any such, the honourable gentleman may be supposed to have a sway—nay, it may be even suspected that he has, under his majesty, the chief direction of each—and therefore he may, some time hereafter, be made to answer for their determinations. But it cannot be suspected that he has the direction of either house of parliament; nor are we to presume that he has any other sway in this house but that which proceeds either from the solidity and strength of his arguments, or from his superior art of persuasion. For which reason he can never be made to answer for any resolution of parliament, or for anything that is done pursuant to the advice of parliament. . . .

---

[4] The first of the following speeches was delivered in the house of commons; the others in the house of lords. They criticized Walpole's conduct of foreign affairs and in particular condemned his refusal to lay diplomatic correspondence before parliament.

The duke of Argyle [1 March 1739]: . . . I remember, my lords, a very good saying of a noble lord, who once sat in this house—it was the late Lord Peterborough. When he was asked by a friend, one day, his opinion of a certain measure, says my lord in some surprise, "This is the first time I ever heard of it." "Impossible," says the other; "why, you are a privy councillor." "So am I," replies his lordship, "and there is a cabinet councillor coming up to us just now. If you ask the same question of him, he will perhaps hold his peace; and then you will think he is in the secret. But if he opens once his mouth about it, you will find he knows as little of it as I do." My lords, it is not being in privy council, or in cabinet council; one must be in the minister's council to know the true motives of our late proceedings. For my own part, my lords, I can only guess at them, but I have disapproved of them these eighteen years; I have disapproved of them in public, in private, and in all companies. Therefore, my lords, what I speak upon this occasion, I speak it as a citizen of the world, and not as a privy councillor. . . .

The duke of Argyle [1 December 1740]: . . . I hope your lordships will indulge me in making a short reply to what has been said by the learned and noble lord who spoke last. Through the whole of what he said upon this new question, he seemed to look upon it as admitted that nothing that required the least secrecy could be safely communicated to this house. From hence your lordships may see how cautious you ought to be of doing anything that may tend toward establishing this as a maxim of our government; for if this should ever come to pass, you will have less confidence from your sovereign, you will be treated in a more contemptible manner by his minister than the writer of the London Gazette. An affair of state may be communicated by way of hint to a gazetier; it may be known to all our news-writers; but the august house of peers will be thought unworthy of being trusted with the secret. If you should ever allow yourselves to be treated in so contemptible a manner by any minister, can you from thenceforth look for any respect from the people? Can you be of any service to your king by advising? Can you be of any service to your country by inquiring?

My lords, the making use of this argument upon any occasion is, in my opinion, the highest indignity that can be offered to this assembly; and therefore I must say I am sorry to see it received with patience. I cannot pretend to any great learning in your journals; but, I am persuaded, many examples may be found where papers of the most secret nature, and of the highest importance, have been communicated to this house when called for. Nay, I have good reason to believe that such motions were always agreed to by the house till the year 1721; because I find among the protests of that year a protest entered against the negative then put upon a motion for laying before this house the instructions given to a noble lord I have in my eye, as his majesty's minister or plenipotentiary to the crown of Sweden or any other of the northern crowns. And that negative is there said to be the first instance to be found in our journals where lords have moved for a sight of instructions of any kind, and have not been supported by the house in that motion.

The year 1721[5] I must therefore, my lords, look on as the fatal era of this modern maxim; which, I confess, has been as inviolably, as imprudently, admitted by the conduct of the house ever since that time. In the same year a negative was put upon a motion for laying the new treaty with Spain before this assembly, and in the same year a negative was put upon the motion for Sir George Byng's instructions, as has been already mentioned. For this last negative the noble lord who moved you this question has, in my opinion, given you what was very probably the true reason. I shall grant that there were several lords at that time in the service of the crown who had been in that service, and some of them perhaps in the administration, in the year 1718. But we are not to suppose that every lord that is in the service of the crown is likewise in the administration of the government; for a lord may be in a very high office under the crown and yet know nothing of what is doing in his majesty's councils. These very instructions to Mr. Vernon, which are now said to contain secrets of such high importance, were made known, I believe, to very few of his majesty's great officers of state. At least I can answer for myself that I never saw them; and yet I was at that time commander-in-chief of his majesty's forces and one of his cabinet council. But your lordships must observe that we have now two cabinet councils in this kingdom: his majesty has one and the minister has another. And I am afraid it often happens that his majesty's cabinet council knows little or nothing of what is doing or intended to be done.

Ibid., X, 591 f., 1136 f.; XI, 763 f.

(F) DEBATE ON THE REMOVAL OF WALPOLE FROM OFFICE (1741)[6]

Lord Carteret: . . . As members of this house, we are in duty bound to have a watchful eye over the public measures his majesty is advised to pursue, and over the chief ministers he is pleased to employ in the administration of public affairs. And when we are of opinion that the measures he is advised to pursue are wrong, or that the ministers he is pleased to employ are weak or wicked, it is our duty and our business, while we sit here, to warn our sovereign of his danger and to remove weak or wicked counsellors from about his throne. As to the parliamentary methods of removing a minister, I need not acquaint your lordships that they are of sev-

---

[5] It was in this year that Walpole gained virtual control of the government.

[6] The first three speeches were delivered in the house of lords; the last in the commons. Walpole was forced to resign just a year after this debate (February, 1742).

eral kinds, and that all but one tend to punish as well as remove. When we proceed by impeachment, by bill of attainder, or by bill of pains and penalties, the design is to punish as well as remove; but there is another way of proceeding in parliament which tends only to remove the minister from the king's counsels without inflicting any real punishment upon him, and that is by an humble address to our sovereign that he would be graciously pleased to remove such a one from his counsels.

I believe, my lords, it will not be questioned that either house of parliament may offer such advice to the crown by way of humble address. I believe it will not be said that it is unusual or unprecedented, and therefore I shall not trouble your lordships with calling to your remembrance any of the precedents that may be found in the journals of parliament. I shall only take notice of the difference between the methods of proceeding by impeachment, by bill of attainder, or bill of pains and penalties, and this method of proceeding by way of humble address to the crown. When we proceed by impeachment, by bill of attainder, or by bill of pains and penalties, some particular criminal facts must be alleged, and there must be some sort of proof of those facts. But when we proceed by way of address to the king, that he would be graciously pleased to remove such a minister from his counsels, a general view of that minister's conduct, a general view of public affairs, may afford just cause for such an address, and common fame is a sufficient proof; for, when no particular fact is insisted on, it is impossible to bring any particular proof. This, my lords, is the difference; and the reason of this difference is very plain. When a man is to be punished, either in his person, his freedom, or estate, some crime or criminal neglect ought to be not only alleged but proved by a legal proof, or by strong presumptions. But as his not being employed in the king's counsels neither affects his person, his freedom, nor his estate, therefore weakness alone, or a general bad character, may be a good cause for removing him. A weak man is certainly in any country very unfit for being in the king's counsels; and in a popular government a man who has incurred the general odium of the people ought not to be continued in the king's counsels, because the unpopularity of the minister may at last affect the throne itself and render the people disaffected to their sovereign.

I must therefore desire your lordships to take particular care to distinguish between the method of proceeding against a minister by impeachment, by bill of attainder, or bill of pains and penalties, and the method of proceeding against a minister by address only; because, if you do not take care to fix this distinction in your minds, you may expect from me what I do not intend to give, and what the nature of the motion I am to make renders it not only unnecessary but unfit for me to give. I am to move only for an humble address to his majesty that he would be graciously pleased to remove a minister—I may say, the minister—from his counsels. . . .

123. PROCEEDINGS IN PARLIAMENT

Duke of Argyle: ... An address ... , my lords, to remove a minister from the king's counsels and presence may be sufficiently founded upon general rumours or general disgusts, and may be agreed to—nay, in many cases ought to be agreed to—without any particular accusation and, consequently, without any proof. A minister's character neither is nor can be affected by such an address; for a man's character depends entirely upon his own conduct and can never be lost by any sort of judicial proceeding. ... For this reason, my lords, I hope we shall have in this motion the concurrence of all those who have a true regard for the character of the minister and, at the same time, a thorough conviction of his innocence. I believe every lord in this house is sensible that he has already lost his character with a great majority of the people of this nation, and that he is generally and violently suspected, not only of great failings, but of heinous crimes. Is not he suspected of having solely engrossed the ear of his sovereign and excluded from his master's presence, as well as confidence, every man that disdains being a slave to him? Is he not suspected of having engrossed the sole disposal of all the favours of the crown, and the sole direction of all the officers of the kingdom? Is he not suspected of having endeavoured to destroy the independency of parliament and the freedom of elections, by making an abject submission to his will and direction the sole title to the obtaining of any favour from the crown or the holding of any post which the crown can take away? Is he not suspected of having applied the public money towards gaining an undue and corrupt influence both in parliament and at elections? Is he not, in general, suspected of having a design, by the continuance and increase of useless offices and the multiplicity of penal laws, to establish in the crown an absolute and uncontrollable power? ...

Does not every one know that the levée of this minister is haunted by lords who, I hope, neither have nor expect any pensions; by land and sea officers who ought not to be allowed to expect any preferment by his favour or recommendation; by lawyers who ought not to be allowed to expect being appointed judges by his means; and by many of the reverend bench and multitudes of other clergymen who, I hope, expect translations or preferments from their piety and learning, and not by neglecting their devotion and trifling away their precious time in attending his levées? My lords, it is needless to deny or disguise this charge. The candidates for preferment have in all countries most excellent noses. They will smell out the proper road to preferment; and when the world sees candidates of all sorts in one road, the world will judge, and most reasonably judge, that to be the sole road to preferment. From hence the general suspicion against this minister has arisen. If the suspicion be well grounded, he is in some degree guilty of high treason by the known laws and constitution of this kingdom, and ought to be impeached as well as removed. But the very suspicion is a sufficient cause for addressing the king to remove him, because the people can never be easy whilst a man is in power who, in their opinion, is a traitor against the laws and constitution of his country; for a man who is in danger of suffering by the law will certainly endeavour to overturn the law. Therefore, to dissipate the fears and jealousies of the people, and to make them easy under the government of their sovereign, such a minister ought to be removed. And after he is removed, the parliament may, without running the risk of being thought corrupted, acquit him, if upon a fair trial he appear to be innocent; and every member may then, without fear, give his vote against him, if he should appear to be guilty.

The next general suspicion I took notice of is his having endeavoured to destroy the independency of parliament and freedom of elections, by disposing of the favours of the crown to such only as vote in parliament or at elections according to his direction, and turning every man out of the employment he holds at the pleasure of the crown, if in either case he disobeys his orders. My lords, the maxim which is the chief corner-stone of our happy constitution is that the king has nothing to do with a man's behaviour in parliament or at elections. King William was so sensible of this that, when his ministers advised him to dismiss an officer of the army for having voted upon some occasion against them in parliament, he answered as every just king ought, and as every wise one will: "The gentleman has always behaved well as an officer of the army, and I have nothing to do with his behaviour as a member of parliament." This, my lords, ought to be the maxim of every king of this country; for if the contrary maxim should ever prevail—if the king should lay it down as a maxim not to bestow a favour upon any one, or continue in commission any officer, but such as vote according to the directions of his ministers—the disposal of the posts and offices necessary for the support of our government must either be taken from the crown, or the crown will take from the parliament its independency, and consequently from our constitution its happiness and freedom. Therefore, I must be of opinion that it is a high degree of treason in any minister to advise the king to lay down such a maxim, or to have any regard to a man's voting in parliament, or at elections, in the distribution of those favours which the crown has to bestow. . . .

The lord chancellor [Hardwicke]: . . . To imagine or suppose that any one minister solely engrosses the ear of his sovereign and usurps the sole disposal of all the favours of the crown is, I am sure, no compliment to the king upon the throne, and it is a supposition that can be made by no man who has the honour of knowing anything of his present majesty's character. His ears, my lords, it is well known, are open not only to all his ministers, but to all his subjects. He is as ready to hear their complaints as he is willing to redress their grievances, and never does bestow any favour without examining, as far as his high station will give him leave, into the character of the person recommended. The minister whose conduct and character is now under our consideration has certainly a great share of his majesty's confidence; but this does not proceed from any blind attachment to him, but from the experience his majesty has had of his fidelity and wisdom. And to those who have the honour to be near his majesty's person, or in his counsels, it is very well known that this minister's recommendation does not always succeed; nor does his opinion always prevail in council. . . . As to the posts, offices, and other favours in the disposal of the crown, it is very well known that he never attempts to recommend any person directly to his majesty, but such as are soliciting for something belonging particularly to his own department. Indeed, as there is and ought and always will be, under a wise king, a very good correspondence between his majesty's ministers, they often recommend to one another; and when a gentleman of the army, navy, or any other sort of business thinks he has a title to the favour of this minister, he may, perhaps, apply to him for his recommendation—not to the crown, but to the minister or great officer whose business and duty it is to recommend to his majesty the most fit and proper person for the office or employment then to be disposed of. Thus, my lords, we may see that this minister's levée may be crowded with suitors of all sorts of characters, without his usurping the disposal of any of the favours of the crown, except such as particularly belong to his own province. . . .

Mr. Sandys: . . . According to our constitution, we can have no sole and prime minister; we ought always to have several prime ministers or officers of state. Every such officer has his own proper department, and no officer ought to meddle in the affairs belonging to the department of another. But it is publicly known that this minister, having obtained a sole influence over all our public counsels, has not only assumed the sole direction of all public affairs, but has got every officer of state removed that would not follow his direction, even in the affairs belonging to his own proper department. By this means he hath monopolized all the favours of the crown and engrossed the sole disposal of all places, pensions, titles, and ribbons, as well as of all preferments, civil, military, or ecclesiastical. This, sir, is of itself a most heinous offence against our constitution. But he has greatly aggravated the heinousness of his crime; for, having thus monopolized all the favours of the crown, he has made a blind submission to his direction at elections and in parliament the only ground to hope for any honours or preferments, and the only tenure by which any gentleman could preserve what he had. . . .

Sir Robert Walpole: . . . It is superfluous to dwell long upon my own vindication; for I have, not only the assistance of my friends, but the concurrence of the parliament to alleviate my task, since all the public transactions have been approved by the legislature which are now charged upon me as instances of ignorance, negligence, or treachery. Upon the modesty or justice of such accusations it is not my business to remark. The vindication of their own honour is properly the business of the parliament. . . .

The gentlemen by whom the motion has been supported have indeed failed in the most essential part of their accusation. They have not yet attempted to prove that I am the author of those measures which they have so clamorously condemned. But surely they cannot be ignorant that, till they have proved the criminal, their declamations upon the crime are empty sounds; that they are arrows shot without a mark, which lose their force in the air or fall down upon those who discharged them. It has indeed, sir, been prudent not to attempt what they are not able to accomplish; for I defy them to show that in any of these transactions I was engaged otherwise than as one among many—as a member of the council in which they were determined on, or of the parliament by which they were approved.

Of the exorbitant power with which I am invested, of the influence which I extend to all parts of the nation, of the tyranny with which I oppress those that oppose, and the liberality with which my followers are rewarded, no instance has been produced—as, indeed, no effects have been felt. But, having first conferred upon me a kind of mock dignity and styled me the prime minister, they carry on the fiction which has once heated their imaginations and impute to me an unpardonable abuse of that chimerical authority which only they have thought it necessary to bestow. . . .

The debate began at eleven in the morning and continued until four the next morning, when, the question being put upon Mr. Sandys' motion, it was resolved in the negative by 290 against 106.

Ibid., XI, 1049-1388.

(G) SIR WILLIAM YONGE ON ANNUAL PARLIAMENTS (1745)

. . . I have always opposed the restoration of triennial parliaments, and consequently must be against annual. Triennial parliaments would, in my opinion, be the cause of great disturbances, but annual would be the cause of absolute confusion. Whether we ever had such a thing as parliaments annually elected is a question too learned for me to determine. It is a question which I shall never dive into for two reasons: first, because I hate poring over musty and obscure records; and, secondly, because I think the question is now of no importance—for, supposing we had such a thing in former ages as annual elections, the thing is now become absolutely impracticable by the great change that has happened in our circumstances. In former ages a seat in parliament was so far from being thought advantageous that it was thought very burdensome upon the person chosen. It was so far from being contended for that it was by many industriously avoided, and was therefore reckoned one of those public offices which a man was obliged to serve, if he happened to be chosen. Frequent elections could therefore in those days occasion no disturbances in the country; but in these our days every one knows the violent contests that are raised in our counties, and many of our populous cities and boroughs, by a general election, especially when party spirit happens to run high and the opposite candidates are pretty nearly equal. These contests are even at this time so violent that the peace of the country is often in danger of being disturbed. How great, how certain, then would the danger be if the heats and animosities raised upon such occasions had no time to subside? It was this danger chiefly that was the occasion of substituting septennial parliaments in the place of triennial. Many of us may remember the mobs and riots that were occasioned by the last two general elections in the queen's reign, and the first after his late majesty's accession. They were such as must make every man tremble that has any regard for the tranquillity of his country; and, as I am old enough to have a very lively and a very terrible impression of them in my mind, I am sure I shall never be for repealing or altering any of those wise regulations by which a happy and a seasonable period was put to them.

Supposing then, sir, that there were no prorogations in the reign of Edward III, that a parliament was then annually held, and that that parliament was annually chosen—and suppose that king to have been, as I believe he really was, one of the greatest and wisest princes that ever swayed the sceptre of this kingdom—yet this is no argument for our doing what he did with respect to parliaments. It might then have been the height of wisdom, and yet now it may be—in my opinion it would be—the height of madness; because it would certainly be attended with great danger, and is neither necessary nor proper for answering the ends proposed. I say, sir, it is not necessary, because in a septennial parliament we may answer all the ends of our institution as well as in a triennial or annual. We are, it is true, the great and general inquisitors of the nation, and consequently are to take notice of, and to lay in a proper manner before our sovereign, all public grievances, as well as those which affect particularly the places we represent. But cannot we do this in septennial parliaments, which meet annually, as well as in parliaments that are annually chosen? Supposing it true that some members never see their constituents from the time they are chosen till they return to solicit their votes at a new election—which I believe is very rarely the case—is there not, or may there not be, a constant intercourse by letters? Are not all letters from or to members of parliament made free of postage for this very purpose? And may not a member of parliament be by letters as fully informed of the sentiments and grievances of his constituents as if he were present among them? As to those grievances which affect the country in general, he can know them no other way but by letters; for he cannot be present in every part of the kingdom. And a member whose constant residence is in London has a better opportunity of being informed and judging of such grievances than one who resides mostly at his seat in any remote part of the kingdom. . . .

And as to our duty with respect to our sovereign, surely, sir, we may perform that duty; we may give our sovereign the fullest information as to the sentiments of our constituents without going down to live among them; because, as regular posts are now established to every part of the kingdom, we may keep a constant correspondence with our constituents, and may know their sentiments of all public measures by their letters with more certainty, I think, than we could do by their conversation. Therefore, if the members of a septennial parliament neglect to inform their sovereign of the murmurings among the people, or if they misrepresent to him the sentiments of the people, it cannot proceed from their ignorance; but from some other cause, which would have the same effect in an annual as it has in a septennial parliament.

Upon this occasion, sir, as upon many others, the word attorney has been artfully brought into the debate, as if the members of this house were nothing more than the attorneys of the particular county, city, or borough they respectively represent. But every one knows that by our constitution, after a gentleman is chosen, he is the representative or, if you please, the attorney of the people of England and as such is at full freedom to act as he thinks best for the people of England in general. He may receive, he may ask, he may even follow the advice of his particular constituents; but he is not obliged, nor ought he to follow their advice, if he thinks it inconsistent with the general interest of his country. He is in some respects, therefore, the attorney or servant of the people in the same manner as an elective king or chief magistrate is the servant of the people; and there is no greater absurdity or impropriety in choosing a representative for a long term of years than in choosing a king or chief magistrate for a long term of years. In both cases, I shall grant, it is an inconvenience, and that the people have often cause to repent of the choice they have made, before the expiration of the term. But this inconvenience must be submitted to for the sake of avoiding a much greater—I mean the continual disturbances that would be occasioned by frequent elections, and the fluctuation in all public measures that must necessarily ensue from a frequent change of public magistrates or representatives. . . .

Now, sir, with regard to the electors—if there must be an increase of corruption in our parliament, or confusion in our government, I think it does not signify much whether the electors be corrupted or no; but if corruption in parliament be increased, can we suppose that corruption at elections would be diminished by the introduction of annual parliaments? The bribes would not, I shall grant, be so high; but they would be much more frequent, and would consequently become more familiar to the people. Therefore, if it be possible to make the people more corrupt than they are, the establishing of annual elections would be the most effectual method we could take for doing it. The gentlemen who argue for such elections seem to be under a very great mistake; they seem to think that it is the highness of the price that corrupts, whereas I think and am certain that corruption proceeds from the nature of the man, and not from the largeness of the price that is offered. A man of a corrupt heart is like a merchant that must sell his goods and has no market but one to sell them at. If he cannot get the price he demands, he must accept of that which is offered. A corrupt man must and will sell his vote; he has no other market for it but the election for the county or corporation of which he is a member. He therefore must and will sell it there at a low price, if he finds he cannot get a high one. If, indeed, he has another interest in view, the case will be different. For example, if he has employment from one candidate and is offered a bribe by another, he will naturally consider which is of the highest value, and will of course refuse the bribe if he thinks it of less value than his employment. But he is never a bit the honester man; nor can such a man's vote be ever of any service to his country, because it never will be directed by the public interest. . . .

Ibid., XIII, 1076 f.

124. RECORDS OF JUDICIAL CASES (1691-1710)

(A) THE CASE OF JOHN ASHTON (1691)[1]

Gentlemen of the jury: You understand that Mr. Ashton is now tried for high treason; it is mentioned in the indictment to be for conspiring the death and deposing the king and queen; and for that purpose he did endeavour to go into France and to carry divers proposals in writing and several memorials to show how this kingdom might be invaded by the French. To prove this, the evidence that has been produced and given by the king's counsel has been long and consists of two parts: witnesses . . . have told how Mr. Ashton designed a voyage to France and that he hired a ship for that purpose, and several papers were taken out of his bosom. . . . At Whitehall this packet [of papers] is opened, and you have several papers produced in evidence and read to you. You have heard what evidence has been given, that these are the very papers that were in the packet thus taken . . . ; so that there can remain no doubt of these being the same papers that were contained in the packet that was taken out of the bosom of Mr. Ashton.

Then, as to the matter of the papers, I think it is plain beyond all contradiction that the import of them is treasonable: they show a design of invading the kingdom by a foreign force and of deposing

---

[1] Ashton, along with Sir Richard Grahme, was arraigned at the Old Bailey, London, on indictment for high treason, 16 January 1691. Grahme, the first to be tried, was convicted on the next day. On 19 January Ashton was brought to trial and likewise found guilty. The following excerpts are from Chief Justice Holt's charge to the jury in the second case.

the king and queen from the government and of setting the late king up on the throne. . . . Gentlemen, there are a great many other particulars, but these are enough—nay, half of them were enough to make any man guilty of treason that was concerned in them or that had a hand in carrying or making use of them. . . . Gentlemen, if there was a design of an invasion—be it by papists or by Protestants —if any act was done tending thereunto, it is high treason within the statute of 25 E[dward III].[2] For purposing and intending to depose the king and queen, manifested by any overt act, hath been always held to be high treason. This, gentlemen, is the sum and substance of the evidence that has been given against the prisoner at the bar.

. . . Gentlemen, if Mr. Ashton had no knowledge upon what design the other persons were to go into France, though he had actually gone into France, it had been a crime in this juncture of affairs, yet not high treason. But to go into France and carry a treasonable scheme of a design and project of an invasion—that is treason. . . . Whether Mr. Ashton went with such a purpose or not you are to consider. I would not lead you into any strain of the evidence, but only state how it stands. . . . Gentlemen, it rests upon you to consider the evidence you have heard, whether it is sufficient to induce you to believe Mr. Ashton was going into France with these papers to carry on the design of deposing the king and queen and invading the kingdom. If you are not satisfied in your consciences that he is guilty, then find him not guilty. On the other side, if you are satisfied that he is guilty, I do not question but you will find him so. . . .

Howell, *State Trials*, XII, 803 f.

(B) BLANKARD V. GALDY (1693)[3]

First: in case of an uninhabited country newly found out by English subjects, all laws in force in England are in force there; so it seemed to be agreed. Secondly: Jamaica being conquered and not pleaded to be parcel of the kingdom of England, but part of the possessions and revenue of the crown of England, the laws of England did not take place there until declared so by the conqueror or his successors. The Isle of Man and Ireland are part of the possessions of the crown of England; yet retain their ancient laws. . . . That it was impossible the laws of this nation, by mere conquest without more, should take place in a conquered country, because for a time there must want officers, without which our laws can have no

---

[2] No. 62F.

[3] The case was tried in the court of king's bench on appeal from Jamaica. In an action for debt on a bond the defendant pleaded that the bond had been given to purchase the office of provost marshal and was void because a statute of Edward VI prohibited the buying of offices concerned with the administration of justice. It was argued for the plaintiff that Jamaica was conquered territory and that the inhabitants were not subject to acts of the English parliament unless specifically named in them. The court found for the plaintiff and the judgment was delivered by Chief Justice Holt. Cf. no. 91C.

force; that, if our law did take place, yet, they in Jamaica having power to make new laws, our general laws may be altered by theirs in particulars. Also they held that in the case of an infidel country their laws by conquest do not entirely cease, but only such as are against the law of God; and that in such cases, where the laws are rejected or silent, the conquered country shall be governed according to the rule of natural equity.

Salkeld, *Reports*, II, 411 f.

(C) ASHBY V. WHITE AND OTHERS (1702-03)[4]

The case is truly stated, and the only question is whether or not, if a burgess of a borough, that has an undoubted right to give his vote for the choosing a burgess of parliament for that borough, is refused giving his vote, [he] has any remedy in the king's courts for this wrong against the wrongdoer. All my brothers agree that he has no remedy; but I differ from them, for I think the action well maintainable that the plaintiff had a right to vote and that, in consequence thereof, the law gives him a remedy if he is obstructed; and this action is the proper remedy. . . .

And here, the plaintiff having this right [of voting by virtue of his burgage tenure], it is apparent that the officer did exclude him from the enjoyment of it; wherein none will say he has done well, but wrong to the plaintiff. And it is not at all material whether the candidate that he would have voted were chosen, or likely to be; for the plaintiff's right is the same and, being hindered of that, he has injury done him for which he ought to have remedy. It is a vain thing to imagine there should be right without a remedy; for want of right and want of remedy are convertibles. If a statute gives a right, the common law will give remedy to maintain it; and wherever there is injury, it imports a damage. And there can be no petition in this case to the parliament; nor can they judge of this injury, or give damages to the plaintiff. Although this matter relates to the parliament, yet it is an injury precedaneous to the parliament; and where parliamentary matters come before us as incident to a cause of action concerning the property of the subject . . . , though the incident matter be parliamentary, we must not be deterred; but are bound by our oaths to determine it. The law consists, not in particular instances, but in the reason that rules them; and if, where a man is injured in one sort of right, he has a good action, why shall he not have it in another? And though the house of commons have right to decide elections, yet

---

[4] In this case, brought in the court of queen's bench, the plaintiff, Matthew Ashby, alleged that in a parliamentary election at Aylesbury he had been illegally excluded from the voting by the defendants, the constables of the borough. Three judges, with Chief Justice Holt dissenting, decided for the defendants on the ground that to interfere would violate the privilege of the commons. On writ of error, the judgment was reversed by the house of lords, thus upholding Holt's opinion, the substance of which follows. See the resolutions of the commons and the lords touching this same matter (no. 123B).

they cannot judge of the charter originally, but secondarily in the determination of the election; and therefore, where an election does not come in debate, as it doth not in this case, they have nothing to do. And we are to exert and vindicate the queen's jurisdiction, and not to be frighted because it may come in question in parliament. And I know nothing to hinder us from judging of matters depending on charter or prescription.

Holt, Reports, pp. 524 f.

(D) The Queen v. Paty and Others (1704)[5]

I am of the opinion that the prosecution of the suit is lawful and no breach of the privilege of that house; nor can their judgment make it so or conclude this court from determining contrary. And when the house of commons exceed their legal bounds and authority, their acts are wrongful and cannot be justified more than the acts of private men. There is no question but their authority is from the law and, as it is circumscribed, so it may be exceeded. If we should say they are judges of their privilege and their own authority, and nobody else, that would make their privileges as they would have them. In such case, if there be a wrongful imprisonment by the house of commons, what court shall deliver the party? Shall we then say there is no redress, and that we are not able to execute those laws on which the liberty of the subject depends? It is true all courts are so far judges of their own privileges that they may punish for contempts; but to make any court final judges of them, exclusive of every other jurisdiction, is to introduce a state of confusion by making every man a judge in his own cause.

It was here a doubt whether any writ of error lay upon a judgment given on a *habeas corpus*. This case went into the house of lords, where it occasioned great debates between the two houses of parliament; but, the parliament being soon after prorogued, the dispute was dropped.

Ibid., pp. 526 f.

(E) The Queen v. Tutchin (1704)[6]

Gentlemen of the jury: This is an information that is preferred by the queen's attorney general against Mr. Tutchin for writing and

---

[5] As a result of the judgment of the house of lords in the case of Ashby v. White, various burgesses of Aylesbury, including Paty, brought suit against the constables who had excluded them, along with Ashby, from voting at the election. The commons, in line with their resolution of 26 January (see no. 123B), committed the plaintiffs to Newgate Prison for breach of privilege. On a writ of *habeas corpus* the legality of this action was brought before the court of queen's bench, which refused to free the prisoners. Chief Justice Holt gave the dissenting opinion that in part follows.

[6] In several numbers of the *Observator* John Tutchin accused various government officials of being in the pay of the king of France and denounced the administration of the navy as being incompetent and corrupt. On prosecution by

composing and publishing, or causing to be writ, composed, or published, several libels against the queen and her government; and all these that are set forth as libels are entitled *The Observator*, and they are in number six. . . . [The defendants] say they are innocent papers and no libels, and they say nothing is a libel but what reflects upon some particular person. But this is a very strange doctrine: to say it is not a libel reflecting on the government, endeavouring to possess the people that the government is maladministered by corrupt persons that are employed in such or such stations either in the navy or army. To say that corrupt officers are appointed to administer affairs is certainly a reflection on the government. If people should not be called to account for possessing the people with an ill opinion of the government, no government can subsist; for it is very necessary for all governments that the people should have a good opinion of it. And nothing can be worse to any government than to endeavour to procure animosities as to the management of it. This has been always looked upon as a crime, and no government can be safe without it be punished.

Now you are to consider whether these words I have read to you do not tend to beget an ill opinion of the administration of the government. . . . Now they, on his behalf, insist on these things. First they say, "You do not prove any crime against him in London." Indeed, it is not proved that he writ them in London; but the question is whether there is not proof of the composing and publishing in London . . . Gentlemen, I must leave it to you. If you are satisfied that he is guilty of the composing and publishing these papers at London, you are to find him guilty.

Howell, State Trials, XIV, 1125 f.

(F) IMPEACHMENT OF SACHEVERELL (1710)[7]

Whereas his late majesty King William III, then prince of Orange, did with an armed force undertake a glorious enterprise for delivering this kingdom from popery and arbitrary power, and divers subjects of this realm, well affected to their country, joined with and assisted his late majesty in the said enterprise and, it having pleased Almighty God to crown the same with success, the late Happy Revolution did take effect and was established; and whereas the said glorious enterprise is approved by several acts of parliament . . . : yet, neverthe-

---

the attorney general, Tutchin was found guilty in the court of queen's bench; but, on account of a technical flaw in the proceedings, the court set aside the verdict and ordered a new trial. As the crown never renewed the prosecution, Tutchin went free. The following extract is from Chief Justice Holt's charge to the jury—a fair statement of the existing law by a liberal-minded judge. Cf. no. 117B.

[7] The facts in this famous case are brought out in the following excerpts: (1) the articles of impeachment presented by the house of commons; (2) the answer drawn up by the defendant; (3) two speeches for the prosecution and one for the defence; (4) the judgment by the lords.

less, the said Henry Sacheverell . . . preached a sermon at the cathedral church of St. Paul before the lord mayor, aldermen, and citizens of London on the 5th day of November last . . . ; which said sermon he, the said Henry Sacheverell, likewise published in print . . . , with a wicked, malicious, and seditious intention to undermine and subvert her majesty's government and the Protestant succession as by law established, to defame her majesty's administration, to asperse the memory of his late majesty, to traduce and condemn the late Happy Revolution, to contradict and arraign the resolutions of both houses of parliament, to create jealousies and divisions amongst her majesty's subjects, and to incite them to sedition and rebellion.

Article I. He, the said Henry Sacheverell, in his said sermon preached at St. Paul's doth suggest and maintain that the necessary means used to bring about the said Happy Revolution were odious and unjustifiable, that his late majesty, in his declaration, disclaimed the least imputation of resistance; and that to impute resistance to the said Revolution is to cast black and odious colours upon his late majesty and the said Revolution.

Article II. He . . . doth suggest and maintain that the foresaid toleration granted by law is unreasonable and the allowance of it unwarrantable; and asserts that he is a false brother, with relation to God, religion, or the Church, who defends toleration and liberty of conscience. . . .

Article III. He . . . doth falsely and seditiously suggest and assert that the Church of England is in a condition of great peril and adversity under her majesty's administration. . . .

Article IV. He . . . doth falsely and maliciously suggest that her majesty's administration, both in ecclesiastical and civil affairs, tends to the destruction of the constitution. . . .

All which crimes and misdemeanours the commons are ready to prove. . . . And the said commons . . . do pray that the said Henry Sacheverell be put to answer to all and every the premises, and that such proceeding, examination, trial, judgment, and exemplary punishment may be thereupon had and executed as is agreeable to law and justice.

To the first part of the first article the said Henry Sacheverell denies that, in his said sermon preached at St. Paul's, he doth suggest and maintain that the necessary means used to bring about the Happy Revolution were odious and unjustifiable. . . . And as to that part of the said article, whereby the said Henry Sacheverell is charged with suggesting and maintaining that his late majesty, in his declaration, disclaimed the least imputation of resistance, the said Henry Sacheverell doth acknowledge himself to have made such suggestion . . . ; the resistance . . . being such a resistance as tended to the conquest of this realm, as plainly appears from . . . his late majesty's declaration. . . .

As to the last charge in the said article, the said Henry Sacheverell denies that he doth, in his said sermon, suggest and maintain that to impute resistance to the said Revolution is to cast black and odious colours upon his late majesty and the said Revolution. The persons whom the said Henry Sacheverell in his sermon describes . . . are . . . those new preachers and new politicians who teach, in contradiction to both Gospel and the laws, that the people have the power vested in them . . . to cancel their allegiance at their pleasure and to call their sovereign to account for high treason against his subjects—nay, and to dethrone and murder him for a criminal, as they did the royal martyr. . . . The said Henry Sacheverell, upon the strictest search into his said sermon . . . , doth not find that he hath given any the least colourable pretence for the accusation exhibited against him in this first article, but barely by his asserting the utter illegality of resistance to the supreme power upon any pretence whatsoever. . . . And the said Henry Sacheverell doth further humbly insist and is advised that the aforesaid assertion is agreeable to and warranted by the common law of England and divers acts of parliament now remaining in full force. The said Henry Sacheverell doth with all humility aver the illegality of resistance on any pretence whatsoever to be the doctrine of the Church of England and to have been the general opinion of our most orthodox and able divines from the time of the Reformation to this day. . . .

To . . . the second article . . . , the said Henry Sacheverell saith that, upon the most diligent inquiry, he hath not been able to inform himself that a toleration hath been granted by law; but admits that an act did pass in the first year of King William and Queen Mary entitled An Act for Exempting Their Majesties' Protestant Subjects Dissenting from the Church of England from the Penalties of Certain Laws—which exemption the said Henry Sacheverell doth not anywhere maintain or suggest to be unreasonable, or that the allowance of it is unwarrantable. . . .

As to . . . the third article . . . , the said Henry Sacheverell denies that he hath either asserted or suggested the Church of England to be in a condition of great peril and adversity under her majesty's administration. But he doth freely acknowledge that he hath in his sermon suggested that, when national sins are ripened up to a full maturity to call down vengeance from Providence on a church and kingdom debauched in principles and corrupted in manners . . . , then we . . . are in danger. . . .

As to the fourth article, it contains charges of a very high and criminal nature of which the said Henry Sacheverell knows his heart to be entirely innocent. And he observes with comfort that . . . in this fourth article he is not accused of maintaining and asserting, but barely suggesting what is therein contained. And he humbly hopes that bare suggestions or insinuations, could they with any colour or probability be made out (as he is fully satisfied they cannot), will not . . . by your lordships . . . be adjudged sufficient to involve an

English subject in the guilt and punishment of high crimes and misdemeanours. . . .

Mr. Lechmere: My lords, I am commanded to assist in stating to your lordships the grounds of the charge of the commons and the nature and tendency of the crimes now before you in judgment. . . . Your lordships will find that the prisoner, in his sermon preached at St. Paul's, has asserted a doctrine in direct defiance and contradiction of that resistance used to bring about the Revolution when he affirms the utter illegality of resistance, on any pretence whatsoever, to be a fundamental of our constitution. And, as your lordships will hear it fully made out from the proofs by those gentlemen to whom that part is assigned, he has also plainly declared himself that even that resistance used at the time of the late Happy Revolution is not to be excepted out of his fundamental rule. My lords, when a preacher of the Gospel and a minister of the Church of England, even under this happy establishment, shall thus publicly condemn the foundations on which it stands, in defiance of her majesty and the great council of the nation then sitting in parliament, it becomes an indispensable duty upon us . . . , not only to demand your lordships' justice on such a criminal, but clearly and openly to assert our foundations. . . . Your lordships on this occasion will again consider the ancient legal constitution of the government of this kingdom; from which it will evidently appear to your lordships that the subjects of this realm had not only a power and right in themselves to make that resistance, but lay under an indispensable obligation to do it. The nature of our constitution is that of a limited monarchy, wherein the supreme power is communicated and divided between queen, lords, and commons, though the executive power and administration be wholly in the crown. The terms of such a constitution . . . express an original contract between the crown and the people. . . . The consequences of such a frame of government are obvious. . . . If the executive part endeavours the subversion and total destruction of the government, the original contract is thereby broke, and the right of allegiance ceases. That part of the government thus fundamentally injured hath a right to save or recover that constitution in which it had an original interest. . . .[8]

Mr. Walpole: My lords, the commons are now making good their charge against Dr. Henry Sacheverell contained in the first article. . . . By what has been already offered to your lordships, I make no doubt but you are fully convinced how injurious these positions must be to the peace and quiet of the kingdom, and how highly they deserve and how loudly call for your lordships' speedy and exemplary justice. The great licentiousness of the press in censuring and reflecting upon all parts of the government has of late given too just cause

---

[8] At the conclusion of this address the commons introduced the evidence against Dr. Sacheverell.

of offence. But when any pamphlets and common libels are matters of complaint, when none but mercenary scribblers and the hackney pens of a discontented party are employed to vent their malice, it is fit to leave them to the common course of the law and to the ordinary proceeding of the courts below. But, my lords, when the trumpet is sounded in Zion; when the pulpit takes up the cudgels; when the cause of the enemies of our government is called the cause of God and of the Church; when this bitter and poisonous pill is gilded over with the specious name of loyalty, and the people are taught for their souls' and consciences' sake to swallow these pernicious doctrines; when, instead of sound religion, divinity, and morality, factious and seditious discourses are become the constant entertainments of some congregations; the commons cannot but think it high time to put a stop to this growing evil, and for the authority of a parliament to interpose and exert itself in defence of the Revolution, the present government, and the Protestant succession. . . .

Sir Simon Harcourt: May it please your lordships, I am counsel for Dr. Sacheverell, who stands impeached in the name of all the commons of Great Britain of high crimes and misdemeanours. The crimes supposed to have been committed by him are contained in four articles. I beg leave to postpone the three last. . . . That which I take to be the main objection in this case is that the doctor's assertion of the illegality of resistance must be necessarily understood with reference to the executive power. And if it be utterly illegal in any case upon any pretence whatsoever, then it was unlawful at the Revolution; and from thence the consequence is drawn that the doctor is guilty of this first charge, of maintaining that the necessary means used to bring about the Happy Revolution were odious and unjustifiable. . . . My lords, I admit the doctor has in general terms asserted this proposition of the illegality of resistance to the supreme power on any pretence whatsoever. . . . It was insisted on the first day that he had not only asserted the utter illegality of resistance to the supreme power on any pretence whatsoever, but also that he had expressly affirmed that the Revolution was not such a case as ought to be excepted out of his general rule. This I deny. If such an expression can be found in the doctor's sermon, I shall think no punishment too great for him. . . . An unlimited passive obedience and non-resistance is a slavish notion. My lords, Dr. Sacheverell does not contend for it. . . . I humbly apprehend, my lords, that extraordinary cases, cases of necessity, are always implied though not expressed, in the general rule. Such a case undoubtedly the Revolution was. . . . Having thus stated to your lordships the question between us . . . , I shall endeavour to satisfy your lordships, first, that the doctor's assertion of the illegality of resistance to the supreme power on any pretence whatsoever, in general terms, without expressing any exception or that any exception is to be made, is warranted by the authority of the Church of England and, secondly, that his manner of expression is agreeable to the law of England. . . .

The lord chancellor . . . : Mr. Speaker, the lords are now ready to proceed to judgment in the case by you mentioned. Dr. Sacheverell, the lords, having found you guilty[9] of high crimes and misdemeanours charged on you by the impeachment of the house of commons . . . , find themselves obliged by law to proceed to judgment against you; which I am ordered to pronounce, and in which you cannot but observe an extreme tenderness towards your character as a minister of the Church of England. Therefore, this high court doth adjudge as followeth:—

That you, Henry Sacheverell, Doctor in Divinity, shall be and you are hereby enjoined not to preach during the term of three years next ensuing; that your two printed sermons, referred to by the impeachment of the house of commons, shall be burnt before the Royal Exchange in London between the hours of one and two o'clock, on the 27th day of this instant March, by the hands of the common hangman in the presence of the lord mayor of the city of London and the sheriffs of London and Middlesex. . . .

Ibid., XV, 37-474.

[9] The vote was 69 to 52.

125. RECORDS CONCERNING COLONIES (1692-1718)

(A) INSTRUCTIONS TO THE GOVERNOR OF NEW YORK (1692)

Instructions for our trusty and well-beloved Benjamin Fletcher. . . . With these our instructions you will receive our commission under our great seal of England, constituting you our captain general and governor-in-chief of our province of New York and the territories depending thereon in America. You are hereupon to fit yourself with all convenient speed to repair to our province of New York in America and, being arrived there, you are to take upon you the execution of the place and trust we have reposed in you, and forthwith to call together the . . . council for that province. . . . You are also to administer unto each of the members of the council as well the oaths appointed by act of parliament . . .[1] as the oath for the due execution of their places and trust.

You are to communicate unto our said council from time to time each and so many of our instructions as you shall find convenient for our service to be imparted unto them. And you are to permit the members of our council to have and enjoy freedom of debate and vote in all things to be debated of in council. . . . You are from time to time to send to us and our committee of trade and plantations the names and qualities of any members by you put into our said council by the first conveniency after your so doing. In the

[1] That is to say, the oaths specified by the Bill of Rights (no. 120A).

choice and nomination of members of our council, as also of the principal officers, judges, assistants, justices, and sheriffs, you are always to take care that they be men of estate and ability, and not necessitous people or much in debt; and that they be persons well affected to our government. You are not to suspend the members of our council without good and sufficient cause; and, in case of suspension of any of them, you are forthwith to transmit unto us and to our said committee your reasons for so doing, together with the charge and proof against the said persons and their answers thereunto.

You are to transmit authentic copies, under the public seal, of all laws, statutes, and ordinances, which at any time shall be made and enacted within our said province, unto us and our committee of trade and plantations, within three months or sooner after their being enacted, together with duplicates thereof . . . , upon pain of our highest displeasure and of the forfeiture of that year's salary wherein you shall . . . omit to send over the said laws and ordinances. . . . And we do particularly require and command that no money or value of money whatsoever be given or granted by any act or order of assembly to any governor, lieutenant governor, or commander-in-chief of our said province which shall not, according to the style of acts of parliament in England be mentioned to be given and granted unto us with the humble desire of such assembly that the same be applied to the use and behoof of such governor, lieutenant governor, or commander-in-chief if we shall think fit. . . . You shall not suffer any public money whatsoever to be issued or disposed of otherwise than by warrant under your hand by and with the advice and consent of the council. You are to cause the accounts of all such money or value of money, attested by you, to be transmitted every half-year to our committee of trade and foreign plantations and to our commissioners of our treasury. . . . And you are particularly not to pass any law or do any act . . . whereby our revenue may be lessened or impaired, without our especial leave or command therein. You are to require the secretary of our said province, or his deputy . . . , to provide . . . a copy of the journals of the assembly, to the end the same may be [sent] unto us and to our committee of trade and foreign plantations. . . .

You shall not displace any of the judges, justices, sheriffs, or ministers within our said province of New York without good and sufficient cause, to be signified unto us and our committee of trade and plantations. . . . You shall not erect any court or office of judicature, not before erected or established, without our special order. . . . Whereas it is necessary that all our rights and dues be received and recovered, and that speedy and effectual justice be administered in all cases concerning our revenue, you are to take care that a court of exchequer be called and do meet at all such times as shall be needful. . . .

You shall take especial care that God Almighty be devoutly and duly served throughout your government, the Book of Common Prayer as it is now established read each Sunday and holy day, and the Blessed Sacrament administered according to the rites of the Church of England. . . . Our will and pleasure is that no minister be preferred by you to any ecclesiastical benefice . . . without a certificate from the right reverend the bishop of London of his being conformable to the doctrine and discipline of the Church of England. . . . You are to take care that drunkenness and debauchery, swearing and blasphemy, be severely punished, and that none be admitted to public trust and employment whose ill fame and conversation may bring scandal thereupon.

You are to take care that no man's life, manor, freehold, or goods be taken away or harmed . . . otherwise than by established and known laws, not repugnant to but—as much as may conveniently be—agreeable to the laws of this our kingdom of England. . . . And you are to permit a liberty of conscience to all persons, except papists, so they be contented with a quiet and peaceable enjoyment of the same, not giving offence or scandal to the government. . . . And that we may be the better informed of the trade of our said province, you are to take care that due entries be made in all ports of all goods and commodities imported and exported . . . ; and that a yearly account thereof be transmitted by you unto us. . . . Forasmuch as great inconveniences may arise by the liberty of printing within our province of New York, you are to provide . . . that no person keep any press for printing, nor that any book, pamphlet, or other matters whatsoever be printed without your especial leave and licence first obtained. . . .

Lastly, if anything shall happen that may be of advantage and security of our said province, which is not herein or by our commission provided for . . . , we do hereby allow unto you, with the advice and consent of our council, to take order for the present therein, giving speedy notice thereof that so you may receive our ratification, if we shall approve of the same. . . .

O'Callaghan, *Documents Relative to New York*, III, 818 f.

(B) ORDER IN COUNCIL ON COLONIAL APPEALS (1696)

[It is ordered] that all appeals from any of the plantations be heard as formerly by a committee who are to report the matter so heard by them with their opinion thereupon to his majesty in council. And in order thereunto his majesty did declare his further pleasure that all the lords of the council, or any three or more of them, be appointed a committee for that purpose.

Acts of the Privy Council, Colonial Series, II, 310.

(C) ORDER ON AN APPEAL FROM CONNECTICUT (1698)

May it please your majesty:—In obedience to your majesty's several orders of council of the 23rd of February last, we have considered the petition of John and Nicholas Hallam and of Edward Palmer and John Hallam, inhabitants of your majesty's colony of Connecticut, thereunto annexed, relating to two particular cases wherein they complain of the obstructions of justice in the said colony. And we thereunto most humbly represent to your majesty that, though the right of either of the said cases do not appear evident to us by any sufficient proofs, and we cannot therefore offer any opinion thereupon, yet nevertheless we humbly conceive that, upon what has been set forth by the forementioned petitions about the denial or obstruction of the course of justice in your majesty's colony of Connecticut, your majesty may fitly require the governor and company of the said colony to take care that no such obstruction of the course of justice be practised or allowed amongst them; but that the respective cases set forth by both the forementioned petitions, and any other cases whatsoever that may hereafter happen upon differences between man and man about private rights, be fairly heard and judged in the proper methods in the courts established in that colony; and that in case the aforesaid petition[er]s, or any of them, or any other persons do think themselves aggrieved by the sentence or sentences which may be there given, they may thereupon be allowed to appeal unto your majesty in council; and that the copies of records and other proceedings in all such respective cases be transmitted hither, in order to a final hearing and determination thereof by your majesty in council, it being the inherent right of your majesty to receive and determine appeals from all your majesty's subjects in America. Which nevertheless is most humbly submitted. Tankerville, Philip Meadows, William Blathwayt, John Pollexfen, Hilary Hill.

His majesty in council, approving of what is proposed by the council of trade in their said representation, is pleased to order that the governor and company of the colony of Connecticut be required to take care that no obstruction of the course of justice be practised or allowed amongst them; but that the respective cases mentioned in the said representation, and any other whatsoever that may hereafter happen upon differences between man and man about private rights, be fairly heard and judged in the proper methods of the courts established in that colony. And in case the petitioners in the aforesaid causes, or any of them, or any other persons shall think themselves aggrieved by the sentence or sentences, which may be there given, they may thereupon be allowed to appeal to his majesty in council. And that copies of all records and other proceedings in all such respective cases be transmitted hither, in order to a final hearing and determination thereof before his majesty in council. And that in all such cases the governor and company of the colony of Connecticut do take notice that it is the inherent right of his majesty to receive and determine appeals from all his majesty's colonies in America; and that they do govern themselves accordingly. And the right honourable the council of trade are to signify this his majesty's pleasure to the governor and company of the colony of Connecticut accordingly.

Macqueen, *Appellate Jurisdiction*, pp. 805 f.

(D) REPORT ON TRADE AND PLANTATIONS (1700)[2]

In obedience to an order of this honourable house, dated the 6th instant, requiring from us an account of what advances we have made towards the improvement of the trade of England, we humbly offer that his majesty was pleased, by a commission dated the 15th of May, 1696, to appoint commissioners for promoting the trade of this kingdom and for inspecting and improving his plantations in America and elsewhere, with several directions and instructions, the chief whereof are as follows: to examine into and take an account of the state and condition of the general trade of England, and of the several particular trades into foreign parts; to examine what trades are or may prove hurtful, and what beneficial, to this kingdom, and by what means the advantageous trades may be improved and those that are prejudicial discouraged; to consider by what means profitable manufactures already settled may be further improved, and how other new and profitable manufactures may be introduced; to consider of proper methods for setting on work and employing the poor, and making them useful to the public; to inquire into the condition of the plantations, as well with regard to the administration of government there as in relation to commerce, and how those colonies may be rendered most beneficial to this kingdom; to inquire what naval stores may be furnished from the plantations, and how the same may be best procured; to prepare instructions for governors and to take account of their administration; to examine the journals of the councils and the acts or laws made by the respective general assemblies, in order to his majesty's approbation or disallowance thereof; to require an account of all money given by the assemblies for public uses, and how the same is expended; and to make representations and reports to his majesty, or the privy council, in writing, as there shall be occasion.

In pursuance whereof, we have proceeded in the manner following.... Having ... observed that several of his majesty's plantations in America applied themselves to the improvement of woolen manufactures in those parts for the supplying of themselves and neighbours, to the hindrance of the exportation of our English manufactures, we prepared a clause for the preventing thereof, which was presented to this honourable house and accordingly received and enacted the last session of parliament; and we have since understood, that the said restraint has had a very good effect. . . .

And, for the better preventing other more general inconveniences apprehended from the East India trade, we did also upon another

---

[2] Presented by the commissioners and ordered laid on the table, to be perused by the members.

occasion humbly propose that the wearing or consumption of the manufactured goods of India, Persia, or China, made of silk or herba, or mixed with either of those materials, as also of painted or stained calicoes, and of all handicraft-wares imported from those parts, should be discouraged and lessened in these kingdoms and in his majesty's plantations. . . .

Upon occasion of the late treaty of peace at Ryswyck,[3] a particular account having been required from us, for the information of his majesty's plenipotentiaries there, of what had been lost or gained in all his majesty's colonies and plantations since the treaty of Breda until that time, we accordingly prepared many particular accounts, not only of what had been lost or gained, as aforesaid, but also of all pretensions and grounds of differences between the French and us, with relation to each particular plantation, as also to Newfoundland, Hudson's Bay, the Royal African Company, etc., which were accordingly transmitted.

Since the conclusion of the peace, we did also, by his majesty's directions, draw up many memorials for the use of the commissioners appointed by his majesty, to treat here with commissioners from France upon all such of the foresaid matters as by the treaty of Ryswyck required any further settlement. . . . We have made representations . . . to promote the *assiento*, or contract for supplying the Spanish West Indies with negroes, not to mention many others upon private cases in matters of trade. . . .

We have made divers representations for the security and improvement of the Newfoundland trade and fishery, as well during the war as since the peace, and have constantly every year examined into and taken an account of the course and progress of that trade; and now particularly formed instructions and heads of inquiries to be given to the commander of the convoy appointed for that fishery, for the due execution of the late act to encourage the trade to Newfoundland, for the better preventing irregularities therein.

We have presented to his majesty a general state of the trade of this kingdom, with observations thereupon how we conceive divers advantageous trades may be improved and prejudicial ones discouraged; a copy whereof has been formerly laid before this honourable house.

As to his majesty's plantations in America, we do further offer that, within the allegiance of the crown of England, there are twenty several colonies—besides Hudson's Bay and Newfoundland, in which last place there is no governor—each whereof have their distinct governments, councils, and assemblies, by whom particular laws and rules of government are passed and enacted; some of which colonies are governed by his majesty's immediate commission, and others by proprietors and charters.

---

[3] Signed with France in 1697. The Peace of Breda was signed with the United Provinces in 1667.

The business relating to these plantations is managed by a constant correspondence with all the governors appointed by his majesty's immediate commission and occasionally with all the rest, in the course whereof they send us journals of their councils, assemblies, and other public proceedings, with accounts of all things whatsoever relating to each of their governments; all which are considered by us for the necessary orders to be returned thereupon. And, more particularly, the many acts or laws of the several assemblies transmitted from thence fall under our examination; and, after our consulting his majesty's counsel learned in the law as to the legal part, our reports are made thereupon to his majesty in his privy council for his royal assent or disallowance thereof, with particular regard to the interest and improvement of the trade of England as well as the good of those plantations.

We have, since our constitution, prepared draughts of commissions and instructions for all the governors of his majesty's plantations.

We have, upon several occasions, proposed to his majesty the appointing of convoys for the plantations, and of ships-of-war necessary to attend and protect the trade of those plantations; and, upon the complaints of the inhabitants there, or merchants in England, of hardships in the pressing of men and otherwise by captains of men-of-war in those parts, we have presented to his majesty regulations therein which have had a good effect.

Upon information from the officers of his majesty's customs in the plantations and others of the partiality of the people there, and more particularly in the propriety governments, in all trials upon the acts of trade wherein their private interest is concerned, and of the difficulties in the obtaining any execution of those acts in the former method, we did represent the usefulness of courts of admiralty in the plantations; upon which such courts have been erected and, where they have not been disputed, have proved of great encouragement to legal trade.

Being informed by many instances of the great countenance given to pirates in some of the plantations—and chiefly in the proprieties and charter-governments, by fitting out their ships from thence and furnishing them with all sorts of provision and ammunition, and receiving them with their plunder and booty at their return and acquitting them upon feigned trials—we did make several representations thereupon and proposed the enacting of laws there for the trial and punishment of pirates, in conformity to a law heretofore passed in Jamaica to that effect; which having been refused in the said proprieties and charter-governments, we proposed, as the only remedy for so great an evil, the offering a bill in parliament for that purpose, wherein we consulted Sir Charles Hedges, judge of his majesty's high court of admiralty, by whose great care and assistance such a bill has been prepared and is now lying before this honourable house.

And, being further sensible of the great irregularities in the proprieties and charter-governments, not only in reference to illegal trade and piracy but otherwise, we have upon several occasions represented the same to his majesty; and an act of parliament having passed, whereby the governors of those plantations are obliged to have his majesty's approbation for their acting in that capacity, we required all the said proprietors and governments to present their respective governors to his majesty and, in order to his approbation of them, to give security for their due observing the acts of trade, according to an address presented to his majesty by the right honourable the house of lords for that purpose. But, all the said proprietors here having declined to give any such security, and only two charter-governments (*viz.,* Connecticut and Rhode Island) having lately done it in America, and not any one of those governors being at present qualified by his majesty's approbation of them as required by the said act of parliament, we do not see anything, without some further provision by parliament, capable to reduce them to a more regular conduct and compliance with their duty in reference to the trade of England.

We have also upon occasion represented the misdemeanours and ill conduct of some governors of plantations acting by his majesty's immediate commission.

We have made many representations in defence of his majesty's title to several islands in America claimed by foreign princes—of which one is a claim made by the elector of Brandenburg to the island of New Tertholen, lying amongst his majesty's Leeward Caribbee Islands; one made by the French king to the island of Santa Lucia, lying amongst the Windward Caribbee Islands; one made by the French king to the island of Tobago, one of the Windward Caribbee Islands; and another by the duke of Courland to the same island.

Having been required this session of parliament by the right honourable the house of lords to lay before their lordships our opinion how consistent the colony at Darien may be with the treaties with Spain and the trade of this kingdom, we did accordingly make our humble report therein; which, we presume, was satisfactory, their lordships having made an address to his majesty to the same effect.

We have made several representations relating to the boundaries between his majesty's plantations and those of the French upon the continent, particularly in the northeastern parts of New England, where they have endeavoured to encroach upon us both as to the land and fishery.

Upon controversies that have happened between some of his majesty's colonies and others relating to their boundaries, especially between his majesty's governments and proprieties, and upon different claims that have been set on foot to some whole provinces, we have examined all their respective titles, and the necessary instructions have been given by his majesty thereupon.

We have often represented the necessity of preserving the friendship of the Five Nations of Indians, which are a barrier between his majesty's plantations and Canada, by treating them kindly and showing them a force constantly maintained in New York, ready to protect them upon all occasions.

We have applied ourselves to the promoting the importation of naval stores from New England and other his majesty's plantations; and, for the carrying on so good a design, his majesty has been pleased, upon our applications, to order the navy board to send commissioners to New England, who have been likewise joined with commissioners of that colony, for the viewing and inspecting the woods lying upon that coast, for providing his majesty's navy with masts and other necessary materials for building of ships, as also with pitch, tar, and resin, of which great quantities may be produced in those parts; and some specimens of each, sent by the said commissioners, are lately arrived and now under the examination of the navy board.

These being the chief particulars about which our time has been and is daily taken up, besides the frequent applications of merchants and of the persons concerned in the plantations, with the constant accession of the like business, we thought it our duty to lay as short an account thereof before this honourable house as the nature of each particular would bear.

All which is humbly submitted.

Journals of the Commons, XIII, 298 f.

(E) COUNCIL PROCEEDINGS ON COLONIAL TRADE (1705-18)

[31 May 1705.] In obedience to your majesty's command, signified to us by the right honourable Mr. Secretary Harley, we have examined a petition of several merchants of Virginia and Maryland complaining of undue practices in Muscovy by some of your majesty's subjects in relation to the vending and manufacture of tobacco there. We have heard the petitioners and likewise Nathaniel Gold, William Dawson, Edward Haistwell, Samuel Heathcote, and others, as also Joseph Martin in behalf of his partners, who are alleged to be concerned in the said practices. And upon the whole matter [we] do find that the said Nathaniel Gold and others, who had made a contract with the czar of Muscovy here in England in the year 1698 for importing certain quantities of tobacco into his dominions (which accordingly they did perform), and wanting a vent for the same (whereby great part of the said tobacco became dry and like to be unfit for sale, unless the same methods as in England were used for the preservation thereof), they had thereupon sent over Peter Marshall and his wife, versed in the cutting and rolling of tobacco, together with instruments and materials necessary thereunto, with a design, as they allege, to recall the said persons immediately after their having performed this particular service, without allowing them the liberty to employ their skill in the rolling or cutting any tobacco of the growth of the dominions of the czar. And we do likewise find that the said Mr. Joseph Martin, merchant of London, by his son Samuel Martin and James Spilman, his correspondents at Moscow, have very lately made a contract with some officers of the czar for the importation of other quantities of tobacco into those dominions from England, as likewise for the sending thither as many persons skilled in the spinning and rolling of tobacco as the czar should require, together with the instruments, engines, materials, and liquors commonly used in that work, to be employed not only for the manufacturing of English tobacco thus imported, but even for the tobacco of the growth of Circassia, a large province appertaining to that prince—by which means his subjects would become equally skilled in that mystery with any of your majesty's subjects, dealers in tobacco. Which proceedings being of the most pernicious consequence to the trade of your majesty's subjects and the welfare of your plantations, we are humbly of opinion that the persons mentioned to have been already sent to Moscow by the first contractors may be immediately recalled by letters of privy seal to be sent to your majesty's envoy for that purpose; and that the engines and materials already there be ordered by your majesty to be broken and destroyed in the presence of your majesty's said envoy; as likewise that the said Martin and correspondents and all other persons whatsoever be directed by your majesty's declaration, in such manner as your majesty shall think proper, not to send any persons versed in this mystery, or any instruments and materials for the same, or employing any persons therein, notwithstanding any clause in his said contract obliging them to a matter so injurious to other your majesty's subjects. And whereas the petitioners, merchants and planters of Virginia and Maryland, do suggest that several persons are soliciting for themselves at Moscow the sole trade and entire importation of tobacco exclusive of all others into those parts: we further humbly offer that your majesty would be pleased to direct your envoy at that court that he be equally and impartially assisting to all your majesty's subjects in the free trade of such tobacco of the growth of your majesty's plantations as shall be imported into the dominions of the czar.

[20 February 1707.] . . . One convoy a year may suffice to carry on this trade [with Virginia and Maryland] during the war; which convoy, as is generally agreed by all the traders, may be appointed to sail about the middle of August or not later than the beginning of September, so as to arrive in the rivers of Virginia in December, that they may have time to unload and distribute the manufactures and other goods from England to the planters, as also to load the tobacco within the several rivers of Virginia and Maryland and to return from thence in the month of May following. By which means the convoy and fleet will avoid the bad seasons in the country and the worm, which in the hot months is so prejudicial to them, and may arrive in England soon enough to go out again with the next convoy at the same season; which method we humbly conceive may best furnish the planters with those European commodities which they stand in need of, and hinder them from applying their labour to any other product or manufacture than that of tobacco.

[9 January 1718. The governor of Jamaica is] particularly enjoined carefully to observe the several instructions given him by his majesty with relation to the passing of laws in that island, more especially in such cases where his majesty's royal prerogative or the trade of Great Britain may be any ways affected; which precaution will be still more necessary in the passing of money bills than those of any other nature, because generally these have their duration but for one year and frequently have their effect before his majesty's royal pleasure can be known concerning them.

[14 May 1718.] Having received from the commissioners of your majesty's customs the extract of a letter to them from Colonel Rhett, surveyor and comptroller of the customs in Carolina, dated in December last—whereby it appears that an act was then passed in that province of a pernicious consequence to the trade and navigation of this kingdom, laying a duty of ten per cent. upon all goods of British manufactory imported into that province from Great Britain—although we do not yet find the said law has hitherto been transmitted to the lords proprietors for their approbation, yet, considering the ill consequences of such an act and that it is of force till repealed, we thought it necessary to have the opinion of your majesty's solicitor general in relation to the said act . . . , who has thereupon reported that, the said law not being consonant to reason nor agreeable to the laws of Britain, he apprehends the power of making laws by the charter to the proprietors is in this instance exceeded. . . . Considering therefore that this law is in force till it shall be repealed, we most humbly offer that your majesty's pleasure be signified to the lords proprietors of Carolina that they immediately send over to that province their disallowance of the same, with directions to their governor there never to give his assent to any law of the like nature for the future.

Acts of the Privy Council, Colonial Series, II, 487 f., 514 f., 729, 740.

SECTION XII

GEORGE III AND GEORGE IV

The scope of the present section, approximately the latter half of the period between the Revolution of 1689 and the great legislative changes of the 1830's, is the classic age of aristocratic government under the unreformed house of commons; the fact that it includes the reigns of two kings is less important. Yet there is a certain convenience in setting as chronological limits the accession of George III and the death of George IV. In the years before 1760, the British aristocracy, controlling both parliament and cabinet through a party system based on family alliance, had gained the dominance of the state. After 1760 this dominance was continuously challenged: first by George III's attempt to pack his councils with "friends" of his own choosing; later by the less direct influences of the French Revolution and the new industrial society. Largely in consequence of foreign war, however, the parliamentary aristocracy survived all such threats in the eighteenth century and, when George IV died in 1830, was still ruling the kingdom in the ancient way.

The bulk of the documents that are here brought together emanate from the long reign of George III. Under no. 126 will be found seventeen of his more important statutes. Three of them (J, K, L) were temporary enactments inspired by the French war. Three (O, P, Q) were regulations of industry necessitated by the growth of factories. Three may be classified as reforms of a more traditional sort: Burke's Place Act, Fox's Libel Act, and the Poor Relief Act of 1795. The remaining eight were all concerned with imperial affairs. The two affecting Ireland (no. 126 G, N), however troublesome they were to prove for British statesmen, are in themselves very simple documents that require no comment here. Of the acts dealing with the colonies, four (A, B, C, E) are included because they illustrate constitutional issues raised by the American Revolution. The Quebec Act deserves a place as the first great statute for the government of a conquered territory. The Canadian Constitution Act of 1791 provided a basis for all the significant experiments in colonial administration made during the next century.

A variety of other parliamentary records are given under no. 128—among them characteristic debates and resolutions on the personal influence of George III and the conduct of his ministers, on the taxation of the colonies, and on the privileges of parliament. Such materials are supplemented by abstracts of several famous trials, particularly those numbered 129A, B, and D. The rest of the cases in the same group turned upon questions of martial law (F, G, H), libel (E, I), and slavery (C). It remains to be noted that the three statutes of George IV (no. 127) anticipated the reform movement that was to achieve noteworthy results in the next generation.

The outstanding discussion of the eighteenth-century constitution, as it was then understood, is that of Sir William Blackstone in his *Commentaries on the Laws of England*; but his treatment is legalistic rather than historical, and his views were criticized in his own day by the great political philosopher, Jeremy Bentham. Modern works dealing with the whole subject or parts of it are T. E. May, *The Constitutional History of England since the Accession of George III*; L. B. Namier, *The Structure of Politics at the Accession of George III*; R. L. Schuyler, *Parliament and the British Empire*; E. and A. Porritt, *The Unreformed House of Commons*; G. S. Veitch, *The Genesis of Parliamentary Reform*; and E. Halévy, *History of the English People in 1815*.

126. GEORGE III: STATUTES

(A) STAMP ACT (1765)

An act for granting and applying certain stamp duties and other duties in the British colonies and plantations in America towards further defraying the expenses of defending, protecting, and securing the same, and for amending such parts of the several acts of parliament relating to the trade and revenues of the said colonies and plantations as direct the manner of determining and recovering the penalties and forfeitures therein mentioned. Whereas, by an act made in the last session of parliament, several duties were granted . . . towards defraying the expenses of defending . . . the British colonies and plantations in America; and whereas it is just and necessary that provision be made for raising a further revenue within your majesty's dominions in America towards defraying the said expenses: we . . . , the commons of Great Britain in parliament assembled, have therefore resolved to give . . . unto your majesty the several rates and duties hereinafter mentioned . . . ; and be it enacted . . . that . . . there shall be raised . . . and paid unto his majesty, his heirs, and successors throughout the colonies and plantations in America . . . , for every skin . . . of vellum . . . or sheet . . . of paper, on which shall be engrossed . . . any declaration . . . or other pleading, or any copy thereof, in any court of law within the British colonies and plantations in America, a stamp duty of 3d. . . .[1]

And be it further enacted . . . that all the moneys which shall arise by the several rates and duties hereby granted, except the necessary charges of raising . . . and accounting for the same, and the necessary charges . . . incurred in relation to this act and the execution thereof, shall be paid into the receipt of his majesty's exchequer, and shall be entered separate and apart from all other moneys, and shall be there reserved to be from time to time disposed of by parliament towards further defraying the necessary expenses of defending, protecting, and securing the said colonies and plantations. . . .

Statutes at Large, XXVI, 179 f.: 5 George III, c. 12.

(B) DECLARATORY ACT (1766)[2]

An act for the better securing the dependency of his majesty's dominions in America upon the crown and parliament of Great Britain. Whereas several of the houses of representatives in his majesty's colonies and plantations in America have of late against law claimed to themselves, or to the general assemblies of the same, the sole and exclusive right of imposing duties and taxes upon his majesty's subjects in the said colonies and plantations; and have in pursuance of such claim passed certain votes, resolutions, and orders derogatory to the legislative authority of parliament and inconsistent with the dependency of the said colonies and plantations upon the crown of Great Britain: . . . be it declared by the king's most excellent majesty, by and with the advice and consent of the lords spiritual and temporal and commons in this present parliament assembled . . . , that the said colonies in America have been, are, and of right ought to be subordinate unto and dependent upon the imperial crown and parliament of Great Britain; and that the king's majesty, by and with the advice and consent of the lords spiritual and temporal and commons of Great Britain in parliament assembled, had, hath, and of right ought to have full power and authority to make laws and statutes of sufficient force and validity to bind the colonies and people of America, subjects of the crown of Great Britain, in all

---

[1] Here follows an elaborate schedule of other stamp duties to be paid on legal documents, calendars, advertisements, playing cards, etc.; together with provisions for enforcement of the act and penalties for its infringement.

[2] Having repealed the Stamp Act, as being "attended with many inconveniences" and likely to be "productive of consequences greatly detrimental to the commercial interests of these kingdoms," parliament then proceeded to make the present declaration.

cases whatsoever. And be it further declared and enacted by the authority aforesaid that all resolutions, votes, orders, and proceedings in any of the said colonies or plantations, whereby the power and authority of the parliament of Great Britain to make laws and statutes as aforesaid is denied or drawn into question, are and are hereby declared to be utterly null and void to all intents and purposes whatsoever.

Ibid., XXVII, 19 f.: 6 George III, c. 12.

(C) TOWNSHEND'S REVENUE ACT (1767)

An act for granting certain duties in the British colonies and plantations in America . . . and for more effectually preventing the clandestine running of goods in the said colonies and plantations. Whereas it is expedient that a revenue should be raised in your majesty's dominions in America for making a more certain and adequate provision for defraying the charge of the administration of justice and the support of civil government in such provinces where it shall be found necessary, and towards further defraying the expenses of defending, protecting, and securing the said dominions: we, your majesty's most dutiful and loyal subjects, the commons of Great Britain in parliament assembled, have therefore resolved to give and grant unto your majesty the several rates and duties hereinafter mentioned. . . .[3]

And, for the more effectual preventing the clandestine running of goods in the British dominions in America, be it further enacted by the authority aforesaid that . . . the master or other person having . . . command of every ship . . . arriving in any British colony or plantation in America shall, before he proceeds with his vessel to the place of unlading, come directly to the custom-house for the port or district where he arrives and make a just and true entry upon oath . . . of the burden, contents, and lading of such ship . . . ; and . . . shall likewise . . . answer upon oath to such questions as shall be demanded of him by the collector or comptroller or other principal officer of the customs . . . concerning such ship . . . or concerning any goods or merchandise that shall or may be laden on board her, upon forfeiture of £100 sterling. . . .

And whereas, by an act of parliament made in the fourteenth year of the reign of Charles II . . . and several other acts now in force, it is lawful for any officer of his majesty's customs, authorized by writ of assistance under the seal of his majesty's court of exchequer, to take a constable . . . or other public officer inhabiting near unto the place and in the daytime to enter . . . any house, shop, cellar, warehouse . . . , or other place and . . . to seize and from thence to bring any kind of goods or merchandise whatsoever prohibited . . . , and to put and secure the same in his majesty's storehouse . . . : be it enacted . . . that . . . such writs of assistance . . . shall and

---

[3] Here follows a schedule of duties to be levied on all sorts of glass, paint, painter's colours, paper, and tea.

may be granted by the . . . supreme court of justice . . . within such colony or plantation. . . .

Ibid., XXVII, 505 f.; 7 George III, c. 46.

(D) Quebec Act (1774)

An act for making more effectual provision for the government of the province of Quebec in North America. Whereas his majesty by his royal proclamation, bearing date the 7th day of October in the third year of his reign, thought fit to declare the provisions which have been made in respect to certain countries, territories, and islands in America, ceded to his majesty by the definitive treaty of peace concluded at Paris . . . ;[4] and whereas, by the arrangements made by the said royal proclamation, a very large extent of country, within which there were several colonies and settlements of the subjects of France who claimed to remain therein under the faith of the said treaty, was left without any provision being made for the administration of civil government therein . . . : be it enacted . . . that all the territories, islands, and countries in North America [as aforesaid] . . .[5] be . . . annexed to and made part and parcel of the province of Quebec. . . . Provided always that nothing herein contained relative to the boundary of the province of Quebec shall in any wise affect the boundaries of any other colony. . . .

And whereas the provisions made by the said proclamation in respect to the civil government of the said province of Quebec . . . have been found upon experience to be inapplicable to . . . the said province, the inhabitants whereof amounted at the conquest to above 65,000 persons, professing the religion of the Church of Rome and enjoying an established form of constitution and system of laws . . . : be it therefore further enacted . . . that the said proclamation, so far as the same relates to the said province of Quebec . . . , be . . . hereby revoked, annulled, and made void. . . .

And, for the more perfect security and ease of the minds of the inhabitants of the said province, it is hereby declared that his majesty's subjects professing the religion of the Church of Rome . . . in the said province of Quebec may have, hold, and enjoy the free exercise of the religion of the Church of Rome, subject to the king's supremacy . . . ;[6] and that the clergy of the said Church may hold, receive, and enjoy their accustomed dues and rights with respect to such persons only as shall profess the said religion. Provided, nevertheless, that it shall be lawful for his majesty, his heirs, or suc-

---

[4] This was the peace of 1763, ending the Seven Years' War. The royal proclamation here referred to set up tentative governments in the recently acquired provinces. See R. Coupland, *The Quebec Act*.

[5] The act here sets precise boundaries for the enlarged province of Quebec—to the southwest the Ohio River, to the west the Mississippi.

[6] As defined in the Act of Supremacy (no. 81A); but Roman Catholics are permitted to take an oath of allegiance in place of the oath of supremacy.

cessors to make such provision out of the rest of the said accustomed dues and rights for the encouragement of the Protestant religion and for the maintenance and support of a Protestant clergy within the said province as he or they shall . . . think necessary and expedient. . . .

And be it further enacted . . . that his majesty's Canadian subjects within the province of Quebec, the religious orders and communities only excepted, may also hold and enjoy their property and possessions . . . and all other their civil rights in as large, ample, and beneficial manner . . . as may consist with their allegiance to his majesty and subjection to the crown and parliament of Great Britain; and that, in all matters of controversy relative to property and civil rights, resort shall be had to the laws of Canada as the rule for the decision of the same . . . , until they shall be . . . altered by any ordinances that shall from time to time be passed in the said province by the governor, lieutenant governor, or commander-in-chief . . . by and with the advice and consent of the legislative council of the same. . . .

And whereas the certainty and lenity of the criminal law of England and the benefits and advantages resulting from the use of it have been sensibly felt by the inhabitants from an experience of more than nine years . . . : be it . . . enacted . . . that the same shall continue to be administered and shall be observed as law in the province of Quebec, as well in the description and quality of the offence as in the method of prosecution and trial . . . ; subject, nevertheless, to such alterations [as aforesaid]. . . .

And whereas it may be necessary to ordain many regulations for the future welfare and good government of the province of Quebec, the occasions of which cannot now be foreseen nor without much delay and inconvenience be provided for, without entrusting that authority . . . to persons resident there; and whereas it is at present inexpedient to call an assembly: be it therefore enacted . . . that it shall and may be lawful for his majesty, his heirs, and successors . . . , with the advice of the privy council, to constitute and appoint a council for the affairs of the province of Quebec, to consist of such persons resident there, not exceeding twenty-three nor less than seventeen, as his majesty, his heirs, and successors shall be pleased to appoint . . . ; which council . . . shall have power and authority to make ordinances for the peace, welfare, and good government of the said province with the consent of his majesty's governor. . . .

Provided always that nothing in this act contained shall extend to . . . empower the said legislative council to lay any taxes or duties within the said province; such rates and taxes only excepted as the inhabitants of any town or district within the province may be authorized by the said council to assess, levy, and apply within the said town or district for the purpose of making roads, erecting and repairing public buildings, or for any other purpose respecting the local convenience and economy of such town or district. Provided also . . . that every ordinance so to be made shall within six months be transmitted by the governor . . . and laid before his majesty for his royal approbation. And if his majesty shall think fit to disallow thereof, the same shall cease and be void from the time that his majesty's order in council thereupon shall be promulgated at Quebec. Provided also that no ordinance touching religion, or by which any punishment may be inflicted greater than fine or imprisonment for three months, shall be of any force or effect until the same shall have received his majesty's approbation. . . .

Provided always . . . that nothing in this act contained shall . . . be construed . . . to repeal or make void, within the said province of Quebec, any act or acts of the parliament of Great Britain heretofore made for . . . regulating the trade or commerce of his majesty's colonies and plantations in America; but that . . . all acts of parliament heretofore made . . . respecting the said colonies and plantations shall be . . . in force within the said province of Quebec. . . .

Ibid., XXX, 549 f.: 14 George III, c. 83.

(E) COLONIAL TAX REPEAL ACT (1778)

An act for removing all doubts and apprehensions concerning taxation by the parliament of Great Britain in any of the colonies, provinces, and plantations in North America and the West Indies. . . . Whereas taxation by the parliament of Great Britain for the purpose of raising a revenue in his majesty's colonies, provinces, and plantations in North America has been found by experience to occasion great uneasinesses and disorders among his majesty's faithful subjects, who may nevertheless be disposed to acknowledge the justice of contributing to the common defence of the empire, provided such contribution should be raised under the authority of the general court or general assembly of each respective colony . . . : it is hereby declared and enacted . . . that, from and after the passing of this act, the king and parliament of Great Britain will not impose any duty, tax, or assessment whatever, payable in any of his majesty's colonies . . . in North America or the West Indies, except only such duties as it may be expedient to impose for the regulation of commerce; the net produce of such duties to be always paid and applied to and for the use of the colony . . . in which the same shall be . . . levied.

And be it further enacted . . . that . . . so much of an act made in the seventh year of his present majesty's reign . . .[7] as imposes a duty on tea imported from Great Britain into any colony . . . in America . . . is hereby repealed. . . .

Ibid., XXXII, 4: 18 George III, c. 12.

---

[7] No. 126c. On account of American protests, all the duties but tea had been repealed in 1770.

(F) BURKE'S PLACE ACT (1782)

An act for better securing the freedom of elections of members to serve in parliament by disabling certain officers employed in the collection or management of his majesty's revenues from giving their votes at such elections. For the better securing the freedom of elections of members to serve in parliament, be it enacted . . . that . . . no commissioner, collector, supervisor, gauger, or other officer or person whatsoever concerned or employed in the charging, collecting, levying, or managing the duties of excise . . . , the customs . . . , the duties on . . . parchment and paper . . . , the duties on salt . . . , the duties on windows or houses . . . , the revenue of the post office . . . , nor any captain, master, or mate of any ship . . . or other vessel employed . . . in conveying the mail to and from foreign ports, shall be capable of giving his vote for the election of any knight of the shire, commissioner, citizen, burgess, or baron to serve in parliament. . . .

Ibid., XXXIV, 48 f.: 22 George III, c. 41.

(G) IRISH APPEALS ACT (1783)

An act for removing and preventing all doubts which may have arisen or might arise concerning the exclusive rights of the parliament and courts of Ireland in matters of legislation and judicature. . . . Whereas, by an act of the last session of this present parliament entitled An Act to Repeal an Act Made in the Sixth Year of . . . George I . . . ,[8] it was enacted that the said last-mentioned act and all matters and things therein contained should be repealed . . . : for removing all doubts respecting the same . . . , be it declared and enacted . . . that the . . . right claimed by the people of Ireland to be bound only by laws enacted by his majesty and the parliament of that kingdom in all cases whatever, and to have all actions and suits at law or in equity which may be instituted in that kingdom decided in his majesty's courts therein finally and without appeal from thence, shall be and it is hereby declared to be established and ascertained forever, and shall at no time hereafter be questioned or questionable. And be it further enacted by the authority aforesaid that no writ of error or appeal shall be received or adjudged, or any other proceeding be had, by or in any of his majesty's courts in this kingdom in any action or suit at law or in equity instituted in any of his majesty's courts in the kingdom of Ireland. . . .

Ibid., XXXIV, 256: 23 George III, c. 28.

(H) CANADIAN CONSTITUTION ACT (1791)

An act to repeal certain parts of an act passed in the fourteenth

---

[8] No. 122c.

year of his majesty's reign . . . and to make further provision for the government of the said provinces. . . .[9]

And whereas his majesty has been pleased to signify, by his message to both houses of parliament, his royal intention to divide his province of Quebec into two separate provinces, to be called the province of Upper Canada and the province of Lower Canada: be it enacted . . . that there shall be within each of the said provinces respectively a legislative council and an assembly . . . ; and that in each of the said provinces respectively his majesty, his heirs, or successors shall have power . . . , by and with the advice and consent of the legislative council and assembly . . . , to make laws for the peace, welfare, and good government thereof, such laws not being repugnant to this act; and that all such laws . . . , assented to by his majesty, his heirs, or successors, or assented to in his majesty's name . . . , shall be . . . valid and binding. . . .

And be it further enacted . . . that, for the purpose of constituting such legislative council as aforesaid . . . , it shall and may be lawful for his majesty, his heirs, or successors . . . to authorize and direct the governor . . . or person administering the government in each of the said provinces respectively . . . to summon to the said legislative council . . . a sufficient number of discreet and proper persons, being not fewer than seven . . . for . . . Upper Canada and not fewer than fifteen . . . for . . . Lower Canada . . . ; and . . . that every member of each of the said legislative councils shall hold his seat therein for the term of his life. . . .

And be it further enacted . . . that, for the purpose of constituting such assembly as aforesaid in each of the said provinces respectively, it shall and may be lawful for his majesty, his heirs, or successors . . . to authorize and direct the governor . . . or person administering the government in each of the said provinces respectively . . . to summon . . . an assembly in and for such province. And be it further enacted . . . that, for the purpose of electing the members of such assemblies respectively, it shall and may be lawful for his majesty, his heirs, or successors . . . to authorize the governor . . . or the person administering the government therein . . . to issue a proclamation dividing such province into districts . . . and towns or townships . . . and declaring . . . the number of representatives to be chosen by each. . . . Provided . . . that the whole number of members to be chosen in the province of Upper Canada shall not be less than sixteen and . . . in the province of Lower Canada shall not be less than fifty. . . .

And be it further enacted . . . that the members for the several districts . . . shall be chosen by the majority of votes of such persons as shall severally be possessed . . . of lands or tenements within

---

[9] The first article of this statute repeals those parts of the Quebec Act (no. 126D) relating to the legislative council.

such district . . . of the yearly value of 40s. sterling or upwards . . . ;[10] and that the members for the several towns or townships . . . shall be chosen by the majority of votes of such persons as either shall severally be possessed . . . of a dwelling-house and lot of ground in such town or township . . . of the yearly value of £5 sterling or upwards, or as, having been resident within the said town or townships for the space of twelve calendar months . . . , shall . . . have paid one year's rent . . . at the rate of £10 sterling per annum or upwards. . . .

And be it enacted . . . that the said legislative council and assembly in each of the said provinces shall be called together once at the least in every twelve calendar months, and that every assembly shall continue for four years . . . , subject, nevertheless, to be sooner prorogued or dissolved by the governor . . . or person administering his majesty's government therein. . . . And be it further enacted . . . that, whenever any bill which has been passed by the legislative council and by the house of assembly . . . shall be presented for his majesty's assent . . . , such governor . . . shall . . . declare . . . that he assents to such bill in his majesty's name, or that he withholds his majesty's assent from such bill, or that he reserves such bill for the signification of his majesty's pleasure thereon. Provided always . . . that, whenever any bill . . . shall . . . have been assented to . . . , such governor . . . shall . . . transmit to one of his majesty's principal secretaries of state an authentic copy of such bill . . . ; and that it shall and may be lawful, at any time within two years . . . , for his majesty, his heirs, or successors . . . to declare his . . . disallowance of such bill. . . .

Be it . . . enacted . . . that nothing in this act contained shall . . . be construed to extend to prevent or affect the execution of any law . . . made by his majesty, his heirs, or successors and the parliament of Great Britain . . . for the regulation of the commerce . . . between the said two provinces, or between either of the said provinces and any other part of his majesty's dominions, or between either of the said provinces and any foreign country. . . . Provided always . . . that the net produce of all duties which shall be so imposed shall . . . be applied to and for the use of each of the provinces respectively, and in such manner only as shall be directed . . . by his majesty, his heirs, or successors by and with the advice and consent of the legislative council and assembly of such province. . . .

Ibid., XXXVII, 294 f.: 31 George III, c. 31.

(I) Fox's Libel Act (1792)[11]

An act to remove doubts respecting the functions of juries in

---

[10] Such land had to be held by some form of free tenure other than leasehold.
[11] Cf. no. 129E, I.

cases of libel. Whereas doubts have arisen whether, on the trial of an indictment or information for the making or publishing any libel . . . , it be competent to the jury . . . to give their verdict upon the whole matter in issue: be it therefore declared and enacted . . . that on every such trial the jury sworn to try the issue may give a general verdict of guilty or not guilty upon the whole matter put in issue upon such indictment or information, and shall not be required or directed by the court or judge . . . to find the defendant or defendants guilty merely on the proof of the publication by such defendant or defendants of the paper charged to be a libel and of the sense ascribed to the same in such indictment or information.

Provided always that on every such trial the court or judge . . . shall, according to their or his discretion, give their or his opinion and directions to the jury on the matter in issue between the king and the defendant or defendants in like manner as in other criminal cases. Provided also that nothing herein contained shall . . . be construed to extend to prevent the jury from finding a special verdict in their discretion, as in other criminal cases. . . .

Ibid., XXXVII, 627 f.: 32 George III, c. 60.

(J) Act Suspending Habeas Corpus in Certain Cases (1794)

An act to empower his majesty to secure and detain such persons as his majesty shall suspect are conspiring against his person and government. Whereas a traitorous and detestable conspiracy has been formed for subverting the existing laws and constitution and for introducing the system of anarchy and confusion which has so fatally prevailed in France: therefore, for the better preservation of his majesty's sacred person and for securing the peace and the laws and liberties of this kingdom, be it enacted . . . that every person or persons that are or shall be in prison within the kingdom of Great Britain at or upon the day on which this act shall receive his majesty's royal assent or after, by warrant of his majesty's most honourable privy council signed by six of the said privy council for high treason or suspicion of high treason or treasonable practices, or by warrant signed by any of his majesty's secretaries of state for such causes as aforesaid, may be detained in safe custody without bail or mainprise until the first day of February, 1795; and that no judge or justice of the peace shall bail or try any such person or persons so committed without order from his said majesty's privy council, signed by six of the said privy council, till the said first day of February, 1795—any law or statute to the contrary notwithstanding. . . .

Provided always and be it enacted that nothing in this act shall be construed to extend to invalidate the ancient rights and privileges of parliament, or to the imprisonment or detaining of any member of either house of parliament, during the sitting of such parliament, until the matter of which he stands suspected be first communicated to the house of which he is a member and the consent of the said house obtained for his commitment or detaining.

Ibid., XXXIX, 556 f.: 34 George III, c. 54.

(K) Treasonable and Seditious Practices Act (1795)

An act for the safety and preservation of his majesty's person and government against treasonable and seditious practices and attempts. . . . Be it enacted . . . that, if any person . . . , during the natural life of our most gracious sovereign lord the king . . . , and until the end of the next session of parliament after a demise of the crown, shall, within the realm or without, compass, imagine, invent, devise, or intend death or destruction, or any bodily harm tending to death or destruction, maim or wounding, imprisonment or restraint of the person of the same our sovereign lord the king, his heirs, and successors; or to deprive or depose him or them from the style, honour, or kingly name of the imperial crown of this realm, or of any other of his majesty's dominions or countries; or to levy war against his majesty, his heirs, and successors within this realm, in order by force or constraint to compel him or them to change his or their measures or counsels, or in order to put any force or constraint upon . . . both houses or either house of parliament, or to move or stir any foreigner or stranger with force to invade this realm or any other his majesty's dominions or countries . . . ; and such . . . intentions . . . shall express, utter, or declare by publishing any printing or writing or by any overt act or deed, being legally convicted thereof upon the oaths of two lawful and credible witnesses upon trial, or otherwise convicted or attainted by due course of law; then every such person and persons so as aforesaid offending shall be deemed, declared, and adjudged to be a traitor and traitors, and shall suffer pains of death, and also lose and forfeit as in cases of high treason.

And be it further enacted . . . that, if any person . . . within that part of Great Britain called England, at any time . . . during three years from the day of passing this act and until the end of the then next session of parliament, shall maliciously and advisedly, by writing, printing, preaching, or other speaking . . . , declare any words or sentences to excite or stir up the people to hatred or contempt of the person of his majesty, his heirs, or successors, or the government and constitution of this realm as by law established, then every such person . . . , being thereof legally convicted, shall be liable to such punishment as may by law be inflicted in cases of high misdemeanours. . . .

Ibid., XL, 561 f.: 36 George III, c. 7.

(L) Seditious Assemblies Act (1795)

An act for the more effectually preventing seditious meetings and assemblies. . . . Be it enacted . . . that no meeting of any description of persons exceeding the number of fifty . . .[12] shall be holden for the purpose or on the pretext of considering of or preparing any petition . . . or other address to the king, or to both houses or either house of parliament, for alteration of matters established in church or state, or for the purpose or on the pretext of deliberating upon any grievance in church or state, unless notice[13] of the intention to hold such meeting . . . shall be given in the names of seven persons at the least, being householders resident within the . . . place where such meeting shall be proposed to be holden. . . . And be it further enacted . . . that all meetings . . . which shall be holden without such previous notice as foresaid . . . shall be deemed and taken to be unlawful assemblies. . . .[14]

And . . . be it . . . enacted . . . that every house, room, field, or other place where lectures or discourses shall be delivered or public debates shall be had on or concerning any supposed public grievance, or any matters relating to the laws, constitution, government, or policy of these kingdoms, for the purpose of raising or collecting money or any other valuable thing from the persons admitted . . . , or, under whatever pretence the same shall be opened or used, to which any person shall be admitted by the payment of money or by tickets sold . . . , unless the opening or using . . . shall have been previously licensed in manner hereinafter mentioned, shall be deemed a disorderly house or place. . . .[15]

Provided, nevertheless, and be it enacted . . . that it shall be lawful for two or more justices of the peace of the . . . place where any house, room, or other building shall be, which any person shall be desirous to open for any of the purposes aforesaid, by writing under their hands and seals . . . to grant a licence to any person or persons desiring the same . . . ; which licence it shall be lawful for the justices of the same . . . place . . . to revoke and declare void. . . .

Provided also that nothing in this act contained shall be construed to extend to any lectures . . . to be delivered in any of the universi-

---

[12] Except courts of counties or towns and their subdivisions, or meetings of corporations lawfully summoned.

[13] Such notice, under a variety of legal formalities, has to be given to the local clerk of the peace or published in a local newspaper.

[14] The following articles apply the provisions of the Riot Act (no. 122A) to such assemblies, and to those of which legal notice has been given, but in which suggestions of revolutionary action are made or proposals tending to incite the people to hatred or contempt of the king or of his government. Persons interfering with the magistrates in the carrying out of this law are to be liable to the death penalty.

[15] The owners, occupiers, superintendents, etc., of such properties, as well as the managers of the meetings there held, are liable to prosecution and a fine of £100 for each offence. The local peace officers may demand admittance to any licensed place of this sort and, if they are not admitted, it shall be considered disorderly.

ties of these kingdoms by any member thereof or any person authorized by the chancellor . . . or other proper officers of such universities. . . .

Ibid., XL, 564 f.: 36 George III, c. 8.

(M) Poor Relief Act (1795)

An act to amend so much of an act made in the ninth year of the reign of King George I . . .[16] as prevents the distributing occasional relief to poor persons in their own houses under certain circumstances and in certain cases. . . . Whereas . . . the act above mentioned has been found to . . . be inconvenient and oppressive, inasmuch as it often prevents an industrious poor person from receiving such occasional relief as is best suited to the peculiar case of such poor person, and inasmuch as in certain cases it holds out conditions of relief injurious to the comfort and domestic situation and happiness of such poor persons: be it therefore enacted . . . that . . . it shall and may be lawful for the overseer or overseers of any parish . . . or place, with the approbation of the parishioners . . . or with the approbation in writing of any of his majesty's . . . justices of the peace . . . , to distribute and pay collection and relief to any industrious poor . . . persons at . . . their homes . . . under certain circumstances of temporary illness or distress. . . .

Provided always that the special cause . . . of ordering and directing collection or relief to any poor person . . . at his . . . house . . . be assigned and written on each order for relief given . . . as aforesaid. And provided always that such order be given for . . . a time not to exceed one month. . . . Provided also that it shall and may be lawful for any two justices as aforesaid to make any further order for the same or like purpose for any further time not exceeding one month . . . , and so on from time to time. . . .

Provided always . . . that nothing in this act contained shall . . . be construed . . . to extend to authorize . . . any . . . overseers or any . . . justices of the peace . . . to distribute . . . any collection or relief to any poor person . . . at his . . . house . . . in any parish . . . or place in or for which any house of industry or other place for the reception and provision of the poor thereof hath been . . . or shall hereafter be erected or provided by and under the authority . . . of an act passed in the twenty-second year of the reign of his present majesty . . . or under the authority . . . of any special act of parliament. . . .[17]

Ibid., XL, 626 f.: 36 George III, c. 23.

---

[16] This was a statute of 1722 which provided that parishes or other units of local government might give the administration of poor relief to a contractor. In that case all persons desiring relief had to reside in the poorhouse maintained by such contractor.

[17] The act of 1782 had authorized owners or occupiers of land in any parish or group of parishes to substitute for the overseers of the poor (see no. 114L) paid

(N) Act of Union with Ireland (1800)

An act for the union of Great Britain and Ireland. Whereas, in pursuance of his majesty's . . . recommendation to the two houses of parliament in Great Britain and Ireland respectively . . . , the two houses of the parliament of Great Britain and the two houses of the parliament of Ireland have severally agreed and resolved that . . . it will be advisable to concur in such measures as may best tend to unite the two kingdoms of Great Britain and Ireland into one kingdom . . . ; and whereas, in furtherance of the same resolution, both houses of the said two parliaments respectively have likewise agreed upon certain articles for effectuating and establishing the said purposes in the tenor following . . . :[18] be it enacted . . . that the said . . . articles . . . be ratified, confirmed, and approved . . . , and they are hereby declared to be the articles of the union of Great Britain and Ireland; and the same shall be in force and have effect forever from the first day of January which shall be in the year of our Lord 1801, provided that before that period an act shall have been passed by the parliament of Ireland for carrying into effect in the like manner the said . . . articles. . . .

[Articles of Union.] Article I. . . . That the said kingdoms of Great Britain and Ireland shall . . . be united into one kingdom by the name of the united kingdom of Great Britain and Ireland. . . .

Article II. . . . That the succession to the imperial crown of the said united kingdom and of the dominions thereunto belonging shall continue limited and settled . . . according to the existing laws and to the terms of union between England and Scotland.

Article III. . . . That the said united kingdom be represented in one and the same parliament. . . .

Article IV. . . . That four lords spiritual of Ireland by rotation of sessions, and twenty-eight lords temporal of Ireland elected for life by the peers of Ireland, shall be the number to sit and vote on the part of Ireland in the house of lords of the parliament of the united kingdom; and one hundred commoners—two for each county of Ireland, two for the city of Dublin, two for the city of Cork, one for the university of Trinity College, and one for each of the thirty-one most considerable cities, towns, and boroughs—be the number to sit and vote on the part of Ireland in the house of commons of the parliament of the united kingdom. That such act as shall be passed in the parliament of Ireland previous to the union to regulate the mode by which the lords spiritual and temporal and the commons, to serve in the parliament of the united kingdom on the part of Ireland, shall be summoned and returned to the said

---

guardians of the poor and governors of the poorhouse. Before 1782 individual parishes had gained equivalent privileges through special acts of parliament. See *Bristol Record Society's Publications*, vol. III, introduction by E. E. Butcher.

[18] For the sake of clarity, the articles of union are placed at the end of the present document.

parliament shall be considered as forming part of the treaty of union. . . . That all questions touching the rotation or election of lords spiritual or temporal of Ireland to sit in the parliament of the united kingdom shall be decided by the house of lords thereof. . . . That all questions touching the election of members to sit on the part of Ireland in the house of commons of the united kingdom shall be heard and decided in the same manner as questions touching such elections in Great Britain now are or at any time hereafter shall by law be heard and decided. . . . That the qualifications in respect of property of the members elected on the part of Ireland to sit in the house of commons of the united kingdom shall be respectively the same as are now provided by law in the cases of elections for counties and cities and boroughs respectively in that part of Great Britain called England, unless any other provision shall hereafter be made in that respect by act of parliament of the united kingdom. . . .

Article V. . . . That the Churches of England and Ireland, as now by law established, be united into one Protestant Episcopal Church, to be called the United Church of England and Ireland; and that the doctrine, worship, discipline, and government of the said United Church shall be and shall remain in full force forever as the same are now by law established for the Church of England; and that the continuance and preservation of the said United Church as the established Church of England and Ireland shall be deemed and taken to be an essential and fundamental part of the union; and that in like manner the doctrine, worship, discipline, and government of the Church of Scotland shall remain and be preserved as the same are now established by law and by the acts for the union of the two kingdoms of England and Scotland.

Article VI. . . . That his majesty's subjects of Great Britain and Ireland shall . . . be entitled to the same privileges . . . as to encouragements and bounties on the like articles, being the growth, produce, or manufacture of either country respectively, and generally in respect of trade and navigation in all ports and places in the united kingdom and its dependencies; and that in all treaties made by his majesty, his heirs, and successors with any foreign power his majesty's subjects of Ireland shall have the same privileges . . . as his majesty's subjects of Great Britain. . . .

Article VII. . . . That the charge arising from the payment of the interest and the sinking fund for the reduction of the principal of the debt incurred in either kingdom before the union shall continue to be separately defrayed by Great Britain and Ireland respectively. . . . That, for the space of twenty years after the union shall take place, the contribution of Great Britain and Ireland respectively towards the expenditure of the united kingdom in each year shall be defrayed in the proportion of fifteen parts for Great Britain, and two parts for Ireland, and that, at the expiration of the said twenty years, the future expenditure of the united kingdom . . . shall be defrayed in such proportion as the parliament of the united kingdom shall deem just and reasonable. . . .

Article VIII. . . . That all laws in force at the time of the union and all the courts of civil and ecclesiastical jurisdiction within the respective kingdoms shall remain as now by law established within the same, subject only to such alterations and regulations from time to time as circumstances may appear to the parliament of the united kingdom to require; provided that all writs of error and appeals, depending at the time of the union or hereafter to be brought, and which might now be finally decided by the house of lords of either kingdom, shall, from and after the union, be finally decided by the house of lords of the united kingdom. . . .

Ibid., XLII, 648 f.: 40 George III, c. 67.

(O) COTTON INDUSTRY ARBITRATION ACT (1800)

An act for settling disputes that may arise between masters and workmen engaged in the cotton manufacture in that part of Great Britain called England. . . . Be it enacted . . . that . . . , in all cases that shall or may arise . . . where the masters and workmen cannot agree respecting the price or prices to be paid for work done or to be done in the said manufacture . . . , and in all cases of dispute or difference arising . . . out of . . . such trade or manufacture which cannot be otherwise mutually adjusted and settled by and between them, it shall . . . be lawful . . . for such masters and workmen . . . , or either of them, to demand and have an arbitration . . . of such . . . matters in dispute, and each of them is hereby authorized and empowered forthwith to nominate and appoint an arbitrator . . . on his . . . behalf. . . . And such arbitrators . . . , after they shall have accepted . . . the business of the said arbitration, are hereby authorized and required to summon before them and examine upon oath the parties and their witnesses . . . , and forthwith to proceed to hear and determine the complaints of the parties and the matter or matters in dispute between them; and the award to be made by such arbitrators shall in all cases be final and conclusive between the parties. But, in case such arbitrators so appointed cannot agree to decide such . . . matters in dispute . . . , and do not make and sign their award within the space of three days after the signing of the said submission . . . , they shall forthwith . . . go before . . . one of his majesty's justices of the peace . . . residing nearest to the place where such dispute shall happen and be referred, and state to such justice the points in difference between them, the said arbitrators; which points in difference the said justice . . . is hereby authorized . . . to hear and determine. Which determination of such justice shall be made and signed within the space of three days after the expiration of the time hereby allowed the arbitrators to make and sign their award, and shall be final and conclusive between the parties so differing as aforesaid. . . .

Ibid., XLII, 792 f.: 39-40 George III, c. 90.

(P) COMBINATION ACT (1800)

An act to repeal an act passed in the last session of parliament . . . and to substitute other provisions in lieu thereof. Whereas it is expedient to explain and amend an act passed in the thirty-ninth year of the reign of his present majesty, entitled An Act to Prevent Unlawful Combinations of Workmen: be it therefore enacted . . . that, from and after the passing of this act, the said act shall be repealed; and that all contracts, covenants, and agreements whatsoever, in writing or not in writing, at any time . . . heretofore made . . . between any journeymen, manufacturers, or other persons within this kingdom for obtaining an advance of wages . . . , or for lessening or altering their . . . usual hours . . . of working, or for decreasing the quantity of work (save and except any contract made or to be made between any master and his journeyman or manufacturer for or on account of the work or service of such journeyman or manufacturer. . . .), or for preventing or hindering any person . . . from employing whomsoever he . . . shall think proper to employ . . . , or for controlling or any way affecting any person . . . carrying on any . . . business in the conduct or management thereof, shall be . . . illegal, null, and void. . . .

And be it further enacted that no journeyman, workman, or other person shall . . . make or enter into . . . any such contract, covenant, or agreement . . . as is hereinbefore declared to be an illegal covenant . . . , and every journeyman . . . or other person who . . . shall be guilty of any of the said offences, being thereof lawfully convicted . . . , shall . . . be committed to . . . the common jail . . . for any time not exceeding three calendar months; or . . . to some house of correction . . . , there to remain and to be kept to hard labour for any time not exceeding two calendar months.

And be it further enacted that every journeyman . . . or other person who shall . . . enter into any combination to obtain an advance of wages . . . or for any other purpose contrary to this act; or who shall, by giving money or . . . by any other means, wilfully and maliciously endeavour to prevent any . . . unemployed journeyman . . . or other person . . . from hiring himself to any manufacturer . . . or person conducting any . . . business; or who shall, for the purpose of obtaining an advance of wages or for any other purpose contrary to the provisions of this act, wilfully and maliciously decoy, persuade, solicit, intimidate, influence, or prevail . . . on any journeyman . . . or other person . . . employed in any such . . . business to quit . . . his work . . . ; or who shall wilfully and maliciously hinder . . . any . . . person from employing . . . such journeymen . . . and other persons as he . . . shall think proper; or who, being . . . employed, shall without any just or reasonable cause refuse to work . . . ; and who shall be lawfully convicted of any of the said offences . . ., shall . . . be committed to . . . the common jail . . . for any time not exceeding three calendar months; or . . . to some house of correction . . . , there to remain and to be kept to hard labour for any time not exceeding two calendar months. . . .[19]

And be it further enacted . . . that all contracts . . . made or to be made by or between any masters or other persons for reducing the wages of workmen, or for adding to or altering the usual hours . . . of working, or for increasing the quantity of work . . . are hereby declared to be illegal, null, and void. . . . And all . . . such masters, being thereof lawfully convicted . . . shall forfeit . . . the sum of £20. . . .

Ibid., XLII, 847 f.: 39-40 George III, c. 106.

(Q) FACTORY ACT (1802)

An act for the preservation of the health and morals of apprentices and others employed in cotton and other mills. . . . Be it enacted that . . . all such mills and factories within Great Britain and Ireland, wherein three or more apprentices or twenty or more other persons shall at any time be employed, shall be subject to the several rules and regulations contained in this act . . . :—

. . . That all and every the rooms and apartments in or belonging to any such mill or factory shall, twice at least in every year, be well and sufficiently washed with quick lime and water over every part of the walls and ceiling thereof; and that due care and attention shall be paid by the master and mistress of such mills or factories to provide a sufficient number of windows and openings in such rooms or apartments, to insure a proper supply of fresh air. . . .

That every such master or mistress shall constantly supply every apprentice . . . with two whole and complete suits of clothing . . . , one new complete suit being delivered to such apprentice once at least in every year. . . .

That no apprentice . . . bound to any such master or mistress shall be employed or compelled to work for more than twelve hours in any one day . . . , exclusive of the time that may be occupied by such apprentice in eating the necessary meals. Provided always that, from and after the first day of June, 1803, no apprentice shall be employed or compelled to work upon any occasion whatever be-

---

[19] Persons attending any meeting for the purposes described above, or soliciting or paying any contribution for such purposes, are to be liable to the same penalties. Elaborate provisions are made for the enforcement of the act. But the settlement of labour disputes by arbitration is continued as allowed by earlier statues (e.g., the previous document) and further articles are added to improve the system.

tween the hours of nine of the clock at night and six of the clock in the morning. . . .

That every such apprentice shall be instructed in some part of every working day, for the first four years at least of his or her apprenticeship . . . , in reading, writing, and arithmetic . . . ; and that the time . . . allotted for such instruction . . . shall be deemed . . . part . . . of the respective periods . . . during which any such apprentice shall be employed or compelled to work. . . .

That the room or apartment in which any male apprentice shall sleep shall be entirely separate and distinct from the room or apartment in which any female apprentice shall sleep, and that not more than two apprentices shall in any case sleep in the same bed. . . .

That every apprentice . . . shall, for the space of one hour at least every Sunday, be instructed and examined in the principles of the Christian religion . . . ; and such master or mistress shall send all his or her apprentices under the care of some proper person, once in a month at least, to attend during divine service in the church of the parish . . . or in some licensed place of divine worship. And in case the apprentices . . . cannot conveniently attend such church or chapel . . . , the master or mistress . . . shall cause divine service to be performed in some convenient room or place in or adjoining to the mill or factory. . . .

And be it further enacted that the justices of the peace for every county . . . shall . . . appoint two persons, not interested in or in any way connected with any such mills or factories, to be visitors . . . ; and the said visitors, or either of them, shall have full power and authority . . . to enter into and inspect any such mill or factory at any time of the day . . . , and . . . shall report from time to time in writing to the quarter sessions of the peace the state and condition of such mills and factories . . . , and whether the same are or not conducted and regulated according to the directions of this act. . . .

Ibid., XLIII, 632 f.: 42 George III, c. 73.

127. GEORGE IV: STATUTES

(A) REPEAL OF THE COMBINATION ACTS (1825)

An act to repeal the laws relating to the combination of workmen and to make other provisions in lieu thereof. . . .[1]

And be it further enacted that, from and after the passing of this act, if any person shall, by violence to the person or property, or by threats or intimidation, or by molesting or in any way obstructing another, force or endeavour to force any journeyman, manufacturer, workman, or other person hired or employed in any manufacture, trade, or business to depart from his hiring, employment,

---

[1] The first three articles repeal all existing laws with regard to combinations of labourers (e.g., no. 126P).

or work or to return his work before the same shall be finished, or prevent or endeavour to prevent any journeyman, manufacturer, workman, or other person not being hired or employed from hiring himself to or from accepting work or employment from any person or persons; or if any person shall use or employ violence to the person or property of another, or threats or intimidation, or shall molest or in any way obstruct another for the purpose of forcing or inducing such person to belong to any club or association, or to contribute to any common fund, or to pay any fine or penalty . . . ; or if any person shall by violence to the person or property of another, or by threats or intimidation, or by molesting or in any way obstructing another, force or endeavour to force any manufacturer or person carrying on any trade or business to make an alteration in his mode of regulating, managing, conducting, or carrying on such manufacture, trade, or business, or to limit the number of his apprentices, or the number or description of his journeymen, workmen, or servants; every person so offending, or aiding, abetting, or assisting therein, being convicted thereof in manner hereinafter mentioned, shall be imprisoned only, or shall and may be imprisoned and kept to hard labour, for any time not exceeding three calendar months.

Provided always, and be it enacted, that this act shall not extend to subject any persons to punishment who shall meet together for the sole purpose of consulting upon and determining the rate of wages or prices which the persons present at such meeting, or any of them, shall require or demand for his or their work, or the hours or time for which he or they will work in any manufacture, trade, or business. . . .

Ibid., LXIII, 1073 f.: 6 George IV, c. 129.

(B) Repeal of the Test and Corporation Acts (1828)

An act for repealing so much of several acts as imposes the necessity of receiving the sacrament of the Lord's Supper as a qualification for certain offices and employments. . . . Be it . . . enacted . . . that so much and such parts of the . . . several acts passed in the thirteenth and twenty-fifth years of the reign of King Charles II . . .[2] as require the person or persons in the said acts respectively described to take or receive the sacrament of the Lord's Supper according to the rites or usage of the Church of England . . . , or as impose upon any such person or persons any penalty, forfeiture, incapacity, or disability whatsoever for or by reason of any neglect or omission to take or receive the said sacrament . . . , be . . . hereby repealed.

And whereas . . . it is just and fitting that, on the repeal of such parts of the said acts . . . , a declaration . . . should be substituted in lieu thereof; be it therefore enacted that every person

---
[2] No. 114J, R.

who shall hereafter be placed, elected, or chosen . . . in or to any office . . . relating to the government of any city, corporation, borough, or Cinque Port within England and Wales . . . shall, within one calendar month next before or upon his admission into any of the aforesaid offices or trusts, make and subscribe the declaration following: "I, A.B., do solemnly and sincerely, in the presence of God, profess, testify, and declare upon the true faith of a Christian that I will never exercise any power, authority, or influence which I may possess by virtue of the office of ―― to injure or weaken the Protestant Church as it is by law established in England, or to disturb the said Church or the bishops and clergy of the said Church in the possession of any rights or privileges to which such Church or the said bishops and clergy are or may be by law entitled" . . .[3]

Ibid., LXV, 22 f.: 9 George IV, c. 17.

(C) ROMAN CATHOLIC EMANCIPATION ACT (1829)

An act for the relief of his majesty's Roman Catholic subjects. Whereas by various acts of parliament certain restraints and disabilities are imposed on the Roman Catholic subjects of his majesty to which other subjects of his majesty are not liable . . . ; and whereas by various acts certain oaths and certain declarations . . . are or may be required to be taken, made, and subscribed by the subjects of his majesty, as qualifications for sitting and voting in parliament, and for the enjoyment of certain offices, franchises, and civil rights: be it enacted . . . that, from and after the commencement of this act, all such parts of the said acts as require the said declarations . . . as a qualification for sitting and voting in parliament, or for the exercise or enjoyment of any office, franchise, or civil right, be and the same are (save as hereinafter provided and excepted) hereby repealed.

And be it enacted that, from and after the commencement of this act, it shall be lawful for any person professing the Roman Catholic religion, being a peer or who shall after the commencement of this act be returned as a member of the house of commons, to sit and vote in either house of parliament respectively, being in all other respects duly qualified to sit and vote therein, upon taking and subscribing the following oath, instead of the oaths of allegiance, supremacy, and abjuration: "I, A.B., do sincerely promise and swear that I will be faithful and bear true allegiance to his majesty King George IV and will defend him to the utmost of my power against all conspiracies and attempts whatever which shall be made against his person, crown, or dignity. . . . And I do faithfullly promise to maintain, support, and defend to the utmost of my power the succession of the crown, which . . . stands limited to the princess Sophia, electress of Hanover, and the heirs of her body being

---

[3] Later articles indemnify all persons holding office under the crown for failure to take the earlier tests, substituting for the latter the declaration already quoted.

Protestants, hereby utterly renouncing and abjuring any obedience or allegiance unto any other person claiming or pretending a right to the crown of this realm. And I do further declare that it is not an article of my faith, and that I do denounce, reject, and abjure the opinion, that princes excommunicated or deprived by the pope, or any other authority of the see of Rome, may be deposed or murdered by their subjects or by any person whatsoever. And I do declare that I do not believe that the pope of Rome or any other foreign prince, prelate, person, state, or potentate hath or ought to have any temporal or civil jurisdiction, power, superiority, or preeminence, directly or indirectly, within this realm. I do swear that I will defend to the utmost of my power the settlement of property within this realm as established by the laws. And I do hereby disclaim, disavow, and solemnly abjure any intention to subvert the present church establishment as settled by law within this realm. And I do solemnly swear that I will never exercise any privilege to which I am or may become entitled, to disturb or weaken the Protestant religion or Protestant government in the united kingdom. . . . So help me God."

And be it further enacted that it shall be lawful for persons professing the Roman Catholic religion to vote at elections of members to serve in parliament for England and for Ireland, and also to vote at the elections of representative peers of Scotland and of Ireland, and to be elected such representative peers, being in all other respects, duly qualified, upon taking and subscribing the oath herein before appointed. . . .

Ibid., LXV, pt. ii, 49 f.: 10 George IV, c. 7.

128. PROCEEDINGS IN PARLIAMENT (1763-84)

(A) Proceedings in the Case of John Wilkes (1763)[1]

[15 November 1763.] Mr. Chancellor of the Exchequer informed the house that he was commanded by the king to acquaint the house that, his majesty having received information that John Wilkes, esquire, a member of this house, was the author of a most seditious and dangerous libel, published since the last session of parliament, he had caused the said John Wilkes, esquire, to be apprehended and secured, in order to his being tried for the same by due course of law. And Mr. Wilkes having been discharged out of custody by the court of common pleas upon account of his privilege as a member of this house, and having, when called upon by the legal process of the court of king's bench, stood out and declined to appear and answer to an information which has since been exhibited against him by his majesty's attorney general for the same offence—in this

---

[1] The following documents are (1) resolutions of the commons occasioned by Wilkes' famous no. 45 of the *North Briton*; (2) a minority protest made by certain lords after the upper house had agreed to the foregoing resolution of the commons.

situation, his majesty being desirous to show all possible attention to the privileges of the house of commons in every instance wherein they can be supposed to be concerned, and at the same time thinking it of the utmost importance not to suffer the public justice of the kingdom to be eluded, has chosen to direct the said libel, and also copies of the examinations upon which Mr. Wilkes was apprehended and secured, to be laid before this house for their consideration. And Mr. Chancellor of the Exchequer delivered the said papers in at the table.

Resolved, *nemine contradicente,* that an humble address be presented to his majesty, to return his majesty the thanks of this house for his most gracious message and for the tender regard therein expressed for the privileges of this house, and to assure his majesty that this house will forthwith take into their most serious consideration the very important matter communicated by his majesty's message. . . . Resolved that the paper entitled the *North Briton,* no. 45, is a false, scandalous, and seditious libel, containing expressions of the most unexampled insolence and contumely towards his majesty, the grossest aspersions upon both houses of parliament, and the most audacious defiance of the authority of the whole legislature; and most manifestly tending to alienate the affections of the people from his majesty, to withdraw them from their obedience to the laws of the realm, and to excite them to traitorous insurrections against his majesty's government. Resolved that the said paper be burnt by the hands of the common hangman. . . .

[24 November 1763.] Resolved that privilege of parliament does not extend to the case of writing and publishing seditious libels, nor ought to be allowed to obstruct the ordinary course of the laws in the speedy and effectual prosecution of so heinous and dangerous an offence.

Journals of the Commons, XXIX, 667, 675.

[29 November.] . . . We cannot hear without the utmost concern and astonishment a doctrine advanced now for the first time in this house, which we apprehend to be new, dangerous, and unwarrantable—*viz.*, that the personal privilege of both houses of parliament has never held and ought not to hold in the case of any criminal prosecution whatsoever—by which all the records of parliament, all history, all the authorities of the gravest and soberest judges are entirely rescinded, and the fundamental principles of the constitution with regard to the independence of parliament torn up and buried under the ruins of our most established rights. We are at a loss to conceive with what view such a sacrifice should be proposed, unless to amplify in effect the jurisdiction of the inferior by annihilating the ancient immunities of this superior court. The very question itself proposed to us from the commons and now agreed to by the lords, from the letter and spirit of it, contradicts this assertion; for, whilst it only narrows privilege in criminal matters, it establishes the principle. . . .

This resolution does not only infringe the privilege of parliament, but points to the restraint of the personal liberty of every common subject in these realms; seeing that it does in effect affirm that all men, without exception, may be bound to the peace for this offence. By this doctrine every man's liberty, privileged as well as unprivileged, is surrendered into the hands of a secretary of state. He is by this means empowered, in the first instance, to pronounce the paper to be a seditious libel—a matter of such difficulty that some have pretended it is too high to be entrusted to a special jury of the first rank and condition. He is to understand and decide by himself the meaning of every innuendo. He is to determine the tendency thereof and brand it with his own epithets. He is to adjudge the party guilty and make him author or publisher, as he sees good. And, lastly, he is to give sentence by committing the party. All these authorities are given to one single magistrate, unassisted by counsel, evidence, or jury, in a case where the law says no action will lie against him because he acts in the capacity of a judge.

From what has been observed, it appears to us that the exception of a seditious libel from privilege is neither founded on usage or written precedents; and therefore this resolution is of the first impression. Nay, it is not only a new law narrowing the known and ancient rule, but it is likewise a law *ex post facto, pendente lite, et ex parte,* now first declared to meet with the circumstances of a particular case. . . .

This method of relaxing the rule of privilege, case by case, is pregnant with this further inconvenience, that it renders the rule precarious and uncertain. Who can foretell where the house will stop, when they have, by one infringement of their own standing orders, made a precedent whereon future infringements may with equal reason be founded? How shall the subject be able to proceed with safety in this perilous business? How can the judges decide, on these or the like questions, if privilege is no longer to be found in records, and journals, and standing orders? Upon any occasion, privilege may be enlarged; no court will venture for the future, without trembling, either to recognize or to deny it.

Journals of the Lords, XXX, 426 f.

(B) MINORITY PROTEST IN THE LORDS ON THE REPEAL OF THE STAMP ACT (1766)[2]

1. Because . . . we are of opinion that the total repealing of that law, especially while such resistance continues, would . . . make the authority of Great Britain contemptible hereafter; and that such a submission of king, lords, and commons, under such circumstances, in so strange and unheard-of a contest, would in effect surrender

---
[2] Cf. No. 126B.

their ancient inalienable rights of supreme jurisdiction and give them exclusively to the subordinate provincial legislatures established by prerogative—which was never intended or thought of and is not in the power of prerogative to bestow, as they are inseparable from the three estates of the realm assembled in parliament.

2. Because the law which this bill now proposes to repeal was passed in the other house with very little opposition, and in this without one dissentient voice . . . ; which, we presume, if it had been wholly and fundamentally wrong, could not possibly have happened. . . .

3. Because, if any particular parts of that law—the principle of which has been experienced and submitted to in this country without repining for near a century past—had been found liable to just and reasonable objections, they might have been altered by a bill to explain and amend it without repealing the whole. . . .

4. Because it appears to us that a most essential branch of that [legislative] authority, the power of taxation, cannot be properly, equitably, or impartially exercised if it does not extend . . . to all the members of the state in proportion to their respective abilities. . . .

5. Because the ability of our North American colonies to bear without inconvenience the proportion laid on them by the Stamp Act of last year appears to us most unquestionable. . . .

6. Because, not only the right, but the expediency and necessity of the supreme legislature's exerting its authority to lay a general tax on our American colonies . . . appears to us undeniable. . . . Every province being separate and independent . . . and having no common council empowered by the constitution of the colonies to act for all or bind all, such a tax cannot regularly or without infinite difficulty be imposed upon them at any time, even for their immediate defence and protection, by their own provincial assemblies; but requires the intervention and superintending power of the parliament of Great Britain. . . .

Ibid., XXXI, 303 f.

(C) PROCEEDINGS ON THE MIDDLESEX ELECTION (1769)[3]

[17 February.] Ordered that the deputy clerk of the crown do attend this house immediately, with the return to the writ for electing a knight of the shire to serve in this present parliament for the county of Middlesex, in the room of John Wilkes, esquire, expelled

---

[3] Having been expelled from the house of commons as unfit to serve, Wilkes offered himself for re-election as a member for Middlesex. He was twice returned unopposed and on each occasion the house annulled the election. On standing for re-election the third time, he was opposed by Colonel Luttrell, who received 296 votes to 1143 for Wilkes. The following documents are (1) the resolutions of the commons barring Wilkes and seating Luttrell; (2) a minority protest signed by forty-two peers when the house of lords refused to condemn the action of the commons.

this house. And the deputy clerk of the crown attending according to order, the said writ and returns were read.

A motion was made, and the question being proposed—that John Wilkes, esquire, having been in this session of parliament expelled this house, was and is incapable of being elected a member to serve in this present parliament—the house was moved that the entry in the journal of the house of the 6th day of March, 1711, in relation to the proceedings of the house upon the return of a burgess to serve ... in the room of Robert Walpole, esquire, expelled the house,[4] might be read. And the same was read accordingly. The house was also moved that the resolution of the house of Friday, the 3d day of this instant February, relating to the expulsion of John Wilkes, esquire, then a member of this house, might be read.

And the same being read accordingly, an amendment was proposed to be made to the question by inserting after the word "house" these words: "for having been the author and publisher of what this house hath resolved to be an insolent, scandalous, and seditious libel; and for having been convicted in the court of king's bench of having printed and published a seditious libel and three obscene and impious libels; and having by the judgment of the said court been sentenced to undergo twenty-two months' imprisonment and being in execution under the said judgment." And the question being put that those words be there inserted ..., it passed in the negative. Then the main question being put ..., it was resolved in the affirmative.

A motion being made [and passed in the affirmative] ..., resolved that the late election of a knight of the shire to serve in this present parliament for the county of Middlesex is a void election. Ordered that Mr. Speaker do issue his warrant to the clerk of the crown to make out a new writ for the electing of a knight of the shire to serve in this present parliament for the county of Middlesex in the room of John Wilkes, esquire, who is adjudged incapable of being elected a member to serve in this present parliament, and whose election for the said county has been declared void. ...

[15 April.] The orders of the day for taking into consideration the poll taken at the last election of a knight of the shire to serve in this present parliament for the county of Middlesex ... being read ..., a motion was made, and the question ... proposed, that Henry Lawes Luttrell, esquire, ought to have been returned a knight of the shire to serve in this present parliament for the county of Middlesex. ... Then the question being put ..., the house divided ... [197 to 143]. So it was resolved in the affirmative. Ordered that the deputy clerk of the crown do amend the return for

---

[4] In January, 1712 (new style), Walpole had been expelled from the house of commons for "a high breach of trust and notorious corruption." In the following March he had been declared "incapable to serve in this present parliament" and a writ had been issued for a new election.

the county of Middlesex by razing out the name of John Wilkes, esquire, and inserting the name of Henry Lawes Luttrell, esquire, instead thereof. And the deputy clerk of the crown, attending according to order, amended the said return accordingly. . . .

[8 May.] A motion being made, and the question being put—that Henry Lawes Luttrell, esquire, is duly elected a knight of the shire to serve in this present parliament for the county of Middlesex—the house divided . . . [221 to 152]. So it was resolved in the affirmative.

Journals of the Commons, XXXII, 228, 386 f., 451.

. . . Then it was moved to resolve that the house of commons, in the exercise of its judicature in matters of election, is bound to judge according to the law of the land and the known and established law and custom of parliament, which is part thereof. Which being objected to, and a question stated thereupon, after debate, the previous question was put. . . . It was resolved in the negative. Dissentient:—

1. Because the resolution proposed was in our judgment highly necessary to lay the foundation of a proceeding which might tend to quiet the minds of the people, by doing them justice at a time when a decision of the other house—which appears to us inconsistent with the principles of the constitution and irreconcilable to the law of the land—has spread so universal an alarm and produced so general a discontent throughout the kingdom.

2. Because, although we do not deny that the determination on the right to a seat in the house of commons is competent to the jurisdiction of that house alone, yet, when to this it is added that whatever they, in the exercise of that jurisdiction, think fit to declare to be law is therefore to be so considered, because there lies no appeal, we conceive ourselves called upon to give that proposition the strongest negative. For, if admitted, the law of the land, by which all courts of judicature without exception are equally bound to proceed, is at once overturned and resolved into the will and pleasure of a majority of one house of parliament, who, in assuming it, assume a power to overrule at pleasure the fundamental right of election, which the constitution has placed in other hands—those of their constituents. And if ever this pretended power should come to be exercised to the full extent of the principle, that house will be no longer a representative of the people, but a separate body, altogether independent of them, self-existing and self-elected.

3. Because, when we are told that expulsion implies incapacity, and the proof insisted upon is that the people have acquiesced in the principle by not re-electing persons who have been expelled, we equally deny the position as false, and reject the proof offered as in no way supporting the position to which it is applied. We are sure the doctrine is not to be **found in any** statute or law book, nor

in the journals of the house of commons; neither is it consonant with any just or known analogy of law. ...

4. Because, as the constitution hath been once already destroyed by the assumption and exercise of the very power which is now claimed, the day may come again when freedom of speech may be criminal in that house, and every member who shall have virtue enough to withstand the usurpations of the time, and assert the rights of the people, will for that offence be expelled by a factious and corrupt majority, and by that expulsion rendered incapable of serving the public. In which case the electors will find themselves reduced to the miserable alternative of giving up altogether their right of election or of choosing only such as are enemies of their country, and will be passive at least, if not active, in subverting the constitution.

5. Because, although it has been objected in the debate that it is unusual and irregular in either house of parliament to examine into the judicial proceedings of the other (whose decisions, as they cannot be drawn into question by appeal, are, it is said, to be submitted to without examination of the principles of them elsewhere), we conceive the argument goes directly to establish the exploded doctrine of passive obedience and non-resistance, which, as applied to the acts of any branch of the supreme power, we hold to be equally dangerous. And though it is generally true that neither house ought lightly and wantonly to interpose even an opinion upon matters which the constitution hath entrusted to the jurisdiction of the other, we conceive it to be no less true that, where under colour of a judicial proceeding either house arrogates to itself the powers of the whole legislature and makes the law which it professes to declare, the other not only may but ought to assert its own right and those of the people; that this house has done so in former instances, particularly in the famous case of Ashby and White. ...[5]

6. Because, upon the whole, we deem the power which the house of commons have assumed to themselves, of creating an incapacity unknown to the law and thereby depriving, in effect, all the electors of Great Britain of their invaluable right of free election confirmed to them by so many solemn statutes, a flagrant usurpation, as highly repugnant to every essential principle of the constitution as the claim of ship money by King Charles I, or that of the suspending and dispensing power by King James II—this being indeed, in our opinion, a suspending and dispensing power assumed and exercised by the house of commons against the ancient and fundamental liberties of the kingdom.

Journals of the Lords, XXXII, 417-18.

(D) COMMONS' DEBATE ON THE REPORTING OF SPEECHES (1778)

[29 January.] Colonel Luttrell . . . complained that in a certain morning paper . . . he had been grossly misrepresented. . . . He

---
[5] See no. 124C.

. . . made many severe strictures on the conduct of the editor of that paper. . . . He considered such conduct as too heinous to be forgiven, and therefore he informed the house that, for his future safety and protection, he was determined to move that the standing order of the house for excluding strangers from the gallery should be strictly carried into execution. . . .

Mr. Fox rose to say . . . he was convinced the true and only method of preventing misrepresentation was by throwing open the gallery and making the debates and decisions of the house as public as possible. There was less danger of misrepresentation in a full company than a thin one, as there would be a greater number of persons to give evidence against the misrepresentation. The shutting of the gallery could not prevent the proceedings of the house from finding their way to public view; for during a certain period, when the gallery was kept empty, the debates were printed, let the manner of obtaining them be what it might. And in fact the public had a right to know what passed in parliament.

The speaker begged to have the sense of the house to direct his future conduct.

Mr. Rigby confessed that he wished to have the gallery shut, not only against gentlemen but ladies, as the latter as well as the former might dabble in party disputes and have their predilections and preferences for one party before another. He thought at this time it was very necessary to exclude every stranger, since in the course of next week a most serious inquiry would take place that might perhaps affect the lives and properties of individuals. He confessed it might be thought odious to make the motion; nevertheless, if the motion was made, he would second it.

Mr. Turner entreated the honourable gentleman to give up his intention of making the motion. He did not like a man that was afraid of having his speech published, a man that weighed his words. He wished to see gentlemen warm when circumstances required it; their fathers were warm before them; they were warm themselves; and he hoped their children would be so after them. For his part, he should be always happy to see the gallery crowded; and if one door was shut to exclude all the men, another should be opened to let in all the women.

The speaker said that the conversation did not a little affect him; for there was a standing order to keep the gallery shut against strangers, and he had, with the acquiescence of the house, relaxed it. He should therefore, as the affair happened to be mentioned, be glad, before the house rose, that they would come to some determination.

Mr. Burke paid a very generous compliment to the speaker for having relaxed in some measure from the rigour of a strict decree; in so doing he had acted wisely and politicly. He was sensible, no doubt, that *summum ius* was *summa iniuria*, and that some laws were better kept in the breach than in the observance. An odium still awaited the exertion of rigorous justice, and to render it respected it must be made gentle. As to the matter then in the contemplation of the house, he had not a doubt about the propriety of opening the doors to strangers, considering it either as the channel of information to the constituents of the members or as a school for the instruction of youth. Nay, as the source of information and amusement to the ladies, it was a matter of very serious concern and ought not to be done away and sported with at pleasure.

Mr. Vyner thought that, while every member had it in his power to order the strangers to withdraw whenever it might be inconvenient for them to remain, either from want of room or from secret business on the tapis, there was no need of taking away the right entirely.

General Conway spoke a few words to the impropriety of shutting the gallery and, as a proof that it was not one individual alone who suffered from newspaper exposure, he mentioned a falsehood asserted of himself, which he laughed at and despised.

Mr. T. Townshend declared it to be unconstitutional to shut the doors of the house generally against the people whom they sat there to represent. He mentioned the exceptions when it was necessary, and the rules of the house could not be dispensed with; and at the same time he passed a very severe censure on all shameful misrepresentations of the proceedings of the house, and of the speeches of members.

Colonel Luttrell owned that the arguments of the honourable gentleman (Mr. Burke) had staggered and influenced his former judgment, and he was now convinced it would be odious to carry the order to its rigour. He therefore should not press his motion. . . .

Cobbett, Parliamentary History, XIX, 647-50.

(E) COMMONS' DEBATE ON NORTH'S GOVERNMENT (1779)

Lord John Cavendish observed . . . he would move an amendment to the question[6] by inserting after the words, "national defence" at the end of the fifth paragraph, these words: "to beseech his majesty to reflect upon the extent of territory, the power, the opulence, the reputation abroad, and the concord at home which distinguished the opening of his majesty's reign and marked it as the most splendid and happy period in the history of this nation; and, when he shall have turned his eyes on the endangered, impoverished, distracted, and even dismembered state of the whole—after all the grants of successive parliaments, liberal to profusion and trusting to the very utmost extent of rational confidence—his majesty will expect to receive the honest opinion of a faithful and affectionate parliament, who should think they betrayed his majesty, and those they represent, if they did not distinctly state to his majesty in words what the world has seen in most calamitous and disgraceful effects, that, if anything can prevent the consummation of public ruin, it can only be by new counsels and

---

[6] A vote of thanks to his majesty for his speech at the opening of parliament.

new counsellors without further loss of time—a real change from a sincere conviction of past errors, and not a mere palliation, which must prove fruitless." . . .

Mr. T. Townshend declared he thought it impossible that we could ever have been brought into the calamitous state in which we were then reduced, if to the inability of our ministers base treachery were not added. Treachery, he was perfectly satisfied, was somewhere lurking in our councils and had surrounded the throne; otherwise, in spite of the blunders of administration, we should be in infinitely a better state of defence than we were. . . . Of late years a most dangerous doctrine had gone forth and been most sedulously propagated by the followers of administration, and perhaps some of its members—though neither had the confidence publicly to avow it—which directly tended to overthrow the constitution: that the king was his own minister, his own admiral-in-chief, his own general, his own secretary, his own president of the council, his own financier. Thus his majesty was made the shield behind which knavery, servility, and every species of folly, treachery, and villainy might screen themselves from punishment. . . . The failure of every measure is thus laid at the door of the sovereign who, according to both the letter and spirit of the constitution, can do no wrong, and the responsibility of the servants transferred to the personal and political character of the master. These were doctrines which afforded but a flimsy and wretched protection from punishment; for an impartial and uncorrupt parliament would know where responsibility ought to rest, would fix it accordingly, and would direct it to the quarter where both justice, the constitution, and the laws pointed, and where at some future day, he predicted, it would be loudly and peremptorily demanded. . . .

Lord North said he rose in this stage of the debate lest his silence should be interpreted as proceeding from a desire to shun the warm conflict so eagerly urged by the noble lord who moved the amendment and the two honourable gentlemen who followed on the same side. An indirect charge of treachery had been made against him by the right honourable gentleman who spoke last. This seemed of late a favourite topic with gentlemen in the opposition. But why did they not pursue their accusations and follow them up with specific proofs, and by so doing endeavour to fix the guilt and bring it home fairly and directly to its proper object and compel the miscreant to undergo that fate which treachery deserves? An honourable gentleman (Mr. J. Grenville) asked him what he would do when he should find himself deserted by his friends in parliament. He was prepared to answer him: he would instantly retire; for, whenever the majority of the house should disapprove of a minister's conduct, he must give way. Like a torrent, their disapprobation must and ought to sweep ministers before it. For God forbid, explained his lordship, that there should be a voice in the nation stronger than that of parliament! Whenever my accounting day shall come, I shall meet it without fear. There are laws for the protection of innocence and, if my accusers are not enemies to law, I am safe. My innocence will be my shield and the laws will defend me. . . . The amendment certainly contained no language that was unparliamentary. It was the duty of parliament to cause ministers to be removed, but justice required that proof should be first made of their delinquency. To remove the servants of the crown without assigning any cause for it, or attributing to them without trial what on trial would be found not imputable to them, would be unjust and unprecedented. Therefore, though he admitted to the fullest extent the right of the house to address the throne for a removal of ministers, as there was nothing specifically charged in the amendment, he certainly would not vote for it. And as it reflected a censure upon him, as included in . . . praying for new counsels and new counsellors, the house, he was sure, would not be surprised that he did not support it. . . .

Mr. Fox . . . [said] he saw very early indeed in the present reign the plan of government which had been laid down and had since been invariably pursued in every department. It was not the mere rumour of the streets that the king was his own minister; the fatal truth was evident and had made itself visible in every circumstance of the war carried on against America and the West Indies. There was not the least intelligence in the West Indies perceptible between the king's officers in the most kindred departments. Had not all such intelligence been destroyed by an invisible cabinet influence, could it ever have happened that there should be in one of our lately captured islands 150 pieces of ordnance and only 40 men to work them? Could there have been in one place cannon without balls, and in another balls without cannon? In short, could mere ignorance in ministers produce of itself so many complicated blunders as the last seven years have furnished, to render the present reign the most disgraceful period in the annals of this country? . . .

The noble lord in the blue ribbon had disclaimed the doctrine held out by the followers of administration relative to the king's being his own minister; but yet it was most certain that such a doctrine was daily dispersed by his followers, probably with an intention of paying their court to him by propagating opinions the most disagreeable to their patron! The doctrine, however, was in itself highly dangerous to the constitution, as it tended to take responsibility from the shoulders of the ministers and place it on a personage who could do no wrong and could not be called to account. However, he would observe that, though in general the evils of a reign were attributed to the wicked counsels of an abandoned ministry, yet, when these evils reached to a certain height, ministers were forgotten and the prince alone was punished. Thus it was with the royal house of Stuart. Charles and his son James had both wicked ministers, to whom, no doubt, the errors of their reigns ought to be chiefly ascribed; and yet they themselves were punished—the one by the loss of life, the other of his crown. This should be a lesson to sovereigns and teach them to check their ministers and not suffer themselves to be blindly led by them, as they themselves may, for their ministers, bear the whole weight of their people's indignation.

There was not, he observed, in the whole history of the country a period that resembled the present, except the reign of the unfortunate Henry VI. His family, like that of his present majesty, did not claim the crown as their hereditary right; it was by revolution that both obtained it. Henry was an amiable and pious prince; so was his present majesty. Henry was the son of the most renowned monarch that had ever sat upon our throne; George was the grandson of a hero. Henry lost all his father's conquests and all his hereditary provinces in France; George had already seen the conquests of his grandfather wrested from him in the West Indies, and his hereditary provinces of America erected into an empire that disclaimed all connection. . . . It was not a secret to that house that the present sovereign's claim to the throne of this country was founded only upon the delinquency of the Stuart family—a circumstance which should never be one moment out of his majesty's recollection. . . .

The house divided: for the amendment 134; against it 233. The original address was then agreed to.

Ibid., XX, 1096-1150.

(F) COMMONS' DEBATE ON DUNNING'S RESOLUTIONS (1780)

[6 April.] The house, according to order, resolved itself into a committee of the whole house to consider of the petition of the gentlemen, clergy, and freeholders of the county of York respecting an economical reform, and also the several other petitions referred to the consideration of the said committee.

The titles of the said petitions being read, in all about forty in number, Mr. Dunning rose and said it was unnecessary to observe that the subject matter to be taken into consideration was the subject matter contained in the petitions. Independent of the great objects which the petitions recommended to the care and attention of parliament, which had been, according to the particular ideas of the several classes of petitioners, of a various nature, there was one great fundamental point on which they hinged: that of setting limits or paring down the increased, dangerous, and alarming influence of the crown, and an economical expenditure of the public money. In one point of view, both these objects might be fairly consolidated into one great principle. For instance, if the public money was faithfully applied and frugally expended, that would reduce the influence of the crown; if, on the other hand, the influence of the crown was restrained within its natural and constitutional limits, it would once more restore that power which the constitution had vested in that house—the inquiring into and controlling the expenditure of public money. . . .[7]

Having endeavoured, as far as lay in my power, to describe what

---

[7] Here Dunning warmly praised the Place Bill recently introduced by Burke; see no. 126F.

the petitioners mean, and what administration mean, on the other hand, give me leave to recur to the ground of my present proposed resolutions. I have already observed that the great objects of the petitioners have been resisted, both in argument and by public avowals, by the minister and his friends. They have told you that the influence of the crown is not too much and ought not, of course, to be lessened; the petitioners have asserted the direct contrary. Ministers have told you that it is not competent for this house to inquire into the expenditure of the civil list; the direct contrary are the sentiments of the petitioners. To talk of petitions or redress is vain, idle, nugatory, and ineffectual while these two points are maintained by those who have the majority of the house. To bring both these points fairly to issue, I mean to frame two propositions, abstracted from the petitions on your table, and take the sense of the committee upon them. . . . My first resolution will be, that it is the opinion of this committee that it is necessary to declare that the influence of the crown has increased, is increasing, and ought to be diminished; my second, that it is competent to this house to examine into and to correct abuses in the expenditure of the civil list revenues, as well as in every other branch of the public revenue, whenever it shall appear expedient to the wisdom of this house so to do. . . .

Earl Nugent: . . . The learned gentleman has produced a proposition that the influence of the crown has increased, is increasing, and ought to be diminished. Has he produced, or so much as promised, a tittle of evidence of the facts so alleged? Not a word of that; but he has said a great deal about the opinions of speculative men, of an eminent lawyer lately deceased, and of two ingenious political writers (Hume and Blackstone). The former says the influence of the crown began to show itself about the year 1742. I was in parliament before that period and remember that clamours and speculations of that kind prevailed long before the year 1742. But I protest that I thought then, as I think now, that they were totally unfounded; and I can fairly affirm that I never felt it myself nor gave a single vote under any influence whatever, but what was necessary for the support of government. But I will go one step further and take the two first assertions in the honourable gentleman's proposition as proved, that the influence of the crown has increased and is increasing. Will the learned gentleman's conclusion follow? May not this increased influence be necessary? Has he ventured to state that it is not? By no means; he declines the fair allegation that it is improper or unconstitutional, and takes a leap to his conclusion by inferring that it ought to be diminished. . . .

Mr. Rous said that gentlemen on the other side of the house had rested their arguments for some time past chiefly on two points: that it was necessary the crown should have influence both within and without that house; and that gentlemen who composed opposition were instigated by motives of ambition. He thought it was necessary to grant both propositions in order to explain the true grounds on which they stood. For his part, he was one who thought that the crown ought to have an influence in that house; but what species of influence? Not surely a corrupt one. By no means; but a fair constitutional influence, an influence arising from a confidence in government, originating in a full conviction that the measures proposed by its subordinate ministers were founded in wisdom . . .—in a thorough conviction that the persons entrusted with the exercise of the executive power were selected for their integrity, talents, and public virtue. This was the influence and the only influence that should ever be felt in that house. But, on the other hand, when the opposite qualities were those which encouraged persons to be candidates for places of the highest trust and confidence under government, who could, without a mixture of indignation and the most ineffable contempt, listen to such as maintained in argument that the friends and supporters of such an administration were not under the dominion of the most corrupt and unconstitutional influence? . . .

At twelve o'clock the committee divided: for Mr. Dunning's [first] motion 233; against it 215. . . . Mr. Dunning made his next motion. . . . The question being called for, the motion was agreed to without a division. . . .

Ibid., XXI, 340-67.

(G) Pitt's Proposals for Reform of Parliament (1783)

Mr. Pitt: An Englishman, who should compare the flourishing state of his country some twenty years ago with the state of humiliation in which he now beholds her, must be convinced that the ruin which he now deplores, having been brought on by slow degrees and almost imperceptibly, proceeded from something radically wrong in the constitution. Of the existence of a radical error no one seemed to doubt; nay, almost all were so clearly satisfied of it that various remedies had been devised by those who wished most heartily to remove it. The house itself had discovered that a secret influence of the crown was sapping the very foundation of liberty by corruption. The influence of the crown had been felt within these walls, and had often been found strong enough to stifle the sense of duty and to overrule the propositions made to satisfy the wishes and desires of the people. The house of commons, in former parliaments, had been base enough to feed the influence that enslaved its members; and thus was at one time the parent and the offspring of corruption. This influence, however, had risen to such a height that men were ashamed any longer to deny its existence, and the house had at length been driven to the necessity of voting that it ought to be diminished. Various were the expedients that had been thought of in order to effect so salutary a purpose as was that of guarding against this influence; of shutting against it the doors of that house, where, if it once got footing, after the resolution alluded to, liberty could no longer find an asylum. The house of commons which, according to the true spirit of the constitution, should be the guardian of the people's freedom, the constitutional check and control over the executive power, would through this influence degenerate into a mere engine of tyranny and oppression, to destroy the constitution in effect, though it should, in its outward form, still remain.

Among the various expedients that had been devised to bar the entrance of such influence into that house, he had heard principally of three. One was to extend the right of voting for members to serve in parliament, which was now so confined, to all the inhabitants of the kingdom indiscriminately; so that every man, without the distinction of freeholder, or freeman of a corporation, should have the franchise of a vote for a person to represent him in parliament—and this mode, he understood, was thought by those who patronized it to be the only one that was consistent with true liberty in a free constitution, where every one ought to be governed by those laws only to which all have actually given their consent, either in person, or by their representative. For himself, he utterly rejected and condemned this mode, which it was impossible for him to adopt without libelling those renowned forefathers who had framed the constitution in the fulness of their wisdom and fashioned it for the government of freemen, not of slaves. If this doctrine should obtain, nearly one-half of the people must in fact be slaves; for it was absolutely impossible that this idea of giving to every man a right of voting, however finely it might appear in theory, could ever be reduced to practice. But, though it were even practicable, still one-half of the nation would be slaves; for all those who vote for the unsuccessful candidates cannot, in the strictness of this doctrine, be said to be represented in parliament, and therefore they are governed by laws to which they give not their assent, either in person or by representatives. Consequently, according to the ideas of the friends to this expedient, all those who vote for unsuccessful candidates must be slaves. Nay, it was oftentimes still harder with those who are members of parliament, who are made slaves also and are governed by laws to which they not only have not given their consent, but against which they have actually voted.

For his part, his idea of representation was this, that the members once chosen and returned to parliament were, in effect, the representatives of the people at large, as well of those who did not vote at all, or who, having voted, gave their votes against them, as of those by whose suffrages they were actually seated in the house. This being therefore his principle, he could not consent to an innovation founded on doctrines subversive of liberty, which in reality went so far as to say that this house of commons was not, and that no house of commons ever had been, a true and constitutional representation of the people; for no house of commons had yet been elected by all the men in the kingdom. The country had long prospered and had even attained the summit of glory, though this doctrine had never been embraced; and he hoped that no one would ever attempt to introduce it into the laws of England, or treat it in any other light than as a mere speculative proposition that may be good in theory but which it would be absurd and chimerical to endeavour to reduce to practice.

The second expedient he had heard of was to abolish the franchise which several boroughs now enjoy of returning members to serve in parliament. These places were known by the favourite, popular appellation of rotten boroughs. He confessed that there was something very plausible in this idea, but still he was not ready to adopt it; he held those boroughs in the light of deformities, which in some degree disfigured the fabric of the constitution, but which he feared could not be removed without endangering the whole pile. It was true that the representation of the people could not be perfect. Nay, it could not be good unless the interests of the representatives and the represented were the same. The moment they became different, from that moment the liberty of the people was in danger; because those who ought to be the guardians of it might find their account in circumscribing it within narrower limits than the constitution marked out, or in carrying through measures which might in the end effectually destroy it. It must be admitted from a variety of circumstances, which it was unnecessary for him at present to explain, that, though the members returned by boroughs might be for the present the brightest patterns of patriotism and liberty, still there was no doubt but that borough members, considered in the abstract, were more liable to the operation of that influence, which every good man wished to see destroyed in that house, than those members who were returned by the counties. And therefore, though he was afraid to cut up the roots of this influence by disfranchising the boroughs—because he was afraid of doing more harm than good by using a remedy that might be thought worse than the disease—still he thought it his duty to counteract, if possible, that influence, the instruments of which he was afraid to remove. The boroughs ought to be considered, not only as places of franchise, but also as places where the franchise was in some measure connected with property by burgage tenure. And therefore, as he was unwilling to dissolve the boroughs, he would endeavour to defeat the effect of undue influence in them by introducing and establishing a counterbalance that should keep it down and prevent it from ruining the country.

This brought him naturally to the third expedient that he had often heard mentioned, which was to add a certain number of members to the house who should be returned by the counties and the metropolis. It was unnecessary for him to say that the county members, in general, were almost necessarily taken from that class and description of gentlemen the least liable to the seduction of corrupt influence, the most deeply interested in the liberty and prosperity of the country, and consequently the most likely to pursue such measures as appeared to them the most salutary to their country. In the hands of such men the liberties of their constituents would be safe, because the interests of such representatives and the represented must necessarily be the same. This expedient appeared to him the most fit to be adopted, because it was the least objectionable. It had the merit of promising an effectual counterbalance to the weight of the boroughs without being an innovation in the form of the constitution. He would not then say what number of members ought to be added to the counties; he would leave that to be inserted in a bill, which, if the resolutions he meant to propose should pass, he intended to move for leave to bring in. He, however, would say that, in his opinion, the number ought not be under one hundred. It was true he thought the house would then be more numerous than he could wish; but still it were better it should be so than that the liberty of the country should be exposed to destruction from the baleful influence of the crown in the boroughs. He was not, however, without an expedient by degrees to reduce the number of members, even after the addition, down to nearly the present number. His expedient was this: that whenever it should be proved before the tribunal, which happily was now established by law to try the merits of contested elections, that the majority of any borough had been bribed and corrupted, the borough should then lose the privilege of sending members of parliament; the corrupt majority should be disfranchised, and the honest minority be permitted to vote at elections for knights of the shire. By this expedient he was sure the boroughs would be preserved free from corruption; or else they must be abolished gradually, and the number of members of that house be reduced to its present standard. This disfranchising of boroughs would be the work of time. The necessity of disfranchising any one, whenever that necessity should appear, would sanctify the measure. It would appear to be what in fact it would then be—an act of justice, not of whim, party, or caprice; as it would be founded, not on surmise, but on the actual proof of guilt.

After amplifying upon this for some time and showing that it was equally founded in policy and in justice, he urgently pressed the necessity of something being done in compliance with the petitions that had been presented, complaining of the present state of the representation; and took abundant pains to caution the house against adopting any extravagant plans of reform that might be suggested by enthusiastic speculatists on the one hand, or obstinately refusing to take any step whatever in compliance with the petitions, under a childish dislike and dread of innovation on the other. After urging very elaborately an infinite variety of arguments, Mr. Pitt said his first resolution was what he conceived every individual member would feel the force [of], and be ready to come into, without a moment's hesitation. Of his second he entertained hopes pretty nearly as sanguine, convinced as he was of its propriety and justice. And with regard to his third, though it might possibly meet with considerable opposition, he was extremely anxious to obtain it the sanction of the house. He then read his three resolutions, which, in substance, were as follows: (1) That it was the opinion of the house that the most effectual and practicable measures ought to be taken for the better prevention both of bribery and expense in the election of members to serve in parliament; (2) That for the future, when the majority of voters for any borough should be convicted of gross and notorious corruption before a select committee of that house appointed to try the merits of any election, such borough should be disfranchised, and the minority of voters, not so convicted, should be entitled to vote for the county in which such borough should be situated; (3) That an addition of knights of the shire, and of representatives of the metropolis, should be added to the state of the representation. . . .

Lord North: . . . They but little know mankind who imagine that a small indulgence will not induce a pressure for greater. A gentleman behind me says, "Give the people fifty knights, and then make your stand." I oppose this idea. Begin with innovation, and there is no knowing where you will stop; like the gravity of a weight in sinking, its velocity increases in proportion to its weight. The addition of one hundred or even fifty county members would give a decided superiority to the landed interest over the commercial; and it is the beauty of the constitution of the house of commons that, like the general fabric of the British legislature, it provides for and preserves the due balance between the several great interests of the empire—the landed, the commercial, and the moneyed. But do not let us begin. *Principiis obsta.* Let us act like men. We are not the deputies, but the representatives of the people. We are not to refer to them before we determine. We stand here as they would stand, to use our own discretion without seeking any other guidance under heaven. In a word, as no defect in the constitution has been proved, as we have heard nothing but declamation and surmise to warrant so awful and so very important a measure as an innovation on the form of the venerable palladium which ages have sanctified down to us, let us again—let me conjure you—act like men and like Britons, and reject what to adopt must inevitably lead to ruin. . . .[8]

Ibid., XXIII, 829-75.

(H) COMMONS' DEBATE ON THE INFLUENCE OF THE CROWN (1783)

Mr. Baker rose again. He observed that . . . an adjournment of a couple of days . . . had given gentlemen time to reflect seriously on the very alarming report that had been for some days in circulation relative to a conference which a noble lord had with a great personage, and the opinion that was said to have been expressed by the latter of the bill which that house had sent up to the lords for vesting the affairs of the East India Company in certain directors. . . . With respect to this rumour he would go so far as to say that, true or false, it had produced very dangerous effects; for he understood that some noble lords, in consequence of it, had taken their proxies from those to whom they had before entrusted them, and given them to noble lords who were known to be hostile to India. He concluded by reading the two following resolutions: (1) That it is now necessary

---

[8] Pitt's motion was lost, 149 to 293.

128. PROCEEDINGS IN PARLIAMENT

to declare that to report any opinion or pretended opinion of his majesty upon any bill or other proceeding depending in either house of parliament, with a view to influence the votes of its members, is a high crime and misdemeanour derogatory to the honour of the crown, a breach of the fundamental privileges of parliament, and subversive of the constitution of this country; (2) That this house will on Monday next resolve itself into a committee of the whole house to consider the state of the nation. Having read the resolutions, Mr. Baker moved the former. . . .

Earl Nugent was never more astonished in his life than with the resolution now moved and seconded. It went, in his opinion, to an utter annihilation of all sovereignty in the country. . . .

Mr. W. Pitt, who had risen at the same time with Lord Nugent, hoped the noble lord would attribute his then getting up to no other motive than that common one which actuated them both—a due attachment to the constitutional independence of parliament and the inalienable right of peers, either individually or collectively, to advise his majesty whenever they thought the situation of public affairs made such a step an essential part of their duty. . . . [The resolution] appeared to him the most unnecessary, the most frivolous and ill-timed, that ever insulted the attention of the national senate. . . . He concluded by moving the order of the day.

Lord Mahon seconded the motion. He began by charging Mr. Secretary Fox with an utter desertion of all principle. He reprobated his East India Bill[9] as the worst and most obnoxious that ever challenged the attention of parliament or roused the indignation of Englishmen. . . .

Lord North . . . contended for the propriety and necessity of the motion; and this he did the more especially as he had been charged, on former occasions, with indifference to the constitution. Had he been silent when such a gross violation of it had met with countenance, he should have thought himself culpable indeed. For what was the influence of the crown—against which on former occasions all these gentlemen had divided against him, and for which he had then deemed it his duty to contend—in comparison of a principle which, once established, would bury in one grave all the privileges of parliament and the rights of the people? He should therefore give the resolution now proposed his most sincere and hearty support. . . .

Mr. Fox spoke to the following effect. I did not intend, sir, to have said anything in addition to what has been already urged so ably in favour of the resolution now agitated. In my own opinion, its importance, propriety, and necessity are completely and substantially established. . . . This rumour has been treated with a levity which amounts to a sarcasm or lampoon on the dignity of the house. But I will tell gentlemen it is not a newspaper; it is not a verbal surmise,

---

[9] A bill to extend control over the East India Company, which had passed the house of commons but had been rejected by the lords.

but something much stronger and more serious; there is a written record to be produced. This letter (pulling it out of his pocket) is not to be put in the balance with the lie of the day. It states that his majesty allowed Earl Temple to say that whoever voted for the India Bill were not only not his friends, but he should consider them as his enemies. And if these words were not strong enough, Earl Temple might use whatever words he might deem stronger or more to the purpose. Is this parliamentary, or is it a truth? Where is the man who dares to affirm the one or deny the other, or to say that he believes in his conscience such a rumour was not calculated to produce an immediate effect? . . . I trust Englishmen will be as jealous of secret influence as superior to open violence. I trust they are not more ready to defend their interests against foreign depredation and insult than to encounter and defeat this midnight conspiracy against the constitution. . . .

Whoever knows the mode of digesting business in the cabinet must be sensible that the least interference with anything pending in parliament must be dangerous to the constitution. The question is not whether his majesty shall avail himself of such advice as no one readily avows, but who is answerable for such advice. Is the honourable gentleman aware that the responsibility of ministers is the only pledge and security the people of England possess against the infinite abuses so natural to the exercise of this power? Once remove this great bulwark of the constitution, and we are in every respect the slaves and property of despotism. And is not this the necessary consequence of secret influence? . . .

Much and gloriously did this house fight and overcome the influence of the crown by purging itself of ministerial dependents. But what was the Contractors Bill, the board of trade, or a vote of the revenue officers compared to a power equal to one-third of the legislature, unanswerable for and unlimited in its acting? Against these we had always to contend. But we knew their strength; we saw their disposition; they fought under no covert; they were a powerful, not a sudden enemy. To compromise the matter therefore, sir, it would become this house to say—rather than yield to a stretch of prerogative thus unprecedented and alarming—"Withdraw your secret influence. . . . Take back those numerous and tried dependents who so often secured you a majority in parliament. We submit to all the mischief which even this accession of strength is likely to produce; but for God's sake strangle us not, in the very moment we look for success and triumph, by an infamous string of bedchamber janissaries! . . ."

I never was the tool of any junto. I accepted of office at the obvious inclination of this house. I shall not hold it a moment after the least hint from them to resume a private station. The honourable gentleman is, however, grasping at place on very different grounds. He is not called to it by a majority of this house; but, in defiance of that majority, stands forth the advocate and candidate for secret influence. . . .

The house divided on the question, that the order of the day be now read: yeas . . . 80; noes . . . 153. Mr. Baker's motion was consequently carried. He then moved his second resolution, which was likewise carried.

Ibid., XXIV, 197-225.

(I) DEBATES ON THE CONTINUANCE OF PITT'S MINISTRY (1784)[10]

[16 January.] Lord Charles Spencer [moved] that, it having been declared to be the opinion of this house that in the present situation of his majesty's dominions it is peculiarly necessary there should be an administration that has the confidence of this house and of the public, and that the appointments of his majesty's present ministers were accompanied by circumstances new and extraordinary and such as do not conciliate or engage the confidence of this house, the continuance of the present ministers in trusts of the highest importance and responsibility is contrary to constitutional principles and injurious to the interests of his majesty and his people. . . .

Mr. Fox observed that political distinctions were by no means involved in the present question. The principles of Whig and Tory, said he, which have given rise to so much difference of sentiment and to so much disputation in the world, have no connection with it. In my conversations with the rankest Whigs, and in the whole course of my reading, I have never found the hardiest of them deny a right inherent in the prerogative to elect its own ministers. On this point all are agreed. But though this be the admitted and established right of the executive branch of the constitution, is it not also the privilege of the house and of parliament to decide on the conduct of administration, on the peculiarity of their introduction into office, and on those circumstances which either entitle them to the confidence or the reprobation of the house? It was on this principle allowed on all hands—and the exercise of which, in various instances, has saved the country from ruin—that the resolutions of last Monday were submitted to the committee, and afterwards received the sanction of this branch of the legislature. But although it is undoubtedly the prerogative of his majesty to appoint his ministers, it may still be a point worthy of consideration how far it may be prudent, wise, and politic in a monarch to continue them

---

[10] This debate took place in the weeks preceding the dissolution of parliament on 25 March. Pitt had taken office in December, 1783, being assured by the king's parliamentary agent, John Robinson, that a favourable majority would be obtained in the next election. Until the voters could be bribed, Pitt had to face the hostile coalition of Fox and North in the commons. But Robinson kept his word and the dissolution brought the promised victory. For full details see W. T. Laprade, *Parliamentary Papers of John Robinson;* also his articles in the *English Historical Review*, XXXI, 224 f., and the *American Historical Review*, XVIII, 155 f.

in power and support them in office, when they are declared by that house to have been elevated to their station by means unconstitutional and such as have rendered them unworthy of confidence. On this question, as I cannot allow myself even to imagine that a monarch would appoint ministers whom he did not think possessed of the confidence of parliament, so I cannot even form an idea that a wise and prudent sovereign would be hardy enough to continue in office those who have been reprobated as undeserving their regard. . . .[11]

[26 January.] Mr. Pitt: He had the profoundest respect for the house, the utmost reverence for their resolutions, being perfectly aware that the house had it in its power at all times to follow up their resolutions with measures that could not fail to render them effectual. That he stood in a situation perfectly new he was ready to admit; but that he stood in that situation in contempt of that house, or as holding himself superior to its authority, he must beg leave to deny. New and extraordinary circumstances might justify new and extraordinary conduct. For any minister who had been declared unworthy the approbation and confidence of that house to remain in office was, he confessed, far from common; but he hoped he should not give offence when he declared that a minister might nevertheless act constitutionally by remaining in office after that house had declared their disapprobation of him. He begged pardon for what he was going to say, but he conceived that, according to the constitution, the immediate appointment or removal of ministers rested not with that house. There was therefore nothing illegal in a minister's remaining in office after that house had declared against him, particularly where immediate resignation would have injured the country; and he hoped a public man might be supposed to act honourably, when, upon public motives, he thought he best served his country by continuing in office after he had been so unfortunate as to lose the confidence of that house. He explained this by declaring that there were acts of duty not the less indispensable because they were disagreeable; that in critical situations it was incumbent on a minister who found he was not approved by that house to look to the probable consequences of his immediate resigning. It behooved him to consider who were likely to be his successors, and whether the country might not receive more detriment than they could possibly derive advantage by his leaving it without any executive government, and thus making room for an administration in whom the crown, the parliament, and the people could not equally repose confidence. . . . To have resigned immediately after the house had come to their resolution on Friday se'nnight would have been to have let in the ministers who, however they might enjoy the confidence of that house, he believed had not the confidence of the nation. Such a change therefore could have done no good to

---

[11] The motion was carried, 205 to 184.

the country. It was true the majority of that house had decided against him; but the sense of the house upon that point did not appear to be grown more and more in the progress of the time that had elapsed since his coming into office. On the contrary, the majority had gradually decreased. . . .

[2 February.] Mr. Coke [moved] that it is the opinion of this house that the continuance of the present ministers in their offices is an obstacle to the formation of such an administration as may enjoy the confidence of this house, and tend to put an end to the unfortunate divisions and distractions of the country.

Mr. Pitt: With regard . . . to the resignation of ministers, he saw no reason for it. If that house insisted upon their going out, there were two constitutional means open to them: either by impeachment to proceed against them for their crimes, if they had committed any, or by an immediate address to the crown to desire their removal. The removal of ministers lay with the crown and not with that house. In remaining in office, therefore, with a view to keep the country from anarchy and confusion and to prevent the government from falling a prey to that administration which had been removed, and suffering them to force themselves upon the sovereign against his will, was neither illegal nor unconstitutional. . . .[12]

[11 February.] Mr. Fox: . . . He would say the only suspicion he entertained, and which had originated in the mode by which the right honourable gentleman obtained and kept possession of power, was that he entertained an opinion that the crown might appoint a ministry, and persist in supporting them, who had not the confidence of the house. He wished he might find the suspicion ill-founded, but he dreaded to find it true; for then a union[13] on such a principle was impossible. It went to deprive this country of an executive government in which the people had any concern, over which they could exercise any control. All the instances of voting money was on a principle of confidence. The minister's influence in the house depended on what confidence they had in him; he was their trustee; to them he was responsible for every article of public expenditure. The very estimates to be considered that night were instances of the same principle in the constitution; and every sum of money voted for the ordnance was voted by gentlemen incapable of judging for themselves whether those sums were properly applied or not; but in confidence that Lord Townshend, the duke of Richmond, or any other whose province it was to direct the business of that very important department, were competent to pronounce on the fitness of the objects for which the money would be applied. . . .

Mr. Pitt: . . . A union might take place in which one minister might look to the right for support and confidence and another to

---

[12] The motion was carried, 223 to 204.
[13] He had been advocating a coalition ministry.

the left, but he thought a minister ought to look to both; he ought to look for the confidence of his sovereign and for the confidence of that house. He would go farther—he ought to look for the confidence of the house of lords and of the people. He had said to the house before, and he would repeat it again, that there was no law in this kingdom which made it criminal in him to remain in office, notwithstanding a resolution of the house of commons. He would, however, admit that the confidence of that house was absolutely necessary, and that an administration could not last that did not possess it. He did not, however, agree with the right honourable gentleman that there was any similitude between the resolution of the 16th January and that principle of confidence on which money was voted in that house. It was certainly necessary that the commons, in matters which, being entirely professional, they were not able to judge of, should confide for the propriety of them in the minister from whose department the estimates came—as, for instance, in the case of the ordnance estimates, which were to be voted that evening, the house must of course repose a confidence in the master-general of the ordnance, whose duty it was to see that the estimates were proper. But surely the right honourable gentleman would not declare that this was the kind of confidence the house had in view when the resolution of the 16th of January passed. . . .

[18 February.] Mr. Pitt . . . declared that his majesty had not yet, in compliance with the resolutions of the house, thought proper to dismiss his present ministers; and that his majesty's ministers had not resigned. This much he thought necessary to say, prior to any discussion on the subject of supplies. . . .

Mr. Fox: He had often stated his conceptions of the prerogatives of the throne. The present question involved them very materially. That his majesty had a legal right to appoint whom he pleased, and even to continue those whom he had appointed to be his ministers, in opposition to the sentiments of this house, he pretended not to dispute; but he was certain, on the other hand, the public money was trusted with the house of commons, whose right to distribute that money was at least not less legal. When, therefore, either the one or the other of these rights were asserted in the extreme, he could consider it in no other light than as a challenge; and the party thus defied was bound in duty to its own honour calmly and deliberately to consider with itself whether it should take up the challenge or not. He did not know that any defiance more explicit and direct could be given to that house than the one which had just come from the right honourable gentleman. He hoped the house was not by any means prepared to accept of it without farther and more sedate consideration. . . .[14]

[1 March.] Mr. Fox: . . . Since the unfortunate reigns of the

---

[14] Grant of supply was postponed by a vote of 208 to 196.

128. PROCEEDINGS IN PARLIAMENT

Stuarts prerogative had never been so much the topic of discussion as it had become of late in parliament. His ideas of whatever the constitution had vested in the crown were no secret; he ever had and ever would avow them. No prerogative of the crown was, in his opinion, distinct or unconnected with the whole of that free and liberal system in which our government chiefly consisted. The people were the great source of all power, and their welfare the sole object for which it was to be exerted; but who in this case were to be the judges? The house of commons undoubtedly were competent to protect the rights of the people, to pronounce on whatever they deemed an encroachment on their privileges; and the moment they could not prevent everything which struck them as such, they were not equal to the design of such an institution. This he called a due seasoning or modification of that enormous power devolved by the constitution on the executive government of the country. The house of commons consequently were possessed of the power of putting a negative on the choice of ministers. They were stationed as sentinels by the people, to watch over whatever could more or less remotely or nearly affect their interest; so that, whenever they discovered in those nominated by his majesty to the several great offices of state want of ability, want of weight to render their situations respectable, or want of such principles as were necessary to give effect to the wishes of the house, in any or all of such cases they were entitled to advise his majesty against employing such persons as his faithful commons could not trust. . . .

Mr. Fox then moved that an humble address be presented to his majesty: . . . That this house with all humility claims it as its right, and on every proper occasion feels it to be their bounden duty, to advise his majesty touching the exercise of any branch of his royal prerogative; that we submit it to his majesty's royal consideration that the continuance of an administration which does not possess the confidence of the representatives of the people must be injurious to the public service; . . . that . . . his majesty's faithful commons . . . find themselves obliged again to beseech his majesty that he would be graciously pleased to lay the foundation of a strong and stable government by the previous removal of his present ministers. . . .

Mr. Pitt: . . . No man was more zealous or more unreserved in admitting and asserting the right of the house to advise the sovereign in the exercise of all his prerogatives than he was. This had always been a sentiment which he had avowed; but that a declaration on the part of the house of their disapprobation of his majesty's ministers should *ipso facto*, in any given instance, bind and compel the sovereign to dismiss those ministers, or oblige them to resign, was a point which he never had admitted and would never allow. . . . Attempts have been made, said Mr. Pitt, to fix imputations of criminality on the present administration. Their sins have been stated; and one of the most glaring of them is that the late ministry were dismissed against the sense of the house. But what is the meaning of this charge? To what conclusion does the argument, when followed up, lead? Does it not fairly admit of this comment, that it is improper for his majesty to dismiss his ministers, provided they are approved of by the house of commons; and that, so long as they act agreeably to its sentiment, so long and no longer are they to enjoy the patronage of the crown and retain the offices of administration? Is this a decent treatment of the prerogative? Is this constitutional doctrine? Is it not degrading the dignity of the sovereign? It is not a transference of the prerogatives of the crown to the house of commons and a placing the royal sceptre under the mace that lies upon the table? The constitution of this country is its glory; but in what a nice adjustment does its excellence consist! Equally free from the distractions of democracy and the tyranny of monarchy, its happiness is to be found in its mixture of parts. It was this mixed government which the prudence of our ancestors devised, and which it will be our wisdom inviolably to support. They experienced all the vicissitudes and distractions of a republic. They felt all the vassalage and despotism of a simple monarchy. They abandoned both and, by blending each together, extracted a system which has been the envy and admiration of the world. It is this scheme of government which constitutes the pride of Englishmen, and which they can never relinquish but with their lives. . . .[15]

Ibid., XXIV, 361-711.

---

[15] The motion was carried, 201 to 189.

129. RECORDS OF JUDICIAL CASES (1763-1820)

(A) HABEAS CORPUS PROCEEDINGS IN WILKES' CASE (1763)

There are two objections taken to the legality of this warrant, and a third matter insisted on for the defendant is privilege of parliament. The first objection is that it does not appear to the court that Mr. Wilkes was charged by any evidence before the secretaries of state that he was the author or publisher of the *North Briton*, no. 45. In answer to this, we are all of opinion that it is not necessary to state in the warrant that Mr. Wilkes was charged by any evidence before the secretaries of state, and that this objection has no weight. . . . The second objection is that the libel ought to be set forth in the warrant *in haec verba*, or at least so much thereof as the secretaries of state deemed infamous, seditious, etc.; that the court may judge whether any such paper ever existed, or, if it does exist,

---

[1] On 30 April 1763 John Wilkes, for having published no. 45 of the *North Briton* (see no. 128A), was arrested on a general warrant (see the following document) signed by the secretaries of state, and was committed to the Tower. On 3 May, after certain legal preliminaries, the question of his liberation on a writ of *habeas corpus* came before the court of common pleas. The decision by Chief Justice Pratt (later Lord Camden) includes a clear statement of the whole case.

whether it be an infamous and seditious libel or not. But we are all of a contrary opinion. . . .

The third matter insisted upon for Mr. Wilkes is that he is a member of parliament—which has been admitted by the king's serjeants—and entitled to privilege to be free from arrests in all cases except treason, felony, and actual breach of the peace, and therefore ought to be discharged from imprisonment without bail. . . . If Mr. Wilkes had been described as a member of parliament in the return, we must have taken notice of the law of privilege of parliament; otherwise the members would be without remedy where they are wrongfully arrested against the law of parliament. We are bound to take notice of their privileges as being part of the law of the land. . . . We are all of opinion that a libel is not a breach of the peace. . . . Suppose a libel be a breach of the peace, yet I think it cannot exclude privilege. . . . Upon the whole it is absurd to require surety of the peace or bail in the case of a libeller, and therefore Mr. Wilkes must be discharged from his imprisonment.

Howell, *State Trials*, XIX, 987 f.

(B) ENTICK V. CARRINGTON (1765)[2]

This record hath set up two defences to the action, on both of which the defendants have relied. The first arises from the facts disclosed in the special verdict, whereby the defendants put their case upon the statute of 24 George II, insisting that they have nothing to do with the legality of the warrants, but that they ought to have been acquitted as officers within the meaning of that act. The second defence stands upon the legality of the warrants. . . .

Upon the whole, we are all of opinion that neither secretary of state nor the messenger are within the meaning of this act of parliament. . . . The defendants, having failed in the attempt made to protect themselves by the statute . . . , are under a necessity to maintain the legality of the warrants under which they have acted and to show that the secretary of state in the instance now before

---

[2] Entick, like Wilkes, had been arrested for publishing a seditious libel on a general warrant issued by the secretaries of state. Since in a number of recent cases the legality of such general warrants had been gravely questioned, Entick brought suit for trespass against Carrington and the other royal messengers who, in making the arrest, had broken into Entick's house and carried off a number of his books and papers. In the course of the trial before the court of common pleas, the facts of the warrant, arrest, seizure, etc., were established by a jury, which awarded the plaintiff £300 damages on condition that the court adjudged the action of the defendant to constitute trespass. As will be seen from the following excerpts, the decision, rendered by Lord Camden, Chief Justice, settled the matter of such general warrants for all time. And by virtue of this opinion, Wilkes in 1769 collected heavy damages from another royal messenger, and from the minister who had ordered the arrest.

us had a jurisdiction to seize the defendant's papers. If he had no such jurisdiction, the law is clear that the officers are as much responsible for the trespass as their superior.

This, though it is not the most difficult, is the most interesting question in the cause; because, if this point should be determined in favour of the jurisdiction, the secret cabinets and bureaus of every subject in this kingdom will be thrown open to the search and inspection of a messenger whenever the secretary of state shall think fit to charge, or even to suspect, a person to be the author, printer, or publisher of a seditious libel. The messenger, under this warrant, is commanded to seize the person described and to bring him with his papers to be examined before the secretary of state. In consequence of this, the house must be searched; the lock and doors of every room, box, or trunk must be broken open; all the papers and books without exception, if the warrant be executed according to its tenor, must be seized and carried away. For it is observable that nothing is left either to the discretion or to the humanity of the officer. . . .

This power, so claimed by the secretary of state, is not supported by one single citation from any law book extant. It is claimed by no other magistrate in this kingdom but himself. . . . The arguments which the defendant's counsel have thought fit to urge in support of this practice are of this kind: that such warrants have issued frequently since the Revolution . . . ; that the case of the warrants bears a resemblance to the case of search for stolen goods. They say too that they have been executed without resistance upon many printers, booksellers, and authors, who have quietly submitted to the authority; that no action hath hitherto been brought to try the right; and that, although they have been often read upon the returns of *habeas corpus,* yet no court of justice has ever declared them illegal. And it is further insisted that this power is essential to government and the only means of quieting clamours and sedition. These arguments, if they can be called arguments, shall be all taken notice of, because upon this question I am desirous of removing every colour or plausibility.

Before I state the question, it will be necessary to describe the power claimed by this warrant in its full extent. If honestly exerted, it is a power to seize that man's papers who is charged upon oath to be the author or publisher of a seditious libel; if oppressively, it acts against every man who is so described in the warrant, though he be innocent. It is executed against the party before he is heard or even summoned. And the information, as well as the informers, is unknown. It is executed by messengers with or without a constable . . . , in the presence or the absence of the party, as the messengers shall think fit, and without a witness to testify what passes at the time of the transaction; so that, when the papers are gone, as the only witnesses are the trespassers, the party injured is left without proof. If this injury falls upon an innocent person, he is as destitute of remedy as the guilty; and the whole transaction is so guarded against discovery that, if the officer should be disposed to carry off a bank-bill, he may do it with impunity, since there is no man capable of proving either the taker or the thing taken. It must not be here forgot that no subject whatsoever is privileged from this search; because both houses of parliament have resolved that there is no privilege in the case of a seditious libel.[3] Nor is there pretence to say that the word "papers" here mentioned ought in point of law to be restrained to the libellous papers only. The word is general, and there is nothing in the warrant to confine it; nay, I am able to affirm, that it has been upon a late occasion executed in its utmost latitude. . . .

Such is the power, and therefore one should naturally expect that the law to warrant it should be clear in proportion as the power is exorbitant. If it is law, it will be found in our books. If it is not to be found there, it is not law. The great end for which men entered into society was to secure their property. That right is preserved sacred and incommunicable in all instances where it has not been taken away or abridged by some public law for the good of the whole. The cases where this right of property is set aside by positive law are various. Distresses, executions, forfeitures, taxes, etc., are all of this description; wherein every man by common consent gives up that right for the sake of justice and the general good. By the laws of England every invasion of private property, be it ever so minute, is a trespass. No man can set his foot upon my ground without my licence but he is liable to an action, though the damage be nothing; which is proved by every declaration in trespass where the defendant is called upon to answer for bruising the grass and even treading upon the soil. If he admits the fact, he is bound to show by way of justification that some positive law has empowered or excused him. The justification is submitted to the judges, who are to look into the books and [find] if such a justification can be maintained by the text of the statute law or by the principles of common law. If no such excuse can be found or produced, the silence of the books is an authority against the defendant, and the plaintiff must have judgment.

According to this reasoning, it is now incumbent upon the defendants to show the law by which this seizure is warranted. If that cannot be done, it is a trespass. Papers are the owner's goods and chattels. They are his dearest property, and are so far from enduring a seizure that they will hardly bear an inspection; and though the eye cannot by the laws of England be guilty of a trespass, yet, where private papers are removed and carried away, the secret nature of those goods will be an aggravation of the trespass and demand more considerable damages in that respect. Where is the written law that gives any magistrate such a power? I can safely answer

---

[3] Cf. No. 128A.

there is none, and therefore it is too much for us without such authority to pronounce a practice legal which would be subversive of all the comforts of society. But though it cannot be maintained by any direct law, yet it bears a resemblance, as was urged, to the known case of search and seizure for stolen goods.

I answer that the difference is apparent. In the one I am permitted to seize my own goods, which are placed in the hands of a public officer till the felon's conviction shall entitle me to restitution. In the other the party's own property is seized before and without conviction, and he has no power to reclaim his goods even after his innocence is cleared by acquittal. The case of searching for stolen goods crept into the law by imperceptible practice. It is the only case of the kind that is to be met with. . . . Observe too the caution with which the law proceeds in this singular case: there must be a full charge upon oath of a theft committed; the owner must swear that the goods are lodged in such a place; he must attend at the execution of the warrant to show them to the officer, who must see that they answer the description; and, lastly, the owner must abide the event at his peril, for if the goods are not found, he is a trespasser and the officer, being an innocent person, will be always a ready and convenient witness against him. On the contrary, in the case before us nothing is described, nor distinguished; no charge is requisite to prove that the party has any criminal papers in his custody; no person [is] present to separate or select, no person to prove in the owner's behalf the officer's misbehaviour. To say the truth, he cannot easily misbehave unless he pilfers, for he cannot take more than all.

If it should be said that the same law, which has with so much circumspection guarded the case of stolen goods from mischief, would likewise in this case protect the subject by adding proper checks—would require proofs beforehand, would call up the servant to stand by and overlook, would require him to take an exact inventory and deliver a copy—my answer is that all these precautions would have been long since established by law if the power itself had been legal; and that the want of them is an undeniable argument against the legality of the thing. What would the parliament say if the judges should take upon themselves to mould an unlawful power into a convenient authority by new restrictions? That would be, not judgment, but legislation.

I come now to the practice since the Revolution, which has been strongly urged with this emphatical addition, that an usage tolerated from the era of liberty, and continued downwards to this time through the best ages of the constitution, must necessarily have a legal commencement. Now, though that pretence can have no place in the question made by this plea—because no such practice is there alleged—yet I will permit the defendant for the present to borrow a fact from the special verdict for the sake of giving it an answer. If the practice began then, it began too late to be law now. If it was more ancient, the Revolution is not to answer for it; and I could have wished that upon this occasion the Revolution had not been considered as the only basis of our liberty. . . .

With respect to the practice itself, if it goes no higher, every lawyer will tell you it is much too modern to be evidence of the common law. And if it should be added that these warrants ought to acquire some strength by the silence of those courts, which have heard them read so often upon returns without censure or animadversion, I am able to borrow my answer to that pretence from the court of king's bench, which lately declared with great unanimity in the case of general warrants that, as no objection was taken to them upon the returns and the matter passed *sub silentio*, the precedents were of no weight. I most heartily concur in that opinion. . . . This is the first instance I have met with where the ancient immemorial law of the land, in a public matter, was attempted to be proved by the practice of a private office. The names and rights of public magistrates, their power and forms of proceeding as they are settled by law, have been long since written and are to be found in books and records. Private customs, indeed, are still to be sought from private tradition. But who ever conceived a notion that any part of the public law could be buried in the obscure practice of a particular person?

To search, seize, and carry away all the papers of the subject upon the first warrant: that such a right should have existed from the time whereof the memory of man runneth not to the contrary, and never yet have found a place in any book of law, is incredible. But if so strange a thing could be supposed, I do not see how we could declare the law upon such evidence. But still it is insisted that there has been a general submission, and no action brought to try the right. . . . As, therefore, no authority in our books can be produced to support such a doctrine, and so many star chamber decrees, ordinances, and acts have been thought necessary to establish a power of search, I cannot be persuaded that such a power can be justified by the common law.

I have now done with the argument which has endeavoured to support this warrant by the practice since the Revolution. It is then said that it is necessary for the ends of government to lodge such a power with a state officer, and that it is better to prevent the publication before than to punish the offender afterwards. I answer, if the [legislature] be of that opinion, they will revive the Licensing Act. But if they have not done that, I conceive they are not of that opinion. And with respect to the argument of state necessity, or a distinction that has been aimed at between state offences and others, the common law does not understand that kind of reasoning, nor do our books take notice of any such distinctions. . . .

Lastly, it is urged, as an argument of utility, that such a search is a means of detecting offenders by discovering evidence. I wish some cases had been shown where the law forceth evidence out of the owner's custody by process. There is no process against papers in civil causes. It has been often tried, but never prevailed. Nay, where the adversary has by force or fraud got possession of your own proper evidence, there is no way to get it back but by action. In the criminal law such a proceeding was never heard of; and yet there are some crimes—such, for instance, as murder, rape, robbery, and house-breaking, to say nothing of forgery and perjury—that are more atrocious than libelling. But our law has provided no paper-search in these cases to help forward the conviction. . . . If, however, a right of search for the sake of discovering evidence ought in any case to be allowed, this crime above all others ought to be excepted, as wanting such a discovery less than any other. It is committed in open daylight and in the face of the world; every act of publication makes new proof; and the solicitor of the treasury, if he pleases, may be the witness himself. . . .

I have now taken notice of everything that has been urged upon the present point; and upon the whole we are all of opinion that the warrant to seize and carry away the party's papers in the case of a seditious libel is illegal and void.

Ibid., XIX, 1044 f.

(C) SOMERSETT'S CASE (1772)[4]

. . . The only question before us is whether the cause on the return is sufficient. If it is, the negro must be remanded; if it is not, he must be discharged. Accordingly, the return states that the slave departed and refused to serve; whereupon he was kept, to be sold abroad. So high an act of dominion must be recognized by the law of the country where it is used. The power of a master over his slave has been extremely different in different countries. The state of slavery is of such a nature that it is incapable of being introduced on any reasons, moral or political, but only by positive law, which preserves its force long after the reasons, occasion, and time itself from whence it was created is erased from memory. It is so odious that nothing can be suffered to support it but positive law. Whatever inconveniences, therefore, may follow from the decision, I cannot say this case is allowed or approved by the law of England; and therefore the black must be discharged.

Ibid., XX, 82 f.

---

[4] James Somersett, a negro slave belonging to Charles Stewart of Jamaica, was brought by his master to England. There Somersett ran away, but he was captured and put for safe-keeping on board a ship lying in the Thames. Friends of Somersett then obtained a writ of *habeas corpus* addressed to the captain of the vessel who, in the return to the writ, set forth the facts as above. Here follows the judgment of the court of king's bench, stated by Chief Justice Mansfield. The counsel for Somersett pointed out that the only form of slavery known to English law was villeinage, which had disappeared from judicial proceedings since 1618 (see no. 91H).

129. JUDICIAL CASES

(D) CAMPBELL V. HALL (1774)[5]

The general question that arises out of all these facts found by the special verdict is this: whether the letters patent under the great seal bearing date the 20th July, 1764, are good and valid to abolish the French duties; and in lieu thereof to impose the 4½ per cent. duty above mentioned, which is paid in all the British Leeward Islands. It has been contended at the bar that the letters patent are void on two points. The first is that, although they had been made before the proclamation of the 7th October, 1763, yet the king could not exercise such a legislative power over a conquered country. The second point is that, though the king had sufficient power and authority before the 7th October, 1763, to do such legislative act, yet before the letters patent of the 20th July, 1764, he had divested himself of that authority.

A great deal has been said and many authorities cited relative to propositions in which both sides seem to be perfectly agreed, and which, indeed, are too clear to be controverted. The stating some of those propositions which we think quite clear will lead us to see with greater perspicuity what is the question upon the first point and upon what hinge it turns. I will state the propositions at large, and the first is this: a country conquered by the British arms becomes a dominion of the king in the right of his crown, and therefore necessarily subject to the legislature, the parliament of Great Britain. The second is that the conquered inhabitants, once received under the king's protection, become subjects and are to be universally considered in that light, not as enemies or aliens. The third [is] that the articles of capitulation upon which the country is surrendered and the articles of peace by which it is ceded are sacred and inviolable according to their true intent and meaning. The fourth [is] that the law and legislative government of every dominion equally affects all persons and all property within the limits thereof, and is the rule of decision for all questions which arise there. . . . The fifth [is] that the laws of a conquered country continue in force until they are altered by the conqueror. . . . The sixth and last proposition is that, if the king—and when I say the king, I always mean the king without the concurrence of parliament—has a power to alter the old and to introduce new laws in a conquered country, this legislation being subordinate (that is, subordinate to his own authority in parliament), he cannot make any new change contrary

---
[5] This was a case brought from Grenada to the court of common pleas. Hall, a tax-collector in the island, had taken a certain amount from Campbell as duty on the export of sugar according to letters patent of the king dated 20 July 1764. Campbell brought suit to recover the money on the ground that the tax was illegal, being imposed by royal prerogative after the king had granted legislative authority within the island to a local assembly. The pertinent facts were established by special verdict of a jury. The judgment of the court on the points of law was rendered by Chief Justice Mansfield. See nos. 91C and 124B.

to fundamental principles. He cannot exempt an inhabitant from that particular dominion . . . or give him privileges exclusive of his other subjects. . . .

But the present change, if it had been made before the 7th October, 1763, would have been made recently after the cession of Grenada by treaty; and is in itself most reasonable, equitable, and political; for it is putting Grenada, as to duties, on the same footing with all the British Leeward Islands. . . . The only question, then, on this first point is whether the king had a power to make such change between the 10th of February, 1763, the day the treaty of peace was signed, and the 7th October, 1763. Taking these propositions to be true which I have stated, the only question is whether the king had of himself that power.

It is left by the constitution to the king's authority to grant or refuse a capitulation. If he refuses and puts the inhabitants to the sword or exterminates them, all the lands belong to him. If he receives the inhabitants under his protection and grants them their property, he has a power to fix such terms and conditions as he thinks proper. He is entrusted with making the treaty of peace; he may yield up the conquest or retain it upon what terms he pleases. These powers no man ever disputed; neither has it hitherto been controverted that the king might change part or the whole of the law or political form of government of a conquered dominion.

. . . But upon the second point, after full consideration, we are of opinion that, before the letters patent of the 20th July, 1764, the king had precluded himself from the exercise of a legislative authority over the island of Grenada. The first and material instrument is the proclamation of the 7th October, 1763. See what it is that the king there says, with what view, and how he engages himself and pledges his word. "For the better security of the liberty and property of those who are or shall become inhabitants of our islands of Grenada, we have declared by this our proclamation that we have commissioned our governor, as soon as the state and circumstances of the colony will admit, to call an assembly to enact laws," etc. With what view is this made? It is to invite settlers and subjects. And why to invite? That they might think their properties, etc., more secure if the legislation was vested in an assembly than under a governor and council only.

Next, having established the constitution, the proclamation of the 20th March, 1764, invites them to come in as purchasers. In further confirmation of all this, on the 9th April, 1764, three months before July, an actual commission is made out to the governor to call an assembly as soon as the state of the island would admit thereof. You observe there is no reservation in the proclamation of any legislature to be exercised by the king, or by the governor and council under his authority in any manner, until the assembly should meet; but rather the contrary. For whatever construction is to be put upon it . . . , it alludes to a government by laws in being and by courts of justice, not by a legislative authority, until an assembly should be called. There does not appear from the special verdict any impediment to the calling an assembly immediately on the arrival of the governor, which was in December, 1764. But no assembly was called then or at any time afterwards, till the end of the year 1765.

We therefore think that, by the two proclamations and the commission to Governor Melville, the king had immediately and irrecoverably granted to all who were or should become inhabitants, or who had or should acquire property in the island of Grenada, or more generally to all whom it might concern, that the subordinate legislation over the island should be exercised by an assembly with the consent of the governor and council, in like manner as the other islands belonging to the king. Therefore, though the abolishing the duties of the French king and the substituting this tax in its stead, which according to the finding in this special verdict is paid in all the British Leeward Islands, is just and equitable with respect to Grenada itself and the other British Leeward Islands, yet, through the inattention of the king's servants in inverting the order in which the instruments should have passed and been notoriously published, the last act is contradictory to and a violation of the first, and is therefore void. How proper soever it may be in respect to the object of the letters patent of the 20th July, 1764, to use the words of Sir Philip Yorke and Sir Clement Wearge, "It can only now be done by the assembly of the island or by an act of the parliament of Great Britain." The consequence is judgment must be given for the plaintiff.

Cowper, *Reports*, I, 208 f.

(E) THE CASE OF THE DEAN OF ST. ASAPH (1784)[6]

... The fundamental definition of trial by jury depends upon a universal maxim that is without an exception. Though a definition or maxim in law without an exception, it is said, is hardly to be found, yet this I take to be a maxim without an exception: *ad quaestionem juris non respondent juratores; ad quaestionem facti non respondent judices*.[7]

---

[6] In 1783 the Reverend William Davies Shipley, dean of St. Asaph, caused to be printed a dialogue written by his brother-in-law advocating parliamentary reform. Being prosecuted before the assizes at Shrewsbury for publishing a seditious libel, he was found guilty of publishing; "but whether a libel or not the jury do not find." Then ensued a wrangle over the propriety of the charge given to the jury and their verdict, and eventually the question came for review to the court of king's bench. Chief Justice Mansfield, giving the judgment of the court, upheld the verdict, as may be seen from the following excerpts, and crown attorneys let the prosecution drop. The case is particularly significant in relation to the bill which Fox was then advocating in parliament (see nos. 126 I, 124E).

[7] Jurors do not answer the question of law; judges do not answer the question of fact.

Where a question can be severed by the form of pleading, the distinction is preserved upon the face of the record, and the jury cannot encroach upon the jurisdiction of the court; where, by the form of pleading, the two questions are blended together and cannot be separated upon the face of the record, the distinction is preserved by the honesty of the jury. The constitution trusts that, under the direction of a judge, they will not usurp a jurisdiction which is not in their province. They do not know and are not presumed to know the law; they are not sworn to decide the law; they are not required to decide the law. If it appears upon the record, they ought to leave it there; or they may find the facts subject to the opinion of the court upon the law. But further, upon the reason of the thing and the eternal principles of justice, the jury ought not to assume the jurisdiction of the law. As I said before, they do not know and are not presumed to know anything of the matter; they do not understand the language in which it is conceived or the meaning of the terms. They have no rule to go by but their affections and wishes. It is said, if a man gives a right sentence upon hearing one side only, he is a wicked judge, because he is right by chance only and has neglected taking the proper method to be informed. So the jury who usurp the judicature of law, though they happen to be right, are themselves wrong, because they are right by chance only and have not taken the constitutional way of deciding the question. It is the duty of the judge in all cases of general justice to tell the jury how to do right, though they have it in their power to do wrong—which is a matter entirely between God and their own consciences.

To be free is to live under a government by law. The liberty of the press consists in printing without any previous licence subject to the consequences of law. The licentiousness of the press is Pandora's box, the source of every evil. Miserable is the condition of individuals, dangerous is the condition of the state, if there is no certain law or—which is the same thing—no certain administration of law to protect individuals or to guard the state. Jealousy of leaving the law to the court, as in other cases so in the case of libels, is now, in the present state of things, puerile rant and declamation. The judges are totally independent of the ministers that may happen to be and of the king himself. Their temptation is rather to the popularity of the day. But I agree with the observation cited by Mr. Cowper from Mr. J. Foster, "that a popular judge is an odious and a pernicious character." The judgment of the court is not final; in the last resort it may be reviewed in the house of lords, where the opinion of all the judges is taken.

In opposition to this what is contended for? That the law shall be in every particular cause what any twelve men, who shall happen to be the jury, shall be inclined to think—liable to no review, and subject to no control, under all the prejudices of the popular cry of the day, and under all the bias of interest in this town, where thousands, more or less, are concerned in the publication of newspapers, paragraphs, and pamphlets. Under such an administration of law, no man could tell, no counsel could advise, whether a paper was or was not punishable.

I am glad that I am not bound to subscribe to such an absurdity, such a solecism in politics. Agreeable to the uniform judicial practice since the Revolution, warranted by the fundamental principles of the constitution, of the trial by jury, and upon the reason and fitness of the thing, we are all of opinion that this motion should be rejected and this rule discharged.

Howell, State Trials, XXI, 1039 f.

(F) Grant v. Gould (1792)[8]

Martial law, such as it is described by Hale and such also as it is marked by Mr. Justice Blackstone, does not exist in England at all. Where martial law is established and prevails in any country, it is of a totally different nature from that which is inaccurately called martial law merely because the decision is by a court martial, but which bears no affinity to that which was formerly attempted to be exercised in this kingdom, which was contrary to the constitution and which has been for a century totally exploded. Where martial law prevails, the authority under which it is exercised claims a jurisdiction over all military persons in all circumstances. Even their debts are subject to inquiry by a military authority. Every species of offence committed by any person who appertains to the army is tried, not by a civil judicature, but by the judicature of the regiment or corps to which he belongs. It extends also to a great variety of cases not relating to the discipline of the army in those states which subsist by military power. Plots against the sovereign, intelligence to the enemy, and the like are all considered as cases within the cognizance of military authority.

In the reign of King William there was a conspiracy against his person in Holland, and the persons guilty of that conspiracy were tried by a council of officers. There was also a conspiracy against him in England, but the conspirators were tried by the common law. And within a very recent period, the incendiaries who attempted to set fire to the docks at Portsmouth were tried by the common law. In this country all the delinquencies of soldiers are not triable, as in most countries in Europe, by martial law; but

---

[8] Grant, while serving as recruiting serjeant in London, was tried by court martial at Chatham and convicted of having persuaded two soldiers to desert the Coldstream Guards and enlist in the forces of the East India Company. Thereupon Grant brought suit in the court of common pleas against the officer who had presided over the court martial, alleging that the latter had in various ways exceeded its lawful powers, especially since Grant was not actually an enlisted soldier. In the judgment, delivered by Chief Justice Loughborough, the court of common pleas upheld the action of the court martial. The chief justice, after holding that Grant was a soldier, proceeded, in the following paragraphs, to explain the whole subject of martial law in England.

where they are ordinary offences against the civil peace, they are tried by the common law courts. Therefore it is totally inaccurate to state martial law as having any place whatever within the realm of Great Britain. But there is, by the providence and wisdom of the legislature, an army established in this country, of which it is necessary to keep up the establishment. The army being established by the authority of the legislature, it is an indispensable requisite of that establishment that there should be order and discipline kept up in it and that the persons who compose the army, for all offences in their military capacity, should be subject to a trial by their officers. That has induced the absolute necessity of a mutiny act accompanying the army. . . .[9]

It is one object of that act to provide for the army; but there is a much greater cause for the existence of a mutiny act, and that is the preservation of the peace and safety of the kingdom. For there is nothing so dangerous to the civil establishment of a state as a licentious and undisciplined army, and every country which has a standing army in it is guarded and protected by a mutiny act. An undisciplined soldiery are apt to be too many for the civil power, but, under the command of officers, those officers are answerable to the civil power, that they are kept in good order and discipline. All history and all experience, particularly the experience of the present moment, give the strongest testimony to this. The object of the mutiny act, therefore, is to create a court invested with authority to try those who are a part of the army, in all their different descriptions of officers and soldiers; and the object of the trial is limited to breaches of military duty. Even by that extensive power granted by the legislature to his majesty to make articles of war, those articles are to be for the better government of his forces and can extend no further than they are thought necessary to the regularity and due discipline of the army.

Henry Blackstone, Reports, II, 98 f.

(G) The Case of Wolfe Tone (1798)[10]

[Mr. Curran, counsel for Tone's father]: I do not pretend to say that Mr. Tone is not guilty of the charges of which he was accused—I presume the officers were honourable men—but it is stated in the affidavit as a solemn fact that Mr. Tone had no commission under his majesty, and therefore no court martial could have cognizance of any crime imputed to him while the court of king's bench sat in the capacity of the great criminal court of the land. In times

---

[9] No. 120B.

[10] Wolfe Tone, an Irish agitator with a commission in the French army, was captured by the British. On Saturday, 10 November 1798, he was tried by court martial in Dublin Barracks, found guilty of high treason, and sentenced to die on the next Monday. On that day, however, the case was brought before the court of king's bench in Ireland through an affidavit of Tone's father. The subsequent proceedings are brought out in the accompanying record.

when war was raging, when man was opposed to man in the field, courts martial might be endured; but every law authority is with me while I stand upon this sacred and immutable principle of the constitution: that martial law and civil law are incompatible, and that the former must cease with the existence of the latter. This is not the time for arguing this momentous question. My client must appear in this court. He is cast for death this day. He may be ordered for execution while I address you. I call on the court to support the law; I move for a *habeas corpus* to be directed to the provost marshal of the barracks of Dublin and Major Sandys to bring up the body of Mr. Tone.

Lord Chief Justice [Kilwarden]: Have a writ instantly prepared.

Mr. Curran: My client may die while this writ is preparing.

Lord Chief Justice: Mr. Sheriff, proceed to the barracks and acquaint the provost marshal that a writ is preparing to suspend Mr. Tone's execution; and see that he be not executed.

[The sheriff's return is awaited.]

Mr. Sheriff: My lords, I have been at the barracks in pursuance of your order. The provost marshal says he must obey Major Sandys. Major Sandys says he must obey Lord Cornwallis.

Mr. Curran: Mr. Tone's father, my lords, returns after serving the *habeas corpus*. He says General Craig will not obey it.

Lord Chief Justice: Mr. Sheriff, take the body of Tone into your custody; take the provost marshal and Major Sandys into custody; and show the order of this court to General Craig.

[The sheriff's return is awaited.]

Mr. Sheriff: I have been at the barracks. Mr. Tone, having cut his throat last night, is not in a condition to be removed. As to the second part of your order, I could not meet the parties. . . .[11]

Lord Chief Justice: Let a rule be made for suspending the execution of Theodore Wolfe Tone, and let it be served on the proper persons.

Howell, *State Trials*, XXVII, 625 f.

(H) WRIGHT V. FITZGERALD (1799)[12]

His lordship said, that the jury were not to imagine that the legislature, by enabling magistrates to justify under the indemnity bill, had released them from the feelings of humanity or permitted them

---

[11] The fact of the prisoner's attempted suicide was sworn to by a surgeon from the barracks. Tone escaped execution, but died of his wound one week later.

[12] Wright, a schoolteacher in the county of Tipperary, brought suit before the assizes of Clonmell to recover damages from Fitzgerald, late sheriff of the county, by whom he charged he had been unjustly imprisoned and flogged. The defendant alleged that his treatment of Wright was justified by the sheriff's duty of putting down rebellion. Here follows Justice Chamberlain's charge to the jury, which found for the plaintiff and awarded him damages of £500.

wantonly to exercise power, even though it were to put down rebellion. No: it expected that in all cases there should be a grave and serious examination into the conduct of the supposed criminal; and every act should show a mind intent to discover guilt, not to inflict torture. By examination or trial he did not mean that sort of examination and trial which they were then engaged in, but such examination and trial the best the nature of the case and the existing circumstances would allow of. That this must have been the intention of the legislature was manifest from the expression, "magistrates and all other persons," which proved that, as every man, whether magistrate or not, was authorized to suppress rebellion and was to be justified by that law for his acts, it is required that he should not exceed the necessity which gave him the power; and that he should show in his justification that he had used every possible means to ascertain the guilt which he had punished; and, above all, no deviation from the common principles of humanity should appear in his conduct.

The plaintiff appeared, by evidence uncontradicted, to be a man of unimpeachable character and to have been grossly and wantonly abused. He was therefore entitled to a compensation in damages—what those damages should be it was not his province to determine. But from the injury proved to have been sustained, if the jury should give the whole damages [£1000] laid in the declaration, he would not think it too much. He thought it but justice to the defendant, to say, that he believed he had done much good in his capacity as sheriff, had suppressed rebellion in his county, and had proved himself to be a man of great courage and intrepidity.

Ibid., XXVII, 765 f.

(I) THE KING v. BURDETT (1820)[13]

We have . . . had allusion to the meeting at Manchester and evidence has been tendered to me for the purpose of showing that the defendant has said nothing but the truth of that which took place there. Nobody knows better than the learned counsel for the defendant that, consistently with my oath, I could not receive that; because if the libel were proved to be true, it cannot bear upon this case. The question is not—nor ever can be, if the liberty of the press is to be supported—whether that which has been written be true or false, because then a man meaning honestly might be convicted for stating an untruth. It is not the truth or falsehood that makes a libel, but the

---

[13] Sir Francis Burdett, for an address to the electors of Westminster on the so-called Massacre of Peterloo, was charged at the Leicester assizes with composing, writing, and publishing a seditious libel. Acting under a charge from Justice Best, the jury found him guilty; whereupon an appeal was made to the court of king's bench, of which Justice Best was a member. After hearing lengthy argument on both sides, that court refused to order a new trial, thus upholding the decisions of both judge and jury at Leicester. The following excerpts are from, first, Justice Best's charge to the Leicester jury; secondly, Justice Best's restatement of his opinion in the court of king's bench.

temper with which it is published. And another ground on which the truth or falsehood cannot be inquired into is this: because, whether it be true or false, no man ought to charge another with crime. That would make the liberty of the press inconsistent with another liberty equally dear to an Englishman—his character. No man's character is to be taken from him by attacks in newspapers or any publication whatever. If they do what is wrong, you were properly told by the learned counsel in the outset, the courts of justice are open to bring them to punishment. It is on these grounds I refused the evidence; because, according to the law of the land, it is not admissible. . . .

. . . Another point on which the motion for a new trial was made was that I took upon myself to lay down the law to the jury as to the libel, and that since the statute 32 George III, c. 60,[14] I was not warranted in so doing. I told the jury that they were to consider whether the paper was published with the intent charged in the information; and that, if they thought it was published with that intent, I was of opinion that it was a libel. I, however, added that they were to decide whether they would adopt my opinion. In forming their opinion on the question of libel, I told the jury that they were to consider whether the paper contained a sober address to the reason of mankind, or whether it was an appeal to their passions, calculated to incite them to acts of violence and outrage. If it was of the former description, it was not a libel; if of the latter description, it was.

It must not be supposed that the statute of George III made the question of libel a question of fact. If it had, instead of removing an anomaly, it would have created one. Libel is a question of law, and the judge is the judge of the law in libel as in all other cases, the jury having the power of acting agreeably to his statement of the law or not. All that the statute does is to prevent the question from being left to the jury in the narrow way in which it was left before that time. The jury were then only to find the fact of the publication and the truth of the innuendoes; for the judges used to tell them that the intent was an inference of law, to be drawn from the paper, with which the jury had nothing to do. The legislature has said that that is not so, but that the whole case is to be left to the jury. But judges are in express terms directed to lay down the law as in other cases. In all cases the jury may find a general verdict; they do so in cases of murder and treason; but there the judge tells them what is the law, though they may find against him, unless they are satisfied with his opinion. And this is plain from the words of the statute, which, after reciting that doubts had arisen whether on the trial of a libel the jury may give their verdict on the whole matter in issue, directs that they "shall not be required or directed by the court or judge to find the defendant guilty, etc., merely on the proof of the publication by such defendant or defendants of the paper charged to be a libel, and of the sense ascribed to the same in such indict-

---
[14] See no. 126 I.

ment." But the statute proceeds expressly to say that, "on every such trial, the court or judge before whom such indictment or information shall be tried shall, according to their or his discretion, give their or his opinion and directions to the jury on the matters in issue between the king and the defendant or defendants, in like manner as in other criminal cases."

That was all that was done on this occasion, and therefore I am of opinion that this objection also fails. As to the libel itself, considering it as the production of a man of large fortune, high rank, and extensive influence, where is the person that can make an observation in favour of any part of it? My opinion of the liberty of the press is that every man ought to be permitted to instruct his fellow subjects; that every man may fearlessly advance any new doctrines, provided he does so with proper respect to the religion and government of the country; that he may point out errors in the measures of public men; but he must not impute criminal conduct to them. The liberty of the press cannot be carried to this extent without violating another equally sacred right; namely, the right of character. This right can only be attacked in a court of justice, where the party attacked has a fair opportunity of defending himself. Where vituperation begins the liberty of the press ends. This maxim was acted upon by the greatest states of antiquity. In our country the liberty of the press allows us to persuade men to use their constitutional influence over their representatives to obtain in the regular parliamentary manner a redress of real or supposed grievances. But this must be done with temper and moderation; otherwise, instead of setting the government in motion for the people, the people may be set in motion against the government. In such a case as this it is fit that the public should know the grounds on which I have acted. . . .

Reports of State Trials, New Series, I, 49, 118 f.

SECTION XIII

WILLIAM IV AND VICTORIA (TO 1880)

So MANY changes in English government have been made during the hundred-odd years since the accession of William IV that, for the purpose of this volume, the period has to be divided. And as the reign of Victoria can be broken without serious inconvenience to the student, the present section has been ended with the year 1880. The half-century thus arbitrarily set apart was dominated by the advance of parliamentary reform. The great act of 1832 entirely reconstructed the house of commons, abandoning a five-hundred-year-old scheme of representation (cf. nos. 49F, 60A), superseding the electoral law of 1429 for the counties (no. 69E), and establishing for the first time a uniform borough franchise. The result was to place the kingdom under control of the middle class—a settlement which continued until Disraeli made his famous "leap" toward democratic suffrage in 1867 (no. 131H).

Meanwhile other articles of the liberals' programme had been carried out. Between 1832 and 1835 slavery was abolished throughout the empire, state supervision of factories was made effective, the administration of poor relief was modernized, and —another innovation—a single plan of municipal government was extended to all the boroughs. No equivalent reform was as yet devised for the counties, but two of Victoria's earlier statutes (no. 131A, D) were preliminary efforts in that direction. The Ballot Act may be regarded as a necessary supplement to the parliamentary franchise law of 1867. By the Education Act, 1870, the state definitely undertook the responsibility of providing schools for the masses. And three years later the Judicature Act, sweeping aside a body of traditions that ran back to the age of Magna Carta, reconstituted the whole English court system.

Another prominent feature of legislation during the middle nineteenth century was the establishment of free trade. This new policy, however, was put into effect through such gradual revision that it cannot be well explained by quoting a few enactments. So the triumph of *laissez faire* principles has been illustrated by the repeal of the ancient statutes limiting commerce by sea (no. 131C). It is likewise impossible in the following pages to give examples of structural changes throughout the empire at large. Most of the British possessions—the military posts, the naval stations, India, and the plantations in the tropics—must here be passed over. But since the British constitution of to-day cannot be understood apart from arrangements made with the great dominions, it has seemed advisable to include the act that created the first of them, Canada (no. 131G). Besides, a number of documents have been added to show how the North American colonies, before their confederation, had come to enjoy responsible government (no. 133).

The reactions of various parliamentary leaders to the new colonial policy will be found in no. 132D. The other discussions under the same heading are mainly concerned with the advance of democracy and its effect upon certain old problems, such as the responsibility of ministers to public opinion and theories of representation. And in this connection it is worth noting that the questions debated in parliament were no longer such as might come before the courts for adjudication. Of the trials briefly reported under no. 134, only Stockdale v. Hansard, with its sequel of the following year, evokes memories of an age when parliamentary privilege was a matter of violent controversy.

In the study of the nineteenth-century constitution the following books, some of which have been cited earlier, are especially important: A. V. Dicey, *The Law of the Constitution,* and *Law and Public Opinion in the Nineteenth Century*; W. R. Anson, *The Law and Custom of the Constitution;* W. Bagehot, *The English Constitution* (edited with an introductory essay by Earl Balfour); T. E. May, *Constitutional History of England* (vol. III by F. Holland); C. S. Emden, *Principles of British Constitutional Law,* and *The People and the Constitution*; E .C. S. Wade and G. C. Phillips, *Constitutional Law;* D. L. Keir and F. H. Lawson, *Cases in Constitutional Law;* G. C. Robertson, *Select Statutes, Cases, and Documents;* D. O. Dykes, *Source Book of Constitutional History from 1660;* A. L. Lowell, *The Government of England;* H. D. Traill, *Central Government;* Sidney and Beatrice Webb, *Local Government;* J. Redlich and F. W. Hirst, *Local Government in England;* C. Seymour,

Electoral Reform in England and Wales; F. Hardie, *The Political Influence of Queen Victoria.*

There are many excellent works dealing with responsible government and imperial federation: among them, A. B. Keith, *Responsible Government in the Dominions;* H. E. Egerton, *Federations and Unions within the British Empire;* C. Martin, *Empire and Commonwealth;* P. Knaplund, *Gladstone and Britain's Imperial Policy;* G. M. Wrong, *Charles Buller and Responsible Government;* K. N. Bell and W. P. Morrell, *Select Documents on British Colonial Policy, 1830-1860;* W. P. M. Kennedy, *The Constitution of Canada.*

130. WILLIAM IV: STATUTES

(A) REFORM ACT (1832)

An act to amend the representation of the people in England and Wales. Whereas it is expedient to take effectual measures for correcting divers abuses that have long prevailed in the choice of members to serve in the commons house of parliament; to deprive many inconsiderable places of the right of returning members; to grant such privilege to large, populous, and wealthy towns; to increase the number of knights of the shire; to extend the elective franchise to many of his majesty's subjects who have not heretofore enjoyed the same; and to diminish the expense of elections: be it therefore enacted . . . that each of the boroughs enumerated in the schedule marked A to this act annexed . . . shall, from and after the end of this present parliament, cease to return any member or members to serve in parliament.

And be it enacted that each of the boroughs enumerated in the schedule marked B . . . shall . . . return one member and no more to serve in parliament.

And be it enacted that each of the places named in the schedule marked C . . . shall for the purpose of this act be a borough, and shall . . . return two members to serve in parliament.

And be it enacted that each of the places named in the schedule marked D . . . shall for the purposes of this act be a borough, and shall . . . return one member to serve in parliament. . . .[1]

And be it enacted that in all future parliaments there shall be six knights of the shire, instead of four, to serve for the county of York . . . ; and . . . that in all future parliaments there shall be four knights of the shire, instead of two, to serve for the county of Lincoln. . . .

---

[1] Schedule A names 56 boroughs; Schedule B, 30 boroughs; Schedule C, 22 places; Schedule D, 20 places. The next seven articles deal with the fixing of boundaries for the boroughs and with qualifications for election officials.

And be it enacted . . . that in all future parliaments there shall be four knights of the shire, instead of two, to serve for each of the . . . counties [enumerated in the schedule marked F] . . . ; and . . . that in all future parliaments there shall be three knights of the shire, instead of two, to serve for each of the counties enumerated in the schedule marked F2 . . . , and two knights of the shire, instead of one, to serve for each of the counties of Carmarthen, Denbigh, and Glamorgan. . . .[2]

And be it enacted that every male person of full age and not subject to any legal incapacity who shall be seised at law or in equity of any lands or tenements of copyhold, or any other tenure whatever except freehold,[3] for his own life or for the life of another or for any lives whatsoever . . . , of the clear yearly value of not less than £10 . . . shall be entitled to vote in the election of a knight or knights of the shire . . . for the county . . . in which such lands or tenements shall be respectively situate.

And be it enacted that every male person of full age and not subject to any legal incapacity who shall be entitled, either as lessee or assignee, to any lands or tenements . . . for the unexpired residue . . . of any term originally created for a period of not less than sixty years . . . of the clear yearly value of not less than £10 . . . , or for the unexpired residue . . . of any term originally created for a period of not less than twenty years . . . of the clear yearly value of not less than £50 . . . , or who shall occupy as tenant any lands or tenements for which he shall be *bona fide* liable to a yearly rent of not less than £50, shall be entitled to vote in the election of a knight or knights of the shire to serve in any future parliament for the county . . . in which such lands . . . shall be respectively situate. . . . And be it enacted that, notwithstanding anything hereinbefore contained, no person shall be entitled to vote in the election of a knight or knights of the shire to serve in any future parliament unless he shall have been duly registered according to the provisions hereinafter contained. . . .[4]

And be it enacted that, in every city or borough which shall return a member or members to serve in any future parliament, every male person of full age and not subject to any legal incapacity who shall occupy within such city or borough . . . , as owner or tenant, any house, warehouse, counting-house, shop, or other building . . . of the clear yearly value of not less than £10 shall, if duly registered according to the provisions hereinafter contained, be entitled to vote in the election of a member or members to serve in any future parliament for such city or borough. Provided always that no such

---

[2] Schedule F names 25 counties; Schedule F2, 7 counties. The next two articles redefine the boundaries of certain counties.

[3] The statute takes for granted the continuance of the 40s. freehold franchise established by the act of 1429 (no. 69E).

[4] Lists of voters are to be kept in each constituency by certain local officials.

person shall be so registered . . . unless he shall have occupied such premises . . . for twelve calendar months . . . ; nor unless such person . . . shall have been rated in respect of such premises to all rates for the relief of the poor . . . made during the time of such his occupation . . . ; nor unless such person shall have paid . . . all the poor's rates and assessed taxes which shall have become payable from him in respect of such premises. . . .

And be it enacted that every person who would have been entitled to vote in the election of a member or members to serve in any future parliament for any city or borough, not included in the schedule marked A . . . , either as a burgess or freeman . . . , if this act had not been passed, shall be entitled to vote in such election, provided such person shall be duly registered. . . .

And be it enacted that . . . all booths erected for the convenience of taking polls shall be erected at the joint and equal expense of the several candidates . . . ; that the expense to be incurred for the booth or booths to be erected at the principal place of election for any county . . . or division of a county . . . shall not exceed the sum of £40 . . . ; and that the expense to be incurred for any booth or booths to be erected for any parish, district, or part of any city or borough shall not exceed the sum of £25. . . .

Provided always . . . that nothing in this act contained shall . . . in any wise affect the election of members to serve in parliament for the universities of Oxford or Cambridge. . . .

Statutes of the United Kingdom, LXXII, 154 f.: 2 William IV, c. 45.

(B) PRIVY COUNCIL APPEALS ACT (1833)

An act for the better administration of justice in his majesty's privy council. . . . Be it . . . enacted . . . that the president for the time being of his majesty's privy council, the lord high chancellor of Great Britain for the time being, and such of the members of his majesty's privy council as shall from time to time hold any of the offices following—that is to say, the office of lord keeper or first lord commissioner of the great seal of Great Britain, lord chief justice or judge of the court of king's bench, master of the rolls, vice-chancellor of England, lord chief justice or judge of the court of common pleas, lord chief baron or baron of the court of exchequer, judge of the prerogative court of the lord archbishop of Canterbury, judge of the high court of admiralty, and chief judge of the court in bankruptcy—and also all persons, members of his majesty's privy council, who shall have been president thereof or held the office of lord chancellor of Great Britain, or shall have held any of the other offices hereinbefore mentioned, shall form a committee of his majesty's said privy council and shall be styled the judicial committee of the privy council. Provided, nevertheless, that it shall be lawful for his majesty from time to time, as and when he shall think fit, by his sign-manual to appoint any two other persons, being privy councillors, to be members of the said committee.

And be it further enacted that . . . all appeals or applications in prize suits and in all other suits or proceedings in the courts of admiralty, or vice-admiralty courts, or any other court in the plantations in America and other his majesty's dominions or elsewhere abroad, which may now by virtue of any law, statute, commission, or usage, be made to the high court of admiralty in England or to the lords commissioners in prize cases, shall be made to his majesty in council. . . .

And be it further enacted that all appeals or complaints in the nature of appeals whatever which either by virtue of this act or of any law, statute, or custom may be brought before his majesty or his majesty in council from or in respect of the determination, sentence, rule, or order of any court, judge, or judicial officer . . . shall . . . be referred by his majesty to the said judicial committee of his privy council. . . .

Ibid., LXXIII, 263 f.: 3-4 William IV, c. 41.

(C) Act Abolishing Slavery (1833)

An act for the abolition of slavery throughout the British colonies. . . . Be it . . . enacted that, subject to the obligations imposed by this act . . . , all . . . persons who on the . . . first day of August, 1834, shall be holden in slavery within any . . . British colony . . . shall upon and from and after the said first day of August, 1834, become and be to all intents and purposes free and discharged of and from all manner of slavery, and shall be absolutely and forever manumitted; and that the children thereafter to be born to any such persons, and the offspring of such children, shall in like manner be free from their birth; and that from and after the said first day of August, 1834, slavery shall be and is hereby utterly and forever abolished and declared unlawful throughout the British colonies, plantations, and possessions abroad. . . .[5]

Ibid., LXXIII, 666 f.: 3-4 William IV, c. 73.

(D) Factory Act (1833)

An act to regulate the labour of children and young persons in the mills and factories of the united kingdom. . . . Be it . . . enacted . . . that . . . no person under eighteen years of age shall be allowed to work in the night—that is to say, between the hours half-past eight o'clock in the evening and half-past five o'clock in the morning— . . . in or about any cotton, woolen, worsted, hemp, flax, tow, linen, or silk mill or factory, wherein steam or water or

---

[5] Existing slaves aged six years and upwards are hereby made apprenticed labourers for limited periods, with the right of purchasing discharge. A sum of £20,000,000 is to be applied to compensating owners for the loss of their slaves. Cf. no. 129C.

any other mechanical power is or shall be used to propel or work the machinery. . . .

And be it further enacted that no person under the age of eighteen years shall be employed in any such mill or factory . . . more than twelve hours in any one day, nor more than sixty-nine hours in any one week. . . . And be it further enacted that there shall be allowed in the course of every day not less than one and a half hours for meals to every such person. . . .

And be it enacted that . . . it shall not be lawful for any person whatsoever to employ in any factory or mill as aforesaid, except in mills for the manufacture of silk, any child who shall not have completed his or her ninth year of age.

And be it further enacted that, from and after the expiration of six months after the passing of this act, it shall not be lawful for any person whatsoever to employ, keep, or allow to remain in any factory or mill as aforesaid for a longer time than forty-eight hours in any one week, nor for a longer time than nine hours in any one day . . . , any child who shall not have completed his or her eleventh year of age; or, after the expiration of eighteen months from the passing of this act, any child who shall not have completed his or her twelfth year of age; or, after the expiration of thirty months from the passing of this act, any child who shall not have completed his or her thirteenth year of age. Provided, nevertheless, that, in mills for the manufacture of silk, children under the age of thirteen years shall be allowed to work ten hours in any one day.[6]

And be it further enacted that all children and young persons whose hours of work are regulated and limited by this act shall be entitled to the following holidays, *viz.*: on Christmas Day and Good Friday, the entire day; and not fewer than eight half-days besides in every year. . . .

And whereas, by an act . . . passed in the forty-second year of the reign of . . . George III,[7] it was . . . provided that the justices of the peace . . . should appoint yearly two persons . . . to be visitors of . . . mills or factories . . . ; and whereas it appears that the provisions of the said act . . . were not duly carried into execution . . . : be it therefore enacted that . . . it shall be lawful for his majesty by warrant under his sign-manual to appoint during his majesty's pleasure four persons to be inspectors of factories and places where the labour of children and young persons under eighteen years of age is employed . . . ; which said several inspectors shall carry into effect the powers, authorities, and provisions of the present act. And such inspectors or any of them are hereby empowered to enter any factory or mill, and any school attached or belonging

---

[6] The act also requires that every child thus employed be provided with a certificate as to his or her strength and appearance, signed by a physician and countersigned by a magistrate.

[7] No. 1269.

thereto at all times and seasons, by day or by night, when such mills or factories are at work; and, having so entered, to examine therein the children and any other person or persons employed therein, and to make inquiry respecting their condition, employment, and education. And such inspectors, or any of them, are hereby empowered to take or call to their aid in such examination and inquiry such persons as they may choose, and to summon and require any person upon the spot or elsewhere to give evidence upon such examinations and inquiry, and to administer to such person an oath. . . .

And be it further enacted that . . . every child hereinbefore restricted to the performance of forty-eight hours of labour in any one week shall, so long as such child shall be within the said restricted age, attend some school. . . .

And be it further enacted that every inspector shall keep full minutes of all his visits and proceedings, and shall report the same to one of his majesty's principal secretaries of state twice in every year, and oftener if required. . . .

And whereas it is expedient that the proceedings, rules, orders, and regulations of the several inspectors appointed under this act should be as nearly alike as is practicable under all circumstances: therefore such inspectors are hereby required, within three months next after they shall have commenced the execution of their several duties and powers under this act, and twice at least in every year afterwards, to meet and confer together respecting their several proceedings, rules, orders, regulations, duties, and powers under this act, and at such meeting to make their proceedings, rules, orders, and regulations as uniform as is expedient and practicable. . . .

Ibid., LXXIII, 985 f.: 3-4 William IV, c. 103.

(E) Poor Law Amendment Act (1834)

An act for the amendment and better administration of the laws relating to the poor in England and Wales. . . . Be it . . . enacted . . . that it shall be lawful for his majesty . . . to appoint three fit persons to be commissioners to carry this act into execution. . . . And be it further enacted that the said commissioners shall be styled the poor law commissioners for England and Wales. . . . And the said commissioners . . . shall be and are hereby empowered, by summons under their hands and seal, to require the attendance of all such persons as they may think fit to call before them upon any question or matter connected with or relating to the administration of the laws for the relief of the poor; and also to make any inquiries and require any answer or returns as to any such question or matter; and also to administer oaths and examine all such persons upon oath, and to require and enforce the production upon oath of books, contracts, agreements, accounts, and writings, or copies thereof respectively, in any wise relating to any such question or matter. . . .

And be it further enacted that, from and after the passing of this act, the administration of relief to the poor throughout England and Wales . . . shall be subject to the direction and control of the said commissioners; and, for executing the powers given to them by this act, the said commissioners shall and are hereby authorized and required . . . to make and issue all such . . . regulations for the management of the poor, for the government of workhouses . . . , for the apprenticing the children of poor persons, and for the guidance and control of all guardians, vestries, and parish officers so far as relates to the management or relief of the poor . . . , and for carrying this act into execution in all other respects, as they shall think proper; and the said commissioners may, at their discretion, from time to time suspend, alter, or rescind such rules, orders, and regulations, or any of them; provided always, that nothing in this act contained shall be construed as enabling the said commissioners or any of them to interfere in any individual case for the purpose of ordering relief. . . .

And be it further enacted that it shall be lawful for the said commissioners, by order under their hands and seal, to declare so many parishes as they may think fit to be united for the administration of the laws for the relief of the poor; and such parishes shall thereupon be deemed a union for such purpose, and thereupon the workhouse or workhouses of such parishes shall be for their common use. . . .

And whereas a practice has obtained of giving relief to persons or their families who, at the time of applying for or receiving such relief, were wholly or partially in the employment of individuals, and the relief of the able-bodied and their families is in many places administered in modes productive of evil in other respects; and whereas difficulty may arise in case any immediate and universal remedy is attempted to be applied in the matters aforesaid: be it further enacted that . . . it shall be lawful for the said commissioners, by such rules, orders, or regulations as they may think fit, to declare to what extent and for what period the relief to be given to able-bodied persons or to their families in any particular parish or union may be administered out of the workhouse of such parish or union. . . .

Ibid., LXXIV, 285 f.: 4-5 William IV, c. 76.

(F) Municipal Corporations Act (1835)

An act to provide for the regulation of municipal corporations in England and Wales. Whereas divers bodies corporate at sundry times have been constituted within the cities, towns, and boroughs of England and Wales, to the intent that the same might forever be and remain well and quietly governed; and it is expedient that the charters by which the said bodies corporate are constituted should be altered in the manner hereinafter mentioned: be it therefore enacted . . . that so much of all laws, statutes, and usages, and so much of all royal and other charters, grants, and letters patent ... relating to the several boroughs named in the schedules A and B to this act annexed ... as are inconsistent with or contrary to the provisions of this act shall be and the same are hereby repealed and annulled. ...

And be it enacted that ... no person shall be elected, made, or admitted a burgess or freeman of any borough by gift or purchase. ... And be it enacted that the town clerk of every borough shall ... make out a list, to be called the freemen's roll, of all persons who, at the time of the passing of this act, shall have been admitted as burgesses or freemen of such borough; and that, whenever any person shall hereafter become entitled to be admitted a burgess or freeman ... of such borough ... and shall claim to be admitted accordingly, the mayor of such borough shall examine into such claim; and, upon such claim being established, every such person shall thereupon be admitted and enrolled by the town clerk of such borough upon the freemen's roll. ...

And be it enacted that, after the first election of councillors under this act in any borough, the body or reputed body corporate named in the said schedules in connection with such borough shall take and bear the name of the mayor, aldermen, and burgesses of such borough; and by that name shall have perpetual succession and shall be capable in law, by the council hereinafter mentioned of such borough, to do and suffer all acts which now lawfully they and their successors respectively may do and suffer by any name or title of incorporation. ...

And be it enacted that every male person of full age who, on the last day of August in any year, shall have occupied any house, warehouse, counting-house, or shop within any borough during that year and the whole of each of the two preceding years, and also during the time of such occupation shall have been an inhabitant householder within the said borough, or within seven miles of the said borough, shall, if duly enrolled in that year according to the provisions hereinafter contained, be a burgess of such borough and member of the body corporate ... of such borough. Provided always that no such person shall be so enrolled in any year unless he shall have been rated in respect of such premises so occupied by him within the borough to all rates made for the relief of the poor of the parish wherein such premises are situated during the time of his occupation as aforesaid, and unless he shall have paid, on or before the last day of August as aforesaid, all such rates—including therein all borough rates, if any, directed to be paid under the provisions of this act—as shall have become payable by him in respect of the said premises. ...

And whereas in divers cities, towns, and boroughs a certain custom hath prevailed, and certain by-laws have been made, that no person, not being free of a city, town, or borough or of certain gilds, mysteries, or trading companies within the same ... shall keep any shop or place for putting to show or sale any or certain wares or merchandise by way of retail or otherwise, or use any or certain trades, occupations, mysteries, or handicrafts ... within the same: be it enacted that, notwithstanding any such custom or by-law, every person in any borough may keep any shop for the sale of all lawful wares and merchandises by wholesale or retail and use every lawful trade, occupation, mystery, and handicraft ... within any borough.

And be it enacted that on the fifth day of September in every year the overseers of the poor of every parish wholly or in part within any borough shall make out an alphabetical list, to be called the burgess list ..., of all persons who shall be entitled to be enrolled ... according to the provisions of this act in respect of property within such parish. ...

And be it enacted that in every borough shall be elected ... one fit person, who shall be ... the mayor of such borough; and a certain number of fit persons who shall be ... aldermen of such borough; and a certain number of other fit persons who shall be ... the councillors of such borough. And such mayor, aldermen, and councillors for the time being shall be ... the council of such borough. ... And the number of persons so to be elected aldermen shall be one-third of the number of persons so to be elected councillors. ... In every third succeeding year the council for the time being of every borough shall elect from the councillors, or from the persons qualified to be councillors, the aldermen of such borough or so many as shall be needed to supply the places of those who shall then go out of office. ... And in every third succeeding year one-half of the ... aldermen of every borough shall go out of office and ... those who shall go out of office shall always be those who have been aldermen for the longest time without re-election. ...

And be it enacted that no person being in holy orders, or being the regular minister of any dissenting congregation, shall be qualified to be ... a councillor ... or an alderman of any such borough; nor shall any person be qualified to be ... a councillor or an alderman of any such borough who shall not be entitled to be on the burgess list of such borough, nor unless he shall be ... possessed of real or personal estate ... to the following amount: that is to say, in all boroughs directed by this act to be divided into four or more wards, to the amount of £1000, or be rated to the relief of the poor of such borough upon the annual value of not less than £30; and in all boroughs directed to be divided into less than four wards, or which shall not be divided into wards, to the amount of £500, or be rated to the relief of the poor in such borough upon the annual value of not less than £15. ... [Nor shall any person be qualified] during such time as he shall hold any office or place of profit, other than that of mayor, in the gift or disposal of the council of such borough; or during such time as he shall have directly or indirectly, by himself or his partner, any share or interest in any contract or employment with, by, or on behalf of such council. . . .

And be it enacted that every burgess of any borough, who shall be enrolled on the burgess roll for the time being of such borough, shall be entitled to vote in the election of councillors and of the auditors and assessors hereinafter mentioned for such borough; and no person who shall not be enrolled in such burgess roll for the time being shall have any voice or be entitled to vote in any such election. . . .

And be it enacted that . . . in every succeeding year one-third . . . of the councillors of every borough shall go out of office, and . . . those who shall so go out of office shall always be the councillors who have been for the longest time in office without re-election. . . .

And be it enacted that . . . in every year the council of the borough shall elect out of the aldermen or councillors of such borough a fit person to be the mayor of such borough, who shall continue in his office for one whole year. . . . And be it enacted that the council of every borough . . . shall appoint a fit person, not being a member of the council, to be the town clerk of such borough, who shall hold his office during pleasure . . . ; and also such other officers . . . as they shall think necessary. . . .

And be it enacted that it shall be lawful for the council of any borough to make such by-laws as to them shall seem meet for the good rule and government of the borough . . . , and to appoint by such by-laws such fines as they shall deem necessary . . . ; provided that no fine so to be appointed shall exceed the sum of £5, and that no such by-law shall be made unless at least two-thirds of the whole number of the council shall be present. Provided that no such by-law shall be of any force until the expiration of forty days after the same or a copy thereof shall have been sent, sealed with the seal of the said borough, to one of his majesty's principal secretaries of state, and shall have been affixed on the outer door of the town hall or in some other public place within such borough. And if, at any time within the said period of forty days, his majesty, with the advice of his privy council, shall disallow the same by-law or any part thereof, such by-law or the part thereof disallowed shall not come into operation. . . .

And be it enacted that it shall be lawful for his majesty from time to time to assign to so many persons as he shall think proper his majesty's commission to act as justices of the peace in and for each borough. . . . And be it enacted that, if the council of any borough shall think it requisite that a salaried police magistrate or magistrates be appointed within such borough, such council is hereby empowered to make a by-law fixing the amount of the salary which he or they are to receive in that behalf; and such by-law so made by any council as aforesaid shall be transmitted to one of his majesty's principal secretaries of state. And it shall be lawful thereupon for his majesty, if he shall think fit, to appoint one or more fit persons, according to the number fixed in the said by-law . . . to be . . . police magistrate or magistrates and a justice or justices of the peace for such borough. . . .

And be it enacted that the council of every borough, which shall be desirous that a separate court of quarter sessions of the peace shall be or continue to be holden in and for such borough, shall signify the same by petition to his majesty in council, setting forth the grounds of the application, the state of the jail, and the salary which they are willing to pay to the recorder in that behalf. And it shall be lawful for his majesty, if he shall be pleased thereupon to grant that a separate court of quarter sessions of the peace shall be thenceforward holden in and for such borough, to appoint for such borough, or for any two or more of such boroughs conjointly, a fit person . . . who shall be and be called the recorder of such borough or boroughs, and shall hold such office during his good behavior. . . .

Ibid., LXXV, 389 f.: 5-6 William IV, c. 76.

131. VICTORIA: STATUTES (1839-76)

(A) Constables Act (1839)

An act for the establishment of county and district constables by the authority of justices of the peace. . . . Be it . . . enacted . . . that, in all cases where it shall be made to appear to the justices of the peace of any county in England or Wales in general or quarter sessions assembled . . . that the ordinary officers appointed for preserving the peace are not sufficient for the preservation of the peace and for the protection of the inhabitants and for the security of property within the county, it shall be lawful for them to set forth the same by a report in writing under the hands of the majority of the justices there present, and to declare how many constables are needed, in their opinion, to be appointed within their county for the purposes aforesaid, and the rates of payment which it would be expedient to pay to the chief and other constables; and every such report shall be sent to one of her majesty's principal secretaries of state. . . .

And whereas it is expedient that the rules for the government, pay, clothing, and accoutrements and necessaries of such constables as may be appointed under this act be uniform, as nearly as may be: be it enacted that such rules shall be from time to time made by one of her majesty's principal secretaries of state, but not so as to increase the number of men proposed to be appointed; and the rules so made shall be sent to the clerk of the peace for each county in which . . . this act shall be in operation. . . .

And be it enacted that, as soon as any such rules, as finally settled, shall have been received from the secretary of state, the justices of the county in general or quarter sessions assembled . . .

shall, subject to the approval of the secretary of state, appoint a person duly qualified according to the rules to be chief constable of the county. . . .

And be it enacted that the salaries and allowances of the chief constable and other constables, and all other expenses incurred in providing them with such clothing, accoutrements, and necessaries as are allowed by the rules, and in putting this act in execution, shall be paid by the treasurer of the county out of the county rate. . . .

Ibid., LXXIX, 508 f.: 2-3 Victoria, c. 93.

(B) DEFENCE ACT (1842)

An act to consolidate and amend the laws relating to the services of the ordnance department and the vesting and purchase of lands and hereditaments for those services and for the defence and security of the realm. . . .[1]

And be it enacted that it shall be lawful for the principal officers of her majesty's ordnance for the time being to enter on, survey, and mark out, or to cause to be surveyed and marked out, any lands, buildings, or other hereditaments or easements wanted for the service of the ordnance department, or for the defence of the realm, or to stop up or divert any public or private foot-paths or bridle-roads, and to treat and agree with the owner or owners of such lands, buildings, hereditaments, or easements, or with any person or persons interested therein, either for the absolute purchase thereof, or for the possession or use thereof during such time as the exigence of the public service shall require. . . .

And be it enacted that, in case any . . . person or persons interested in any such lands, buildings, or other hereditaments, which shall be so marked out and surveyed as aforesaid, shall . . . refuse or decline to treat or agree; or by reason of absence shall be prevented from treating or agreeing with the said principal officers; or shall refuse to accept such sum of money as shall be offered by the said principal officers as the consideration for the absolute purchase of such lands, buildings, or other hereditaments, or such annual rent or sum as shall be offered for the hire thereof . . . ; then . . . it shall be lawful for the said principal officers to require two or more justices of the peace . . . to put the said principal officers . . . into immediate possession of such lands, buildings, or other hereditaments, which such justices . . . are hereby required to do . . . and shall also issue their warrants to the sheriff of the county . . . to summon a jury. . . . And the jury, on hearing any witnesses and evidence that may be produced, shall on their oaths . . . find the compensation to be paid. . . .

Ibid., LXXXII, 793 f.: 5-6 Victoria, c. 94.

---

[1] The earlier articles of this act repeal a long series of statutes running back to 1708; cf. no. 139E.

(C) REPEAL OF THE NAVIGATION ACTS (1849)

An act to amend the laws in force for the encouragement of British shipping and navigation. . . . Be it enacted . . . that, from and after the first day of January, 1850, the following acts and parts of acts shall be repealed. . . .[2]

And be it enacted that no goods or passengers shall be carried coastwise from one part of the united kingdom to another . . . except in British ships. . . . And be it enacted that no goods or passengers shall be carried from one part of any British possession in Asia, Africa, or America to another part of the same possession except in British ships. Provided always and be it enacted that, if the legislature . . . of any such British possession shall present an address to her majesty praying her majesty to authorize . . . the conveyance of goods or passengers from one part of such possession to another part thereof in other than British ships, or if the legislatures of any two or more possessions, which . . . her majesty in council shall declare to be neighbouring possessions, shall present addresses . . . praying her majesty to place the trade between them on the footing of a coasting trade . . . , it shall thereupon be lawful for her majesty by order in council so to authorize. . . .

And be it enacted that, in case it shall be made to appear to her majesty that British vessels are subject in any foreign country to any prohibitions or restrictions as to the voyages in which they may engage, or as to the articles which they may import into or export from such country, it shall be lawful for her majesty . . . by order in council to impose such prohibitions or restrictions . . . as her majesty may think fit . . . , to place the ships of such country on as nearly as possible the same footing in British ports. . . .

Ibid., LXXXIX, 70 f.: 12-13 Victoria, c. 29.

(D) COUNTY AND BOROUGH POLICE ACT (1856)

An act to render more effectual the police in counties and boroughs in England and Wales. . . . Be it . . . enacted . . . as follows:—

In every county in which a constabulary has not been already established for the whole of such county under the . . . acts of the second and third and third and fourth years of her majesty . . .[3] the justices of such county, at the general or quarter sessions . . . , shall proceed to establish a sufficient police force for the whole of such county. . . .

It shall be lawful for her majesty, by warrant under her royal sign-manual, to appoint during her majesty's pleasure three persons as inspectors under this act, to visit and inquire into the state and

---

[2] Here are enumerated sections of eleven statutes running back to 1797. These statutes had modified the earlier Navigation Acts, such as no. 114D.

[3] For the first of these statutes, see no. 131A. The other statute was a supplementary enactment. The procedure for setting up a police force in a county remains the same under the present act.

the efficiency of the police appointed for every county and borough, and whether the provisions of the acts under which such police are appointed are duly observed and carried into effect . . . ; and each of the inspectors so appointed shall report generally upon such matters to one of her majesty's principal secretaries of state, who shall cause such reports to be laid before parliament. And such inspectors shall be paid, out of such money as may be provided by parliament for the purpose, such salaries and allowances as shall be determined by the commissioners of her majesty's treasury.

Upon the certificate of one of her majesty's principal secretaries of state that the police of any county or borough established under the provisions of the said acts and this act, or any of them, has been maintained in a state of efficiency in point of numbers and discipline for the year ending on the 29th of September then last past, it shall be lawful for the commissioners of her majesty's treasury to pay from time to time, out of the moneys provided by parliament for the purpose, such sum toward the expenses of such police for the year mentioned in such certificate as shall not exceed one-fourth of the charge for their pay and clothing. . . .

Ibid., XCVI, 360 f.: 19-20 Victoria, c. 69.

(E) PETITIONS OF RIGHT ACT (1860)

An act to amend the law relating to petitions of right, to simplify the proceedings, and to make provisions for the costs thereof. Whereas it is expedient to amend the law relating to petitions of right . . . and to assimilate the proceedings as nearly as may be to the course of practice and procedure now in force in actions and suits between subject and subject: be it therefore enacted . . . as follows:—

A petition of right may, if the suppliant think fit, be intituled in any one of the superior courts . . . at Westminster in which the subject matter of such petition, or any material part thereof, would have been cognizable if the same had been a matter in dispute between subject and subject . . . , and shall set forth with convenient certainty the facts entitling the suppliant to relief, and shall be signed by such suppliant, his counsel, or attorney. The said petition shall be left with the secretary of state for the home department in order that the same may be submitted to her majesty for her majesty's gracious consideration, and in order that her majesty, if she shall think fit, may grant her fiat that right be done; and no fee or sum of money shall be payable by the suppliant on so leaving such petition, or upon his receiving back the same. Upon her majesty's fiat being obtained to such petition, a copy of such petition and fiat shall be left at the office of the solicitor to the treasury with an endorsement thereon . . . praying for a plea or answer on behalf of her majesty within twenty-eight days; and it shall thereupon be the duty of the said solicitor to transmit such petition to the particular department to which the subject matter of such petition may relate, and the same shall be prosecuted in the court in which the same shall be intituled or in such other court as the lord chancellor may direct. . . .

Upon every such petition of right the . . . judgment . . . shall be that the suppliant is or is not entitled either to the whole or to some portion of the relief sought by his petition, or such other relief as the court may think right; and such court may give a . . . judgment that the suppliant is entitled to such relief, and upon such terms and conditions, if any, as such court shall think just. . . . Whenever, upon any such petition of right, a judgment . . . shall be given . . . that the suppliant is entitled to relief . . . , any one of the judges of the court in which such petition shall have been prosecuted shall and may, upon application in behalf of the suppliant . . . , certify to the commissioners of her majesty's treasury or to the treasurer of her majesty's household . . . the tenor and purport of the same. . . .

It shall be lawful for the commissioners of her majesty's treasury, and they are hereby required to pay the amount of any moneys and costs . . . out of any moneys in their hands for the time being legally applicable thereto, or which may be hereafter voted by parliament for that purpose; provided such petition shall relate to any public matter. And in case the same shall relate to . . . any matter affecting her majesty in her private capacity . . . , the amount to which the suppliant is entitled shall be paid to him out of such funds or moneys as her majesty shall be graciously pleased to direct to be applied for that purpose. . . .

Ibid., C, 117 f.: 23-24 Victoria, c. 34.

(F) Colonial Laws Validity Act (1865)

An act to remove doubts as to the validity of colonial laws. . . . Be it . . . enacted . . . as follows:—

The term "colony" shall in this act include all of her majesty's possessions abroad in which there shall exist a legislature, as hereinafter defined, except the Channel Islands, the Isle of Man, and such territories as may for the time being be vested in her majesty under or by virtue of any act of parliament for the government of India. The terms "legislature" and "colonial legislature" shall severally signify the authority, other than the imperial parliament or her majesty in council, competent to make laws for any colony. The term "representative legislature" shall signify any colonial legislature which shall comprise a legislative body of which one-half are elected by inhabitants of the colony. The term "colonial law" shall include laws made for any colony either by such legislature as aforesaid or by her majesty in council. An act of parliament, or any provision thereof, shall, in construing this act, be said to extend to any colony when it is made applicable to such colony by the express words or necessary intendment of any act of parliament. The term "governor" shall mean the officer lawfully administering the government of any colony. The term "letters patent" shall mean letters patent under the great seal of the united kingdom of Great Britain and Ireland.

Any colonial law which is or shall be in any respect repugnant to the provisions of any act of parliament extending to the colony to which such law may relate, or repugnant to any order or regulation made under authority of such act of parliament, or having in the colony the force and effect of such act, shall be read subject to such act, order, or regulation, and shall, to the extent of such repugnancy, but not otherwise, be and remain absolutely void and inoperative. No colonial law shall be or be deemed to have been void or inoperative on the ground of repugnancy to the law of England, unless the same shall be repugnant to the provisions of some such act of parliament, order, or regulation as aforesaid. No colonial law passed with the concurrence of or assented to by the governor of any colony, or to be hereafter so passed or assented to, shall be or be deemed to have been void or inoperative by reason only of any instructions with reference to such law or the subject thereof which may have been given to such governor by or on behalf of her majesty by any instrument other than the letters patent or instrument authorizing such governor to concur in passing or to assent to laws for the peace, order, and good government of such colony, even though such instructions may be referred to in such letters patent or last-mentioned instrument.

Every colonial legislature shall have, and be deemed at all times to have had, full power within its jurisdiction to establish courts of judicature, and to abolish and reconstitute the same, and to alter the constitution thereof, and to make provision for the administration of justice therein; and every representative legislature shall, in respect to the colony under its jurisdiction, have and be deemed at all times to have had full power to make laws respecting the constitution, powers, and procedure of such legislature; provided that such laws shall have been passed in such manner and form as may from time to time be required by any act of parliament, letters patent, order in council, or colonial law for the time being in force in the said colony.

Ibid., CV, 129 f.: 28-29 Victoria, c. 63.

(G) BRITISH NORTH AMERICA ACT (1867)

An act for the union of Canada, Nova Scotia, and New Brunswick, and the government thereof, and for purposes connected therewith. Whereas the provinces of Canada, Nova Scotia, and New Brunswick have expressed their desire to be federally united into one dominion under the crown of the united kingdom of Great Britain and Ireland, with a constitution similar in principle to that of the united kingdom; and whereas such a union would conduce to the welfare of the provinces and promote the interests of the British Empire; and whereas, on the establishment of the union by authority of parliament, it is expedient, not only that the constitution of the legislative authority in the dominion be provided for, but also that the nature of the executive government therein be declared; and whereas it is expedient that provision be made for the eventual admission into the union of other parts of British North America: be it therefore enacted . . . as follows:—

I. Preliminary. This act may be cited as the British North America Act, 1867. The provisions of the act referring to her majesty the queen extend also to the heirs and successors of her majesty, kings and queens of the united kingdom of Great Britain and Ireland.

II. Union. It shall be lawful for the queen, by and with the advice of her majesty's most honourable privy council, to declare by proclamation that on and after a day therein appointed, not being more than six months after the passing of this act, the provinces of Canada, Nova Scotia, and New Brunswick shall form and be one dominion under the name of Canada; and on and after that day those three provinces shall form and be one dominion under that name accordingly. . . . Canada shall be divided into four provinces: named Ontario, Quebec, Nova Scotia, and New Brunswick. The parts of the province of Canada (as it exists at the passing of this act) which formerly constituted respectively the provinces of Upper Canada and Lower Canada shall be deemed to be severed, and shall form two separate provinces: . . . the province of Ontario and . . . the province of Quebec. . . .

III. Executive Power. The executive government and authority of and over Canada is hereby declared to continue and be vested in the queen.

The provisions of this act referring to the governor general extend and apply to the governor general for the time being of Canada. . . . There shall be a council to aid and advise in the government of Canada, to be styled the queen's privy council for Canada; and the persons who are to be members of that council shall be from time to time chosen and summoned by the governor general and sworn in as privy councillors, and members thereof may be from time to time removed by the governor general.

All powers, authorities, and functions which under any act of the parliament of Great Britain, or of the parliament of the united kingdom of Great Britain and Ireland, or of the legislature of Upper Canada, Lower Canada, Canada, Nova Scotia, or New Brunswick, are at the union vested in or exercisable by the respective governors or lieutenant governors . . . individually, shall, as far as the same continue in existence and capable of being exercised after the union in relation to the government of Canada, be vested in and exercisable by the governor general with the advice, or with the advice and consent of, or in conjunction with the queen's privy council for Canada or any members thereof, or by the governor general individually, as the case requires; subject nevertheless (except with respect to such as exist under acts of the parliament of Great Britain or of the parliament of the united kingdom of Great Britain and Ireland) to be abolished or altered by the parliament of Canada. . . .

The command-in-chief of the land and naval militia, and of all naval and military forces of and in Canada, is hereby declared to continue and be vested in the queen.

IV. Legislative Power. There shall be one parliament for Canada, consisting of the queen, an upper house styled the senate, and the house of commons. The privileges, immunities, and powers to be . . . exercised by the senate and by the house of commons . . . shall be such as are from time to time defined by act of the parliament of Canada, but so that the same shall never exceed those at the passing of this act . . . exercised by the commons house of parliament of the united kingdom. . . .

The senate shall, subject to the provisions of this act, consist of seventy-two members who shall be styled senators. In relation to the constitution of the senate, Canada shall be deemed to consist of three divisions: (1) Ontario; (2) Quebec; (3) the maritime provinces, Nova Scotia and New Brunswick. Which three divisions shall . . . be equally represented in the senate as follows: Ontario by twenty-four senators; Quebec by twenty-four senators; and the maritime provinces by twenty-four senators, twelve thereof representing Nova Scotia and twelve thereof representing New Brunswick.

The qualifications of a senator shall be as follows: (1) He shall be of the full age of thirty years; (2) He shall be either a natural-born subject of the queen naturalized by an act of the parliament of Great Britain . . . or of the legislature of one of the provinces . . . before the union, or of the parliament of Canada after the union; (3) He shall be legally or equitably seised as of freehold for his own use and benefit of lands or tenements . . . within the province for which he is appointed of the value of $4000 over and above all rents, dues, debts, charges, mortgages, and incumbrances . . . charged on or affecting the same; (4) His real and personal property shall be together worth $4000 over and above his debts and liabilities; (5) He shall be resident in the province for which he is appointed. . . .

The governor general shall from time to time, in the queen's name . . . , summon qualified persons to the senate. . . . The number of senators shall not at any time exceed seventy-eight. A senator shall, subject to the provisions of this act,[4] hold his place in the senate for life. . . .

The house of commons shall, subject to the provisions of this act, consist of 181 members, of whom 82 shall be elected for Ontario, 65 for Quebec, 19 for Nova Scotia, and 15 for New Brunswick. . . .[5]

Until the parliament of Canada otherwise provides, all laws in force in the several provinces at the union relative to . . . the qualifications . . . of persons to be elected or to sit or vote as members of the house of assembly . . . in the several provinces . . . shall

---

[4] A senator is disqualified by loss of his property qualification, failure to attend two consecutive sessions of parliament, bankruptcy, or conviction of treason, felony, or infamous crime.

[5] The following articles divide the provinces into single member districts and provide for a readjustment of representation every ten years.

respectively apply to elections of members to serve in the house of commons. . . . The number of members of the house of commons may be from time to time increased by the parliament of Canada, provided the proportionate representation . . . prescribed by this act is not thereby disturbed.

Bills for appropriating any part of the public revenue, or for imposing any tax or impost, shall originate in the house of commons. It shall not be lawful for the house of commons to adopt or pass any vote, resolution, address, or bill for the appropriation of any part of the public revenue, or of any tax or impost, to any purpose that has not been first recommended to that house by message of the governor general in the session in which such vote, resolution, address, or bill is proposed.

Where a bill passed by the houses of the parliament is presented to the governor general for the queen's assent, he shall declare, according to his discretion, but subject to the provisions of this act and to her majesty's instructions, either that he assents thereto in the queen's name, or that he withholds the queen's assent, or that he reserves the bill for the signification of the queen's pleasure. Where the governor general assents to a bill in the queen's name, he shall by the first convenient opportunity send an authentic copy of the act to one of her majesty's principal secretaries of state; and, if the queen in council within two years after receipt thereof by the secretary of state thinks fit to disallow the act, such disallowance . . . shall annul the act from and after the day of such signification. A bill reserved for the signification of the queen's pleasure shall not have any force unless and until, within two years from the day on which it was presented to the governor general for the queen's assent, the governor general signifies, by speech or message to each of the houses of parliament or by proclamation, that it has received the assent of the queen in council.

V. Provincial Constitutions. For each province there shall be an officer styled the lieutenant governor, appointed by the governor general in council by instrument under the great seal of Canada. A lieutenant governor shall hold office during the pleasure of the governor general; but any lieutenant governor appointed after the commencement of the first session of the parliament of Canada shall not be removable within five years from his appointment, except for cause assigned. . . .

The executive council of Ontario and Quebec shall be composed of such persons as the lieutenant governor from time to time thinks fit and, in the first instance, of the following officers: namely, the attorney general, the secretary and registrar of the province, the treasurer of the province, the commissioner of crown lands, and the commissioner of agriculture and public works, with, in Quebec, the speaker of the legislative council and the solicitor general. The constitution of the executive authority in each of the provinces of Nova

Scotia and New Brunswick shall . . . continue as it exists at the union until altered under the authority of this act.

There shall be a legislature for Ontario, consisting of the lieutenant governor and of one house styled the assembly of Ontario. The legislative assembly of Ontario shall be composed of eighty-two members, to be elected to represent the eighty-two electoral districts set forth in the first schedule to this act. There shall be a legislature for Quebec, consisting of the lieutenant governor and of two houses, styled the legislative council of Quebec and the legislative assembly of Quebec. The constitution of the legislature of each of the provinces of Nova Scotia and New Brunswick shall . . . continue as it exists at the union until altered under the authority of this act. . . .

The following provisions of this act respecting the parliament of Canada—namely, the provisions relating to appropriation and tax bills, the recommendation of money bills, the assent to bills, the disallowance of acts, and the signification of pleasure on bills reserved—shall extend and apply to the legislatures of the several provinces as if those provisions were here re-enacted and made applicable in terms to the respective provinces and the legislatures thereof. . . .

VI. Distribution of Legislative Powers. It shall be lawful for the queen, by and with the advice and consent of the senate and house of commons, to make laws for the peace, order, and good government of Canada in relation to all matters not coming within the classes of subjects by this act assigned exclusively to the legislatures of the provinces; and for greater certainty, but not so as to restrict the generality of the foregoing terms of this section, it is hereby declared that . . . the exclusive legislative authority of the parliament of Canada extends to all matters coming within the classes of subjects next hereinafter enumerated: that is to say, (1) the public debt and property; (2) the regulation of trade and commerce; (3) the raising of money by any mode or system of taxation; (4) the borrowing of money on the public credit; (5) postal service; (6) the census and statistics; (7) militia, military and naval service, and defence; (8) the fixing of and providing for salaries and allowances of civil and other officers of the government of Canada; (9) beacons, buoys, lighthouses, and Sable Island; (10) navigation and shipping; (11) quarantine and the establishment and maintenance of marine hospitals; (12) sea-coast and inland fisheries; (13) ferries between a province and any British or foreign country or between two provinces; (14) currency and coinage; (15) banking, incorporation of banks, and the issue of paper money; (16) savings banks; (17) weights and measures; (18) bills of exchange and promissory notes; (19) interest; (20) legal tender; (21) bankruptcy and insolvency; (22) patents of invention and discovery; (23) copyrights; (24) Indians and lands reserved for the Indians; (25) naturalization and aliens; (26) marriage and divorce; (27) the criminal law except the constitution of courts of criminal jurisdiction, but including the procedure in criminal matters; (28) the establishment, maintenance, and management of penitentiaries; (29) such classes of subjects as are expressly excepted in the enumeration of the classes of subjects by this act assigned exclusively to the legislatures of the provinces. And any matter coming within any of the classes of subjects enumerated in this section shall not be deemed to come within the class of matters of a local or private nature comprised in the enumeration of the classes of subjects by this act assigned exclusively to the legislatures of the provinces.

In each province the legislature may exclusively make laws in relation to matters coming within the classes of subjects next hereinafter enumerated: that is to say, (1) the amendment from time to time . . . of the constitution of the province, except as regards the office of lieutenant governor; (2) direct taxation within the province in order to the raising of a revenue for provincial purposes; (3) the borrowing of money on the sole credit of the province; (4) the establishment and tenure of provincial offices and the appointment and payment of provincial officers; (5) the management and sale of the public lands belonging to the province and of the timber and wood thereon; (6) the establishment, maintenance, and management of public and reformatory prisons in and for the province; (7) the establishment, maintenance, and management of hospitals, asylums, charities, and eleemosynary institutions in and for the province other than marine hospitals; (8) municipal institutions in the province; (9) shop, saloon, tavern, auctioneer, and other licences, in order to the raising of a revenue for provincial, local, or municipal purposes; (10) local works and undertakings other than such as are of the following classes—(a) lines of steam or other ships, railways, canals, telegraphs, and other works and undertakings connecting the province with any other or others of the provinces or extending beyond the limits of the province; (b) lines of steamships between the province and any British or foreign country; (c) such works as, although wholly situate within the province, are before or after their execution declared by the parliament of Canada to be for the general advantage of Canada or for the advantage of two or more of the provinces—; (11) the incorporation of companies with provincial objects; (12) the solemnization of marriage within the province; (13) property and civil rights in the province; (14) the administration of justice in the province, including the constitution, maintenance, and organization of provincial courts both of civil and of criminal jurisdiction, and including procedure in civil matters in those courts; (15) the imposition of punishment by fine, penalty, or imprisonment for enforcing any law of the province made in relation to any matter coming within any of the classes of subjects enumerated in this division; (16) generally all matters of a merely local or private nature in the province.

In and for each province the legislature may exclusively make laws in relation to education. . . .[6] In each province the legislature may make laws in relation to agriculture in the province, and to immigration into the province. And it is hereby declared that the parliament of Canada may from time to time make laws in relation to agriculture in all or any of the provinces and to immigration into all or any of the provinces; and any law of the legislature of a province relative to agriculture or to immigration shall have effect in and for the province as long and as far only as it is not repugnant to any act of the parliament of Canada.

VII. Judicature. The governor general shall appoint the judges of the superior, district, and county courts in each province, except those of the courts of probate in Nova Scotia and New Brunswick. . . . The parliament of Canada may, notwithstanding anything in this act, from time to time provide for the constitution, maintenance, and organization of a general court of appeal for Canada, and for the establishment of any additional courts for the better administration of the laws of Canada. . . .

XI. Admission of Other Colonies. It shall be lawful for the queen, by and with the advice of her majesty's most honourable privy council, on addresses from the houses of the parliament of Canada, and from the houses of the respective legislatures of the colonies or provinces of Newfoundland, Prince Edward Island, and British Columbia, to admit those colonies or provinces, or any of them, into the union; and on address from the houses of the parliament of Canada to admit Rupert's Land and the Northwestern Territory, or either of them, into the union, on such terms and conditions in each case as are in the addresses expressed and as the queen thinks fit to approve, subject to the provisions of this act. And the provisions of any order in council in that behalf shall have effect as if they had been enacted by the parliament of the united kingdom of Great Britain and Ireland. . . .

Public General Statutes, II, 5 f.: 30 Victoria, c. 3.

(H) Representation of the People Act (1867)

An act further to amend the laws relating to the representation of the people in England and Wales. . . . Be it enacted . . . as follows:—

Every man shall, in and after the year 1868, be entitled to be registered as a voter and, when registered, to vote for a member or members to serve in parliament for a borough, who is qualified as follows: that is to say, (1) is of full age, and not subject to any legal incapacity; and (2) is on the last day of July in any year and has during . . . the preceding twelve calendar months been an inhabitant occupier, as owner or tenant, of any dwelling-house within the bor-

---

[6] Subject to certain provisions guaranteeing equal rights to Catholic and Protestant schools.

ough; and (3) has during the time of such occupation been rated as an ordinary occupier in respect of the premises so occupied by him within the borough to all rates, if any, made for the relief of the poor in respect of such premises; and (4) has, on or before the twentieth day of July in the same year, *bona fide* paid an equal amount in the pound to that payable by other ordinary occupiers in respect of all poor rates that have become payable by him in respect of the said premises up to the preceding fifth day of January. Provided, that no man shall under this section be entitled to be registered as a voter by reason of his being a joint occupier of any dwelling-house.

Every man shall, in and after the year 1868, be entitled to be registered as a voter and, when registered, to vote for a member or members to serve in parliament for a borough, who is qualified as follows: that is to say, (1) is of full age and not subject to any legal incapacity; and (2) as a lodger has occupied in the same borough separately and as sole tenant for the twelve months preceding the last day of July in any year the same lodgings, such lodgings being part of one and the same dwelling-house, and of a clear yearly value, if let unfurnished, of £10 or upwards; and (3) has resided in such lodgings during the twelve months immediately preceding the last day of July, and has claimed to be registered as a voter at the next ensuing registration of voters.

Every man shall, in and after the year 1868, be entitled to be registered as a voter and, when registered, to vote for a member or members to serve in parliament for a county, who is qualified as follows. . . .[7]

From and after the end of this present parliament, no borough which had a less population than 10,000 at the census of 1861 shall return more than one member to serve in parliament. . . .[8]

In all future parliaments the university of London shall return one member to serve in parliament. Every man whose name is for the time being on the register of graduates constituting the convocation of the university of London shall, if of full age and not subject to any legal incapacity, be entitled to vote in the election of a member to serve in any future parliament for the said university. . . .[9]

Whereas great inconveniences may arise from the enactments now in force limiting the duration of the parliament in being at the demise

---

[7] The county franchises of 1832 (see no. 130A) are now reduced to two: freehold, copyhold, and leasehold for a term of sixty years of lands or tenements of the annual value of £5 and upwards; and occupation of lands or tenements of the ratable value of £12 and upwards.

[8] Thirty-eight such boroughs are listed. Furthermore, Manchester, Birmingham, and Leeds are each given an additional representative; a number of new boroughs are created; and certain counties are divided to form new constituencies.

[9] The universities of Oxford and Cambridge continue to be represented as before.

of the crown: be it therefore enacted that the parliament in being at any future demise of the crown shall not be determined or dissolved by such demise, but shall continue so long as it would have continued but for such demise, unless it should be sooner prorogued or dissolved by the crown—anything in the act passed in the sixth year of her late majesty Queen Anne . . . in any way notwithstanding.[10]

Whereas it is expedient to amend the law relating to offices of profit the acceptance of which from the crown vacates the seats of members accepting the same, but does not render them incapable of being re-elected: be it enacted that, where a person has been returned as a member to serve in parliament since the acceptance by him from the crown of any office described in schedule H to this act annexed, the subsequent acceptance by him from the crown of any other office or offices described in such schedule in lieu of and in immediate succession the one to the other shall not vacate his seat. . . .

Schedule H: Offices of Profit Referred to in This Act:—
  Lord High Treasurer
  Commissioner for Executing the Offices of Treasurer of the Exchequer of Great Britain and Lord High Treasurer of Ireland
  President of the Privy Council
  Vice-President of the Committee of Council for Education
  Comptroller of Her Majesty's Household
  Treasurer of Her Majesty's Household
  Vice-Chamberlain of Her Majesty's Household
  Equerry or Groom in Waiting on Her Majesty
  Any Principal Secretary of State
  Chancellor and Under-Treasurer of Her Majesty's Exchequer
  Paymaster General
  Postmaster General
  Lord High Admiral
  Commissioner for Executing the Office of Lord High Admiral
  Commissioner of Her Majesty's Works and Public Buildings
  President of the Committee of Privy Council for Trade and Plantations
  Chief Secretary for Ireland
  Commissioner for Administering the Laws for the Relief of the Poor in England
  Chancellor of the Duchy of Lancaster
  Judge Advocate General
  Attorney General for England
  Solicitor General for England
  Lord Advocate for Scotland
  Solicitor General for Scotland
  Attorney General for Ireland
  Solicitor General for Ireland

Ibid., II, 1082 f.: 30-31 Victoria, c. 102.

---
[10] No. 121B.

(I) EDUCATION ACT (1870)

An act to provide for public elementary education in England and Wales. Be it enacted . . . as follows:—

. . . There shall be provided for every school district a sufficient amount of accommodation in public elementary schools, as hereinafter defined, available for all the children resident in such district for whose elementary education efficient and suitable provision is not otherwise made, and where there is an insufficient amount of such accommodation . . . , the deficiency shall be supplied in manner provided by this act. Where the education department . . . are satisfied and have given public notice that there is an insufficient amount of public school accommodation for any school district, and the deficiency is not supplied as hereinafter required, a school board shall be formed for such district and shall supply such deficiency; and, in case of default by the school board, the education department shall cause the duty of such board to be performed in manner provided by this act. . . .

Every public elementary school shall be conducted in accordance with the following regulations . . . : namely, (1) It shall not be required, as a condition of any child being admitted into or continuing in the school, that he shall attend or abstain from attending . . . any religious observance or any instruction in religious subjects, in the school or elsewhere . . . ; (2) The time or times during which any religious observance is practised or instruction in religious subjects is given at any meeting of the school shall be either at the beginning or at the end . . . of such meeting . . . ; (3) The school shall be open at all times to the inspection of any of her majesty's inspectors . . . ; (4) The school shall be conducted in accordance with the conditions required to be fulfilled by an elementary school in order to obtain an annual parliamentary grant.

For the purpose of determining with respect to every school district the amount of public school accommodation, if any, required for such district, the education department . . . shall consider whether any and what public school accommodation is required for such district; and in so doing they shall take into consideration every school . . . , whether actually situated in the school district or not, which in their opinion gives . . . efficient elementary education to . . . the children of such district.

The education department shall publish a notice of their decision as to the public school accommodation for any school district. . . . If any persons, being either ratepayers of the district . . . or the managers of any elementary school in the district, feel aggrieved by such decision, such persons may . . . apply in writing to the education department for, and the education department shall direct the holding of, a public inquiry. . . . If no public inquiry is directed, or after the receipt of the report made after such inquiry . . . , the education department may, if they think that the amount of public school accommodation for the district is insufficient, publish a final notice ... directing that the public accommodation therein mentioned ... be supplied. If, after the expiration of a time not exceeding six months ... , the education department are satisfied that all the public school accommodation required by the final notice ... has not been so supplied, nor is in course of being supplied ... , the education department shall cause a school board to be formed for the district, as provided in this act; and shall send a requisition to the school board ... requiring them to take proceedings forthwith for supplying the public school accommodation mentioned in the requisition. ...

Every school provided by a school board shall be conducted under the control and management of such board in accordance with the following regulations: the school shall be a public elementary school within the meaning of this act; no religious catechism or religious formulary, which is distinctive of any particular denomination, shall be taught in the school. ... Every child attending a school provided by any school board shall pay such weekly fee as may be prescribed by the school board, with the consent of the education department; but the school board may from time to time, for a renewable period not exceeding six months, remit the whole or any part of such fee in the case of any child when they are of opinion that the parent of such child is unable from poverty to pay the same. ...

The school board shall be elected in manner provided by this act: in a borough by the persons whose names are on the burgess roll of such borough for the time being in force, and in a parish not situate in the metropolis by the ratepayers. ... The number of members of a school board shall be such number, not less than five nor more than fifteen, as may be determined in the first instance by the education department and afterwards, from time to time, by a resolution of the school board approved by the education department. ...[11]

The expenses of the school board ... shall be paid out of a fund called the school fund. There shall be carried to the school fund all moneys ... in any manner whatever received by the school board. ... Any sum required to meet any deficiency in the school fund ... shall be paid by the rating authority out of the local rate. The school board may serve their precept on the rating authority, requiring such authority to pay the amount specified therein. ...

Every school board may from time to time, with the approval of the education department, make by-laws for all or any of the following purposes: (1) requiring the parents of children of such age, not less than five years nor more than thirteen years, as may be fixed by the by-laws to cause such children, unless there is some reasonable excuse, to attend school; (2) determining the time during which children are so to attend school ... ; (3) providing for the remission or payment of the whole or any part of the fees of any

---

[11] Elaborate provisions are made for the organizing of school districts in the metropolis and, when expedient, for combining two or more districts.

child . . . ; (4) imposing penalties for the breach of any by-laws. . . . Any of the following reasons shall be a reasonable excuse: namely, (1) that the child is under efficient instruction in some other manner; (2) that the child has been prevented from attending school by sickness or any unavoidable cause; (3) that there is no public elementary school open which the child can attend within such distance, not exceeding three miles . . . , as the by-laws may prescribe.

The school board, not less than one month before submitting any by-law under this section for the approval of the education department, shall deposit a printed copy of the proposed by-laws at their office for inspection by any ratepayer and supply a printed copy thereof gratis to any ratepayer, and shall publish a notice of such deposit. The education department, before approving of any by-laws, shall be satisfied that such deposit has been made and notice published, and shall cause such inquiry to be made in the school district as they think requisite. Any proceeding to enforce any by-law may be taken and any penalty for the breach of any by-law may be recovered in a summary manner; but no penalty imposed for the breach of any by-law shall exceed such amount as with the costs will amount to 5s. for each offence; and such by-laws shall not come into operation until they have been sanctioned by her majesty in council.

Ibid., V, 443 f.: 33-34 Victoria, c. 75.

(J) Ballot Act (1872)

An act to amend the law relating to procedure at parliamentary and municipal elections. . . . Be it enacted . . . as follows:—

. . . In the case of a poll at an election the votes shall be given by ballot. The ballot of each voter shall consist of a paper . . . showing the names and description of the candidates. Each ballot paper shall have a number printed on the back and shall have attached a counterfoil with the same number printed on the face. At the time of voting the ballot paper shall be marked on both sides with an official mark and delivered to the voter within the polling station; and the number of such voter on the register of voters shall be marked on the counterfoil; and the voter, having secretly marked his vote on the paper and folded it up so as to conceal his vote, shall place it in a closed box in the presence of the officer presiding at the polling station . . . , after having shown to him the official mark on the back. . . .

Every officer, clerk, and agent in attendance at a polling station shall maintain and aid in maintaining the secrecy of the voting in such station and shall not communicate, except for some purpose authorized by law, before the poll is closed, to any person any information as to the name or number on the register of voters of any elector who has or has not applied for a ballot paper or voted at that station, or as to the official mark. And no such officer, clerk, or agent, and no person whosoever, shall interfere with or attempt to interfere with a voter when marking his vote, or otherwise attempt to obtain in the polling station information as to the candidate for whom any voter in such station is about to vote or has voted, or communicate at any time to any person any information obtained in a polling station as to the candidate for whom any voter in such station is about to vote or has voted, or as to the number on the back of the ballot paper given to any voter at such station. . . .

Ibid., VII, 193 f.: 35-36 Victoria, c. 33.

(K) Judicature Act (1873)

An act for the constitution of a supreme court and for other purposes relating to the better administration of justice in England. . . . Be it enacted . . . as follows:—

From and after the time appointed for the commencement of this act, the several courts hereinafter mentioned—that is to say, the high court of chancery of England, the court of queen's bench, the court of common pleas at Westminster, the court of exchequer, the high court of admiralty, the court of probate, the court for divorce and matrimonial causes, and the London court of bankruptcy—shall be united and consolidated together, and shall constitute, under and subject to the provisions of this act, one supreme court of judicature in England.

The said supreme court shall consist of two permanent divisions, one of which, under the name of Her Majesty's High Court of Justice, shall have and exercise original jurisdiction, with such appellate jurisdiction from inferior courts as is hereinafter mentioned, and the other of which, under the name of Her Majesty's Court of Appeal, shall have and exercise appellate jurisdiction, with such original jurisdiction, as hereinafter mentioned, as may be incident to the determination of any appeal.

Her majesty's high court of justice shall be constituted as follows. . . .[12] Subject to the provisions hereinafter contained, whenever the office of a judge of the said high court shall become vacant, a new judge may be appointed thereto by her majesty by letters patent. All persons to be hereafter appointed to fill the places of the lord chief justice of England, the master of the rolls, the lord chief justice of the common pleas, and the lord chief baron . . . shall continue to be appointed to the same respective offices with the same precedence and by the same respective titles . . . as heretofore. . . . All the judges of the said court shall have in all respects, save as in this act is otherwise expressly provided, equal power, authority, and jurisdiction. . . . The lord chief justice of England . . . shall be president of the said high court of justice in the absence of the lord chancellor.

Her majesty's court of appeal shall be constituted as follows:— There shall be five *ex officio* judges thereof and also so many ordinary

---

[12] The members are the judges of the courts enumerated above, except such as may be appointed ordinary judges in the court of appeal.

judges, not exceeding nine at any one time, as her majesty shall from time to time appoint. The *ex officio* judges shall be the lord chancellor, the lord chief justice of England, the master of the rolls, the lord chief justice of the common pleas, and the lord chief baron of the exchequer. . . . The lord chancellor . . . shall be president of the court of appeal. . . .

The high court of justice shall be a superior court of record and, subject as in this act mentioned, there shall be transferred to and vested in the said high court of justice the jurisdiction which, at the commencement of this act, was vested in . . . all or any of the courts following. . . .[13]

There shall not be transferred to or vested in the said high court of justice, by virtue of this act, (1) any appellate jurisdiction of the court of appeal in chancery or of the same court sitting as a court of appeal in bankruptcy; (2) any jurisdiction of the court of appeal in chancery of the county palatine of Lancaster; (3) any jurisdiction usually vested in the lord chancellor or in the lords justices of appeal in chancery . . . in relation to the custody of the persons and estates of idiots, lunatics, and persons of unsound mind; (4) any jurisdiction vested in the lord chancellor in relation to grants of letters patent or the issue of commissions or other writings to be passed under the great seal of the united kingdom; (5) any jurisdiction exercised by the lord chancellor in right of or on behalf of her majesty as visitor of any college or of any charitable or other foundation; (6) any jurisdiction of the master of the rolls in relation to records in London or elsewhere in England.

The court of appeal established by this act shall be a superior court of record, and there shall be transferred to and vested in such court all jurisdiction and powers of the courts following: that is to say, (1) all jurisdiction and powers of the lord chancellor and of the court of appeal in chancery in the exercise of his and its appellate jurisdiction, and of the same court as a court of appeal in bankruptcy; (2) all jurisdiction and powers of the court of appeal in chancery of the county palatine of Lancaster . . . ; (3) all jurisdiction and powers of the court of the lord warden of the stannaries, assisted by his assessors . . . ; (4) all jurisdiction and powers of the court of exchequer chamber; (5) all jurisdiction vested in or capable of being exercised by her majesty in council, or the judicial committee of her majesty's privy council, upon appeal from any judgment or order of the high court of admiralty or from any order in lunacy made by the lord chancellor or any other person having jurisdiction in lunacy.

The said court of appeal shall have jurisdiction and power to hear and determine appeals from any judgment or order, save as hereinafter mentioned, of her majesty's high court of justice, or of any

---

[13] Those mentioned at the beginning of the act, together with certain minor courts.

judges or judge thereof, subject to the provisions of this act, and to such rules and orders of court, for regulating the terms and conditions on which such appeals shall be allowed, as may be made pursuant to this act. For all the purposes of and incidental to the hearing and determination of any appeal within its jurisdiction and the amendment, execution, and enforcement of any judgment or order made on any such appeal, and for the purpose of every other authority expressly given to the court of appeal by this act, the said court of appeal shall have all the power, authority, and jurisdiction by this act vested in the high court of justice. . . .

No error or appeal shall be brought from any judgment or order of the high court of justice or of the court of appeal . . . to the house of lords or to the judicial committee of her majesty's privy council. . . .[14]

In every civil cause or matter commenced in the high court of justice, law and equity shall be administered by the high court of justice and the court of appeal respectively. . . .

Her majesty by commission of assize or by any other commission, either general or special, may assign to any judge or judges of the high court of justice or other persons usually named in commissions of assize, the duty of trying and determining within any place or district specially fixed for that purpose by such commission . . . any cause or matter depending in the said high court or the exercise of any civil or criminal jurisdiction capable of being exercised by the said high court. . . . And any commissioner or commissioners appointed in pursuance of this section shall, when engaged in the exercise of any jurisdiction assigned to him or them in pursuance of this act, be deemed to constitute a court of the said high court of justice. . . .

For the more convenient dispatch of business in the said high court of justice . . . , there shall be in the said high court five divisions . . . , called respectively the Chancery Division, the Queen's Bench Division, the Common Pleas Division, the Exchequer Division, and the Probate, Divorce, and Admiralty Division. . . . His majesty in council may from time to time, upon any report or recommendation of the council of judges of the supreme court . . . , order that any reduction or increase in the number of divisions of the high court of justice, or in the number of the judges of the said high court . . . may . . . be carried into effect. . . .

All appeals from petty or quarter sessions, from a county court, or from any other inferior court, which might before the passing of this act have been brought to any court or judge whose jurisdiction is by this act transferred to the high court of justice, may be heard and determined by divisional courts of the said high court of justice. . . . The determination of such appeals respectively by such divisional

---

[14] But see the following statute.

courts shall be final, unless special leave to appeal from the same to the court of appeal shall be given. . . .[15]

Ibid., VIII, 306 f.: 36-37 Victoria, c. 66.

(L) APPELLATE JURISDICTION ACT (1876)

An act for amending the law in respect of the appellate jurisdiction of the house of lords and for other purposes. Be it enacted . . . as follows:—

. . . Subject as in this act mentioned, an appeal shall lie to the house of lords from any order or judgment of any of the courts following: that is to say, (1) of her majesty's court of appeal in England; and (2) of any court in Scotland from which error or an appeal, at or immediately before the commencement of this act, lay to the house of lords by common law or by statute; and (3) of any court in Ireland from which error or an appeal, at or immediately before the commencement of this act, lay to the house of lords by common law or by statute.

Every appeal shall be brought by way of petition to the house of lords, praying that the matter of the order or judgment appealed against may be reviewed before her majesty the queen in her court of parliament, in order that the said court may determine what of right and according to the law and custom of this realm ought to be done in the subject matter of such appeal.

An appeal shall not be heard and determined by the house of lords unless there are present at such hearing and determination not less than three of the following persons, in this act designated lords of appeal: that is to say, (1) the lord chancellor of Great Britain for the time being; and (2) the lords of appeal in ordinary to be appointed as in this act mentioned; and (3) such peers of parliament as are for the time being holding or have held any of the offices in this act described as high judicial offices.

For the purpose of aiding the house of lords in the hearing and determination of appeals, her majesty may, at any time after the passing of this act, by letters patent appoint two qualified persons to be lords of appeal in ordinary, but such appointment shall not take effect until the commencement of this act. A person shall not be qualified to be appointed by her majesty a lord of appeal in ordinary unless he has been, at or before the time of his appointment, the holder for a period of not less than two years of some one or more of the offices in this act described as high judicial offices, or has been, at or before such time as aforesaid, for not less than fifteen years, a practising barrister in England or Ireland or a practising advocate in Scotland. Every lord of appeal in ordinary shall hold his office during good behaviour, and shall continue to hold the same notwith-

---

[15] The detailed provisions concerning the jurisdiction of the divisional courts and the procedure followed there and in the court of appeal are here omitted.

standing the demise of the crown; but he may be removed from such office on the address of both houses of parliament. There shall be paid to every lord of appeal in ordinary a salary of £6000 a year.

Every lord of appeal in ordinary, unless he is otherwise entitled to sit as a member of the house of lords, shall, by virtue and according to the date of his appointment, be entitled during his life to rank as a baron by such style as her majesty may be pleased to appoint, and shall during the time that he continues in his office as a lord of appeal in ordinary, and no longer, be entitled to a writ of summons to attend and to sit and vote in the house of lords. His dignity as a lord of parliament shall not descend to his heirs. On any lord of appeal in ordinary vacating his office by death, resignation, or otherwise, her majesty may fill up the vacancy by the appointment of another qualified person.

A lord of appeal in ordinary shall, if a privy councillor, be a member of the judicial committee of the privy council, and, subject to the due performance by a lord of appeal in ordinary of his duties as to the hearing and determining of appeals in the house of lords, it shall be his duty, being a privy councillor, to sit and act as a member of the judicial committee of the privy council. . . .

For preventing delay in the administration of justice, the house of lords may sit and act for the purpose of hearing and determining appeals, and also for the purpose of lords of appeal in ordinary taking their seats and the oaths, during any prorogation of parliament. . . . If on occasion of a dissolution of parliament her majesty is graciously pleased to think that it would be expedient, with a view to prevent delay in the administration of justice, to provide for the hearing and determination of appeals during such dissolution, it shall be lawful for her majesty, by writing under her sign-manual, to authorize the lords of appeal, in the name of the house of lords, to hear and determine appeals during the dissolution of parliament. . . .

An appeal shall not be entertained by the house of lords without the consent of the attorney general or other law officer of the crown in any case where proceedings in error or on appeal could not hitherto have been had in the house of lords without the fiat or consent of such officer. . . .

Be it enacted that, whenever any two of the paid judges of the judicial committee of the privy council have died or resigned, her majesty may appoint a third lord of appeal in ordinary in addition to the lords of appeal in ordinary hereinbefore authorized to be appointed. And on the death or resignation of the remaining two paid judges of the judicial committee of the privy council, her majesty may appoint a fourth lord of appeal in ordinary. . . .[16]

Ibid., XI, 380 f.: 39-40 Victoria, c. 59.

---

[16] Such lords of appeal in ordinary, on being made privy councillors, would become members of the judicial committee of the privy council; see the third paragraph above.

132. PROCEEDINGS IN PARLIAMENT (1831-66)
(A) Debates on the Reform Bill (1831)[1]

[1 March.] Lord John Russell: . . . The measure I have now to bring forward is a measure, not of mine, but of the government in whose name I appear—the deliberate measure of a whole cabinet, unanimous upon this subject and resolved to place their measure before this house in redemption of their pledge to their sovereign, the parliament, and to their country. . . .

It will not be necessary on this occasion that I should go over the arguments which have been so often urged in favour of parliamentary reform; but it is due to the question that I should state shortly the chief points of the general argument on which the reformers rest their claim. Looking at the question then as a question of right, the ancient statutes of Edward I contain the germ and vital principle of our political constitution. The 25th of Edward I, c. 6,[2] declares in the name of the king that "for no business from henceforth we should take such manner of aids, tasks, nor prises, but by the common assent of the realm and for the common profit thereof, saving the ancient aids and prises due and accustomed." The 34th Edward I, commonly called the Statute de Tallagio Concedendo,[3] provides "that no tallage or aid shall be taken or levied by us or our heirs in our realm without the good will and assent of archbishops, bishops, earls, barons, knights, burgesses, and other freemen of the land." Although some historical doubts have been thrown upon the authenticity of this statute, its validity in point of law is asserted in the Petition of Rights,[4] was allowed by the judges in the case of Hampden,[5] and is, in fact, the foundation of the constitution as it has existed since the days of the Stuarts.

To revert again for a moment to ancient times, the assent of the commonalty of the land, thus declared necessary for the grant of any aid or tax, was collected from their representatives consisting of two knights from each county, from each city two citizens, and from every borough two burgesses. For 250 years the constant number of boroughs so sending their representatives was about 120.

---

[1] In 1830, on the defeat of Wellington's Tory ministry, Earl Grey became head of a new government pledged to reform parliament. Accordingly, in March of the next year, Lord John Russell, leader of the majority in the house of commons, introduced such a bill. Dispute over the bill led to the dissolution of parliament in April. Having won a large majority in the ensuing election, the government resumed its efforts to secure reform in the new parliament. Finally, in June 1832, an amended form of the bill passed both houses and received the royal assent (see no. 130A). The following extracts are from speeches by Russell and Peel in the commons and by Melbourne and Wellington in the lords.
[2] No. 51A.
[3] See p. 165, n. 1.
[4] No. 92D.
[5] No. 94C.

Some thirty or forty others occasionally exercised or discontinued that practice or privilege, as they rose or fell in wealth and importance. How this construction of the house of commons underwent various changes, till the principle on which it was founded was lost sight of, I will not now detain the house by explaining. There can be no doubt, however, that at the beginning of the period I have alluded to, the house of commons did represent the people of England. No man of common sense pretends that this assembly now represents the commonalty or people of England. If it be a question of right, therefore, right is in favour of reform.

Let us now look at the question as one of reason. Allow me to imagine, for a moment, a stranger from some distant country, who should arrive in England to examine our institutions.... He would have been told that the proudest boast of this celebrated country was its political freedom. If, in addition to this, he had heard that once in six years this country, so wise, so renowned, so free, chose its representatives to sit in the great council where all the ministerial affairs were discussed and determined, he would not be a little curious to see the process by which so important and solemn an operation was effected. What then would be his surprise if he were taken by his guide, whom he had asked to conduct him to one of the places of election, to a green mound and told that this green mound sent two members to parliament, or to be taken to a stone wall with three niches in it and told that these three niches sent two members to parliament; or, if he were shown a green park with many signs of flourishing vegetable life, but none of human habitation, and told that this green park sent two members to parliament! But his surprise would increase to astonishment if he were carried into the north of England, where he would see large flourishing towns, full of trade and activity, containing vast magazines of wealth and manufactures, and were told that these places had no representatives in the assembly which was said to represent the people. Suppose him, after all, for I will not disguise any part of the case—suppose him to ask for a specimen of popular election, and to be carried for that purpose to Liverpool; his surprise would be turned into disgust at the gross venality and corruption which he would find to pervade the electors. After seeing all this, would he not wonder that a nation which had made such progress in every kind of knowledge, and which valued itself for its freedom, should permit so absurd and defective a system of representation any longer to prevail? But whenever arguments of this kind have been urged, it has been replied—and Mr. Canning placed his opposition to reform on this ground—"We agree that the house of commons is not, in fact, sent here by the people; we agree that, in point of reason, the system by which it is sent is full of anomaly and absurdity; but government is a matter of experience, and so long as the people are satisfied with the actual working of the house of commons, it would be unwise to embark in theoretical change." Of this argument, I confess, I always felt the weight, and so long as the people did not answer the appeals of the friends of reform, it was indeed an argument not to be resisted. But what is the case at this moment? The whole people call loudly for reform. . . . The chief grievances of which the people complain are these: first, the nomination of members by individuals; second, the elections by close corporations; third, the expense of elections. . . .[6]

Having now, sir, gone through the principal provisions of the bill which I propose to introduce, I cannot but take notice of some particulars in which, perhaps, this measure will be considered by many to be defective. In the first place, there is no provision for the shorter duration of parliaments. That subject has been considered by his majesty's ministers; but upon the whole we thought that it would be better to leave it to be brought before the house by any member who may choose to take it up, than to bring it in at the end of a bill regulating matters totally distinct. . . . There is another question, sir, of which no mention is made in this bill, although it at present occupies very much the attention of the country—I mean the question of vote by ballot. Sir, there can be no doubt that that mode of election has much to recommend it. The arguments I have heard advanced in its favour are as ingenuous as any that ever fell under my observation on any subject. But at the same time I am bound to say that this house ought to pause before it gives its sanction to that measure. . . .

I arrive at last at the objections which may be made to the plan we propose. I shall be told, in the first place, that we overturn the institutions of our ancestors. I maintain that, in departing from the letter, we preserve the spirit of those institutions. Our opponents say our ancestors gave Old Sarum representatives; therefore we should give Old Sarum representatives. We say our ancestors gave Old Sarum representatives because it *was* a large town; therefore we give representatives to Manchester, which *is* a large town. . . . It has been asserted also, if a reform were to be effected, that many men of great talents, who now get into this house for close boroughs, would not be able to procure seats. I have never entertained any apprehensions of the sort, for I believe that no reform that can be introduced will have the effect of preventing wealth, probity, learning, and wit from having their proper influence upon elections. . . . It may be said, too, that one great and injurious effect of the measures I propose will be to destroy the power and privileges of the aristocracy. This I deny. . . . Wherever the aristocracy reside, receiving large incomes, performing important duties, relieving the poor by charity, and evincing private worth and public virtue, it is not in human nature that they should not possess a great influence upon public opinion and have an equal weight in

---

[6] Russell here takes up these grievances in order and shows how the proposed bill meets them.

electing persons to serve their country in parliament. Though such persons may not have the direct nomination of members under this bill, I contend that they will have as much influence as they ought to have. But if by aristocracy those persons are meant who do not live among the people, who know nothing of the people, and who care nothing for them—who seek honours without merit, places without duty, and pensions without service—for such an aristocracy I have no sympathy; and I think the sooner its influence is carried away, with the corruption on which it has thriven, the better for the country. . . .

To establish the constitution on a firm basis, you must show that you are determined not to be the representatives of a small class or of a particular interest, but to form a body who, representing the people, springing from the people, and sympathizing with the people, can fairly call on the people to support the future burdens of the country and to struggle with the future difficulties which it may have to encounter. . . . I conclude, sir, by moving for leave to bring in a bill for amending the state of the representation in England and Wales.

[6 July.] Sir Robert Peel: . . . I do not admit . . . that the settled opinion of this country is fixed, and permanently decided, in favour of this bill. I would advise those who assert it not to rely too confidently on the duration of the present excitement, to bear in mind the causes which have combined to foment it, and to consider whether they are of lasting operation. Our sober judgment has been disturbed by the recent events in France, by sympathy in the triumph of liberal opinions, and by a natural indignation at the illegal exercise of authority. While those feelings are at their height, a government is formed pledged to reform, and they redeem that pledge by a more extensive measure of reform than was expected by the most sanguine reformer. They dissolve the parliament in order to take the opinion of an already excited people on a question of all others the most requiring sober and dispassionate inquiry, and they superadd to every other cause of agitation an appeal to the personal wishes and opinions of the king. With regard to the dissolution of the parliament, it might be right or it might be wrong; but nothing could be more unwise than to countenance the popular belief that the king was personally interested in the question of reform. I do not for a moment call in question the undoubted prerogative of the crown to dissolve the late parliament; but I do call in question the prudence with which that prerogative was exercised, the time and mode of its exercise, and above all the lavish use of his majesty's name and authority with the view of influencing election contests. I regret most deeply that through their organs of the press the government condescended to the humiliation of propagating tales which could only be addressed and suited to the lowest and most vulgar class of minds. I regret most deeply that they should, for any purpose whatever, have resorted to the dangerous expedient of teaching the people to associate loyalty to their king with hostility to the constitution of parliament. I do not think it a happy circumstance that the feelings of the people have been thus excited; I doubt the existence of an unanimous feeling as connected with this measure on their part; and I deeply regret that the sober and temperate judgment of the people has been disturbed by a variety of causes. But, sir, if this feeling be such as we have heard it represented, and if it shall permanently endure, I am then ready to admit that no government can go on without enacting such measures as shall alleviate and remove that intense feeling. . . .

[20 July.] Sir Robert Peel: . . . The noble lord said that, when they looked at the measure as a whole, they would see that its object was to give to the people a full and fair representation in parliament, and that, as such, it might be justly described as a restoration of the ancient principles of the constitution; for that those principles were that the people should be fully and fairly represented in the commons house of parliament. Now that involved the fallacy that the people of this country ever had the right which it was proposed to give them by this bill. He would deny that the phrase, the people of England, ever meant the people of England as they were polled by this bill. What was meant by the people of England, when we spoke of the representation of the people of England in ancient times, consisted in the great corporate bodies and those great classes of the community to whom the franchise was entrusted and of whom the members sent to parliament were the representatives. But the word people was never used then as it was in the present bill—it was never used so as to mean £10 householders who had never hitherto possessed a right to that franchise which it was now proposed to give them. The elective franchise, as it had been established in England in former times, had never existed in the form in which the present bill proposed to establish it, but in a much better, more practical, and more beneficial form. . . . So far as burgage-tenure boroughs were concerned, they certainly could not be described as any usurpation on the rights of the people. It was said that the possession of such boroughs could not be advantageous to the aristocracy and, indeed, the lord advocate of Scotland has argued upon a former night that, as the right of returning members from such boroughs was vested in individuals, it was not probable that it could be exercised for the benefit of the general body, and that, in fact, the possession of such boroughs was disadvantageous to the interests of the aristocracy at large. But though the power might be vested in the hands of a single individual, was it to be supposed that it ever would be used by him for the promotion of his individual and personal interests, and not for the promotion and support of the interests of the general body to which he belonged? If, for instance, they should give members to Birmingham, was it probable that those members would attend only to the interests of Birmingham, and not to the interests of the iron-manufacturers at large? Now those nomination boroughs served the same purpose exactly with respect to the property and interests of the aristocracy. . . .

[4 October.] Viscount Melbourne: . . . My lords, we have been told by one of your lordships that we ought not to yield to popular opinion . . . , and that it frequently becomes the duty of legislative and representative bodies, and of all those having authority, to resist the will of the people. I readily admit the truth of that proposition. Else why have a representative body at all? The wildest democrat in existence, those who assert that all power is derived from the people, would hardly deny the proposition. No man can suppose for one moment that it is the duty of a legislative body to yield to every gust of the popular breath. No man can suppose that in questions involving the immediate petty interests of the people this should be done, much less in making those fundamental changes which affect the whole interests of a great country and of which the people are necessarily very incompetent judges. But, my lords, although it may be our duty to resist the will of the people for a time, is it possible to resist it forever? Have we not in this case resisted it long enough? . . .

The noble lord has asked what is the basis of the measure, and whether it is not population. Population is not the basis of the measure. It was necessary that we should have, for the purposes of disfranchisement, some practical rule, and therefore the want of population was adopted as the rule to disfranchise nomination boroughs. But there is nothing about population on the face of the bill. . . . We never intended that population should be the basis of the representation of the country. The whole measure goes to effect an extension of the present system of representation and adapts it more completely to the circumstances and situation of the country; but it looks at property, at different interests, and at different classes, as well as at population. . . .

The duke of Wellington: . . . A bill was introduced into the other house of parliament . . . , which after long discussion was read a second time by the decision of a small majority. This measure altered everything; it changed or destroyed every interest in the country. Instead of proceeding upon the basis of the established institutions, it destroyed them all and, among other things, altered the relative numbers of the representatives in parliament from the different kingdoms of the united empire. It was proposed in the house of commons that the proportion of representatives for England should not be diminished; to which proposition, after long debate, the house of commons agreed by a majority of seven. The principle of the noble lord's bill had been agreed to. Why did not the noble lords persevere and carry through their bill, making such

132. PROCEEDINGS IN PARLIAMENT

alterations as might render it palatable to the house of commons and consistent with the established practice of the constitution? This did not suit their purpose. They dissolved the parliament and advised their sovereign to appeal to his people. I attribute all our misfortunes to that event.

The noble lords advised their sovereign upon that occasion to come to parliament and to make this speech: "I have come to meet you for the purpose of proroguing this parliament with a view to its immediate dissolution. I have been induced to resort to this measure for the purpose of ascertaining the sense of my people in the way in which it may be most constitutionally and authentically expressed on the expediency of making such changes in the representation as circumstances may seem to require; and which, founded upon the acknowledged principles of the constitution, may tend at once to uphold the just rights and prerogatives of the crown and to give security to the liberties of my people."

The dissolution then made and the speech delivered by his majesty were both upon a principle entirely different from that of the precedents according to which the measure was adopted. In 1784 the king, George III, differed from his ministers upon a great question. They retired from his service, and his majesty appointed other ministers. Those ministers did not enjoy the confidence of the house of commons, and the king dissolved his parliament and put an end to the session in the words which I am about to read to your lordships: "On a full consideration of the present situation of affairs and of the extraordinary circumstances which have produced it, I am induced to put an end to this session of parliament. I feel it a duty which I owe to the constitution and to the country in such a situation to recur as speedily as possible to the sense of my people by calling a new parliament. I trust that this measure will tend to obviate the mischiefs arising from the unhappy divisions and distractions which have lately subsisted, and that the various important objects which will require consideration may be afterwards proceeded upon with less interruption and with happier effect. I can have no other object but to preserve the true principles of our free and happy constitution and to employ the powers entrusted to me by law for the only end for which they were given—the good of my people."

I will not give your lordships the trouble of listening to the perusal of the case of 1807, which stands precisely upon the same principle as that of 1784. In both the king differed in opinion with his ministers and with the parliament upon measures upon which his majesty had decided, and he appealed to the sense of his people and called upon them to elect a parliament which should give their confidence to the ministers of his choice in carrying on the measures which he approved. The transaction was brought to a close before the appeal was made to the people. The people were not called upon to deliberate upon any measure, but the appeal to them was rather, it may be said, in favour of the men whom his majesty had named as his ministers. In the case of 1831, however, the noble lords have advised their sovereign to refer for discussion to the people, not whether the king was to be supported in naming his ministers—not whether parliament is to be reformed, because upon the principle of reform there was a majority in the late house of commons—but upon a particular plan of reform which was accordingly discussed throughout the country.

It is on the ground of the dissolution and of this speech from the throne that I charge the noble lords with having excited the spirit which existed in the country at the period of the last general election, and with having been the cause of the unconstitutional practice hitherto unknown of electing delegates for a particular purpose to parliament—delegates to obey the daily instructions of their constituents and to be cashiered if they should disobey them, whatever may be their own opinion, instead of being, as they have been hitherto, independent members of parliament to deliberate with their colleagues upon matters of common concern and to decide according to the best of their judgment after such deliberation and debate. This is an evil of which the country will long feel the consequences, whatever may be the result of these discussions. . . .

Parliamentary Debates, Third Series, II, 1061-89; IV, 891 f.;
V, 114 f.; VII, 1177-82, 1191-93.

(B) DEBATE ON MELBOURNE'S GOVERNMENT (1841)

Sir Robert Peel [moving a vote of no confidence in the ministry] : . . . The interests of the crown and the interests of the house of commons are identical. You cannot strike a blow at the house of commons in its just and legitimate authority without at the same time striking a blow at the monarchy of this country. But can it be said to add to the authority of the monarchy that its ministers and representatives . . . counsel measures in this house on the authority of the crown? Can it be supposed that the sorry triumph of being maintained in power by the crown is a compensation for the delays, for the spectacle of insufficiency and want of authority in the government we have recently beheld? It may be said, "True, we may not have the confidence of the house of commons; but perhaps, as Mr. Pitt was able to say—though Mr. Fox denied it—if we fail in the house of commons, there are sufficient indications that we possess the confidence of the country." First, however, I should say with Mr. Fox it is dangerous to admit any other recognized organ of public opinion than the house of commons. It is dangerous to set up the implied or supposed opinions of constituencies against their declared and authorized organ, the house of commons. The house and the constituencies should not be brought into this unseemly contest. But if you deny the force of that argument, if you hold that it is right to refer to the opinions of the constituencies, can you, I ask, show me in the elections that have recently taken place any just ground for the boast that the confidence withheld from you by the house has been extended to you by the constituencies of the empire? I know not exactly how many vacancies have occurred since the commencement of the present parliament; I believe them to have been upwards of one hundred. But this I can say with confidence: that upon the general balance there have been twenty elections in which there have been changes of the former members, and of those twenty—embracing large towns, boroughs, agricultural districts, in fact, every kind and description of constituency—out of those twenty in which changes have taken place, sixteen have been averse to you and four only have been in your favour; so that upon the whole, in those places where changes have taken place during the present parliament, there has been a positive loss of not less than twelve members. I say, then, whatever may be the object you expect from an appeal to the people—if that be the course you are meditating—you have no right to say from the result of the elections hitherto that the opinion of the constituencies differs from that of their representatives. I know it will be said that all my general doctrines may be true, that it is right under ordinary circumstances that ministers should have the confidence of the house of commons—"But there are special and peculiar circumstances," her majesty's ministers might say, "that except us from the ordinary rule and entitle us to continue in office." Now it is perfectly obvious that this plea will apply in fact to all times. Who can deny that in the important position of this country, with such complicated affairs to be administered, there must be at all times special and peculiar circumstances connected with the executive government of the day, and that you (the government), being the judges, will be enabled to discover special and peculiar circumstances why you should be exempted from the ordinary principle; so that, in fact, there will be no limit to the application of that principle? The men who have to determine are not quite impartial judges as to the urgency of the circumstances which constitute the special case. Perhaps, however, it may be said that you contemplate an appeal to the people, and that you are holding office for the purpose of making that appeal. I know nothing whatever upon that subject. As a member of the house of commons, I can have no evidence of the intentions of the crown. But I see you repeatedly in minorities; I see indications that you have not the confidence of this house. I know that you have power, at any time, to dissolve. I know, too, that you can choose the most favourable time for a dissolution. No doubt that is the prerogative of the crown—a prerogative of a delicate nature for the house of commons to meddle with. But all this does not relieve me from the performance of what I conceive to be a duty in calling upon the house of commons to say if her majesty's government possess their confidence or not. And here, too, I will say that I shall have no additional confidence if, after exciting the public mind upon such a subject as the sustenance of the people, you then make your appeal to the country by a dissolution. I believe that you are not, by that course, advancing the measure which you advocate. . . .

Sir John Hobhouse: The right honourable gentleman has taunted us with wishing an appeal to be made to the people at an inopportune time, but what degree of weight there is in the argument I cannot see. If we propose what we consider to be measures which would give the greatest possible relief to the suffering industry of the country and those measures are opposed, and we think that the country are with us, is there any harm in having our schemes and reasons and our principles fairly laid before the country? It seems to me there is not. Surely the agitation, if agitation there is to be, is no fault of ours. The question is a great fiscal question of monopoly or no monopoly. It is a question whether or not we shall, by adopting a new scheme, relieve the industry of the country and at the same time increase the revenue, and thereby render any additional burden on the people unnecessary; or whether the present system shall be maintained—that is to say, whether a reduction of duties shall take place, and thereby supply the deficiency of the revenue, or whether that deficiency shall be made up by the ordinary mode of imposing fresh taxes on the people. This is the point which the country have to determine. If the people feel a lively interest in the determination of this question, I cannot help it. If the industrious classes are anxious to remove the burdens they now labour under, and are desirous of eating cheaper bread and cheaper sugar and of obtaining cheaper timber than they are now capable of obtaining, we cannot be held responsible for it. And if this strong wish for a reduction of the prices of those articles is agitation, and if the fact of asking the people whether or not they think that these fiscal schemes are right and that they think we are doing our duty in proposing them is agitation, then I am afraid we must plead guilty to having excited that agitation. But this is not, I beg leave to inform [the] honourable gentlemen opposite, a fault resting with us alone. I could quote very recent instances where agitation had been called in to bear upon elections. (Cheers.) The honourable gentleman cheers out of place. I do not deny that agitation has been used for the purpose of acting on the feelings and prepossessions of the people on our side; but I do not see that any great backwardness has been evinced on that score by [the] honourable gentlemen opposite. I never saw, in my experience, any reluctance on their side to avail themselves of that mode of carrying any question which they advocated. The right honourable baronet has said, now that the appeal is made, and now that we are to go to the country, that he shall not make any particular exposition of his principles. But when the right honourable baronet came into office in 1834, he thought differently. He then thought it right to make an exposition of his political principles in his famous Tamworth Manifesto[7]—at a time, too, when parliament was not sitting. He did not then deem it improper to make an appeal to the country. And then again at a subsequent period, at the Mansion House, he did not object to a mode of proceeding which he now seems so much to eschew. And I recollect well that some things dropped from him on those occasions which looked very like what the right honourable baronet now calls bidding for the favour of the people. Moreover, he did make so high a bidding that I and my friends were at the time not a little apprehensive of the result. Now, however, he takes, and is to take, a totally different course. . . .

Mr. Macaulay: It was the first duty of the ministers of the crown to administer the existing law. If the house of commons did not place sufficient confidence in the government for this purpose, it might express its opinion, either indirectly by the rejection of all the propositions of the administration, or directly, as was the case in the instance alluded to by the right honourable baronet, Sir Robert Walpole. The proceedings in either case sufficiently marked the want of confidence of the house of commons in the government. Under such circumstances, there was only the one or other constitutional course to pursue: namely, either to retire from office, or to dissolve the parliament. He denied, however, that it could be called a want of confidence, if the house withheld its assent from any new legislative measure, or refused to sanction the alteration of an old law. . . . For himself, he did not hold that any government was bound to resign because it could not carry legislative changes, except in particular cases, where they were impressed with the conviction that, without such and such a law, they could not carry on the public service; and then this was a case which did not depend upon whether the hindrance arose from king, lords, or commons. He was quite sure that on both sides of the house gentlemen would feel that there were many ways in which it might be ascertained whether the house did or did not repose confidence in a ministry, without putting on the records of the house so ill-advised and unsound a resolution as this, declaring that such and such were the principles of the constitution.

Sir Robert Peel: . . . Can any man survey the course of government in this country and not see that acts of legislation are so interwoven with acts of administration as to render it utterly impossible to draw a line of distinction between them? Nay, I go further and say that the character of an administration, that their claim upon public confidence, is infinitely stronger on account of their legislative measures than on account of their administrative acts. If mere departmental administration, not liable to question, is a sufficient ground for a government to retain office and to be re-

---

[7] A statement of what were to be the guiding principles of the Conservative Party, issued by Peel in 1834.

gardless of legislative defeats, it is pretty clear that there need be no union or concert among ministers. I dare say in ordinary times, when questions of peace or war are not in agitation, it may be tolerably easy to fill the departments of office with honest, respectable, and sufficiently competent men who, each in his department, would be able to conduct the duties devolving on him in such a manner as not to be much liable to question by the house of commons, and no matter what opinions such men may entertain upon the legislative policy of the country. They may either avoid legislation altogether or take the safer course—propose measures and, being defeated, fall back upon their acts of administration. But, I say, survey the course of the legislative and executive administration of this country and look at the great measures which the government have had to consider of late years, and see whether the character and vigour of a government do not depend upon its legislative more than upon its executive administration. Take the measures which the noble lord has referred to with so much pride and satisfaction. Take the removal of the Roman Catholic disabilities as affecting Ireland. Take the repeal of the Test and Corporation Acts, as affecting this country. Take the reform of parliament; take the poor law bill; take the municipal bill; take the proposition for the repeal or alteration of the corn laws—are not these the great questions by which the character of administrations has been judged and determined? And is it possible to contend in a reformed parliament, with these great measures in our view, that a government can be safely indifferent to the success or failure of its legislative acts? See what the inevitable consequence would be if such a doctrine were to prevail. See what an inducement would be given, both to the crown and to the house of commons, to depart from the sphere of their proper respective functions. The crown would, or might, be constantly attempting to place the house of commons in the wrong by proposing popular legislative measures and throwing upon the house of commons the odium of rejecting them. The crown might constantly labour to place the house of commons in opposition to the constituent body and to lower the character of the house of commons by inducing it to reject popular measures, purposely proposed with that view. If the doctrine of the right honourable gentleman were to prevail, all that the crown would have to do, in order to stop the useful functions of the house of commons, would be to say: "Legislative measures are matters of indifference; the government I have chosen shall remain in office in spite of the rejection of the measures they have proposed; and we, the crown and the government, shall have credit with the country for propounding popular measures which you, the house of commons, have rejected." Such would be the effect as regarded the crown. Then see what an inducement you would give to the house of commons to step beyond its functions, and thwart the executive. If the government say: "We are independent of the legislative measures and decisions of this house; that which is your peculiar function we will disregard; our fate shall not depend upon your decisions; nothing but your interference with our executive administration shall influence our retention of power"—what an inducement do you not hold out to the house of commons to interfere with the prerogatives of the crown! The house of commons then, knowing that the only way in which it could influence the fate of the government was by interfering with its administrative functions, would press for the production of dispatches the production of which possibly may be injurious to the public service, or would protest against appointments made by the crown! In short, knowing that by the exercise of its ordinary legislative control it could not affect the government, the doctrine of the right honourable gentleman would present to the house of commons the greatest inducement to depart from its proper sphere and to interfere with the most important functions of the executive.

Ibid., LVIII, 817 f., 850 f., 881, 885, 1224 f.

(C) DISRAELI ON THE WORK OF THE COMMONS (1848)

... Perhaps it would not be uninteresting to the house and to the country that I should state what, independent of our debates, this house of commons, which it is the fashion to blame at present, has really done; and, in doing so, I will refer to a short paragraph in the report of the committee on public business, which, though already laid on the table of the house, has accidentally not been circulated among members. It appears from that report that there have been this year forty-five public committees, some of more than usual importance, with an average number of fifteen members serving on each committee. Then there have been twenty-eight election committees, with five members serving on each committee; fourteen groups on railway bills, with five members on each group; seventeen groups on private bills, with five members on each group. And there have been also one hundred and eleven other committees on private business. Of the public committees, that on commercial distress sat thirty-nine days; that on sugar and coffee planting, thirty-nine days; that on the navy, army, and ordnance expenditure, forty days; and that on the miscellaneous expenditure, thirty-seven days. There have, besides, been presented this year upwards of 18,500 petitions, showing an increase of 25 per cent. above the greatest number presented in any former year, except 1843.

Here I would make one observation on these petitions, since considerable error exists out of doors among our constituents on the subject. There is an idea that the presentation of a petition is an empty form, that it is ordered to lie on the table and is never heard of again. Now it is as well that our constituents should know that every petition laid on the table is scrutinized by a select committee of the most experienced and influential members of this house; that every petition which, from the importance of its subject or the ability of its statements, appears to merit more particular notice is printed at the public cost and afterwards circulated among the members. And I believe that at this moment the right of petition, although it is not permitted to make speeches on every petition, is a more important and efficient right than has ever been enjoyed at any time by the people of England in this respect. . . .

Ibid., CI, 672 f.

(D) Debate on the Rebellion Losses Bill of Canada (1849)[8]

[22 March.] Mr. Gladstone said he would take this opportunity, in consequence of the intelligence lately received from Canada, of asking her majesty's government the two questions of which he had given notice. The first was whether any instructions have been given to the governor general of Canada as to the course which he is to pursue, in the event of its being proposed to him by his advisers to allow them to introduce into the house of assembly any bill giving compensation to any persons known to have been implicated in the rebellions of 1837 or 1838 on account of the damage sustained by them in those rebellions, or in the event of the passing of any such bill through the two houses of the provincial legislature. His second question was whether, according to the usage of Canada, if any such bill should have passed through both houses of the legislature, and should have become an act by the governor general's assent without a suspending clause, the money thereby authorized to be paid would be payable forthwith, or before her majesty's servants had had an opportunity of advising her majesty with respect to the allowance or disallowance of such act. And perhaps, for the convenience of the house, he had better put a third question: namely, whether any official information had been received by her majesty's government from Canada with regard to these proceedings; and if so, whether they had any objection to place it upon the table of this house.

Mr. Hawes said, in answer to the question of the right honourable gentleman, he had to state that no instructions whatsoever were given to the noble lord at the head of the Canadian government with reference to the introduction of this bill or in contemplation of any such measures. His noble friend (Earl Grey) had entire confidence in the noble lord the governor general's judgment and discretion, and was not in the habit of giving him instructions of that kind. With regard to the second question of the right honourable gentleman, who had himself filled the office of secretary of state for the colonies, he had to state that all colonial laws . . . , having passed through their formal stages and received the assent of

[8] An act recently passed by the Canadian parliament to compensate those who had suffered damages during the Rebellion of 1837-38. The following extracts are (1) from proceedings in the house of commons and (2) from those in the house of lords. With the defeat of Lord Brougham's resolutions, debate on the matter came to an end. For earlier discussions of responsible government, see no. 133.

the crown through her majesty's representative in the colony, come into immediate operation unless they contain a suspending clause. This would apply, of course, to all acts, whether they were for the appropriation of money or not; and therefore, from the passing of such a bill, of course the act would come into operation and would continue to have the force of law unless disallowed by her majesty. In that case, it would only cease to be law upon the arrival of the specification of her majesty's disallowance in the colony. With regard to the right honourable gentleman's third question, he had to say that no dispatch whatever had been received from the earl of Elgin with reference to this transaction. . . . He used the word dispatch advisedly. His noble friend (Earl Grey) had a private letter from Canada, which he only received yesterday; but, with regard to any public dispatch, nothing of the kind had been received. . . .

Mr. Robinson wished to know if the honourable gentleman the under-secretary for the colonies, when he made use of the expression, "when the measure receives the assent of the crown it will come into immediate operation," meant the governor general.

Mr. Hawes had said that, when the measure received the assent of the representative of the queen in the colony, it would come into immediate operation.

Subject dropped. . . .

[19 June.] Lord Brougham: I rise to bring before your lordships a subject of very great interest and fully equal importance. . . . I mean the later affairs of the province of Canada. . . .

A notion sprung up at one time which was very much encouraged by Lord Durham and his council, and which goes by the name of responsible government. If I were to say that I clearly understand what is meant by the term, I should be arrogating to myself a degree of perspicacity to which I have no right; I should, moreover, be invidiously placing my intellect in contact with that of my noble friend at the head of the government. The principle of responsible government is this, that whosoever governs a colony . . . shall be bound to choose as his ministers whomsoever the legislature of the colony is disposed to give its confidence to. And further, whatever be his opinions of their conduct, so long as the confidence continues, he cannot remove them. . . . Such is the construction put upon responsible government in the colonies; and Lord Elgin, I see, has put this construction upon it. Indeed, but for such a construction, nobody could ever have dreamt of appointing Mr. Lafontaine. He was first appointed in the time of Sir Charles Bagot, who was, I believe, an able governor. . . . He was, however, in very bad health during the greater part of his government—which thus added to the weight and influence of his ministers. He appointed Mr. Lafontaine because responsible government had become the order of the day. . . . Then came Lord Metcalfe, a most excellent governor. . . .

Soon after Lord Metcalfe assumed the reins of power, he dismissed the government which he found in office; and I can well believe that he was most anxious and willing to part with Mr. Lafontaine. But there came afterwards another change, and the doctrine of responsible government was applied, in the utmost rigour of its absurd interpretation, by the new governor, Lord Elgin. He restored Mr. Lafontaine and his friends to office.

This notion of responsible government, as applied to the colonies, almost passes my powers of comprehension. It is utterly inapplicable in the colonies—that is, as it is upheld in the mother country. It is no doubt to a certain limited extent applicable, but only to a limited extent. I would, for my part, interfere as little as possible with the powers and workings of the colonial assemblies in respect to the making of roads, bridges, and canals, and as to all matters of a like nature; but in matters that touch in the slightest degree the honour of the crown, or the interests of the imperial government, I deny that you can have responsible colonial government. According to that theory, it is said that whatever the majority of a colony may choose to do, their acts are always to bind the minority, without the power of appeal to the crown. I, for one, say that, if that is to be the rule, gross injustice will be done, frightful cruelty will be exercised. . . .

Now, having stated this, and before I come to consider the bill in question, I shall only refer . . . to one of the ablest state papers which I ever recollect to have proceeded from a statesman. It is a dispatch dated the 14th October, 1839, sent by the Lord John Russell to the right honourable Poulett Thomson. . . .[9] But he, perspicacious as he is, and imaginative to conceive cases that might arise, could not anticipate this other case which has arisen—where British loyalists are taxed to pay French rebels for losses which they, the rebels, sustained in a rebellion that was crushed by those loyalists. . . .

Mr. Lafontaine asked for a creation of new peers. . . . He gets the governor to send home—because the governor, according to this doctrine of responsible government, is a mere tool or puppet in the hands of the colonial ministers—he gets the governor to send home and obtain blank tickets for peerages, and he uses them at his will. Having thus prepared everything for their movement, they bring in their bill; and I venture to say that such a bill was never before produced before any assembly. . . . It is a bill of compensation for losses sustained by rebels. Allow me now to refer your lordships to the dispatch of Lord Elgin. . . . In it Lord Elgin says: "I shall not fail by the first mail to furnish you with full information respecting its character and objects, the circumstances which led to its introduction, and the grounds on which I resolved, after much reflection, to sanction it." This is after he had given his assent to the bill. . . .

---

[9] Brougham here quotes parts of the dispatch (no. 133c).

I have now, my lords, got to a close. I am perfectly certain that there cannot be a more fatal error than carrying to the extreme to which it has been carried the doctrine of responsible government. . . . Let us therefore come to the consideration of this question uninfluenced by the farce of responsible government, so well exposed to ridicule and reprobation in the dispatch of Lord John Russell which I have read. . . . It is ill adapted where there is not the check of a house of lords, where the colonial assembly is small in point of numbers and may be therefore packed, as I have shown that the Canadian parliament is packed. . . . I do not call upon you absolutely to refuse assent to this bill. I do not ask you to interfere with the royal prerogative by addressing the crown to withhold that assent; but I ask you to take care that the bill should be made clear and plain and intelligible . . . , and that in the meanwhile the bill shall be suspended, not refused, in order that due time may be afforded for making the amendments.

It is impossible, my lords, to know the strong and sincere feelings of loyalty which pervade masses of your fellow subjects and not be sensible to know how cruel it would be to take any steps which would throw them into the hands of the Americans. . . . My lords, you are not to hasten that catastrophe. I call upon you to save them from it. I implore you to save your Canadian fellow subjects from being made a sacrifice to this whim of responsible government. . . . I therefore implore your lordships to adopt these resolutions which, I am positively certain, will act like oil poured upon the troubled waters, and will restore peace and concord. I move your lordships to resolve that, by an act passed in the parliament of Canada entitled An Act to Provide for the Indemnification of Parties in Lower Canada . . . , no security is afforded against compensation for losses sustained in the rebellion in Canada in 1837 and 1838 being given to persons engaged in the said rebellion; that it is just and necessary, either by recommending a further and amending bill to the legislature of Canada or by such other means as may be effectual, to provide security against any compensation for losses sustained in the said rebellion being given to persons engaged in or having aided or abetted the same.

Earl Grey: I have listened, my lords, most attentively to the very able and elaborate speech which the noble and learned lord has just addressed to the house; but I confess that at the close of it I am as utterly unable as I was at the beginning to comprehend what is the great public object, and what is the great public interest, which the noble and learned lord thinks will be answered by this house assenting to the resolutions he has moved. . . . I have heard no explanations from the noble and learned lord of how he considers the government of the province could advantageously be carried on after the wishes of the great majority of its representatives had been set at naught by a resolution of this house. . . .

In calling upon your lordships to reject the resolution of the noble and learned lord, I do so far less by way of asking you to express an opinion upon the details of this bill than to say that this was a subject upon which the wishes of the people of Canada have been shown by their representatives, and that no grounds have been made out for calling upon her majesty to interfere to prevent the making of an act which the people in Canada, as shown by two-thirds of their representatives, think ought to become law. . . . The question whether the measure is a right one or a wrong one has now merged in the larger and much more important question of whether it is politic, when the parliament of Canada has passed a measure, the minority should be allowed to appeal to the crown to overrule the decision of the majority. That is the point now to be considered; that is the large and important question we are now at issue upon; that is the question upon which the great majority of the inhabitants of the province—of whatever religion, of whatever rank, and, I believe, of whatever political opinions—are at variance with the noble and learned lord, who says, if we adopt this resolution we shall be throwing oil upon the troubled waves, and produce a calm upon the agitated ocean of Canadian politics. Instead, however, of that being true, it is my firm conviction that, by passing a resolution of this kind, we shall be endangering the connection between this country and Canada by shaking the confidence which all persons cherish in the system of government now happily established there. . . . If therefore, my lords, you adopt these resolutions, you will be striking a grievous blow at our Canadian possessions; and it is upon that ground that I oppose the resolutions, and I hope and trust your lordships will concur with me in that opinion. . . .

Their lordships divided. The numbers were: . . . content 96; not content . . . 99. . . .

Ibid., CIII, 1124 f.; CVI, 450-547.

(E) LORD JOHN RUSSELL ON PALMERSTON'S DISMISSAL (1852)[10]

. . . It is as well that I should state what I conceive to be the position of a secretary of state as regards the crown in the administration of foreign affairs, and what I conceive to be the position of a secretary of state for foreign affairs as regards the prime minister of this country. I think that when, on the one hand, the crown, in consequence of a vote of the house of commons, places its constitutional confidence in a minister, that minister is bound, on the other hand, to the crown to the most frank and full detail of every measure that is taken, and is bound either to obey the sanction of the crown or to leave to the crown that full liberty

---

[10] In December, 1851, Lord Palmerston, foreign secretary in Russell's government, expressed his personal approbation of the *coup d'état* by which President Bonaparte had overturned the republican constitution of France. How this indiscretion led to his dismissal from office is explained in the following excerpt from a speech in the commons by the prime minister.

132. PROCEEDINGS IN PARLIAMENT

which the crown must possess, of no longer continuing that minister in office. Such, sir, I hold to be the general doctrine. But, with regard to my noble friend, it did so happen that in 1850 precise terms were laid down, in a communication to my noble friend, with respect to the transaction of business between the crown and the secretary of state for foreign affairs.

I became the organ of making that communication to my noble friend, and thus became responsible for the sanction of the document I am about to read. I shall refer only to that part of the document which has reference to the subject now under consideration: "The queen requires, first, that Lord Palmerston will distinctly state what he proposes in a given case, in order that the queen may know as distinctly to what she is giving her royal sanction; secondly, having once given her sanction to a measure, that it be not arbitrarily altered or modified by the minister. Such an act she must consider as failing in sincerity towards the crown, and justly to be visited by the exercise of her constitutional right of dismissing that minister. She expects to be kept informed of what passes between him and the foreign ministers before important decisions are taken, based upon that intercourse; to receive the foreign dispatches in good time; and to have the drafts for her approval sent to her in sufficient time to make herself acquainted with their contents before they must be sent off. The queen thinks it best that Lord John Russell should show this letter to Lord Palmerston." I sent that accordingly, and received a letter from my noble friend to the following effect: "I have taken a copy of this memorandum of the queen and will not fail to attend to the directions which it contains." I conceive those directions were such as should be maintained between the foreign secretary and the crown.

And now, sir, I will state what is the duty of the prime minister; and I will state it, not in my own words, but in the words which were used by the late Sir Robert Peel in giving evidence before the committee of this house with respect to official salaries. The words are: "Take the case of the prime minister. You must presume that he reads every important dispatch from every foreign court. He cannot consult with the secretary for foreign affairs, and exercise the influence which he ought to have with respect to the conduct of foreign affairs, unless he be master of everything of real importance passing in that department." I conceive Sir Robert Peel there lays down the duty of a prime minister and makes him responsible for the business of the country. I may say, likewise, that I was informed both by her majesty and Sir Robert Peel that Sir Robert Peel had advised her majesty to consult me whenever a question should arise with respect to foreign affairs, and to take my advice on such question. Such, then, being the state of the relations which I held towards the crown on the one hand and to my noble friend on the other, I must say I have found the situation one of great difficulty. When my noble friend first held the seals of the foreign office, he was placed under Earl Grey, a statesman of age and experience, to whom my noble friend, then young in that particular office, would no doubt readily defer. When Lord Melbourne was at the head of the government, that noble lord's long intimacy and connection with my noble friend would naturally incline him to place some confidence in the conduct of my noble friend. Without either of these advantages I have certainly found, from time to time, that those relations were very difficult to maintain; while, at the same time, I felt that great responsibility devolved upon me. . . .[11]

When this took place . . . , it appeared to me that I had no other course than to inform my noble friend that, while I held office, he could no longer hold the seals of the foreign office. Later in the day, and after I had formed that resolution, I received a long letter from my noble friend, stating the reasons why he approved of the act of the president of France. But it appeared to me that those reasons no longer touched the case, because the real question now was whether the secretary of state was entitled, of his own authority, to write a dispatch as the organ of the queen's government in which his colleagues had never concurred, and to which the queen had never given her royal sanction. It appeared to me that, without degrading the crown, I could not advise her majesty to retain that minister in the foreign department of her government. I at the same time informed her majesty that a correspondence had taken place between Lord Palmerston and myself with respect to her majesty's wishes on the subject of dispatches and diplomatic notes. This was on the Wednesday. I waited until the Saturday following in order to consider and reconsider the matter before I finally resolved to submit this correspondence to her majesty. On Thursday I informed my noble friend that I should wait until that day, as I thought it possible that he might either propose some course or suggest some course by which a separation might be avoided. Nothing of that kind, however, occurred and, being then as fully convinced as before, I on Saturday, the 20th, wrote to her majesty conveying copies of the correspondence which had passed and likewise intimating my advice to her majesty that my noble friend should be required to give up the seals of the foreign office. In coming to a decision so weighty, by which I must be separated from a colleague with whom I had acted so long, whose abilities I admired and whose policies I had approved, I felt fully—whether I was right or wrong in so acting I do not say—that it was one which I was bound to take by myself, and one upon which I ought not to consult any of my colleagues, and one for which, in order to avoid

---

[11] Russell here explains at length how Palmerston had embarrassed the government by expressing, without the concurrence of the cabinet and without the sanction of the crown, his approval of Bonaparte's action.

anything which might hereafter be tortured into the appearance of a cabal, I ought to assume the sole and entire responsibility. . . .

Ibid., CXIX, 89-99.

(F) GLADSTONE ON THE ADVANCE OF THE WORKING CLASS (1866)

. . . Since 1832 every kind of beneficial change has been in operation in favour of the working classes. There never was a period in which religious influences were more active than in the period I now name. It is hardly an exaggeration to say that within that time the civilizing and training powers of education have for all practical purposes been not so much improved as, I might almost say, brought into existence, as far as the mass of the people is concerned. As regards the press, an emancipation and extension have taken place to which it would be difficult to find a parallel. I will not believe that the mass of gentlemen opposite are really insensible to the enormous benefit that has been effected by that emancipation of the press—when, for the humble sum of a penny or for even less, newspapers are circulated from day to day by the million rather than by the thousand, in numbers almost defying the powers of statistics to follow, and carrying home to all classes of our fellow-countrymen accounts of public affairs; enabling them to feel a new interest in the transaction of those affairs and containing articles which, I must say, are written in a spirit, with an ability, with a sound moral sense, and with a refinement that have made the penny press of England the worthy companion—I may indeed say the worthy rival—of those dearer and older papers which have long secured for British journalism a renown perhaps without parallel in the world. By external and material as well as by higher means, by measures relating to labour, to police, and to sanitary arrangements, parliament has been labouring, has been striving to raise the level of the working community, and has been so striving with admitted success. And there is not a call which has been made upon the self-improving powers of the working community which has not been fully answered. Take, for instance, the working men's free libraries and institutes throughout the country. Take, as an example of the class, Liverpool. Who are the frequenters of that institution? I believe that the majority of the careful, honest, painstaking students who crowd that library are men belonging to the working classes, a large number of whom cannot attend without making some considerable sacrifice. Then again, sir, we called upon them to be provident; we instituted for them post-office savings banks, which may now be said to have been in full operation for four years. And what has been the result? During these four years we have received these names at the rate of thousands by the week, and there are now 650,000 depositors in those savings banks. This, then, is the way in which parliament has been acting towards the working classes. But what is the meaning of all this? Parliament has been striving to make the working classes progressively fitter and fitter for the franchise. And can anything be more unwise, not to say more senseless, than to persevere from year to year in this plan, and then blindly to refuse to recognize its legitimate upshot—namely, the increased fitness of the working classes for the exercise of political power? . . .

Ibid., CLXXXII, 1132 f.

133. RECORDS CONCERNING CANADA (1839-59)
(A) THE DURHAM REPORT (1839)

Report on the affairs of British North America from the earl of Durham.[1] . . . The preceding pages have sufficiently pointed out the nature of those evils to the extensive operation of which I attribute the various practical grievances and the present unsatisfactory condition of the North American colonies. It is not by weakening but strengthening the influence of the people on its government, by confining within much narrower bounds than those hitherto allotted to it, and not by extending the interference of the imperial authorities in the details of colonial affairs, that I believe that harmony is to be restored where dissension has so long prevailed, and a regularity and vigour, hitherto unknown, introduced into the administration of these provinces. It needs no change in the principles of government, no invention of a new constitutional theory, to supply the remedy which would, in my opinion, completely remove the existing political disorders. It needs but to follow out consistently the principles of the British constitution and introduce into the government of these great colonies those wise provisions by which alone the working of the representative system can in any country be rendered harmonious and efficient. We are not now to consider the policy of establishing representative government in the North American colonies. That has been irrevocably done, and the experiment of depriving the people of their present constitutional power is not to be thought of. To conduct their government harmoniously in accordance with its established principles is now the business of its rulers and I know not how it is possible to secure that harmony in any other way than by administering the government on those principles which have been found perfectly efficacious in Great Britain. I would not impair a single prerogative of the crown; on the contrary, I believe that the interests of the people of these colonies require the protection of prerogatives which have not hitherto been exercised. But the crown must, on the other hand, submit to the necessary consequences of representative institutions; and, if it has to carry on the government in unison with a representative body, it must consent to carry it on by means of those in whom that representative body has confidence. . . .

[1] Lord Durham, a Radical Whig and the son-in-law of Earl Grey, was sent to Canada in 1838 to investigate the conditions that had given rise to the rebellion of the previous year.

An elective executive council would not only be utterly inconsistent with monarchical government, but would really, under the nominal authority of the crown, deprive the community of one of the great advantages of an hereditary monarchy. Every purpose of popular control might be combined with every advantage of vesting the immediate choice of advisers in the crown, were the colonial governor to be instructed to secure the co-operation of the assembly in his policy by entrusting its administration to such men as could command a majority, and if he were given to understand that he need count on no aid from home in any difference with the assembly that should not directly involve the relations between the mother country and the colony. This change might be effected by a single dispatch containing such instructions; or, if any legal enactment were requisite, it would only be one that would render it necessary that the official acts of the governor should be countersigned by some public functionary. This would induce responsibility for every act of the government; and, as a natural consequence, it would necessitate the substitution of a system of administration by means of competent heads of departments for the present rude machinery of an executive council. The governor, if he wished to retain advisers not possessing the confidence of the existing assembly, might rely on the effect of an appeal to the people, and, if unsuccessful, he might be coerced by a refusal of supplies, or his advisers might be terrified by the prospect of impeachment. But there can be no reason for apprehending that either party would enter on a contest when each would find its interest in the maintenance of harmony, and the abuse of the powers which each would constitutionally possess would cease when the struggle for larger powers became unnecessary. Nor can I conceive that it would be found impossible or difficult to conduct a colonial government with precisely that limitation of the respective powers which has been so long and so easily maintained in Great Britain.

I know that it has been urged that the principles which are productive of harmony and good government in the mother country are by no means applicable to a colonial dependency. It is said that it is necessary that the administration of a colony should be carried on by persons nominated without any reference to the wishes of its people; that they have to carry into effect the policy, not of that people, but of the authorities at home; and that a colony which should name all its own administrative functionaries would, in fact, cease to be dependent. I admit that the system which I propose would, in fact, place the internal government of the colony in the hands of the colonists themselves, and that we should thus leave to them the execution of the laws of which we have long entrusted the making solely to them. Perfectly aware of the value of our colonial possessions, and strongly impressed with the necessity of maintaining our connection with them, I know not in what respect it can be desirable that we should interfere with their internal legislation in matters which do not affect their relations with the mother country. The matters which so concern us are very few. The constitution of the form of government, the regulation of foreign relations and of trade with the mother country, the other British colonies, and foreign nations, and the disposal of the public lands are the only points on which the mother country requires a control. This control is now sufficiently secured by the authority of the imperial legislature, by the protection which the colony derives from us against foreign enemies, by the beneficial terms which our laws secure to its trade, and by its share of the reciprocal benefits which would be conferred by a wise system of colonization. A perfect subordination on the part of the colony on these points is secured by the advantages which it finds in the continuance of its connections with the empire. It certainly is not strengthened, but greatly weakened, by a vexatious interference on the part of the home government with the enactment of laws for regulating the internal concerns of the colony, or in the selection of the persons entrusted with their execution. The colonists may not always know what laws are best for them, or which of their countrymen are the fittest for conducting their affairs; but, at least, they have a greater interest in coming to a right judgment on these points, and will take greater pains to do so, than those whose welfare is very remotely and slightly affected by the good or bad legislation of these portions of the empire. If the colonists make bad laws and select improper persons to conduct their affairs, they will generally be the only, always the greatest, sufferers; and, like the people of other countries, they must bear the ills which they bring on themselves until they choose to apply the remedy. But it surely cannot be the duty or the interest of Great Britain to keep a most expensive military possession of these colonies in order that a governor or secretary of state may be able to confer colonial appointments on one rather than another set of persons in the colonies. For this is really the only question at issue. . . .

A plan by which it is proposed to insure the tranquil government of Lower Canada must include in itself the means of putting an end to the agitation of national disputes in the legislature, by settling at once and forever the national character of the province. I entertain no doubts as to the national character which must be given to Lower Canada; it must be that of the British Empire, that of the majority of the population of British America, that of the great race which must, in the lapse of no long period of time, be predominant over the whole North American continent. Without effecting the change so rapidly or so roughly as to shock the feelings and trample on the welfare of the existing generation, it must henceforth be the first and steady purpose of the British government to establish an English population, with English laws and language, in this province, and to trust its government to none but a decidedly English legislature. . . .

I am far from wishing to encourage indiscriminately these pretensions to superiority on the part of any particular race; but while the greater part of every portion of the American continent is still uncleared and unoccupied, and while the English exhibit such constant and marked activity in colonization, so long will it be idle to imagine that there is any portion of that continent into which that race will not penetrate, or in which, when it has penetrated, it will not predominate. It is but a question of time and mode; it is but to determine whether the small number of French who now inhabit Lower Canada shall be made English, under a government which can protect them, or whether the process shall be delayed until a much larger number shall have to undergo, at the rude hands of its uncontrolled rivals, the extinction of a nationality strengthened and embittered by continuance. . . .

Parliamentary Papers, 1839, no. 3, pp. 1, 100 f.

(B) LETTER OF HOWE TO RUSSELL (18 SEPTEMBER 1839)[2]

The [Durham] report has circulated for some months in the colonies, and I feel it a duty to state the grounds of my belief that his lordship, in attributing many if not all of our colonial evils and disputes to the absence of responsibility in our rulers to those whom they are called to govern, is entirely warranted by the knowledge of every intelligent colonist; that the remedy pointed out, while it possesses the merits of being extremely simple and eminently British—making them so responsible—is the only cure for those evils short of arrant quackery, the only secure foundation upon which the power of the crown can be established on this continent, so as to defy internal machination and foreign assault.

It appears to me that a very absurd opinion has long prevailed among many worthy people on both sides of the Atlantic, that the selection of an executive council, who upon most points of domestic policy will differ from the great body of the inhabitants and the majority of their representatives, is indispensable to the very existence of colonial constitutions; and that, if it were otherwise, the colony would fly off, by the operation of some latent principle of mischief which I have never seen very clearly defined. By those who entertain this view, it is assumed that Great Britain is indebted for the preservation of her colonies, not to the natural affection of their inhabitants—to their pride in her history, to their participation in the benefit of her warlike, scientific, or literary achievements—but to the disinterested patriotism of a dozen or two persons, whose names are scarcely known in England, except by the clerks in Downing Street; who are remarkable for nothing above their neighbours in the colony, except perhaps the enjoyment of offices too richly endowed, or their zealous efforts to annoy, by the distri-

---

[2] Written from Halifax by Joseph Howe, a prominent citizen of Nova Scotia, to Lord John Russell, secretary of state for war and the colonies.

bution of patronage and the management of public affairs, the great body of inhabitants, whose sentiments they cannot change.

I have ever held, my lord, and still hold to the belief that the population of British North America are sincerely attached to the parent state; that they are proud of their origin, deeply interested in the integrity of the empire and not anxious for the establishment of any other form of government here than that which you enjoy at home—which, while it has stood the test of ages and purified itself by successive peaceful revolutions, has so developed the intellectual, moral, and natural resources of two small islands as to enable a people, once comparatively far behind their neighbours in influence and improvement, to combine and wield the energies of a dominion more vast in extent and complicated in all its relations than any other in ancient or modern times. Why should we desire a severance of old ties that are more honourable than any new ones we can form? Why should we covet institutions more perfect than those which have worked so well and produced such admirable results? Until it can be shown that there are forms of government, combining stronger executive power with more of individual liberty —offering nobler incitements to honourable ambition and more security to unaspiring ease and humble industry—why should it be taken for granted, either by our friends in England or our enemies elsewhere, that we are panting for new experiments; or are disposed to repudiate and cast aside the principles of that excellent constitution, cemented by the blood and the long experience of our fathers, and upon which the vigorous energies of our brethren, driven to apply new principles to a field of boundless resources, have failed to improve? This suspicion is a libel upon the colonist and upon the constitution he claims as his inheritance, and the principles of which he believes to be as applicable to all the exigencies of the country where he resides as they have proved to be to those of the fortunate islands in which they were first developed. . . .

Chisholm, *Speeches and Letters of Joseph Howe*, I, 223.

(C) DISPATCHES OF RUSSELL TO POULETT THOMSON (1839)[3]

[14 October.] Sir: it appears from Sir George Arthur's dispatches that you may encounter much difficulty in subduing the excitement which prevails on the question of what is called "responsible government." I have to instruct you, however, to refuse any explanation which may be construed to imply an acquiescence in the petitions and addresses upon this subject. . . .

It does not appear, indeed, that any very definite meaning is generally agreed upon by those who call themselves the advocates of this principle; but its very vagueness is a source of delusion and,

---

[3] Sir Charles Poulett Thomson, later Lord Sydenham, was at this time governor general of Canada. On the importance of this and the following dispatch, see P. Knaplund in the *Canadian Historical Review*, V, 26 f.

133. RECORDS CONCERNING CANADA

if at all encouraged, would prove the cause of embarrassment and danger. The constitution of England, after long struggles and alternate success, has settled into a form of government in which the prerogative of the crown is undisputed, but is never exercised without advice. Hence the exercise only is questioned and, however the use of the authority may be condemned, the authority itself remains untouched. This is the practical solution of a great problem, the result of a contest which from 1640 to 1690 shook the monarchy and disturbed the peace of the country. But if we seek to apply such a practice to a colony, we shall at once find ourselves at fault. The power for which a minister is responsible in England is not his own power, but the power of the crown of which he is for the time the organ. It is obvious that the executive councillor of a colony is in a situation totally different. The governor, under whom he serves, receives his orders from the crown of England. But can the colonial council be the advisers of the crown of England? Evidently not, for the crown has other advisers for the same functions, and with superior authority. It may happen, therefore, that the governor receives at one and the same time instructions from the queen, and advice from his executive council, totally at variance with each other. If he is to obey his instructions from England, the parallel of constitutional responsibility entirely fails; if, on the other hand, he is to follow the advice of his council, he is no longer a subordinate officer, but an independent sovereign.

There are some cases in which the force of these objections is so manifest that those who at first made no distinction between the constitution of the united kingdom and that of the colonists admit their strength. I allude to the questions of foreign war and international relations, whether of trade or diplomacy. It is now said that internal government is alone intended. But there are some cases of internal government in which the honour of the crown, or the faith of parliament, or the safety of the state, are so seriously involved that it would not be possible for her majesty to delegate her authority to a ministry in a colony. . . .

While I thus see insuperable objections to the adoption of the principle as it has been stated, I see little or none to the practical views of colonial government recommended by Lord Durham, as I understand them. The queen's government have no desire to thwart the representative assemblies of British North America in their measures of reform and improvement. They have no wish to make those provinces the resource for patronage at home. They are earnestly intent on giving to the talent and character of leading persons in the colonies advantages similar to those which talent and character, employed in the public service, obtain in the united kingdom. Her majesty has no desire to maintain any system of policy among her North American subjects which opinion condemns. In receiving the queen's commands, therefore, to protest against any declaration at variance with the honour of the crown and the unity of the empire, you are at the same time instructed to announce her majesty's gracious intention to look to the affectionate attachment of her people in North America, as the best security for permanent dominion.

It is necessary for this purpose that no official misconduct should be screened by her majesty's representative in the provinces; and that no private interests should be allowed to compete with the general good. Your excellency is fully in possession of the principles which have guided her majesty's advisers on this subject; and you must be aware that there is no surer way of earning the approbation of the queen, than by maintaining the harmony of the executive with the legislative authorities.

While I have thus cautioned you against any declaration from which dangerous consequences might hereafter flow, and instructed you as to the general line of your conduct, it may be said that I have not drawn any specific line beyond which the power of the governor on the one hand, and the privileges of the assembly on the other, ought not to extend. But this must be the case in any mixed government. Every political constitution in which different bodies share the supreme power is only enabled to exist by the forbearance of those among whom this power is distributed. In this respect the example of England may well be imitated. The sovereign using the prerogative of the crown to the utmost extent, and the house of commons exerting its power of the purse to carry all its resolutions into immediate effect, would produce confusion in the country in less than a twelvemonth. So in a colony: the governor thwarting every legitimate proposition of the assembly, and the assembly continually recurring to its power of refusing supplies, can but disturb all political relations, embarrass trade, and retard the prosperity of the people. Each must exercise a wise moderation. The governor must only oppose the wishes of the assembly where the honour of the crown or the interests of the empire are deeply concerned, and the assembly must be ready to modify some of its measures for the sake of harmony and from a reverent attachment to the authority of Great Britain. . . .

[16 October.] Sir: I am desirous of directing your attention to the tenure on which public offices in the gift of the crown appear to be held throughout the British colonies. I find that the governor himself and every person serving under him are appointed during the royal pleasure, but with this important difference. The governor's commission is, in fact, revoked whenever the interests of the public service are supposed to require such a change in the administration of local affairs. But the commissions of all other public officers are very rarely indeed recalled, except for positive misconduct. . . . This system of converting a tenure at pleasure into a tenure for life originated probably in the practice, which formerly prevailed, of selecting all the higher class of colonial functionaries

133. RECORDS CONCERNING CANADA

from persons who at the time of their appointment were resident in this country. . . . But the habit, which has obtained of late years, of preferring as far as possible, for places of trust in the colonies, persons resident there has taken away the strongest motive which could thus be alleged in favour of a practice to which there are many objections of the greatest weight. It is time, therefore, that a different course should be followed; and the object of my present communication is to announce to you the rules which will be hereafter observed on this subject in the province of Lower Canada.

You will understand, and will cause it to be made generally known, that hereafter the tenure of colonial offices held during her majesty's pleasure will not be regarded as equivalent to a tenure during good behaviour; but that not only will such officers be called upon to retire from the public service as often as any sufficient motives of public policy may suggest the expediency of that measure, but that a change in the person of the governor will be considered as a sufficient reason for any alterations which his successor may deem it expedient to make in the list of public functionaries, subject of course to the future confirmation of the sovereign.

These remarks do not extend to judicial offices, nor are they meant to apply to places which are altogether ministerial and which do not devolve upon the holders of them duties in the right discharge of which the character and policy of the government are directly involved. They are intended to apply rather to the heads of departments than to persons serving as clerks or in similar capacities under them. Neither do they extend to officers in the service of the lords commissioners of the treasury. The functionaries who will be chiefly though not exclusively affected by them are the colonial secretary, the treasurer or receiver general, the surveyor general, the attorney and solicitor general, the sheriff or provost marshal, and other officers who, under different designations from these, are entrusted with the same or similar duties. To this list must also be added the members of the council, especially in those colonies in which the legislative and executive councils are distinct bodies. . . .

Parliamentary Papers, 1847-48, no. 621, pp. 3-5.

(D) DISPATCH OF STANLEY TO BAGOT (8 OCTOBER 1841)[4]

. . . You cannot too early and too distinctly give it to be understood that you enter the province with the determination to know no distinctions of national origin or religious creed; to consult in your legislative capacity the happiness, and—so far as may be consistent with your duty to your sovereign and your responsibility to her constitutional advisers—the wishes of the mass of the community; and in your executive capacity to administer the laws firmly, moderately, and impartially. You will invite to aid you, in your

---

[4] Lord Stanley was secretary of state for war and the colonies; Sir Charles Bagot was governor general of Canada (1841-43).

labours for the welfare of the province, all classes of the inhabitants; you will consider it your bounden duty to be accessible to the representations, and prepared to listen to the complaints, or the statements of the views, of all; and the only passports to your favour will be loyalty to the queen, attachment to British connection, and an efficient and faithful discharge of public duty.

You will give every encouragement in your power to the extension, within the province, of religious education and of secular instruction. And you will not fail to bear in mind that the habits and opinions of the people of Canada are, in the main, averse from the absolute predominance of any single church; and that, while the Churches of England and of Scotland are by law established and endowed and must be steadily upheld and anxiously cherished, the Church of Rome also, to which a large portion of the population belongs, is recognized by the law and secured in the enjoyment of rights, which you will be bound to protect; and that the co-operation of Wesleyan Methodists and Protestant dissenters is not to be refused or discouraged by the executive.

In civil matters it must be your policy to seek to withdraw the legislature, and the population generally, from the discussion of abstract and theoretical questions—by which the government of Canada in former times has been too often and too seriously embarrassed—to the calm and dispassionate consideration of practical measures for the improvement and advancement of the internal prosperity of the province. In maturing measures of this description, you will endeavour to avail yourself of the advice and services of the ablest men without reference to distinctions of local party, which upon every occasion you will do your utmost to discourage; and, in framing them for the consideration of the provincial legislature, you will endeavour to present them in the form in which they are most likely to be favourably received by the house of assembly.

I do not, of course, intend to institute a precise analogy between the functions of that house and those of the house of commons; but I should strongly impress upon you my opinion that, on matters purely domestic, or where you are not bound either by absolute instructions or by a sense of the paramount duty which you owe to imperial interests, it would be matter of great regret that measures should be repeatedly and deliberately affirmed by large majorities of the assembly and subsequently rejected by the legislative council. Your efforts will, on all occasions, be directed to promoting and maintaining harmonious action between the two branches of the legislature. Questions may undoubtedly arise on which you may feel it absolutely inconsistent with your duty to sanction measures approved by one or even by both houses; but I would hope that they may be of very rare occurrence and that, when they arise, you may be enabled temperately and firmly to reconcile the performance of your duty, upon your responsibility to the crown, with that respect which, I am sure, you will be on all occasions desirous of showing to the expressed wishes of the representatives of the people. . . .

Bell and Morrell, Select Documents, pp. 45 f.

(E) Dispatch of Metcalfe to Stanley (5 August 1843)[5]

. . . My objects are to govern the country for its own welfare and to engage its attachment to the parent state. For these purposes it is my wish to conciliate all parties; and, although this might be difficult, I do not perceive that it would be impracticable, if the governor were free to act thoroughly in that spirit. But the accomplishment of that wish seems almost impossible when the governor is trammelled with a council deeming it necessary for their existence that their own party alone should be considered. Sooner than abandon myself as a partisan to such a course, I would dismiss the council and take the consequences; but it is scarcely possible to avoid the influence of party spirit in an administration in which every adviser and every executive officer is guided by it; and the chief difficulty of my position, I conceive, is to act according to my own sense of what is right and in opposition to this party spirit, without thereby breaking with the council and the majority that at present support them. The form of administration adopted by Lord Sydenham appears to me to have put heavy shackles on any governor who means to act with prudence and would not recklessly incur the consequences of a rupture with the majority in the popular assembly. The meeting of the legislature will probably enable me to see my position more clearly. It is at present far from certain that a change of councillors would produce any beneficial alteration in respect to the difficulty noticed; for any council appointed on the principle of Canada responsible government would most probably have similar party views and the same pressure on them from their partisans. . . .

It becomes a question whether party government can be avoided. The experiment of responsible government in this colony hitherto would indicate that it cannot. It seems to be inevitable in free and independent states where responsible government exists, and the same causes are likely to produce similar effects everywhere; but there is a wide difference between an independent state and a colony. In an independent state all parties must generally desire the welfare of the state. In a colony subordinate to an imperial government, it may happen that the predominant party is hostile in its feelings to the mother country or has ulterior views inconsistent with her interests. In such a case, to be obliged to co-operate with that party and to permit party government to crush those who are best affected, would be a strange position for the mother country to be placed in and a strange part for her to act. This ought to have been well considered before the particular system which has obtained the name

---

[5] Sir Charles Metcalfe was governor general of Canada (1843-45).

of responsible government was established. It is now, perhaps, too late to remedy the evil. . . .

Kaye, *Papers of Lord Metcalfe*, pp. 411-18.

(F) DISPATCHES OF GREY TO HARVEY (1846-47)[6]

[3 November 1846.] . . . Of whatsoever party your council may be composed, it will be your duty to act strictly upon the principle you have yourself laid down in the memorandum delivered to the gentlemen with whom you have communicated—that, namely, "of not identifying yourself with any one party," but, instead of this, "making yourself both a mediator and a moderator between the influential of all parties." In giving, therefore, all fair and proper support to your council for the time being, you will carefully avoid any acts which can possibly be supposed to imply the slightest personal objection to their opponents, and also refuse to assent to any measures which may be proposed to you by your council, which may appear to you to involve an improper exercise of the authority of the crown for party rather than for public objects. In exercising, however, this power of refusing to sanction measures which may be submitted to you by your council, you must recollect that this power of opposing a check upon extreme measures proposed by the party for the time in the government depends entirely for its efficacy upon its being used sparingly and with the greatest possible discretion. A refusal to accept advice tendered to you by your council is a legitimate ground for its members to tender to you their resignations—a course they would doubtless adopt, should they feel that the subject on which a difference had arisen between you and themselves was one upon which public opinion would be in their favour. Should it prove to be so, concession to their views must sooner or later become inevitable; since it cannot be too distinctly acknowledged that it is neither possible nor desirable to carry on the government of any of the British provinces in North America in opposition to the opinion of the inhabitants.

Clearly understanding, therefore, that refusing to accede to the advice of your council for the time being, upon a point on which they consider it their duty to insist, must lead to the question at issue being brought ultimately under the decision of public opinion, you will carefully avoid allowing any matter not of very grave concern, or upon which you cannot reasonably calculate upon being in the end supported by that opinion, to be made the subject of such a difference. And if, unfortunately, such a difference should arise,

---

[6] Earl Grey was secretary of state for war and the colonies; Sir John Harvey was lieutenant governor of Nova Scotia. On the significance of this and the following dispatch, see Chester Martin, "Nova Scotian and Canadian Reformers of 1848," in the *Transactions of the Royal Society of Canada*, Third Series, XXIII, sect. ii, 1-16.

you will take equal care that its cause and the grounds of your own decision are made clearly to appear in written documents capable of being publicly quoted.

The adoption of this principle of action by no means involves the necessity of a blind obedience to the wishes and opinions of the members of your council. On the contrary, I have no doubt that, if they see clearly that your conduct is guided, not by personal favour to any particular men or party, but by a sincere desire to promote the public good, your objections to any measures proposed will have great weight with the council—or, should they prove unreasonable, with the assembly, or in last resort with the public. Such are the general principles upon which the constitutions granted to the North American colonies render it necessary that their government should be conducted. . . .

[31 March 1847.] . . . There is scarcely any part of the system of government in this country which I consider of greater value than that which—though not enforced by any written law, but deriving its authority from usage and public opinion—makes the tenure of the great majority of officers in the public service to depend upon good behaviour. Although, with the exception of those who hold the higher judicial situations or situations in which judicial independence has been considered necessary, the whole body of public servants in the united kingdom hold their offices technically during the pleasure of the crown, in practice all but the very small proportion of offices which are distinguished as political are held independently of party changes. Nor are those who have once been appointed to them ever in point of fact removed except in consequence of very obvious misconduct or unfitness. Thus, in fact, though the legal tenure "during good behaviour" is rare, tenure during good behaviour, in the popular sense of the term, may be said to be the general rule of our public service.

The exception is in the case of those high public servants whom it is necessary to invest with such discretion as really to leave in their hands the whole direction of the policy of the empire in all its various departments. Such power must, with a representative government, be subject to constant control by parliament, and is therefore administered only by such persons as from time to time enjoy the confidence of parliament as well as of the crown. These heads of departments or ministers, together with their immediate subordinates who are required to represent or support them in parliament, are almost invariably members of one or other house and hold their offices only as long as they enjoy the confidence of parliament. . . .

The system with regard to the tenure of office, which has been found to work so well here, seems well worthy of imitation in the British American colonies; and the small population and limited revenue of Nova Scotia, as well as the general occupation and social state of the community, are in my opinion additional reasons for abstaining, so far as regards that province, from going further than can be avoided, without giving up the principle of executive responsibility, in making the tenure of offices in the public service dependent upon the result of party contests. In order to keep the executive government in harmony with the legislature, it is doubtless necessary that the direction of the internal policy of the colony should be entrusted to those who enjoy the confidence of the provincial parliament; but it is of great moment not to carry the practice of changing public officers further than is absolutely necessary for the attainment of that end, lest the administration of public affairs should be deranged by increasing the bitterness of party spirit and subjecting the whole machinery of government to perpetual change and uncertainty. . . .

The question how many of the public officers in Nova Scotia ought to be regarded as political is one to be determined on the general principles I have before laid down. . . . The practical end of responsible government would be satisfied by the removability of a single public officer, provided that through him public opinion could influence the general administration of affairs. Without quite assenting to the too modest estimate, which your present council have given, of the resources of the province, I admit that the smallness of the community, its want of wealth, and the comparative deficiency of a class possessing leisure and independent incomes preclude it from at present enjoying a very perfect division of public employments. Small and poor communities must be content to have their work cheaply and somewhat roughly done. Of the present members of your council, the attorney general and provincial secretary, to whom the solicitor general should perhaps be added, appear to me sufficient to constitute the responsible advisers of the governor. The holders of these offices should henceforth regard them as held on a political tenure. And with a view to that end, the provincial secretary should be prepared, in the event of any change, to disconnect from his office that of the clerkship of the council, which seems to be one that should on every account be held on a more permanent tenure. . . .

You will observe that in the preceding observations I have assumed that those only of the public servants who are to be regarded as removable on losing the confidence of the public legislature are to be members of the executive council. This I consider to follow from the principles I have laid down. Those public servants who hold their offices permanently must, upon that very ground, be regarded as subordinate, and ought not to be members of either house of the legislature—by which they would necessarily be more or less mixed up in party struggles. And, on the other hand, those who are to have the general direction of affairs exercise that function by virtue of their responsibility to the legislature—which implies their being removable from office, and also that they should be members either of

133. RECORDS CONCERNING CANADA

the assembly or of the legislative council. But this general direction of affairs and the control of all subordinate officers it is the duty of the governor to exercise through the executive council. Hence the seats in that council must be considered as in the nature of political offices and, if held in connection with other offices, must give to these also a political character. . . .

Parliamentary Papers, 1847-48, no. 621, pp. 7 f., 29 f.

(G) DISPATCH OF ELGIN TO GREY (1847)[7]

. . . My course . . . is, I think, clear and plain. It may be somewhat difficult to follow occasionally, but I feel no doubt as to the direction in which it lies. I give to my ministers all constitutional support frankly and without reserve, and the benefit of the best advice that I can afford them in their difficulties. In return for this I expect that they will, in so far as it is possible for them to do so, carry out my views for the maintenance of the connection with Great Britain and the advancement of the interests of the province. On this tacit understanding we have acted together harmoniously up to this time, although I have never concealed from them that I intend to do nothing which may prevent me from working cordially with their opponents, if they are forced upon me. That ministries and oppositions should occasionally change places is of the very essence of our constitutional system, and it is probably the most conservative element which it contains. By subjecting all sections of politicians in their turn to official responsibilities, it obliges heated partisans to place some restraint on passion and to confine within the bounds of decency the patriotic zeal with which, when out of place, they are wont to be animated. In order, however, to secure these advantages, it is indispensable that the head of the government should show that he has confidence in the loyalty of all the influential parties with which he has to deal, and that he should have no personal antipathies to prevent him from acting with leading men.

I feel very strongly that a governor general, by acting upon these views with tact and firmness, may hope to establish a moral influence in the province, which will go far to compensate for the loss of power consequent on the surrender of patronage to an executive responsible to the local parliament. Until, however, the functions of his office, under our amended colonial constitution, are more clearly defined—until that middle term which shall reconcile the faithful discharge of his responsibility to the imperial government and the province with the maintenance of the quasi-monarchical relation in which he now stands towards the community over which he presides be discovered and agreed upon—he must be content to tread along a path which is somewhat narrow and slippery, and to find that incessant watchfulness and some dexterity are requisite to prevent him from falling,

---

[7] Lord Elgin was governor general of Canada (1847-54).

on the one side into the *néant* of mock sovereignty, or on the other into the dirt and confusion of local factions.

Walrond, Letters of Elgin, pp. 40 f.

(H) LETTER OF GREY TO ELGIN (22 FEBRUARY 1848)

... I can have no doubt that you must accept such a council as the newly elected parliament will support and that, however unwise as relates to the real interests of Canada their measures may be, they must be acquiesced in, until it shall pretty clearly appear that public opinion will support a resistance to them. There is no middle course between this line of policy and that which involves in the last resort an appeal to parliament to overrule the wishes of the Canadians—and this I agree with both Gladstone and Stanley in thinking impracticable. If we overrule the local legislature, we must be prepared to support our authority by force; and, in the present state of the world and of Canada, he must in my opinion be an insane politician who would think of doing so. It does not, however, follow that you are by any means powerless; if your advisers insist upon an improper course of proceeding, the line to take is freely to place before them the objections of it, but to yield if they insist up to the point when they have put themselves so clearly in the wrong that public opinion will support you in resistance, taking the greatest care to carry concession to them as far as possible.

Bell and Morrell, Select Documents, p. 107.

(I) DISPATCH OF ELGIN TO NEWCASTLE (26 MARCH 1853)[8]

... It is argued that, by the severance of the connection, British statesmen would be relieved of an onerous responsibility for colonial acts of which they cannot otherwise rid themselves. Is there not, however, some fallacy in this? If, by conceding absolute independence, the British parliament can acquit itself of the obligation to impose its will upon the colonists in the matter, for instance, of a church establishment, can it not attain the same end by declaring that, as respects such local questions, the colonists are free to judge for themselves? How can it be justifiable to adopt the former of these expedients, and so sacrilegious to act upon the latter?

The true policy, in my humble judgment, is to throw the whole weight of responsibility on those who exercise the real power—for, after all, the sense of responsibility is the best security against the abuse of power—and, as respects the connection, to act and speak on this hypothesis, that there is nothing in it to check the development of healthy national life in these young communities. I believe that this policy will be found to be not only the safest, but also—an important consideration in these days—the most economical. ...

Walrond, Letters of Elgin, pp. 121 f.

---

[8] The duke of Newcastle was secretary of state for war and the colonies.

133. RECORDS CONCERNING CANADA

(J) THE GALT MEMORANDUM (1859)[9]

Report of the Rt. Hon. A. T. Galt to the duke of Newcastle. The minister of finance has the honour respectfully to submit certain remarks and statements upon the dispatch of his grace the duke of Newcastle, dated 13 August, and upon the memorial of the chamber of commerce of Sheffield, dated 1 August transmitted therewith.

It is to be deeply regretted that his grace should have given to so great a degree the weight of his sanction to the statements in the memorial, without having previously afforded to the government of Canada the opportunity of explaining the fiscal policy of the province and the grounds upon which it rests. The representations upon which his grace appears to have formed his opinions are those of a provincial town in England, professedly actuated by selfish motives; and it may fairly be claimed for Canada that the deliberate acts of its legislature, representing nearly three millions of people, should not have been condemned by the imperial government on such authority until the fullest opportunity of explanation had been afforded. It is believed that nothing in the legislation of Canada warrants the expressions of disapproval which are contained in the dispatch of his grace, but that on the contrary due regard has been had to the welfare and prosperity of her majesty's Canadian subjects.

From expressions used by his grace in reference to the sanction of the Provincial Customs Act, it would appear that he had even entertained the suggestion of its disallowance. And though happily her majesty has not been so advised, yet—the question having been thus raised, and the consequences of such a step, if ever adopted, being of the most serious character—it becomes the duty of the provincial government distinctly to state what they consider to be the position and rights of the Canadian legislature.

Respect to the imperial government must always dictate the desire to satisfy them that the policy of this country is neither hastily nor unwisely formed, and that due regard is had to the interests of the mother country as well as of the province. But the government of Canada acting for its legislature and people cannot, through those feelings of deference which they owe to the imperial authorities, in any manner waive or diminish the right of the people of Canada to decide for themselves both as to the mode and extent to which taxation shall be imposed. The provincial ministry are at all times ready to afford explanations in regard to the acts of the legislature to which they are party; but, subject to their duty and allegiance to her majesty, their responsibility in all general questions of policy must be to the provincial parliament, by whose confidence they administer the affairs of the country. And in the imposition of taxation it is so plainly necessary that the administration and the people

[9] Sir Alexander Galt, minister of finance in the Canadian government, here answers a British protest against the tariff bill prepared by him and recently passed by the Canadian parliament.

should be in accord, that the former cannot admit responsibility or require approval beyond that of the local legislature. Self-government would be utterly annihilated if the views of the imperial government were to be preferred to those of the people of Canada. It is, therefore, the duty of the present government distinctly to affirm the right of the Canadian legislature to adjust the taxation of the people in the way they deem best, even if it should unfortunately happen to meet the disapproval of the imperial ministry. Her majesty cannot be advised to disallow such acts, unless her advisers are prepared to assume the administration of the affairs of the colony irrespective of the views of its inhabitants.

The imperial government are not responsible for the debts and engagements of Canada. They do not maintain its judicial, educational, or civil service; they contribute nothing to the internal government of the country; and the provincial legislature, acting through a ministry directly responsible to it, has to make provision for all these wants. They must necessarily claim and exercise the widest latitude as to the nature and extent of the burdens to be placed upon the industry of the people. The provincial government believes that his grace must share their own convictions on this important subject; but, as serious evil would have resulted had his grace taken a different course, it is wiser to prevent future complication by distinctly stating the position that must be maintained by every Canadian administration. . . .

Parliamentary Papers, 1864, no. 400, pp. 11 f.

134. RECORDS OF JUDICIAL CASES (1832-76)

(A) CHARGE TO THE BRISTOL GRAND JURY (1832)[1]

It has been well said, that the use of the law consists, first, in preserving men's persons from death and violence; next, in securing to them the free enjoyment of their property. And although every single act of violence and each individual breach of the law tends to counteract and destroy this, its primary use and object, yet do general risings and tumultuous meetings of the people in a more especial and particular manner produce this effect—not only removing all security, both from the persons and property of men, but for the time putting down the law itself and daring to usurp its place. The law of England hath accordingly, in proportion to the danger which it attaches to riotous and disorderly meetings of the people, made ample provision for preventing such offences and for the prompt and effectual suppression of them whenever they arise; and I think it may not be unsuitable to the present occasion, if I proceed to call

---

[1] On the occasion of the reform bill serious rioting had broken out at Bristol, and to try persons arrested in that connection a special commission had been set up by the government. As head of the commission, Chief Justice Tindal gave the following charge to the local grand jury.

your attention, with some degree of detail, to the various provisions
of the law for carrying that purpose into effect.

In the first place, by the common law, every private person may
lawfully endeavour, of his own authority, and without any warrant
or sanction of the magistrate, to suppress a riot by every means in
his power. He may disperse, or assist in dispersing, those who are
assembled; he may stay those who are engaged in it from executing
their purpose; he may stop and prevent others whom he shall see
coming up from joining the rest. And not only has he the authority,
but it is his bounden duty as a good subject of the king, to perform
this to the utmost of his ability. If the riot be general and dangerous,
he may arm himself against the evil-doers to keep the peace. . . . If
the occasion demands immediate action, and no opportunity is given
for procuring the advice or sanction of the magistrate, it is the
duty of every subject to act for himself and upon his own responsibility in suppressing a riotous and tumultuous assembly; and he may
be assured that whatever is honestly done by him in the execution
of that object will be supported and justified by the common law.
And whilst I am stating the obligation imposed by the law on every
subject of the realm, I wish to observe that the law acknowledges no
distinction in this respect between the soldier and the private individual. The soldier is still a citizen, lying under the same obligation
and invested with the same authority to preserve the peace of the
king as any other subject. . . .

Still further, by the common law, not only is each private subject
bound to exert himself to the utmost, but every sheriff, constable, and
other peace officer is called upon to do all that in them lies for the
suppression of riot, and each has authority to command all other
subjects of the king to assist them in that undertaking. . . . And
here I most distinctly observe that it is not left to the choice or will
of the subject, as some have erroneously supposed, to attend or not
to the call of the magistrate as they think proper; but every man is
bound when called upon, under pain of fine and imprisonment, to
yield a ready and implicit obedience to the call of the magistrate,
and to do his utmost in assisting him to suppress any tumultuous
assembly. . . .

In later times the course has been for the magistrate, on occasions
of actual riot and confusion, to call in the aid of such persons as he
thought necessary, and to swear them as special constables. . . .
Again, that this call of the magistrate is compulsory, and not left
to the choice of the party to obey or not, appears from the express
enactment . . . that, if he disobeys, unless legally exempted, he is
liable to the penalties and punishments therein specified. But the
most important provision of the law for the suppression of riots is to
be found in the statute 1 George I, st. 2, c. 5, by which it is enacted. . . .[2]

---

[2] No. 122A.

Such are the different provisions of the law of England for the putting down of tumultuary meetings; and it is not too much to affirm that, if the means provided by the law are promptly and judiciously enforced by the magistrate and honestly seconded by the co-operation of his fellow subjects, very few and rare would be the instances in which tumultuous assemblages of the people would be able to hold defiance to the laws.

Carrington and Payne, *Reports,* V, 556 note.

(B) STOCKDALE v. HANSARD (1839)[3]

Lord Denman, C. J.: This was an action for a publication defaming the plaintiff's character by imputing that he had published an obscene libel. The plea was that the inspectors of prisons made a report to the secretary of state, in which improper books were said to be permitted in the prison of Newgate; that the court of aldermen wrote an answer to that part of the report and the inspectors replied, repeating the statements and adding that the improper books were published by the plaintiff; that all these documents were printed by and under orders from the house of commons. . . .

The plea, it is contended, establishes a good defence to the action on various grounds. (1) The grievance complained of appears to be an act done by order of the house of commons, a court superior to any court of law, and none of whose proceedings are to be questioned in any way. . . . It is a claim for an arbitrary power to authorize the commission of any act whatever on behalf of a body which in the same argument is admitted not to be the supreme power in the state. The supremacy of parliament, the foundation on which the claim is made to rest, appears to me completely to overturn it; because the house of commons is not the parliament, but only a co-ordinate and component part of the parliament. That sovereign power can make and unmake the laws, but the concurrence of the three legislative estates is necessary; the resolution of any one of them cannot alter the law or place any one beyond its control. The proposition is therefore wholly untenable and abhorrent to the first principles of the constitution of England.

(2) The next defence involved in this plea is that the defendant committed the grievance by order of the house of commons in a case of privilege, and that each house of parliament is the sole judge of its own privileges. This last proposition requires to be first considered. For, if the attorney general was right in contending—as he

---

[3] This was a suit brought in the court of queen's bench by Stockdale, a publisher, against James Hansard and others, a firm which had been employed by the house of commons to print various papers. Among the latter was a report of certain prison commissioners, declaring that a book published by Stockdale, though purporting to be of a scientific nature, was indecent and obscene. The principal issues in the case are reviewed in the opinions of Chief Justice Denman and Judge Patteson, which in part follow. The court ruled for the plaintiff.

did more than once in express terms—that the house of commons, by claiming anything as its privilege, thereby makes it a matter of privilege, and also that its own decision upon its own claim is binding and conclusive, then plainly this court cannot proceed in any inquiry into the matter, and has nothing else to do but declare the claim well founded because it has been made.

This is the form in which I understand the committee of a late house of commons to have asserted the privileges of both houses of parliament; and we are informed that a large majority of that house adopted the assertion. It is not without the utmost respect and deference that I proceed to examine what has been promulgated by such high authority; most willingly would I decline to enter upon an inquiry which may lead to my differing from that great and powerful assembly. But, when one of my fellow subjects presents himself before me in this court, demanding justice for an injury, it is not at all at my option to grant or withhold redress; I am bound to afford it if the law declares him entitled to it. I must then ascertain how the law stands, and, whatever defence may be made for the wrongdoer, I must examine its validity. The learned counsel for the defendant contends for his legal right to be protected against all consequences of acting under an order issued by the house of commons in conformity with what that house asserts to be its privilege; nor can I avoid, then, the question whether the defendant possesses that legal right or not. . . .[4]

In truth, no practical difference can be drawn between the right to sanction all things under the name of privilege and the right to sanction all things whatever by merely ordering them to be done. The second proposition differs from the first in words only. In both cases the law would be superseded by one assembly; and, however dignified and respectable that body, in whatever degree superior to all temptations of abusing their power, the power claimed is arbitrary and irresponsible, in itself the most monstrous and intolerable of all abuses. . . .

(3) I come at length to consider whether this privilege of publication exists. The plea states the resolution of the house that all parliamentary reports printed for the use of the house should be sold to the public and that these several papers were ordered to be printed, not however stating that they were printed for the use of the house. . . . The difference between the extent of publication formerly practised and the uncontrolled sale of all that the house may choose to print in order to raise a fund for paying its officers cannot fail to strike every unbiased understanding. I must add that the evidence on this subject set forth in the report convinces me that publication has never been by way of exercising any of its privileges, nor the fruit

---

[4] The chief justice here enters into a long consideration of cases involving parliamentary privilege in the past, including the Aylesbury election cases (no. 124C, D).

of deliberation to what extent it ought to be carried and within what bounds restrained. With very different objects the practice was originally introduced; it grew imperceptibly into a perquisite; and I venture to believe that it was raised into a traffic and a means of levying money without much consideration. . . .

I am of opinion, upon the whole case, that the defence pleaded is no defence in law, and that our judgment must be for the plaintiff. . . .

Patteson, J.: . . . It is further argued that the courts of law are inferior courts to the court of parliament and to the court of the house of commons, and cannot form any judgment as to the acts and resolutions of their superiors. I admit fully that the court of parliament is superior to the courts of law, and in that sense they are inferior courts; but the house of commons by itself is not the court of parliament. Further, I admit that the house of commons, being one branch of the legislature to which legislature belongs the making of laws, is superior in dignity to the courts of law, to whom it belongs to carry those laws into effect and, in so doing, of necessity to interpret and ascertain the meaning of those laws. It is superior also in this, that it is the grand inquest of the nation and may inquire into all alleged abuses and misconduct in any quarter . . . ; but it cannot, by itself, correct or punish any such abuses or misconduct. It can but accuse or institute proceedings against the supposed delinquents in some court of law or, conjointly with the other branches of the legislature, may remedy the mischief by a new law. With respect to the interpretation and declaration of what is the existing law, the house of lords is doubtless a superior court to the courts of law. And those courts are bound by a decision of the house of lords expressed judicially upon a writ of error or appeal in a regular action at law or suit in equity. But I deny that a mere resolution of the house of lords, or even a decision of that house in a suit originally brought there—if any such thing should occur, which it never will, though formerly attempted—would be binding upon the courts of law, even if it were accompanied by a resolution that they had power to entertain original suits. Much less can a resolution of the house of commons, which is not a court of judicature for the decision of any question either of law or fact between litigant parties except in regard to the election of its members, be binding upon the courts of law. And it should be observed that, in making this resolution, the house of commons was not acting as a court either legislative, judicial, or inquisitorial, or of any other description. . . .

Upon the whole, the true doctrine appears to me to be this: that every court in which an action is brought upon a subject matter generally and *prima facie* within its jurisdiction, and in which by the course of the proceedings in that action the powers and privileges and jurisdiction of another court come into question, must of necessity determine as to the extent of those powers, privileges, and jurisdiction; that the decisions of that court whose powers, privileges, and jurisdiction are so brought into question, as to their extent, are authorities and, if I may so say, evidences in law upon the subject but not conclusive. In the present case, therefore, both upon principle and authority, I conceive that this court is not precluded by the resolution of the house of commons of May, 1837, from inquiring into the legality of the act complained of, although we are bound to treat that resolution with all possible respect, and not by any means to come to a decision contrary to that resolution unless we find ourselves compelled to do so by the law of the land, gathered from the principles of the common law, so far as they are applicable to the case, and from the authority of decided cases and the judgments of our predecessors, if any be found which bear upon the question. . . .

Privileges—that is, immunities and safeguards—are necessary for the protection of the house of commons in the exercise of its high functions. All the subjects of this realm have derived, are deriving, and I trust and believe will continue to derive, the greatest benefits from the exercise of those functions. All persons ought to be very tender in preserving to the house all privileges which may be necessary for their exercise, and to place the most implicit confidence in their representatives as to the due exercise of those privileges. But power, and especially the power of invading the rights of others, is a very different thing. It is to be regarded, not with tenderness, but with jealousy; and, unless the legality of it be most clearly established, those who act under it must be answerable for the consequences. The onus of showing the existence and legality of the power now claimed lies upon the defendants. It appears to me, after a full and anxious consideration of the reasons and authorities adduced by the attorney general in his learned argument, and after much reflection upon the subject, that they have entirely failed to do so. And I am therefore of opinion that the plaintiff is entitled to our judgment in his favour.

Adolphus and Ellis, *Reports,* IX, 78-214.

(C) The Case of the Sheriff of Middlesex (1840)[5]

The only question upon the present return is whether the commitment is sustained by a legal warrant. Three objections have been taken to the warrant in point of form merely. . . . The verbal criticisms therefore fall to the ground. The great objection remains behind,

---

[5] As a consequence of the judgment in Stockdale v. Hansard (the case preceding), the sheriff of Middlesex sought to execute a writ whereby Stockdale might collect the damages awarded by the court. The house of commons then issued a warrant ordering the imprisonment of the sheriff, "as having been guilty of a contempt and breach of the privileges of this house." The legality of the imprisonment came before the court of queen's bench through *habeas corpus* proceedings on behalf of the sheriff. The judgment, as delivered by Chief Justice Denman, in part follows.

that the facts which constitute the alleged contempt are not shown by the warrant....

It is unnecessary to discuss the question whether each house of parliament be or be not a court; it is clear that they cannot exercise their proper functions without the power of protecting themselves against interference.... And we must presume that what any court, much more what either house of parliament, acting on great legal authority, takes upon it to pronounce a contempt is so.... On the motion for a *habeas corpus* there must be an affidavit from the party applying; but the return, if it discloses a sufficient answer, puts an end to the case. And I think the production of a good warrant is a sufficient answer. Seeing that, we cannot go into the question of contempt on affidavit nor discuss the motives which may be alleged. Indeed, as the courts have said in some of the cases, it would be unseemly to suspect that a body, acting under such sanctions as a house of parliament, would in making its warrant suppress facts which, if discussed, might entitle the person committed to his liberty. If they ever did act so, I am persuaded that, on further consideration, they would repudiate such a course of proceeding....

In the present case I am obliged to say that I find no authority under which we are entitled to discharge these gentlemen[6] from their imprisonment.

Ibid., XI, 287-92.

(D) Wason v. Walter (1868)[7]

The main question for our decision is whether a faithful report in a public newspaper of a debate in either house of parliament, containing matter disparaging to the character of an individual, as having been spoken in the course of the debate, is actionable at the suit of the party whose character has thus been called in question. We are of opinion that it is not.

Important as the question is, it comes now for the first time before a court of law for decision. Numerous as are the instances in which the conduct and character of individuals have been called in question in parliament during the many years that parliamentary debates have been reported in the public journals, this is the first instance in which an action of libel founded on a report of a parliamentary debate has

---

[6] Two men holding the one office of sheriff.

[7] In the course of a debate in the house of lords over the presentation of a petition, Lord Derby, the prime minister, declared the petition was "slanderous, calumnious, and unfounded." Walter printed an accurate account of the debate in the London *Times*, together with editorial comment upon it. Thereupon Wason, the author of the petition, sued Walter for libel. In the ensuing trial the jury rendered a verdict for Walter, and Wason then sought an order for a new trial from the court of queen's bench. This court refused, on the grounds stated by Chief Justice Cockburn in the following judgment.

come before a court of law. There is, therefore, a total absence of
direct authority to guide us. . . . Decided cases thus leaving us
without authority on which to proceed in the present instance, we
must have recourse to principle in order to arrive at a solution of
the question before us, and fortunately we have not far to seek before we find principles in our opinion applicable to the case, and which
will afford a safe and sure foundation for our judgment.

It is now well established that faithful and fair reports of the
proceedings of courts of justice, though the character of individuals
may incidentally suffer, are privileged, and that for the publication of
such reports the publishers are neither criminally nor civilly responsible. The immunity thus afforded in respect of the publication of the
proceedings of courts of justice rests upon a twofold ground. In the
English law of libel, malice is said to be the gist of an action for
defamation. . . . It is thus that in the case of reports of proceedings
of courts of justice, though individuals may occasionally suffer from
them, yet, as they are published without any reference to the individuals concerned, but solely to afford information to the public and
for the benefit of society, the presumption of malice is rebutted and
such publications are held to be privileged. The other and the broader
principle on which this exception to the general law of libel is
founded is that the advantage to the community from publicity being
given to the proceedings of courts of justice is so great that the occasional inconvenience to individuals arising from it must yield to the
general good . . .

Both the principles on which the exemption from legal consequences is thus extended to the publication of the proceedings of
courts of justice appear to us to be applicable to the case before
us. . . . It seems to us impossible to doubt that it is of paramount
public and national importance that the proceedings of the houses of
parliament shall be communicated to the public, who have the deepest
interest in knowing what passes within their walls, seeing that on
what is there said and done the welfare of the community depends.
Where would be our confidence in the government of the country . . . where would be our attachment to the constitution under
which we live—if the proceedings of the great council of the realm
were shrouded in secrecy and concealed from the knowledge of the
nation? How could the communications between the representatives
of the people and their constituents, which are so essential to the
working of the representative system, be usefully carried on if the
constituencies were kept in ignorance of what their representatives
are doing? What would become of the right of petitioning on all
measures pending in parliament, the undoubted right of the subject,
if the people are to be kept in ignorance of what is passing in either
house? Can any man bring himself to doubt that the publicity given in
modern times to what passes in parliament is essential to the maintenance of the relations subsisting between the government, the legislature, and the country at large? It may, no doubt, be said that, while

it may be necessary as a matter of national interest that the proceedings of parliament should in general be made public, yet that debates in which the character of individuals is brought into question ought to be suppressed. But to this, in addition to the difficulty in which parties publishing parliamentary reports would be placed, if this distinction were to be enforced and every debate had to be critically scanned to see whether it contained defamatory matter, it may be further answered that there is perhaps no subject in which the public have a deeper interest than in all that relates to the conduct of public servants of the state—no subject of parliamentary discussion which more requires to be made known than an inquiry relating to it. Of this no better illustration could possibly be given than is afforded by the case before us. A distinguished counsel (Sir Fitzroy Kelly), whose qualification for the judicial bench had been abundantly tested by a long career of forensic eminence, is promoted to a high judicial office, and the profession and the public are satisfied that in a most important post the services of a most competent and valuable public servant have been secured. An individual comes forward and calls upon the house of lords to take measures for removing the judge, in all other respects so well qualified for his office, by reason that on an important occasion he had exhibited so total a disregard of truth as to render him unfit to fill an office for which a sense of the solemn obligations of truth and honour is an essential qualification. Can it be said that such a subject is not one in which the public has a deep interest, and as to which it ought not to be informed of what passes in debate? Lastly, what greater anomaly or more flagrant injustice could present itself than that, while from a sense of the importance of giving publicity to their proceedings, the houses of parliament not only sanction the reporting of their debates, but also take measures for giving facility to those who report them, while every member of the educated portion of the community from the highest to the lowest looks with eager interest to the debates of either house, and considers it a part of the duty of the public journals to furnish an account of what passes there, we were to hold that a party publishing a parliamentary debate is to be held liable to legal proceedings because the conduct of a particular individual may happen to be called in question? . . .

Whatever disadvantages attach to a system of unwritten law—and of these we are fully sensible—it has at least this advantage, that its elasticity enables those who administer it to adapt it to the varying conditions of society . . . , so as to avoid the inconsistencies and injustice which arise when the law is no longer in harmony with the wants and usages and interests of the generation to which it is immediately applied. Our law of libel has, in many respects, only gradually developed itself into anything like a satisfactory and settled form. The full liberty of public writers to comment on the conduct and motives of public men has only in very recent times been recognized. Comments on government, on ministers and officers of state, on members of both houses of parliament, on judges and other public functionaries, are now made every day, which half a century ago would have . . . brought down fine and imprisonment on publishers and authors. . . . Again, the recognition of the right to publish the proceedings of courts of justice has been of modern growth. Till a comparatively recent time the sanction of the judges was thought necessary even for the publication of the decisions of the courts upon points of law. . . .

It is to be observed that, the analogy between the case of reports of proceedings of courts of justice and those of proceedings in parliament being complete, all the limitations placed on the one to prevent injustice to individuals will necessarily attach on the other. A garbled or partial report, or of detached parts of proceedings, published with intent to injure individuals, will equally be disentitled to protection.

It only remains to advert to an argument urged against the legality of the publication of parliamentary proceedings: namely, that such publication is illegal as being in contravention of the standing orders of both houses of parliament. The fact no doubt is that each house of parliament does, by its standing orders, prohibit the publication of its debates. But practically each house not only permits but also sanctions and encourages the publication of its proceedings, and actually gives every facility to those who report them. Individual members correct their speeches for publication in Hansard or the public journals, and in every debate reports of former speeches contained therein are constantly referred to. Collectively, as well as individually, the members of both houses would deplore as a national misfortune the withholding their debates from the country at large. Practically speaking, therefore, it is idle to say that the publication of parliamentary proceedings is prohibited by parliament. The standing orders which prohibit it are obviously maintained only to give to each house the control over the publication of its proceedings, and the power of preventing or correcting any abuse of the facility afforded. Independently of the orders of the houses, there is nothing unlawful in publishing reports of parliamentary proceedings. Practically, such publication is sanctioned by parliament; it is essential to the working of our parliamentary system and to the welfare of the nation. Any argument founded on its alleged illegality appears to us, therefore, entirely to fail. . . .

Law Reports, Queen's Bench, IV, 73 f.

(E) RUSTOMJEE V. THE QUEEN (1876)[8]

The making of peace and the making of war, as they are the undoubted, so they are perhaps the highest, acts of the prerogative of

---

[8] The plaintiff asserted that a Chinese firm had owed him a large sum of money; that the justice of this claim had been recognized by agents of the English government; that, by a treaty made between the queen of England and the emperor of China, $3,000,000 had been paid by the latter to meet

the crown. The terms on which peace is made are in the absolute discretion of the sovereign. If Captain Elliot did . . . promise that the queen would compel the Chinese government to pay these claims when terms of peace were arranged, if Sir Henry Pottinger did promise that these claims should be insisted on and should be paid, they both exceeded their authority and promised what they had no power to perform or to pledge the queen to perform. The queen might or not, as she thought fit, have made peace at all; she might or not, as she thought fit, have insisted on this money being paid her. She acted throughout the making of the treaty and in relation to each and every of its stipulations in her sovereign character and by her own inherent authority; and as in making the treaty, so in performing the treaty, she is beyond the control of municipal law, and her acts are not to be examined in her own courts. It is a treaty between herself as sovereign, and the emperor of China as sovereign; and though he might complain of the infraction, if infraction there were, of its provisions, her subjects cannot. We do not say that under no circumstances can the crown be a trustee; we do not even say that under no circumstances can the crown be an agent; but it seems clear to us that in all that relates to the making and performance of a treaty with another sovereign the crown is not, and cannot be, either a trustee or an agent for any subject whatever.

We do not, indeed, doubt that, on the payment of the money by the emperor of China, there was a duty on the part of the English sovereign to administer the money so received according to the stipulations of the treaty. But it was a duty to do justice to her subjects according to the advice of her responsible ministers; not the duty of an agent . . . or of a trustee. . . . If there has been a failure to perform that duty, which we only suggest for the sake of argument, it is one which parliament can and will correct; not one with which the courts of law can deal. . . .

Law Reports, Queen's Bench Division, II, 73 f.

---

the claims of such merchants as were then owed money by Chinese; and that, accordingly, he was entitled to reimbursement by the queen. The case was taken from the court of queen's bench to the court of appeal. The following excerpt is from the judgment delivered by Chief Justice Coleridge.

SECTION XIV

VICTORIA (1880) TO GEORGE VI

A GLANCE at the contents of this final section can hardly fail to give an impression of remarkable legislative progress. And the impression will be strengthened when it is realized that only a meagre selection of important acts is included here—most of them in skeleton form. The work accomplished by the British parliament since 1880 has indeed been astonishing, not only in its bulk and variety, but also in its revolutionary character. Almost without exception the radical statutes of the previous fifty years have been superseded by others, infinitely more radical. For example, Disraeli's reform of parliament was first supplemented by Gladstone's measures of 1884-85 (no. 135A, B), and then entirely replaced by the Representation of the People Act of 1918. This in turn was amended by conferring complete equality of suffrage upon women (no. 137K). Meanwhile the constitution of parliament had been altered by three other measures: one curtailing the ancient powers of the upper house, another permitting a member of the lower house to accept office under the crown without seeking re-election, and a third granting certain legislative powers to a Church of England assembly (no. 137A, E, G).

Equally great changes were made in local government by devising, after the pattern of municipal corporations, a uniform system of elected county councils and giving them the administration of the poor law, the care of public health, and numerous other functions (nos. 135D, 137L). But this was only one of many ways whereby the state was attempting to improve the material welfare of the people. Measures such as the Allotments Act of 1887 authorized boroughs to acquire land and build houses for occupation by labourers. Ten years later the Workmen's Compensation Act inaugurated a programme of social insurance, which in 1911 was extended to provide security against unemployment and sickness (no. 137B). The Trade Disputes Act of 1906 modified the law for the benefit of labour unions—and so much so that in 1927 it was felt necessary to curb their political influence (no. 137J).

These, it should be remembered, are merely scattered examples of parliament's increasing activity in the economic sphere—a socialistic tendency that has enormously widened the scope of the British government and has constantly imposed heavier burdens on its officials, both central and local. The routine work of administering the state has, in fact, grown so rapidly that much of it has had to be delegated to a variety of departments, commissions, and boards. And under the pressure of war or other emergencies, broad discretionary authority has been conferred on the executive (no. 137C, H). The creation of such agencies, ordinary or extraordinary, has inevitably raised many new questions of constitutional law, some of which are discussed in the reports of cases numbered 139B-E.

Of much greater concern to British subjects throughout the world has been the problem of imperial organization. Following the precedent set by the British North America Act of 1867, parliament in 1900 established the commonwealth of Australia, and in 1909 the union of South Africa. The constitutions of both dominions (nos. 135F, 136B) are here given in outline because the former, though federal, differs greatly from that of Canada, while the latter is fundamentally unlike the other two in not being federal at all. No attempt, however, has been made to set forth the complicated history of the Irish Free State, aside from presenting the agreement by which the dominion was first recognized and the judgment acknowledging its complete autonomy (nos. 137 I, 139F)—an inevitable decision, once the recommendations of the imperial conference had been incorporated in the momentous Statute of Westminster (nos. 140, 137M).

In this section, as in those preceding, it has been impossible to trace the devious course of party politics. But a few vivid glimpses of the rival leaders in parliament can be obtained from no. 138, as well as a direct introduction to several famous controversies of the twentieth century. Still more recent developments are illustrated by the closing extracts in the book. No. 141 is a picture—no less graphic because it is official—of the British government in 1936. No. 142 contains, not only a very important statute, but also the most intimate account of the relations between king and cabinet that has ever appeared in a formal record. And it is wholly fitting that a volume dealing with English constitutional history should end with a document emphasizing its continuity. Despite all change of form, the coronation oath of

George VI remains substantially that of William and Mary, of Edward II, and of Edgar (nos. 120C, 55, 10).

Little by way of special bibliography needs to be given for this section. The following works, as distinguished from those cited above (p. 722), deal more particularly with recent developments: M. Amos, *The English Constitution;* F. A. Ogg, *English Government and Politics;* R. Muir, *How Britain is Governed;* W. I. Jennings, *Cabinet Government;* A. B. Keith, *The King and the Imperial Crown;* F. J. Port, *Administrative Law;* G. B. Adams, *Constitutional History of England* (concluding chapters in the revised edition by R. L. Schuyler).

135. VICTORIA: STATUTES (1884-1900)

(A) Representation of the People Act (1884)

An act to amend the law relating to the representation of the people of the united kingdom. Be it enacted . . . as follows:—

A uniform household franchise and a uniform lodger franchise at elections shall be established in all counties and boroughs throughout the united kingdom, and every man possessed of a household qualification or a lodger qualification shall, if the qualifying premises be situate in a county in England or Scotland, be entitled to be registered as a voter and when registered to vote at an election for such county; and if the qualifying premises be situate in a county or borough in Ireland, be entitled to be registered as a voter and when registered to vote at an election for such county or borough. . . .

Every man occupying any land or tenement in a county or borough in the united kingdom of a clear yearly value of not less than £10 shall be entitled to be registered as a voter and when registered to vote at an election for such county or borough in respect of such occupation subject to the like conditions respectively as a man is, at the passing of this act, entitled to be registered as a voter and to vote at an election for such county in respect of the county occupation franchise, and at an election for such borough in respect of the borough occupation franchise.

In this act the expression "a household qualification" means, as respects England and Ireland, the qualification enacted by the third section of the Representation of the People Act, 1867. . . .[1]

Public General Statutes, XXI, 3 f.: 48 Victoria, c. 3.

(B) Redistribution of Seats Act (1885)

An act for the redistribution of seats at parliamentary elections and for other purposes. Be it enacted . . . as follows:—

---

[1] No. 131H.

... From and after the end of this present parliament, the parliamentary boroughs named in the first part of the first schedule to this act shall cease as boroughs to return any member. Each of the counties of cities and towns in the second part of the said schedule named shall, for the purpose of parliamentary elections, be included in the county at large named opposite thereto. . . .[2]

From and after the end of this present parliament, the city of London shall return two members and no more, and each of the parliamentary boroughs named in the second schedule to this act shall return one member and no more.[3]

From and after the end of this present parliament each of the parliamentary boroughs named in the third schedule to this act shall return the number of members named opposite to such borough. . . .[4]

From and after the end of this present parliament, each of the towns and places named in the fourth schedule to this act shall be a parliamentary borough and return the number of members specified. . . .[5]

From and after the end of this present parliament, each of the parliamentary boroughs named in the fifth schedule to this act shall, for all purposes of and relating to parliamentary elections, include the places and be comprised within the boundaries which are respectively specified and described in the said schedule. . . .[6]

From and after the end of this present parliament, each of the parliamentary boroughs mentioned in the sixth schedule to this act shall, for the purpose of returning members . . . , be divided into divisions. The number of members for each division and the number, names, contents, and boundaries of such divisions respectively shall be those specified in the said schedule. . . .[7]

From and after the end of this present parliament, each of the counties at large named in the seventh schedule to this act shall return the number of members in that behalf named in the said schedule; and for the purpose of returning such members, if more than one, shall be divided into the same number of divisions as the number of members. . . .[8]

Ibid., XXI, 128 f.: 48-49 Victoria, c. 23.

(C) ALLOTMENTS ACT (1887)

An act to facilitate the provision of allotments for the labouring classes. Be it enacted . . . as follows:—

---

[2] The first part lists 103 boroughs; the second part lists five counties.
[3] Thirty-nine boroughs are named.
[4] Nineteen boroughs are named with from two to nine members each.
[5] Thirty-three towns and places are named, with from one to four members each. Some of these new boroughs were really extensions of old parliamentary boroughs.
[6] Forty-six old boroughs are given new boundaries.
[7] Here is given a list of single member districts for the large boroughs.
[8] Here is given a list of the counties with their divisions.

On a representation in writing to the sanitary authority of any urban or rural district by any six registered parliamentary electors or ratepayers . . . that the circumstances of the urban district or parish are such that it is the duty of the sanitary authority to take proceedings under this act therein, the sanitary authority shall take such representation into consideration. If the sanitary authority of any urban or rural district are of opinion, either after inquiry made in consequence of such representation or otherwise, that there is a demand for allotments for the labouring population in such urban district, or in any parish in such rural district, and that such allotments cannot be obtained at a reasonable rent and on reasonable conditions by voluntary arrangement between the owners of land suitable for such allotments and the applicants for the same, the sanitary authority, subject to the provisions of this act, shall by purchase or hire acquire any suitable land which may be available . . . , and shall let such land in allotments to persons belonging to the labouring population resident in the said district or parish and desiring to take the same. A sanitary authority shall not under this act acquire land for allotments save at such price or rent that, in the opinion of the sanitary authority, all expenses . . . incurred by the sanitary authority in acquiring the land and otherwise in relation to the allotments may reasonably be expected to be recouped out of the rents obtained in respect thereof. . . .

If a sanitary authority are unable by hiring or purchase by agreement to acquire suitable land sufficient for allotments under this act for any district or parish at a reasonable price or rent and subject to reasonable conditions, such authority may petition the county authority . . . and the county authority may make a provisional order authorizing the sanitary authority to put in force, as respects the land mentioned in the order, the provisions of the Lands Clauses Consolidation Act, 1845. . . .[9]

Subject to the provisions of this act, the sanitary authority may from time to time make, revoke, and vary such regulations as appear to be necessary or proper for regulating the letting of allotments under this act, and for preventing any undue preference in the letting thereof, and generally for carrying the provisions of this act into effect. . . . Provided . . . that all regulations made under this section shall not be of any force unless and until they have been confirmed by the local government board. . . .

Where allotments have been provided under this act for a parish in any rural district, a petition to the sanitary authority may be presented by a number of the electors of allotment managers in such parish, not being less than one sixth of the whole number of such electors, praying for the election of allotment managers in such parish, and thereupon the sanitary authority shall order such

---

[9] That is to say, the sanitary authority might take the necessary land, leaving the price to be determined by arbitration.

election, and the allotment managers so elected shall be the allotment managers appointed by the sanitary authority, who, on an election under this act, shall cease to hold office. . . .

The electors of allotment managers shall be the parliamentary electors in the parish. . . .

Ibid., XXIV, 196 f.: 50-51 Victoria, c. 48.

(D) LOCAL GOVERNMENT ACT (1888)

An act to amend the laws relating to local government in England and Wales and for other purposes connected therewith. Be it enacted . . . as follows:—

A council shall be established in every administrative county as defined by this act and be entrusted with the management of the administrative and financial business of that county, and shall consist of the chairman, aldermen, and councillors. The council of a county and the members thereof shall be constituted and elected and conduct their proceedings in like manner and be in the like position in all respects as the council of a borough divided into wards, subject nevertheless to the provisions of this act and in particular to the following provisions. . . .

As respects the aldermen or councillors: clerks in holy orders and other ministers of religion shall not be disqualified for being elected . . . ; a person shall be qualified . . . who . . . is a peer owning property in the county or is registered as a parliamentary voter in respect of the ownership of property of whatsoever tenure situate in the county . . . ; the county councillors shall be elected for a term of three years . . . ; the divisions of the county for the purpose of the election of county councillors shall be called electoral divisions . . . and one county councillor only shall be elected for each electoral division.

As respects the number of the county councillors and the boundaries of the electoral divisions in every county: the number of the county councillors and their apportionment . . . shall be such as the local government board may determine; and any borough returning one councillor only shall be an electoral division; and in the rest of the county the electoral divisions shall be such as, in the case of a borough returning more than one councillor, the council of the borough and, in the rest of the county, the quarter sessions for the county may determine. . . .

As respects the electors of the county councillors: the persons entitled to vote at their election shall be, in a borough, the burgesses enrolled in pursuance of the Municipal Corporations Act, 1882, and the acts amending the same, and elsewhere the persons registered as county electors under the County Electors Act, 1888.[10]

---

[10] These acts had extended the parliamentary franchises of 1867 and 1884 to elections in boroughs and counties.

As respects the chairman of the county council: he shall . . . , by virtue of his office, be a justice of the peace for the county. . . .

There shall be transferred to the council of each county, on and after the appointed day, the administrative business of the justices of the county in quarter sessions assembled, that is to say, all business done by the quarter sessions or any committee appointed by the quarter sessions, in respect of the several matters following: namely, the making, assessing, and levying of county, police, hundred, and all rates and the application and expenditure thereof . . . ; the borrowing of money; the passing of the accounts of . . . the county treasurer; . . . county buildings, works, and property . . . ; the licensing under any general act of houses and other places for music or for dancing, and the granting of licences under the Racecourses Licensing Act, 1879; the provision, enlargement, maintenance, management, and visitation of . . . asylums for pauper lunatics; the establishment and maintenance of and the contribution to reformatory and industrial schools; bridges and roads repairable with bridges and any powers vested by the Highways and Locomotives (Amendment) Act, 1878, in the county authority . . . ; the appointment, removal, and determination of salaries of the county treasurer, the county surveyor, the public analysts . . . , and any officers whose remuneration is paid out of the county rate, other than the clerk of the peace and the clerks of the justices . . . ; the execution as local authority of the acts relating to contagious diseases of animals, to destructive insects, to fish-conservancy, to wild birds, to weights and measures, and to gas meters . . . ; any other business transferred by this act.

After the appointed day a coroner for a county shall not be elected by the freeholders of the county, and on any vacancy occurring in the office of a coroner for a county, who is elected to that office . . . , the county council shall thereupon appoint a fit person, not being a county alderman or county councillor, to fill such office, and in the case of a county divided into coroner's districts shall assign him a district. . . .

Nothing in this act shall transfer to a county council any business of the quarter sessions or justices in relation to appeals by any overseers or persons against the basis or standard for the county rate or against that or any other rate. All business of the quarter sessions or any committees thereof not transferred by or in pursuance of this act to the county council shall be reserved to and transacted by the quarter sessions or committee thereof in the same manner, as far as circumstances admit, as if this act had not passed. The powers, duties, and liabilities of quarter sessions and of justices out of session with respect to the county police shall, on and after the appointed day, vest in and attach to the quarter sessions and the county council jointly. . . . Nothing in this act shall affect the powers, duties, and liabilities of justices of the peace as conservators of the peace, or the obligation of the chief constable or other constables to obey their lawful orders given in that behalf. . . .

Each of the boroughs named in the third schedule to this act, being a borough which, on the first day of June, 1888, either had a population of not less than 50,000 or was a county of itself, shall . . . be for the purposes of this act an administrative county of itself. . . .[11] The mayor, aldermen, and burgesses of each county borough, acting by the council, shall . . . have and be subject to all the powers, duties, and liabilities of a county council under this act. . . .

Ibid., XXV, 231 f.: 51-52 Victoria, c. 41.

(E) Workmen's Compensation Act (1897)

An act to amend the law with respect to compensation to workmen for accidental injuries suffered in the course of their employment. Be it enacted . . . as follows:—

If in any employment to which this act applies personal injury by accident arising out of and in the course of the employment is caused to a workman, his employer shall, subject as hereinafter mentioned, be liable to pay compensation in accordance with the first schedule to this act. Provided that (a) the employer shall not be liable under this act in respect of any injury which does not disable the workman for a period of at least two weeks from earning full wages at the work at which he was employed; (b) when the injury was caused by the personal negligence or wilful act of the employer, or of some person for whose act or default the employer is responsible, nothing in this act shall affect any civil liability of the employer, but in that case the workman may, at his option, either claim compensation under this act, or take the same proceedings as were open to him before the commencement of this act . . . ; (c) if it is proved that the injury to a workman is attributable to the serious and wilful misconduct of that workman, any compensation claimed in respect of that injury shall be disallowed.

If any question arises in any proceedings under this act as to the liability to pay compensation under this act . . . , or as to the amount or duration of compensation under this act, the question, if not settled by agreement, shall . . . be settled by arbitration in accordance with the second schedule to this act. . . .

If the registrar of friendly societies, after taking steps to ascertain the views of the employer and workmen, certifies that any scheme of compensation, benefit, or insurance for the workmen of an employer in any employment, whether or not such scheme includes other employers and their workmen, is on the whole not less favourable to the general body of workmen and their dependants than the provisions of this act, the employer may, until the certificate is revoked, contract with any of those workmen that the provisions of the scheme shall be substituted for the provisions of this act, and thereupon the employer shall be liable only in accordance with the scheme; but, save as aforesaid, this act shall apply notwithstanding

---

[11] Sixty-one boroughs are named.

any contract to the contrary made after the commencement of this act. . . .

This act shall apply only to employment . . . on or in or about a railway, factory, mine, quarry, or engineering work, and to employment . . . on, in, or about any building which exceeds thirty feet in height and is either being constructed or repaired by means of a scaffolding, or being demolished, or on which machinery driven by steam, water, or other mechanical power is being used for the purpose of the construction, repair, or demolition thereof. . . .

Ibid., XXXIV, 53 f.: 60-61 Victoria, c. 37.

(F) COMMONWEALTH OF AUSTRALIA ACT (1900)

An act to constitute the commonwealth of Australia. Whereas the people of New South Wales, Victoria, South Australia, Queensland, and Tasmania, humbly relying on the blessing of Almighty God, have agreed to unite in one indissoluble federal commonwealth under the crown of the united kingdom of Great Britain and Ireland and under the constitution hereby established; and whereas it is expedient to provide for the admission into the commonwealth of other Australasian colonies and possessions of the queen: be it therefore enacted . . . as follows:—

. . . It shall be lawful for the queen with the advice of the privy council, to declare by proclamation that, on and after a day therein appointed, not being later than one year after the passing of this act, the people of New South Wales, Victoria, South Australia, Queensland, and Tasmania, and also, if her majesty is satisfied that the people of Western Australia have agreed thereto, of Western Australia, shall be united in a federal commonwealth under the name of the commonwealth of Australia. But the queen may, at any time after the proclamation, appoint a governor general for the commonwealth. . . .

"The commonwealth" shall mean the commonwealth of Australia as established under this act. "The states" shall mean such of the colonies of New South Wales, New Zealand, Queensland, Tasmania, Victoria, Western Australia, and South Australia, including the northern territory of South Australia, as for the time being are parts of the commonwealth, and such colonies and territories as may be admitted into or established by the commonwealth as states. . . . "Original states" shall mean such states as are parts of the commonwealth at its establishment. . . .

Chapter I: The Parliament. The legislative power of the commonwealth shall be vested in a federal parliament which shall consist of the queen, a senate, and a house of representatives, and which is hereinafter called "the parliament" or "the parliament of the commonwealth."

A governor general appointed by the queen shall be her majesty's representative in the commonwealth, and shall have and may exercise in the commonwealth during the queen's pleasure, but subject to this constitution, such powers and functions of the queen as her majesty may be pleased to assign to him. . . . The governor general may appoint such times for holding the sessions of the parliament as he thinks fit and may also from time to time . . . prorogue the parliament and . . . dissolve the house of representatives. . . . There shall be a session of the parliament once at least in every year; so that twelve months shall not intervene between the last sitting of the parliament in one session and its first sitting in the next session. . . .

The senate shall be composed of senators for each state, directly chosen by the people of the state, voting, until the parliament otherwise provides, as one electorate. . . . Until the parliament otherwise provides, there shall be six senators for each original state. The parliament may make laws increasing or diminishing the number of senators for each state, but so that equal representation of the several original states shall be maintained and that no original state shall have less than six senators. The senators shall be chosen for a term of six years, and the names of the senators chosen for each state shall be certified by the governor to the governor general. . . . Until the parliament otherwise provides, but subject to this constitution, the laws in force in each state for the time being relating to elections for the more numerous house of the parliament of the state shall, as nearly as practicable, apply to elections of senators for the state. . . . The qualifications of a senator shall be the same as those of a member of the house of representatives. . . .

The house of representatives shall be composed of members directly chosen by the people of the commonwealth, and the number of such members shall be, as nearly as practicable, twice the number of the senators. The number of members chosen in the several states shall be in proportion to the respective numbers of their people. . . . But . . . five members at least shall be chosen in each original state. . . . Until the parliament otherwise provides, the qualification of electors of members of the house of representatives shall be in each state that which is prescribed by the law of the state as the qualification of electors of the more numerous house of parliament of the state. . . .

Until the parliament otherwise provides, the qualifications of a member of the house of representatives shall be as follows: (1) He must be of the full age of twenty-one years, and must be an elector entitled to vote at the election of members of the house of representatives . . . and must have been for three years at the least a resident within the limits of the commonwealth as existing at the time when he is chosen. (2) He must be a subject of the queen, either natural-born or for at least five years naturalized under a law of the united kingdom, or of a colony which has become or becomes a state, or of the commonwealth, or of a state. . . .

The parliament shall, subject to this constitution, have power to make laws for the peace, order, and good government of the commonwealth with respect to (1) trade and commerce with other countries and among the states; (2) taxation, but so as not to discriminate between states or parts of states; (3) bounties on the production or export of goods, but so that such bounties shall be uniform throughout the commonwealth; (4) borrowing money on the public credit of the commonwealth; (5) postal, telegraphic, telephonic, and other like services; (6) the naval and military defence of the commonwealth and of the several states and the control of the forces to execute and maintain the laws of the commonwealth; (7) lighthouses, lightships, beacons, and buoys; (8) astronomical and meteorological observations; (9) quarantine; (10) fisheries in Australian waters beyond territorial limits; (11) census and statistics; (12) currency, coinage, and legal tender; (13) banking other than state banking, also state banking extending beyond the limits of the state concerned, the incorporation of banks, and the issue of paper money; (14) insurance other than state insurance, also state insurance extending beyond the limits of the state concerned; (15) weights and measures; (16) bills of exchange and promissory notes; (17) bankruptcy and insolvency; (18) copyrights, patents of inventions and designs, and trade marks; (19) naturalization and aliens; (20) foreign corporations and trading or financial corporations formed within the limits of the commonwealth; (21) marriage; (22) divorce and matrimonial causes and, in relation thereto, parental rights and the custody and guardianship of infants; (23) invalid and old age pensions; (24) the service and execution throughout the commonwealth of the civil and criminal process and the judgments of the courts of the states; (25) the recognition throughout the commonwealth of the laws, the public acts and records, and the judicial proceedings of the states; (26) the people of any race, other than the aboriginal race in any state, for whom it is deemed necessary to make special laws; (27) immigration and emigration; (28) the influx of criminals; (29) external affairs; (30) the relations of the commonwealth with the islands of the Pacific; (31) the acquisition of property on just terms from any state or person for any purpose in respect of which the parliament has power to make laws; (32) the control of railways with respect to transport for the naval and military purposes of the commonwealth; (33) the acquisition with the consent of a state of any railways of the state . . . ; (34) railway construction and extension in any state, with the consent of that state; (35) conciliation and arbitration for the prevention and settlement of industrial disputes extending beyond the limits of any one state. . . .

Proposed laws appropriating revenue or moneys, or imposing taxation, shall not originate in the senate. . . . The senate may not amend proposed laws imposing taxation or proposed laws appropriating revenue or moneys for the ordinary annual services of the government. The senate may not amend any proposed law so as to increase any proposed charge or burden on the people. The senate may at any stage return to the house of representatives any proposed law which the senate may not amend, requesting by message the omission or amendment of any items or provisions therein. . . . Except as provided in this section, the senate shall have equal power with the house of representatives in respect of all proposed laws. . . .

When a proposed law passed by both houses of the parliament is presented to the governor general for the queen's assent, he shall declare, according to his discretion but subject to this constitution, that he assents in the queen's name, or that he withholds assent, or that he reserves the law for the queen's pleasure. The governor general may return to the house in which it originated any proposed law so presented to him and may transmit therewith any amendments which he may recommend, and the houses may deal with the recommendation. The queen may disallow any law within one year from the governor general's assent, and such disallowance, on being made known by the governor general by speech or message to each of the houses of parliament or by proclamation, shall annul the law from the day when the disallowance is so made known. A proposed law reserved for the queen's pleasure shall not have any force unless and until, within two years from the day on which it was presented to the governor general for the queen's assent, the governor general makes known, by speech or message to each of the houses of the parliament or by proclamation, that it has received the queen's assent.

Chapter II: The Executive Government. The executive power of the commonwealth is vested in the queen and is exercisable by the governor general as the queen's representative, and extends to the execution and maintenance of this constitution and of the laws of the commonwealth. There shall be a federal executive council to advise the governor general in the government of the commonwealth, and the members of the council shall be chosen and summoned by the governor general and sworn as executive councillors and shall hold office during his pleasure. . . . The governor general may appoint officers to administer such departments of state of the commonwealth as the governor general in council may establish. Such officers shall hold office during the pleasure of the governor general. They shall be members of the federal executive council and shall be the queen's ministers of state for the commonwealth. . . . Until the parliament otherwise provides, the ministers of state shall not exceed seven in number and shall hold such offices as the parliament prescribes or, in the absence of provision, as the governor general directs. . . . The command-in-chief of the naval and military forces of the commonwealth is vested in the governor general as the queen's representative. . . .

Chapter III: The Judicature. The judicial power of the commonwealth shall be vested in a federal supreme court, to be called the high court of Australia, and in such other federal courts as the parliament creates, and in such other courts as it invests with federal jurisdiction. The high court shall consist of a chief justice and so many other justices, not less than two, as the parliament prescribes.

The justices of the high court and of the other courts created by the parliament (1) shall be appointed by the governor general in council; (2) shall not be removed except by the governor general in council on an address from both houses of the parliament in the same session, praying for such removal on the ground of proved misbehaviour or incapacity. . . .

The high court shall have jurisdiction, with such exceptions and subject to such regulations as the parliament prescribes, to hear and determine appeals from all judgments, decrees, orders, and sentences of any justice or justices exercising the original jurisdiction of the high court; of any other federal court or court exercising federal jurisdiction, or of the supreme court of any state, or of any other court of any state from which, at the establishment of the commonwealth, an appeal lies to the queen in council. . . . No appeal shall be permitted to the queen in council from a decision of the high court upon any question, howsoever arising, as to the limits *inter se* of the constitutional powers of the commonwealth and those of any state or states, or as to the limits *inter se* of the constitutional powers of any two or more states, unless the high court shall certify that the question is one which ought to be determined by her majesty in council. The high court may so certify if satisfied that for any special reason the certificate should be granted, and thereupon an appeal shall lie to her majesty in council on the question without further leave.

Except as provided in this section, this constitution shall not impair any right which the queen may be pleased to exercise by virtue of her royal prerogative to grant special leave of appeal from the high court to her majesty in council. The parliament may make laws limiting the matters in which such leave may be asked, but proposed laws containing any such limitation shall be reserved by the governor general for her majesty's pleasure.

In all matters arising under any treaty, affecting consuls or other representatives of other countries, in which the commonwealth or a person suing or being sued on behalf of the commonwealth is a party, between states or between residents of different states or between a state and a resident of another state, in which a writ of mandamus or prohibition or an injunction is sought against an officer of the commonwealth, the high court shall have original jurisdiction. The parliament may make laws conferring original jurisdiction on the high court in any matter arising under this constitution or involving its interpretation; arising under any laws made by the parliament; of admiralty and maritime jurisdiction; relating to the same subject matter claimed under the laws of different states. . . .

Chapter IV: Finance and Trade. All revenues or moneys raised or received by the executive government of the commonwealth shall form one consolidated revenue fund, to be appropriated for the purposes of the commonwealth. . . . No money shall be drawn from the treasury of the commonwealth except under appropriation made by law. . . .

Uniform duties of customs shall be imposed within two years after the establishment of the commonwealth. . . . On the imposition of uniform duties . . . trade, commerce, and intercourse among the states . . . shall be absolutely free. . . .

Chapter V: The States. The constitution of each state of the commonwealth shall, subject to this constitution, continue as at the establishment of the commonwealth, or as at the admission or establishment of the state, as the case may be, until altered in accordance with the constitution of the state. Every power of the parliament of a colony which has become or becomes a state shall, unless it is by this constitution exclusively vested in the parliament of the commonwealth or withdrawn from the parliament of the state, continue as at the establishment of the commonwealth, or as at the admission or establishment of the state, as the case may be. . . . When a law of a state is inconsistent with a law of the commonwealth, the latter shall prevail and the former shall, to the extent of the inconsistency, be invalid. . . .

Chapter VI: New States. The parliament may admit to the commonwealth or establish new states, and may upon such admission or establishment make or impose such terms and conditions, including the extent of representation in either house of the parliament, as it thinks fit. . . .

Chapter VIII: Alteration of the Constitution. This constitution shall not be altered except in the following manner. The proposed law for the alteration thereof must be passed by an absolute majority of each house of the parliament, and not less than two nor more than six months after its passage through both houses the proposed law shall be submitted in each state to the electors qualified to vote for the election of members of the house of representatives. But if either house passes any such proposed law by an absolute majority, and the other house rejects or fails to pass it or passes it with any amendment to which the first-mentioned house will not agree, and if after an interval of three months the first-mentioned house in the same or the next session again passes the proposed law by an absolute majority with or without any amendment which has been made or agreed to by the other house, and such other house rejects or fails to pass it or passes it with any amendment to which the first-mentioned house will not agree, the governor general may submit the proposed law as last proposed by the first-mentioned house, and either with or without any amendments subsequently agreed to by both houses, to the electors in each state qualified to vote for the election of the house of representatives.

When a proposed law is submitted to the electors, the vote shall be taken in such manner as the parliament prescribes. . . . And if in a majority of the states a majority of the electors voting approve the proposed law, and if a majority of all the electors voting also approve the proposed law, it shall be presented to the governor general for the queen's assent. No alteration diminishing the proportionate representation of any state in either house of the parliament, or the minimum number of representatives of a state in the house of representatives, or increasing, diminishing, or otherwise altering the limits of the state, or in any manner affecting the provisions of the constitution in relation thereto, shall become law unless the majority of the electors voting in that state approve the proposed law.

Ibid., XXXVIII, 24 f.: 63-64 Victoria, c. 12.

136. EDWARD VII: STATUTES

(A) TRADE DISPUTES ACT (1906)

An act to provide for the regulation of trades unions and trade disputes Be it enacted . . . as follows:—

The following paragraph shall be added as a new paragraph after the first paragraph of section three of the Conspiracy and Protection of Property Act, 1875: "An act done in pursuance of an agreement or combination by two or more persons shall, if done in contemplation or furtherance of a trade dispute, not be actionable unless the act, if done without any such agreement or combination, would be actionable."

It shall be lawful for one or more persons, acting on their own behalf or on behalf of a trade union or of an individual employer or firm in contemplation or furtherance of a trade dispute, to attend at or near a house or place where a person resides or works or carries on business or happens to be, if they so attend merely for the purpose of peacefully obtaining or communicating information or of peacefully persuading any person to work or abstain from working. . . .

An act done by a person in contemplation or furtherance of a trade dispute shall not be actionable on the ground only that it induces some other person to break a contract of employment or that it is an interference with the trade, business, or employment of some other person, or with the right of some other person to dispose of his capital or his labour as he wills.

An action against a trade union, whether of workmen or masters or against any members or officials thereof on behalf of themselves and all other members of the trade union in respect of any tortious act alleged to have been committed by or on behalf of the trade union, shall not be entertained by any court. . . .

Ibid., XLIV, 246 f.: 6 Edward VII, c. 47.

(B) UNION OF SOUTH AFRICA ACT (1909)

An act to constitute the union of South Africa. Whereas it is desirable for the welfare and future progress of South Africa that the several British colonies therein should be united under one government in a legislative union under the crown of Great Britain and Ireland; and whereas it is expedient to make provision for the union of the colonies of the Cape of Good Hope, Natal, the Transvaal, and the Orange River Colony on terms and conditions to which they have agreed by resolution of their respective parliaments . . . : be it therefore enacted . . . as follows:—

I. Preliminary. . . . In this act, unless it is otherwise expressed or implied, the words "the union" shall be taken to mean the union of South Africa as constituted under this act; and the words "houses of parliament," "house of parliament," or "parliament" shall be taken to mean the parliament of the union. . . .

II. The Union. It shall be lawful for the king, with the advice of the privy council, to declare by proclamation that, on and after a day therein appointed, not being later than one year after the passing of this act, the colonies of the Cape of Good Hope, Natal, the Transvaal, and the Orange River Colony, hereinafter called the colonies, shall be united in a legislative union under one government under the name of the union of South Africa. On and after the day appointed by such proclamation, the government and parliament of the union shall have full power and authority within the limits of the colonies, but the king may at any time after the proclamation appoint a governor general for the union. . . . The colonies mentioned . . . shall become original provinces of the union. . . . Upon any colony entering the union . . . , every . . . act applying to any of the colonies as being self-governing colonies or colonies with responsible government shall cease to apply to that colony; but, as from the date when this act takes effect, every such act of parliament shall apply to the union.

III. Executive Government. The executive government of the union is vested in the king and shall be administered by his majesty in person or by a governor general as his representative. . . .

There shall be an executive council to advise the governor general in the government of the union, and the members of the council shall be chosen and summoned by the governor general and sworn as executive councillors and shall hold office during his pleasure. . . . The governor general may appoint officers, not exceeding ten in number, to administer such departments of state of the union as the governor general in council may establish. Such officers shall hold office during the pleasure of the governor general. They shall be members of the executive council and shall be the king's ministers of state for the union. After the first general election of members of the house of assembly . . . , no minister shall hold office for a longer period than three months unless he is or becomes a member of either house of parliament.

The appointment and removal of all officers of the public service of the union shall be vested in the governor general in council, unless the appointment is delegated by the governor general in council, or by this act or by a law of parliament, to some other authority. All powers, authorities, and functions which at the establishment of the union are in any of the colonies vested in the governor, or in the governor in council, or in any authority of the colony, shall . . . be vested in the governor general, or in the governor general in council, or in the authority exercising similar powers under the union . . . , except such powers and functions as are by this act or may by a law of parliament be vested in some other authority. The command-in-chief of the naval and military forces within the union is vested in the king or in the governor general as his representative. . . .

IV. Parliament. The legislative power of the union shall be vested in the parliament of the union . . . , which shall consist of the king, a senate, and a house of assembly. The governor general may appoint such times for holding the sessions of parliament as he thinks fit, and may also from time to time . . . prorogue parliament, and may . . . dissolve the senate and the house of assembly. . . . There shall be a session of parliament once at least in every year. . . .

For ten years after the establishment of the union, the constitution of the senate shall . . . be as follows. . . .[1] Parliament may provide for the manner in which the senate shall be constituted after the expiration of ten years. . . .

The qualifications of a senator shall be as follows: he must be not less than thirty years of age; be qualified to be registered as a voter for the election of members of the house of assembly in one of the provinces; have resided for five years within the limits of the union . . . ; be a British subject of European descent; in the case of an elected senator, be the registered owner of immovable property within the union of the value of not less than £500 over and above any special mortgages thereon. . . .

The house of assembly shall be composed of members directly chosen by the voters of the union in electoral divisions delimited as hereinafter provided. . . .[2] Parliament may by law prescribe the qualifications which shall be necessary to entitle persons to vote at the election of members of the house of assembly. . . . No person who, at the passing of any such law, is registered as a voter in any province shall be removed from the register by reason only of any disqualification based on race or colour. . . . Between the date of the passing of this act and the date fixed for the establishment of the union, the governor in council of each of the colonies shall nominate a judge . . . , and the judges so nominated shall . . . form a joint commission . . . for the purpose of the first division of the provinces into electoral divisions. . . . The commission shall divide each province into electoral divisions, each returning one member. . . . As soon as may be after every quinquennial census, the

---

[1] Eight senators are to be nominated by the governor general in council and eight are to be elected by each colonial legislature.

[2] The representation of a province is roughly proportioned to the number of European male adults there resident. Provision is made for a reallotment of seats on the basis of a new census every five years.

governor general in council shall appoint a commission consisting of three judges of the supreme court of South Africa to carry out any redivision which may have become necessary. . . .

The qualifications of a member of the house of assembly shall be as follows: he must be qualified to be registered as a voter for the election of members of the house of assembly in one of the provinces; have resided for five years within the limits of the union . . . ; be a British subject of European descent. . . .

Parliament shall have full power to make laws for the peace, order, and good government of the union. Bills appropriating revenue or moneys or imposing taxation shall originate only in the house of assembly. . . . The senate may not amend any bills so far as they impose taxation or appropriate revenue or moneys for the services of the government. The senate may not amend any bill so as to increase any proposed charges or burdens on the people. . . .

When a bill is presented to the governor general for the king's assent,[3] he shall declare according to his discretion . . . that he assents in the king's name, or that he withholds assent, or that he reserves the bill for the signification of the king's pleasure. . . . The king may disallow any law within one year after it has been assented to by the governor general. . . . A bill reserved for the king's pleasure shall not have any force unless and until, within one year from the day on which it was presented to the governor general for the king's assent, the governor general makes known . . . that it has received the king's assent. . . .

V. The Provinces. In each province there shall be a chief executive officer appointed by the governor general in council, who shall be styled the administrator of the province, and in whose name all executive acts relating to provincial affairs therein shall be done. . . . There shall be a provincial council in each province, consisting of the same number of members as are elected in the province for the house of assembly. . . . The members of the provincial council shall be elected by the persons qualified to vote for the election of members of the house of assembly. . . . Each provincial council shall continue for three years from the date of its first meeting and shall not be subject to dissolution. . . .

Subject to the provisions of this act and the assent of the governor general in council . . . , the provincial council may make ordinances in relation to matters coming within the following classes of subjects: that is to say, (1) direct taxation within the province in order to raise a revenue for provincial purposes; (2) the borrowing of money on the sole credit of the province . . . ; (3) education other than higher education . . . ; (4) agriculture to the extent and subject to the conditions to be defined by parliament; (5) the establish-

---

[3] Normally bills have to receive a majority in both houses; but in case of a prolonged deadlock on any measure, it may be passed by the two houses in joint session called by the governor general.

ment, maintenance, and management of hospitals and charitable institutions; (6) municipal institutions . . . and other local institutions of a similar nature . . . ; (7) local works and undertakings within the province other than railways and harbours and other than such works as extend beyond the borders of the province . . . ; (8) roads . . . and bridges . . . ; (9) markets and pounds; (10) fish and game preservation; (11) the imposition of punishment . . . for enforcing any law or any ordinance of the province . . . ; (12) generally all matters which, in the opinion of the governor general in council, are of a merely local or private nature in the province; (13) all other subjects in respect of which parliament shall by any law delegate the power of making ordinances to the provincial council. . . .

VI. The Supreme Court of South Africa. There shall be a supreme court of South Africa, consisting of a chief justice of South Africa, the ordinary judges of appeal, and the other judges of the several divisions of the supreme court of South Africa in the provinces. There shall be an appellate division of the supreme court consisting of the chief justice of South Africa, two ordinary judges of appeal, and two additional judges of appeal. . . . The several supreme courts of the Cape of Good Hope, Natal, and the Transvaal and the high court of the Orange River Colony shall, on the establishment of the union, become provincial divisions of the supreme court of South Africa. . . . The chief justice of South Africa, the ordinary judges of appeal, and all other judges of the supreme court of South Africa . . . shall be appointed by the governor general in council. . . . The chief justice of South Africa and other judges of the supreme court of South Africa shall not be removed from office except by the governor general in council on an address from both houses of parliament in the same session praying for such removal on the ground of misbehaviour or incapacity. . . .

In every case, civil or criminal, in which at the establishment of the union an appeal might have been made . . . to a superior court in any of the colonies, the appeal shall be made to the corresponding division of the supreme court of South Africa; but there shall be no further appeal against any judgment given on appeal by such division except to the appellate division, and then only if the appellate division shall have given special leave to appeal. There shall be no appeal from the supreme court of South Africa or from any division thereof to the king in council; but nothing herein contained shall be construed to impair any right which the king in council may be pleased to exercise to grant special leave to appeal from the appellate division to the king in council. Parliament may make laws limiting the matters in respect of which such special leave may be asked. . . .

IX. New Provinces and Territories. Parliament may alter the boundaries of any province . . . on the petition of the provincial council of every province whose boundaries are affected thereby. The king, with the advice of the privy council, may, on addresses from the houses of parliament of the union, admit into the union the territories administered by the British South Africa Company. . . .

X. Amendment of Act. Parliament may by law repeal or alter any of the provisions of this act, provided that no provision thereof for the operation of which a definite period of time is prescribed shall during such period be repealed or altered. . . .

Ibid., XLVII, 42 f.: 9 Edward VII, c. 9.

137. GEORGE V: STATUTES

(A) PARLIAMENT ACT (1911)[1]

An act to make provision with respect to the powers of the house of lords in relation to those of the house of commons and to limit the duration of parliament. Whereas it is expedient that provision should be made for regulating the relations between the two houses of parliament; and whereas it is intended to substitute for the house of lords as it at present exists a second chamber constituted on a popular instead of hereditary basis, but such substitution cannot be immediately brought into operation; and whereas provision will require hereafter to be made by parliament in a measure effecting such substitution for limiting and defining the powers of the new second chamber, but it is expedient to make such provision as in this act appears for restricting the existing powers of the house of lords: be it therefore enacted . . . as follows:—

If a money bill, having been passed by the house of commons and sent up to the house of lords at least one month before the end of the session, is not passed by the house of lords without amendment within one month after it is so sent up to that house, the bill shall, unless the house of commons direct to the contrary, be presented to his majesty and become an act of parliament on the royal assent being signified, notwithstanding that the house of lords have not consented to the bill. A money bill means a public bill which in the opinion of the speaker of the house of commons contains only provisions dealing with all or any of the following subjects: namely, the imposition, repeal, remission, alteration, or regulation of taxation; the imposition for the payment of debt or other financial purposes of charges on the consolidated fund, or on money provided by parliament, or the variation or repeal of any such charges; supply; the appropriation, receipt, custody, issue, or audit of accounts of public money; the raising or guarantee of any loan or the repayment thereof; or subordinate matters incidental to those subjects or any of them. In this sub-section the expressions, "taxation," "public money," and "loan" respectively, do not include any taxation, money, or loan raised by local authorities or bodies for local purposes. There shall be

---

[1] Cf. no. 138A-C.

endorsed on every money bill when it is sent up to the house of lords
and when it is presented to his majesty for assent the certificate of
the speaker of the house of commons signed by him that it is a
money bill. . . .

If any public bill (other than a money bill or a bill containing any
provision to extend the maximum duration of parliament beyond five
years) is passed by the house of commons in three successive sessions (whether of the same parliament or not), and, having been
sent up to the house of lords at least one month before the end of
the session, is rejected by the house of lords in each of those sessions, that bill shall, on its rejection for the third time by the house
of lords, unless the house of commons direct to the contrary, be
presented to his majesty and become an act of parliament on the
royal assent being signified thereto, notwithstanding that the house
of lords have not consented to the bill. Provided that this provision
shall not take effect unless two years have elapsed between the date
of the second reading in the first of those sessions of the bill in the
house of commons and the date on which it passes the house of commons in the third of those sessions. When a bill is presented to his
majesty for assent in pursuance of the provisions of this section,
there shall be endorsed on the bill the certificate of the speaker of
the house of commons signed by him that the provisions of this section have been duly complied with. A bill shall be deemed to be rejected by the house of lords if it is not passed by the house of lords
either without amendment or with such amendments only as may be
agreed to by both houses. A bill shall be deemed to be the same
bill as a former bill sent up to the house of lords in the preceding
session if, when it is sent up to the house of lords, it is identical
with the former bill or contains only such alterations as are certified
by the speaker of the house of commons to be necessary owing to
the time which has elapsed since the date of the former bill, or to
represent any amendments which have been made by the house of
lords in the former bill in the preceding session, and any amendments which are certified by the speaker to have been made by the
house of lords in the third session and agreed to by the house of
commons shall be inserted in the bill as presented for royal assent
in pursuance of this section. . . .

Any certificate of the speaker of the house of commons given
under this act shall be conclusive for all purposes, and shall not be
questioned in any court of law.

In every bill presented to his majesty under the preceding provisions of this act, the words of enactment shall be as follows, that is
to say: "Be it enacted by the king's most excellent majesty, by and
with the advice and consent of the commons in this present parliament assembled, in accordance with the provisions of the Parliament
Act, 1911, and by authority of the same, as follows." . . .

Five years shall be substituted for seven years as the time fixed for the maximum duration of parliament under the Septennial Act, 1715. . . .²

Ibid., XLIX, 38 f.: 1-2 George V, c. 13.

(B) NATIONAL INSURANCE ACT (1911)

An act to provide for insurance against loss of health and for the prevention and cure of sickness and for insurance against unemployment, and for purposes incidental thereto. Be it enacted . . . as follows:—

Part I: National Health Insurance. Subject to the provisions of this act, all persons of the age of sixteen and upwards who are employed within the meaning of this part of this act shall be, and any such persons who are not so employed but who possess the qualifications hereinafter mentioned may be, insured in manner provided in this part of this act, and all persons so insured (in this act called "insured persons") shall be entitled in the manner and subject to the conditions provided in this act to the benefits in respect of health insurance and prevention of sickness conferred by this part of this act. The persons employed within the meaning of this part of this act (in this act referred to as "employed contributors") shall include all persons of either sex, whether British subjects or not, who are engaged in any of the employments specified in Part I of the first schedule to this act, not being employments specified in Part II of that schedule. . . .³

Except as otherwise provided by this act, the funds for providing the benefits conferred by this part of this act and defraying the expenses of the administration of those benefits shall be derived as to seven-ninths (or, in the case of women, three-fourths) thereof from contributions made by or in respect of the contributors by themselves or their employers, and as to the remaining two-ninths (or, in the case of women, one-quarter) thereof from moneys provided by parliament. The contributions payable in respect of employed contributors shall be at the rate specified in Part I of the second schedule to this act (hereinafter referred to as the employed rate), and shall comprise contributions by the contributors and contributions by their employers at the rates specified in that part of that schedule, and shall be payable at weekly or other prescribed intervals. . . . The employer shall, in the first instance, pay both the contributions payable by himself (in this act referred to as the employer's contributions) and also, on behalf of the employed contributor, the contributions payable by such contributor, and shall be entitled to recover from the contributor by deduction from his wages or otherwise

---

² No. 122B.

³ Part I lays down the principle that in general the labouring class shall be insured under the act. The persons excepted in Part II are mainly government employees, salaried officials, teachers, workers hired for casual employment, and those earning more than £160 a year otherwise than by manual labour.

the amount of the contributions so paid by him on behalf of the contributor, in accordance with the rules set out in the third schedule to this act. . . .

Subject to the provisions of this act, the benefits conferred by this act upon insured persons are (a) medical treatment and attendance . . . (in this act called "medical benefit"); (b) treatment in sanatoria or other institutions . . . (in this act called "sanatorium benefit"); (c) periodical payments whilst rendered incapable of work by . . . bodily or mental disablement . . . , continuing for a period not exceeding twenty-six weeks (in this act called "sickness benefit"); (d) in the case of the disease or disablement continuing after the determination of sickness benefit, periodical payments so long as so rendered incapable of work . . . (in this act called "disablement benefit"); (e) payment in the case of the confinement of the wife . . . of an insured person, or of any other woman who is an insured person, of a sum of 30s. (in this act called "maternity benefit"). . . .

Every insurance committee shall, for the purpose of administering medical benefit, make arrangements with duly qualified medical practitioners in accordance with regulations made by the insurance commissioners.[4] The regulations made by the insurance commissioners shall provide for the arrangements made being subject to the approval of the insurance commissioners and being such as to secure that insured persons shall . . . receive adequate medical attendance and treatment from the medical practitioners with whom arrangements are so made, and shall require the adoption by every insurance committee of such system as will secure (a) the preparation and publication of lists of medical practitioners who have agreed to attend and treat insured persons whose medical benefit is administered by the committee; (b) a right on the part of any duly qualified medical practitioner who is desirous of being included in any such list as aforesaid of being so included . . . ; (c) a right on the part of any insured person of selecting, at such periods as may be prescribed, from the appropriate list the practitioner by whom he wishes to be attended and treated, and, subject to the consent of the practitioner so selected, of being attended and treated by him; (d) the distribution amongst . . . the several practitioners, whose names are on the lists, of the insured persons who after due notice have failed to make any selection, or who have been refused by the practitioner whom they have selected. . . .

Part II: Unemployment Insurance. Every workman who, having been employed in a trade mentioned in the sixth schedule to this act[5]

---

[4] The insurance commissioners were officials appointed by the crown for the general administration of the act. Within each county an insurance committee, of from forty to eighty members, was to supervise the payment of benefits.

[5] The principal trades mentioned are building, construction of works, shipbuilding, mechanical engineering, ironfounding, and construction of vehicles.

(in this act referred to as "an insured trade"), is unemployed, and in whose case the conditions laid down by this part of this act (in this act referred to as "statutory conditions") are fulfilled, shall be entitled . . . to receive payments (in this act referred to as "unemployment benefit") at weekly or other prescribed intervals at such rates and for such periods as are authorized by or under the seventh schedule to this act. . . .

The sums required for the payment of unemployment benefit under this act shall be derived partly from contributions by workmen in the insured trades and partly from contributions by employers of such workmen and partly from moneys provided by parliament. Subject to the provisions of this part of this act, every workman employed within the united kingdom in an insured trade and every employer of any such workman shall be liable to pay contributions at the rates specified in the eighth schedule to this act. Except where the regulations under this part of this act otherwise prescribe, the employer shall, in the first instance, be liable to pay both the contribution payable by himself and also, on behalf of and to the exclusion of the workman, the contribution payable by such workman; and, subject to such regulations, shall be entitled, notwithstanding the provisions of any act or any contract to the contrary, to recover from the workman by deductions from the workman's wages or from any other payment due from him to the workman the amount of the contributions so paid by him on behalf of the workman. . . .

For the purposes of this part of this act, there shall be established under the control and management of the board of trade a fund called the unemployment fund, into which shall be paid all contributions payable under this part of this act by employers and workmen and out of moneys provided by parliament, and out of which shall be paid all claims for unemployment benefit and any other payments which under this part of this act are payable out of the fund. . . . The treasury may out of the consolidated fund or the growing produce thereof advance, on the security of the unemployment fund, any sums required for the purpose of discharging the liabilities of that fund under this part of this act; provided that the total amount of advances outstanding at any time shall not exceed £3,000,000. . . .

Ibid., XLIX, 337 f.: 1-2 George V, c. 55.

(C) Defence of the Realm Consolidation Act (1914)

An act to consolidate and amend the Defence of the Realm Acts. Be it enacted . . . as follows:—

His majesty in council has power, during the continuance of the present war, to issue regulations for securing the public safety and the defence of the realm and as to the powers and duties for that purpose of the admiralty and army council and of the members of his majesty's forces and other persons acting in his behalf; and may, by such regulations, authorize the trial by courts martial, or in the case of minor offences by courts of summary jurisdiction, and punishment of persons committing offences against the regulations and in particular against any of the provisions of such regulations designed (a) to prevent persons communicating with the enemy or obtaining information for that purpose or any purpose calculated to jeopardize the success of the operations of any of his majesty's forces or the forces of his allies or to assist the enemy; or (b) to secure the safety of his majesty's forces and ships and the safety of any means of communication and of railways, ports, and harbours; or (c) to prevent the spread of false reports or reports likely to cause disaffection to his majesty or to interfere with the success of his majesty's forces by land or sea or to prejudice his majesty's relations with foreign powers; or (d) to secure the navigation of vessels in accordance with directions given by or under the authority of the admiralty; or (e) otherwise to prevent assistance being given to the enemy or the successful prosecution of the war being endangered.

Any such regulations may provide for the suspension of any restrictions on the acquisition or use of land, or the exercise of the power of making by-laws or any other power under the Defence Acts, 1842 to 1875. . . .[6] It shall be lawful for the admiralty or army council to require that there shall be placed at their disposal the whole or any part of the output of any factory or workshop in which arms, ammunition, or warlike stores or equipment, or any articles required for the production thereof, are manufactured; to take possession of and use for the purpose of his majesty's naval or military service any such factory or workshop. . . .

The Defence of the Realm Act, 1914, and the Defence of the Realm (No. 2) Act, 1914, are hereby repealed; but nothing in this repeal shall affect any orders in council made thereunder. . . .

Ibid., LIII, 21 f.: 5 George V, c. 8.

(D) REPRESENTATION OF THE PEOPLE ACT (1918)

An act to amend the law with respect to parliamentary and local government franchises and the registration of parliamentary and local government electors and the conduct of elections, and to provide for the redistribution of seats at parliamentary elections and for other purposes connected therewith. Be it enacted . . . as follows:—

A man shall be entitled to be registered as a parliamentary elector for a constituency (other than a university constituency) if he is of full age and not subject to any legal incapacity, and has the requisite residence qualification or has the requisite business premises qualification. A man, in order to have the requisite residence qualification or business premises qualification for a constituency, must on the last day of the qualifying period be residing in premises in the constituency or occupying business premises in the constituency, as the case may be, and must during the whole of the qualifying period have resided in premises or occupied business premises, as the case may

---

[6] Cf. nos. 131B, 139D, E.

be, in the constituency or in another constituency within the same parliamentary borough or parliamentary county, or within a parliamentary borough or parliamentary county contiguous to that borough or county. . . . The expression "business premises" in this section means land or other premises of the yearly value of not less than £10 occupied for the purpose of the business, profession, or trade of the person to be registered. A man shall be entitled to be registered as a parliamentary elector for a university constituency if he is of full age and not subject to any legal incapacity and has received a degree (other than an honorary degree) at any university forming, or forming part of, the constituency. . . . A man shall be entitled to be registered as a local government elector for a local government electoral area, if he is of full age and not subject to any legal incapacity and is on the last day of the qualifying period occupying, as owner or tenant, any land or premises in that area and has, during the whole of the qualifying period, so occupied any land or premises in that area. . . .

A woman shall be entitled to be registered as a parliamentary elector for a constituency (other than a university constituency) if she has attained the age of thirty years and is not subject to any legal incapacity and is entitled to be registered as a local government elector in respect of the occupation in that constituency of land or premises (not being a dwelling-house) of a yearly value of not less than £5 or of a dwelling-house, or is the wife of a husband entitled to be so registered. A woman shall be entitled to be registered as a parliamentary elector for a university constituency if she has attained the age of thirty years and either would be entitled to be so registered if she were a man, or has been admitted to and passed the final examination, and kept under the conditions required of women by the university the period of residence necessary for a man to obtain a degree at any university forming, or forming part of, a university constituency which did not at the time the examination was passed admit women to degrees. A woman shall be entitled to be registered as a local government elector for any local government electoral area where she would be entitled to be so registered if she were a man, and where she is the wife of a man who is entitled to be so registered in respect of premises in which they both reside, and she has attained the age of thirty years and is not subject to any legal incapacity. . . .

Every person registered as a parliamentary elector for any constituency shall . . . be entitled to vote at an election of a member to serve in parliament for that constituency; but a man shall not vote at a general election for more than one constituency for which he is registered by virtue of a residence qualification or for more than one constituency for which he is registered by virtue of other qualifications of whatever kind, and a woman shall not vote at a general election for more than one constituency for which she is registered by virtue of her own or her husband's local government qualification, or for more than one constituency for which she is registered by virtue of any other qualification. . . . A person shall not be disqualified from being registered or from voting as a parliamentary or local government elector by reason that he or some person for whose maintenance he is responsible has received poor relief or other alms. . . .

Each of the areas mentioned in the first column of the first part of the ninth schedule to this act shall be a parliamentary borough returning the number of members specified opposite thereto in the said schedule, and where so provided in the schedule shall be divided into the divisions specified therein, and each such division shall return one member. Each of the areas mentioned in the first column of the second part of the ninth schedule to this act shall be a parliamentary county returning the number of members specified opposite thereto in the said schedule, and where so provided in the schedule shall be divided into the divisions specified therein, and each such division shall return one member. Each of the universities and combinations of universities mentioned in the third part of the ninth schedule to this act shall be a constituency returning the number of members specified opposite thereto in the said schedule. The distribution of seats in Great Britain under this part of this act shall take the place of the distribution of seats existing at the time of the passing of this act. . . .[7]

Ibid., LV, 253 f.: 7-8 George V, c. 64.

(E) Re-election of Ministers Act (1919)

An act to make provision for restricting the necessity of the re-election of members of the house of commons on acceptance of office and to make provision as to the right of certain ministers to sit in the house of commons. Be it enacted . . . as follows:—

Notwithstanding anything in any act, a member of the commons house of parliament shall not vacate his seat by reason only of his acceptance of an office of profit if that office is an office the holder of which is capable of being elected to or sitting or voting in that house, and if such acceptance has taken place within nine months after the issue of a proclamation summoning a new parliament.[8] Provided that this section shall not apply to the acceptance of any office mentioned in the schedule to this act;[9] nor shall it affect the provisions of any act imposing a limit on the number of secretaries or under-secretaries of state who may sit and vote in the commons house of parliament. . . .

Where, before or after the passing of this act, a member of his

---

[7] The ninth schedule contains a complete amended list of the constituencies in the united kingdom.

[8] This restriction was repealed in 1926.

[9] The schedule names two offices: steward or bailiff of his majesty's three Chiltern hundreds of Stoke, Desborough, and Burnham; steward or bailiff of the manors of East Hendred, Northstead, or Hempholme.

majesty's privy council has been or is appointed to be a minister of the crown at a salary, without any other office being assigned to him, he shall not by reason thereof be deemed to have been or to be incapable of being elected to or of sitting or voting in the commons house of parliament, and the office of such minister shall be deemed to be an office included in the above-mentioned schedules. Provided that not more than three ministers to whom this section applies shall sit as members of that house at the same time. . . .

Ibid., LVII, 4 f.: 9 George V, c. 2.

(F) SEX-DISQUALIFICATION REMOVAL ACT (1919)

An act to amend the law with respect to disqualifications on account of sex. Be it enacted . . . as follows:—

A person shall not be disqualified by sex or marriage from the exercise of any public function, or from being appointed to or holding any civil or judicial office or post, or from entering or assuming or carrying on any civil profession or vocation, or for admission to any incorporated society . . . and a person shall not be exempted by sex or marriage from the liability to serve as a juror.

Provided that, notwithstanding anything in this section, his majesty may by order in council authorize regulations to be made providing for and prescribing the mode of the admission of women to the civil service of his majesty . . . and giving power to reserve to men any branch of or posts in the civil service in any of his majesty's possessions overseas, or in any foreign country; and any judge, chairman of quarter sessions, recorder or other person before whom a case is or may be heard may, in his discretion, on an application made by or on behalf of the parties . . . make an order that the jury shall be composed of men only or of women only as the case may require, or may, on an application made by a woman to be exempted from service on a jury in respect of any case by reason of the nature of the evidence to be given or of the issues to be tried, grant such exemption. . . .

Nothing in the statutes or charter of any university shall be deemed to preclude the authorities of such university from making such provision as they shall think fit for the admission of women to membership thereof, or to any degree, right, or privilege therein or in connection therewith. . . .

Ibid., LVII, 325 f.: 9-10 George V, c. 71.

(G) CHURCH OF ENGLAND ASSEMBLY ACT (1919)

An act to confer powers on the national assembly of the Church of England . . . and for other purposes connected therewith. Whereas the convocations of Canterbury and York have recommended . . . that, subject to the control and authority of his majesty and of the two houses of parliament, powers in regard to legislation touching matters concerning the Church of England shall be conferred on the national assembly of the Church of England . . . ; and whereas it is expedient, subject to such control and authority as aforesaid, that such powers should be conferred on the Church assembly so constituted: be it therefore enacted . . . as follows:—

. . . There shall be a committee of members of both houses of parliament styled the ecclesiastical committee. The ecclesiastical committee shall consist of fifteen members of the house of lords, nominated by the lord chancellor, and fifteen members of the house of commons, nominated by the speaker of the house of commons, to be appointed . . . at the commencement of each parliament to serve for the duration of that parliament. . . . The powers and duties of the ecclesiastical committee may be exercised and discharged by any twelve members thereof, and the committee shall be entitled to sit and to transact business whether parliament be sitting or not and notwithstanding a vacancy in the membership of the committee. Subject to the provisions of this act, the ecclesiastical committee may regulate its own procedure.

Every measure passed by the Church assembly[10] shall be submitted by the legislative committee to the ecclesiastical committee, together with such comments and explanations as the legislative committee may deem it expedient or be directed by the Church assembly to add. The ecclesiastical committee shall thereupon consider the measure so submitted to it and may . . . invite the legislative committee to a conference to discuss the provisions thereof, and thereupon a conference of the two committees shall be held accordingly. After considering the measure, the ecclesiastical committee shall draft a report thereon to parliament stating the nature and legal effect of the measure and its views as to the expediency thereof, especially with relation to the constitutional rights of all his majesty's subjects. The ecclesiastical committee shall communicate its report in draft to the legislative committee, but shall not present it to parliament until the legislative committee signify its desire that it should be so presented.

At any time before the presentation of the report to parliament the legislative committee may, either on its own motion or by direction of the Church assembly, withdraw a measure from further consideration by the ecclesiastical committee; but the legislative committee shall have no power to vary a measure of the Church assembly either before or after conference with the ecclesiastical committee. A measure may relate to any matter concerning the Church of England, and may extend to the amendment or repeal in whole or in part of any act of parliament, including this act. Provided that a measure shall not make any alteration in the composition or powers

---

[10] The two convocations had established a single national assembly for the Church of England consisting of a house of bishops, a house of clergy, and a house of laity.

or duties of the ecclesiastical committee, or in the procedure in parliament prescribed by . . . this act.

When the ecclesiastical committee shall have reported to parliament on any measure submitted by the legislative committee, the report, together with the text of such measure, shall be laid before both houses of parliament forthwith, if parliament be then sitting, or, if not, then immediately after the next meeting of parliament, and thereupon, on a resolution being passed by each house of parliament directing that such measure in the form laid before parliament should be presented to his majesty, such measure shall be presented to his majesty, and shall have the force and effect of an act of parliament on the royal assent being signified thereto in the same manner as to acts of parliament. . . .

Ibid., LVII, 348 f.: 9-10 George V, c. 76.

(H) EMERGENCY POWERS ACT (1920)

An act to make exceptional provision for the protection of the community in cases of emergency. Be it enacted . . . as follows:—

If at any time it appears to his majesty that any action has been taken or is immediately threatened by any persons or body of persons of such a nature and on so extensive a scale as to be calculated, by interfering with the supply and distribution of food, water, fuel, or light, or with the means of locomotion, to deprive the community, or any substantial portion of the community, of the essentials of life, his majesty may by proclamation . . . declare that a state of emergency exists. No such proclamation shall be in force for more than one month, without prejudice to the issue of another proclamation at or before the end of that period. Where a proclamation of emergency has been made, the occasion thereof shall forthwith be communicated to parliament and, if parliament is then separated by such adjournment or prorogation as will not expire within five days, a proclamation shall be issued for the meeting of parliament within five days, and parliament shall accordingly meet and sit upon the day appointed by that proclamation. . . .

Where a proclamation of emergency has been made, and so long as the proclamation is in force, it shall be lawful for his majesty in council by order to make regulations for securing the essentials of life to the community; and those regulations may confer or impose on a secretary of state or other government department, or any other persons in his majesty's service or acting on his majesty's behalf, such powers and duties as his majesty may deem necessary for the preservation of the peace, for securing and regulating the supply and distribution of food, water, fuel, light, and other necessities, for maintaining the means of transit or locomotion, and for any other purposes essential to the public safety and the life of the community; and may make such provisions incidental to the powers aforesaid as may appear to his majesty to be required for making the exercise of those powers effective.

Provided that nothing in this act shall be construed to authorize the making of any regulations imposing any form of compulsory military service or industrial conscription. Provided also that no such regulation shall make it an offence for any person or persons to take part in a strike, or peacefully to persuade any other person or persons to take part in a strike. Any regulations so made shall be laid before parliament as soon as may be after they are made, and shall not continue in force after the expiration of seven days from the time when they are so laid unless a resolution is passed by both houses providing for the continuance thereof.

The regulations may provide for the trial, by courts of summary jurisdiction, of persons guilty of offences against the regulations; so, however, that the maximum penalty which may be inflicted for any offence against any such regulations shall be imprisonment with or without hard labour for a term of three months, or a fine of £100 or both such imprisonment and fine, together with the forfeiture of any goods or money in respect of which the offence has been committed. Provided that no such regulations shall alter any existing procedure in criminal cases or confer any right to punish by fine or imprisonment without trial. . . .

This act shall not apply to Ireland.

Ibid., LVIII, 345 f.: 10-11 George V, c. 55.

(I) IRISH FREE STATE AGREEMENT ACT (1922)

An act to give the force of law to certain articles of agreement for a treaty between Great Britain and Ireland and to enable effect to be given thereto, and for other purposes incidental thereto and consequential thereon. Be it enacted . . . as follows:—

The articles of agreement for a treaty between Great Britain and Ireland set forth in the schedule to this act shall have the force of law as from the date of the passing of this act. For the purpose of giving effect to article 17 of the said agreement, orders in council may be made transferring to the provisional government established under that article the powers and machinery therein referred to; and, as soon as may be and not later than four months after the passing of this act, the parliament of Southern Ireland shall be dissolved and such steps shall be taken as may be necessary for holding . . . an election of members for the constituencies which would have been entitled to elect members to that parliament, and the members so elected shall constitute the house of the parliament to which the provisional government shall be responsible, and that parliament shall, as respects matters within the jurisdiction of the provisional government, have power to make laws in like manner as the parliament of the Irish Free State when constituted. . . . No writ shall be issued after the passing of this act for the election of a member to serve in the commons house of parliament for a constituency in Ireland other than a constituency in Northern Ireland. . . .

Articles of Agreement. . . . 1. Ireland shall have the same constitutional status, in the community of nations known as the British Empire, as the dominion of Canada, the commonwealth of Australia, the dominion of New Zealand, and the union of South Africa, with a parliament having powers to make laws for the peace, order, and good government of Ireland, and an executive responsible to that parliament, and shall be styled and known as the Irish Free State.

2. Subject to the provisions hereinafter set out, the position of the Irish Free State in relation to the imperial parliament and government and otherwise shall be that of the dominion of Canada, and the law, practice, and constitutional usage governing the relationship of the crown or the representative of the crown and of the imperial parliament to the dominion of Canada shall govern their relationship to the Irish Free State.

3. The representative of the crown in Ireland shall be appointed in like manner as the governor general of Canada and in accordance with the practice observed in the making of such appointments.

4. The oath to be taken by members of the parliament of the Irish Free State shall be in the following form:—

"I, ———, do solemnly swear true faith and allegiance to the constitution of the Irish Free State as by law established, and that I will be faithful to his majesty King George V, his heirs, and successors by law, in virtue of the common citizenship of Ireland with Great Britain and her adherence to and membership of the group of nations forming the British Commonwealth of Nations." . . .

11. Until the expiration of one month from the passing of the act of parliament for the ratification of this instrument, the powers of the parliament and the government of the Irish Free State shall not be exercisable as respects Northern Ireland. . . .

12. If, before the expiration of the said month, an address is presented to his majesty by both houses of the parliament of Northern Ireland to that effect, the powers of the parliament and government of the Irish Free State shall no longer extend to Northern Ireland. . . .[11]

16. Neither the parliament of the Irish Free State nor the parliament of Northern Ireland shall make any law so as either directly or indirectly to endow any religion, or prohibit or restrict the free exercise thereof, or give any preference or impose any disability on account of religious belief or religious status, or affect prejudicially the right of any child to attend a school receiving public money without attending the religious instruction at the school, or make any discrimination as respects state aid between schools under the management

---

[11] Since an address to this effect was presented, a number of articles contemplating the subordination of Northern Ireland to the Free State remained without force.

of different religious denominations, or divert from any religious denomination or any educational institution any of its property except for public utility purposes and on payment of compensation.

17. By way of provisional arrangement for the administration of Southern Ireland during the interval which must elapse between the date hereof and the constitution of a parliament and government of the Irish Free State in accordance therewith, steps shall be taken forthwith for summoning a meeting of members of parliament elected for constituencies in Southern Ireland since the passing of the Government of Ireland Act, 1920, and for constituting a provisional government, and the British government shall take the steps necessary to transfer to such provisional government the powers and machinery requisite for the discharge of its duties, provided that every member of such provisional government shall have signified in writing his or her acceptance of this instrument. But this arrangement shall not continue in force beyond the expiration of twelve months from the date hereof. . . .

Ibid., LX, 4 f.: 12 George V, c. 4.

(J) TRADE DISPUTES AND TRADE UNIONS ACT (1927)

An act to declare and amend the law relating to trade disputes and trade unions . . . and for other purposes connected with the purposes aforesaid. Be it enacted . . . as follows:—

. . . Any strike is illegal if it has any object other than or in addition to the furtherance of a trade dispute within the trade or industry in which the strikers are engaged, and is a strike designed or calculated to coerce the government either directly or by inflicting hardship upon the community. . . .[12]

The provisions of the Trade Disputes Act, 1906, shall not, nor shall the second proviso to sub-section 1 of section 2 of the Emergency Powers Act, 1920,[13] apply to any act done in contemplation or furtherance of a strike or lockout which is by this act declared to be illegal, and any such act shall not be deemed for the purposes of any enactment to be done in contemplation or furtherance of a trade dispute. Provided that no person shall be deemed to have committed an offence under any regulations made under the Emergency Powers Act, 1920, by reason only of his having ceased work or having refused to continue to work or to accept employment.

No person refusing to take part or to continue to take part in any strike or lockout which is by this act declared to be illegal, shall be, by reason of such refusal or by reason of any action taken by him under this section, subject to expulsion from any trade union or society, or to any fine or penalty, or to deprivation of any right or benefit to which he or his legal personal representatives would otherwise be entitled, or liable to be placed in any respect either directly

---

[12] Exactly the same provisions are applied to lockouts.
[13] See nos. 136A, 137H.

or indirectly under any disability or at any disadvantage as compared with other members of the union or society, anything to the contrary in the rules of a trade union or society notwithstanding. . . .

It is hereby declared that it is unlawful for one or more persons (whether acting on their own behalf or on behalf of a trade union or of an individual employer or firm, and notwithstanding that they may be acting in contemplation or furtherance of a trade dispute) to attend at or near a house or place where a person resides or works or carries on business, or happens to be, for the purpose of obtaining or communicating information or of persuading or inducing any person to work or to abstain from working, if they so attend in such numbers or otherwise in such manner as to be calculated to intimidate any person in that house or place, or to obstruct the approach thereto or egress therefrom, or to lead to a breach of the peace. . . .

It shall not be lawful to require any member of a trade union to make any contribution to the political fund of a trade union unless he has . . . delivered at the head office or some branch office of the trade union notice in writing . . . of his willingness to contribute to that fund. . . .

Amongst the regulations as to the conditions of service in his majesty's civil establishments there shall be included regulations prohibiting established civil servants from being members, delegates, or representatives of any organization of which the primary object is to influence or affect the remuneration and conditions of employment of its members, unless the organization is an organization of which the membership is confined to persons employed by or under the crown. . . .

It shall not be lawful for any local or other public authority to make it a condition of the employment or continuance in employment of any person that he shall or shall not be a member of a trade union, or to impose any condition upon persons employed by the authority whereby employees who are or who are not members of a trade union are liable to be placed in any respect either directly or indirectly under any disability or disadvantage as compared with other employees. It shall not be lawful for any local or other public authority to make it a condition of any contract made or proposed to be made with the authority, or of the consideration or acceptance of any tender in connection with such a contract, that any person to be employed by any party to the contract shall or shall not be a member of a trade union. . . . There shall be added to section 5 of the Conspiracy and Protection of Property Act, 1875, the following provision, that is to say: "If any person employed by a local or other public authority wilfully breaks a contract of service with that authority, knowing or having reasonable cause to believe that the probable consequence of his so doing, either alone or in combination with others, will be to cause injury or danger or grave inconvenience to the community, he shall be liable, on summary conviction, to a fine not exceeding £10 or to imprisonment for a term not exceeding three months." . . .

Public General Acts, 1927, 328 f.: 17-18 George V, c. 22.

(K) EQUAL FRANCHISE ACT (1928)

An act to assimilate the franchises for men and women in respect of parliamentary and local government elections, and for purposes consequential thereon. Be it enacted . . . as follows:—

For the purpose of providing that the parliamentary franchise shall be the same for men and women, sub-sections 1 and 2 of section 4 of the Representation of the People Act, 1918 (in this act referred to as the principal act), shall be repealed, and the following sections shall be substituted for sections 1 and 2 of that act:—

. . . "1. A person shall be entitled to be registered as a parliamentary elector for a constituency (other than a university constituency) if he or she is of full age and not subject to any legal incapacity and has the requisite residence qualification, or has the requisite business premises qualification, or is the husband or wife of a person entitled to be so registered in respect of a business premises qualification. . . ."

"2. A person shall be entitled to be registered as a parliamentary elector for a university constituency if he or she is of full age and not subject to any legal incapacity and has received a degree (other than an honorary degree) at any university forming, or forming part of, the constituency. . . ."

For the purpose of providing that the local government franchise shall be the same for men and women, sub-section 3 of section 4 of the principal act shall be repealed, and the following section shall be substituted for section 3 of that act:—

"A person shall be entitled to be registered as a local government elector for a local government electoral area if he or she is of full age and not subject to any legal incapacity and is on the last day of the qualifying period occupying as owner or tenant any land or premises in that area, and has during the whole of the qualifying period so occupied any land or premises in that area . . . , or is the husband or wife of a person entitled to be so registered in respect of premises in which both the person so entitled and the husband or wife, as the case may be, reside. . . ."

Ibid., 1928, 27 f.: 18-19 George V, c. **12.**

(L) LOCAL GOVERNMENT ACT (1929)

An act to amend the law relating to the administration of poor relief, registration of births, deaths, and marriages, highways, town-planning, and local government . . . , and for purposes consequential on the matters aforesaid. Be it enacted . . . as follows:—

On the appointed day the functions of each poor law authority shall, subject to the provisions of this act . . . , be transferred to the council of the county or county borough comprising the poor law area for which the poor law authority acts . . . and, as from the appointed day, all the then existing poor law authorities shall cease to exist.

As from the appointed day the following provisions shall have effect with respect to functions relating to infant life, protection, and vaccination formerly discharged by poor law authorities: functions under Part I of the Children Act, 1908, shall be discharged by the councils of counties and county boroughs as functions under the Maternity and Child Welfare Act, 1918, except that where the council of a district have established a maternity and child welfare committee the said functions shall, in that district, be discharged by the council of the district and not by the county council; and functions relating to vaccination shall be discharged by the councils of counties and county boroughs as functions relating to public health. . . .

The council of every county and county borough shall prepare and, within six months after the commencement of this act, submit to the minister a scheme . . . of the administrative arrangements proposed to be made for discharging the functions transferred to the council under this part of this act. . . . A council, in preparing an administrative scheme, shall have regard to the desirability of securing that, as soon as circumstances permit, all assistance which can lawfully be provided otherwise than by way of poor relief shall be so provided . . . ; but nothing in this sub-section or in any scheme shall diminish or otherwise affect the duty of a council under section 34 of the Poor Law Act, 1927, to provide relief for the poor. For the purpose of this sub-section, the expression "assistance" includes maintenance and treatment at hospitals and other places, the education of children, and any other services which could, after the appointed day, be provided either by way of poor relief or by virtue of any of the above-mentioned acts. . . .

An administrative scheme shall provide for the constitution of a committee of the council (hereinafter referred to as the public assistance committee) and may provide (a) that any other committee of the council shall act as the public assistance committee, or that the members for the time being of any other such committee shall so act; and (b) for the inclusion in the public assistance committee, or among any members of another committee acting as such, of persons who are not members of the council, some of whom shall be women— so, however, that of the whole number of members of the public assistance committee, or committee or body acting as such, two-thirds at least shall be members of the council. . . .

In the case of a county the administrative scheme shall provide for the division of the county into areas, each area consisting of one or more districts, and for the constitution for each such area of a local sub-committee of the public assistance committee (to be called the guardians committee of the area) consisting of not more than thirty-six nor less than twelve members . . . ; for the discharge, subject to such general or special restrictions or conditions as the county council may from time to time impose, by each guardians committee, or a sub-committee thereof, of such of the functions transferred to the council under this part of this act as relate to the following matters:—the consideration and examination of applications for relief; the determination of the nature and amount of the relief, if any, to be given to such applicants; the determination of the amount, if any, to be paid by any recipient of relief, or the persons liable for his maintenance, towards reimbursing the council the amount expended by them on his relief; the visiting inspection or management, if the public assistance committee so request, of any poor law institutions in the area for which the guardians committee is appointed—so, however, that the functions to be delegated under this sub-section shall not include the appointment or dismissal of any officer. . . . No scheme so submitted to the minister shall be of any effect unless and until it has been approved by the minister. . . .

The council of every county shall be the highway authority as respects every road in the county which at the appointed day is a main road, or which would, apart from this section, at any time thereafter have become a main road. . . .

Where after the appointed day the council of a county and any local authority or local authorities under the Town Planning Act, 1925, are desirous of acting jointly in the preparation or adoption of a town planning scheme, they shall be entitled to do so. . . .

Ibid., 1928-29, 49 f.: 19 George V, c. 17.

(M) STATUTE OF WESTMINSTER (1931)

An act to give effect to certain resolutions passed by imperial conferences held in the years 1926 and 1930. Whereas the delegates of his majesty's governments in the united kingdom, the dominion of Canada, the commonwealth of Australia, the dominion of New Zealand, the union of South Africa, the Irish Free State, and Newfoundland, at imperial conferences holden at Westminster in the years of our Lord 1926 and 1930, did concur in making the declarations and resolutions set forth in the reports of the said conferences; and whereas it is meet and proper to set out by way of preamble to this act that, inasmuch as the crown is the symbol of the free association of the members of the British Commonwealth of Nations, and as they are united by a common allegiance to the crown, it would be in accord with the established constitutional position of all the members of the commonwealth in relation to one another that any alteration in the law touching the succession to the throne or the royal style and titles shall hereafter require the assent as well of the parliaments of all the dominions as of the parliament of the united kingdom; and whereas it is in accord with the established constitutional position that no law hereafter made by the parliament of the united kingdom shall extend to any of the said dominions as part of the law of that dominion otherwise than at the request and with the consent of that dominion; and whereas it is necessary for the ratifying, confirming, and establishing of certain of the said declarations and resolutions of the said conferences that a law be made and enacted in due form by authority of the parliament of the united kingdom; and whereas the dominion of Canada, the commonwealth of Australia, the dominion of New Zealand, the union of South Africa, the Irish Free State, and Newfoundland have severally requested and consented to the submission of a measure to the parliament of the united kingdom for making such provision with regard to the matters aforesaid as is hereafter in this act contained: now, therefore, be it enacted . . . as follows:—

In this act the expression dominion means any of the following dominions: that is to say, the dominion of Canada, the commonwealth of Australia, the dominion of New Zealand, the union of South Africa, the Irish Free State, and Newfoundland. The Colonial Laws Validity Act, 1865,[14] shall not apply to any law made after the commencement of this act by the parliament of a dominion. No law and no provision of any law made after the commencement of this act by the parliament of a dominion shall be void or inoperative on the ground that it is repugnant to the law of England, or to the provisions of any existing or future act of parliament of the united kingdom, or to any order, rule, or regulation made under any such act, and the powers of the parliament of a dominion shall include the power to repeal or amend any such act, order, rule, or regulation in so far as the same is part of the law of the dominion. It is hereby declared and enacted that the parliament of a dominion has full power to make laws having extra-territorial operation. No act of parliament of the united kingdom passed after the commencement of this act shall extend, or be deemed to extend, to a dominion as part of the law of that dominion, unless it is expressly declared in that act that that dominion has requested, and consented to, the enactment thereof. . . .

Nothing in this act shall be deemed to apply to the repeal, amendment, or alteration of the British North America Acts, 1867 to 1930, or any order, rule, or regulation made thereunder. The provisions of section 2 of this act shall extend to laws made by any of the provinces of Canada and to the powers of the legislatures of such provinces. The powers conferred by this act upon the parliament of Canada or upon the legislatures of the provinces shall be restricted to the enactment of laws in relation to matters within the competence of the parliament of Canada or of any of the legislatures of the provinces respectively. Nothing in this act shall be deemed to confer any power to repeal or alter the constitution or the Constitution Act of the commonwealth of Australia or the Constitution Act of the dominion of New Zealand otherwise than in accordance with the law existing before the commencement of this act.

---

[14] No. 131F.

Nothing in this act shall be deemed to authorize the parliament of the commonwealth of Australia to make laws on any matter within the authority of the states of Australia, not being a matter within the authority of the parliament or government of the commonwealth of Australia. Nothing in this act shall be deemed to require the concurrence of the parliament or government of the commonwealth of Australia in any law made by the parliament of the united kingdom with respect to any matter within the authority of the states of Australia, not being a matter within the authority of the parliament or government of the commonwealth of Australia, in any case where it would have been in accordance with the constitutional practice existing before the commencement of this act that the parliament of the united kingdom should make that law without such concurrence. . . .

Ibid., 1932, 13 f.: 22 George V, c. 4.

138. PROCEEDINGS IN PARLIAMENT (1909-32)

(A) DEBATE ON THE BUDGET (1909)[1]

[2 December.] The prime minister (Mr. Asquith) moved that the action of the house of lords in refusing to pass into law the financial provision made by this house for the service of the year is a breach of the constitution and a usurpation of the rights of the commons.

We are met here this afternoon under circumstances which are unexampled in the history of the British parliament. Nearly ten months ago the sovereign in a paragraph in the gracious speech from the throne addressed to the house of commons, and to the house of commons alone, invited us to make provision for the heavy additional expenditure which is due to necessities of social reform and of national defence. In a session which—if not for the actual length of its duration, certainly for the strenuousness of its labours—is, I believe, almost without a rival we have addressed ourselves to that task. . . . When a short time ago the Finance Bill received its third reading, and as it left this house, it represented, I believe, in a greater degree than can be said of any measure of our time the matured, the well sifted, the deliberate work of an overwhelming majority of the representatives of the people upon a matter which, by the custom of generations and by the course of a practically unbroken authority, is the province of this house, and of this house alone. In the course of a week, or little more than a week, the whole of this fabric has been thrown to the ground. For the first time in English history the grant of the whole of the ways and means for the supply and service of the year—a grant made at the request of the crown to the crown by the commons—has been intercepted and nullified by a body which admittedly has not the power to increase or diminish one single tax,

---

[1] On 4 November the commons, by a vote of 379 to 149, had passed the budget introduced by Lloyd George, chancellor of the exchequer. Principally because the bill included a new tax on the unearned increment of land, it had been rejected by the house of lords on 30 November.

or to propose any substitute or alternative for any one of the taxes. The house of commons would, in the judgment of his majesty's government, be unworthy of its past and of the traditions of which it is the custodian and the trustee, if it allowed another day to pass without making it clear that it does not mean to brook the greatest indignity and, I will add, the most arrogant usurpation to which, for more than two centuries, it has been asked to submit. . . .

I may be pardoned if, in passing, I refer at this point to two suggestions which have been made, proceeding from very opposite quarters, and both of them, I think, for obvious but very different reasons untenable. The first is that the executive should continue to demand and enforce the new taxes sanctioned by resolution, notwithstanding the prorogation of parliament. It is frankly admitted by those who put that suggestion forward that it is a revolutionary proposal. It would certainly bring any one who adopted it into rapid collision with the courts of law, and it does not commend itself to the judgment of his majesty's government. The second suggestion . . . is that here and now, before the present session closes, the government should bring in a new budget and submit it for approval or rejection to the house of lords. . . . It would be a pretty pass indeed for the house of commons if, after having for the first time been offered by the other house the indignity of the summary rejection of the whole of the financial arrangements of the year, it were then to stoop spontaneously to the humiliation of presenting to the same house, for its criticism and sanction, an amended budget, pruned and trimmed and refurbished to suit its scruples and to meet its tastes. . . . No minister who ventured to make such a proposal to the house of commons would deserve, and certainly no minister would retain for five minutes, the confidence of this assembly. It would be, in fact, a recognition of the right of the house of lords, not only to reject, but also to amend the financial arrangements of the year.

I dismiss these impossible suggestions, and I come to the course—the only course—which in the circumstances it is open to the government, without either breaking the law or sacrificing constitutional principle, to pursue. That course is to advise, as we have advised the crown, to dissolve this parliament at the earliest possible moment. His majesty has been graciously pleased to accept that advice, and the result, I trust, will be that the new house of commons will assemble at such time as to make it possible for it to provide, both retrospectively and prospectively, for the needs of the current financial year. If we are fortunate enough to enjoy its confidence, its first act will be to reimpose, as from this week, all taxes and duties which were embodied in the Finance Bill and to validate all past collections and deductions. . . .

But I go on now to say that the purpose of my motion to-day is not to complain of the financial and administrative hardship which the house of lords has so heedlessly inflicted upon us. . . . No; mine is a totally different purpose. It is to ask the house, in vindication of the first principles of the constitution and in assertion of its own immemorial rights, to enter a prompt and solemn protest against the whole proceeding. We live in this country, and we have lived for centuries past, under an unwritten constitution. . . . It is of course true that we have upon the statute book great instruments like Magna Carta itself, the Petition of Rights, and the Bill of Rights, which define and secure many of our rights and privileges; but the great bulk of our constitutional liberties—and, I would add, of our constitutional practices—do not derive their validity and sanction from any bill which has received the formal assent of king, lords, and commons. They rest upon usage, upon custom, upon convention. . . . And let me point out further it is an essential incident of such an unwritten constitution that there should be powers which are legal powers . . . , yet which in the course of time . . . first of all came to be fitfully and intermittently used, and finally . . . became dormant, moribund, and for all practical purposes dead.

A familiar illustration of this, well known to everybody, is the veto of the crown. There is nothing whatever to prevent me, or any other minister, from advising his majesty to-morrow to refuse his assent to a bill which has passed through both the house of commons and the house of lords. And if his majesty were to take that advice, and so refuse his assent, that bill could not take its place on the statute book and would not have its effect in law. I think, however, the minister who gave that advice would deserve to be impeached, although in point of law the right of the crown to veto a bill is just as unquestionable to-day as it was in the time of Queen Elizabeth. But two hundred years of desuetude and contrary practice have made it a legal right not constitutionally exercised or followed now. . . .

Tried by the test which I have been endeavouring to describe—the test of usage, the test of convention, the test of unbroken understanding—does not the recent action of the house of lords in rejecting the Finance Bill deserve the description which I have given to it in my resolution? Is it not a breach of the constitution? No one will deny that the house of lords has a technical right to reject a finance bill or any other bill. . . . But ever since 1628 . . . , when by the advice of the greatest lawyers of that day, the mention of the lords was deliberately omitted from the granting words in the preamble of supply bills, this house has asserted with ever-growing emphasis its own exclusive right to determine the taxation and the expenditure of the country. . . .

I am not going to discuss in reference to this unprecedented act the merits of the Finance Bill with the house of lords, but I think it is only right and fair, before I bring my case to a conclusion, that I should examine such justifications as have been put forward for the action which has been taken. In the first place, I have seen it suggested . . . that this bill was not a finance bill at all, and that therefore the constitutional rule does not apply. That, of course, is one of the most absurd contentions which has ever been advanced by a bankrupt controversialist. Here is a bill of nearly one hundred clauses, which imposed ten or eleven different sets of taxes. I will undertake to say there was not a single clause which was not relevant to its primary and governing purpose—namely, the raising of revenue. . . .

But there is another reason which is put forward by way of justification, which I think demands rather fuller scrutiny. The house of lords or their apologists tell us that they have not rejected this bill; all they have done is to refer it to the people. . . . This newfangled Caesarism which converts the house of lords into a kind of plebiscitory organ is one of the quaintest inventions of our time. Let us see what it is. . . . The theory is that the people require to be protected against their own elected representatives, especially —may I not say exclusively?—when the majority of those representatives happen to belong to the Liberal Party. By whom is the protection to be afforded? In what quarter is it to be found? Here the theory goes on that Providence, as in so many other ways, has been exceptionally kind. It has supplied us with exactly the kind of thing we want for the purpose by an unforeseen and unforeseeable evolution in our ancient house of lords. . . .

The truth is that all this talk about the duty or the right of the house of lords to refer measures to the people is, in the light of our practical and actual experience, the hollowest outcry of political cant. We never hear of it . . . when a Tory government is in power. . . . It is simply a thin rhetorical veneer, by which it is sought to gloss over the partisan, and in this case the unconstitutional, action of a purely partisan chamber. The sum and substance of the matter is that the house of lords rejected the Finance Bill last Tuesday, not because they love the people, but because they hate the budget. . . . This motion . . . is confined in terms to the new and unprecedented claim made by the house of lords to interfere with finance. . . . It represents a stage—a momentous and perhaps a decisive stage—in a protracted controversy which is drawing to a close. The real question which emerged from the political struggles in this country for the last thirty years is not whether you will have a single or a double chamber system of government, but whether, when the Tory Party is in power, the house of commons shall be omnipotent, and whether, when the Liberal Party is in power, the house of lords shall be omnipotent. . . .

The house of lords have deliberately chosen their ground. They have elected to set at naught, in regard to finance, the unwritten and time-honoured conventions of our constitution. In so doing, whether they foresaw it or not, they have opened out a wider and more far-reaching issue. We have not provoked the challenge, but we welcome it. We believe that the first principles of representative government, as embodied in our slow and ordered but everbroadening constitutional development, are at stake, and we ask the house of commons by this resolution to-day, as at the earliest possible moment we shall ask the constituencies of the country, to declare that the organ, the voice of the free people of this country, is to be found in the elective representatives of the nation.

Mr. A. J. Balfour: . . . The right honourable gentleman and his party have a perfect passion for these abstract resolutions. They bring them forward at intervals. They bind nobody; they help nobody; they hurt nobody. I doubt whether they encourage anybody, and I am sure that they do not frighten anybody. Least of all, are these resolutions likely to prove formidable to enemies or encouraging to friends, when they are made by the last dying breath of the house of commons. . . . I greatly regret that we should go down, so to speak, to our political friends uttering so gross a misrepresentation of the constitution of this country. . . . The right honourable gentleman moved easily and quickly through large spaces of English history; he went back to 1628 and he came down to the paper duties. Did he give a single argument indicating that the course which the house of lords has recently pursued is a course which, in the language of the resolution, is a breach of the constitution and a usurpation of the rights of the commons? The right honourable gentleman really never touched that point. He based his observations, as I understood him, upon a distinction between that which is technically within the law and that which is substantially within the constitution. And he said that he did not deny that rejection by the house of lords was technically within the law. He did deny that it, in no substantial sense, was within the limits of the constitution. I think the right honourable gentleman is absolutely wrong—not in drawing a distinction between that part of our constitution which is written on the statute book and that part of our constitution which is not written on the statute book; of course there is that distinction. But within the constitution which is not written on the statute book there are some things which are technically possible, which substantially nobody would recommend. There are other things which are done every day. And there is a third class belonging neither to the first nor to the second class of things —things which certainly ought not to be part of our every-day practice, but which are clearly within not merely the written law of the constitution, but within its spirit interpreted in any broad and statesmanlike way.

I do not know why the right honourable gentleman should have so deliberately ignored some of the points which he must know lie on the very face of this constitutional discussion. . . . Take so important a point as this, that the house of commons . . . as against the lords admitted in terms that the house of lords had a right to reject. . . .[2] If the very original resolution on which all our claims are based . . . bears on the face of it that admission, gratuitously made by the house of commons, why are we to go back on that,

---

[2] Balfour does not cite the resolution, but it is no. 116E.

and why are we now to alter, not the written law, but the substance of the constitution . . . ? The right honourable gentleman tells us that there is an unbroken tradition under which the house of lords has never rejected the financial proposals of the year. . . . How long has that unbroken tradition continued? It evidently could not go back before the period when all our provisions for taxation were embodied in one bill, and that is within the memory of men living. . . . The English constitution did not begin in 1860, but before that. It is quite true that the budget embodying the taxes of the year was never rejected, because there never was a budget bill embodying them; it is an entirely modern invention. . . .

Has the house of lords, in declaring that the constituencies must be consulted on this measure, gone beyond the functions which we ought to leave to a second chamber, however rarely it may be proper that they should be exercised? That is the real point. . . . That is the point which the country will have to determine. On that point I individually have no doubts whatever. . . . I shall never waver in the belief that in the exercise of its power—a power which, I grant, has been rarely exercised, but which has never been abandoned—the second chamber have shown a perfectly clear and sound instinct of what it is the duty of a second chamber to do. They have done it fearlessly, and I believe they will be supported by the country. . . .

The house divided: Ayes, 349; Noes, 134.

Parliamentary Debates, House of Commons, N.S., XIII, 546-78.

(B) DEBATE ON REFORM OF THE HOUSE OF LORDS (1910)

[29 March.] The prime minister (Mr. Asquith) moved that this house will immediately resolve itself into a committee to consider the relations between the two houses of parliament and the question of the duration of parliament. . . .

We have had within the last six months, first, and by way of climax to a long series of acts by which the decisions of this house have been flouted and set at naught, an encroachment by the house of lords upon a domain which has come to be regarded by universal consent as entirely outside their constitutional province. Next, we have had an election in which, if our interpretation of it is correct, a large majority of the representatives of the people have come here with the direct and express authority of their constituents to bring this state of things, both as regards finance and legislation, to the earliest possible close. And, lastly, we have the acknowledgment of the lords themselves that, with all the virtues and all the wisdom which they are conscious of possessing, they are, like a certain class of heroines in fiction, "not fully understood." . . .

As a necessary preliminary to the working out of our declared policy, we have as a first and urgent step to deal with things as they are, and in particular to deal with the house of lords as it is and to prevent a repetition of the unconstitutional raid of last year into the domain of finance. We have to secure, as against the house of lords, that the wish of the people, as expressed by the mature and reiterated decisions of their elected representatives, shall in all legislation be predominant. We have, as I think, at the same time to provide by adequate safeguards that the elected house shall not outstay its authority. . . . These are all matters which were clearly brought before the constituencies at the last election, and on which we believe this house is prepared to pass an immediate verdict. The resolutions for the consideration of which I am asking the house to go into committee, are of necessity couched in general terms. They are not to be treated as clauses in a bill. They are, on the contrary, the broad basis on which a bill is to be built up. . . .

I am sorry to have detained the house so long in dealing with the details of these resolutions. We put them forward to deal with the emergency which confronts us, not as purporting to be a full or adequate solution of the whole problem or as exhausting the policy of the government. We put them forward as the first and indispensable step to the emancipation of the house of commons and to rescue from something like paralysis the principles of popular government. Further, we put them forward as a demand sanctioned, as we believe, by a large majority of the representatives of the people chosen at the recent general election, themselves representing a large majority of the electorate.

Fundamental changes in this country, as nothing illustrates more clearly than this controversy, are slow to bring into effect. There was a story current of the last parliament, which in this connection bears repetition. It was told of a new member of the then house of commons, that in 1906 he witnessed for the first time the ceremony of opening parliament. . . . He was a man of very advanced views and, as he gazed upon that unique and impressive spectacle, felt constrained to mutter to a neighbour, a man of like opinions with himself, "This will take a lot of abolishing." So it will. It was a very shrewd observation; but I am not sure he had mastered the real lesson of the occasion. So far as outward vision goes, one would seem no doubt, in the presence of such a ceremony as that, to be transplanted to the days of the Plantagenets. The framework is the same; the setting is almost the same; the very figures of the picture—kings, peers, judges, commons—are the same, at any rate, in name. But that external and superficial identity masks a series of the greatest transformations that have been recorded in the constitutional experience of mankind.

The sovereign sits there on the throne of Queen Elizabeth who, as history tells us, on one occasion at the end of a single session opposed the royal veto to no less than forty-eight out of ninety-one bills which had received the assent of both houses of parliament. That royal veto, then and for long afterwards an active and potent enemy of popular rights, is literally as dead as Queen Anne. Yes, sir—and has the monarchy suffered? . . . There is not a man among us, in whatever quarter of the house he sits, who does not know the crown of this realm, with its hereditary succession, its prerogatives adjusted from generation to generation to the needs of the people and the calls of the empire, is held by our gracious sovereign by a far securer tenure than ever fell to the lot of any of his Tudor or Stuart ancestors. The liberties, again, of the commons which you, sir, only a month ago once more claimed and asserted at the same bar in time-honoured phrases . . . —the liberties of the commons, slowly and patiently won, in these days newly threatened and invaded . . . —are only in danger if, unlike our forefathers here, we refuse to take the necessary steps to make them safe. . . . The absolute veto of the lords must follow the veto of the crown before the road can be clear for the advent of full-grown and unfettered democracy.

Mr. A. J. Balfour: There were phrases in the peroration of the right honourable gentleman which suggested that he had approached the great constitutional issue, which he has raised by these resolutions, in the spirit of a constitutional minister. But I confess that, neither in the proposals themselves nor in the arguments by which in the main he has supported them, do I see any of that wise power of adapting institutions to the changing needs of the community which has been the glory of this country. . . .

Every country, when it has got a written constitution, takes care to protect that constitution and surrounds it with safeguards. We have not got a written constitution; we have no safeguards. The changes which have taken place—the right honourable gentleman has not exaggerated them—have been great and profound. They have been going on to the present time. The greatest of them has gone on without the sort of wretched legislation which you now propose. Those changes have been gradual in their growth, and we have hitherto not been threatened by those violent processes. We are threatened by them now. Some of us desire these revolutions; some of us fear them. I say, whether we desire them or whether we fear them, we are not doing our duty by the constitution which we have inherited, if we leave it to the power of the majority of this house, without the deliberate assent of the people to these changes, to carry them into effect over the heads of another place. . . .

It is madness for us to make a change in the constitution which may entirely remove all the safeguards which the right honourable gentleman himself thinks ought to exist as regards legislation in general; it is madness to remove them in regard to finance. I agree that their exercise ought to be rare, that they should be used with the utmost caution and circumspection; but that we should make it impossible that they should ever be used . . . seems to me to be the height of folly. And let me say that the opinion I venture to express upon this point is the opinion which, as far as I know, is held by all the free self-governing communities of the world. It is held by the United States of America; it is held by France; it is held by Germany; it is held by Italy; it is held by every one of our colonies, as far as I know. . . .

I must say I do not think the full absurdity of these resolutions can have occurred to those who framed them. What do they amount to? Parliament has now to last for five years—that is to say, five years is to be the limit of its legal existence. Presumably its existence will be about four years. . . . That four years is to be divided constitutionally into two periods: a one-chamber period and a two-chamber period. During the first of these periods we shall be governed by Costa Rica; we shall have a single chamber, and only a single chamber. During the second of these periods we shall revert to the traditional practice sanctioned by centuries in the British constitution and imitated in almost every civilized country in the world. Can anything be more grotesque than this double constitution under which we shall henceforth live? Like Harlequin, half will be black and half white. . . .

It is an old failing of the party which the right honourable gentleman leads, to suppose that by upsetting something which exists you are going to reform some evil of which you disapprove. . . . I think from every point of view the government are ill-advised in the course which they are taking. They are ill-advised because, I think, their change of the constitution, on their own showing, is not the one they ought to have begun. They ought, on their own showing, to have begun by reforming the house of lords. It is ill-advised because the actual alterations in their functions proposed by these resolutions are in themselves absurd and grotesque. . . . I can only say, for my own part, that, both on the demerits of these proposals themselves and on their indirect effects upon the legislation of this country, I shall offer them at every stage the strongest opposition which it is in my power to give. . . .

[14 April.] The chairman, pursuant to the order of the house of the 5th day of April, reported the resolutions to the house[3] . . . :—

1. That it is expedient that the house of lords be disabled by law from rejecting or amending a money bill, but that any such limitation by law shall not be taken to diminish or qualify the existing rights and privileges of the house of commons. For the purpose of this resolution a bill shall be considered a money bill if, in the opinion of the speaker, it contains only provisions dealing with all or any of the following subjects: namely, the imposition, repeal, remission, alteration, or regulation of taxation; charges on the consolidated fund or the provision of money by parliament; supply; the appropriation, control, or regulation of public money; the raising or guarantee of any loan or the repayment thereof; or matters incidental to those subjects or any of them. Question put, that this house doth agree with the committee in the said resolution. The house divided: Ayes, 340; Noes, 241. . . .

---

[3] Cf. no. 137A.

2. That it is expedient that the powers of the house of lords as respects bills [other] than money bills be restricted by law, so that any such bill, which has passed the house of commons in three successive sessions and, having been sent up to the house of lords at least one month before the end of the session, has been rejected by that house in each of those sessions, shall become law without the consent of the house of lords on the royal assent being declared; provided that at least two years shall have elapsed between the date of the first introduction of the bill in the house of commons and the date on which it passes the house of commons for the third time. For the purposes of this resolution, a bill shall be treated as rejected by the house of lords if it has not been passed by the house of lords either without amendment or with such amendments only as may be agreed upon by both houses. Question put, that this house doth agree with the committee in the said resolution. The house divided: Ayes, 346; Noes, 243. . . .

3. That it is expedient to limit the duration of parliament to five years. Question put, that this house doth agree with the committee in the said resolution. The house divided: Ayes, 347; Noes, 244. . . .

Ibid., XV, 1162-98; XVI, 1531-42.

(C) RESOLUTIONS OF THE HOUSE OF LORDS (1910)[4]

I. Reform of the house of lords. (1) That a strong and efficient second chamber is not merely an integral part of the British constitution, but is necessary to the well-being of the state and to the balance of parliament. (2) That such a chamber can best be obtained by the reform and reconstitution of the house of lords. (3) That a necessary preliminary of such reform and reconstitution is the acceptance of the principle that the possession of a peerage should no longer of itself give the right to sit and vote in the house of lords. (4) That in future the house of lords shall consist of lords of parliament, (a) chosen by the whole body of hereditary peers from among themselves and by nomination by the crown, (b) sitting by virtue of offices and of qualifications held by them, (c) chosen from outside.

II. Relations between the two houses of parliament. (1) That, in the opinion of this house, it is desirable that provision should be made for settling differences which may arise between the house of commons and this house, reconstituted and reduced in numbers in accordance with the recent resolutions of this house. (2) That, as to bills other than money bills, such provision should be upon the fol-

---

[4] These resolutions were finally adopted by the lords after protracted debate on certain motions of Lord Rosebery, and were sent to the commons in November, 1910. That house, however, had already adopted entirely different resolutions of its own (see the preceding document). The latter programme was carried through in the following year after the government had retained its majority in another general election, and after Prime Minister Asquith had announced that the king would, if necessary, create enough peers to force the Parliament Bill (no. 137A) through the upper house.

lowing lines: if a difference arises between the two houses with regard to any bill other than a money bill in two successive sessions, and with an interval of not less than one year, and such difference cannot be adjusted by any other means, it shall be settled in a joint sitting composed of members of the two houses; provided that, if the difference relates to a matter which is of great gravity and has not been adequately submitted for the judgment of the people, it shall not be referred to the joint sitting, but shall be submitted for decision to the electors by referendum. (3) That, as to money bills, such provision should be upon the following lines: the lords are prepared to forgo their constitutional right to reject or amend money bills which are purely financial in character; provided that effectual provision is made against tacking, and provided that, if any question arises as to whether a bill or any provisions thereof are purely financial in character, that question be referred to a joint committee of both houses, with the speaker of the house of commons as chairman, who shall have a casting vote only. If the committee hold that the bill or provisions in question are not purely financial in character, they shall be dealt with forthwith in a joint sitting of the two houses.

Ibid., XX, 457 f.

(D) DEBATE IN THE COMMONS ON CABINET RESPONSIBILITY (1932)

[8 February.] Mr. Lansbury: I beg to move that this house can have no confidence in a government which confesses its inability to decide upon a united policy and proposes to violate the long-established constitutional principle of cabinet responsibility by embarking upon tariff measures of far-reaching effect which several of his majesty's ministers declare will be disastrous to the trade and industry of the country. . . .

In regard to the general question, we shall be told, I have no doubt, that this is quite an exception. I will come to that in a minute. I want now to say that we are not opposing this procedure because we think that such procedure should not take place on occasion, or because we are opposed to the members of the government having freedom of action. I do not understand that the lord president is going to say to-day that the government propose permanently to alter the procedure that has been followed for the last hundred years with regard to cabinet responsibility. If, because of the conditions prevailing in the country, the cabinet had come to the conclusion that we ought to have a change in this matter, I think he would have found us quite ready not only to discuss but to support very drastic changes both in the methods of procedure in this house and certainly in the relationship which should exist between the cabinet and the government. No one, I think, has ever argued that a cabinet of twenty men, or even a dozen or three men, would always say aye or no on any particular question under discussion, or at all times. We are not arguing that to-day, or that a government should not, in some circumstances, make an exception, as is proposed now.

The point that we want to make in that connection is that, so far, we know that the government have no intention of asking parliament to change the present position. There is no proposal to abolish the constitutional practice which, in spite of the present cabinet decision, still remains the custom and unwritten law of the land. At the risk of being charged with not being a constitutional lawyer, I will, in the presence of the attorney general, state what the ordinary person like myself thinks the position is. Members of the cabinet are members of the privy council. They are sworn in before they take office. They are appointed by the prime minister, who is appointed by the crown, and not by this house. The prime minister, in turn, submits the names of his colleagues to his majesty. Of course, in the acceptance of a cabinet, his majesty has to take account of opinion in this house and relies on the advice of such of his advisers as he thinks necessary to call in to advise him. Therefore, the cabinet is not something which is appointed by this house, but the constitutional practice is that the cabinet is approved by the king but appointed and chosen by the prime minister. . . .

The further point I want to make is that the cabinet does not of itself resign. It is the prime minister who resigns and, by doing so, the cabinet comes to an end. It is necessary that that should be understood, because in this matter we have not heard the prime minister. I regret the cause of his absence and hope that he will soon be recovered. We do not know at present on which side of the question the prime minister stands, and if it should be that he is on the side of the dissentients, then we have the extraordinary position of a cabinet being divided, and the head being on one side and, I suppose, the body on the other. I want also to say that the cabinet is looked upon as a unit; that the one person who represents the cabinet is the prime minister; and that the prime minister is the one person who represents to the crown the decision of the cabinet.

About that there is not any question: "The cabinet is a unit—a unit as regards the sovereign and a unit as regards the legislature." It is not maintained by the authorities that you can have two voices in regard to the cabinet in this house: "Its views are laid before the sovereign and before parliament as if they were the views of one man. It gives its advice as a single whole, both in the royal closet and in the hereditary or the representative house." That is the statement, not of a theorist, but of a man well versed in practical affairs, and recognized as an authority on these matters.

I should have thought the minister of education would have considered that the late Lord Morley was a respectable authority on such a matter. But Todd's *Parliamentary Government* also says on this question: "It is not therefore allowable for a cabinet minister to oppose the measures of government, to shrink from an unqualified responsibility in respect to the same,"—this is a point which the home secretary might take to heart—"to refrain from assisting his colleagues in the advocacy of their particular measures in parliament, or to omit the performance of any administrative act which may be necessary to carry out a decision of the government, even though he may not have been a consenting party thereto. A minister who infringes any one of these rules is bound to tender his immediate resignation of office." . . .

The government on Thursday put up three of their spokesmen. The first was the chancellor, who made a very able and lucid speech and argued that only the policy of protection could save the nation. He was followed by the home secretary, equally lucid and equally convincing, who informed the nation that, if the policy set forth by the chancellor was carried, not prosperity but ruin would descend upon us. As I listened to him I thought that, from the point of view of capitalist business, there was no answer to it. Later we had a speech from the financial secretary of the treasury who in turn made mincemeat of the home secretary. Now we are told that in the sacred name of national unity these men must always play the game of "Let us pretend," and that on all other questions they are united—we do not know that at all—and that, because they may or may not be united on some other questions, they must remain the rulers of the country and break the constitutional position that they believe in. . . .

Mr. Baldwin: To-day, whatever the right honourable gentleman may say, we have a national government. In other words, it is not the government of one party. It is a government consisting of representatives of the three parties. (Honourable members: "No!") Secondly, if we look for a moment at the enormous majority which supports the government, it is perfectly true to say of many of them that we should not have had the pleasure of their company here if they had not stood as supporting a national government. Therefore, the great principle for which the fight for a century and more went on is not at stake here. The fate of no party is at stake in making a fresh precedent for a national government. Had the precedent been made for a party government, it would have been quite new, and it would have been absolutely dangerous for that party. Domestically, the tariff issue is one of great importance. Internationally, for the government the world problems are infinitely more difficult, and, whatever the right honourable gentleman may say, we believe that it would have been a grave matter for the world at large if, within a few months of the inauguration of this government, there had been a secession of any section of its members. It is very interesting that all the dissentient voices in this matter come from those who would like to see the government split. You ask, "Is what we are doing constitutional?" I remember very well—and it shows how at times questions are asked and at other times silence is maintained—after the general election of 1929, having a discussion with many of my friends as to whether we should resign at once or meet parliament. Some of my friends, perhaps with greater knowledge of the constitution than I, took the view that the constitutional position was to meet parliament and accept our dismissal by parliament. I took the view that, whatever had been the constitutional position, under universal suffrage the situation had altered; that the people of this country had shown plainly that, whether they wanted honourable members opposite or not, they certainly did not want me, and I was going to get out as soon as I could. My colleagues agreed with me, but I do not remember right honourable gentlemen opposite asking me whether I behaved constitutionally. They were getting into our places before we had time to move. Is our action constitutional? Who can say what is constitutional in the conduct of a national government? It is a precedent, an experiment, a new practice, to meet a new emergency, a new condition of things. . . .

Sir Donald Maclean: My colleagues and I joined the government on the specific definite basis of the manifesto which we laid before the country and of the manifesto of the prime minister. Those of us who accepted the invitation of the prime minister to join his cabinet can, I think, claim that we were not lacking in loyal co-operation in any of the proposals which were laid before the cabinet and subsequently before the house. Some of these were matters which were extremely distasteful to us, and we accepted them because they constituted part of the policy of dealing with an abnormal situation by emergency measures. I am no authority on cabinets, notwithstanding the long experience I have had in this house on the back benches and on both front benches, and the very happy times I have had in the chair assisting former speakers; but I think I can say that it was a very remarkable achievement to keep cabinet unity on so vast a range of subjects. That unity did not develop out of ease and compromise, but out of real difficulties, out of great dangers, and not out of safety.

Why is this debate taking place to-day? It is for the simple reason that the present proposals before the house and the country, in the view of myself and my colleagues, constitute an acceptance of a permanent protectionist policy; also that it carries with it, at any rate for the time being, a complete reversal of the practice of free trade. Some day, I hope and believe, somebody will stand at this box and propose the wiping away of these duties. You never know. That reversal will come in one of two ways: either by a party that sets itself out definitely to make the reversal, or—what I am sure my conservative friends would much prefer—by a world recognition of the harm and the disastrous damage wrought by hostile tariffs. There was no alternative for us but that of resignation, and it is no secret to say, as my right honourable friend the home secretary has said, that we did tender our resignations to the prime minister.

It is a very proper question to ask what I am doing at this box. Nobody suggests that we could not be very easily replaced. It is not a suggestion of any of my right honourable friends, certainly not of my own, that there is any special virtue in us individually which could not be more than amply made up for by those who could take our places. We only say that we are of the average capacity of dullness which usually follows the assumption of office—varied, as a wit once said, by occasional flashes of mediocrity. I have had no experience of cabinets, but I very much doubt whether any one in the government was ever present at more remarkable gatherings than those of the cabinet, dominated as they are, not with an atmosphere of self-seeking on the part of anybody, but of a very earnest desire to seek the public good. We made our response to that—all of us with some knowledge and some with considerable knowledge indeed of parliamentary life—knowing the difficulties which it has brought and will bring. In those difficulties we shall, quite naturally, bear the greater share of the burden. . . .

Earl Winterton: The doctrine of cabinet responsibility is not a mere abstract constitutional theory. It has been found to be a practical necessity in order that administrative action and legislation may have a fair chance of success. If a minority of members of the cabinet are at liberty to criticize the action of the majority of their colleagues on a matter of prime importance, the policy dealing with it is subjected from the start to an unfair handicap. . . .

Mr. Boothby: The national government was formed, and received a mandate from the country and the electorate at the last election, to put into operation a national economic policy. Of that there can be no doubt. Every national candidate of whom I heard pledged himself at the election to approach the whole economic question with an open mind, to accept the decision of the government once it was reached, and loyally to support the government subsequently. I think the right honourable gentleman, the secretary of state for the home department, is guilty of some breach of the pledges that he and his party gave at the election. The government came to a decision, by a majority of the cabinet, I agree; but at the election we knew nothing about this new doctrine of cabinet irresponsibility. . . .

Mr. de Rothschild: At the general election the fiscal policy was not part of the policy put forward either by the prime minister or the lord president of the council. It was not regarded as a paramount issue. The paramount issue was: Shall we or shall we not have a national government to tackle these great problems which face the country to-day—war debts, reparations, currency, disarmament? . . . The national government was elected in order that more than one point of view should be put forward at cabinet meetings and thus each member of the government owes it to the country to voice his own conception. If members of the government believe that the fiscal policy has an important bearing on questions of world peace, disarmament, war debts, and reparations, or if they believe that the new fiscal system will prevent the countries of the world arriving at a settlement, then it becomes their duty to put forward their views in regard to any fiscal changes proposed by the government. It is the will of the nation that all these views should be expressed. . . .

Sir Thomas Inskip: . . . The practice of so-called cabinet unanimity is certainly no older than the fiscal system which we have been discussing in the last few days in this house. Some parliamentary institutions have grown up with the nation, but this particular tradition of government unanimity or government solidarity, has certainly been the growth of no more than a hundred years, as my right honourable friend, the lord president of the council, pointed out. The fact is, as everybody knows, that it is a custom that has only developed since governments began to take their shape on hard and fast party lines. It was a practice formulated and adopted, not so much in the national interest, as in the party interest. Now, as we all know, the events of the last six months, or rather of the late summer of last year, were events which made everybody, every thinking person, appreciate that it was not a time when the best results could be obtained from the party system. The decision to form a national government was, I think, applauded in every party in the state, and I believe that everybody realized that, if we were to come through the troubles that then suddenly confronted us, there must be a drawing together of men of good will in all parties. I think a great many people in the Labour Party regretted that there was such a manifestation of the most acid and bitter party spirit in the discussions that took place immediately following the formation of that government. But when that decision to form a national government was taken, it is not surprising that the nation's necessities compelled us to consider whether the old constitutional precedents need to be followed with the same rigidity and exactness as had been customary. . . .

Speaking for the government, as I do this evening, I say the government have deliberately come to the decision that in the very special circumstances of this kind it is better that they should openly and honestly disagree upon this one topic than that there should be any pretence of agreement while all the time there is a festering sore of disagreement in the ranks of the cabinet. . . . There is no intention of any substantial breach or any other breaches of what is, of course, a rule of common sense—that men who are going to act together shall be substantially agreed upon the policy which they have to carry through. Let us consider the nature of this question upon which there has been a measure of division. The tariff question has been with us for some twenty-five or thirty years. It is a question that has a peculiar flavour. It excites passionate feelings. It recalls "far off things and battles long ago." It is charged with emotion. It is a question upon which people do not readily surrender their convictions. Some of my right honourable friends here have anchored their views to free trade, just as some of us have anchored ours to protection.

Is it to be said that in this crisis of the nation's history it was quite impossible for anybody who had formed a definite opinion upon this great controversy to get together with others who disagree with him on that question and to unite with them in preparing measures which will bring the nation through its crisis? Of course it may be said that it is impossible; but we believe, contrary to what the honour-

able gentleman has said, that it is not impossible. By adopting a method of which the country has approved with an amazing measure of unanimity—the proposal that there shall be disagreement and an opportunity of expressing it on the part of four or five members of the government—we can have an agreement upon the whole policy of the government except upon this one topic; and upon this topic effect is to be given to what is the view of the majority of the cabinet and also, I believe, of the party. . . .
Parliamentary Debates, House of Commons, Fifth Series, CCLXI, 515-624.

139. RECORDS OF JUDICIAL CASES (1884-1935)

(A) BRADLAUGH V. GOSSETT (1884)[1]

. . . The resolution of the house of commons of the 9th of July, 1883, read with the correspondence between the speaker and Mr. Bradlaugh, shows that for reasons which are not before us the house of commons resolved that Mr. Bradlaugh, who had been duly elected member for Northampton, should not be permitted to take the oath prescribed by law for members duly elected, and that he should be excluded, if necessary, by actual force from the house, unless he would engage not to do so. We are asked to declare this order void, and to restrain the serjeant-at-arms from enforcing it.

I may observe, before considering this question, that but for the amendment made at the hearing I, at least, should have felt bound to decide the case on a much narrower ground than that on which I think we ought to deal with it. Taken by itself, the order of the 9th of July states nothing except that the house had by resolution excluded a member, who in the judgment of the house had disturbed its proceedings, till he undertook not further to disturb it. It is obvious that we could not interfere with what might be a mere measure

---

[1] In 1880, on being elected to parliament and on coming before the speaker to be sworn in, Charles Bradlaugh sought to substitute an affirmation for an oath. This he held he might do by virtue of the Parliamentary Oaths Act of 1866, which allowed such substitution on the part of members already entitled to make affirmation in ordinary legal proceedings. The house, however, by majority vote denied him the privilege, on the ground that he had not been permitted to make affirmation in legal proceedings until after the year 1866. Then, when Bradlaugh offered to take the oath, the majority adjudged him incompetent to do so because he had abandoned that procedure in the courts. He vainly tried other means of inducing the house to admit him—including the administration of the oath to himself. Ultimately, he went to law, bringing suit against Gossett, serjeant-at-arms of the commons, to prevent the latter from enforcing the exclusion order. The following excerpt from the judgment of Justice Stephen in the queen's bench division shows why the court refused to interfere in the matter. Though frequently re-elected, Bradlaugh did not gain admission to the house until 1886, when a new speaker asserted the right of every member to take an oath when he chose to do so. In 1891 the commons unanimously voted to strike the earlier exclusion order from the journals of the house. Cf. no. 134B, C.

of internal discipline. The order as it stands is consistent with the supposition that Mr. Bradlaugh, on presenting himself to take the oath, had in some way misconducted himself, and that the house had ordered him to be excluded till he promised not to repeat his misconduct. With such a measure of internal discipline we obviously could not interfere. The correspondence with the speaker certainly sets the matter in a different light. I cannot read the statement of claim as asserting less or interpret the demurrer as admitting less than what I have already stated; and this raises the question which the parties probably wished to have decided in a very broad way.

The legal question which this statement of the case appears to me to raise for our decision is this: Suppose that the house of commons forbids one of its members to do that which an act of parliament requires him to do, and, in order to enforce its prohibition, directs its executive officer to exclude him from the house by force if necessary; is such an order one which we can declare to be void and restrain the executive officer of the house from carrying out? In my opinion, we have no such power. I think that the house of commons is not subject to the control of her majesty's courts in its administration of that part of the statute law which has relation to its own internal proceedings, and that the use of such actual force as may be necessary to carry into effect such a resolution as the one before us is justifiable. . . .

The Parliamentary Oaths Act prescribes the course of proceeding to be followed on the occasion of the election of a member of parliament. In order to raise the question now before us, it is necessary to assume that the house of commons has come to a resolution inconsistent with the act; for, if the resolution and the act are not inconsistent, the plaintiff has obviously no grievance. We must, of course, face this supposition and give our decision upon the hypothesis of its truth. But it would be indecent and improper to make the further supposition that the house of commons deliberately and intentionally defies and breaks the statute law. The more decent, and I may add, the more natural and probable supposition is that, for reasons which are not before us and of which we are therefore unable to judge, the house of commons considers that there is no inconsistency between the act and the resolution. They may think there is some implied exception to the act. They may think that what the plaintiff proposes to do is not in compliance with its directions. With this we have nothing to do. Whatever may be the reasons of the house of commons for their conduct, it would be impossible for us to do justice without hearing and considering those reasons; but it would be equally impossible for the house, with any regard for its own dignity and independence, to suffer its reasons to be laid before us for that purpose, or to accept our interpretation of the law in preference to its own. It seems to follow that the house of commons has the exclusive power of interpreting the statute, so far as the regulation of its own proceedings within its own walls is concerned; and that, even if that interpretation should be erroneous, this court has no power to interfere with it directly or indirectly. . . .

The plaintiff argued his own case before us at length. It is due to him to state the reasons why his arguments do not convince me. He referred to a great number of authorities; but his argument was in substance short and simple. He said that the resolution of the house of commons was illegal, as the house had no power to alter the law of the land by resolution; and, admitting that the house has power to regulate its own procedure, he contended that in preventing him from taking his seat, the house went beyond matter of internal regulation and procedure, as they deprived both him and the electors of Northampton of a right recognized by law, which ought to be protected by the law; and so inflicted upon him and them wrongs which would be without a remedy if we failed to apply one. I think that each part of this argument requires a plain, direct answer.

It is certainly true that a resolution of the house of commons cannot alter the law. If it were ever necessary to do so, this court would assert this doctrine to the full extent to which it was asserted in Stockdale v. Hansard. The statement that the resolution of the house of commons was illegal must, I think, be assumed to be true, for the purposes of the present case. The demurrer for those purposes admits it. We decide nothing unless we decide that, even if it is illegal in the sense of being opposed to the Parliamentary Oaths Act, it does not entitle the plaintiff to the relief sought. . . . I do not say that the resolution of the house is the judgment of a court not subject to our revision; but it has much in common with such a judgment. The house of commons is not a court of justice; but the effect of its privilege to regulate its own internal concerns practically invests it with a judicial character when it has to apply to particular cases the provisions of acts of parliament. We must presume that it discharges this function properly and with due regard to the laws, in the making of which it has so great a share. If its determination is not in accordance with law, this resembles the case of an error by a judge whose decision is not subject to appeal. There is nothing startling in the recognition of the fact that such an error is possible. If, for instance, a jury in a criminal case give a perverse verdict, the law has provided no remedy. The maxim that there is no wrong without a remedy does not mean, as it is sometimes supposed, that there is a legal remedy for every moral or political wrong. If this were its meaning, it would be manifestly untrue. There is no legal remedy for the breach of a solemn promise not under seal and made without consideration; nor for many kinds of verbal slander, though each may involve utter ruin; nor for oppressive legislation, though it may reduce men practically to slavery; nor for the worst damage to person and property inflicted by the most unjust and cruel war. The maxim means only that legal wrong and legal remedy are correlative terms; and it would be more intelligibly and correctly stated, if it were reversed, so as to stand, "Where there is no legal remedy, there is no legal wrong."

The assertion that the resolution of the house goes beyond matter of procedure, and that it does in effect deprive both Mr. Bradlaugh himself and his constituents of legal rights of great value, is undoubtedly true if the word "procedure" is construed in the sense in which we speak of civil procedure and criminal procedure, by way of opposition to the substantive law which systems of procedure apply to particular cases. No doubt, the right of the burgesses of Northampton to be represented in parliament, and the right of their duly elected representative to sit and vote in parliament and to enjoy the other rights incidental to his position upon the terms provided by law are in the most emphatic sense legal rights, legal rights of the highest importance, and in the strictest sense of the words. Some of these rights are to be exercised out of parliament, others within the walls of the house of commons. Those which are to be exercised out of parliament are under the protection of this court, which, as has been shown in many cases, will apply proper remedies if they are in any way invaded, and will in so doing be bound, not by resolutions of either house of parliament, but by its own judgment as to the law of the land, of which the privileges of parliament form a part. Others must be exercised, if at all, within the walls of the house of commons; and it seems to me that, from the nature of the case, such rights must be dependent upon the resolutions of the house. In my opinion the house stands with relation to such rights and to the resolutions which affect their exercise, in precisely the same relation as we, the judges of this court, stand in to the laws which regulate the rights of which we are the guardians, and to the judgments which apply them to particular cases; that is to say, they are bound by the most solemn obligations which can bind men to any course of conduct whatever, to guide their conduct by the law as they understand it. If they misunderstand it or (I apologize for the supposition) wilfully disregard it, they resemble mistaken or unjust judges; but in either case there is, in my judgment, no appeal from their decision. The law of the land gives no such appeal; no precedent has been or can be produced in which any court has ever interfered with the internal affairs of either house of parliament, though the cases are no doubt numerous in which the courts have declared the limits of their powers outside of their respective houses. This is enough to justify the conclusion at which I arrive.

We ought not to try to make new laws, under the pretence of declaring the existing law. But I must add that this is not a case in which I at least feel tempted to do so. It seems to me that, if we were to attempt to erect ourselves into a court of appeal from the house of commons, we should consult neither the public interest, nor the interests of parliament and the constitution, nor our own dignity. We should provoke a conflict between the house of commons and this court, which in itself would be a great evil; and, even upon the most improbable supposition of their acquiescence in our adverse decision, an appeal would lie from that decision to the court of appeal, and thence to the house of lords, which would thus become the judge in the last resort of the powers and privileges of the house of commons.

For these reasons I am of opinion that there must be judgment for the defendant.

Law Reports, Queen's Bench Division, XII, 277 f.

(B) KRUSE V. JOHNSON (1898)[2]

The county council of Kent, claiming to act under their statutory powers, made the following by-law: "No person shall sound or play upon any musical or noisy instrument or sing in any public place or highway within fifty yards of any dwelling-house after being required by any constable, or by an inmate of such house personally, or by his or her servant, to desist."

The appellant was summoned before the magistrates for offending against this by-law, when it was proved that, on October 17, 1897, he persisted in singing in a public highway within fifty yards of a dwelling-house, after having been required by a police constable to desist. It was further proved by the occupier of the dwelling-house that the singing of the appellant and those with him was an annoyance to such occupier. The occupier had not, on the day in question, set the constable in motion, but he had on previous occasions complained to the police of the appellant's singing. The magistrates convicted the appellant, and against that conviction the present appeal is brought.

The question reserved for this court is whether the by-law is valid. If valid, the conviction is to stand. It is objected that the by-law is *ultra vires*, on the ground that it is unreasonable and therefore bad. It is necessary, therefore, to see what is the authority under which the by-law in question has been made, and what are the relations between its framers and those affected by it. But first it seems necessary to consider what is a by-law. A by-law of the class we are here considering I take to be an ordinance affecting the public, or some portion of the public, imposed by some authority clothed with statutory powers ordering something to be done or not to be done, and accompanied by some sanction or penalty for its non-observance. It necessarily involves restriction of liberty of action by persons who come under its operation as to acts which, but for the by-law, they would be free to do or not do as they pleased. Further, it involves this consequence: that, if validly made, it has the force of law within the sphere of its legitimate operation.

In the present case we are dealing with a by-law made by a local representative body, namely, the county council of Kent, which is

---

[2] The facts in this case are fully stated in the following judgment, given by Lord Russell of Killowen, Chief Justice, in the queen's bench division of the high court, to which Kruse, a holder of religious meetings, had appealed after conviction before the local magistrates.

created under the Local Government Act, 1888,[3] and is endowed with the powers of making by-laws given to municipal corporate bodies under the Municipal Corporations Act, 1882.[4] Section 16 of the Local Government Act, 1888, provides that a county council shall have the same power of making by-laws in relation to their county as the council of a borough have in relation to their borough; and it further provides that section 187 of the Public Health Act of 1875[5] shall apply to such by-laws. I will take these statutes in the order of time.

Section 182 of the act of 1875 provides that all by-laws made by a local authority under that act shall be under their common seal, and may be altered or repealed by a subsequent by-law; but no by-law shall be repugnant to the laws of England or to the provisions of the act. Section 183 gives power to impose penalties. Section 184 provides that by-laws shall not take effect until confirmed by the local government board, which may allow or disallow them, and before their confirmation notice of intention to apply for confirmation must be advertised, and for a month at least before such application a copy of the proposed by-laws must have been kept at the office of the local authority for the inspection of ratepayers, and the clerk of the local authority is bound to furnish on application a copy of the proposed by-laws, or a part of them, to any ratepayer on a certain payment being made. Section 23 of the act of 1882 provides that the council of the borough may from time to time make such by-laws as to them seem meet for the good rule and government of the borough, and for the prevention and suppression of nuisances not already punishable in a summary manner, and they may, by such by-laws, appoint such fines, not exceeding £5, as they deem necessary for the prevention of offences against the by-laws. It is under this authority that the by-law in question was framed.

What are the checks or safeguards under which this very wide authority of making by-laws is exercisable? The same section 23 further provides that no by-law can be made unless two-thirds of the whole number of the council are present; and, when so made, it shall not come into force until the expiration of forty days after a copy thereof has been fixed on the town hall; and it shall not come into force until the expiration of forty days after a copy sealed with the corporate seal has been sent to the secretary of state; and if, within those forty days, the queen, with the advice of her privy council, disallows a proposed by-law or part thereof, such by-law, or such part, shall not come into force, and the queen may, within the forty days, enlarge the time within which the by-law shall not come into

---

[3] No. 135D.

[4] By this act the powers of municipal corporations, as reformed in 1835 (see L.O. 130F), were further defined, particularly in relation to the authority of the central government.

[5] A codification which displaced all earlier legislation concerning public health.

force. We thus find that parliament has thought fit to delegate to representative public bodies in towns and cities, and also in counties, the power of exercising their own judgment as to what are the by-laws which to them seem proper to be made for good rule and government in their own localities. But that power is accompanied by certain safeguards. . . .

I agree that the presence of these safeguards in no way relieves the court of the responsibility of inquiring into the validity of by-laws where they are brought in question, or in any way affects the authority of the court in the determination of their validity or invalidity. It is to be observed, moreover, that the by-laws, having come into force . . . are not unchangeable. The power is to make by-laws from time to time as to the authority shall seem meet; and if experience shows that in any respect existing by-laws work hardly or inconveniently, the local authority, acted upon by the public opinion, as it must necessarily be, of those concerned, has full power to repeal or alter them. It need hardly be added that, should experience warrant that course, the legislature which has given may modify or take away the powers they have delegated.

I have thought it well to deal with these points in some detail, and for this reason, that the great majority of the cases in which the question of by-laws has been discussed are not cases of by-laws of bodies of a public representative character entrusted by parliament with delegated authority, but are for the most part cases of railway companies, dock companies, or other like companies, which carry on their business for their own profit, although incidentally for the advantage of the public. In this class of case it is right that the courts should jealously watch the exercise of these powers and guard against their unnecessary or unreasonable exercise to the public disadvantage. But when the court is called upon to consider the by-laws of public representative bodies, clothed with the ample authority which I have described and exercising that authority accompanied by the checks and safeguards which have been mentioned, I think the consideration of such by-laws ought to be approached from a different standpoint. They ought to be supported if possible. They ought to be, as has been said, "benevolently" interpreted, and credit ought to be given to those who have to administer them that they will be reasonably administered. This involves the introduction of no new canon of construction. But, further, looking to the character of the body legislating under the delegated authority of parliament, to the subject matter of such legislation, and to the nature and extent of the authority given to deal with matters which concern them, and in the manner which to them shall seem meet, I think courts of justice ought to be slow to condemn as invalid any by-law, so made under such conditions, on the ground of supposed unreasonableness. . . .

I do not mean to say that there may not be cases in which it would be the duty of the court to condemn by-laws, made under such authority as these were made, as invalid because unreasonable. But unreasonable in what sense? If, for instance, they were found to be partial and unequal in their operation as between different classes; if they were manifestly unjust; if they disclosed bad faith; if they involved such oppressive or gratuitous interference with the rights of those subject to them as could find no justification in the minds of reasonable men; the court might well say, "Parliament never intended to give authority to make such rules; they are unreasonable and *ultra vires.*" But it is in this sense, and in this sense only, as I conceive, that the question of unreasonableness can properly be regarded. A by-law is not unreasonable merely because particular judges may think that it goes further than is prudent or necessary or convenient, or because it is not accompanied by a qualification or an exception which some judges may think ought to be there. Surely it is not too much to say that in matters which directly and mainly concern the people of the county, who have the right to choose those whom they think best fitted to represent them in their local government bodies, such representatives may be trusted to understand their own requirements better than judges. . . .

In my opinion, judged by the test of reasonableness, even in its narrower sense, this is a reasonable by-law; but, whether I am right or wrong in this view, I am clearly of opinion that no court of law can properly say that it is invalid. In the result the conviction appealed from must, in my opinion, be affirmed.

Ibid., 1898, II, 96-103.

(C) LOCAL GOVERNMENT BOARD V. ARLIDGE (1915)[6]

. . . Which of these opinions (expressed by judges in the court of appeals) was right can only be determined by referring to the language of the legislature. Here, as in other cases, we have simply to construe that language and to abstain from guessing at what parliament had in its mind, excepting so far as the language enables us to do so. There is no doubt that the question is one affecting property and the liberty of a man to do what he chooses with what is his own. Such rights are not to be affected unless parliament has said so. But parliament, in what it considers higher interests than those of the individual, has so often interfered with such rights on other occasions that it is dangerous for judges to lay much stress on what a hundred years ago would have been a presumption consider-

---

[6] Arlidge, the holder of a lease on a dwelling-house, brought suit against the local government board (established in 1871) for having, as he alleged, prohibited the use of his house for habitation without duly observing the provisions of the Housing and Town-Planning Act of 1909. Having lost the decision in the divisional court, he took the case to the court of appeal, where a majority of the judges rendered judgment in his favour, although a minority expressed decided views on the other side. Thereupon the local government board appealed to the house of lords. The unanimous opinion of that court, as delivered by Viscount Haldane, will appear from the accompanying extracts.

ably stronger than it is to-day. I therefore turn to the acts of parliament which are relevant with the sense that there is little justification for looking in advance for the embodiment of one scheme as more probable than the embodiment of another.

The closing of dwelling-houses as being dangerous or injurious to health, or unfit for habitation, is no new jurisdiction. The Housing of the Working Classes Act, 1890, gave to the local authority the power to take proceedings to enforce penalties and closing orders before courts of summary jurisdiction, to be followed, in certain circumstances, by demolition orders. Under that act the owner of the house had an appeal to quarter sessions. This power of closing was somewhat extended by the Housing of the Working Classes Act, 1903, but the principle of the application being to a court of justice remained the same. A change of this principle was introduced in the Housing and Town-Planning Act, 1909. The local authority was empowered itself to make the closing order, certain conditions having been complied with, and it was given power to determine the closing order if satisfied that the house in respect of which the order had been made had subsequently been rendered fit for habitation. In respect of both a closing order and a determining order, the owner was given a right of appeal. But the appeal was to be, not as before to quarter sessions, but to the local government board. Stringent powers of inspection were given to both the local authority and the local government board. In the case of an appeal, the procedure as to everything, including costs, was to be such as the board might by rules determine. The board was to have power to make such order on any appeal as it should think equitable. It could state a case, but only on a question of law, for the opinion of the high court, and could be compelled by the high court to do so. The rules were to provide that the board should not dismiss any appeal without having first held a public local inquiry. . . . My lords, it is obvious that the act of 1909 introduced a change of policy. The jurisdiction, both as regards original applications and as regards appeals, was in England transferred from courts of justice to the local authority and the local government board, both of them administrative bodies, and it is necessary to consider what consequences this change of policy imported.

My lords, when the duty of deciding an appeal is imposed, those whose duty it is to decide it must act judicially. They must deal with the question referred to them without bias, and they must give to each of the parties the opportunity of adequately presenting the case made. The decision must be come to in the spirit and with the sense of responsibility of a tribunal whose duty it is to mete out justice. But it does not follow that the procedure of every such tribunal must be the same. In the case of a court of law, tradition in this country has prescribed certain principles to which in the main the procedure must conform. But what that procedure is to be in detail must depend on the nature of the tribunal. In modern times it has become increasingly common for parliament to give an appeal in matters which really pertain to administration, rather than to the exercise of the judicial functions of an ordinary court, to authorities whose functions are administrative and not in the ordinary sense judicial. Such a body as the local government board has the duty of enforcing obligations on the individual which are imposed in the interests of the community. Its character is that of an organization with executive functions. In this it resembles other great departments of the state. When, therefore, parliament entrusts it with judicial duties, parliament must be taken, in the absence of any declaration to the contrary, to have intended it to follow the procedure which is its own, and is necessary if it is to be capable of doing its work efficiently.

I agree with the view expressed in an analogous case by my noble and learned friend Lord Loreburn. . . . He laid down that, in disposing of a question which was the subject of an appeal to it, the board of education was under a duty to act in good faith and to listen fairly to both sides, inasmuch as that was a duty which lay on every one who decided anything. But he went on to say that he did not think it was bound to treat such a question as though it were a trial. The board had no power to administer an oath, and need not examine witnesses. It could, he thought, obtain information in any way it thought best, always giving a fair opportunity to those who were parties in the controversy to correct or contradict any relevant statement prejudicial to their view. If the board failed in this duty, its order might be the subject of *certiorari* and it must itself be the subject of *mandamus*.[7]

My lords, I concur in this view of the position of an administrative body to which the decision of a question in dispute between parties has been entrusted. The result of its inquiry must, as I have said, be taken, in the absence of directions in the statute to the contrary, to be intended to be reached by its ordinary procedure. In the case of the local government board it is not doubtful what this procedure is. The minister at the head of the board is directly responsible to parliament like other ministers. He is responsible not only for what he himself does but for all that is done in his department. The volume of work entrusted to him is very great and he cannot do the great bulk of it himself. He is expected to obtain his materials vicariously through his officials, and he has discharged his duty if he sees that they obtain these materials for him properly. To try to extend his duty beyond this and to insist that he and other members of the board should do everything personally would be to impair his efficiency. Unlike a judge in a court, he is not only at liberty but is compelled to rely on the assistance of his staff. When, therefore, the board is directed to dispose of an appeal, that

---

[7] Writs through which its decisions might be subjected to judicial review.

does not mean that any particular official of the board is to dispose of it. . . .

Provided the work is done judicially and fairly in the sense indicated by Lord Loreburn, the only authority that can review what has been done is the parliament to which the minister in charge is responsible. . . . So long as the board followed a procedure which was usual and not calculated to violate the tests to which I have already referred, I think that the board was discharging the duty imposed on it in the fashion parliament must be taken to have contemplated when it deliberately transferred the jurisdiction, first, from a court of summary jurisdiction to the local authority, and then, for the purposes of all appeals, from quarter sessions to an administrative department of the state. . . .

For the reasons I have given, I have arrived at the conclusion that . . . the order of the divisional court should be restored.

Law Reports, Appeal Cases, 1915, pp. 130 f.

(D) THE KING v. HALLIDAY (1917)[8]

My lords, the appellant in this case is a naturalized British subject of German birth who has been interned by an order made by the secretary of state under the powers of regulation 14 B, which was made under the Defence of the Realm Consolidation Act, 1914.[9] It was contended that regulation 14 B was not authorized by the act and was *ultra vires.*

It is beyond all dispute that parliament has power to authorize the making of such a regulation. The only question is whether on a true construction of the act it has done so. The relevant part of the act in question is section 1, sub-section 1:—

"His majesty in council has power during the continuance of the present war to issue regulations for securing the public safety and the defence of the realm, and as to the powers and duties for that purpose of the admiralty and army council and of the members of his majesty's forces and other persons acting in his behalf; and may by such regulations authorize the trial by courts martial, or in the case of minor offences by courts of summary jurisdiction, and punishment of persons committing offences against the regulations, and in particular against any of the provisions of such regulations designed (a) to prevent persons communicating with the enemy or obtaining information for that purpose or any purpose calculated to jeopardize the success of the operations of any of his majesty's forces or the forces of his allies or to assist the enemy; or (b) to secure the safety of his majesty's forces and ships and the safety

---

[8] This was an *ex parte* action, brought in the king's name on behalf of one Zadig, interned during the war with Germany. The facts in the case are all set forth in the judgment delivered in the house of lords by Lord Chancellor Finlay.

[9] No. 137c.

of any means of communication and of railways, ports, and harbours; or (c) to prevent the spread of false reports or reports likely to cause disaffection to his majesty or to interfere with the success of his majesty's forces by land or sea or to prejudice his majesty's relations with foreign powers; or (d) to secure the navigation of vessels in accordance with directions given by or under the authority of the admiralty; or (e) otherwise to prevent assistance being given to the enemy or the successful prosecution of the war being endangered."

The power conferred on his majesty is limited to the duration of the war and is to issue regulations for securing the public safety and the defence of the realm. The sub-section goes on to provide that his majesty may by such regulations authorize the trial and punishment of persons committing offences against the regulations, and especially against regulations designed for any of the purposes enumerated under heads (a), (b), (c), (d), and (e). . . . On the face of it, the statute authorizes in this sub-section provisions of two kinds: for prevention and for punishment. Any preventive measures, even if they involve some restraint or hardship upon individuals, do not partake in any way of the nature of punishment, but are taken by way of precaution to prevent mischief to the state. Any one who infringes such regulations will become the proper subject of punishment.

The regulation in question made under this statute is regulation 14 B of the Defence of the Realm (Consolidation) Regulations. It is as follows:—

"Where, on the recommendation of a competent naval or military authority or of one of the advisory committees hereinafter mentioned, it appears to the secretary of state that, for securing the public safety or the defence of the realm, it is expedient, in view of the hostile origin or associations of any person, that he shall be subjected to such obligations and restrictions as are hereinafter mentioned, the secretary of state may by order require that person forthwith, or from time to time, either to remain in, or to proceed to and reside in, such place as may be specified in the order, and to comply with such directions as to reporting to the police, restriction of movement, and otherwise as may be specified in the order, or to be interned in such place as may be specified in the order: provided that any such order shall, in the case of any person who is not a subject of a state at war with his majesty, include express provision for the due consideration by one of such advisory committees of any representations he may make against the order. . . . The advisory committees for the purposes of this regulation shall be such advisory committees as are appointed for the purpose of advising the secretary of state with respect to the internment and deportation of aliens, each of such committees being presided over by a person who holds or has held high judicial office. . . .

It will be observed that any action of the secretary of state under this regulation is to be upon the recommendation of a competent naval or military authority or of an advisory committee. If on such recommendation it appears to the secretary of state that, for securing the public safety or the defence of the realm, it is expedient so to do, he may subject any person of hostile origin or associations to certain restrictions, one of which is internment. The order must, however, include provision in the case of any person, not being an enemy subject, for consideration of any representation which the person affected may make against the order by an advisory committee, which is to be presided over by a person who holds or has held high judicial office. The regulation, therefore, provides means for ascertaining whether any complaint against the justice or necessity of the order is well founded.

The order complained of was made by the home secretary on October 15, 1915, and is as follows:—

"Whereas, on the recommendation of a competent military authority appointed under the Defence of the Realm Regulations, it appears to me that, for securing the public safety and the defence of the realm, it is expedient that Arthur Zadig, of 56 Portsdown Road, Maida Vale, W., should, in view of his hostile origin and associations, be subjected to such obligations and restrictions as are hereinafter mentioned: I hereby order that the said Arthur Zadig shall be interned in the institution in Cornwallis Road, Islington, which is now used as a place of internment, and shall be subject to all the rules and conditions applicable to aliens there interned. If, within seven days from the date on which this order is served on the said Arthur Zadig, he shall submit to me any representations against the provisions of this order, such representations will be referred to the advisory committee appointed for the purpose of advising me with respect to the internment and deportation of aliens and presided over by a judge of the high court, and will be duly considered by the committee. If I am satisfied by the report of the said committee that this order may be revoked or varied without injury to the public safety or the defence of the realm, I will revoke or vary the order by a further order in writing under my hand. Failing such revocation or variation, this order shall remain in force. (Signed) John Simon, one of his majesty's principal secretaries of state. Whitehall, 15th October, 1915."

The truth of the recital that Zadig is a person of hostile origin and associations was not questioned, but it was insisted that parliament had not conferred the power to make such an order in the interest of the public safety against such persons. The order provides for representations being made against it and for their consideration by an advisory committee presided over by a judge of the high court, and states that, if the home secretary is satisfied by the report of such committee that the order may be revoked or varied without injury to the public safety and the defence of the realm, he will revoke or vary the order. As I have stated, the power of parliament to authorize such a proceeding was not and could not be disputed. The only question is as to the construction of the act.

It was contended (1) that some limitation must be put upon the general words of the statute; (2) that there is no provision for imprisonment without trial; (3) that the provisions made by the Defence of the Realm Act, 1915, for the trial of British subjects by a civil court with a jury strengthened the contention of the appellant; (4) that general words in a statute could not take away the vested rights of the subject or alter the fundamental law of the constitution; (5) that the statute is in its nature penal and must be strictly construed; (6) that a construction said to be repugnant to the constitutional traditions of this country could not be adopted. Reference was made by the appellant's counsel to the history of the various interferences with a right to *habeas corpus* in times of public danger, and it was urged that, if it had been intended to interfere with personal liberty, this is the course which would have been adopted.

I am unable to accede to any of the arguments urged on behalf of the appellant. It was not, as I understand the argument, contended that the words of the statute are not in their natural meaning wide enough to authorize such a regulation as regulation 14 B, but it was strongly contended that some limitation must be put upon these words, as an unrestricted interpretation might involve extreme consequences—such as, it was suggested, the infliction of the punishment of death without trial. It appears to me to be a sufficient answer to this argument that it may be necessary in a time of great public danger to entrust great powers to his majesty in council and that parliament may do so, feeling certain that such powers will be reasonably exercised. . . .

One of the most obvious means of taking precautions against dangers such as are enumerated is to impose some restriction on the freedom of movement of persons whom there may be any reason to suspect of being disposed to help the enemy. It is to this that regulation 14 B is directed. The measure is not punitive but precautionary. It was strongly urged that no such restraint should be imposed except as the result of a judicial inquiry, and indeed counsel for the appellant went so far as to contend that no regulation could be made forbidding access to the seashore by suspected persons. It seems obvious that no tribunal for investigating the question, whether circumstances of suspicion exist warranting some restraint, can be imagined less appropriate than a court of law. No crime is charged. The question is whether there is ground for suspicion that a particular person may be disposed to help the enemy. The duty of deciding this question is by the order thrown upon the secretary of state, and an advisory committee presided over by a judge of the high court is provided to bring before him any grounds for thinking that the order may properly be revoked or varied.

The statute was passed at a time of supreme national danger, which still exists. The danger of espionage and of damage by secret agents to ships, railways, munition works, bridges, etc., had to be guarded against. The restraint imposed may be a necessary measure of precaution, and in the interests of the whole nation it may be regarded as expedient that such an order should be made in suitable cases. This appears to me to be the meaning of the statute. Every reasonable precaution to obviate hardship which is consistent with the object of the regulation appears to have been taken. It was urged that, if the legislature had intended to interfere with personal liberty, it would have provided, as on previous occasions of national danger, for suspension of the rights of the subject as to a writ of *habeas corpus*. The answer is simple. The legislature has selected another way of achieving the same purposes, probably milder as well as more effectual than those adopted on the occasion of previous wars. The suggested rule as to construing penal statutes and the provision as to trial of British subjects by jury made by the Defence of the Realm Act, 1915, have no relevance in dealing with an executive measure by way of preventing a public danger.

The application of the present appellant was rejected by the divisional court, consisting of five members, and by the court of appeal, and in my opinion the present appeal ought to be dismissed.

Ibid., 1917, pp. 264-270.

(E) ATTORNEY GENERAL v. DE KEYSER'S ROYAL HOTEL (1920)[10]

My lords: The present appeal is in the matter of petition of right presented by De Keyser's Royal Hotel, Ltd., the owners of the well-known hotel of that name, for compensation for the compulsory occupation of certain parts of their premises by the war office acting in the name and on behalf of the crown for purposes connected with the defence of the realm during the late war. The crown contests the right of the suppliants to compensation for such compulsory occupation, and pleads that it was an exercise of the royal prerogative and gave no right of compensation.

The facts of the case are not substantially in dispute, the real issue being a question of law of great and general importance. . . . In deciding the issues raised herein between the crown and the suppliants, the first question to be settled in the present case might be, to my mind, treated as a question of fact: namely, was possession in fact taken under the royal prerogative or under special statutory powers giving to the crown the requisite authority? Regarded as a question of fact, this is a matter which does not admit of doubt. Possession was expressly taken under statutory powers. The letter of May 1, 1916, from the representative of the army council to Mr. Whinney says: "I am instructed by the army council to take pos-

---

[10] This was another case brought on appeal to the house of lords. All the pertinent facts are presented in the opinion of Lord Moulton—a judgment in which the other lords concurred.

session of the above property under the Defence of the Realm Regulations." It was in response to this demand that possession was given. It is not competent to the crown, who took and retained such possession, to deny that their representative was acting under the powers given to it by these regulations, the validity of which rests entirely on statute. . . .

But when the crown elects to act under the authority of a statute, it, like any other person, must take the powers that it thus uses *cum onere*. It cannot take the powers without fulfilling the condition that the statute imposes on the use of such powers.

The Defence of the Realm Consolidation Act, 1914,[11] commenced by enacting that "his majesty in council has power to issue regulations for securing the public safety and the defence of the realm, and as to the powers and duties for that purpose of the admiralty and army council and of the members of his majesty's forces and other persons acting on his behalf." It then goes on to particularize certain subjects to which these regulations may relate, and in subsection 2 it deals with the question of the acquisition of land as follows: "Any such regulations may provide for the suspension of any restrictions on the acquisition or user of land or the exercise of the power of making by-laws, or any other power under the Defence Acts, 1842 to 1875, or the Military Lands Acts, 1891 to 1903."

The Defence Act, 1842,[12] . . . is the last of a series of acts regulating the acquisition of lands and interests in land for purposes of the defence of the realm. These acts commence in 1708, and occur at intervals up to 1842. . . . But it is not necessary to dwell on their provisions, seeing that the Defence Act, 1842, repealed all such existing acts and laid down general provisions which have regulated since that time the procedure for the acquisition by the crown of land for such purposes. This act gives very wide powers to the crown. It has unrestricted powers of selection of the necessary lands, buildings, etc., to be taken. It contemplates in the first instance voluntary purchase, but, if that cannot be arranged, then the lands, etc., may be acquired compulsorily subject to certain certificates being obtained as to the necessity or expediency of the acquisition or in case of actual invasion. I am satisfied that it enables the crown to acquire either the property or the possession or use of it as it may need. In all cases compensation is to be paid by the crown, the amount to be settled by a jury.

The regulations and the act under which they are made must, of course, be read together, and it is in my opinion a sound inference from the language of sub-section 2 that the legislature intended that, so far as the acquisition or user of land was concerned, the regulations should take the form of action under the Defence Act,

---

[11] No. 137C.
[12] No. 131B.

1842, facilitated by the suspension of some or all of the restrictions which it imposes. The particular provisions relating to the taking of land or buildings are to be found in section 2 of the regulations. They empower the military authorities to take possession of any land or of any buildings where for the purposes of the defence of the realm it is necessary so to do. These are very wide powers, but so general are the powers of the Defence Act, 1842, that they would be attained by simply suspending the restrictions therein contained and allowing its powers to be put in force without them. Reading, therefore, this regulation with sub-section 2 of the act, I think it is clear that, in the case of acquisition and user of land under the regulations, we ought to consider them as authorizing action being taken under the Defence Act, 1842, save that no restrictions therein appearing are to be enforced. The duty of paying compensation cannot be regarded as a restriction. It is a consequence of the taking, but in no way restricts it, and, therefore, as the acquisition is made under the Defence Act, 1842, the suppliants are entitled to the compensation provided by that act.

On these grounds, therefore, I am of opinion that the suppliants are entitled to our judgment in this appeal. But it would be unsatisfactory in a case of such general importance to leave unconsidered the question whether, apart from the fact that the crown expressly purported to be acting under powers given to it by statute, the suppliants' claim could be maintained. To decide this question, one must consider the nature and extent of the so-called royal prerogative in the matter of taking or occupying land for the better defence of the realm. I have no doubt that in early days, when war was carried on in a simpler fashion and on a smaller scale than is the case in modern times, the crown, to whom the defence of the realm was entrusted, had wide prerogative powers as to taking or using the lands of its subjects for the defence of the realm when the necessity arose. But such necessity would be in general an actual and immediate necessity arising in face of the enemy. . . . The necessity would in almost all cases be local, and no one could deny the right of the crown to raise fortifications on or otherwise occupy the land of the subject in the face of the enemy, if it were necessary so to do.

Nor have I any doubt that in those days the subjects who had suffered in this way in war would not have been held to have any claim against the crown for compensation in respect of the damage they had thus suffered. It must not be forgotten that in those days the costs of war were mainly borne by the royal revenues, so that the king himself was the heaviest sufferer. The limited and necessary interference with the property of the subjects, of which I have spoken, would have been looked upon as part of the damage done by the war, which it had fallen to their lot to bear, and there is no reason to think that any one would have thought that he had a claim against the crown in respect of it. Certainly no trace of any such claim having been put forward is to be found.

This state of things lasted for several centuries. . . . But in the last three centuries very important changes have occurred, which have completely altered the position of the crown in such matters. In the first place, war has become far more complicated, and necessitates costly and elaborate preparations in the form of permanent fortifications, and otherwise, which must be made in times of peace. In the second place, the cost of war has become too great to be borne by the royal revenues; so that the money for it has to come from the people through the legislature, which long ago assumed, and has since retained, the command of all national resources. In the third place, the feeling that it was equitable that burdens borne for the good of the nation should be distributed over the whole nation and should not be allowed to fall on particular individuals has grown to be a national sentiment. The effect of these changes is seen in the long series of statutes relating to the occupation of land for the purposes of fortifications or otherwise for national defence, to which I have already referred and which cover the last two centuries. In all these acts provision was made for compensation to the individual whose lands were taken or used, and indeed there is clear evidence that for many years, prior to the first of these statutes, the crown acted on this principle. It is not necessary to examine these acts in detail. They were mostly local in their operation and frequently temporary, and usually related to specific fortifications which it was proposed to erect.

But towards the beginning of the last century the acts take on a more general and permanent form, and eventually they culminate in the Defence Act, 1842, which gives to the crown, through its properly appointed officials, the widest possible powers of taking land and buildings needed for the defence of the realm under a minutely defined procedure set out in the act. It contemplates, as I have already said, that the acquisition shall, as a rule, be by agreement; but it gives ample powers of compulsory acquisition if the necessity be duly vouched, or in case of an actual invasion. In all cases compensation for the taking or using of the land by the crown is to be assessed by a jury who (in the words of the act) have to find "the compensation to be paid, either for the absolute purchase of such lands, buildings, or other hereditaments, or for the possession or use thereof, as the case may be." This act was not limited either in time or place, and with small modifications, which are not material for our present purpose, is still in force.

What effect has this course of legislation upon the royal prerogative? I do not think that it can be said to have abrogated that prerogative in any way, but it has given to the crown statutory powers which render the exercise of that prerogative unnecessary, because the statutory powers that have been conferred upon it are wider and more comprehensive than those of the prerogative itself. But it has done more than this. It has indicated unmistakably that it is the intention of the nation that the powers of the crown in these respects should be exercised in the equitable manner set forth in the statute; so that the burden shall not fall on the individual, but shall be borne by the community.

This being so, when powers covered by this statute are exercised by the crown, it must be presumed that they are so exercised under the statute, and therefore subject to the equitable provision for compensation which is to be found in it. There can be no excuse for reverting to prerogative powers *simpliciter*, if indeed they ever did exist in such a form as would cover the proposed acquisition— a matter which is far from clear in such a case as the present, when the legislature has given to the crown statutory powers which are wider even than any one pretends that it possessed under the prerogative, and which cover all that can be necessary for the defence of the nation, and which are moreover accompanied by safeguards to the individual which are in agreement with the demands of justice. Accordingly, if the commandeering of the buildings in this case had not been expressly done under statutory powers, I should have held that the crown must be presumed to have acted under these statutory powers, and thus given to the subject the statutory right to compensation. . . .

I am therefore of opinion that the suppliants are entitled to the declaration in the form approved of by the court below, and that this appeal should be dismissed with costs.

Ibid., 1920, pp. 546 f.

(F) MOORE AND OTHERS V. THE ATTORNEY GENERAL OF THE IRISH FREE STATE (1935)[13] *

. . . The petitioners claim to be owners of a fishery in the tidal waters of the River Erne in Ireland. They had brought an action in the Irish courts to enforce their claim and had succeeded before the trial judge. On appeal to the supreme court, that judgment was reversed on July 31, 1933, by a majority. The petitioners then presented to the privy council their petition for special leave to appeal, the grant of which leave was on October 9, 1933, advised by this board, and on November 10, 1933, an order granting such leave was made by the king in council. But on November 15, 1933, an act was passed by the . . . parliament of the Irish Free State, hereinafter called the *oireachtas*, providing that no appeal should lie to his majesty in council from any court in the Irish Free State. This enactment was also expressed to apply to appeals then pending. The petitioners thereupon brought this petition praying to have it

---

[13] The accompanying excerpts are from the judgment rendered by the judicial committee of the privy council, delivered by the lord chancellor, Viscount Sankey.

declared that the enactment was void and did not bar their appeal. . . .

For the decision of these questions it is necessary to consider the mode in which the constitution of the Irish Free State was established. On December 6, 1921, there were signed, in London, Articles of an Agreement for a Treaty between Great Britain and Ireland (this instrument will hereinafter be referred to as the Treaty). It was signed by representatives of Great Britain on the one hand and of the Irish Free State (or what became the Irish Free State) on the other. On March 31, 1922, an act of the imperial parliament was passed. It was entitled the Irish Free State (Agreement) Act, 1922,[14] and . . . it provided that, as from the date of that act, the treaty which was scheduled to it should have the force of law. It also provided . . . that there should be elected certain members of a body to be called the House of the Parliament, to which the provisional government should be responsible and which should have power, as respects matters within the jurisdiction of that government, to make laws in like manner as the parliament of the Irish Free State when constituted. . . .

In due course the House of the Parliament, which was a single chamber body, was elected, and met on September 9, 1922. It proceeded to sit as a constituent assembly for the settlement of the constitution of the Irish Free State. The measure which it so passed was scheduled to an act of the imperial parliament entitled the Irish Free State Constitution Act, 1922, which received the royal assent on December 5, 1922; and which described the measure as the Constituent Act and by section 1 provided as follows:—

"The constitution set forth in the first schedule to the Constituent Act shall, subject to the provisions to which the same is by the Constituent Act so made subject as aforesaid, be the constitution of the Irish Free State, and shall come into operation on the same being proclaimed by his majesty in accordance with article 83 of the said constitution; but his majesty may at any time after the proclamation appoint a governor general for the Irish Free State."

The provisions to which the constitution was made subject by the Constituent Act were recited in the act. . . . Thus the treaty received the force of law, both in the united kingdom and in Ireland, by reason of the passing of an act of the imperial parliament; and the Constituent Act owed its validity to the same authority. . . . Of the articles of the constitution the following are so material in this matter that they should be set out here in full. . . .[15]

---

[14] No. 137 I.

[15] Article 12 creates a two-house legislature (*oireachtas*) with the "sole and exclusive power of making laws" for the Free State. Article 50 provides that the constitution may be amended "within the terms of the scheduled treaty" by an act of the *oireachtas* when ratified by popular referendum. Article 66 establishes a supreme court, the decision of which shall be "final and conclusive," but with the proviso "that nothing in this constitution shall impair the right of

On December 6, 1922, there was issued a proclamation of his majesty announcing the passing and adoption of the constitution, and thereafter the House of Parliament . . . was in due course dissolved, and a parliament called the *oireachtas* for the Irish Free State was elected. . . .

On December 11, 1931, the Statute of Westminster,[16] hereinafter called the Statute, was enacted. It was the result of the proceedings at the Imperial Conference, 1930, in which representatives of the Irish Free State took part together with the delegates of the other dominions. . . . Section 1 includes in the expression dominion (with the other dominions) the Irish Free State. Of the other sections, that which is most relevant in these proceedings is section 2, which is in the following terms: "The Colonial Laws Validity Act, 1865, shall not apply to any law made after the commencement of this act by the parliament of a dominion. No law and no provision of any law made after the commencement of this act by the parliament of a dominion shall be void or inoperative on the ground that it is repugnant to the law of England, or to the provisions of any existing or future act of parliament of the united kingdom, or to any order, rule, or regulation made under any such act, and the powers of the parliament of a dominion shall include the power to repeal or amend any such act, order, rule, or regulation in so far as the same is part of the law of the dominion." . . .

On May 3, 1933, the *oireachtas* passed an act, no. 6 of 1933, entitled the Constitution (Removal of Oath) Act, 1933. That act . . . provided . . . that article 50 of the constitution should be amended by deleting the words "within the terms of the scheduled treaty." Finally, on November 15, 1933, the *oireachtas*, as already stated, enacted the Constitution (Amendment No. 22) Act, 1933, amending article 66 of the constitution so as to terminate the right of appeal to his majesty in council.

It is clear that, if this last-mentioned amending act is valid, the petition must fail, because the amendment of the constitution embodied in that act must bar the right of appeal to the king in council, if it is effective. But it cannot be effective unless the earlier act (no. 6 of 1933) is also valid; namely, that which is directed to removing from article 50 the condition that there can be no amendment of the constitution unless it is within the terms of the scheduled treaty. . . .

In their [lordships'] opinion, the Constituent Act and the constitution of the Irish Free State derived their validity from the act of the imperial parliament, the Irish Free State Constitution Act, 1922. This act established that the constitution, subject to the provisions of the Constituent Act, should be the constitution of the

---

any person to petition his majesty for special leave to appeal from the supreme court to his majesty in council, or the right of his majesty to grant such leave."
[16] No. 137M.

Irish Free State and should come into operation upon being proclaimed by his majesty, as was done on December 6, 1922. The action of the House of Parliament was thereby ratified; apart from such ratification that body had no authority to make a constitution. . . . It has been pointed out in the foregoing statement that in the Statute the Irish Free State was treated as one of the dominions, the delegates of which took part in the Imperial Conference of 1930. The Irish Free State is, in their lordships' judgment, bound by the acts of the imperial parliament in the same way as any other of the dominions; if it were not for section 2 of the Statute, the *oireachtas* would have had no power to amend or repeal an act of the imperial parliament. . . . Hence the act no. 6 of 1933 and the amendment no. 22 of 1933 . . . are valid acts of the *oireachtas* only in virtue of the Statute. . . . It follows that, by virtue of the Statute, article 66 of the constitution has been validly amended, with the result that the proviso to that article is removed and appeals to the king in council are now prohibited.

The position may be summed up as follows:—(1) The Treaty and Constituent Act respectively form parts of the statute law of the united kingdom, each of them being parts of an imperial act. (2) Before the passing of the Statute of Westminster it was not competent for the Irish Free State parliament to pass an act abrogating the treaty because the Colonial Laws Validity Act forbade a dominion legislature to pass a law repugnant to an imperial act. (3) The effect of the Statute of Westminster was to remove the fetter which lay upon the Irish Free State legislature by reason of the Colonial Laws Validity Act. That legislature can now pass acts repugnant to an imperial act. In this case they have done so. . . .

In the result their lordships are of opinion that the petition should fail and be dismissed. They will humbly so advise his majesty.

Ibid., 1935, pp. 489-99.

140. RECORDS OF THE IMPERIAL CONFERENCE (1926)[1]

Report of the inter-imperial relations committee. . . . II. Status of Great Britain and the dominions. The committee are of opinion that nothing would be gained by attempting to lay down a constitution for the British Empire. Its widely scattered parts have very different characteristics, very different histories, and are at very different stages of evolution; while, considered as a whole, it defies classification and bears no real resemblance to any other political organization which now exists or has ever yet been tried. There is, however, one most important element in it which, from a strictly constitutional point of view, has now, as regards all vital matters, reached its full development—we refer to the group of self-govern-

---

[1] Since the close of the nineteenth century regular conferences had been held between the British government and representatives of the dominions for the discussion of imperial questions.

ing communities composed of Great Britain and the dominions. Their position and mutual relation may be readily defined. They are autonomous communities within the British Empire, equal in status, in no way subordinate one to another in any aspect of their domestic or external affairs, though united by a common allegiance to the crown, and freely associated as members of the British Commonwealth of Nations.

A foreigner endeavouring to understand the true character of the British Empire by the aid of this formula alone would be tempted to think that it was devised rather to make mutual interference impossible than to make mutual co-operation easy. Such a criticism, however, completely ignores the historic situation. The rapid evolution of the oversea dominions during the last fifty years has involved many complicated adjustments of old political machinery to changing conditions. The tendency towards equality of status was both right and inevitable. Geographical and other conditions made this impossible of attainment by the way of federation. The only alternative was by the way of autonomy; and along this road it has been steadily sought. Every self-governing member of the empire is now the master of its destiny. In fact, if not always in form, it is subject to no compulsion whatever.

But no account, however accurate, of the negative relations in which Great Britain and the dominions stand to each other can do more than express a portion of the truth. The British Empire is not founded upon negations. It depends essentially, if not formally, on positive ideals. Free institutions are its life-blood. Free co-operation is its instrument. Peace, security, and progress are among its objects. Aspects of all these great themes have been discussed at the present conference; excellent results have been thereby obtained. And, though every dominion is now and must always remain the sole judge of the nature and extent of its co-operation, no common cause will, in our opinion, be thereby imperilled.

Equality of status, so far as Britain and the dominions are concerned, is thus the root principle governing our inter-imperial relations. But the principles of equality and similarity appropriate to status do not universally extend to function. Here we require something more than immutable dogmas. For example, to deal with questions of diplomacy and questions of defence, we require also flexible machinery—machinery which can, from time to time, be adapted to the changing circumstances of the world. This subject also has occupied our attention. The rest of this report will show how we have endeavoured, not only to state political theory, but to apply it to our common needs. . . .

IV. Relations between the various parts of the British Empire. Existing administrative, legislative, and judicial forms are admittedly not wholly in accord with the position as described in section II of this report. This is inevitable, since most of these forms date back to a time well antecedent to the present stage of constitutional development. Our first task then was to examine these forms with special reference to any cases where the want of adaptation of practice to principle caused or might be thought to cause inconvenience in the conduct of inter-imperial relations.

(a) *The title of his majesty the king.* The title of his majesty the king is of special importance and concern to all parts of his majesty's dominions. Twice within the last fifty years has the royal title been altered to suit changed conditions and constitutional developments. The present title, which is that proclaimed under the Royal Titles Act of 1901, is as follows: "George V, by the Grace of God, of the United Kingdom of Great Britain and Ireland and of the British Dominions beyond the Seas King, Defender of the Faith, Emperor of India."

Some time before the conference met, it had been recognized that this form of title hardly accorded with the altered state of affairs arising from the establishment of the Irish Free State as a dominion. It had further been ascertained that it would be in accordance with his majesty's wishes that any recommendation for change should be submitted to him as the result of discussion at the conference. . . . We recommend that, subject to his majesty's approval, the necessary legislative action should be taken to secure that his majesty's title should henceforward read: "George V, by the Grace of God, of Great Britain, Ireland, and the British Dominions beyond the Seas King, Defender of the Faith, Emperor of India."

(b) *Position of governors general.* We proceeded to consider whether it was desirable formally to place on record a definition of the position held by the governor general as his majesty's representative in the dominions. That position, though now generally well recognized, undoubtedly represents a development from an earlier stage when the governor general was appointed solely on the advice of his majesty's ministers in London and acted also as their representative. In our opinion it is an essential consequence of the equality of status existing among the members of the British Commonwealth of Nations that the governor general of a dominion is the representative of the crown, holding in all essential respects the same position in relation to the administration of public affairs in the dominion as is held by his majesty the king in Great Britain, and that he is not the representative or agent of his majesty's government in Great Britain or of any department of that government.

It seemed to us to follow that the practice whereby the governor general of a dominion is the formal official channel of communication between his majesty's government in Great Britain and his governments in the dominions might be regarded as no longer wholly in accordance with the constitutional position of the governor general. It was thought that the recognized official channel of communication should be in future between government and government direct. The representatives of Great Britain readily recognized that the existing procedure might be open to criticism and accepted the proposed change in principle in relation to any of the dominions which desired it. Details were left for settlement as soon as possible after the conference had completed its work, but it was recognized by the committee, as an essential feature of any change or development in the channels of communication, that a governor general should be supplied with copies of all documents of importance and in general should be kept as fully informed as is his majesty in Great Britain of cabinet business and public affairs.

(c) Operation of dominion legislation. Our attention was also called to various points in connection with the operation of dominion legislation, which, it was suggested, required clarification. The particular points involved were (1) the present practice under which acts of the dominion parliaments are sent each year to London and it is intimated, through the secretary of state for dominion affairs, that "his majesty will not be advised to exercise his powers of disallowance" with regard to them; (2) the reservation of dominion legislation in certain circumstances for the signification of his majesty's pleasure, which is signified on advice tendered by his majesty's government in Great Britain; (3) the difference between the legislative competence of the parliament at Westminster and of the dominion parliaments in that acts passed by the latter operate as a general rule only within the territorial area of the dominion concerned; (4) the operation of legislation passed by the parliament at Westminster in relation to the dominions. In this connection special attention was called to such statutes as the Colonial Laws Validity Act.[2] It was suggested that in future uniformity of legislation as between Great Britain and the dominions could best be secured by the enactment of reciprocal statutes based upon consultation and agreement.

We gave these matters the best consideration possible in the limited time at our disposal, but came to the conclusion that the issues involved were so complex that there would be grave danger in attempting any immediate pronouncement other than a statement of certain principles which, in our opinion, underlie the whole question of the operation of dominion legislation. We felt that, for the rest, it would be necessary to obtain expert guidance as a preliminary to further consideration by his majesty's governments in Great Britain and the dominions. . . .

On the question raised with regard to the legislative competence of members of the British Commonwealth of Nations other than Great Britain, and in particular to the desirability of those members being enabled to legislate with extra-territorial effect, we think that it should similarly be placed on record that the constitutional practice is that legislation by the parliament at Westminster applying to a dominion would only be passed with the consent of the dominion concerned. . . .

---

[2] No. 131F.

(e) *Appeals to the judicial committee of the privy council.* Another matter which we discussed, in which a general constitutional principle was raised, concerned the conditions governing appeals from judgments in the dominions to the judicial committee of the privy council. From these discussions it became clear that it was no part of the policy of his majesty's government in Great Britain that questions affecting judicial appeals should be determined otherwise than in accordance with the wishes of the part of the empire primarily affected. It was, however, generally recognized that, where changes in the existing system were proposed which, while primarily affecting one part, raised issues in which other parts were also concerned, such changes ought only to be carried out after consultation and discussion. . . .

V. *Relations with foreign countries.* . . . It was agreed in 1923 that any of the governments of the empire contemplating the negotiation of a treaty should give due consideration to its possible effect upon other governments and should take steps to inform governments likely to be interested of its intention. This rule should be understood as applying to any negotiations which any government intends to conduct, so as to leave it to the other governments to say whether they are likely to be interested. When a government has received information of the intention of any other government to conduct negotiations, it is incumbent upon it to indicate its attitude with reasonable promptitude. So long as the initiating government receives no adverse comments, and so long as its policy involves no active obligations on the part of the other governments, it may proceed on the assumption that its policy is generally acceptable. It must, however, before taking any steps which might involve the other governments in any active obligations, obtain their definite assent.

Where by the nature of the treaty it is desirable that it should be ratified on behalf of all the governments of the empire, the initiating government may assume that a government which has had full opportunity of indicating its attitude and has made no adverse comments will concur in the ratification of the treaty. In the case of a government that prefers not to concur in the ratification of a treaty unless it has been signed by a plenipotentiary authorized to act on its behalf, it will advise the appointment of a plenipotentiary so to act. . . .

It was frankly recognized that in this sphere, as in the sphere of defence, the major share of responsibility rests now and must for some time continue to rest with his majesty's government in Great Britain. Nevertheless, practically all the dominions are engaged to some extent, and some to a considerable extent, in the conduct of foreign relations, particularly those with foreign countries on their borders. A particular instance of this is the growing work in connection with the relations between Canada and the United States of America, which has led to the necessity for the appointment of a minister plenipotentiary to represent the Canadian government in

Washington. We felt that the governing consideration underlying all discussions of this problem must be that neither Great Britain nor the dominions could be committed to the acceptance of active obligations except with the definite assent of their own governments. . . .

Parliamentary Papers, 1926, vol. XI.

141. HIS MAJESTY'S GOVERNMENT (1936)

The Cabinet

Prime Minister, First Lord of the Treasury and Leader of the House of Commons—Rt. Hon. Stanley Baldwin, M.P.
Lord President of the Council—Rt. Hon. James Ramsay MacDonald, M.P.
Chancellor of the Exchequer—Rt. Hon. Neville Chamberlain, M.P.
Lord Chancellor—Rt. Hon. Viscount Hailsham.
Secretary of State for the Home Department and Deputy Leader of the House of Commons—Rt. Hon. Sir John Simon, G.C.S.I., K.C.V.O., O.B.E., K.C., M.P.
Secretary of State for Foreign Affairs—Rt. Hon. Robert Anthony Eden, M.C., M.P.
Lord Privy Seal and Leader of the House of Lords—Rt. Hon. Viscount Halifax, K.G., G.C.S.I., G.C.I.E., T.D.
Secretary of State for Dominion Affairs—Rt. Hon. Malcolm John MacDonald, M.P.
Secretary of State for the Colonies—Rt. Hon. William George Arthur Ormsby-Gore, M.P.
Secretary of State for War—Rt. Hon. Alfred Duff Cooper, D.S.O., M.P.
Secretary of State for India—Most Hon. the Marquess of Zetland, G.C.S.I., G.C.I.E.
Secretary of State for Air—Rt. Hon. Viscount Swinton, G.B.E., M.C.
Secretary of State for Scotland—Rt. Hon. Walter E. Elliot, M.C., M.P.
President of the Board of Trade—Rt. Hon. Walter Runciman, M.P.
First Lord of the Admiralty—Rt. Hon. Sir Samuel Hoare, Bt., G.C.S.I., G.B.E., C.M.G., M.P.
Minister for the Co-ordination of Defence—Rt. Hon. Sir Thomas Walker Hobart Inskip, C.B.E., K.C., M.P.
Minister of Agriculture and Fisheries—Rt. Hon. William Shepherd Morrison, M.C., K.C., M.P.
President of the Board of Education—Rt. Hon. Oliver Frederick George Stanley, M.C., M.P.
Minister of Health—Rt. Hon. Sir H. Kingsley Wood, M.P.
Minister of Labour—Rt. Hon. Alfred Ernest Brown, M.C., M.P.
First Commissioner of Works—Rt. Hon. the Earl Stanhope, K.G., D.S.O., M.C.
Minister of Transport—Rt. Hon. Leslie Hore-Belisha, M.P.

Departments of State

Home Affairs: Secretary of State . . . ; Under-Secretary of State. . . .
Foreign Affairs: Secretary of State . . . ; Under-Secretaries of State. . . .
Overseas Trade Department, Secretary . . . (Representing Foreign Office and Board of Trade).
Dominion Affairs: Secretary of State . . . ; Under-Secretary of State. . . .
Colonial Office: Secretary of State . . . ; Under-Secretary of State. . . .
War Office: Secretary of State . . . ; Under-Secretary of State . . . ; Financial Secretary. . . .
Air Ministry: Secretary of State . . . ; Under-Secretary of State. . . .
Lord President of the Council. . . .
Lord Privy Seal. . . .
India Office: Secretary of State . . . ; Under-Secretary of State. . . .
Admiralty: First Lord . . . ; Parliamentary and Financial Secretary . . . ; Civil Lord. . . .
Minister for the Co-ordination of Defence. . . .
Board of Trade: President . . . ; Parliamentary Secretary . . . ; Mines Department, Parliamentary Secretary . . . ; Department of Overseas Trade, Secretary . . . (Representing Foreign Office and Board of Trade).
Ministry of Health: Minister . . . ; Parliamentary Secretary. . . .
Ministry of Transport: Minister . . . ; Parliamentary Secretary. . . .
Board of Education: President . . . ; Parliamentary Secretary. . . .
Ministry of Labour: Minister . . . ; Parliamentary Secretary. . . .
Ministry of Pensions: Minister. . . .
Ministry of Agriculture and Fisheries: Minister . . . ; Parliamentary Secretary. . . .
Chancellor of the Duchy of Lancaster. . . .
First Commissioner of Works. . . .
Attorney General. . . .
Solicitor General. . . .
General Post Office: Postmaster General . . . ; Assistant-Postmaster General. . . .
Paymaster General. . . .
Treasury: Chancellor of the Exchequer . . . ; Parliamentary Secretary. . . ; Financial Secretary . . . ; Lords Commissioners . . . ; Assistant Whips (unpaid). . . .
Scotland: Secretary of State . . . ; Under-Secretary of State . . . ; Lord Advocate . . . ; Solicitor General. . . .
His Majesty's Household: Lord Chamberlain . . . ; Lord Stew-

ard . . . ; Master of the Horse . . . ; Treasurer . . . ; Comptroller . . . ; Vice-Chamberlain . . . ; Captain of the Honourable Corps of Gentlemen-at-Arms . . . ; Captain of the King's Bodyguard of the Yeomen of the Guard . . . ; Lords-in-Waiting. . . .

Parliamentary Debates, Fifth Series, CCCXVIII, i f.

142. RECORDS OF EDWARD VIII'S ABDICATION (1936)

(A) Speech by Prime Minister Baldwin

[10 December.] The prime minister (Mr. Baldwin) at the bar acquainted the house that he had a message from his majesty the king to this house, signed by his majesty's own hand. And he presented the same to the house and it was read out by Mr. Speaker as followeth, all the members of the house being uncovered:—

Fort Belvedere,
Sunningdale,
Berkshire.

Members of the House of Commons:

After long and anxious consideration, I have determined to renounce the throne to which I succeeded on the death of my father, and I am now communicating this, my final and irrevocable decision. Realizing as I do the gravity of this step, I can only hope that I shall have the understanding of my peoples in the decision I have taken and the reasons which have led me to take it. I will not enter now into my private feelings, but I would beg that it should be remembered that the burden which constantly rests upon the shoulders of a sovereign is so heavy that it can only be borne in circumstances different from those in which I now find myself. I conceive that I am not overlooking the duty that rests on me to place in the forefront the public interest, when I declare that I am conscious that I can no longer discharge this heavy task with efficiency or with satisfaction to myself.

I have accordingly this morning executed an Instrument of Abdication in the terms following: "I, Edward VIII, of Great Britain, Ireland, and the British Dominions beyond the Seas, King, Emperor of India, do hereby declare my irrevocable determination to renounce the throne for myself and for my descendants and my desire that effect should be given to this Instrument of Abdication immediately. In token whereof I have hereunto set my hand this 10th day December, 1936, in the presence of the witnesses whose signatures are subscribed. (signed) Edward, R.I." My execution of this instrument has been witnessed by my three brothers, their royal highnesses the duke of York, the duke of Gloucester, and the duke of Kent.

I deeply appreciate the spirit which has actuated the appeals which have been made to me to take a different decision and I have, before reaching my final determination, most fully pondered over them. But my mind is made up. Moreover, further delay cannot but be most injurious to the peoples whom I have tried to serve as prince of Wales and as king, and whose future happiness and prosperity are the constant wish of my heart.

I take my leave of them in the confident hope that the course which I have thought it right to follow is that which is best for the stability of the throne and empire, and the happiness of my peoples. I am deeply sensible of the consideration which they have always extended to me both before and after my accession to the throne, and which I know they will extend in full measure to my successor.

I am most anxious that there should be no delay of any kind in giving effect to the instrument which I have executed, and that all necessary steps should be taken immediately to secure that my lawful successor, my brother, his royal highness the duke of York, should ascend the throne.

Edward, R.I.

The prime minister: I beg to move that his majesty's most gracious message be now considered. No more grave message has ever been received by parliament and no more difficult, I may almost say repugnant, task has ever been imposed upon a prime minister. . . . I should like to say at the start that his majesty, as prince of Wales, has honoured me for many years with a friendship which I value, and I know that he would agree with me in saying to you that it was not only a friendship but, between man and man, a friendship of affection. . . .

Now, sir, the house will want to know how it was that I had my first interview with his majesty. I may say that his majesty has been most generous in allowing me to tell the house the pertinent parts of the discussions which took place between us. As the house is aware, I had been ordered in August and September a complete rest. . . . When October came . . . I felt that I could not in fairness to my work take a further holiday. . . . There were two things that disquieted me at that moment. There was coming to my office a vast volume of correspondence . . . expressing perturbation and uneasiness at what was then appearing in the American press. I was aware also that there was in the near future a divorce case coming on as a result of which I realized that possibly a difficult situation might arise later; and I felt that it was essential that some one should see his majesty and warn him of the difficult situation that might arise later, if occasion was given for a continuation of this kind of gossip. . . . I felt that in the circumstances there was only one man who could speak to him and talk the matter over with him, and that man was the prime minister. I felt doubly bound to do it by my duty as I conceived it to the country and my duty to him, not only as a counsellor, but as a friend. I consulted, I am ashamed to say—and they have forgiven me,—none of my colleagues. . . .

I communicated with him through his secretary and stated that I desired to see him—this is the first and only occasion on which I was the one who asked for an interview—that I desired to see him, that the matter was urgent. I told him what it was. I expressed my willingness to come to Sandringham on Tuesday the 20th, but I said that I thought it wiser, if his majesty thought fit, to see me at Fort Belvedere; for I was anxious that no one at that time should know of my visit, and that at any rate our first talk should be in complete privacy. The reply came from his majesty that he would motor back on the Monday, 19th October, to Fort Belvedere, and he would see me on the Tuesday morning. And on the Tuesday morning I saw him.

Sir, I may say, before I proceed to the details of the conversation, that an adviser to the crown can be of no possible service to his master unless he tells him at all times the truth as he sees it, whether that truth be welcome or not. And let me say here, as I may say several times before I finish, that during those talks, when I look back, there is nothing I have not told his majesty of which I felt he ought to be aware—nothing. His majesty's attitude all through has been—let me put it in this way: never has he shown any sign of offence, of being hurt at anything I have said to him. The whole of our discussions have been carried out, as I have said, with an increase if possible of that mutual respect and regard in which we stood.

I told his majesty that I had two great anxieties. One [was] the effect of a continuance of the kind of criticism that at that time was proceeding in the American press, the effect it would have in the dominions and particularly in Canada, where it was widespread—the effect it would have in this country. That was the first anxiety. And then I reminded him of what I had often told him and his brothers in the past: the British monarchy is a unique institution. The crown in this country through the centuries has been deprived of many of its prerogatives; but to-day, while that is true, it stands for far more than it ever has done in its history. The importance of its integrity is, beyond all question, far greater than it ever has been, being as it is not only the last link of empire that is left, but the guarantee in this country, so long as it exists in that integrity, against many evils that have affected and afflicted other countries. There is no man in this country, to whatever party he may belong, who would not subscribe to that. But while this feeling largely depends on the respect that has grown up in the last three generations for the monarchy, it might not take so long, in the face of the kind of criticisms to which it was being exposed, to lose that power far more rapidly than it was built up; and once lost, I doubt if anything could restore it. . . .

I told him I had come—naturally, I was his prime minister—but I wanted to talk it over with him as a friend, to see if I could help him in this matter. . . . He said to me, not once but many times . . . : "You and I must settle this matter together; I will not have any one interfering." I then pointed out the danger of the divorce proceedings; that, if a verdict was given in that case that left the matter in suspense for some time, that period of suspense might be dangerous, because then every one would be talking. And when once the press began—as it must begin some time in this country—a most difficult situation would arise for me [and] for him. . . . I said that I pressed him for no kind of answer; but would he consider everything I had said?

The next time I saw him was on Monday, 16th November. That was at Buckingham Palace. By that date the decree *nisi* had been pronounced in the divorce case. His majesty had sent for me on that occasion. . . . I felt it my duty to begin the conversation, and I spoke with him for a quarter of an hour, or twenty minutes, on the question of marriage. Again, we must remember that the cabinet had not been in this at all. I had reported to about four of my senior colleagues the conversation at Fort Belvedere. I saw the king on Monday, 16th November, and I began by giving him my view of a possible marriage. I told him that I did not think that a particular marriage was one that would receive the approbation of the country. That marriage would have involved the lady becoming queen. I did tell his majesty once that I might be a remnant of the old Victorians, but that my worst enemy would not say of me that I did not know what the reaction of the English people would be to any particular course of action. And I told him that, so far as they went, I was certain that that would be impracticable. . . . I pointed out to him that the position of the king's wife was different from the position of the wife of any other citizen in the country; it was part of the price which the king has to pay. His wife becomes queen; the queen becomes the queen of the country. And therefore, in the choice of a queen, the voice of the people must be heard. Then his majesty said to me—I have his permission to state this—that he wanted to tell me something that he had long wanted to tell me. He said, "I am going to marry Mrs. Simpson, and I am prepared to go." I said, "Sir, that is most grievous news and it is impossible for me to make any comment on it to-day." . . .

He sent for me again on Wednesday, 25th November. In the meantime a suggestion had been made to me that a possible compromise might be arranged to avoid those two possibilities that had been seen. . . . The compromise was that the king should marry; that parliament should pass an act enabling the lady to be the king's wife without the position of queen. And when I saw his majesty on 25th November, he asked me whether that proposition had been put to me; and I said Yes. He asked me what I thought of it. I told him that I had not considered it. I said, "I can give you no considered opinion." If he asked me my first reaction informally, my first reaction was that parliament would never pass such a bill. But I said that, if he desired it, I would examine it formally. He said he did so desire. Then I said, "It will mean my putting that formally before the whole cabinet and communicating with the prime ministers of all the dominions." And was that his wish? He told me that it was. I said that I would do it.

On 2nd December the king asked me to go and see him. Again I had intended asking for an audience later that week, because such inquiries as I thought proper to make I had not completed. The inquiries had gone far enough to show that neither in the dominions nor here would there be any prospect of such legislation being accepted. His majesty asked me if I could answer his question. I gave him the reply that I was afraid it was impracticable for those reasons. . . . His majesty said he was not surprised at that answer. He took my answer with no question and he never recurred to it again. . . . That decision was of course a formal decision, and that was the only formal decision of any kind taken by the cabinet until I come to the history of yesterday. When we had finished that conversation, I pointed out that the possible alternatives had been narrowed and that it really had brought him into the position that he would be placed in a grievous situation between two conflicting loyalties in his own heart: either complete abandonment of the project on which his heart was set, and remaining as king, or doing as he intimated to me that he was prepared to do . . . , going and later on contracting that marriage if it were possible. ... .

I would say a word or two on the king's position. The king cannot speak for himself. The king has told us that he cannot carry . . . these almost intolerable burdens of kingship without a woman at his side, and we know that. This crisis, if I may use the word, has arisen now, rather than later, from that very frankness of his majesty's character which is one of many of his attractions. It would have been perfectly possible for his majesty not to have told me of this at the date when he did, and not to have told me for some months to come. But he realized the damage that might be done in the interval by gossip, rumours, and talk; and he made that declaration to me when he did on purpose to avoid what he felt might be dangerous, not only here but throughout the empire, to the moral force of the crown which we are all determined to sustain.

He told me his intentions and he has never wavered from them. I want the house to understand that. He felt it his duty to take into his anxious consideration all the representations that his advisers might give him; and not until he had fully considered them did he make public his decision. There has been no kind of conflict in this matter. My efforts during these last days have been directed, as have been the efforts of those most closely round him, in trying to help him to make the choice which he has not made, and we have failed. The king has made his decision to take this moment to send this gracious message, because of his confident hope that by that he will preserve the unity of this country and of the whole empire. . . .

Yesterday morning, when the cabinet received the king's final and definite answer officially, they passed a minute and, in accordance with it, I sent a message to his majesty which he has been good enough to permit me to read to the house with his reply. "Mr. Baldwin, with his humble duty to the king. This morning Mr. Baldwin reported to the cabinet his interview with your majesty yesterday and informed his colleagues that your majesty then communicated to him informally your firm and definite intention to renounce the throne. The cabinet received this statement of your majesty's intention with profound regret, and wished Mr. Baldwin to convey to your majesty immediately the unanimous feeling of your majesty's servants. Ministers are reluctant to believe that your majesty's resolve is irrevocable and still venture to hope that, before your majesty pronounces any formal decision, your majesty may be pleased to reconsider an intention which must so deeply distress and so vitally affect all your majesty's subjects. Mr. Baldwin is at once communicating with the dominion prime ministers for the purpose of letting them know that your majesty has now made to him the informal intimation of your majesty's intention."

His majesty's reply was received last night: "The king has received the prime minister's letter of the 9th December, 1936, informing him of the views of the cabinet. His majesty has given the matter his further consideration, but regrets that he is unable to alter his decision." . . .

Ibid., CCCXVIII, 2175 f.

(B) Declaration of Abdication Act

An act to give effect to his majesty's declaration of abdication, and for purposes connected therewith. Whereas his majesty by his royal message of the 10th day of December in this present year has been pleased to declare that he is irrevocably determined to renounce the throne for himself and his descendants, and has for that purpose executed the Instrument of Abdication set out in the schedule to this act, and has signified his desire that effect thereto should be given immediately; and whereas, following upon the communication to his dominions of his majesty's said declaration and desire, the dominion of Canada, pursuant to the provisions of section 4 of the Statute of Westminster, 1931, has requested and consented to the enactment of this act, and the commonwealth of Australia, the dominion of New Zealand, and the union of South Africa have assented thereto: be it therefore enacted . . . as follows:—

Immediately upon the royal assent being signified to this act, the Instrument of Abdication executed by his present majesty on the 10th day of December, 1936, set out in the schedule to this act, shall have effect, and thereupon his majesty shall cease to be king and there shall be a demise of the crown, and accordingly the member of the royal family then next in succession to the throne shall succeed thereto and to all the rights, privileges, and dignities thereunto belonging. His majesty, his issue, if any, and the descendants of that issue, shall not after his majesty's abdication have any right, title, or interest in or to the succession to the throne, and section 1 of the

Act of Settlement shall be construed accordingly. The Royal Marriages Act, 1772, shall not apply to his majesty after his abdication nor to the issue, if any, of his majesty or the descendants of that issue. . . .

Public General Acts, 1936: 1 Edward VIII, c. 3.

143. GEORGE VI: CORONATION OATH (1937)

. . . Then shall the archbishop go to the king and, standing before him, administer the coronation oath; first asking the king, "Sir, is your majesty willing to take the oath?" And the king answering, "I am willing," the archbishop shall minister these questions; and the king, having a book in his hands, shall answer each question severally as follows:—

Archbishop: "Will you solemnly promise and swear to govern the peoples of Great Britain, Ireland, Canada, Australia, New Zealand, and the union of South Africa, of your possessions and the other territories to any of them belonging or pertaining, and of your empire of India according to their respective laws and customs?" King: "I solemnly promise so to do."

Archbishop: "Will you to your power cause law and justice, in mercy, to be executed in all your judgments?" King: "I will."

Archbishop: "Will you to the utmost of your power maintain the laws of God and the true profession of the Gospel? Will you to the utmost of your power maintain in the united kingdom the Protestant Reformed religion established by law? And will you maintain and preserve inviolably the settlement of the Church of England and the doctrine, worship, discipline, and government thereof, as by law established in England? And will you preserve unto the bishops and clergy of England, and to the churches there committed to their charge, all such rights and privileges as by law do or shall appertain to them or any of them?" King: "All this I promise to do."

Then the king, arising out of his chair, supported as before and assisted by the lord great chamberlain, the sword of state being carried before him, shall go to the altar and, there being uncovered, make his solemn oath in the sight of all the people to observe the premises; laying his hand upon the Holy Gospel in the great Bible . . . , saying these words: "The things which I have here before promised I will perform and keep. So help me God." Then the king shall kiss the Book and sign the oath. . . .

Form and Order of the Coronation, pp. 13 f.

SAINTS' DAYS AND OTHER FESTIVALS MENTIONED IN THE FOREGOING DOCUMENTS

All Saints: 1 November
All Souls: 2 November
Annunciation of the Virgin, The: 25 March
Ascension of the Lord, The: the fortieth day after Easter
Ash Wednesday: the first day of Lent
Assumption of the Virgin, The: 15 August
Bartholomew, St.: 24 August
Candlemas: 2 February
Chair of St. Peter, The: 18 January
Close of Easter, The: the Sunday after Easter
Conception of the Virgin, The: 8 December
Corpus Christi: the first Thursday after Trinity Sunday
Cuthbert, St.: 20 March
Dunstan, St.: 19 May
Easter: the first Sunday after the first full moon after the vernal equinox (21 March)
Edmund the King, St.: 20 November
Edward the Confessor, St.: 13 October
Epiphany: 6 January
Exaltation of the Holy Cross, The: 14 September
Faith, St.: 1 August
Giles, St.: 1 September
Gregory the Great, St.: 3 November
Helen, St.: 18 August
Hilary, St.: 13 January
Hokeday: the second Tuesday after Easter
James the Apostle, St.: 25 July
John, St.: 27 December
John the Baptist, St.: 24 June
Lent: the forty week-days preceding Easter
Martin, St.: 12 November
Matthew, St.: 21 September
Michael, St. (Michaelmas): 29 September
Mid-Lent: the fourth Sunday in Lent
Nativity of the Lord, The (Christmas): 25 December

SAINTS' DAYS

Nativity of the Virgin, The: 8 September
Pentecost: the seventh Sunday after Easter
Peter and Paul, Sts.: 29 June
Purification of the Virgin, The: 2 February
Rogation Days: the three days before the feast of the Ascension
Simon and Jude, Sts.: 28 October
Stephen, St.: 26 December
Thomas the Martyr, St.: 6 September
Trinity, The Holy: the eighth Sunday after Easter
Vincent, the Martyr, St.: 22 January
Whitsuntide (Whit Sunday): the seventh Sunday after Easter

GENERAL BIBLIOGRAPHY

This list includes only those works that have been cited in the preceding pages. For additional titles, the student is referred to C. Gross, *Sources and Literature of English History from the Earliest Times to about 1485*, Second Edition (London, 1915); C. Read, *Bibliography of British History: Tudor Period* (Oxford, 1933); G. Davies, *Bibliography of British History: Stuart Period* (Cambridge, 1918); H. M. Cam and A. S. Turberville, *Bibliography of English Constitutional History*, Historical Association Leaflet no. 75 (London, 1929). Useful bibliographies are also appended to A. B. White, *The Making of the English Constitution*, Second Edition (New York, 1925); W. A. Morris, *The Constitutional History of England to 1216* (New York, 1930); G. B. Adams, *Constitutional History of England*, Revised Edition (New York, 1934); and many of the more specialized books already mentioned in the introductory notes to the various sections.

Acts of the Privy Council. Colonial Series. 6 vols. Hereford, 1908-12.

Acts of the Privy Council. New Series. London, 1890————.

Adams, G. B. *Constitutional History of England.* Revised edition, by R. L. Schuyler. New York, 1934.

Adams, G. B. *The Origin of the English Constitution.* New edition. New Haven, 1920.

Adolphus, J. L., and Ellis, T. F. *Reports.* (See *English Reports.*)

American Historical Review, The. New York, 1895————.

Amos, M. *The English Constitution.* London, 1930.

Anniversary Essays in Mediaeval History by Students of C. H. Haskins. Boston, 1929.

Anonimalle Chronicle, The. Edited by V. H. Galbraith. Manchester, 1927.

Anson, W. R. *The Law and Custom of the Constitution.* Fourth edition. 2 vols. Oxford, 1935.

Archaeologia Aeliana. Fourth Series. Newcastle-upon-Tyne, 1925————.

Atkinson, J. C. (editor). *Quarter Sessions Records.* North Riding Record Society, vols. I-IX. London, 1884-92.

GENERAL BIBLIOGRAPHY 895

Attenborough, F. L. (editor). *The Laws of the Earliest English Kings*. Cambridge, 1922.

Bagehot, W. *The English Constitution*. With an introduction by the earl of Balfour. London, 1933.

Baildon, W. P. (editor). *Select Cases in Chancery, 1364-1471*. Selden Society, vol. X. London, 1896.

Baldwin, J. F. *The King's Council in England during the Middle Ages*. Oxford, 1913.

Ballard, A., and Tait, J. (editors). *British Borough Charters*. 2 vols. Cambridge, 1913-22.

Bateson, M. (editor). *Records of the Borough of Leicester, 1103-1603*. 3 vols. Cambridge, 1899-1905.

Bateson, M. (editor). *Borough Customs*. Selden Society, vols. XVIII, XXI. London, 1904-06.

Bell, K. N., and Morrell, W. P. (editors). *Select Documents on British Colonial Policy, 1830-1860*. Oxford, 1928.

Bigelow, M. M. (editor). *Placita Anglo-Normannica*. Boston, 1879.

Birch, W. de Gray (editor). *Cartularium Saxonicum*. 3 vols. London, 1885-93.

Blackstone, H. *Reports*. (See *English Reports*.)

Blackstone, W. *Commentaries on the Laws of England*. 2 vols. London, 1914.

Blauvelt, M. T. *The Development of Cabinet Government in England*. New York, 1902.

Brady, R. *An Historical Treatise of Cities and Burghs or Boroughs*. New edition. London, 1777.

Bristol Record Society Publications. Bristol, 1930——.

Bryant, A. (editor). *The Letters, Speeches, and Declarations of King Charles II*. London, 1935.

Bulletin of the Institute of Historical Research (University of London). London, 1925——.

Calendar of the Charter Rolls. Rolls Series. London, 1903——.

Calendar of the Patent Rolls. Rolls Series. London, 1891——.

Calendar of Treasury Books. Rolls Series. London, 1904——.

Cam, H. M. *The Hundred and the Hundred Rolls*. London, 1930.

Cam, H. M. *Local Government in Francia and England*. London, 1912.

Cambridge History of the British Empire, The. 8 vols. Cambridge, 1929-36.

Cambridge Medieval History, The. 8 vols. Cambridge, 1911-36.
Canadian Historical Review, The. Toronto, 1920——.
Carrington, F. A., and Payne, J. *Reports of Cases.* . . . 9 vols. Philadelphia, 1856.
Chadwick, H. M. *Studies on Anglo-Saxon Institutions.* Cambridge, 1905.
Charters Granted to the East India Company from 1601. London, 1773.
Cheyney, E. P. *History of England from the Defeat of the Spanish Armada to the Death of Elizabeth.* 2 vols. New York, 1914-26.
Chisholm, J. A. (editor). *Speeches and Public Letters of Joseph Howe.* 2 vols. Halifax, 1909.
Chrimes, S. *English Constitutional Ideas in the Fifteenth Century.* Cambridge, 1935.
Clarke, M. V. *Medieval Representation and Consent.* London, 1936.
Close Rolls of the Reign of Henry III. Rolls Series. London, 1902——.
Cobbett, W. (editor). *Parliamentary History of England.* 36 vols. London, 1806-20.
Coke, E. *Reports.* (See *English Reports.*)
Collections for a History of Staffordshire. William Salt Archaeological Society. New Series. London, 1898——.
Coupland, R. *The Quebec Act.* Oxford, 1925.
Cowper, H. *Reports.* (See *English Reports.*)
Cunningham, W. *Growth of English Industry and Commerce.* Fifth edition. 2 vols. Cambridge, 1910-12.
Davies, G. *Bibliography of British History: Stuart Period.* Oxford, 1928.
Davies, J. C. *The Baronial Opposition to Edward II.* Cambridge, 1918.
Davis, H. W. C. (editor). *Regesta Regum Anglo-Normannorum, 1066-1154.* Vol. I. Oxford, 1913.
D'Ewes, Simonds. *Journals of All the Parliaments during the Reign of Queen Elizabeth.* London, 1682.
Dialogus de Scaccario. Edited by C. G. Crump, A. Hughes, and C. Johnson. Oxford, 1902.
Dicey, A. V. *Introduction to the Study of the Law of the Constitution.* London, 1902.
Dicey, A. V. *Lectures on the Relation between Law and Public Opinion in England during the Nineteenth Century.* London, 1905.

GENERAL BIBLIOGRAPHY 897

Dicey, A. V., and Rait, R. S. *Thoughts on the Union of England and Scotland.* London, 1920.

Domesday Book seu Liber Censualis Wilhelmi Primi Regis Angliae. Record Commission. 2 vols. London, 1783.

Dykes, D. O. (editor). *Source Book of English Constitutional History from 1660.* London, 1930.

Egerton, H. E. *Federations and Unions within the British Empire.* Second edition. Oxford, 1924.

Elyot, Thomas. *The Boke Named the Governour.* Edited by H. H. S. Croft. 2 vols. London, 1883.

Emden, C. S. *The People and the Constitution.* Oxford, 1933.

Emden, C. S. *Principles of British Constitutional Law.* London, 1925.

English Historical Review, The. London, 1886——.

English Reports, The. 176 vols. Edinburgh, 1900-30. (A full reprint with the paging of the original editions—to which paging reference is made in the foregoing citations.)

Firth, C. H. *The House of Lords during the Civil War.* London, 1910.

Firth, C. H. *Last Years of the Protectorate.* 2 vols. London, 1929.

Firth, C. H., and Rait, R. S. (editors). *Acts and Ordinances of the Interregnum, 1642-1660.* 3 vols. London, 1911.

Form and Order of the Service for the Coronation of Their Majesties King George VI and Queen Elizabeth, The. London, 1937.

Fortescue, John. *The Governance of England.* Edited by C. Plummer. Oxford, 1885.

Furnivall, F. J. (editor). *Life Records of Chaucer.* Chaucer Society. London, 1876.

Gardiner, S. R. (editor). *Constitutional Documents of the Puritan Revolution, 1625-1660.* Third edition. Oxford, 1906.

Gardiner, S. R. *History of England ... , 1603-1642.* 10 vols. London, 1883-85.

Gardiner, S. R. (editor). *Parliamentary Debates in 1610.* Camden Society, vol. LXXXI. London, 1862.

Gardiner, S. R. *History of the Commonwealth and Protectorate, 1649-1660.* 3 vols. London, 1894-1903.

Gardiner, S. R. *History of the Great Civil War, 1642-1649.* 3 vols. London, 1886-91.

Gardiner, S. R. (editor). *Reports of Cases in the Courts of Star*

Chamber and High Commission. Camden Society, New Series, vol. XXXIX. London, 1886.

Gee, H., and Hardy, W. T. (editors). *Documents Illustrative of English Church History.* London, 1896.

Glanville, Ranulf de. *Tractatus de Legibus et Consuetudinibus Regni Angliae.* Edited by G. E. Woodbine. New Haven, 1932.

Gooch, G. P. *English Democratic Ideas in the Seventeenth Century.* Second edition, by H. J. Laski. Cambridge, 1927.

Gras, N. S. B. *The Early English Customs System.* Cambridge, Mass., 1918.

Gray, H. L. *The Influence of the Commons on Early Legislation.* Cambridge, Mass., 1932.

Grey, A. (editor). *Debates of the House of Commons from the Year 1667 to the Year 1694.* 10 vols. London, 1763.

Grose, F. *Military Antiquities Respecting a History of the English Army.* New edition. 2 vols. London, 1801.

Gross, C. *The Gild Merchant.* 2 vols. Oxford, 1890.

Gross, C. (editor). *Select Cases from Coroners' Rolls, 1270-1638.* Selden Society, vol. IX. London, 1896.

Hakluyt, R. *Principal Navigations. . . .* Hakluyt Society. 12 vols. Glasgow, 1903-05.

Halévy, E. *History of the English People in 1815.* Translated by E. I. Watkins and D. A. Barker. London, 1924.

Halmota Prioratus Dunelmensis. Surtees Society, vol. LXXXII. Durham, 1889.

Hamilton, N. E. S. A. (editor). *Inquisitio Comitatus Cantabrigiensis.* Royal Society of Literature. London, 1876.

Hardie, F. *The Political Influence of Queen Victoria, 1861-1901.* London, 1935.

Harding, N. D. (editor). *Bristol Charters, 1155-1373.* Bristol Record Society, vol. I. Bristol, 1930.

Harland, J. *The Lancashire Lieutenancy.* Chetham Society, vols. XLIX-L. Manchester, 1859.

Hatsell, J. *Precedents and Proceedings in the House of Commons.* 4 vols. Dublin, 1786-96.

Historical Essays in Honour of James Tait. Manchester, 1933.

Holdsworth, W. S. *A History of English Law.* 9 vols. London, 1903-26.

Holt, F. L. *Reports.* (See *English Reports.*)

Howell, T. B. (editor). *A Complete Collection of State Trials to 1783; Continued to the Present Time.* Second edition. 33 vols. London, 1816-26.

Jenkinson, H., and Formoy, B. E. R. (editors). *Select Cases in the Exchequer of Pleas.* Selden Society, vol. XLVIII. London, 1932.

Jenks, E. *The Constitutional Experiments of the Commonwealth.* Cambridge, 1890.

Jennings, W. I. *Cabinet Government.* Cambridge, 1936.

Journals of the House of Commons. 117 vols. London, 1803-63.

Journals of the House of Lords. 119 vols. London, ? -1887.

Kaye, J. W. (editor). *Selections from the Papers of Lord Metcalfe.* London, 1855.

Keir, D. L., and Lawson, F. H. (editors). *Cases in Constitutional Law.* Oxford, 1928.

Keith, A. B. *Constitutional History of the First British Empire.* Oxford, 1930.

Keith, A. B. *The King and the Imperial Crown.* London, 1936.

Keith, A. B. *Responsible Government in the Dominions.* Second edition. Oxford, 1929.

Kemble, J. M. (editor). *Codex Diplomaticus Aevi Saxonici.* English Historical Society. 6 vols. London, 1839-48.

Kennedy, W. P. M. *The Constitution of Canada.* London, 1922.

Knaplund, P. *Gladstone and Britain's Imperial Policy.* New York, 1935.

Lambarde, William. *Eirenarcha, or the Office of the Justices of Peace.* London, 1581.

Laprade, W. T. (editor). *Parliamentary Papers of John Robinson, 1774-1784.* Camden Society, Third Series, vol. XXXIII. London, 1922.

Laud, William. *Works.* Edited by W. Scott and J. Bliss. 7 vols. Oxford, 1847-60.

Law Reports: Appeal Cases. London, 1875———.

Law Reports: Court of Queen's Bench. 10 vols. London, 1865-75.

Law Reports: Queen's Bench Division. London, 1876———.

Leadam, I. S. (editor). *Select Cases before the King's Council in the Star Chamber, A.D. 1477-1544.* Selden Society, vols. XVI, XXV. London, 1903-11.

Leadam, I. S., and Baldwin, J. F. (editors). *Select Cases before* the King's Council, 1243-1482. Selden Society, vol. XXXV. London, 1918.

Lecky, W. E. H. *A History of England in the Eighteenth Century.* 7 vols. London, 1892.

Liber Niger Scaccarii. Edited by T. Hearne. Oxford, 1728.

Liebermann, F. (editor). *Gesetze der Angelsachsen.* 3 vols. Halle, 1903-16.

Liebermann, F. *The National Assembly in the Anglo-Saxon Period.* Halle, 1913.

Lodge, E. C., and Thornton, G. A. (editors). *English Constitutional Documents, 1307-1485.* Cambridge, 1935.

Lowell, A. L. *The Government of England.* New edition. 2 vols. New York, 1912.

McIlwain, C. H. *The High Court of Parliament and Its Supremacy.* New Haven, 1910.

McIlwain, C. H. (editor). *Political Works of James I.* Cambridge, Mass., 1918.

Macqueen, J. *A Practical Treatise on the Appellate Jurisdiction of the House of Lords and Privy Council.* London, 1842.

McKechnie, W. S. *Magna Carta.* Second edition. Glasgow, 1914.

McKisack, M. *The Parliamentary Representation of the English Boroughs during the Middle Ages.* London, 1932.

Magna Carta Commemoration Essays. Royal Historical Society. London, 1917.

Maitland, F. W. *Domesday Book and Beyond.* Cambridge, 1897.

Maitland, F. W. (editor). *Memoranda de Parliamento.* Rolls Series. London, 1893.

Maitland, F. W. (editor). *Three Rolls of the King's Court, 1194-1195.* Pipe Roll Society, vol. XIV. London, 1891.

Maitland, F. W. (editor). *Select Pleas of the Crown, 1200-1225.* Selden Society, vol. I. London, 1888.

Maitland, F. W. (editor). *Select Pleas in Manorial and Other Seignorial Courts.* Selden Society, vol. II. London, 1889.

Martin, C. B. *Empire and Commonwealth.* Oxford, 1929.

May, T. E. *The Constitutional History of England since the Accession of George III.* Continued to 1911 by F. Holland. 3 vols. London, 1912.

Mitchell, S. K. *Studies in Taxation under John and Henry III.* New Haven, 1914.

More, Thomas. *Utopia.* Edited and translated by J. H. Lupton. Oxford, 1895.
Morris, W. A. *The Early English County Court.* Berkeley, 1926.
Morris, W. A. *The Frankpledge System.* London, 1910.
Morris, W. A. *The Mediaeval English Sheriff to 1300.* Manchester, 1927.
Muir, R. *How Britain Is Governed.* Third edition. Boston, 1935.
Munimenta Gildhallae Londoniensis. Edited by H. T. Riley. Rolls Series. 3 vols. London, 1859-62.
Murray, K. M. E. *Constitutional History of the Cinque Ports.* Manchester, 1935.
Namier, L. B. *The Structure of Politics at the Accession of George III.* London, 1929.
Nicholas, E. *Proceedings and Debates in the House of Commons in 1620 and 1621.* 2 vols. Oxford, 1766.
Nicolas, H. *Proceedings and Ordinances of the Privy Council of England.* Record Commission. 7 vols. London, 1834-37.
Notestein, W. (editor). *The Journal of Sir Simonds D'Ewes.* New Haven, 1923.
Notestein, W., and Relf, F. H. (editors). *Commons Debates for 1629.* Minneapolis, 1921.
Notestein, W., Relf, F. H., and Simpson, H. (editors). *Commons Debates, 1621.* 7 vols. New Haven, 1935.
Noy, W. *Reports.* (See *English Reports.*)
O'Callaghan, E. B. (editor). *Documents relative to the Colonial History of New York.* 10 vols. Albany, 1856-58.
Ogg, D. *England in the Reign of Charles II.* 2 vols. Oxford, 1934.
Ogg, F. A. *English Government and Politics.* New York, 1934.
Oliver, G. (editor). *Monasticon Dioecesis Exoniensis.* Exeter, 1846.
Oxford Essays in Mediaeval History Presented to H. E. Salter. Oxford, 1934.
Page, W. *London: Its Origin and Early Development.* London, 1929.
Palgrave, F. (editor). *Parliamentary Writs.* Record Commission. 2 vols. London, 1827-34.
Parliamentary Debates. (Four series of debates in both houses, 1803-1908.) London, 1812-1908.
Parliamentary Debates: House of Commons. London, 1909———.
Parliamentary Debates: House of Lords. London, 1909———.

Parliamentary Papers. (An enormous collection of bills, reports, and other documents ordered printed by the house of commons. For complete description, see the Alphabetical Lists from time to time published by official order.)

Pasquet, D. *Essay on the Origins of the English House of Commons.* Translated by R. G. D. Laffan, with a preface and notes by G. Lapsley. Cambridge, 1925.

Patent Rolls, 1216-1225. Rolls Series. London, 1901.

Pease, T. C. *The Leveller Movement.* Washington, 1916.

Petit-Dutaillis, C., and Lefebvre, G. *Studies and Notes Supplementary to Stubbs' Constitutional History.* Manchester, 1930.

Pickthorn, K. W. M. *Early Tudor Government: Henry VII.* Cambridge, 1934.

Pickthorn, K. W. M. *Early Tudor Government: Henry VIII.* Cambridge, 1934.

Pipe Roll of 31 Henry I. Record Commission. London, 1833. Reprinted by the Pipe Roll Society. London, 1929.

Pipe Roll of 33 Henry II. Pipe Roll Society, vol. XXXVII. London, 1915.

Pollard, A. F. *England under Protector Somerset.* London, 1900.

Pollard, A. F. *The Evolution of Parliament.* London, 1920.

Pollock, F., and Maitland, F. W. *History of English Law.* Second edition. 2 vols. Cambridge, 1899.

Poole, R. L. *The Exchequer in the Twelfth Century.* Oxford, 1912.

Poore, B. P. (editor). *The Federal and State Constitutions, Colonial Charters, and Other Organic Laws of the . . . United States.* Second edition. 2 vols. Washington, 1878.

Porritt, E. and A. G. *The Unreformed House of Commons.* 2 vols. Cambridge, 1903.

Port, F. J. *Administrative Law.* London, 1929.

Proceedings of the British Academy. London, 1903———.

Prothero, G. W. (editor). *Select Statutes and Other Constitutional Documents Illustrative of the Reigns of Elizabeth and James I.* Oxford, 1894.

Public General Acts. London, 1926———.

Public General Statutes. 63 vols. London, 1866-1925.

Read, C. *Bibliography of British History: Tudor Period, 1485-1603.* Oxford, 1933.

GENERAL BIBLIOGRAPHY

Red Book of the Exchequer, The. Edited by H. Hall. Rolls Series. 3 vols. London, 1896.

Redlich, J., and Hirst, F. W. *Local Government in England.* 2 vols. London, 1903.

Reid, R. R. *The King's Council in the North.* London, 1921.

Relf, F. H. *The Petition of Right.* Minneapolis, 1917.

Reports from the Lords' Committees . . . Touching the Dignity of a Peer. 5 vols. London, 1820-29.

Reports of the Royal Commission on Historical Manuscripts. Reports I-XX. London, 1874-1928.

Reports of State Trials. New Series. 8 vols. London, 1888-98.

Richardson, H. G., and Sayles, G. *Rotuli Parliamentorum Anglie hactenus Inediti, MCCLXXIX-MCCCLXXIII.* Camden Society, Third Series, vol. LI. London, 1935.

Robertson, A. J. (editor). *Anglo-Saxon Charters.* Announced by the Cambridge University Press.

Robertson, A. J. (editor). *The Laws of the Kings of England from Edmund to Henry I.* Cambridge, 1925.

Robertson, C. G. (editor). *Select Statutes, Cases, and Documents to Illustrate English Constitutional History, 1660-1832; with a Supplement from 1832-1894.* London, 1904.

Rotuli de Liberate ac de Misis et Praestitis Regnante Johanne. Record Commission. London, 1844.

Rotuli Litterarum Clausarum. Record Commission. 2 vols. London, 1833-44.

Rotuli Litterarum Patentium, 1201-1216. Record Commission. London, 1835.

Rotuli Parliamentorum. 6 vols. (London, 1776-77.)

Round, J. H. (editor). *Ancient Charters, Royal and Private, Prior to 1200.* Pipe Roll Society, vol. X. London, 1888.

Round, J. H. *The Commune of London and Other Studies.* Westminster, 1899.

Round, J. H. *Feudal England.* London, 1895.

Round, J. H. *Geoffrey de Mandeville.* London, 1892.

Round, J. H. *The King's Serjeants and Officers of State.* London, 1911.

Round, J. H. *Studies on the Red Book of the Exchequer.* London, 1898.

Rushworth, J. (editor). *Historical Collections, 1618-1648.* 8 vols. London, 1721.

Rymer, T. (editor). *Foedera, Conventiones, Litterae, et . . . Acta Publica.* . . . 20 vols. London, 1704-35. (Vols. XVI-XX edited by R. Sanderson.)

Salkeld, W. *Reports.* (See *English Reports.*)

Sayles, G. O. (editor). *Select Cases in the Court of King's Bench under Edward I.* Selden Society, vol. LV. London, 1936.

Schuyler, R. L. *Parliament and the British Empire.* New York, 1929.

Seymour, C. *Electoral Reform in England and Wales.* New Haven, 1915.

Smith, Thomas. *De Republica Anglorum.* Edited by L. Alston. Cambridge, 1906.

Speculum: A Journal of Mediaeval Studies. Cambridge, Mass., 1926——.

State Papers: Henry VIII. Rolls Series. 11 vols. London, 1830-52.

Statutes at Large. 105 vols. Cambridge, 1762-1865.

Statutes at Large: Ireland. 8 vols. Dublin, 1765.

Statutes of the Realm. Record Commission. 11 vols. London, 1810-28.

Statutes of the United Kingdom of Great Britain and Ireland. 59 vols., London, 1807-65.

Stenton, F. M. *The First Century of English Feudalism, 1066-1166.* Oxford, 1932.

Stenton, F. M. *Norman London.* Historical Association Leaflet no. 93. London, 1934.

Stephenson, C. *Borough and Town.* Cambridge, Mass., 1933.

Stevenson, W. H. (editor). *Records of the Borough of Nottingham.* 5 vols. London, 1882-1900.

Stith, W. *History of the First Discovery and Settlement of Virginia.* Williamsburg, 1747.

Stocks, J. E. (editor). *Records of the Borough of Leicester.* 4 vols. London, 1899-1923. (A continuation of Mary Bateson's work.)

Strype, J. *Life and Acts of Matthew Parker.* 3 vols. Oxford, 1821.

Strype. J. *Life and Acts of John Whitgift.* 3 vols. Oxford, 1822.

Stubbs, W. *Constitutional History of England.* Fifth edition. 3 vols. Oxford, 1891-96.

Stubbs, W. (editor). *Select Charters and Other Illustrations of*

English Constitutional History. Ninth edition, by H. W. C. Davis. Oxford, 1913.

Tait, J. (editor). *The Domesday Survey of Cheshire.* Chetham Society, New Series, vol. LXXV. Manchester, 1916.

Tait, J. *The Medieval English Borough.* Manchester, 1936.

Tanner, J. R. (editor). *Constitutional Documents of the Reign of James I, A.D. 1603-1625.* Cambridge, 1930.

Tanner, J. R. *English Constitutional Conflicts of the Seventeenth Century, 1603-1689.* Cambridge, 1928.

Tanner, J. R. (editor). *Tudor Constitutional Documents, 1485-1603.* Cambridge, 1922.

Thompson, F. *The First Century of Magna Carta.* Minneapolis, 1925.

Thomson, G. S. *Lords Lieutenants in the Sixteenth Century.* London, 1923.

Thorpe, B. (editor). *Diplomatarium Anglicum Aevi Saxonici.* London, 1865.

Thorpe, F. N. (editor). *The Federal and State Constitutions, Colonial Charters, and Other Organic Laws of the . . . United States.* 7 vols. Washington, 1909.

Tout, T. F. *Chapters in the Administrative History of Mediaeval England.* 6 vols. Manchester, 1920-33.

Tout, T. F. *The Place of the Reign of Edward II in English History.* Manchester, 1914.

Traill, H. D. *Central Government.* London, 1881.

Transactions of the Royal Historical Society. Fourth Series. London, 1918———.

Transactions of the Royal Society of Canada. Montreal, 1883———.

Trevelyan, G. M. *England under Queen Anne.* 3 vols. London, 1930-34.

Tudor Studies Presented by the Board of Studies in History in the University of London to A. F. Pollard. London, 1924.

Turberville, A. S. *The House of Lords in the Eighteenth Century.* Oxford, 1927.

Turner, E. R. *The Privy Council of England in the Seventeenth and Eighteenth Centuries, 1603-1784.* 2 vols. Baltimore, 1927-28.

Turner, G. J. (editor). *Select Pleas of the Forest.* Selden Society, vol. XIII. London, 1901.

Usher, R. G. *The Rise and Fall of the High Commission.* Oxford, 1913.

Veitch, G. S. *The Genesis of Parliamentary Reform.* London, 1913.

Victoria History of the Counties of England, The. Westminster, 1900——.

Vinogradoff, P. *Villainage in England.* Oxford, 1892.

Wade, E. C. S., and Phillips, G. C. *Constitutional Law.* London, 1931.

Walrond, T. (editor). *Letters and Journals of James, Eighth Earl of Elgin.* London, 1872.

Webb, S. and B. *English Local Government.* 6 vols. London, 1906-29.

Weinbaum, M. *The Incorporation of Boroughs.* Manchester, 1937.

Weinbaum, M. *London unter Eduard I und II.* 2 vols., Stuttgart, 1923.

Weinbaum, M. *Verfassungsgeschichte Londons, 1066-1268.* Stuttgart, 1929.

White, A. B. *Self-Government at the King's Command.* Minneapolis, 1933.

Wilkins, D. (editor). *Concilia Magnae Britanniae et Hiberniae.* 4 vols. London, 1737.

Willard, J. F. *Parliamentary Taxes on Personal Property, 1290-1334.* Cambridge, Mass., 1934.

Willson, D. H. (editor). *The Parliamentary Diary of Robert Bowyer, 1606-1607.* Minneapolis, 1931.

Worcestershire Quarter Sessions Papers. (Worcestershire County Records, Division I.) Vol. I. Worcester, 1900.

Wright, H. G. *Life and Works of Arthur Hall.* Manchester, 1919.

Wrong, E. M. *Charles Buller and Responsible Government.* Oxford, 1926.

Date Due